'Thou art a retailer of phrases, and dost deal in
remnants of remnants'
William Congreve, *The Way of the World* (1700)

'False English, bad pronunciation, old sayings and
common proverbs; which are so many proofs of
having kept bad and low company'
4th Earl of Chesterfield, A*dvice to his Son on Men
and Manners* (1775)

'Sir, it [an earthquake] will be much exaggerated in
popular talk; for, in the first place, the common
people do not accurately adapt their thoughts to the
objects; nor, secondly, do they accurately adapt their
words to their thoughts: they do not mean to lie;
but, taking no pains to be exact, they give you very
false accounts. A great part of their language is
proverbial, If anything rocks at all, they say it *rocks
like a cradle*; and in this way they go on'
Samuel Johnson, quoted in James Boswell, *The Life
of Samuel Johnson* (1791) – for 14 September 1777

'Blank cheques of intellectual bankruptcy'
A definition of catchphrases attributed to Oliver
Wendell Holmes (1809–94)

'What do I mean by a phrase? A clutch of words that
gives you a clutch at the heart'
Robert Frost, interviewed in the Sat*urday Evening
Post* (16 November 1960)

Nigel Rees is one of the world's leading authorities on popular phrases and sayings.

Born near Liverpool in 1944, he went to the Merchant Taylors' School, Crosby, and then took a degree in English at Oxford. On graduating, he joined Granada Television in Manchester and made his first appearances on local programmes in 1967 before moving to London as a freelance.

He reported for ITN's *News at Ten* and then became involved in a wide range of programmes for BBC Radio – news, current affairs, arts and entertainment – including two years as co-presenter of the breakfast-time *Today* programme on Radio 4.

As a broadcaster, he has since become best known as the deviser and presenter of BBC Radio's 'Quote . . . Unquote', a 'quiz-anthology' that has been delighting audiences worldwide for thirty years. Unusually, he has combined his more serious broadcasting work with appearances in radio and TV comedy shows.

As an author, he has written upwards of fifty books – mostly devoted to quotations, anecdotes and aspects of the popular use of the English language. Always emphasizing the humour in his subject, his works have included studies of the origin and use of allusions, catchphrases, clichés, family sayings, idioms, graffiti, nicknames, politically correct language and slogans.

He lives with his wife in Notting Hill, London. In 1981, he was honoured to receive a Heineken Award for 'refreshing the parts' of the British nation.

A WORD IN YOUR SHELL-like

6,000 Curious & Everyday Phrases Explained

NIGEL REES

Collins

HarperCollins*Publishers*
Westerhill Road, Glasgow G64 2QT

The Collins website address is www.collins.co.uk

© Nigel Rees 2004

Reprint 10 9 8 7 6 5 4 3 2 1 0

ISBN 0 00 715593 X

A catalogue record for this book is available from the British
Library

Text design by Clare Crawford.

Printed and bound in Great Britain by Clays Ltd, St Ives plc.

Introduction

A Word in Your Shell-like is an extensive examination of more than 6,000 phrases, detailing their origins, dates, meanings and use. But what is a 'phrase'? Although it is technically possible for a phrase to consist of one word, I have mostly limited myself to *clusters* of two or more words and left analysis of single words to the etymologists and lexicographers. Within this definition of a phrase, however, fall idiomatic expressions, proverbial sayings, stock and format phrases, catchphrases, clichés, journalese, headline fodder, slogans, advertising lines, as well as titles of books and entertainments which either quote a specific source or themselves create a form of words. There is also a number of 'short quotations' – phrases derived from famous sayings that may be said to have a life of their own.

As to my choice of phrases for inclusion, I have simply concentrated on those about which there is something interesting to say with regard to their origins and use. I have not always restricted myself to phrases that have caught on in an enduring fashion – which might be the criterion for inclusion in a more formal dictionary – but I also look at phrases that may have had only a brief flowering. This is because to record them here may help to explain an allusion that might puzzle the reader of a novel or other work. In addition, even a briefly popular phrase can help to evoke a period and thus should be examined as part of the social history of the language.

These are the main types of phrase that I have explored in this book:

Catchphrase: simply a phrase that has 'caught on' with the public and is, or has been, in frequent use. It might have originated with a particular person – like CALL ME MADAM – or it might not be traceable to a particular source – like BACK TO THE DRAWING-BOARD!

Cliché: a worn or hackneyed phrase. There are some who would say that the clichés of journalism are used in such a way that they amount to a special language – journalese – which does not deserve to be condemned. I disagree.

Euphemisms: phrases used when you are trying to be gentle – or, in modern guise – when you are trying to be politically correct. The word 'loophemism' coined by Frank Deakin of Wilmslow in 1995 describes the largest number of such phrases in this book, having to do with going to the lavatory: (GO AND) SEE A MAN ABOUT A DOG.

Nannyisms: usually of a cautionary nature, these sayings may have been handed down by actual nannies or by grown-ups of a nannyish tendency: BACK IN THE KNIFE-BOX, LITTLE MISS SHARP.

Format phrase: a basic phrase or sentence structure capable of infinite variation by the insertion of new words – like ONE SMALL STEP FOR ——, ONE GIANT LEAP FOR —— where the sentence structure can be adapted to suit the speaker's purpose.

Idiom: a picturesque expression that is used to convey a metaphorical meaning different from its literal one – or, as *The Oxford Dictionary of Current Idiomatic English* puts it, that has a meaning 'not deducible from those of the separate words'. For example, if I say someone is a SQUARE PEG IN A ROUND HOLE it is obvious he or she cannot literally be such a thing. My hearers will know exactly what I mean, although I have not told them directly. Like the term 'catchphrase', 'idiom' could be applied to most of the phrases in this book, but I have tried to restrict its use to those that conform to the above definition.

Quotation, short: a number of phrases that are parts of quotations – e.g. WINTER OF DISCONTENT – are also included, especially when they have been used as the titles of popular books or films. Equally, when original phrases chosen as titles have become part of popular speech, they also are covered.

Saying, brief: this is what is sometimes called 'a well-known phrase or saying' (as in 're-arrange these words into a well-known phrase or saying') but, unlike a formal 'quotation', is probably not attributable to a precise source, be it speaker, book or show. Proverbial expressions most commonly fall into this category.

Slogan: a phrase designed to promote a product, idea or cause – or which has this effect. However, at times I have employed it rather loosely to cover any phrase that is used in advertising – in headlines, footnotes, but not necessarily in a selling line that names the product. BODY ODOUR (or BO) could hardly be described as a slogan in itself, but as an advertising line it did help to promote a product.

Stock phrase: a regularly used phrase that can't be said to have 'caught on' like a full-blooded catchphrase – for example, a celebrity's verbal mannerism (CAN WE TALK?), by which he or she is known but which can't be said to have 'caught on' with the public as a proper catchphrase should. It also refers to phrases which get regularly trotted out but which, again, cannot be said to have passed into the language generally.

A word about dating: Eric Partridge was always 'game' (as someone once felicitously put it) to try to pinpoint when a phrase came into use, though many of his stabs at it were no more than guesses. Using the citations that I have accumulated, I have tried to be a little more precise in this area. When I say that a phrase was '*Current* in 1975', I mean that I simply have a record of its use then – *not* that I think it was first used in that year. It may also have been current long after that date. When I say that a phrase was '*Quoted* in 1981', I mean precisely that – not that it was originated in that year. It might have been coined long before. On the whole I have not indulged in speculation about when a phrase might have entered the language but have simply recorded hard and fast examples of its use.

In case you find my interpretation of alphabetical order puzzling, the phrases are listed in what is known as 'letter by letter' order – that is to say, in alphabetical order of letters within the whole phrase exactly as it is written. Thus, for example, **nicest things come in smallest parcels** appears before **nice work if you can get it!** and **move the goalposts** before **Mr**.

Cross-references to other entries are made in SMALL CAPITALS.

Acknowledgements

I am indebted to the authors and publishers of books quoted in the text and to the editors and journalists of the many newspapers and magazines who have provided citations.

Many people have helped me with the entries in this book, either by giving me their reactions when the phrases have been featured on my BBC Radio 4 programme *Quote . . . Unquote* (on the air since 1976) or through the pages of *The "Quote . . . Unquote" Newsletter*, a subscription quarterly (first published in 1992). Many have also contributed via its associated website, www.btwebworld.com/quote-unquote. I am most grateful to them all. They are mentioned in the individual entries alongside the information with which they have supplied me, but there are some people who have been so generally supportive (sometimes without really knowing it) that an expression of my especial thanks is only proper here. These include: Dr J. K. Aronson, Ralph Berry, Marian Bock, W. P. Brown, Paul Cloutman, Leslie Dunkling, T. A. Dyer, David Elias, Jaap Engelsman, Jean English, Mark English, Carl Faulkner, Thomas D. Fuller, Jane Gregory, W. Eric Gustafson, Patricia M. Guy, Dick Hallson, Dr Henry Hardy, Donald Hickling, the late Sir David Hunt, Antony Jay, Miss M. L. King, Joe Kralich, Morton Kupperman, Dennis K. Lien, Michael R. Lewis, Professor Wolfgang Mieder, the late Frank Muir, Michael and Valerie Grosvenor Myer, James Nation, the late Vernon Noble, Denis Norden, Michael Quinnion – World Wide Words, Tony Ring – the P. G. Wodehouse Society (UK), Antony Percy, Derek Robinson, Leen Verhoeff.

In particular, I should like to remember with gratitude my collaboration with the late Paul Beale, reviser of Eric Partridge's *Dictionary of Slang and Unconventional English* and *Dictionary of Catch Phrases*, for his selfless encouragement and for his willingness to share his unpublished materials with me. Any mistakes are, however, entirely my own responsibility and I gratefully anticipate their being pointed out to me.

NIGEL REES
London, 2004

Abbreviations

Apperson: G. L. Apperson, *English Proverbs and Proverbial Phrases,* 1929
Bartlett: *Bartlett's Familiar Quotations* (15th edn), 1980, (16th edn), 1992, (17th edn), 2002
Benham: *Benham's Book of Quotations,* 1907, 1948, 1960
Bible: The Authorized Version, 1611 (except where stated otherwise)
Brewer: *Brewer's Dictionary of Phrase and Fable,* (2nd edn), 1894, (3rd edn), 1923, (13th edn), 1975, (14th edn), 1989
Burnam: Tom Burnam, *The Dictionary of Misinformation,* 1975; *More Misinformation,* 1980
Casson/Grenfell: Sir Hugh Casson & Joyce Grenfell, *Nanny Says* (ed. Diana, Lady Avebury), 1982
CODP: *The Concise Oxford Dictionary of Proverbs,* 1982
DOAS: Wentworth & Flexner, *Dictionary of American Slang,* 1960 (1975 revision and 1987 edition, ed. Robert L. Chapman)
DNB: *The Dictionary of National Biography*
Flexner: Stuart Berg Flexner, *I Hear America Talking,* 1976; *Listening to America,* 1982
Grose: Francis Grose, *Dictionary of the Vulgar Tongue,* 1785–1823
Mencken: *H. L. Mencken's Dictionary of Quotations,* 1942
Morris: William and Mary Morris, *Morris Dictionary of Word and Phrase Origins,* 1977
ODP: *The Oxford Dictionary of Proverbs* (3rd edn), 1970
ODQ: *The Oxford Dictionary of Quotations* (2nd edn), 1953, (3rd edn), 1979, (4th edn), 1992, (5th edn), 1999
OED2: *The Oxford English Dictionary* (2nd ed,) 1989, (CD-ROM version 3.0), 2002
Partridge/Catch Phrases: Eric Partridge, *A Dictionary of Catch Phrases* (2nd edn, edited by Paul Beale), 1985
Partridge/Slang: Eric Partridge, *A Dictionary of Slang and Unconventional English* (8th edn, edited by Paul Beale), 1984
Safire: William Safire, *Safire's Political Dictionary,* 1978
Shakespeare: The Arden Shakespeare (2nd series)
Slanguage: Brigid McCoville & John Shearlaw, *The Slanguage of Sex,* 1984
Street Talk: *Street Talk: The Language of Coronation Street,* eds Jeffrey Miller & Graham Nown, 1986

A

abandon hope all ye who enter here!
Ironic but good-humoured welcoming
phrase – a popular mistranslation of the
words written over the entrance to Hell in
Dante's *Divina Commedia* (*circa* 1320).
'All hope abandon, ye who enter here!'
would be a more accurate translation of
the Italian, '*lasciate ogni speranza voi
ch'entrate*!'

—— abhors a vacuum PHRASES A format
based on the maxim, 'Nature abhors a
vacuum,' that François Rabelais quotes in
its original Latin form '*natura abhorret
vacuum*' in his *Gargantua* (1535). Galileo
(1564–1642) asserted that it was the reason
mercury rises in a barometer. An early
appearance in English is, 'The Effatum,
That Nature abhors a Vacuum', from
Robert Boyle, *A Free Enquiry Into the
Vulgarly Receiv'd Notion of Nature* (1685).
'Nature abhors a straight line' was a saying
of the English garden landscaper Capabil-
ity Brown (1715–83). Clare Boothe Luce,
the American writer and socialite (1903–
87), is supposed to have said, 'Nature
abhors a virgin', but this may just be a
version of the line in her play *The Women*
(1936): 'I'm what nature abhors – an old
maid. A frozen asset.' 'Nature abhors a
vacuum and what appears ultimately to
concern the Reagan Administration most of
all is the possibility that President
Mitterrand's France will gradually abandon
its traditional military protection of central
Africa and the Sahara' – *Financial Times*
(12 August 1983); 'Though I like Scalia's
principles better, I prefer Wilkey's conclusions. Law, like nature, abhors a vacuum.
It seems wise to extend the protection of
the law to those who are left out in the
cold of a legal no-man's land' – *Financial
Times* (14 March 1985); 'I quickly developed a pearshaped figure that testified to
my indolent lifestyle. I became the archetypal also-ran that PE masters could barely
bring themselves to talk to without risk of
life-threatening apoplexy: they abhorred
my idleness as Nature abhors a vacuum' –
The Guardian (24 June 1986).

above and beyond (the call of duty)
Phrase expressing an outstanding level of
service, used in tributes and such like.
OED2 has several 'above and beyonds' but
not this precise one. *Above and Beyond*
was the title of an American TV series of
military stories (*circa* 1996).

Abraham's bosom Where the dead sleep
contentedly. From Luke 16:23: 'And it
came to pass, that the beggar died, and
was carried by the angels into Abraham's
bosom.' The phrase alludes to Abraham,
first of the Hebrew patriarchs. Compare
ARTHUR'S BOSOM.

**absolutely, Mister Gallagher! / positively,
Mister Shean!** Phrases of agreement;
roundabout ways of saying 'yes', taken
from the American vaudevillians (Ed)
Gallagher and (Al) Shean whose act
flourished in the early part of the 20th
century. The exchange was included in a
popular song 'Mr Gallagher and Mister
Shean' (1922) though, in that song, the
order of words was 'positively, Mister
Gallagher / absolutely, Mr Shean'. Each
syllable of the adverbs is emphasized –
e.g. 'pos-it-ive-ly', 'ab-so-lute-ly'.

**accidents will occur in the best-regu-
lated families** A catchphrase used lightly
to cover any domestic upset. The basic
proverbial expression, 'Accidents will
happen' was known by the 1760s; this full
version by the 1810s. Best known in the
form delivered by Mr Micawber in Charles
Dickens, *David Copperfield* (Chap. 28,
1850): '"Copperfield," said Mr. Micawber,
"accidents will occur in the best-regulated
families; and in families not regulated by
. . . the influence of Woman, in the lofty
character of Wife, they may be expected
with confidence, and must be borne with
philosophy".' Dickens had earlier used the
saying in *Pickwick Papers* (1836–7) and
Dombey and Son (1844–6).

(an) accident waiting to happen
Hindsight phrase, frequently used in the
wake of a disaster. This is the survivors'
and experts' way of pointing to what, to

them, seems the foreseeable and inevitable result of lax safety standards that will now probably be corrected only *as a result* of the tragedy. Much used in relation to the late 1980s spate of disasters in the UK (Bradford City football ground fire, Zeebrugge ferry overturning, Piper Alpha oil-rig explosion, Kings Cross Tube fire, Hillsborough football stadium crowd deaths). Used as the title of a 1989 book on the subject by Judith Cook. 'Ignorance and neglect cost 51 lives [in the *Marchioness* boat disaster] . . . "You don't need the benefit of hindsight to say this was an accident waiting to happen," he said' – *Today* (16 August 1991).

according to Cocker By strict calculation, exactly. Edward Cocker (1631–75) was an arithmetician who is believed to have written down the rules of arithmetic in a popular guide.

according to Hoyle Exactly; correctly; according to the recognized rules; according to the highest authority. The phrase comes from the name of the, at one time, standard authority on the game of whist (and other card games). Edmond Hoyle was the author of *A Short Treatise on the Game of Whist* (1742). 'If everything goes according to Hoyle, I'll go into semi-retirement there' – *Melody Maker* (21 August 1971).

(an) ace in the hole A hidden advantage or secret source of power. An American phrase used as the title of a Cole Porter song in the show *Let's Face It* (1941), of a Billy Wilder film (US 1951) and of an Annie Proulx novel, *That Old Ace In the Hole* (2002). It came originally from the game of stud poker. A 'hole' card is one that is not revealed until the betting has taken place. If it is an ace, so much the better. *DOAS* dates the use of the expression, in a poker context, to the 1920s, *OED2* to 1915. In British English, the nearest equivalent would be to talk of having **an ace up one's sleeve**. 'In the long haul . . . AM's ace in the hole may be the $213 million net operating loss carry-forward it still has left from its 1981–2 losses' – *The New York Times* (6 May 1984).

(an) Achilles' heel The vulnerable point of any person or thing. Referring to

Achilles, the foremost warrior in the Trojan war, who sulked in his tent, was hero of the *Iliad* and was vulnerable only at the heel (in allusion to the story of the dipping of Achilles' heel in the river Styx). 'Divorce is the Achilles' heel of marriage' – Bernard Shaw, letter (2 July 1897). It was cited as a 'dying metaphor' by George Orwell, 'Politics and the English Language' in *Horizon* (April 1946). 'If Oppenheimer has an "Achilles" heel, it is his overriding loyalty to his friends' – Arthur Holly Compton, *Atomic Quest* (1956); 'It is the refusal to condemn which is the Achilles heel of contemporary Christian psychology' – *Catholic Herald* (28 January 1972).

(an) acid test A crucial test. Originally an 'acid test' involved the use of aqua fortis to test for gold. Cited as a 'lump of verbal refuse' by George Orwell, 'Politics and the English Language' in *Horizon* (April 1946). 'The treatment accorded Russia by her sister nations in the months to come will be the acid test of their good will' – President Woodrow Wilson, quoted in *The Times* (9 January 1918); 'The acid test of any political decision is, "What is the alternative?"' – Lord Trend, quoted in *The Observer* (21 December 1975); 'Let's get South Africa working. For we must together and without delay begin to build a better life for all South Africans. This is going to be the acid test of the government of national unity' – Nelson Mandela, quoted in *Financial Times* (3 May 1994); 'If the same weight is not given to the improvement of human capital as to market share, profit and other organisational priorities, small wonder the human resources function is often viewed as unrelated to the "real" goals of the company. The acid test here is: do the job descriptions of all staff (board of directors, executive, administration) include meaningful percentages of weights and time spent in subordinate development with examples of what this means in practice?' – *Financial Times* (6 May 1994).

(an) action man A person who is given more to action than to thought, named after a boy's doll that could be dressed in various military-type costumes with appropriate accoutrements. Prior to his marriage in 1981, Charles, Prince of Wales, was noted for his enthusiastic sporting activities in many fields. Coupled with his active service in the Royal Navy, such expenditure of energy caused him to be accorded this nickname. A report of a General Medical Council disciplinary inquiry in *The Independent* (29 March 1990) stated: 'He told the hearing: "Mr Bewick is an Action Man, not a philosopher. Action Man's advantage is that at the drop of a hat, he can go anywhere and do anything".'

action this day   Instruction phrase, for office use. 'ACTION THIS DAY', 'REPORT IN THREE DAYS' and 'REPORT PROGRESS IN ONE WEEK' were printed tags that Winston Churchill started using in February 1940 to glue on to memos at the Admiralty. Subtitled 'Working with Churchill', the book *Action This Day* (1968) is a collection of the reminiscences of those who had been closely associated with Churchill during the Second World War. 'She [Margaret Thatcher] had the draft of that circular on her desk that night. She said "Action this day" and she got it. We didn't stop to argue' – Hugo Young, *One of Us*, Chap. 6 (1989).

(an) actor laddie   An actor with the booming voice and declamatory manner of the Victorian and Edwardian stage. The expression presumably derives from the habit of adding the somewhat patronizing endearment 'laddie' when talking to junior members of their companies. The playwright Ronald Harwood singled out Frank G. Carillo as an example of the breed, from the early 1900s: '[He] intoned rather than talked, in a deep, trembling voice ideally suited to melodrama and he used it with equal fortissimo both on and off the stage.' Sir Donald Wolfit, himself somewhat prone to this manner, described Carillo as one of the few actors he had actually heard use the word 'laddie'.

actress   See AS THE BISHOP.

act your age (also **be your age)!**   Grow up, behave in a manner more befitting your years. Probably from the US and in use by the 1920s. An elaboration heard in the UK (1985) – **act your age, not your shoe size** (normal shoe sizes in the UK are in the range 4–12).

Adam's rib   The film *Adam's Rib* (US 1949) is about husband and wife lawyers opposing each other in court and stars Spencer Tracy and Katharine Hepburn. It is also the title of a 1923 Cecil B. de Mille film about marriage, with biblical flashbacks. The phrase alludes to Genesis 2:21–2, which states that God made woman from one of Adam's ribs. Compare SPARE RIB.

adjust   See DO NOT.

(an) admirable Crichton   A resourceful servant. Also applied – broadly – to anyone of intellectual accomplishment. *The Admirable Crichton* has been the title of a novel by Harrison Ainsworth (1837) and of J. M. Barrie's play (1902; films UK 1918, 1957), the latter about a butler who succours his shipwrecked aristocratic employer on a desert island. The term had originally been applied to James Crichton (1560–85), Scottish traveller and scholar, by Sir Thomas Urquhart in *The Jewel* (1652).

adopt, adapt, improve   Motto of the National Association of Round Tables of Great Britain and Ireland, from 1927 onwards. The Prince of Wales (later Edward VIII) had said in a speech at the British Industries Fair in Birmingham (1927): 'The young business and professional men of this country must get together round the table, adopt methods that have proved sound in the past, adapt them to the changing needs of the times and, whenever possible, improve them.' The Round Table movement is a social and charitable organization for young professional and business men under the age of forty (after which age Rotary takes over).

adrift   See CAST ADRIFT.

advance Australia   Motto of the Commonwealth of Australia when the states united in 1901. In the 1970s and 1980s, as republicanism grew, it acquired the force of a slogan and was used in various campaigns to promote national pride (sometimes as 'Let's Advance Australia'). In 1984, 'Advance Australia Fair', slightly adapted, superseded 'God Save the Queen' as the country's national anthem. This song, by Peter Dodds McCormick, had first been performed in Sydney in 1878, though the alliterative slogan 'Advance Australia' apparently existed earlier when Michael Massey Robinson wrote in the *Sydney Gazette* (1 February 1826): '"Advance Then, Australia", / Be this thy proud gala / . . . And thy watch-word be "Freedom, For Ever!"'

advise and consent The title of Allen Drury's novel about Washington politics *Advise and Consent* (1959; film US 1962) (not 'advice') is taken from US Senate Rule 38: 'The final question on every nomination shall be, "Will the Senate advise and consent to this nomination?"' In the US Constitution (Art. II, Sect. 2), dealing with the Senate's powers as a check on the President's appointive and treaty-making powers, the phrase includes the noun rather than the verb, '*Advice* and consent'. Originally, George Washington as President went in person to the Senate Chamber (22 August 1789) to receive 'advice and consent' about treaty provisions with the Creek Indians. Vice-President Adams used the words, 'Do you advise and consent?' Subsequent administrations have sent written requests.

(the) affluent society Label applied to Western society in the mid-20th century. John Kenneth Galbraith's book *The Affluent Society* (1958) is about the effect of high living standards on economic theories that had been created to deal with scarcity and poverty. The resulting 'private affluence and public squalor' stemmed from an imbalance between private and public sector output. For example, there might be more cars and TV sets but not enough police to prevent them from being stolen. The Revd Dr Martin Luther King Jnr, in a 1963 letter from gaol, used the phrase thus: 'When you see the vast majority of your twenty million Negro brothers smouldering in an airtight cage of poverty in the midst of an affluent society . . . then you will understand why we find it difficult to wait.' The notion was not new to the mid-20th century. Tacitus, in his *Annals* (*circa* AD 115) noted that 'many, amid great affluence, are utterly miserable' and Cato the Younger (95–46 BC), when denouncing the contemporary state of Rome said: '*Habemus publice egestatem, privatim opulentiam* [public

want, private wealth].' The punning tag of the **effluent society**, a commonplace by the 1980s, had appeared in Stan Gooch's poem 'Never So Good' in 1964, and indeed before that.

after I've shampooed my hair, I can't do a thing with it (or **I washed my hair last night – and now . . .)!** Commonplace excuse for one's less than good appearance and a domestic conversational cliché. In *Are You a Bromide?* (1907), the American writer Gelett Burgess castigated people who spoke in what he called 'Bromidioms', like this one. The second part is sometimes given as a chorused response as though anticipating the cliché involved.

after the Lord Mayor's show comes the shit-cart A reference to the anti-climactic appearance of a dust-cart and operative to clean up the horse manure that is left behind after the Lord Mayor's annual show (really a procession) in the City of London. *Partridge/Catch Phrases* suggests that it is a late 19th century Cockney observation and one that could be applied to other from-the-sublime-to-the-ridiculous situations.

after you, Claude! / no, after you, Cecil! Catchphrase exchange spoken by Horace Percival and Jack Train playing two over-polite handymen, Cecil and Claude, in the BBC radio show *ITMA* (1939–49). It still survives in pockets as an admirable way of overcoming social awkwardness in such matters as deciding who should first go through a door. In the early 1900s, the American cartoonist Fred Opper created a pair of excessively polite Frenchmen called Alphonse and Gaston who had the similar exchange: 'You first, my dear Alphonse' – 'No, no, you first, my dear Gaston.'

afternoon men Drunkards ('afternoon', presumably because they have imbibed a liquid lunch). 'As if they had heard that enchanted horn of Astolpho, that English duke in Ariosto, which never sounded but all his auditors were mad, and for fear ready to make away [with] themselves . . . . They are a company of giddy-heads, afternoon men.' This is the final part of the quotation given by Anthony Powell as the epigraph to his novel *Afternoon Men* (1931). He gives the source as Burton's

Anatomy of Melancholy. The only other use found of the term 'afternoon men' is from the same work. In the introductory 'Democritus to the Reader', Burton has: 'Beroaldus will have drunkards, afternoon men, and such as more than ordinarily delight in drink, to be mad.'

age See ACT YOUR.

age before beauty! A phrase used (like AFTER YOU . . .) when inviting another person to go through a door before you. In the famous story, Clare Boothe Luce said it to Dorothy Parker, ushering her ahead. Parker assented, saying, 'Pearls before swine.' Mrs Luce described this account as completely apocryphal in answer to a question from John Keats, Parker's biographer, for his book *You Might as Well Live* (1970). The saying presumably originated when people first started worrying about the etiquette of going through doors. It does not occur in Jonathan Swift's *Polite Conversation* (1738), as one might have expected. A variant reported from New Zealand (1987) is **dirt before the broom**, though *Partridge/Catch Phrases* has this as the *response* to 'Age before beauty' (which it describes as a 'mock courtesy'). Other versions are **dust before the broom** (recorded in Dublin, 1948) and **the dog follows its master**. Whichever phrase is used, it usually precipitates a response. An exchange between two boozy buffoons at a pub door in Posy Simmonds's cartoon strip in *The Guardian* (19 May 1985) included these phrases: '"Certainly! Dogs follow their master!" "Dirt before the broom!" "Shepherd before sheep!" "Shit before shovel!"' Another phrase to offer in reply is: **grace before meat!**

(the) age of anxiety Label for the mid-20th century. It was the title of a long poem by W. H. Auden, written 1944–6 – an expression of loneliness in the mid-century. It was the inspiration of Leonard Bernstein's second symphony (1947–9), which became known as 'The Age of Anxiety', and was used as the score for a ballet (US 1950), also with the title.

(the) age of Aquarius The astrological age, lasting two thousand years, which was said to be beginning in the 1960s (following the Piscean Age). 'This is the dawning of the Age of Aquarius,' sang the cast of the 'American tribal love-rock musical' *Hair* (1968), in what was to become something of a hippy anthem. This new age held forth the promise of more liberal values, world freedom and brotherhood, as well as promoting general optimism.

(the) age of innocence *The Age of Innocence* was the title of a novel published in 1920 by the American writer Edith Wharton. In it, she looked back on the New York of her youth and told the story of a love affair frustrated by the morals of the time. Presumably, the description 'age of innocence' is ironically applied to this earlier period.

(an) age of kings *An Age of Kings* was the title of a fifteen-part fortnightly BBC TV serialization of Shakespeare's history plays from *Richard II* to *Richard III*, transmitted live in 1960. The phrase does not appear to have been used before. TV parodist Alan Melville came up with a version entitled 'An *Eternity* of Kings'.

(the) age of miracles is past As with **(the) age of chivalry is past**, this proverb is now used more often in the ironic *negative*, i.e. when saying 'the age of miracles is *not* past' or 'the age of chivalry is *not* dead' out of feigned gratitude for a stroke of good fortune or an unexpected courtesy. In its original positive form, 'miracles' was current by 1602. 'The age of chivalry is gone' occurs in Edmund Burke's *Reflections on the Revolution in France* (1790). In about 1900, Oscar Wilde wrote in a letter: '[Frank Harris] keeps Bosie in order: clearly the age of miracles is not over.' In Ira Gershwin's lyric for the song 'A Foggy Day (in London Town)' (1937) are the lines: 'I viewed the morning with alarm. / The British Museum had lost its charm. / How long, I wondered, could this thing last? / But the age of miracles hadn't passed.'

(the) age of reason Label for the 18th century as a period when philosophy was a predominant force in Europe – hence also the name **age of enlightenment**. *The Age of Reason* was the title of Thomas Paine's book (1793), an attack on Christianity and the Bible. English-born Paine went to America and encouraged the fight for independence.

(the) age of uncertainty Label for the second half of the 20th century. *The Age of Uncertainty* was the title given by J.K. Galbraith to his 1976 TV series (and accompanying book) on 'the rise and crisis in industrial society seen in the light of economic factors'. It contrasted the great certainties in economic thought of the 19th century with the uncertainties of the second half of the 20th.

à go-go PHRASES Meaning, 'in abundance', 'no end of'. Known by 1965. Possibly derived from 'Whisky à gogo' – a name given to night clubs all over France since the 1960s. Curiously, these take the name from the French title of the film *Whisky Galore* (UK 1948) – source Philip Kemp, *Lethal Innocence: The Cinema of Alexander Mackendrick* (1991). 'This is really nothing but Leninism à go-go!' – *The New York Times* (24 September 1966).

—— agonistes PHRASES The title of John Milton's poem *Samson Agonistes* (1671) refers to the biblical Samson coupled with the Greek word for 'champion/combatant'. T. S. Eliot used the format for his own poetic drama *Sweeney Agonistes* (1932), where the proletarian hero is called Sweeney.

(an) agonizing reappraisal A process of reconsideration in politics, possibly before a decision is taken to make a U-turn. The reassessment of position has usually been forced on the reappraiser. The modern use stems from a speech that John Foster Dulles, US Secretary of State, made to the National Press Club, Washington DC, in December 1953: 'When I was in Paris last week, I said that . . . the United States would have to undertake an agonizing reappraisal of basic foreign policy in relation to Europe.' Further examples: 'As in response to new directions from an agonising reappraisal in MCC's room at lunch, the scoring spurted as Cowdrey twice swung Benaud to the leg fence' – *Star* (9 December 1958); 'The nation's rogue elephants rampage, shattering complacency and compelling many to an agonizing reappraisal' – Kenneth Gregory, *The First Cuckoo* (1978); 'He forecast a

period of agonizing reappraisal for Nato. The flexible response strategy was now clearly untenable for many reasons, so a new approach would be essential' – *The Times* (27 June 1987).

(the) agony and the ecstasy Phrase for the supposed turmoil of artistic expression – a colourful coinage, now used only in mockery. *The Agony and the Ecstasy* is the title of a novel (1961; film US 1965) by Irving Stone, about Michelangelo and the painting of the Sistine Chapel. Compare what the novelist William Faulkner said in his speech accepting the Nobel Prize for Literature (10 December 1950): '[Whatever was] worth the agony and the sweat [was worth writing about].'

(an) agony aunt One who answers questions about personal problems posed by readers of a newspaper or magazine. Hence the term **agony column**, originally applied to what would now be called a 'personal column' in newspapers, containing messages for missing relatives (by the 1860s). From the 1930s onwards, the name has been given to the space in which 'advice' journalism appears. Neither phrase was in wide use until the 1970s, and neither is much used outside Britain. **Sob sister** is a similar term for one who allows readers to weep on his or her shoulder. Although the name may be of American invention, such an adviser has long been known in British women's magazines, the subjects formerly being household management, etiquette and bringing up the family. Such columnists proliferated after the Second World War and some achieved eminence for sympathetic advice and information. See also MISS LONELYHEARTS.

aha, me proud beauty (I've got you where I want you)! A phrase suggestive of 19th-century melodramas or, at least, parodies of their style. Dryden has the phrase 'proud beauty' in *Oedipus* (1679).

ahh, Bisto! Advertising line for Bisto gravy browning, which has been promoted with this cry in the UK since 1919. The name 'Bisto' is a hidden slogan, too. When the Cerebos company first put it on the market in 1910, the product did not have a name. According to legend, the initial letters of the proposed slogan 'Browns, Seasons, Thickens In One' were rearranged to produce 'BISTO'. The Bisto Kids, drawn by Will Owen, first appeared in 1919, sniffing a wisp of gravy aroma and murmuring, 'Ahh Bisto!' This is a phrase much played on in political cartoon captions over the years – 'Ah, Blitzo!'; 'Ah, Bizerta!'; 'Ah, Crippso!'; 'Ah! Winston!'; 'Ah! Coupon free!', and so on.

ah, Woodbine – a great little cigarette!
A slogan current in 1957. Norman Hackforth – the Mystery Voice from BBC radio's *Twenty Questions* – spoke the line memorably in TV ads.

—— Aid PHRASES
In the mid-1980s, it became fashionable to give names with the suffix ' —— aid' to charitable fund-raising events. This stemmed from the first such event – the recording of 'Do They Know It's Christmas', performed in 1984 by an ad hoc group of pop singers and musicians called **Band Aid**, in punning allusion to the Band-Aid brand of medical dressing. This record, successfully drawing attention to those suffering in the Ethiopian civil war and famine, prepared the way for the notable foundation of the **Live Aid** rock concert of July 1985. Similar, though in some cases much smaller-scale, events followed, including Sport Aid (sponsored athletes), Mandarin Aid (civil servants), School Aid (children), Fashion Aid, Academy Aid (painters), Sheep Aid (agricultural events in Yorkshire) and Deaf Aid (no, only joking).

ain't it a shame, eh? ain't it a shame?
Catchphrase spoken by Carleton Hobbs as a nameless man who told banal tales ('I waited for hours in the fish queue . . . and a man took my plaice'), in the BBC radio show *ITMA* (1939–49). He always prefaced and concluded his remarks with, 'Ain't it a shame?'

ain't it grand to be bloomin' well dead?
Title line of a song (1932) by Leslie Sarony, the British entertainer and writer (1897–1985).

aisle See GO UP THE.

Ajax defying the lightning
Phrase for a particular artistic pose in 19th-century sculpture or painting. From Charles Dickens, *Bleak House*, Chap. 18 (1853): 'Well!' said Mr Boythorn . . . I am looked upon about here, as a second Ajax defying the lightning. Ha ha ha ha!' From Oscar Wilde's New York lecture 'The English Renaissance of Art' (9 January 1882): 'The English [artists'] models form a class entirely by themselves. They are not so picturesque as the Italian, nor so clever as the French, and they have absolutely no tradition, so to speak, of their order. Now and then some old veteran knocks at the studio door, and proposes to sit as Ajax defying the lightning, or as King Lear upon the blasted heath.' The Ajax referred to in this is not the warrior of the siege of Troy but Ajax the Lesser who was at the siege nevertheless and raped Priam's daughter Cassandra after dragging her from a statue of Athena. This so annoyed the goddess that she shipwrecked Ajax on his way home. He clung to a rock, defied the goddess, not to mention the lightning, and was eventually washed off and drowned by Neptune. So, how and when did the allusion turn into a phrase? In the description of Ajax's death in Homer's *Odyssey*, the lightning incident is not mentioned. So is it from a later re-telling? Virgil's *Aeneid* (Bk 1, line 42-) does show him being dealt with by Zeus's bolts. Earlier, the matter was mentioned, though less specifically, by Euripides in his *Trojan Women* and in Ovid's *Metamorphoses* (Bk 14; translated by Dryden, Pope and others). There are a number of representations in art of Ajax the Lesser going about his rapes and so on, but the search is still on for the lightning-defying pose. Was there a particular painting or a sculpture of the event that so fixed the defiant image that it was readily evoked thereafter?

alarums and excursions (sometimes alarms . . .)
Confused noise and activity after the varying use of the phrase in the stage directions of Shakespeare's history plays, notably *Henry VI, Part 3* and *Richard III,* especially during battle scenes. 'Alarum' is a form of 'alarm' (meaning a call to arms) and an 'excursion' is a sally against the enemy. Now used about any sort of confused situation. 'I was a happy child, skipping through the fifties, a time of calm and convention for the middle

classes, with parents thankful for routine and certainty after the alarms and excursions of war' – Kate Adie, *The Kindness of Strangers*, Chap. 2 (2002).

(The) Albany Whether this is a phrase or not rests on one's response to a supposed solecism: is it correct to use the 'The' or not to use the 'The' when talking about Albany, a grand apartment block in Piccadilly, London? Oscar Wilde uses the full phrase 'The Albany' no fewer than three times in *The Importance of Earnest* (1895). He also used it earlier in *The Picture of Dorian Gray*, Chap. 3 (1890). The earliest use so far found of the 'the' being apparently correct usage is in the title of a novel by Marmion Savage, *The Bachelor of the Albany* (1848). Anthony Trollope, *The Small House at Allington*, Chap. 43 (1864), has: 'Plantagenet Palliser . . . felt, as he sat in his chambers in the Albany, that something else was wanting to his happiness.' Charles Dickens describes the character 'Fascination' Fledgeby as living there in *Our Mutual Friend*, Pt 2, Chap. 5 (1865): 'He lived in chambers in the Albany, did Fledgeby, and maintained a spruce appearance'. A resident's letterhead dating from 1888 is shown in Harry Furniss, *Paradise in Piccadilly: the Story of Albany,* but the title of that book (published in 1925) is – so far – the earliest example found of the 'the' being deliberately excluded. Later, Terence Rattigan (who lived in the chambers for a while) gave this description of the setting for Act 1 of his play *While the Sun Shines* (1943): 'The sitting-room of Lord Harpenden's chambers in Albany, London.' So what was it that happened between 1898 and 1925 to give rise to the change? Indeed, what is one to make of the whole question? Perhaps H. Montgomery Hyde has the simplest explanation in *The Annotated Oscar Wilde* (1982): 'The Albany refers to the exclusive apartments off Piccadilly, very popular with bachelors, that had been converted in the early nineteenth century from the Duke of York and Albany's large private house. About the turn of the century it became the custom to allude to it as "Albany" instead of "the" Albany, probably because the latter sounded like a club or pub.'

Alexander weeping for want of worlds to conquer The allusion is, undoubtedly, to Plutarch's wonderful vignette of Alexander the Great to be found in 'Of the Tranquillity of the Mind': 'So reason makes all sorts of life easy, and every change pleasant. Alexander wept when he heard from Anaxarchus that there was an infinite number of worlds, and his friends asking him if any accident had befallen him, he returns this answer: Do not you think it is a matter worthy of lamentation, that, when there is such a vast multitude of them, we have not yet conquered one? But Crates with only his scrip and tattered cloak laughed out his life jocosely, as if he had been always at a festival.' So it was not so much that Alexander wept because he had run out of worlds to conquer but because he felt that he had not even managed to conquer this one.

(an) Alice-blue gown The colour of the garment, a light-greenish blue, takes its name from a particular Alice – daughter of President Theodore Roosevelt. The song 'Alice-blue Gown' was written for her by Joseph McCarthy and Harry Tierney in 1900, when she was sixteen, though apparently it was not published until 1919. In the late 1930s, there was another (British) song, called 'The Girl in the Alice-blue Gown'.

Alice in Wonderland Quoted from almost as extensively as Shakespeare and the Bible, *Alice's Adventures in Wonderland* (1865) and *Through the Looking Glass and What Alice Found There* (1872), both by Lewis Carroll, are alluded to for their particular characters and incidents and as a whole, to denote a mad, fantastic world. From *Chips: the Diaries of Sir Henry Channon*, entry for 30 July 1940 (1967): 'The big FO debate began with an absurd Alice in Wonderland wrangle about procedure which lasted from 3.45 until 5.30 . . . in war time! it was ludicrous in the extreme.'

(is) alive and well and living in —— This format phrase probably began in a perfectly natural way – 'What's happened to old so-and-so?' 'Oh, he's still alive and well and living in Godalming' etc. In the preface to *His Last Bow* (1917), Conan

Doyle wrote: 'The Friends of Mr Sherlock Holmes will be glad to learn that he is still alive and well . . .' The extended form was given a tremendous fillip when the Belgian-born songwriter and singer Jacques Brel (1929–78) became the subject of an off-Broadway musical show entitled *Jacques Brel is Alive and Well and Living in Paris* (1968–72). Quite why M. Brel should have merited this WHERE ARE THEY NOW? treatment is not too apparent, but the format caught on. *The Listener* (3 October 1968), quoting the *Daily Mail*, stated: 'The *Goon Show* is not dead. It is alive and well, living in Yorkshire and operating under the name of BBC Radio Leeds.' The format had earlier probably been used in religious sloganeering, possibly prompted by *Time* Magazine's famous cover (*circa* 1966), 'IS GOD DEAD?' The *New Statesman* (26 August 1966) quoted a graffito, 'God is alive and living in Argentina'. This suggests that the formula might have been used originally in connection with Nazi war criminals who had escaped prosecution and lived unharmed in South America. Other graffiti have included: 'God is not Dead – but Alive and Well and working on a Much Less Ambitious Project' – quoted in *The Guardian* (27 November 1975); 'Jesus Christ is alive and well and signing copies of the Bible at Foyles' (quoted in 1980). A headline from *The Independent* (25 June 1990): 'Socialism is alive and well and living in Moscow'. In a letter to *The Independent* Magazine (13 March 1993), M. H. I. Wright wrote: 'When I was a medical student and young house physician 50 years ago, we had to write very detailed case-sheets on every patient admitted. Under the heading "Family History", we detailed each member of his family – for example, "Father, died of heart diseases in 1935; Mother, alive and well and living in London." One pedantic consultant insisted we drop the word "alive" because, as he said, how could the relative be "dead and well"?' On the other hand, a US film in 1975 was burdened with the title *Sheila Devine Is Dead and Living in New York*. 'The last English eccentric is alive and well and living comfortably in Oakland' – *Time* Magazine (5 September 1977); 'The golden age detective story is alive and well' – review in *The Times* of Ruth Rendell's *Put*

On By Cunning (1981); 'Socialism is alive and well and living in Moscow' – *The Independent* (25 June 1990).

all animals are equal but some animals are more equal than others A fictional slogan from George Orwell's *Animal Farm* (1945), his commentary on the totalitarian excesses of Communism. It had been anticipated: Hesketh Pearson recalled in his biography of the actor/manager Sir Herbert Beerbohm Tree (1956) that Tree wished to insert one of his own epigrams in a play by Stephen Phillips called *Nero*, produced in 1906. It was: 'All men are equal – except myself.' In Noël Coward's *This Year of Grace* (1928), there is this exchange – *Pellet:* 'Men are all alike.' *Wendle:* 'Only some more than others.' The saying alludes, of course, to Thomas Jefferson's 'All men are created equal and independent', from the Preamble to the American Declaration of Independence (1776). It has, perhaps, the makings of a format phrase in that it is more likely to be used to refer to humans than to animals. Only the second half of the phrase need actually be spoken, the first half being understood: 'You-Know-Who [Mrs Thatcher] is against the idea [televising parliament]. There aren't card votes at Westminster, but some votes are more equal than others' – *The Guardian* (15 February 1989).

all balls and bang me arse! Sheer nonsense. An intensifier of the basic **all balls!** British use, probably since the 1910s.

(I'm) all behind like the cow's tail What people say when they are behind with their tasks. The expression 'all behind like a cow's tail' has also been used to describe a person who is always last or is of a daydreaming disposition. 'C. H. Rolph' wrote in *London Particulars* (1980): 'Grandma Hewitt [his grandmother] was a walking repository, rather than a dictionary, of clichés and catchphrases; and I have often wished she could have been known to Mr Eric Partridge during the compilation of his delectable dictionaries. Both she and I . . . could pre-date many of [his] attributions. Here are four examples . . . all of which were common currency in my Edwardian childhood: "Just what the doctor ordered", "Are you kidding?", "Cheats never prosper", and "All behind like a cow's tail".' There is also, of course, the expression 'All behind like Barney's bull'.

all bitter and twisted Said about someone who is psychologically mixed-up and shows it. Sometimes made light of in the form 'all twitter and bisted'. Since the 1940s, at least.

all contributions gratefully received As with **please give generously/all you can**, this is a standard phrase from charitable appeals for money. But it is also used jokingly when accepting gifts of almost anything – another helping of food, even a sexual favour. Probably since the first half of the 20th century.

——, all day! A response to the question 'What day is it?' or 'What's the date?' For example, 'Tuesday/the 13th . . . all day!' In use since the late 19th century.

(it's) all done and dusted Meaning, 'that task has been completed'. Heard in a Yorkshire hotel in 1996, but much older.

(it's) all done with mirrors Used as a way of describing how anything has been accomplished when the method is not obvious. Originally, a way of explaining how conjuring tricks and stage illusions were performed when some, indeed, were done using mirrors – but without going into detail. Admiration, but also a suspicion of trickery, is implicit in the phrase. Noël Coward uses it in *Private Lives* (1930); *They Do It With Mirrors* is the title of an Agatha Christie thriller (1952). Compare SMOKE AND MIRRORS.

all dressed up and nowhere to go A phrase used to describe forlorn indecision comes (slightly altered) from a song popularized by the American comedian Raymond Hitchcock in *The Beauty Shop* (New York 1914) and *Mr Manhattan* (London 1915): 'When you're all dressed up and no place to go, / Life seems dreary, weary and slow.' The words gained further emphasis when they were used by William Allen White to describe the Progressive Party following Theodore Roosevelt's decision to retire from presidential competition in 1916. He said it was: 'All dressed up with nowhere to go.'

The *OED2* has the phrase starting life in a song by 'G. Whiting' (1912), 'When You're All Dressed Up and Have No Place to Go'. But Lowe's *Directory of Popular Music* ascribes the song to Silvio Hein and Benjamin Burt.

all dressed up like a Christmas tree Gaudily attired – not a compliment. Since the late 19th century.

all dressed up like a pox-doctor's clerk Flashily attired – not a compliment. Since the late 19th century. Presumably the implication is that a pox-doctor's clerk would have plenty of money and that he would not spend on tasteful clothing.

allegedly A single word slipped into libellous statements to defuse them on the BBC TV topical quiz, *Have I Got News For You* (1990–). Principally employed by the original host, Angus Deayton. The approach had much earlier been used by David Frost on BBC TV, *That Was The Week That Was* (1962–4).

alley See I WOULDN'T LIKE TO MEET.

all for one and one for all [*tous pour un, un pour tous*] The motto of the Three Musketeers in the novel *Les Trois Mousquetaires* (1844–5) by Alexandre Dumas. It had appeared earlier in Shakespeare's *Lucrece*, lines 141–4 (1594), as: 'The aim of all is but to nurse the life / With honour, wealth and ease, in waning age; / And in this aim there is much thwarting strife / That *one for all, or all for one* we gage [= pledge].' Dumas apparently derived the motto from a form of words he recorded in an account of a journey to Switzerland (1833). In the Berne Parliament, the pledge given by representatives of the regions who formed the basis of the Swiss federation in AD 1291 is rendered as '*Einer für alle, alle für einen.*' Compare 'Each for all and all for each' – Co-Operative Wholesale Society (UK, 20th century).

all fur coat and no knickers Given to show and having no modesty; poverty concealed in an effort to keep up appearances; elegant on the outside but sleazy underneath, when describing a certain type of woman. Encountered in a Welsh context (1988), it was also the title of play that toured the UK in the same year. A variant (1993), said to come from Lanca-shire (or, at least, from the North of England), is: 'Red hat, no knickers'. A similar expression is **all kid gloves and no drawers** This last was given as an example of colourful Cockney bubble-pricking by the actor Kenneth Williams in *Just Williams* (1985). He said it was used in his youth (1930s) to denote the meretri-cious. 'Silk stockings and no knickers' is another version.

all gas and gaiters To do with the church, especially the higher clergy. *All Gas and Gaiters* was the title of a BBC TV comedy series about the clergy (1966–70). The title was taken from Charles Dickens, *Nicholas Nickleby*, Chap. 49 (1838–9): 'All is gas and gaiters.' Gaiters (leg coverings below the knee) have been traditionally associated with bishops. 'Gas' presumably hints at their accustomed volubility.

all gong and no dinner All talk and no action. What you would say of a loud-mouthed person, somewhat short on achievement. Current by the mid-20th century. *Partridge/Slang* has a citation from BBC Radio's *The Archers* in 1981. Michael Grosvenor Myer, Cambridgeshire (1999), produced a Texan variant: 'All hat and no cattle.'

all good things must come to an end A proverbial expression meaning 'pleasure cannot go on for ever'. Spoken at the completion of absolutely any activity that is enjoyable (but usually said with a touch of piety). *CODP* points out that the addition of the word 'good' to this proverb is a recent development. 'To all things must be an end' can be traced back to the 15th century. There is a version from 1440, and, as 'Everything has an end', the idea appears in Chaucer's *Troilus and Criseyde* (1385). The Book of Common Prayer version of Psalm 119:96 is: 'I see that all things come to an end.'

all hands on deck! Everybody help. Obviously of naval origin – but now used in any emergency, serious or slight, domestic or otherwise. Since the 19th century?

all hell broke loose Pandemonium broke out. This descriptive phrase probably derives its popularity from its use in

Milton's *Paradise Lost*, Bk. 4, line 917 (1667), when the Archangel Gabriel speaks to Satan: 'Wherefore with thee / Came not all hell broke loose.' But Milton had been anticipated in this by the author of a Puritan pamphlet, *Hell Broke Loose: or, a Catalogue of Many of the Spreading Errors, Heresies and Blasphemies of These Times, for Which We are to be Humbled* (1646). Also, in Robert Greene's play *Friar Bacon and Friar Bungay* (*circa* 1589), the character Miles has the line: 'Master, master, master up! Hell's broken loose.' And, as 'I thinke, hell breake louse', it occurs in a play called *Misogonus* (1577). As an idiomatic phrase it was certainly well established by 1738 when Jonathan Swift compiled his *Polite Conversation*. There is 'A great Noise below' and Lady Smart exclaims: 'Hey, what a clattering is there; one would think Hell was broke loose'.

all human life is there Advertising line used to promote the *News of the World* newspaper (*circa* 1958) and taken from Henry James, 'Madonna of the Future' (1879): 'Cats and monkeys, monkeys and cats – all human life is there.' In 1981, Maurice Smelt, the advertising copywriter, commented: '"All human life is there" was my idea, but I don't, of course, pretend that they were my words. I simply lifted them from *The Oxford Dictionary of Quotations*. I didn't bother to tell the client that they were from Henry James, suspect-ing that, after the "Henry James – who he?" stage, he would come up with tiresome arguments about being too high-hat for his readership. I did check whether we were clear on copyright, which we were by a year or two . . . I do recall its use as baseline in a tiny little campaign trailing a series that earned the *News of the World* a much-publicized but toothless rebuke from the Press Council. The headline of that campaign was: '"I've been a naughty girl," says Diana Dors". The meiosis worked, as the *News of the World* knew it would. They ran an extra million copies of the first issue of the series.'

all I know is what I read in the papers I'm just an ordinary guy. From a saying much used by Will Rogers, the American cowboy comedian of the 1920s. For example, from *The Letters of a Self-Made Diplomat to His President* (1927): 'Dear Mr Coolidge: Well all I know is just what I read in the papers.'

(it's) all in a lifetime (or **all in one's lifetime**). 'That's life, IT'S ALL PART OF LIFE'S RICH PAGEANT' – reflective, philosophical phrase, implying resignation to whatever happens or has happened. Mostly American use? Since 1849. P. G. Wodehouse concludes a letter (23 July 1923) in which he describes how he was knocked down by a car: 'Byt, my gosh! doesn't it just show that we are here today and gone tomorrow! . . . Oh, well, it's all in a lifetime!' Hence, the title of Walter Allen's novel *All In a Lifetime* (1959).

(it's) all in the family A saying with the implication that there's no need to be over-punctilious or stand on ceremony, or fuss too much about obligations, because nobody outside the family is affected and those who are in the family will understand. For example, 'it's okay for me to borrow money or clothing from my sister without asking her first . . . because it's all in the family.' Compare, 'We are all friends here!' *All In the Family* was the title of the American TV version (1971–83) of the BBC's sitcom *Till Death Us Do Part*. The respective main characters were Archie Bunker and Alf Garnett, racists and bigots both. The phrase had a double meaning as the show's title: that Archie's rants would be mortifying if overheard by anyone outside the family and that such wildly different types of people find themselves related to each other. There is not a trace of the phrase in the *OED2*. However, there is an 1874 citation, 'all *outside* the family, tribe or nation were usually held as enemies', which may hint at the possible existence of an opposite construction. The phrase occurs in Chap. 25 of James Fenimore Cooper, *The Pioneers* (1823): 'David says, in the Psalms – no, it was Solomon, but it was all in the family – Solomon said, there was a time for all things; and, in my humble opinion, a fishing party is not the moment for discussing important subjects.' Then there is Herman Melville, *Moby Dick*, Chap. 21 (1851) in which Elijah is trying to warn Ishmael and Queequeg against the *Pequod*

and its captain: '"Morning to ye! morning to ye!" he rejoined, again moving off. "Oh! I was going to warn ye against – but never mind, never mind – it's all one, all in the family too; – sharp frost this morning, ain't it?"' From Robert Louis Stevenson, *Catriona*, Chap. 9 (1893): 'It was old Lovat that managed the Lady Grange affair; if young Lovat is to handle yours, it'll be all in the family.' From Bret Harte, *A Ward of Colonel Starbottle's* (1903): '"Don't mind us, Colonel," said Judge Beeswinger, "it's all in the family here, you know! And – now I look at the girl – hang it all! she does favor you, old man. Ha! ha!"' From Jack London, *The Sea-Wolf,* Chap. 32 (1904): 'All hands went over the side, and there I was, marooned on my own vessel. It was Death's turn, and it's all in the family anyway.' All these citations – even the Stevenson – confirm a likely American origin for the phrase. It is hardly known elsewhere.

all jam and Jerusalem A popular misconception of the local Women's Institute groups in the UK is that their members are solely concerned with making jam, flower arranging and singing the Blake/Parry anthem 'Jerusalem'. This encapsulation is said to date from the 1920s. Simon Goodenough's history of the movement was called *Jam and Jerusalem* (1977).

all joints on the table shall/will be carved Table manners instruction, i.e. elbows off the table. *Casson/Grenfell* (1982) has it – as well as, 'No uncooked joints on the table, please.'

all mouth and trousers Describing a type of man who is 'all talk' rather than sexually active or successful (compare the earlier 'all prick and breeches'). Since the mid-20th century? *Slanguage* describes it now as 'an insulting (non-sexual) catch phrase'. From BBC radio's *Round the Horne* (15 May 1966): 'There he goes, his kilt swinging in the breeze – all mouth music and no trousers.'

all my eye and Betty Martin Meaning, 'nonsense'. *OED2* finds a letter written in 1781 by one 'S. Crispe' stating: 'Physic, to old, crazy Frames like ours, is all my eye and Betty Martin – (a sea phrase that Admiral Jemm frequently makes use of)'.

Grose (1785) has 'That's my eye betty martin, an answer to any one that attempts to impose or humbug.' The phrase is used in *Punch* (11 December 1841). *Apperson* has 'Only your eye and Miss Elizabeth Martin' in 1851. The shorter expressions 'all my eye' or 'my eye' predate this. As to how it originated, *Brewer* (1894) has the suggestion (from Joe Miller, 1739) that it was a British sailor's garbled version of words heard in an Italian church: '*O, mihi, beate Martine* [Oh, grant me, blessed St Martin]', but this sounds too ingenious and, besides, no prayer is known along those lines. Probably there *was* a Betty Martin of renown in the 18th century (*Partridge/Catch Phrases* finds mention of an actress with the name whose favourite expression is supposed to have been 'My eye!') and her name was co-opted for popular use. Some people use a 'Peggy Martin' version.

all of a doodah   In a state of dithering excitement. Known by 1915. From P. G. Wodehouse, *Jeeves and the Feudal Spirit*, Chap. 14 (1954): 'A glance was enough to show me that he [Uncle Tom] was all of a doodah.'

all of a tiswas   Meaning, 'confused, in a state'. Known by 1960. This might be from an elaboration of 'tizz' or 'tizzy' and there may be a hint of 'dizziness' trying to get in. But no one really knows. The acronym of 'Today Is Saturday, Wear A Smile' seems not to have anything to do with the meaning of the word and to have been imposed later. The acronym-slogan was the apparent reason for the title *Tiswas* being given to a children's TV show (UK 1974–82), famous for its buckets-of-water-throwing and general air of mayhem. Broadcast on Saturday mornings, its atmosphere was certainly noisy and confused.

all one's Christmasses have come at once   When one has benefited from lots of luck or been snowed under with gifts. Since the second half of the 20th century?

(to say that) all one's geese are swans Meaning, 'to exaggerate or overestimate the worth of one's children/pupils/anyone dear to one – and to see them in an especially rosy light.' Burton's *The Anatomy of Melancholy*, 'Democritus to the Reader' (1621), has 'All his Geese are swannes'. The actor David Garrick wrote to the Duke of Devonshire about a visit to Milan (1763) and the warmth of his reception by the Governor of Lombardy: 'You would think, as You Us'd to say to me, that all my Geese were Swans . . . there was no Civility that I did not receive from him.' Horace Walpole wrote of Sir Joshua Reynolds (in a letter of 1786): 'All his own geese are swans, as the swans of others are geese.'

all our yesterdays   From Macbeth's speech in Shakespeare's *Macbeth*, V.v.22 (1606): 'To-morrow, and to-morrow, and to-morrow,/ Creeps in this petty pace from day to day, / To the last syllable of re-corded time; / And all our yesterdays have lighted fools / The way to dusty death. Out, out, brief candle! / Life's but a walking shadow; a poor player,/ That struts and frets his hour upon the stage,/ And then is heard no more: it is a tale/ Told by an idiot, full of sound and fury,/ Signifying nothing.' This speech has proved a rich source of title phrases. *Tomorrow and Tomorrow* was a film (US 1932); *All Our Yesterdays* was the title of Granada TV's programme (1960–73) devoted to old newsreels and of the actor Edward G. Robinson's memoirs (1974); *The Way to Dusty Death* was the title of a 1973 novel by Alastair Maclean; *Brief Candles* was the title of a collection of short stories (1930) by Aldous Huxley; *Told By an Idiot* was a 1923 novel by Rose Macaulay; 'full of sound and fury' is echoed in the title of William Faulkner's novel *The Sound and The Fury* (1929).

all over bar the shouting   Almost com-pletely over, finished or decided, except for any talking and argument that will not alter the outcome. Said of a contest or event. Of sporting origin, with the shout-ing, say, the appeal against a referee's decision in boxing. Known since 1842 (in the form '. . . *but* the shouting'). Groucho Marx says 'All over but the shooting' in *The Cocoanuts* (US 1929). A Cole Porter song (1937) has the title 'It's All Over But the Shouting'. 'But if the Rhodesia affair is all over bar the shouting, can the same be said about South Africa?' – *Western Morn-*

ing News (25 September 1976); 'Fewer than half of the trusts had made 3 per cent offers and only half of those were without strings. "He seems to be giving the impression the pay round is all over bar the shouting. He couldn't be more wrong," she said' – *The Times* (15 May 1995).

all over the place like a mad woman's underclothes In her book *Daddy, We Hardly Knew You* (1989), the writer Germaine Greer recalls that, when she was growing up in Australia in the 1940s, this was her mother's phrase to describe an untidy room. In consequence, Greer used *The Madwoman's Underclothes* as the title of a collection of her assorted writings (1986). *Partridge/Slang* does not find this precise expression but in discussing the phrase 'all over the place like a mad woman's shit' points to the euphemistic variants cited by G.A. Wilkes in *A Dictionary of Australian Colloquialisms* (1978): '. . . like a mad woman's knitting . . . custard . . . lunch box.' So, Australian it seems to be.

all passion spent 'And calm of mind, all passion spent' – line 1758 (the last line) of Milton's dramatic poem *Samson Agonistes* (1671). Hence, *All Passion Spent*, the title of a novel (1931) by Vita Sackville-West (a study of ageing and independence in old age). 'The story of it belongs to a later and final book still to be written: of our hero, ambition laid aside, all passion spent, learning to accept defeat, growing old gracefully' – Arthur Bryant, *Samuel Pepys: The Saviour of the Navy*, Preface (1949 edn).

all piss and wind Empty, vacuous – of a man prone to bombast and no achievement. Apparently derived from the earlier saying, 'All wind and piss like a barber's cat', known by 1800.

all publicity is good publicity A modern proverb dating from at least the 1960s, but probably as old as the public relations industry. Alternative forms include: **there's no such thing as bad publicity**; **there's no such thing as over-exposure – only bad exposure**; **don't read it – measure it**; and **I don't care what the papers say about me as long as they spell my name right**. The latter saying has been attributed to the American Tammany leader 'Big Tim'

Sullivan. *CODP* includes it in the form 'Any publicity is good publicity' and finds no example before 1974. In Dominic Behan's *My Brother Brendan* (1965), however, the Irish playwright is quoted as saying, 'There is no such thing as bad publicity except your own obituary.' James Agate in *Ego 7* (for 19 February 1944) quotes Arnold Bennett as having said, 'All praise is good,' and adds: 'I suppose the same could be said about publicity.'

all quiet on the Western Front A familiar phrase from military communiqués and newspaper reports on the Allied side in the First World War. Also taken up jocularly by men in the trenches to describe peaceful inactivity. It was used as the title of the English translation of the novel *Im Westen nichts Neues* [From the Western Front – Nothing to Report] (1929; film US 1930) by the German writer Erich Maria Remarque. The title is ironic – a whole generation was being destroyed while newspapers reported that there was 'no news in the west'. *Partridge/Catch Phrases* hears in it echoes of 'All quiet on the Shipka Pass' – cartoons of the 1877–8 Russo-Turkish War that Partridge says had a vogue in 1915–6, though he never heard the allusion made himself. For no very good reason, Partridge rules out any connection with the American song 'All Quiet Along the Potomac'. This, in turn, came from a poem called 'The Picket Guard' (1861) by Ethel Lynn Beers, a sarcastic commentary on General Brinton McClellan's policy of delay at the start of the Civil War. The phrase (alluding to the Potomac River which runs through Washington DC) had been used in reports from McLellan's Union headquarters and put in Northern newspaper headlines. **All quiet along the Potomac** continues to have some use as a portentous way of saying that nothing is happening.

all right for some! Meaning, 'some people have all the luck!' – a good-humoured expression of envy. 'I'm just off to the West Indies for an all-expenses paid holiday' – 'All right for some!' From the mid-20th century.

all roads lead to Rome Whatever route you follow (especially in thinking), you will reach a common objective. The earliest use of this proverb in English is in a treatise by Chaucer on the astrolabe (1391), in which he states, 'Right as diverse paths leden diverse folk the righte way to Rome'. In Medieval Latin, this was expressed as: *'mille vie ducunt hominem per secula Romam* [a thousand roads lead man for ever towards Rome].' This reflects the geographical fact that the Roman road system did indeed seem to radiate outwards from Rome.

all rowed fast, but none so fast as stroke A nonsensical compliment relating to effort. In *Sandford of Merton*, Chap. 12 (1903), Desmond Coke wrote: 'His blade struck the water a full second before any other: the lad had started well. Nor did he flag as the race wore on: as the others tired, he seemed to grow more fresh, until at length, as the boats began to near the winning-post, his oar was dipping into the water nearly twice as often as any other.' This is deemed to be the original of the modern proverbial saying – which is used, for example, in its 'all rowed fast' form in 'The Challenge' episode of the TV adaptation of *The Forsyte Saga* (1967). The 'misquotation' is sometimes thought to have been a deliberate distortion of something written earlier than Coke, by Ouida, 'designed to demonstrate the lady's ignorance of rowing, or indeed of any male activity' – Peter Farrer in *Oxford Today* (Hilary, 1992). The *Oxford Companion to English Literature* (1985) refers to the ridicule Ouida suffered for 'her inaccuracies in matters of men's sports and occupations', of which this might be one.

all's fair in love, war and —— The basic proverb here is 'All is fair in love and war', which *CODP* finds in the form 'Love and war are all one' by 1620 and as well established by the 19th century. But nowadays the extended form – to include almost anything that the speaker might wish, most frequently politics – is more common. In 1982, Leonard Miall concluded a BBC radio talk ('Byways in a Broadcasting Career') with: 'I suppose that all's fair in love, war and party politicals [i.e. broadcasts].' Michael Foot MP was quoted in 1986 as having said, 'I had better recall before someone else does,

that I said on one occasion that all was fair in love, war and parliamentary procedure.' 'The Shadow Chancellor, Mr John Smith . . . said he did not expect to receive any special favours from his political opponents. "All is fair in love, war and parliamentary politics," he added' – *The Guardian* (23 January 1989).

all-singing, all-dancing The worlds of computing and finance have both taken to using a phrase whose origins are pure Hollywood. For once, it is possible to be very precise about the source of a piece of popular phraseology. First, the computing use. From a report in *The Guardian* (3 October 1984) about a new police computer called 'Holmes': 'Sir Lawrence Byford is proud that Britain got there first. Holmes, he claims, is unique. "It should provide our detectives with unrivalled facilities when dealing with crimes such as homicides and serious sexual offences . . . it's the all-singing all-dancing act." The only thing it can't do, it seems, is play the violin.' And from a special report on computers in the same paper (24 June 1985): 'I'm knocking these present notes together on the word-processor incorporated into Jazz, the all-singing, all-dancing "integrated" package from the Lotus Development Corporation.' *Partridge/Catch Phrases* dates the start of the computing use to about 1970. The phrase is used every bit as much when writing about financial 'packages'. From a special report in *The Times* (8 November 1985): 'The City's financial institutions have been busily preparing themselves for the changes. Many of the large stockbroking firms have forged links with banks: conceding their independence but benefiting from the massive capital injection which many believe will be necessary to cope with the new look all-singing-and-dancing exchange.' The meaning is reasonably clear. What you should anticipate getting in each sphere is a multipurpose something or other, with every possible feature, that may or may not 'perform' well. A dictionary of jargon (1984) goes so far as to give the general business meaning as 'super-glamorised, gimmicky, flashy', when referring to a version of any stock product. As such, the phrase has been used in many other fields as well – not least in show business. The source? In 1929, when sound came to the movies, the very first Hollywood musical, MGM's *Broadway Melody*, was promoted with posters bearing the slogan: '*The New Wonder of the Screen!* / ALL TALKING / ALL SINGING / ALL DANCING / *Dramatic Sensation.*' Oddly enough, in that same year, two rival studios both hit on the same selling pitch. Alice White in *Broadway Babes* (using Warners' Vitaphone system) was '100% TALKING, SINGING, DANCING'. And Radio Picture's *Rio Rita* (with Bebe Daniels) was billed as 'ZIEGFELD'S FABULOUS ALL-TALKING, ALL-SINGING SUPER SCREEN SPECTACLE'. It was natural that the studios should wish to promote the most obvious aspect of the new sound cinema but it is curious that they should all have used much the same phrase.

all Sir Garnet Meaning 'all correct', this phrase alludes to Sir Garnet Wolseley (1833–1913), a soldier noted for his organizational powers, who led several successful military expeditions 1852–5 and helped improve the lot of the Other Ranks. The expression was known by 1894. Wolseley is also celebrated as 'The Modern Major-General' in Gilbert and Sullivan's *Pirates of Penzance* (1879). From the same source, *Sir Garnet* is the name of a boat in *Coot Club*, the novel (1934) by Arthur Ransome.

all sorts *Street Talk* (1986) defines this as 'all sorts of people, things or activities. Often said pejoratively of people, as in, "You get all sorts in a neighbourhood like that".' The proverb 'It takes all sorts to make a world' was known by 1620. There may also be a modern allusion to Bassett's Liquorice Allsorts, the brand of confectionery that comes in many different colours and shapes.

all's well that ends well The Reverend Francis Kilvert's diary entry for 1 January 1878 noted: 'The hind axle broke and they thought they would have to spend the night on the road . . . All's well that ends well and they arrived safe and sound.' Is the allusion to the title of Shakespeare's play *All's Well That Ends Well* (*circa* 1603) or to something else? In fact, it was a proverbial expression before Shakespeare

used it. *CODP* finds 'If the ende be wele, than is alle wele' in 1381, and points to the earlier form 'Wel is him that wel ende mai'. See also under WAR AND PEACE.

all systems go! In a state of readiness to begin an enterprise. From the US space programme of the 1960s.

all that heaven allows Peggy Fenwick's script for the film with this title (US 1955) has widow Cary (Jayne Wyman) falling for her gardener, Ron (Rock Hudson), to the consternation of her class-conscious friends. Despite Wyman's quoting a hefty chunk from Thoreau's *Walden*, no hint is given as to where the title of the film comes from. In fact, it comes from the poem 'Love and Life' by John Wilmot, Earl of Rochester (1647–80). This was included in Quiller-Couch's *Oxford Book of English Verse* (1900) – that great repository of quotations later to be used as film titles: 'Then talk not of inconstancy, / False hearts, and broken vows; / If I by miracle can be / This live-long minute true to thee, / 'Tis all that Heaven allows.'

all the news that's fit to print This slogan was devised by Adolph S. Ochs when he bought *The New York Times*, and it has been used in every edition since – at first on the editorial page, on 25 October 1896, and from the following February on the front page near the masthead. It became the paper's war cry in its 1890s' battle against formidable competition in New York City from the *World*, the *Herald* and the *Journal*. At worst, it sounds like a slogan for the suppression of news. However, no newspaper prints everything. It has been parodied by Howard Dietz as 'All the news *that fits* we print'.

all the President's men Carl Bernstein and Bob Woodward gave the title *All the President's Men* to their first Watergate book (1974; film US 1976). It might seem to allude to the lines from the nursery rhyme 'Humpty Dumpty' (first recorded in 1803): 'All the king's horses / And all the king's men, / Couldn't put Humpty together again.' There is also a Robert Penn Warren novel (1946; filmed US 1949), *All the King's Men*, based on the life of the southern demagogue Huey 'Kingfish' Long. More directly, the Watergate book took its title from a saying of Henry Kissinger's at the time of the 1970 Cambodia invasion: 'We are all the President's men and we must behave accordingly' – quoted in Kalb and Kalb, *Kissinger* (1974).

all the world and his wife   Meaning, 'everybody' – though the phrase is in decline now after the feminism of the 1970s. Christopher Anstey in *The New Bath Guide* (1766) has: 'How he welcomes at once all the world and his wife, / And how civil to folk he ne'er saw in his life.' Jonathan Swift included it in *Polite Conversation* (1738): 'Who were the Company? – Why; there was all the World and his Wife.' There is an equivalent French expression: 'All the world and his father'. A letter from Lord Byron to Thomas Moore (29 February 1816) has: 'I am at war with "all the world and his wife" or rather, "all the world and *my* wife" are at war with me.' From F. Scott Fitzgerald, *The Great Gatsby*, Chap. 4 (1926): 'On Sunday morning while church bells rang in the villages alongshore, the world and its mistress returned to Gatsby's house and twinkled hilariously on his lawn.'

all the world loves a lover   This modernish proverbial saying was used by James Agate in a speech on 17 December 1941 (reported in *Ego 5*, 1942). It would appear to be an adaptation of the established expression, 'Everybody/all the world loves a lord' (current by 1869) – not forgetting what the 1st Duke of Wellington apparently once said: 'Soldiers dearly love a lord'. Almost a format saying: Stephen Leacock in *Essays and Literary Studies* (1916) has: 'All the world loves a grafter – at least a genial and ingenious grafter – a Robin Hood who plunders an abbot to feed a beggar'; 'All the world loves a dancer' – the Fred Astaire character in the film *Swing Time* (US 1936).

all things bright and beautiful   The popular hymn (1848) by Mrs Cecil Frances Alexander, of which this is the first line, is still notorious for its other famous lines about (THE) RICH MAN IN HIS CASTLE (THE POOR MAN AT HIS GATE. It also provided the author James Herriot with new titles for his collected volumes about life as a vet – books originally called *It Shouldn't Happen To a Vet, Let Sleeping Vets Lie, Vets Might*

Fly, etc. When these titles were coupled together in three omnibus editions especially for the US market (from 1972), Mrs Alexander's hymn was plundered and they became *All Things Bright and Beautiful, All Creatures Great and Small*, and *All Things Wise and Wonderful. The Lord God Made Them All* was given to a further original volume.

all this and Heaven too   As acknowledged in Rachel Fields's novel with the title *All This and Heaven Too* (1939; film US 1940), Matthew Henry, the English Bible commentator (d. 1714), ascribed the saying to his minister father in his own *Life of Mr Philip Henry* (1698). Compare the film title *All This and World War II* (US 1976) and the classic *Daily Express* newspaper headline on Queen Elizabeth II's Coronation day (2 June 1953): 'ALL THIS – AND EVEREST TOO', announcing the conquest of the world's highest mountain by a British-led expedition.

(an) all-time low   Meaning, 'to the lowest point on record'. Probably American in origin, by the early 20th century. Could the phrase have first referred to weather temperatures? Conversely, there is also **(an) all-time high**, but perhaps less frequently. 'Brings cost of power to new all-time low' – *Saturday Evening Post* (10 June 1933); 'British prestige sunk to yet another all-time low' is included in the parody of sportswriters' clichés by David Frost and Peter Cook included in the book *That Was The Week That Was* (1963); 'A new all-time low in political scurviness, hoodlumism' – Germaine Greer, *The Female Eunuch* (1970); 'Tory MP Phil Gallie was even prompted to predict the party could gain a seat, despite pundits' claims of likely Tory losses and the party's crushing all-time low of 13% in the polls' – *The Sunday Times* (1 May 1994); 'What is also significant about BP's share rise to 386p last week is that it has brought the prospect of a serious assault on the all-time high of 418p much nearer the day' – *The Observer* (1 May 1994).

all we want is the facts, ma'am (or **just the facts, ma'am**). From the American TV series *Dragnet* (1951–8, revived 1967–9). Sgt Joe Friday (played by Jack Webb) had a staccato style of questioning. These were probably the first big phrases to catch on in Britain after the start of commercial TV in 1955. The phrase 'all we want is the facts' was, however, already a cliché when importunate journalists were represented in theatrical sketches. In 'Long-Distance Divorce', a revue sketch from *Nine Sharp* (1938), Herbert Farjeon put the phrase in the mouth of a British reporter interviewing a Hollywood star.

all women look the same in the dark
Contemptuous male view of women as sexual objects – sometimes, 'they all the look the same in the dark'. An established view by the mid-20th century at least. The least politically correct phrase in this book. Compare the similar expression **you don't look at the mantelpiece when you're poking the fire** (an old joke revived by John Osborne in *The Entertainer*, 1957); Ovid's more felicitous and diplomatic version in his *Ars Amatoria* (*circa* 2 BC); 'The dark makes every woman beautiful'; and the English proverb (known by 1546), 'All cats are grey in the dark'. Robert Herrick appeared to say much the same in 'No Difference i' th' Dark' (1648): 'Night makes no difference 'twixt the Priest and the Clerk; / Joan as my Lady is as good i' th' dark.'

(the) almighty dollar An early indication of the currency's all-powerful role in American life. 'The almighty dollar is the only object of worship' – *Philadelphia Public Ledger* (2 December 1836). In fact, this possible first use of the term 'almighty dollar' had just been preceded by Washington Irving's statement in *Knickerbocker Magazine* (12 November 1836): 'The almighty dollar, that great object of universal devotion throughout our land.' Mark Twain took up the theme in his *Notebooks* (1935): 'We Americans worship the almighty dollar! Well, it is a worthier god than Hereditary Privilege.' Earlier, Ben Jonson in his poem 'Epistle to Elizabeth, Countess of Rutland' from *The Forest* (1616) wrote of 'almighty gold'.

almost a gentleman Bill matter (i.e. the descriptive line that appeared on posters) of the British music-hall comedian Billy Bennett (1887–1942). John Osborne took it as the title of his second volume of

memoirs (1991). Compare Daisy Ashford, *The Young Visiters*, Chap. 1 (1919): 'I am not quite a gentleman but you would hardly notice it but can't be helped anyhow.'

along came a spider The title of a cop film (US 2001) starring Morgan Freeman is taken from the nursery rhyme 'Little Miss Muffet', known since 1805 and containing the lines (properly), 'There came a big spider / Who sat down beside her / And frightened Miss Muffet away.' 'Along came a spider' is the more usual American version, however. People like to think that Miss Muffet was Patience, the daughter of Dr Thomas Muffet, an entomologist who died in 1604. If he had been an arachnologist, that would have been even neater.

altered See CASE IS.

altered states Where drugs take you to. *Altered States* is the title of a novel (1979; film US 1980) by Paddy Chayevsky (screen credit as 'Sidney Aaron'). This is a sci-fi thriller about genetic experimentation or, as one of the film guides puts it, about a 'psychophysiologist who hallucinates himself back into primitive states of human evolution, in which guise he emerges to kill'. Might there be a connection with what Dr Albert Hofmann observed of his discovery, the psychedelic drug LSD? He noted in his diary for 1943: 'An intense stimulation of the imagination and *an altered state of awareness of the world*.'

although I says it as shouldn't Phrase of excuse before uttering an indiscretion. Since the 17th century.

always leave them wanting more
Proverbial expression in the world of entertainment. From *The Independent* (8 May 1996): 'Franz Welser-Möst will doubtless have seen the irony in stepping down as music director of the London Philharmonic with a Requiem . . . But there is an old theatrical adage that says "Always leave them wanting more". And – surprise, surprise – I do believe he has.'

always merry and bright The British comedian Alfred Lester (1872–1925) is principally associated with this phrase, although it crops up in all sorts of other places. As 'Peter Doody', a lugubrious jockey in the Lionel Monckton/Howard Talbot/Arthur Wimperis musical comedy *The Arcadians* (1909), he had it as his motto in a song, 'My Motter'. *Punch* quoted the phrase on 26 October 1910. Somerset Maugham in a letter to a friend (1915) wrote: 'I am back on a fortnight's leave, very merry and bright, but frantically busy – I wish it were all over.' An edition of *The Magnet* from 1920 carried an ad for *Merry and Bright* – a comic paper. P. G. Wodehouse used the phrase in *The Indiscretions of Archie* (1921). Larry Grayson suggested that it was used as the billing for Billy Danvers (1884–1964), the British variety entertainer, and so it was, but he may also have used 'Cheeky, Cheery and Chubby'.

always partridge See SEMPER PERDRIX.

always steer towards the gunfire Tackle matters head on. Originally from naval warfare. Or is it 'head towards'?

always true to you in my fashion The song with this title by Cole Porter from *Kiss Me Kate* (1948) echoes, consciously or unconsciously, the line 'I have been faithful to thee, Cynara! in my fashion' from the poem *'Non Sum Qualis Eram'* (1896) by Ernest Dowson.

always verify your references In 1949 Winston Churchill gave an inaccurate account to the House of Commons of when he had first heard the words 'unconditional surrender' from President Roosevelt. Subsequently, in his *The Second World War*, Vol. 4 (1951), Churchill wrote: 'It was only when I got home and searched my archives that I found the facts as they have been set out here. I am reminded of the professor who in his declining hours was asked by his devoted pupils for his final counsel. He replied, "Verify your quotations".' Well, not exactly a 'professor', and not exactly his dying words, and not 'quotations' either. Dr Martin Routh (1755–1854) was President of Magdalen College, Oxford, for sixty-three years. Of the many stories told about Routh, Churchill was groping towards the one where he was asked what precept could serve as a rule of life to an aspiring young man. Said Routh: 'You will find it a

very good practice *always to verify your references, Sir!*' The story was first recorded in this form in July 1878, as Churchill and his amanuenses might themselves have verified. In 1847, Routh gave the advice to John Burgon, later a noted Dean of Chichester, who ascribed it to Routh in an article in the *Quarterly Review* (and subsequently in his *Lives of Twelve Good Men*, 1888 edn). Perhaps Churchill was recalling instead the Earl of Rosebery's version, given in a speech on 23 November 1897: 'Another confirmation of the advice given by one aged sage to somebody who sought his guidance in life, namely, "Always wind up your watch and verify your quotations".'

amazing grace Most people are familiar with the hymn 'Amazing Grace' from the great popular success it had when sung and recorded by Judy Collins in the early 1970s, but it is quite wrong for record companies to label the song 'Trad.'. The words of the hymn were written in the 17th century by John Newton (1725–1807), a reformed slave-trafficker. He (together with the poet William Cowper) wrote the *Olney Hymnbook* of 1779, and this is but one example from that work. The slightly complicated thing is that the *tune* to which 'Amazing Grace' now gets sung *is* a traditional tune – it is an old American one, though some say that it was an anonymous *Scottish* tune before this.

amber nectar Nectar was the (sweet) drink of the gods in classical mythology. 'Amber fluid' and 'amber liquid' are both Australianisms acknowledged by the *Macquarie Dictionary* (1981) for beer (particularly amber-coloured lager). Put all this together and you have the term 'amber nectar' used by Paul Hogan in 1980s' TV commercials in Britain for Foster's. Earlier examples: in 1713, the *London and Country Brewer* was referring to 'the amber-coloured Malt'; 'Barrel of amber' and 'amber fluid' are terms used about beer in *Chicago Gang Wars in Pictures, X Marks the Spot* (1930); 'Amber-coloured fluid' was a term for cocktails used in the novels of the British-born writer E. Phillips Oppenheim (1866–1946).

Amen Corner (1) A place near St Paul's

Cathedral, London, where monks would conclude saying the Pater Noster as they processed on Corpus Christi Day. Hence the other place names: Paternoster Row, Ave Maria Lane, Creed Lane. (2) (in US use by 1860) the name given to the part of a church or meeting house where people sat who used to assist the preacher by calling out the responses, especially 'Amen'. (3) The name of a British pop group of the late 1960s.

America can't stand pat 'To stand pat', meaning 'to keep a fixed position or belief, to stand fast', may have originated in the game of poker, in which you can decline to exchange the cards you are dealt. A 'pat hand' is one that is exactly suited to your purpose. In the 1960 US presidential election, John F. Kennedy pointed to the old slogan 'Stand pat with McKinley' as an example of Republican reaction. Richard Nixon countered with 'America can't stand pat' – until it was politely pointed out to him that he was married to a woman with that name. 'America can't stand still' was rapidly substituted.

American as apple pie The *OED2* does not find this expression before 1977. However, *Flexner* (1976) adds that 'the apple itself is even more American than apple pie and Americans have used the word often'. Confirming the position of the apple as central to American life, *Flexner* also adds: 'Until the 20th century citrus boom, apples – raw, in cider, and cooked in many dishes – were the most popular and talked about fruit in America.'

(the) American dream An expression used to describe the ideals of democracy and standards of living that inspired the founding of the United States. Probably coined by J.T. Adams in *The Epic of America* (1931). Before that, in 'America the Beautiful' (1893), Katharine Lee Bates had written of a 'patriot dream that sees beyond the years'. *The American Dream* is the title of a play (1961) by Edward Albee, and *An American Dream* (1965) is a novel by Norman Mailer.

American Gothic Title of a painting (1930) by Grant Wood (1892–1942) that shows an American farm couple posing

stiffly in front of their Gothic house. The man in overalls carries a pitchfork. The equally dour woman wears an apron. It has been asserted that she is supposed to be his daughter rather than wife. Whatever the case, the artist used his own sister and his dentist as models. Wood's treatment of them has been described as 'half epic, half ironic'. Hence, *American Gothic* – the title of a horror movie (US 1988).

American pie *American Pie* was the title of a rites-of-passage film (US 1999) that follows the famous song 'American Pie' (1971), written and performed by Don McLean. This was a tribute to Buddy Holly and full of allusions to 1960s' America. It has been claimed that 'American Pie' was the name of the aircraft in which Holly was flying when he died but this has been specifically denied by Don McLean. Presumably, if any particular pie was being evoked it was apple pie. See also under JACOB'S JOIN.

amid the glare of television lights See UNDER THE GLARE.

am I not a man and a brother? Accompanying a picture of a kneeling Negro slave in chains, this slogan appeared on a pottery cameo made by Josiah Wedgwood in about 1790. Subsequently, it was frequently reproduced during the fight against slavery and adopted by the Anti-Slavery Society. It also appears in Chap. 6 of Charles Kingsley, *The Water Babies* (1863).

am I right, or am I right? An expression brooking no debate. From American show biz, one suspects. In P. G. Wodehouse & Guy Bolton, *Bring On the Girls*, Chap. 9 (1954) there is: '"It's no good for a revue, Flo [Ziegfeld]. It needs a situation back of it. It needs a guy named Bill and the girl who loves him." He turned to Plum [Wodehouse]. "Am I right or am I right?"' It is also in the script of the films *Gypsy* (US 1962) and *Shampoo* (US 1975). Compare: 'Am I wet, or am I wet?' from Henry Reed, *A Very Great Man Indeed* (1953) and what Mae West asks in *I'm No Angel* (1933): 'Is that elegant, or is that elegant?' It builds of course on the more usual expression 'am I wrong or am I right?' The format endures: 'Is that funny or is that funny?' – from the

BBC radio show *Round the Horne* (10 April 1966); '[Of a dog] is he great or is he great?' – Thames TV, *Rock Follies* (2 March 1976); 'Is that a great theme or is that a great theme?' – same show (9 March 1976).

amor vincit omnia [love conquers all]
One of the best-known proverbial expressions of all. It is from Virgil's *Eclogues*, No. 10, line 69. Chaucer's Prioress had it on her brooch, as mentioned in 'The General Prologue' to *The Canterbury Tales*.

(—— don't) amount to a hill of beans
Meaning, '—— don't amount to anything.' One of the most remembered lines from the film *Casablanca* (US 1942) is the one in which Rick (Humphrey Bogart) says: 'Ilsa, I'm no good at being noble, but it doesn't take much to see that the problems of three little people don't amount to a hill of beans in this crazy world.' An earlier use of the 'hill of beans' phrase – 'Ancestors are a poor excuse for not amounting to a hill of beans' – is quoted in Wolfgang Mieder, *Talk Less and Say More: Vermont Proverbs* (1986) and *OED2* has an 1863 (US) citation of this same version. A parallel expression has 'row of beans'. From P. G. Wodehouse, *Psmith Journalist*, Chap. 9 (1915): 'Look at *Everybody's Magazine*. They didn't amount to a row of beans till Lawson started his "Frenzied Finance" articles.'

Amplex See EVEN YOUR BEST.

amusing, awful and artificial This is reputedly King James II's description of St Paul's Cathedral, London, using three words whose meanings have since changed. He meant that it was 'pleasing, awe-inspiring, and skilfully achieved.' The earliest citation found is in Simeon Potter's *Our Language* (1976). But in William Kent's *An Encyclopedia of London* (1937), it is rather Charles II who in 1675 approved a new design for St Paul's because it was 'very artificial, proper and useful.' As all monarchs from King James I to Queen Anne seem to have had the remark ascribed to them, perhaps a true source for this phrase will never be found.

(the) anatomy of—— A title format, of which the first notable use is *The Anatomy of Melancholy* (1621) by Robert Burton.

That book used the word 'anatomy' in an appropriate manner, its subject being a medical condition (*anatome* is the Greek word for dissection). The modern vogue for 'anatomies' of this and that began with the film *Anatomy of a Murder* (US 1959) and was followed by Anthony Sampson's book *Anatomy of Britain*, first published in 1962 and revised a number of times since.

ancestral vices/voices *Ancestral Vices* is the title of a novel (1980) by Tom Sharpe; *Ancestral Voices* is the title of the first volume of diaries (1975) by the architectural historian James Lees-Milne (1908–97). Both allude to the poem 'Kubla Khan' (1798) by Samuel Taylor Coleridge, which contains the lines: '. . . Five miles meandering with a mazy motion / Through wood and dale the sacred river ran, / Then reach'd the caverns measureless to man, / And sank in tumult to a lifeless ocean: / And 'mid this tumult Kubla heard from far / Ancestral voices prophesying war! / The shadow of the dome of pleasure / Floated midway on the waves; / Where was heard the mingled measure / From the fountain and the caves. / It was a miracle of rare device, / A sunny pleasure-dome with caves of ice!' The poem as a whole has been ransacked for all subsequent titles of Lees-Milne's published diaries: *Prophesying Peace* (1977), *Caves of Ice* (1983), *Midway on the Waves* (1985), *A Mingled Measure* (1994), *Ancient As the Hills* (1997), *Through Wood and Dale* (1998), *Deep Romantic Chasm* (2000), *Holy Dread* (2001), *Beneath a Waning Moon* (2003). Compare STATELY PLEASURE DOME.

and all because the lady loves Milk Tray
Cadbury's Milk Tray chocolates have been promoted with this line since 1968. On British TV, the line was the pay-off to action adverts showing feats of James Bond-style daring that climaxed with the presentation of a box of the chocolates to a suitably alluring female.

—— and all that 'And all that sort of thing.' Apparently the phrase was in the language before Sellar and Yeatman used it in the title of their cod volume of English history, *1066 And All That* (1930). See also GOODBYE TO ALL THAT.

and all that jazz 'And all that stuff, the rest, etcetera' – often with the dismissive suggestion 'and all that nonsense, rubbish'. American in origin, popular since 1959. From Gore Vidal, *Myra Breckinridge*, Chap. 6 (1968): 'He [was] so pleased to have me "on the team" and me so happy to be able to do work in Hollywood, California, a life's dream come true and – as they used to say in the early Sixties – all that jazz.' *All That Jazz* was the title of a film (US 1979) about the life and death of a choreographer.

and a special goodnight to you Before becoming a disc jockey on British radio, David Hamilton (b. 1939) was an announcer with a number of independent television companies, including Tyne Tees, ABC and Thames. In the days when TV schedules ended round about midnight, his romantic sign-off became so distinctive that he even made a record with the title – 'A Special Goodnight to You' (*circa* 1967). At about the same time, the sign-off was also used by Barry Aldiss ('B. A.') on Radio Luxembourg and subsequently by several other broadcasters.

and awa-a-aay we go! On the *Jackie Gleason Show* on US television (1952–70), the rotund comic hosted variety acts and would always use this phrase to lead into the first sketch. He had a special pose to accompany it – head turned to face left, one leg raised ready to shoot off in the same direction. Gleason's other stock (perhaps catch) phrases were **how sweet it is!**; **baby, you're the greatest!**; **one of these days . . . one of these days . . .**; and **pow! right in the kisser!** He also popularized the word 'labonza' for posterior, as in 'a kick in the labonza'. In *The Life of Riley* (1949–50), Gleason's phrase after some stroke of fate was **what a revoltin' development this is!**, though this appears to have been taken over by William Bendix, who followed him in the part.

and Death shall have no dominion The title of the notable poem (1936) on immortality by Dylan Thomas is a straightforward allusion to Romans 6:9: 'Christ being raised from the dead dieth no more: death hath no more dominion over him.'

and finally . . . Introduction to the final light or amusing story on Independent Television News's *News at Ten* bulletin (in the UK) and chiefly noticed when Reginald Bosanquet was newscasting in the 1970s. This kind of 'tailpiece' had first been established by ITN in the 1950s. A book called *And Finally* (edited by Martyn Lewis) collected some of these tailpieces and was published in 1984.

and how! An intensifying phrase of agreement, almost certainly of American origin from, probably, the 1920s. '"I should say she was pretty," said a loud and cheery voice just behind him . . . "Pneumatic too. And how!"' – Aldous Huxley, *Brave New World*, Chap. 4 (1932).

and I don't mean maybe! An intensifier to show that the speaker has just issued a command, not simply expressed a wish. *Mencken* lists it as an 'American saying *circa* 1920'. The second line of the song 'Yes, Sir, That's My Baby' (*circa* 1922) is: '. . . No, sir, don't mean maybe'. *OED2* has it by 1926, and it is in James Joyce, *Anna Livia Plurabelle* (1928).

and I'm like, hello? An expression of mock incredulity, popularized in the mid-1990s by the American TV show *Friends*. 'Did you see that vicar the other day who made all the kiddies cry by telling them that Father Christmas couldn't possibly exist – I mean, I was like, hello, why don't you tell us about your boss, then, and how he manages?' – *The Independent* (17 December 2002).

and in a packed programme tonight . . . A worn-out TV presentation phrase gently mocked by Ronnie Barker at the start of each edition of the BBC TV comedy show *The Two Ronnies* (1971–88). Compare his similar mocking of the dual presenters' IT's GOODNIGHT FROM ME . . .

and I quote Rather portentous indication of a quoted remark coming up – as though putting spoken quotation marks around whatever it is the speaker is about to say. *The Complete Naff Guide* (1983) lists it under 'Naff Expressions'. Fritz Spiegl commented in *MediaSpeak* (1989): 'On TV, "and I quote" may be replaced by the now fashionable, quaint "I quote" gesture: both hands raised aloft, first and second fingers sticking up like rabbit's ears and brought down once or twice to meet the thumb.' These finger-waggling 'air quotes' were known by 1977.

and justice for all This phrase comes from the Pledge of Allegiance to the Flag (put into its final form by Francis Bellamy in 1892, though further amended in the 1920s and 50s): 'I pledge allegiance to the flag of the United States of America and to the republic for which it stands, one nation under God, indivisible, with liberty and justice for all.' The idea of 'justice for all' is, however, one that goes back to the Greeks. It also gave rise to the remark by Lord Justice Sir James Mathew (d. 1908): 'In England, justice is open to all, like the Ritz Hotel.' *And Justice for All* was the title of a film (1979) about the US legal system. See also ONE NATION UNDER GOD.

and no heavy lifting Phrase used in a jokey description of the demands made – or not made – by a job, usually in politics. In an interview with Hunter Davies in *The Independent* (18 January 1994), Diane Abbott, the British Labour politician, said: 'Being an MP is a good job, the sort of job all working-class parents want for their children – clean, indoors and no heavy lifting. What could be nicer?' Much the same claim had earlier been made by Senator Robert Dole about the US vice-presidency (ABC TV broadcast, 24 July 1988): 'It is inside work with no heavy lifting.' And then J. K. Galbraith, *Name-Dropping*, Chap. 8 (1999), had: '[John F.] Kennedy also knew how to identify himself with an audience and with the larger electorate. At the end of his 1960 campaign, he addressed a vast crowd in the old Boston Garden. As a member of his campaign staff, I was there. He asked himself, as though from the floor, why he was running for president. In reply, he listed some issues, all relevant to his audience, that needed attention; then he ended by saying that the presidency was a well-paid job with no heavy lifting. The largely working-class gathering responded with appreciation, affection and joy. He was one of them.'

——, and no mistake! An intensifying phrase of affirmation, dating from the 1810s.

and now a word from our sponsor One of the various ways of getting into a commercial break, taken from American radio and television and much employed in British parodies of same in the 1950s and 60s – though never used in earnest in the UK (for the simple reason that sponsored TV of any type was not permitted until much later).

and now for something completely different ... Catchphrase from BBC TV, *Monty Python's Flying Circus* (1969–74) and used as the title of the comedy team's first cinema feature in 1971. Like most graduate comedy shows of the 1960s and 70s, *Monty Python* rather frowned upon the use of catchphrases as something belonging to another type of show business. Usually delivered by John Cleese as a dinner-jacketed BBC announcer, seated before a microphone on a desk in some unlikely setting, the phrase had hitherto been a slightly arch 'link' much loved by magazine programme presenters. These people were thus deprived of a very useful phrase. After all, there is not much else you can say to get from an interview with the Prime Minister to an item about beer-drinking budgerigars. The children's BBC TV series *Blue Peter* is sometimes said to have provoked the *Python* use of the phrase. It was first delivered by Eric Idle in the second edition of *Python* (12 October 1969), though it had also featured in some of the same team's earlier series, *At Last the 1948 Show*, on ITV (1967), where it was uttered by 'the lovely Aimi Macdonald' in her introductions.

and now, her nibs, Miss Georgia Gibbs! The standard introduction to the singer of that name on the US radio show *The Camel Caravan* (1943–7).

and pigs might fly (or **a pig may fly**). An expression of the unlikelihood or impossibility of something actually taking place. Thomas Fuller, the proverb collector, had 'That is as likely as to see an hog fly' in 1732 though, earlier, *The Spectator* (2 April 1711) was bemoaning absurd inn signs including 'flying Pigs', which would seem to refer to this saying. From Lewis Carroll, *Alice's Adventures in Wonderland*, Chap. 9 (1865): '"I've a right to think," said Alice ...

"Just about as much right," said the Duchess, "as pigs have to fly".'

and so forth 'And similarly, and then onwards' – now mostly used after breaking off a list or quotation. This is a very old phrase indeed. Aelfric was writing 'And swa forþ' *circa* AD 1000 (see YE OLDE TEA SHOPPE). A would-be humorous elaboration of it, dating from the mid-20th century, is **and so forth and so fifth!**

and so it goes Mildly irritated or amused and philosophical phrase used when presented with yet another example of the way things are in the world. A catchphrase in Kurt Vonnegut's novel *Slaughterhouse-Five* (1969). *So It Goes* was the title of a British TV pop show devoted mainly to punk (by 1976). 'And so it goes: hassle, hassle, hassle, one horrible death after another, and yet the put-upon lad's soul is a butterfly that transmutes (on the spiritual sphere, you understand) into an Airfix Spitfire. By MTV standards, Hirst could be the next Francis Ford Coppola' – *The Observer* (25 February 1996); 'Sausages are brilliant all-rounders, everyone knows that. Fried up for breakfast, sandwiched between two slices of bread at lunch, grilled with mustard and mash for supper, cold on sticks at children's parties, hot on sticks with a spicy dip at grown-up dos, and so it goes' – *The Sunday Times* (25 February 1996).

and so to bed Samuel Pepys's famous signing-off line in his diary entries appears first on 15 January 1660. However, on that particular occasion, they are not quite his last words. He writes: 'I went to supper, and after that to make an end of this week's notes in this book, and so to bed.' Then he adds: 'It being a cold day and a great snow, my physic did not work so well as it should have done'. *And So To Bed* was the title of a play (1926) by J. B. Fagan, which was then turned into a musical by Vivian Ellis (1951).

and so we say farewell ... The travelogues made by James A. Fitzpatrick (1902–80) were a supporting feature of cinema programmes from 1925 onwards. With the advent of sound, the commentaries to 'Fitzpatrick Traveltalks' became noted for their closing words: 'And it's

from this paradise of the Canadian Rockies that we reluctantly say farewell to Beautiful Banff . . . / And as the midnight sun lingers on the skyline of the city, we most reluctantly say farewell to Stockholm, Venice of the North . . . / With its picturesque impressions indelibly fixed in our memory, it is time to conclude our visit and reluctantly say farewell to Hong Kong, the hub of the Orient . . .' Frank Muir and Denis Norden's notable parody of the genre – 'Bal-ham – Gateway to the South' – first written for radio *circa* 1948 and later performed on a record album by Peter Sellers (1958) accordingly contained the words, 'And so we say farewell to this historic borough . . .'

and still they come ... Phrase for the remorseless oncoming of those you (probably) don't like. From John Greenleaf Whittier's poem 'The King's Missive' (1881): 'The pestilent Quakers are in my path! / Some we have scourged, and banished some, / Some hanged, more doomed, and still they come.' The chorus from 'The Astronomer' in Jeff Wayne's musical album *The War of the Worlds* (1978) is: 'The chances of anything coming from Mars / Are a million to one, but still, they come . . .' The title of a book by Elliott Barkan is *And Still They Come: Immigrants and American Society, 1920 to the 1990s* (1998). One is also reminded of Lewis Carroll's lines about the oysters in 'The Walrus and the Carpenter': 'And thick and fast they came at last, / And more, and more, and more.' Then there is this from Shakespeare, *Macbeth*, V.v.1 (1606): 'Hang out our banners on the outward walls; / The cry is still, "They come!"' 'One million. And still they came' – headline over peace march report in *The Observer* (16 February 2003).

and that ain't hay! Meaning, 'And that's not to be sniffed at/that isn't negligible' – often with reference to money. The title of the 1943 Abbott and Costello film that is said to have popularized this (almost exclusively US) exclamation was *It Ain't Hay*. But in the same year Mickey Rooney exclaimed 'And that ain't hay!' as he went into the big 'I Got Rhythm' number (choreographed by Busby Berkeley) in the film *Girl Crazy* (the scene being set, appropriately, in an agricultural college).

and that, my dears, is how I came to marry your grandfather As though at the end of a long and rambling reminiscence by an old woman. Also used by the American humorist Robert Benchley (1889–1945) – possibly in capsule criticism of the play *Abie's Irish Rose* – and so quoted by Diana Rigg in *No Turn Unstoned* (1982).

and that's official Journalistic formula used when conveying, say, the findings of some newly published report. The aim, presumably, is to dignify the fact(s) so presented but also to do it in a not too daunting manner. A cliché condemned by Keith Waterhouse in *Daily Mirror Style* (1981). 'Yes, the Prime Minister's condition is "satisfactory" – and that's official!' – *Private Eye* (1962); 'In America, there are no bad people, only people who think badly of themselves. And that's official. California has a state commission to promote self-esteem, there is a National Council for Self-Esteem with its own bulletin . . .' – *Independent on Sunday* (8 May 1994).

and that's the way it is The authoritative but avuncular TV anchorman Walter Cronkite (b. 1916) retired from anchoring the CBS TV *Evening News* after nineteen years – for most of which he had concluded with these words. On the final occasion, he said: 'And that's the way it is, Friday March 6, 1981. Goodnight.'

and the band played on . . . Things went on as usual, no notice was taken. A phrase from a song, 'The Band Played On', written by John F. Palmer in 1895. A nonfiction book by Randy Shilts about the first years of AIDS was called *And the Band Played On* and filmed (US 1993). This title presumably alludes to the earlier play by Mart Crowley, *The Boys in the Band*, also about male homosexuals (filmed US 1970).

and the best of luck! Ironic encouragement. Frankie Howerd, the British comedian (?1917–92), claimed in his autobiography, *On the Way I Lost It* (1976), to have given this phrase to the language: 'It came about when I introduced into radio *Variety Bandbox* [late 1940s] those appallingly badly sung mock operas starring . . . Madame Vera Roper (soprano) . . . Vera

would pause for breath before a high C and as she mustered herself for this musical Everest I would mutter, "And the best of luck!" Later it became, "**And the best of British luck**!" The phrase is so common now that I frequently surprise people when I tell them it was my catchphrase on *Variety Bandbox*.' *Partridge/Catch Phrases* suggests, however, that the 'British luck' version had already been a Second World War army phrase meaning the exact opposite of what it appeared to say and compares it with a line from a First World War song: 'Over the top with the best of luck / Parley-voo'.

and the next object is —— In the radio quiz *Twenty Questions*, broadcast by the BBC from 1947 to 1976, a mystery voice – most memorably Norman Hackforth's – would inform listeners in advance about the object the panellists would then try to identify by asking no more than twenty questions. Hackforth would intone in his deep, fruity voice: 'And the next object is "The odour in the larder" [or some such poser].'

and the next *Tonight* will be tomorrow night . . . The stock concluding phrase of the original BBC TV early evening magazine *Tonight* (1957–65). Cliff Michelmore, who used to say 'And the next *Tonight* will be tomorrow night . . . good night!', commented (1979): 'The combined brains of Alasdair Milne, Donald Baverstock, myself and three others were employed to come up with the phrase. There were at least ten others tried and permed. At least we cared . . . !'

and thereby hangs a tale As a storytelling device, this is still very much in use to indicate that some tasty titbit is about to be revealed. It occurs a number of times in Shakespeare. In *As You Like It*, II.vii.28 (1598) Jaques, reporting the words of a motley fool (Touchstone), says: 'And so from hour to hour, we ripe and ripe, / And then, from hour to hour, we rot and rot: / And thereby hangs a tale.' Other examples occur in *The Merry Wives of Windsor* (I.iv.143) and *The Taming of the Shrew* (IV.i.50). In *Othello* (III.i.8), the Clown says, 'O, thereby hangs a tail,' emphasizing the innuendo that may or may not be present in the other examples.

and there's more where that came from Catchphrase from the BBC radio *Goon Show* (1951–60). This was sometimes said by Major Denis Bloodnok (Peter Sellers) and occasionally by Wallace Greenslade (a BBC staff announcer who, like his senior colleague, John Snagge, was allowed to let his hair down on the show). An example occurs in 'The Call of the West' (20 January 1959). The origins of the phrase probably lie in some music-hall comedian's patter, uttered after a particular joke had gone well. Charles Dickens in Chapter 11 of *Martin Chuzzlewit* (1843–4) shows that the phrase was established in other contexts first: 'Mr Jonas filled the young ladies' glasses, calling on them not to spare it, as they might be certain there was plenty more where that came from.' Jimmy Cricket, a British comedian, was exclaiming simply, 'And there's *more*!' by 1986.

and they all lived happily ever after The traditional ending to 'fairy' tales is not quite so frequently used as ONCE UPON A TIME, but it is present (more or less) in five of *The Classic Fairy Tales* gathered in their earliest known English forms by Iona and Peter Opie (1974). 'Jack and the Giants' (*circa* 1760) ends: 'He and his Lady lived the Residue of their Days in great Joy and Happiness.' 'Jack and the Bean-Stalk' (1807) ends: 'His mother and he lived together a great many years, and continued always to be very happy.' A translation of 'Snow White and the Seven Dwarfs' by the brothers Grimm (1823) ends: 'Snow-drop and the prince lived and reigned happily over that land many many years.' A translation of 'The Frog-Prince' ends: 'They arrived safely, and lived happily a great many years.' A Scottish version of 'Cinderella' (collected 1878) has: 'They lived happily all their days.' The concluding words of Winston Churchill's *My Early Life* (1930) are: '. . . September 1908, when I married and lived happily ever afterwards.'

and this is where the story really starts . . . Catchphrase from BBC radio's *The Goon Show* (1951–60), usually uttered by the announcer/narrator, Wallace Greenslade, and especially in 'Dishonoured – Again' (26 January 1959).

and this too shall pass away Chuck Berry spoke the words of a 'song' called 'Pass Away' (1979) that told of a Persian king who had had carved the words 'Even this shall pass away'. George Harrison had earlier called his first (mostly solo) record album 'All Things Must Pass' (1970). These musicians were by no means the first people to be drawn to this saying. As Abraham Lincoln explained in an address to the Wisconsin State Agricultural Society (1859): 'An Eastern monarch once charged his wise men to invent him a sentence to be ever in view, and which should be true and appropriate in all times and situations. They presented him with the words, "And this, too, shall pass away". How much it expresses! How chastening in the hour of pride! How consoling in the depths of affliction!' But who was the oriental monarch? *Benham* (1948) says the phrase was an inscription on a ring – 'according to an oriental tale' – and the phrase was given by Solomon to a Sultan who 'desired that the words should be appropriate at all time'. In 1860, Nathaniel Hawthorne wrote in *The Marble Faun* of the 'greatest mortal consolation, which we derive from the transitoriness of all things – from the right of saying, in every conjuncture, "This, too, will pass away".'

and when did you last see your father? There can be few paintings where the title is as important as (and as well known as) the actual picture. This one was even turned into a tableau at Madame Tussaud's where it remained until 1989. It was in 1878 that William Frederick Yeames RA first exhibited his painting with this title at the Royal Academy; the original is now in the Walker Art Gallery, Liverpool. The title of the painting has become a kind of joke catchphrase, sometimes used nudgingly and often allusively – as in the title of Christopher Hampton's 1964 play *When Did You Last See My Mother?* and the 1986 farce by Ray Galton and John Antrobus, *When Did You Last See Your . . . Trousers?* Tom Lubbock writing in the *Independent on Sunday* (8 November 1992) commented on the fact that the title tends to be remembered wrongly: 'But the *And* matters. It turns the title from an abrupt demand into a slyly casual inquiry . . . [But] the title will probably outlast the image, just as a form of words that rings some distant bell. On green cashpoint screens you now find the query "When did you last update your insurance?" I'm sure the forgotten Yeames is ultimately responsible.'

and with that, I return you to the studio! Catchphrase from the BBC radio show *Beyond Our Ken* (1958–64). Hugh Paddick played Cecil Snaith, a hush-voiced BBC outside broadcasts commentator. After some disaster in which he had figured, he would give this as the punchline, in a deadpan manner. The show's host, Kenneth Horne, apparently suggested the line. In its straight form, many TV and radio news reporters use the phrase in live spots even today.

(the) Angel of Death A nickname bestowed in the Second World War upon Dr Joseph Mengele, the German concentration camp doctor who experimented on inmates – 'for his power to pick who would live and die in Auschwitz by the wave of his hand' (*Time* Magazine, 17 June 1985). 'Angel of death' as an expression for a bringer of ills is not a biblical phrase and does not appear to have arisen until the 18th century. Samuel Johnson used it in *The Rambler* in 1752.

angels dancing on the head of a pin *Benham* (1948) went into this thoroughly but did not provide an actual example of what it gives as a head phrase, namely, 'A company of angels can dance on the point of a needle'. Nevertheless, it glosses the phrase thus: 'Saying attrib. with variations to St Thomas Aquinas (*circa* 1227–74) [who] in *Summae Theologiae* devotes superabundant space to fanciful conjectures about the nature of angels . . . "Whether an angel can be in several places at once" . . . "Whether several angels can be in one place at the same time" . . . He expends much laboured argument on this and similar problems.' Correspondents in *The Times* (20/21 November 1975) seemed to suggest that the attribution to Thomas Aquinas had been mistakenly made by Isaac Disraeli. Mention was made of the 14th-century tractate *Swester Katrei* – wrongly ascribed to Meister Eckhart – which contains this passage: 'Doctors declare that in heaven a thousand angels can stand on the point of a needle.' *Mencken* (1942) has 'How many angels can dance upon the point of a needle?' – 'ascribed to various medieval theologians, *c*. 1400.'

angels one five In Royal Air Force jargon, 'angels' means height measured in units of a thousand feet; 'one five' stands for fifteen; so '20 MEs at Angels One Five' means 'Twenty Messerschmitts at 15,000 feet'. *Angels One Five* was the title of a film (UK 1952) about RAF fighter pilots during the Second World War.

Anglo-Saxon attitudes Typically English behaviour. The title of Angus Wilson's novel (1956) about a historian investigating a possible archaeological forgery comes from Lewis Carroll's *Through the Looking Glass*, Chap. 7 (1872). Alice observes the Messenger 'skipping up and down, and wriggling like an eel, as he came along'. When she expresses surprise, the King explains: 'He's an Anglo-Saxon Messenger – and those are Anglo-Saxon attitudes.' Harry Morgan Ayres in *Carroll's Alice* (1936) suggests that the author may have been spoofing the Anglo-Saxon scholarship of his day. He also reproduces drawings of Anglo-Saxons in various costumes and attitudes from the Caedmon manuscript in the Bodleian Library, Oxford.

(the) Angry Decade A decade label for the 1950s though it is not certain that this had any wide circulation beyond being the title of Kenneth Allsopp's book – a cultural survey (1958). Obviously it derived from:

(an) angry young man Label for any writer in the mid-1950s who showed a social awareness and expressed dissatisfaction with conventional values and with the Establishment – John Osborne, Kingsley Amis and Colin Wilson among them. Leslie Paul, a social philosopher, had called his autobiography *Angry Young Man* in 1951, but the popular use of the phrase stems from *Look Back in Anger*, the 1956 play by John Osborne that featured an anti-hero called Jimmy Porter. The phrase did not occur in the play but was applied to the playwright by George Fearon in publicity material sent out by the Royal Court

Theatre, London. Fearon later told *The Daily Telegraph* (2 October 1957): 'I ventured to prophesy that [Osborne's] generation would praise his play while mine would, in general, dislike it . . . "If this happens," I told him, "you would become known as the Angry Young Man." In fact, we decided then and there that henceforth he was to be known as that.'

anguish turned to joy (and *vice versa***)**   A journalistic cliché noticed as such by the 1970s: 'A young mother's anguish turns to joy . . .' and so on. 'Joy has turned to anguish for the parents of British student Colin Shingler aged 20, who was trapped in the Romano during the earthquake. Only hours after hearing that he had been rescued they were told that surgeons had to amputate his left hand' – *The Times* (23 September 1985); 'Meanwhile, that anguish had turned to joy among the 250 Brechin fans at Hamilton. The players took a salute and then it was Clyde's turn to be acclaimed, with the championship trophy being paraded round the ground' – *The Herald* (Glasgow) (17 May 1993).

animal, vegetable and mineral   Not a quotation from anyone in particular, merely a way of describing three types of matter. And yet, why does the phrase trip off the tongue so? Edward Phillips, *The New World of English Words* (ed. Kersey) (1706) has: 'Chymists . . . call the three Orders of Natural Bodies, viz. Animal, Vegetable, and Mineral, by the name of Kingdoms.' But why not 'animal, *mineral*, vegetable'? Or '*vegetable*, animal, mineral'? Perhaps because these variants are harder to say, although in W. S. Gilbert's lyrics for *The Pirates of Penzance* (1879), Major-General Stanley does manage to sing: 'But still in matters vegetable, animal, and mineral, / I am the very model of a modern Major-General.' For BBC television viewers, the order was clearly stated in the title of the long-running archaeological quiz *Animal, Vegetable, Mineral?* (established by 1956) in which eminent university dons had to identify ancient artefacts just by looking at them. The trio of words was also evoked in the long-running radio series *Twenty Questions*. This originated on the Mutual Radio Network in the US in 1946, having been created by Fred Van De

Venter and family – who transferred with the show to NBC TV, from 1949 to 1955. *Twenty Questions* ran on BBC radio from 1947 to 1976. Panellists simply had to guess the identity of a 'mystery object' by asking up to twenty questions. A fourth category – 'abstract' – was added later. In 1973–4, a version of this game made for BBC World Service was actually called *Animal, Vegetable or Mineral*. The key to the matter is that the original American show was admittedly based on the old parlour game of 'Animal, Vegetable [and/or] Mineral'. This seems to have been known on both sides of the Atlantic in the 19th century. In *Charles Dickens: His Tragedy and Triumph* by Edgar Johnson, we find (1839–41): 'Dickens was brilliant in routing everybody at "Animal, Vegetable, or Mineral", although he himself failed to guess a vegetable object mentioned in "mythological history" and belonging to a queen, and was chagrined to have it identified as the tarts made by the Queen of Hearts.' In the same book, in a chapter on the period 1858–65, we also read: '[Dickens] was swift and intuitive in "Twenty Questions" . . . On one occasion, he failed to guess "The powder in the Gunpowder Plot", although he succeeded in reaching Guy Fawkes.' Presumably, then, the game was known by both names, though Dickens also refers to a version of it as 'Yes and No' in *A Christmas Carol* (1843). 'Twenty Questions' is referred to as such in a letter from Hannah Moore as early as 1786. Yet another name for this sort of game (by 1883) appears to have been 'Clumps' or 'Clubs'.

animals   See ALL ANIMALS.

(the) Animated Meringue   Nickname of (Dame) Barbara Cartland (1902–2000), British romantic novelist and health food champion, who employed a chalky style of make-up in addition to driving around in a pink and white Rolls-Royce. She was thus dubbed by Arthur Marshall who said that far from taking offence, Miss Cartland sent him a telegram of thanks. Compare: 'At dinner that night it was Eleanor herself who mentioned the name of a certain statesman, who may be decently covered under the disguise of X. "X.," said Arlington Stringham, "has the soul of a meringue"' – Saki, *The Chronicles of Clovis*, 'The Jesting of Arlington Stringham' (1911).

annus mirabilis Phrase for a remarkable or auspicious year, in modern (as opposed to classical) Latin. Dryden's *Annus Mirabilis: the year of wonders* was published in 1666, but the idea was known before this, viz. *Mirabilis annus secundus; or, the Second year of prodigies: Being a true and impartial collection of many strange signes and apparitions, which have this last year been seen in the heavens, and in the earth, and in the waters* (1662). In the Netherlands, 1566 used to be known (but not until the mid-19th century) as *wonderjaar*, because of its crucial role in the start of the Dutch revolt. The opposite term – **annus horribilis** – was popularized by Queen Elizabeth II in a speech in the City of London (24 November 1992) to mark her fortieth year on the British throne: '1992 is not a year I shall look back on with undiluted pleasure. In the words of one of my more sympathetic correspondents, it has turned out to be an *Annus Horribilis*.' She was reflecting her current mood: she had a cold, part of Windsor Castle had been burned down four days previously and the marriages of three of her children had collapsed or were collapsing. She states that she had the phrase from a correspondent. It seems more likely that it was inserted by the Queen's private secretary and speechwriter, Sir Robert Fellowes, having been written in a Christmas card sent to Her Majesty by her former Principal Private Secretary, Sir Edward Ford.

another See HERE'S A FUNNY.

another country Julian Mitchell's play *Another Country* (1981; film UK 1984) shows how the seeds of defection to Soviet Russia were sown in a group of boys at an English public school. The title comes not, as might be thought, from the celebrated line in Christopher Marlowe's *The Jew of Malta* (*circa* 1592): 'Fornication: but that was in another country; / And besides the wench is dead.' Rather, as the playwright has confirmed, it is taken from the second verse of Sir Cecil Spring Rice's patriotic 'Last Poem' (1918), which begins 'I vow to thee, my country' and continues 'And there's another country, I've heard of

long ago – / Most dear to them that love her, most great to them that know.' In the original context, the 'other country' is Heaven, rather than the Soviet Union, of course. *Another Country* had earlier been used as the title of a novel (1962) by James Baldwin.

another day – another dollar! What one says to oneself at the conclusion of toil. Obviously of American origin but now as well known in the UK where there does not appear to be an equivalent expression using 'pound' instead of 'dollar'. *Partridge/ Catch Phrases* dates the phrase from the 1940s in the UK and from *circa* 1910 in the US.

another little drink wouldn't do us any harm This boozer's jocular justification for another snort is rather more than a catchphrase. Allusion is made to it in Edith Sitwell's bizarre lyrics for 'Scotch Rhapsody' in *Façade* (1922): 'There is a hotel at Ostend / Cold as the wind, without an end, / Haunted by ghostly poor relations . . . / And "Another little drink wouldn't do us any harm," / Pierces through the sabbatical calm.' The actual origin is in a song with the phrase as title, written by Clifford Grey to music by Nat D. Ayer and sung by George Robey in the show *The Bing Boys Are Here* (1916). It includes a reference to the well-known fact that Prime Minister Asquith was at times the worse for wear when on the Treasury Bench: 'Mr Asquith says in a manner sweet and calm: / And another little drink wouldn't do us any harm.'

(that's) another meal the Germans won't have Dismissive catchphrase on finishing a meal. 'When my (French) wife arrived in this country some thirty years ago, she surprised me by remarking, after a particularly good meal, "*Voilà, un autre repas que les Allemands n'auront pas.*" This saying apparently derived from her mother, or indeed her grandmother, who suffered in the Occupation. To my astonishment, on a trip to Avignon ten years ago, after an exceptional banquet, a young French lad aged about 25, turned to my wife and made the same remark. It would seem that this has now become a French proverb' – Raymond Harris (1995). Confirmation comes from *The Sunday Times* (23

March 1997): 'Older Frenchmen admitted they sometimes still use the toast, when raising their glasses, of "This is one the *Boches* won't get".' And from even further back: 'On his first visit to Germany nearly forty years later, [Matisse] told one of his students that . . . he never forgot his mother repeating like a grace at meals: "Here's another one the Germans won't lay their hands on". The phrase would become a familiar refrain throughout the region during the incursions of the next seventy-five years and more' – Hilary Spurling, *The Unknown Matisse*, Vol. 1 (1998), referring to the Prussians who passed through north-eastern France in the 1871 Franco-Prussian war.

another opening, another show! Show business exclamation – perhaps uttered ironically, like ON WITH THE MOTLEY! 'Another Op'nin, Another Show' is the title of a song sung by the members of a theatrical troupe in Cole Porter's musical *Kiss Me Kate* (1948).

another page turned in the book of life Conversational reflection on someone's death. One of the numerous clichés of bereavement, designed to keep the awfulness of death at bay by means of comfortingly trite remarks. A cliché from by about 1960. However, the notion of life as a book whose pages turn can be invoked on other occasions as well. On 1 September 1872, the Reverend Francis Kilvert wrote in his diary: 'Left Clyro for ever. A chapter of life closed and a leaf in the Book of Life turned over.' In its original biblical sense, the said book is a record of those who will inherit eternal life (as in Philippians 4:3 and Revelation 20:12).

another part of the wood Title of the first volume of (Lord) Kenneth Clark's autobiography (1974) and taken from the stage direction to Act 3, Sc. 2 of Shakespeare's *A Midsummer Night's Dream*. Scene locations such as this were mostly not of Shakespeare's own devising but were added by later editors. Clark said he wished also to allude to the opening of Dante's *Inferno*: 'I found myself in a dark wood where the straight way was lost.' Lillian Hellman had earlier entitled one of

her plays *Another Part of the Forest* (1946) and Beryl Bainbridge, a novel, *Another Part of the Wood* (1968).

another Sunday and sweet FA This phrase was used as the title of a Granada TV play by Jack Rosenthal (UK 1972) about the struggles of a referee during an (amateur) Sunday-morning football game. But was it a phrase before the play? Compare the (subsequent) diary of a member of the British forces in the Falklands conflict, found on the internet. On Sunday 16 May 1982, he wrote: 'All I can say about today is another bloody Sunday and sweet FA. We were due to be linked up with the rest of the task force during the night but due to the extreme bad weather all ships have had to slow down.'

answer See IS THE RIGHT.

(the) answer is in the plural and they bounce That is to say, 'balls!' – reputedly the response given by the architect Sir Edwin Lutyens to a Royal Commission. However, according to Robert Jackson, *The Chief* (1959), when Gordon (later Lord) Hewart was in the House of Commons, he was answering questions on behalf of David Lloyd George. For some time, one afternoon, he had given answers in the customary brief parliamentary manner – 'The answer is in the affirmative' or 'The answer is in the negative'. After one such non-committal reply, several members arose to bait Hewart with a series of rapid supplementary questions. He waited until they had all finished and then replied: 'The answer is in the plural!'

(the) answer's a lemon! Fobbing-off phrase. 'My Cumbrian grandmother when asked a question would reply, "The answer's a lemon". "Why?" we asked – "**Suck it and see**," was her response' – Janet C. Egan (2000). This exchange brings together two well-known expressions. 'The answer is a lemon', being a non-answer to a question or a refusal to do something requested of one, is probably of American origin and seems to have been in use by 1910. A lemon is acidic and sour, and there are several other American phrases in which a lemon suggests that something is unsatisfactory or not working properly. The lemon is also the least valuable object on a fruit machine. 'Suck it and see', meaning 'try out', presumably derives from what you would say about a sweet – 'suck it and see whether you like the taste of it'. It was used as a catchphrase by Charlie Naughton of the Crazy Gang, though it is probably of earlier music-hall origin – at least according to W. Buchanan-Taylor, *One More Shake* (1944). *Partridge/Slang* dates it from the 1890s. A correspondent, H. E. Johnson, suggested (1999) that it started with a *Punch* cartoon at the turn of the 19th/20th century, with the caption: *First urchin:* 'I don't know if this here's a plum or a beetle.' *Second urchin:* 'Suck it and see.'

(to) answer the call of nature A lavatorial euphemism known since 1761 when Laurence Sterne's *Tristram Shandy* had that someone 'hearkened to the call of nature.' 'The calls of nature are permitted and Clerical Staff may use the garden below the second gate' – *Tailor & Cutter* (1852). 'Call of nature "sent [Robert] Maxwell overboard" . . . He would frequently get up in the middle of the night and found it more convenient, as a lot of men do on a boat, to relieve themselves over the side as it was moving' – headline and text, *The Independent* (21 October 1995). There is also the variant, '(to) answer a certain requirement of nature.' The **call of the great outdoors** may also be used in the same way. Originally the phrase 'great outdoors' was used simply to describe 'great open space' (by 1932).

(the) answer to a maiden's prayer An eligible bachelor – especially one who is young, good-looking and wealthy. Perhaps a Victorian coinage, now used only ironically or somewhat mockingly and also used in a wider sense to refer to anything one might have been searching for. There is an ancient tradition that maidens prayed to St Agnes (patron saint of virgins) on 20 January, in the hope of being granted a vision of their future husbands. Hence, the poem by John Keats, 'The Eve of St Agnes' (1820). 'The Maiden's Prayer' was the translated title given to the piano solo popular in Victorian drawing-rooms, 'Molitwa dziewicy' by the Polish composer Thekla Badarzewska (1834–61). 'Here, you Freshmen, Seniors, et al, is the answer to a

maiden's prayer' – *Mademoiselle* Magazine (15 August 1935).

anxiety See AGE OF.

any colour so long as it's black An expression used to convey that there is, in fact, no choice. This originated with Henry Ford, who is supposed to have said it about the Model T Ford that came out in 1909 and is quoted in his *My Life and Work* (written with Henry Crowther, 1922). Hill and Nevins in *Ford: Expansion and Challenge* (1957) have him saying: 'People can have it any colour – so long as it's black.' However, in 1925, the company had to bow to the inevitable and offer a choice of colours. Dr Harry Corbett commented (1996): 'Initially, the T model was available in several colours but when Ford changed to a different painting technique the product used was only available in the colour black. The early finishing technique was a carryover from the carriage industry and resulted in curing times of up to four weeks. This meant that huge numbers of cars had to be stored during the finishing process. From what I can gather, Ford changed to a faster drying product – which was only available in black – to rid himself of the warehousing difficulties.'

any gum, chum? Remark addressed to American GIs based in Britain during the Second World War. 'Crowds of small boys gathered outside American clubs to pester them for gifts, or called out as American lorries passed: "Any gum, chum?" which rapidly became a national catchphrase' – Norman Longmate, *How We Lived Then* (1971).

any more for the *Skylark*? The age-old cry of swarthy fishing-folk inviting seaside visitors to take a trip around the bay but now domesticated into a 'generalised invitation', as *Partridge/Catch Phrases* puts it. But how did it get into the language in the first place? A pamphlet (undated) entitled 'Any More for the Skylark? The Story of Bournemouth's Pleasure Boats' by L. Chalk tells of a whole series of 'Skylark' vessels run by a certain Jake Bolson at that seaside resort from 1914 to 1947. There is, however, a much earlier source. A researcher at the Brighton Fishing Museum disclosed that a boat owner/skipper of those parts called Captain Fred Collins had owned many 'Skylarks' in his career. As he died in 1912, Collins was clearly ahead of the Bournemouth boats. Indeed, the *Brighton Gazette* had mentioned a 'new pleasure yacht, "The Skylark"' arriving from the builders in May 1852. The *Gazette*'s earliest citation of the actual phrase 'Any more for the Skylark' occurs in the edition of 17 November 1928 (in an article concerning Joseph Pierce, who took over from Collins). This does not explain how the phrase caught on beyond Brighton (perhaps through a song or stage-show sketch?) The edition of 8 May 1948 placed it among other pleasure boat cries: 'Brighton's fishermen . . . will take their boats down to the sea and the summer season chorus of "Any more for the Skylark," "Half-way to China," "Motor boat going" and "Lovely ride out" will start again.' A variation, **all aboard the Sky-lark!**, was apparently popularized by *Noah and Nelly*, an animated British TV children's programme of the mid-1970s.

(is there/have you) any more, Mrs Moore?   Elaborations of 'any more?', from the British music-hall song 'Don't Have Any More, Mrs Moore!' – written by Castling & Walsh (early 1900s) and performed by Lily Morris.

anyone for tennis?   This perkily expressed inquiry from a character entering through French windows and carrying a tennis racquet has become established as typical of the 'teacup' theatre of the 1920s and 30s (as also in the forms **who's for tennis?** and **tennis, anyone?**). A clear example of it being used has proved elusive, however, although there are many near misses. The opening lines of Part II of Strindberg's *Dance of Death* (1901) are (in translation): 'Why don't you come and play tennis?' A *very* near miss occurs in the first act of Shaw's *Misalliance* (1910) in which a character asks: 'Anybody on for a game of tennis?' Teddie in Somerset Maugham's *The Circle* (1921) always seems on the verge of saying it, but only manages, 'I say, what about this tennis?' Myra in Noël Coward's *Hay Fever* (1925) says, 'What a pity it's raining, we might have had some tennis.' Perhaps it is just another

of those phrases that was never actually said in the form popularly remembered. Unfortunately, a terrible wild-goose chase was launched by Jonah Ruddy and Jonathan Hill in their book *Bogey: The Man, The Actor, The Legend* (1965). Describing Humphrey Bogart's early career as a stage actor (*circa* 1921) they said: 'In those early Broadway days he didn't play menace parts. "I always made my entrance carrying a tennis racquet, baseball bat, or golf club. I was the athletic type, with hair slicked back and wrapped in a blazer. The only line I didn't say was, 'Give me the ball, coach, I'll take it through.' Yes, sir, I was Joe College or Joe Country Club all the time." It was hard to imagine him as the originator of that famous theatrical line – "Tennis anyone?" – but he was.' It is clear from this extract that the authors were merely adding their own gloss to what Bogart had said. *Bartlett* (1968) joined in and said it was his 'sole line in his first play'. But Bogart (who died in 1957) had already denied ever saying it (quoted in Goodman, *Bogey: The Good-Bad Boy* and in an ABC TV documentary of 1974 using old film of him doing so). Alistair Cooke in *Six Men* (1977) is more cautious: 'It is said he appeared in an ascot and blue blazer and tossed off the invitation Tennis, anyone?' – and adds that Bogart probably did not coin the phrase. In British show business, it has been suggested that Leon Quatermaine, a leading man of the 1920s and 30s, was the first man to say it. In the form 'Anyone for tennis?' the phrase was used by J. B. Priestley as the title of a 1968 television play, and in 1981 it was converted into *Anyone for Denis?* by John Wells as the title of a farce guying Margaret Thatcher's husband.

anyone we know?   Originally, a straightforward request for information when told, say, that someone you know is getting married and you want to know to whom. Then it became a playful catchphrase: 'She's going to have a baby' – 'Who's the father – anyone we know?' The joke use certainly existed in the 1930s. In the film *The Gay Divorcee* (US 1934), Ginger Rogers states: 'A man tore my dress off.' A woman friend asks: 'Anyone we know?'

'The moment from which many of us date the genre was when the curtain rose on a production by Harry Kupfer in the late 1970s – I think of a work by Richard Strauss – to reveal a set dominated by a huge phallus, occasioning, from one male in the stalls to his gentleman friend, the loud whisper: "Anyone we know, duckie?"' – *The Times* (17 May 1986).

any one who . . . can't be all bad Format phrase suggesting that something about which doubt has been expressed is really rather good. Perhaps the original is what Leo Rosten said about W. C. Fields (and not, as is sometimes reported, what Fields himself said of another): 'Any man who hates children and dogs can't be all bad' (*or* 'Anybody who hates dogs and babies can't be all bad'). This was at a Masquers' Club dinner (16 February 1939). Subsequently: 'Anyone with a name like Hitler can't be all that bad' – Spike Milligan, *The Last Goon Show of All* (1972); 'All the same, Garland and Rooney as *Babes In Arms* . . . plus long-lost tracks from *Band Wagon* and *Good News* and *Brigadoon* and *It's Always Fair Weather*, can't be all bad' – Sheridan Morley in *Theatreprint*, Vol. 5, No. 95 (May 1995).

any port in a storm Meaning, metaphorically, 'any roof over your head is better than none' or 'you can't be choosy about shelter in adversity'. The phrase makes an early appearance in John Cleland's *Fanny Hill* (1749): 'I feeling pretty sensibly that it [her lover's member] was going by the right door, and knocking desperately at the wrong one, I told him of it: "Pooh, says he, my dear, any port in a storm".'

anything can happen and probably will The standard opening announcement of the BBC radio show *Take It From Here* (1948–59) was that it was a comedy programme 'in which anything can happen and probably will.' The show was based on literate scripts by Frank Muir (1920–98) and Denis Norden (b. 1922) and featured Jimmy Edwards (1920–88), Dick Bentley (1907–95) and June Whitfield (b. 1926) (who succeeded Joy Nichols).

anything for a laugh Casual reason given for doing something a little out of the ordinary, since the 1930s. P. G. Wode-

house, *Laughing Gas* (1936): '"Anything for a laugh" is your motto.' In the 1980s it was combined with the similar phrases **good for a laugh** (itself used as the title of a book by Bennett Cerf in 1952) and **game for anything** to produce the title of the British TV show *Game For a Laugh* (1981–5). This consisted of various stunts and had elements of *Candid Camera* as it persuaded members of the public to take part in stunts both in and out of the studio. The title was much repeated by the presenters of the show, as in 'Let's see if so-and-so is **game for a laugh** . . .'

anything for a quiet life The Jacobean playwright Thomas Heywood used this proverbial phrase in his play *Captives*, Act 3, Sc. 3 (1624), but Thomas Middleton had actually entitled a play *Anything For a Quiet Life* (possibly written with John Webster) in about 1620. Swift included the phrase in *Polite Conversation* (1738) and Dickens incorporated it as a Wellerism in *The Pickwick Papers*, Chap. 43 (1837): 'But anythin' for a quiet life, as the man said wen he took the sitivation at the lighthouse.'

anything goes! Meaning, 'there are no rules and restrictions here, you can do whatever you like.' Popularized by the song and musical show with the title written by Cole Porter (1934). Compare the much older **this is/it's Liberty Hall**, which was probably coined by Oliver Goldsmith in *She Stoops To Conquer*, Act 2 (1773): 'This is Liberty-hall, gentlemen. You may do just as you please.' W. W. Reade wrote a book with the title *Liberty Hall* (1860).

anything you say may be taken down and used in evidence against you The police 'caution' to a person who may be charged with a crime has had various forms in the UK. The version you might expect from reading fiction would go something like: 'You are not obliged to say anything unless you wish to do so but, I must warn you, whatever you do say will be taken down and may be given in evidence *against you*.' But this does not conform with modern practice. British police are advised that care should be taken to avoid any suggestion that evidence might only be used *against* a person, as this could prevent an innocent person making a statement that might help clear him of a charge. Old habits die hard, however. The phrase is etched on the national consciousness, and it must have been said at one time. Charles Dickens in *Our Mutual Friend* (1864–5) has Mr Inspector (an early example of a police officer in fiction) give 'the caution' (which he refers to as such) in these words: 'It's my duty to inform you that whatever you say, will be used against you' (Bk 4, Chap. 12). Earlier, Dickens had Mr Bucket saying in *Bleak House*, Chap. 49 (1852–3): 'It's my duty to inform you that any observation you may make will be liable to be used against you.' Examples of the 'against you' caution also appear in Sherlock Holmes short stories by Conan Doyle (1905 and 1917). In the US, the phrase may still be found. In *Will* (1980), G. Gordon Liddy describes what he said during a raid on Dr Timothy Leary's house in connection with drugs charges (in March 1966): 'I want you to understand that you don't have to make any statement, and any statement you do make may be used against you in a court of law.' A decision of the US Supreme Court (*Miranda v. Arizona*, 1966) – known as the Miranda Decision – requires law enforcement officials to tell anyone taken into custody that, *inter alia*, anything the person says can be used against them.

any time, any place, anywhere A line from Martini advertisements in the UK from the early 1970s. Barry Day of the McCann-Erickson advertising agency that coined the phrase agreed (1981) that there is more than a hint of Bogart in the line, but adds: 'As a Bogart fan of some standing, with my union dues all paid up, I think I would have known if I had lifted from one of his utterances, but I honestly can't place it.' Possibly there is a hint of Harry Lime, too. In the film *The Third Man* (1949), Lime says (in the run-up to the famous cuckoo-clock speech): 'When you make up your mind, send me a message – I'll meet you any place, any time . . .' Two popular songs of the 1920s were 'Anytime, Any Day, Anywhere' and 'Anytime, Anywhere, Any Place – I Don't Care'. The exact phrase 'any time, any place, anywhere' had occurred, however, before the

Martini ads in the song 'I Love To Cry at Weddings' from the musical *Sweet Charity* (1966) and in the film script of Tennessee Williams's *Cat on a Hot Tin Roof* (US 1958). Precisely as 'Anytime, Anyplace, Anywhere', it was the title of an R&B hit for Joe Morris in the US (1950) – sung by Little Laurie Tate. Even earlier it was spoken in the film *The Strawberry Blonde* (US 1941) of which the last lines are: 'When I want to kiss my wife, I'll kiss her anytime, anyplace, anywhere. That's the kind of hairpin I am' – this was written by the Epstein brothers who co-wrote *Casablanca*, so perhaps that is the Bogart connection? And then in *His Girl Friday* (US 1940), Cary Grant says to Rosalind Russell: 'I'd know you anytime, anyplace, anywhere' – having just re-met his ex-wife, he is recalling a line he had used to her on the night he proposed. In April 1987, a woman called Marion Joannou was jailed at the Old Bailey for protecting the man who had strangled her husband. She was nicknamed 'Martini Marion' because, apparently, she would have sex 'any time, any place, anywhere'.

a-okay Another way of saying 'OK' or 'All systems working'. From NASA engineers in the early days of the US space effort 'who used to say it during radio transmission tests because the sharper sound of "A" cut through the static better than "O"' – Tom Wolfe, *The Right Stuff* (1979). Now largely redundant, it seems never to have been used by astronauts themselves. President Reagan, emerging from a day of medical tests at a naval hospital in June 1986, pronounced himself 'A-OK'. Another derivation is that 'a-okay' is a melding of 'A1' and 'OK'.

'appen 'It may happen; happen it may; maybe; perhaps' – a North of England dialect expression, used for example by Uncle Mort (Robin Bailey), the scuffling, seedy old misogynist in Peter Tinniswood's funereal Yorkshire comedy series *I Didn't Know You Cared* on BBC TV (1975–9).

apple See AMERICAN AS.

(to be the) apple of one's eye To be what one cherishes most or holds most dear. The pupil of the eye has long been known as the 'apple' because of its supposed round, solid shape. To be deprived of the apple is to be blinded and lose something extremely valuable. The Bible has: 'He kept him as the apple of his eye' in Deuteronomy 32:10.

apple-pie order Meaning 'with everything in place; smart', this expression (known since 1780) possibly derives from the French *cap-à-pied*, wearing armour 'from head to foot'. Another suggested French origin is from *nappe pliée*, a folded tablecloth or sheet – though this seems a more likely source for the term **apple-pie bed**, known since 1781, for a bed made so that you can't get into it. On the other hand, a folded cloth or napkin does convey the idea of crispness and smartness.

(an) appointment in Samarra An appointment with Death, or one that simply cannot be avoided. The novel *Appointment in Samarra* (1934) by John O'Hara alludes to the incident – described also by W. Somerset Maugham in his play *Sheppey* (1933) – in which a servant is jostled by Death in the market at Baghdad. Terrified, he jumps on a horse and rides to Samarra (a city in northern Iraq) where he thinks Death will not be able to find him. When the servant's master asks Death why he treated him in this manner, Death replies that he had merely been surprised to encounter the servant in Baghdad . . . 'I had an appointment with him tonight in Samarra.' The story appears earlier in Jean Cocteau, *Le Grand Écart* (1923) – translator not known: 'A young Persian gardener said to his Prince: "Save me! I met Death in the garden this morning, and he gave me a threatening look. I wish that by tonight, by some miracle, I might be far away, in Ispahan." The Prince lent him his swiftest horse. That afternoon, as he was walking in the garden, the Prince came face to face with Death. "Why," he asked, "did you give my gardener a threatening look this morning?" "It was not a threatening look," replied Death. "It was an expression of surprise. For I saw him there this morning, and I knew that I would take him in Ispahan tonight".'

approbation from Sir Hubert Stanley is praise indeed Ironic comment on the source of praise or compliment. There is no actual Sir Hubert Stanley in *Who Was Who* or the *DNB*. However, there is a Sir *Herbert* Stanley, colonial administrator (1872–1955) who might fit the bill. But no, the origin of this remark is the line 'Approbation from Sir Hubert Stanley is praise indeed' which comes from the play *A Cure for the Heartache*, Act 5, Sc. 2 (1797) by the English playwright Thomas Morton (?1764–1838). Charles Dickens has 'Praise from Sir Hubert Stanley' in *Dombey and Son*, Chap. 1 (1846–8). P. G. Wodehouse uses the expression as 'this is praise from Sir Hubert Stanley' in both *Psmith Journalist*, Chap. 15 (1915) and *Piccadilly Jim*, Chap. 18 (1918). It is alluded to in Dorothy L. Sayers, *Gaudy Night*, Chap. 15 (1935): 'At the end of the first few pages [Lord Peter Wimsey] looked up to remark: "I'll say one thing for the writing of detective fiction: you know how to put your story together; how to arrange the evidence." "Thank you," said Harriet drily; "praise from Sir Hubert is praise indeed".'

après nous le déluge **[after us, the flood]** The Marquise de Pompadour's celebrated remark to Louis XV was made on 5 November 1757 after Frederick the Great had defeated the French and Austrian armies at the Battle of Rossbach. It carries with it the suggestion that nothing matters once you are dead and has also been interpreted as a premonition of the French Revolution. *Bartlett* (1980) notes that this 'reputed reply' by the king's mistress was recorded by three authorities, though a fourth gives it to the king himself. *Bartlett* then claims the saying was not original anyway but 'an old French proverb'. However, the *ODP* has as an English proverb, 'After us the deluge' . . . deriving from Mme de Pompadour. Its only citation is Burnaby's *Ride to Khiva* (1876): 'Our rulers did not trouble their heads much about the matter. "India will last my time . . . and after me the Deluge".' Metternich, the Austrian diplomat and chancellor, may later have said *'après moi le déluge'*, meaning that everything would grind to a halt when he stopped controlling it. The deluge alluded to in all cases is a dire event like the Great Flood or 'universal deluge' of Noah's time.

Aquarius See AGE OF.

Arabs See FOLD ONE'S TENTS.

aren't plums cheap? Catchphrase of the British music-hall 'Naval Comic', Bob Nelson, of whom no other information is to hand. In *The Bandsman's Daughter* (1979), Irene Thomas recalls, 'One comedian acrobat who towards the end of his act used to do a handstand balanced on the back of a chair. Then, upside down, he'd turn his poor old beetroot coloured face towards the audience and croak, *apropos* nothing, "Aren't plums cheap today?"'

aren't we all? In Frederick Lonsdale's play *Aren't We All?* (1924) – the title proving that the phrase was well established by then – the Vicar says, 'Grenham, you called me a bloody old fool,' and Lord Grenham replies, 'But aren't we all, old friend?' Ray Henderson composed the song 'I'm a Dreamer, Aren't We All' in 1929. The collusive use has possibly weakened and the phrase become a simple jokey retort or a way of coping with an unintentional *double entendre*: 'I'm afraid I'm coming out of my trousers' – 'Aren't we all, dear, aren't we all?'

aren't you the lucky one? Congratulatory phrase from the 1920s, tinged with mockery but no envy.

are there any more at home like you? *Partridge/Catch Phrases* traces this chat-up line to the musical comedy *Floradora* (1899), which contains the song (written by Leslie Stuart) 'Tell Me, Pretty Maiden (Are There Any More At Home Like You?)' *Partridge* adds that the line was 'obsolete by 1970 – except among those with long memories'. Indeed, Tom Jones may be heard saying it to a member of the audience on the album *Tom Jones Live at Caesar's Palace Las Vegas* (1971).

are we downhearted? – no! A morale-boosting phrase connected with the early stages of the First World War but having political origins before that. The politician Joseph Chamberlain said in a 1906 speech: 'We are not downhearted. The only trouble is, we cannot understand what is happening to our neighbours.' The day after he was defeated as candidate in the Stepney Borough Council election of 1909, Clement Attlee, the future British Prime Minister, was greeted by a colleague with the cry, 'Are we downhearted?' (He replied, 'Of course, we are.') On 18 August 1914, the *Daily Mail* reported: 'For two days the finest troops England has ever sent across the sea have been marching through the narrow streets of old Boulogne in solid columns of khaki . . . waving as they say that new slogan of Englishmen: "Are we downhearted? . . . Nooooo!" "Shall we win? . . . Yessss!"' Horatio Nicholls (Lawrence Wright) incorporated the phrase into a song (1917).

are yer courtin' [are you courting]? Stock phrase from the BBC radio show *Have A Go* (1946–67) – what the host, Wilfred Pickles, would say when chatting up unmarried women contestants of any age ('from nineteen to ninety').

are you all right? Fanny's all right! Stock phrase of the American actress, comedienne and singer Fanny Brice (1891–1951).

are you a man or a mouse? Usually said by a female disparagingly of a timorous male, this seems to have originated in the US, by the 1930s. A correspondent, Irene Summers (1998), remembered it being a feature of an Eddie Cantor film, *Strike Me Pink* (1935): 'Eddie played a coward as usual, working in a dry cleaners. He triumphed in the end, beat the bullies and got the girl. When we came out, the attendants gave us little coins, with a mouse on one side and a man on the other, with the words, "Are you a man or a mouse?" and "See Eddie Condon in 'Strike Me Pink'".' In the Marx Bros' film *A Day At the Races* (1937) Alan Jones asks it of Groucho, who replies: 'You put a piece of cheese down here and you'll find out.' Later on, the fondly remembered Sabrina recorded the song 'Man Not a Mouse' from the 1950s' musical *Grab Me a Gondola*. In BBC TV, *Yes, Minister* (1980s), a minister overridden by a spokesman is asked, 'Are you a man or a *mouth?*'

are you going to pardon me? Catchphrase from the BBC radio show *Ray's a Laugh* (1949–60), spoken by Charles Hawtrey as Mr Muggs.

are you looking for a punch up the bracket? Stock phrase of Tony Hancock in his BBC radio show, *Hancock's Half-Hour* (1954–9), though merely popularized and not coined by him. For no accountable reason, 'bracket' refers to the nose and mouth, but really the target area is unspecified. Compare: **a punch up the conk**, where the nose is obviously specified – as in the BBC radio *Goon Show*, 'The Mysterious Punch-Up-the-Conker' (7 February 1957).

are you now or have you ever been (a member of the Communist Party)?
The stock phrase of McCarthyism, the pursuit and public ostracism of suspected US Communist sympathizers at the time of the war with Korea in the early 1950s. Senator Joseph McCarthy was the instigator of the 'witch hunts', which led to the blacklisting of people in various walks of life, notably the film business. Those appearing at hearings of the House of Representatives Committee on UnAmerican Activities (1947-*circa* 1957) were customarily challenged with the full question. *Are You Now Or Have You Ever Been?* was the title of a radio/stage play (1978) by Eric Bentley.

are you ready, Eddie? Slogan for the *Today* newspaper in the UK (1986). Not an immortal slogan but worth mentioning for what it illustrates about advertising agencies and the way they work. *Today*, a new national newspaper using the latest production technology, was launched by Eddie Shah, hitherto known as a union-busting printer and publisher of provincial papers. In its collective wisdom, the Wight Collins Rutherford Scott agency, charged with promoting the new paper's launch, built the whole campaign around the above slogan. Why had they chosen it? Starting with the name 'Eddie' – Mr Shah being thought of as a folk hero in some quarters – the agency found that it rhymed with 'ready'. So the man was featured in TV ads being asked this important question by his staff. Unfortunately, the ad agency had zeroed in all too well on the most pertinent aspect of the new paper's launch. *Today* was *not* ready, and the slogan echoed hollowly from the paper's disastrous start to the point at which Mr Shah withdrew. The phrase had earlier been used as the title of a track on the Emerson, Lake and Palmer album *Tarkus* (1971), where it referred to the recording engineer, Eddie Offord (to whom it had,

presumably, been addressed). The same rhyme occurs in **ready for Freddie**, meaning 'ready for the unexpected, the unknown or the unusual' (according to *DOAS*, 1960), and was a phrase that came out of the 'L'il Abner' comic strip of the 1930s; **are you ready for Freddy?** was used as a slogan to promote the film *Nightmare on Elm Street – Part 4* (US 1989) – referring to the gruesome character, Freddy Krueger.

are you ready to take the challenge?
This was used in some marketing tests in 1990–1 for an unidentifed product – 'I fill out a form and stand in line. When it came to my turn I was presented with a tray on which stood two unmarked beakers and two upturned tubs. My jolly uniformed woman smiled and said: "Are you ready to take the challenge?"' – *Independent on Sunday* (23 September 1990). Taking up a challenge was originally a procedure in medieval chivalry. The knight making the challenge would throw down his gauntlet. The person accepting the challenge would formally pick it up. Mostly in political and business use, there is the phrase **to meet the challenge** – a cliché by the mid-20th century. It occurs along with other rhetorical clichés during the 'Party Political Speech' (written by Max Schreiner) on the Peter Sellers' comedy album *The Best of Sellers* (1958): 'If any part of what I say is challenged, I am more than ready to meet that challenge'. 'Meet the challenge, make the change' – slogan, Labour Party Conference (1989); 'With the Tories reeling from their worst nationwide election defeat in modern times, the Prime Minister [John Major] marched out to Downing Street to promise: "I will meet a challenge whenever it comes"' – *Evening Standard* (London) (6 May 1994); 'The World Bank reports: "Deficiencies in the system of legal education and training and a dearth in appropriate standards of professional ethics, have left legal practitioners complacent and unprepared to meet the challenge of their business clients competing in a global economy"' – *Financial Times* (15 July 1994).

are you sitting comfortably? – then I'll begin This was the customary way of beginning stories on BBC radio's daily programme for small children, *Listen with Mother*. The phrase was used from the programme's inception in January 1950. Julia Lang, the original presenter, recalled in 1982: 'The first day it came out inadvertently. I just said it. The next day I didn't. Then there was a flood of letters from children saying, "I couldn't listen because I wasn't ready".' It remained a more or less essential part of the proceedings until the programme ended in 1982. Sometimes Lang said, '. . . then *we'll* begin.' In the archive recording of 7 February 1950, Lang says, 'Are you sitting *quite* comfortably, then I'll begin.' In the *Times* obituary (18 January 1988) of Frieda Fordham, an analytical psychologist, it was stated that *she* had actually coined the phrase when advising the BBC's producers. From the same programme came the stock phrase **and when it/the music stops**, [Daphne Oxenford, or some other] **will be here to tell you a story**.

are you there, Moriarty? Name of a rather rough party game that has probably been played since the early 20th century, if not earlier. Why it is called this is not known, though perhaps it might have something to do with the evil ex-Professor James Moriarty, arch-enemy of Sherlock Holmes and the man who apparently killed him off. In the game, two blindfolded individuals lie on the floor, facing each other and holding left hand to left hand. In their free hands they hold rolled-up newspapers or magazines. One says, 'Are you there, Moriarty?' The other answers, 'Yes' or 'I am here', and the first then attempts to hit him on the head, if he can locate it. Obviously, the person about to be hit can attempt to move his head out of the line of fire. It takes all people . . .

'arf a mo', Kaiser! A 1915–16 recruiting poster during the First World War showed a British 'Tommy' lighting a pipe prior to going into action, with this caption underneath. The phrase caught on from there. A photograph of a handwritten sign from the start of the Second World War shows it declaring, ''Arf a mo, 'itler!' In 1939, there was also a short documentary produced by British Paramount News with the title *'Arf a Mo' Hitler*.

Argentina See DON'T CRY.

arm See CHANCE ONE'S.

(to cost an) arm and a leg A measurement of (high) cost, as in 'That'll cost you an arm and a leg'. Probably of American origin, mid-20th century. Compare this with B. H. Malkin's 1809 translation of Le Sage's *Gil Blas*: 'He was short in his reckoning by an arm and a leg.'

armed to the teeth Heavily armed, alluding to the fact that pirates are sometimes portrayed as carrying a knife or sabre held between the teeth. 'Is there any reason why we should be armed to the teeth?' – Richard Cobden, *Speeches* (1849); 'Mujahedin . . . played a major role in bringing down the Shah and armed to the teeth' – *The Daily Telegraph* (21 August 1979); 'Once upon a time it would have been pirates fighting over buried treasure. Nowadays it's redneck firemen (Bill Paxton and William Sadler) under siege from a posse of drug dealers (headed by rappers Ice T and Ice Cube) who are armed to the teeth with guns and mobile phones' – *The Sunday Telegraph* (9 May 1993).

armpit See MAKES YOUR.

arms and the man The title of George Bernard Shaw's play *Arms and the Man* (1894) comes from the first line of Virgil's *Aeneid*: '*Arma virumque cano* [Of arms and the man, I sing]' or rather from Dryden's translation of the same: 'Arms, and the man I sing.' Earlier than Shaw, Thomas Carlyle, suggesting in *Past and Present* (1843) that a true modern epic was technological rather than military, had written: 'For we are to bethink us that the Epic verily is not *Arms and the Man*, but *Tools and the Man*.'

(the) army game *The Army Game* was an immensely popular British TV comedy series (1957–62). Its title homed in on a phrase that seemed to sum up the attitude of those condemned to spend their lives in the ranks. Apparently of American origin, possibly by 1900, 'it's the old army game' refers to the military system as it works to the disadvantage of those in the lower ranks. From Theodore Fredenburgh's *Soldiers March* (1930): 'I get the idea. It's the old army game: first, pass the buck, second . . .' The phrase also occurs in the film *You Can't Take It With You* (US 1938). Compare **war game** (known by 1900), a theoretical way of fighting battles (and a type of chess). *The War Game* (1965) was the title of a TV film by Peter Watkins that was for a long time not shown because of its vivid depiction of the effect of nuclear war on the civilian population.

(the) arrogance of power *The Arrogance of Power* (1967) was the title of a book by the American Democratic politician J. William Fulbright. It questioned the basis of US foreign policy, particularly in Vietnam and the Dominican Republic. In the previous year, Fulbright, the Democratic chairman of the Senate Foreign Relations Committee, had given lectures establishing his theme: 'A psychological need that nations seem to have . . . to prove that they are bigger, better or stronger than other nations.'

arse See ALL BALLS; DOESN'T KNOW HIS.

arsehole See FROM ARSEHOLE.

arsenic and old lace Title of a play (1941) by Joseph Kesselring (filmed US 1941) about two old ladies who poison elderly gentlemen. It plays upon the earlier **lavender and old lace**, itself used as the title of sentimental novel (1902) by Myrtle Reed. That phrase came to be used as a way of indicating old-fashioned gentility.

ars gratia artis Motto of the Metro-Goldwyn-Mayer film company. Howard Dietz, director of publicity and advertising with the original Goldwyn Pictures company, had left Columbia University not long before creating it *circa* 1916. When asked to design a trademark, he based it on the university's lion and added the Latin words meaning 'art for art's sake' underneath. The trademark and motto were carried over when Samuel Goldwyn retired to make way for the merger of Metropolitan with the interests of Louis B. Mayer in what has become known since as Metro-Goldwyn-Mayer. Goldwyn may never have subscribed to the sentiment it expressed. Most of his working life was spent as an independent producer, famously more interested in money than art.

art See AS THE ART.

Arthur See BIG-HEARTED.

Arthur's bosom A malapropism for ABRAHAM'S BOSOM from Shakespeare's *Henry V*, II.iii.9 (1599). The Hostess (formerly Mistress Quickly) says of the dead Falstaff: 'Nay, sure, he's not in hell: he's in Arthur's bosom, if ever man went to Arthur's bosom.'

artificial See AMUSING.

(the) art of the possible What politics is said to be. A phrase used as the title of memoirs (1971) by R. A. (Lord) Butler, the British Conservative politician. In the preface to the paperback edition of *The Art of the Possible*, Butler noted that this definition of politics appears first to have been used in modern times by Bismarck in 1866–7 (in conversation with Meyer von Waldeck: '*Die Politik ist keine exakte Wissenschaft, wie viele der Herren Professoren sich einbilden, sondern eine Kunst* [politics are not a science, as many professors declare, but an art]'). If he said precisely the phrase as used by Butler, it would have been: '*Die Politik ist die Lehr vom Möglichen*'. Others who have touched on the idea included Cavour, Salvador de Madriaga, Pindar and Camus. To these might be added J.K. Galbraith's rebuttal: 'Politics is not the art of the possible. It consists in choosing between the disastrous and the unpalatable' – letter to President Kennedy (March 1962), quoted in *Ambassador's Journal* (1969).

art thou weary? From a hymn 'translated from the Greek' by the Reverend J. M. Neale (1818–66). It continues: '. . . art thou languid, / art thou sore distressed?' Compare: 'Art thou troubled? / Music will calm thee. Art thou weary . . .' – an aria from Handel's opera *Rodelinda* (1725), with libretto by Salvi.

as any fule kno [as any fool know] A stock phrase of the schoolboy character Nigel Molesworth in the books written by Geoffrey Willans and illustrated by Ronald Searle in the 1950s. The books retained the schoolboy spelling of the 'Curse of St Custard's'. From *Down With Skool!* (1953): 'A chiz is a swiz or swindle as any fule kno.' The phrase had a revival from the 1980s onwards when the books were republished.

as awkward as a pig with side pockets
(Of a person) very awkward. *Apperson*
finds 'as much need of it as a toad of a
side pocket, said of a person who desires
anything for which he has no real occasion', by 1785, and 'as much use as a cow
has for side pockets', in *Cheshire Proverbs*
(1917). Compare **as awkward as a cow
with a musket**.

as black as Egypt's night Very black
indeed. The allusion is biblical. Exodus
10:21 mentions the plague of 'darkness
which may be felt' (a sandstorm, perhaps),
that Moses imposed on the Pharaoh in
response to the Lord's instruction. Samuel
Wesley (d. 1837) had: 'Gloomy and dark as
Hell's or Egypt's night'; and John and
Charles Wesley's version of Psalm 55
contains (although the Bible doesn't): 'And
horror deep as Egypt's night, or hell's
tremendous gloom.' A more benign view
of Egypt's night occurs in Kipling's 'The
White Man's Burden' (1899) where the
people of India complain of British
colonization: 'Why brought ye us from
bondage, / Our loved Egyptian night?' –
where the reference is to civilized Egypt.
In the poem 'Riding Down from Bangor',
written by the American Louis Shreve
Osborne and anthologized by 1897, a
bearded student and a village maiden
make the most of it when the railway train
in which they are travelling enters a
tunnel: 'Whiz! Slap! Bang! into the tunnel
quite / Into glorious darkness, black as
Egypt's night . . .'

as black as Newgate knocker This
comparison meaning 'extremely black' and
known by 1881 alludes to Newgate gaol,
the notorious prison for the City of London
until 1880. It must have had a very formidable and notable knocker because not
only do we have this expression but a
'Newgate knocker' was the name given to
a lock of hair twisted to look like a
knocker.

as black as the Devil's nutting bag
Apperson has this by 1866. Mrs Jean
Wigget wrote (1995) that her mother used
to say that 'Dirty hands looked "like the
colour of Old Nick's nutting bag".'

**as busy as a one-armed paperhanger
with the itch** Colourful comparison,
listed by *Mencken* (1942) as an 'American
saying'. 'As busy as a one-armed man with
the nettle-rash pasting on wall-paper'
appears in O. Henry, *Gentle Grafter: The
Ethics of Pig* (1908). The supply is endless,
but here are a few more: 'as scarce as
rocking-horse manure' (an example from
Australia); 'as lonely as a country dunny'
(ditto); 'as mad as a gumtree full of galahs'
(ditto); 'as inconspicuous as Liberace at a
wharfies' picnic' (ditto); 'as black as an
Abo's arsehole' (ditto); 'as easy as juggling
with soot'; 'as jumpy as a one-legged cat in
a sandbox'; 'as much chance as a fart in a
windstorm'; 'as much use as a one-legged
man at an arse-kicking contest' (or 'a
legless man in a pants-kicking contest' –
Gore Vidal, *Life* Magazine (9 June 1961);
'as likely as a snowstorm in Karachi'. In his
1973 novel *Red Shift*, Alan Garner has
'you're as much use as a chocolate teapot';
'as useless as a chocolate kettle' (of a UK
football team, quoted on BBC Radio *Quote
. . . Unquote* (1986).

as cold as charity Ironic description of
charity that is grudgingly given or dis-
pensed without warmth – particularly by
the public charities of the Victorian era. In
1382, John Wycliffe translated Matthew
24:12 as: 'The charite of many schal wexe
coold.' Robert Southey, *The Soldier's Wife*
(1721), has: 'Cold is thy heart and as
frozen as charity'. Anthony Trollope, *Can
You Forgive Her?*, Chap. 43 (1865) has:
'The wind is as cold as charity.'

as dark as the inside of a cow As dark
as it can possibly be. A likely first appearance of this phrase is in Mark Twain,
Roughing It, Chap. 4 (1891). He puts it
within quotes, thus: '. . . made the place
"dark as the inside of a cow," as the
conductor phrased it in his picturesque
way.' So probably an American coinage. A
few years later Somerville & Ross were
writing in *Some Experiences of an Irish RM*,
Chap. 10 (1899): 'As black as the inside of
a cow'.

as different as chalk from cheese Very
different indeed (despite the superficial
similarity that they both look whitish). In
use since the 16th century, although the
pairing of the alliterative chalk and cheese
has been known since 1393. Sometimes
found as 'not to know chalk from cheese'

– unable to tell the difference – or 'to be able to tell chalk from cheese' – to have good sense.

as dim as a Toc H lamp Very dim (unintelligent). Dates from the First World War in which there was a Christian social centre for British 'other ranks' opened at Talbot House in Poperinghe, Belgium, in 1915 and named after an officer who was killed – G. W. L. Talbot, son of a Bishop of Winchester. 'Toc H' was signalese for 'Talbot House'. The institute continued long after the war under its founder, the Reverend P. B. ('Tubby') Clayton. A lamp was its symbol.

as Dorothy Parker once said . . . The title of a stage show (*circa* 1975), devoted to the wit of Dorothy Parker and performed by Libby Morris. This is testimony to the fact that Parker is undoubtedly the most quoted woman of the 20th century. It is probably an allusion to the verse of Cole Porter's song 'Just One of Those Things' (1935), that begins: 'As Dorothy Parker once said to her boy friend, "Fare thee well" . . .'

as easy as falling off a log Very simple. This citation from the New Orleans *Picayune* (29 March 1839) suggests a North American origin and the quotation marks, that it was reasonably well established by that date: 'He gradually went away from the Lubber, and won the heat, "just as easy as falling off a log".'

as every schoolboy knows 'It is a well-known fact' – a consciously archaic use. Robert Burton wrote 'Every schoolboy hath . . .' in *The Anatomy of Melancholy* (1621) and Bishop Jeremy Taylor used the expression 'every schoolboy knows it' in 1654. In the next century, Jonathan Swift had, 'I might have told how oft Dean Perceval / Displayed his pedantry unmerciful, / How haughtily he cocks his nose, / To tell what every schoolboy knows', in his poem 'The Country Life' (1722). But the most noted user of this rather patronizing phrase was Lord Macaulay, the historian, who would say things like, 'Every schoolboy knows who imprisoned Montezuma, and who strangled Atahualpa' (essay on 'Lord Clive', January 1840). But do they still?

as if I cared . . . Catchphrase from the 1940s BBC radio series *ITMA*. Sam Fairfechan (Hugh Morton) would say, 'Good morning, how are you today?' and immediately add, 'As if I cared . . .' The character took his name from Llanfairfechan, a seaside resort in North Wales, where Ted Kavanagh, *ITMA*'s scriptwriter, lived when the BBC Variety Department was evacuated to nearby Bangor during the early part of the Second World War.

as it happens A verbal tic of the British disc jockey Jimmy Savile (later Sir James Savile OBE) (b. 1926). He used it as the title of his autobiography in 1974. However, when the book came out in paperback the title had been changed to *Love Is an Uphill Thing* because (or so it was explained) the word 'love' in the title would ensure extra sales. After dance-hall exposure, Savile began his broadcasting career with Radio Luxembourg in the 1950s. His other stock phrase **how's about that then, guys and gals?** started then. For example, on Radio Luxembourg, *The Teen and Twenty Disc Club*, he certainly said, 'Hi, there, guys and gals, welcome to the . . .'

as I was saying before I was so rudely interrupted . . . A humorous phrase used when resuming an activity after an enforced break. In September 1946, Cassandra (William O'Connor) resumed his column in the *Daily Mirror* after it had been suspended for the duration of the Second World War, with: 'As I was saying when I was interrupted, it is a powerful hard thing to please all the people all the time.' In June of that same year, announcer Leslie Mitchell is reported to have begun BBC TV's resumed transmissions with: 'As I was saying before I was so rudely interrupted.' The phrase sounds as if it might have originated in music-hall routines of the I DON'T WISH TO KNOW THAT, KINDLY LEAVE THE STAGE type. Compare A. A. Milne, *Winnie-the-Pooh* (1926): '"AS – I – WAS – SAYING," said Eeyore loudly and sternly, "as I was saying when I was interrupted by various Loud Sounds, I feel that – ".' Fary Luis de León, the Spanish poet and religious writer, is believed to have resumed a lecture at Salamanca University in 1577 with, '*Dicebamus* *hesterno die* . . . [We were saying yester-day].' He had been in prison for five years.

as I walked out one midsummer morning The title of Laurie Lee's memoir *As I Walked Out One Midsummer Morning* (1969) uses a format phrase that occurs in a number of English folk songs. Indeed, in his earlier *Cider With Rosie*, Lee refers to an old song with the line, 'As I walked out one May morning'. Another folk song begins, 'As I rode out one midsummer's morning.' Compare the line from the Robert Burns' poem, 'As I went out ae [= one] May morning' (which is based on an old Scottish song).

ask See DON'T.

ask a silly question (get a silly answer) A response to an answer that is less than helpful or amounts to a put-down. The second part is often not spoken, just inferred. Probably since the late 19th century.

ask the man who owns one This slogan for Packard motors, in the USA from *circa* 1902, originated with James Ward Packard, the founder of the company, and appeared for many years in all Packard advertising and sales material. Someone had written asking for more information about his motors. Packard told his secretary: 'Tell him that we have no literature – we aren't that big yet – but if he wants to know how good an automobile the Packard is, tell him to ask the man who owns one.' A 1903 Packard placard is the first printed evidence of the slogan in use. It lasted for more than 35 years.

as lazy as Ludlum's dog who lay down to bark Very lazy. *Partridge/Slang* has 'lazy as Ludlum's/(David) Laurence's/Lumley's dog . . . meaning extremely lazy . . . According to the [old] proverb, this admirable creature leant against a wall to bark' and compares the 19th-century 'lazy as Joe the marine who laid down his musket to fart' and 'lazy as the tinker who laid his budget to fart'. *Apperson* finds 'lazy as *Ludlam's* dog, that leant his head against a wall to bark' in Ray's proverb collection (1670).

as long as you've got your health, that's the main thing A resounding cliché –

uttered in BBC TV, *Hancock*, 'The Blood Donor' (23 June 1961). The corollary: 'If you haven't got your health, you haven't got anything.'

as many —— as you've had hot dinners Originally perhaps 'I've had as many women . . .', this is an experienced person's boast to one less so. Well established by the mid-20th century, then subjected to endless variation. 'I've had more gala luncheons than you've had hot dinners' – BBC TV, *Monty Python's Flying Circus* (12 October 1969); 'If I agreed to these sorts of requests my name would be on more notepaper than you've had hot dinners' – letter from Kenneth Williams (16 July 1975) in *The Kenneth Williams Letters* (1994).

as near as damn is to swearing Very close indeed. First heard from a Liverpool optician in 1963. No confirmation from any other source.

as night follows day . . . Inevitably. Possibly a Shakespearean coinage – in *Hamlet* (I.iii.78) (1600), Polonius says: 'This above all: to thine own self be true, / And it must follow as the night the day / Thou canst not then be false to any man'. Further examples: 'Because, if incomes run ahead of production, it will follow as night follows day, that the only result will be higher prices and no lasting improvement in living standards' – Harold Wilson in a speech to the Shopworkers' Union Conference (1965); 'As surely as night follows day, the pompous, the pretentious and the politically correct will seize the lion's share of the money available' – leading article, *Daily Mail* (28 April 1995).

as one does A slightly destabilizing comment in conversation. Indentified by Miles Kington in *The Independent* (2 May 2000): 'One recent expression that has caught on in a big way is: "As one does," or variants of it. Someone says, "I was going along the Piccadilly the other day wearing one green, one brown sock," and while all the other listeners are waiting patiently to hear why this happened and whether it can be made funny, there is always one smart alec who pipes up: "As one does." That is still very trendy, and I wish it wasn't.' Another version is **as you**

do. 'The couple retain a pad in Canada as well as homes in London, New York and Palm Beach, and it's to Toronto that Lady Black "flies to get her hair cut". As you do' – *The Guardian* (26 August 2002).

as pleased as Punch   The earliest citation for this phrase is in a letter from the poet Thomas Moore to Lady Donegal in 1813: 'I was (as the poet says) as pleased as Punch.' Obviously this alludes to the appearance of Mr Punch, a character known in England from the time of the Restoration (1660). As his face is carved on wood, it never changes expression and is always beaming. The *Longman Dictionary of English Idioms* (1979) is thus clearly wrong in attributing the *origin* of the phrase to 'the cheerful pictures of the character Punch, who appeared on the covers of *Punch* magazine in the 1840s'. Even earlier, there was the expression **as proud as punch**. A description of a visit by George III and his Queen to Wilton House in 1778 is contained in a letter from a Dr Eyre to Lord Herbert (1 January 1779). He says: 'The Blue Closet within was for her Majesty's private purposes, where there was a red new velvet Close Stool, and a very handsome China Jordan, which I had the honour to produce from an old collection, & you may be sure, I am proud as Punch, that her Majesty condescended to piss in it.' This version – 'as proud as Punch' – would now seem to have died out, more or less, although Christy Brown, *Down All the Days*, Chap. 17 (1970) has, 'Every man-jack of them sitting there proud as punch with their sons . . .'

as queer as Dick's hatband (it went round twice and then didn't meet or **wouldn't tie)**   Very odd. Numerous versions of this saying have been recorded but all indicate that something is not right with a person or thing. 'A botched-up job done with insufficient materials was "like Dick's hat-band that went half-way round and tucked"' – according to Flora Thompson, *Lark Rise*, Chap. 3 (1939). The *OED2* gives the phrase thus: 'as queer (tight, odd, etc.) as Dick's (or Nick's) hatband', and adds: 'Dick or Nick was probably some local character or half-wit, whose droll sayings were repeated.'

Partridge/Slang describes it as 'an intensive tag of chameleonic sense and problematic origin' and dating it from the mid-18th to the early 19th century, finds a Cheshire phrase, 'all my eye and Dick's hatband', and also a version that went, 'as queer as Dick's hatband, that went nine times round and wouldn't meet.' In *Grose* (1796) is the definition: 'I am as queer as Dick's hatband; that is, out of spirits, or don't know what ails me.' But who was Dick, if anybody? *Brewer* (1894) was confident that it knew the answer: Richard Cromwell (1626–1712), who succeeded Oliver, his father, as Lord Protector in 1658 and did not make a very good job of it. Hence, 'Dick's hatband' was his 'crown', as in the following expressions: *Dick's hatband was made of sand* ('his regal honours were a "rope of sand"'), *as queer as Dick's hatband* ('few things have been more ridiculous than the exaltation and abdication of Oliver's son') and *as tight as Dick's hatband* ('the crown was too tight for him to wear with safety').

as right as ninepence   Very right, proper, correct, in order. But why ninepence? Once again, the lure of alliteration lead to the (probably) earlier phrase 'as nice as ninepence', and then the slightly less happy phrase resulted when someone was coining an 'as right as' comparison. In any case, the word 'ninepence' occurs in a number of proverbial phrases ('as like as nine pence to nothing', 'as neat as ninepence'), dating from the time when this was a more substantial amount of money than it now is.

as seen on TV   A line used in print advertising to underline a connection with products already shown in TV commercials. Presumably of American origin and dating from the 1940s/50s. Now also used to promote almost anything – books, people – that has ever had the slightest TV exposure. From *Joyce Grenfell Requests the Pleasure* (1976): 'There was sponge cake of the most satisfactory consistency. Unlike the bready stuff that passes for sponge cake today (machine-made, packaged to be stirred up, as seen on TV) . . .'

as sure as eggs is eggs   Absolutely certain. *A New Dictionary of the Terms Ancient and Modern of the Canting Crew* by 'B.E.' has 'As sure as eggs be eggs' in 1699. There is no very obvious reason why eggs should be 'sure', unless the saying is a corruption of the mathematician or logician's '*x* is *x*'. But by the 18th century, the saying was being shortened to 'as sure as eggs', which might dispose of that theory. Known by 1680. It occurs also in Charles Dickens, *The Pickwick Papers*, Chap.43 (1836–7). Compare the rather different **like as one egg to another** (i.e. very like) which dates from Plautus in Latin but can be found in English forms from 1542. Shakespeare, *The Winter's Tale*, I.ii.129 (1611) has: 'Yet they say we are / Almost as like as eggs.'

as sure as I'm riding this bicycle A rather meaningless assertion of certainty or truth, not to be taken too seriously. Michael Flanders says, 'Absolutely true, as sure as I'm riding this bicycle', in his explanation following the song 'Commonwealth Fair' on the record album *Tried By the Centre Court* (1977). This was obviously a questionable assertion as he was sitting in his wheel-chair at the time. Similar expressions, to be believed or not, include 'True as I'm strangling this ferret' in BBC radio's *I'm Sorry I'll Read That Again* (1960s), 'as true as the gospel' (earliest citation 1873), 'as true as I live' (1640), 'as true as steel/velvet' (1607).

(the) Assyrian came down like a wolf on the fold An allusion to Byron's line, 'The Assyrian came down like the wolf on the fold' from 'The Destruction of Sennacherib', St. 1 (1815). Byron based his poem on 2 Chronicles 32 and 2 Kings 19, in which Sennacherib, King of Assyria, gets his comeuppance for besieging Jerusalem in this manner.

as the art mistress said to the gardener! Monica (Beryl Reid), the posh schoolgirl friend of Archie Andrews in the BBC radio show, *Educating Archie* (1950–60), used this as an alternative to the traditional:

as the Bishop said to the actress (or *vice versa***)!** A device for turning a perfectly innocent preceding remark into a *double entendre* (e.g. 'I've never seen a female "Bottom" . . . as the Bishop said to the actress'). The phrase was established by 1930 when Leslie Charteris used it no fewer than five times in *Enter the Saint*, including: '"I should be charmed to oblige you – as the actress said to the bishop," replied the Saint'; '"There's something I particularly want to do to-night." "As the bishop said to the actress," murmured the girl'; and, '"You're getting on – as the actress said to the bishop," he murmured.'

as the crow flies The shortest distance between two points. Known by 1800. In fact, crows seldom fly in a straight line but the point of the expression is to express how *any* bird might fly without having to follow the wanderings of a road (as an earthbound traveller would have to do).

as the monkey said . . . Introductory phrase to a form of Wellerism. For example, if a child says it can't wait for something, the parent says: 'Well, as the monkey said when the train ran over its tail, "It won't be long now".' According to *Partridge/Slang*, there is any number of 'as the monkey said' remarks in which there is always a simple pun at stake: e.g. '"They're off!" shrieked the monkey, as he slid down the razor blade.'

as the poet has it/says A quoter's phrase, exhibiting either a knowing vagueness or actual ignorance. 'As the poet says' was being used in 1608. This is in a letter from the poet Thomas Moore to Lady Donegal in 1813: 'I was (as the poet says) as pleased as Punch.' When Margaret Thatcher was British Prime Minister, she was interviewed on radio (7 March 1982) about how she felt when her son, Mark, was believed lost on the Trans-Sahara car rally. She realized then, she said, that all the little things people worried about really were not worth it . . . 'As the poet said, "One clear morn is boon enough for being born," and so it is.' (In this case, she might be forgiven for using the phrase, as the authorship of the poem is not known.) The phrase can also be used to dignify an undistinguished quotation (rather as PARDON MY FRENCH excuses swearing): P. G. Wodehouse, *Mike* (1909): 'As the poet has it, "Pleasure is pleasure, and biz is biz".'

as the saying is Boniface, the landlord in George Farquhar's play *The Beaux' Stratagem* (1707), has a curious verbal mannerism. After almost every phrase, he adds, 'As the saying is . . .', but this was in itself a well-established phrase even then. In 1548, Hugh Latimer in *The Sermon on the Ploughers* had: 'And I fear me this land is not yet ripe to be ploughed. For as the saying is: it lacketh weathering.' Nowadays, 'as the saying goes' seems to be preferred. From R. L. Stevenson, *Treasure Island*, Chap. 4 (1883): 'There were moments when, as the saying goes, I jumped in my skin for terror.' Stevenson also uses 'as the saying is', however. Another, less common, form occurs in Mervyn Jones, *John and Mary*, Chap. 1 (1966): 'She gave herself, as the phrase goes. It wouldn't normally be said that I gave myself: I took her, as the phrase goes.'

as thick as two short planks   Very thick (or stupid) indeed. Of course, the length of the planks is not material here, but never mind. *OED2*'s sole mention of the phrase dates only from 1987. *Partridge/Slang* dates the expression from 1950.

as though there were no tomorrow Meaning, 'recklessly, with no regard to the future' or 'with desperate vigour' (especially the spending of money), as Paul Beale glosses it in his revision of *Partridge/Slang*, suggesting that it was adopted from the US in the late 1970s. However, it had been known since 1862. 'The free travel scheme aimed at encouraging cyclists to use trains unearthed a biking underground which took to the trains like there was no tomorrow' – *Time Out* (4 January 1980); 'Oil supplies that Americans at home continue to consume as though there were no tomorrow' – *Guardian Weekly* (3 February 1980); 'The evidence from the last major redrawing of council boundaries is mixed. Some authorities did go for broke, and spent their capital reserves as though there were no tomorrow' – *The Times* (9 June 1994).

astonish me!   A cultured variant of the more popular **amaze me!** or **surprise me!** inserted into conversation, for example, when the other speaker has just said something like, 'I don't know whether you will approve of what I've done . . .' In some cases, an allusion to the remark made by Serge Diaghilev, the Russian ballet impresario, to Jean Cocteau, the

French writer and designer, in Paris in 1912. Cocteau had complained to Diaghilev that he was not getting enough encouragement and the Russian exhorted him with the words, '*Étonne-moi!* I'll wait for you to astound me' – recorded in Cocteau's *Journals* (1956).

as we know it   'Politics as we know it will never be the same again' – *Private Eye* (4 December 1981). This simple intensifier has long been with us, however. From *Grove's Dictionary of Music* (1883): 'The Song as we know it in his [Schubert's] hands . . . such songs were his and his alone.' From a David Frost/Peter Cook sketch on sport clichés (BBC TV, *That Was the Week That Was*, 1962–3 series): 'The ghastly war which was to bring an end to organised athletics as we knew it.'

as we say in the trade   A slightly self-conscious (even camp) tag after the speaker has uttered a piece of jargon or something unusually grandiloquent. First noticed in the 1960s and probably of American origin. From the record album *Snagglepuss Tells the Story of the Wizard of Oz* (1966): '"Once upon a time", as we say in the trade . . .' Compare the older **as we say in France**, after slipping a French phrase into English speech (from the 19th century) – and compare THAT'S YOUR ACTUAL FRENCH.

at a stroke   Although this expression for 'with a single blow, all at once' can be traced back to Chaucer, the allusion latterly has been to the supposed words of Edward Heath, in the run-up to the British General Election of 1970. 'This would, at a stroke, reduce the rise in prices, increase productivity and reduce unemployment' are words contained in a press release (No. G.E. 228), from Conservative Central Office, dated 16 June 1970, that was concerned with tax cuts and a freeze on prices by nationalized industries. The perceived promise of 'at a stroke', though never actually spoken by Heath, came to haunt him when he became Prime Minister two days later.

at daggers drawn   Meaning, 'hostile to each other'. Formerly, 'at daggers' drawing' – when quarrels were settled by fights with daggers. Known by 1668 but common

only from the 19th century. 'Three ladies . . .
talked of for his second wife, all at daggers
drawn with each other' – Maria Edgeworth, *Castle Rackrent* (1801). 'It just
might be different this time, however,
because of a dimension that, amid all the
nuclear brouhaha, has received much less
attention than it merits. The two Korean
governments may be at daggers drawn,
but this has not stopped their companies
from doing business' – *The Independent*
(28 June 1994); 'The trick will be shown
on The Andrew Newton Hypnotic Experience which starts on BSkyB next Friday
and will have fellow illusionist Paul
McKenna glued to his seat – the pair have
been at daggers drawn for years' – *Today*
(8 October 1994).

(the) Athens of the North Nickname for
Edinburgh, presumably earned by the city
because of its reputation as a seat of
learning. It has many long-established
educational institutions and a university
founded in 1583. In addition, when the
'New Town' was constructed in the early
1800s, the city took on a fine classical
aspect. As such, it might remind spectators
of the Greek capital with its ancient
reputation for scholastic and artistic
achievement. Calling the Scottish capital
either 'Athens of the North' or 'Modern
Athens' seems always to have occasioned
some slight unease. James Hannay, writing
'On Edinburgh' (*circa* 1860), said: 'Pompous the boast, and yet a truth it speaks: /
A Modern Athens – fit for modern Greeks.'
Most such phrases date from the 19th
century, though this kind of comparison
has now become the prerogative of travel
writers and journalists. Paris has been
called the 'Athens of Europe', Belfast the
'Athens of Ireland', Boston, Mass., the
'Athens of the New World', and Cordoba,
Spain, the 'Athens of the West'. In one of
James A. Fitzpatrick's 'Traveltalks' – a
supporting feature of cinema programmes
from 1925 onwards – the commentator
said: 'And as the midnight sun lingers on
the skyline of the city, we most reluctantly
say farewell to Stockholm, Venice of the
North . . .' From Tom Stoppard's play
Jumpers (1972): 'McFee's dead . . . he took
offence at my description of Edinburgh as
the Reykjavik of the South.' 'All those

colorful canals, criss-crossing the city, that
had made travel agents abroad burble
about Bangkok as the Venice of the East' –
National Geographic Magazine (July
1967); 'Vallam is a religious spot, once
known as the Mount Athos of the North' –
Duncan Fallowell, *One Hot Summer in St
Petersburg* (1994).

at one fell swoop In a single movement
or action, all at once. A Shakespearean
coinage. In *Macbeth* (IV.iii.219), Macduff is
reacting to being told of the deaths of his
wife and all his children: 'Did you say all?
– O Hell-kite! – All? / What, all my pretty
chickens, and their dam, / At one fell
swoop?' So the image is that of a kite
swooping on its prey. 'Fell' here means
'fierce, ruthless'.

at one with the universe Meaning, 'in
harmony with the rest of mankind' or, at
least, 'in touch with what is going on in
some larger sphere'. When the Quaker
George Fox (1624–91) consented to take a
puff from a tobacco pipe, he said no one
could accuse him of 'not being at one with
the universe'. Sometimes the phrase is 'at-
oneness with the universe'. Compare, from
Gore Vidal, *Myra Breckinridge*, Chap. 13
(1968): '[With a hangover from gin and
marijuana] I lay in that empty bathtub with
the two rings, [and] looking up at the
single electric light bulb, I did have the
sense that I was at one with all creation.'

attention all shipping! For many years
on BBC radio, the shipping (weather)
forecasts were preceded by this call when
rough seas were imminent. Then would
follow: 'The following Gale Warning was
issued by the Meterological Office at 0600
hours GMT today . . .' (or whatever).

at the crack of dawn (or day) Meaning,
'at the break of day, dawn', but often used
jovially in the sense of unpleasantly early,
as when complaining of having to get up
early to carry out some task. Apparently of
US origin (by 1887), 'crack of day' seems
to have come before 'crack of dawn'.

at the drop of a hat Originally an
American expression meaning 'at a given
signal' – when the dropping of a hat was
the signal to start a fight or race. The
phrase has come to mean something more
like 'without needing encouragement,

without delay.' For example, 'He'll sit down and write a witty song for you at the drop of a hat.' Hence, the title of a revue *At the Drop of a Hat* (1957) featuring Michael Flanders and Donald Swann – who followed it up with *At the Drop of Another Hat* (1963).

at the end of the day This must have been a good phrase once – alluding perhaps to the end of the day's fighting or hunting. It appeared, for example, in Donald O'Keeffe's 1951 song, 'At the End of the Day, I Kneel and Pray'. But it was used in epidemic quantities during the 1970s and 1980s, and was particularly beloved of British trade unionists and politicians, indeed anyone wishing to tread verbal water. It was recognized as a hackneyed phrase by 1974, at least. Anthony Howard, a journalist, interviewing some BBC bigwig in *Radio Times* (March 1982), asked, 'At the end of the day one individual surely has to take responsibility, even if it has to be after the transmission has gone out?' Patrick Bishop, writing in *The Observer* (4 September 1983), said: 'Many of the participants feel at the end of the day, the effects of the affair [the abortion debate in the Irish Republic] will stretch beyond the mere question of amendment.' And Queen Elizabeth II, opening the Barbican Centre in March 1982, also used it. But it *is* the Queen's English, so perhaps she is entitled to do what she likes with it.

at the grassroots (or from the grassroots) A political cliché, used when supposedly reflecting the opinions of the 'rank and file' and the 'ordinary voter' rather than the leadership of the political parties 'at national level'. The full phrase is 'from the grassroots up' and has been used to describe anything of a fundamental nature since *circa* 1900 and specifically in politics from *circa* 1912 – originally in the US. A cliché in the UK since the late 1960s. A BBC Radio programme *From the Grassroots* started in 1970. Katherine Moore writing to Joyce Grenfell in *An Invisible Friendship* (letter of 13 October 1973): 'Talking of writing – why have roots now always got to be *grass* roots? And what a lot of them seem to be about.' 'In spite of official discouragement and some genuine

disquiet at the grassroots in both parties, 21 such joint administrations have been operating in counties, districts and boroughs over the past year' – *The Guardian* (10 May 1995); 'The mood of the grassroots party, and much of Westminster too, is for an end of big government, substantial cuts in taxation, cuts in public spending, toughness on crime, immigration and social-security spending, and as little Europe as possible' – *The Guardian* (10 May 1995).

at the midnight hour The 'midnight hour' phrase may first have occurred in the poetry of Robert Southey. *Thalaba the Destroyer* (written 1799–1800, published 1801), a romance set in medieval Arabia, contains (Bk 8): 'But when the Cryer from the Minaret / Proclaims the midnight hour, / Hast thou a heart to see her?' Charles Lamb's friend 'Ralph Bigod' [John Fenwick] in his essay 'The two Races of Men' (1820) has: 'How magnificent, how *ideal* he was; how great at the midnight hour . . .' In the same year, John Keats, 'Ode to Psyche', has: 'Temple thou hast none, nor / Virgin-choir to make delicious moan / *Upon the* midnight hours'. Keats also wrote of, '[Sleep] embalmer of the still midnight', and so on. Edward Lear's poem 'The Dong With the Luminous Nose' (1871) has 'at *that* midnight hour'. The full phrase 'at the midnight hour' is a quotation from the Weston & Lee song 'With Her Head Tucked Underneath Her Arm (She Walks the Bloody Tower)' (1934), as notably performed by Stanley Holloway. In a speech to the Indian Constituent Assembly (14 August 1947), Jawharlal Nehru said: '*At the stroke of the* midnight hour, while the world sleeps, India will awake to life and freedom.' Wilson Pickett, the American soul singer, established the phrase '*In the Midnight Hour*' with his hit single of that title (1965).

at the psychological moment Now rather loosely used to describe an opportune moment when something can be done or achieved. It is a mistranslation of the German phrase *das psychologische Moment* (which was, rather, about momentum) used by a German journalist during the 1870 siege of Paris. He was thought to be discussing the moment when the

Parisians would most likely be demoralized by bombardment. With or without the idea of a mind being in a state of receptivity to some persuasion, a cliché by 1900. 'The Prince is always in the background, and turns up at the psychological moment – to use a very hard-worked and sometimes misused phrase' – *Westminster Gazette* (30 October 1897); *The Psychological Moment* – title of a book (1994) by Robert McCrum; 'Indeed, some would argue that the end of hanging in 1969 was the psychological moment at which we ceased to take crime as a whole seriously, putting the liberal-humanitarian "conscience" first' – *Daily Mail* (27 August 1994).

at this moment in time (or **at this point in time**) I.e. 'now'. Ranks with AT THE END OF THE DAY near the top of the colloquial clichés' poll. From its periphrastic use of five words where one would do, it would be reasonable to suspect an American origin. Picked up with vigour by British trade unionists for their ad-lib wafflings, it was already being scorned by 1971: 'What comes across vis-à-vis the non-ambulant linguistic confrontation is a getting to-gether of defensible media people at this moment in time. I am personally oriented towards helpless laughter at the postures of these bizarre communicators' – letter to *The Times* from J. R. Barnes (2 December 1971); 'The usual stuff about meaningful relationships taking place . . . at this moment in time' – *The Guardian* (12 March 1973); 'There were five similar towers . . . but at this moment in time, they were only of passing interest' – Clive Eagleton, *October Plot* (1974); 'The phrase "at that point of time" . . . quickly became an early trademark of the whole Watergate affair' – *Atlantic Monthly* (January 1975); 'At this point in time' was described by Eric Partridge in the preface to the 5th edition of his *A Dictionary of Clichés* (1978) as the 'mentally retarded offspring' of IN THIS DAY AND AGE. 'The Marines, of course, had other ideas, but fortune was not favouring them at this moment in time' – R. McGowan and J. Hands, *Don't Cry for Me, Sergeant Major* (1983); 'Thoroughly agree with you about the lowering of standards in English usage on the BBC. "At this moment of time" instead of "Now" is

outrageous' – Kenneth Williams, letter of 8 October 1976, in *The Kenneth Williams Letters* (1994); 'At this point in time the private rented sector of the housing market was shrinking' – *The Irish Times* (8 June 1977).

attitudes See ANGLO-SAXON.

at your throat or at your feet Either attacking you or in submissive mode. Working backwards through the citations: according to J. R. Colombo's *Popcorn in Paradise* (1979), Ava Gardner said about a well-known American film critic: 'Rex Reed is either at your feet or at your throat.' From Marlon Brando in *Playboy* (January 1979): 'Chaplin reminded me of what Churchill said about the Germans: either at your feet or at your throat.' In fact, almost every use of the phrase tends to mention Winston Churchill. He said in a speech to the US Congress (19 May 1943): 'The proud German Army by its sudden col-lapse, sudden crumbling and breaking up, has once again proved the truth of the saying "The Hun is always either at your throat or at your feet".' That is as far back as the phrase has been traced, though Dorothy L. Sayers, *Have His Carcase*, Chap. 12 (1932), has the similar: 'Like collies – lick your boots one minute and bite you the next.'

August See MAKES YOUR ARMPIT.

auld lang syne Meaning, 'long ago' (literally, 'old long since'). 'Syne' should be pronounced with an 's' sound and not as 'zyne'. In 1788, Robert Burns adapted 'Auld Lang Syne' from 'an old man's singing'. The title, first line and refrain had all appeared before as the work of other poets. Nevertheless, what Burns put together is what people should sing on New Year's Eve. Here is the first verse and the chorus: 'Should auld acquaintance be forgot, / And never brought to min[d]? / Should auld acquaintance be forgot, / And days of o' lang syne. / (*Chorus*) For auld lang syne, my dear / For auld syne, / We'll take a cup o' kindness yet / For auld lang syne.' 'For *the sake of* auld lang syne' should *not* be substituted at the end of verse and chorus.

aunt See AGONY; MY GIDDY.

Aunt Edna During the revolution in British drama of the 1950s, this term was called into play by the new wave of 'angry young' dramatists and their supporters to describe the more conservative theatre-goer – the type who preferred comfortable three-act plays of the Shaftesbury Avenue kind. Ironically, the term was coined in self-defence by Terence Rattigan, one of the generation of dramatists they sought to replace. In the preface to Vol. II of his *Collected Plays* (1953) he had written of: 'A nice, respectable, middle-class, middle-aged maiden lady, with time on her hands and the money to help her pass it . . . Let us call her Aunt Edna . . . Now Aunt Edna does not appreciate Kafka . . . She is, in short, a hopeless lowbrow . . . Aunt Edna is universal, and to those who may feel that all the problems of the modern theatre might be solved by her liquidation, let me add that . . . she is also immortal.'

Auntie/Aunty BBC (or plain **Auntie/ Aunty)** The BBC was mocked in this way by newspaper columnists, TV critics and her own employees, most noticeably from about 1955 at the start of commercial television – the Corporation supposedly being staid, over-cautious, prim and unambitious by comparison. A BBC spokesman countered with, 'An Auntie is often a much loved member of the family.' The corporation assimilated the nickname to such effect that when arrangements were made to supply wine to BBC clubs in London direct from vineyards in Burgundy, it was bottled under the name *Tantine*. In 1979, the comedian Arthur Askey claimed that he had originated the term during the *Band Waggon* programme as early as the late 1930s. While quite probable, the widespread use of the nickname is more likely to have occurred at the time suggested above. Wallace Reyburn in his book *Gilbert Harding – A Candid Portrayal* (1978) ascribes the phrase to the 1950s' radio and TV personality. The actor Peter Bull in *I Know the Face, But . . .* (1959) writes: 'I would be doing my "nut" and probably my swansong for Auntie BBC.' The politician Iain Macleod used the phrase when editing *The Spectator* in the 1960s. Jack de Manio, the broadcaster, entitled his memoirs *To Auntie With Love*

(1967), and the comedian Ben Elton had a BBC TV show *The Man from Auntie* (1990–4).

au reservoir! A jokey valediction (obviously based on *au revoir*) popularized by E. F. Benson in his *Lucia* novels of the 1920s. The phrase may have existed before this, possibly dating from a *Punch* joke of the 1890s.

(an) auspicious occasion Cliché used in speech-making or at any time when portentousness or pomposity is demanded. In fact, almost any use of the word 'auspicious' is a candidate for clichédom: 'Drinking around the imposing stone in order to celebrate some auspicious occasion' – Charles T. Jacobi, *The Printers' Vocabulary* (1888); 'An auspicious debut on the platform was made the other day by Mr Winston Churchill, elder son of the late Lord Randolph Churchill' – *Lady* (5 August 1897); 'What about a glass of sherry to celebrate the auspicious occasion?' – 'Taffrail', *Pincher Martin* (1916); 'The longer the game wore on the more obvious it became that Forest could not even rise to this auspicious occasion, much as they yearned to give their manager the mother and father of all send-offs' – *The Sunday Times* (2 May 1993).

Australia See ADVANCE.

author! author! The traditional cry of an audience summoning the playwright whose work it has just watched to come on the stage and receive its plaudits. Date of origin unknown. 'After the final curtain [at the first night of *Lady Windermere's Fan* (1892)] the applause was long and hearty, and Wilde came forward from the wings to cries of "Author!"' – Richard Ellman, *Oscar Wilde*, Chap. 14 (1987); *Author! Author!* – title of a book (1962) by P. G. Wodehouse.

avoid 'five o'clock shadow' The expression 'five o'clock shadow' for the stubbly growth that some dark-haired men acquire on their faces towards the end of the day would appear to have originated in adverts for Gem Razors and Blades in the USA before the Second World War. A 1937 advert added: 'That unsightly beard growth which appears prematurely at about 5 pm looks bad.' The most noted sufferer was

Richard Nixon, who may have lost the TV debates in his US presidential race against John F. Kennedy in 1960 as a result. In his *Memoirs* (1978), Nixon wrote: 'Kennedy arrived . . . looking tanned, rested and fit. My television adviser, Ted Rodgers, recommended that I use television make-up, but unwisely I refused, permitting only a little "beard stick" on my perpetual five o'clock shadow.'

(to) avoid —— like the plague   To avoid completely, to shun. The *OED2* finds the poet Thomas Moore in 1835 writing, 'Saint Augustine . . . avoided the school as the plague'. The 4th-century St Jerome is also said to have quipped, 'Avoid as you would the plague, a clergyman who is also a man of business.' A well-established cliché by the mid-20th century. It may have been Arthur Christiansen, one of the numerous former editors of the *Daily Express* about that time, who once posted a sign in the office saying: 'ALL CLICHÉS SHOULD BE AVOIDED LIKE THE PLAGUE.'

Avon calling!   A slogan first used in the USA in 1886. The first Avon Lady, Mrs P. F. A. Allre, was employed by the firm's founder, D. H. McConnell, to visit customers at home and sell them cosmetics.

award-winning ——   As used in promotion, especially of theatre, films and publishing. Depressing because it does not describe its subject in any useful way. Almost any actor in a leading role is likely to have received one of the many theatrical awards available at some time, just as any writer may (however illegitimately) be called a 'best-selling author' if more than just a few copies of his or her books have been sold. The phrase was in use by 1962. From the *Evening Standard* (London) (17 February 1993): 'Why go on about the latest "award-winning documentary maker"? If you get a documentary on television, you win an award: it goes with the territory.' 'Giles Cooper, who died nearly twenty years ago, is described in today's *Times* as "award-winning playwright Giles Cooper". I'd have thought one of the few things to be said in favour of death was that it extinguished all that' – Alan Bennett, diary entry for 30 June 1984, quoted in *Writing Home* (1994); 'Award-

winning actor Michael Gambon can also be seen . . . David Hare has written many successful plays and screenplays, including his award-winning trilogy . . . the Pulitzer Prize winning author, John Updike . . .' – Royal National Theatre brochure (26 June–28 August 1995); 'We also introduce some new writers this week. Allison Pearson, the award-winning TV Critic of the year, joins us from the *Independent on Sunday* . . . Kenneth Roy, another new award-winning voice . . . will be writing a personal weekly peripatetic notebook' – *The Observer* (27 August 1995).

away   See AND AWAY.

aw, don't embarrass me!   British ventriloquist Terry Hall (b. 1926) first created his doll, Lenny the Lion, from a bundle of fox fur and papier-mâché – with a golf ball for a nose – in 1954. He gave his new partner a gentle lisping voice, and added a few mannerisms and a stock phrase that emerged thus: 'He's ferocious! (*drum roll*) / He's courageous! (*drum roll*) / He's the king of the jungle! (*drum roll*) / – Aw, don't embarrass me! (*said with a modest paw over one eye*).' Unusually for the originator of a successful phrase, Terry Hall said (in 1979) that he made sure he did not overuse it and rested it from time to time.

awful   See AMUSING.

awkward   See AS AWKWARD.

(the) awkward age   Adolescence – when one is no longer a child but not yet a fully fledged adult. Current by the late 19th century and possibly a development of the French *l'âge ingrat*. Hence, *The Awkward Age*, the title of a novel (1899) by Henry James.

(the) awkward squad   Of military origin and used to denote a group of difficult, uncooperative people, the phrase originally referred to a squad that consisted of raw recruits and older hands who were put in it for punishment. The phrase may also have been applied to a group of soldiers who are briefed to behave awkwardly and in an undisciplined fashion in order to test the drilling capabilities of an officer under training. Sloppy in *Our Mutual Friend* (1864–5) is described by Charles Dickens as 'Full-Private Number One in the Awkward Squad of the rank and file of life'. The dying words of the Scots poet Robert Burns in 1796 are said to have been, 'John, don't let the awkward squad fire over me' – presumably referring to his fear that literary opponents might metaphorically fire a volley of respect, as soldiers sometimes do over a new grave.

(I) awoke one morning and found myself famous Byron's famous comment on the success of the first two cantos of *Childe Harold* in 1812 has become an expression in its own right. It was first quoted in Thomas Moore, *The Letters and Journals of Lord Byron* (1830).

AWOL 'Absent WithOut Leave' – unwarranted absence from the military for a short period but falling short of actual desertion. This expression dates from the American Civil War when offenders had to wear a placard with these initials printed on it. During the First World War, the initials were still being pronounced individually. Not until just before the Second World War was it pronounced as the acronym 'Awol'. It does not mean 'absent without *official* leave'.

(to have an) axe to grind The expression meaning 'to have an ulterior motive, a private end to serve' would appear to have originated with an anecdote related by Benjamin Franklin in his essay 'Too Much for Your Whistle'. A man showed interest in young Franklin's grindstone and asked how it worked. In the process of explaining, Franklin – using much energy – sharpened up the visitor's axe for him. This was clearly what the visitor had had in mind all along. Subsequently, Franklin (who died in 1790) had to ask himself

whether other people he encountered had 'another axe to grind'. Cited as a 'dying metaphor' by George Orwell in 'Politics and the English Language' in *Horizon* (April 1946). 'Manhattan Cable showed that some of the most ordinary people are very good on TV. In Britain, where the idea of access is a familiar one, it's still a very mediated and restricted thing where you have to have a politically correct axe to grind' – *The Guardian* (24 October 1991).

aye, aye, that's yer lot! Signing-off line of Jimmy Wheeler (1910–73), a British Cockney comedian with a fruity voice redolent of beer, jellied eels and winkles. He would appear in a bookmaker's suit, complete with spiv moustache and hat, and play the violin. At the end of his concluding fiddle piece, he would break off and intone these words.

aye, well – ye ken noo! 'Well, you know better now, don't you!' – said after someone has admitted ignorance or has retold an experience that taught a lesson. It is the punch line of an old Scottish story about a Presbyterian minister preaching a hell-fire sermon whose peroration went something like this: 'And in the last days ye'll look up from the bottomless pit and ye'll cry, "Lord, Lord, we did na ken [we did not know]", and the Guid Lord in his infinite mercy will reply . . . "Aye, well – ye ken noo!"'

ay thang yew! A distinctive pronunciation of 'I thank you!' picked up from the cry of London bus conductors by Arthur Askey for the BBC radio show *Band Waggon* (1938–39) and used by him thereafter. He commented (1979): 'I didn't know I was saying it till people started to shout it at *me*.' Later, as *I Thank You*, it became the title of one of Askey's films (1941).

B

(a')babbled of green fields One of the most pleasing touches to be found in all of Shakespeare may not have been his at all. In *Henry V* (II.iii.17), the Hostess (formerly Mistress Quickly) relates the death of

Falstaff: 'A'parted ev'n just between twelve and one, ev'n at the turning o' th' tide: for after I saw him fumble with the sheets and play with flowers and smile upon his fingers' end, I knew there was but one way; for his nose was as sharp as a pen, and a'babbled of green fields.' The 1623 Folio of Shakespeare's plays renders the last phrase as 'and a Table of green fields', which makes no sense, though some editors put 'as sharp as a pen, on a table of green field' (taking 'green field' to mean green cloth.) Shakespeare may well have handwritten 'babld' and the printer read this as 'table' – a reminder that the text of the plays is far from carved in stone and a prey to mishaps in the printing process, as are all books and newspapers. The generally accepted version was inserted by Lewis Theobald in his 1733 edition. As the 1954 Arden edition comments: '"Babbled of green fields" is surely more in character with the Falstaff who quoted the Scriptures . . . and who lost his voice hallooing of anthems. Now he is in the valley of the shadow, the "green pasture" of Psalm 23 might well be on his lips.' Francis Kilvert, the diarist, makes a pleasant allusion to the phrase in his entry for 15 May 1875: 'At the house where I lodge there is a poor captive thrush who fills the street with his singing as he "babbles of green fields".'

babes in the wood (1) Simple, inexperienced, trustful people who are easily fooled. Known by 1866. So called by way of allusion to 'The Children in the Wood', an old ballad based on the case of two Norfolk children whose uncle plotted to kill them in order to obtain their inheritance. But one of the ruffians employed to do the deed prevented it, and the children were left in a wood to perish. The story (sometimes held to be true and to have taken place in Wayland Wood near Watton) was published in Norwich by Thomas Millington in 1595. In ballad form, it is mentioned in a play by Rob Yarrington (1601) and in *Percy's Reliques* (1765). The story also forms the basis of the popular British pantomime format, *Babes in the Wood*. (2) The name has also been applied to Irish ruffians who ranged the Wicklow mountains and the Enniscorthy woods towards the end of the 18th century. (3) It was also given to men in the (wooden) stocks or pillory.

babies See KILL YOUR DARLINGS.

baby See DON'T THROW.

—— Babylon PHRASES. Used to describe groups of people or whole societies where high living and scandals abound. The link to the biblical Babylon is not direct. Although heathen, that was rather a place of magnificence and luxury. In 588BC, Nebuchadnezzar, King of Babylon, took Jerusalem and carried away many of the inhabitants to Babylon where they became slaves. These somewhat stuffy Jews reacted strongly to the amorality of the Babylonians (described by Herodotus), and Babylon became a byword for cruelty and vice. When the Romans took Jerusalem in AD 70, some Jewish writers (including the author of the Book of Revelation) referred to Rome as Babylon. The modern connotation of Babylon probably goes back at least as far as Disraeli, who wrote in *Lothair* (1847): 'London is a modern Babylon'. Dickens has Mr Micawber make the same comparison in *David Copperfield* (1850), but here Babylon is evoked only to signify a magnificent, big city. So *Brewer* (1894) may have been a touch off the mark in saying that 'The Modern Babylon' is 'London . . . on account of its wealth, luxury and *dissipation*'. The key to why, since film-maker Kenneth Anger entitled his book of movie scandals *Hollywood Babylon* in 1975, we have had a spate of titles like *Rock'n'Roll Babylon* (1982), *Washington Babylon* (1996), *TV Babylon* (1997) and *Hamptons Babylon* (1997) seems to lie in the popularization of the idea of Babylon as a city of decadence promoted by D. W. Griffith in his film *Intolerance* (US 1916). The Anger book is prefaced by a poem by Don Blanding 'as recited by Leo Carillo in the 1935 musical *Star Night at the Cocoanut Grove*': 'Hollywood, Hollywood . . . / Fabulous Hollywood . . . / Celluloid Babylon, / Glorious, glamorous . . . / City delirious, / Frivolous, serious . . . / Bold and ambitious, / And vicious and glamorous . . .' This led to Gary Herman, for example, writing of the original Babylon in his preface to *Rock'n'Roll Babylon*: '[It] was the capital of a vast and profligate empire. [Similarly] in the rock world, its citizens may start from humble beginnings, but soon they are ushered into lush hanging gardens where there are no dreams of democracy and change, only dreams of power, wealth and the perfect tan.' In a separate develop-ment, because the Babylonians had enslaved the Israelites, Afro-Caribbean people with a history of enslavement have taken to referring to their oppressors – and by extension prosperous and privileged members of racist white society – as 'Babylon'. In particular, 'The Babylon' means the police. A No.1 hit of 1977 for Boney M, the West Indies group, was 'Rivers of Babylon', based on 'By the rivers of Babylon, there we sat down, yea, and wept' (Psalm 137:1) – which in the Book of Common Prayer is, 'By the waters of Babylon we sat down and wept.' But, equally, this Babylonic allusion has also been used in what would seem to be the more traditional sense: in 1945, Elizabeth Smart likened New York to Babylon in the title of her novel, *By Grand Central Station I Sat Down and Wept*. This was a short, fictionalized account of a love affair, written in 'poetic prose'. Much earlier, in a letter of 12 June 1775, Horace Walpole wrote: 'By the waters of Babylon we sit down and weep, when we think of thee, O America!'

(a) bachelor gay Someone who puts himself about in a way characteristic of the unmarried male. 'A Bachelor Gay (Am I)' is the title of a song by James W. Tate in *The Maid of the Mountains* (1917). An arch phrase, to be used only within quotation marks, even before the change in meaning of 'gay' from the 1960s onwards. '"He was a bachelor gay," says Diana. "He left his first wife and small child, years before I knew him . . . After that he'd lived at separate times with two other women and walked out on both of them. He said to me: "You must appreciate I've been around a lot." It was part of the appeal' – *Daily Mail* (29 November 1993).

back See — IS BACK.

back in the knife-box, little Miss Sharp! A nannyism addressed to a person with a sharp tongue. Compare the similar **you're so sharp you'll be cutting yourself**. *Casson/Grenfell* also has: 'Very sharp we are today, we must have slept in the knife box / we must have slept on father's razor case / we must have been up to Sheffield'. Also there is **Mr Sharp from Sheffield,**

straight out of the knife-box! Paul Beale found a homely example of the knife-box version in Donald Davie's autobiographical study *These the Companions* (1982): 'More than twenty-five years ago I [composed] a poem which has for epigraph what I remember my mother [in Barnsley, York-shire] saying when I was too cocky as a child: "Mr Sharp from Sheffield, straight out of the knife-box!"' Earlier than all this, Murdstone referred to David – Charles Dickens, *David Copperfield*, Chap. 2 (1849) – as 'Mr Brooks of Sheffield', to indicate that he was 'sharp'. There was indeed a firm of cutlery makers called Brookes of Sheffield – a city that has for centuries been the centre of the English cutlery trade.

back of a lorry See FELL OFF THE.

backroom boys Nickname given to scientists and boffins – and specifically to those relied on to produce inventions and new gadgets for weaponry and navigation in the Second World War. Compare *The Small Back Room*, the title of a novel (1943) by Nigel Balchin. The phrase was originated, in this sense, by Lord Beaverbrook as Minister of Aircraft Pro-duction when he paid tribute to his research department in a broadcast on 19 March 1941: 'Let me say that the credit belongs to the boys in the backrooms [*sic*]. It isn't the man who sits in the limelight who should have the praise. It is not the men who sit in prominent places. It is the men in the backrooms.' In the US, the phrase 'backroom boys' can be traced to the 1870s at least, but Beaverbrook can be credited with the modern application to scientists and boffins. The inspiration quite obviously was his favourite film, *Destry Rides Again* (1939), in which Marlene Dietrich jumped on the bar of the Last Chance saloon and sang the Frank Loesser song 'See What the Boys in the Back Room Will Have'.

(with our) backs to the wall This expression, meaning 'up against it', dates back to 1535 at least but was memorably used when the Germans launched their last great offensive of the First World War. On 12 April 1918, Sir Douglas Haig, the British Commander-in-Chief on the West-ern Front, issued an order for his troops to stand firm: 'Every position must be held to the last man: there must be no retirement. With our backs to the wall, and believing in the justice of our cause, each one us must fight on to the end.' A. J. P. Taylor in his *English History 1914–45* (1966) commented: 'In England this sentence was ranked with Nelson's last message. At the front, the prospect of staff officers fighting with their backs to the walls of their luxurious chateaux had less effect.'

back to basics John Major, the British Prime Minister, launched this ill-fated slogan in a speech to the Conservative Party Conference in 1993: 'The message from this Conference is clear and simple. We must go back to basics . . . The Conservative Party will lead the country back to these basics, right across the board: sound money, free trade; traditional teaching; respect for the family and the law.' A number of government scandals in the ensuing months exposed the slogan as hard to interpret or, at worst, suggesting rather a return to 'the bad old days'. The alliterative phrase (sometimes 'back to *the* basics') may first have surfaced in the USA where it was the mid-1970s' slogan of a movement in education to give priority to the teaching of the fundamentals of reading, writing and arithmetic.

back to normalcy Together with 'Return to normalcy with Harding', this was a slogan effectively used by US President Warren G. Harding. Both were based on a word extracted from a speech he had made in Boston during May 1920: 'America's present need is not heroics but healing, not nostrums but normalcy, not revolution but restoration, not agitation but adjustment, not surgery but serenity, not the dramatic but the dispassionate, not experiment but equipoise, not submergence in internationality but sustainment in triumphant nationality.' Out of such an alliterative bog stuck the word 'normalcy' – a perfectly good Americanism, though it has been suggested that Harding was actually mispronouncing the word 'normality'. He himself claimed that 'normalcy' was what he had meant to say, having come across it in a dictionary.

back to square one Meaning 'back to the beginning', this phrase is sometimes said

to have gained currency in the 1930s through its use by football commentators on British radio. *Radio Times* used to print a map of the football field divided into numbered squares to which commentators would refer. Thus: 'Cresswell's going to make it – FIVE. There it goes, slap into the middle of the goal – SEVEN. Cann's header there – EIGHT. The ball comes out to Britton. Britton manoeuvres. The centre goes right in – BACK TO EIGHT. Comes on to Marshall – SIX' (an extract from the BBC commentary on the 1933 Cup Final between Everton and Manchester City). The idea had largely been abandoned by 1940. Against this proposition is the fact that square 'one' was nowhere near the beginning. The game began at the centre spot, which was at the meeting point of squares three, four, five and six. On the other hand, when the ball was passed to the goal-keeper (an event far commoner than a re-start after a goal), then this would indeed have been 'back to square one' (though, equally, two, seven or eight). Indeed, *Partridge/Catch Phrases* prefers an earlier origin in the children's game of hopscotch or in the board game Snakes and Ladders. If a player was unlucky and his or her counter landed on the snake's head in Square 97 or thereabouts, it had to make the long journey 'back to square one'.

(ah, well,) back to the drawing-board! Meaning 'We've got to start again from scratch', this is usually said after the original plan has been aborted. It is just possible this phrase began life in the caption to a cartoon by Peter Arno that appeared in *The New Yorker* (3 January 1941). An official, with a rolled-up engineering plan under his arm, is walking away from a recently crashed plane and saying: 'Well, back to the old drawing board.'

back to the jungle A return to primitive conditions, nearly always used figuratively (as in 'a return to the Dark Ages'). Winston Churchill, in a speech about post-Revolution Russia on 3 January 1920, referred to a recent visitor to that country: 'Colonel John Ward . . . has seen these things for many months with his own eyes . . . [and] has summed all up in one biting, blasting phrase – "Back to the jungle".'

back to the land The cry 'Back to the land!' was first heard at the end of the 19th century when it was realized that the Industrial Revolution and the transfer of the population towards non-agricultural work had starved farming of labour. From *The Times* (25 October 1894): 'All present were interested in the common practice that it was desirable, if possible, to bring the people back to the land.' At about this time, a Wickham Market farmer wrote to Sir Henry Rider Haggard, who was making an inventory of the decline, published as *Rural England* (1902): 'The labourers "back to the land". That is the cry of the press and the fancy of the people. Well, I do not think that they will ever come back; certainly no legislation will ever bring them. Some of the rising generation may be induced to stay, but it will be by training them to the use of machinery and paying them higher wages. It should be remembered that the most intelligent men have gone: these will never come back, but the rising generation may stay as competition in the town increases, and the young men of the country are better paid.' By 1905, the *Spectator* (23 December) was saying: '"Back-to-the-land" is a cry full not only of pathos, but of cogency.' In the 1970s, a British TV comedy series was called *Backs to the Land*, playing on the phrase to provide an innuendo about its heroines – 'Land Girls', members of the Women's Land Army conscripted to work on the land during the Second World War (though the WLA had first been established in the First World War.)

(either) back us or sack us From a speech by James Callaghan, when British Prime Minister, at the Labour Party Conference (5 October 1977). This became a format phrase in British politics, usually spoken by an individual rather than a whole government. From *The Independent* (25 October 1989): 'The Chancellor of the Exchequer [Nigel Lawson] was last night challenged by the Opposition to stand up to the Prime Minister, say "Back me or sack me" and end confusion over who is running the economy . . . "It is time to say (to the Prime Minister) either back me or sack me" . . . Mr Smith said.' Compare PUT UP OR SHUT UP.

bacon See BRING HOME THE.

bad See ANYONE WHO; CAN'T BE.

badger See BALD AS A.

(a) bad hair day A day on which you feel depressed, possibly because – as it used to be put – you 'can't do a thing' with your hair. American origin, early 1990s. 'I'm fine, but you're obviously having a bad hair day' – line delivered by Kristy Swanson in the film *Buffy, The Vampire Slayer* (US 1992); '"Having a bad hair day", in the fast-changing slang favoured by Californian teenagers, is how you feel when you don't want to leave the house: out of sorts, ugly and a bit depressed . . . having a bad hair day is meant to be a metaphor for a bad mood' – *The Daily Telegraph* (19 December 1992); 'The Chanel public relations director is having what Manhattanites describe as a bad hair day. But, somewhat perversely, she is quite enjoying herself' – *The Times* (13 January 1993); '[Hillary Clinton] stopped saying "two-fer-one" and "vote for him, you get me" – but still, one bad hair day was following the next. Soon she started making jokes about it with her campaign staff. "How 'bout it?" she'd say. "Another bad hair day?"' – *The Guardian* (19 January 1993).

bah, humbug! Dismissive catchphrase, derived from Charles Dickens, *A Christmas Carol*, Stave 1 (1843): '"Bah," said Scrooge. "Humbug!"' Ebenezer Scrooge, an old curmudgeon, userer and miser, has this view of the Christmas spirit until frightened into changing his ways by the appearance of visions and a ghost. The derivation of the word 'humbug' meaning 'deception, sham' is uncertain but it suddenly came into vogue *circa* 1750.

(a) baker's dozen Thirteen. In use by the 16th century, this phrase may have originated with the medieval baker's habit of giving away an extra loaf with every twelve to avoid being fined for providing underweight produce. The surplus was known as 'inbread' and the thirteenth loaf, the 'vantage loaf'. A **devil's dozen** is also thirteen – the number of witches who would gather when summoned by the devil.

(the) balance of power The promotion of peace through parity of strength in rival groups – an expression used by the British Prime Minister, Sir Robert Walpole, in the House of Commons (13 February 1741). *Safire* (1978) states that the phrase had earlier been used in international diplomacy by 1700. Initially, the phrase appears to have been 'the balance of power in Europe'. In 1715, Alexander Pope wrote a poem with the title 'The Balance of Europe': 'Now Europe's balanc'd, neither side prevails; / For nothing's left in either of the scales.'

bald See FIGHT BETWEEN.

(as) bald as a badger/bandicoot/coot Completely bald. 'Bald as a coot' has been known since 1430. The aquatic coot, known as the bald coot, has the appearance of being bald. The Australian marsupial, the bandicoot, is not bald but is presumably evoked purely for the alliteration and because the basic 'coot' expression is being alluded to. As for badger, the full expression is 'bald as a badger's bum'. There was once a belief that bristles for shaving brushes were plucked from this area. Christy Brown, *Down All the Days* (1970), has, rather, 'bald as a baby's bum'.

bald-headed See GO AT SOMETHING.

(Mr) Balfour's poodle A reference to the House of Lords. David Lloyd George spoke in the House of Commons on 26 June 1907 in the controversy over the power of the upper house. He questioned the Lords' role as a 'watchdog' of the constitution and suggested that A. J. Balfour, the Conservative leader, was using the party's majority in the upper chamber to block legislation by the Liberal government (in which Lloyd George was President of the Board of Trade). He said: '[The House of Lords] is the leal and trusty mastiff which is to watch over our interests, but which runs away at the first snarl of the trade unions. A mastiff? It is the Right Honourable Gentleman's poodle. It fetches and carries for him. It bites anybody that he sets it on to.' Hence, all subsequent ' —— 's poodle' jibes usually applied to one politician's (or government's) subservience to another. 'Ninety per cent of respondents feared military

action against Baghdad would result in more September 11-style attacks on the West, while 54 per cent thought it fair to describe Mr Blair as "Bush's poodle"' – *The Age* (Australia) (13 August 2002).

(the) ball of clay I.e. 'planet earth, the world'. Known by 1635. Also in the song 'Look for Small Pleasures' ('. . . upon this ball of clay') written by Michaels/Sandrich for the musical *Ben Franklin in Paris* (Broadway 1964). Compare WHOLE BALL OF WAX.

balloon See GO DOWN.

(the) balloon's gone up Current by 1924 and meaning 'the action or excitement has commenced', particularly in military activities. The expression derives from the sending up of barrage balloons (introduced during the First World War) to protect targets from air raids. The fact that these balloons – or manned observation balloons – had 'gone up' would signal that some form of action was imminent. C. H. Rolph in *London Particulars* (1980) suggests that the phrase was in use earlier, by 1903–4.

ballroom See IS SHE A.

balls See ALL; COLD ENOUGH TO.

balm in Gilead See IS THERE NO.

(the) banality of evil 'The fearsome word-and-thought-defying banality of evil' was how the German-born philosopher Hannah Arendt summed up the lessons to be learned from the trial of Adolf Eichmann, the Nazi official who was executed in Israel as a war criminal in 1962. Her book *Eichmann in Jerusalem* (1963) was subtitled 'A Report on the Banality of Evil' and caused controversy because it seemed to suggest that Eichmann was not personally responsible for his deeds during the Holocaust.

band See AND THE.

(a) band of brothers *Band of Brothers* was the title of a Steven Spielberg TV film series (US 2001) based on a non-fiction book (1992) by Stephen E. Ambrose that told the history of a single company in the 101st US Airborne Division 1942–5. It comes from Shakespeare, *Henry V*, IV.iii.60 (1599), where the King says before the

Battle of Agincourt: 'We few, we happy few, we band of brothers . . . / And gentlemen in England now a-bed / Shall think themselves accurs'd they were not here.'

bang   See ALL BALLS.

bang, bang, you're dead!   A child's apt summary of the manner of TV Westerns, probably dating from the 1950s. Compare the slightly later KISS-KISS, BANG-BANG.

bang goes sixpence!   A lightly joking remark about one's own or another person's unwillingness to spend money. The origins of this lie in the caption to a *Punch* cartoon (5 December 1868). A Scotsman who has just been on a visit to London says: 'Mun, a had na' been the-rre abune two hours when – bang – went saxpence!' *Benham* (1948) has it that the story was communicated to the cartoonist Charles Keene by Birket Foster who had it from Sir John Gilbert. The saying was re-popularized by Sir Harry Lauder, the professional stage Scotsman (1870–1950).

(she) bangs like a shithouse door   She copulates regularly and noisily. Australian, 1930s. A variation is **(she) bangs like a shithouse rat**.

bang to rights   As in 'You've got me bang to rights!' said by a criminal to an arresting policeman, this is an alternative to 'It's a fair cop [You are quite right to have caught me, constable]!' There is also an element of 'You've caught me red-handed, in an indefensible position'. *Partridge/Slang* dates this from the 1930s, but *OED2* finds a US example in 1904. Possibly derived from 19th-century usage – from the idea of being 'bang-on right' in absolute certainty. Compare the somewhat rare Americanism 'bang' for a criminal charge or arrest, as in 'it's a bum bang', that may have been coined with reference to the banging of a cell door.

bank   See CRY ALL THE WAY TO.

ban the bomb   One of the simplest and best-known alliterative slogans, current in the US from 1953 and marginally afterwards in the UK. The (British) Campaign for Nuclear Disarmament – whose semi-official slogan it became – was not publicly launched until February 1958. The phrase was in use by 1960. (Richard Crossman referred to 'Scrap the Bomb' in a 1957 press article.)

Banzai!   From a hundred war films and cheap comics we are familiar with the cry used by Japanese forces in the Second World War, meaning '[May you live] ten thousand years!' During the war – and after it – this traditional cry came to mean 'Ten thousand years to the Emperor' or to 'Japan'. M. R. Lewis observed (1986): 'The root of the problem is that a language written in the Chinese ideographic characters is often difficult to translate sensibly into a West European language, because it is often not apparent when the literal meaning is intended and when the figurative. "*Banzai*" literally means no more than "ten thousand years", but what it more usually means is "for a long time". So, a pen in Japanese is, when literally translated, a "ten thousand year writing brush", which is gibberish in any language! What it actually means is "a long-lasting writing instrument" . . . For the suicide pilots, the ritual shout of "*Banzai!*" swept up many layers of meaning, of which the most immediate was undoubtedly "*Tenno heika banzai*" – "Long live the Emperor", a phrase which goes back into the mists of Japanese history, despite its appropriation by the nationalist movements of the 1930s. The phrase is still in use on such occasions as the Emperor's birthday, as I can testify from recent experience. When he stepped out on to the balcony and the shouts rose around me, I began to feel that I was in the wrong movie! As for the oddity of the phrase – if literally translated, is it really so different from: "Zadok the priest, and Nathan the prophet, anointed Solomon king. And all the people rejoiced and said, God save the king. Long live the king, *may the king live for ever*. Amen. Alleluia" – which has been sung at the coronation of almost every English sovereign since William of Normandy was crowned in Westminster Abbey on Christmas Day 1066?' Jonathan Swift includes **may you live a thousand years** among the conversational chestnuts in *Polite Conversation* (1738). The Sergeant in Charles Dickens, *Great Expectations*, Chap. 5 (1860–1), incorporates it in a toast.

(a) baptism of fire A testing initial experience. Originally the phrase described a soldier's first time in battle (compare the French *baptême du feu*) and is said to derive from ecclesiastical Greek. Matthew 3:11 has 'I [John the Baptist] indeed baptize you with water . . . but he that cometh after me . . . shall baptize you with the Holy Ghost and with fire.' 'The first American troops to receive a baptism of fire in Europe in this war were the men of the United States Ranger Battalion who fought in the Dieppe raid today' – *The New York Times* (20 August 1942); 'The past four months have been a baptism of fire for Mr Georges-Christian Chazot, Eurotunnel's chief executive. Appointed in January to turn a large construction project into a profitable transport undertaking, he has been faced with a succession of postponements to the start of commercial operations' – *Financial Times* (6 May 1994); 'I was in the Dundee Repertory Theatre when I had a call asking me to test for *For Them That Trespass*. To my amazement I got the part and starred in the first film I ever made. It certainly was a baptism of fire but I was very lucky because my producer, Victor Skutezky, and the director Alberto Cavalcanti took me in hand' – Richard Todd, quoted in *The Daily Telegraph* (14 May 1994).

bar See ALL OVER.

(the) barbarians are at the gates Meaning, 'the end of civilization is at hand'. Hyperbole. In 1990, *Barbarians at the Gate* was used as the title of a book by Bryan Burrough (filmed US 1993). Subtitled 'The Fall of RJR Nabisco', it was about goings-on in Wall Street – suggesting that unregulated, or at least ungentlemanly, behaviour had broken out. Appropriately enough, the phrase is used literally in Edward Gibbon's *Decline and Fall of the Roman Empire*, I.303 (1776–88): 'Such was the public consternation when the barbarians were hourly expected at the gates of Rome.' Compare, from the journal *Queen* (5 September 1914): 'Stand up and meet the war. The Hun is at the gate!'

(the) Bard of Avon One of several sobriquets for William Shakespeare and alluding to the river running through the town of his birth, Stratford in Warwick-shire. Ben Jonson called Shakespeare 'Sweet Swan of Avon' (in a verse prefacing the First Folio of plays, 1623), and David Garrick, who excelled in Shakespearean parts at the Drury Lane Theatre, London, felt intimate enough to nickname him 'Avonian Willy'. **The Bard** on its own is also, unfortunately, common, though anything is better than the assumed familiarity, chiefly among actors, of 'Will' or 'Bill' Shakespeare. 'Pen introduced [the topic of Shakespeare because he] professed an uncommon respect for the bard of Avon' – William Thackeray, *Pendennis*, Chap. 6 (1848–50); 'But there may well be more subtle influences at work than the Bard of Avon was aware of. An American scientist has recently published results which suggest that the rate at which human beings procreate is influenced by variations in terrestrial magnetism no matter how constant the human or animal attractiveness may be' – *Irish Times* (3 October 1994); 'This man who killed two people in his former life as a numbers racketeer in Cleveland . . . acquired the rudiments of a classical education. I once heard him react to an English accent with the line: 'As yo' great Bard of Avon truly said, "To be or not to be – that's what they askin', baby"' – *The Mail on Sunday* (26 March 1995).

barefaced cheek Assertive behaviour that is accomplished without a blush of embarrassment. A cliché by the late 1980s. *Barefaced Cheek* – title of book about Rupert Murdoch by Michael Leapman (1983); 'Garden-rustling is Britain's fastest-growing crime, as thieves twig that all you need to nurture a flourishing fortune is a spade – and a wheelbarrow-load of barefaced cheek' – *Today* (25 May 1993); 'When it was announced recently that HM the Q had graciously consented to allow taxpayers to view their own property for £8 a head . . . It was left to newspaper cartoonists to characterize it as the kind of barefaced cheek which could only happen in a country which, as Cobbett observed, has a Royal Mint but a National Debt' – *The Observer* (6 June 1993).

(the) bare necessities The minimum requirements needed to keep alive – food, drink and possibly a roof over one's head.

Known by 1913, when *Punch* (10 December) referred to 'The Bare Necessity Supply Association [having] the honour to announce their list of Daintiest Recencies for the Yule-Tide Season'. A cliché not so much in its original form but as a veiled allusion to the song 'Bare Necessities' in the Walt Disney film of Kipling's *The Jungle Book* (US 1967) – which was sung by a *bear*. 'Profits in the bare necessities of life' – headline in *The Independent* (13 May 1995).

Barkis is willing A catchphrase that derives from Charles Dickens, *David Copperfield*, Chap. 5 (1850). Mr Barkis, a Yarmouth carrier, asks young David Copperfield to convey his willingness to marry Peggotty, in the words, 'Barkis is willin'.' Eventually they do marry.

(to) bark up the wrong tree This phrase meaning 'to follow a false scent' is of US origin (by 1832) and is said to come from racoon hunting. As this activity is done at night (racoons being nocturnal animals) and as, if chased, racoons run up trees, it would be quite possible for a dog to bark mistakenly under the wrong tree.

barmy See I'VE GOT A LETTER.

(to) bash the bishop (or flog the bishop) Meaning, 'to masturbate'. *Partridge/Slang* dates this from the late 19th century and suggests it derives from the resemblance between the penis and a chess bishop or a bishop in ecclesiastical mitre. It was unfortunate, therefore, that Labour MPs should have accused the Conservative minister, John Selwyn Gummer MP, of **bishop-bashing** when he was involved in criticisms of various Anglican bishops in March 1988. The —— **bashing** phrases had been used before, of course – as in the practice of **Paki-bashing** *circa* 1970 (i.e. subjecting Pakistani immigrants to physical assault) and as in the old 'square-bashing' (army slang for drill).

basics See BACK TO.

(a) basket case This phrase now has two applications – firstly, to describe a mental or physical cripple and, secondly, a totally ruined enterprise. Either way, it seems to be an American term, and the *OED2*'s earliest citation is from the *U.S. Official*

Bulletin (28 March 1919) in the aftermath of the First World War: 'The Surgeon General of the Army . . . denies . . . that there is any foundation for the stories that have been circulated . . . of the existence of "basket cases" in our hospitals.' Indeed, another definition of the term is 'a soldier who has lost all four limbs' – thus, presumably, requiring transportation in something like a basket. To complicate matters, *Flexner* (1976) describes this as being originally *British* Army slang. It has been suggested, probably misguidedly, that the association with mental disability comes from the fact that basket-weaving is an activity sometimes carried out in mental hospitals. The second meaning was established by about 1973 and is still frequently used in business journalism when describing doomed ventures: 'On a continent that is full of economic basket cases, the small, landlocked nation is virtually debt free' – *Newsweek* (11 January 1982). Here, one might guess that the original phrase has been hi-jacked and the implication changed. What the writer is now referring to is something that is so useless that it is fit only to be thrown into a waste-paper basket.

bath See DON'T THROW.

(to have) bats in the belfry Meaning 'to be mentally deficient, harmlessly insane, mad, batty', this expression conveys the idea that a person behaves in a wildly disturbed manner, like bats disturbed by the ringing of bells. Stephen Graham wrote in *London Nights* (1925): 'There is a set of jokes which are the common property of all the comedians. You may hear them as easily in Leicester Square as in Mile End Road. It strikes the unwonted visitor to the Pavilion as very original when Stanley Lupino says of some one: "He has bats in the belfry." It is not always grasped that the expression belongs to the music hall at large.' Attempts have been made to derive 'batty', in particular, from the name of William Battie (1704–76), author of a *Treatise on Madness*, though this seems a little harsh, given that he was the psychiatrist and not the patient. On the other hand, there was a Fitzherbert Batty, barrister of Spanish Town, Jamaica, who made news when he was certified insane in London in 1839. The names of these two gentlemen merely, and coincidentally, reinforce the 'bats in the belfry' idea – but there do not seem to be any examples of either expression in use before 1900.

(a) bat's squeak of sexuality Use of this phrase probably derives from Evelyn Waugh, *Brideshead Revisited*, Chap. 3 (1945): 'As I took the cigarette from my lips and put it in hers, I caught a thin bat's squeak of sexuality, inaudible to any but me' (Charles Ryder of Lady Julia). A later use of 'bat's squeak', not otherwise much recorded: at the Conservative Party Conference in 1981, a then upwardly rising politician called Edwina Currie was taking part in a debate on law and order. To illustrate some point, she held aloft a pair of handcuffs. Subsequently, the Earl of Gowrie admitted to having felt 'a bat's squeak of desire' for Mrs Currie at that moment.

(the) Battle of Britain The urge to give names to battles – even before they are fought and won – is well exemplified by Winston Churchill's coinage of 18 June 1940: 'What General Weygand called the Battle of France is over. I expect that the Battle of Britain is about to begin.' It duly became the name by which the decisive overthrowing of German invasion plans by 'the Few' is known. The order of the day, read aloud to every pilot on 10 July, contained the words: 'The Battle of Britain is about to begin. Members of the Royal Air Force, the fate of generations is in your hands.' Another Churchill coinage – 'The Battle of Egypt' (speech, 10 November 1942) – caught on less well.

(to wage a) battle royal Meaning 'to take part in a keenly fought contest, a general free-for-all', this term originated in cockfighting, or at least has been specifically used in that sport. In the first round, sixteen birds would be put into a pit to fight each other until only half the number was left. The knock-out competition would then continue until there was only one survivor. *OED2* finds the phrase for general use by 1672; by 1860 for cockfighting.

battle-scarred (veterans) A mostly journalistic cliché. 'Our leaders battle-scarred' wrote Oliver Wendell Holmes in

an open letter *To General Grant* (1865). In Nat J. Ferber, *I Found Out* (1939), it is related that once on the New York *American* the printing error 'battle-scared hero' was hastily corrected in a later edition and came out reading 'bottle-scarred hero'. 'Can a bunch of battle-scarred old pols . . . gang up to stop a brash young lawyer named Brian Mulroney?' – *Toronto Star* (14 February 1976); 'The man who made it possible – bringing a new lease of life to his own political career in the process – was Mr Peres, one of the most battle-scarred veterans of Israeli politics' – *The Sunday Telegraph* (5 September 1993); '"Just be the benevolent old maestro, Bob, battle-scarred and wordly-wise in the ways of the biz," Moir advised' – Bob Monkhouse, *Crying With Laughter* (1993); 'Battle-scarred veterans of the women's movement can be forgiven for sighing wearily at some of this; like the youngsters who "think sex was invented the year they reached puberty," she seems unaware that the Sixties movement was greatly about women's right to love freely' – *The Observer* (5 December 1993); 'Okay, so he has more important priorities in life now like setting up a new wine bar with a partner, and the Dump Truck and his fellow young professional monsters will never have to worry about a 36-year-old battle-scarred dad-of-three from England, but he reckons he could make a sizeable mark in the amateur ranks for a couple of years' – *The Sunday Times* (27 November 1994).

BBC See AUNTIE.

be afraid – be very afraid Slogan for film *The Fly* (US 1986) and also included as a line spoken by Geena Davis (Veronica) to a date of Seth Brundle's (he is the man who half-turns into a fly): 'No. Be afraid. Be very afraid.'

beam me up, Scotty! Catchphrase popularly associated with the US TV science-fiction series *Star Trek* (1966–9). According to Trekkers, however, Capt. Kirk (William Shatner) never actually said to Lt. Commander 'Scotty' Scott, the chief engineer, 'Beam me up, Scotty!' – which meant that he should transpose body into matter, or transport someone from planet to spaceship, or some such thing. In the fourth episode, however, he may have said, 'Scotty, beam me up!' The more usual form of the injunction was, '*Enterprise*, beam us up' or, 'Beam us up, Mr Scott.'

beans See AMOUNT TO.

Beanz meanz Heinz This slogan for Heinz Baked Beans in the UK (from 1967) is the type of advertising line that annoys teachers because it appears to condone wrong spelling. Johnny Johnson wrote the music for the jingle that went: 'A million housewives every day / Pick up a tin of beans and say / Beanz meanz Heinz.' 'I created the line at Young & Rubicam,' copywriter Maurice Drake stated in 1981. 'It was in fact written – although after much thinking – over two pints of bitter in the Victoria pub in Mornington Crescent.'

bear See GLADLY MY CROSS-EYED.

(to) beard the lion in his den To confront a person with impunity. This phrase derives from the notion of taking a lion by the beard and partly from the use of the word 'beard' to mean the face. Shakespeare, *Henry VI, Part 1*, IV.i.12 (1591), has: 'No man so potent breathes upon the ground, / But I will beard him', but the 'lion' image seems first to have been employed in Tobias Smollet, *Regicide*, II.vii (1777): 'Sooner wouldst thou beard The lion in his rage.' W. S. Gilbert, *Iolanthe* (1882) has: 'Beard the lion in his lair – None but the brave deserve the fair.' R. D. Blackmore, *Perlycross*, II.iv.68 (1894), has the complete phrase: 'Nothing less would satisfy her than to beard – if the metaphor applies to ladies – the lion in the den, the arch-accuser, in the very court of judgment.'

—— bears eloquent testimony Pompous phrase used by writers of opinion columns and by speech-makers. Date of origin unknown. Listed in *The Independent* (24 December 1994) as a cliché of newspaper editorials and well established as such by that date. 'Mr Hamilton said last night: "I entirely refute the allegations and the writ will make that perfectly clear." When asked if there was any grain of truth in the Guardian report Mr Hamilton said: "My writ I think is eloquent testimony to the view that I have as to their veracity.

Nobody issues a writ to launch a libel action for fun"' – *The Times* (21 October 1994).

(the) beast of —— Nickname formula. (1) The 'Beast of Belsen' was Josef Kramer, German commandant of the Belsen concentration camp during the worst period of its history from December 1944 to the end of the Second World War. He was executed for his crimes in 1945. (2) The 'Beast/Bitch of Buchenwald' was Ilse Koch (d. 1967), wife of the commandant of the concentration camp near Weimar. Infamous for having had lampshades made out of the skin of her victims. (3) The 'Beast of Bolsover' is Dennis Skinner (b. 1932), the aggressive and outspoken Labour MP for Bolsover in Derbyshire (since 1970). Noted for interrupting speeches and making loud comments in the House of Commons. (4) The 'Beast of Jersey' was E. J. L. (Ted) Paisnel, convicted of 13 sex offences against children and sentenced to 30 years imprisonment in 1971. The name was applied to him during the 11 years he evaded arrest on the island.

(to) beat a path to someone's door Sarah Yule claimed (1889) that she had heard Ralph Waldo Emerson say the following in a lecture: 'If a man write a better book, preach a better sermon, or make a better mousetrap than his neighbour, 'tho he build his house in the woods, the world will make a beaten path to his door.' Elbert Hubbard also claimed authorship. Either way, this is a remark alluded to when people talk of 'beating a path to someone's door' or a **better mousetrap**. In his journal for February 1855, Emerson had certainly entertained the thought: 'If a man . . . can make better chairs or knives . . . than anybody else, you will find a broad hard-beaten road to his house, though it be in the woods.'

beaten the panel See IS IT BIGGER.

(the) Beat Generation 'Beatniks' were young people who opted out of normal society in the 1950s (first of all in the USA) because they were unable or unwilling to conform to conventional standards. Careless of appearance, critical of the Establishment, they were less intellectual than the average angry young man, but rebellious like the teddy boys who preceded them (in the UK) and the hippies who followed. The name with its Yiddish or Russian suffix (compare the Russian *sputnik* satellite orbiting the earth in 1957) derived from the phrase 'Beat Generation', coinage of which is usually credited to Jack Kerouac, although in his book *The Origins of the Beat Generation*, he admitted to borrowing the phrase from a drug addict called Herbert Huncke. In Randy Nelson's *The Almanac of American Letters* (1981), there is a description of the moment of coinage. Kerouac is quoted as saying: 'John Clellon Holmes . . . and I were sitting around trying to think up the meaning of the lost generation and the subsequent existentialism and I said: "You know, this is really a beat generation," and he leapt up and said: "That's it, that's right".' Holmes himself attributed the phrase directly to Kerouac in *The New York Times* Magazine of 16 November 1952.

beautiful See ALL THINGS; BUT MISS.

(the) beautiful game Football. This description is usually credited to the Brazilian player Pelé, and his autobiography (written with Robert L. Fish) has the English title *My Life and the Beautiful Game* (1977). But whether he said it first in Portuguese (*o jogo lindo*) or in English is not known. *The Beautiful Game* was the title of a musical (London 2000) about football and the sectarian divide in Northern Ireland (book by Ben Elton, music by Andrew Lloyd Webber). The phrase had much earlier been applied to *cricket* by Arnold Wall (1869–1966) in a poem called 'A Time Will Come' during the First World War.

(the) beautiful people Coinage of this term is credited in *Current Biography* (1978) to the American fashion journalist Diana Vreeland (*circa* 1903–89). Whether she deserves this or not is open to question, although she does seem to have helped launch the similar term SWINGING LONDON. The earliest *OED2* citation with capital letters for each word is from 1966, though there is a *Vogue* use from 15 February 1964 that would appear to support the link to Vreeland. The *OED2* makes the phrase refer primarily to

'"flower people", hippies' though the 1981 *Macquarie Dictionary*'s less narrow definition of 'fashionable social set of wealthy, well-groomed, usually young people' is preferable. The Lennon and McCartney song 'Baby You're a Rich Man' (released in July 1967) contains the line 'How does it feel to be one of the beautiful people?' William Saroyan's play *The Beautiful People* had first been performed long before all this, in 1941, and Oscar Wilde in a letter to Harold Boulton (December 1879) wrote: 'I could have introduced you to some very beautiful people. Mrs Langtry and Lady Lonsdale and a lot of clever beings who were at tea with me.'

beauty See AGE BEFORE; AHA, ME.

beauty and the beast The story of the beast who insists on marrying a beautiful princess is one of the classic fairy tales. One version is that of Marie Leprince (or Le Prince) de Beaumont, a French governess working in London, who published *Le Magasin des enfans* (1756–7), a booklet in French with dialogues meant for educating young girls. The fifth dialogue of Vol. 1 is '*La Belle et la Bête*'. The title and version (though much shortened) were mostly taken from another French author, Gabrielle-Suzanne de Villeneuve in *Les Contes Marins* (1740), which in turn harks back to Straparola's telling in *Piacevoli Notti* (1550) and the traditional story of Amor and Psyche. The Villeneuve story (which was the first with the title *La Belle et la Bête*) was not apparently intended for children. Where the Leprince version has the Beast saying, 'Would you be my wife?', Villeneuve has him saying he wants to go to bed with her. When she finally agrees, all the Beast does is sleep and snore, and wake up a beautiful prince. Jean Cocteau made a film version of the story, as *La Belle et la Bête* (France 1946) and a Disney animated musical *Beauty and the Beast* (US 1991) has kept the story alive. The phrase might now be used to describe a couple where the woman is good looking and the man is definitely not.

beauty sleep 'Sleep before midnight, supposedly conducive to good looks and health', according to *Partridge/Slang*. Apparently, this phrase appeared in Frank

Smedley's novel, *Frank Fairleigh* (1850). It was certainly in Charles Kingsley, *Two Years Ago* (1857).

Beaver! (1) The cry identifying a man with a beard appears to have been common among children in the 1910s and 1920s, though it is now obsolete. In 1922, *Punch* had several jokes and cartoons on the theme and noted (19 July) in a caption: 'To Oxford is attributed the credit of inventing the game of "Beaver" in which you score points for spotting bearded men.' But why *beaver*? *Flexner* (1976) notes the use of the animal's name to describe a high, sheared-fur hat in the USA. The beaver's thick dark-brown fur, he says, also refers 'to a well-haired pudendum or a picture showing it, which in pornography is called a "beaver shot".' Beaver for beard may derive rather from the Middle Ages when the 'beaver' was the part of a soldier's helmet which lay around the chin as a face-guard (the 'vizor' was the bit brought down from the forehead). In Shakespeare's *Hamlet*, I.ii.228 (1600), the Prince asks: 'Then saw you not his face?' (that of his father's ghost). Horatio replies: 'O yes, my lord, he wore his beaver up.' (2) Nickname of William Maxwell Aitken, 1st Baron Beaverbrook (1879–1964), newspaper magnate and politician in Britain. He took his title from the town in New Brunswick, Canada, where he had a home. Called 'Max' by his friends, he was known to his staff as 'the Beaver', a name explained by Tom Driberg (his first 'William Hickey' columnist on the *Daily Express*) as being a 'zoological symbol of tireless industry'.

be British! Jingoistic phrase. In 1912, Captain Edward Smith reputedly said, 'Be British, boys, be British' to his crew some time in the hours between his command, the *Titanic*, hitting the iceberg and his going down with the ship. Michael Davie in his book on the disaster describes the evidence for this as 'flimsy', but the legend was rapidly established. 'Be British! was the cry as the ship went down' is the first line of a commemorative song, 'Be British', written and composed by Lawrence Wright and Paul Pelham. In 1914, when a statue to Smith was erected in Lichfield, it had 'Be British' as part of the inscription.

because I'm worth it! Phrase from TV commercial for L'Oréal hair products. 'Shamelessly vainglorious claim voiced by a succession of blandly pretty actresses (and the French football Adonis, David Ginola) on a TV commercial to justify, implicitly, the shockingly exorbitant price of L'Oréal hair products' – John Walsh in *The Independent* (2 December 2000). By October 2002, in the UK, there was a poster ad proclaiming, 'Discover the beauty of science. Because you're worth it. L'Oréal.' The French version, seen in 2003, was: *'Les progrès de la science se reflètent dans vos cheveux. Parce que vous le valez bien.'*

because it's there As a flippant justification for doing anything, this makes use of a phrase chiefly associated with the British mountaineer George Leigh Mallory (1886–1924). He disappeared on his last attempt to climb Mount Everest. The previous year, during a lecture tour in the USA, he had frequently been asked why he wanted to achieve the goal. He replied, 'Because it is there.' The saying has become a catchphrase in situations where the speaker wishes to dismiss an impossible question about motives and also to express acceptance of a challenge that is in some way daunting or foolish. There have been many variations (and misattributions). Sir Edmund Hillary repeated it regarding his own successful attempt on Everest in 1953. From *Private Eye* (*circa* April 1962): 'Someone once asked me why I married the Queen. And I replied "Because she was there"' – caption to a cartoon of the Duke of Edinburgh.

because the scenery is better An overworked and inevitable argument in promoting the superior imaginative qualities of radio as a medium. It supposedly originated in a letter to *Radio Times* in the 1920s, quoting a child who had said rather: 'The pictures are better'. A cliché by the 1970s. 'Do you ever listen [to the radio]? I do. I like it best. As a child I know says: "I see it much better on radio than on TV"' – Joyce Grenfell in a letter of 22 September 1962 and included in *An Invisible Friendship* (1981); '"I like the wireless better than the theatre," one London child wrote in a now legendary letter, "because the scenery is better"' –

Derek Parker, *Radio: The Great Years* (1977); 'By way of illustration a young lad was quoted as saying he preferred radio to television – because the scenery is better. A proof of the power of imagination!' – Prayer Book Society *Newsletter* (August 1995).

Becket See DO A THOMAS.

bed See AND SO TO; HE CAN LEAVE.

bedpost See BETWEEN YOU AND ME.

(to have) been and gone and done it Emphatic form of expression suggesting that one has finally done something and from which there may be no escape – for example, getting married. P. G. Wodehouse describes it as 'language of the man of the street' in his *Tales of St Austin's* (1903). Even earlier, W. S. Gilbert has: 'The padre said, "Whatever have you been and gone and done?"' in *The Bab Ballads*, 'Gentle Alice Brown' (1869).

(to have) been there To have shared in or to have knowledge of some experience – often of an emotional nature. Of American origin. 'Some reasons why I left off drinking whiskey, by one who has been there' – headline in the *Saturday Evening Post* (1877). Whether the title of the film *Being There* (US 1980) is related is not clear. 'The agony and ecstasy of *La bohème* are the agony and ecstasy of adolescence . . . one reason why we weep harder at *La bohème* than at any other opera is that we were all there once' – Germaine Greer, quoted in Glyndebourne Festival Opera programme (2003). As for, **been there, done that . . .**: 'Michael Caine was once asked if he had a motto: "Yeah – Been There, Done That. It'll certainly be on my tombstone. It'll just say, 'Been There, Done That'"' – quoted in Elaine Gallagher *et al*, *Candidly Caine* (1990). This is what might be called a T-shirt motto and is certainly not original to Caine. Ian Dury used the phrase 'been there' in the song 'Laughter' (*The Ian Dury Songbook*, 1979) to indicate that a seduction has been accomplished, but the motto is not solely concerned with sex. It can cover all human activity. About 1989 there were T-shirts for jaded travellers with the words: 'Been there, done that, **got the T-shirt**.'

(I have) been to the mountain top As in Dr Martin Luther King Jr's speech at Memphis (3 April 1968), the night before he was assassinated: 'I've been to the mountain top . . . I've looked over, and I've seen the promised land.' The original **promised land** (not called as such in the Bible but referring to Canaan, western Palestine, and by association, Heaven) was promised to the descendants of Abraham, Isaac and Jacob. In Numbers 14:39–40: 'Moses told these sayings unto all the children of Israel . . . And they rose up early in the morning and gat them up into the top of the mountain, saying, Lo, we be here, and will go up unto the place which the Lord hath promised.'

beer See I'M ONLY HERE.

beer and sandwiches at No. 10 An encapsulation of the informal (and often eleventh-hour) style of negotiation held at senior level (and quite often at the Prime Minister's residence, No. 10, Downing Street) between British trade unionists and politicians to avert threatened strikes and stoppages. These only really took place under the Labour administrations of Harold Wilson (1964–70, 1974–6). Nothing like it was known under Margaret Thatcher, who seldom, if ever, conversed with union leaders, let alone offered them any form of hospitality. Some called it a pragmatic approach; others viewed it less favourably. Phillip Whitehead (a one-time Labour MP) was quoted in *The Independent* (25 April 1988) as having said of Wilson that he 'bought the hours with beer and sandwiches at No. 10 and the years with Royal Commissions'. Compare 'coffee and Danish at the White House' – an expression from the Carter administration for the breakfasts of coffee and Danish pastries offered by the President to Congressional leaders and others to win them over.

(life isn't all) beer and skittles An apparently late-appearing proverb (1855), urging that life is not just about simple pleasures or unalloyed enjoyment – specifically the drinks and games you would find in a pub, the British yeoman's idea of heaven on earth. From Thomas Hughes, *Tom Brown's Schooldays* (1857): 'Life isn't all beer and skittles, – but beer and skittles, or something better of the same sort, must form a good part of every Englishman's education.'

(the) beer that made Milwaukee famous The Schlitz Brewing Company had its roots in an operation begun in Milwaukee in 1849. By 1871, the year of the great Chicago fire, it was a thriving concern. The fire left Chicago thirsty; the city was desperately short of drinking water, and its breweries had virtually been destroyed. So Joseph Schlitz floated a shipload of beer down Lake Michigan to refresh his parched neighbours. They liked and remembered Milwaukee beer long after the crisis passed. It is not known who coined the phrase, but this is the incident that inspired it. The slogan was incorporated and registered in 1895, and was in use until production ceased in the 1980s.

(the) bee's knees 'The very best around; absolutely top hole'. There has always been a fascination with bees' knees. In the 18th century there was the expression 'as big as a bee's knee' and, in the 19th, 'as weak as a bee's knee'. But the bee whose knees became celebrated in US slang by 1923 was probably only there because of the rhyme. At about the same time, we find **the kipper's knickers**, **the cat's whiskers** (perhaps because of the importance of these in tuning wireless crystal sets in the 1920s), **the cat's pyjamas** (still new enough to be daring), 'the cat's miaow/eyebrows/ankles/tonsils/adenoids/galoshes/cufflinks/roller skates'. Not to mention 'the snake's hips', 'the clam's garter', 'the eel's ankle', 'the elephant's instep', 'the tiger's spots', 'the flea's eyebrows', 'the canary's tusks', 'the leopard's stripes', 'the sardine's whiskers', 'the pig's wings' – 'and just about any combination of animal, fish, or fowl with a part of the body or clothing that was inappropriate for it' – *Flexner* (1976).

before See HERE AND NOW.

before one can say 'Jack Robinson' (or **as quick as . . .**) This expression, meaning 'immediately; straight away', appears to have been alluded to by Richard Brinsley Sheridan in the House of Commons (some time after 1780) to avoid using a fellow member's name (as was, and is partly still,

the custom there). Having made a derogatory reference to the Secretary to the Treasury, John Robinson, and been asked by members shouting 'Name, name' to disclose the person he was referring to, Sheridan said, 'You know I cannot name him, but I could – as soon as I can say Jack Robinson' – quoted in Hesketh Pearson, *Lives of the Wits* (1962). Clearly, Sheridan was alluding to an already established expression. Neil Ewart in *Everyday Phrases* (1983) cites the theory that it 'refers to an erratic [18th-century] gentleman of that name who rushed around to visit his neighbours, rang the front-door bell, and then changed his mind and dashed off before the servant had time to announce his name'. Eric Partridge in his *Name Into Word* (1949) suggests that it was a made-up name using very common first and last elements. Fanny Burney has 'I'll do it as soon as say Jack Robinson' in her novel *Evelina*, Letter 82 (1778), so that pushes back the date somewhat. A promising explanation is that the phrase may have something to do with Sir John Robinson who was Officer Commanding the Tower of London 1660–79. In that case, the original reference may have been to the speed of beheading with an axe – as discussed in *The Observer* (24 April 1988).

(it) beggars all description A light literary turn of phrase for what is indescribable and originating with the meaning of the verb 'to beggar' in the sense 'to exhaust the resources of'. Apparently this was an original coinage of Shakespeare in *Antony and Cleopatra*, II.ii.197 (1607), where Enobarbus says of Cleopatra: 'For her own person, / It beggar'd all description'. 'Let us begin the tale in 1755 when an entranced visitor to the park [Painshill] wrote: "Pray follow me to Mr Hamilton's. I must tell you it beggars all description, the art of hiding art is here in such sweet perfection"' – *Financial Times* (23 April 1988); 'A place which beggars all description' – Mrs Piozzi, *Observations and Reflections Made in the Course of a Journey Through France &c.* (1789); 'Of the massacre itself that followed, where shall I begin and what shall I tell? It simply beggars all description. Occidentals of the

19th century cannot comprehend it. Still, I will try to give a few facts' – *The Times* (29 March 1895).

be good – and if you can't be good be careful! A nudging farewell, possibly originating with the American song 'Be Good! If You Can't Be Good, Be Careful!' (1907). It is the same sort of farewell remark as **don't do anything I wouldn't do!** that probably dates from the same period.

be good but not so frightfully good that someone says to you, 'Ah, and now what mischief are you up to?' A rather extended catchphrase. On the BBC radio *Children's Hour* by 1932 and into the early 1940s, there was a man called Commander Stephen King Hall who gave talks in an unhurried, avuncular voice, explaining current events (of which there were quite a few in those days) to his young listeners. And at the end he would sign off in this characteristic way. On 17 February 1941, after talking about the progress of the war, he ended: 'And now I think I'll give you a saying which some of you will know: Be Good but not so frightfully good that someone at once says, "Mmm, and now what mischief are you up to?" Well, goodbye and good luck.'

be good to yourself Sign-off from Don McNeill, homely American radio star, on the air 1934–68.

(to) beg the question Nowadays an expression frequently misused in place of 'to pose a question'. For example, 'I had a ghastly holiday in France which begs the question of why I went there in the first place.' The phrase (in English by 1581) really means 'to take for granted the matter in dispute, to assume without proof.' Or, more precisely, 'to take into consideration as part of your proof the thing you are trying to prove'. The process is apparent from these two exchanges: '*Q.* Why do parallel lines never meet?' '*A.* Because they are parallel.' '*Q.* Why do you think police series on TV are so popular?' '*A.* Because people like them.' H. W. Fowler in *Modern Engish Usage* (1965 Gowers' edn) relates the matter to *petitio principii* – 'the fallacy of founding a conclusion on the basis that as much needs to be proved as the

conclusion itself' and includes under 'Misapprehensions' that 'to beg a question is to avoid giving a straight answer.'

behind See ALL BEHIND.

behind closed doors Secretively, out of sight. There was a novel entitled *Behind Closed Doors* (1888) by A. K. Kreen, but the phrase does not seem to have caught on until the 1920s. *Washington: Behind Closed Doors* was the title of a fictional TV series about presidential politics (US 1977–8) – based on the Watergate affair; 'Strange goings-on behind the closed doors of that exotic building just off Great Queen Street, Covent Garden . . . Freemasons' Hall they call it, a secret world, a world of secrets' – *The Independent* (19 May 1995); 'This unique and fascinating tour uncovers a Venice normally hidden behind closed doors' – Ultimate Travel Company brochure (January 2003).

behind every —— man stands a —— woman A much used, unascribed format that is probably most often encountered nowadays in parodied versions. Working backwards, here are some of the parodies: 'Behind every good man is a good woman – I mean an exhausted one' – the Duchess of York, speech, September 1987. 'As usual there's a great woman behind every idiot' – John Lennon (quoted 1979). 'Behind every successful man you'll find a woman who has nothing to wear' – L. Grant Glickman (quoted 1977) *or* James Stewart (quoted 1979). 'We in the industry know that behind every successful screenwriter stands a woman. And behind her stands his wife' – Groucho Marx (quoted 1977). 'The road to success is filled with women pushing their husbands along' – Lord (Thomas R.) Dewar, quoted in Stevenson, *The Home Book of Quotations* (1967). 'And behind every man who is a *failure* there's a woman, too!' – John Ruge, cartoon caption, *Playboy* (March 1967). 'Behind every successful man stands a surprised mother-in-law' – Hubert Humphrey, speech (1964). An early example of the original expression occurs in an interview with Lady Dorothy Macmillan, wife of the then just retired British Prime Minister (7 December 1963). In the *Daily Sketch*, Godfrey Winn concluded his piece with the typical sentiment (his capitals): 'NO MAN SUCCEEDS WITHOUT A GOOD WOMAN BEHIND HIM. WIFE OR MOTHER. IF IT IS BOTH, HE IS TWICE BLESSED INDEED.' The *Evening Standard* (London) (18 April 1961) carried an advertisement showing a spaceman (Yuri Gargarin was in the news at that time) drifting off into space with the slogan, 'Behind every great man there's a bottle of Green Shield' (Worthington beer). In the film *The Country Girl* (US 1954), William Holden spoke the lines: 'That's what my ex-wife used to keep reminding me of, tearfully. She had a theory that behind every great man there was a great woman.' In *Love All*, a little known play by Dorothy L. Sayers, that opened at the Torch Theatre, Knightsbridge, London, on 9 April 1940 and closed before the end of the month, was this: 'Every great man has a woman behind him . . . And every great woman has some man or other in front of her, tripping her up.' Even earlier, Sayers herself referred to it as an 'old saying' in *Gaudy Night*, Chap. 3 (1935). Harriet Vane is talking to herself, musing on the problems of the great woman who must either die unwed or find a still greater man to marry her: 'Wherever you find a great man, you will find a great mother or a great wife standing behind him – or so they used to say. It would be interesting to know how many great women have had great fathers and husbands behind them.'

behind me   See GET THEE.

behind you   See OH NO THERE ISN'T.

being for the benefit of ——   A standard 19th-century phrase used in advertising for 'testimonial' performances. The title of Chapter 48 of *Nicholas Nickleby* (1838–9) by Charles Dickens is: 'Being for the benefit of Mr Vincent Crummles, and Positively his last Appearance on this Stage.' 'Being for the Benefit of Mr Kite' is the title of a track on the Beatles' *Seageant Pepper* album (1967). The lyrics, largely written by John Lennon, though credited jointly to him and Paul McCartney, derive almost word for word, as Lennon acknowledged, from the wording of a Victorian circus poster dated 1843 and in his possession.

belfry   See BATS IN THE.

Belgium   See IF IT'S TUESDAY.

believe it or not!   This exclamation was used as the title of a long-running syndicated newspaper feature, and radio and TV series, in the USA. Robert Leroy Ripley (1893–1949) created and illustrated a comic strip, *Ripley's Believe It or Not* (*circa* 1923), but citations for the phrase before this are lacking.

believe only half of what you see and nothing that you hear   *Mencken* (1942) finds an early quotation of this proverbial saying in *A Woman's Thoughts* by Dinah Mulock Craik (1858) where it is described as a 'cynical saying, and yet less bitter than at first appears'. As such, it builds upon the simpler 'Don't believe all you hear', which *CODP* finds in some form before 1300, perhaps even as a proverb of King Alfred the Great's.

be like dad, keep mum   British security slogan of the Second World War, emanating from the Ministry of Information in 1941. Another version was **keep mum, she's not so dumb** and showed a very un-Mum-like blonde being ogled by representatives of the three services. The security theme was paramount in both the UK and US wartime propaganda. Civilians as well as military personnel were urged not to talk about war-related matters lest the enemy somehow got to hear. Compare MUM'S THE WORD.

be like that (as also **be that way)!**   A joshing remark made to someone who has said something, or is doing something, of which you disapprove. American and British use by the mid-20th century.

bell, book and candle   Phrase from a solemn form of excommunication from the Roman Catholic Church. *Bartlett* (1980) says the ceremony has been current since the 8th century AD. There is a version dating from AD 1200 which goes: 'Do to the book [meaning, close it], quench the candle, ring the bell.' These actions symbolize the spiritual darkness the person is condemned to when denied further participation in the sacraments of the church. Sir Thomas Malory in *Le Morte d'Arthur* (1485) has: 'I shall curse you with book and bell and candle.' Shakespeare has the modern configuration in *King John*, III.ii.22 (1595): 'Bell, book and candle shall not drive me back.' *Bell, Book and Candle* was the title of John Van Druten's play (1950; filmed US 1958) about a publisher who discovers that his girlfriend is a witch.

(the/la) belle époque Literally 'the beautiful time, fine era', this phrase is used to describe the period of assured and comfortable living, particularly in France, from the last years of the 19th century until the outbreak of the First World War. It is particularly applied to the life of artistic and literary people of the time. Catalogues show that the phrase appears – first of all in French book titles – around 1948, with one possible case in 1936. From 1948 onwards it became generally known. The phrase without its modern meaning has been current since at least the late 18th century, in the more general sense of 'the best period' of, for example, Egyptian or mediaeval art, or the happiest days in someone's life. Victor Hugo, in a letter written before 1848, put: *'Quoi qu'on en dise, l'époque où nous vivons est une belle époque.'*

bells and smells Phrase characterizing Anglo-Catholicism or the 'High' Anglican church with its emphasis on incense-burning and other rites more usually associated with Roman Catholicism. Sometimes given as 'bells and *spells*', the phrase was established by the early 1980s. Such rites (and their adherents) are also described as **way up the candle**.

(the) bells! the bells! Supposed cry of Mathias, a burgomaster, who constantly sees visions of a man that he long ago murdered and robbed, in *The Bells*, an adaptation by Leopold Lewis of Erckmann-Chatrian's play *Le Juif Polonais*. Chiefly associated with the actor (Sir) Henry Irving who had his first great success with it when it was produced at the Lyceum Theatre, London, in 1871. Impressions of Irving invariably include the line in which Mathias is haunted by the sound of the sledge bells of the man he murdered. In *Bring On the Girls* (1954), P. G. Wodehouse reproduces this as: 'Eah! daun't you hear . . . the sund of bell–ll–s?'

(to) bell the cat To undertake a dangerous mission. This expression derives from the fable (told, for example, in *Piers Plowman, circa* 1377) about the old mouse who suggested putting a bell round the neck of a cat so that mice would be warned of its approach. It was generally agreed among the mice that this was a very good idea – except that one young mouse pointed out the only flaw in it: 'But who shall hang the bell about the cat's neck?' The nickname 'bell-the-cat' was applied to Archibald Douglas, 5th Earl of Angus (*circa* 1450–1514) who earned it by devising a scheme to get rid of Robert Cochrane, hated favourite of James III of Scotland. He is reputed to have said that he would 'bell the cat', and he began the attack by pulling Cochrane's gold chain from his neck. Cochrane and others were hanged. Douglas switched his allegiance and was a leader in the rebellion against James.

belly See BETTER THAN A SLAP.

—— belongs to —— A modestly used but memorable format for titles. *London Belongs To Me* was the title of a novel (1945) by Norman Collins (filmed UK 1948 but known in the US as *Dulcimer Street*). *Paris Belongs To Us* was the English title of Jacques Rivette's film *Paris nous appartient* (France 1960).

belt and braces A term applied to a system with its own back-up, suggesting that if one part falls down, the other will stay up; a double check. It is an engineer's expression, used for example by a BBC man to describe the two microphones placed side-by-side when broadcasting the sovereign's Christmas message. In the days when this was broadcast live, it ensured radio transmission. Belt and Braces was the name of a British theatre group of the 1970s. An Australian engineer commented (1993) that some of his colleagues would talk of 'belt, braces and bowyangs, too' – 'bowyangs' being ties round a worker's trousers to keep out cold and mud.

be my guest *American Speech* in 1955 had 'be my guest' as a way of saying 'go right ahead; do as you wish'. Hilton hotels may also have used 'be my guest' as a slogan at some time. Certainly, *Be My*

Guest was the title of a book (1957) by the hotelier, Conrad Hilton. What is not clear is when the phrase originated.

bend   See CLEANS ROUND.

benefit   See BEING FOR THE.

benign neglect   When he was a counsellor to President Nixon, the American Democratic politician Daniel Patrick Moynihan (1927–2003) quoted this phrase in a memorandum dated 2 March 1970: 'The time may have come when the issue of race could benefit from a period of "benign neglect". The subject has been too much talked about . . . We may need a period in which negro progress continues and racial rhetoric fades.' This was leaked to *The New York Times* and the inevitable furore ensued, though all Moynihan suggested was that racial tensions would be lessened if people on both sides were to lower their voices a little. He was repeating an 1839 phrase of an Earl of Durham to Queen Victoria regarding Canada. It had done so well 'through a period of benign neglect' by the mother country, the Earl said, that it should be granted self-government.

Bentley   See BLACK MARK.

be prepared   The motto of the Boy Scout movement (founded 1908), which shares its initials with the movement's founder, Sir Robert Baden-Powell. With permission, the words were subsequently used as an advertising slogan for Pears' soap. They were also used, as a motto, by police in South Africa.

(a right) berk   *Morris* (1977) cites Dudley Moore as saying of Peter Cook (in a magazine interview): 'It is hard to distinguish sometimes whether Peter is being playful or merely a berk.' *Morris* then goes on, coyly, to say '*berk* is British slang – originally a bit of Cockney rhyming slang – meaning "fool"' – and leaves it at that. In fact, 'berk' is short for 'Berkeley/Berkshire Hunt', which is rhyming slang for 'cunt'. Spelling the word 'birk' or 'burk(e)' helps obscure the origin. Theoretically, if it comes from this source, the word should be pronounced 'bark'. The use probably does not date from before 1900.

Bernie, the bolt!   Bob Monkhouse, host of ATV's game show *The Golden Shot* 1967–75, explained in 1979: 'Lew Grade had bought the Swiss-German TV success *The Golden Shot* and the host had to repeat one line in each show – the word of instruction to the technician to load the dangerous crossbow and simultaneously warn the studio of the fact that the weapon was armed . . . "Heinz, the bolt!" [was the original phrase]. When I took over in 1967, Heinz went home. He stayed long enough to train an ATV technician, Derek Young. I said, "'Derek, the bolt' sounds lousy. Let's make it alliterative. What's funny and begins with B?" We were reckoning without the man himself. Derek liked Derek. "Well, you think of a name that begins with B and won't embarrass you," I said. And Bernie it became. I found out later that his wife liked it. Certainly the audience did. Only blokes called Bernie grew to loathe it. Thousands of letters were addressed simply to "Bernie the Bolt, ITV".' The phrase stayed the same even when Derek was replaced by another technician. At one time, viewers watching the programme at home could ring and instruct the operator to aim the gun. Hence: **Left a bit, – stop! Down a bit, – stop! Up a bit, – stop! Fire!** This acquired a kind of catchphrase status, not least because of the possible *double entendre*.

be soon   See SHE KNOWS YOU KNOW.

best   See IT'S ALL DONE.

(the) best and the brightest   This alliterative combination is almost traditional: 'Political writers, who will not suffer the best and brightest of characters . . . to take a single right step for the honour or interest of the nation' – *Letters of Junius* (1769); 'Best and brightest, come away!' – Shelley, 'To Jane: The Invitation' (1822); 'Brightest and best of the sons of the morning' – from the hymn by Bishop Heber (1827); 'The best, the brightest, the cleverest of them all!' – Anthony Trollope, *Dr Thorne*, Chap. 25 (1858); 'So we lose five thousand of the best and brightest [i.e. coins/money] – P. G. Wodehouse, 'Anselm Gets His Chance' (1930). In David Halberstam's book *The Best and the Brightest* (1972), the phrase applies to those young men from business, industry and the academic world whom John F. Kennedy brought into government in the early 1960s but who were ultimately responsible for the quagmire of American involvement in the Vietnam War.

best beloved Term of endearment (also 'O My Best Beloved' and 'O Best Beloved') addressed to the reader of Rudyard Kipling's *Just So Stories* (1902). These comic fables explaining the distinguishing characteristics of animals ('How the Camel Got His Hump' and so on) were originally told by Kipling to his own children.

(to put one's) best foot forward Meaning 'to walk as fast as possible; to make a good impression', this probably derives from an earlier form: 'To put one's best foot/leg foremost'. In Shakespeare's *King John*, IV.ii.170 (1595), we find: 'Nay, but make haste; the better foot before' The *right* foot has from ancient times been regarded as the best foot, right being associated with rationality, the left with emotion. To put your right foot forward is thus to guard against ill-luck.

best friends See EVEN YOUR.

(the) best fucks are always after a good cry A seldom recorded observation. In *Peter Hall's Diaries* (1983) – entry for 22 May 1979 – it is quoted as having been said at Glyndebourne after Elizabeth Söderström had burst into tears at being given tough direction and then gone on to give 'a very good first act'.

be still, my beating heart! A common phrase from 19th-century verse, now only used in parody or as a cynical comment on an account of young love or a romantic incident. 'My beating heart', on its own, appears in innumerable verses between 1700 and 1900. Compare: 'Lo, where he comes! – Be still, my heart! they are / Thy foes, must be thy victims: wilt thou beat / For those who almost broke thee?' – Byron, *The Two Foscari*, Act 1 (1821). But, in particular, 'Be still, my beating heart, be still!' is the first line of 'All One' by Mary Elizabeth Coleridge (1861–1907). 'Oh my soul, my beating heart' is in Mark Twain, *Innocents Abroad* (1869). Dr James Beattie's 'Elegy: Written in the Year 1758' has: 'But peace, bold thought! Be still, my bursting heart!' W. S. Gilbert, in *The*

Sorcerer, Act 1 (1877), has Dr Daly say, 'Be still, my fluttering heart!' Since he is a middle-aged clergyman, might the joke not lie in the audience being familiar with it from a heroine of one of the Victorian melodramas? In *HMS Pinafore*, Act 1 (1878), Gilbert puts: 'Oh, my heart, my beating heart'. A little later than all this, there was a song entitled 'Be Still, My Heart! (I Can Tell Who's Knocking At My Door)' (1934).

(the) best-kept secret In its original form, about any well-withheld information, this was a cliché by the mid-20th century, but as used by travel-writers to describe a holiday destination, it was included in the 'travel scribes' armoury' compiled from competition entries in *The Guardian* (10 April 1993). 'Seeing that in the last month Lasmo's share price has drifted northwards from 114p to a peak of 169p (now 149.5p) this was hardly the world's best-kept secret' – *The Observer* (1 May 1994); 'If this punchy little two-hander from Footpaul Productions of South Africa has ambitions to being the best kept secret of this year's Mayfest, then it won't work because word-of-mouth will acclaim it for the gem it is' – *The Herald* (Glasgow) (11 May 1994); 'Once known as "Europe's best kept secret", the secret leaked out and now much of [the Algarve's] wonderful Atlantic coast has been obscured by a wall of concrete – *The Herald* (Glasgow) (28 May 1994).

(to make the) best of both worlds Meaning, 'to have the benefits of two contrasting or separate ways of life or circumstances.' The expression appears to have originated in the title of a book by the Congregationalist preacher Thomas Binney (1798–1874), *Is It Possible To Make the Best of Both Worlds? A Book for Young Men* (1853). Binney answers his own question affirmatively: not only is it possible for a good Christian to lead a happy life on earth, such a life is even the best preparation for life after death. Released from its religious origins, the phrase became increasingly popular from the 1960s onwards (Robert Palmer had a modest hit with the song 'Best of Both Worlds' in 1978), and then an explosion of popularity after 1990.

(the) best Prime Minister we have (or **never had)** R. A. (later Lord) Butler (d. 1982) has sometimes been known as 'the best Prime Minister we never had' (so have others, like Denis Healey, for example), and it is to Butler that we probably owe both the positive and the negative formats. In December 1955, having (not for the last time) been passed over for the Conservative leadership, he was confronted by a Press Association reporter just as he was about to board an aircraft at London airport. As criticism was growing over the performance of Anthony Eden, the Prime Minister, the reporter asked: 'Mr Butler, would you say that this [Eden] is the best Prime Minister we have?' Butler assented to this 'well-meant but meaningless proposition . . . indeed it was fathered upon me. I don't think it did Anthony any good. It did not do me any good either' – *The Art of the Possible* (1973).

best-regulated See ACCIDENTS.

(to give something one's) best shot To try as hard as possible, to do one's very best. An American idiom known by 1951 when, in the film *His Kind of Woman*, Robert Mitchum said, during a card game, 'Take your best shot.' Presumably the expression derives from the sporting sense of 'shot' (as in golf) rather than the gun sense. '"We're not able to adequately counsel the farmer with the present plan," he said. "With this, we'll be able to give him our best shot"' – *The Washington Post* (13 February 1984); 'The editor must keep his powder dry. He is there to sell newspapers and his best shot is to find and project material denied to his rivals' – *The Guardian* (14 May 1984); the film *Hoosiers* (US 1986), about a basketball team, was also known as *Best Shot*; 'For Clinton and the Democrats, the issue his candidacy continues to pose is electability. His primary claim to the nomination lies not in ideology and political correctness but in being the Democrat who has the best shot at winning in November' – *The Washington Post* (31 January 1992); '[Imran Khan] had prepared for marriage like a cricket match. He had no guarantees it would work but he would give it his "best shot"' – *The Independent* (21 June 1995).

(the) best swordsman in —— (or **finest swordsman . . .)** Latterly a cliché of swashbuckling epics, this phrase has quite a history. John Aubrey in his *Brief Lives* (*circa* 1697) has a literal use: 'Sir John Digby yielded to be the best swordsman of his time.' Charles Dickens, *Barnaby Rudge*, Chap. 27 (1841), has a relatively unselfconscious use: 'I have been tempted in these two short interviews, to draw upon that fellow, fifty times. Five men in six would have yielded to the impulse. By suppressing mine, I wound him deeper and more keenly than if I were the best swordsman in all Europe.' In the film *Son of Monte Cristo* (US 1940), Louis Hayward as the Count of Monte Cristo says: 'Don't worry. My father was the best swordsman in France!' 'He thinks that will protect him against me – the finest swordsman in Bavaria' is spoken in the film *A Night in Casablanca* (US 1946). 'He is the fastest sword in the whole of France' – spoken by Ernie Wise in a 'Three Musketeers' sketch on BBC TV *The Morecambe and Wise Christmas Show* (1970). *The Finest Swordsman in All France* is the title of a book (1984) by Keith Miles on the subject of clichés in general.

(the) best things in life are free A modern proverb that really does seem to have started life with the song of the title (1927) by De Sylva, Brown and Henderson – featured in the show *Good News* (filmed US 1930 and 1947).

better See COULD IT GET.

better and better See EVERY DAY.

(one's) better half One's spouse or partner. General use and pretty inoffensive except to the politically correct who might jib at implied inequality of any kind in a married relationship (even if the better of the two people is invariably the woman). Of long standing: 'My dear, my better half (said he) I find I must now leave thee' – Argalus to his wife, in Sir Philip Sidney, *Arcadia* (1580).

better out than in What you say having belched. Quoted in Mary Killen, *Best Behaviour* (1990). Or when farting, according to *Partridge/Catch Phrases*, in which Paul Beale dates it to the 1950s.

better red than dead A slogan used by some (mainly British) nuclear disarmers. Bertrand Russell wrote in 1958: 'If no alternative remains except communist domination or the extinction of the human race, the former alternative is the lesser of two evils'. *Time* Magazine (15 September 1961) gave 'I'd rather be Red than dead' as a slogan of Britain's Campaign for Nuclear Disarmament. The counter-cry: 'Better dead than red' may also have had some currency. In the film *Love With a Proper Stranger* (US 1964), Steve McQueen proposed to Natalie Wood with a picket sign stating 'Better Wed Than Dead'.

(well, it's) better than a poke in the eye with a sharp stick What you say to someone who is hesitating over accepting something – a small tip, say, or an equivocal compliment: it is 'better than nothing.' Certainly established usage by the time it was uttered on BBC Radio, *Round the Horne* (15 February 1967). Indeed, *Partridge/Catch Phrases* dates it and other similar phrases to '*circa* 1920' and adds: 'Most seem to have originated late in C19. Compare *Grose* (1788): "*this is better than a thump on the back with a stone*".' An English Midlands variant, dating from the mid-20th century is: 'Better than a poke in the eye with a hedge stake' (which is, of course, a sharp stick). Compare also:

(well, it's) better than a slap in your belly with a wet fish What you say to someone who may be hesitating over accepting something. *Partridge/Catch Phrases* has ' . . . than a slap across the kisser'. The art critic Brian Sewell revealed on BBC Radio *Quote . . . Unquote* (12 April 1994) that his nurse, when bathing him, would not only inquire 'Have you done down there?' but also command him to stand up at the conclusion of the proceedings and whack him with a sopping wet flannel, saying, 'There's a slap in the belly with a wet fish.'

(it is) better to die on your feet than live on your knees A Republican slogan from the Spanish Civil War, 1936. Dolores Ibarruri ('La Pasionaria') said it in a radio speech from Paris calling on the women of Spain to help defend the Republic (3 September 1936). According to her autobi-

ography (1966), she had used the words earlier, on 18 July, when broadcasting in Spain. Emiliano Zapata (*circa* 1877–1919), the Mexican guerilla leader, had used the expression long before her in 1910: 'Men of the South! It is better to die on your feet than to live on your knees [. . . *Es mejor preferible morir a pie que vivir en rodillas*]!' Franklin D. Roosevelt later picked up the expression in his message accepting an honorary degree from Oxford University (19 June 1941): 'We, too, are born to freedom, and believing in freedom, are willing to fight to maintain freedom. We, and all others who believe as we do, would rather die on our feet than live on our knees.'

Betty See ALL MY EYE.

between a rock and a hard place In a position impossible to get out of, literally or metaphorically. Popular in the 1970s and almost certainly of North American origin, despite its almost biblical resonance. The UK/Canada group Cutting Crew had a song with the title, '(Between a Rock) And A Hard Place', in 1989. An early appearance is in John Buchan, *The Courts of the Morning* (1929), but the phrase was being discussed in *Dialect Notes*, No. 5 (1921), where it was defined as 'to be bankrupt . . . Common in Arizona in recent panics; sporadic in California'. Some have attempted to suggest that it is a modern version of **between Scylla and Charybdis** where Scylla was a sea monster on a rock and Charybdis was a whirlpool – two equal dangers one could not avoid. This is not the meaning of 'between a rock and a hard place' – besides, a whirlpool is not exactly a 'hard' place, except in the sense of a problematical one to get out of. A few years ago, the late King Hussein of Jordan (or P.L.K. = Plucky Little King) was said to be 'Between Iraq and a Hard Place.'

between you and me and the gatepost (or bedpost or doorpost) Confidentially – a phrase suggesting (lightly and not very seriously) that a secret is about to be imparted and that it should be kept. Known by 1832. Charles Dickens, *Nicholas Nickleby*, Chap. 10 (1839), has: 'Between you and me and the post, sir, it will be a very nice portrait.' The previous year, Dickens had written in a letter: 'Between you and me and the general post.'

betwixt the devil and the deep blue sea Meaning, 'having two courses of action open to one, both of them dangerous' (as with the classical Scylla and Charybdis, see just above). The phrase should not be taken too literally. The 'devil' here may refer to the seam of a wooden ship's hull or to a plank fastened to the side of a ship as a support for guns. Either of these was difficult of access, a perilous place to be, but better than in the deep blue sea. An earlier form was 'between the devil and the Dead Sea' (known by 1894).

bet you can't eat just one A slogan for Lay's potato chips in the USA (quoted in 1981). By 1982, **bet you can't eat three** was being used by the cricketer Ian Botham to promote Shredded Wheat in the UK.

Beulah – peel me a grape! A catchphrase expressing dismissive unconcern, first uttered by Mae West to a black maid in the film *I'm No Angel* (1933), after a male admirer has stormed out on her. It has had some wider currency since then but is nearly always used as a conscious quotation.

be upstairs ready, my angel See BURMA.

beware Greeks bearing gifts A warning against trickery, this is an allusion to the most famous Greek gift of all – the large wooden horse that was built as an offering to the gods before the Greeks were about to return home after besieging Troy unsuccessfully for ten years. When it was taken within the city walls of Troy, men leapt out from it, opened the gates and helped destroy the city. Virgil in the *Aeneid* (II.49) has Laocoön warn the Trojans not to admit the horse, saying '*timeo Danaos et dona ferentes* [I still fear the Greeks, even when they offer gifts].' 'Upon my admiring some gooseberry wine at dinner, she turned to the Butler, and ordered him to send half-a-dozen to the Parsonage the following day, which I did all I could to decline, under the old feeling, Timeo Danaos et dona ferentes' – Reverend John Skinner, diary entry for 28 April 1822 (*Journal of a Somerset Rector 1803–1834*, pub. 1930/1971).

beyond See ABOVE AND.

beyond the Fringe *Beyond the Fringe* was the title of a trend-setting, somewhat satirical, revue (London 1961 and then on Broadway). It had first been shown, however, at the 1960 Edinburgh Festival as part of the main programme of events, where it was 'beyond' the unofficial series of theatrical manifestations at Edinburgh known as the 'Fringe'. Note also an allusion to the following:

beyond the pale Meaning, 'outside the bounds of acceptable behaviour'. The Pale was the area of English settlement around Dublin in Ireland, dating from the 14th century, in which English law had to be obeyed, but there have also been areas known as pales in Scotland, around Calais and in Russia. The derivation is from the Latin *palus*, meaning 'a stake'. Anyone who lived outside this fence was thought to be beyond the bounds of civilization. The allusive use does not appear earlier than the mid-19th century.

BFN See MORNING ALL.

bicycle See AS SURE.

(the) Big Apple As a nickname for New York City, this expression seems to have arisen in the 1920s/30s. There are various possible explanations: the Spanish word for a block of houses between two streets is *manzana* which is also the word for apple; in the mid-1930s there was a Harlem night club called 'The Big Apple', which was a mecca for jazz musicians; there was also a jitterbugging dance from the swing era (*circa* 1936) that took its name from the nightclub; 'big apple' was racetrack argot, and New York City had a good reputation in this field – hence, the phrase was used to describe the city's metropolitan racing (as in a column 'On the Big Apple' by John J. Fitzgerald in the *Morning Telegraph*, mid-1920s.) OED2 has 'Big Apple' for New York City in 1928 *before* the dance explanation, but *Safire* plumps for the jazz version, recalling a 1944 jive 'handbook' defining 'apple' as: 'the earth, the universe, this planet. Any place that's large. A big Northern city'. Hence, you called New York City the Big Apple if you considered it to be the centre of the universe. In 1971, Charles Gillett, president of the New York Convention and Visitors Bureau, attempted to revitalize NYC's economy by re-popularizing it as 'the Big Apple' (compare I LOVE NEW YORK). In the 18th century, Horace Walpole had called London 'The Strawberry' because of its freshness and cleanliness in comparison with foreign cities.

(a) big boy did it and ran away The classic child's excuse when insisting that something which has happened is not its fault. Hence, *A Big Boy Did It and Ran Away*, the title of a novel (2001) by Christopher Brookmyre.

Big Brother is watching you A fictional slogan from George Orwell's novel *Nineteen Eighty-Four* (1948). In a dictatorial state, every citizen is regimented and observed by a spying TV set in the home. The line became a popular catchphrase following a sensational BBC TV dramatization of the novel in 1954. Aspects of the Ministry of Truth in the novel were derived not only from Orwell's knowledge of the BBC (where he worked) but also from his first wife Eileen's work at the Ministry of Food, preparing 'Kitchen Front' broadcasts during the Second World War (*circa* 1942–4). From 2000, Channel 4 in the UK showed an annual series of *Big Brother*, a so-called 'reality' TV programme in which the behaviour of a group of people contained in a house was continuously recorded and shown in edited excerpts.

(a) big butter and egg man This description of a small-town businessman trying to prove himself a big shot in the city was much used by Texas Guinan, the US nightclub hostess (d. 1933). Cyril Connolly in his *Journals* (1983) characterized the man in question as a small-town success, often a farmer who produced such commodities as butter and eggs, and who attempted to pass for a sophisticate in the big city. Finding it first in the 1920s, *OED2* emphasizes that the man in question – 'wealthy, unsophisticated' – spends his money freely. *The Butter and Egg Man* was the title of a play (1925) by George S. Kaufman.

big conk, big cock (or **big nose, big cock)!** A phrase expressing the age-old superstition that there is a correlation

between the size of a man's nose and his penis. Erasmus (1466–1536), of all people, is supposed to have included the aphorism (in Latin) in one of his works, as '*Bene nasati, bene menticulati*'. Compare **large feet, large cock** and its corollary, **small feet, small cock** – recorded in my book *The Gift of the Gab* (1985). Hence, the playful exchange in the film *Notting Hill* (UK 1999): *Anna:* 'You have big feet.' *William:* 'Yes, always have had.' *Anna:* 'You know what they say about men with big feet?' *William:* 'No, what's that?' *Anna:* 'Big feet, large shoes.'

big deal! A deflating (mostly American) exclamation. *DOAS* has it in 'wide student use since *circa* 1940' and 'popularized by comedian Arnold Stang in the Henry Morgan network radio program *circa* 1946 and on the Milton Berle network program *circa* 1950'. Leo Rosten in *Hooray for Yiddish!* (1982) emphasizes its similarity with sarcastic, derisive Jewish phrases and notes how 'it is uttered with emphasis on the "big", in a dry disenchanted tone'.

(the) Big Enchilada Nickname of John Mitchell (1913–88), US Attorney General, who led President Nixon's re-election campaign in 1972 and subsequently was sentenced to a gaol term for associated offences. An enchilada is a Mexican dish. The term was evoked (like 'Big Cheese') by a Nixon aide, John Ehrlichman, during a 1973 taped conversation in the White House. He sought to describe the size of the sacrificial victim who was being thrown to the wolves.

(the) Big Fellow (or **Big Fella)** Nickname of Michael Collins (1890–1922), the Irish politician and Sinn Fein leader. Tim Pat Coogan in his biography (1990) notes that the sobriquet indicated: 'Swollen-headedness as much as height, just under six feet.' Sometimes also known as **the Long Fellow**.

(too) big for one's boots Meaning, 'conceited'. In use by 1879. Perhaps originally '. . . for one's breeches' (US by 1835). An example: in 1948, reports of a speech by Harold Wilson, then President of the Board of Trade, wrongly suggested he had claimed that when at school, some of his classmates had gone barefoot. Ivor

Bulmer-Thomas consequently remarked at the 1949 Conservative Party Conference: 'If ever he went to school without any boots it was because he was too big for them.' This remark is often wrongly attributed to Harold Macmillan.

bigger See IS IT.

(a) bigger splash Title of David Hockney's 1967 painting – one of his California swimming pool series – that shows a splash as a diver enters the water but does not show his body. Accordingly, *A Bigger Splash* became the title of a 1973 British documentary for the cinema about Hockney's life as an artist and as a homosexual.

(the) bigger they come, the harder they fall A proverbial phrase often attributed to Bob Fitzsimmons (1862–1917), a British-born boxer in the USA, referring to an opponent of larger build (James L. Jeffries), prior to a fight in San Francisco (9 June 1899). This was quoted in the *Brooklyn Daily Eagle* (11 August 1900) as, 'The bigger they are, the further they have to fall.' Also attributed to the boxer John L. Sullivan but probably of earlier proverbial origin in any case. Hence, presumably, *The Harder They Fall*, title of a novel by Budd Schulberg and a film (US 1956) about boxing. *The Harder They Come* was also the title of a film (US 1973).

(a) big girl's blouse Phrase used about a man who is not as manly as he might be. A rather odd expression, possibly of Welsh origin, and suggesting what an effeminate football or rugby player might wear instead of a proper jersey. Could it have something to do with the wobbliness of the image conjured up? *Street Talk* (1986) states that it 'describes an adult male who has a low pain threshold, a "sissy". When trying to remove a splinter someone might say: "Hold still you big girl's blouse. It won't hurt".' Confirming its mostly North country use, the phrase has also been associated with the British comedienne Hylda Baker (1908–86) in the form 'You big girl's blouse', probably in the situation comedy *Nearest and Dearest* (ITV 1968–73). From *The Guardian* (20 December 1986) – about a nativity play: 'The house is utterly still (except where Balthazar is

trying to screw the spout of his frankincense pot into Melchior's ear, to even things up for being called a big girl's blouse on the way in from the dressing room.)' From *The Herald* (Glasgow) (20 October 1994): 'His acid-tongued father [Prince Philip] might be reinforced in his view of him as a big girl's blouse, but Prince Charles is actually a big boy now. His children, locked away in the posh equivalent of care, are not.' From *The Sunday Times* (6 November 1994): 'Men, quite naturally, are equally unwilling to accept paternity leave, because of the fear that this will mark them for ever as a great big girl's blouse.'

big head (or big 'ead)! Said of a conceited person and achieving catchphrase status when spoken by Max Bygraves in the BBC radio show *Educating Archie* (mid-1950s). He ran into trouble with educationists for not pronouncing the 'h', but he persisted and also recorded a song with the refrain 'Why does everybody call me "Big 'ead"?'

big-hearted Arthur, that's me! Arthur Askey (1900–82) has good cause to be acclaimed as the father of the British radio catchphrase. He had such a profusion of them from the BBC's *Band Waggon* (1938–39) onwards, that he may be said to have popularized the notion that broadcast comedians were somehow incomplete *without* a catchphrase. 'There had been radio comedians before this who used catchphrases,' he commented in 1979, 'like Sandy Powell, but ours was the first show which really made a thing of them. I was the one who was on the air most and kept banging them in.' *Band Waggon* was the first BBC comedy show specifically tailored for radio – as opposed to being made up of variety acts. The basic format was that of a magazine, but the best-remembered segment is that in which Askey shared a flat with Richard Murdoch (1907–90) on the top of Broadcasting House in London, bringing added meaning to the term 'resident comedians'. A catchphrase that stayed with Askey for the rest of his life was spoken in the first edition of the show on 5 January 1938. 'I have always used this expression – even when I was at school. When playing cricket, you know, if the ball was hit to the boundary and nobody would go and fetch it – I would . . . saying "Big-hearted Arthur, that's me!"' 'Big-Hearted Arthur' was also Askey's bill matter.

(the) big lie From the German *grosse Lüge* – a distortion of the truth so brazen that it cannot fail to be accepted, a technique that was the cornerstone of Nazi propaganda. Adolf Hitler wrote in *Mein Kampf* (1925): 'The great mass of the people . . . will more easily fall victims to a big lie than to a small one.' Together with Josef Goebbels, his propaganda chief, Hitler perceived that the bigger a lie was and the more frequently it was told, the greater was the likelihood of its mass acceptance.

(the) big one This boast, beloved – in particular – of a certain type of advertiser, almost certainly dates back to 1907 when, in the USA, Ringling Brothers Circus bought up its rival, Barnum and Bailey. The two together were billed, understandably, as 'The Big One'. When the outfit closed in 1956, the *New York Post* had the headline, 'THE BIG ONE IS NO MORE!' The term may be applied to any product or event that an advertiser wishes to promote as important. From the BBC radio show *Round the Horne* (14 May 1967): '*Rousing fanfare:* "This is the big one" – "Watch out for it" – "It's coming your way" – "It's coming soon" – "Don't miss it".' From advertising for the film *The Bridges of Madison County* (September 1995): '"THIS IS THE BIG ONE!" – Joel Siegel, *Good Morning America*, ABC-TV.' Since the 1960s at least, the phrase 'Big One' has also been applied to the feared and inevitable major earthquake expected in southern California, of which there have been several harbingers. From *The Washington Post* (2 October 1987): 'Shaken Californians' Thoughts Turn To The Future "Big One" – . . . Southern Californians spent most of their day today reliving the earthquake and almost everybody's wild fear that this would be what is generally referred to in this state as "the Big One" . . . a reference to the earthquake all Californians know has been building for decades along the San Andreas Fault, and which is predicted, when it hits, to cause massive

devastation along the West Coast.' The British TV commentator David Vine caused a good deal of inappropriate laughter in about 1974 when, at athletic competitions, he would talk of competitors 'pulling out the big one' – i.e. making the supreme effort. Note also a 'big one' in the sense of a drink offered as a thank-you, literally or metaphorically. From Christopher Ogden, *Life of the Party* (1994): 'Pamela had introduced Clinton to the Washington power circuit and she had helped organize and pay for the overhaul of the Democratic party. The president-elect owed her a big one.' *DOAS* points out that a 'big one' is also a $1,000 bill (from gambling) [£100 in the UK] and a nursery euphemism for a bowel movement. *Partridge/Slang* has 'big one' or 'big 'un' for 'a notable person' and dates it from between 1800 and 1850. Pierce Egan in *Boxiana* (1829) has: 'Jem had now reduced the "big one" to his own weight, and had also placed him upon the stand-still system.'

(a) big shot A powerful man, especially in the worlds of crime, politics and business. Of American origin, since about 1929, it carries a suggestion of disapproval. From Norman Lewis, *The Honoured Society* (1964): 'By 1914, and the outbreak of the First World War, Zu Calo was the undisputed head of the Mafia of the province of Caltanisetta, and as such, in Mafia jargon, a *pezzo di novanta* [gun of ninety] – a term of honour derived from an unwieldy but impressive piece of siege artillery of the epoch of Garibaldi, firing a shell 90 millimetres in diameter (hence the translated Americanism, "big shot") . . .'

(the) big sleep A synonym for death, as in the title of the novel *The Big Sleep* (1939; filmed US 1946 and 1977) by Raymond Chandler.

(the) Big Yin Nickname of Billy Connolly, the Scots comedian (b. 1942). It means 'Big One' and probably derives from a routine he did in the early 1970s called 'Last Supper and Crucifixion' in which he referred to Christ as such.

Bill's mother's See IT'S DARK.

bill stickers will be prosecuted Form of words that used to appear on advertisement hoardings or board fencing in the UK in an attempt to discourage fly-posting. The notice is shown in a *Punch* cartoon in the edition of 26 April 1939. The term 'bill-sticker' has been known since 1774 at least. Perhaps the phrase has fallen out of use because of the graffitoed addition, recorded in the 1970s: '. . . Bill Stickers is innocent.'

Bingo! A generalized exclamation on achieving anything, similar to 'Eureka!'. In 1919, at a carnival near Jacksonville, Florida, Edwin Lowe saw people playing what they called 'bean-o' – putting beans on a numbered card. This game of chance was already established elsewhere under the names 'Keno', 'Loo', and 'Housey-Housey'. Lowe developed the idea and launched a craze that netted him a fortune. One of his friends stuttered, 'B–b–bingo!' on winning, and that is how the game is said to have got its name. The word had already been applied to brandy in the 17th century, but – as a result of this develop-ment from 'bean-o' – it turned not only into an exclamation on winning Lowe's game but also into a generalized cry of success.

bird See GET THE.

(the) birds of the air This is essentially a biblical phrase – for example, Matthew 8:20: 'The foxes have holes, and the birds of the air have nests; but the Son of man hath not where to lay his head.' However, it makes a later notable appearance in the rhyme 'Who Killed Cock Robin?' (first recorded in the 18th century): 'All the birds of the air / Fell a-sighing and a-sobbing, / When they heard the bell toll / For poor Cock Robin.' *The Birds of the Air* is the title of a novel (1980) by Alice Thomas Ellis. A variant is 'fowl(s) of the air' (Genesis 1:26), though much more commonly one finds 'fowls of the heavens' in (mostly) the Old Testament. The 'fish(es) of the sea' occurs at least three times in the Old Testament (e.g. Genesis 1:26). 'All the beasts of the forest' is biblical, too (Psalms 104:20), though more frequent is **beasts of the field** (e.g. Psalms 8:7).

birth pangs Denoting initial difficulties in any sphere of activity, as though comparable to those experienced when a mother gives birth. Date of origin unknown. 'The

inevitable transformation of universities everywhere into "multi-versities" is being achieved with appalling birth pangs in the University of California' – *The Guardian* (30 November 1968); 'The boom in DIY retailing in the 1980s had been fuelled by the growth in home ownership and the number of house moves. Once that engine was switched off, retail price wars and "20pc off everything" promotions fol-lowed. Do It All, still in its painful birth pangs, was thrust into the firing line' – *The Daily Telegraph* (7 May 1994).

bishop See AS THE BISHOP; BASH THE; DO YOU KNOW.

Bisto See AHH!

bitch See EVERY DOG.

(the) bitch-goddess Success This phrase was coined by the American psychologist William James (1842–1910) in a letter to H. G. Wells (11 September 1906): 'The moral flabbiness born of the exclusive worship of the bitch-goddess Success. That – with the squalid cash interpretation put on the word success – is our national disease.' In *Lady Chatterley's Lover* (1928), D. H. Lawrence uses the term 'bitch-goddess Success' on no fewer than ten occasions – and then attributes it to William James's brother, Henry . . .

(to) bite the bullet Meaning, 'to face up to adversity with courage'. The phrase probably derives from the days of field surgery in battle before anaesthesia was available. A wounded man would literally be given a bullet to bite on to distract him from the pain. 'Brace up and bite the bullet. I'm afraid I've bad news for you' – P. G. Wodehouse, *The Inimitable Jeeves*, Chap. 2 (1923).

bite the dust See KICK THE BUCKET.

bitter See ALL.

(the) bitter end Meaning, 'the last extremity; the absolute limit', and a common phrase by the mid-19th century. Bitterness doesn't really enter into it: the nautical 'bitt' is a bollard on the deck of a ship around which cables and ropes are wound. The end of the cable that is wrapped round or otherwise secured to the bollard is the 'bitter end'. On the other hand, ends have – for possibly longer – been described as bitter in other senses. Proverbs 5:4 has: 'But her end is bitter as wormwood, sharp as a two-edged sword'. 'The rather shallow stretch of water we call "la Manche" has always masked a gaping chasm of a different sort – between the island and the Continent (what a strange word!) in general, and France in particular. Right to the bitter end, some island fundamentalists have feared that the tunnel will bring some foreign plague or other, be it rabies, frogs' legs or garlic' – *The Guardian* (6 May 1994); 'The maverick anti-Maastricht MP, Denzil Davies, indicated that he would continue fighting for nominations until the bitter end. The former Treasury minister and MP for Llanelli is not expected to attract more than a handful' – *The Independent* (16 June 1994).

bitter experience An inevitable pairing of words. Date of origin unknown. A cliché by the 1920s/30s and listed in *The Independent* (24 December 1994) as a cliché of newspaper editorials. 'Breeders know from bitter experience that matings do not always "nick" and that . . . they are sure to suffer many a disappointment' – *The Daily Telegraph* (4 January 1971); 'The bitter experience of 1960 affected Nixon deeply. Watergate was born in the way the Kennedys and the Kennedy money treated him then. Nobody was ever going to cheat him again' – *The Scotsman* (2 May 1994); 'The battery alone in my laptop weighs just marginally less than the combined weight of a Psion computer and modem – and I know from bitter experience you always have to carry at least one spare battery' – *Lloyd's List* (28 June 1994).

black See ANY COLOUR; AS BLACK.

(the) blackboard jungle One of several phrases that suggest that there are urban areas where the 'law of the jungle' may apply – in this case, the educational system. *The Blackboard Jungle* was the title of a novel (1954; film US 1955) by Evan Hunter. Earlier, there had been W. R. Burnett's novel *The Asphalt Jungle* (1949), though *OED2* finds that phrase in use in 1920. A little later, in 1969, came references to 'the concrete jungle'.

(a) black box After a plane crash there is usually a scramble to retrieve the aircraft's 'black box' – or, more properly, its 'flight data recorder'. This contains detailed recordings of the aircraft's performance prior to the crash and can be of value in determining what went wrong. The name has been used since the Second World War. Originally it was RAF slang for a box containing intricate navigational equipment. Flight recorders are in fact *orange* so as to be more easily seen. The popular name arose probably because black is a more mysterious colour, appropriate for a box containing 'secret' equipment (Pye produced a record player with the name in the 1950s) and because of the alliteration.

black-coated workers Referring to prunes as laxatives, this term, of earlier origin, was popularized from 1941 onwards in an early-morning BBC programme *The Kitchen Front* by the 'Radio Doctor', Charles (later Lord) Hill. He noted in his autobiography, *Both Sides of the Hill* (1964): 'I remember calling on the Principal Medical Officer of the Board of Education . . . At the end of the interview this shy and solemn man diffidently suggested that the prune was a black-coated worker and that this phrase might be useful to me. It was.' Earlier, the diarist MP Chips Channon was using the phrase in a literal sense concerning the clerical and professional class when he wrote (8 April 1937): 'The subject was "Widows and Orphans", the Old Age Pensions Bill, a measure which affects Southend and its black-coated workers' – *Chips: The Diaries of Sir Henry Channon*, ed. Robert Rhodes James (1967).

(the) black dog Used notably by Winston Churchill to describe the fits of depression to which he was sometimes subjected, this is an old phrase. It was known by the late 18th century, as in the country/nursery saying about a sullen child: 'The black dog is on his back'. *Brewer* (1894) has the alternative, 'a black dog has walked over him'. The reference here is to the devil, as in J. B. Priestley's *The Good Companions* (1929): 'He [Jess Oakroyd] was troubled by a vague foreboding. It was just as if a demoniac black dog went trotting everywhere at his heels.' A perfect explanation appears in a letter from Samuel Johnson to Mrs Thrale (28 June 1783): 'The black Dog I hope always to resist, and in time to drive though I am deprived of almost all those that used to help me . . . Mrs Allen is dead . . . Mrs Williams is so weak that she can be a companion no longer. When I rise my breakfast is solitary, the black dog waits to share it . . .'

black dwarf See POISONED CHALICE.

Black Friday Originally this was a description of Good Friday, when clergymen wore dark vestments. However, there have been any number of specific 'Black Fridays' so designated. In Britain, on one such day (15 April 1921), certain trade unions withdrew support from the hard-pressed miners, a general strike was cancelled, and this is recalled in the Labour movement as a day of betrayal. In the USA, the 'first' Black Friday was on 24 September 1929 when panic broke out on the stock market. During the Wall Street crash there were similarly a **Black Wednesday**, a **Black Thursday** – the actual day of the crash – and a **Black Tuesday**. In 1988, on stock markets round the world, there was a **Black Monday** (October 19) and another Black Thursday (October 22).

(a) black hole A term in astronomy for what is left when a star collapses gravitationally, thus leaving a field from which neither matter nor radiation can escape. The term was in use by 1968 and is sometimes used figuratively to describe the place to which a person has gone who has inexplicably just disappeared.

(the) Black Hole of Calcutta In 1756, 146 Europeans, including one woman, were condemned by the Nawab of Bengal to spend a night in the 'Black-Hole' prison of Fort William, Calcutta, after it had been captured. Only 23, including the woman, survived till morning. Subsequently the phrase has been applied to any place of confinement or any airless, dark place. From Francis Kilvert's diary entry for 27 October 1874 (about a Church Missionary Society meeting): 'The weather was close, warm and muggy, the room crowded to suffocation and frightfully hot, like the Black Hole of Calcutta, though the doors

and all the windows were wide open' (*Kilvert's Diary*, Vols.1–3, ed. William Plomer, 1961).

black is beautiful The Reverend Dr Martin Luther King Jnr launched a poster campaign based on these words in 1967, but Stokely Carmichael had used the phrase earlier at a Memphis Civil Rights rally in 1966, and it had appeared in *Liberation* (NY) on 25 September 1965. The phrase may have had its origins in the Song of Solomon 1:5: 'I am black, but comely.'

black list See ENEMIES LIST.

black mark, Bentley! Jimmy Edwards chiding Dick Bentley in the BBC radio show *Take It From Here* (1948–59). Frank Muir, the co-scriptwriter, commented (1979) that it arose from the use of 'black mark!' by James Robertson Justice in Peter Ustinov's film of *Vice Versa* (UK 1947).

black power A slogan encompassing just about anything that people want it to mean, from simple pride in the black race to a threat of violence. Adam Clayton Powell Jnr, the Harlem congressman, said in a baccalaureate address at Howard University in May 1966: 'To demand these God-given rights is to seek black power – what I call audacious power – the power to build black institutions of splendid achievement.' On 6 June the same year, James Meredith, the first black person to integrate the University of Mississippi (in 1962), was shot and wounded during a civil rights march. Stokely Carmichael, heading the Student Non-violent Coordinating Committee, continued the march, during which his contingent first used the phrase as a shout. Carmichael used it in a speech at Greenwood, Mississippi, the same month. It was also adopted as a slogan by the Congress for Racial Equality. However, the notion was not new in the 1960s. Langston Hughes had written in *Simple Takes a Wife* (1953): 'Negro blood is so powerful – because just *one* drop of black blood makes a coloured man – *one* drop – you are a Negro! . . . Black is powerful.'

black velvet Name of a drink made up of equal parts of champagne and stout (especially Guinness) and which derives from its appearance and taste. Also used to describe the sexual attributes of a black woman, according to *Partridge/Slang*. Known by 1930 in both senses.

blah-blah-blah 'Blah' or 'blah-blah', signifying 'empty talk; airy mouthings', are phrases that have been around (originally in the USA) since the end of the First World War. More recently the tripartite version (although known by 1924) has become marginally more frequent to denote words omitted or as another way of saying 'and so on'. Ira and George Gershwin wrote a song called 'Blah, Blah, Blah' for a film called *Delicious* (1931) which contains such lines as 'Blah, blah, blah, blah moon . . . Blah, blah, blah, blah croon'. Other examples are: '*Burt* [a journalist]: "You wouldn't object to that angle for the piece? Here's what he says: The Family bla-bla-bla, here's how he lives . . ."' – Peter Nichols, *Chez Nous* (1974); 'Saul Kelner, 19 . . . was the first person in line to see the president. He arrived at the White House . . . 11¹/₂ hours before the open house was to begin. "We didn't sleep," he said. "What we did, we circulated a list to ensure our places on line. 'We the people, blah, blah, blah,' and we all signed it"' – *The Washington Post* (22 January 1989); 'Bush referred to the diplomatic language [after a NATO summit conference in Bonn] in casual slang as "blah, blah"' – *The Washington Post* (31 May 1989). The latter caused foreign journalists problems: 'After all, how do you translate "blah, blah" into Italian?'

(the) bland leading the bland This coinage is anonymous and is quoted in Leslie Halliwell, *The Filmgoer's Book of Quotes* (1973). It probably alludes to 'Television is the bland leading the bland', which occurs in Murray Schumach, *The Face on the Cutting Room Floor* (1964). The trope also occurs in J. K. Galbraith, *The Affluent Society* (1958): 'These are the days when men of all social disciplines and all political faiths seek the comfortable and the accepted; when the man of controversy is looked upon as a disturbing influence; when originality is taken to be a mark of instability; and when, in minor modification, the bland lead the bland.' That same year (2 November 1958), *The*

Sunday Times reported critic Kenneth Tynan's view on his joining another paper: 'They say the *New Yorker* is the bland leading the bland . . . I don't know if I'm bland enough.' Compare (THE) BLIND LEADING THE BLIND.

(to kiss the) Blarney Stone Meaning, to bestow on oneself the gift of the gab. The custom of kissing (the somewhat inaccessible) stone at Blarney Castle near Cork in Ireland is of relatively recent origin, having not been mentioned in print until the late 18th century. The word 'blarney' seems, however, to have entered the language a little while before. The origin traditionally given is that in 1602, during the reign of Queen Elizabeth I, one Cormac Macarthy (or Dermot McCarthy) was required to surrender the castle as proof of his loyalty. He prevaricated and came up with so many excuses that (it is said) the Queen herself exclaimed: 'Odds bodikins, more Blarney talk'.

(a) blazing inferno An inevitable pairing, especially in journalistic use. Date of origin unknown. Singled out as a media cliché by Malcolm Bradbury in *Tatler* (March 1980) in the form: 'As I stand here in the blazing inferno that was once called Saigon/ Beirut/ Belfast . . .' 'Hex's favourite Stephen Jones hats remain the series of fabulous kitchen follies which included a frying-pan (complete with bacon and eggs) and a colander brimming with vegetables. Does Jones have a particular favourite? From a blazing inferno in his showroom he might try to save a gigantic layered tulle confection' – *The Scotsman* (11 May 1994); 'In June a 13-year-old schoolgirl died as she saved her two young sisters and brother after a massive gas explosion ripped through their home. The blast turned their home in Ramsgate, Kent, into a blazing inferno' – *Daily Mirror* (29 December 1994).

bleats See EVERY TIME.

bless (his) little cotton socks A pleasant remark to make about a child, meaning, 'Isn't (he) sweet, such a dear little thing'. As 'bless your little cotton socks', it just means 'thank you'. *Partridge/Slang* dates the expression from *circa* 1900 and labels it heavily 'middle-class'.

(a) blessing in disguise Meaning 'a misfortune that turns out to be beneficial', this phrase has been in existence since the early 18th century. A perfect example is provided by the noted exchange between Winston Churchill and his wife, Clementine. Attempting to console him after his defeat in the 1945 General Election, she said: 'It may well be a blessing in disguise.' To which he replied: 'At the moment, it seems quite effectively disguised.' Despite this comment, Churchill seems to have come round to something like his wife's point of view. On 5 September 1945, he wrote to her from an Italian holiday: 'This is the first time for very many years that I have been completely out of the world . . . Others having to face the hideous problems of the aftermath . . . It may all indeed be "a blessing in disguise".'

blind See LIKE TAKING MONEY.

(the) blind leading the blind Ineffectual leadership. 'They be blind leaders of the blind. And if the blind lead the blind, both shall fall into the ditch' (Matthew 15:4).

(a) blind man on a galloping horse could see that It is very obvious indeed. Swift has 'a blind man would be glad to see that' in *Polite Conversation* (1738), and *Apperson* finds 'A blind man on a galloping horse would be glad to see it' by 1894. Former Beatle Paul McCartney on the similarity between the sound of the Fab Four and the much later group Oasis: 'You would have to be a blind man on a galloping horse not to see it' – quoted by the Press Association (5 September 1996). Compare the Australianism **even blind Freddie could see that**, for what is blindingly obvious, a phrase since the 1930s.

(a) blinking idiot Term of abuse where 'blinking' is a euphemism for 'bloody'. However, Shakespeare coined the phrase in *The Merchant of Venice*, II.ix.54 (1596), where the Prince of Arragon opens the silver casket and exclaims: 'What's here? the portrait of a blinking idiot / Presenting me a schedule.' This is probably a more literal suggestion of an idiot whose eyes blink as a token of his madness.

bliss beyond compare See OH JOY.

block See CHIP OFF THE OLD.

(a) blonde bombshell A journalistic cliché now used to describe *any* (however vaguely) blonde woman but especially if she has a dynamic personality and is a film star, show business figure or model. In June 1975, Margo Macdonald complained of being described by the *Daily Mirror* as 'the blonde bombshell MP' who 'hits the House of Commons today'. The original was Jean Harlow, who appeared in the 1933 US film *Bombshell*. In the UK – presumably so as not to suggest that it was a war film – the title was changed to *Blonde Bombshell*.

blondes See IS IT TRUE.

blood all over the walls See SHIT HITS.

(through) blood and fire Motto of the Salvation Army, founded by General William Booth in 1878. The conjunction of blood and fire has appropriate biblical origins. In Joel 2:30, God says: 'And I will shew wonders in the heavens and in the earth, blood, and fire, and pillars of smoke.'

blood and iron When Bismarck addressed the Budget Commission of the Prussian House of Delegates on 30 September 1862, what he said was: 'It is desirable and it is necessary that the condition of affairs in Germany and of her constitutional relations should be improved; but this cannot be accomplished by speeches and resolutions of a majority, but only by iron and blood [*Eisen und Blut*].' On 28 January 1886, speaking to the Prussian House of Deputies, he did, however, use the words in the more familiar order: 'This policy cannot succeed through speeches, and shooting-matches and songs; it can only be carried out through blood and iron [*Blut und Eisen*].' The words may have achieved their more familiar order, at least to English ears, through their use by A. C. Swinburne in his poem 'A Word for the Country' (1884): 'Not with dreams, but with blood and with iron, shall a nation be moulded at last.' (Eric Partridge, while identifying this source correctly in *A Dictionary of Clichés*, 1966 edn, ascribes the authorship to Tennyson.) On the other hand, the Roman orator Quintillian (1st century AD) used the exact phrase *sanguinem et ferrum*.

blood and sand *Blood and Sand* was the title of a silent film (US 1922) starring Rudolph Valentino as a matador. It was adapted from a play with the title by Tom Cushing, in turn adapted from a novel about bull-fighting, *Sangre y Arena* (which means the same thing) by Vicente Blasco Ibáñez. It was later re-made with Tyrone Power (US 1941).

blood and thunder Bloodshed and violence – especially as found in 'blood-and-thunder' books, films and tales (especially in the USA, where the coinage originated by 1852). However, the conjunction occurred before this in England as an oath. Byron's *Don Juan*, Canto 8, St. 1 (1822), has the line: 'Oh, blood and thunder! and oh, blood and wounds! / These are but vulgar oaths.' The melodramatic, violent, bloody and sensational tales are sometimes called 'thud and blunder', if they are ineptly done.

(a) blood libel Name given to accusations by medieval anti-Semites that Jews had crucified Christian children and drunk their blood at Passover. In September 1982, following allegations that Israeli forces in Lebanon had allowed massacres to take place in refugee camps, the Israeli government invoked the phrase in a statement headed: 'BLOOD LIBEL. On the New Year (Rosh Hashana), a blood libel was levelled against the Jewish state, its government and the Israel Defense Forces . . .'

(to pay the) blood price To be willing to sustain casualties by going to war. The British Prime Minister, Tony Blair, said that he was prepared to send troops and 'pay the blood price' of Britain's special relationship with America by attacking President Hussein of Iraq (in a BBC 2 TV interview, 8 September 2002). In fact, the phrase had been fed to him by the interviewer, quoting Robert McNamara, Lyndon Johnson's Defense secretary in the Vietnam War. The phrase occurs much earlier, in Spenser, *The Faerie Queene*, I.v.26 (1590): 'The man that made Sansfoy to fall, / Shall with his owne blood price that he hath spilt.'

bloodstained tyrannies Cited as the phrase of a 'tired hack' by George Orwell, 'Politics and the English Language' in *Horizon* (April 1946). 'The Prime Minister [Mrs Thatcher] welcomed Romania to "the family of free nations" and promised help for its people. She praised the Romanian "heroes" who had not been prepared to "knuckle under in a bloodstained tyranny"' – *The Guardian* (23 December 1989).

blood, sweat and tears In his classic speech to the House of Commons on 13 May 1940, upon becoming Prime Minister, Winston Churchill said: 'I would say to the House, as I said to those who have joined this Government: I have nothing to offer but blood, toil, tears and sweat.' Ever since then, people have had difficulty getting the order of his words right. The natural inclination is to put 'blood', 'sweat' then 'tears' together – as did Byron in 1823 with 'blood, sweat and tear-wrung millions' and as did the Canadian/US rock group Blood Sweat and Tears in the late 1960s and 70s. Much earlier, however, there had been yet another combination of the words in John Donne's *An Anatomy of the World* (1611): ''Tis in vain to do so or to mollify it with thy tears, or sweat, or blood.' Churchill seemed consciously to avoid these configurations. In 1931, he had written of the Tsarist armies: 'Their sweat, their tears, their blood bedewed the endless plain.' Having launched his version of the phrase in 1940, he referred to it five more times during the course of the war.

bloody See CAN A BLOODY.

bloody but unbowed Often used as an unascribed quotation, meaning 'determined after having suffered a defeat'. From W. E. Henley's poem 'Invictus. In Memoriam R.T.H.B.' (1888): 'In the fell clutch of circumstance, / I have not winced nor cried aloud: / Under the bludgeonings of chance / My head is bloody but unbowed.' 'Bloody but unbowed, veteran discount retailers Gerald and Vera Weisfeld have hit out at the new £56m rescue deal agreed between struggling Poundstretcher owner Brown & Jackson and South African group Pepkor' – *Daily Mail* (10 May 1994); 'Bloody but unbowed, Dungannon had several heroes. Johns lorded the lineouts; while Beggs and Willie Dunne scrapped for everything' – *The Irish Times* (17 October 1994); 'Charles Scott, acting chairman of

Saatchi & Saatchi, now renamed Cordiant, survived his first shareholders' meeting since the upheavals at the top of the advertising combine bloody but unbowed, with investors' vitriol shared out fairly equally between him, the Saatchi brothers and David Herro, the Chicago investor' – *The Times* (17 March 1995).

(the) bloody deed was done　The provenance of this phrase has proved elusive. In Shakespeare, the phrase 'bloody deed' occurs several times and, what with Macbeth's 'I have done the deed' and the almost immediate references to 'blood', not to mention Rosse's 'Is't known who did this more than bloody deed?' (II.iv.22), might well have produced this conflation. The nearest one gets is *Richard III*, IV.iii.1(1592–3): 'The tyrannous and bloody act is done' – which is what Tyrrel says about the murder of the Princes in the Tower. As with 'the bloody dog is dead' from the end of the same play (V.v.2), we are almost there, but the exact phrase remains untraced – except in the works of lesser poets of the 17th to 19th centuries: 'Here through my bosom run / Your sword, and when the bloody deed is done, / When your steel smoaks with my hearts reeking Gore, / Bid me be well as e're I was before' – from Anon., *Sophonisba, or Hannibal's Overthrow: a Tragedy*, Act 2, Sc 1 (1676); 'Pallid grew every face; and man on man, / Speechless with horror, looked; for well they knew / The bloody deed was done' – Edwin Atherstone, *The Fall of Nineveh*, Bk 24 (1868). These quotations, taken together, encourage one to think that the original coinage will not be found: it is simply a proverbial expression.

Bloody Sunday　As with BLACK FRIDAY, there have been a number of these. On 13 November 1887, two men died during a baton charge on a prohibited socialist demonstration in Trafalgar Square, London. On 22 January 1905, hundreds of unarmed peasants were mown down when they marched to petition the Tsar in St Petersburg. In Irish history, there was a Bloody Sunday on 21 November 1920 when, among other incidents, fourteen undercover British intelligence agents in Dublin were shot by Sinn Fein. More

recently, the name was applied to Sunday 30 January 1972 when British troops killed thirteen Catholics after a protest rally in Londonderry, Northern Ireland. Perhaps the epithet sprang to mind readily on this last occasion because of the film *Sunday Bloody Sunday* (UK 1971). This story had a screenplay by Penelope Gilliatt. It was about a *ménage à trois* and, although not explained explicitly, the title probably referred to the pivotal day on which the relationships ran further into the sand. Since the 19th century there has been the exclamation 'Sunday, *bloody* Sunday!' to express the gloom and despondency of the day. In 1973, the UK/US group Black Sabbath released an album with the title *Sabbath Bloody Sabbath*.

blooming　See AIN'T IT.

(to) blot one's copybook　To make a serious blunder, misdemeanour or gaffe that affects one's hitherto good record – as though one had spilled ink on a copybook, which was an aid to learning handwriting much in use until the mid-20th century. The student would imitate writing sentences in the correct style, in spaces below what was printed on the page. A 'copy book' is mentioned in Shakespeare's *Love's Labour's Lost* (1588) and Dorothy L. Sayers has the expression in *Gaudy Night*, Chap. 5 (1935): 'Now, it was the College that had blotted its copybook and had called her in as one calls in a specialist.'

(a) blot on one's escutcheon　A stain on one's character or reputation. An escutcheon is a shield with armorial bearings on it. The earliest appearance would seem to be in John Dryden, *Virgil*, II, 'Dedication' (1697): 'The banishment of Ovid was a blot in his escutcheon.' *A Blot In the 'Scutcheon* is the title of a play (1843) by Robert Browning. In W. S. Gilbert, *The Sorcerer*, Act 1 (1877), Sir Marmaduke Pointdextre says: 'Aline is rich, and she comes of a sufficiently old family, for she is the seven thousand and thirty-seventh in direct descent from Helen of Troy. True, there was a blot on the escutcheon of that lady – that affair with Paris – but where is the family, other than my own, in which there is no flaw?'

(a) blot on the landscape Anything that spoils or disfigures a view in an unsightly way (not least a person), or, figuratively, that is simply objectionable. Since the 16th century, 'blot' on its own was used in this sense. The first citation to have the whole phrase is in a letter from T. E. Lawrence (dated 20 February 1938): 'His two Kufti people . . . will be rather a blot on the landscape.' A Baumer cartoon in *Punch* uses it (25 April 1934). From P. G. Wodehouse, *Jeeves in the Offing*, Chap. 1 (1960): '"And a rousing toodle-oo to you, you young blot on the landscape," she replied cordially.' Tom Sharpe's novel *Blot on the Landscape* (1975) features a character called 'Blott'. 'Their makeshift shanties have always been a blot on the landscape (they creep right up to the hard shoulder of the motorway that brings visitors in from the airport) and they are now not only a blot on the conscience but a blot, too, on the immediate scrutiny of the immaculate dream to which some whites still subscribe' – *The Times* (9 December 1995). 'It is a blot on the landscape – and it's lost its flavour. Now Wrigley, the chewing-gum manufacturer, is trying to teach Britain's estimated 22 million chewers where not to stick the gluey residue' – *The Sunday Telegraph* (11 February 1996).

blouse See BIG GIRL'S.

blow See DON'T BLOW.

(to) blow a raspberry To make a farting noise by blowing through the lips. This is rhyming slang, raspberry tart = fart. From Barrère & Leland, *Dictionary of Slang* (1890): 'The tongue is inserted in the left cheek and forced through the lips, producing a peculiarly squashy noise that is extremely irritating. It is termed, I believe, a *raspberry*, and when not employed for the purpose of testing horseflesh, is regarded rather as an expression of contempt than of admiration.'

(to) blow hot and cold Meaning 'to vacillate between enthusiasm and apathy', this expression has been known in English since 1577 and is to be found in one of Aesop's *Fables*. On a cold day, a satyr comes across a man blowing his fingers to make them warm. He takes the man home

and gives him a bowl of hot soup. The man blows on the soup, to cool it. At this, the satyr throws him out, exclaiming that he wants nothing to do with a man who can 'blow hot and cold from the same mouth'.

(to) blow one's own trumpet Meaning, 'to boast of one's own achievements'. This is sometimes said to have originated with the statue of 'Fame' on the parapet of Wilton House, near Salisbury. The figure – positioned after a fire in 1647 – originally held a trumpet in each hand. But why does one need a precise origin? Besides, the *OED2* cites Abraham Fleming, *A Panoplie of Epistles* (1576) – 'I will . . . sound the trumpet of mine owne merites', which is virtually the modern phrase. Henry Fielding, *Joseph Andrews*, Chap 5. (1742), has, 'Fame blew her brazen trumpet'. *Apperson* has an example of 'blowing the trumpet of my own praise' from 1799. *Brewer* (1894), more reasonably, states that in 'to sound one's own trumpet', the 'allusion is to heralds, who used to announce with a flourish of trumpets the knights who entered a list' (as, for example, in jousting). It is also possible that Diogenianus (2nd century AD) originated the expression (unverified). Lord Beaverbrook used to say that if you did not blow your own trumpet, no one else would do it for you – quoted in *The Observer* (12 March 1989).

blow some my way A slogan used from 1926 when a woman made her first appearance in US cigarette advertising (some thought suggestively). The brand was Chesterfield whose other slogan, 'I'll tell the world – they satisfy', was current the same year.

(to) blow the gaff Meaning, 'to blab about something; to let the secret out; give the game away.' An earlier (18th-century) form was 'to blow the gab' and, conceivably, 'gaff' could have developed from that. 'Gaff' may here mean 'mouth' (like gab/gob) and, coupled with 'blow', gives the idea of expelling air through it and letting things out. Known by 1812. 'As she invariably uses her travels with a friend as the basis for her pieces, I really do not see why there needed to be any hiatus. Or has she found someone else to travel with and does not want to blow the gaff?' – *The Sunday Times* (29 October 1995).

(to) blow the whistle on Meaning, 'to call a halt to something by exposing it' (alluding to the police use of whistles). 'Now that the whistle has been blown on his speech . . .' – P. G. Wodehouse, *Right Ho, Jeeves*, Chap. 17 (1934). More recently, *The Listener* (3 January 1980) reported: 'English as she is murdered on radio became an issue once more. Alvar Liddell stamped his foot and blew the whistle in *The Listener*.' Sir Robert Armstrong was quoted in *The Observer* (2 March 1986) as saying: 'I do not think there could be a duty on a civil servant to blow the whistle on his Minister.'

blue See ENOUGH.

(the) blue bird (of happiness) An allusion to the title of a children's play, *L'Oiseau bleu* by Maurice Maeterlinck, that was translated as *The Blue Bird* in 1909. Hence, the prevalence of Blue Bird cafés, Blue Bird toffees and song lyrics such as 'There'll be blue birds over / The White Cliffs of Dover . . .' (1941).

blue for a boy, pink for a girl Colour coding for babies along these lines may be comparatively recent. Although the *Daily Chronicle* (18 November 1909) had 'Brief drawing-room appearances in a nurse's arms with robes and tie-ups – blue for a boy, pink for a girl', according to *The Independent* (7 February 1994), 'there are also indications that the Women's Institute were advising *blue* for girls and *pink* for boys as late as 1920'. Indeed, blue has for centuries been the colour of the Virgin Mary's robe. Possibly it is the case that greetings card manufacturers happened upon the revised guidelines by emphasizing the alliterative qualities of 'blue for a boy'.

blue murder See GET AWAY.

(to) blue-pencil To censor. In the BBC wartime radio series *Garrison Theatre* (first broadcast 1939), Jack Warner as 'Private Warner' helped further popularize this well-established synonym (the *OED2*'s first citation is an American one from 1888). In reading blue-pencilled letters from his

brother at the Front, expletives were deleted ('not blue pencil likely!') and Warner's actual mother boasted that, 'My John with his blue-pencil gag has stopped the whole nation from swearing.' In his autobiography, Warner recalled a constable giving evidence at a London police court about stopping 'Mr Warner', a lorry driver. The magistrate inquired, 'Did he ask what the blue pencil you wanted?' 'No, sir,' replied the constable, 'this was a different Mr Warner . . .' It is said that when the Lord Chamberlain exercised powers of censorship over the British stage (until 1968), his emendations to scripts were, indeed, marked with a blue pencil.

(the) blue-rinse brigade (or set) A blue rinse is a hair preparation (known since the 1930s) designed to disguise grey or white hair with a temporary blue tint. As this is favoured by middle-class women of advancing years, the term has come to be applied to them collectively, suggesting their respectable, conservative tastes and views. 'The blue-rinse vote went down the drain' – *Punch* (28 October 1964). 'During his 16-year tenure with the Los Angeles Philharmonic, Mehta was at once a matinée idol of the blue-rinse brigade and a favorite target of critical barbs' – *Los Angeles Times* (16 August 1986).

(a) blue stocking Denoting 'a literary or studious woman', this phrase derived from the gatherings of cultivated females and a few eminent men at the home of Elizabeth Montagu in London around 1750. Boswell in his *Life of Johnson* (1791) explains that a certain Benjamin Stillingfleet was a popular guest, soberly dressed but wearing blue stockings: 'Such was the excellence of his conversation, that his absence was felt as so great a loss, that it used to be said, "We can do nothing without the blue stockings," and thus by degrees the title was established.'

blue velvet A film (US 1986), directed by David Lynch, about drugs and menace, has the title *Blue Velvet*. This alludes firstly to the song 'Blue Velvet' (1951), written by Wayne and Morris, which is sung by the night-club singer heroine in the film, and secondly – as *DOAS* describes – to the name for 'a mixture of paregoric, which contains opium and . . . an antihistamine, to be injected', which is also relevant to the film.

boats See BURN ONE'S.

(and) Bob's your uncle! An almost meaningless expression of the type that takes hold from time to time. It is another way of saying 'there you are; there you have it; simple as that'. It was current by the 1880s but doesn't appear to be of any hard and fast origin. It is basically a British expression – and somewhat baffling to Americans. There is the story of one such [the director and playwright Burt Shevelove – according to Kenneth Williams on BBC Radio *Quote . . . Unquote* (24 July 1980)] who went into a London shop, had it said to him, and exclaimed: 'But how on earth do you know – I do have an Uncle Bob!?' In 1886, Arthur Balfour rose meteorically from the Scottish Office to be Chief Secretary for Ireland. He was appointed by *his* uncle, *Robert* Arthur Talbot Gascoyne-Cecil, 3rd Marquis of Salisbury. Could this be a possible source? There is slang use, too, of the expression 'one's uncle', meaning a pawnbroker, which might perhaps be linked.

(the) bodger on the bonce Referring to the horn of a rhinoceros, as in the Flanders and Swann song 'The Rhinoceros' (1956): '(*Chorus*) Oh the Bodger on the Bonce! / The Bodger on the Bonce! / Oh pity the poor old Rhino with / The Bodger on the Bonce!'. Few dictionaries seem to have recorded the word 'bodger' in the sense of a pointed instrument, though it has long been used to mean a stick for picking up litter or for a tool used to make holes in the ground for seeds. And 'to bodge' is Black Country dialect for poking or making a hole. A link between bodgers in this sense and with the name given to skilled, itinerant wood-turners who worked in the beech woods on the chalk hills of the Chilterns and who led to the establishment of the chair-making trade in the High Wycombe area has yet to be proved. Or with 'The Bodgers' as the nickname of the Wycombe Wanderers football team and with bodgers as the name given to people who do a bodged job (a variation on 'botchers').

(a) body blow Meaning 'a severe knock to one's esteem or activities', this clearly derives from boxing. 'That body-blow left Joe's head unguarded' – Thomas Hughes, *Tom Brown* (1857). 'Its latest action is a body-blow to the growers' – *Daily Chronicle* (24 August 1908); 'Criminalizing squatters, New Age travellers and the like is hardly a body-blow to the well-established underworld. No matter how many times Mr Howard says the word "people" (count it, next time you hear him), he will not convince me that he is really going to deal with the real problems of crime in this country' – *Independent on Sunday* (1 May 1994); 'The conclusions of Lonrho's report . . . destroyed Bond's credibility. In unambiguous terms they declared he was technically bust, and so it proved. It was a body blow from which Bond never recovered' – *The Sunday Times* (6 November 1994).

(a) body count A phrase from the Vietnam War (in use by 1968), referring to the number of enemy dead. In 1981, the American horror film *Friday the 13th Part II* was promoted with the line, 'The body count continues'. From *Time* Magazine (15 April 1985): 'In the field, the Americans were encouraged to lie about their "body counts" (measuring progress in the war by lives taken, not land taken).' Later, used less literally to describe the number of people (not necessarily dead) in a specific situation.

body fascism In July 1980, Anna Ford, then a television newcaster with ITN, popularized this phrase in a speech given to the Women in Media group in London. Attacking the obsession with the looks and clothes of women who appear on television, she added: 'Nobody takes pictures of Richard Baker's ankles or claims that Peter Woods only got his job because of the bags under his eyes.' Ford did not invent the feminist phrase, however. It is not a very clear one, except that 'fascism' is often invoked simply to describe something that the speaker dislikes. 'Sexism' and 'lookism' would have conveyed what Ford meant; possibly even 'glamour-abuse'.

body odour (or BO) This worrying concept was used to promote Lifebuoy soap, initially in the USA, and was current by 1933. In early American radio jingles, the initials 'BO' were sung *basso profundo*, emphasizing the horror of the offence: 'Singing in the bathtub, singing for joy, / Living a life of Lifebuoy – / Can't help singing, 'cos I know / That Lifebuoy really stops BO.' In the UK, TV ads showed pairs of male or female friends out on a spree, intending to attract partners. When one of the pair was seen to have a problem, the other whispered helpfully, 'BO'.

(the) body politic   The nation in its corporate character, the state-organized society. In a legal document of 1532, in the reign of King Henry VIII, there is the usage: 'This Realm of England is an Empire . . . governed by one supreme Head and King . . . unto whom a Body politick, compact of all Sorts and Degrees of people . . .' Compare the **soul politic**, a phrase used by Margaret Thatcher in speeches in the 1980s. But Thomas Carlyle had anticipated her in *Signs of the Times* (1829).

boets and bainters   The *ODQ* has long had the remark 'I hate all Boets and Bainters' ascribed to King George I (1660–1727), finding it in Lord Campbell, *Lives of the Chief Justices* (1849). However, as it is said that George I never learned to speak English (even German-accented), a more believable account is that George II (1683–1760), who did speak English, was the one who actually said it. And as it is given that, whichever George it was, he was discussing Hogarth's print 'The March to Finchley' at the time – a picture not published until 1750/1 – this would square better with the dates. John Ireland's *Hogarth Illustrated* (2nd edn, 1793) specifically records that the picture was brought to *George II*: 'Before publication it was inscribed to his late Majesty, and the picture taken to St James's, in the hope of royal approbation. George the Second was an honest man, and a soldier, but not a judge of either a work of humour, or a work of art . . . [Hence] his disappointment on viewing the delineation. His first question was addressed to a nobleman in waiting – "Pray, who is this Hogarth?" "A painter, my liege." "I hate bainting and boetry too! neither the one nor the other ever did any good! Does

the fellow mean to laugh at my guards?"' The print was returned to Hogarth, who dedicated it instead to the King of Prussia. Obviously this was a story that could have been aimed at both father and son (in Lord Campbell's *Lives of the Justices*, George I has 'I hate all Boets and Bainters' attached to him in the context of a *poem* being read), but Ireland's anecdote is rooted in a particular circumstance and is written closer to the events described, so it is to be favoured.

bog standard   Average. From the 1980s on. Tony Thorne defines 'bog-standard' in his *Dictionary of Contemporary Slang* (1990) as, 'Totally unexceptional, normal and unremarkable. Bog is here used as an otherwise meaningless intensifier.' It has been suggested that before the Second World War, 'bog' was an acronym for 'British Or German', as a mark of *distinction* in a product, but there is no confirmation of this unpromising theory.

(the) bohemian life   Life as lived by artists and writers, often poverty-stricken and amoral. Puccini's opera *La Bohème* (1896) was based on Henry Murger's novel *Scènes de la Vie de Bohème* (1847), set in the Latin Quarter of Paris. At first, the term 'Bohemian' was applied to gypsies because they were thought to come from Bohemia (in what is now the Czech Republic) or, at least, because the first to come to France had passed through Bohemia. The connection between the irregular life of gypsies and that of artists is just about understandable – they are on the margins of society.

boil your head   See GO AND.

bold   See OH HELLO.

(as) bold as brass   Very bold indeed, possibly also reflecting that brass was sometimes looked upon as a cheap substitute for gold. Obviously the alliteration is attractive, but the word brass may have been chosen because of its connection with 'brazen', meaning 'flagrant, shameless' (the Old English word *braesen* actually means brass). The *OED2*'s earliest citation is from 1789, which is interesting because there is a colourful explanation that the phrase derives from a Lord Mayor of London called 'Brass Crosby' who died in 1793. He was sent to the Tower for refusing to sentence a printer for the unlawful act of publishing Parliamentary debates and, some believe, 'bold as brass' became a popular turn of phrase for the way he supported reforms. There may, however, be no connection.

boldness be my friend Used as the title of a book (1953) by Richard Pape about his exploits in the Second World War, this phrase is taken from what Iachimo says when he sets off to pursue Imogen in Shakespeare's *Cymbeline*, I.vii.18 (1609–10): 'Boldness be my friend! / Arm me, Audacity, from head to foot'. In 1977, Richard Boston wrote a book called *Baldness Be My Friend*, partly about his own lack of hair.

bomb See BAN THE; GO DOWN A.

bombshell See BLONDE.

BOMFOG An acronym for a pompous, meaningless generality. When Governor Nelson Rockefeller was competing against Barry Goldwater for the US Republican presidential nomination in 1964, reporters latched on to a favourite saying of the candidate – 'the brotherhood of man under the fatherhood of God' – and rendered it with the acronym BOMFOG. In fact, according to *Safire*, they had been beaten to it by Hy Sheffer, a stenotypist on the Governor's staff who had found the abbreviation convenient for the previous five or six years. The words come from a much quoted saying of John D. Rockefeller: 'These are the principles upon which alone a new world recognizing the brotherhood of man and the fatherhood of God can be established . . .' Later, BOMFOG was used by feminists to denote the use of language that they thought demeaned women by reflecting patrician attitudes. The individual phrases 'brotherhood of man' and 'fatherhood of God' do not appear before the 19th century. In *As We Are*, Chap. 13 (1932), E. F. Benson has: 'The Fatherhood of God fared no better than the brotherhood of man . . . His protective paternity had proved that these privileges must be heavily paid for in advance.'

— bonanza PHRASES A journalistic cliché, used to describe any wildly lucra- tive deal. Of American origin and known since the 1840s, the derivation is from the Spanish word for 'fair weather, prosperity'. Initially used by miners with reference to good luck in finding a body of rich ore. Used figuratively, a good deal later. Specifically 'pay bonanza' is listed as a cliché to be avoided by Keith Waterhouse in *Daily Mirror Style* (1981). 'The show is still, as topical entertainment, a real bonanza' – *The Listener* (10 January 1963); 'Jobs bonanza for ex-ministers . . . Former Cabinet ministers who served under Margaret Thatcher and John Major hold a total of 125 directorships and 30 consultan- cies' – *The Independent* (2 May 1995).

bonce See BODGER ON THE.

(the) Boneless Wonder A spineless character named after a fairground freak, notably evoked by Winston Churchill in an attack on Ramsay MacDonald in the House of Commons (28 January 1931). During a debate on the Trades Disputes Act, Churchill referred to recent efforts by the Prime Minister to conciliate Roman Catho- lic opinion regarding education reform (including the lowering of the school- leaving age to fifteen): 'I remember when I was a child, being taken to the celebrated Barnum's Circus which contained an exhibition of freaks and monstrosities, but the exhibit on the programme which I most desired to see was the one described as the Boneless Wonder. My parents judged that the spectacle would be too revolting and demoralizing for my youthful eyes, and I have waited fifty years to see the Boneless Wonder sitting on the Treas- ury bench.' There have been several circus or fairground attractions with this bill matter. The specific one may be that of 'Valentine', who died in 1907.

Boney will get you! A curiously enduring threat. Although Napoleon died in 1821 (and all possibility of invasion had evapo- rated long before that), it was still being made to children in the early 20th century. In 1985, the actor Sir Anthony Quayle recalled it from his youth and, in 1990, John Julius Norwich remembered the husband of his nanny (from Grantham) saying it to him in the 1930s. He added: 'And a Mexican friend of mine told me that when she was a little girl her nanny or mother or whoever it was used to say, "*Il Drake* will get you" – and that was Sir Francis Drake!'

(the) bonfire of the vanities The title of Tom Wolfe's 1987 novel *The Bonfire of the Vanities* is derived from Savonarola's 'burning of the vanities' at Florence in 1497. The religious reformer – 'the puritan of Catholicism' – enacted various laws for the restraint of vice and folly. Gambling was prohibited, and Savonarola's followers helped people burn their costly ornaments and extravagant clothes.

(to cast/throw one's) bonnet over the windmill To act unrestrainedly and defiantly; to throw caution to the winds. This is a translation of the French expression *'jeter son bonnet par-dessus les moulins'* that had entered the English language by 1885 as 'flung his cap over the windmill'. According to Valerie Grove, *Dear Dodie* (1996), when Dodie Smith entitled one of her plays *Bonnet Over the Windmill* (in 1937), 'she enlisted Sir Ambrose Heal's help in establishing where the expression . . . came from.' A London University professor 'reported that the phrase . . . was originally a lazy way of finishing off a story for children.'

book See ANOTHER PAGE; EVERYONE HAS ONE.

book 'em, Danno! A stock phrase from the American TV series *Hawaii Five-O* (1968–80). On making an arrest, Detective Steve McGarrett (Jack Lord) would say to Detective 'Danno' Williams (James MacArthur), 'Book 'em, Danno!' – adding 'Murder One' if the crime required that charge.

boom, boom! Verbal underlining to the punchline of a gag. Comedian Ernie Wise commented (1979) that it was like the drum-thud or trumpet-sting used, particularly by American entertainers, to point a joke. Music-hall star Billy Bennett (1887–1942) may have been the first to use this device, in the UK, to emphasize his comic couplets. Morecambe and Wise, Basil Brush (the fox puppet on British TV), and many others, took it up later. 'Boom boom' has also been used as a slang/*lingua franca* expression for sexual intercourse, especially by Americans in South-East Asia during the Vietnam War.

(a) boon companion Literally, 'a good fellow' and used originally in a jovial bacchanalian sense. Now only used in a consciously archaic manner and referring to a close companion of either sex. 'With such boon companions Pepys loved to broach a vessel of ale and be merry' – Arthur Bryant, *Samuel Pepys: The Man in the Making*, Chap. 5 (1933); 'Only after Saudi pressure, it is said, did the president relent and two months ago allow Rifaat to return from six months in exile. The Saudi crown prince, Abdullah, is a brother-in-law and boon companion of Rifaat, and the Saudis like Rifaat's pro-western views' – *The Economist* (26 January 1985).

boop-boop-a-doop This phrase originated in the Kalmar/Stothart/Ruby song 'I Wanna Be Loved By You', sung by the 'Boop Boop a Doop' girl, Helen Kane, in a 1928 musical. Then 'Betty Boop' became a cartoon character – sexy, baby-faced, baby-voiced – in Max Fleischer cinema cartoons of the 1930s. Marilyn Monroe sang the song in the film *Some Like It Hot* (US 1959). More recently there was a British pop singer who called herself 'Betty Boo'.

boots See BIG FOR ONE'S; DIE WITH ONE'S; HE CAN LEAVE.

border See BREAK FOR THE.

bored! Jo Ann Worley used to exclaim this loudly on NBC TV, *Rowan and Martin's Laugh-In* (1967–73). Could this be connected with 'bor-ring!' said by people in a sonorous, two-note sing-song way at about this time?

bored stiff Meaning, 'extremely bored' (possibly a pun on 'stiff as a board'). Known by 1918, according to the *OED2*, which is unable to find citations for *any* of the various boredom phrases before the 20th century: **'bored rigid'** (earliest citation 1972), **'bored to death'** (1966), **'bored to hell'** (1962), **'(to) bore the pants off'** (1958) and **'crashing bore'** (1928). There are no citations at all for **'bored to tears'**, **'bored out of one's mind/skull'**, or **'bored to distraction'**. What does this have to tell us – that before the 20th century there was no expectation that you shouldn't be bored? Or were the Victorians so bored that they couldn't even be bothered to find words for it? Either way, there are one or two relatively new arrivals in the field. To say that something is '**as exciting as watching paint dry**', though popular, does not seem very old. The earliest citation to hand is of a graffito from 1981, which stated that 'Living in Croydon is about as exciting as watching paint dry'. As for '**boring as a wet weekend in Wigan**', referring to the town in the north-west of England, the earliest use found is in the *Today* newspaper for 16 July 1991. As so often, alliteration is the main force behind this piece of phrase-making. 'Wet weekends' have long been abhorred, but Wigan appears to have been tacked on because it has a downbeat sound, it alliterates and because people recall the old music-hall joke about there being a WIGAN PIER.

born-again Applied to evangelical and fundamentalist Christians in the Southern USA since the 1960s, this adjective derives from the story of Jesus Christ and Nicodemus in John 3 ('Ye must be born again'). Originally suggesting a re-conversion or first conversion to Christianity, this adjectival phrase took on a figurative sense of 're-vitalized', 'zealous', 'newly converted' around the time when Jimmy Carter, from a born-again Baptist background in the South, was running for the US presidency in 1976. Carter said in an interview with Robert L. Turner (16 March 1976): 'We believe that the first time we're born, as children, it's human life given to us; and when we accept Jesus as our Saviour, it's a new life. That's what "born again" means.' Hence, usages like 'born-again automobiles' (for reconditioned ones) and such like.

born 1820 – still going strong Johnnie Walker whisky has used this advertising line since 1910. There *was* a John Walker but he was not born in 1820 – that was the year he set up a grocery, wine and spirit business in Kilmarnock. In 1908, Sir Alexander Walker decided to incorporate a portrait of his grandfather in the firm's advertising. Tom Browne, a commercial artist, was commissioned to draw the firm's founder as he might have appeared in 1820. Lord Stevenson, a colleague of Sir Alexander, scribbled the phrase 'Johnnie Walker, born 1820 – still going strong'

alongside the artist's sketch of a striding, cheerful Regency figure. It has been in use ever since. From Randolph Quirk, *Style and Communication in the English Language* (1983): 'English lexicography knocks Johnnie Walker into a tricuspidal fedora. Over four hundred years, and going stronger than ever.'

bosom See ABRAHAM'S.

boss, boss, sumpin' terrible's happened! From the BBC radio show *ITMA* (1939–49). Spoken in a gangster drawl by Sam Scram (Sydney Keith), Tommy Handley's henchman.

(the) Boston Strangler Nickname of Albert de Salvo, who strangled thirteen women during 1962–4 in the Boston, Mass., area. Not forgotten, the man's reputation led to the creation of a joke format: from *Today* (24 May 1987), 'Liberal David Steel said earlier this year: "Mrs Thatcher seems to have done for women in politics what the Boston Strangler did for door-to-door salesmen".' From *The Independent* (20 January 1989): 'Mr Healey also had a pithy word for President Reagan: "He has done for monetarism what the Boston Strangler did for door-to-door salesmen".' From *The Washington Post* (16 October 1991): 'Shields introduced Hatch, the starched shirt of the Senate hearings, as "the man who has done for bipartisanship what the Boston Strangler did for door-to-door salesmen".' From *The Sunday Times* (9 February 1992): 'Denis Healey, who claimed to have tried to do for economic forecasters what the Boston Strangler did for door-to-door salesmen . . .'

(the) bottomless pit A description of Hell from Revelation 20:1: 'And I saw an angel come down from heaven, having the key of the bottomless pit'; also in Milton, *Paradise Lost*, Bk 6, line 864 (1671): 'Headlong themselves they threw / Down from the verge of Heaven, eternal wrath / Burnt after them to the bottomless pit.' William Pitt the Younger, British Prime Minister in the years 1783–1801 and 1804–6, was nicknamed 'the Bottomless Pitt', on account of his thinness. A caricature with this title, attributed to Gillray, shows Pitt as Chancellor of the Exchequer introducing his 1792 budget. His bottom is non-existent.

(the) bottom line The ultimate, most important outcome. Originally an American expression referring to the last line of a financial statement that shows whether there has been profit or loss – and still very much in use ('They're only interested in the bottom line, those investors') – but also used in the figurative sense of the final analysis or determining factor; the point, the crux of the argument. 'George Murphy and Ronald Reagan certainly qualified because they have gotten elected. I think that's the bottom line' – *San Francisco Examiner* (8 September 1967); in the 1970s, Henry Kissinger spoke of the 'bottom line' as the eventual outcome of political negotiations, disregarding the intermediate arguments; 'Our "bottom-line" has always been to protect jobs and services in our boroughs. In London, with a good deal of help from the GLC, we should survive' – *The Guardian* (21 June 1985); 'The bottom line / Protecting Miami's heritage . . . The billboard's pro-tan message in the era of thinning ozone layers is no longer consistent with Coppertone's new emphasis on sunscreens . . . Baring little girls' bottoms is not so politically correct either' – headline and text, *The Economist* (14 September 1991); Arthur Jacobs took an *Independent* editorial to task for a 'splendidly meaningless example [on 14 April 1995]: "The bottom line is that there are too many boats chasing too few fish". Surely this, as the statement of the problem, would be a top line and a true bottom line would be the solution.' 'According to a leaked memo seen by *The Independent* . . . "The bottom line is that the waste cannot be dumped at sea. The only option is to take ashore and treat' – *The Independent* (20 June 1995); 'The IRA's bottom line is a united Ireland, so what happens when they realise they're not going to get that?' – *The Independent* (1 September 1995).

bounce See ANSWER IS.

bounden duty A consciously archaic phrase, meaning 'conduct that is expected of one or to which one is bound by honour or position'. Best known from its use in the Anglican *Book of Common Prayer* (1662): 'It is very meet, right, and our bounden duty, that we should at all times, and in all places, give thanks unto thee, O Lord' – though the phrase predates this. 'Had Evan Hunter been dealing with the Lizzie Borden case under his other hat as Ed McBain it would have been one's bounden duty to keep the solution dark' – *The Guardian* (23 August 1984); 'These were the people who promoted and supported public libraries, municipal swimming baths and playing fields, museums and art galleries, free access to which was part of the spiritual provision the Victorians saw as their bounden duty towards their fellow citizens' – *The Sunday Telegraph* (6 May 1990); 'John Nott also wished to resign. But I told him straight that when the fleet had put to sea he had a bounden duty to stay and see the whole thing through' – Margaret Thatcher, *The Downing Street Years* (1993).

bourgeois See DISCREET CHARM.

Bovril prevents that sinking feeling Slogan for Bovril (meat extract) in the UK. This line first appeared in 1920. On H. H. Harris's cheery poster of a pyjama-clad man astride a jar of Bovril in the sea, However, the slogan was born in a golfing booklet issued by Bovril in 1890 that included the commendation: 'Unquestionably, Bovril . . . supplies . . . the nourishment which is so much needed by all players at the critical intermediate hour between breakfast and luncheon, when the *sinking feeling* engendered by an empty stomach is so distressing, and so fruitful of deteriorated play.' It is said that Bovril had intended to use the phrase earlier but withheld it because of the *Titanic* disaster of 1912. With updated illustrations, it lasted until 1958. Heading from *The Independent* (12 April 1989): 'Crucible challenge for a champion [Steve Davis, snooker player] who thinks rivals under the table before relishing that sinking feeling.'

(the) box A slightly passé term for a TV set (having earlier been applied to wire-lesses and gramophones) and one of several derogatory epithets that were applied during the medium's rise to mass popularity in the 1940s and 50s. Groucho Marx used the expression in a letter (1950). Maurice Richardson, sometime TV critic of *The Observer*, apparently coined the epithet **idiot's lantern** prior to 1957.

Box and Cox Meaning, 'by turns, turn and turn about, or alternately.' From a story (originally French) about a deceitful lodging-house keeper who lets the same room to two men, Box and Cox. Unbeknown to each other, one occupies it during the day and the other during the night. J. M. Morton's farce *Box and Cox* was staged in 1847. A short musical version called *Cox and Box* with music by Sullivan and lyrics – not by W. S. Gilbert but by F. C. Burnand – followed in 1867.

(it's a) box of birds (or **box of fluffy ducks)** A New Zealandism/Australianism for 'fine, excellent, OK'. Known by 1943.

box-office poison Meaning (of a film star, in particular) that he or she is capable of repulsing potential film-goers through his or her reputation. A term perhaps applied in the first instance to Katharine Hepburn in 1938 by members of the Independent Motion Picture Theatre Proprietors organization in the USA. Alexander Walker in *Stardom* (1970) refers, however, to 'the notorious red-bordered advertisement placed by a group of exhibitors in a trade paper which listed the stars [*sic*] who were deemed to be "box-office poison".' So perhaps she was not alone. 'British films are box-office poison' – Michael Caine, quoted in *Screen International* (29 July 1978).

boy See BIG BOY.

(the) boy done well Although now used in any context (for example as the headline to an article about Rod Stewart, the singer, in *The Independent* on 4 April 1991), this phrase of approbation is unquestionably of sporting origin. The question is, which sport? It sounds like the kind of thing a boxer's manager might say – 'All right, he got KO'd in the first round – but my boy done well . . .' – although the citations obtained so far are from every sport *but* boxing. Working backwards: 'Back on dry land he took victory well and, like all good managers had words of praise for his team, in this case Derek Clark. "It's a good result, they done well the lads," he said. "Class will always tell and it did today but everything happened

that quick I didn't have time to enjoy it." The boy Ron done well' – 'Cowes Diary' (yachting), *The Times* (7 August 1991); 'Particularly noteworthy were two goals by Mark Robins, one with his right, then a left-foot chip. It prompted manager Alex Ferguson to utter the immortal words: "The boy has done well"' – 'Football Focus', *The Sunday Times* (9 September 1990); 'The boy Domingo done good. The boy Carreras done well. The boy Pavarotti done great' – TV operatic concert review, *The Guardian* (9 July 1990); 'It wasn't all death and destruction . . . England reached the quarter finals of the World Cup [football]. The boy Lineker – the competition's top scorer – done well . . . The boy Andrew done well, too. Sarah Ferguson, proved a popular bride' – 'Review of the Year', *The Guardian* (31 December 1986). Quite the best suggestion for an origin was Fagin in *Oliver Twist*, but, no, he did not say it. Compare this letter to *The Guardian* on the ungrammatical World Cup TV commentaries of Emlyn Hughes and Mike Channon (1986): 'Conjugate the verb "done great": I done great. He done great. We done great. They done great. The boy Lineker done great.'

boy meets girl Short form of what might seem to be the most popular plot in all fiction: 'Boy meets girl. Boy woos girl. Boy marries girl.' Known as a concept by 1945 and possibly originating in discussion of Hollywood movies in the 1930s. In a letter from P. G. Wodehouse (24 August 1932): 'Don't you find that the chief difficulty in writing novels is getting the love interest set? Boy meets girl. Right. But what happens then?'

(the) boy next door Admirably defined by *Photoplay* (October 1958) as: 'The boy who's within reach of every girl fan' – hence, a straightforward, unsophisticated young man figuring in a conventional romance, particularly on the cinema screen. The female equivalent, **girl next door**, seems to have emerged a fraction later. From the *Times Educational Supplement* (23 February 1968): 'Diana Quick's Ophelia was very much the girl-next-door.'

(a) boy's best friend is his mother Norman Bates in the Hitchcock film

Psycho (1960) gets to say 'A boy's best friend is his mother' – with good reason, but we won't go into all that – and, indeed, the line was used to promote the picture. It has been suggested that earlier the line was originally 'a *girl's* best friend is her mother'. Either way, the saying seems to have been set in concrete – if not in treacle – by an American songwriter called Henry Miller in 1883. The music was by the prolific Joseph P. Skelly, who was also a plumber. Their song with the expression as title contains the chorus: 'Then cherish her with care, / And smooth her sil'vry hair, / When gone you will never get another. / And wherever we may turn, / This lesson we shall learn, / A boy's best friend is his Mother.' There are no citations for the phrase earlier than this.

boys will be boys! A comment on the inevitability of youthful male behaviour. Thackeray has it in *Vanity Fair* (1848).

(the) boy who put his finger in the dike A figure of speech for someone who staves off disaster through a simple (albeit temporary) gesture. Hans Brinker is the hero of the children's book *Hans Brinker, or the Silver Skates* (1865) by the American author Mary Mapes Dodge. What he is not – as often erroneously asserted – is 'the boy who put his finger in the dike.' The connection is that the tale of the (nameless) legendary Dutch boy who spotted a tiny leak in his local dam, or dike, and stuck his finger in it and stopped it from getting worse, is related in Chapter 18 of *Hans Brinker*: 'He looked up and saw a small hole in the dike through which a tiny stream was flowing. Quick as a flash, he saw his duty. His chubby finger was thrust in, the flowing was stopped! "Ah!" he thought, with a chuckle of boyish delight, "the angry waters must stay back now! Haarlem shall not be drowned while *I* am here!"' Mary Mapes Dodge (who had never been to Holland) included the story of this 'Hero of Haarlem' in her novel and, as a result, various Dutch towns claimed the boy as their own. A statue was erected to him – but he was never more than a legend. Hence, however, from *The Times* (9 October 1986): 'To try to stand in front of the markets like the Little Dutch Boy with his finger in the dike would have

been an act of folly if the Government were not convinced that the dike was fundamentally sound'; (27 July 1989): '"It was finger-in-the-dike stuff for us throughout the match," the Oxbridge coach, Tony Rodgers, said. "Ultimately the flood walls cracked".'

boy wonder See HOLY —.

bra See BURN YOUR.

bracket See ARE YOU LOOKING.

brain(s) trust *The Brains Trust* was the title of a BBC radio discussion programme (1941 onwards), originating from the American term for a group of people who give advice or who comment on current issues. In his first campaign in 1932, President Franklin D. Roosevelt set up a circle of advisers which became known as his '*brain* trust'. In Britain, the term was borrowed and turned into '*brains* trust'. Curiously, the Roosevelt coinage, attributed to James Michael Kieran Jnr, was at first 'the *brains* trust' also.

brand new (or bran ...) This expression for 'very new' comes from the old word meaning 'to burn' (just as a 'brand' is a form of torch). A metal that was brand (*or* bran) new had been taken out of the flames, having just been forged. Shakespeare has the variation 'fire-new' – e.g. in *Love's Labour's Lost*, I.i.177 (1592–3) – which points more directly to the phrase's origin.

brandy–y–y–y! Catchphrase from the BBC radio *Goon Show* (1951–60). Accompanied by the sound of rushing footsteps, this was the show's beloved way of getting anybody out of a situation that was proving too much for him. Most often, however, it was shouted by Neddie Seagoon (Harry Secombe) as a signal to clear off before the musical interludes of Max Geldray (harmonica). The Goons – Peter Sellers, Harry Secombe and Spike Milligan – first appeared in a BBC radio show called *Crazy People* in May 1951. At that time, Michael Bentine was also of their number. *The Goon Show* proper ran from 1952 to 1960, with one extra programme in 1972 and numerous re-runs. The humour was zany, often taking basic music-hall jokes and giving them further infusions of surrealism. The cast of three did all the funny voices, though Harry Secombe concentrated on the main character, Neddie Seagoon.

brass See BOLD AS; COLD ENOUGH TO.

(to get down to) brass tacks Probably of US origin, this phrase means 'to get down to essentials' and has been known since 1897, at least. There are various theories as to why we say it, including: (1) In old stores, brass tacks were positioned a yard apart for measuring. When a customer 'got down to brass tacks', it meant he or she was serious about making a purchase. (2) Brass tacks were a fundamental element in 19th-century upholstery, hence this expression meant to deal with a fault in the furniture by getting down to basics. (3) 'Brass tacks' is rhyming slang for 'facts', though the version 'to get down to brass nails' would contradict this.

(the) brat pack Name for a group of young Hollywood actors in the mid-1980s who tended to behave in a spoiled, unruly fashion. Coined by David Blum in *New York* Magazine (10 June 1985) and fashioned after **rat pack**, the name given in the 1950s to the then young Frank Sinatra, Peter Lawford, Sammy Davis Jnr, etc. Has also been applied to other young cliques of writers, performers. The original brat-packers, including Emilio Estevez, Matt Dillon, Patrick Swayze and Tom Cruise, had all appeared together in Francis Ford Coppola's film *The Outsiders* (1983).

(a) brave new world A future state, particularly one where 'progress' has produced nightmarish conditions. Nowadays a slightly ironic term for some new and exciting aspect of modern life. *Brave New World* was the title of a futuristic novel (1932) by Aldous Huxley. It is taken from Miranda's exclamation in Shakespeare's *The Tempest*, V.i.183 (1612): 'O brave new world, / That has such people in't!' 'Perhaps as much a cliché as it is a vogue-term' – Eric Partridge, *Usage and Abusage* (1947). 'Its title is now a pervasive media catch phrase, automatically invoked in connection with any development viewed as ultra-modern, ineffably zany or involving a potential threat to human liberty' – David Bradshaw, Intro-

duction to a 1994 edition of Huxley's novel. 'Consequently, when the pair signed to Virgin a couple of years back, the record company was keen to talk them up as a multi-media outfit, the kind of band best suited to the brave new world of interactive CDs' – *The Observer* (1 May 1994); 'Will there still be a [BBC radio] drama department in 10 years or, in the multi-skilled brave new world, will producers be billeted on different departments and everyone else be casualised?' – *The Guardian* (13 March 1995).

breach See CUSTOM MORE.

bread See CAST ONE'S.

bread and butter! Phrase uttered when two people – who are a couple – walk along and come to an obstacle and separate to go round it. Mostly American usage, though a Russian origin has been suggested. Marian Bock remembered (2002) saying it in the 1960s: 'Approaching we would say, "Bread and butter" and rejoining hands on the other side of the obstacle we would say, "All good wishes come true". I was grown before I realized that my sisters were in the habit of *making* a wish in the interim.' There is obviously a superstition involved, but why say 'bread and butter' (or 'salt and pepper', another version)? Is it because these are things that *belong together*? Apparently, the expression occurs in a number of Hollywood films of the 1930s/40s.

bread and butter issues Fundamental matters of direct concern to ordinary people – as important to them as the basic food they eat. Of quite recent origin and a cliché by about 1990. 'The second problem is more fundamental: what does the party stand for? The dilemma was highlighted in a thoughtful speech to a fringe meeting by Mr Matthew Taylor, MP for Truro, who pointed out that "we have a higher profile on Bosnia than on any bread-and-butter domestic policy issue that determines how people vote"' – *Financial Times* (14 March 1994); 'This is precisely why Tony Blair has devoted much time and thought to softening up the ground to be more fertile to accept the reasons for widespread change in the way the country is governed. It is very much a bread and butter issue' – letter to the editor, *The Guardian* (3 January 1995).

bread and circuses What the citizen is chiefly concerned about, having been bribed by whoever is in office with public entertainments and free food, as a way of avoiding popular discontent. Coined as *panem et circenses* by the Roman satirist, Juvenal (*circa* AD 60-*circa* 130) in his *Satires*, No. 10. Circuses here means chariot races and games in a stadium. The Circus was an oval-shaped racecourse.

bread and pullet (or pullit) Grown-up's fobbing-off phrase, when asked, usually by a small person, 'What's for tea?' – according to the writer Christopher Matthew on BBC Radio *Quote . . . Unquote* (16 May 1995) and confirmed by many others. 'My mother used to say "Bread and Pullett", supposedly a reference to a poor family who had to take the bread and pull it to make it go round' – Sylvia Dowling (1998). 'I recently came across a Victorian recipe for "Pulled Bread". The white crumb was peeled from the middle of a freshly baked, still warm loaf. This was then put in the oven until golden brown' – John Smart (2000). The basic phrase would seem to refer to bread without any addition of butter or jam, just plain fare.

breadbox See IS IT BIGGER.

break a leg! A traditional theatrical greeting given before a performance, especially a first night, because it is considered bad luck to wish anyone 'good luck' directly. Another version is **snap a wrist!** *Partridge/Slang* has 'to break a leg' as 'to give birth to a bastard', dating from the 17th century, but that is probably unconnected. As also is the fact that John Wilkes Booth, an actor, broke his leg after assassinating President Lincoln in a theatre. *Morris* (1977) has it based on a German good luck expression, *Hals und Beinbruch* [May you break your neck and your leg]. Perhaps this entered theatrical speech (like several other expressions) via Yiddish. Compare SEE YOU ON THE ICE! Other theatrical good-luck expressions include **merde!** [French: shit!], TOY! TOY! and **in bocca del lupo** [Italian: into the wolf's jaws], although this last has also been heard in the form '*bocc' al lupo*'.

breakfast See CONDEMNED MAN; DOG'S.

break for the border This alliterative phrase has been used as (1) the title of a radio programme presented by the disc jockey Andy Kershaw on the British Forces Broadcasting Service (1987–90); (2) the title of various recorded musical numbers, from 1990 onwards; (3) the name of a group of restaurant/bars in the UK and Ireland in the 1990s. Its origin has not been found (and Andy Kershaw is unable to remember why his programme was called that . . .)

breakfast of champions An advertising line used to promote Wheaties breakfast cereal in the USA, since 1950 at least. In the 1980s, a series of ads featuring sporting champions showed, for example, 'Jackie Robinson – one of the greatest names in baseball . . . this Dodgers star is a Wheaties man: "A lot of us ball players go for milk, fruit and Wheaties," says Jackie . . . Had *your* Wheaties today?' Kurt Vonnegut used the phrase as the title of a novel (1973). In 1960s' Australia it was also used as a slang expression for sexual intercourse on awakening – specifically cunnilingus.

(the) breaking of nations The title of Thomas Hardy's poem 'In Time of "The Breaking of Nations"' (conceived at the time of the Franco-Prussian War of 1870 and written during the First World War) alludes to Jeremiah 51:20: 'Thou art my battle axe and weapons of war: for with thee will I break in pieces the nations, and with thee will I destroy kingdoms.'

(to) break the mould 'To start afresh from fundamentals'. When the Social Democratic Party was established in 1981, there was much talk of it 'breaking the mould of British politics' – i.e. doing away with the traditional system of one government and one chief opposition party. But this was by no means a new way of describing political change and getting rid of an old system for good in a way that prevents it being reconstituted. In *What Matters Now* (1972), Roy Jenkins, one of the new party's founders, had quoted Andrew Marvell's 'Horatian Ode Upon Cromwell's Return from Ireland' (1650): 'And cast the kingdoms old, / Into another mould.' In a speech at a House of Commons Press Gallery lunch on 8 June 1960, Jenkins had also said: 'The politics of the left and centre of this country are frozen in an out-of-date mould which is bad for the political and economic health of Britain and increasingly inhibiting for those who live within the mould. Can it be broken?' A. J. P. Taylor, in his *English History 1914–1945* (1965), had earlier written: 'Lloyd George needed a new crisis to break the mould of political and economic habit'. The image evoked, as in the days of the Luddites, is of breaking the mould from which iron machinery is cast – so completely that the machinery has to be re-cast from scratch.

breath See DON'T HOLD YOUR.

breathing space A phrase generally used to denote a pause in time for consideration when some outside pressure has been taken off. Date of origin uncertain. 'Their crowd expects results, speed and guts, and particularly results. Playing in Europe, where even the most demanding crowd realizes guile is all, has given Arsenal the breathing space to develop different ideas' – *The Sunday Times* (1 May 1994); 'Alexon Group, the women's wear retailer, has secured financial breathing-space by striking an agreement with its bankers for a new two-year facility. The shares responded by rising 4p to 26p' – *Financial Times* (31 March 1995).

brewed, saucered and blowed A drink of tea that is now ready for drinking – because it has been brewed, poured into a saucer and blown on to cool it a little. A British expression, probably in use by the mid-20th century.

brick See CAN'T THROW A BRICK.

(the) bridegroom on the wedding cake A memorable insult, this phrase is usually attributed to Alice Roosevelt Longworth (1884–1980). She said that Thomas Dewey, who was challenging Harry S Truman for the US presidency in 1948, looked like the 'bridegroom' or just 'the man' 'on the wedding cake'. Dewey did indeed have a wooden, dark appearance and a black moustache.

(a) bridge over troubled water 'Like a bridge over troubled water, / I will ease your mind' comes from the song 'Bridge Over Troubled Water' (1970), by the American singer/songwriter Paul Simon. It sounds positively biblical – but although waters are troubled in Psalm 46:3 and John 5:7, the word 'bridge' occurs nowhere in the Bible. In fact, the phrase may have been influenced by 'I'll be a bridge over deep water if you trust my name', spoken by the Reverend Claude Jeter, lead singer of the Swan Silvertones gospel group, in 'O Mary Don't You Weep'.

(a) bridge too far A phrase sometimes used allusively when warning of an unwise move or regretting one that has already been made. The clichéd use derives from the title of Cornelius Ryan's book *A Bridge Too Far* (1974; film UK/US 1977) about the 1944 airborne landings in Holland. These were designed to capture eleven bridges needed for the Allied invasion of Germany – an attempt that came to grief at Arnhem, the Allies suffering more casualties there than in the Normandy landings. In advance of the action, Lieutenant-General Sir Frederick Browning was reported to have protested to Field-Marshal Montgomery, who was in overall command: 'But, sir, we may be going a bridge too far.' More recent research has established that Browning did not see Montgomery before the operation and most likely did not make this comment to him. 'A BRIDGE TOO NEAR. A public inquiry opened yesterday into plans to re-span the Ironbridge Gorge in Shropshire' – *The Times* (20 June 1990); 'Ratners: A bid too far?' – *The Observer* (8 July 1990); 'The Government is poised to announce legislation to ban [pub lotteries], but is its decision justified? Fran Abrams asks why ministers believe that this is a punt too far' – *The Independent* (13 November 1997); 'In *The Path to Power* [Lady Thatcher] describes Maastricht as "a treaty too far" and calls for the rolling back of European Union law' – *The Independent* (22 May 1995).

bright-eyed and bushy-tailed Alert, especially like a squirrel. The expression appears to have been used in connection with US astronauts (*circa* 1967). *Partridge/Slang* suggests a Canadian 1930s' origin.

But the great popularizer must have been
B. Merrill's song with the title in 1953: 'If
the fox in the bush and the squirr'l in the
tree be / Why in the world can't you and
me be / Bright eyed and bushy tailed and
sparkelly as we can be?'

bright   See ALL THINGS; ALWAYS MERRY.

bright young things   Young socialites of
the 1920s and early 30s whose reaction to
the rigours of the First World War was to
give parties and dance away the night,
copied in more modest style by their
poorer contemporaries. During a short
period of frivolity, such people disre-
garded the poverty and unemployment
around them and flouted convention. The
females were also known as 'flappers'. The
phrase in this form was known by 1927,
but *Punch* (4 August 1926) has: 'The
energies of that exuberant coterie known
as the "Bright Young People" whose
romps, practical jokes . . . have contributed to the liveliness of London during the
last few months.' Indeed, 'Bright Young
People' would appear to be the original
form of the phrase, and Evelyn Waugh, in
his novel *Vile Bodies* (1930), continues to
call them this, with capital first letters.
However, when Waugh's novel was filmed
(UK 2003), it was given the title *Bright
Young Things*.

bring back the cat   Long the cry of
corporal punishment enthusiasts in Britain
demanding the return of beating as an
official punishment. Usually associated
with right-wing 'hangers and floggers'
within the Conservative Party who seldom
miss their chance to utter the cry (though
not in so many words) at their annual
conference. The cat-o'-nine-tails was the
nine-thong whip once used to enforce
discipline in the Royal Navy. A female jury
member utters the cry in BBC TV,
Hancock, 'Twelve Angry Men' (16 October
1959). In a now published letter (19 June
1970), Philip Larkin wrote: 'Remember my
song, How To Win The Next Election?
"Prison for Strikers, Bring back the cat,
Kick out the niggers, How about that?"'

(to) bring home the bacon   Meaning 'to
be successful in a venture', this may have
to do with the **Dunmow Flitch**, a tradition
established in AD 1111 at Great Dunmow

in Essex. Married couples who can prove
they have lived for a year and a day
without quarrelling or without wishing to
be unmarried can claim a gammon of
bacon. Also, country fairs used to have
competitions that involved catching a
greased pig. If you 'brought home the
bacon', you won. In 1910, when Jack
Johnson, the American negro boxer, won
the World Heavyweight boxing championship, his mother exlaimed: 'He said he'd
bring home the bacon, and the honey boy
has gone and done it.' The *Oxford Companion to American History* suggests that
this 'added a new phrase to the vernacular'. Unlikely, given the Dunmow Flitch
connection, and yet the *OED2*'s earliest
citation is not until 1924 (in P. G.
Wodehouse).

bring on the girls (or **dancing girls)!**
Let's move on to something more entertaining. What any host might say to cheer
up his guests, but probably originating in a
literal suggestion from some bored American impresario as to what was needed to
pep up a show in the 1920s. From P. G.
Wodehouse and Guy Bolton, *Bring On the
Girls*, Chap. 1 (1954): '[There is] a dull spot
in the second act . . . Lending to the
discussion the authority of long experience
and uttering the slogan which he probably
learned at his mother's knee, [the impresa-
rio] says, "Bring on the girls!" It is the
panacea that never fails. It dates back,
according to the great Bert Williams, to the
days of ancient Egypt . . .'

bring out your dead   This was the cry of
the carters who went about at night
collecting corpses during the Great Plague
of London in 1665. Source not found.
Quoted in Rudyard Kipling, *Stalky & Co.*,
'An Unsavoury Interlude' (1899).

Britain can take it   During the Second
World War, slogans rained down upon the
hapless British as profusely as German
bombs. The Ministry of Information, in
blunderbuss fashion, fired away with as
much material as possible in the hope of
hitting something. Some of the slogans
were brilliant, others were quite the
reverse – hence the Ministry's abandonment of 'Britain can take it' in December
1941. 'While the public appreciated due

recognition of their resolute qualities,' wrote Ian McLaine in *Ministry of Morale* (1979), 'they resented too great an emphasis on the stereotyped image of the Britisher in adversity as a wise-cracking Cockney. They were irritated by the propaganda which represented their grim experience as a sort of particularly torrid Rugby match.' The notion was resurrected by Winston Churchill in May 1945 in a tribute to Cockney fortitude: 'No one ever asked for peace because London was suffering. London was like a great rhinoceros, a great hippopotamus, saying: "Let them do their worst. London can take it." London could take anything.'

British See BE BRITISH.

(the) British are coming, the British are coming! Doubt has been cast on Paul Revere's reputed cry to warn people of approaching British troops during the American War of Independence. On his night ride of 18 April 1775, from Boston to Lexington, it is more likely that he cried 'The regulars are out' and, besides, there were many other night-riders involved. Hence, however, *The Russians Are Coming, The Russians Are Coming*, the title of a film (US 1966). Although this was an obvious allusion to Revere's cry, it has also been said that these were the last words uttered by US Secretary of Defense, James Forrestal, before he committed suicide by jumping from his office window at the Pentagon in 1949. In fact, two months *after* being replaced as Defense Secretary, Forrestal did commit suicide, but by jumping from a 16th-floor window at the National Naval Medical Center in Bethesda, Maryland, where he was being treated for depression. It is not recorded that he said any words before jumping. All that is known is that he broke off from copying out a translation of Sophocles before killing himself. It is, however, apparently true (at least according to Daniel Yergin, *The Shattered Peace*, 1977) that within a week of losing his job, Forrestal became deranged and walked the streets saying, 'The Russians are coming! I've seen Russian soldiers!'

(a) broad church A body or group or organization, of any kind, that takes a liberal and tolerant attitude to its members' beliefs or activities. The use derives from the designation 'Broad Church' as applied to the Church of England from the mid-19th century onwards, meaning that it was broad enough to encompass a wide variety of beliefs and attitudes. According to Benjamin Jowett, the Master of Balliol College, Oxford, the term in relation to the Church of England was coined by the poet Arthur Hugh Clough.

broad sunlit uplands In Winston Churchill's long speaking career, there was one thematic device he frequently resorted to for his perorations. It appears in many forms but may be summarized as the 'broad, sunlit uplands' approach. In his collected speeches, there are some thirteen occasions when he made use of the construction. 'The level plain . . . a land of peace and plenty . . . the sunshine of a more gentle and a more generous age' (1906); 'I earnestly trust . . . that by your efforts our country may emerge from this period of darkness and peril once more in the sunlight of a peaceful time' (at the end of a speech on 19 September 1915 when Churchill's own position was precarious following the failure of the Gallipoli campaign); in his 'finest hour' speech, Churchill hoped that, 'The life of the world may move forward into broad, sunlit uplands' (1940); 'It is an uphill road we have to tread, but if we reject the cramping, narrowing path of socialist restrictions, we shall surely find a way – and a wise and tolerant government – to those broad uplands where plenty, peace and justice reign' (1951, prior to the General Election).

broke See ALL HELL.

(a) broken reed A weak support; something not to be trusted or leant on. In Isaiah 36:6, it is said that Hezekiah could not put his trust in Egypt if the Assyrians made war on Jerusalem: 'Lo, thou trustest in the staff of this broken reed . . . whereon if a man lean, it will go into his hand, and pierce it.' In II Kings 18:21, a similar passage has 'bruised reed'.

(a) Bronx cheer A noise of derisive disapproval. *DOAS* suggests that this form of criticism (known by 1929) originated at the National Theater in the Bronx, New

York City, although the Yankee baseball stadium is also in the same area.

broom   See AGE BEFORE.

broomstick   See LIVE OVER THE.

brother   See AM I NOT; BIG BROTHER.

brother of the more famous Jack
Brother of the More Famous Jack is the title of a novel (1982) by the English novelist Barbara Trapido (b. 1941). It refers neither to characters in the book nor to Robert and John F. Kennedy (as perhaps might be supposed). No, Chap. 4 has: 'Yeats, William Butler . . . Brother of the more famous Jack, of course.' The Irish poet W. B. Yeats did indeed have a brother, Jack, who was a leading artist. Often alluded to. From Robert Stephens, *Knight Errant* (1995): 'The stars were Claude Hulbert, brother of the more famous Jack, his wife Delia Trevor, and another fine comedian called Sonny Hale.' From Michael Kerrigan, *Who Lies Where* (1995): 'Bankside was, of course, theatreland in the seventeenth century. Edmund Shakespeare, brother of the more famous William, is buried here.'

brothers   See BAND OF.

brought to a satisfactory conclusion
'Satisfactory conclusion' on its own was known by 1825. The full phrase was cited as a 'resounding commonplace' by George Orwell, 'Politics and the English Language' in *Horizon* (April 1946). 'There Richard Cattell, who had unique experience in repairing inadvertently damaged common bile ducts, brought this sad episode to a more or less satisfactory conclusion' – *The Daily Telegraph* (19 May 1994); 'Andrew Cohen, Betterware's chief executive says: "Hopefully, this saga has been now brought to a conclusion satisfactory to all parties"' – *The Sunday Telegraph* (17 July 1994).

brown   See DON'T SAY.

(to earn/win) brownie points   Originating in American business or the military and certainly recorded before 1963, this has nothing to do with Brownies, the junior branch of the Girl Guides, and the points they might or might not gain for doing their 'good deed for the day'. Oh no! This has a scatological origin, not unconnected with brown-nosing, brown-tonguing, arse-licking and other unsavoury methods of sucking up to someone important. Note also the American term 'Brownie', an award for doing something *wrong*. According to *DOAS*, 'I got a pair of Brownies for that one' (1942) refers to a system of disciplinary demerits on the railroads. The name was derived from the inventor of the system, presumably a Mr Brown.

(to be in a) brown study   To be in idle or purposeless reverie. Originally from the sense of brown = gloomy and has been so since 1532: 'Lack of company will soon lead a man into a brown study.' Samuel Johnson defined the term as 'gloomy meditation'.

brush   See DAFT AS A; LIVE OVER THE.

(a) brush off   Meaning 'a rebuff', this noun is said to derive from a habit of Pullman porters in the USA who, if they thought you were a poor tipper, gave you a quick brush over the shoulders and passed on to the next customer. However, perhaps the mere action of brushing unwanted dirt off clothing is sufficient reason for the expression. Known by 1941. 'Later when she began to hate her job at the *Evening Standard* and made plans to leave, she gave Robert Lutyens the brush-off. She no longer needed him' – Christopher Ogden, *Life of the Party* (1994).

brute force and ignorance   What is needed to get, say, a recalcitrant machine to work again. Sometimes pronounced 'hignorance'; sometimes abbreviated to 'BF & I'. Known by 1930.

(the) buck stops here   Harry S Truman (US President 1945–53) had a sign on his desk bearing these words, indicating that the Oval Office was where the passing of the buck had to cease. It appears to be a saying of his own invention. 'Passing the buck' is a poker player's expression. It refers to a marker that can be passed on by someone who does not wish to deal. Later, Jimmy Carter restored Truman's motto to the Oval Office. Listed in *The Independent* (24 December 1994) in the form 'the buck must stop here' as a cliché of newspaper editorials. When President Nixon published his memoirs (1978), people opposed to its sale went around wearing buttons that said 'The book stops here'.

buds See DARLING.

bugger Bognor! What King George V said in reply to a suggestion that his favourite watering place be dubbed Bognor Regis (*circa* 1929). They are not his dying words, as often supposed – for example by Auberon Waugh in his *Private Eye* diary entry (9 August 1975) that stated: 'Shortly before the King died, a sycophantic courtier said he was looking so much better he should soon be well enough for another visit to Bognor, to which the old brute replied "Bugger Bognor" and expired.' The first recorded telling of this incorrect version that I have found is in a letter from R. K. Parkes to the *New Statesman* (3 March 1967). The correct dating and occasion is given by Kenneth Rose in his biography *George V* (1983) where it is linked to the King's recuperative visit to Bognor after a serious illness in the winter of 1928–9: 'A happier version of the legend rests on the authority of Sir Owen Morshead, the King's librarian. As the time of the King's departure from Bognor drew near, a deputation of leading citizens came to ask that their salubrious town should henceforth be known as Bognor Regis. They were received by Stamfordham, the King's private secretary, who, having heard their petition, invited them to wait while he consulted the King in another room. The sovereign responded with the celebrated obscenity, which Stamfordham deftly translated for the benefit of the delegation. His Majesty, they were told, would be graciously pleased to grant their request.'

bugger's grips The short whiskers on the cheeks of Old Salts (in the British navy) – fancifully supposed to be useful for a bugger to hold on to. By the early 20th century. Compare **love handles**, a possibly more heterosexual term for excess folds of fat above the hips, also presumed useful to hold on to during sexual intercourse. A noticeably popular usage in the 1990s but probably dating from the 1950s. *Slanguage* (1984) comments: 'Affectionate usage, often by females describing their own

bodies. "I *haven't* put on weight, these are my love handles." Synonymous is **side steaks**.'

Buggins' turn (more correctly **Buggins's turn**) This expression gives the reason for a job appointment having been made – when it is somebody's turn to get the job rather than because the person is especially well qualified to do so. The name Buggins is used because it sounds suitably dull and humdrum ('Joseph Buggins, Esq. J.P. for the borough' appears in one of G. W. E. Russell's *Collections and Recollections*, 1898. Trollope gives the name to a civil servant in *Framley Parsonage*, 1861. The similar sounding 'Muggins', self-applied to a foolish person, goes back to 1855, at least). The earliest recorded use of the phrase 'Buggins's turn' is by Admiral Fisher, later First Sea Lord, in a letter of 1901. Later, in a letter of 1917 (printed in his *Memories*, 1919), Fisher wrote: 'Some day the Empire will go down because it is Buggins's turn.' It is impossible to say whether Fisher coined the phrase, though he always spoke and wrote in a colourful fashion. But what do people with the name Buggins think of it? In February 1986, a Mr Geoffrey Buggins was reported to be threatening legal action over a cartoon that had appeared in the London *Evening Standard*. It showed the husband of Margaret Thatcher looking through the New Year's Honours List and asking, 'What did Buggins do to get an MBE?' She replies: 'He thought up all those excuses for not giving one to Bob Geldof' (the pop star and fund raiser who only later received an Honorary KBE). The real-life Mr Buggins (who had been awarded an MBE for services to export in 1969) said from his home near Lisbon, Portugal: 'I am taking this action because I want to protect the name of Buggins and also on behalf of the Muddles, Winterbottoms and the Sillitoes of this world.' The editor of the *Standard* said: 'We had no idea there was a Mr Buggins who had the MBE. I feel sorry for his predicament, but if we are to delete Buggins's turn from the English language perhaps he could suggest an alternative.'

(the) bulldog breed In 1857, Charles Kingsley wrote of: 'The original British bulldog breed, which, once stroked against the hair, shows his teeth at you for ever afterwards.' In 1897, the British were called 'boys of the bulldog breed' in a music-hall song, 'Sons of the Sea, All British Born', by Felix McGlennon. At the outbreak of the First World War in 1914, Winston Churchill spoke at a 'Call to Arms' meeting at the London Opera House. 'Mr Churchill has made a speech of tremendous voltage and carrying power,' the *Manchester Guardian* reported. 'His comparison of the British navy to a bulldog – "the nose of the bulldog has been turned backwards so that he can breathe without letting go" – will live. At the moment of delivery, with extraordinary appositeness, it was particularly vivid, as the speaker was able by some histrionic gift to suggest quite the bulldog as he spoke.' Indeed, during the Second World War, small model bulldogs were manufactured bearing Churchill's facial pout and wearing a tin helmet. **John Bull** as a symbol and personification of Britain (sometimes shown accompanied by a bulldog) dates from before John Arbuthnot's *The History of John Bull* (1712), which was an anti-French tract. The organist and composer John Bull (1563–1628) is believed to have composed the first national anthem. Cartoonists built up an image of a stolid, fearless (sometimes boorish) country gentleman in riding jacket and top boots. Pamphleteers credited him with rugged common sense, patriotism and affability.

bullet See BITE THE.

(a) bull in a china shop A clumsy person. This is a proverbial saying in many languages but, apart from English, the animal named is invariably an elephant. From Captain Marryat, *Jacob Faith*, Chap. 15 (1834): 'Whatever it is that smashes, Mrs. T. always swears it was the *most valuable* thing in the room. I'm like a bull in a china-shop.'

bully for you! A congratulatory phrase, latterly perhaps used a touch resentfully and ironically. 'I've just won the lottery and married the woman of my dreams . . .' 'Bully for you!' Established by the mid-19th century. A *Punch* cartoon (5 March 1881)

drawn by Gerald du Maurier has the caption 'Bully for little Timpkins!'

(a) bumper bundle From the radio record request shows *Family Favourites* and *Two-Way Family Favourites* on the BBC (1945–84). Cliff Michelmore, who used to introduce the programme from Hamburg, and later met and married the London presenter, Jean Metcalfe, recalled the origin of the phrase (in 1979): 'It was invented by Jean. Her road to Damascus was at the crossroads on Banstead Heath one Sunday morning when driving in to do the programme. It was used to describe a large number of requests all for the same record, especially "Top Ten" hits, *circa* 1952–3.'

buried their own See THEY CAME.

Burleigh's nod A significant nod of the head, whose meaning may be explained in any way. Referring to William Cecil (1st Lord Burleigh), the English courtier and politician (1520–98). Within R. B. Sheridan's play *The Critic* (1779), there is a performance of a mock-tragedy on the Spanish Armada. Burleigh is represented as too preoccupied with affairs of state to be able to say anything, so he shakes his head and the character Puff explains what he means: 'Why by that shake of the head, he gave you to understand that even though they had more justice in their cause and wisdom in their measures – yet, if there was not a greater spirit shown on the part of the people – the country would at last fall a sacrifice to the hostile ambition of the Spanish monarchy . . .' 'The devil! – did he mean all that by shaking his head?' 'Every word of it – if he shook his head as I taught him.' Hence, also, the expression 'To be as significant as the shake of Lord Burleigh's head'.

(a) Burlington Bertie A swell gentleman, named after the one with the 'Hyde Park drawl and the Bond Street crawl', commemorated in a song with words and music by Harry B. Norris (first published 1900) and performed by Vesta Tilley. Not to be confused with 'Burlington Bertie from Bow', a parody written in 1915 by William Hargreaves for his wife, Ella Shields, the male impersonator. In this song, now the better remembered of the two, Bertie is a more down-at-heel character.

BURMA Meaning, 'Be Upstairs Ready, My Angel'. Lovers' acronym for use in correspondence and to avoid military censorship. Probably in use by the First World War.

burn, baby, burn! A black extremists' slogan that arose from the August 1965 riots in the Watts district of Los Angeles when 34 people were killed and entire blocks burnt. The 1974 song with this title by Hudson-Ford had other connotations. Indeed, it has been suggested that the phrase arose as a joke expression of sexual encouragement a year or so before the riots. Popularized by the Black disc jockey Magnificent Montague, it was called out by audiences to singers and musicians.

(to) burn daylight To waste time. Shakespeare twice uses this expression. In *The Merry Wives of Windsor*, II.i.52 (1601), Mistress Ford says: 'We burn daylight.' In *Romeo and Juliet*, I.iv.43 (1594), Mercutio says, 'Come, we burn daylight, ho . . . I mean, sir, in delay / We waste our lights in vain, light lights by day.' Hence, *Burning Daylight*, the title of a novel (1910) by Jack London.

(a) burning question The subject of the hour; what really needs to be addressed. Popular from the 19th century onwards. Benjamin Disraeli used the phrase in 1873. 'The source of the Boulangist election expenditure is a burning question in France' – *St James's Gazette* (16 January 1889). 'The burning question of the week has been whether a school teacher, now dead, beat boys during the 1960s. More than a quarter of the *Times*'s letters page was devoted to this urgent subject on Thursday, and nearly as much again on Friday' – *Independent on Sunday* (1 May 1994).

(to) burn one's boats To close off all one's avenues of retreat. The *OED2* is hopeless on this point – it's earliest citation is from only 1886. *Brewer* (1894) has a short piece concentrating on the meaning and origin – 'The allusion is to Julius Caesar and other generals, who burned their boats or ships when they invaded a foreign country, in order that their soldiers might feel that they must either conquer the country or die, as retreat would be impossible.' So to *Notes and Queries*, which had a look at the matter three times between 1922 and 1932 and, first of all, found two allusions to the act (if not an actual use of the phrase) in Gibbon's *Decline and Fall of the Roman Empire* (1776). In Chap. 13, Asclepiodotus does it, acting for Constantius in the recovery of Britain from the usurper Allectus (*circa* AD 296), and in Chap. 56: Robert Guiscard proposes this measure before the battle of Durazzo in October 1081 – whether it was carried out is not very clear. Then Edward J. G. Forse contributes this: 'The gentleman who "burnt his boats" was Agathocles, Tyrant of Syracuse. The details will be found in Smith's *Dictionary of Biography*. This is worth recording, for most dictionaries (even Weekley) give all sorts of more recent instances, and some years ago I had an infinity of trouble in tracing the phrase back to what seems to be the original incident that started the expression.' Compare **(to) burn one's bridges**, meaning exactly the same thing. The earliest citation for this is Mark Twain in 1892.

(to) burn the midnight oil To sit up and work beyond midnight; to slave over something. Known by 1744. 'Mr Moore, a council member since the mid-1970s, said: "I have three partners (one of whom is about to be a council member of the Irish institute), and I get tremendous support from them. But it does mean that I have to burn a lot of midnight oil to keep my end going"' – *The Independent* (3 May 1994); 'At a time of year when students and staff used to be in the classroom, students are now wandering around like lost sheep while the staff burn the midnight oil trying to get marking completed in a week' – letter to the editor, *Times Higher Education Supplement* (24 February 1995).

burn your bra! A feminist slogan from America, *circa* 1970, encouraging women to destroy an item of apparel quite clearly designed by a male chauvinist and likely to make a woman more of a sex object. There is an analogy with the burning of draft-cards as a protest against the Vietnam War.

(to) bury the hatchet Meaning, to settle an argument – after the American Indian ritual of burying *two* axes to seal a peace treaty. Recorded by 1680.

business as usual   The standard declaration posted when a shop has suffered some misfortune like a fire or is undergoing alterations. However, in the First World War the phrase was adopted in a more general sense. Herbert Morgan, an advertising man, promoted the slogan – that had 'quite a vogue till it fell terribly out of favour as being, firstly, terribly untrue and, secondly, hopelessly inappropriate' – Eric Field, *Advertising: the forgotten years* (1959). In a Guildhall speech on 9 November 1914, Winston Churchill said: 'The maxim of the British people is "Business as usual".' Rather curiously, a cartoon appeared in *Punch* on 12 August 1914 (i.e. just as war was breaking out) that showed a group of builders renovating a pub (and sitting around drinking thereat) with the caption: 'BUSINESS AS USUAL DURING ALTERATIONS'. The first occurrence of the phrase (though not used in this way) appears to be in Daniel Defoe, *A Journal of the Plague Year* (1722): '. . . the Apprehensions of its being the Infection went also quite away with my Illness, and I went about my Business as usual.' Dickens, Thackeray and Samuel Butler all used the phrase in the 19th century, but again not quite in this manner.

business before pleasure   A golden rule, known by 1767, but in this precise form only since 1837.

(a) busman's holiday   A holiday or break spent doing much the same as you do for a living – as though a bus driver were to go on a motoring holiday. Recorded by 1893. Oddly, the word 'busman' has virtually no existence outside this phrase.

bustling nightlife   'Bustling trade' was probably the forerunner of this travel writer's cliché. 'Bustling nightlife' was listed in *The Independent* 'DIY travel writers' cliché kit' (31 December 1988). 'I had now seen both sides of Ibiza – the bustling nightlife for which it is justly famed, and the less well-known northern coastline where white sandy beaches, hidden coves, beautiful countryside and clean shallow waters makes it an ideal family holiday haven' – *Today* (8 May

1993); 'Suffering businesses have hit on a plan to restore Asakusa's bustling trade and jazzy nightlife. They have pooled £300,000 to open a geisha school' – *The Daily Telegraph* (29 December 1993).

busy   See AS BUSY.

(the) Butcher   Nickname of Ulysses S. Grant (1822–85), commander-in-chief of Union forces in the American Civil War and 18th President of the US (1869–77). His opponents in the North called him this because they thought he was careless of the lives of men in his army. Critics opposed to tyrannical ways and his running for a third presidential term dubbed him **American Caesar**.

but I'm all right now   Catchphrase from the BBC radio show *ITMA* (1939–49). Sophie Tuckshop (Hattie Jacques) was always stuffing herself and giggling and pretending to suffer. Then, with a squeal, she would say this.

(the) butler did it!   The origins of this phrase – an (often ironic) suggested solution to detective stories in their 1920s and 30s heyday – remain a complete blank. A review of Edgar Wallace's play *The Man Who Changed His Name* in *Punch* (28 March 1928) appears to be alluding to the idea: 'For a long time, I must say, I thought the butler had something to do with it . . . I think the play would have been subtler if the unravelling of the mystery had included the butler.' A possible earlier sighting was recalled by a correspondent (1983) who said he had heard it spoken by a member of the audience after a showing of the last episode of the film series *The Exploits of Elaine* at a London cinema in *circa* 1916. Joseph R. Sandy noted: 'The detective was called Craig Kennedy and the butler's name was Bennet. I do not remember who played the parts (except the heroine, who was Pearl White) or anything much more about the serial.' Mary Roberts Rinehart, the American novelist (1878–1938), is sometimes credited with the phrase, though she does not actually use it in *The Circular Staircase* (1908) or *The Door* (1930) where butlers may be the guilty parties. The Georgette Heyer thriller *Why Shoot a Butler?* (1933) manages to avoid any mention of the phrase. Later, however, in Patricia Wentworth's *The Ivory Dagger* (1951) the butler really *does* do it. The earliest use of the phrase it is possible to give chapter and verse for is the caption to a *Punch* cartoon by Norman Mansbridge in the issue of 14 September 1938. Two policemen are shown standing outside a cinema that is showing *The Mansion Murder* and on the posters it asks 'Who killed the duke?' One policeman is saying to the other: 'I guessed the butler did it.' In 1956, Robert Robinson made an allusion in his Oxford thriller *Landscape With Dead Dons*: '"Well, well," said the Inspector, handing his coffee cup to Dimbleby, who was passing with a tray, "it always turns out to be the butler in the end".' The film *My Man Godfrey* (1957 – not the 1936 original), which is not even a whodunnit, contains the line: 'The butler did it! He made every lady in the house, oh, so very happy!' P. G. Wodehouse wrote *The Butler Did It* (1957), but this was known as *Something Fishy* in the UK.

but, Miss ——, you're beautiful (without your glasses on)! Were these phrases (or something like them) ever actually delivered in a Hollywood movie – or only in later parodies of the situation where a boss or producer discovers that his glasses-wearing secretary or auditionee is unexpectedly attractive when she takes them off? In Act 2 of William Inge's 1953 play *Picnic*, a Mrs Potts delivers the following speech, having just seen the plainer of two teenage daughters get dressed up: 'It's a miracle, that's what it is! I never knew Millie could look so pretty. It's just like a movie I saw once with Betty Grable – or was it Lana Turner? Anyway, she played the part of a secretary to some very important businessman. She wore glasses and did her hair real plain and men didn't pay any attention to her at all. Then one day she took off her glasses and her boss wanted to marry her right away! Now all the boys are going to fall in love with Millie!' So, a search was on for a Turner or Grable movie that fitted the bill. In a pictorial history of Paramount, the plot of *Thrill of a Lifetime* (US 1937) is summarized as: 'A prim secretary's yearning for her playwright boss is unrequited until she

takes off her glasses. (It was the boss, Leif Erickson, who needed them, considering she had been Betty Grable all along).' But the script of the movie does not contain anything approaching the key line. Following an earlier glasses-off moment, Dick Powell says to Ruby Keeler in *Footlight Parade* (US 1933), 'Oh, but what a change, you're beautiful.' Katharine Hepburn might seem to be alluding to the line when she comments to Cary Grant in *Bringing Up Baby* (US 1938), 'You're so good-looking without your glasses.' There is a particularly delicious moment between Humphrey Bogart and Dorothy Malone when, as a bookseller, she takes her glasses off and lets down her hair in *The Big Sleep* (US 1946), but the line itself is left unspoken. Indeed, the line only comes into its own when conscious allusions and parodies of the situation begin to occur in Hollywood movies – as, for example, in *The Bandwagon* (US 1953). In addition, a Peter Arno cartoon appeared in *The New Yorker* (20 May 1950) that shows a director on a movie set instructing an actor in his role *viz-à-vis* a hugely sexy actress: 'You've never noticed her, see? She's just an ordinary Plain Jane an' you're oblivious to her. Then alluva sudden she happens t'take off her glasses . . .' In fact, one doubts whether the *line* as such was ever actually spoken in the movies – only in parodies and allusions back to the *situation*. The line is cited in the song 'I Love a Film Cliché' by Dick Vosburgh and Trevor Lyttleton from the show *A Day in Hollywood, A Night in the Ukraine* (1980) in the form, 'Why, Miss Murray, without your glasses, you're . . . BEAUTIFUL!' In his introduction to *The Faber Book of Movie Verse* (1993), Philip French has the cliché as 'You look beautiful without your glasses' – 'a line that in endless variations reaches down to the 1992 Australian film *Strictly Ballroom*.'

but not in the South . . . A phrase with which to deflate or obstruct someone you are talking to. *Lifemanship* (1950) was the second volume of Stephen Potter's humorous exploration of the art of 'One-Upmanship', which he defined as 'how to make the other man feel that something has gone wrong, however slightly'. In discussing ways of putting down experts while in conversation with them, Potter introduces this 'blocking phrase' with which to disconcert, if not totally silence, them: '"Yes, but not in the South", with slight adjustments will do for any argument about any place, if not about any person.' In a footnote, Potter remarks: 'I am required to state that World Copyright of this phrase is owned by its brilliant inventor, Mr Pound' – though which 'Pound' he does not reveal. Indeed, the blocking move was known before this. Richard Usborne wrote of it in a piece called 'Not in the South' that is included in *The Pick of 'Punch'* (1941). He introduced a character called Eustace who had found a formula 'for appearing to be a European, and world, pundit. It was a formula that let me off the boredom of finding out facts and retaining knowledge.' It was to remark, 'Not in the South.'

butter   See BIG BUTTER; FINE WORDS.

butter fingers!   What you cry when a person has dropped something. Date of origin unknown but first found in connection with a cricketer who lets the ball slip through his fingers. 'At every bad attempt to catch, and every failure to stop the ball, he launched his personal displeasure at the head of the devoted individual in such denunciations as . . . butter-fingers, muff, humbug, and so forth' – Charles Dickens, *The Pickwick Papers*, Chap. 7 (1837); 'Swinging the hammer with a will, [he] discharged a smashing blow on his own knuckles . . . He crushed down an oath and substituted the harmless comment, "butter fingers!"' – R. L. Stevenson & Lloyd Osbourne, *The Wrong Box*, Chap. 5 (1889).

(the) butterfly effect   'Predictability: Does the Flap of a Butterfly's Wings in Brazil Set Off a Tornado in Texas?' was the title of a paper on predictability in weather forecasting delivered to the American Association for the Advancement of Science, Washington DC, on 29 December 1979 by Edward Lorenz (b. 1917), an American meteorologist. Apparently, Lorenz had originally used the image of a *seagull's* wing flapping. What is now called 'The Butterfly Effect' – how small acts lead to large – appeals to chaos theorists, who

view the physical universe as largely irregular and unpredictable. J. Gleick gives another example in *Chaos: Making a New Theory* (1988), also from weather forecasting: 'The notion that a butterfly stirring the air today in Peking can transform storm systems next month in New York.'

(to look as if) butter wouldn't melt in one's mouth   A phrase used critically of people who appear more innocent, harmless or demure than they can possibly be. A surprisingly ancient expression: 'He maketh as thoughe butter wolde nat melte in his mouthe' – Jehan Palsgrave, *Lesclarcissement de la langue françoyse* (1530). Presumably the suggestion is that the person so described looks so impossibly 'cool' that if butter was put in the (warm) mouth it still would not melt. Perhaps mostly used about women – as in Swift's *Polite Conversation* (1738)? Elsa Lanchester is supposed to have said of her fellow actress Maureen O'Hara: 'She looked as though butter wouldn't melt in her mouth. Or anywhere else' – quoted in *News Summaries* (30 January 1950).

but that's another story   Phrase with which (amusingly) to break off a narrative on the grounds of assumed irrelevance. The popularity of this catchphrase around 1900 derived from Rudyard Kipling. He used it in *Plain Tales from the Hills* (1888), but it had appeared earlier elsewhere. For example, in Laurence Sterne's *Tristram Shandy* (1760), it is intended to preclude one of the many digressions of which that novel is full.

buy some for Lulu   See WOT A LOT.

by and large   Meaning, 'generally speaking'. Originally this was a nautical term: to sail by and large meant to keep a ship on course so that it was sailing at a good speed even though the direction of the wind was changing. *Brewer* (1999) defines it thus: 'To sail close to the wind and slightly off it, so making it easier for the helmsman to steer and less likely for the vessel to be taken aback.' The nautical sense was current by 1669, the general sense by 1706.

—— by Christmas   PHRASES. At first, it was thought that the First World War would not last very long. Having started in August 1914, it would be 'over by Christmas', hence the unofficial, anti-German slogan **Berlin by Christmas**. The phrase **all over by Christmas** was used by some optimists as it had been in several previous wars – none of which was over by the Christmas in question. The fact that this promise was not fulfilled did not prevent Henry Ford from saying, as he tried to stop the war a year later: 'We're going to try to get the boys out of the trenches before Christmas. I've chartered a ship, and some of us are going to Europe.' He was not referring to American boys because the United States had not joined the war at this stage. The *New York Tribune* announced: 'GREAT WAR ENDS CHRISTMAS DAY. FORD TO STOP IT.' In her *Autobiography* (1977), Agatha Christie remembered that the South African War would 'all be over in a few weeks'. She went on: 'In 1914 we heard the same phrase. "All over by Christmas". In 1940, "Not much point in storing the carpets with mothballs" – this when the Admiralty took over my house – "It won't last over the winter".' In *Tribune* (28 April 1944), George Orwell recalled a young man 'on the night in 1940 when the big ack-ack barrage was fired over London for the first time', insisting, 'I tell you, it'll all be over by Christmas.' In his diary for 28 November 1950, Harold Nicolson wrote, 'Only a few days ago [General] MacArthur was saying, "Home by Christmas," and now he is saying, "This is a new war [Korea]".' *Flexner* (1976) comments: '*The war will be over by Christmas* was a popular 1861 expression [in the American Civil War]. Since then several generals and politicians have used the phrase or variations of it, in World War I, World War II, and the Korean war – and none of the wars was over by Christmas.' (Clever-clogs are apt to point out, however, that all wars are eventually over by *a* Christmas . . .)

bye bye, everyone See IZZY-WIZZY.

(a) bygone era Meaning, simply, 'a period in the past.' Date of origin unknown. A cliché, especially in tourist promotions, by the 1980s.

by Grand Central Station I sat down and wept See under —— BABYLON.

by gum, she's a hot 'un! Characteristic phrase of the (very) North of England comedian Frank Randle (1902–57) one of whose turns was as a randy old hitchhiker chiefly interested in girls' legs and ale. Randle was an earthy Lancastrian who did not travel well as a performer but has acquired something of a cult following now that he is safely dead. His other phrases included: **any more fer sailing?** and **by gum, ah've supped sum ale toneet** (compare WE'VE SOOPED SOME STOOFF . . . under RIGHT MONKEY!) Also: **would y'care for a Woodbine?** a cigarette-offering joke, believed to have been perpetrated by Randle in the film *Somewhere in England* (UK 1940). A correspondent suggests that what he actually said was 'Would you care for a Woodbine? Go on, take a big one' – and then offered a tin full of fag-ends. For 'by gum', see EE, BAH GUM.

by hook or by crook *OED2*, while finding a couple of references in the works of John Wycliffe around 1380, states firmly that while there are 'many theories', there is no firm evidence for the origin of this phrase meaning 'by some means or another'. In fact, the only real theory is the one about peasants in feudal times being allowed to take for firewood only those tree branches that they could pull down 'by hook or by crook' – 'crook' here meaning the hooked staff carried by shepherds (and also, symbolically, by bishops). 'By hook or by crook **I'll be last in this book**' is the cliché you append to the final page of an autograph book when asked to contribute a little something more than your signature.

by jingo! Now a mild and meaningless oath, this phrase derived its popularity from G. W. Hunt's notable anti-Russian music-hall song 'We Don't Want to Fight (But By Jingo If We Do . . .)' (1877). The song gave the words 'jingo' and 'jingoism' their modern meaning (excessive patriotism), but the oath had existed before this. *Punch* (3 February 1872) had a cartoon caption, 'Ghosts, by Jingo!' Motteux in his translation of Rabelais in 1694 put 'by jingo' for '*par dieu*', and there is some evidence to show that 'jingo' was conjuror's gibberish dating from a decade or two before.

by Jove, I needed that!   Used by several comedians, as though after consuming long-awaited alcoholic refreshment. Ken Dodd said it (1960s/70s) after a quick burst on the banjo to relieve tension. It may also have been used in the BBC radio *Goon Show*.

by their fruits shall ye know them
Meaning, 'you can judge people by the results they produce'. A direct quotation from Matthew 7:20 in the part of the Sermon on the Mount about being wary of false prophets.

by the pale moonlight (sometimes **in the pale moonlight)**   Poetic phrase, first found in Sir Walter Scott, *The Lay of the Last Minstrel*, Canto 2, St. 1 (1805): 'If thou would'st view fair Melrose aright, / Go visit it by the pale moonlight.' Next, 'in the pale moonlight' occurs in Charles Dickens, *The Old Curiosity Shop*, Chap. 43 (1840). Then from the song 'Who Were You With Last Night?' (1912), written by the British composer of music-hall songs Fred Godfrey (1889–1953) with Mark Sheridan: 'Who were you with last night? / Out in the pale moonlight'. John Masefield's 'Captain Stratton's Fancy' (1903) has: 'And some are all for dancing by the pale moonlight'; and from the much later film *Batman* (US 1989): 'Have you ever danced with the devil in the pale moonlight?'

(to get/have someone) by the short and curlies   To have someone in a metaphorical position from which it is impossible to escape – from the fact that if someone is holding you by the short (and sometimes curly) hairs on the back of the neck, it is very painful. The phrase probably does not have anything to do with pubic hairs. Recorded by Eric Partridge as British forces' slang in 1948 and dated by him to about 1935. This would seem to be an extension of **to get/have someone by the short hairs**, which dates from 1905 at least and possibly back to the 1890s.

by the sword divided   Consciously archaic phrase devised for the title of the BBC TV historical drama *By the Sword Divided* (1983–5). Set in the English Civil War, this series was created by John Hawkesworth who commented (1991): 'When I first wrote down the idea for a story about the Civil War I called it *The Laceys of Arnescote* . . . [but] I decided the title didn't convey the sort of Hentyish swashbuckling style that we were aiming at, so I thought again. The title *By the Sword Divided* came to me as I was walking along a beach in Wales.' Earlier, in dealing with the Civil War period, Macaulay had written in his *History of England*, Chaps. 1–2 (1848): 'Thirteen years followed during which England was . . . really governed by the sword'; 'the whole nation was sick of government by the sword'; 'anomalies and abuses . . . which had been destroyed by the sword'.

C

cabbage-looking   See I'M NOT SO.

Cabbage Patch Kids   Millions of soft, ugly dolls with this name were sold in 1983–4. Created by American entrepreneur Xavier Roberts, they became a craze around the world. People did not purchase them but, tweely, 'adopted' them. Whereas, in Britain, babies that are not delivered **by the stork** are found **under a gooseberry bush**, in the USA, they are found in 'cabbage patches'. The 'stork' and 'cabbage-patch' theories of childbirth were known by 1923; the 'gooseberry-bush' by 1903. Compare *Mrs Wiggs of the Cabbage Patch* (1901), the title of a US children's novel by Alice Hegan Rice.

cabbages and kings   Phrase from Lewis Carroll's 'Walrus and the Carpenter' episode in *Through the Looking Glass and What Alice Found There*, Chap. 4 (1871): 'The time has come,' the Walrus said, / 'To talk of many things: / Of shoes – and ships – and sealing-wax – / Of cabbages and kings . . .'. The American writer O. Henry took *Cabbages and Kings* as the title of his first collection of short stories (1904), and there is a book, *Of Kennedys and Kings: making sense of the Sixties* by Harris Wofford (1980). However, the alliterative conjunction of 'cabbages' and 'kings' pre-dates Carroll. In Hesketh Pearson's *Smith of Smiths*, a biography of the Reverend Sydney Smith (d. 1845), he quotes Smith as saying about a certain Mrs George Groce: 'She had innumerable hobbies, among them horticulture and democracy, defined by Sydney as "the most approved methods of growing cabbages and destroying kings".'

Caesar's wife must be above suspicion
An example of this phrase occurs in Lord Chesterfield's letters (*circa* 1740): 'Your moral character must be not only pure, but, like Caesar's wife, unsuspected.' Originally, it was Julius Caesar himself who said this of his wife, Pompeia, when he divorced her in 62 BC. In North's translation of Plutarch's *Lives* – which is how the saying came into English in 1570 – Caesar is quoted thus: 'I will not, sayd he, that my wife be so much as suspected.' Pompeia was Caesar's second wife, and, according to Suetonius, in 61 BC she took part in the women-only rites of the Feast of the Great Goddess. But it was rumoured that a profligate called Publius Clodius attended, wearing women's clothes, and that he committed adultery with Pompeia. Caesar divorced Pompeia and at the subsequent inquiry into the desecration was asked why he had done so. 'Caesar's wife must be above suspicion,' he replied. He later married Calphurnia.

ça ira ... à la lanterne 'Ah! Ah! ça ira, ça ira / Les aristocrates à la lanterne' is the refrain of the French revolutionary song, first heard when the Parisians marched on Versailles (5–6 October 1789). *Ça ira*, though almost impossible to translate, means something like 'That will certainly happen', 'It will go', 'Things will work out.' *À la lanterne* is the equivalent of the modern 'string 'em up' (*lanterne* being a street lamp in Paris useful for hanging aristocrats from). The inspiration for the first line of the refrain *may* have been Benjamin Franklin's recent use of the phrase in connection with the American Revolu-

tion of 1776. After the French Revolution, the phrase *Ça ira* caught on quickly in Britain and the song was included in an opera at Covent Garden in 1790.

cakes and ale A synonym for 'enjoyment', as in the expression 'life isn't all cakes and ale'. On 4 May 1876, the Reverend Francis Kilvert wrote in his diary: 'The clerk's wife brought out some cakes and ale and pressed me to eat and drink. I was to have returned to Llysdinam to luncheon . . . but as I wanted to see more of the country and the people I decided to let the train go by, accept the hospitality of my hostess and the cakes and ale which life offered, and walk home quietly in the course of the afternoon' – a neat demonstration of the literal and metaphorical uses of the phrase. *Cakes and Ale* is the title of a novel (1930) by W. Somerset Maugham. The phrase comes from Sir Toby Belch's remark to Malvolio in Shakespeare's *Twelfth Night*, II.iii.114 (1600): 'Does thou think, because thou art virtuous, there shall be no more cakes and ale?'. The Arden edition comments that cakes and ale were 'traditionally associated with festivity, and disliked by Puritans both on this account and because of their association with weddings, saints' days, and holy days'.

Calcutta See BLACK HOLE; OH!

call See ANSWER THE; DON'T CALL US.

(to) call a spade a spade To speak bluntly, to call things by their proper names without resorting to euphemisms. But why a spade? Said to have arisen when Erasmus mistranslated a passage in Plutarch's *Apophthegmata* where the object that 'Macedonians had not the wit to call a spade by any other name than a spade' was rather a trough, basin, bowl or boat in the original Greek. The phrase was in the English language, however, by 1539.

calling all cars, calling all cars! What the police controller says over the radio to patrolmen in American cop films and TV series of the 1950s. For some reason, it is the archetypal cop phrase of the period, and evocative. However, the formula had obviously been known before this if the British film titles *Calling All Stars* (1937),

Calling All Ma's (1937) and *Calling All Cars* (1954) are anything to go by. Indeed, the phrase appears in an American advertisement for Western Electric radio equipment, dated 1936.

call me madam When Frances Perkins was appointed Secretary of Labor by President Roosevelt in 1933, she became the first American woman to hold Cabinet rank. It was told that when she had been asked *in Cabinet* how she wished to be addressed, she had replied: 'Call me Madam.' She denied that she had done this, however. It was *after* her first Cabinet meeting when reporters asked how they should address her. The Speaker-elect of the House of Representatives, Henry T. Rainey, answered for her: 'When the Secretary of Labor is a lady, she should be addressed with the same general formalities as the Secretary of Labor who is a gentleman. You call him "Mr Secretary". You will call her "Madam Secretary". You gentlemen know that when a lady is presiding over a meeting, she is referred to as "Madam Chairman" when you rise to address the chair' – quoted in George Martin, *Madam Secretary – Frances Perkins* (1976). Some of the reporters put this ruling into Perkins's own mouth and that presumably is how the misquotation occurred. Irving Berlin's musical *Call Me Madam* was first performed on Broadway in 1950, starring Ethel Merman as a woman ambassador appointed to represent the USA in a tiny European state. It was inspired by the case of Pearl Mesta, the society hostess whom Harry Truman had appointed as US Ambassador to Luxembourg.

(the) call of the unknown (or **challenge ...)** Not recorded in *OED2*. Found in the speech that the Norwegian explorer Fridtjof Nansen gave when he was installed as Rector of the University of Aberdeen in November 1926: 'We will find in the lives of men who have done anything, of those whom we call great men, that it is this spirit of adventure, the call of the unknown, that has lured and urged them along on their course . . .'

(a) callow youth An immature, inexperienced young person (in slightly archaic

use). 'One overhears a callow youth of twenty address a still fascinating belle of forty' – A. M. Binstead, *More Gal's Gossip* (1901); 'There is a slightly awkward father-and-son relationship here between the gullible, disapproving, callow youth who lived and the sophisticated man who writes, and it is the open unresolvability of this tension which makes the book so recognisable and so true' – *The Guardian* (17 May 1994); 'On his first ever visit to the regal ski resort of St Moritz, King Farouk of Egypt, then a callow youth, felt a sartorial fool. He had arrived at the Suvretta House Hotel wearing a black morning suit and nervelessly flicked back the tails as he helped his mother' – *Daily Mail* (24 December 1994).

(the) camera cannot lie (or **does not lie** or **never lies)** A 20th-century proverb, though its origins have not been recorded. In the script for the commentary of a film ('Six Commissioned Texts', I., 1962), W. H. Auden wrote: 'The camera's eye / Does not lie, / But it cannot show / The life within.' 'The camera cannot lie. But it can be an accessory to the untruth' – Harold Evans, *Pictures on a Page* (1978).

camel See EYE OF.

came the dawn (or **comes the dawn)** A stock phrase of romantic fiction in the early 20th century – also reported to have been a subtitle or inter-title from the early days of cinema. C. A. Lejeune wrote that it was one of the screen title captions illustrated by Alfred Hitchcock in his early days in the cinema, 'in black letters on a white ground.' This is confirmed by François Truffaut's *Hitchcock* (English version, 1968) in which Hitchcock refers to it as 'narrative title'. He also mentions a similar title phrase: 'The next morning . . .' 'Came the Dawn' was the title of a P. G. Wodehouse short story reprinted in *Mulliner Omnibus* (1927). The phrase is spoken by Tony Cavendish in the George S. Kaufman/Edna Ferber play *The Royal Family* (1927), in which he is a swashbuckling silent film actor, given to speaking in the clichés of screen titling. Again, the line is spoken in the film *The Bad and the Beautiful* (US 1952) to describe the change of scene the morning after a party and a gambling loss. It is quoted as 'Comes the Dawn' in *Flexner* (1982). Before the coming of film sound, it was possible for a catchphrase to emerge from this kind of use. In *A Fool There Was* (US 1914), Theda Bara 'spoke' the inter-title **kiss me, my fool**, and this was taken up as a fad expression. Similarly, Jacqueline Logan 'said' **harness my zebras** in Cecil B. De Mille's *King of Kings* (US 1925). This became a fad expression for 'let's leave' or as a way of expressing amazement – 'Well, harness my zebras!'

(as) camp as a row of tents Extremely affected, outrageous, over the top. A pun on the word 'camp', which came into general use in the 1960s to describe the manner and behaviour of (especially) one type of homosexual male. As it happens, one of the suggested origins for the word 'camp' in this sense is that it derives from 'camp followers', the female prostitutes who would accompany an army on its journeyings to service the troops in or adjacent to their tents.

can a (bloody) duck swim! (sometimes **does/will a fish swim!**) This is said by way of meaning 'You bet!', 'Of course, I will'. *ODP* has 'Will a duck swim?' in 1842. Winston Churchill claimed he said the 'can' version to Stanley Baldwin when the Prime Minister asked if he would accept the post of Chancellor of the Exchequer in the 1924 government. Lady Violet Bonham Carter spoke the phrase *to* Churchill when he asked her to serve as a Governor of the BBC in 1941. After this, he referred to her as his 'Bloody Duck', and she had to sign her letters to him, 'Your BD'.

(he/she) can dish it out but can't take it in Said of people who are unable to accept the kind of criticism they dispense to others. A reader's letter to *Time* Magazine (4 January 1988) remarked of comedienne Joan Rivers's action in suing a magazine for misquoting her about her late husband: 'For years she has made big money at the expense of others with her caustic remarks. Obviously Rivers can dish it out but can't take it in.' The idiomatic phrase was established by the 1930s. In the film *Little Caesar* (US 1931), Edward G. Robinson says, 'He could dish it out but he

couldn't take it in.' In the film *49th Parallel* (1941), Raymond Massey, as a Canadian soldier, apparently plays with the phrase when he says to a Nazi, 'When things go wrong, we can take it. We can dish it out, too.'

candle See CARE OF; HOLD A.

(a) candle in the wind The song 'Candle in the Wind' (1973) has words by Bernie Taupin and music by Elton John. The opening words 'Goodbye Norma Jean' refer to Marilyn Monroe (who was born Norma Jean Mortenson/Baker): 'It seems to me you lived your life / Like a candle in the wind. / Never knowing who to cling to / When the rain set in. / And I would have liked to have known you / But I was just a kid / That candle burned out long before / Your legend ever did.' Elton John sang a revised version of the song at the funeral of Princess Diana (7 September 1997): 'Goodbye England's rose; / May you ever grow in our hearts . . ./ And it seems to me you lived your life / Like a candle in the wind; / Never fading with the sunset / When the rain set in.' But where did the original title phrase come from? *Mencken* (1942) gives 'Man's life is like a candle in the wind' as a 'Chinese proverb'. A French dictionary of proverbs lists *'La vie de l'homme est comme une chandelle dans le vent'* as Chinese. A Dutch collection of Oriental quotations has: 'What is the life of Man? A candle in the wind, hoar frost on the roof, the spasm of a fish in the frying pan.' A poem by the Chinese poet Bai Juyi (772–846) describing the illusory character of reality contains the phrase 'a candle's flame in the wind.' A Latin emblem book by the French author Denis Lebey de Batilly (1596 edn) has a picture of a man seated at a table amidst classicist architecture. On the table is not a candle but a classical oil-lamp with burning wick. Big clouds with faces and puffed-up cheeks blow at the flame. The Latin motto is (in corrected form): *'QUID EST HOMO SICVT LVCERNA IN VENTO POSITA* [what is Man but a lamp in the wind].' The four-line Latin commentary says, in translation (from German): 'Man is like a small lamp, which in the dark night is exposed to the winds blowing from all sides. His flame of life feeds on such meagre, such unreliable oil

– it is extinguished when the gale of Death grabs it.' The English novelist George Meredith later majored in wind-blown candle images in several of his novels. 'The light of every soul burns upward. Of course, most of them are candles in the wind. Let us allow for atmospheric disturbance' is from his novel, *Diana of the Crossways*, Chap. 39 (1885), where it is spoken by the heroine. Charles Joaquin Quirk, an American Catholic priest and a professor at Loyola University, published a book with the title *Candles in the Wind* in 1931. There is also a book with the same title by Maud Diver (1909). Alexander Solzhenitsyn wrote a play entitled *Candle in the Wind* (1960) about moral choices in any society, either communist or capitalist. The original Russian title was *Svecha na vetru: (svet kotoryj v tebe)* [(A) candle in the wind: (the light which is in thee)], which refers to Luke 11:35. Of course, Taupin may not have been aware of any of these earlier uses. Indeed, according to Philip Norman's biography of Elton John, *Elton* (1991), Taupin heard that someone had applied the phrase to the singer Janis Joplin (1943–70), 'also doomed to early death from drugs', and took it on from there.

can do! 'Yes, I can do it!' in a sort of Pidgin English, popular in the Royal Navy before the First World War. The opposite **no can do** was established by the time of the Second World War.

can I do you now, sir? From *ITMA*, and one of the two greatest catchphrases from the BBC radio show (1939–49). It was spoken by Mrs Mopp (Dorothy Summers), the hoarse-voiced charlady or 'Corporation Cleanser', when entering the office of Tommy Handley, as the Mayor. Curiously, the first time Mrs Mopp used the phrase, on 10 October 1940, she said, 'Can I do *for* you now, sir?' This was soon replaced by the familiar emphases of 'Can I *do* you *now*, sir?' that people could still be heard using decades later. Bob Monkhouse recalled (1979) that Dorothy Summers said: 'Oh, I do wish people wouldn't expect me to be only Mrs Mopp. That awful char. I never wanted to say it in the first place. I think it was rather distasteful.' She seems to have been the only person to detect any double meaning in it.

can I phone a friend? Contestant to host (Chris Tarrant) in the original British version of the TV quiz *Who Wants To Be a Millionaire?* (1999–). Before answering questions, contestants were encouraged to firm up their resolve by consulting the studio audience or by phoning a friend who had been lined up in advance.

cannon fodder Soldiers regarded as people whose only purpose is to get killed in battle. This may be seen as a translation of the German *Kanonenfutter* (known by the 1840s) or the French *chair à canon* (current at about the same time). However, a letter from Captain Richard Pope, describing Marlborough's cavalry in 1703, uses the phrase with confidence, suggesting that it was an established concept even then: 'Such a set of ruffians and imbeciles you never beheld, you may call them cannon fodder, but never soldiers.' Indeed, Shakespeare has the phrase 'food for powder', meaning the same thing, in *Henry IV, Part 1*, IV.ii.65 (1597).

(a) can of worms An unpleasantly complicated problem, as in such phrases as 'that's another can of worms', 'let's not open that can of worms'. The image is that of opening a can of tinned food only to find that it is full of writhing maggots. So the implication is that it would be better not to look into something in case it presents unexpected problems. Probably of American origin, by the late 1940s. 'Mr Berger has opened, in an old American phrase, a fine can of worms. He is suggesting that an impeached President, should he be found guilty, could appeal to the Supreme Court' – *The Times* (22 May 1973).

can't be bad! Congratulatory response to good news, popular in Britain in the 1970s – 'I've made a date with that well-stacked blonde in the typing pool' – 'Can't be bad!' Possibly linked to the usage in the Beatles' song 'She Loves You' (1963): 'Because she loves you / And you know that can't be bad . . .' 'Further up the pecking order is the 27-ish woman who left to set up a gilt-trading operation at a rival for £300,000. "She's nothing special, but she'll stay three years and do an okay job for them, and from her point of view it can't be bad"' –

The Independent (13 May 1994); 'Colin Montgomerie three-putted for the first time in the week as he shot a 72 for 279, but he insisted: "After taking four weeks off and tying for 17th place in America, that can't be bad"' – *Daily Record* (6 March 1995); 'Uncomfortable parallels between Dracula and Nicolae Ceausescu, the former Stalinist dictator, meant that such a gathering was impossible in the Communist era. But now Europe's second poorest country after Albania can cash in on the legend. Can't be bad for garlic growers either' – *Financial Times* (22 May 1995).

(he) can't chew gum and fart at the same time He is really stupid and incapable. The most notable use of this (presumably traditional American) jibe was by President Lyndon Johnson about the man who was eventually to turn into another US President: 'That Gerald Ford. He can't fart and chew gum at the same time' – quoted in Richard Reeves, *A Ford Not a Lincoln* (1975), and in J. K. Galbraith, *A Life in Our Times* (1981). This is the correct version of the euphemistic: 'He couldn't walk and chew gum at the same time.'

can't pay, won't pay Slogan adopted by those objecting to the British government's Community Charge or 'poll tax' in 1990 and by other similar protest groups. *Can't Pay, Won't Pay* was the English title of the play *Non Si Paga! Non Si Paga!* (1974) by Dario Fo, as translated by Lino Pertile (1981).

(you) can't throw a brick without hitting ... It is very easy to do something because you can't miss. 'Combe Regis is just the place for you. Perfect hot-bed of golf. Full of the finest players. Can't throw a brick without hitting an amateur champion' – P. G. Wodehouse, *Love Among the Chickens*, Chap. 2 (1906/1921). 'In a Lancashire cotton-town you could probably go for months on end without once hearing an "educated" accent, whereas there can hardly be a town in the South of England where you could throw a brick without hitting the niece of a bishop – George Orwell, *The Road to Wigan Pier* (1937). Obviously, this is a development of what appears in Mark Twain, *The Inno-*

cents Abroad, Chap. 37 (1869): 'I could throw a rock here without hitting a captain . . . You'd fetch the captain of the watch, maybe.'

can we talk? Stock phrase of Joan Rivers, the American comedienne and TV chat-show host, by 1984.

(the) canyons of your mind Title phrase of Vivian Stanshall's 1968 hit song 'Canyons of Your Mind' (with the Bonzo Dog Band): 'In the canyons of your mind / I will wander through your brain / To the ventricles of your heart, my dear / I'm in love with you again.' Curiously, the phrase was taken from the 1966 Val Doonican hit 'Elusive Butterfly' (written by Bob Lind, who had recorded it himself in 1965): 'You might have heard my footsteps / Echo softly through the distance / In the canyons of your mind.'

can you hear me, mother? The British comedian Sandy Powell (1900–82) recalled in 1979: 'It was in about 1932/3, when I was doing an hour's show on the radio, live, from Broadcasting House in London. I was doing a sketch called "Sandy at the North Pole". I was supposed to be broadcasting home and wanting to speak to my mother. When I got to the line, "Can you hear me, mother?" I dropped my script on the studio floor. While I was picking up the sheets all I could do was repeat the phrase over and over. Well, that was on a Saturday night. The following week I was appearing at the Hippodrome, Coventry, and the manager came to me at the band rehearsal with a request: "You'll say that, tonight, won't you?" I said, "What?" He said, "'Can you hear me, mother?' Everybody's saying it. Say it and see." So I did and the whole audience joined in and I've been stuck with it ever since. Even abroad – New Zealand, South Africa, Rhodesia, they've all heard it. I'm not saying it was the first radio catchphrase – they were all trying them out – but it was the first to catch on.'

can you tell Stork from butter? Slogan for Stork margarine in the UK from *circa* 1956. One of the earliest slogans on British commercial TV, it was invariably alluded to in parodies of TV advertising. In the original ads, housewives were shown taking part in comparative tests and tasting pieces of bread spread with either real butter or with Stork.

captains courageous The phrase comes from a ballad, 'Mary Ambree', included in Thomas Percy's *Reliques* (1765): 'When captains courageous whom death could not daunt, / Did march to the siege of the city of Gaunt, / They mustered their soldiers by two and by three, / And the foremost in battle was Mary Ambree.' Hence, *Captains Courageous*, title of a novel (1897) by Rudyard Kipling.

captains of industry Prominent figures in business and commerce. 'Captains of Industry' was a heading in Thomas Carlyle's *Past and Present* (1843). 'A hardnosed captain of industry who wanted a pretty mannequin from tidewater aristoc-racy' – D. Anthony, *Long Hard Cure* (1979); 'So where are the captains of industry, the entrepreneurs and knights of yesteryear – the modern equivalents of those Victorian worthies who steered the once-great civic authorities? Are local councils dying, victims of local apathy and central government emasculation?' – *Independent on Sunday* (1 May 1994); 'He has created his own brand of lobbying where prospective clients are wooed by conversation littered with the names of MPs and ministers, captains of industry and mandarins and the endless parties and lunches which they all attend' – *Daily Telegraph* (21 October 1994).

caravan See DOGS BARK.

carbon-copy murders Killings that replicate other recent crimes and may have been inspired by them. Journalistic cliché by the 1950s/60s. Listed by Keith Waterhouse as a cliché to be avoided in *Daily Mirror Style* (1981). But who knows what carbon paper is nowadays? 'Victim of the week-old "carbon copy" murder' – *Daily Telegraph* (3 April 1961); 'Detectives probing that crime revealed they are checking for possible links with the "carbon copy" murder of housewife Wendy Speakes at Wakefield, Yorkshire, a year ago . . . A spokesman for Lincolnshire police said last night: "We have requested the file on the Wakefield case because of the similarities with our inquiry. It appears

to be a carbon copy murder"' – *Daily Mirror* (12 October 1994).

carcase See HABEAS.

card-carrying Paid-up, committed members of any movement (but mostly political or social). 'The most dangerous Communists in the nation today are not the open, avowed, card-carrying party members' – Bert Andrews, *Washington Witch Hunt*, Chap. 2 (1948).

cared See AS IF I.

careful See BE GOOD AND.

careless talk costs lives Security slogan, during the war, in the UK, from mid-1940. This became the most enduring of security slogans, especially when accompanied by Fougasse cartoons – showing two men in a club, for example, one saying to the other '. . . strictly between four walls' (behind them is a painting through which Hitler's head is peeping), or two women gossiping in front of Hitler wallpaper. Compare **loose talk costs lives** – security slogan (USA only) from the same war.

care of candle ends Proverbial expres-sion for making petty economies. It is possible to melt the stubs of candles down and make new candles from the wax. The *OED2* has a citation from 1668, referring to filching candle ends and laying them away, which is not conclusive. But the following citation from 1732 is quite clearly an allusion: 'When Hopkins dies, a thousand lights attend / Who living, sav'd a candle's end" – Alexander Pope *Moral Essays – Epistle III to Allen Lord Bathhurst* (1732). In the days when candles were a major expense in grand houses, the candle ends were a perquisite of certain servants, to be re-used or sold. British Prime Ministers W. E. Gladstone and John Major seem to have defended themselves from accusations of 'saving candle ends' by arguing that 'many a mickle maks a muckle'. 'There were scenes of wild enthusiasm, bordering on delirium, in the streets of London yesterday as [Prime Minister] John Major spoke out once more – with all the passion at his command – on the topic of the Citizen's Charter. Oh, yes. It has been criticised for dealing with a lot of little things. But, said Mr Major, quoting the less colourful Mr Gladstone, ". . . if you add the candle ends together you get a whole candle'" – *The Guardian* (4 December 1992).

caring and sharing The word 'caring' – to describe official 'care' of the disadvantaged – was stretched almost to breaking point during the 1980s to embrace almost anybody concerned with social and welfare services, in all sorts of combinations that sought to manipulate the hearer. Marginally worse was the facile rhyme of 'caring and sharing' used, for example, to promote a Telethon-type fund-raiser in Melbourne, Australia (November 1981). The phrase is probably of American origin: 'The love I feel for our adopted children is in no way less strong than the love I feel for the three children in our family who were born to us . . . It is the caring and sharing that count' – Claudia L. Jewett, *Adopting the Older Child* (1978); 'Jeffrey, a very famous model, was walking along a sandy beach, the salt wind ruffling his hair, a small boy on his shoulders. "Caring and sharing, you see," murmured Geary' – *Daily Telegraph* (11 June 1994).

carpe diem Motto meaning 'enjoy the day while you have the chance' or 'make the most of the present time, seize the opportunity.' From the *Odes* of the Roman poet Horace. Another translation of the relevant passage is: 'While we're talking, envious time is fleeing: / Seize the day, put no trust in the future.'

(to) carry a torch for (someone) To love someone who does not reciprocate. Since the 1920s. Perhaps because Venus is sometimes depicted as carrying a torch. 'When a fellow "carries the torch" it doesn't simply imply that he is "lit up" or drunk, but girl-less. His steady has quit him for another or he is lonesome for her' – *Vanity Fair* (NY) (November 1927).

carry on —— It is fitting that the injunction to 'carry on', a staple part of several catch- and stock phrases, should have been celebrated in the more than thirty titles of British film comedies in the *Carry On* series. The very first of the films showed the origin: *Carry On, Sergeant* (1958) was about a sergeant attempting to discipline a platoon of extremely raw recruits. 'Carry on, sergeant' is what an officer would say, having addressed some homily to the ranks before walking off and leaving the sergeant to get on with his drill, or whatever. The actual services origin of the phrase is, however, nautical. From the *Daily Chronicle* (24 July 1909): '"Carry on!" is a word they have in the Navy. It is the "great word" of the service . . . To-morrow the workaday life of the Fleet begins again and the word will be, "Carry on!"' Other citings: *Carry On, Jeeves* – as the title of P. G. Wodehouse's collection of stories (1925); in 1936, when President F. D. Roosevelt was seeking re-election, a Democratic slogan was 'Carry on, Roosevelt'. A cable from the Caribbean was received in Whitehall during the summer of 1940: 'Carry on, Britain! Barbados is behind you!' When Sub-Lieutenant Eric Barker (1912–90) starred in the Royal Navy version of the BBC radio show *Merry Go Round* (*circa* 1945), his favourite command to others was, 'Carry on, smokin'!' Jimmy Jewel (1912–95) of the double-act Jewel and Warriss would refer to Ben Warriss (d. 1993) as 'Harry Boy' and say 'Carry on, 'Arry Boy! Tell 'em, boy. Has Harry Boy been up to something naughty?' When some dreadful tale had been unfolded, Jewel would cap it with 'What a carry on!' This last phrase became the title of a film the two comedians made in 1949. In his autobiography (1982), Jewel remarked that Tommy Trinder 'stole' the line 'and later we almost came to blows over it'.

carry on, London! At the end of the BBC radio topical interview show *In Town Tonight* (1933–60), a stentorian voice would bellow this to get the traffic moving again. Various people were 'The Voice', but Freddie Grisewood may have been the first. See also ONCE AGAIN WE STOP THE MIGHTY ROAR . . .

(to) carry the can To bear responsibility; take the blame; become a scapegoat. This is possibly a military term, referring to the duties of the man chosen to get beer for a group. He would have to carry a container of beer to the group and then carry it back when it was empty. Some consider it to be precisely naval in origin; no example before 1936. Alternatively, it could refer to the man who had to remove 'night soil' from earth closets – literally, carrying the can – and leave an empty can in its place. Or then again, it could have to do with the 'custom of miners carrying explosives to the coal face in a tin can (hence everyone's reluctance to "carry the can")' – *Street Talk* (1986).

cart See IN THE.

carved See ALL JOINTS.

casbah See COME WITH ME.

(a) case of the tail wagging the dog
Phrase suggesting that the proper roles in a situation have been reversed. Known by 1907. 'The tail wagged the dog in this case and it still often does' – William Hollingsworth Whyte, *The Organization Man* (1956); 'This film came with a seal of approval, from Peter Benchley, the man who wrote *Jaws*, which is a bit like Michael Crichton rubber-stamping a scientist's findings on the stegosaurus. Given that the novelist whose thrills are drawn from the natural world is reliant on the knowledge of experts, this was a particularly implausible case of the tail wagging the dog' – *The Independent* (15 April 1995).

(the) case is altered
Sometimes '"The case is altered", quoth Plowden' – a proverbial expression derived from a law case in which the lawyer Edmund Plowden himself featured. A Roman Catholic, Plowden was arrested some time after 1570 for the treasonable offence of attending a surreptitious mass. He defended himself and was able to prove that the priest who had presided over the mass in question was an agent provocateur. Accordingly, he argued that a true mass could not be celebrated by an impostor – so 'the case is altered' – and was acquitted. Another, less likely, origin is given by Henry G. Bohn in *A Hand-Book of Proverbs* (1855): 'Plowden being asked by a neighbour of his, what remedy there was in law against his neighbour for some hogs that had trespassed his ground, answered, he might have very good remedy; but the other replying, that they were his [i.e. Plowden's] hogs, Nay then, neighbour, (quoth he), the case is altered.' The phrase

was much quoted. In Shakespeare's *King Henry VI, Part 3*, IV.iii.30 (1590–1) there occurs the following exchange: *King Edward*: 'Why, Warwick, when we parted, / Thou call'dst me King.' / *Warwick*: 'Ay, but the case is alter'd: / When you disgrac'd me in my embassade, / Then I degraded you from being King, / And come now to create you Duke of York.' It occurs in Thomas Kyd, *Soliman and Perseda*, II.i.292 (1592), and Ben Jonson's play with the title *The Case Is Altered* (1598–9). The dying Queen Elizabeth I is sometimes quoted as having said in 1603: 'I am tied, I am tied, and the case is altered with me' – Elizabeth Jenkins, *Elizabeth the Great* (1958). From all this, The Case Is Altered is also the name given to a number of public houses in Britain though it is sometimes erroneously said to be a corruption of the Spanish *casa alta* (high house). In addition, 'The Case is Altered' was the provisional title of J. M. Barrie's play *The Admirable Crichton* (1902) – an allusion surviving in the line 'Circumstances might alter cases' (Act 1, Sc. 1). It is also the title of a book (1932) by William Plomer.

(to) cash/throw in one's chips/checks
Meaning, originally, 'to stop gambling' but then 'to die' and, as *DOAS* has it: 'to terminate a business transaction, sell one's share of, or stock in, a business, or the like, in order to realize one's cash profits'. It also may mean 'to make a final gesture'. Tom Mangold wrote in *The Listener* (8 September 1983) concerning the US arms race in space: 'Under malign command, a technological guarantee of invulnerability could induce the holder to cash his chips and go for a pre-emptive first strike.'

cast adrift in an open boat This is listed as a film cliché by Leslie Halliwell in *The Filmgoer's Book of Quotes* (1978 edition), though it is not one really. It cannot have been used sufficiently for it to become a worn-out phrase even though the combination of words does have a certain inevitability. The words are used in the film *Mutiny on the Bounty* (US 1935) concerning the fate of Captain Bligh. The phrase recurs in the BBC radio *Goon Show*, 'Drums Along the Mersey' (11 October 1956).

(with a) cast of thousands Now only used jokingly and ironically, this type of film promotion line *may* have made its first appearance in connection with the 1927 version of *Ben Hur* where the boast was, 'Cast of 125,000'!

(to) cast one's bread upon the waters Meaning 'to reap as you shall sow', after Ecclesiastes 11:1: 'Cast thy bread upon the waters: for thou shalt find it after many days.' Oddly expressed, the idea is that if you sow seed or corn in a generous fashion now, you will reap the benefits in due course. The New English Bible translates this passage more straightfor- wardly as, 'Send your grain across the seas, and in time you will get a return'.

cat See BRING BACK THE.

(to) catch a falling star To perform something miraculous. After John Donne, 'Go, and catch a falling star / Get with child a mandrake root, / Tell me, where all past years are. / Or who cleft the Devil's foot' – 'Song' in *Songs and Sonnets* (1611). Since at least 1563 a 'falling star' has been another name for a meteor or shooting star. Here, the catching is clearly just one of four impossible tasks. 'Catch a falling star' was also the title of a 1958 song popularized by Perry Como: 'Catch a falling star / And put it in your pocket, / Never let it fade away.'

catch as catch can Another alliterative phrase, one of many that expresses the getting hold of things in any way you can. These have been around since the 14th century (compare 'by hook or by crook'). Compare 'catch me who can' (in a steam engine advert, 1803) and the film titles *Catch Us If You Can* (UK 1965) and *Catch Me If You Can* (about a confidence trick- ster) (US 2002).

(a/the) catcher in the rye *The Catcher in the Rye* is the title of a novel (1951) by J. D. Salinger, about the emergent seven- teen-year-old Holden Caulfield. As ex- plained in Chap. 22, it comes from a vision he has of standing in a field of rye below a cliff where he will catch any children who fall off. He wishes to protect innocent children from disillusionment with the world of grown-ups. The phrase comes from a misreading of the song 'Comin'

Thro' the Rye' by Robert Burns that contains the lines: 'Gin a body meet a body / Comin' thro' the rye.'

Catch-22 Phrase encapsulating the popular view that 'there's always a catch' – some underlying law that defeats people by its brutal, ubiquitous logic. *Catch-22* was the title of a novel (1961; film US 1970) by Joseph Heller about a group of US fliers in the Second World War. 'It was a Catch-22 situation,' people will say, as if resorting to a quasi-proverbial expression like 'Heads you win, tails I lose' or 'Damned if you do, damned if you don't'. Oddly, though, Heller had originally numbered it 18 (apparently *Catch-18* was dropped to avoid confusion with Leon Uris's novel *Mila-18*). In the book, the idea is explored several times. Captain Yossarian, a US Air Force bombardier, does not wish to fly any more missions. He goes to see the group's MO, Doc Daneeka, about getting grounded on the grounds that he is crazy: *Daneeka:* 'There's a rule saying I have to ground anyone who's crazy.' *Yossarian:* 'Then why can't you ground me? I'm crazy.' *Daneeka:* 'Anyone who wants to get out of combat duty isn't really crazy.' 'This is the catch – Catch-22.'

(a) categorical denial An inevitable pairing, date of origin unknown. A cliché by the 1970s in public relations, political and journalistic use. 'Mr Weisfeld said he had "reason to believe" that Philip Green, the former chairman of Amber Day, was connected with the Pepkor bid. This is despite a categorical denial of such a link from Pepkor . . . He had asked Pepkor if Mr Green was linked with its bid. The reply was a categorical denial. And a categorical denial from a man like Pepkor's chairman, Christo Wiese, has to be taken seriously' – *The Independent* (10 May 1994); 'But Price Waterhouse in London issued a categorical denial. A spokesman said the firm was "extremely upset" about the reports' – *The Sunday Telegraph* (12 March 1995).

(has the) cat got your tongue? Question put to a person (usually young) who is not saying anything, presumably through guilt. Since the mid-19th century and a prime example of nanny-speak, as in *Casson/ Grenfell*. A challenge to the mute. The *OED2*'s earliest citation is H. H. Harper, *Bob Chadwick* (1911): 'I was so angry at her that I . . . made no answer . . . Presently she said, "Has the cat got your tongue?"'

(a) cat has nine lives   A proverbial saying (known by 1546). But why so many? While cats have an obvious capacity for getting out of scrapes – literally 'landing on their feet' in most cases – in ancient Egypt, they were venerated for ridding the country of a plague of rats and were linked to the trinity of Mother, Father and Son. 'To figure out how many extra lives the cat had, the Egyptians multiplied the sacred number three, three times, and arrived at nine' – Robert L. Shook, *The Book of Why* (1983).

catholic   See IS THE POPE.

(a) cat house   A brothel. In *Catwatching* (1986), Desmond Morris traces this term (mostly US use) from the fact that prostitutes have been called 'cats' since the 15th century, 'for the simple reason that the urban female cat attracts many toms when it is on heat and mates with them one after the other'. As early as 1401, Morris adds, men were warned of the risk of chasing 'cat's tail' – women. Hence the slang word 'tail' to denote the female genitals (and compare 'pussy').

(not to have a) cat in Hell's chance   Meaning, 'to have no chance whatsoever' – the full expression makes the phrase clear: 'No more chance than a cat in hell *without claws*' – which is recorded in *Grose* (1796).

cat on a hot tin roof   From the (mostly US) expression 'as nervous as a cat on a hot tin roof' that derives from the common English expression 'like a cat on hot bricks', meaning 'ill-at-ease, jumpy'. John Ray in his *Collection of English Proverbs* (1670–8) has 'to go like a cat upon a hot bake stone'. Another English proverbial expression (known by 1903) is 'Nervous as cats'. In the play *Cat On a Hot Tin Roof* (1955; film US 1958) by Tennessee Williams, the 'cat' is Maggie, Brick's wife, 'whose frayed vivacity', wrote Kenneth Tynan, 'derives from the fact that she is sexually ignored by her husband'.

cat's eyes   Lines of light-reflecting studs placed to demarcate traffic lanes at night. Known as such by 1940. Hence, 'Cat's Eyes' Cunningham, nickname of Group Capt. John Cunningham (1917–2002), distinguished RAF night fighter pilot in the Second World War. Even when navigational aids were not available he managed to shoot down twelve German aircraft.

(a) cat's paw   Meaning 'someone used as a tool by another', this term was known in Britain by 1657 and chiefly derives from one of La Fontaine's fables, 'The Monkey and the Cat', in which a monkey persuades a cat to pick up chestnuts off a hot stove. 'The Cat's Paw' is the title of a painting (1824) by Sir Edwin Landseer, illustrating the story. In nautical use, a 'cat's paw' is the mark made by a puff or gust of wind on an otherwise calm sea – possibly an allusion to cats dabbing at the surface of fish ponds.

(a) cat that walks alone   A self-possessed, independent person. 'I am the cat that walks alone' was a favourite expression of the newspaper magnate Lord Beaverbrook (1879–1964). He was alluding to 'The Cat That Walked By Himself' in *The Just-So Stories* (1902) by Rudyard Kipling.

caught in the act   Caught in the very act for which retribution will be forthcoming. Known by 1655. In Jane Austen's novel *Persuasion* (1818), there is rather 'caught in the *fact*'. Compare **caught red-handed**, where a murderer still has blood on his hands.

caught up in a sinister maze (or web) of plot and double-cross   Publishing and book-reviewing cliché (in various combinations) when promoting and discussing (usually) spy fiction and thrillers. 'A sinister web of power, lust and perversion binds the psychotic killer hunting him down to the traumatic childhood murder of his mother' – *The Times* (19 November 1994); 'Turow and Grisham are often lumped together as operators in the same territory, but separately they tend very different gardens: where Turow lures the reader into an intricate and sinister maze, with Grisham you never get beyond raking and hoeing and pulling up the weeds' – *Sunday Times* (22 January 1995); 'Giorgio

Ambrosoli, the young Milanese lawyer whose sleuthing, begun in 1974, brought down the Sicilian banking tycoon Michele Sindona. The latter's sinister web linked the Vatican, the Mafia, the Christian Democrat Party, and the secret P2 masonic lodge' – *The European* (7 April 1995); 'Niamh went for one more session. "They promised me the sun, moon and stars. They said I'd be put in touch with other women and that, they would pass on information as it became available." She heard nothing. "They left me in darkness and in fear." By the time the results of the virus test arrived, the sense of being in a sinister maze had deepened' – *The Irish Times* (8 April 1995); 'Secret government papers released today at the Public Record Office in Kew reveal a web of intrigue and deceit by state and monarchy that has remained hidden for 66 years' – *The Independent* (30 January 2003).

causing grave concern Journalistic and official cliché – when warning of some imminent unpleasantness, especially a person's death. 'While neither of the men involved in either of the Bishops Avenue deals is in any way crooked, the astonishing scale of the Eastern bloc spending spree is causing grave concern among the capital's most senior crime fighters, who fear it signals the arrival of the Russian mafia, or the Organizatsiya, as it is known and feared on the violent streets of Moscow' – *Evening Standard* (London) (6 May 1994); 'As air traffic within Europe is predicted to rise by around 60 per cent over the next ten years, the potential for future problems is still a grave concern' – *The European* (10 June 1994); 'The Glasgow women's rights campaigner Sheena Duncan said the sheriff's remarks had caused grave concern. She added: "It is a simplistic analysis of the problem, particularly when you think about what women suffer"' – *The Scotsman* (24 June 1994); 'A public meeting in Bansha, Co Tipperary, resolved on June 26th, 1926: "That we the citizens desire to express our grave concern at the circulation of undesirable literature, which constitutes a grave danger to the moral and national welfare of the country, and we urge upon the Government the need for immediate legislation on

the lines recommended by the Catholic Truth Society of Ireland, or on other equally adequate lines" – *The Irish Times* (2 January 1995); 'Listen, for instance, to Father Diarmuid Connolly, chairman of the board of management of St Brigid's School (which has 930 children on the roll) and parish priest of Castleknock, who says: "The current use of the land as playing pitches has been a real safety valve and the proposal to sell them for housing is causing us grave concern"' – *The Irish Times* (28 January 1995).

caviare to the general A famously misunderstood phrase meaning 'of no interest to common folk'. It has nothing to do with giving expensive presents of caviare to unappreciative military gentlemen. In Shakespeare's *Hamlet*, II.ii.434, the Prince refers to a play which, he recalls, 'pleased not the million, 'twas caviare to the general' (the general public, in other words). The Arden edition notes that in *circa* 1600, when the play was written, caviare was a novel delicacy. It was probably inedible to those who had not yet acquired a taste for it.

Cecil See AFTER YOU.

(the) centre of the universe Label applied to a place where it's all happening though, originally, applied to the Almighty: 'God is the centre of the universe' – Bailey, *Centration* (1730–6). Compare HUB OF THE UNIVERSE.

(the) century of the common man Label applied to the 20th century (not entirely successfully) by Henry Wallace (1888–1965), American Democratic Vice-President. 'The century on which we are entering – the century which will come out of this war – can be and must be the century of the common man' – speech (8 May 1942).

certain substances A police euphemism for drugs, chiefly used in the UK where restrictions are placed on the reporting of criminal activity before a charge has been made. Starting in the 1960s, newspapers would report raids on pop stars' houses and conclude: 'Certain substances were taken away for analysis.' From the episode of BBC TV's *Monty Python's Flying Circus* broadcast on 16 November 1969: *Police-*

man: 'I must warn you, sir, that outside I have police dog Josephine, who is not only armed, and trained to sniff out certain substances, but is also a junkie.'

(a) chain reaction A series of linked events, a self-maintaining process. Originally scientific: 'a chemical or nuclear reaction forming intermediate products which react with the original substance and are repeatedly renewed'. Known by the 1930s. 'If you publish a candid article about any community, giving actual names of people . . . you are . . . braving a chain reaction of lawsuits, riots and civil commotion' – *Saturday Evening Post* (22 March 1947); 'If we think they can be helped by exercise, we prescribe it. As a result, they are often encouraged to improve their diet and lifestyle and give up smoking. They can also improve their self-image. It's a chain reaction' – *The Independent* (3 May 1994); 'Scotsman John Cleland was the unluckiest man of the day after powering his Vauxhall Cavalier into the lead, passing Radisich and Soper from the standing start. Four cars were involved in a chain reaction accident which led to the red flag being brought out to halt the race' – *Daily Telegraph* (17 October 1994).

chalk See AS DIFFERENT.

(to) chalk something up to experience (or **put down to . . .**) What you are advised to do when a mistake has been made that cannot be rectified and a situation has been created that cannot be redeemed. Possibly since the 19th century and deriving from the slate in a public house upon which a drinker's credit or debit is displayed.

challenge See ARE YOU READY.

—— challenged PHRASES. A suffix designed to convey a personal problem or disadvantage in a more positive light. Originating in the USA, the first such coinage would appear to have been 'physically challenged' in the sense of disabled: 'This bestselling author [Richard Simmons] of *The Never Say Diet Book* creates a comprehensive fitness program for the physically challenged' – *Publishers Weekly* (10 January 1986). Actual '—— challenged' coinages are now far outnumbered by jocular inventions, many aimed at discrediting the proponents of politically correct terminology. Among the many suggested in Britain and the USA are: 'aesthetically challenged' for 'ugly'; 'chronologically challenged' for 'old'; and, 'follicularly challenged' for 'bald'.

champagne corks will be popping Journalistic cliché to denote celebration. 'On Tuesday, when the industry reports on the amount of business it handled last year, the champagne corks will be popping in the City' – *The Observer* (18 June 1995); 'When Hong Kong's last British financial secretary takes his leave of the colony next week the traditional popping of Champagne corks will be missing' – *The Independent* (1 September 1995); 'After a gap of almost 100 years, the champagne corks have been popping again in the Budapest underground railway' – *The Independent* (2 October 1995).

champagne socialism The holding of socialist beliefs by people who are conspicuous consumers of the good things in life. The most obvious example of a **champagne socialist** is (Sir) John Mortimer, the prolific British playwright, novelist and lawyer (b. 1923), who may indeed have used it about himself. The earliest use of the term appears to have been in connection with 'Robert Maxwell, *Daily Mirror* newspaper tycoon and possibly the best known Czech in Britain after Ivan Lendl, [who] has long been renowned for his champagne socialist beliefs' – *The Times* (2 July 1987). However, a similar appellation was earlier applied to the Labour politician Aneurin Bevan. Randolph Churchill (who was, rather, a champagne *Conservative*) recalled how Brendan Bracken once attacked Bevan: '"You Bollinger Bolshevik, you ritzy Robespierre, you lounge-lizard Lenin," he roared at Bevan one night, gesturing, as he went on, somewhat in the manner of a domesticated orang-utang. "Look at you, swilling Max [Beaverbrook]'s champagne and calling yourself a socialist"' – *Evening Standard* (London) (8 August 1958).

champions See BREAKFAST OF.

(to) chance one's arm Meaning, 'to perform an action in the face of probable failure; to take one's chance of doing something successfully' – *OED2* (which finds it first in an 1889 slang dictionary and in some unspecified tailoring context). In January 1997, the Bishop of Swindon's newsletter carried this account of how the phrase may have come about: 'In 1492 there was a bitter feud between two Dublin families, and the leader of one fled for his life and with his followers took refuge in the Cathedral chapter house. As the siege wore on, the leader of the other family began to realise the foolishness of their quarrel. He called to those behind the bolted door, to come and no harm would befall them. His enemies didn't believe him, and stayed put. Getting no response he seized his spear, cut a hole in the door, and thrust his arm through – no sword, no clenched fist, just hand which the others could have cut off. It was grasped by another hand on the other side, the door was opened, the two leaders embraced, and the feud was brought to an end.' This would appear to be one of those retrospectively imposed origins on a phrase that hardly requires such explaining. Other suggestions include, that it refers to risking a court-martial where all the stripes could be taken off a soldier's sleeve, and something to do with boxing (that's Eric Partridge's guess).

chance would be a fine thing!   Self-consolatory (or -deceiving) remark made when people are examining the prospect of enjoying an opportunity that is unlikely to come their way. Certainly in use by the 1900s and probably much older, especially in the sexual sense. Also used as a put-down: a woman might say disapprovingly of a man that she wouldn't sleep with him even if he asked. Then another might respond, 'Chance'd be a fine thing!' – that is, 'You can say that, given that you won't ever get the opportunity.' 'How many of us have said something not particularly amusing, only to have it turned into a joke of sorts by someone else saying, "Chance would be a fine thing"' – Miles Kington, *The Independent* (2 May 2000).

change and decay   A phrase from the hymn 'Abide With Me' (*circa* 1847) by H. F. Lyte, the English clergyman and hymn writer (1793–1847): 'Change and decay in all around I see; / O Thou, who changest

not, abide with me.' (The title phrase **abide with me** was possibly inspired by Luke 24:29: 'Abide with us: for it is toward evening, and the day is far spent.') Hence, *Change and Decay In All Around I See*, the title of a novel (1978) by Allan Massie.

Channel   See CONTINENT ISOLATED.

(a) chapter of accidents   A series of unforeseen happenings or misfortunes. The 4th Earl of Chesterfield used the phrase in a letter to his son in 1753. In 1837, John Wilkes was quoted by Southey as saying: 'The chapter of accidents is the longest chapter in the book'. 'A Chapter of Accidents' is the heading of Pt 1, Chap. 9 of Thomas Hughes, *Tom Brown's Schooldays* (1857). *A Chapter of Accidents* was the title of the autobiography (1972) of Goronwy Rees, the writer.

chariots of fire   *Chariots of Fire* was the title given to a film (UK 1981) about the inner drives of two athletes (one a future missionary) in the 1924 Olympics. Appropriately for a film whose basic themes included Englishness, Christianity and Judaism, the title comes from William Blake's poem, which is sung in Parry's setting 'Jerusalem' at the climax of the film. Note the singular 'chariot' in the original: 'Bring me my bow of burning gold, / Bring me my arrow of desire / Bring me my spear! Oh, clouds unfold / Bring me my chariot of fire.' 'Chariots of fire' in the plural occurs in 2 Kings 6:17: 'And the Lord opened the eyes of the young man; and he saw: and, behold, the mountain was full of horses and chariots of fire round about Elisha.'

(a) charisma bypass (operation)   An expression at one time in general joke use, especially in show business and politics, to describe the reason why someone is unimpressive at self-projection. Originally rather a good joke. The earliest use found in the press is in *The Washington Post* (2 May 1986) concerning a Texas gubernatorial primary: 'When Loeffler started the campaign, his name recognition was well under 10% . . . Part of the problem, according to one Republican consultant, is his rather plodding nature. "The guy is in desperate need of a charisma bypass," said the consultant. "But if he gets into the runoff against Clements, he might get some charisma in a hurry".' 'Politicians fall victim to a quick swipe with a well-turned phrase, such as the "charisma bypass", which the unfortunate Premier of New South Wales is said to have undergone' – *The Daily Telegraph* (14 February 1987); 'When Betty Ford slipped quietly into hospital for a heart operation, the surgeon told her he had carried out Richard Nixon's charisma bypass' – *Today* (25 November 1987); '[Of Steve Davis, snooker player] "Oh yes, we say he had a charisma bypass when he was 17," said Barry Hearn [manager] last week, without bothering to get involved in any defence of his protégé' – *The Sunday Times* (11 December 1988).

charity begins at home The idea behind this proverb is expressed by Wyclif, *circa* 1383, but may also be traced back to Theocritus and Terence. The meaning was originally, 'Set an example of charity in your home and spread it out from there' – it does not end there – but nowadays it is sometimes used as an excuse for not giving to causes farther afield. From Sheridan, *The School for Scandal*, Act 5, Sc. 1 (1777): 'Yet he has a string of charitable sentiments, I suppose, at his fingers' ends.' 'Or, rather, at his tongue's end . . . for I believe there is no sentiment he has such faith in as that "Charity begins at home".'

Charley See CLAP HANDS.

Charlie See COME TO; HOLD MY HAND.

Charlie! / 'Allo, what do you want, Ingrid? An exchange between Pat Hayes and Fred Yule from the BBC radio show, *Ray's a Laugh* (1949–60). 'Charlie' was pronounced 'Char–har–lie'.

Charlie Farnsbarns A foolish person whose name one cannot remember or does not care to. Although this moderately well-known expression escaped Eric Partridge and his reviser, Paul Beale, in *Partridge/Slang*, Beale commented (1985): 'Charlie Farnsbarns was a very popular equivalent of e.g. "Mrs Thing" or "Old Ooja", i.e. "Old whatsisname". Much play was made with the name in [the BBC radio show] *Much Binding In the Marsh*, but whether Murdoch and Horne actually invented it, or whether they borrowed it "out of the air", I'm afraid I don't know.

They would mention especially, I remember, a magnificent motorcar called a "Farnsbarns Special" or something like, say, a "Farnsbarns Straight Eight". This was in the period, roughly, 1945–50, while I was at school – I recall a very jolly aunt of mine who was vastly amused by the name and used it a lot.' Of course, a 'Charlie' (as in CHASE ME CHARLIE, PROPER CHARLIE and RIGHT CHARLIE) has long been a slightly derogative name to apply to an ordinary bloke. In Australia, it may also be a shortening of 'Charlie Wheeler', rhyming slang for 'Sheila', a girl (recorded in Sydney Baker, *The Australian Language*, 1945). 'Farnsbarns' has the numbing assonance needed to describe a bit of a nonentity. The phrase probably came out of the services (possibly RAF) in the Second World War.

Charlie's dead Cry indicating that a woman's slip or petticoat is showing below the hem of her dress. Known by the 1940s at least. Could it be that it looks like a flag flying at half-mast because Charlie is dead?

(a) charmed life A life in which luck and ease are in full measure. 'Let fall thy blade on vulnerable crests; / I bear a charmed life' – Shakespeare, *Macbeth*, V.viii.12 (1606). *Charmed Life* – title of a book by Mary McCarthy (1956). '"Actually, the goaltender led a charmed life. Most of the danger was involved with the fellow who played between point and cover-point' – *The Globe and Mail* (Toronto) (16 May 1967); 'The sport remains intensely and inherently dangerous. There have been narrow escapes in recent years. But there is little doubt that Formula One had begun to think it led a charmed life. The trouble with the charmed life was that it coincided with the sport becoming more boring' – *The Guardian* (2 May 1994); 'They were married the following year and lived happily ever after. "I think they had a charmed life," says Hagerty. "They were both passionate about photography and the landscape"' – *The Guardian* (9 July 1994).

(a) charm offensive A happy coinage (along the lines of 'peace offensive') for the gregarious and open tactics towards the West of the Soviet leader Mikhail Gorbachev, around 1986. These tactics contrasted greatly with the frosty style of his predecessors. Later used to describe glad-handing by anybody, especially if this marks a change of tactics. 'Now enraged beyond all reason, the furious drummer launches a widespread charm offensive and appears on all daytime chat shows to promote his rotten new record' – *The Spectator* (7 December 2002).

chase See CUT TO THE.

chase me, (Charlie) 'Chase me' has been the catchphrase of the camp British comedian Duncan Norvelle since before 1986. 'Chase me, Charlie', as the title of a song from Noël Coward's *Ace of Clubs* (1950) was not original. It had also been the title of a popular song current in 1900.

(the) chattering classes A term for those newspaper journalists and broadcasters who are paid to discuss topics of current interest, the opinion-formers, but also those – usually of a liberal bent – who simply like to talk about them. The phrase first registered when Alan Watkins used it in *The Observer* (4 August 1985): 'At the beginning of the week the *Daily Mail* published, over several days, a *mélange* of popular attitudes towards Mrs Thatcher. Even though it contained little that was surprising or new, it was much discussed among the chattering classes.' The following weekend (on 11 August), a *Sunday Times* editorial went thus: 'The BBC and the weather have been the only two stories in town this silly season. But the outlook for British broadcasting is actually rather cheery, despite all the wailing and gnashing of teeth among the chattering classes.' Subsequently, Watkins described (in *The Guardian*, 25 November 1989) how the phrase had been coined by the rightish political commentator Frank Johnson in conversation with Watkins in the early years of Margaret Thatcher's prime ministership (i.e. *circa* 1980). Johnson believes he first used the phrase in *Now!* Magazine in 1981.

cheap and cheerful A self-deprecatingly compensatory phrase in middle-class British use since the 1950s. Used when showing clothes or furniture or home when these are not of the high standards that one would like. 'Do you like my new flat? It's cheap and cheerful – but it's *home*!'

(it would be) cheap at half the price Cheap, very reasonable. Not a totally sensible phrase, dating probably from the 19th century. Presumably what it means is that the purchase in question would still be cheap and a bargain if it was *twice* the price that was being asked. Some consider that the expression does make sense if 'cheap' is taken as meaning 'of poor quality', in other words, 'it would still be a poor bargain if it was only half the price.' Another interpretation is that the market trader means that his product is 'cheap, at half the price it ought to be.' The rest of us are not convinced by such arguments. In his *Memoirs* (1991), Kingsley Amis comments on phrases like this that perform semantic somersaults and manage to convey meanings quite the reverse of their literal ones. He cites from a soldier: 'I'd rather sleep with her with no clothes on than you in your best suit.'

cheeky monkey! See RIGHT MONKEY!

cheerful Charlie See PROPER CHARLIE.

cheese See AS DIFFERENT; HELLISH DARK.

(to be) cheesed off (or browned off) 'To be fed up' – both terms known since 1941. 'Cheese' and 'off-ness' rather go together, so one might think of cheese as having an undesirable quality. Also, when cheese is subjected to heat, it goes brown, or gets 'browned off'. On the other hand, the phrase could derive from 'cheese off', an expression like 'fuck off', designed to make a person go away. 'Cheesed off' may just be a state of rejection, like 'pissed off'.

(a) chequered career A working life that is full of ups and downs. Book title: *A Chequered Career, or Fifteen Years in Australia and New Zealand* by H. W. Nesfield (1881). 'My career with 20th Century Fox was somewhat chequered' – *The Listener* (17 August 1967); 'It is the latest blow to Mr Tapie's much chequered career. This year he has been prosecuted by Customs over his yacht, been accused of match rigging and seen Olympique Marseille relegated to the second division' – *The Daily Telegraph* (21 May 1994); 'Myers has spent two episodes of his chequered career with Widnes, but he rarely enjoyed the freedom in their colours that he discovered playing against their sadly depleted current line-up yesterday' – *The Independent* (12 September 1994).

cherchez la femme [look for the woman]! The key to a problem, the answer to some mystery, is the involvement of a woman. Attributed in this form to Joseph Fouché, the French revolutionary and politician (1763–1820). The first citation, however, is *'cherchons la femme* [let us look for the woman]', from Alexandre Dumas (*père*) in his novel *Les Mohicans de Paris* (1854–5). 'There's a quarrel – a scandal – cherchez la femme – always a woman at the bottom of it' – Bernard Shaw, *The Philanderer* (1898).

(a) cherished belief A belief that one holds dear. Date of origin unknown. 'I brought him up to think for himself and to challenge things if I said something was true. I wanted him to say what he felt even if it was against my most cherished belief' – *The Daily Telegraph* (12 July 1994); 'The dream is for the duvet-cover or the pillow-case to spring to life – "I want Mark's baby," said one girl with shocking candour. The most cherished belief is that if the object of desire could just single out her face from the crowd, then she would be the one he would choose' – *The Daily Telegraph* (29 August 1994).

che sera sera The proverbial saying 'What must be, must be' can be found as far back as Chaucer's 'Knight's Tale' (*circa* 1390): 'When a thyng is shapen, it shal be.' But what of this foreign version, as sung, for example, by Doris Day in her 1956 hit song 'Whatever Will Be Will Be'? She also sang it in the remake of Alfred Hitchcock's *The Man Who Knew Too Much* in the same year. Ten years later, Geno Washington and the Ram Jam Band had a hit with a song entitled *'Que Sera Sera'*. So is it *che* or *que*? There is no such phrase as *che sera sera* in modern Spanish or Italian, though *che* is an Italian word and *será* is a Spanish one. What we have here is an Old French or Old Italian spelling of what would be, in modern Italian, *che sara, sara*. This is the form in which the Duke of Bedford's motto has always been written.

(to grin like a) Cheshire Cat To smile very broadly. The Cheshire Cat is most famous from its appearances in Lewis

Carroll's *Alice's Adventures in Wonderland* (1865) – where it has the ability to disappear, leaving only its grin behind – but the beast had been known since about 1770. Carroll, who was born in Cheshire, probably knew that Cheshire cheeses were at one time moulded in the shape of a grinning cat. 'British power was slowly disappearing during the Churchillian Era, leaving, like the Cheshire Cat, only a wide smile behind' – Andrew Roberts, *Eminent Churchillians* (1994).

chew See HE CAN'T.

(to) chew the cud Meaning, 'to think deeply about something, especially the past'. This figurative expression (in use by 1382) refers to the ruminative look cows have when they chew their 'cud' – that is, bring back food from their first stomachs and chew it in their mouths again. 'Cud' comes from Old English *cwidu*, meaning 'what is chewed'.

(to) chew the rag 'To chew something over; to grouse or grumble over something at length, to discuss matters with a degree of thoroughness' (compare 'to chew the fat'). Known by 1885. As in the expression 'to chew something over', the word 'chew' here means simply 'to say' – that is, it is something carried on in the mouth like eating. The 'rag' part relates to an old meaning of that word, in the sense 'to scold' or 'reprove severely'. 'Rag' was also once a slang word for 'the tongue' (from 'red rag', probably).

chicken à la King Cooked chicken breast served in a cream sauce with mushrooms and peppers. No royal origin – rather, it is said to have been named after E. Clark King, a hotel proprietor in New York, where the dish was introduced in the 1880s. Another story is that it was dreamed up at Delmonico's restaurant by Foxhall Keene, son of the Wall Street operator and sportsman J. R. Keene, and served as *chicken à la Keene*. Yet another version is that the dish was created at Claridge's in London for J. R. Keene himself after his horse won the Grand Prix.

(a) chicken and egg situation A problem where cause and effect are in dispute, from the ancient question 'Which came first, the chicken or the egg?' The construction was known by 1959. 'The chicken-and-egg attitude towards the home background of addicts' – *The Guardian* (24 February 1967); 'She sees no problem in finding enough readers; she sees the problem as a general lack of left-wing publishing in this country. "If you want a good read, you don't think of buying a left magazine," she says. "It is a chicken-and-egg situation. *New Statesman* is the only other independent around and they have welcomed *Red Pepper*. They think we will help to open up the market' – *The Guardian* (4 May 1994); 'The other members objected to this formula because, as a rule, UN member states will not volunteer troops unless there is a definite Security Council mandate. "It was a chicken and egg situation," said one diplomat' – *The Independent* (18 May 1994).

(the) chief cook and bottle-washer (sometimes **head cook . . .**) 'A person put in charge of running something; a factotum' (known by 1887). What may be an early form of the phrase occurs in Schikaneder's libretto for Mozart's *Die Zauberflöte*, II.xix. (1791). Papageno says: 'Here's to the head cook and the head butler [*Der Herr Koch und der Herr Kellermeister sollen leben*]!'

(appeals to the) child in all of us A cringe-making assertion made about certain types of entertainment or about occasions like Christmas. Noticed with some frequency in the 1980s. 'In *Back to the Future*, [Robert Zemeckis] scores by adhering to the first rule of [Steven] Spielbergism: appeal to the child in all of us' – *The Sunday Times* (18 August 1985); '*The Wind in the Willows* appeals to the child in all of us, so we adults have accorded it the status of "a children's classic"' – *The Sunday Times* (22 June 1986); 'Growing up tends to hurt. And the child in all of us wants a Daddy/Mummy figure to rub our legs and give us aspirin when growing pains become acute' – *The Guardian* (28 July 1986).

children should be seen and not heard This proverbial expression was, according to *CODP*, originally applied to young *women*. 'A mayde schuld be seen, but not herd' was described as an 'old' saying in *circa* 1400. It was not until the 19th

century that a general application to children of both sexes became common, though Thackeray in *Roundabout Papers* (1860–3) still has: 'Little boys should not loll on chairs . . . Little girls should be seen and not heard.'

(the) children's hour When the long-running and fondly remembered BBC radio programme *Children's Hour* began in 1922, it was known as '*The* Children's Hour', which suggests that it ultimately derived from the title of a poem by Longfellow (1863): 'Between the dark and the daylight, / When the night is beginning to lower, / Comes a pause in the day's occupations, / That is known as the Children's Hour.' This became the name for the period between afternoon tea and dressing for dinner, particularly in Edwardian England. Lillian Hellman also wrote a play called *The Children's Hour* (1934), variously filmed, about a schoolgirl's allegations of her teachers' lesbianism.

children's shoes have far to go Slogan for Start-Rite children's shoes in the UK, current by 1946. The idea of the boy and girl 'twins' walking up the middle of a road between rows of beech trees came to the company's advertising agent as he drove back to London from a meeting at Start-Rite's Norwich offices. He was reminded of the illustration in Kipling's *Just So Stories* of 'the cat who walked by himself' and developed the idea from there – despite many subsequent suggestions from the public that walking down the middle of the road would not enable children, or their shoes, to get very far.

chill out! Calm down, act cool. Originally US black person's slang of the 1970s. Latterly used by both black persons and whites. Whoopi Goldberg says it in the film *Ghost* (US 1990).

(to apply for the) Chiltern Hundreds Originally, a hundred was a division of a shire and long ago a steward was appointed to deal with robbers in three hundreds of the Chiltern Hills in southern England. Then, in the days when to hold an office of profit under the crown involved having to resign from the House of Commons, the process of applying for the stewardship of the Chiltern Hundreds was used as a way of resigning from parliament because this had become necessary for some other reason – a scandal, for example. William Douglas-Home's play entitled *The Chiltern Hundreds* (1947) was set on the day the Conservative Party lost the 1945 British General Election to Labour.

Chinese See DAMNED CLEVER.

Chinese whispers 'Inaccurate gossip' – a phrase deriving from the name of a children's party game. Seated in a circle, the children whisper a message to each other until it arrives back at the person who started, usually with the meaning changed out of all recognition. An alternative name for the game is 'Russian Scandal', which *OED2* finds in 1873, (or 'Russian Gossip' or 'Russian Rumour(s)'). Presumably, Chinese and Russian are mentioned because of their exotic 19th-century connotations, the difficulty of both languages, and because the process of whispering might sound reminiscent of both the languages when spoken. 'The words "Air Red, Air Red," had become confused as they were passed down the line, and by the time they reached the end had been changed to "Galtieri dead, Galtieri dead" . . . It was later pointed out that a message had been similarly misjudged in an earlier war. "Send reinforcements, the regiment is going to advance," had been received as "Send three and four pence, the regiment is going to a dance"' – McGowan & Hands, *Don't Cry for Me, Sergeant-Major* (1983) (about the Falklands war).

(a) chip of(f) the old block (or same block) Referring to a child having the same qualities as its parent, this expression's use was established by the 1620s. Edmund Burke said of the first speech in the House of Commons by William Pitt the Younger (in 1781): 'Not merely a chip of the old "block", but the old block itself' (that is, William Pitt the Elder, 1st Earl of Chatham).

(to have a) chip on one's shoulder Meaning 'to bear a grudge in a defensive manner', the expression originated in the USA where it was known by the early 19th century. The *Long Island Telegraph*

explained in 1830: 'When two churlish boys were determined to fight, a chip [of wood] would be placed on the shoulder of one, and the other [was] demanded to knock it off at his peril.'

chips See CASH IN ONE'S.

(when the) chips are down Meaning 'at a crucial stage in a situation', this phrase alludes to the chips used in betting games. The bets are placed when they are down, but the outcome is still unknown. 'If when the chips are down, the world's most powerful nation . . . acts like a pitiful helpless giant, the forces of totalitarianism and anarchy will threaten free nations and free institutions throughout the world' – Richard M. Nixon, TV speech (30 April 1970); 'There is a substantial body of opinion in Britain – and in Chobham – that holds that Lloyd's Names deserve all the suffering they have got. In a sense, it is this factor that has turned their calamity into a tragedy. Now that the chips are down, communities aren't rallying round' – *Independent on Sunday* (19 March 1995).

chips with everything Phrase descriptive of British working-class life and used as the title of a play (1962) by Arnold Wesker about class attitudes in the RAF during National Service. Alluding to the belief that the working classes tend to have chips (potatoes) as the accompaniment to almost every dish at mealtimes. Indeed, the play contains the line: 'You breed babies and you eat chips with everything.' Earlier, in an essay published as part of *Declaration* (1957), the film director Lindsay Anderson had written: 'Coming back to Britain is always something of an ordeal. It ought not to be, but it is. And you don't have to be a snob to feel it. It isn't just the food, the sauce bottles on the cafe tables, and the chips with everything. It isn't just saying goodbye to wine, goodbye to sunshine . . .'

chivalry See AGE OF.

(a) chocolate soldier Bernard Shaw's play *Arms and the Man* (1894) was turned into a musical in Germany, *Der Tapfere Soldat* [Brave Soldier] (1908). The title of the English version of this musical (New York, 1909) was *The Chocolate Soldier*. The story concerns Captain Bluntschli, a Swiss officer, who gets the better of a professional cavalry soldier. Shaw's phrase for Bluntschli was, rather, 'the chocolate cream soldier'. Later, during the First World War, 'chocolate soldier' seems to have become a term of abuse about a certain type of recruit who complained of the conditions. This was not how Shaw viewed Bluntschli. The character was not a coward but an admirable, realistic soldier who saw the sense of keeping alive. That was why he carried chocolate creams, not bullets. Subsequently, the Australian Army of the Second World War, the Militia (who volunteered to serve only within Australia) were known as the Chocolate Soldiers because of their chocolate-coloured shoulder patches. Ian Fleming, the creator of James Bond, was nicknamed the 'chocolate sailor' during the Second World War because, though a Commander of the RNVR, he never actually went to sea. In 2002, during a court case, the model Naomi Campbell mistakenly sensed that a journalist who had described her as a 'chocolate soldier' was indulging in racist abuse. As someone commented at the time, the reference was more probably to the expression 'as much use as a chocolate teapot/kettle', i.e. useless. In 1943, there was an American song 'Chocolate Soldier from the USA' that did describe a black soldier fighting for his country and so was not considered derogatory.

Christmas See ALL DRESSED; BY CHRISTMAS; DO THEY KNOW.

'Christmas comes but once a year' – thank God! The allusion is to a 16th-century rhyme ('. . . and when it comes it brings good cheer'); the sour comment – presumably from someone objecting to the commercialization of the season or the exhaustion of having to organize the festivities – was known by the 1940s.

Christmas has come early this year Meaning, 'We have had some good fortune or welcome [usually financial] news'. Beginning a report in *The Guardian* (8 April 1988), Michael Smith wrote of the Volvo purchase of the Leyland Bus operation: 'Christmas has come early for management and staff at Leyland Bus, the sole UK manufacturers of buses which changed

hands last week' – they stood to enjoy a windfall of £19 million. The previous week, Lord Williams had said of another sale – that of Rover to British Aerospace: 'Christmas has come rather early this year.' From McGowan & Hands's *Don't Cry for Me, Sergeant-Major* (1983) (about the Falklands war): 'De-briefings afterwards . . . related that the SAS "thought Christmas had come early". They couldn't believe their luck. There were at least eleven Argentine aircraft virtually unguarded.'

Christmasses See ALL OF.

chuck it ——! Meaning, 'Abandon that line of reasoning, that posturing'. An example from the BBC's *World at One* radio programme in May 1983 during the run-up to the General Election: Roy Hattersley complained that he was being questioned only on the ten per cent of the Labour Party manifesto with which he disagreed. Robin Day, the interviewer, replied: 'Chuck it, Hattersley!' This format was used earlier and notably by G. K. Chesterton. In his 'Antichrist, or the Reunion of Christendom' (1912), he satirized the pontificating of F. E. Smith (later 1st Earl of Birkenhead) on the Welsh Disestablishment Bill: 'Talk about the pews and steeples / And the cash that goes therewith! / But the souls of Christian peoples . . . / Chuck it, Smith!'

cigar See END OF ME; GIVE THE MAN.

cigarette See AH, WOODBINE.

Cinderella See COULD MAKE ANY.

circumstances See DUE TO.

circuses See BREAD AND.

(a) citizen of the world Cicero has this phrase as '*civem totius mundi*', meaning 'one who is cosmopolitan, at home anywhere'. Similarly, Socrates said, 'I am a citizen, not of Athens or Greece, but of the world.' The *OED2* finds the English phrase in Caxton (1474) and, 'If a man be gracious and courteous to strangers, it shows he is a citizen of the world' in Francis Bacon's 'Goodness, and Goodness of Nature' (1625). *The Citizen of the World* was the title of a collection of letters by Oliver Goldsmith purporting to be those of Lien Chi Altangi, a philosophic Chinaman living in London and commenting on English life and characters. They were first published as 'Chinese Letters' in the *Public Ledger* (1760–1), and then again under this title in 1762. James Boswell, not untypically, in his *Journal of a Tour to the Hebrides* (1786) reflects: 'I am, I flatter myself, completely a citizen of the world . . . In my travels through Holland, Germany, Switzerland, Italy, Corsica, France, I never felt myself from home; and I sincerely love "every kindred and tongue and people and nation".'

—— **City** PHRASES. The suffix '—— City', applied since the 1960s, is a way of elevating a place or situation, concrete or abstract, to a higher status. 'Fat City', meaning 'an ideal situation' or 'wealth' (often illegally gained), however, may have been around since the 1940s. *Fat City* was the title of a film with a boxing theme (US 1972). 'Nose City' featured in the BBC Radio show *The Burkiss Way* (20 December 1977). 'Cardboard city' was the name applied to an area on London's South Bank where homeless people would shelter in cardboard boxes (1980s). 'Depression City – one of a number of wholly imaginary localities invented in the early 1980s, as the symbolic dwelling places of people in certain states of mind. It originated as the obverse of "Fun City", as New York was christened in 1966 by a *Herald Tribune* journalist at the start of Mayor John V. Lindsay's tenure in office. In the same vicinity you may find the ironically named Thrill Central, the neighbouring state of Dullsville, Arizona, and the inhabitants of Loser's Lane' – John Walsh in *The Independent* (2 December 2000).

civilisation   See END OF.

clanger   See DROP.

clap hands, here comes Charley   This apparently nonsensical catchphrase, popular at one time in Britain, appears to derive from a song used as the signature tune of Charlie Kunz (1896–1958). Born in the USA, Kunz became a feathery-fingered, insistently rhythmic pianist popular on British radio in the 1930s/40s. The song went, 'Clap hands, here comes Charley . . . here comes Charley now.' With lyrics by Billy Rose and Ballard MacDonald, and

music by Joseph Meyer, it was first recorded in the USA in 1925. According to *The Book of Sex Lists*, the song was written 'in honour of a local chorine, first-named Charline, who had given many of the music publishers' contact men (song pluggers) cases of gonorrhoea – a venereal disease commonly known as "the clap".' *Partridge/Slang* adds that 'to do a clap hands Charlie' was 1940s' RAF slang for flying an aircraft in such a way as to make its wings seem to meet overhead.

Claude   See AFTER YOU.

clay   See BALL OF.

cleanliness is next to godliness   Although this phrase appears within quotation marks in Sermon 88 'On Dress' by John Wesley, the Methodist evangelist (1703–91), it is without attribution. *Brewer* (1989) claims that it is to be found in the writings of Phinehas ben Yair, a rabbi (*circa* 150–200). In fact, the inspiration appears to be the Talmud: 'The doctrines of religion are resolved into carefulness . . . abstemiousness into cleanliness; cleanliness into godliness.' So the saying is not from the Bible, as might be supposed. Wesley might have found it, however, in Francis Bacon, *The Advancement of Learning*, Bk 2 (1605): 'Cleanliness of body was ever deemed to proceed from due reverence to God.' Thomas J. Barratt, one of the fathers of modern advertising, seized upon the phrase to promote Pears' Soap, chiefly in the UK. On a visit to the USA in the 1880s, he sought a testimonial from a man of distinction. Shrinking from an approach to President Grant, he ensnared the eminent divine Henry Ward Beecher. Beecher happily complied with Barratt's request and wrote a short text beginning: 'If cleanliness is next to godliness . . .' and received no more for his pains than Barratt's 'hearty thanks'.

cleans round the bend   Harpic lavatory cleaner used this slogan in the UK from the 1930s onwards, but it is not the origin of the idiom 'round the bend', meaning 'mad'. The *OED2* cites F. C. Bowen in *Sea Slang* (1929) as defining that, thus: 'An old naval term for anybody who is mad'.

clear and present danger   A phrase taken from a ruling by the US Supreme

Court justice Oliver Wendell Holmes Jr in the case of Schenk *v.* United States (1919). This concerned free speech and included Holmes's claim that the most stringent protection of same would not protect a man who falsely shouted fire in a theatre and caused panic: 'The question in every case is whether the words used are used in such circumstances and are of such a nature as to create a clear and present danger that they will bring about the evils that Congress has a right to prevent.' A film with the title *Clear and Present Danger* (US 1994) was about a CIA agent in conflict with his political masters in Washington.

(as) clear as mud I.e. not clear at all. Current since the early 19th century.

(in a) cleft stick In a position from which it is impossible to advance or retreat – in a dilemma, fix or jam. 'We are squeezed to death, between the two sides of that sort of alternative which is commonly called a cleft stick' – in a letter from the poet William Cowper (1782). The word 'cleft' is of the same derivation as 'cleave' or 'cloven'. A literal use of a 'cleft stick' – as a piece of wood with a hole chopped out – in which an African bearer might carry messages famously occurs in Evelyn Waugh, *Scoop*, Bk 2, Chap. 2, Pt 4, (1938): 'She went over to the pile of cleft sticks. "How do you use these?" "They are for sending messages." . . . Lord Copper said I was to send my messages with them".'

clerk See ALL DRESSED.

clever See DAMNED.

(a) clever clogs (or **clever boots)** An overly clever person. Since the 1940s. It is not clear what the footware has to do with the cleverness. 'Clever clogs fly BIA to Amsterdam' – British Island Airways advertisement (mid-1970s).

(the) cleverest young man in England An unofficial title bestowed semi-humorously from time to time. In 1976, the recipient was Peter Jay (b. 1937), then an economics journalist on *The Times*. He was called this in an article so headed (with the saving grace of a question mark) by *The Sunday Times* Magazine (2 May). Two years earlier he had been included in *Time* Magazine's list of the 150 people 'most likely to achieve leadership in Europe'. He became Britain's Ambassador to Washington at the age of 40, at which point people stopped calling him one of the most promising of his generation. In September 1938, at the League of Nations, Chips Channon had written in his diary of: 'John Foster, that dark handsome young intellectual . . . Fellow of All Souls, prospective candidate, and altogether one of the cleverest young men in England.' This was presumably the person who became Sir John Foster QC, a Tory MP. *Punch* (12 September 1874), in a cartoon caption, has: 'Now look at Gladstone, the cleverest man in all England!' Compare also Gladstone's remark that Mary Sedgwick, mother of the fabulous Benson brothers – A. C., E. F. and so on – was 'the cleverest woman in Europe'.

(the) climate of opinion The prevailing view that may dictate public decisions and actions. A phrase since 1661. 'To us he [Freud] is no more a person / now but a whole climate of opinion' – W. H. Auden, poem 'In Memory of Sigmund Freud' in *Another Time* (1940); 'He likes saving causes . . . he's brilliant at forming what they call now "climates of opinion"' – Angus Wilson, *Hemlock and After* (1952); 'Mrs Thatcher as premier was more made by the anti-statist climate of opinion in the 1970s and 1980s than vice versa. It is a truth about her often overlooked, not least by her admirers' – *The Daily Telegraph* (4 May 1994); 'But the public can look, learn, comment, write and agitate if it feels like it, make its input as the project moves from winning entry to final design, and help create a climate of opinion that will affect future competitions' – *The Sunday Times* (4 December 1994).

(to) climb aboard the gravy train To gain access to a money-spinning scheme. This was an American expression originally – *DOAS* suggests that it started in sporting circles. An alternative version is 'to climb aboard the gravy *boat*', which is a bit easier to understand. Gravy boats exist for holding gravy in and take their name from their shape. So, if money is perceived as being like gravy, it is not hard to see how the expression arose.

According to *Webster's Dictionary*, the 'train' and 'boat' forms are equally popular in the USA (and have been since the 1920s). 'Boat' is probably less popular in the UK.

(to) climb on the bandwagon (or **jump on the bandwagon)** To join something that is already an established success. Principally in the USA, circuses had bandwagons. They had 'high decks so that musicians could be seen and heard by street crowds', according to *Flexner* (1982). Barnum and Bailey had an elaborately decorated one in 1855 for use in circus parades. Politicians in the USA also had bandwagons which would lead the procession when votes were being canvassed. Those who jumped, climbed or hopped aboard were those who were leading the support for the candidate. Since then, a slight shift in meaning has bandwagon-jumpers as people who give support once success has been assured.

clinging to the wreckage *Clinging to the Wreckage* was the title of the autobiography (1982) of the playwright, novelist and lawyer (Sir) John Mortimer. He explained its significance in an epigraphic paragraph or two: 'A man with a bristling grey beard [a yachtsman, said:] "I made up my mind, when I bought my first boat, never to learn to swim . . . When you're in a spot of trouble, if you can swim you try to strike out for the shore. You invariably drown. As I can't swim, I cling to the wreckage and they send a helicopter out for me. That's my tip, if you ever find yourself in trouble, cling to the wreckage!"' Mortimer concludes: 'It was advice that I thought I'd been taking for most of my life.'

close See GIVE THE MAN.

(a) close encounter of the —— kind An expression derived from the title of Steven Spielberg's film *Close Encounters of the Third Kind* (US 1977) that, in turn, is said to be taken from the categories used in the American forces to denote UFOs. A 'close encounter 1' would be a simple UFO sighting; a 'close encounter 2', evidence of an alien landing; and a 'close encounter 3', actual contact with aliens. The categories were devised by a UFO researcher called J. Allen Hynek – source: Rick Meyers, *The*

Great Science Fiction Films. Used allusively to describe intimacy: 'For a close encounter of the fourth kind, ring ****'; 'Polanski's new movie – Close Encounters with the Third Grade' – graffiti, quoted 1982.

(a) closely knit community (or **tightly knit community)** Cliché phrase invariably invoked whenever a community is hit by trouble or tragedy. By the 1980s. 'A local SDLP councillor, Ms Margaret Ritchie, also condemned the killing but said it would not shatter the community which had always been very closely knit' – *The Irish Times* (9 August 1994); 'When you have a community as closely knit as this one, what you do to one person affects everybody else. You can't threaten to evict somebody and not expect to get everybody's blood pressure up, but Schelly doesn't seem to understand that' – *The Herald* (Glasgow) (2 November 1994); '"Everyone will be touched by this [coach crash]," said Bill McLeod, 52, owner of a local guesthouse, "It's such a tight-knit community . . . that everyone will know someone who was killed or injured"' – *The Independent* (25 May 1995); 'Relatives and friends of the Royal Welch Fusiliers held hostage in Bosnia anxiously awaited news of their fate yesterday. The 300-year-old regiment is based in the tightly knit community of Wrexham in Clwyd' – *The Independent* (29 May 1995).

close-run See DAMN.

close your eyes and think of England The source that *Partridge/Catch Phrases* gives for this saying – in the sense of advice to women when confronted with the inevitability of sexual intercourse, or jocularly to either sex about doing anything unpalatable – is the *Journal* (1912) of Alice, Lady Hillingdon: 'I am happy now that Charles calls on my bedchamber less frequently than of old. As it is, I now endure but two calls a week and when I hear his steps outside my door I lie down on my bed, close my eyes, open my legs and think of England.' There *was* an Alice, Lady Hillingdon (1857–1940). She married the 2nd Baron in 1886. He was Conservative MP for West Kent (1885–92) and, according to *Who's Who*, owned 'about 4,500 acres' when he died (in 1919). A portrait of Lady Hillingdon was painted by Sir Frank Dicksee PRA in 1904. The rose 'Climbing Lady Hillingdon' may also have been named after her. But where her journals are, if indeed they ever existed, is not known. Jonathan Gathorne-Hardy, repeating the quotation in *The Rise and Fall of the British Nanny* (1972), calls her Lady Hilling*ham*, which only further makes one doubt that a woman with any such a name was coiner of the phrase. *Salome Dear, Not In the Fridge* (ed. Arthur Marshall, 1968) has it instead that the newly wedded Mrs Stanley Baldwin was supposed to have declared: 'I shut my eyes tight and thought of the Empire.' We may discount Bob Chieger's assumption in *Was It Good for You, Too?* (1983) that 'Close your eyes and think of England' was advice given to Queen Victoria 'on her wedding night'. Sometimes the phrase occurs in the form **lie back and think of England**, but this probably comes from confusion with SHE SHOULD LIE BACK AND ENJOY IT. In 1977, a long-running play by John Chapman and Anthony Marriott opened in London with the title *Shut Your Eyes and Think of England*.

cloth-eared Phrase used to describe someone who is somewhat deaf and thus, in a transferred sense, has no taste in matters musical. Known by 1912. It is not completely obvious why 'cloth' is used in this phrase – maybe in contrast with a richer material.

cloud See GET OFF MY.

(to live in) cloud-cuckoo land Meaning 'to have impractical ideas', the expression comes from the name *Nephelococcygia*, suggested for the capital city of the birds (in the air) in *The Birds* by Aristophanes. Listed as a current cliché in *The Times* (28 May 1984). 'The decision to standardize the names of authors may be a big stride for the book world. But it is only a small step towards that cloud-cuckoo-land where everybody speaks and writes English according to the same rules' – *The Times* (30 May 1994); 'Fund managers have questioned RJB's assessment of the market after 1998 when contracts with power generators, coal's biggest customer, expire. One banker advising an under-bidder said

the RJB predictions "were in cloud-cuckoo-land"' – *The Sunday Times* (27 November 1994); 'Mr Watkinson said that the RMT's claim for 6 per cent [pay rise] meant that the [union's] leadership was "living in cloud cuckoo land"' – *The Independent* (27 May 1995).

(on) cloud nine (or **cloud seven)**
Meaning, 'in a euphoric state'. Both forms have existed since the 1950s. The derivation appears to be from terminology used by the US Weather Bureau. Cloud nine is the cumulonimbus, which may reach 30–40,000 feet. *Morris* notes, 'If one is upon cloud nine, one is high indeed,' and also records the reason for cloud nine being more memorable than cloud seven: 'The popularity . . . may be credited to the *Johnny Dollar* radio show of the 1950s. There was one recurring episode . . . Every time the hero was knocked unconscious – which was often – he was transported to cloud nine. There Johnny could start talking again.' 'Nurse John McGuinness Shares Double Rollover Lottery Jackpot . . . "It still hasn't sunk in and I've been on cloud nine since the draw"' – *Daily Mirror* (29 January 1996); 'Scotland's rugby centre Scott Hastings is on cloud nine after becoming a father for the second time. The newest arrival to the Hastings clan, Kerry Anne, was not expected until later in the week but she was born on Sunday night, weighing in at 7lb 2oz' – *The Herald* (Glasgow) (7 February 1996).

(a) cloud no bigger than a man's hand
When something is described as such, it is not yet very threatening – as though a man could obliterate a cloud in the sky by holding up a hand in front of his face. The phrase is biblical: 'Behold, there ariseth a little cloud out of the sea, like a man's hand' (1 Kings 18:44). The Reverend Francis Kilvert, on 9 August 1871, has: 'Not a cloud was in the sky as big as a man's hand.' In a letter to Winston Churchill on 14 December 1952, Bob Boothby MP wrote of a dinner at Chartwell: 'It took me back to the old carefree days when I was your Parliamentary Private Secretary, and there seemed to be no cloud on the horizon; and on to the fateful days when the cloud was no bigger than a man's

hand, and there was still time to save the sum of things.'

club See IN THE.

clumsy clot! Catchphrase from the BBC radio show *Take It From Here* (1948–59). A hangover from wartime slang.

clunk, click, every trip Accompanied by the sound of a car door closing and of a seat belt being fastened, this was used as a slogan in British road safety ads featuring Jimmy Savile from 1971. In 1979, someone wrote the slogan on a museum cabinet containing a chastity belt.

c'mere, big boy! Stock phrase of Florence Halop as Hotbreath Houlihan, a sexpot in the American radio show *The Camel Caravan* (1943–7).

coach See DRIVE A COACH.

coat See GET YOUR COAT.

cock See BIG CONK.

(a) cock-and-bull story A long, rambling, unbelievable tale, as used notably in Laurence Sterne's *Tristram Shandy* (1760–7). The last words of the novel are: "'L—d!" said my mother, "what is all this story about?' – "A cock and a bull," said Yorick, "And one of the best of its kind, I ever heard".' Suggested origins are that the phrase comes from: old fables in general that have animals talking, going right back to Aesop – confirmed perhaps by the equivalent French phrase '*coq à l'âne*' [literally 'cock to donkey']; Samuel Fisher's 1660 story about a cock and a bull being transformed into a single animal – which people may have thought pretty improbable; somehow from the Cock and the Bull public houses, which are but a few doors apart in Stony Stratford, Buckinghamshire. The *OED2*'s earliest citation in this precise form is from the Philadelphia *Gazette of the United States* (1795): 'a long cock-and-bull story about the Columbianum' (a proposed national college). Motteux's 1700 translation of Cervantes, *Don Quixote* (Pt 1, Bk 3, Chap. 17), has: 'don't trouble me with your foolish stories of a cock and a bull'. *Apperson* trumps all with a 1608 citation – from John Day's play, *Law Trickes or who would have thought it*, IV.ii: 'What a tale of a cock and a bull he tolde my father.'

(to) cock a snook A snook is the derisive gesture made with thumb and hand held out from the nose (though the phrase is also used figuratively for a cheeky gesture). 'To take a sight' is an alternative phrase. Both were known by the mid-19th century; indeed, *OED2* has 'cock snooks' in 1791. The game of snooker derives its name not from this but rather from the military nickname for a raw recruit.

cocked hat See KNOCK SOMETHING.

Cocker See ACCORDING TO.

(a) cock-up on the catering front Catchphrase from the BBC TV series *The Fall and Rise of Reginald Perrin* (1976–9) written by David Nobbs. Reggie's brother-in-law, Jimmy Anderson (played by Geoffrey Palmer) had a military background and, in civilian life, used military turns of phrase to explain things away. For example, 'No food. Bit of a cock-up on the catering front . . .' Really something of a format phrase.

(the) cocks may crow but it's the hen that lays the egg Informal proverb. Uttered by Margaret Thatcher, when British Prime Minister, at a private dinner party in 1987 (according to Robert Skidelsky in *The Sunday Times*, Books (9 April 1989). A London News Radio phone-in (December 1994) had this version: 'The cock does all the crowing but the hen lays all the eggs.' 'My grandmother's all-embracing put down of males: "He's a clever old cock, but he can't lay eggs"' – Margaret Rawles (2000). *Apperson* finds the obvious original, 'The cock crows but the hen goes', in use by 1659.

cocoa See GRATEFUL.

coconut See GIVE THE MAN.

coffin See DRIVE A NAIL.

coffin nails Derogatory name for cigarettes, from a 1957 British newsreel, but *Partridge/Slang* suggests an origin *circa* 1885 and in catchphrase form – 'Another nail in your coffin!' (said to someone lighting up). *OED2* has it from Texas in 1888. Indeed, it is possibly American – Mieder & Co.'s *Dictionary of American Proverbs* (1992) has two (undated) entries of the 'Every cigarette is a nail in your coffin' type. The journal *Proverbium* (1992) also suggests that 'Cigarettes are coffin nails' may have originated in Kentucky.

cold See AS COLD; IN THE.

cold enough to freeze the balls off a brass monkey The derivation of this phrase meaning 'extremely cold' (known by 1835) may have nothing to do with any animal. A brass monkey was the name given to the plate on a warship's deck on which cannon balls (or other ammunition) were stacked. In cold weather the brass would contract, tending to cause the stack to fall down. 'Monkey' appears to have been a common slang word in gunnery days (and not just at sea) – there was a type of gun or cannon known as a 'monkey' and a 'powder monkey' was the name for a boy who carried powder to the guns. Philip Holberton challenged this theory (1998): 'Why would anyone use an expensive metal like brass on which to stack cannon balls? If the stack is going to collapse in cold weather, what will happen to it in a seaway? In pictures I have seen, the bottom row of a stack of cannon balls fitted into a wooden grid or a series of hollows like an old-fashioned egg-rack.' Brian J. Goggin (1999) said no evidence had been found of the phrase in any nautical writings from the era of warships with cannon.

cold hands, warm heart A forgiving little phrase, for when having shaken hands and found the other person's to be cold. A proverb first recorded in 1903 (*CODP*).

(to give someone the) cold shoulder Meaning, 'to be studiedly indifferent towards someone'. Known by 1820, this expression is said to have originated with the medieval French custom of serving guests a hot roast. When they had outstayed their welcome, the host would pointedly produce a cold shoulder of mutton to get them on their way.

(a) cold war Any tension between powers, short of all-out war, but specifically that between the Soviet Union and the West following the Second World War. This latter use was popularized by Bernard Baruch, the US financier and presidential adviser, in a speech in South Carolina (16 April 1947): 'Let us not be deceived – we are today in the midst of a cold war.' The phrase was suggested to him by the speechwriter Herbert Bayard Swope, who had been using it privately since 1940.

collapse of stout party A catchphrase that might be used as the tag-line to a story about the humbling of a pompous person. It has long been associated with *Punch* and was thought to have occurred in the wordy captions given to that magazine's cartoons. But as Ronald Pearsall explains in his book with the title *Collapse of Stout Party* (1975): 'To many people Victorian wit and humour is summed up by *Punch* when every joke is supposed to end with "Collapse of Stout Party", though this phrase tends to be as elusive as "Elementary, my dear Watson" in the Sherlock Holmes sagas.' At least *OED2* manages to find a reference to a 'Stout Party' in the caption to a cartoon in the edition of *Punch* dated 25 August 1855.

colour See ANY COLOUR.

(a/the) colour bar Name given to the divisions, legal and social, between white people and 'people of colour' in the first half of the 20th century. Known by 1913.

Columbus and the egg A reference to the anecdote of Christopher Columbus's egg. Someone, jealous of his success, pointed out that if he had not discovered the New World someone else would have done so. Columbus did not reply directly but asked the other people present if they could make an egg stand on its end. When they failed, he broke the end of the egg and stood it up that way. The moral was plain: once he had shown the way, anyone could do it. From Margery Allingham, *Death of a Ghost,* Chap. 1 (1934): '"Ah," said Mr Potter, "remember Columbus and the egg. They could all make it stand up after he'd shown them how to crack it at one end. The secret was simple, you see, but Columbus thought of it first".'

column See AGONY.

comb See FIGHT BETWEEN; FINE-TOOTH.

come See AND STILL THEY.

(to) come a cropper (or **fall/get)**   To have a bad fall (physically) or, in a transferred sense, to run into major misfortune, particularly when things seem to be going well. Possibly from a horse-riding accident where the rider might fall with a crop (handle of a whip) in the hand. Also the phrase 'neck and crop' means 'completely'. Known by the mid-19th century. R. S. Surtees, *Ask Mamma*, Chap. 53 (1858): '[He] rode at an impracticable fence, and got a cropper for his pains.' Anthony Trollope, *The Way We Live Now* (1875): 'He would "be coming a cropper rather", were he to marry Melmotte's daughter for her money, and then find that she had got none.'

come again?   'Repeat what you have just said, please!' Usually uttered, not when the speaker has failed to hear the foregoing but cannot believe or understand it. British and American use by the 1930s, at least.

(the) comedy is ended   The last words of François Rabelais (who died about 1550) are supposed to have been: '*Tirez le rideau, la farce est jouée* [bring down the curtain, the farce is played out].' The attribution is made, hedged about with disclaimers, in Jean Fleury's *Rabelais et ses oeuvres* (1877) and also in the edition of Rabelais by Motteux (1693). In Lermontov's novel *A Hero of Our Time* (1840), a character says: '*Finita la commedia*'. At the end of Ruggiero Leoncavallo's opera *Il Pagliacci* [The Clowns] (1892), Canio exclaims: '*La commedia è finita* [the comedy is finished/over].'

come back, all is forgiven   See WHERE ARE THEY NOW?

come hell and high water   Meaning 'come what may', this phrase is mentioned in *Partridge/Slang* as a cliché but, as such phrases go, is curiously lacking in citations. *OED2* finds no examples earlier than the 20th century. *Come Hell or High Water* was used as the title of a book by yachtswoman Clare Francis in 1977. She followed it in 1978 with *Come Wind or Weather*. *Hell and High Water* was the title of a US film in 1954. Graeme Donald in *Today* (26 April 1986) linked it to punishments meted out to witches in the Middle Ages: 'Lesser transgressions only warranted the miscreant being obliged to stand in boiling water, the depth of which was directly proportional to the crime. Hence the expression "From Hell and high water, may the good Lord deliver us".' This is rather fanciful. Perhaps he was thinking of the so-called Thieves' Litany **from Hull, Hell and Halifax, good Lord deliver us** (known by 1594, because the gibbet was much used in these places in the 16th and 17th centuries). 'Charged him with caring only about conquering the Valley on 13,455ft Mount Kinabalu "come hell or high water"' – *Daily Record* (21 September 1994); 'The shares are then held, come hell or high water, for a year. Then the process is repeated and a new portfolio is bought' – *The Independent* (1 April 1995).

come in, number ——, your time is up!   Mimicking the kind of thing the hirers of pleasure boats say, this is sometimes applied in other contexts to people who are overstaying their welcome. By the mid-20th century, at least.

come on down!   In the American TV consumer game *The Price is Right* (from 1957), the host (Bill Cullen was the first) would appear to summon contestants from the studio audience by saying '[name], come on down!' This procedure was reproduced when the quiz was broadcast on British ITV 1984 –8, with Leslie Crowther uttering the words.

comfortably   See ARE YOU SITTING.

(to) come out fighting   Not to take something lying down, responding to a challenge. Date of origin unknown. 'We'll get to the sea and we're coming out fighting' – film *Retreat, Hell!* (US 1952).

(to) come over on the last boat   Phrase used in response to someone who has doubted your wisdom – 'I didn't come over on the last boat, you know.' *Partridge/Catch Phrases* has 'I didn't *come up* with the last boat' as a Royal Navy phrase from the mid-1940s, but also 'I didn't come up in the last bucket' and 'I didn't just get off the boat, y'know', for similar situations.

come the revolution ...   Introductory phrase to some prediction (often ironic) of what life would hold when (usually

Communist) revolution swept the world. Second half of the 20th century. Compare the joke ascribed to the American comedian Willis Howard: 'Come the revolution, everyone will eat strawberries and cream' – 'But, Comrade, I don't *like* strawberries and cream' – 'Come the revolution, *everyone* will eat strawberries and cream!'

cometh the hour, cometh the man An expression that appears from a survey of ten British newspapers in recent years to be a weapon (or cliché), especially in the sportswriter's armoury. From *Today* (22 June 1986): 'Beating England may not be winning the World Cup, but, for obvious reasons, it would come a pretty close second back in Buenos Aires. Cometh the hour, cometh the man? Destiny beckons. England beware.' From *The Times* (13 August 1991): '"Graham [Gooch] is a very special guy," [Ted] Dexter said. "It has been a case of 'Cometh the hour, cometh the man.' I do not know anyone who would have taken the tough times in Australia harder than he did".' From the *Scotsman* (29 February 1992): 'In the maxim of "Cometh the hour, cometh the man," both the Scotland [Rugby Union] manager, Duncan Paterson, and forwards coach, Richie Dixon, indicated yesterday the need to look to the future.' But where does the phrase come from? John 4:23 has 'But the hour cometh, and now is' and there is an English proverb 'Opportunity makes the man' (though originally, in the 14th century, it was 'makes the *thief*'). Harriet Martineau entitled her biography of Toussaint L'Ouverture (1840) *The Hour and the Man*. An American, William Yancey, said about Jefferson Davis, President-elect of the Confederacy in 1861: 'The man and the hour have met,' which says the same thing in a different way. P. G. Wodehouse in *Aunts Aren't Gentlemen* (1974) has: 'And the hour . . . produced the man.' Earlier, at the climax of Sir Walter Scott's novel *Guy Mannering*, Chap. 54 (1815), Meg Merrilies says, 'Because the Hour's come, and the Man.' In the first edition and in the *magnum opus* edition that Scott supervised in his last years, the phrase is emphasized by putting it in italics. Then, in 1818, Scott used 'The hour's come, but not [*sic*] the man' as the

fourth chapter heading in *The Heart of Midlothian*, adding in a footnote: 'There is a tradition, that while a little stream was swollen into a torrent by recent showers, the discontented voice of the Water Spirit [or Kelpie] was heard to pronounce these words. At the same moment a man, urged on by his fate, or, in Scottish language, *fey*, arrived at a gallop, and prepared to cross the water. No remonstrance from the bystanders was of power to stop him – he plunged into the stream, and perished.' Both these examples appear to be hinting at some earlier core saying that remains untraced.

(to) come to a grinding halt General use, meaning 'to come to a sudden and spectacular stop' – and not usually in a vehicular sense. Date of origin unknown. Perhaps from the sound made by a railway train stopping in an emergency? Identified as a current cliché in *The Times* (17 March 1995). 'Unfortunately, things did not go quite according to plan. "We came to a grinding halt pretty quickly," he admitted' – *The Herald* (Glasgow) (15 December 1994); 'So this is Christmas . . . Police had a field day, towing away 14 cars. Princes Street came grinding to a halt and the city's car parks also did a roaring trade' – *Sunday Mail* (18 December 1994).

come to Charlie! In about 1952, following the success of his BBC radio show *Stand Easy*, Charlie Chester (1914–97) had another programme with the title *Come to Charlie* – that grew out of his catchphrase. He recalled (1979): 'I would talk to somebody from the stage and say, "Are you all right, Ada? Speak to Charlee–ee. Charlie spoke to *you*!" . . . You'd be surprised how many people still ask, "Say that phrase for me – say, "come to Charlee–ee!" It's just one of those things they like to hear.' In his later role as a BBC Radio 2 presenter, latterly on *Sunday Soapbox*, Chester developed an elaborate sign-off (from about 1970): **there we are, dear friends, both home, overseas and over the borders**.

come up and see me sometime Mae West (1892–1980) had a notable stage hit on Broadway with her play *Diamond Lil* (first performed 9 April 1928). When she appeared in the 1933 film version entitled *She Done Him Wrong*, what she said to a very young Cary Grant (playing a coy undercover policeman) was: 'You know I always did like a man in uniform. And that one fits you grand. Why don't you come up some time and see me? I'm home every evening.' As a catchphrase, the words have been rearranged to make them easier to say. That is how W. C. Fields says them *to* Mae West in the film *My Little Chickadee* (1939), and she herself took to saying them in the re-arranged version. Even so, she was merely using an established expression. The American author Gelett Burgess in *Are You a Bromide?* (1907) lists among his 'bromidioms': 'Come up and see us any time. You'll have to take pot luck, but you're always welcome.'

come up and see my etchings Nudging invitation from a man to a woman, as though he were an artist plotting to seduce her. By the 1920s, at least. A bit puzzling why he should choose 'etchings' rather than anything else? There is a James Thurber cartoon of a man and a woman in a hotel lobby, to which the caption is: 'You wait here and I'll bring the etchings down.'

come with me to the Casbah A line forever associated with the film *Algiers* (1938) and its star, Charles Boyer. He is supposed to have said it to Hedy Lamarr. Boyer impersonators used it, the film was laughed at because of it, but nowhere was it said in the film. It was simply a Hollywood legend that grew up. Boyer himself denied he had ever said it and thought it had been invented by a press agent. In *Daddy, We Hardly Knew You* (1989), Germaine Greer writes of the early 1940s: 'Frightened and revolted the Australians fled for the nearest watering-hole [in the Middle East]. "Kem wiz me to ze Casbah," Daddy used to say, in his Charles Boyer imitation. Poor Daddy. He was too frightened ever to go there.'

coming   See BRITISH ARE.

(where one is) coming from   Listed in *The Complete Naff Guide*, 'Naff Expressions' (1983), this means 'the origin of one's stance, one's motivation in doing whatever it is one is doing'.

coming in on a wing and a prayer   A popular US song of the Second World War (published in 1943) supposedly took its title from an alleged remark by an actual pilot who was coming in to land with a badly damaged plane. Harold Adamson's lyrics include the lines: 'Tho' there's one motor gone, we can still carry on / Comin' In On A Wing And A Pray'r.' A film about life on an aircraft carrier (US 1944) was called simply *Wing and a Prayer*.

(the) commanding heights of the economy   In a speech to the Labour Party conference in November 1959, Aneurin Bevan said: 'Yesterday, Barbara [Castle] quoted from a speech which I made some years ago, and she said that I believed that socialism in the context of modern society meant the conquest of the commanding heights of the economy . . .' Alan Watkins in a throwaway line in his *Observer* column (28 September 1987) said 'the phrase was originally Lenin's'. At the Labour Party Conference in October 1989, Neil Kinnock revived the phrase in saying that education and training were 'the commanding heights of every modern economy'. The true source remains untraced.

common   See CENTURY OF THE.

common decency   The accepted standard of propriety in behaviour and taste. A common pairing. 'There is one branch of learning without which learning itself cannot be railed at with common decency, namely, spelling' – S. T. Coleridge, *The Friend* (1809–10). 'Even though he [E. M. Forster] never renounced the ideal which suffuses his novels, that of society being guided by a principle of common decency, he was undoubtedly cast adrift by the war and the end of England' – *The Scotsman* (8 May 1993); 'Now we know. How many more examples of deceit, immorality, financial impropriety and lack of common decency will have to pass before the bemused gaze of the electorate before this ragbag administration finally runs out of credit?' – letter to the editor, *The Observer* (22 May 1994).

common or garden   Common, ordinary. Since 1892. 'I have – to use a common or garden expression – been "rushed" in this matter' – *Westminster Gazette* (4 August 1897); 'I wonder if it's possible that I'm all wrong about our friend Victor Dean. Can it be that he was merely a common or garden blackmailer, intent on turning his colleague's human weaknesses to his own advantage?' –Dorothy L. Sayers, *Murder Must Advertise*, Chap. 13 (1933); 'The APT is going to be the common or garden inter-city train of the future' – *New Scientist* (10 June 1971).

(the) common pursuit '[The critic] must compose his differences with as many of his fellows as possible in the common pursuit of true judgement' – T. S. Eliot, 'The Function of Criticism' (1923). Hence, *The Common Pursuit*, title of a book of essays (1952) by the critic F. R. Leavis. In turn, it became the title of a play (1984) by Simon Gray about a group of Cambridge undergraduates and graduates who produce a literary magazine called *The Common Pursuit*.

communist See ARE YOU NOW.

compassion fatigue Reluctance to contribute further to charities and good causes because of the many demands made upon one's compassion. A coinage of the 1980s when numerous fund-raising events, such as Live Aid for famine relief, led to instances of public withdrawal from giving. Originally used in the USA regarding refugee appeals. Derived from 'metal fatigue'. A variant was **donor fatigue**. 'Geldof, the Irish rock musician who conceived the event [Live Aid] and spearheaded its hasty implementation, said that he "wanted to get this done before compassion fatigue set in"' – *The New York Times* (22 September 1985); 'What the refugee workers call "compassion fatigue" has set in. Back in the 1970s, when the boat people were on the front page, the world was eager to help. But now the boat people are old news' – *The Listener* (29 October 1987).

(a/the) competitive edge The quality that gives a product or service the ability to defeat its rivals. 'Banks and securities firms lag behind their rivals elsewhere in innovation, and have lost what competitive edge Japan's relatively low interest rates and strong currency gave them abroad a

few years ago' – *The Economist* (1 May 1993); 'Over the coming months all Harris Semiconductors' employees around the world – from managers to office cleaners – will play the game to experience for themselves the tough business decisions executives must make to maintain their competitive edge' – *The Daily Telegraph* (6 May 1995).

concentrated cacophony! Catchphrase from the BBC radio show *ITMA* (1939–49). Deryck Guyler's archetypical scouser, 'Frisby Dyke', found this a bit hard to understand. After a noisy burst of music, the show's star, Tommy Handley might say, 'Never in the whole of my three hundred *ITMA*'s have I ever heard such a piece of concentrated cacophony.' Dyke: 'What's "concentrated cacophony"?'

(the) concrete jungle Deprived urban areas where the 'law of the jungle' may apply. Known by 1969. Compare the similar **asphalt jungle** and BLACKBOARD JUNGLE [i.e. the educational system]. The 'asphalt' phrase was in use by 1920 though it was further popularized by W. R. Burnett's novel *The Asphalt Jungle* (1949). 'The May sun beats down upon the Glasgow Deccan, the hot tarmac plains that stretch to the east, to the fringe of the steaming concrete jungle' – *The Scotsman* (8 May 1994); 'Sir: Roy Porter's comments ("Frankly we don't give a hoot for barn owls", 19 October) might impress some fellow townies and lovers of the concrete jungle, but this anti-rural spleen does not fool those who better understand the countryside' – letter to the editor, *The Independent* (21 October 1994).

(the) condemned man ate a hearty breakfast Meaning that someone in apparently deep trouble has managed to make an ostentatious display of not worrying about it. The tradition has been established that a condemned man can have anything he desires for his last meal. Boswell in his *Life of Johnson* (for 27 June 1784) has General Paoli saying: 'There is a humane custom in Italy, by which persons [sentenced to death] are indulged with having whatever they like best to eat and drink, even with expensive delicacies'. This, presumably, was not then an English custom or Paoli would not have bothered to mention it, nor Boswell to repeat it. As to the origin of the cliché, it presumably lies in ghoulish newspaper reports of the events surrounding executions in the days of capital punishment in Britain. There was a vast amount of popular literature concerning prominent criminals and public executions, especially in the late 18th and early 19th centuries, but so far citations of this date only from the 20th and tend to be of a metaphorical nature. A book of short stories about the Royal Navy by 'Bartimeus', called *Naval Occasions and Some Traits of the Sailor* (1914), has: 'The Indiarubber Man opposite feigned breathless interest in his actions, and murmured something into his cup about condemned men partaking of hearty breakfasts.' The tone of this suggests it was, indeed, getting on for a cliché even then. *The Prisoner Ate a Hearty Breakfast* is the title of a novel (1940) written by Jerome Ellison. In the film *Kind Hearts and Coronets* (1949), Louis Mazzini, on the evening of his supposed execution, disavows his intention of eating 'the conventional hearty breakfast'. In *No Chip on My Shoulder* (1957), Eric Maschwitz writes: 'Far from closing for ever, *Balalaika* [was merely to be] withdrawn for a fortnight during which time a revolving stage was to be installed at Her Majesty's! It was almost ridiculously like an episode from fiction, the condemned man, in the midst of eating that famous "hearty breakfast", suddenly restored to life and liberty.' 'As tradition would have it, the condemned man ate a hearty breakfast. Lennie Lawrence, the Charlton manager, tucked into his scrambled egg and sausages before the match at Maine Road and said that to lose against fellow regulation contenders Manchester City would leave him with a "massive, massive task"' – *The Sunday Times* (25 February 1990).

conduct unbecoming The full phrase is 'conduct unbecoming the character of an officer and a gentleman' and seems to have appeared first in the (British) Naval Discipline Act, Article 24 (10 August 1860), though the notion has also been included in disciplinary regulations of other services, and in other countries, if not in quite these

words. *Conduct Unbecoming* is the title of a play by Barry England (1969; film UK 1975) and obviously was drawn from this same source, as was the title of the film *An Officer and a Gentleman* (US 1982).

(a) confederacy of dunces A phrase that comes from Jonathan Swift: 'Many a true genius appears in the world – you may know him by this sign, that the dunces are all in confederacy against him' – *Thoughts on Various Subjects* (1706). Hence, *A Confederacy of Dunces*, the title of a novel (1980) by John Kennedy Toole.

confirmed bachelor See NOT THE MARRYING SORT.

confusion to his enemies British naval toast to the king, possibly first used in the 17th century. A schedule of naval toasts included: 'Monday Night – Our Ships at sea; Thursday Night – Confusion to our enemies, or, A bloody war, or, more selectively, Death to the French!' Other versions are 'Confusion to the enemy' and 'Confusion to the French' (perhaps the original form). From Tom Higgs, *300 Years of Mitcham Cricket*: 'Lord Nelson, when watching the cricket match on Mitcham Green before travelling to Portsmouth, his ship "Victory" and the Battle of Trafalgar (October 1805), gave John Bowyer (aged fifteen) a shilling: "To drink confusion to the French". The traditional song 'Here's a Health unto His Majesty', continues: 'With a fal lal la la la la la! / Confusion to his enemies / With a fal lal la la la la la!' A nautical dictionary, this definition of a Fire Ship: 'A ship which has been deliberately set on fire to cause damage and *confusion to the enemy*.' Compare the infrequently sung second verse of 'God Save the King': 'O Lord our God, arise, / Scatter his enemies . . .

conk See ARE YOU LOOKING; BIG CONK.

conquer See ALEXANDER WEEPING.

consent See ADVISE AND.

(a) conspiracy theory A belief that a happening (usually political) is the result of a group of people conspiring together rather than the activity of a lone individual or the result of sheer chance or accident. The phrase arose in the mid-1960s when arguments raged over whether the 1963 assassination of President John F. Kennedy was the work of one man – Lee Harvey Oswald – working on his own or was the result of a plot by organized crime, the Soviet Union, the FBI, or any number of bodies. Now inevitably invoked whenever causes of events are being investigated. Sometimes people say that they prefer the 'cock-up theory' of history rather than conspiracies. 'Conspiracy theories are often framed after the deaths of famous people. Like a kaleidoscope, the conspiracy theory can create satisfying shapes and patterns from even the most random details . . . Others said Lincoln had been killed on the orders of his cabinet, or by Roman Catholics or Southerners' – *The Times* (12 November 1991); *Conspiracy Theory* – title of film (US 1997).

(to) contain the seeds of (something's) own destruction (sometimes **germs . . .)** An allusion to Karl Marx's observation: 'Not only has the bourgeoisie forged the weapons that bring death to itself; it has also called into existence the men who are to wield those weapons – the modern working class – the proletarians' – *The Communist Manifesto*, Pt I (1848). Or to this from Vol. 1, Chap. 32 of *Das Kapital*: 'The capitalist mode of appropriation, the result of the capitalist mode of production, produces capitalist private property. This is the first negation of individual private property, as founded on the labour of the proprietor. But capitalist production begets, with the inexorability of a law of nature, its own negation. It is the negation of negation . . .' Compare 'He bears the seed of ruin in himself' – Matthew Arnold, *Merope* (1858).

continent isolated In Maurice Bowra's *Memories 1898–1939* (1966) he recalls how Ernst Kantorowicz, a refugee from Germany in the 1930s, 'liked the insularity of England and was much pleased by the newspaper headline, "Channel storms. Continent isolated", just as he liked the imagery in, "Shepherd's Bush combed for dead girl's body".' As an indicator of English isolationism, the 'Continent isolated' headline does indeed seem to have surfaced in the 1930s. John Gunther, *Inside Europe* (1938 edn), has: 'Two or three winters ago a heavy storm com-

pletely blocked traffic across the Channel. "CONTINENT ISOLATED," the newspapers couldn't help saying.' The cartoonist Russell Brockbank drew a newspaper placard stating 'FOG IN CHANNEL – CONTINENT ISOLATED' (as shown in his book *Round the Bend with Brockbank*, published by Temple Press, 1948). By the 1960s and 1970s, and by the time of Britain's attempts to join the European Community, the headline was more often invoked as: 'FOG IN CHANNEL. EUROPE ISOLATED.'

continong   See MORNING ALL.

contributions   See ALL.

(to go on a) Cook's tour   To travel in an organized manner, possibly on a tour of rather greater extent than originally intended (compare MAGICAL MYSTERY TOUR). Thomas Cook was the founder of the world's original travel agency. His first tour was in 1841 when he took a party of fellow teetotallers on a railway trip in the British Midlands. Alas, there has always been a certain amount of prejudice against the organized tour. Amelia B. Edwards, the Victorian Egyptologist, is suitably caustic in *A Thousand Miles Up the Nile* (1877): '[The newcomer in Cairo soon] distinguishes at first sight between a Cook's tourist and an independent traveller'.

cool as a cucumber   (Of a person) very calm and collected, not nervous. The first recorded use is in a poem (1732) by John Gay: 'I, cool as a cucumber, could see the rest of womankind.'

cool as a mountain stream   A slogan for Consulate (menthol) cigarettes, in the UK from the early 1960s.

cool Britannia   Britain's Labour Government (elected in 1997) briefly flirted with this concept slogan during its first year in office, then ditched it (perhaps mindful of how its predecessor's BACK TO BASICS' cry ultimately did it more harm than good). The idea had been to promote a more up-to-date image of Britain and not one of a country stuck in the past, a heritage theme park of castles and villages. The origin of the pun on 'Rule Britannia' was quickly located in the title and lyrics of Vivian Stanshall's song for the Bonzo Dog Doo Dah Band record album *Gorilla* (1968):

'Cool Britannia, Britannia you are cool, take a trip . . . / Britons ever, ever, ever shall be hip (hit me, hit me!)' However, a more pertinent and more recent cue for the phrase may have come from the name of a strawberry and chocolate ice manufactured by Ben & Jerry's. That name was coined by the winner of a competition to come up with a new flavour in 1996. Ben & Jerry ditched it, too.

(a) cool hundred/thousand/million
OED2 says drily that the 'cool' gives emphasis to the (large) amount. Is this because a large amount of money is rather chilling, lacking in warmth, or because of the calm way the money is paid out? Perhaps the word 'cool' in this context anticipates its more modern connection with jazz, as something thrilling, to be admired and approved of. In Henry Fielding's *Tom Jones* (1749), we read: 'Watson rose from the table in some heat and declared he had lost a cool hundred . . .' In Charles Dickens's *Great Expectations* (1861): 'She had wrote a little [codicil] . . . leaving a cool four thousand to Mr Mathew Pocket.' *A Cool Million* is the title of a satire by Nathaniel West (1934), and in Anthony Powell's *Hearing Secret Harmonies* (1975), Lord Widmerpool comments on a smoke bomb let off at a literary prize-giving: 'I wouldn't have missed that for a cool million.'

(the) corridors of power A phrase that had become established for the machinations of government, especially in Whitehall, by the time C. P. Snow chose it for the title of his novel *Corridors of Power* (1964). Earlier, Snow had written in *Homecomings* (1956): 'The official world, the corridors of power, the dilemmas of conscience and egotism – she disliked them all.' 'Boffins at daggers drawn in corridors of power' – headline in *The Times* (8 April 1965).

cor – strike a light! An exclamation now mainly used by way of parody of what a Cockney character might say. *Brewer* (1923) has 'strike-a-light' as a noun for the flint used in striking fire from a tinderbox and also as 'an exclamation of surprise'. *Partridge/Slang* has it as a phrase meaning 'to commence work' and says it comes from sheet metal workers' language.

Partridge also has 'light' as a slang word for 'credit' and 'to strike a light' as 'to open an account' of the small sort (as on a slate at a pub). Of the exclamation, *Partridge* just has it 'probably from the imperative of the literal Standard English phrase'. The *OED2* finds it as a 'mild imprecation' (mostly from Australia and New Zealand), with its earliest citation from 1936. A suggested origin is that it derives from the fact that if you strike a match in a lavatory (or outdoor privy) it kills any unpleasant odour (by burning off the methane).

così fan tutte Literally, 'thus do all' in Italian but understood to refer to women, specifically referring to their infidelity. Hence, the phrase is taken to mean 'That's what all women do' or 'Women are like that.' Mozart's opera with the title was first performed in 1790. The phrase had appeared earlier in Lorenzo Da Ponte's libretto for Mozart's *Le nozze di Figaro* (1778). In that opera, Don Basilio sings, '*Così fan tutte le belle, non c'è alcuna novità* [that's what all beautiful women do, there's nothing new in that].'

cost See ARM AND A LEG.

cotton See BLESS HIS LITTLE.

(a) couch potato Pejorative term for an addictive, uncritical (and possibly fat) TV viewer. Said to have been coined in the late 1970s by Tom Iacino in southern California. *Sunday Today* was only getting round to explaining the word to British readers on 27 July 1986. But why potato? Is it because of the shape of a fat person slouched on a couch? Or does it allude to the consumption of potato crisps, or to behaviour like that of a 'vegetable'? It seems the phrase may be a complicated pun on the phrase 'boob-tube' (US slang for TV, not an article of clothing) and 'tuber', meaning a root vegetable.

coughin' well tonight The British comedian George Formby Snr (1877–1921) used to make this tragically true remark about himself. He had a convulsive cough, the result of a tubercular condition, and it eventually killed him. He was ironically known as 'The Wigan Nightingale'.

coughs and sneezes spread diseases A British Ministry of Health warning from about 1942, coupled with the line, 'Trap the germs in your handkerchief'.

could it get any better than this? 'A popular phrase with [TV] presenters this year; particularly those facing the unpredictable mobs who turn up for reality show live broadcasts' – *The Independent* (1 January 2003). 'The first night swung, the audience stood at the end, and we were home and I should be saying to myself "It doesn't get any better than this," but maybe it gets different' – Richard Eyre, *National Service* (2003), diary entry for 20 December 1996. Compare **as good as it gets** (probably a contraction of the question 'Is this as good as it gets?'). *As Good As It Gets* was the title of a film (US 1997); 'David Aaronovitch regards the Government's Sustainable Communities Plan as "about as good as it's going to get"' – *The Observer* (16 February 2003).

could make any ordinary girl feel like a princess (or **could make you feel like Cinderella before the clock struck)** Testaments to male prowess of one sort or another, though these are phrases likely to occur more to journalists than mere mortals. In February 1983, the Press Council reported on the curious case of Miss Carol Ann Jones and the *News of the World*. Miss Jones had been quoted as having said that Peter Sutcliffe, the Yorkshire Ripper, 'could make any ordinary girl from a mill town feel like a princess. Even now I have a place in my heart for him'. The Press Council felt that 'some words attributed to her as direct quotations were ones she was unlikely to have used'.

(you) couldn't knock the skin off a rice pudding Said to a weak person or to a big-headed person. *Partridge/Catch Phrases* dates it from the First World War.

(you) couldn't run a whelk-stall A way of describing incompetence, this appears to have originated with John Burns, the Labour MP: 'From whom am I to take my marching orders? From men who fancy they are Admirable Crichtons . . . but who have not got sufficient brains and ability to run a whelk-stall?' – *South-Western Star* (13 January 1894). *Partridge/Slang* has 'no way to run a whelk-stall' as the UK equivalent of the US '[that's] a hell of a

way to run a railroad' and dates it from later, in the 20th century. The phrases **couldn't organize a piss-up in a brewery** and **couldn't fight his/her way out of a paper bag** are more likely to be employed nowadays.

(a) counter-factual proposition Meaning, 'a lie' – a joke coinage from *The New York Times* (22 March 1991) – though probably more to do with the art of bureaucratic euphemism than with mainstream political correctness.

(two) countries separated by a common language Referring to England and America, was this said by Shaw or Wilde? Wilde wrote: 'We have really everything in common with America nowadays except, of course, language' – *The Canterville Ghost* (1887). However, the 1951 *Treasury of Humorous Quotations* (eds Esar & Bentley), quotes Shaw as saying: 'England and America are two countries separated by the same language,' without giving a source. A radio talk prepared by Dylan Thomas shortly before his death (and published after it in *The Listener*, April 1954), contained an observation about European writers and scholars in America 'up against the barrier of a common language'.

country See ANOTHER; FROM A FAR; IN THE.

country folk See EVERY DAY.

(a) country mile A long distance, from the fact that covering a mile in the country seems to take longer than it would in a built-up area. It is often to be observed that mileages given on signposts in the country seem to be underestimates of the distance it feels as though you are travelling. Probably since the late 1940s and of American origin. 'South Africa normally the league leader by a country mile in the coins business . . .' – *The Herald* (Glasgow) (4 June 1986); 'Irish coach Dick Best had nothing but admiration for Northampton. "That was the best [Rugby Union] team we have played against this season by a country mile' – *Daily Mirror* (27 January 2000).

courage, mon brave! Encouragement associated with French swashbuckling romances, though perhaps more to be found in film versions and parodies than in the originals. Nevertheless, Alexandre Dumas, *Vingt ans après*, Chap. 26 (1845), has: '*D'Artagnan se tourna vers Porthos, et crut remarquer qu'il était agité d'un léger tremblement. Il sourit, et s'approchant de son oreille, il lui dit: – Bon courage, mon brave ami! ne soyez pas intimidé.*' Charles Nodier, *Contes*, Chap. 13 (1830–3), has it precisely: '*Courage, mon brave, dit-il en me frappant sur l'épaule avec un air tout riant.*'

course you can, Malcolm   One of those advertising phrases that, for no accountable reason, caught on for a while. From British TV ads for Vick's Sinex (nasal spray). In February 1994, after the ads had been relaunched, starring the original 1970s' cast, the manufacturers released a dance single recording the adventures of Malcolm, the youth in the TV commercials.

courting   See ARE YER.

(the) courts of the morning   The somewhat obscure title of John Buchan's adventure novel *The Courts of the Morning* (1929) is a translation of *Los Patios de la Mañana*, a geographical hill feature in the fictitious South-American republic of Olifa, where the book is set: 'In the Courts of the Morning there was still peace. The brooding heats, the dust-storms, the steaming deluges of the lowlands were unknown. The air was that of a tonic and gracious autumn slowly moving to the renewal of spring.' It is not known whether the name has anywhere been given to actual hills.

cow   See ALL BEHIND; AS DARK; EVERYBODY TO THEIR.

cowabunga!   This cry was re-popularized by the Teenage Mutant Ninja Turtles phenomenon of the early 1990s but had been around since the 1950s when, in the American cartoon series *The Howdy Doody Show*, it was used as an expression of anger – 'kowa-bunga' or 'Kawabonga' – by Chief Thunderthud. In the 1960s it transferred to *Gidget*, the American TV series about a surfer, as a cry of exhilaration when cresting a wave and was taken into surfing slang. In the 1970s, the phrase graduated to TV's *Sesame Street*.

cowardy, cowardy custard!   One child's taunt to another who is holding back from some activity or who runs away. First recorded in 1836. The original rhyme was, 'Cowardy, cowardy custard / Can't eat bread and mustard.' 'Costard' was an old contemptuous name for a 'head', which may be relevant. Cowardice is often associated with the colour yellow, of course. A revue devoted to the songs of Noël Coward was presented in London with the title *Cowardy Custard* in 1972, with no reflection on his moral standing.

crack   See AT THE CRACK.

crackerjack!   In the USA, this word has the meaning 'excellent' and has also been used as the name of a brand of popcorn and syrup. *Crackerjack* was the title of a BBC TV children's programme (from 1955) which had a noisy studio audience of youngsters who had only to hear the word 'Crackerjack' for them to scream back 'CRACKERJACK!' It was probably not a word known to them before.

crafty as a wagon-load of monkeys   Very cunning. Mid-20th century. Compare the (apparently unconnected) cry to a group of people waiting to depart in a bus or coach: 'a cartload of monkeys and the wheel won't turn' – that *Partridge/Catch Phrases* suggests was current by 1890.

crazy like a fox   I.e. 'apparently crazy but with far more method than madness' – *Partridge/Catch Phrases*. Craziness is hardly a quality one associates with foxes, so the expression was perhaps merely formed in parallel with the older 'cunning as a fox'. The similar 'crazy *as* a fox', also of US origin, was known by the mid-1930s. Foxes always seem to get into expressions like these. In a 1980 radio interview, the actress Judy Carne was asked about Goldie Hawn, her one-time colleague on *Laugh-In*. Carne said: 'She's not a dizzy blonde. She's about as *dumb* as a fox. She's incredibly bright.' *Crazy Like a Fox* was the title of a US TV series about a 'sloppy old private eye' and his 'smart lawyer son' (from 1984). Before that, it was used as the title of a book by S. J. Perelman (1945).

(a) creaking gate hangs longest   Of a (complaining) person in poor health who outlives an apparently healthier person. *Apperson* finds 'a creaking gate (or door) hangs long' by 1776. Other variants are: 'A creaking cart goes long on the wheels' (quoted as a common proverb in 1900) and 'creaking carts go a long way.'

(the) cream of the crop The very best of anything. Date of origin unknown. And which crop produces cream, one wonders? 'As a matter of opinion I think he's the tops / My opinion is he's the cream of the crop' – song 'My Guy' by Smokey Robinson (1964); 'Recipe: Cream of the crop – Edward Hardy on a sauce that's so good for the sole' – headline in *The Guardian* (16 July 1994); 'Reporting on the Lincoln Center controversy, Greg Thomas in *The Guardian* said that to call the jazz programme racist was "patently ridiculous". He also made the point that to discuss jazz musicians in this way should be unnecessary, since in jazz history, "like post-Fifties basketball, the cream of the crop have always risen"' – *The Times* (16 July 1994); 'Football: Cream Of The Crop: John Spencer Shows Off New Hairstyle' – headline in *The People* (13 November 1994).

creative accountancy (or accounting) A term for ingenious manipulation of accounts that may or may not actually be illegal. An early example of the phrase occurs in the film *The Producers* (US 1968): 'It's simply a matter of creative accounting. Let's assume for a moment that you are a dishonest man . . . It's very easy. You simply raise more money than you need.' The film's subject is such accountancy applied to the world of the theatrical angel.

(a/the) credibility gap The difference between what is claimed as fact and what is actually fact. It dates from the time in the Vietnam war when, despite claims to the contrary by the Johnson administration, an escalation of US participation was taking place. 'Dilemma in "Credibility Gap"' was the headline over a report on the matter in *The Washington Post* (13 May 1965).

(la) crème de la crème The elite; the very pick of any group in society. *OED2* claims that this expression was first used of the Austrians by the actress and author Fanny Kemble in a letter of 22 January 1848. Another claim is that it was introduced by Fanny Trollope in her travel book *Vienna and the Austrians* (1838). 'I am putting old

heads on your young shoulders . . . and all my pupils are the crème de la crème' – Muriel Spark, *The Prime of Miss Jean Brodie*, Chap. 1 (1961).

(a) crew cut A brush-like short haircut popular with the US military but apparently first adopted by oarsmen at Harvard and Yale Universities (hence the 'crew') and athletes who no doubt appreciated its aerodynamic qualities. Known since 1942.

Crichton See ADMIRABLE.

crime doesn't pay A slogan used variously by the FBI and by the cartoon character Dick Tracy. Known by 1927. *Crime Does Not Pay* was the title of a series of two-reel cinema shorts made by MGM between 1935 and 1947. 'You been reading a lot of stuff about "Crime don't pay". Don't be a sucker. That's for yaps and small-timers on shoestrings. Not for people like us' – gangster Rocky Sullivan (James Cagney) in *Angels With Dirty Faces* (US 1938). 'Crime never pays, not even life insurance benefits' – Zelda Popkin, *No Crime For a Lady* (1942). 'Crime doesn't pay' – *Punch* (22 August 1945).

crimes and misdemeanors A phrase from the Constitution of the United States, Article II, Sect. 4 (1787): 'The President, Vice-President, and all civil officers of the United States, shall be removed from office on impeachment for, and conviction of, treason, bribery, or other high crimes and misdemeanors.' Hence, *Crimes and Misdemeanors*, the title of a Woody Allen film (US 1989).

criminal folly An inevitable pairing of words meaning 'folly that has deeply serious implications or is sufficient to be likened to a criminal act'. Known in the 19th century. Listed in *The Independent* (24 December 1994) as a cliché of newspaper editorials. 'Miners' lamps . . . so convenient . . . that it would really seem to be nothing short of criminal folly to run the slightest risk with flame lamps' – *Daily News* (10 May 1888); 'He condemned the 1982 Israeli invasion of Lebanon as a "criminal folly" and used the same words yesterday to describe the Israeli bombardment of the villages of southern Lebanon last July' – *The Independent* (7 September 1993); 'He also warned Unionists not to entertain ideas of an independent Ulster. "In Ulster, the greater number who may still have to contend with terrorism would be guilty of criminal folly if they opened up a second front with Britain as the other enemy'" – *The Sunday Telegraph* (16 October 1994).

criminals return to the scene of the crime (sometimes **murderers ...)** There is no obvious source for this proverbial saying. A French propaganda poster from the First World War has the slogan: '*Les assassins reviennent toujours . . . sur les lieux de leur crime.*' In fiction, Raskolnikov does indeed return to the scene of *his* crime in Dostoevsky's *Crime and Punishment* (1866), though the phrase is not used. From H. B. Creswell, *Thomas*, Chap. 5 (1918): 'I crept out of the house like a murderer fascinated by the scene of his crime'. From Dorothy L. Sayers, *Unnatural Death*, Chap. 6 (1927): 'It is a well-established psychological fact that criminals . . . revisit the place of the crime.' In *The Laurel-Hardy Murder Case* (US 1930), a policeman says: 'I believe that the criminal always returns to the scene of his crime.' From the BBC radio *Goon Show* (15 October 1954): 'We all know that a criminal always returns to the scene of the crime.' There may be a slight allusion to Proverbs 26:11: 'As a dog returneth to his vomit, so a fool returneth to his folly'.

crisis, what crisis? The British Prime Minister James Callaghan may be said to have been eased out of office by a phrase he did not (precisely) speak. Returning from a sunny summit meeting in Guadeloupe to Britain's 'winter of discontent' on 10 January 1979, he was asked by a journalist at a London airport press conference: 'What is your general approach and view of the mounting chaos in the country at the moment?' Callaghan replied: 'Well, that's a judgement that you are making. I promise you that if you look at it from the outside (and perhaps you are taking rather a parochial view), I don't think that other people in the world would share the view that there is mounting chaos.' Next day, *The Sun* carried the headline: 'Crisis? What crisis?' Callaghan lost the May 1979 General Election. The editor of *The Sun* was given a knighthood by the incoming Prime

Minister. Some people insist on recalling that Callaghan said something much more like 'Crisis? What crisis?' on the TV news. When told that these words do not survive on film, these people begin to talk about conspiracy theories. But the impression he created was a strong one. In *The Diaries of Kenneth Williams* (1993), the comedian noted in his entry for 10 January 1979 (the day of Callaghan's return and not of the *Sun* headline, which he would not have seen anyway): 'Saw the news. Callaghan arrived back from Guadeloupe saying, "There is no chaos" which is a euphemistic way of talking about the lorry drivers ruining all production and work in the entire country, but one admires his phlegm.'

crocodile tears A false display of sorrow. The legend that crocodiles shed tears in order to lure victims to their deaths was established by the year 1400. In an account of a 1565 voyage by Sir John Hawkins (published by Richard Hakluyt, 1600), there is: 'In this river we saw many crocodiles . . . His nature is ever when he would have his prey, to cry and sob like a Christian body, to provoke them to come to him, and then he snatcheth at them.' Shakespeare makes reference to crocodile tears in *Antony and Cleopatra*, *Othello* and *Henry VI*.

crop See CREAM OF THE.

cropper See COME A.

(a) cross of gold William Jennings Bryan's speech to the Democratic Convention in July 1896 contained an impassioned attack on supporters of the gold standard: 'You shall not press down upon the brow of labour this crown of thorns. You shall not crucify mankind upon a cross of gold.' Bryan had said virtually the same in a speech to the House of Representatives on 22 December 1894. He won the nomination and fought the presidential election against William J. McKinley, who supported the gold standard but lost. A 'cross of gold'-type speech is sometimes called for when a politician (like Edward Kennedy in 1980) is required to sweep a convention with his eloquence.

crossroads See DIRTY WORK.

(to) cross the Rubicon To make a significant decision from which there is no turning back. An allusion to Julius Caesar's crossing the stream of that name in 49 BC, which meant that he passed from Cisalpine Gaul into Italy and thus became an invader. Known by 1626. Hence also this limited application: "'I've been to Paris with Fulke Warwick . . .' 'Talk about crossing the Rubicon.' 'Crossing the Rubicon' was deb talk for going all the way' – Christopher Ogden, *Life of the Party* (1994).

crow See AS THE.

(a) crowd pleaser Any form of art and entertainment that contains obviously popular elements inserted simply with the intention of 'playing to the gallery'. Known by 1943 in North America. 'George Eliot and Charles Dickens are the giants of the Victorian novel. Eliot was an uncompromising highbrow; Dickens a shameless crowd-pleaser. In the end, only the quality matters' – *Evening Standard* (London) (30 June 1994); 'The wish to increase the number of available third level places is a noble one and a sure fire crowd pleaser, but unless the Department of Education is willing to put its money where its mouth is by extending college facilities and employing more staff, the admission of yet more young hopefuls would be lunacy' – *The Irish Times* (29 August 1994).

crown imperial 'Crown Imperial' was the title given to Sir William Walton's march, which was composed for the coronation of King George VI in 1936. 'Orb and Sceptre' followed for that of Queen Elizabeth II in 1953. In a television interview, Walton said that if he lived to write a march for a third coronation it would be called 'Sword and Mace'. He was alluding to the passage from Shakespeare, *Henry V*, IV.i.266 (1599): ''Tis not the balm, the sceptre and the ball, / The sword, the mace, the crown imperial / . . . That beats upon the high shore of this world.' Oddly enough, the orchestral parts of 'Crown Imperial' bear a different quotation: 'In beauty bearing the crown imperial' from the poem 'In Honour of the City' by William Dunbar. This is what Walton must have begun with, subsequently discovering the Shakespeare sequence.

(the) crowning glory Meaning, 'whatever puts the final touches to a triumph or is the culmination of a series of triumphs or outstanding features'. Known by 1902. 'Gerty's crowning glory was her wealth of wonderful hair' – James Joyce, *Ulysses* (1922). 'Tennis . . . It is as though the subjects of the Queen of Eastbourne reached a collective decision at the beginning of the week to offer the 37-year-old a final crowning glory before she bids farewell to the place she has made her own' – *The Times* (16 June 1994); 'That was the era when Coney Island was billed as The Eighth Wonder Of The World. Brooklyn was the second largest city in America, and Coney was its crowning glory' – *The Sunday Times* (4 September 1994).

(the) crown jewels Anything of great value, so named after the British Crown Jewels stored in the Tower of London. 'Crown jewels . . . the male genitals' – Julia P. Stanley, 'Homosexual Slang', *American Speech*, xlv (1970); 'Material so sensitive that national security demands that the material is not exposed to the public . . . It was necessary for the jury to examine in detail the material – called "the Crown Jewels" – in order that it might understand the full facts' – *The Guardian* (29 January 1985); 'Move to safeguard TV "crown jewels" [important programmes]' – headline in *The Guardian* (17 January 1996).

crucial A 1980s' vogue word, used by the young to convey the same as 'great', 'fantastic'. It came into British slang – from American hip hop, apparently – through its use as a catchphrase of Delbert Wilkins, a creation of the British comedian Lenny Henry (b. 1958). As presenter of a record programme on BBC Radio 1 in 1982, Henry portrayed 'Wilkins' as a garrulous DJ from a Brixton pirate radio station. 'Well, basic, well, crucial, man!' he would say. He also used the word **wicked** to mean 'wonderful', 'splendid', and this also passed into youth slang. His exclamation **diamond!** did not. Henry first came to notice as a 16-year-old on ITV's *New Faces*. His send-up of a woolly-hatted Rastafarian – Algernon Winston Spencer Churchill Gladstone Disraeli Pitt the Younger Razzmatazz – gave the West Indian catchphrase **Ooookaaay!** to a generation of schoolchildren. On ITV's *O.T.T.* (1982), Henry introduced another black character, 'Joshua

Yarlog', with the catchphrase **Katanga!** (which, as one paper commented, 'half the population already seems to have taken up in an attempt to drive the other half mad').

cruellest See IS THE.

(the) crux of the matter (or case or problem) The central or divisive point of interest, especially in argument or debate. Date of origin unknown. 'The crux of the matter is that the behaviour under consideration must pass through the needle's eye of social acceptance' – Ruth Benedict, *Patterns of Culture* (1934); '"Precisely," answered the officer, "and that brings us to the crux of the matter. Namely, that the Eurocorps is a historical or political symbol, but remains a military nonentity' – *The European* (22 July 1994); 'The crux of the matter is that the Europeans believe that the Bosnians are almost certain to be the losers even if the arms embargo is lifted, while the Americans profess to believe that the Bosnians could beat the Serbs if there was equality in weaponry' – *The Guardian* (29 November 1994).

(to) cry all the way to the bank Meaning 'to be in a position to ignore criticism', this expression was certainly popularized, if not actually invented, by the flamboyant pianist Liberace (1919–87). In his autobiography (1973), Liberace wrote: 'When the reviews are bad I tell my staff that they can join me as I cry all the way to the bank.' Liberace was using the expression by 1954. In Alfred Hitchcock's film *North by Northwest* (US 1959), the Cary Grant character gets to say: '. . . while we cry about it all the way to the bank'. (A less pointed version is, 'to *laugh* all the way to the bank'.) Liberace was as famous for his phrases in the 1950s as he was for his candelabra. He seemed to say 'ladies and gentlemen' between every sentence, frequently mentioned his 'Mom', and thanked audiences on behalf of **my brother George**.

(to) cry budget (or cry mum) To keep quiet. Compare the more common 'keep mum'. In Ngaio Marsh's *A Wreath for Riviera* (1949), Inspector Alleyn whispers, 'You cry mum and I'll cry budget', when hiding from a villain. The allusion is to Shakespeare, *The Merry Wives of Windsor*,

V.ii.6 (1600–1), in which Slender's ludicrous planned elopement with Anne Page is to be carried out by their finding each other in the crowd with the greeting 'Mum' to be answered by 'Budget' – 'and by that we know one another'. The Arden edition of Shakespeare adds the gloss: 'An appropriately childish greeting. "Mumbudget" . . . was used of an inability or a refusal to speak . . . *OED* conjectures, with convincing citations, that it was "the name of some children's game in which silence was required". Thomas Hardy later uses "to come mumbudgeting" in the sense of "to come secretly".'

crystal clear This phrase is about as clear (in meaning) as it is possible to get. Known in connection with glass (Browning, 1845) and water (1859). Identified as a current cliché in *The Times* (17 March 1995). 'The Administration was never crystal-clear on exactly how we would massively retaliate with nuclear weapons' – *The Listener* (29 March 1962); 'In this book we have the service itself and the crystal clear explanations of Raymond Chapman as to the meaning of various passages and who does what and why' – advertisement for book *Draw Near With Faith* (1995).

(a/the) cultural cringe A belief that one's own country's culture is inferior to that of others. This phrase is probably Australian in origin and is certainly well known in that country. Arthur Angell Phillips wrote in 1950: 'Above our writers – and other artists – looms the intimidating mass of Anglo-Saxon culture. Such a situation almost inevitably produces the characteristic Australian Cultural Cringe – appearing either as the Cringe Direct, or as the Cringe Inverted, in the attitude of the Blatant Blatherskite, the God's-Own-Country and I'm-a-better-man-than-you-are Australian bore.'

(a) culture vulture Slightly mocking name for a person who gobbles up artistic experiences, especially as a tourist. *DOAS* has it by 1947 and, indeed, it is probably an American coinage.

cunning plan See I HAVE.

cupboard love Devotion to people because of the material things, notably food, that they can provide. Originally, perhaps, from the display of love by children towards the cook in a household – love that is based on this kind of self-interest. From the middle of the 18th century. Later also known as **lump-love**, where the real object of affection is a lump of food.

(my) cup runneth over Meaning 'I'm overjoyed; my blessings are numerous', the expression derives from Psalms 23:5: 'Thou preparest a table before me in the presence of mine enemies: thou anointest my head with oil; my cup runneth over.' Shirley Polykoff, the advertising executive, recounts in her book *Does She . . . Or Doesn't She?* (1975) that she once jestingly proposed 'Her cup runneth over' as a slogan for a corset manufacturer. 'It took an hour to unsell him,' she adds.

(the) cup that cheers The reference here is to tea (taken in preference to alcohol). The phrase originated in 'The Winter Evening' from William Cowper's *The Task* (1783), where it is in the plural: 'Now stir the fire, and close the shutters fast, / Let fall the curtains, wheel the sofa round, / And, while the bubbling and loud-hissing urn / Throws up a steamy column, and the cups, / That cheer but not inebriate, wait on each, / So let us welcome peaceful ev'ning in.' Eric Partridge listed 'cups that cheer but not inebriate' in his *Dictionary of Clichés* (1940) and noted that earlier, in *Siris* (1744), Bishop Berkeley had said of tar water that it had a nature 'so mild and benign and proportioned to the human constitution, as to warm without heating, to cheer but not inebriate'. In *Three Men In a Boat*, Chap. 2 (1889), Jerome K. Jerome puts the phrase into reverse: 'Luckily you have a bottle of the stuff that cheers and inebriates, if taken in proper quantity, and this restores to you sufficient interest in life.'

(like a) curate's egg Meaning, 'patchy, good in parts, of unequal quality', the phrase comes from the caption to a *Punch* cartoon entitled 'TRUE HUMILITY' (9 November 1895) in which a 'Right Reverend Host' (a bishop at the breakfast table) is saying: 'I'm afraid you've got a bad egg, Mr Jones!' The nervous young curate, keen not to say anything critical, flannels the reply: 'Oh no, my Lord, I assure you! Parts of it are excellent.' Hence the expression, although the point of the cartoon is rather that the egg is completely bad and the curate is seeking a way of softening any criticism implied by pointing this out in circumstances that are inexpedient. The cartoon was drawn by George Du Maurier, the French-born British artist and novelist (1834–96) during the last year of his life.

curlies See BY THE SHORT.

(the) curse of Scotland The nine of diamonds (playing card). As to why this should be, there are up to eight reasons advanced. The most popular of these is probably that which asserts that the Duke of Cumberland wrote his 'no quarter' command after the Battle of Culloden (1746) on the back of a nine of diamonds card. The slaughter of Jacobites at and after the battle by this 'Butcher' has never been forgotten in Scotland. However, the term for the playing card was already known by this date.

(a) curtain lecture (or Caudle lecture) Meaning 'a private reproof given by a wife to her husband', this phrase refers to the scolding that took place after the curtains round the bed (as on a four-poster) had been drawn. Known as such by 1633. The 'Caudle' variation derives from Douglas Jerrold's *Mrs Caudle's Curtain Lectures*, a series published by *Punch* in 1846 in which Mr Caudle suffered the naggings of his wife after they had gone to bed. Another early version of the idea is contained in the phrase 'boulster lecture' (1640). Lady Diana Cooper in a letter of 12 January 1944 wrote: 'Clemmie has given him [Winston Churchill] a Caudle curtain lecture on the importance of not quarrelling with Wormwood.'

(the) customer is always right Gordon Selfridge (1856–1947) was an American who, after a spell with the Marshall Field store in Chicago came to Britain and introduced the idea of the monster department store to London. It appears that he was the first to assert that 'the customer is always right' and many other phrases now generally associated with the business of selling through stores. *Punch* had the phrase as a cartoon heading on 25 April 1934. However, the hotelier César Ritz was being credited with the saying 'the customer is never wrong' by 1908.

(a) custom more honour'd in the breach Usually taken to mean that whatever custom is under consideration has fallen into sad neglect. But in Shakespeare's *Hamlet*, I.iv.16 (1600–1), the Prince tells Horatio that the King's drunken revelry is a custom that would be *better* 'honour'd' if it were not followed at all.

(to) cut and run Meaning, 'to escape; run away'. The phrase has a nautical origin (recorded in 1704). In order to make a quick getaway, instead of the lengthy process of hauling up a ship's anchor, the ship's cable was simply cut. This was easy to do when the anchor was attached to a hemp rope rather than a chain. The figurative use was established by 1861.

(to) cut no ice with someone To make no impression whatsoever. Of American origin. Known by 1895. 'Such speeches! Eloquence cut no ice at *that* dinner' – J. S. Wood, *Yale Yarns* (1895).

(to) cut off at the pass Phrase from Western films, meaning 'to intercept, ambush' (sometimes in the form **head 'em off at the pass**). It resurfaced as one of the milder sayings in the transcripts of the Watergate tapes (published as *The White House Transcripts*, 1974). As used by President Nixon it meant simply, 'We will use certain tactics to stop them'. The phrase occurred in a crucial exchange in the White House Oval Office on 21 March 1973 between the President and his Special Counsel, John Dean: *Nixon*: 'You are a lawyer, you were a counsel . . . What would you go to jail for?' *Dean*: 'The obstruction of justice.' *Nixon*: 'The obstruction of justice?' *Dean*: 'That is the only one that bothers me.' *Nixon*: 'Well, I don't know. I think that one . . . I feel it could be cut off at the pass, maybe, the obstruction of justice.' Sometime after 1954, C. A. Lejeune wrote an article entitled 'Head 'em off at Eagle Pass' for *Good Housekeeping* in which she told a story about the actor Charles Bickford, a standard villain in many Westerns, who claimed to have been saying the line for fifteen years.

(to) cut off your nose to spite your face To perform a self-defeating action. The expression may have originated in 1593 when King Henry IV of France seemed willing to sacrifice the city of Paris because of its citizens' objections to his being monarch. One of his own men had the temerity to suggest that destroying Paris would be like cutting off his nose to spite his face. The phrase seems not to have taken hold in English until the mid-19th century.

(to) cut the mustard To succeed, to have the ability to do what's necessary. One might say of someone 'He didn't cut much mustard.' An American phrase dating from about 1900 when 'mustard' was slang for the 'real thing', 'the best' or the 'genuine article', and this may have contributed to the coinage. Alternatively, as mustard is a notoriously difficult crop to harvest, if you can't cut it or hack it, then your vigour has disappeared and you are not up to scratch. Another theory is that the phrase is a mishearing of 'cut the muster', a military phrase meaning 'well-turned-out' both in appearance and timeliness. Whether there is any connection with the phrase KEEN AS MUSTARD is unclear. 'Boss Finley's too old to cut the mustard [i.e. perform sexually]' – Tennessee Williams, *Sweet Bird of Youth* (1959); 'So few now bother to attend the Church of England that the ancient title Defender of the Faith – so important in its historical context – cuts little mustard' – Polly Toynbee in *Radio Times* (22 July 1995).

(the) cutting edge That which is considered to be at the centre of attention or activity. The term is derived from the ancient notion that the sharp edge is the most important part of a blade, but the earliest example in the *OED2* is only from 1966. Before it had been watered down by overuse, Dr Jacob Bronowski used the phrase in his TV series *The Ascent of Man* (1973): 'The hand is more important than the eye . . . The hand is the cutting edge of the mind.' A cliché by the late 1980s. In its original sense (of the business end of a blade), it occurs in the first line of John Masefield's poem 'To-morrow' (1921). 'Yet something has changed. Sex – except perhaps, and necessarily, for lesbians and gay men – is no longer at the cutting edge of politics, especially for women' – *The Guardian* (14 March 1989); 'His apologists would no doubt claim Nyman as a cutting-edge post-modernist, knowingly subverting the traditional genre and exposing the hollowness within; but what is the difference?' – *Financial Times* (19 April 1995); 'Barbara Kohnstamm believes we may be at the cutting edge of mother-son relationships' – *The Irish Times* (26 April 1995).

cutting room   See FACE ON.

(to) cut to the chase   Meaning 'to cut out the unnecessary chit-chat and get to the point', the phrase obviously comes from film editing but the transferred use became popular only in the 1990s. There is a literal first use of the phrase in a film editing context in Joseph Patrick McEvoy, *Hollywood Girl* (1929): 'Jannings escapes . . .

Cut to chase.' But even the more recent allusive uses are either *in* films or bound up with them. The phrase occurs in William Goldman's Hollywood novel *Tinsel* (1979); 'Darryl Zanuck used to tell film makers, "If you're in trouble, cut to the chase"' – *The New York Times* (6 November 1981); in the film *The Presidio* (US 1988), Donna Caldwell (Meg Ryan) says seductively to a cop: 'We can sit here and talk for a couple of hours and wonder what it would be like to be alone together . . . or . . . we could just cut to the chase'; from Madonna's diary of filming *Evita*, published in *Vanity Fair* (November 1996): meeting President Menem to get permission for her to sing 'Don't Cry For Me, Argentina' on the actual balcony of the Casa Rosada, Madonna evidently overturned diplomatic niceties and said, 'Let's cut to the chase here. Do we have the balcony or don't we?' Menem replied: 'You can have the balcony.'

D

daddy   See DON'T GO DOWN.

Dad's Army   The long-running BBC TV comedy series *Dad's Army* (1968–77) established in general use a nickname for the Local Defence Volunteers (LDV), formed in Britain at the outbreak of the Second World War and soon renamed the Home Guard. 'Dad's Army' was a posthumous nickname given by those looking back on the exploits of this civilian force (though its members were uniformed and attached to army units). Many of the members were elderly men.

daft   See EE, ISN'T IT.

daft as a brush   Meaning 'stupid', this expression was adapted from the northern English **soft as a brush** by the comedian Ken Platt (1921–98), who said in 1979: 'I started saying daft as a brush when I was doing shows in the Army in the 1940s. People used to write and tell me I'd got it wrong!' (*Partridge/Slang* suggests that 'daft . . .' was in use before this, however, and Paul Beale reports the full version – 'daft

as a brush without bristles' – from the 1920s.)

daggers   See AT DAGGERS.

Damascus   See ROAD TO DAMASCUS.

damn   See AS NEAR AS.

(a) damn close-run thing   A narrow victory. What the 1st Duke of Wellington actually told the memoirist Thomas Creevey about the outcome of the Battle of Waterloo was: 'It has been a damned serious business. Blucher and I have lost 30,000 men. It has been a damned nice thing – the nearest run thing you ever saw in your life' (18 June 1815). The *Creevey Papers* in which this account appears were not published until 1903. Somehow out of this description a conflated version arose, with someone else presumably supplying the 'close-run'.

damn(ed) clever these Chinese (or dead clever chaps/devils these Chinese)   Referring to a reputation for wiliness rather than skill. A Second World War phrase taken up from time to time by the BBC radio *Goon Show* (1951–60). Compare the line 'Damn clever, these *Armenians*' uttered by Claudette Colbert in the film *It Happened One Night* (US 1934).

damned if you do and damned if you don't   A modern version of 'betwixt the devil and the deep blue sea' – possibly of American origin. From *The Guardian* (1 July 1992): 'It's still very much a thing with women that you're damned if you do and damned if you don't. If women choose to stay at home and look after their children, now they're accused of opting out of the workforce and decision-making because they're afraid to look up to it.'

damn fine cup of coffee – and hot!   'Kyle Maclachlan, who plays the FBI Special Agent Dale Cooper in *Twin Peaks* . . . is one of TV's true originals. His much loved and oft-repeated catchphrase "Damn fine cup of coffee, and hot!" has indeed caught on and Maclachlan himself parodies it crisply in a TV commercial' – *Radio Times* (15–21 June 1991). Other food-related exclamations by 'Coop' included: 'Had a slice of cherry pie – *incredible!*' and (confronted with a table of doughnuts), 'A policeman's dream!' The American TV series *Twin Peaks* was first aired in 1990.

damn the torpedoes – full speed ahead!   Meaning, 'never mind the risks [torpedoes = mines], we'll go ahead any way'. A historical quotation. David Glasgow Farragut, the American admiral, said it on 5 August 1864 at the Battle of Mobile Bay during the Civil War.

(a) damsel in distress   A young maiden in difficulty or in an embarrassing position and in need of rescue by a knight in shining armour, by way of allusion to supposed situations in medieval romances. Date of origin unknown. From Tobias Smollett, *Roderick Random*, Chap. 22 (1748): 'Coming to the relief of a damsel in distress.' The P. G. Wodehouse novel *A Damsel in Distress* (1919) eventually became a film musical (US 1937).

(the) dance of the seven veils   Salome so beguiled Herod by her seductive dancing that he gave her the head of St John the Baptist, as she requested. In neither

Matthew 14:6 nor Mark 6:22 is she referred to by name – only 'as the daughter of Herodias'. The name Salome was supplied by Josephus, a 2nd-century Jewish historian. Nor is the nature of her dancing described. One must assume that the particular nature of the dance originated with Oscar Wilde in whose play *Salomé* (pub. 1893) appears the stage direction: '*Salomé dances the dance of the seven veils.*' Originally, Wilde's play was written in French). Richard Strauss took the idea for his opera *Salome* (1905) from it. However, a little earlier, in Gustave Flaubert's 'Hérodias' in *Trois contes* (1877) only one veil is mentioned.

dancing   See ALL-DANCING; ANGELS; BRING ON THE.

(to get one's) dander up   Meaning 'to get ruffled or angry', the expression occurs in William Thackeray's *Pendennis,* Chap. 44 (1848–50): 'Don't talk to me about daring to do this thing or t'other, or when my dander is up it's the very thing to urge me on.' Apparently of US origin (known by 1831), where 'dander' was either a 'calcined cinder' or 'dandruff'. It is hard to see how the expression develops from either of these meanings. The Dutch word *donder*, meaning 'thunder', or 'dunder', a Scottish dialect word for 'ferment', may be more relevant.

(the) dangerous age   The title of an early (and very mild) Dudley Moore film comedy of 1967 was *Thirty Is a Dangerous Age, Cynthia*. This would seem to allude, however distantly and unknowingly, to *Den farlige alder* [The dangerous age], a book in Danish by Karin Michaelis (1910). In that instance, the dangerous age was forty. In the Moore film, it was very important for him to write a musical, or perhaps get married, before he was *thirty*. In fact, the 'dangerous age' is whatever the speaker thinks it is. It might be said of teenagers first encountering the opposite sex, 'Well, that's the dangerous age, of course' as much as it might be said of married folk experiencing the SEVEN YEAR ITCH.

Darby Kelly (or Derby Kelly)   Rhyming slang for 'belly', known in the USA but probably more so in the UK, chiefly through the song 'Boiled Beef and Carrots', popularised by Harry Champion (1866–1942): 'Boiled beef and carrots – that's the stuff for yer darby kel, / Makes yer fat an' keeps yer well . . .' But who was he? A likely person features in a marching/recruiting song that probably dates from the Napoleonic Wars – as it refers back to the singer's grandfather's involvement with the Duke of Marlborough as well as to the Duke of Wellington between the Peninsular Campaign and Waterloo: 'My grandsire beat the drum complete / His name was Darby Kelly-o, / None smart as he at rat-tat-too, / At roll-call or reveille-o.' Thomas Dibdin has been credited with the words of a song entitled 'Darby Kelly' and dated 1820. Whether this is the same, is not known.

(the) daring young man on the flying trapeze The original person featured in the song 'The Man on the Flying Trapeze' by George Leybourne and Alfred Lee (1868) was Jules Léotard (d. 1880), the French trapeze artist. He also gave his name to the tight, one-piece garment worn by ballet dancers, acrobats and other performers. *The Daring Young Man on the Flying Trapeze* was the title of a volume of short stories (1934) by William Saroyan.

dark See ALL WOMEN; AS DARK.

(the) dark continent (and darkest Africa) In 1878, H. M. Stanley, the journalist who discovered Dr Livingstone, published *Through the Dark Continent* and followed it, in 1890, with *Through Darkest Africa*. It was from these two titles that we appear to get the expressions 'dark continent' and 'darkest —' to describe not only Africa but almost anywhere remote and uncivilized. Additionally, *Flexner* (1982) suggests that 'In darkest Africa' was a screen caption in a silent film of the period 1910–14.

(the) darkest hour comes just before the dawn A proverb of the 'things will get worse before they get better' variety. Terence Rattigan used it in his play *The Winslow Boy* (1946). *Mencken* finds it in Thomas Fuller's *A Pisgah-Sight of Palestine* (1650): 'It is always darkest just before the day dawneth.' Whether there is any little literal truth in it is another matter.

(a) dark horse Figuratively, the phrase refers to a runner about whom everyone is 'in the dark' until he comes from nowhere and wins the race – of whatever kind. It is possible the term originated in Benjamin Disraeli's novel *The Young Duke: A Moral Tale Though Gay* (1831) in which 'a dark horse, which had never been thought of . . . rushed past the grandstand in sweeping triumph.' It is used especially in political contexts. 'Rank dark horse in bid to run lottery . . . Brian Newman, lottery follower at Henderson Crosthwaite, says: "Because of its low profile, Rank was unfancied at the outset. But it has emerged as the dark horse"' – *The Sunday Times* (15 May 1994); 'The biggest challenges to Britain appear likely to come from Australia and the United States, with South Africa, back in both events for the first time since 1976, emerging as a possible dark horse' – *The Times* (30 December 1994).

(the) dark lady of the sonnets Nickname of the beauty to whom Shakespeare addressed some of his sonnets (from no. 128 onwards). Her eyes were 'raven black' and so was her hair. Her identity has been a subject for literary detectives for many years, and the candidates are numerous. She was referred to as the 'Dark Lady' in literary criticism by 1901 but the full phrase seems to have been coined by Bernard Shaw as the title of a short play in which the Dark Lady and Shakespeare are both characters. *The Dark Lady of the Sonnets* was first performed in 1914.

darkness and gnashing of teeth A humorous phrase for where there is unhappiness and dissatisfaction. Taken from Matthew 8:12: 'But the children of the kingdom shall be cast out into outer darkness: there shall be weeping and gnashing of teeth.' '[Rogers] had candles placed all round the dining room, in order to show off the pictures. "I asked [the Reverend Sydney] Smith how he liked the plan." "Not at all," he replied, "above there is a blaze of light, and below, nothing but darkness and gnashing of teeth"' – quoted in *Rogers's Table Talk*, ed. A. Dyce (1856).

darkness at noon *Darkness at Noon, or the Great Solar Eclipse of the 16th June 1806* was the title of an anonymous booklet published in Boston (1806). Arthur

Koestler's novel *Darkness at Noon* (1940) (originally written in German but apparently with the title in English) is about the imprisonment, trial and execution of a Communist who has betrayed the Party. It echoes Milton's *Samson Agonistes* (1671): 'O dark, dark, dark, amid the blaze of noon.'

(a) dark night of the soul Mental and spiritual suffering prior to some big step. The phrase '*La Noche oscura del alma*' was used as the title of a work in Spanish by St John of the Cross. This was a treatise based on his poem 'Songs of the Soul Which Rejoices at Having Reached Union with God by the Road of Spiritual Negation' (*circa* 1578). In *The Crack-up* (1936), F. Scott Fitzgerald wrote: 'In a real dark night of the soul it is always three o'clock in the morning, day after day.' Douglas Adams wrote *The Long Dark Tea-time of the Soul* (1988), a novel.

darling See DON'T GO NEAR.

(the) darling buds of May Shakespeare's Sonnet 18 contains the lines: 'Shall I compare thee to a summer's day? / Thou art more lovely and more temperate. / Rough winds do shake the darling buds of May, / And summer's lease hath all too short a date.' Hence, the titles of two modern novels. In H. E. Bates, *The Darling Buds of May* (1958), Charlie the tax inspector recites the poem when he is drunkenly pursuing the lovely Mariette. John Mortimer's *Summer's Lease* (1988) is about goings-on in a villa rented by English visitors to Tuscany.

(the) Darling of the Halls (Sir) George Robey, the British music-hall comedian, was sometimes known as 'the Darling of the Halls'. The appellation derived from the possibly apocryphal exchange between the lawyer F. E. Smith (later Lord Birkenhead) (1872–1930) and a judge. In the way judges have of affecting ignorance of popular culture (compare WHO ARE THE BEATLES?), the judge asked who George Robey was and Smith replied: 'Mr George Robey is the Darling of the music halls, m'lud.' This gains added sense when you know that the judge was Mr Justice *Darling* whose own witticisms attracted much publicity.

Darth Vader Applied to any dark, menacing person, this name derives from a character in the film *Star Wars* (US 1977) and its prequels and sequels. He was a fallen Jedi knight who had turned to evil, appeared totally in shiny black, all skin hidden, and spoke with a distorted voice. 'Mr Lorenzo, who in some circles is viewed as the "Darth Vader" of the industry, has shown nothing but contempt for Eastern [Airlines'] employees, both union and non-contract' – *Palm Beach Post* (5 March 1989).

dash my wig! An archaic oath. The writer and jazz singer George Melly described on BBC Radio *Quote . . . Unquote* (27 May 1997) how his paternal grandmother exclaimed on being offered some (then rare) Danish Blue cheese in the late 1940s: 'Dash me wig, where did you get that?' This turned into a Melly family saying. When cheese was fancied, they said, 'I'll have a bit of dash-me-wig.' *OED2* has 'dash my wig' as a 'mild imprecation' by 1797. As 'dash my vig' the exclamation appears in R. S. Surtees, *Handley Cross*, Chap. 50 (1843). From *Punch* (20 February 1864): 'New Danish oath – "Dash my Schles-wig!"' *Brewer* (1894) finds in addition 'Dash my buttons!' and explains: '*Dash* is a euphemism for a common oath; and *wig*, buttons, etc., are relics of a common fashion at one time adopted in comedies and by "mashers" of swearing without using profane language.'

(a) date with destiny Alliterative cliché. 'Cheers and tears at Ark Royal's date with destiny' – headline in *The Observer* (12 January 2003). Compare: 'They had a date with fate in . . . *Casablanca*' – poster slogan for the film (US 1941).

daughter See DON'T GO NEAR.

(a) daunting prospect (or task) A very difficult prospect/task in prospect. Date of origin unknown, but this inevitable pairing of words was a cliché by the mid-20th century. 'Reclaiming prostitutes was a daunting prospect for charitable women however tough-minded' – F. K. Prochaska, *Women and Philanthropy in Nineteenth Century England* (1980); 'She's always been honest with me. When I was about 21 I cooked dinner for her, which was a daunting prospect. I made a salmon souffle which I thought was rather good, but she said: 'This is disgusting' – *Daily Mail* (24 January 1995); 'Owning a second home is an attractive, but daunting, prospect. However, a Scottish property firm believes that it has the answer at its holiday cottages in St Andrews in Fife and Drummore, near Portpatrick' – *The Herald* (Glasgow) (22 February 1995); 'Jane Forder rings to see whether I will still produce "HBR" diary entries to run alongside those of James Lees-Milne . . . It's a very daunting task' – *National Trust Magazine* (Summer 1995).

dawn   See AT THE CRACK; CAME THE; DARKEST HOUR.

(the) dawn's early light   Phrase from 'The Star-Spangled Banner' (1814) – latterly an American national anthem – by Francis Scott Key: 'O, say, can you see, by the dawn's early light, / What so proudly we hailed at the twilight's last gleaming.' Hence, also, *So Proudly We Hail*, title of a film (US 1943), and *Twilight's Last Gleaming*, title of a film (US/West Germany 1977).

day   See ALL; ANOTHER DAY; AS NIGHT; HAPPY AS THE.

day and age   See IN THIS.

day for night   A film-maker's term for shooting a scene during the day and then tinting it dark to make it look like night. Hence, *Day for Night* – the English title given to François Truffaut's film about film-making (1973) whose original title *La Nuit Américaine* [American Night], is the equivalent phrase in French film-making.

(a) day in the life   'A Day in the Life', the most remembered track from the Beatles' *Sgt. Pepper* album (1967), presumably took its name from that type of magazine article and film documentary that strives to depict 24 hours in the life of a particular person or organization. In 1959, Richard Cawston produced a TV documentary that took this form, with the title *This Is the BBC*. The English title of a novel (1962; film UK 1971) by Alexander Solzhenitsyn was *One Day in the Life of Ivan Denisovich*. John Lennon and Paul McCartney's use of the phrase 'A Day in the Life' for the descrip-

tion of incidents in the life of a drug-taker may have led to the *Sunday Times* Magazine feature 'A Life in the Day' (running since the 1960s) and the play title *A Day in the Death of Joe Egg* by Peter Nichols (1967; film UK 1971).

(a) day late and a dollar short   When describing people, this means they are unprepared and undependable, irresponsible and disorganized. By extension, to include those who habitually miss out on life's opportunities. Confined almost exclusively to the USA, the expression seems to have arisen in the mid-20th century. There was a song, 'Day Late and a Dollar Short', recorded by Billy Barton in 1959. Terry McMillan wrote a novel, *A Day Late and a Dollar Short*, in 2001. A possible origin has been suggested – that the saying derives from field workers who were paid on a daily basis or at the end of their work period. If workers were too tired or too lazy to get in line, they lost out on that day's wages. Compare, perhaps, TOO LITTLE, TOO LATE.

daylight robbery   Flagrant over-charging – a phrase in use by the 1940s and building upon the simple 'it's robbery' to describe the same thing, dating from the mid-19th century. Application of the phrase in Britain to the Window Tax (1691–1851) that led to the blocking up of windows – and thus to a literal form of daylight robbery – appears to be retrospective.

day of destiny   See RENDEZVOUS.

daylight   See BURN.

(the) day of the locust   The relevance of the title *The Day of the Locust* to Nathanael West's novel (1939) about the emptiness of life in Hollywood in the 1930s is not totally clear. Locusts are, however, usually associated with times when waste, poverty or hardship are in evidence. They also go about in swarms, committing great ravages on crops. The climax of the novel is a scene in which Tod, the hero, gets crushed by a Hollywood mob. In the Bible, Joel 2:25 has: 'And I will restore to you the years that the locust hath eaten'; Revelation 9:3: 'There came out of the smoke locusts upon the earth: and unto them we give power'; Revelation 9:4: 'locusts give power to hurt only those men which have not the seal of God in their foreheads'.

days See HAPPIEST.

(the) days of wine and roses Ernest Dowson wrote the lines: 'They are not long, the weeping and the laughter, / Love and desire and hate . . . / They are not long the days of wine and roses; / Out of a misty dream / Our path emerges for a while, then closes / Within a dream' in '*Vitae Summa Brevis Spem Nos Vetar Incohare Longam*' (1896). Hence, *The Days of Wine and Roses*, title of a film (US 1962) about an alcoholic (though the phrase is often used to evoke romance). Hence, also, *The Weeping and the Laughter*, the title of a novel (1988) by Noel Barber, and of autobiographies by J. Maclaren-Ross (1953) and Viva King (1976).

(the) day that the rains came down A line from the song 'The Day the Rains Came', written by Carl Sigman and Gilbert Bécaud. Jane Morgan had a hit with it in 1958.

(the) day war broke out A catchphrase from the Second World War radio monologues of the British comedian Robb Wilton (1881–1957): 'The day war broke out . . . my missus said to me, "It's up to you . . . you've got to stop it." I said, "Stop what?" She said, "The war."' Later, when circumstances changed, the phrase became 'the day *peace* broke out'.

dead See AIN'T IT; BRING OUT YOUR.

dead and gone See HERE'S A FUNNY.

dead – and never called me mother This line is recalled as typical of the three-volume sentimental Victorian novel, yet it does not appear in Mrs Henry Wood's *East Lynne* (1861) as is often supposed. Nevertheless, it was inserted in one of the numerous stage versions of the novel (that by T. A. Palmer in 1874) which were made before the end of the century. The line occurs in a scene when an errant but penitent mother who has returned in the guise of a governess to East Lynne, her former home, has to watch the slow death of her eight-year-old son ('Little Willie'), but is unable to reveal her true identity.

dead as a doornail Completely dead. In the Middle Ages, the doornail was the name given to the knob on which the knocker struck: 'As this is frequently knocked on the head, it cannot be supposed to have much life in it' – *Brewer* (1894). The phrase occurs as early as 1350, then again in Langland's *Piers Plowman* (1362). Shakespeare uses it a couple of times, in the usual form and, as in *Henry IV, Part 2*, V.iii.117 (1597): *Falstaff:* 'What, is the old king dead!' *Pistol:* 'As nail in door!'

(he's) dead but he won't lie down *Partridge/Catch Phrases* dates this saying from around 1910. A song with the title 'He's Dead But He Won't Lie Down' was written by Will Haines, James Harpur and Maurice Beresford for Gracie Fields to sing in the film *Looking on the Bright Side* (UK 1931). A separate song with this title was written by Johnny Mercer (with music by Hoagy Carmichael) for the film *Timberjack* (1955).

dead in the water Helpless, lacking support, finished. Suddenly popular in the late 1980s and undoubtedly of North American origin. In other words, an opponent or antagonist is like a dead fish. He is still in the water and not swimming anywhere. 'Mr John Leese, editor of both the *Standard* and the *Evening News*, replied: "This obviously means that Mr Maxwell's [news]paper is dead in the water"' – *The Guardian* (2 March 1987).

deadlier than the male See FEMALE OF THE SPECIES.

deadly earnest Really serious. Known by 1880. A cliché phrase by the mid-20th century. 'A recital which had more of the air of friendly music-making at home than the deadly earnest aspiration usually encountered on this platform' – *The Times* (1963); '*The Getaway* is in deadly earnest about its deadly games. Without a trace of irony, it often looks crude and cruel' – *Independent on Sunday* (3 July 1994); 'All good knockabout stuff, but Elvis is in deadly earnest about his new venture' – *The Sunday Times* (27 November 1994).

(to wait for) dead men's shoes To wait for someone to die in order to inherit his possessions or position. Known by 1530.

'Who waitth for dead men shoen, shall go long barefoote' – included in John Heywood, *Proverbs* (1546).

dead men tell no tales A proverbial phrase that, oddly, does not seem to have been used as the title of a film (yet), though there was a TV movie (US 1971) with it, based on a novel by Kelly Roos. *Apperson* has it first appearing in the form 'The dead can tell no tales' in 1681. E. W. Hornung entitled a novel *Dead Men Tell No Tales* in 1899. 'Dead men don't tell tales' appears in Walter de la Mare, *The Return*, Chap. 27 (1910).

(a) dead parrot Meaning, 'something that is quite incapable of resuscitation'. This expression derives from the most famous of all *Monty Python's Flying Circus* sketches, first shown on BBC TV (7 December 1969). A man (named 'Praline' in the script) who has just bought a parrot that turns out to be dead, registers a complaint with the pet shop owner in these words: 'This parrot is no more. It's ceased to be. It's expired. It's gone to meet its maker. This is a late parrot. It's a stiff. Bereft of life it rests in peace. It would be pushing up the daisies if you hadn't nailed it to the perch. It's rung down the curtain and joined the choir invisible. It's an ex-parrot.' In early 1988, there were signs of the phrase becoming an established idiom when it was applied to a controversial policy document drawn up as the basis for a merged Liberal/Social Democratic Party. Then *The Observer* commented (8 May 1988): 'Mr Steel's future – like his document – was widely regarded as a "dead parrot". Surely this was the end of his 12-year reign as Liberal leader?' In October 1990, Margaret Thatcher belatedly came round to the phrase (fed by a speechwriter, no doubt) and called the Liberal Democrats a 'dead parrot', at the Tory Party Conference. When the Liberals won a by-election at Eastbourne the same month, the Tory party chairman Kenneth Baker said the 'dead parrot' had 'twitched'. Whether the phrase will have much further life, ONLY TIME WILL TELL. As indeed it did: on 6 October 1998, *The Sun* carried a front page photo of a dead parrot with the head of the Conservative Party leader William Hague superimposed. The headline was:

'This party is no more . . . it has ceased to be . . . this is an EX-party.'

(a) dead ringer Meaning 'one person closely resembling another', the expression derives from horse-racing in the USA, where a 'ringer' has been used since the 19th century to describe a horse fraudulently substituted for another in a race. 'Dead' here means 'exact', as in 'dead heat'. *Dead Ringers* was the title of a BBC Radio 4 comedy series (from 2000) featuring topical impersonations.

(a) deafening silence A silence that by being so noticeable is significant. Known by 1968. 'Conservative and Labour MPs have complained of a "deafening silence" over the affair' – *The Times* (28 August 1985); 'Many in the Rosyth area would like to know why he has maintained a deafening silence on the issue since it was first mooted in 1986' – letter to the editor in *The Scotsman* (19 August 1994); 'As the internationals begin to multiply in the run-up to the World Cup, it is deflating to realise that in too many aspects, the game in Britain is in a mess. The deafening silence which has greeted a sequence of discreditable events in recent months is shaming enough' – *The Daily Telegraph* (5 November 1994).

deal See BIG DEAL.

dear boy Mode of address, now considered rather affected and often employed when poking fun at the speech of actors and similar folk. If the many people who have tried to imitate Noël Coward's clipped delivery over the years are to be believed, the words he uttered most often in his career were 'Dear boy'. His friend Cole Lesley claimed, however, in *The Life of Noël Coward* (1978) that, 'He rarely used this endearment, though I expect it is now too late for me to be believed.' William Fairchild, who wrote dialogue for the part of Coward in the film *Star!* (US 1968), was informed by the Master, after he had checked the script: 'Too many Dear Boys, dear boy.'

dear John Name for a type of letter sent by a woman to a man and telling him that she is breaking off their relationship. Its origins are said to lie in US and Canadian armed forces' slang of the Second World

War when faithless girls back home had to find a way to admit they were carrying on with or maybe had become pregnant by other men. It subsequently became the name of a letter informing a man that he had given the woman VD. Perhaps even AIDS? Known by 1945.

dear mother   See SELL THE PIG.

death   See AND DEATH; ANGEL OF; HIS.

death and the maiden   A phrase originally made famous by *'Der Tod und das Mädchen'* – a song (D. 531) by Schubert (1817), which was a setting of a poem by Matthias Claudius (a brief exchange between the Maiden and Death). The theme was a subject that fascinated northern European painters in the 14th/15th centuries, especially Hans Baldung Grien, whose *Death and the Maiden* (1517) is now to be seen at Basel. It was later re-used by Schubert as the title of his notable String Quartet in D Minor (D. 810). More recently, *Death and the Maiden* was the title of a play (1992; filmed UK/US/France 1994) by Ariel Dorfman. His original version was in Spanish and called *La Muerta y la doncella*.

death by chocolate   Name of a recipe for an extremely rich type of chocolate cake, described as a 'cake/mousse dessert' – probably of US origin. Gallows humour by chocoholics who are happily aware of the possible consequence of overindulgence in their favourite food. Known by 1990. By 2003, there were signs that, possibly in emulation of this coinage, a format phrase 'death by — ' was emerging. TV programmes were entitled *Death By Home* and *Death By Gardening* (showing video clips of household mishaps) and headlines included 'Death by indifference' and 'Death by embarrassment'.

(a/the) death knell   Meaning, 'an event that signals the end or destruction of something'. Originally, the tolling of a bell that signalled a person's death. The figurative use has been known since the 19th century. 'A slogan cry which would . . . sound the death-knell of ascendancy and West Britishism in this country' – *Dundalk Examiner* (1895); 'Boston's union longshoremen have sounded the death knell of their traditional but unwieldy dock

shape-up' – *Boston Sunday Herald* (30 April 1967); 'The Polish Parliament . . . yesterday voted . . . for a new trade union law that sounds the death knell of Solidarity' – *The Times* (9 October 1982); 'This announcement will almost certainly be the death-knell to the 25-square-mile site' – *The Scotsman* (9 February 1995); 'The European Union and Canada yesterday ended their six-week fishing dispute with a deal hailed in Ottawa as a "victory for conservation" but condemned in Spain as the "death knell for the fishing industry"' – *The Times* (17 April 1995).

deathless prose/verse   An (often ironical) description of writing, sometimes used self-deprecatingly about one's own poor stuff. 'He would embody the suggestion about the nose in deathless verse' – Rudyard Kipling, 'Slaves of the Lamp, Part 1' (1897); 'Robert Burns once expressed in deathless verse a Great Wish. His wish, translated into my far from deathless prose, was to the effect . . .' – Collie Knox, *For Ever England* (1943); 'A passionate devotion to your deathless prose' – a 1963 letter from M. Lincoln Schuster to Groucho Marx in *The Groucho Letters* (1967); 'No piece of prose, however deathless, is worth a human life' – Kenneth Tynan in *The Observer* (13 March 1966). From an actor's diary: 'The writer . . . concentrates his most vicious verbal gymnastics [in these scenes]. After we've mangled the deathless prose we have another cup of tea' – *Independent on Sunday* (13 May 1990).

(a/the) death of a thousand cuts (or by a thousand cuts)   Meaning, 'the destruction of something by the cumulative effect of snipping rather than by one big blow'. In February 1989, Robert Runcie, Archbishop of Canterbury, told the General Synod: 'If the Government does not take the axe to the BBC, there is surely here the shadow of death by a thousand cuts.' The allusion may be to a literal death of this kind, as shown in the proverbial saying from an English translation of Chairman Mao's *Little Red Book* (1966): 'He who is not afraid of death by a thousand cuts dares to unhorse the emperor.' An eastern source for the phrase may be hinted at in what Jaffar the villainous magician (Conrad Veidt) says in the 1940 film version of *The Thief of*

Baghdad: 'In the morning they die the death of a thousand cuts.' *Carry on Up the Khyber* (1968) has the phrase, too.

(the) death sentence I.e. the spoken order for execution. In English law, it really was a sentence, but quite a long one, and capable of variation. When William Corder was found guilty of the murder of Maria Marten at the Red Barn, Polstead, Suffolk, the Lord Chief Baron said: '. . . that sentence is, that you be taken back to the prison from which you came, and that you be taken thence, on Monday next, to the place of execution, and there be hanged by the neck till you are dead, and that your body shall afterwards be dissected and anatomized, and the Lord God Almighty have mercy on your soul' – reported in *The Times* (9 August 1828). By 1910, when Dr Harvey Crippen was being sentenced to death for the murder of his wife by poisoning, the Lord Chief Justice (Lord Alverstone), having assumed the black cap, was solemnly saying this: 'The sentence of the Law is that you be taken from this place to a lawful prison, and thence to a place of execution, that you be there hanged by the neck until you are dead, and that your body be buried within the precincts of the prison in which you will be confined before your execution. And may the Lord have mercy on your soul!' This formula had been adopted in 1903. Ultimately it derives from and expands the medieval death sentence – '*Suspendatur per collum* [Let him be hanged by the neck].' Along the way, it had been able to accommodate all the grisly demands made by the Law. Thus, for example, in the 17th century: 'The Court doth award that you be drawn upon a hurdle to the place of execution and there shall be hanged by the neck, and, being alive, shall be cut down and your entrails to be taken out of your body, and, you living, the same to be burnt before your eyes, and your head to be cut off, your body divided into four quarters, and head and quarters to be disposed of at the pleasure of the King's Majesty: and the Lord have mercy on your soul.' The last execution was ordered in Britain in 1964. The death penalty was abolished in 1970. The *OED2* does not find the actual phrase

'death sentence' until 1943, but in Edgar Allan Poe's story 'The Pit and the Pendulum' (1843) he writes of 'the dread sentence of death'.

death where is thy sting? The basic element here is from 1 Corinthians 15:55: 'O death, where is thy sting? O grave, where is thy victory?' There is a parody: 'The bells of hell go ting-a-ling-a-ling / For you but not for me, / Oh death, where is thy sting-a-ling-a-ling, / Or grave, thy victory?' This was notably used by Brendan Behan in Act 3 of his play *The Hostage* (1958), but he was, in fact, merely adopting a song popular in the British Army 1914–18. Even before that, though, it had been sung – just like this – as a Sunday School chorus. It may have been in a Sankey and Moody hymnal, though it has not been traced. 'There was a death-where-is-thy-sting-fullness about her manner which I found distasteful' – P. G. Wodehouse, *Right Ho, Jeeves*, Chap. 9 (1934).

(a) death wish In the original, psychological sense of the phrase, it may be one's own death that is being wished for. In 1913, Sigmund Freud suggested that people have an innate tendency to revert to their original state. This could be self-destructive, although the death wish towards parents might also be strong. Accordingly, the phrase in its psychological sense is a translation of the German *Todeswunsch*, although the two words had come together in English by 1896. The film *Death Wish* (US 1974) and its several sequels is concerned with the death of others by way of retribution. 'Anyone who willingly jumps from an aeroplane at 3,000 feet might be accused of having a death wish. Or perhaps it might be because two successive defeats have undermined his club's dream of promotion. Jim Duffy would argue differently. The fact of the matter is that the Dundee manager is neither a vicarious thrill-seeker nor a crackpot in urgent need of medical assistance' – *Daily Mail* (3 May 1995).

(the) debate continues Concluding phrase from BBC radio news reports of parliamentary proceedings in the 1940s/50s. *The Debate Continues* was also used as the title of a programme in which pundits in the studio would pick over the subjects of parliamentary debates. Compare **(the) case/hunt/ search continues** at the conclusion of similar broadcast (and newspaper) reports on court proceedings, escaped prisoners and missing people.

decisions, decisions! What a harried person might exclaim over having to make even a trivial choice. This is listed among the 'Naff Expressions' in *The Complete Naff Guide* (1983). It is used precisely in this way as a headline in *Punch* (17 June 1970). *Partridge/Catch Phrases* offers about 1955 as a possible starting date. There is perhaps in it an echo of the perpetually fraught White Rabbit in *Alice's Adventures In Wonderland*. Although he doesn't utter this actual phrase, he does mutter: 'Oh my ears and whiskers, how late it's getting.'

deck See ALL HANDS.

decline and fall The title of the novel (1928) by Evelyn Waugh was ludicrously extended to *Decline and Fall . . . of a Birdwatcher!* when filmed (UK 1968). As with all such titles, the origin is *The History of the Decline and Fall of the Roman Empire* (1766–88) by Edward Gibbon. Compare the numerous variations on the **rise and fall of ——** theme: *The Rise and Fall of Legs Diamond* (film US 1960); *The Rise and Fall of the Man of Letters* – a book (1969) by John Gross; *The Fall and Rise of Reginald Perrin* –BBC TV comedy series (1976–80); *The Rise and Rise of Michael Rimmer* (film UK 1970).

decus et tutamen This is the inscription to be found on the rim of the British one pound (£1) coin which replaced the banknote of that denomination in 1983. The same words, suggested by John Evelyn the diarist, had appeared on the rim of a Charles II crown of 1662/3 (its purpose then was as a safeguard against clipping). Translated as 'an ornament and a safeguard' – referring to the inscription rather than the coin – the words come from Virgil's *Aeneid* (Bk 5) '*Decus et tutamen in armis*'. In its full form, this is the motto of the Feltmakers' Company (incorporated 1604).

deed See BLOODY DEED.

—— deeply regret(s) any embarrassment (or inconvenience) caused A cliché of apology. The standard form is something like: '—— apologizes for the late running of this train and for any inconvenience that may have been caused' (never mind the pain of having to listen to the apology being trotted routinely out). Incidentally, when giving apologies it is important never to be explicit as to the cause. If trains arrive late it is 'because of late departure' (but no apology for that); at airports, planes are late taking off 'because of the late arrival of the incoming plane'. Or, in other words, things happen – or, rather, don't happen, 'for operational reasons'. Lieutenant Colonel Sitiveni Rabuka, leader of a coup in Fiji (May 1987), was quoted as saying, 'We apologize for any inconvenience caused.'

Deep Throat This has come to mean 'a person within an organization who supplies information anonymously about wrongdoing by his colleagues'. It was originally the nickname given to the source within the Nixon White House who fed *Washington Post* journalists Carl Bernstein and Bob Woodward with information that helped in their Watergate investigations (1972–4). It has been alleged that 'Deep Throat' never existed but was a cover for unjustified suppositions. The journalists have declined to reveal his identity before he dies. The nickname was derived from *Deep Throat* (US 1972), a notorious porno movie concerning a woman, played by Linda Lovelace, whose clitoris is located in the back of her throat.

(a/the) defining moment (or defining ——) Meaning, 'a time when the nature or purpose of something is made abundantly clear; a moment that encapsulates what something is all about or shapes our perception of it'. Used especially in British politics, though probably of American origin. According to William Safire in *The New York Times* Magazine (10 May 1998), the first person to use 'defining moment' in print was Howell Raines of the same paper in 1983. Identified as a current cliché in *The Times* (17 March 1995). 'The political advisers of Vice-President George Bush claim that his confrontation on Monday with Mr Dan Rather, the CBS

Television news anchorman, was a "defining moment" which has galvanized his campaign for the Republican Party's presidential nomination' – *Financial Times* (28 January 1988); 'Mary Lamb, in a fit of insanity, attacked and killed her mother. It was the defining crisis of Charles Lamb's early life, which shaped his whole future' – Richard Holmes, *Coleridge: Early Visions*, Chap. 6 (1989). In fact, any use of the word 'defining' now borders on the cliché: 'Today we bear witness to an extraordinary act in one of history's defining dramas, a drama that began in a time of our ancestors when the word went forth from a sliver of land between the River Jordan and the Mediterranean Sea' – President Clinton, speech at signing of Middle East peace accord (13 September 1993); 'Bosnian Serb television yesterday showed dramatic footage, likely to be remembered among the defining images of the war, of UN military observers chained to poles beside ammunition dumps and key bridges' – *The Independent* (27 May 1995); 'But Marlowe's *Edward II*, the defining role in McKellen's career 26 years ago, makes spiritual and technical demands beyond this performer's capacity' – *The Observer* (28 May 1995).

de gustibus non [est] disputandum [there is no accounting for/arguing about tastes] This is a proverb and not a quotation or classical Latin. One source describes it as a 'medieval scholastic joke'. Sometimes it is given as *de gustibus et coloribus* [about colours (or perhaps) beauty] *non est disputandum*.

Delenda est Carthago [Carthage must be destroyed] Cato the Elder (or 'the Censor'), the Roman politician and orator (234–149 BC), punctuated or ended his speeches to the Roman Senate with this slogan for eight years around 157 BC, realizing the threat that the other state posed. It worked – Carthage was destroyed (in 146 BC) and Rome reigned supreme, though Cato had not lived to see the effect of his challenge. He did have the decency to precede the slogan with the words '*ceterum censeo* [in my opinion]'.

deliberate See THIS WEEK'S.

delightful weather we're having for the time of year Genteel conversational

gambit, possibly from the 19th century. In parody, often used as a way of changing the subject from something embarrassing. An example occurs in J. B. Priestley, *When We Are Married*, Act 1 (1938).

de mortuis nil nisi bonum [of the dead, speak kindly or not at all] Sometimes ascribed to Solon (*circa* 600 BC), this version of 'speak not evil of the dead' was also a saying of Chilo(n) of Sparta (one of the Seven Sages (6th century BC). Later, Sextus Propertius (who died in AD 2) wrote: '*Absenti nemo non nocuisse velit* [let no one be willing to speak ill of the absent].' Sometimes simply referred to in the form '*de mortuis . . .*', it is a proverb that appears in some form in most European languages.

den See BEARD THE LION.

Dennis the Menace This name has been applied to two separate comic book characters, one British and one American, but both have given a phrase to describe any badly behaved boy (and, by transference, person). The British Dennis was created by David Law in the *Beano* in 1951 and the American one by Hank Ketcham in the same year. What a coincidence. '*Dennis the Menace Comes in From the Cold*. Can Newt Gingrich save the GOP House Minority from irrelevance?' – headline in *US News & World Report* (27 March 1989).

de profundis The title of Oscar Wilde's letter of self-justification following his imprisonment (published 1905) comes from the Latin words for 'out of the depths' (Psalm 130).

(the) desert and the sown Phrase contrasting the desert and ground that has been seeded. Date of origin not known. 'With me along some Strip of Herbage strown / That just divides the desert from the sown' – Edward Fitzgerald, *The Rubáiyát of Omar Khayyám*, St. 10 (1859); 'The difference between Hejaz and Syria was the difference between the desert and the sown' – T. E. Lawrence, *Seven Pillars of Wisdom*, V.lviii (1935).

Desert Storm 'Operation Desert Storm' was the code name bestowed by its American leadership on the Allied military operation whose aim was to reverse the 1990 Iraqi occupation of Kuwait. Curiously, a desert storm is the worst climatic condition under which to launch a military operation. The conflict came to be more widely known as the **Gulf War** (by 22 January 1991) and was concluded by March 1991.

deserves See EVERY GOOD BOY.

designer — PHRASES. This adjective was applied to clothes and fashion accessories in the 1960s/70s. It suggested that they carried the label of a particular designer, were not just mass-produced and, consequently, had extra prestige and were worth coveting. 'Designer jeans' (by 1978) were what probably caused people to notice the usage, bringing together, as they did, the extremes of a 'name' designer and mass production. Then came the jokes: fashionable Perrier was being called 'designer water' by 1984; studied lack of facial shaving by men left them with what was known as 'designer stubble' by 1989.

design for living *Design for Living* was the title of a play (1932) by Noël Coward. This, although dealing with what later would be called 'trendy' people, had nothing to do with fashion. It was about a *ménage-à-trois*, so the 'living' was in that sense. However, the phrase is often used in magazine journalism for headlines when the practical aspects of furniture and even clothes design are being discussed. The Flanders and Swann song 'Design for Living' in *At The Drop of a Hat* (1957) concerned trendy interior decorating and furnishing. *Slanguage* has it as a US slang expression for 'group sex between three people'.

desist! As in 'desist, curb your hilarity' or 'desist, refrain and cease', mock-disapproving phrases employed by the British music-hall comedian (Sir) George Robey (1869–1954), **the Prime Minister of Mirth** (his bill matter). When disapproving of ribald laughter he had provoked, he would say things like: 'If there is any more hilarity, you must leave. Pray temper your hilarity with a modicum of reserve. Desist! And I am surprised at you, Agnes [pronounced Ag–er–ness]!' Also 'Go *out*!' or 'Get *out*!' or simply '*Out*!'

desperate diseases require desperate remedies Proverbial saying commonly ascribed to Guy Fawkes on 6 November 1605 (when he was arrested the day after attempting to blow up the Houses of Parliament). 'A desperate disease requires a dangerous remedy' (the version according to the *DNB*) was apparently said by him to James I, one of his intended victims. The king asked if he did not regret his proposed attack on the Royal Family. Fawkes replied that one of his objects was to blow the Royal Family back to Scotland. He was subsequently tried and put to death. What he said, however, appears to have been a version of an established proverbial saying. In the form: 'Strong disease requireth a strong medicine', *ODP* traces it to 1539. In Shakespeare's *Romeo and Juliet*, IV.i.68 (1594), there is: 'I do spy a kind of hope, / Which craves as desperate an execution / As that which we would prevent.' Shakespeare also alludes to the saying on two other occasions.

desperation, pacification, expectation, acclamation, realization – 'it's Fry's' In the UK, advertisements for Fry's chocolate for many years after the First World War featured the faces of five boys anticipating a bite and coupled them with these descriptive words.

destiny See DATE WITH.

***Deutschland über Alles* [Germany before/ beyond everything]** National slogan in Germany by 1900. '*Deutschland, Deutschland über Alles*' was originally the title of a poem (1841) by August Heinrich Hoffmann von Fallersleben (1798–1874). Sung to Haydn's tune for the Austrian national anthem, the poem became the German national anthem between 1922 and 1945. It was reinstated in 1952 as the national anthem of the German Federal Republic after an attempt to introduce another anthem had failed. Of the original three stanzas, only the third was retained '*Einigkeit und Recht und Freiheit . . .*' – according to G. Taddey, *Lexikon der deutschen Geschichte*. Chiefly, the *über Alles* disappeared.

devices and desires Phrase from the General Confession in the Anglican Book of Common Prayer: 'We have followed too much the devices and desires of our own hearts.' *Devices and Desires* is the title of a crime novel (1989) by P. D. James.

devil See AS BLACK AS; BETWIXT THE.

(the) devil can cite scripture for his own purposes Meaning 'an ill-disposed person may turn even good things to his own advantage', and in this precise form this is an allusion to Antonio the Merchant in Shakespeare's *The Merchant of Venice*, I.iii.93 (1596) who says it because Shylock has just been doing so.

(the) Devil made me do it! The American comedian Flip Wilson became famous for saying this, wide-eyed, about any supposed misdemeanour, when host of a TV comedy and variety hour (1970–4).

(a/the) devil's advocate Originally, a person who advanced arguments, as though on the part of the Devil, *against* the canonization of a particular saint. In Latin, this role was known as *advocatus diaboli*. Now it is used in a very general way about someone who outlines the opposite (and probably unpopular) point of view when something is being discussed. It was being used in this way by 1760. 'The father made it a point of honour to defend the *Enquirer*, the son played devil's advocate' – J. Bonar, *Malthus*, I.i. (1885).

(there'll be the) devil to pay There will be a terrible penalty to pay for pursuing this course of action. Presumably referring to the pacts that people are said to have made with the Devil which always end with the Devil exacting his side of the bargain. It has also been suggested that it has to do with 'paying' or 'caulking the devil', a seam near a ship's keel – hence the longer form, 'The devil to pay and no pitch hot'. 'And then there will be the devil and all to pay' – Jonathan Swift, *Journal to Stella* (letter of 28 September 1711). *The Devil to Pay* is the title of a ballad opera (1731) by Charles Coffey.

diametrically opposed (or opposite or antagonistic) Completely opposed and with no overlapping of views. Kn own by 1645. 'A sense of determinism that is diametrically opposed to the ruler-class "law-and-order and individualism"' – *Black*

World (December 1973); 'Confusion surrounding the US action in Haiti has not destroyed optimism . . . but the existence of two diametrically opposed political camps did not dampen the euphoria in Port-au-Prince last week' – *Financial Times* (24 September 1994); 'Economists undeniably have a bad name. Blamed for the nation's economic ills . . . they are regarded as reliable only for the capacity to come up with diametrically opposed views on any question put to them' – *The Observer* (15 January 1995).

(a) diamond is forever Originally an advertising slogan, this phrase now has an almost proverbial feel to it. In 1939, the South African-based De Beers Consolidated Mines launched a campaign to promote further the tradition of diamond engagement rings. The N. W. Ayer agency of Chicago (copywriter B. J. Kidd) came up with this phrase. It passed easily into the language. Ian Fleming gave a variation of the phrase as the title of his 1956 James Bond novel, *Diamonds are Forever*. Technically speaking, however, they are not. It takes a very high temperature, but, being of pure carbon, diamonds *will* burn. Anita Loos in *Gentlemen Prefer Blondes* (1925) had already enshrined something like the idea in: 'Kissing your hand may make you feel very, very good but a diamond and safire bracelet lasts for ever' (**diamonds are a girl's best friend** comes not from the Anita Loos novel but from the Jule Styne/Leo Robin song with this title in the 1949 stage musical and 1953 film based on the book).

Dick See AS QUEER AS.

Dickie's meadow See END UP.

diddy See HOW TICKLED.

did I ever tell you about the time I was in Sidi Barrani? Catchphrase from the BBC radio show *Much Binding in the Marsh* (1947–53). The programme starred the urbane Kenneth Horne and Richard Murdoch, and this phrase was used by way of introduction to a boring anecdote, perhaps as a way of changing the subject.

didn't he do well? From the BBC TV show *The Generation Game* when presented (1971–8) by Bruce Forsyth (b. 1928) who soon had the nation parroting this and other catchphrases. 'Didn't he do well?' first arose when a contestant re-called almost all the items that had passed before him on a conveyor belt (in a version of 'Kim's Game'). However, it is also said to have originated in about 1973 with what a studio attendant used to shout down from the lighting grid during re-hearsals. Thirty years later, Forsyth was introducing yet another game show on BBC TV, with the title *Didn't They Do Well?* **Good game ... good game!** was encour-agement to contestants. **Nice to see you, to see you ... / Nice!** was the opening exchange of greetings with the studio audience (they supplied the rejoinder). Forsyth would also say **Anthea, give us a twirl** – an invitation to the hostess, Anthea Redfern (to whom he was briefly married), to show off her skirt of the week.

did she fall or was she pushed? The original form of this inquiry is said to date from the 1890s when it had to do with loss of virginity. Then it was supposedly used in newspaper reports (*circa* 1908) of a woman's death on cliffs near Beachy Head. Thorne Smith alluded to the phrase in the title of a novel *Did She Fall?* (1936). In *You Only Live Twice*, Chap. 2 (1964), Ian Fleming had: 'The coroner gave an open verdict of the "Fell Or Was Pushed" variety.' The line 'Was she pushed or did she jump?' occurred in the song 'Well! Well! Well! (My Cat Fell Down the Well)' by Shand/Moll/Robertson (1970s). Now applied to both sexes, the formula usually inquires whether they departed from a job of their own volition or whether they were eased out by others. (Hence, the 1970s graffito, 'Humpty Dumpty was pushed . . . by the CIA'.)

did the earth move for you? Now only jokingly addressed to one's partner after sexual intercourse, this appears to have originated as 'Did thee feel the earth move?' in Ernest Hemingway's novel *For Whom the Bell Tolls* (1940). It is not uttered in the 1943 film version, however. Head-line from *The Sport* (22 February 1989): 'Sport Sexclusive On A Bonk That Will Make The Earth Move'.

did you spot this week's deliberate mistake? As a way of covering up a mistake that was *not* deliberate, this expression arose from the BBC radio series *Monday Night at Seven* (later *Eight*) in *circa* 1938. Ronnie Waldman had taken over as deviser of the 'Puzzle Corner' part of the programme which was presented by Lionel Gamlin. 'Through my oversight a mistake crept into "Puzzle Corner" one night,' Waldman recalled in 1954, 'and when Broadcasting House was besieged by telephone callers putting us right, Harry Pepper [the producer] concluded that such "listener participation" was worth exploit-ing as a regular thing. "Let's always put in a deliberate mistake," he suggested.' Waldman revived the idea when he himself presented 'Puzzle Corner' as part of *Kaleidoscope* on BBC Television in the early 1950s, and the phrase 'this week's deliberate mistake' has continued to be used jokingly as a cover for ineptitude.

die See BETTER TO.

die another day When the makers of the James Bond movies finally exhausted the title phrases supplied by Ian Fleming, the character's creator, some tantalizing new ones emerged (see TOMORROW NEVER DIES; WORLD IS NOT ENOUGH). As for *Die Another Day* (UK/US 2002), it might just be a quotation from A. E. Housman's poem *A Shropshire Lad*, No. 56 (1896): 'But since the man that runs away / Lives to die another day . . .'

(the) die is cast The fateful decision has been made, there is no turning back now. Here 'die' is the singular of 'dice', and the expression has been known in English since at least 1634. When Julius Caesar crossed the Rubicon, he is supposed to have said '*Jacta alea est*' – 'the dice have been thrown' (although he actually said it in Greek). 'At 4 a.m. on June 5 the die was irrevocably cast: the invasion would be launched on June 6 [1944: the D-Day landings in Normandy]' – Winston S. Churchill, *The Second World War* (Vol. 5, 1952); 'Making reality take over in take-overs . . . Whatever finance directors may argue, the die is cast and they will have to comply from next year' – *The Times* (22 September 1994); 'Ardiles might still be at Tottenham – in one capacity or another – had he buried his pride and accepted a sideways shift after the 3–0 Coca-Cola Cup humiliation at Notts County last Wednesday that, he conceded, ended his Spurs career; "the die was cast" even before Saturday's home win over West Ham' – *The Guardian* (2 November 1994).

(to) die with one's boots on (sometimes **die in one's boots/shoes)** Meaning, to die violently or to be hanged summarily. Used in England by the 18th century and in the American West by the 1870s. From Mark Twain, *Roughing It*, Chap. 48 (1872): 'They killed each other on slight provocation, and hoped and expected to be killed themselves – for they held it almost shame to die otherwise than "with their boots on," as they expressed it.' The American Western use was firmly ensconced in the language by the time of the 1941 Errol Flynn film *They Died With Their Boots On*, about General Custer and his death at Little Big Horn. The title of a porn film with Vivien Neves was *She Died With Her Boots On* (UK 1970s). In one sense, the phrase can suggest an ignominious death (say, by hanging) but in a general way it can refer to someone who dies 'in harness', going about his work, like a soldier in the course of duty. 'To die with one's boots *off*' suggests, rather, that one dies in bed.

different See AND NOW FOR; AS DIFFERENT.

(to march to a) different drummer To act in a way expressive of one's own individualism. The concept comes from Henry David Thoreau in *Walden* (1854): 'If a man does not keep pace with his companions, perhaps it is because he hears a different drummer. Let him step to the music which he hears, however measured or far away.' Hence, presumably: *Different Drummer*, a ballet (1984) choreographed by Kenneth MacMillan; *The Different Drum* (1987), a work of popular psychotherapy by M. Scott Peck; and *Different Drummer*, a BBC TV series (1991) about eccentric American outsiders.

different strokes for different folks This means 'different people have different requirements'. The proverb is repeated several times in the song 'Everyday People' (1968) sung by Sly and the Family Stone. *Diff'rent Strokes* was the title of a US TV series (from 1978 onwards) about a

widowed millionaire who adopts two black boys. Wolfgang Mieder in *Proverbs Are Never Out of Season* (1993), welcoming this relatively new coinage from the southern USA of the 1950s, comments: 'It expresses the liberating idea that people ought to have the opportunity to live their lives according to their own wishes. For once we have a proverb that is not prescriptive or didactic. Instead, it expresses the American worldview that individuals have the right to at least some free choice.'

(the) difficult we do immediately – the impossible takes a little longer *Bartlett* (1980) reported that the motto, now widespread in this form, was used by the US Army Service Forces. The idea has, however, been traced back to Charles Alexandre de Calonne (d. 1802), who said: '*Madame, si c'est possible, c'est fait; impossible, impossible? cela se fera* [Madame, if it is possible, it is done; if it is impossible, it will be done].' Henry Kissinger once joked: 'The illegal we do immediately, the unconstitutional takes a little longer' – quoted in William Shawcross, *Sideshow* (1979).

dig for victory Shortage of foodstuffs was an immediate concern in the UK upon the outbreak of the 1939–45 war. On 4 October 1939, Sir Reginald Dorman Smith, the Minister of Agriculture, broadcast these words: 'Half a million more allotments, properly worked, will provide potatoes and vegetables that will feed another million adults and one-and-a-half million children for eight months out of twelve . . . So, let's get going. Let "Dig for victory" be the motto of everyone with a garden and of every able-bodied man and woman capable of digging an allotment in their spare time.' A poster bearing the slogan showed a booted foot pushing a spade into earth. Consequently, the number of allotments rose from 815,000 in 1939 to 1,400,000 in 1943.

dignity in destiny See RENDEZVOUS.

(the) dignity of labour This phrase refers especially to manual labour, but citations have proved a touch elusive. In his 1887 short story 'The Model Millionaire', Oscar Wilde has the artist Alan

Trevor say: 'Why, look at the trouble of laying on the paint alone, and standing all day long at one's easel! It's all very well, Hughie, for you to talk, but I assure you that there are moments when Art almost attains to the dignity of manual labour.' At the close of Wilde's *The Picture of Dorian Gray*, Chap. 1 (1890), Lord Henry Wotton congratulates himself on missing an engagement: 'Had he gone to his aunt's, he would have been sure to have met Lord Goodbody there, and the whole conversation would have been about the feeding of the poor . . . The rich would have spoken on the value of thrift, and the idle grown eloquent over the dignity of labour.' Wilde also states in his essay 'The Soul of Man Under Socialism' (1891) that 'a great deal of nonsense is being written and talked nowadays about the dignity of manual labour'. Booker T. Washington, the Afro-American writer, alludes to the notion in *Up from Slavery* (1901): 'No race can prosper till it learns that there is as much dignity in tilling a field as in writing a poem.' Bernard Shaw, in his play *Man and Superman*, Act 2 (1903), has the exchange: 'I believe most intensely in the dignity of labour' / 'That's because you never done any, Mr Robinson.' Dorothy L. Sayers has the exact phrase in *Gaudy Night*, Chap. 3 (1935). The similar **honest toil** is almost as elusive. Thomas Gray in his 'Elegy' (1751) spoke of the **useful toil** of the 'rude forefathers' in the countryside. 'Useful Work *versus* Useless Toil' was the title of a lecture by William Morris (1880s). *Useful Toil* was the title of a book comprising 'autobiographies of working people from the 1820s to the 1920s' (published 1974). The *OED2* finds 'honest labour' in 1941. Thomas Carlyle spoke of 'honest work' in 1866. 'Honourable toil' appears in the play *Two Noble Kinsmen* (possibly by John Fletcher and William Shakespeare, published 1634).

dim   See AS DIM.

diminishes   See HIS DEATH.

dinner   See ALL GONG; DOG'S.

dinners   See AS MANY.

dire straits   Meaning, 'desperate trouble, circumstances'. A cliché phrase by the

early 1980s when this inevitable coupling was compounded by the name Dire Straits being taken by a successful British pop group. 'In fact, as a Mori survey in one of the Sunday newspapers pointed out, the middle classes in Britain have seldom been in such dire straits' – *The Daily Telegraph* (29 June 1994); 'War heroes' rents soar . . . In Staffordshire, another St Dunstaner blinded by shell fire at Normandy in 1944, said: "I can't understand how they have got into such dire straits"' – *The Mail on Sunday* (2 April 1995).

dirt   See AGE BEFORE.

dirty   See DOM.

dirty work at the crossroads   Meaning 'despicable behaviour; foul play' (in any location), this is mostly a Hollywood idiom but not quite a cliché. The earliest film citation found is from *Flying Down to Rio* (US 1933), although P. G. Wodehouse had it in the book *Man Upstairs* in 1914 and Walter Melville, a 19th-century melodramist, is said to have had it in *The Girl Who Took the Wrong Turning, or, No Wedding Bells for Him* (no date). A *Notes and Queries* discussion of the phrase in 1917 threw up the view that it might have occurred in a music-hall sketch of the 1880s and that the chief allusion was to the activities of highwaymen. *Brewer* (1999) suggests that it might have something to do with the old custom of burying people at crossroads. 'Why couch it in arcane, ridiculous questions? If you think there is dirty work at the crossroads, say so. Don't shilly shally, don't ask the minister concerned what information he possesses about what may have occurred at the crossroads on such and such a date' – Peter McKay, *Evening Standard* (London) (13 July 1994); 'Miss Downs's withdrawal upset the congregation. "This was dirty work at the crossroads and gross discrimination of the worst kind," a man who attended the service, but refused to take communion, said yesterday' – *The Independent* (5 August 1994).

(the) discreet charm of the bourgeoisie   A tantalizing title devised by the writer/ director Luis Buñuel (1900–83) for his France/Spain/Italy film (1972). In its original French: *Le charme discret de la* *bourgeoisie*. In his native Spanish: *El discreto encanto de la burgesía*.

(to) discuss Ugandan affairs To have sexual intercourse. In *Private Eye* No. 293 (9 March 1973), there appeared a gossip item that launched this euphemism: 'I can reveal that the expression "Talking about Uganda" has acquired a new meaning. I first heard it myself at a fashionable party given recently by media-people Neal and Corinna Ascherson. As I was sipping my Campari on the ground floor I was informed by my charming hostess that I was missing out on a meaningful confrontation upstairs where a former cabinet colleague of President Obote was "talking about Uganda". Eager, as ever, to learn the latest news from the Dark Continent I rushed upstairs to discover the dusky statesman "talking about Uganda" in a highly compromising manner to vivacious former features editor, Mary Kenny . . . I understand that "Long John" and Miss Kenny both rang up later to ascertain each other's names.' Later, references to 'Ugandan practices' or 'Ugandan discussions' came to be used – though probably not far beyond the readership of *Private Eye*. In a letter to *The Times* (13 September 1983), Corinna Ascherson (now signing herself Corinna Adam) identified the coiner of the phrase as the poet and critic James Fenton. Richard Ingrams (editor of *Private Eye* at the time) added the interesting footnote in *The Observer* (2 April 1989) that the original Ugandan was 'a one-legged former Minister in President Obote's Government. When the *New Statesman* found out that the *Eye* was going to refer to the incident, representations were made to the effect that the Minister, on the run from Obote, would be in danger if identified. The detail of the wooden leg was therefore omitted, but the expression passed into the language.' As a further footnote, Nicholas Wollaston wrote to *The Observer* (9 April 1989) and pointed out that the one-legged performer *wasn't* on the run from President Obote but 'the much-loved chairman of the Uganda Electricity Board, also of the Uganda Red Cross, and an exile for seven years from the tyranny of Idi Amin. When he died in 1986, it was reported that 10,000 people attended his funeral . . . and a memorial service at St Martin-in-the-Fields was packed with his friends, among them several who remembered their discussions on Uganda with him, the artificial limb notwithstanding, with much pleasure.'

diseases See DESPERATE.

disgusted, Tunbridge Wells When it was announced in February 1978 that a Radio 4 programme was to be launched with the title *Disgusted, Tunbridge Wells* (providing a platform for listeners' views on broadcasting), there was consternation in the Kent township (properly, Royal Tunbridge Wells). The title was intended to evoke the sort of letter fired off to the press between the wars when the writer did not want to give his/her name and so signed 'Mother of Three', 'Angry Ratepayer', 'Serving Policeman', etc. Tunbridge Wells has long been held as the source of reactionary, blimpish views. Derek Robinson, the presenter of the programme, while disliking its title, commented (1989): 'Why Tunbridge Wells was considered to be stuffier than, say, Virginia Water or Maidenhead, I don't know. It's just one of those libels, like tightfisted Aberdeen, that some places get lumbered with.' The *Kent Courier* (24 February 1978) reported the 'disgust' that the 'Disgusted' label had stirred up in the town. Some people interviewed thought the tag had originated with Richard Murdoch in the BBC radio show *Much Binding in the Marsh* in which 'he made much use of his connections with the town' and was always mentioning it. Frank Muir confirmed, however, in 1997, that 'Disgusted Tunbridge Wells' was the name of a character played by Wallas Eaton – with an outraged tone of voice – in *Take It from Here* (1948–59). Can the phrase ever have been seriously used outside the confines of that programme? Earlier citations are lacking.

dish See CAN DISH IT.

ditchwater See DULL AS.

diver See DON'T FORGET.

divide and rule A way of overcoming opposition – by breaking it down and then conquering it. Originally expressed in Latin: *divide et impera*. Philip of Macedon and Louis XI of France are among the many who have subscribed to it, but Machiavelli is generally credited with having popularized the maxim.

divine discontent Dissatisfaction with life as it is but which can give rise to hope. Most often used in a religious context and frequently attributed to St Augustine who does not, however, appear to have used the phrase, although at the start of his *Confessions* he did write: 'Thou awakest us to delight in Thy praise; for Thou madest us for Thyself, and our heart is *restless*, until it repose in Thee.' The earliest citation to hand is from Charles Kingsley in a pamphlet *Health and Education* (1874): 'To be discontented with the divine discontent, and to be ashamed with the noble shame, is the very germ and first upgrowth of all virtue.' There is a 'divine despair' in Tennyson's *The Princess* (1847). '[Of Mole] Spring was moving in the air above and in the earth below and around him, penetrating even his dark and lowly little house with its spirit of divine discontent and longing' – Kenneth Grahame, *The Wind In the Willows*, Chap. 1 (1908).

dizzy heights Meaning, 'a position of success' (while hinting at its dangers). Date of origin unknown. A cliché by the mid-20th century. Sometimes used non-figuratively: 'Steel-erectors . . . walk along girders at dizzy heights as though they were strolling along Piccadilly' – *Radio Times* (25 July 1958); 'But with Saints on a roll, Ball dearly wants to climb even further from their dizzy heights of eighth spot, Everton will find it tough' – *Daily Mirror* (8 October 1994); 'Poor Kylie's having a tough time. Her new single entered the charts at the dizzy heights of number 17, the Virgin 1215 poster campaign screaming "We've done something to improve Kylie's songs. Banned them" started, and now she's being sued over her last single "Confide In Me"' – *Daily Record* (26 November 1994); 'If the comparisons are extreme it is because England's cricket has had so little to commend it, or to truly excite its audience, that the dizzy heights of Gough's daring retaliation deserved exaggeration' – *The Daily Telegraph* (3 January 1995).

(to) do a Thomas à Becket This phrase is used to suggest a possible course of action, in a general sense, that is then interpreted by others more positively than might have been the speaker's actual intention. King Henry II's rhetorical question regarding Thomas à Becket, 'Will no man rid me of this turbulent priest?' (which was acted upon by the Archbishop's murderers in 1170) is ascribed to 'oral tradition' by *ODQ* in the form: 'Will no one revenge me of the injuries I have sustained from one turbulent priest?' The young king, who was in Normandy, had received reports that the Archbishop was ready 'to tear the crown from' his head. 'What a pack of fools and cowards I have nourished in my house,' he cried, according to another version, 'that not one of them will avenge me of this turbulent priest!' Yet another version has, '. . . of this upstart clerk'. An example of the phrase used allusively in a tape-recorded conversation was played at the conspiracy-to-murder trial involving Jeremy Thorpe MP in 1979. Andrew Newton was heard to say, speaking of the alleged plot: 'They feel a Thomas à Becket was done, you know, with Thorpe sort of raving, "Would nobody rid me of this man?"' The name is now more commonly written 'Thomas Becket'.

(to) do a two six 'To do something very speedily and promptly'. Mr E. Pettinger, Lanarkshire, inquired (1993) about a saying 'which was common among RAF ground staff when I was serving between 1945 and 1948. It was said when help was required in opening or closing the big hangar doors – "Two Six on the hangar doors!" I can still visualise the response following the shout. One had to stop what one was doing and help to push the enormous sliding doors.' *Partridge/Slang* dates it from 1930. Compare **one-two, one-two**, which a military person might bark with the same intention. Possibly from gun-drill – the number of a command in an instruction booklet? Paul Beale commented: 'Numbers Two and Six were part of the guncrew in Nelson's navy, or soon after, whose arduous task it was to heave the cannon back after firing so that Number something-else could swab it out, and yet another Number reload for (probably) Number One to light and fire again.'

doctor See IS THERE A.

Doctor Greasepaint (or Doctor Theatre) will cure me Both versions of this theatrical saying were quoted in obituaries for the actress Irene Handl in November 1987 as phrases that had been used by her. The saying suggests that acting is not only a cure for ailments but also that actors *have* to be well most of the time to be able to perform their function. The actor Bernard Bresslaw commented in 1991 that his preference was for **Doctor Footlights will cure me**. Compare **(the) best doctors in the world are Doctor Diet, Doctor Quiet and Doctor Merryman**. This nannyish sentiment goes back to Jonathan Swift who included it among the clichés of *Polite Conversation* (1738). Nay, even further: *Apperson* has a citation from 1558 and the idea may be found in a poem by Lidgate (1449). The creation of an imaginary doctor's name can also be found in the nickname **Dr Brighton** for the healthy seaside resort.

Doctor Livingstone, I presume? Now a catchphrase used on meeting someone unexpectedly or after an arduous journey, this famous greeting was put by (Sir) Henry Morton Stanley, the explorer and journalist, to the explorer and missionary Dr David Livingstone at Ujiji, Lake Tanganyika, on 10 November 1871. Stanley had been sent by the *New York Herald* to look for Livingstone, who was missing on a journey in central Africa. In *How I Found Livingstone* (1872), Stanley described the moment: 'I would have run to him, only I was a coward in the presence of such a mob – would have embraced him, only, he being an Englishman, I did not know how he would receive me; so I did what cowardice and false pride suggested was the best thing – walked deliberately to him, took off my hat and said: "Dr Livingstone, I presume?" "Yes," said he, with a kind smile, lifting his cap slightly.'

doctors wear scarlet Phrase put on invitations to university gatherings – 'Evening dress with decorations, doctors wear scarlet' – referring to the scarlet academic robes worn by doctors of law and divinity, and so on. *Doctors Wear Scarlet* is the title of a novel (1960) by Simon Raven and is set in Cambridge University, involving certain bloody goings-on thereat.

dodgy! Rather as the British upper classes tend to rely on two adjectives – 'fascinating' and 'boring' – so, too, did the comedian Norman Vaughan (1923–2002) in the 1960s. Accompanied by an upward gesture of the thumb, his **swinging!** was the equivalent of upper-class 'fascinating' and (with a downward gesture of the thumb) his 'dodgy!', the equivalent of their 'boring'. Vaughan commented in 1979: 'The words "swinging" and "dodgy" came originally from my association with jazz musicians and just seemed to creep into everyday conversation. Then when I got the big break at the Palladium [introducing ITV's *Sunday Night at the London Palladium* in 1962] they were the first catchphrases that the papers and then the public seized upon.' According to Anthony Howard and Richard West, *The Making of the Prime Minister 1964*, the Labour Party considered using the word 'swinging' with an upraised thumb as the basis of its advertising campaign prior to the 1964 General Election. Doubts were expressed, however, whether everyone would get the allusion and only the thumb was used. Although not, of course, the first person to use the word, Vaughan's use of 'swinging' helped to characterize an era – the SWINGING SIXTIES. During his Palladium stint he also introduced the format phrase **a touch of the ——** ('A touch of the Nelson Riddles' etc.) Later, he had a TV series called *A Touch of the Norman Vaughans*. This was established by May 1965 when an undergraduate revue at Oxford was entitled *A Touch of the Etceteras* ('The Etceteras' being a hoped-for Oxford equivalent of the Cambridge Footlights).

does he take sugar? A principal failing of people when dealing with the physically disabled is encapsulated in the title of the BBC Radio series *Does He Take Sugar?* This phrase, pinpointed originally by social workers in the title of a booklet, 'Does he take sugar in his tea?', was used from the programme's inception in 1978. It represents the unthinking attitude that leads people to talk to the companions or relatives of those with physical disabilities rather than directly to the people themselves. From 'Guide to the Representation of People With Disabilities in Programmes' (compiled by Geoffrey Prout, BBC, 1990): 'For the record, [the title] has nothing to do with diabetes. It refers to the tendency of able-bodied people to speak over the heads of those with a disability and assume that they are brain-dead. In fact the vast majority of people, no matter what their disability, are perfectly able and willing to speak for themselves. In particular, we should not assume that people with a mental handicap are inarticulate.'

does my bum look big in this? See SUITS YOU, SIR.

doesn't it make you want to spit! An Arthur Askey catchphrase from the BBC radio show *Band Waggon* (1938–39) and subsequently. Askey commented (1979) that he was rapped over the knuckles for introducing this 'unpleasant expression': '[Sir John] Reith [the BBC Director-General] thought it a bit vulgar but I was in the driving seat. The show was so popular, he couldn't fire me. I suppose I said it all the more!'

(he) doesn't know his ass from a hole in the ground One of numerous 'doesn't know' phrases designed to describe another person's ignorance or stupidity. Mostly American, dating perhaps from the early 1900s and mostly featuring the word arse/ass. The format 'Doesn't know . . . from a hole in the ground' is used in the film *Mr Smith Goes to Washington* (US 1939). **(He) doesn't know whether to shit or light a fire** is about a person who can't make up his mind, and apparently this refers to soldiers who, at the end of a long day's march can't decide whether to warm up first, or . . . Surprisingly, Eric Partridge (with his army background) does not appear to know this expression. However, he did include (to describe ignorance rather than indecision): 'He doesn't know whether to shit or go blind/whether he wants a shit or a haircut/whether to scratch his watch or wind his ass', some of which are American in origin. A similar British expression is **(he) doesn't know pussy from a bull's foot** – referring to someone

who doesn't know what he is talking about or is ignorant. *Partridge/Slang* has **doesn't know a great A from a bull's foot** and 'does not know A from a battledore/windmill/the gable-end' (these last two versions known since 1401). There is also 'doesn't know B from a bull's foot' (1401), 'battledor' (1565) and 'broomstick' (undated). ' So we are definitely talking about the letter 'A' rather than hay. All this means is that somebody cannot distinguish between the letter in a child's alphabet book and the object in question.

doesn't time fly when you're having fun (or **enjoying yourself)?** Nowadays, an expression more often used ironically when work is hard, boredom rife or there is some other reason for not using the expression straightforwardly. Even in Act 2 of W. S. Gilbert's *The Mikado* (1885), it is used ironically. Yum-Yum is to marry Nanki-Poo, but her joy is somewhat tempered by the thought that he is to be beheaded at the end of the month. Nanki-Poo tries to cheer her up by saying that they should call each hour a day, each day a year – 'At that rate we've about thirty years of married happiness before us!' Yum-Yum ('*still sobbing*') says: 'Yes. How time flies when one is thoroughly enjoying oneself.' From *The Scotsman* (21 November 1991): 'Can it really be a year since [Margaret Thatcher] became politically semi-detached . . . Doesn't time fly when you're having more fun than you've been allowed for a decade and more.' Another laconic use of the phrase, from *The Times* (30 October 1985): 'I go home and look for the invoice. Find it. It was not three months ago but ten months. Doesn't time fly when your car is falling to bits?' Of course, 'Doesn't time fly?', on its own, is a version of the ancient *tempus fugit* [time flies], and the original 'doesn't time fly when . . .' is an old thought. In Shakespeare's *Othello*, II.iii.369 (1604), Iago says: 'Pleasure, and action, make the hours seem short.'

does she . . . or doesn't she? This innuendo-laden phrase began life selling Clairol hair dye in 1955. The brainchild of Shirley Polykoff (who entitled her advertising memoirs *Does She . . . or Doesn't She?* in 1975), the question first arose at a party when a girl arrived with flaming red hair. Polykoff involuntarily uttered the line to her husband, George. As she tells it, however, her mother-in-law takes some of the credit for planting the words in her mind some twenty years previously. George told Shirley of his mother's first reaction on meeting her: 'She says you paint your hair. Well, do you?' When Ms Polykoff submitted the slogan at the Foote Cone & Belding agency in New York (together with two ideas she wished to have rejected), she suggested it be followed by the phrase 'Only her mother knows for sure!' or 'So natural, only her mother knows for sure'. She felt she might have to change 'mother' to 'hairdresser' so as not to offend beauty salons, and **only her hairdresser knows for sure** was eventually chosen. It was felt, however, that the double meaning in the main slogan would cause the line to be rejected. Indeed, *Life* Magazine would not take the ad. But subsequent research at *Life* failed to turn up a single female staff member who admitted detecting any innuendo and the phrases were locked into the form they kept for the next 18 years. 'J', author of *The Sensuous Woman* (1969), did find a double meaning, as shown by this comment: 'Our world has changed. It's no longer a question of "Does she or doesn't she?" We all know she wants to, is about to, or does.' A New York graffito, quoted in 1974, stated: 'Only *his* hairdresser knows for sure.'

does your mother know you're out?

Put-down addressed to a stupid or presumptuous young person, implying that he or she should not be around without parental supervision. *Benham* (1948) notes that it: 'Occurs in verses by Gerald Griffin (author of "The Collegians") about 1827. It is stated by Griffin's biographer that the saying was then "a cant phrase in the Metropolis." It occurs also in a poem in "The Mirror," 28 April, 1838.' A hugely popular and enduring catchphrase thereafter. Perhaps more recently a chat-up line addressed to a seemingly under-age girl.

dog See AGE BEFORE; AS LAZY AS; EVERY.

(the) dog beneath the skin

The Dog Beneath the Skin was the title of a play (1935) by W. H. Auden and Christopher Isherwood. According to Humphrey Carpenter's biography of Auden (1981), the title was suggested by Rupert Doone and probable alludes to T. S. Eliot, 'Whispers of Immortality' (1920): 'Webster was much possessed by death / And saw the skull beneath the skin; / And breastless creatures under ground / Leaned backwards with a lipless grin.' Hence, also, *The Skull Beneath the Skin*, title of a crime novel (1982) by P. D. James.

(a) dog collar Name applied to the distinctive white collar worn (as though back to front) by a clergyman – a clerical collar. Known as such by 1860s in the UK. Compare **putting on the dog**, which means putting on airs, fine clothes, and so on. This appears to be an American expression dating from the 1870s – perhaps among college students (especially at Yale) who had to wear stiff, high collars (jokily also known as dog-collars) on formal occasions. Sometimes the phrase is 'to put on dog', without the definite article.

dog days Nothing to do with dogs getting hot under the collar, contracting rabies, or anything like that. The ancients applied this label to the period between 3 July and 11 August when the Dog-star, Sirius, rises at the same time as the sun. At one time, this seemed to coincide with the overwhelmingly hot days of high summer. Known as such from ancient times but in English by 1597.

dog eat dog Ruthless, cut-throat competition. Significantly, *Brewer* (1923) only has the expression 'dog *don't* eat dog' and compares it to 'there's honour among thieves.' *CODP* has 'dog does not eat dog' in English by 1543 and in Latin – *canis caninam non est* – in Varro, *De Lingua Latina*. So, the principal proverb is well established and 'dog eat dog' a modern development to describe a situation that is so bad, a dog would eat dog in it. *OED2*'s earliest citation is from 1931. 'What makes a man turn animal on a Rugby field when off it he's gentle and softly spoken? Clarke explains: "Rugby League is a game of survival. It's dog eat dog"' – *Sunday People* (24 November 1974).

dogged determination An alliterative inevitable, meaning 'grimly tenacious' (like a dog holding on to something). Known by 1902. A cliché by the mid-20th century. 'Before Boycott's appointment can be confirmed, the problem of reconciling his media role with the coaching job needs to be resolved. Given his dogged determination, no one should be surprised if he manages to juggle both roles – unlike his future boss, Illingworth, who had to give up his column in the *Daily Express*' – *The Sunday Telegraph* (30 April 1995); 'As opinion polls provided the relentless message of a ruling party up to 30 points behind Labour, a dogged determination reigned at Conservative Central Office' – *Financial Times* (4 May 1995).

(to be in the) dog house To be in disgrace, out of favour. An American expression (known by 1932), as is shown by the use of 'dog house' rather than 'kennel'. It seems to be no more than coincidence that in J. M. Barrie's *Peter Pan and Wendy* (1911), it is said of Mr Darling, who literally ends up in a dog house: 'In the bitterness of his remorse he swore that he would never leave the kennel until his children came back.'

(a) dog in the manger Someone who will not allow another to use something that he has, although he does not use it himself. The allusion is to the fable (in Aesop) about the dog who occupied a manger and would not allow an ox or horse to come and get its hay. One version: 'A dog, lying in a manger, would neither eat the barley herself nor allow the horse, which could eat it, to come near it.' It is one of the shortest of the fables and does not even have a moral attached. 'We find Eamonn de Valera, then the Irish Prime Minister, playing dog-in-the-manger by pointing out a change to the monarchy would require the sanction of the Irish Free State, still a dominion' – *The Independent* (30 January 2003).

(the) dogs bark – but the caravan passes by Meaning 'critics make a noise, but it does not last'. Sir Peter Hall, the theatre director, was given to quoting this 'Turkish proverb' during outbursts of public hostility in the mid-1970s. In *Within a Budding Grove* – the 1924 translation of Marcel Proust's *A l'Ombre des Jeunes Filles en Fleurs* (1918) – C. K. Scott Moncrieff

has: 'The fine Arab proverb, "The dogs may bark; the caravan goes on!"' In the film *The Lives of a Bengal Lancer* (US 1934), 'Mohammed Khan' quotes a proverb, 'The little jackal barks, but the caravan passes.' Truman Capote entitled a book, *The Dogs Bark: Public People and Private Places* (1973).

(looking/dressed up like a) dog's breakfast (or **dinner)** When the first saying (known by 1937) suggests something *scrappy* and the second (known by 1934) something *showy*, what are we led to conclude about the differing nature of a dog's breakfast and dinner? A dog's breakfast might well have consisted (before the invention of tinned dog food) of the left-over scraps of the household from the night before. So that takes care of that, except that there is also the phrase **cat's breakfast**, meaning a mess. Could both these derive from a belief that dogs and cats on occasions eat their own sick? A dog's dinner might well not have differed very much (and, on occasions, can mean the same as a dog's breakfast) except for the case described in 2 Kings 9 where it says of Jezebel that, after many years leading Ahab astray, she 'painted her face and tired her head' but failed to impress Jehu, whose messy disposal of her fulfilled Elijah's prophecy that the 'dogs shall eat Jezebel by the wall of Jezreel'. Quite how one should distinguish between the two remains a problem, as is shown by this use of both phrases in a letter from Sir Huw Wheldon (23 July 1977), published in the book *Sir Huge* (1990) and concerning his TV series *Royal Heritage*: 'It was very difficult, and I feared it would be a Dog's Dinner. There was so much . . . to draw upon . . . I think it matriculated, in the event, into a Dog's Breakfast, more or less, & I was content.'

(the) dogs of war Phrase from Shakespeare's *Julius Caesar*, III.i.273 (1599): 'Cry havoc and let slip the dogs of war'. Used as the title of a Frederick Forsyth novel (1974; film UK 1980). Compare the title of the book *Cry Havoc!* (1933) by Beverley Nichols and the film *Cry Havoc* (US 1943).

doh (or **d'oh)!** Exclamation made famous by Homer Simpson in the TV series *The Simpsons* (1996–) when admitting his own foolishness or expressing his frustration at the way things have turned out. Of course, he wasn't the first person to use the word in this way or any other. And it may be the case that it was originally said by one person expressing irritation at *someone else's* foolishness. It used to be spelt 'Duh!' and dates from the 1940s/50s. The *OED* in an update defined this version as, 'Expressing inarticulacy or incomprehension. Also implying that the person has said something foolish or extremely obvious.' Working backwards in time: in the 1960s, Peter Glaze used to say 'Doh!' in sketches with Leslie Crowther in the children's TV show *Crackerjack*, as would the Walter Gabriel character in radio's *The Archers*; in Anthony Buckeridge's 'Jennings at school' stories (1950s), Jennings's form master, Mr Wilkins, would say: 'Doh! You stupid boy!'; in the 1940s' radio series *ITMA*, Miss Hotchkiss (played by Diana Morrison) would express exasperation at her boss, Tommy Handley, with a simple 'Doh!' In the 1930s, the Scots actor James Finlayson, who appeared in many of the Laurel and Hardy films, would similarly sound off at the duo's behaviour. In fact, Dan Castellaneta, who provides the voice for Homer Simpson, has apparently said that he based his 'doh!' on James Finlayson's rendering – which is where we came in.

—— do it ——ly Joke slogan format. On 26 April 1979, the British *Sun* newspaper was offering a variety of T-shirts with nudging 'do it' slogans inscribed upon them. The craze was said to have started in the USA. Whatever the case, scores of slogans 'promoting' various groups with this allusion to performing the sexual act appeared over the next several years on T-shirts, lapel buttons, bumper stickers and car-window stickers. In the *Graffiti* books (1979–86), some seventy were recorded, among them: 'Charles and Di do it by Royal Appointment'; 'Donyatt Dog Club does it with discipline and kindness'; 'Linguists do it orally'; 'Footballers do it in the bath afterwards'; 'Gordon does it in a flash'; 'Chinese want to do it again after twenty minutes'; 'City planners do it with their eyes shut'; 'Builders do it with erections'; 'Windsurfers do it standing up'; 'Printers do it and don't wrinkle the

sheets'. All this from simple exploitation of the innuendo in the phrase 'do it', which had perhaps first been seized on by Cole Porter in the song 'Let's Do It, Let's Fall in Love' (1928): 'In shady shoals, English soles do it, / Goldfish in the privacy of bowls do it . . .', and then in a more personal parody by Noël Coward (1940s): 'Our leading writers in swarms do it / Somerset and all the Maughams do it . . .' Much later came the advertising slogan 'You can do it in an M.G.' (quoted in 1983).

(la) dolce vita The title of Federico Fellini's 1960 Italian film *La Dolce Vita* passed into English as a phrase suggesting a high-society life of luxury, pleasure and self-indulgence. Meaning simply 'the sweet life', it is not clear how much of a set phrase it was in Italian before it was taken up by everybody else. Compare **dolce far niente** [sweet idleness].

dollar See ALMIGHTY; ANOTHER DAY.

(I'll bet/lay you) dollars to doughnuts *Flexner* (1982) states: 'The almost forgotten terms *dollars-to-buttons* and *dollars-to-dumplings* appeared in the 1880s, meaning "almost certain" and usually used in "I'll bet you dollars-to-buttons/dumplings" or "you can bet dollars-to-buttons/dumplings." They were replaced by 1890 with the more popular *dollars-to-doughnuts* (a 1904 variation, *dollars-to-cobwebs*, never became very common, perhaps because it didn't alliterate).' Now obsolete.

DOM Abbreviation of '*Deo, Optimo, Maximo* [To God, most good, most great]' – what you find inscribed on bottles of Benedictine liqueur. Since the 16th century. Also short for **Dirty Old Man**. 'Poor Shirley, she thought, Harry is going to become a prize D.O.M.' – Will Camp, *Ruling Passion*, Chap. 12 (1959). This abusive phrase written out in full goes back farther: 'Mum think's he's harmless . . . In fact she was quite umbrageous with me when I called him a dirty old man' – Rosamond Lehmann, *Invitation to the Waltz*, Pt 3, Chap. 14 (1932). In the BBC TV sitcom *Steptoe and Son* (1962–5, 1970–74), the younger Steptoe (Harry H. Corbett) would say to his father (Wilfred Brambell), **'You dirty old man'**, at the slightest hint of any impropriety on his part.

dominion See AND DEATH.

(the) domino theory The old simile of falling over 'like a stack of dominoes' was first used in the context of Communist takeovers by the American political commentator Joseph Alsop. Then President Eisenhower said at a press conference in April 1954: 'You have broader considerations that might follow what you might call the "falling domino" principle. You have a row of dominoes set up. You knock over the first one, and what will happen to the last one is that it will go over very quickly.' In South-East Asia, the theory was proved true to an extent in the 1970s. When South Vietnam collapsed, Cambodia then fell to the Khmer Rouge and Laos was taken over by the Communist-led Pathet Lao. In 1989, when one Eastern European country after another *renounced* Communism, there was talk of 'reverse domino theory'.

done See ALL; BOY DONE WELL.

donkey's years As in, 'I haven't seen her for donkey's years' – i.e. for a very long time. Current by 1916. It is not very hard to see that what we have here is a distortion of the phrase 'donkey's *ears*' (which are, indeed, long). As such, what we have is a form of rhyming slang: donkey's = donkey's ears = years. (*Brewer*, however, at one time gave the less enjoyable explanation that 'donkey's years' is an allusion to the 'old tradition' that one never sees a dead donkey.) This also helps to explain the alternative expression (known since the 1960s), 'I haven't seen her **for yonks**', where 'yonks' may well be a distortion of 'year' and 'donk(ey)s'.

(la) donna è mobile [woman is fickle]
From the Duke of Mantua's aria in Act 3 of Verdi's opera *Rigoletto* (1851), also translated as: 'Woman is wayward / As a feather in the breeze / Capricious is the word'. The libretto is by Francesco Maria Piave (1810–76).

donor fatigue See COMPASSION FATIGUE.

do not adjust your set In the early days of British television, particularly in the late 1940s and early 1950s, technical breakdowns were a common feature of the evening's viewing. The BBC's caption *normal service will be resumed as soon as possible* became a familiar sight. The wording is still sometimes used in other contexts. As standards improved, it was replaced by the (usually more briefly displayed) phrase, 'There is a fault – do not adjust your set'. *Do Not Adjust Your Set* was the title of a children's comedy series on ITV in 1968, devised in part by some of the future *Monty Python* team.

do not fold, spindle or mutilate Phrase used when punched computer cards began to accompany bills and statements in the 1950s, though *Bartlett* used to date this somewhat bossy injunction to the 1930s. By the 1960s, the words evoked a machine age that was taking over. By the 1980s, the cards were no longer necessary. A slogan of the 1960s' student revolution [as seen for example at the Berkeley riots of 1964] was: 'I am a human being – do not fold, spindle or mutilate me.' A graffito (quoted 1974) read: 'I am a masochist – please spindle, fold or mutilate.' *Do Not Fold Spindle or Mutilate* was the title of a film (US 1971).

do not pass 'Go' An enduring phrase from Monopoly, the name of a board game invented by an unemployed salesman, Charles Darrow, in 1929, the year of the Wall Street crash. It is based on fantasies of buying up real estate in Atlantic City. Players begin on the square marked 'Go', may possibly return to that square to 'collect $200 salary as you pass', or land on the 'Go to jail' square, or draw a 'Chance' card with the penalty: 'GO TO JAIL / MOVE DIRECTLY TO JAIL / DO NOT PASS "GO" / DO NOT COLLECT $200.' In the UK version, the sum is £200. A *Sunday Mirror* editorial (3 May 1981) stated: 'The laws of contempt are the ones under which editors and other media folk can be sent straight to jail without passing Go.' A businessman said to a woman who had paid for her husband to be beaten up: 'If the police find out you are paying, you will go to jail, directly to jail, you will not pass "go" or collect £200' – report of trial in *The Times* (30 November 1982).

don't ask! Phrase usually inserted in parentheses to warn the reader or listener not to inquire too deeply about a piece of information that is being given – because it might be irrelevant to the main point of what is being related or may reveal a fact that is embarrassing to somebody. Noticed by the late 1990s. 'So whose pointy-headed children did Pendennis spot arriving at the exclusive – £7,000 a year – Dragon School in Oxford the other day? Don't ask!' – *The Observer* (9 February 2003).

don't ask the price – it's a penny An early slogan from the great British store Marks & Spencer. The firm had its origins in a stall set up at Leeds market in 1884 by a 21-year-old Jewish refugee from Poland. Michael Marks's slogan has become part of commercial folklore. It was written on a sign over the penny section – not all his goods were that cheap. He had simply hit upon the idea of classifying goods according to price.

don't be filthy! Don't use bad language or make obscene suggestions – but an expression usually applied following a *double entendre* or something quite innocent. Used by Arthur Askey in the BBC radio show *Band Waggon* (from 1938).

don't be fright! Catchphrase of Sirdani, the British radio magician (*sic*) in *circa* 1944.

don't be misled See READY AYE READY.

don't be vague – ask for Haig Slogan for Haig whisky since about 1936. The origin is to some extent lost in a Scotch mist because many of the John Haig & Co. archives were destroyed during the Second World War. However, the agency thought to be responsible was C. J. Lytle Ltd. An ad survives from 1933 with the wording, 'Don't be vague, order Haig'; another from 1935 with 'Why be vague? Ask for Haig'; and it seems that the enduring form arose shortly after this. It has been jocularly suggested that Haig's premium brand Dimple (which is sold as Pinch in North America) should be promoted with the slogan, 'Don't be simple, ask for Dimple'.

don't blow on it, Herbert, fan it with your hat What you say to someone who is attempting to drink very hot tea or soup – usually pronounced, 'Don't blow on it, 'Erbert, fan it wiv yer 'at.' As so often, the origin seems to lie with *Punch,* in particular F. H. Townsend's cartoon from the issue of 9 May 1906. Two young women are seated, for no apparent reason, in front of a labelled bust of Hogarth (locating the scene in Leicester Square, London, where Joseph Durham's 1875 bust is still in place), and one says: 'Such a nice young man took me out to dinner last night – such a well-mannered man. D'you know, when the coffee come and 'e'd poured it on 'is saucer, instead of blowing on it like a common person, 'e fanned it with 'is 'at!' The instruction specifically to Herbert may have been inserted in a later music-hall song. A similar line occurs in the Judy Garland movie *The Harvey Girls* (US 1946).

don't call us, we'll call you What theatre directors reputedly say to auditionees, the implication being that 'we' will never actually get round to calling 'you'. Now more widely applied to anyone unwelcome who is seeking a favour. *OED2* finds no example before 1969. However, a *Punch* cartoon on 11 October 1961 showed the European Council of Ministers saying to a British diplomat: 'Thank you. Don't call us: we'll call you'; and in the film *The Barefoot Contessa* (US 1954), a show business character says: 'Don't call me, I'll call you.' In *Some Like It Hot* (US 1959), there is a 'Don't call us, we'll call you.' Also used in a situation like this is the phrase: **we'll let you know** – as during an audition in the BBC radio show *Round the Horne* (6 June 1966).

don't come the raw prawn (with me)! 'Don't try to put one over on me, delude or deceive me' – the archetypal Australianism, dating from around the time of the Second World War. A raw prawn is presumably held to be less palatable than a cooked one, but lurking in the background is the abusive Australian use of 'you prawn!' to signify that someone is, like a prawn, sexless.

don't cry for me, Argentina Title phrase of a song from the Tim Rice/Andrew Lloyd Webber musical *Evita* (1976). There is an unexplained conjunction between this line and the inscription (in Spanish) which appears on Eva Perón's bronze tomb in Recoleta cemetery, Buenos Aires, and begins with words to the effect, 'Do not cry for me when I am far away.' But Eva's body was not returned to Argentina until 1976, and the inscription (of which there is more than one) in Recoleta cemetery bears the date '1982'. Could it have been inspired by the song rather than the other way round? Hence, however, *Don't Cry for Me, Sergeant Major*, title of a book (1983) by Robert McGowan and Jeremy Hands, giving an 'other ranks' view of the Falklands conflict between Britain and Argentina.

don't fire until you see the whites of their eyes A suggestion that you should not use up your ammunition (metaphorically speaking) before it can be effective. Or, wait until you are right up close to a problem before you begin to deal with it. In origin, a historical quotation. At the Battle of Bunker Hill (17 June 1775) in the American War of Independence, the instruction given by either US General Israel Pitman or, more likely, Colonel William Prescott was: 'Men, you are all marksmen – don't one of you fire until you see the whites of their eyes.' However, Frederick the Great had earlier said something very similar at Prague on 6 May 1757.

don't force it, Phoebe! A catchphrase from the British comedian Charlie Chester (1914–97) in his BBC radio show *Stand Easy* (1946–50). From that show also came the name **Whippit Kwick**, a cat burglar in a 'radio strip cartoon'. Leslie Bridgmont, the producer, recalled in *Leslie Bridgmont Presents* (1949) how the name swept the country. Wherever he went on bus, Tube or train he would hear someone say, 'Who's that over there?', to which the reply would come, 'Whippit Kwick!' Chester remembered (1979): 'Bruce Woodcock, the boxer, used to run around the streets chanting the jungle chants from the same strip cartoon: **Down in the jungle, living in a tent, / Better than a pre-fab – no rent!** – that sort of thing. Once at Wembley, just before he threw a right to put the other fellow out for the count, some wag in the audience yelled out, "Whippit Kwick!" he did – and it went in.' Also from *Stand Easy* came **wotcher, Tish! / wotcher, Tosh!** – an exchange between two barrow boys, and yet another catchphrase: 'This

was really a joke on my missus. My wife broke her arm and was sitting in the audience. I told Len Marten to keep coming up to me with the line **I say, what a smasher!** Then, at the end of the programme, the resolving gag was: "Len, what do you mean by all this, 'I say, what a smasher' business?" He said, "The blonde in the third row!" And there's this broken arm sticking out like a beacon. Strangely enough, I went down to Butlin's not long after and somebody dropped a pile of crockery. Of course the noise resounded all over the place and everybody shouted "I say, what a smasher!"' *Partridge/Catch Phrases* finds the phrase earlier in a 1940 ad for Kolynos toothpaste, and Partridge's *Dictionary of Forces' Slang* (1948) has the word 'smasher', meaning an attractive girl, as coming from the Scots 'a wee smasher'. Iona and Peter Opie in *The Lore and Language of Schoolchildren* (1959) show how the phrase penetrated, firstly, to 'Girls, 13, Swansea, 1952' who recited: 'I say, what a smasher, / Betty Grable's getting fatter, / Pick a brick and throw it at her. / If you wish to steal a kiss, / I say, what a smasher.' And, secondly, to 'Boy, 11, Birmingham': 'I say what a smasher / Pick it up and slosh it at her. / If you miss / Give her a kiss / I say what a smasher.' Chester also used the phrase **I can hear you!** which first arose when he noticed somebody talking about him in a rehearsal room.

don't forget the diver! Of all the many catchphrases sired by the BBC radio show *ITMA* (1939–49), the one with the most interesting origin was spoken by Horace Percival as the Diver. It was derived from memories that the star of the show, Tommy Handley, had of an actual man who used to dive off the pier at New Brighton, on the River Mersey, in the 1920s/30s. 'Don't forget the diver, sir, don't forget the diver,' the man would say, collecting money. 'Every penny makes the water warmer, sir.' The radio character first appeared in 1940 and no lift went down for the next few years without somebody using the Diver's main catchphrase or his other one, **I'm going down now, sir!** – which bomber pilots in the Second World War would also use when about to make a descent. From *ITMA*'s VE-Day edition (1945): *Effects: Knocking – Handley:* 'Who's that knocking on the tank?' *The Diver:* 'Don't forget the diver, sir – don't forget the diver.' *Handley:* 'Lumme, it's Deepend Dan. Listen, as the war's over, what are you doing?' *The Diver:* 'I'm going down now, sir.' *Effects: Bubbles*. But who was the original diver? James Gashram wrote to *The Listener* (21 August 1980): 'My grandfather McMaster, who came from a farm near the small village of Rathmullen, in County Donegal, knew Michael Shaughnessy, the one-legged ex-soldier, in the late 1890s, before he left for the Boer War and the fighting that cost him his leg. About 1910, Shaughnessy, then married to a Chester girl, settled in Bebington on the Wirral peninsula . . . Before the internal combustion engine, [he] used to get a lift every weekday from Bebington to New Brighton in a horse-drawn bread-cart owned by the Bromborough firm of Bernard Hughes. The driver of that cart, apparently, was always envious of the "easy" money Shaughnessy got at New Brighton – sometimes up to two pounds a day in the summer – and would invariably say to him on the return to Bebington, 'Don't forget the *driver*'. Shaughnessy rarely did forget. It was many years later, some time in the early 1930s, that, remembering the phrase so well, he adapted it to his own purposes by changing it to "Don't forget the diver", and shouted it to the people arriving from Liverpool.'

don't forget the fruit gums, mum! A slogan for Rowntree's Fruit Gums (1958–61) in the UK and coined by copywriter Roger Musgrave at the S. T. Garland agency. Market research showed that most fruit gums were bought by women but eaten by children. Later on, the line fell foul of advertising watchdogs keen to save parents from nagging. Accordingly, 'Mum' became 'chum'.

don't get mad, get even One of several axioms said to come from the Boston-Irish political jungle or, more precisely, from Joseph P. Kennedy (1888–1969), father of President Kennedy. *Don't Get Mad Get Even* is the title of a book (1983) – 'a manual for retaliation' – by Alan Abel.

don't get me mad, see! Phrase frequently used by those impersonating the actor James Cagney (1899–1986) in gangster mode, but it is not possible to say which of his films he says it in. Sometimes remembered as, 'Jest don't make me mad, see?'

don't get your knickers in a twist! 'Don't make a drama out of a crisis; don't get worked up or confused about something; don't get excited or you'll make the problem worse.' As 'knickers' (for female underwear) is solely a Britishism, this phrase has not travelled. In use by 1971.

don't go down the mine, Daddy A phrase used as a warning to anyone against doing something. When Winston Churchill visited Berlin in 1945 and was preparing to enter Hitler's bunker, his daughter Mary said to him, 'Don't go down the mine, Daddy.' It comes from a tearjerking ballad popular with soldiers during the First World War and written by Will Geddes and Robert Donnelly in 1910. The title is, correctly, 'Don't Go Down *In* the Mine, *Dad*'.

don't go near the water Phrase (one of two) derived from the nursery rhyme (best known in the USA): 'Mother, may I go out to swim? / **Yes, my darling daughter**; / Hang your clothes on a hickory limb, / But don't go near the water.' Even Peter and Iona Opie were unable to date this rhyme, but it may not go back beyond 1900. *Don't Go Near the Water* was the title of a film (US 1957) about sailors stationed on a South Pacific island – based on a William Brinkley novel. 'Yes, My Darling Daughter' was a popular song of 1941 – the Andrews Sisters recorded it – and there was also a play with the title in the late 1930s, subsequently filmed (US 1939). *No, My Darling Daughter* was the title of a film comedy (UK 1961).

(you) don't have to be snippy about it An expression used on a famous occasion. During the night after the US presidential election of November 2000, the Democratic candidate, Al Gore, had phoned his Republican rival, George W. Bush, and announced that he was withdrawing his concession of victory (because of voting irregularities that subsequently delayed a final result for several days). *The New York Times* reported that Bush said: 'You mean to tell me, Mr Vice President, that you're retracting your concession?' To which Gore responded, 'You don't have to be snippy about it.' The *Times*'s word expert, William Safire, glossed 'snippy' as 'given to cutting off tiny pieces', thereby seeming 'curt, fault-finding, supercilious' and hence 'touchy, disrespectful, on your high horse, having an attitude.' In its original citation by John Bartlett, *A Dictionary of Americanisms* (1848), 'snippy' was categorised as a 'woman's word'. It has remained an exclusively American expression since then.

don't hold your breath! 'Don't expect results too soon.' Perhaps related to the child's threat 'I'll hold my breath until you . . .' Not noted before the 1970s. 'I think the recession's over, you know' – 'I'm not holding my breath.'

don't just stand there: do something! An amusing exhortation dating from the 1940s, perhaps from services' slang. Now sometimes reversed: 'Don't do anything – just stand there!'

don't leave home without it   Slogan for the American Express credit card. Current in the USA by 1981. Bob Hope once did a parody on a TV special in which he appeared as the Pope carrying his Vatican Express card ('Don't leave Rome without it').

don't make me laugh   Derisive response to something said or suggested. Possibly a shortened version of 'don't make me laugh **. . . I've got a cracked lip/split lip/cut my lip.**' *Partridge/Catch Phrases* suggests that these longer phrases, known by the early 1900s, were moribund by the 1940s.

don't mention the war! Instruction from Basil Fawlty (John Cleese) to the staff of his hotel in BBC TV *Fawlty Towers*, 'The Germans', Series 1, Episode 6 (24 October 1975). Needless to say, he and they go right ahead and do so in this, probably the most remembered episode of the comedy series. It has become a sort of catchphrase. For example, when the England football team defeated Germany 5–1 in a World Cup qualifying game (1 September 2001), both the *News of the World* and the *Independent on Sunday*, headlined the story, 'Don't mention the score!'

don't panic!   Injunction written on the cover of the eponymous fictional guide featured in *The Hitch Hiker's Guide to the Galaxy*, the radio series (1978) and in the preface to the novel (1979) by Douglas Adams. See also under PERMISSION TO SPEAK, SIR!

don't quote me!   Injunction, usually given in a light and informal manner, when advancing a possibly unreliable fact or opinion. Possibly from no earlier than the mid-20th century. 'Of course, I *may* be wrong – don't quote me, for Heaven's sake' – Agatha Christie, *A Pocket Full of Rye* (1953).

don't say Brown – say Hovis   Slogan for Hovis bread, from the mid-1930s. One of the firm's paper bags of that period shows a radio announcer saying, 'Here's a rather important correction . . . I should have said Hovis and not just "brown".' The slogan was used in its final form from 1956 to 1964. It still reverberates: in May 1981, when a British golfer, Ken Brown, was deserted by his caddie during a championship, the *Sunday Mirror* headline was, 'Don't Say Brown, Say Novice'.

don't shoot the pianist!   Injunction, in the form of an allusion. Oscar Wilde reported having seen the notice 'Please do not shoot the pianist. He is doing his best' in a bar or dancing saloon in the Rocky Mountains – 'Leadville' from *Impressions of America* (1882–3). Hence, the title of the film *Tirez Sur Le Pianiste* (France 1960), translated as 'Shoot the Pianist/Piano-Player' and Elton John's 1972 record album, *Don't Shoot Me, I'm Only the Piano-Player*.

don't some mothers have 'em?   Comment about a stupid person. The British comedian Jimmy Clitheroe (1916–73) was a person of restricted growth and with a high-pitched voice who played the part of a naughty schoolboy until the day he died. The BBC radio comedy programme *The Clitheroe Kid*, which ran from 1957 to 1972, popularized an old Lancashire – and possibly general North Country – saying, 'Don't some mothers have 'em?' In the form 'Some mothers do 'ave 'em', the phrase was used in the very first edition of TV's *Coronation Street* (9 December 1960) and later as the title of a series on BBC TV (1974–9) in which Michael Crawford played an accident-prone character, Frank Spencer.

don't speak to the man at the wheel Injunction to persons travelling by boat or ship not to distract the helmsman. There are numerous references to this phrase in *Punch* during the 1880s. All is explained by Lewis Carroll in his Preface to *The Hunting of the Snark* (1876) where, commenting on the line, 'Then the bowsprit got mixed with the rudder sometimes', he notes: 'The helmsman used to stand by with tears in his eyes: *he* knew it was all wrong, but alas! Rule 42 of the [Naval] Code [containing Admiralty Instructions], "*No one shall speak to the Man at the Helm,*" had been completed by the Bellman himself with the words, "*and the Man at the Helm shall speak to no one.*" So remonstrance was impossible, and no steering could be done until the next varnishing day. During these intervals the ship usually sailed backwards.' So, the phrase was merely the shipboard equivalent of the modern instruction not to speak to the driver [of a bus] when the vehicle is in motion. When Stanley Baldwin stepped down as Prime Minister, flushed with (short-lived) success over his handling of the Abdication crisis, he made this statement to the Cabinet (28 May 1937) and later released it to the press: 'Once I leave, I leave. I am not going to speak to the man on the bridge, and I am not going to spit on the deck.' Earlier, at his inauguration as Rector of Edinburgh University in 1925, Baldwin had expressed a view of the limitations on the freedom of a former Prime Minister in similar terms: 'A sailor does not spit on the deck, thereby strengthening his control and saving unnecessary work for someone else; nor does he speak to the man at the wheel, thereby leaving him to devote his whole time to his task and increasing the probability of the ship arriving at or near her destination.' When Harold Wilson resigned as Prime Minister, he duly quoted Baldwin's 'Once I leave . . .' words in his own statement to the Cabinet (16 March 1976) and also later released them to the press.

don't spit – remember the Johnstown flood This Americanism is an admonition against spitting. The Johnstown flood of 31 May 1889 entered US folklore when a dam burst near Johnstown, Pennsylvania, and 2,200 died. A silent film, *The Johnstown Flood*, was made in the USA in 1926. *Partridge/Catch Phrases* finds that notices bearing this joke were exhibited in bars before Prohibition started in 1919. *Safire* quotes William Allen White's comment on the defeat of Alfred Landon in the 1936 US presidential election: 'It was not an election the country has just undergone, but a political Johnstown flood.'

don't teach your grandmother to suck eggs Meaning, 'don't try to tell people things which, given their age and experience, they might be expected to know anyway'. According to *Partridge/Slang*, variations of this very old expression include advice against instructing grandmothers to 'grope ducks', 'grope a goose', 'sup sour milk', 'spin' and 'roast eggs'. In 1738, Jonathan Swift's *Polite Conversation* had 'Go teach your grannam to suck eggs'. It has been suggested that, in olden days, sucking eggs would be a particularly important thing for a grandmother to be able to do because, without teeth, it would be all she was capable of. Known since the late 17th century.

don't throw the baby out with the bath water Meaning, 'don't get rid of the essential when disposing of the inessential'. There are several similar English expressions, including 'to throw away the wheat with the chaff', 'to throw away the good with the bad', but this one seems to have caught on following its translation from the German by Thomas Carlyle in 1849. According to Wolfgang Mieder in *Western Folklore* (October 1991), the first written occurrence appears in the satirical book *Narrenbeschwörung* (1512). Chap. 81 is entitled '*Das kindt mit dem bad vß schitten* [to throw the baby out with the bath water].'

don't try this at home Injunction, usually to young television viewers, not to try to replicate stunts and dangerous activities they have just been shown. Accordingly, *Don't Try This At Home*

became the title of a British TV programme of which *The Guardian* (25
January 1999) said: '[It] takes itself seriously. Large lumps of the programme are
devoted to repeating the title in case
viewers try to kill themselves.' At about
this time, the catchphrase warning was
noticed in a Dutch text (but in English)
describing a somewhat dangerous sexual
position. Earlier: 'As one baffled scientist
told his peers over the electronic mail,
"Remember, kids, don't try this at home,
unless you want your baby brother to have
three arms"' – *The Guardian* (12 April 1989).

don't want it good – want it Tuesday
Journalistic motto of editors – and quoted
by journalists – suggesting that actual
delivery of copy is more important than
striving after quality. British, mid-20th
century. Compare: 'Don't get it right, just
get it written' – James Thurber, *Fables of
Our Time*, 'The Sheep In Wolf's Clothing'
(1940).

don't worry, be happy
Injunction. Bobby
McFerrin's song with this title became
George Bush's unofficial campaign theme
in the presidential election of 1988 and
won the Grammy award for the year's best
song. 'The landlord says the rent is late, he
might have to litigate, but don't worry, be
happy,' sang McFerrin, in a song which
became a minor national anthem, reflecting a feeling in the USA at the time. *The
Times* (8 March 1989) noted: 'The song has
spawned a whole "happy" industry and relaunched the Smiley face emblem that
emerged in America in the late 1960s and
was taken up in Britain by the acid-house
scene last year. Bloomingdales, the Manhattan department store, now features a
"Don't worry, be happy shop".' In the
form, 'Be happy, don't worry', it was
earlier a saying of Meher Baba (1894–
1969), the so-called Indian God-Man.

don't you just love being in control?
Slogan from TV advertising for British Gas
from 1991. Originally, the 'control' was
seen to come from the fact that a gas
appliance responds more quickly to its
operator's demands than does an electrical
one, but the saying soon achieved brief
catchphrase status in the UK, not least
because of its scope for sexual innuendo.

From *The Independent* (19 October 1992):
'England signally failed to achieve their
stated [rugby union] goals. Perhaps disar-
ranged by their new surroundings, England, who just love being in control, were
frustrated by the resilience and organisation of the Canadians.' From *The Daily
Telegraph* (5 April 1993): 'Most annoying
of all is the circle of fire [in a National
Theatre production of *Macbeth*], like a
giant gas ring, which whooshes into jets of
flame at certain key moments. It is ludicrously obtrusive and sometimes it doesn't
seem to be working properly, adding to
the viewer's sense of fretful alienation. As
Alan Howard stands in the middle of it,
looking haggard, you suddenly wonder if
the whole dire production is actually an
advertisement for British Gas. Will he
suddenly flick his thumb and say "Don't
you just love being in control?"'

don't you know there's a war on?
Reproof delivered in response to complaints and used by (Will) Hatton and
(Ethel) Manners portraying a Cockney
chappie and a Lancashire lass in their
British variety act of the 1940s. Fairly
widely taken up, ironically *after* the
Second World War. Somehow or other it
found its way into the script of the US film
It's A Wonderful Life (1946), where it is
exclaimed by James Stewart. *Partridge/
Catch Phrases* has the similar 'Remember
there's a war on' dating from the First
World War. In a letter to Cyril Connolly on
19 October 1939, John Betjeman wrote:
'We must all do our bit. *There's a war on,
you know.*'

don't you pour that tea, there will be ginger twins!
Injunction expounding the
curious superstition that the person who
has made a pot of tea should be the one
to pour it out. If it was poured by another
it would bring ginger twins into the family.
There are, in fact, several superstitions
concerning the pouring out of tea, especially if it involves two people. Another is
that it is bad luck for two people to pour
out of the same pot. The journal *Folklore*
(in 1940) reported this as follows: 'I have
often heard . . . that two women should
not catch hold of a teapot at once or one
of them will have ginger-headed twins
within the year.'

doodah See ALL OF.

doolally tap Mad, of unbalanced mind. 'Tap' here is in the sense of 'heat, fever' and 'doolally' is the spoken form of the Marashtra (India) word '*deolali*'. Fraser & Gibbons, *Soldier & Sailor Words* (1925), state: '*Deolali tap* (otherwise *doolally tap*), mad, off one's head. Old Army.' *Street* (1986) describes Deolali as 'a turn-of-the-century Bombay sanatorium where many British soldiers were detained before being shipped home.'

doom and gloom (or **gloom and doom**) **(merchants)** The basic rhyming phrase became especially popular in the 1970s/80s and a cliché almost simultaneously. 'Doom and gloom merchants' was part of the 'travel scribes' armoury' compiled from a competition in *The Guardian* (10 April 1993). An early appearance was in the musical *Finian's Rainbow* (1947; film US 1968) in which Og, a pessimistic leprechaun, uses it repeatedly, as in: 'I told you that gold could only bring you doom and gloom, gloom and doom.' 'It was only last month that Mr Alex Park, chief executive of British Leyland, was attacking the news media for "pouring out gloom and doom about the car industry"' – BBC Radio 4, *Between the Lines* (9 October 1976); 'Amongst all the recent talk of doom and gloom one thing has been largely overlooked . . .' – *Daily Telegraph* (7 November 1987); 'The doom-and-gloom merchants would have us convinced that only an idiot would ever invest another hard-earned penny in property' – *Daily Record* (7 March 1995); 'Yet athletics usually gets its own back on the doom-and-gloom merchants, and can do so here when people such as Privalova and Johnson take the stage' – *The Guardian* (10 March 1995).

doomed See MANY MANY TIMES.

(to) do one's own thing A 1960s' expression, meaning 'establish your own identity/follow your own star', which is said to have been anticipated by Ralph Waldo Emerson (1803–82), the American poet and essayist. The passage from his 'Essay on Self Reliance' actually states: 'If you maintain a dead church, contribute to a dead Bible-society, vote with a great party either for the government or against it . . . under all these screens, I have difficulty to detect the precise man you are . . . But do your [. . .] thing, and I shall know you.' 'With surpassing ease and a cool sense of authority, the children of plenty have voiced an intention to live by a different ethical standard than their parents accepted . . . To do one's own thing is a greater duty than to be a useful citizen' – *Time* Magazine (29 August 1969).

doornail See DEAD AS A.

doors See BEHIND CLOSED.

(the) doors of perception Phrase from William Blake, *The Marriage of Heaven and Hell* (*circa* 1790): 'If the doors of perception [i.e. the senses] were cleansed, every thing would appear to man as it is, infinite.' This view was seized upon by proponents of drug culture in the 1960s. *The Doors of Perception* had been the title given to Aldous Huxley's book (1954) about his experiments with mescalin and LSD. From the phrase was also derived the name of the US vocal/instrumental group The Doors.

Dorothy See IS SHE A.

do that thing (or **small thing)!** 'How nice of you to offer to do that!' Or, 'Please go ahead!' Or 'Thanks, yes!' Current in the UK 1950s/60s.

do the right thing *Do the Right Thing* was the title of a film (US 1989) about Afro-American people in a Brooklyn slum. From *Harper's Index* (January 1990): 'Number of times the phrase "do the right thing" has been used in Congress since Spike Lee's film was released last June: 67 / Number of times the phrase was used in reference to congressional pay rise: 16 / Number of times it was used in reference to racial issues: 1.' The British English equivalent would be **do the decent thing** (known by 1914), although 'do the right thing' seems almost as well established (known by the 1880s). Is there a connection with First World War epitaphs, 'He trusted in God and tried to do the right' or with the older motto 'Trust in God, and do the Right'?

do they know it's Christmas? Referring to those suffering from famine. This was the question posed in the title of a song written by Bob Geldof and Midge Ure in 1984. Performed by Band Aid – an ad hoc group of pop singers and musicians – it became the UK Christmas No. 1 record in 1984 and again in 1989. In 1984, by drawing attention to those suffering in the Ethiopian civil war and famine, it gave rise to the Band Aid concert in July 1985.

(a) Double Diamond works wonders
Slogan for Double Diamond beer in the UK, from 1952. The double alliteration may have a lot to do with it, but it was surely the singing of the slogan to the tune of 'There's a Hole in my Bucket' that made it one of the best-known of all beer slogans.

(a) double whammy A two-part or two-pronged blow, difficulty or disadvantage. Until the General Election of 1992, few people in Britain were familiar with the phrase. Then the Conservative Party introduced a poster showing a boxer wearing two enormous boxing gloves, labelled '1. More tax' and '2. Higher prices'. The overall slogan was 'LABOUR'S DOUBLE WHAMMY'. This caused a good deal of puzzlement in Britain, though the concept of a 'double whammy' had been known in the USA since the 1950s. *DOAS* traces the word to Al Capp's 'L'il Abner' comic strip where a 'whammy' was the evil-eyed stare of the character Eagle Eye Feegle. He was able to render people motionless and speechless merely by looking at them. A stare with one eye was called a 'whammy', but in emergencies he could use both eyes, hence 'double whammy'. Whatever the origin, the Conservatives were returned to power.

double your pleasure, double your fun
Slogan for Wrigley's Doublemint chewing gum, in the USA from 1959. However, about the same time, the signature tune of ITV's *Double Your Money* quiz included the line, 'Double your money, and double your fun'. The show was first transmitted in 1955.

(a) doubting Thomas A sceptic who has to be given evidence in order to believe. An allusion to Saint Thomas, the apostle, who would not believe that Christ had risen from the dead until he had actually

seen and touched the wounds from the Crucifixion (John 20:25). The phrase is a relatively late coinage (known by 1883), having been preceded by such usages as 'wavering Thomas' and 'unbelieving Thomas'.

doughnuts See DOLLARS TO.

down among the dead men Dead drunk – where you would be down among the empty bottles and underneath the table. The phrase occurs in an English folk song/ drinking song: 'Come let's drink it while we have breath / For there's no drinking after death / And he that will his health deny, / Down, down, down, down / Down among the dead men let him lie.' The words are said to be by John Dyer, an English poet (1699–1757). The music was notably arranged by Ralph Vaughan Williams. The phrase occurs in Cuthbert Bede, *The Adventures of Mr Verdant Green* (1853–7). Hence, also, *Down Among the Dead Men*, the title of a science-fantasy novel (1993) by Simon R. Green. *Down Among the Z-Men* was the title of a film (UK 1952) featuring all the original members of the BBC radio *Goon Show*.

downhearted See ARE WE.

down in the dumps Melancholy, depressed, dejected, in low spirits. Often at one time 'in the doleful dumps'. But apart from being an appropriate sounding word, what is/are 'dumps'? Possibly, in this context, 'mental haze or mist', after the Dutch word *domp* [exhalation, haze, mist]. Known as such since the early 16th century, presumably suggesting that the mind is befogged. 'When I come home she is in the dumps' – *The Spectator*, No. 176 (1711). It had become 'down in the dumps' by the time of *Grose* (1785).

down in the forest something stirred A gently mocking suggestion merely that something has happened (perhaps after prolonged inactivity) – and not without possible innuendo. The line comes from the song 'Down in the Forest' (1915) with words by H. Simpson and music by Sir Landon Ronald. And what was it that stirred? 'It was only the note of a bird.'

down memory lane Journalistic cliché, though once a pleasant phrase referring to where you go, figuratively, for a reminiscent, nostalgic trip. The phrase seems to have developed from 'Memory Lane', the title of a popular waltz (1924) written by Buddy De Sylva, Larry Spier, and Con Conrad – not to be confused with 'Down Forget-Me-Not Lane' by Horatio Nicholls, Charlie Chester and Reg Morgan (1941). *Down Memory Lane* was the title of a compilation of Mack Sennett comedy shorts (US 1949). *OED2* gives 'Down Memory Lane' as a 'title by Dannet and Rachel' (1954). 'The Ding-Dong special that spelled love for Sid and Jan Parker will take a trip down memory lane . . . to celebrate their 25th wedding anniversary. The happy couple will kiss and cuddle on the top deck of the No. 44 bus, just like they did when they were courting' – *The Sun* (15 October 1983); 'Our opponents began this campaign hoping that America has a poor memory. Well, let's take them on a little stroll down memory lane. Let's remind them of how a 4.8-percent inflation rate in 1976 became back-to-back years of double-digit inflation' – Ronald Reagan, speech accepting the GOP Presidential Nomination, Dallas, Texas (23 August 1984); 'NWPC: Hear Them Roar . . . The women last night sure thought so. Everything was wonderful. Whoops, cheers and standing ovations were politically correct and enthusiastically bestowed for even the bumpiest ride down memory lane' – *The Washington Post* (12 July 1991).

down the garden path See UP THE.

down the hatch! Drinker's phrase before pouring the liquid down the throat. Possibly ex-Navy. Recorded by 1931.

down the little red lane Down the throat. Now chiefly baby talk, but 'red lane' for throat is in *Grose* (1785).

down the rabbit hole Phrase to explain where anything disappears. Bruce Rodgers, *The Queen's Vernacular – A Gay Lexicon* (1972), has it meaning 'into the mouth and down the gullet' as a US gay term for fellatio.

down the Swanee See SOLD DOWN.

down to the wire Right up to the last possible moment. From the imaginary line marking the finishing mark of a horse race. Horses would 'pass under the wire'. Of American origin. 'The Greentree filly outgamed Rosetown in a thrilling battle to the wire' – *The Sun* (Baltimore) (14 June 1940).

down under In Australia. 'A few more hours and we were to bid adieu to the "Australasian", her light-souled but good and clever captain, her ever kind and attentive officers. She had carried us safely down under, as the Square gardener put it to me afterwards in London, scarcely able to believe it could be reality' – James Anthony Froude, *Oceana and Her Colonies* (1886) – the first recorded use of the term. 'Down under may be the place to make money, but up over is the place to spend it!' – *Time* Magazine (14 June 1971).

do you come here often? Traditional chatting up line, common by the 1920s/30s.

do you know me? See THAT'LL DO NICELY.

do you know —? / no, but if you hum it, I'll pick out the tune (or fake it) A comic exchange, current in the US and the UK by the 1960s. From BBC radio *Round the Horne* (29 May 1966): 'Do you know Limehouse?'/'No, but if you hum a few bars, I'll soon pick it up.' Compare the caption from a cartoon in *Punch* (26 October 1872) in which a 'Kirk Elder' asks, 'My friend, do you know the chief end of man?' A Scots piper replies, 'Na, I dinae mind the chune! Can you whistle it?' Then later in *Punch* (16 April 1887) came this under the heading 'Conversational Inanities' – *He*: 'Of course, you know the "Heir of Redclyffe"?' *She*: 'I'm not sure. Would you mind just humming it?' [It's a novel by C. M. Yonge . . .]

do you know the Bishop of Norwich? A question traditionally addressed to a port drinker who is holding on to the bottle and not passing it round. *Partridge/Slang* lists a 'norwicher' as 'one who drinks too much from a shared jug . . . an unfair drinker'. Perhaps this is a subtle way of calling somebody such? *Brewer* (1894) also has the version: 'Do you know Dr Wright of Norwich?' Had there been a Dr Wright who was Bishop of Norwich? The nearest was Dr White (d. 1632). Amy Mellars (1999) reported that she had come across the similar saying, 'The Bishop has put his foot in it', meaning 'I have burned the custard'.

do you mind! Catchphrase from the BBC radio show, *Ray's a Laugh* (1949–60), spoken by Kenneth Connor as 'Sidney Mincing'. Appearing in a different situation each week, Mincing was usually some sort of unhelpful, downbeat shop assistant and was introduced, for example, thus, by Ted Ray in a furniture store: 'It looks like a contemptuous lamp-standard with a weird-looking shade.' Mincing: 'Do you mind! My name is Sidney Mincing and I happen to be the proprietor of this dish pans, frying pans and Peter Pans (as it's all on the Never-Never) emporium. What can I do for you?'

do you see who I see? See LOOK WHO IT ISN'T.

do you sincerely want to be rich? Question posed to his salesmen, during training, by Bernie Cornfeld (1928–95), who made a name and a fortune selling investment plans in the 1960s. He spent eleven months in a Swiss jail before fraud charges against him were dropped. *Do You Sincerely Want To Be Rich?* was the title of a book about the phenomenon (1972) by Charles Raw *et al*.

dozen See BAKER'S.

draconian powers Very harsh or severe powers, chiefly legal ones. Named after Draco, the 7th century BC Athenian legislator. A cliché by the mid-20th century. 'Dean Marsh, solicitor (advises on music licences): 'It's a further infringement of civil liberties. It gives the police draconian powers to seize equipment they consider to be involved and there seems to be no provision for these to be returned' – *The Independent* (3 November 1994); 'In a speech yesterday, Mr Mandela made an apparently veiled threat that he might be forced to use draconian powers to clamp down on violence in the troubled province of KwaZulu/Natal' – *The Times* (25 February 1995). Similarly there is also the phrase **drastic powers**. 'The central government has no authority in law for doing that, and, whatever might happen in the house of commons, new legislation for any such drastic powers would face stiff opposition in the lords' – *The Economist* (21 Septem-

ber 1985); 'Caracas attacked over drastic powers' – headline in *Financial Times* (29 June 1994).

(to) drag (someone/thing) kicking and screaming into the twentieth century Format phrase to describe the forced abandonment of reactionary postures and practices. The nascent form can be found in a 1913 article by J. B. Priestley in *London Opinion*: '[By listening to ragtime] he felt literally dragged out of the nineteenth into the twentieth century.' (His use of 'literally' suggests that the idea of being dragged from one century to another was already an established one.) 'A change, slight but unmistakable, has taken place; the English theatre has been dragged, as Adlai Stevenson once said of the Republican Party, kicking and screaming into the twentieth century' – article by Kenneth Tynan written in 1959 and collected in *Curtains* (1961); 'It is given to Bristol in this election to wrench the parliamentary system away from its feudal origins, and pitchfork it kicking and screaming into the twentieth century' – Tony Benn during a by-election, fought on his right to renounce a peerage (May 1961); 'Should we force science down the throats of those that have no taste for it? Is it our duty to drag them kicking and screaming into the twentieth century? I am afraid it is' – speech by Nobel chemist Sir George Porter (September 1986). As a format phrase, it is also liable to playful modification: 'The loveable cockney sparrer . . . drags us kicking and screaming back into the nineteenth century' – sketch by Keith Waterhouse and Willis Hall in BBC TV, *That Was the Week That Was* (1962–3 series); 'Mr Ian McIntyre, whose ambition was to bring Radio 4 kicking and screaming into the 1970s . . .' – *The Daily Telegraph* (11 September 1979); 'All [President Reagan] said before he was dragged kicking and screaming into the East Room was that he wouldn't call the Soviet Union an "evil empire" any more' – *The Washington Post* (19 January 1984); 'Still, Jones and Hawke, prodded by other corporate-minded partners, have dragged Arnold & Porter – sometimes kicking and screaming – into a 21st century mode of thinking, which they believe will position the firm to compete with firms that already have more than 1,000 lawyers' – *The Washington Post* (19 December 1988).

(the) Dragon Lady Nickname applied to a fearsome woman. Nancy Reagan, when US First Lady in the 1980s, was known as such. She attracted criticism for what was perceived as being her manipulative and frosty style and was given this nickname, as also were Imelda Marcos, wife of Ferdinand Marcos, ruler of the Philippines until his ousting in 1986, and Michele Duvalier, wife of 'Baby Doc' Duvalier, ruler of Haiti until his fall from power, also in 1986. The original 'Dragon Lady' was a beautiful Chinese temptress in the American comic strip 'Terry and the Pirates' (1934–73).

(to sow) dragon's teeth To stir up trouble – especially by doing something that appears designed to bring about the opposite. From the Greek myth of Cadmus who, having killed the dragon guarding the fountain of Dirce, sowed its teeth. These sprang up as fierce warriors. Milton alludes to the story in *Areopagitica* (1644).

drama queen See TRAGEDY QUEEN.

drawing board See BACK TO THE.

(the) dreaded lurgi A fictional allergy that featured in more than one episode of the BBC radio *Goon Show* (1951–60). It is pronounced 'lurgy' (with a hard 'g'), despite the soft 'g' of allergy. 'Lurgi Strikes Britain' (aka 'Lurgi Strikes Again') is the title applied to the episode of 9 November 1954 in which this line is spoken: 'On the Isle of Ewe the dreaded lurgi struck.' It became a catchphrase used when referring to colds or 'flu – 'Oh, I've got the dreaded lurgi!'

dream See AMERICAN.

(the) dream is over A phrase very much associated with John Lennon. He used it in his song 'God' (1970): 'And so, dear friends, you'll just have to carry on, the dream is over.' Also, in the 1970s he reflected on the split-up of the Beatles and the end of the 1960s: 'And so, dear friends, you'll just have to carry on. The dream is over . . . nothing's changed. Just a few of us are walking around with longer hair.' Compare the **dream is ended**. From C. S.

Lewis, *The Last Battle* (1956): 'The term is over: the holidays have begun. The dream is ended: this is the morning.'

dream on, baby, dream on Meaning, 'if you really believe that, then carry on kidding yourself'. One would suspect a black American blues origin if not in fact a Country and Western musical one. As simply *Dream On*, the phrase became the title of an 'American adult [TV] comedy series', broadcast in the UK in 1991–2, while 'Dream On' has been the title of songs from Lynn Anderson (1990) right back to Herman's Hermits (1965). 'Dream On Baby' was recorded by Rosco Gordon in Memphis, Tenn. in the 1950s, while 'Dream On, My Love, Dream On' was recorded by The Four Lads in 1955. Colin Clark, in *The Prince, the Showgirl and Me* (1995), includes his diary entry for 15 August 1956: 'What fun it might have been to make a movie with [Marilyn Monroe] when she felt everyone around was her friend. Dream on, Colin.' A prostitute cries 'Dream on!' in the film *Pretty Woman* (US 1990). Clearly there was a revival of the phrase in the early 1990s. From the *Independent on Sunday* (24 November 1991), here is the country and western singer Tammy Wynette talking about an embarrassing encounter with an ex-husband who came up and asked her to autograph a photo for him: 'I thought, "Now what do I say here?" and then it hit me like a light and I wrote – "Dream on, baby, dream on!" . . . Sweet revenge at last.'

(to) dream the impossible dream The expression derives from a line in the song 'The Impossible Dream' in the musical about Don Quixote, *Man of La Mancha* (1965; film US 1972).

(a) dream ticket An ideal pairing of politicians standing for election. Of American origin and used in connection with presidential and vice-presidential contenders whose combination of qualities – age/youth, North/South affiliations, right-wing/liberal views, religious leanings – will, it is hoped, appeal to the largest number of electors in order to ensure their victory. In use by 1960. In British politics, the term was introduced when the Labour Party was choosing its leader and deputy leader in 1983. 'Mr Kinnock, a leading left-winger, and Mr Hattersley, an outspoken figure on Labour's Centre-Right, have been described as the dream ticket because they would form a team uniting both wings of the Labour Party' – *The Sunday Telegraph* (2 October 1983); 'Staring down at Bill [Clinton] and Al [Gore] on the Madison Square Garden podium, she could see how they complemented one another. Suddenly, the two looked like a dream ticket' – Christopher Ogden, *Life of the Party* (1994).

(a) dream turned to nightmare Journalistic cliché – employed when any happy situation turns to bad. Known by the 1960s. 'He said yesterday: "It was supposed be a dream holiday but it turned into a nightmare and I lost three months of my life"' – *Today* (16 March 1995); 'Continue the process with a tram or taxi to a communist industrial dream-turned-nightmare: the Nowa Huta suburb, in which more than 200,000 people live and work, producing over half of Poland's steel – a living relic of Stalinist town planning' – *The European* (7 April 1995).

dressed See ALL.

dressed (or **got up) like a pox doctor's clerk** Dressed showily. *Partridge/Slang* defines this as 'in a smart civilian suit' and describes it as a Royal Navy phrase of the 20th century. A vivid, if rather extraordinary, image. Presumably the clerk or assistant of a doctor treating venereal diseases would be well off, as the doctor would have plenty of patients.

dressed to kill Dressed extremely smartly, very fashionably, so that you are capable of making a 'kill' or conquest of a member of the opposite sex. The film *Dressed to Kill* (US 1980), being a thriller, took the phrase literally: the murderer wore the clothes of the opposite sex. 'One chap was dressed to kill for the King in Bombastes' – John Keats, in a letter (23 January 1818); '"I am dressed to kill," as the recruit said when he donned his uniform' – *Cambridge Tribune* (US newspaper) (10 November 1881).

dressed up to the nines Very smartly dressed. This may have come to us through a pronunciation shift. If you were to say dressed up 'to then eyne', that would mean, in Old English, 'dressed up to the eyes' (*eyne* being the old plural of eye). The snag with this is that no examples of the phrase occur before the 18th century. One does not accept the *Longman Dictionary of English Idioms* (1979) definition, which suggests that it refers to the setting of a standard with ten as the highest point you can reach. If you were up to nine, you were very nearly the best. Compare the expression, 'How would you rate it/her/anything ON A SCALE OF ONE TO TEN?' or 'she's a ten', which was all the rage after the film *10* in 1979. Nor agree with Neil Ewart, *Everyday Phrases* (1983), that it has anything to do with setting oneself up to match the Nine Muses of classical mythology. Nor with *Partridge/Slang* that it has to do with the mystic number nine. Nor with whoever suggested that as the 99th Regiment of Foot was renowned for smartness of dress, anyone well turned out was 'dressed up [to equal] the nines'. The origin remains a mystery.

drink See ANOTHER LITTLE.

Drinka Pinta Milka Day Slogan for milk in the UK, 1950s. The target was to get everyone drinking one pint of milk a day, and the slogan was a piece of bath-tub inspiration that came to the client, namely Bertrand Whitehead, executive officer of the National Milk Publicity Council of England and Wales in 1958. The creative department of Mather & Crowther took an instant dislike to it, but Francis Ogilvy, the agency chairman, insisted on its being used despite the protests. It was the kind of coinage to drive teachers and pedants mad, but eventually 'a pinta' achieved a kind of respectability when accorded an entry in *Chambers' Twentieth Century Dictionary* and others (the *OED2* in due course).

drink Camp See READY AYE READY.

drinking in the last-chance saloon
Description of a person who has run out of options and is making some desperate move or one that could prove terminal. It is not clear where precisely this metaphor comes from except a vague view of film Westerns where the Last Chance Saloon was indeed the last opportunity to get a

drink before going into remote territory (like the fuel stations that announce they are the last chance to fill up before going on a motorway). The Last Chance Saloon was the location of a famous Marlene Dietrich song (and much other action) in the film *Destry Rides Again* (US 1939). In Eugene O'Neill's play *The Iceman Cometh* (1946), there is the similar line, 'It's the No Chance Saloon.' A cliché by the late 1980s. The second citation may be the coinage: 'The authority of the Takeover Panel and its shadowy status within our legal system are once again under threat. But this time the battle resembles a shoot-out at the last-chance saloon' – *The Times* (19 January 1988); 'I do believe the popular press is drinking in the last-chance saloon' – David Mellor, quoted in *The Times* (22 December 1989) (this was the Home Office minister responsible for the press, warning that Britain's popular papers had had their last chance of avoiding legislation); 'John Major's last-chance saloon' – headline, *The Independent* (23 June 1995) (when the British Prime Minister gambled over his re-election as party leader in order to silence his critics)

(to) drive a coach and horses through something   Meaning, 'to overturn something wantonly, and to render it useless'. Sir Stephen Rice (1637–1715), a Roman Catholic Chief Baron of the Exchequer, is quoted as saying in 1672: 'I will drive a coach and six horses through the Act of Settlement.' It is clear that by the late 17th century this was based on a common metaphor (usually mentioning *six* horses) for something large: in Sir John Vanbrugh's play *The Relapse*, Act II (1696), there is: *Seringe (viewing his wound)* 'Oons, what a gash is here! Why, sir, a man may drive a coach and six horses into your body.' The modern equivalent probably involves a bus or a tank. In 1843 Charles Dickens wrote in *A Christmas Carol*: 'You may talk vaguely about driving a coach-and-six up a good old flight of stairs, or through a bad young Act of Parliament' (which might seem to allude to the first example). '[Jubilation which was] to drive a number of coaches and horses through the contempt laws: the popular press seems to have decided that this was such a fantastic story that they would publish what they wanted and let the lawyers pick up the pieces later' – leading article in *The Times* (January 1981); 'Labour lawyers argued that Mr Justice Mervyn Davies had "driven a coach and horses" through Conservative legislation designed to limit the scope of trade disputes and outlaw political strikes, by refusing to ban the "blacking" of Mercury' – *The Times* (22 October 1983).

(to) drive another nail into the coffin of ——   To bring something even nearer to its end if not to its actual death. Known by 1824 – Sir Walter Scott, *Redgauntlet*. A cliché by the 1880s. '"The Candidate" . . . is one more nail in the coffin of slow acting' – *The Illustrated London News* (29 November 1884); 'An aesthete? One of those scruffy long-haired fellows in peculiar garb, lisping about art for art's sake? . . . Old Oscar screwed the last nail in the aesthete's coffin' – Harold Acton, *Memoirs of an Aesthete* (1948). Included in the parody of sportswriters' clichés by David Frost and Peter Cook in the book *That Was The Week That Was* (1963) was: 'This British soccerbluesday – there is no other word for it – drove another nail into the tottering coffin of Britain's barons of ball and caliphs of kick'. 'And this is another nail in the Tory coffin' – *Daily Record* (5 April 1995); 'To gag the Press would be another nail in the coffin of democracy. We have every moral right to know what people we have elected into power are up to. They should live with dignity' – letter to the editor in *Today* (15 April 1995).

(to) drive/go/ride/sail/wander off into the sunset   To end happily and probably romantically. Derived from the visual cliché of the silent film era when a united couple would often do just this at the end of a story. In P. G. Wodehouse, *The Heart of a Goof*, Chap. 4 (1926), the concluding sentence regarding an about-to-be married couple is: 'And together they wandered off into the sunset.' *OED2*'s first citation is from 1967. Used inevitably when Ronald Reagan retired from the White House: 'As Reagan rides off into the sunset we offer two opposing verdicts on his eight years in office . . .' – *The Observer* (15 January 1989).

droit de seigneur   Phrase used when a man tries to exercise some imagined 'right' in order to force a woman to go to bed with him, as perhaps a boss might do with a secretary. The general assumption is that this 'right' dates from the days when medieval barons would claim first go at the newly wedded daughters of their vassals – under the so-called **ius primae noctis** [law of the first night]. In the play *Le Mariage de Figaro* (1784) by Beaumarchais, the Count has just renounced his right and is beginning to regret it. In March 1988, it was reported that Dr Wilhelm Schmidt-Bleibtreu of Bonn had looked into the matter very thoroughly and discovered there was never any such legal right and that reliable records of it ever happening were rare. He concluded that the whole thing was really a male fantasy – and it was exclusively men who had used the phrase – though he didn't rule out the possibility that sex of the kind *had* taken place between lords and new brides in one or two cases, legally or otherwise. 'There was also something called the *jus primae noctis*, which would probably not be mentioned in a textbook for children. It was the law by which every capitalist had the right to sleep with any woman working in one of his factories' – George Orwell, *Nineteen Eighty-Four*, Pt 1, Chap. 7 (1949).

drop   See AT THE DROP.

(to) drop a clanger   'To say something socially embarrassing or commit an act of similar kind.' According to a photograph caption in *The Sunday Times* Magazine (30 January 1983): 'The nerveless men who worked on the construction of New York's Woolworth Building in 1912 had nightmares of dropping a girder, or "clanger" in the phrase they gave to the language.' *Partridge/Slang* calls 'clanger' here a synonym for 'testicle', but derives it from the inoffensive 'drop a brick'. *OED2*'s first citation is from 1958.

drop dead!   Said by (mostly) young persons in almost any situation to someone with whom they are in disagreement. *Partridge/Catch Phrases* correctly notes that it is short for 'Why don't you drop dead!' and dates it from the USA of the late 1930s. The earliest *OED2* citation is from a John O'Hara story of 1934. Leo Rosten in *Hooray for Yiddish* (1982) draws attention to the Yiddish equivalent, *Ver derharget!*, meaning 'get yourself killed'. As he also suggests, this is a vigorous version of 'Fuck you!' and the more useful because its component words are perfectly respectable. He points to the enormously impactful use of the phrase as the Act Two curtain line of Garson Kanin's play *Born Yesterday* (1946). Judy Holliday said 'Du-rop du-ead!' – and 'the slow, sweet, studied rendition was stupendous. Waspish ladies have been tossing "Drop dead!" into their phones (to obscene callers) and as retorts (to abusive cabbies) ever since.'

drop-dead gorgeous   Phrase describing (usually) a woman's good looks – the sort sufficient to stop the traffic if not actually to terminate the beholder with extreme prejudice. 'In *No Mercy* . . . Jillette, a maverick Chicago cop . . . hears that the woman (Kim Basinger) is drop-dead gorgeous. That's all Jillette needs to hear. He's that kind of guy' – *The Washington Post* (23 December 1986); 'Today's 12-year-olds . . . [have] an insatiable appetite for snog-worthy dream-guys. All groovin', slammin', drop-dead gorgeous kickin' lads – for in the stylised world of the teenage magazines, no young man is ever simply good-looking' – *The Guardian* (16 June 1990); 'Take the issue of [Michelle Pfeiffer's] beauty, for example. She is indeed drop-dead-gorgeous with flawless, natural beauty which is different from the striking, often eccentric looks you find among top models' – *The Sunday Telegraph* (5 January 1992); *Drop Dead Gorgeous* became the title of a film (US 1999) about a beauty pageant.

dropping the pilot   Dispensing with a valued leader. This phrase comes from the caption to a *Punch* cartoon (29 March 1890) by Sir John Tenniel that showed Kaiser Wilhelm II leaning over the side of a ship as his recently disposed-of Chancellor, Otto von Bismarck, dressed as a pilot, walked down steps to disembark. Bismarck had been forced to resign following disagreements over home and foreign policy. The phrase was also used as the title of a poem on the same subject. From

The Independent (12 May 1990): 'Kenneth Baker, the Conservative chairman, yesterday called on Tories to stop idle speculation about the party leadership . . . "We have moved through difficult waters . . . We should not, we must not, we will not drop the pilot."'

drop the gun, Looey!   Catchphrase wrongly associated with Humphrey Bogart. Alistair Cooke writing in *Six Men* (1977) remarked of Bogart: 'He gave currency to another phrase with which the small fry of the English-speaking world brought the neighbourhood sneak to heel: "Drop the gun, Looey!"' Quite how Bogart did this, Cooke does not reveal. We have Bogart's word for it: 'I never said, "Drop the gun, Louie"' – quoted in Ezra Goodman, *Bogey: The Good-Bad Guy* (1965). It's just another of those lines that people would like to have heard spoken but which never were. At the end of *Casablanca* (1942) what Bogart says to Claude Rains (playing Captain Louis Renault) is: 'Not so fast, Louis.' Ironically, it is *Renault* who says: 'Put that gun down.'

drop the other shoe!   Meaning, 'go ahead and say the next obvious thing' and/or 'end the suspense'. The first of these definitions comes from *Partridge/Catch Phrases* where he says it has been rarely heard since the 1930s. The second is from *Morris* (1971 edn). The Morrises continue: 'There are various stories to account for its origin, but our own favourite comes from Kiyoaki Murata, managing editor of the *Tokyo Times*: "A traveler came to an inn late at night and asked for a room. There was only one available and he was told to be very careful because the guest in the next room was a very light sleeper. So the new guest made every effort to be silent as he got ready for bed, but because he was so nervous he dropped one shoe, making a crashing sound. Sure enough, it wakened the man next door and the new guest could hear him toss and turn. So he managed to get the other shoe off in silence and got into bed. Toward dawn he heard his neighbor still tossing about and finally, just about daybreak, he heard a pounding on the wall and a shout: 'When are you going to drop the other shoe?'"' A

cartoon about Hitler in *New York World-Telegram* (15 February 1943) was entitled 'Waiting for That Other Shoe to Drop!'

(his whole life passes before the eyes of a) drowning man   A common belief, origins unknown. 'It is said that a drowning man sees the whole of his life in a flash' – James Agate, *Ego* (1935); '[Attended] *a ball*, my dearest Colonel . . . I must say I felt like a drowning man, the whole of my past life was there' – letter from Nancy Mitford (3 February 1946).

drummer   See DIFFERENT.

(a) drunken stupor   A helpless state brought about by alcohol consumption. Date of origin unknown. 'A policeman who had mistaken an Insulin coma for a drunken stupor' – Monica Dickens, *One Pair of Feet* (1942); 'The episode is significant: first, because a fire in these circumstances is notoriously associated with drunken stupor, and – secondly – because Ronnie Welsh, whose role in McRae's death is significant and strange, has since vanished' – *The Herald* (Glasgow) (27 March 1995); 'He fell into a drunken stupor, but before he did, one of the old prophecies of Nostradamus floated through his head. ". . . A pearled isle will give birth to a leader, a man of the circus, and he shall destroy a nation"' – short story in *The Herald* (Glasgow) (25 April 1995).

duck   See DYING; HONEY.

ducks   See GET YOUR; LOVELY WEATHER.

duck soup   An American phrase, meaning 'anything simple or easy, a cinch' or 'a gullible person, easily victimized, a pushover'. A little hard to explain this one. The first recorded use is in a Tad Dorgan cartoon of 1902 that shows a man deftly juggling a number of miscellaneous items. When *Duck Soup* was used as the title of a Marx Brothers' movie (US 1933), Groucho admitted that he did not understand it. Nevertheless, he explained: 'Take two turkeys, one goose, four cabbages, but no duck, and mix them together. After one taste, you'll duck soup for the rest of your life.' The film's director, Leo McCarey, had earlier made a Laurel and Hardy picture with the same title (US 1927).

due to circumstances beyond our control Cliché of apology. The 1st Duke of Wellington used the phrase, 'Circumstances over which I have no control', in an 1839 letter. Charles Dickens had Mr Micawber talk of 'circumstances beyond my individual control' in *David Copperfield* (1849–50). The broadcaster Fred W. Friendly entitled a critical survey of American TV *Due to Circumstances Beyond Our Control* (1967), presumably from the TV announcer's 'We regret we are unable to proceed withP the scheduled programme, due to . . .'

dulce et decorum (est pro patria mori) Meaning, 'it is sweet and honourable to die for one's country'. From Horace, *Odes*, III.ii.13. Frequently put in the shortened form '*pro patria mori*' on the graves of those killed on active service. Also used as a family motto. Wilfred Owen treated the saying with savage irony in his 1917 poem 'Dulce et Decorum est': 'If you could hear, at every jolt, the blood / Come gargling from the froth-corrupted lungs, / Obscene as cancer, bitter as the cud / Of vile, incurable sores on innocent tongues, – / My friend, you would not tell with such high zest / To children ardent for some desperate glory, / The old Lie: Dulce et decorum est / Pro patria mori.'

dulcet tones A person's speaking voice. Sometimes used ironically. Known by 1800. 'I suspect I will not have been alone in watching Sky's pictures but occasionally turning down the sound in favour of the Test Match Special team on Radio 5 Live and the dulcet tones of Christopher Martin-Jenkins, Jonathan Agnew and Neville Oliver and the rather less dulcet views of Geoffrey Boycott' – *The Times* (28 November 1994); '"Guess what I've just done," said my friend Jane one Sunday morning over the phone. We'd been gossiping, and this came out of the blue. "What?" I said, expecting to hear about some new illicit sex romp. "Cindy," she said sheepishly. She'd just spent the morning on her living room floor toiling away to Cindy Crawford's dulcet tones' – *The Independent* (8 December 1994).

(as) dull as dishwater Extremely dull, boring. This is taken to be a modern mishearing of the older 'dead/dull/flat as *ditchwater*'. The earliest citation for the original construction is a 1725 translation of Erasmus. David Garrick wrote in a 1772 letter: '*The Grecian Daughter*'s being as dead as dishwater after the first act.' Charles Dickens, *Our Mutual Friend*, Pt 3, Chap. 10 (1865), has: 'He'd be sharper than the serpent's tooth, if he wasn't as dull as ditchwater.' Ditchwater suggests a muddy colour; dishwater a grey, dingy colour, as of water in which dishes have been washed.

dull it isn't Slogan for London's Metropolitan police, 1972. The day after the brief TV and poster campaign using this curiously memorable slogan started, it was apparent that the phrase was catching on. A senior Scotland Yard officer has told how a young policeman went to break up a fight at White Hart Lane football ground. Having seized a young hooligan, the constable emerged, dishevelled but triumphant from the mêlée. A voice from the crowd cried out, 'Dull it effing isn't, eh?' The format still sometimes appears: '*Casualty* it isn't' – from the front cover of *Radio Times* (16 April 1994). It may derive ultimately from a Yiddish construction. In *The Joys of Yiddish* (1968), Leo Rosten has the phrase 'smart he isn't . . .'

dumbing down Crass simplification, reducing to the lowest standards. This nicely alliterative phrase was apparently coined to describe a tendency in the American education system in about 1986, as the first citation explains. The usage spread to Britain, most notably with regard to broadcast programming in 1997. 'America's knowledge vacuum is largely caused by what has been called the "dumbing down" of school curricula and textbooks over recent years. Books have been made bland and easy, partly in an effort to appease militant interest groups, partly because the act of reading is given more importance than the matter that is read, partly in the name of "social relevance" (whatever that is)' – *The Economist* (19 September 1987); 'The BBC is about to axe 30 programmes on Radio 4 as part of the most significant shake-up in the network's history. The changes have already prompted critics to accuse the corporation of "dumbing down" large swathes of its output' – *The Sunday Times* (13 July 1997).

dumps See DOWN IN THE.

(the) Dunkirk spirit National resolve after a significant defeat. *OED2* does not find this phrase until 1956, though it does find 'to do a Dunkirk' (meaning 'to extract oneself from disaster') as early as 1944. Both phrases allude to the evacuation from the northern French town of Dunkerque/ Dunkirk in May-June 1940. Retreating in the face of the German advance, British and Allied troops had a remarkable escape in an *ad hoc* rescue by small boats. About 338,000 were rescued in this way. It was, in anybody's language, a defeat but almost at once was seen as a triumph. Harold Nicolson wrote to his wife on 31 May: 'It is a magnificent feat once you admit the initial misery of the thing.' Winston Churchill, in his 'We shall never surrender' speech to the House of Commons on 4 June, warned: 'We must be very careful not to assign to this deliverance the attributes of a victory. Wars are not won by evacuations. But there was a victory inside this deliverance which should be noted.' Harold Wilson said in the House of Commons (26 July 1961): 'I have always deprecated . . . in crisis after crisis, appeals to the Dunkirk spirit as an answer to our problems.' No sooner had he become Prime Minister than he said in a speech to the Labour Party Conference (12 December 1964): 'I believe that the spirit of Dunkirk will once again carry us through to success.'

(in) durance vile 'In awful forced confinement, imprisonment, constraint' – a quasi-legal expression. Samuel Butler has 'durance base' in 1663 and Edmund Burke, 'vile durance' in 1770. 'Temperate Jack is swilling Hogsheads of Claret in Boeotia, Poor Pistol is in Durance Vile' – *Daily Gazette* (5 September 1745); 'A Workhouse! ah, that sound awakes my woes, / And pillows on the thorn my racked repose! / In durance vile here must I wake and weep, / And all my frowzy couch in sorrow steep' – Robert Burns, 'Epistle from Esopus to Maria' (1795–6); 'It was nice to

feel that I had got my bedroom to myself for a few minutes, but against that you had to put the fact that I was in what is known as durance vile and not likely to get out of it' – P. G. Wodehouse, *The Code of the Woosters* (1938).

dust See AGE BEFORE; KICK THE BUCKET.

(the) dustbin of history (or dustheap/ scrapheap . . .) The fate to which you might wish to consign your opponents or their ideas. The phrase was used by Trotsky in his *History of the Russian Revolution*, Vol. 3, Chap. 10 (1933): 'You [the Mensheviks] are pitiful isolated individuals; you are bankrupts; your role is played out. Go where you belong from now on – into the dustbin of history.' In a similar coinage, Charles Dickens reflected on Sir Robert Peel's death in 1850: 'He was a man of merit who could ill be spared from the Great Dust Heap down at Westminster.' Augustine Birrell, politician and writer (d. 1933), wrote of 'that great dustheap called "history"' in his essay on Carlyle.

dusted See ALL DONE.

dyed in the wool Rigid in opinions, not susceptible to persuasion. Wool that is dyed before it is treated or made up into a garment retains the dye more thoroughly. Known since 1830 in the USA but the idea was written down in England in 1579.

(like a) dying duck in a thunderstorm As a description of a person's forlorn appearance, *OED2* finds 'like a duck in thunder' in 1802, and 'like a dying fowl . . . like a duck in a thunderstorm' in Sir Walter Scott's *Peveril of the Peak*, Chap. 11 (1822). By 1843–4, the phrase was sufficiently well known for Charles Dickens to allude to it in *Martin Chuzzlewit* (Chap. 10): 'His eye . . . with something of that expression which the poetry of ages has attributed to a domestic bird, when breathing its last amid the ravages of an electric storm.' The equivalent expression in German is apparently: *Ey – da Stehen die Ochsen wieder am Berge* [like an ox with a hill in front of it].

E

each and every one of you   Mostly American and especially political periphrastic use – dating from the Nixon era at least. 'Each and every' on its own was known by the 17th century. Eric Partridge, *A Dictionary of Clichés* (5th edn, 1978), lists 'each and every one' as late 19th to 20th century. 'Each and every of the said Articles . . . and all and singular matters . . . therein contained' – *Articles of Confederation of the U.S.* (1781); 'There are people who strictly deprive themselves of each and every eatable' – Mark Twain, *Autobiography* (1897); 'I'm a peacemaker who reaches out to each and every one of you' – Harold Washington, on becoming Mayor of Chicago (May 1983).

(the) Eagle has landed   In July 1969, when the lunar module bearing Neil Armstrong touched down for the first ever moon visit, he declared: 'Tranquillity Base here – the Eagle has landed' ('Eagle' was the name of the craft, after the US national symbol). Subsequently and rather inappropriately, *The Eagle Has Landed* became the title of a novel (1975; film UK 1976). Jack Higgins fancifully suggested in an Author's Note that Heinrich Himmler was informed on 6 November 1943 that 'The Eagle has landed' – meaning that a small force of German paratroops had safely landed in England in order to kidnap Winston Churchill. A headline from *The Observer Magazine* (24 June 1990) – over a profile of the tycoon and crook, Robert Maxwell – 'The Ego Has Landed'.

(an) eagle's breakfast   Nothing – from 'an eagle's breakfast: a shit and a good look round', known in Australia by 1992.

ear   See IN YOUE.

earlier   See HERE'S ONE I MADE.

early bath   See UP AND UNDER.

earth shattering   Of earthquake-like importance. Date of origin unknown. 'According to their style guru Veronica Manussis, these rings can be casual on the beach, eye-catching at a rave or "incredibly dressy for playing bridge". That's the other earth-shattering thing about plastic: it will go out with anyone' – *The Guardian* (22 April 1995); 'Today will probably not be as earth-shattering for Hiroshi Nakajima, controversial head of the World Health Organization, as some Geneva-watchers make out. For despite calls from African members of the WHO for his resignation – over allegedly racist remarks – Nakajima looks set to live to fight another day' – *Financial Times* (11 May 1995).

(with an) ear to the ground   In close touch with what is happening – presumably alluding to the way in which a Native Indian or other tracker would be able to tell what was happening elsewhere by sound carried through the ground. Hence these developments: a critic – possibly a Welsh church leader – said of Randall Davidson, Archbishop of Canterbury from 1903–28, that he became used to 'to sitting on the fence with both ears to the ground' – told in *The Monarch Book of Christian Wisdom*, ed. Robert Paterson (1997). This criticism resurfaced in connection with Robert Runcie, the later Archbishop of Canterbury. In *The Observer* (8 September 1996), George Austin, an archdeacon, wrote that, 'Runcie was once described in the General Synod by the then Bishop of Leicester as a man who enjoyed "sitting on the fence with both ears to the ground". It helped him to accommodate both sides in every argument, but in the long term had the effect of destroying trust in his own statements.' However, this may simply be an established expression ever in search of someone to be attached to. 'A politician is an animal who can sit on a fence and yet keep both ears to the ground' is from Anon. in *Mencken* (1942). Compare the definition of an American politician that J. K. Galbraith ascribed to J. M. Keynes on the TV programme *Horizon* (6 January 1981): 'A man with his ears so close to the ground that he cannot hear the words of an upright man.'

east is east   A phrase from Rudyard Kipling, 'The Ballad of East and West' (1889): 'Oh, East is East, and West is West, and never the twain shall meet, / Till Earth and Sky stand presently at God's great Judgement Seat; / But there is neither East nor West, Border, nor Breed, nor Birth, / When two strong men stand face to face, though they come from the ends of the earth!' Kipling had a curious ability to coin popular phrases, of which 'East is East and West is West' is but one. George Orwell noted in *Horizon* (February 1942): 'Kipling is the only English writer of our time who has added phrases to the language. The phrases and neologisms which we take over and use without remembering their origin do not always come from writers we admire . . . [but] Kipling deals in thoughts that are both vulgar and permanent.' Hence, *East Is East*, the title of a film (UK 1999) about a Pakistani family living in England.

(the) East is red A theme song of the Chinese Cultural Revolution (1966–9). When the first Chinese space satellite was launched in April 1970, it circled the earth, broadcasting the message: '*Tung fang hung – Mao Tse-tung* [The east is red – Mao Tse-tung].' The song begins: 'The East turns red, day is breaking, / Mao Tse-tung arises over Chinese soil . . .'

East of Suez Territory, especially that belonging to the British Empire as it was in India and the East, and usually reached through the Suez Canal (opened in 1869). In the poem 'Mandalay' (1892), Rudyard Kipling wrote: 'Ship me somewhere east of Suez', and that would appear to be the origin of the phrase. Somerset Maugham entitled a play *East of Suez* (1922), while John Osborne wrote a play set on a 'sub-tropical island, neither Africa nor Europe' with the title *West of Suez* (1971).

(the) east wind An ill wind. 'When the wind is in the east, / It's good for neither man nor beast' – proverb (1600). 'To us in Britain, the east wind is held for evil, as in the proverb' – Francis Bacon, *Historia Ventorum* (1622). In scripture, the east wind is always bad news. In Christian eschatology, it represents judgement: 'The East Wind is the wind of judgement that will blow before the New Day' – George Kirkpatrick. Voltaire quotes an 18th-century English court physician who said,

'The nameless east wind that blows over London only in the months of November and March' caused 'black melancholy to spread over the nation. Dozens of dispirited Londoners hanged themselves, animals became unruly, people grew dim and desperate. Because of the east wind, said the doctor, Charles I was beheaded and James II deposed.' In Charles Dickens, *Bleak House* (1852–3), the character John Jarndyce blames the east wind for his bad moods. '"Learn what is true, in order to do what is right," is the summing up of the whole duty of man, for all who are unable to satisfy their mental hunger with the east wind of authority' – T. H. Huxley. 'There is no good in arguing with the inevitable. The only argument available with an east wind is to put on your overcoat' – J. R. Lowell. There is a slightly obscure allusion to all this in Lord Halifax's diary entry for 17 October 1941 in which, as British Ambassador to Washington, he describes entertaining the Duke and Duchess of Windsor to lunch. He writes that he was, 'Impressed by her general dignity and behaviour and . . . adroit good manners . . . She conversed quite easily . . . and never said anything that had any east wind in it – again a mark of wisdom.' This may mean that the Duchess was careful never to assume a tone of judgement or an air of authority to which she was barely entitled. But this is rather a long way from the traditional attributes of the east wind.

easy See AS EASY AS.

ea–sy, ea–sy! Crowd chant, most usually heard at football matches in the UK. The Scotland World Cup Squad recorded a song called 'Easy, Easy' in 1974. The phrase was also chanted by supporters of candidates at the declaration of the Hillhead, Glasgow by-election (1982).

eat See BET YOU CAN'T.

(to) eat crow Meaning, 'to have to do something distasteful or humiliating' – like recanting. This expression refers to an incident in the British-American war of 1812–14. During a ceasefire, a New England soldier went hunting and crossed over into British lines where, finding no better game, he shot a crow. An unarmed British officer encountered the American and, by way of admiring his gun, took hold of it. He then turned it on him and forced him to eat part of the crow. Known since 1851. Around the 1870s, there was an 'eat *boiled* crow' version, but obviously in the original incident, boiling was not involved.

eat, drink and be merry (for tomorrow we die) *Brewer* (1923) comments: 'A traditional saying of the Egyptians who, at their banquets, exhibited a skeleton to the guests to remind them of the brevity of life.' From Isaiah 22:13: 'Let us eat and drink, for tomorrow we shall die.' Ecclesiastes 8:15 has: 'A man hath no better thing under the sun, than to eat, and to drink, and to be merry,' and Luke 12:19: 'Take thine ease, eat, drink and be merry.'

(to) eat humble pie Meaning, 'to submit to humiliation' – the 'humbles' or 'umbles' were those less appealing parts of a deer (or other animal) killed in a hunt. They would be given to those of lower rank and perhaps served as 'humble pie' or 'umble pie'. Appropriately, it is Uriah Heep in Charles Dickens, *David Copperfield*, Chap. 39 (1849–50), who says: 'I got to know what umbleness did, and I took to it. I ate umble pie with an appetite.'

eating people is wrong A maxim from the song 'The Reluctant Cannibal' by Michael Flanders and Donald Swann, featured in the revue *At the Drop of a Hat* (1956). *Eating People is Wrong* became the title of a novel (1959) by Malcolm Bradbury.

eat my shorts! Catchphrase from 20th-Century Fox's TV cartoon series *The Simpsons* (US 1989–). It became a threatening imperative (shorts = underpants), having previously been popular in the 1980s with high school and college kids. Other phrases from the show include: **I'm Bart Simpson – who the hell are you?** The skateboard-toting teenage son of Homer and Marge became the first media hero of the 1990s. His vocabulary was colourful, if not always comprehensible: **yo, dude!**; **aye caramba!**; **whoa, mama!**; **au contraire, mon frère**; and **don't have a cow, man!** These all sounded as if they had been plucked straight off the streets but probably weren't – even if they soon

found their way there on a host of T-shirts, buttons and bumper stickers. His **underachiever and proud of it** became a curiously potent slogan.

(to) eat someone out of house and home To finish off all the food available in a house that one is visiting and cause unsustainable expense to the host. A proverbial expression, known since 1400. It occurs, for example, in Shakespeare, *Henry IV, Part 2*, II.i.72 (1597) – *Hostess (of Falstaff)*: 'He hath eaten me out of house and home, he hath put all my substance into that fat belly of his.'

——, eat your heart out! A minor singer having just finished a powerful ballad might exult defiantly, 'Frank Sinatra, eat your heart out!' *Partridge/Catch Phrases* glosses it as: 'Doesn't *that* make you jealous, fella!' As something said *to* another person, this expression acquired popularity in the mid-20th century largely through its American show business use. As such, it is probably another Jewish expression. Originally, as 'to eat one's (own) heart out' – simply meaning 'to pine' – it was current in English by the 16th century. Leo Rosten in *Hooray for Yiddish* (1983) finds it in the Yiddish *Es dir oys s'harts*. Apparently, Diogenes Laertius ascribed to Pythagoras the saying 'Do not eat your heart', meaning 'do not waste your life in worrying'.

(to) echo these fears Pompous phrase in opinion writing. Date of origin unknown. Listed in *The Independent* (24 December 1994) as a cliché of newspaper editorials. 'To many outside observers these allegations will appear ridiculous, but they echo the fears of many Asian families in the East End that their tradional way of life is threatened by the "Western disease"' – *The Observer* (1 March 1992); 'A Shanghai newspaper, Wenhuibao, last week expressed its fears about the consequences of these changes, in words that will echo eerily in other parts of the world' – *The Economist* (12 June 1993).

ecky thump! (1) Supposedly a North of England exclamation uttered in place of an actual oath. From *The Guardian* (21 March 1991): '"Jackanory stuff is for wimps," says [Bernard] Manning. "Grown men that work on building sites don't want to hear ecky thump and ooh dammit. They don't talk like that on building sites".' The derivation of this euphemistic phrase is a mystery. (2) An adjectival phrase used to describe whatever is characteristic of North of England culture, i.e. brass bands, slag heaps, flat caps, *Coronation Street*, black puddings, ferrets down the trouser, and so on. In about 1974, a senior BBC executive who, like several of his ilk, was a Hungarian refugee, opined that something was 'a bit ecky thump'. One concluded that he had been completely assimilated into British culture. J. Wright's *English Dialect Dictionary* (*circa* 1900) gives 'ecky' as a 'mild oath or rather meaningless expression . . . "the ecky", "go to ecky" . . .', but gives no clue as to how the 'thump' came to be grafted on to the expression. Note, however, that 'thump' is a Yorkshire word for a festival, wake or feast, and there is also an obsolete expression (though not Yorkshire) 'to cry thump', meaning 'to make a thumping sound'.

(to be) economical with the truth To dissemble, tell a lie. On 18 November 1986, the British Cabinet Secretary, Sir Robert Armstrong, was being cross-examined in the Supreme Court of New South Wales. The British Government was attempting to prevent publication in Australia of a book about MI5, the British Secret Service. Defence counsel Malcolm Turnbull asked Sir Robert about the contents of a letter he had written that had been intended to convey a misleading impression. 'What's a "misleading impression"?' inquired Turnbull. 'A sort of bent untruth?' Sir Robert replied: 'It is perhaps being economical with the truth.' This explanation was greeted with derision not only in the court but in the world beyond, and it looked as though a new euphemism for lying had been coined. In fact, Sir Robert had prefaced his remark with, 'As one person said . . .' and, when the court apparently found cause for laughter in what he said, added: 'It is not very original, I'm afraid.' In March 1988, (by now) Lord Armstrong said in a TV interview that he had no regrets about using the phrase. He said, again, it was not his own, but Edmund Burke's, though an earlier use is by Samuel Pepys in 1669/70.

economy See COMMANDING HEIGHTS.

ecstasy See AGONY AND.

Eddie See ARE YOU READY.

Edmond See MILK?

Edna See AUNT EDNA.

ee, bah gum! A Lancastrian/North of England version – though probably more often attributed mockingly by outsiders – of the old oath 'by gum' (possibly a contraction of 'by God Almighty' and known by 1806). The Yorkshire comedian Dick Henderson used it in a monologue about first meeting his wife (probably in the 1920s): 'Apart from that she has one very good point – ee, by gum, she can cook.' In 1994, a 'Yorkshire playground rhyme' was reported: 'Eeh bah gum / I saw me father's bum. / I carved a slice / And it were nice / Eeh bah gum!'

ee, in't it grand to be daft Catchphrase of Albert Modley (1901–79), the Northern English comedian who achieved nationwide fame through BBC radio's *Variety Bandbox* in the late 1940s. A former railway porter, he employed several Northern expressions of the 'Heee!' and 'Flippin' 'eck!' variety. In *Roy Hudd's Book of Music-Hall, Variety and Showbiz Anecdotes* (1993), the phrase is given, rather, as 'Eeeh, intit grand when you're daft!' Towards the end of Modley's life, he referred (on TV's *Looks Familiar, circa* 1979) to an inexplicable catchphrase he had used on BBC radio's *Variety Bandbox*: **ninety-two!**

ee, wot a geezer! Catchphrase of the Glasgow-born comedian Harold Berens (1903–95). Often believed to be a Cockney, he became known through the late 1940s' BBC radio show *Ignorance is Bliss*. He said (1979) that when he was living near the Bayswater Road in London he would buy his daily newspaper from a vendor who always asked him what the latest joke was. When told, his customary reaction was, 'Ee, wot a geezer.' 'Wot a Geezer!' became his bill matter. Berens acquired another of his catchphrases from a woman who used to sell him carnation buttonholes. To everything he said she would reply, **now, there's a coincidence!**

effect See I THOUGHT.

efficiency See MISS EFFICIENCY.

effluent See AFFLUENT SOCIETY.

egg See COLUMBUSES'S; CURATE'S.

eggs See AS SURE AS; DON'T TEACH.

Egypt See AS BLACK AS.

eheu fugaces From Horace's lament for
the passing of time in his *Odes*, II.xiv.1:
'*Eheu fugaces, Postume, Postume, /
Labuntur anni* [Ah me, Postumus,
Postumus, the fleeting years are slipping
by].' Note how Byron quoted it in his diary
(22 January 1821): 'It is three minutes past
twelve . . . and I am now thirty-three!
*Eheu, fugaces, Posthume, Posthume, /
Labuntur anni*, – but I don't regret them
so much for what I have done, as for what
I *might* have done.'

eh-oh! 'Hello!' from the very young
children's TV series *Teletubbies*, first
broadcast on British TV by the BBC in
1997. 'Teletubbies Say Eh-Oh!' was the title
of a No. 1 record in the British charts at
Christmas in that year.

eighty in the shade A phrase used to
express extremely hot weather. The song
'Charming Weather' in *The Arcadians*
(1908) has the lines: 'Very, very warm for
May / Eighty in the shade they say, / Just
fancy!' However, one notes that it is
alluded to comically with regard to age
rather than temperature in Gilbert and
Sullivan's *The Mikado* (1885). Ko-Ko asks
Katisha: 'Are you old enough to marry, do
you think? / Won't you wait till you are
eighty in the shade?' *Eighty in the Shade* is
the title of a play by Clemence Dane
(published 1959). *Ninety in the Shade*
(1915) was the title of a musical by Guy
Bolton and Jerome Kern.

**(to give someone the big) elbow (or big
E)** To dispose of someone's services, to
get rid of them, i.e. by elbowing them
aside. The 'big E' version was current in
show business circles by 1971.

(an) elder statesman Meaning, a 'person
of ripe years and experience whose
counsel is sought and valued', especially a
former leading politician. The expression
is derived from the Japanese *Genro*.

Known in English by 1921. 'Balfour, the
Elder Statesman' – heading in *The Illustrated London News* (15 January 1937); *The
Elder Statesman* – title of play by T. S. Eliot
(1958); 'Nixon, whom Bill Rogers . . .
referred to as the world's youngest elder
statesman, had acquired enormous stature
in world affairs' – *Billings Gazette* (Montana) (20 June 1976); 'Chingford's Elder
Statesman [Lord Tebbit] repeatedly urged
his party to campaign on their traditional –
and popular – strengths: United Kingdom
sovereignty, strict immigration control,
adequate defence and police forces' –
letter to the editor in *The Sunday Telegraph* (19 April 1992).

(an) elegant sufficiency When declining
an offer of more food, people say, 'No,
thank you, I have had an elegant sufficiency'. Or '. . . I have had an *ample*
sufficiency' (as in the second episode of
the TV *Forsyte Saga*, 1967). Paul Beale's
*Concise Dictionary of Slang and Uncon-
ventional English* (1989) describes this as a
'jocular indication, mocking lower-middle-
class gentility, that one has had enough to
eat or drink, as "I've had an elegant
sufficiency, ta!" since *circa* 1950.' It is in
fact a quotation – from James Thomson,
The Seasons, 'Spring' (1746): 'An elegant
sufficiency, content, / Retirement, rural
quiet, friendship, books.' 'I once heard two
elderly ladies trying to piece together a
much longer version of this, which went
something like "I have had an elegant
sufficiency of the appetising comestibles
which you in your gracious hospitality so
generously have provided", but I doubt if
that is an accurate version as the only
thing they could agree on was that it
ended, "In other words – I'm full!"' – Sylvia
Dowling (1998). Indeed, there would seem
to be other jokey and verbose variations.

elementary, my dear Watson! The
Sherlock Holmes phrase appears nowhere
in the writings of Sir Arthur Conan Doyle
(1859–1930), though the great detective
does exclaim 'Elementary' to Dr Watson in
The Memoirs of Sherlock Holmes, 'The
Crooked Man' (1894) and 'Ho! (*Sneer.*)
Elementary! The child's play of deduction!'
in the play *Sherlock Holmes*, written with
William Gillette in 1901 (1922 revision).
Conan Doyle brought out his last Holmes

book in 1927. His son Adrian (in collaboration with John Dickson Carr) was one of those who used the phrase in follow-up stories – as have adapters of the stories in film and broadcast versions. In the 1929 film *The Return of Sherlock Holmes* – the first with sound – the final lines of dialogue are: *Watson:* 'Amazing, Holmes!' *Holmes:* 'Elementary, my dear Watson, elementary.' This may have put the catchphrase squarely in the language, but it appears already to have been known by 1915: in *Psmith Journalist*, Chap. 19, P. G. Wodehouse wrote: '"Elementary, my dear Watson, elementary," murmured Psmith.' Even earlier, in *Psmith in the City*, Chap. 8 (1910), Psmith is already reaching towards the finished phrase: 'Then I am prepared to bet a small sum that he is nuts on Manchester United. My dear Holmes, how — ! Elementary, my dear fellow, quite elementary.'

(the) Elephant and Castle Name given to a British public house in central London, south of the River Thames, and thereafter to the adjoining area (not before the 17th century). The sign of the pub (now pulled down) probably showed an elephant with a fortified howdah containing armed soldiers on its back, as was customary in ancient times. A suggestion that the phrase is a corruption of *Infanta de Castile* – Eleanor of Castile, wife of Edward I – is entertaining but fanciful. 'The Elephant' (simply) was known as a pub name by Shakespeare's time and one is mentioned in *Twelfth Night* (1600).

(the) elephant in one's drawing room (or sitting room or living room) Meaning, an enormous problem that is wilfully overlooked by some although it is obvious to everyone else. *An Elephant In the Living Room* was the title of a book by Jilly Hastings (1984), using a metaphor created by people involved in drug and alcohol recovery to describe a phenomenon typically observable in the dysfunctional family. Perhaps first used in connection with Alcoholics Anonymous? As a Northern Ireland expression, it was quoted in *The Guardian* (26 June 1988) to the effect that **the Troubles** were 'the elephant in your drawing room' – referring to the debilitating effect of sectarian hostility and violence

in the province. A TV movie on this theme and based on a story by Bernard MacLaverty was entitled *Elephant* (UK 1989). Before the present round of civil strife in Northern Ireland started in 1969, 'The Troubles' had been applied specifically to the outburst of Civil War in southern Ireland (1919–23) but was also applied generally to any nationalist unrest – even to events as far back as 1641.

(an) elephant never forgets What one might say of oneself when complimented on remembering a piece of information forgotten by others. It is based on the view that elephants are supposed to remember trainers, keepers, and so on, especially those who have been *unkind* to them. A song with the title 'The Elephant Never Forgets' was featured in the play *The Golden Toy* by Carl Zuckmayer (London, 1934) and recorded by Lupino Lane. *Stevenson's Book of Proverbs, Maxims and Familiar Phrases* (1949) has that it derives from a Greek proverb: 'The camel [*sic*] never forgets an injury.' Compare Saki, *Reginald* (1904): 'Women and elephants never forget an injury'. The P. G. Wodehouse story 'Monkey Business' (1932) has this: 'There suddenly flashed upon him the recollection of an old saw which he had heard in his infancy – The Gorilla Never Forgets. In other words, Do the square thing by gorillas, and they will do the square thing by you.'

(an) elephants' graveyard A place to which people go to retire or, more loosely, any place where the formerly important now languish. *Partridge/Slang* prefers 'the elephants' burial ground', referring to Petersfield in Hampshire where 'vast legions of retired admirals' live (an expression dating from the 1940s). The allusion is probably to the known death rituals of elephants, who tend to congregate when one of their number is on the way out – sometimes standing around and providing the pachyderm equivalent of hospital screens.

(the) eleventh commandment *Mencken* has that this is 'Mind your own business' as 'borrowed from Cervantes, *Don Quixote*, 1605' but also records 'The Eleventh Commandment: Thou shalt not be found out – George Whyte-Melville, *Holmby House*, 1860', and that is the much more usual meaning. Hence, the title of Brandon Fleming's play *The Eleventh Commandment* (1922). *OED2* adds from the *Pall Mall Gazette* (10 September 1884): 'The new and great commandment that nothing succeeds like success' and, from *Paston Carew* (1886) by Mrs Lynn Lynton, that the eleventh commandment was 'Do not tell tales out of school'. In 1850, Charles Kingsley suggested that it was: **buy cheap, sell dear**. *Brewer* (1923) has: 'Don't tell tales out of school', 'Nothing succeeds like success', as well as, 'Thou shalt not be found out'. The 1981 remake of the film *The Postman Always Rings Twice* was promoted with the slogan: 'If there was an 11th Commandment, they would have broken that too'.

(at the) eleventh hour Meaning 'at the last moment', this phrase's origin lies in the parable of the labourers, of whom the last 'were hired at the eleventh hour' (Matthew 20:9). It was used with a different resonance at the end of the First World War. The Armistice was signed at 5 a.m. on 11 November 1918 and came into force at 11 a.m. – 'at the eleventh hour of the eleventh day of the eleventh month'. 'Relays of writers try to think of a way out, and give it up. Then at the eleventh hour the missing author returns' – E. S. Turner, *Boys Will Be Boys* (1948).

eloquent See BEARS ELOQUENT.

embarrass See AW DON'T.

embarrassing See HAVE YOU EVER HAD.

(an) éminence grise This nickname is given to any shadowy figure who exercises power or influence. It was first applied to François Leclerc du Tremblay (d. 1638), known as Père Joseph, private secretary to Cardinal Richelieu. Hence, *Grey Eminence*, title of a biography of Father Joseph (1941) by Aldous Huxley. Richelieu, statesman and principal adviser to Louis XIII of France, was something of an '*éminence grise*' himself and virtually ruled France from 1624 until his death. He was known, however, as the **Red Cardinal** or as '*L'Eminence Rouge*'. Du Tremblay, who dressed in grey, became known, first of all, as 'the Grey Cardinal'

because – although not a cardinal – he exercised the power of one through his influence on Richelieu. Later, the Nazi Martin Bormann was sometimes known as the **Brown Eminence**, probably because of his 'Brownshirt' background.

Emma Peel The name of a self-sufficient female character played by Diana Rigg in the British TV series *The Avengers*. The part was introduced *circa* 1965 and the name derives from the producers' desire to give the programme 'M appeal' (or **man appeal**, as a phrase from Oxo advertising had been putting it since 1958).

(the) emperor's new clothes Describing a person's imaginary qualities whose fictitiousness other people forbear to point out. The origin of this expression lies in a story called 'The Emperor's New Clothes' (1835) by Hans Christian Andersen, in which tailors gull an emperor into wearing a new suit of clothes, invisible to unworthy people but which does not, in fact, exist at all. None of the emperor's subjects dares point out that this renders him naked – until an innocent boy does just that.

(The) Empire Strikes Back Title of a sci-fi movie (US 1980), the first sequel to George Lucas's *Star Wars*. This was the fictional EVIL EMPIRE vaguely alluded to by Ronald Reagan in his remarks about the Soviet Union. The phrase caught on in other ways, too. In *circa* 1981, the proprietors of an Indian restaurant in Drury Lane, London, considered it as a name before rejecting it in favour of 'The Last Days of the Raj'. 'Chalk Dust – The Umpire Strikes Back' was the title of a record by Roger Kitter (UK 1982) guying John McEnroe's behaviour towards tennis umpires.

(the) empire upon which the sun never sets The British Empire, which was so widespread at its apogee that the sun was always up on some part of it. 'John Wilson' (Christoper North) wrote in *Noctes Ambrosianae*, No. 20 (April 1829), of: 'His Majesty's dominions, on which the sun never sets.' Earlier, the idea had been widely applied to the Spanish Empire. In 1641, the English explorer and writer Captain John Smith (of Pocahontas fame) asked in *Advertisements for the Unexperi-*

enced, Etc.: 'Why should the brave Spanish soldier brag the sun never sets in the Spanish dominions, but ever shineth on one part or other we have conquered for our king?' Ascribed to 'Duncan Spaeth' (is this John Duncan Spaeth, the US educator?) in Nancy McPhee *The Book of Insults* (1978) is the saying: 'I know why the sun never sets on the British Empire: God wouldn't trust an Englishman in the dark.'

encounter See CLOSE ENCOUNTER.

end See ALL GOOD THINGS; AT THE END.

(an/the) end game An expression describing the final stages of a chess game when few pieces remain. *End Game* is the English title of *Fin de Partie*, a play (1957) by Samuel Beckett. Compare **checkmate** – also used as the title of a ballet by Ninette de Valois and Arthur Bliss (1937) – from the term for the actual end of a game of chess, which has been etymologized as from the Arabic *Shah-mat* [the Shah/King is dead].

(the) end is nigh Traditional slogan of placard-bearing religious fanatics – sometimes, in full, 'The End of the World Is Nigh'. It refers to the end of the world and the day of judgement. But, although 'nigh' is a biblical word, the phrase does not occur as such in the Authorized Version. Rather: 'The day of the Lord . . . is nigh at hand' (Joel 2:1); 'the kingdom of God is nigh at hand' (Luke 21:31); 'the end of all things is at hand' (1 Peter 4:7). Charles Hill, the British Conservative politician, gave a party political broadcast in 1951 in the course of which he said, apropos his Labour opponent, Aneurin (Nye) Bevan, 'The end is Nye'.

(the) end of an era Journalistic cliché that is trotted out when an important or influential person dies, when a long-established institution shuts its doors or when some chapter of human experience is closed. Date of origin unknown but certainly around by the 1980s.

(the) end of civilization as we know it A supposed Hollywood cliché (and the title of an announced but unreleased film, US 1977) – the kind of thing said when people are under threat from invaders from Mars, or wherever: 'This could mean the end of civilization as we know it . . .' A citation from sci-fi films is not to hand, but the deathless phrase does get uttered in *Citizen Kane* (1941). Orson Welles as the newspaper magnate Kane is shown giving a pre-war press conference: 'I've talked with the responsible leaders of the Great Powers – England, France, Germany, and Italy. They're too intelligent to embark on a project which would mean the end of civilization as we now know it. You can take my word for it: there'll be no war!' From *The Independent* Magazine (4 February 1989): '[A second Danish television channel] was about to take to the air, with the certain result that culture would be relegated to the dustbin . . . In short, it will be for Danes the end of civilisation as they know it.'

(the) end of history A concept that was promoted by Francis Fukuyama, a US State Department official, in a 1989 article to describe Western democracy's perceived triumph over Communism in Eastern Europe: 'What we may be witnessing is not the end of the Cold War but the end of history as such: that is, the end point of man's evolution and the universalisation of Western liberal democracy.' Compare the title of Daniel Bell's book *The End of Ideology* (1960).

(the) end of me old cigar 'The End of My Old Cigar' was the title of a mildly suggestive music-hall song (1914) by R. P. Weston and Worton David, performed by Harry Champion. Sample verse and chorus: 'To help the Prince of Wales' Fund, and do our little share, / We gave a swell bazaar down at the mission room, and there / My wife was selling kisses to the dukes and earls, it's true. / She charged them half a sov'reign each, and I was helping too / [*Chorus*] With the end of my old cigar – Hoorah! hoorah! hoorah! / We got the Prince of Wales a thousand pounds at our bazaar. / The wife was selling kisses to the swells at "half a bar", / And I was running a peepshow with the end of my old cigar.' In his play *The Entertainer* (1957), John Osborne quoted it thus: 'Oh, the end of me old cigar, cigar, the end of me old cigar, I turned 'em round and touched 'em up with the end of me old cigar' – though these words do not appear in the published lyric. *The End of Me Old Cigar* was also the title of a play (1975) by Osborne.

(the) end of the beginning Something of a catchphrase, popularized when used by Winston Churchill in a speech at the Mansion House, London (10 November 1942). Of the Battle of Egypt, he said: 'Now this is not the end. It is not even the beginning of the end. But it is, perhaps, the end of the beginning.' The formula seems to have a particular appeal, judging by the number of times it has been recalled. One occasion that comes to mind is when Ian Smith, the Rhodesian leader, broadcast a speech containing – or so it seemed at the time – a commitment to majority rule, after Dr Henry Kissinger's shuttle diplomacy in the autumn of 1976. Note that Talleyrand went only halfway when he said, 'It is the beginning of the end [*Voilà le commencement de la fin*]' either after Napoleon's defeat at Borodino (1812) or during the Hundred Days (20 March – 28 June 1815). In *F. E. Smith, First Earl of Birkenhead* (1983), John Campbell observes that Churchill was sitting next to F.E. when Smith addressed an all-party meeting in London on 11 September 1914. The battle of the Marne, Smith said, was not the beginning of the end, 'it is only the end of the beginning'. And, Campbell suggests, Churchill 'remembered and tucked [it] away for use again twenty-seven years later'.

(to) end up in Dickie's meadow To end up in bad trouble. The allusion is to Bosworth Field where King Richard III was famously defeated and killed in 1485. However, a simpler explanation has also been offered. *Grose* (1811) defines 'dickie' as a 'donkey', so if you are in dickie's meadow you are in the mire.

enemies See CONFUSION TO.

(the) enemies' list The list of one's opponents who are ripe for harrassment – after the list maintained by President Richard M. Nixon and revealed by John Dean during the Watergate hearings (1974). Compare such terms as **black list** (people who have incurred disfavour, suspicion, censure or punishment and who may be discriminated against on this basis)

(by 1718), **hit list** (people who are to be assassinated) (by 1976) and **shit list** (people in one's bad books, who have offended one in some way and are in line for retribution) (by the 1940s). 'The bizarre phony-bomb incident got cops shuffling through their list of Gotti's enemies once again . . . an enemies list the size of a small-town phone directory' – *New York Post* (27 March 1989).

(an) enemy of the people Henrik Ibsen's play *En Folkefiende* (1882), translated as *An Enemy of the People*, is about a health resort where a doctor warns that the water is polluted. He is seen as an enemy of the people for obstructing the town's economic development. Ibsen made the phrase famous, but it had occurred earlier in Norwegian, for example in a newspaper debate in 1843, and had been used by totalitarian regimes. It later, of course, became popular in the Soviet Union, where anyone whom the authorities didn't like could be branded 'an enemy of the people', though it seems unlikely that this was inspired by Ibsen's ironic use of the phrase. 'The purge against Trotskyists and the hunt for "enemies of the people and socialism"' – *Encyclopedia Book of the Year 1938*. Earlier than all this, Jeremy Bentham wrote in 1828: 'The enemies of the people may be divided into two classes. The *depredationists* . . . and the *oppressionists*.' Ultimately, the origin may lie in French and in the Revolution. Marat used it in a 1790 pamphlet against Necker. Marat had been publishing a paper with the title *L'Ami du peuple* since the previous year. On 10 June 1794, a notorious law was passed by the National Convention, proposed by Robespierre and Couthon, making the action of the existing Revolutionary Tribunal more rigorous and ruthless. Article 4 states: '*Le Tribunal révolutionnaire est institué pour punir les ennemis du peuple.*' Almost anybody could be an enemy of the people, and the rights of the accused were negligible. The members of the jury were expected to judge on the basis of what their conscience told them, enlightened by love for the fatherland. The only possible punishment was the guillotine. This started the Great Terror, which ended July 28 with the execution of Robespierre and Couthon (and over 1,300 others in the meantime). But the phrase also occurs in French texts from the early 18th century, i.e before the Revolution.

(the) enemy within An internal rather than external threat. It may be a shortened version of 'the enemy/traitor within the gate(s)' – i.e. one who acts, or is thought to act, against the interests of the family, group, society, etc., of which he is a member. As for its particular modern use, on 22 January 1983 *The Economist* wrote of the industrial relations' scene in Britain: 'The government may be trusting that public outrage will increasingly be its ally. Fresh from the Falklands, Mrs Thatcher may even relish a punch-up with the enemy within to enhance her "resolute approach" further.' Seven months later, Margaret Thatcher was using exactly the same phrase and context regarding the British miners' strike. In a speech to the 1922 Committee (19 July 1984), she said: 'We had to fight the enemy without in the Falklands. We always have to be aware of the enemy within which is more difficult to fight and more dangerous to liberty.' Earlier, in 1980, Julian Mitchell had used the phrase as the title of a play about anorexia. It was also the title of a Tony Garnett BBC TV play in 1974, of a stage play by Brian Friel in 1962 and of a 1960 book by Robert F. Kennedy about 'organized corruption' in the US labour movement. A 1957 film had a title *The Enemy Below* and a 1978 TV film *The Enemy at the Door*. In 1940, Winston Churchill said of the BBC that it was 'an enemy within the gates, doing more harm than good'. The earliest citation of the phrase in the *OED2* dates from 1608: 'The enemy within . . . sporteth herself in the consumption of those vital parts, which waste and wear away by yielding to her unpacifiable teeth' – Edward Topsell, *The Historie of Serpents*. Charles Welsey's hymn 'None Is Like Jeshurun's God' (1742) contains the lines: 'God is thine; disdain to fear/ The enemy within: / God shall in thy flesh appear, / And make an end of sin . . .' Compare also Cicero on the Catilinarian conspiracy to launch a *coup d'état*: '*Intus est hostis*' – *In Catilinam*, II.v.11.

engage brain before speaking! Admonition, current in the UK by 1980.

England See CLOSE YOUR EYES.

England expects Admiral Horatio Lord Nelson's signal to his fleet before the Battle of Trafalgar on 21 October 1805 was 'England expects that every man will do his duty'. At 11.30 a.m., the fleet approached Napoleon's combined French and Spanish fleets before the Battle of Trafalgar. Nelson told one of his captains: 'I will now amuse the fleet with a signal.' At first it was to be 'Nelson confides that every man will do his duty', but it was suggested that 'England' would be better than 'Nelson'. Flag Lieutenant Pasco then pointed out that the word 'expects' was common enough to be in the signal book, whereas 'confides' would have to be spelt out letter by letter and would require seven flags, not one. When Admiral Lord Collingwood saw the signal coming from HMS *Victory*, he remarked: 'I wish Nelson would stop signalling, as we all know well enough what we have to do.' *Mencken* found a US saying from 1917 – during the First World War: 'England expects every American to do his duty'. In Britain at about the same time, there was a recruiting slogan: 'England Expects that Every Man Will Do His Duty and Join the Army Today'.

England, home and beauty Phrase derived from one of the most popular songs of the 19th century, 'The Death of Nelson' by John Braham and S. J. Arnold. It is from their opera *The Americans* (1811), though the words do not appear exactly in the above order: 'Our Nelson mark'd them on the wave, / Three cheers our gallant Seamen gave, / Nor thought of home or beauty (*rpt.*) / Along the line this signal ran, / "England expects that every man / This day will do his duty!" (*rpt.*)' Charles Dickens has Captain Cuttle quote, 'Though lost to sight, to memory dear, and England, Home, and Beauty!' in *Dombey and Son*, Chap. 48 (1844–6), though these words do not appear in the text consulted (there may be other versions). Braham was not alone in perceiving the rhyming delights of 'duty' and 'beauty'. In Gilbert and Sullivan's *Trial by Jury* (1875), 'Time may do his duty' is rhymed with 'Winter hath a beauty', at which point, Ian Bradley in his annotated edition remarks: 'This is the first of no fewer than fifteen occasions, exclusive of repetitions, when the words "duty" and "beauty" are rhymed in the Savoy Operas . . . *HMS Pinafore* holds the record with four separate songs in which the words are rhymed.' *Home and Beauty* (simply) was the title of a play (1919) by Somerset Maugham, concerning the complications surrounding a First World War 'widow' who remarries and whose original husband then turns up (in the USA the play was known as *Too Many Husbands*).

England, my England Phrase from a poem by W. E. Henley called 'For England's Sake' (1892): 'What have I done for you, / England, my England? / What is there I would not do, / England, my own?' *England My England* was used as the title of a book of short stories by D. H. Lawrence (1922). Compare A. G. MacDonell's satire on country life, *England, Their England* (1933), and a book of George Orwell's essays, *England, Your England* (1953). *England, Our England* was the title of a revue by Keith Waterhouse and Willis Hall (London, 1962).

English as she is spoke Phrase now used to show how the language might be spoken by foreigners or the illiterate. Its origin lies in an English edition of a book of selections (1883) from the notorious French-Portuguese phrasebook *O Novo Guia da Conversação em frances e portuguez* by José da Fonseca, which had been published in Paris in 1836. The original text was in parallel columns; then, in 1865, a third column, carrying English translations, was added by one Pedro Carolino. Field and Tuer's English book, *English As She Is Spoke*, took its title from a phrase in the chapter on 'Familiar Dialogues'. In 1883, Mark Twain also introduced an edition of the complete work in the USA.

enjoying a well-deserved (or well-earned) break (or rest) A cliché, especially in journalistic use. 'The statesman is now enjoying a well-earned rest' was dated 'ca. 1880' by Eric Partridge in *A Dictionary of Clichés* (5th edition, 1978).

'He could not enjoy his well earned rest' – Mark Twain, *A Tramp Abroad*, Chap. 15 (1880). 'Meanwhile, although enjoying a well-earned rest before being geared up for her autumn campaign, Balanchine was still very much in the limelight after Cezanne, who led her in all her work before the Oaks and Irish Derby, had come to the rescue of beleaguered York bookies by outgalloping the heavily-backed favourite, Midnight Legend, in the Magnet Cup' – *The Sunday Times* (10 July 1994); 'The Courtyard also has a soft play area which is ideal for the tiny tots. They can romp safely while Mum and Dad take a well-earned rest!' – *Daily Mirror* (21 March 1995); 'Savouring the moment: Normandy veterans in Hyde Park take a well-earned break yesterday' – photo caption, *The Observer* (7 May 1995); 'Sophie Grigson is taking a well-deserved holiday' – *The Sunday Times* Magazine (10 September 1995).

enlightenment See AGE OF.

enough blue to make a pair of sailor's trousers This saying is listed in *Casson/Grenfell* (1972) as an example of 'nanny philosophy': 'If there's enough blue sky to make a pair of sailor's trousers then you can go out.' *Brewer* (1989) glosses it as 'two patches of blue appearing in a stormy sky giving the promise of better weather' and notes the alternative 'Dutchman's breeches' for 'sailor's trousers'. Indeed, 'Dutchman's breeches' would seem to be the original version, as stated in Smyth, *Sailor's Wordbook* (1867): '*Dutchman's breeches*, the patch of blue sky often seen when a gale is breaking, is said to be, however small, "enough to make a pair of breeches for a Dutchman".'

enough is enough! A basic expression of exasperation, this is often trotted out in political personality clashes – though usually without result. 'What matters is that Mr Macmillan has let Mr [Selwyn] Lloyd know that at the Foreign Office, in these troubled times, enough is enough' – *The Times* (1 June 1959). Having fed the story to *The Times*, Macmillan was prevented by the fuss it caused from firing Lloyd, and the Foreign Secretary remained in place for a further year. On 10 May 1968, the

Daily Mirror carried a front page headline, 'Enough is Enough', referring to the Labour government of Harold Wilson. It was over an article by Cecil H. King, Chairman of the International Publishing Corporation, but it led to *his* fall from power, however, and not the government's.

enough of this ——, let's ——! Format catchphrase used particularly regarding sex. 'Enough of this bourgeois love-making, let's fuck!' is said to be the punch line of a joke about a female Russian soldier in the Second World War who makes an innocuous remark to a male Russian soldier. A milder version from the 1980s: **enough with the small talk, off with the clothes!**

enough said! Agreement has been reached, let us not prolong discussion of these matters. Also in the abbreviated form **nuff said!** (or 'nuff ced' or 'N.C.' or 'N.S.'– especially in the USA where these variations date from the 1840s).

(it's) enough to make a parson swear A mild way of expressing genuine aggravation, annoyance or irritation. Edward Ward used it in *Hudibras Redivivus* (1706): 'Your Folly makes me stare; / Such talk would make a Parson swear.' It also appears in Swift's *Polite Conversation* (1738).

e *pluribus unum* [one out of many] Motto of the United States, with the force of a slogan, in use since 1776. It is a phrase from Virgil's *Moretum*, chosen by Benjamin Franklin, Thomas Jefferson and John Adams. It appears on the Great Seal of the United States and on all coins and banknotes, although 'In God We Trust' was formally adopted by Congress as the country's motto in 1956.

Epps See GRATEFUL AND COMFORTING.

equal See ALL ANIMALS ARE.

equal opportunity In the 1970s this phrase came mostly to refer to employment opportunities for women. Originally, as 'equality of opportunity', the term referred to general social mobility. Then, as 'equal opportunity', it seems to have resurfaced in the USA with specific reference to racial prejudice and discrimination. 'A sufficient measure of social justice, to ensure health, education, and a measure of

equality of opportunity' – H. G. Wells, *The Outline of History* (1920); 'Equal opportunity for all, under free institutions and equal laws – there is the banner for which we will do battle against all rubber-stamp bureaucracies or dictatorships' – Winston Churchill, *Victory* (1946); 'I define integration not as a flattening process of assimilation but as equal opportunity accompanied by cultural diversity in an atmosphere of mutual tolerance' – *The Listener* (26 December 1968); 'N.Y. Hilton . . . An equal opportunity employer' – *The New York Times* (3 November 1972); '*Equality of opportunity* . . . can be glossed as "equal opportunity to become unequal" – Raymond Williams, *Keywords* (1976); '"Equal opportunities!" said Norman. "That's one of the things we men prefer to leave to the ladies!"' – Barbara Pym, *Quartet in Autumn* (1977); the UK Equal Opportunities Commission was established in 1975; 'The Thatcherite view accepts the . . . thesis that "equality of opportunity means equal opportunity to be unequal"'– John Boyd-Carpenter, *Way of Life* (1980).

equal pay for equal work A modern feminist slogan dating from the 1970s, though echoing a cry of teacheßßßrs' organizations in the late 19th century. The phrase 'equal pay' on its own was known by 1923.

'er indoors Meaning 'the wife' (unseen, but domineering), this expression was popularized by George Cole as Arthur Daley in the British TV series *Minder* (1979–85; 1988–94). The series, which was created by Leon Griffiths, had a field day with (predominantly) London slang. When he died, his obituarist in *The Independent* wrote (10 June 1992): 'Once Griffiths gave me the inside story on the expression "'Er indoors". A taxi-driver drinking companion of his always referred to his never-to-be-seen wife as "'Er Indoors" . . . When the series was eventually screened, Griffiths was terrified the taxi-driver would be upset. He need not have bothered for he soon realised that the taxi-driver firmly believed all husbands never took their wives to a pub and always called them "'Er Indoors". I even know someone who pays tribute to Griffiths by calling his cat "'Er Outdoors".' 'I'm talking about Lodge Hill estate, in Bucks. This lies cheek-by-jowl with Chequers . . . the country seat of Her Indoors [i.e. Mrs Thatcher], and it's up for sale' – *The Guardian* (25 January 1989).

escutcheon   See BLOT ON.

etchings   See COME UP AND SEE.

(the) eternal triangle   The traditional struggle and rivalry in a relationship between two persons of one sex and one of the other – often where a couple, married or not, has to relate to a third party. One of the most common situations in fiction and in fact. Known since 1907, though one would think it older. 'Mrs Dudeney's novel . . . deals with the eternal triangle, which, in this case, consists of two men and one woman' – *Daily Chronicle* (5 December 1907).

et in Arcadia ego   This inscription on a tomb means either that, in death, the dead person is in Arcadia, or that he was formerly there. '*Et in Arcadia ego vixi* [. . . I lived]' or '*Et in Arcadia fui pastor* [. . . I was a shepherd]' are variants. Or, more likely, it is Death itself speaking – 'Even in Arcadia, I, Death, cannot be avoided.' Arcadia is the Greek name for a place of rural peace and calm taken from an actual area in the Peloponnese but used generally since classical times. '*Et in Arcadia ego*' is a phrase associated with tombs, skulls and Arcadian shepherds in classical paintings but not before the 17th century. Most notably the phrase occurs in two paintings by the French artist Nicolas Poussin (1594–1665), both of which depict shepherds reading the words carved on a tomb.

et tu, Brute [even you, Brutus]?   Julius Caesar's supposed dying words to Brutus, on realizing that his old friend was one of his assassins in 44 BC, were made famous through Shakespeare's use of '*Et tu, Brute? – Then fall Caesar!*' in the play *Julius Caesar*, III.i.77 (1599). The Latin words are not found in any classical source, but they do occur in English drama just before Shakespeare. *The True Tragedie of Richard Duke of Yorke* (printed in 1595) has 'Et tu, Brute, wilt thou stab Caesar too?' The origin of the phrase lies probably in Suetonius's account of the assassination in which Caesar is made to say, in *Greek*,

'Even you, my son?' The 'son' has been taken literally – as, according to Suetonius, Caesar had had an intrigue with Brutus's mother and looked upon Brutus as his likely son. Chips Channon wrote in his diary (7 April 1939): 'The Italians are occupying Albania . . . "Et tu Benito?" – for Mussolini had only recently assured us that he had no territorial claims whatsoever on Albania.'

even unto half my kingdom   In precisely this form, the phrase derives from Lord Alfred Douglas's 1894 translation of the Oscar Wilde play *Salomé* (from which Richard Strauss later took his opera). Herod says to Salomé: 'If you dance for me you may ask of me what you will, and I will give it you, even unto the half of my kingdom.' In the protracted negotiations that follow, Herod also says, 'even the half of my kingdom', then 'even to the half of my kingdom' and, again, 'even to the half of my kingdom'. Mark 6:23 (the original telling of the Salome story) merely has: 'And he sware unto her, whatsoever thou shalt ask of me, I will give it thee, unto the half of my kingdom.' P. G. Wodehouse frequently alludes to the headword version. Similar phrases in the Bible occur in the Book of Esther, 5:3, 5:6 and 7:2 (where it appears in the Authorized Version as 'even to the half of the kingdom').

evenin' all!   Accompanied by a shaky salute to the helmet, PC George Dixon (Jack Warner) would bid viewers welcome with this phrase through many episodes of *Dixon of Dock Green* on BBC TV (1955–76). His farewell, **mind how you go!**, achieved equal status as the phrase that all real policemen ought to say, even if not all of them do.

eventually – why not now?   Slogan for Gold Medal Flour in the USA, from *circa* 1907. The story has it that when Benjamin S. Bull, advertising manager of the Washburn Crosby company, requested members of his department to suggest catchphrases to be used in support of the flour, nobody came up with anything worthwhile. Mr Bull demanded, 'When are you going to give me a decent slogan?' His underlings staved him off by saying, 'Eventually.' 'Eventually!' thundered Mr Bull, 'Why not now?'

even your best friends won't tell you
Advertising line that originated in the
famous Listerine mouthwash advertisement
headed OFTEN A BRIDESMAID BUT
NEVER A BRIDE (US, 1920s), though the
idea may have been used to promote
another such product in the UK – Lifebuoy
soap, perhaps – in the late 1950s. Originally, the line in the Listerine copy was
**and even your closest friends won't tell
you**. *Partridge/Catch Phrases* suggests that
it became a catchphrase in the form **your
best friend(s) won't tell you** (= 'you
stink!'). In the film *A Day at the Races* (US
1935), Groucho Marx says the line, 'Even
my best friends don't know . . .' and in
Dangerous Moonlight (UK 1941), the
Anton Walbrook character says to a man
putting on hair oil (in New York), 'Even
your best friend won't *smell* you.' This
helps with the dating but does not really
confirm the American origin as the film
was made and scripted in England. A
similar idea was used by Amplex, the
breath purifier, in advertisements (current
in the UK, 1957) showing two people
reacting to a smelly colleague with the
slogan **someone isn't using Amplex**. This
was parodied in a *Private Eye* cartoon
(1964/5) showing Soviet leaders watching
a May Day parade. Or perhaps it was
'somebody's not using Amplex', as reported in *The Lyttelton Hart-Davis Letters*,
Vol. 2 (1979) – for 5 January 1957.

ever See AND THEY ALL.

(the) ever-open door Slogan phrase
used to describe Dr Barnado's Homes, the
orphaned children's charity in the UK (by
the 1910s). There appears to have been a
play with the title in 1913, and *Punch* had
a political cartoon with it as the caption
(26 November 1913). However, one can
recall it being applied to the insatiable
mouth, representing the appetite of an un-
orphaned youth (me), in the 1950s. A
correspondent recalls a mother calling her
son (b. 1900) 'the ever-open door'. And
note this, from Alexander Pope's translation of the *Iliad*, VI.14 (1715–20): 'He held
his seat; a friend to human race / Fast by
the road, his ever-open door / Obliged the
wealthy and relieved the poor.'

everybody has one book in them A
cliché of the publishing world – or perhaps not, for it advances a popular belief
that publishers might well disagree with.
Presumably, the idea behind the saying is
that all people have one story that they
alone can tell – namely, the story of their
life. Known by the 1940s. 'It is commonly
said that every human being has in him
the material for one good book, which is
true in the same sense as it is true that
every block of stone contains a statue' –
George Orwell in *New Statesman and
Nation* (7 December 1940); 'Every one, it
is said, has one good book inside him, and,
if this be so, it would be unkind to suggest
that Mr James Agate is the exception that
proves the rule. All one can in fairness say
is that his good book is not among the
thirty-six he has so far produced' – *Punch*
book review, quoted in James Agate, *Ego 6*
(entry for 12 November 1942).

everybody out! Catchphrase from the TV
sitcom *The Rag Trade*, written by Ronald
Wolfe and Ronald Chesney, which had the
unusual, though not unique, experience of
running on BBC TV from 1961 to 1965 and
then being revived on London Weekend
Television from 1977. Miriam Karlin in her
best flame-thrower voice as Paddy, the
Cockney shop steward, would shout the
phrase at every opportunity. Now connected in the public mind with all strike-
happy trade union leaders.

**everybody to their liking, as the old lady
said when she kissed the cow** Wellerism.
There are venerable early uses for this
formula. Heywood's *Proverbs* (1546) has:
'Quoth the good man whan that he kyst
his coowe.' Swift's *Polite Conversation*
(1738) has: 'Why; every one as they like;
as the good Woman said, when she kiss'd
her Cow'. In Sir Walter Scott's *Peveril of the
Peak*, Chap. 7 (1823), we find: '"She hath a
right to follow her fancy," as the dame said
who kissed her cow.'

everybody wants to get into the act
See GOODNIGHT MRS CALABASH.

**every day and in every way I am getting
better and better (**sometimes **every day
in every way . . .** or **day by day in every
way . . .)** Slogan or, as we would now
say, mantra. The French psychologist
Emile Coué was the originator of a system
of 'Self-Mastery Through Conscious Auto-

Suggestion' that had a brief vogue in the early 1920s. His patients had to repeat this phrase over and over, and it became a popular catchphrase of the time, though physical improvement did not necessarily follow. The French original was: '*Tous les jours, à tous les points de vue, je vais de mieux en mieux.*' Couéism died with its inventor in 1926, though there have been attempted revivals. John Lennon alludes to the slogan in his song 'Beautiful Boy' (1980).

(an) everyday story of country-folk
Explanatory line about *The Archers*, the BBC radio agricultural soap opera that has been running on national radio since 1951.

every dog has its day – and a bitch two afternoons! *Apperson* finds the second half of this proverbial saying being added by 1896 and – earlier, by 1864 – the 'Essex saying', 'Every dog has his day, and a cat has two Sundays.'

every —— gets the —— it deserves
Format phrase that probably derives from a quotation. Joseph de Maistre said, 'Every country has the government it deserves', in *Lettres et Opscules Inédits* (15 August 1811). From *Today* (10 June 1993), concerning Jeffrey Archer: 'It's said that a nation gets the politicians it deserves . . .'

Every Good Boy Deserves Favour
Mnemonic for remembering, in ascending order, the five horizontal black lines of the treble clef – signifying the notes E, G, B, D and F. The four spaces between the lines are for the notes F, A, C and E, which hardly need a mnemonic. Also used as the title of a Moody Blues LP (1971) and of a Tom Stoppard play for speaker and orchestra (1977).

every home should have one All-purpose slogan probably deriving from American advertising in the 1920s/30s. Used as the title of a British film about an advertising man in 1970. Against the American origin, is the fact that *Punch* (18 October 1905) had a cartoon whose caption contained the interesting variation: 'The Portable Gramophone . . . no country house should be without it.'

every inch a gentleman A complete gentleman. The basic expression occurs,

for example, in William Thackeray, *Pendennis*, Chap. 54 (1848–50). 'Every inch a man' was a proverbial expression by 1576. Shakespeare, *King Lear*, IV.vi.107 (1605), has 'Every inch a king'. *Every Other Inch a Lady* was the UK title of the film *Dancing Co-Ed* (US 1939) and also of the autobiography (1973) of Beatrice Lillie, the actress who was Lady Peel in private life. 'For all his reputation [he] is not a bounder. He is every other inch a gentleman' – R. E. Drennan in *Wit's End* (1973) quotes Alexander Woollcott as having said this of Michael Arlen. The same remark about Arlen has also been attributed to Rebecca West (by Ted Morgan in *Somerset Maugham*, 1980).

every little helps – as the old lady said when she piddled into the sea One of the best-known Wellerisms. As '"Every little helps," quoth the wren when she pissed in the sea', it occurs in William Camden's *Remains Concerning Britaine* (1605). The slightly politer, '"Every little bit helps," said the lady, as she spit in the ocean', is in John Dutton, *Letters from New England* (1867).

every man has his price *Mencken* says of this proverb: 'Ascribed to Robert Walpole *circa* 1740 in William Coxe, *Memoirs of the Life and Administration of Robert Walpole*, 1798.' There the form was: 'All those men have their price.' But *CODP* finds W. Wyndham in *The Bee* (1734) saying: 'It is an old Maxim, that every Man has his Price, if you can but come up to it.'

every one a coconut (or **every time . . .**)
Every time you try, you'll gain success. From the fairground barker's traditional cry at the coconut shy.

every picture tells a story A modern proverb and derived from a slogan used to promote Doan's Backache Kidney Pills (not 'Sloane's', as in the *Penguin Dictionary of Modern Quotations*, 1980), and current in 1904. The picture showed a person bent over with pain. In 1847, Charlotte Brontë had placed the same thought in *Jane Eyre*: 'The letter-press . . . I cared little for . . . Each picture told a story.'

everything in the garden's lovely
Meaning, 'all is well', in a general sense. The saying comes from the title of a song

(1898), written by G. LeBrunn & J. P. Harrington and made popular by Marie Lloyd. *Everything in the Garden* was the title of a stage play (1962) by Giles Cooper, about suburban housewives turning to prostitution.

everything's coming up roses All is well, prospects are good, everything's blooming. The phrase is used as the title of a song with words by Stephen Sondheim in the musical *Gypsy* (1959). But did the expression exist before this? *Partridge/Catchphrases* guesses that it was already current *circa* 1950. It is possibly adapted from the expression 'to come out of something smelling of roses', but there do not even seem to be any examples of *that* in use before the date of the Sondheim song.

everything you always wanted to know about —— but were afraid to ask Format phrase inspired by the title *Everything You Always Wanted To Know About Sex But Were Afraid to Ask*, a book published in 1970 by David Reuben MD. The use was popularized even further when Woody Allen entitled a film *Everything You Always Wanted To Know About Sex, But Were Afraid To Ask* (US 1972) – though, in fact, he simply bought the title of the book and none of its contents. The format soon became a cliché, and almost any subject you can think of has been inserted into the sentence. An advertisement for the UK *Video Today* Magazine (December 1981) promised: 'All you ever wanted to know about video but were afraid to ask.' In 1984, it was possible to draw up this short list from the scores of books that bore similar titles: *Everything That Linguists Have Always Wanted to Know About Logic But Were Ashamed To Ask*; *Everything You Always Wanted to Know About Drinking Problems And Then a Few Things You Didn't Want to Know*; *Everything You Always Wanted to Know About Elementary Statistics But Were Afraid to Ask*; *Everything You Always Wanted to Know About Mergers, Acquisitions and Divestitures But Didn't Know Whom to Ask*; *Everything You Wanted to Know About Stars But Didn't Know Where to Ask*; *Everything You Wanted to Know About the Catholic Church But Were Too Pious to Ask*; *Every-thing You Wanted to Know About the Catholic Church But Were Too Weak to Ask* . . . Compare the later title of a book by Robert Goldenson and Kenneth Anderson: *Everything You Ever Wanted to Know About Sex – But Never Dared Ask* (1988) – which is surely where we came in.

every time a sheep bleats it loses a nibble Sometimes rendered as 'Every time a sheep ba's it loses a bite'. *Mencken* (1942) has this as an English proverb in the form 'Every time the sheep bleats it loses a mouthful' and states that it was 'apparently borrowed from the Italian and familiar since the 17th century'. In this form it certainly appears in Thomas Fuller's *Gnomologia* (1732). *CODP* finds a version in 1599 and seems to prefer 'A bleating sheep loses a bite', explaining this as 'opportunities are missed through too much chatter.'

evidence See ANYTHING YOU SAY; I SWEAR.

evil See BANALITY OF.

(an) evil empire The Soviet Union was so described by President Reagan in a speech to the National Association of Evangelicals at Orlando, Florida (8 March 1983): 'In your discussions of the nuclear freeze proposals, I urge you to beware the temptation of pride – the temptation blithely to declare yourselves above it all and label both sides equally at fault, to ignore the facts of history and the aggressive impulses of an *evil empire* . . .' It is a reasonable assumption that the President's use of the phrase 'evil empire' was influenced by George Lucas's film *Star Wars* (US 1977) in which reference is made to an 'evil galactic empire'. From *The Independent* (19 May 1990): 'Frank Salmon, an East End protection racketeer who built an "evil empire" on violence and fear, was yesterday jailed for $7^1/_2$ years at the Old Bailey.'

evil under the sun Phrase used as the title of an Agatha Christie thriller about murder in a holiday hotel (1941; film UK 1982). It is not explained in the text, though Hercule Poirot, the detective, remarks before any evil has been committed: 'The sun shines. The sea is blue . . . but there is evil everywhere under the sun.' Shortly afterwards, another character remarks: 'I was interested, M. Poirot, in something you said just now . . . It was almost a quotation from Ecclesiastes . . . "Yea, also the heart of the sons of men is full of evil, and madness is in their heart while they live".' But Ecclesiastes (which finds everything 'under the sun') gets nearer than that: 'There is a sore evil which I have seen under the sun, namely, riches kept for the owners thereof to their hurt' (5:13) and: 'There is an evil which I have seen under the sun' (6:1, 10:1). Were it not for the clue about Ecclesiastes, one might be tempted to think that Christie had once more turned to an old English rhyme for one of her titles. In this one, the phrase appears exactly: 'For every evil under the sun, / There is a remedy or there is none; / If there be one, try and find it; / If there be none, never mind it.' See also NOTHING NEW UNDER THE SUN.

exactly   See IT DOES.

excellent   See NOT!

excuse me, sir, do you think that's wise? Catchphrase from the BBC TV comedy series *Dad's Army* (1968–77). Sergeant Wilson (John le Mesurier) would quietly inquire this of Captain Mainwaring (Arthur Lowe).

excuse stinkers   Smoker's phrase from the 1920s/30s when lighting up an inferior brand. As Robert Graves and Alan Hodge explain in *The Long Week-End* (1940), cigarettes made from Virginia tobacco were, at that time, considered by fashionable women to be a little vulgar. A common catchphrase when offering them was was 'I hope you don't mind; it's only a Virgin', or, more pointedly, 'Excuse stinkers'.

(to) exercise the ferret   Euphemism for sexual intercourse, recorded in 1985. Robert Burchfield, *The English Language* (1985), mentions 'to exercise the armadillo' as a memorable piece of Australian slang spotted in the 1970s.

existing conditions   An inevitable pairing, known in the USA by 1858. It occurs along with other rhetorical clichés during the 'Party Political Speech' (written by Max Schreiner) on the Peter Sellers' comedy album *The Best of Sellers* (1958):

'My friends, in the light of present-day developments, let me say right away that I do not regard existing conditions likely.' 'Among the national claims are increasing pay equity between men and women, the regulation of fixed-term and casual contracts, codification of existing conditions where these are not already covered under an industrial award, and greater flexibility in working hours for staff with families' – *The Times Higher Education Supplement* (25 November 1994).

exit pursued by a bear   Famous stage direction, from Shakespeare, *The Winter's Tale*, III.iii.58 (1611). It refers to the fate of Antigonus who is on the (in fact, non-existent) sea coast of Bohemia. Most of Shakespeare's stage directions are additions by later editors, but this one may be original. The bear could have been real (as bear-baiting was common in places adjacent to Shakespeare's theatres) or a man in costume.

exit stage left   Spoken aloud stage direction. Something that the cartoon character Snagglepuss used to say. Compare the fact that in the BBC radio *Goon Show*, Bluebottle (Peter Sellers) also tended to speak his own stage directions – 'Enter Bluebottle', 'Exit Bluebottle'. In addition, Neddie Seagoon (Harry Secombe) says, 'Ellington, play while I meditate. Exit left, smoking' in the edition of 15 October 1954.

experience   See CHALK IT UP TO.

(the) —— experience   A cliché of 1980s' marketing, particularly of 'heritage' material. It suggests that by going to some historical site or theme park you will have a life-enhancing visit and not just an ordinary day out. From the *Independent on Sunday* (25 April 1993): 'At Land's End, for instance, there's the *Land's End Experience*, a multi-media retelling of our island story, in which visions of Excalibur gleam through dry ice, waves crash and – for that extra tang of actuality – visitors are lightly-moistened with simulated sea-spray. A curious thing: to go to the sea-side to get wet indoors.' A few miles away it was possible, in the same year, to have the *Minack Experience* – a rather unnecessary indoor display attached to a wonderful open-air theatre (which truly is an experience). From *The Independent* (20 August 1992): 'The *Dracula Experience* exhibition in Whitby, North Yorkshire, is for sale . . . The exhibit, in the town that inspired Bram Stoker, author of the legend, attracts 80,000 visitors a year.' 'The Definitive Perlman Experience' – title of series of concerts by Itzhak Perlman at the Royal Festival Hall, London (June 1995); 'Leave your worries and the traffic behind and enjoy the Cotswold Experience . . . For your Cotswold Experience leaflet and booking details, just give us a call' – advertisement in *The Observer* (27 August 1995). Could the popularity of this usage somehow lie with the 'Jimi Hendrix Experience', the name given to the 1960s' rock musician's group?

expletive deleted The American way of indicating that an obscenity or blasphemous remark has been left out of a printed document. The phrase became general elsewhere during Watergate upon the release of transcripts of conversations between President Nixon and his aides – published as *The White House Transcripts* (1974). The documents also used 'expletive removed', 'adjective omitted', 'characterization omitted'. British practice had been to rely on **** (asterisks) or . . . (dots) or — (dashes) for sensitive deletions. Note this from a 1937 *Time* review of Hemingway's *To Have and Have Not*: 'No matter how a man alone ain't got no bloody (Obscenity deleted) chance.' For a while after Watergate people even exclaimed 'Expletive deleted!' instead of swearing.

(to) explore every avenue Political, rhetorical use, known by 1922. Cited as a 'silly expression' that had recently been 'killed by the jeers of a few journalists' by George Orwell, 'Politics and the English Language' in *Horizon* (April 1946). Earlier, A. P. Herbert in *What a Word!* (1935) had thought it was disappearing. In *Usage and Abusage* (last revised 1957) Eric Partridge called it a 'fly-blown phrase'. Still with us. 'Fancy picture of an eminent politician in search of a formula, leaving no stone unturned while exploring every avenue' – caption to cartoon, *Punch* (2 December 1931); 'In war-time we are bound to

explore every avenue, whether it's likely to be productive or not' – Nancy Mitford, *Pigeon Pie* (1940); 'To achieve our ultimate aim of Grand Slam and World Cup victories we must explore every avenue, not least in the mind. Far from being an admission of weakness, talking to a psychologist is simply striving for the best in oneself and for the team' – *The Independent* (18 February 1995); 'There was, however, a "moral obligation to explore every avenue to reduce the numbers out of work", she added. Work-sharing should aim to secure "a fairer distribution of the income which a job brings, and as a corollary, reduce the unequal burden of unemployment"' – *The Irish Times* (29 March 1995)

exporting is fun A Harold Macmillan slogan that misfired, though in this instance he never actually 'said' it. The phrase was included in a 1960 address to businessmen by the then British Prime Minister, but when he came to the passage he left out what was later considered to be a rather patronizing remark. The press, however, printed what was in the advance text of the speech as though he had actually said it. Compare the earlier **we must export – or die**, which arose out of a severe balance of payments problem under the Labour government in 1945/6.

exposed to the ravages of — Date of origin unknown. 'Mr Derek Hodgson, deputy general secretary of the UCW postal workers' union, attacked Post Office management for promoting privatisation. "They are a disgrace," he said. "The Post Office does not need to be exposed to the ravages of money-grabbing speculators" – *Financial Times* (6 October 1994); 'The mermaid, originally believed to be a siren who enticed seamen to their doom, has been exposed as the harmless, placid and less than seductive manatee, a species of sea cow increasingly vulnerable to the ravages of the powerboat propeller' – *The Sunday Telegraph* (26 February 1995); 'The [Churchill] graves are exposed to the ravages of thousands of tourists every year' – ITN news (28 April 1995).

exterminate, exterminate! The science fiction TV series *Dr Who* has given rise to numerous beasties since its inception on BBC TV in 1963 but none more successful than the Daleks (who arrived in 1964) – deadly, mobile pepper pots whose metallic voices rasped out 'Exterminate, exterminate!' as they set about doing so with ray guns. Much imitated by children.

extra mile See GO THE.

—— extraordinaire! A format phrase, current by 1940, and now a cliché. '[Culture Club's] flexible eight-piece includes Steve Grainger's sax, Terry Bailey's trumpet, Phil Pickett's keyboards, and their secret weapon, Helen Terry, a backing singer extraordinaire' – Max Bell in *The Times* (27 September 1983); '"If not Ivan the Terrible, then a Terrible Ivan", in the catchy phrase coined by US defence lawyer extraordinaire, Alan Dershowitz' – *Financial Times* (28 May 1994); 'I dropped in on fund-raiser extraordinaire, Dr Jerry Nims' – *The Observer* (30 September 1984); 'Even the peacemaker extraordinaire, former president Jimmy Carter, has offered his services – yet while Haiti, the Middle East and Bosnia were soothed by his touch, baseball would not budge' – *The Guardian* (29 March 1995).

eyaydon, yauden, yaydon, negidicrop dibombit! Catchphrase from the Navy version of BBC radio's *Merry Go Round* (1943–8) in which Jon Pertwee (1919–96) portrayed Svenson, a Norwegian stoker, whose cod Norwegian (based on close scrutiny of wartime news broadcasts) always ended up with these words. Paul Beale in *Partridge/Catch Phrases* adds that this was 'much imitated at the time'. In the same show, Pertwee also played Weatherby Wett (who later became Commander Weatherby in *The Navy Lark*). He would say **dabra, dabra!** (followed by stuttering). Then there was an inefficient character whose watchword was **the efficiency's the ticket**, and, in *Mediterranean Merry Go Round*, a Devonshire bugler at Plymouth barracks who eventually became a postman in *Waterlogged Spa* – not to mention thirteenth trombonist in the Spa Symphony Orchestra. At one concert he became bored with the slow movement of a symphony and broke into 'Tiger Rag'. When Eric Barker remonstrated

with him, he said: 'Ah, me old darling, but it tore 'em through, didn't it?' Barker: 'Well, er, yes . . .' Postman: 'Well, **what does it matter what you do as long as you tear 'em up?** Pertwee explained in *Pick of the Week* (4 July 1975) that all this was derived from a character he had known as a boy in the West Country, a postman who used to get drunk on cider and throw all the letters away.

eye See ALL MY; APPLE OF ONE'S; DON'T FIRE UNTIL.

eyeball to eyeball Meaning, 'in close confrontation'. Use of this expression is of comparatively recent origin. In the missile crisis of October 1962, the USA took a tough line when the Soviet Union placed missiles on Cuban soil. After a tense few days, the Soviets withdrew. *Safire* records that Secretary of State Dean Rusk (1909–94) was speaking to an ABC news correspondent, John Scali, on 24 October and said: 'Remember, when you report this, that, eyeball to eyeball, they blinked first.' Columnists Charles Bartlett and Stewart Alsop then helped to popularize this as, 'We're eyeball to eyeball and the other fellow just blinked.' Before this, 'eyeball to eyeball' was a black American serviceman's idiom. *Safire* quotes a reply given by the all-black 24th Infantry Regiment to an inquiry from General MacArthur's HQ in Korea (November 1950): 'Do you have contact with the enemy?' 'We is eyeball to eyeball.'

eyeless in Gaza Phrase from John Milton's *Samson Agonistes* (1671): 'Ask for this great deliverer now, and find him / Eyeless in Gaza, at the mill with slaves.' *Eyeless in Gaza* is the title of a book (1936) by Aldous Huxley.

(through the) eye of a needle . . . This biblical phrase from Matthew 19:24 and Mark 10:25 comes from the saying: 'it is easier for a camel to go through the eye of a needle than for a rich man to enter into the kingdom of God'. The Koran contains a similar view and in Rabbinical writings there is the expression 'to make an *elephant* pass through the eye of a needle' – which also appears in an Arab proverb. So why this camel/elephant confusion? Probably because the word for 'camel' in older Germanic languages, including Old English, was almost like the modern word for 'elephant' (OE *olfend*, 'camel'). In this biblical saying, however, it is probable that neither camel nor elephant was intended. The original Greek word should probably have been read as *kamilos*, 'a rope, cable', rather than *kamelos*, 'a camel'. The impossibility of threading a rope through the eye of a needle makes a much neater image. Another theory is that Christ was alluding to the Needle's Eye, a name given to a narrow defensive postern in the walls of Jerusalem, which admitted one man at a time. Or, as Lord Nugent's *Travels* mentions, to a similar gate at Hebron of the same name. But perhaps these gates were named by allusion to this remark rather than the other way round?

eyes See HERE AND NOW.

(the) eyes and ears of the world Slogan promoting the cinema newsreel Paramount News, 1927–57. Not Gaumont British News, as in *Partridge/Slang*.

(the) eyes are windows of the soul A person's eyes tell us a lot about the person. In *Zuleika Dobson* (1911), Max Beerbohm wrote: 'It needs no dictionary of quotations to remind me that the eyes are the windows of the soul.' But who was credited with that coinage in his dictionary of quotations? It has been suggested that

Plato originated the concept in the *Dialogues*, which in Jowett's translation reads: 'So does the stream of beauty, passing through the eyes which are the windows of the soul, come back to the beautiful one.' Another writer to speak along these lines was Guillaume du Bartas (1544–90), who wrote in 1578 of 'These lovely lamps, these windows of the soul.' Shakespeare, *Richard III*, V.iii.116 (1592–3), has Richmond mention, 'The windows of mine eyes' (but here windows = eyelids, and the eyes are being looked out of rather than in through). Théophile Gautier combined the notions in '*À deux beaux yeux* [Two Beautiful Eyes] (1833–8): *'Ils sont si transparents qu'ils lassient voir votre âme* [Eyes so transparent that they permit your soul to be seen].' And then there is this from William Blake: 'This life's five windows of the soul / Distort the Heavens from pole to pole, / And leads you to believe a lie / When you see with, not thro', the eye' – *The Everlasting Gospel* (*circa* 1818). Here, Blake seems to be saying that the five *senses* (or perhaps two eyes, two ears and a nose?) are the windows of the soul. In some texts, it is 'life's dim windows of the soul'. Compare: 'Everyone notices nice shoes. They are like windows to the soul' – Natasha Hamilton of Atomic Kitten, quoted in *The Independent*, 'Quotes of the Week' (7 December 2002).

F

(the) Fab Four An early nickname of The Beatles (1962–70). 'Fab' was a vogue word, short for fabulous, and current by 1963. It is said by some to have originated in Liverpool lingo, but *Partridge/Slang* has it in general teenage use by the late 1950s.

face See HIS FACE.

(the) face grows to fit the mask This notion goes back to Max Beerbohm's long short story *The Happy Hypocrite* (1897). Regency reprobate Lord George Hell dons a mask to woo operetta artiste Jenny Mere, who has told him he can never be her husband because his face is not saintly enough. His wax saint's mask does the trick, and he marries her in it. Happily,

when he is unmasked, his actual face is found to have grown saintly to match his reformed character. 'I perceived in this moment that when the white man turns tyrant it is his own freedom that he destroys. He becomes a sort of hollow, posing dummy, the conventionalized figure of a sahib. For it is the condition of his rule that he shall spend his life in trying to impress the "natives" and so in every crisis he has got to do what the "natives" expect of him. He wears a mask, and his face grows to fit it' – from George Orwell's essay 'Shooting an Elephant' (1936).

(a) face like a well-kept grave In recent times this descriptive phrase was applied by Jack Leach (a sportswriter) to Lester Piggott, the famously cadaverous English jockey. But earlier, W. C. Fields as 'The Great "Mark Antony" McGonigle' says to an elderly lady that she is 'All dressed up like a well-kept grave' in the film *The Old-Fashioned Way* (US 1934).

(the) —— faces of —— Journalistic format phrase with the number of faces variable. The origin lies in the book and film title *The Three Faces of Eve* (US 1957) – a story concerning a schizophrenic. In Fritz Spiegl's *Keep Taking the Tabloids* (1983), he concluded wrongly that the film title was *The Four Faces of Eve* on the basis of a newspaper headline, 'The Four Faces Of Steve'. When BBC2 TV started transmissions in 1964 each evening's viewing had its own theme – education, entertainment, minorities – and this scheduling was billed as 'The Seven Faces of the Week' (and was soon abandoned, as it was ratings death). Walter Terry in the *Daily Mail* (19 June 1964) listed the 'Ten faces of Harold [Wilson]' – 'Little Englander Harold, Capitalist Harold, Russian Harold . . .' etc.

(the) face on the cutting-room floor An actor or actress cut out of a film after it has been completed. Used as the title of a novel by Cameron McCabe in 1937 and possibly related to the ballad known as 'The Face on the Bar-room Floor' by H. Antoine d'Arcy (though he insisted the title was simply 'The Face on the Floor'). Now the 'cutting-room floor' tends to be invoked as the place where any unwanted material ends up – and not only with reference to media matters. From Josephine Tey, *A Shilling for Candles* (1936): 'Treating me like bits on the cutting-room floor.'

(the) face that launch'd a thousand ships An impressive compliment to female beauty, much alluded to. Originally, Christopher Marlowe's mighty line in *Dr Faustus* (*circa* 1594) referred to Helen of Troy: 'Was this the face that launch'd a thousand ships?' Earlier, Marlowe had said something similar in *Tamburlaine the Great* (1587): 'Helen, whose beauty . . . drew a thousand ships to Tenedos.' Shakespeare must have been alluding to Marlowe's line when, in *Troilus and Cressida* (*circa* 1601), he said of Helen:

'Why she is a pearl / Whose price hath launch'd above a thousand ships.' He also alludes to it in *All's Well That Ends Well* (1603). The consistent feature of these mentions is the figure of a 'thousand', which was a round number probably derived from the accounts of Ovid and Virgil. Chips Channon records (23 April 1953) in the House of Commons: '[Aneurin] Bevan looked at poor, plain Florence Horsburgh [Independent MP for the Combined English Universities] and hailed her with the words "That's the face that sank a thousand scholarships".' To Jack de Manio, the broadcaster, is attributed a more recent version. Of Glenda Jackson, the actress, he is alleged to have said, in the 1970s: 'Her face could launch a thousand dredgers.'

(to) face the music Meaning 'to face whatever punishment is coming' and known by 1850, this saying has two possible origins. An actor or entertainer must not only accept the judgement of the audience but also of the (often hard-to-impress) musicians in the orchestra in front of him. He literally faces the music. More likely is the second explanation, that it is akin to the expression 'to be **drummed out of**' something. At one time, if a soldier was dismissed from the army for dishonourable conduct, he would be drummed out in a ceremony that included having a description of his crime read out and his insignia stripped from his uniform.

face to face Looking another person in the face, possibly close up. Known since 1300. In the 1960s, the phrase was used as the title of a BBC Television interview series, conducted by John Freeman, in which the interviewer was not seen, only his subject – an appropriate use as there is a proverb that states, in full, 'Face to face, the truth comes out' (known by 1732).

(that) face would stop a clock *Partridge/Catch Phrases* gives a date of 1890 for this phrase and suggests that it would be applied only to a female.

(the) fact of the matter is . . . Journalistic and rhetorical use. Date of origin unknown. Identified as a current cliché in *The Times* (17 March 1995). 'Pressed as to how farmers could produce leaner carcasses, Prof James said: "It's a complex inter-play between breeding, earlier slaughter and feeding. The fact of the matter is that successive support measures have persuaded farmers to keep cattle longer than they should just to gain extra weight and therefore a seemingly greater reward'" – *The Scotsman* (8 November 1994); 'Anyone who willingly jumps from an aeroplane at 3,000 feet might be accused of having a death wish. Or perhaps it might be because two successive defeats have undermined his club's dream of promotion. Jim Duffy would argue differently. The fact of the matter is that the Dundee manager is neither a vicarious thrill-seeker nor a crackpot in urgent need of medical assistance' – *Daily Mail* (3 May 1995).

(the) —— factor Journalistic phrase and also a cliché of book titles since the early 1980s, when the alliterative lure of the 'Falklands Factor' gave rise to numerous other inventions. This 'factor' was the apparent reason for the supposed improvement in Margaret Thatcher's fortunes in the 1983 British General Election following her 'victory' in the previous year's conflict with Argentina over the Falklands. Indeed, in the 1980s, almost any phenomenon was liable to be dignified by the '—— factor' suffix. It gave a spurious sense of science – or at least journalistic weight – to almost any theory or tendency that had been spotted. '[Geraldine] Ferraro's "sleaze factor" . . . Anything questionable which emerges subsequently about their background becomes known as the "sleaze factor"' – *The Observer* (19 August 1984); 'The Chernobyl factor appears to have cast its shadow over not just British lamb, but the homes of those unfortunate to live near the four areas shortlisted for the NIREX nuclear dumping site' – *The Daily Telegraph* (3 July 1986); 'Liz Howell, the woman behind GMTV, admits that when Fiona Armstrong was employed she was asked to have an image makeover – shorter skirts, shorter hair and a big flirtatious smile that could give her the F-Factor (F for fanciability) rating they wanted' – *Today* (6 January 1993); 'Fiona Armstrong, Good Morning TV's new presenter, has it. Her co-host, Michael

Wilson, is on the way to having it. GMTV swears by it. "It" is the F-Factor, where "F" stands, officially at least, for "fanciability"' – *The Times* (6 January 1993); 'To be greeted by Paul Johnson as a Christian gentleman who has no time for class politics and understands that public spending must be controlled contributes nicely to the ripple effect Blair seeks to spread across the surface of politics, dispelling the fear factor which lurks in the stagnant depths. The fear factor was a killer in 1992. Anything that accelerates the party's move out of the time-warp is a contribution' – *The Guardian* (11 April 1995); '[Joan Littlewood] scorns the "elocution" of Edith Evans but is a sucker for the Gielgud factor' – *The Independent* (18 June 1995).

facts See ALL WE WANT.

faint from lack of nourishment See I WANT ME TEA.

fair See ALL'S FAIR.

(a) fair crack of the whip What one should give to people in order that they may have a fair chance or, at least, an opportunity, to do something. Known by 1929. The origin is obvious: in the days of horse-drawn transport, whoever had the whip was also holding the reins and therefore in charge of the vehicle's progress.

(a) fair day's wages for a fair day's work Slogan of 19th-century British origin. T. Attwood in a speech in the House of Commons (14 June 1839) said: 'They only ask for a fair day's wages for a fair day's work.' This is picked up by Charles Dickens in *Our Mutual Friend*, Bk 1, Chap. 13 (1864–5): 'A fair day's wages for a fair day's work is ever my partner's motto.'

(a) fair deal 'Every segment of our population and every individual has a right to expect from this government a Fair Deal' – from President Truman's State of the Union message (1949), introducing a package of measures including legislation on civil rights and fair employment practices. The two words had, however, been together since 1600.

(off/away with the) fairies In a dazed state of mind. Known in Australia and Britain by the 1980s.

(the) fair sex The female sex. Known by 1688, a cliché by 1900, and a phrase only to be used with caution following the rise of feminism in the 1970s and the politically correct movement in the 1990s. 'The aspirin age needed its drugs largely because the fair sex tried so hard to look anything but' – *News Chronicle* (27 July 1960); 'Since Dale Reid and Corinne Dibnah won the [golf] title in crushing style in 1990, the fair sex have seen their handicap allowance cut. "We keep telling them but they won't listen," Ms Moon complained. "It was just too long for us"' – *The Independent* (23 March 1995).

fairy-tale See LIKE A.

faithful unto death Epitaphic phrase of biblical origin – Revelation 2:10 has: 'Be thou faithful unto death and I will give thee a crown of life.' The phrase was also used as the title of a famous painting (1865) by Sir Edward John Poynter PRA that shows a centurion staying at his sentry post during the eruption of Vesuvius which destroyed Pompeii in AD 79. In the background, citizens are panicking as molten lava falls upon them. The picture was inspired by the discovery of an actual skeleton of a soldier in full armour excavated at Pompeii in the late 18th or early 19th century. Many such remains were found of people 'frozen' in the positions they had held as they died. Bulwer-Lytton described what might have happened to the soldier in his *Last Days of Pompeii* (1834). The painting hangs in the Walker Art Gallery, Liverpool.

fall See BIGGER THEY COME; DID SHE FALL.

falling See AS EASY AS; CATCH A.

falling towards England Phrase, probably derived from W. H. Auden's poem 'O Love, the interest itself' (1936): 'And make us as Newton was, who in his garden watching / The apple falling towards England, became aware between himself and her of an eternal tie.' Used as the title of the second volume of memoirs (1985) by the Australian-born writer Clive James, though he does not acknowledge it. Julian Mitchell's 1994 play about a family in the early part of the 20th century has the similar title, *Falling Over England*.

fame and fortune An inevitable alliterative pairing. 'Lingering in suspense, whilst his fame and fortune are *sub judice*' – General C. Lee, *Memoirs* (1778/1792); 'The ladder by which he climbed to fame and fortune was runged by indomitable perseverance' – Macleod, *Clyde District Dumbarton* (1886); 'Mac McGowan was to . . . drop his silver talent into the slit of the slot-machine of fame and fortune that gives up reputation and dough' – O. Henry, *Rolling Stones* (1912); '"Will you wait for me, Muriel? . . . Call it six months or a year. By that time I shall have won fame and fortune"' – P. G. Wodehouse, *Lord Emsworth and Others*, Chap. 2 (1937); 'Elizabeth's mother discovered the full story of the tragic end of the young girl who had set out from her Nottingham home aged 17 hoping for fame and fortune' – *The Observer* (5 January 2003).

fame at last! Ironic exclamation on finding one's name in print – especially in an unflattering context, say in a list of chores. From the 1940s onwards.

fame is the spur Phrase from Milton's 'Lycidas' (1637): 'Fame is the spur that the clear spirit doth raise / (That last infirmity of noble mind) / To scorn delights, and live laborious days.' Used as the title of a novel (1940; film UK 1946) by Howard Spring about an aspiring politician.

families See ACCIDENTS WILL.

family See ALL IN THE; IN THE FAMILY.

(the) family jewels (1) A 'jocular CIA phrase for its own most embarrassing secrets', according to *Safire* (1978). Director of Central Intelligence William Colby, reflecting on his predecessor's attempts to unearth CIA activities that were outside its charter, noted in his book *Honorable Men* (1978): 'They were promptly dubbed by a wag the "family jewels"; I referred to them as "our skeletons in the closet".' (2) The testicles or the whole 'male sexual apparatus'. *Partridge/Slang* finds this in services' use in the Second World War and probably earlier, back to the 1920s.

(not in a) family newspaper Journalistic humbug of the OUR REPORTER MADE AN EXCUSE AND LEFT variety. The reporter sails as close to the wind as he can and then states, 'She committed an act which we cannot describe in a family newspaper', or some such. Claud Cockburn in *I, Claud* (1967) said, 'the Bowdlers – "can't put that in a family newspaper" – were on the job everywhere, swabbing down the lavatory walls'. The idea of a 'family' newspaper goes back as far as the first edition of *The Observer* (4 December 1791) in which the 'Address to the Public' stated: 'Servants also, as the *Observer* cannot fail of becoming a favourite family Paper, will find it their peculiar interest to give it their decided preference.' The notion has now spread to broadcasting – 'This is a family show, so I couldn't possibly tell you what happened . . .'

(the) family that prays together stays together Slogan, devised by Al Scalpone of the Roman Catholic Rosary Crusade in the USA. The crusade began in 1942, and the slogan was first broadcast on 6 March 1947, according to Father Patrick Peyton, *All For Her* (1967). The slogan is quoted in Joseph Heller, *Catch-22* (1961), which is set in the period 1944–5, but this may simply be an anachronism. It has been the inspiration of many humorous variants: 'The family that shoots together loots together', 'The family that flays together stays together', etc.

famous See AWOKE ONE MORNING.

famous for being famous Phrase used to describe people who are celebrated by the media although it is difficult to work out precisely what it is they have done to deserve such attention. Nowadays, these 'celebrities' appear as guests on TV quiz shows, participate in charity telethons and – as they have always done – feature on guest lists for first nights and film premieres. The phrase probably dates from the 1960s/70s. 'With Christine Keeler in person . . . and with the attendant chorus of showbiz froth and nonentities famous for being famous, the film's premiere brazenly upheld all the meretricious values' – *Daily Mail* (4 March 1989). Daniel J. Boorstin in *The Image* (1962) noted: 'The celebrity is a person who is known for his well-knownness.'

(to be) famous for fifteen minutes Meaning 'to have transitory fame' of the

type prevalent in the 20th century, this expression comes from the celebrated words in a catalogue for an exhibition of Andy Warhol's work in Stockholm (1968). The artist wrote: 'In the future everyone will be world-famous for fifteen minutes.' It is often to be found used allusively, e.g.: 'He's had his fifteen minutes', etc. *Famous for Fifteen Minutes* was the title of a series of, naturally, fifteen-minute programmes on BBC Radio 4 (from 1990) in which yesterday's headline-makers were recalled from obscurity. In Warhol's published diaries (for 27 July 1978), he wrote: 'After work I just stayed in. Watched *20/20* and instead of saying, "In the future everyone will be famous for fifteen minutes," it was so funny to hear Hugh Downs say, "As Andy Warhol once said, in fifteen minutes everybody will be famous." People on TV always get some part wrong, like – "In the future fifteen people will be famous".' 'So spectacular was the [tree] fall that the local NBC affiliate did a live broadcast from [our neighbourhood]. Alas, none of us had the electricity to savour our 15 minutes-worth as it happened' – *The Independent* (22 September 2003).

famous last words! This is the kind of response given to someone who has just made a rash statement, tempting providence, of the type: 'I always drive better when I've got a few drinks inside me.' The phrase was first recorded by Eric Partridge in his *Dictionary of Forces' Slang* (1948) where it is described as a catchphrase rejoinder to such fatuous statements as, 'Flak's [anti-aircraft fire's] not really dangerous.' *OED2*, defining the phrase as 'a remark or prediction likely to be proved wrong by events', also gives an example from *Shell Aviation News*, No. 117 (1948): 'Leopoldville is easy to find because you cannot miss the Congo River. (Famous last words!)' A book with the title *Famous Last Words* by Barnaby Conrad (1962) was the first of a number of such works using the phrase in a non-ironic sense and recording the notable dying words of celebrities. 'Mr Campbell recently said he believed the Government had overcome its reputation for "spin". But he added: "Famous last words"' – *The Independent* (11 December 2002). Compare **you have been warned!** A book made up entirely of motorists' boasts, with illustrations by Fougasse, was entitled *You Have Been Warned* (1936). This second phrase comes from what *Partridge/Catch Phrases* describes as the 1930s' 'familiar police admonition'. On 11 February 1931, *Punch* was running a cartoon parodying a series of warning notices erected by the 'Car Society' (i.e. the AA or RAC): 'Very Dangerous Bend', 'You Have Been Warned', 'There! We Told You So.'

fancy-free Not in love with anyone; without commitments. Apparently, this phrase makes its first appearance in Shakespeare, *A Midsummer Night's Dream*, II.i.163 (1595): 'And the imperial votress passed on, / In maiden meditation, fancy-free.' More recently, the saying is the alliterative 'foot-loose and fancy-free'. 'I'm travelling around, you see. Footloose and fancy free, you might call me. I've no special ties anywhere' – E. Candy, *Words for Murder Perhaps*, Chap. 11 (1971).

Fanny See ARE YOU ALL RIGHT; MY GIDDY.

far See FROM A.

(the) far end of the fart 'My mother, who was born in Lincolnshire, was wont to say of a person she considered too inquisitive: "He always wants to know the far end of the fart and where the stink goes"' – W. G. Wayman (1993). Compare this from Anne Marie Hawkins (1994): 'My grandmother said of an inquisitive woman of her acquaintance: "She wanted to know the far end of a goose's trump, how many ounces it weighed, and which way the stink blew".'

farewell See AND SO WE SAY.

farewell cruel world (or goodbye . . .)! Poetic cry, used now only in parody. Bluebottle (Peter Sellers) said 'Farewell, cruel world' having just been 'deaded' (as he so often was) in an edition of the BBC radio *Goon Show* entitled 'The Vanishing Room' (13 October 1958). In 1961, an American singer called James Darren had a minor hit with a song entitled 'Goodbye, cruel world'. It famously went on: '. . . I'm off to join the circus.' Thirty years later, Shakespear Sister also entered the charts with this title (but it was not the same

song). The only citation to hand of the original, straightforward cry is from Monk Lewis's poem 'The Orphan's Prayer' (1812): 'Farewell, thou cruel world! – To-morrow / No more thy scorn my heart shall tear; / The grave will shield the child of sorrow, / And Heaven will hear the Orphan's prayer.'

(a) farewell to arms Title of a novel (1929) by Ernest Hemingway. Borrowed from the title applied to George Peele's sonnet beginning 'His golden locks time hath to silver turn'd . . .' (1590). Found by Hemingway when trawling through Sir Arthur Quiller-Couch's *Oxford Book of English Verse* (1900) searching for a title. The phrase 'a farewell to arms' also occurs in D. B. Haseler's poem beginning, 'Now that the king has no more need of me' (1919).

farewell to the flesh Supposed derivation of the word 'carnival', meaning the period leading up to Shrove Tuesday and the beginning of Lent, when flesh as food is put away or removed. The etymology of this would rely on the Latin *vale* (farewell) and *carne* (flesh), but – as the *OED2* declares – this belongs to the domain of popular etymology. The more likely derivation is as a corruption of Latin *carnem levare* or Italian *carne levare* (putting away or removal of flesh as food). Hence, however, *Farewell to the Flesh*, title of a novel (1998) by Gemma O'Connor.

far from the madding crowd Phrase from Thomas Gray's 'Elegy Written in a Country Church-Yard' (1751): 'Far from the madding crowd's ignoble strife / Their sober wishes never learn'd to stray.' Hence, the title of Thomas Hardy's novel (1874; film UK 1967). 'Madding' here means 'frenzied, mad' – not 'maddening'.

Farmer Giles The personification of the (British) country farmer, possibly named after the subject of Robert Bloomfield's poem *The Farmer's Boy* (1800) (although he is a labourer rather than a farmer). Coincidentally or not, Isaac Bickerstaff in *The Maid of the Mill* (1765) has: 'I am determined farmer Giles shall not stay a moment on my estate, after next quarter day.' Accordingly, 'farmers' is rhyming slang for piles (haemorrhoids). 'You find yourself remembering how Farmer Giles did you down over the sale of your pig, and Farmer Giles finds himself remembering that it was your son, Ernest, who bunged the half-brick at his horse on the second Sunday before Septuagesima' – P. G. Wodehouse, *Very Good, Jeeves,* 'The Ordeal of Young Tuppy' (1930). *Farmer Giles of Ham* was the title of a story (1949) by J. R. R. Tolkien.

Farnsbarns See CHARLIE.

fart See CAN'T EAT GUM; FAR END OF; HE CAN'T.

fashion See ALWAYS TRUE.

(a) fashion victim A person (usually female) who wears clothes solely to be fashionable and without consideration as to whether the particular items are suitable for her figure. Possibly a coinage of the American journal *Women's Wear Daily* and current by the early 1970s. There is also the phrase **a martyr to be smarter** that *Partridge/Slang* locates mid-20th century and which seems to be describing the same affliction.

fast See ALL ROWED; FLYING FICKLE.

faster than a speeding bullet! The comic-strip hero Superman was the brainchild of a teenage science-fiction addict Jerry Siegel in 1933. Five years later, Superman appeared on the cover of the first issue of *Action Comics*. In 1940, he took to the radio airwaves in the USA on the Mutual Network, with Clayton 'Bud' Collyer as the journalist Clark Kent who can turn into the Man of Steel whenever he is in a tight spot: 'This looks like a job for . . . Superman! Now, off with these clothes! **Up, up and awa-a-a-ay!**' After appearing in film cartoons, Superman finally appeared as a live-action hero on the screen in a 15-episode serial in 1948. He was still on the big screen in the 1970s and 80s. It was from the radio series, however, that the exciting phrases came: *Announcer:* 'Kellogg's Pep . . . the super-delicious cereal . . . presents . . . *The Adventures of Superman!* Faster than a speeding bullet! [*ricochet*] More powerful than a locomotive! [*locomotive roar*] Able to leap tall buildings at a single bound! [*rushing wind*] Look! Up in the sky!' *Voice 1:* '**It's a bird!**' *Voice 2:* '**It's a plane!**' *Voice 3:* '**It's Super-**

man!' *Announcer:* 'Yes, it's Superman – a strange visitor from another planet, who came to earth with powers and abilities far beyond those of mortal men. Superman! – who can change the course of mighty rivers, bend steel with his bare hands, and who – disguised as Clark Kent, mild-mannered reporter for a great metropolitan newspaper – fights **a never-ending battle for truth, justice and the American way**.' 'Up, up, and away!' was used by Jim Webb as the title of a song in 1967 and, in the same year, was incorporated in the airline slogan 'Up, up and away with TWA'.

fat cats Moneyed and probably complacent people. Originally, the term was popularized by Frank R. Kent of the *Baltimore Sun* in his 1928 book, *Political Behavior,* to describe major contributors to political campaign funds. 'I've always wondered why the Democrats call supporters of the Republican party "fat cats" but their own contributors are called "public spirited philanthropists"' – attributed to Ronald Reagan.

father See AND WHEN DID YOU.

fat lady sings See OPERA AIN'T OVER.

(the) Fat Controller Name of a character in the *Thomas the Tank Engine* series of children's books by the Reverend W(ilbert) Awdry (1911–97). He has twice undergone a name change. From the Introduction to *James the Red Engine* (1948): 'We [British Rail] are nationalised now, but the same engines still work the Region. I am glad, too, to tell you that the Fat Director, who understands our friends' ways, is still in charge, but is now the Fat Controller.' Initially, indeed, he was shown very much as a director of a private railway company, wearing striped pants, tail coat and top hat. In the 1990s, when hugely successful TV film series were made of the stories, sales to the politically correct US market necessitated that the character be referred to, not by this fat-ist name, but as 'Sir Topham Hat' – which was actually Awdry's original name for him.

(a) fate worse than death Originally referring to loss of virginity or rape, this is an expression dating from the days when such dishonour for a woman would, indeed, have seemed so. In John Cleland's

Memoirs of a Woman of Pleasure (1748–9), Fanny Hill talks of a 'dread of worse than death'. Thomas Morell's libretto for Handel's oratorio *Theodora* (1749) has this exchange in Act 1: *Septimius*: 'Death is not yet thy doom, / But worse than death to such a virtuous mind; / Lady, these guards are ordered to convey / You to the vile place, / As a prostitute to devote your charms.' *Theodora*: 'Oh worse than death indeed!' *OED2* has the phrase in its original sense by 1810. In *The Trumpet-Major* (1882), Thomas Hardy reproduces what purports to be a document headed 'Address to All Ranks and Descriptions of Englishmen' dating from the time of Napoleonic invasion scares: 'You will find your best Recompense,' it concludes, '. . . in having protected your Wives and Children from death, or worse than Death, which will follow the Success of such Inveterate Foes.' Now used jokingly of any situation one might wish to avoid. 'You are fully aware that should the evil spread . . . Bertram Wooster will be faced with the fate that is worse than death – viz. marriage' – P. G. Wodehouse, *The Mating Season*, Chap. 12 (1949).

fat, fair and forty Alliterative phrase of some antiquity. 'Fat, fair and forty were all the toast of the young men' – John O'Keeffe, *The Irish Mimic* (or *Irish Minnie*), Act 2 Sc. 3 (1795); '"Fat, fair, and forty," said Mr Winterblossom; "that's all I know of her – a mercantile person"' – Walter Scott, *St Ronan's Well*, Chap. 7 (1823); '[A Frenchwoman] remembered an anecdote of George the Fourth [and one of his mistresses] which had led to a phrase, now passed into a proverb, always pleasantly recalled by beauties of a certain age. "Faat, farre, and forté"' – Fanny Trollope, *Hargrave* (1843).

(the) father of his country Sobriquet, notably applied to George Washington (1732–99), 1st President of the USA (1789–97). First used on a 1778 calendar, published in Pennsylvania, in German: '*Das Landes Vater*'.

(a) Faustian pact A bargain of the type where one sells one's soul to the devil, and so named after Johann Faust(us), a German astrologer and necromancer (d. 1541) who is reputed to have practised the black arts and was later celebrated in several plays including Christoper Marlowe's *The Tragical History of Dr Faustus* (*circa* 1592) and Goethe's *Faust* (1772–1831). In these plays Faust exchanges his soul for a longer life in which all pleasure and knowledge are his for the asking. *A Faustian Pact* was the title of a book (1983) by Anthony Beevor.

fay ce que voudras (or **fais ce que voudras)** Meaning, '**do what you will**; do as you please'. This is an appealing motto and one that has been adopted by more than one free-living soul. It appeared first in Bk 1 of *Gargantua and Pantagruel* (1532) by Rabelais. Then, in the 18th century, it was the motto of the Monks of Medmenham, better known as the Hell Fire Club. Sir Francis Dashwood founded a mock Franciscan order at Medmenham Abbey in Buckinghamshire in 1745, and the members of the Club were said to get up to all sorts of disgraceful activities, orgies, black masses, and the like. The politician John Wilkes was of their number. The motto was written up over the ruined door of the abbey. Aleister Crowley (*circa* 1876–1947), the satanist who experimented in necromancy, the black arts, sex and drugs, also picked up the motto. Of his 'misunderstood commandment', Germaine Greer comments in *The Female Eunuch* (1970): '*Do as thou wilt* is a warning not to delude yourself that you can do otherwise, and to take full responsibility for what you do. When one has genuinely chosen a course for oneself it cannot be possible to hold another responsible for it.'

fear and loathing in —— Format phrase based on *Fear and Loathing in Las Vegas*, the title of a book (1972) by the US writer Hunter S. Thompson, describing a visit to a motorbike race outside the gambling city while under the influence of a variety of mind-expanding drugs. Thompson also wrote *Fear and Loathing on the Campaign Trail, '72* (1972) and 'Fear and Loathing at the Superbowl' (in *Rolling Stone*, 15 February 1973). Apart from having a much quoted title, the book is a prime example of what Thompson calls **gonzo journalism**, in which the writer chronicles his own role in the events he is reporting and doesn't worry too much about the facts. The word may be the same as Italian *gonzo* [a fool; foolish], though Thompson is quoted as saying, 'It's a Portuguese word, and it translates almost exactly into what the Hell's Angels would have said was off the wall.'

(to have a) feather in one's cap Meaning 'to have an honour or achievement of which one can be proud', the expression (known by 1700) probably dates from 1346, when the Black Prince was awarded the crest of John, King of Bohemia, which showed three ostrich feathers, after he had distinguished himself at the Battle of Crécy. This symbol has since been carried by every Prince of Wales. Later, any knight who had fought well might wear a feather in his helmet. 'It could be argued that when Logan struck the penalty that drew Stirling level, 6–6, after Stark had been caught offside, it was another feather in his cap' – *The Scotsman* (26 February 1995).

(a) feeding frenzy Meaning, 'furious media attention'. The image here is of fish swimming to retrieve bait thrown to them by a fisherman, or of homing in on any potential food. An article by Professor Perry W. Gilbert in *Scientific American* (July 1962) has this: 'As the blood and body juices of the marlin flow from the wound, the other sharks in the pack become more and more agitated and move in rapidly for their share of the meal. Frequently three or four sharks will attack the marlin simultaneously. A wild scene sometimes called a "feeding frenzy" now ensues.' As William Safire observed in *The New York Times* Magazine (in September 1988), packs of journalists in the USA had come to be described by that time as 'in a piranha-like feeding frenzy' or behaving like 'sharks in a feeding frenzy'. Alliteration rules once more: '[Hunter S. Thompson's] forthcoming trial has the makings of an international media circus – or "feeding frenzy", as Thompson would put it' – *The Independent* (14 April 1990).

(it's just like) feeding time at the zoo A meal or any event where there is no discipline, especially when involving young children. Since the 1950s/60s?

(the) feel-good factor Mostly political use to describe a type of feeling in the electorate whose presence may inhibit people from voting for change or whose absence encourages dissatisfaction with the *status quo*. As an example of the first type, it was advanced by Neil Kinnock, British Labour Party leader, as a reason why he was unable to defeat the long-running Conservative government in the election of 1987. As an example of the latter type, it was frequently evoked in 1994–5 to explain the continuing lack of popularity of the Conservative government. Identified as a current cliché in *The Times* (17 March 1995). As for the element 'feel good', this had been established earlier and was already something of a cliché before it was added to the 'factor'. Coined in the USA, the phrase for the idea of 'feeling good with yourself' was a way of describing your 'quality of life', which, in due course, became a very politically correct thing to have. Was the name of the British vocal and instrumental group Dr Feelgood (late 1970s) some influence on this or was it, in turn, derived from the earlier use of the phrase? 'Then there are the "Mr Feel Good" labels. These assure you a position in lefty heaven because you have bought yogurt from Fred, "made with loving care and pure Jersey milk from a nearby farm" or politically-correct coffee beans made by workers in Nicaragua who will never use Hair Salad on contras' – *The Washington Post* (27 December 1987); 'Shadow Scottish Secretary George Robertson disagreed. "Ian Lang must be living on another planet to everyone else. The Secretary of State may think everything in the garden is rosy, but for the thousands of ordinary Scots the "feel good factor" is nothing but a cruel joke' – *The Herald* (Glasgow) (13 December 1994).

feet See AT YOUR THROAT; GET ONE'S FEET.

fell See AT ONE FELL.

(it) fell off the back of a lorry The traditional response of a man suspected of stealing something and who is challenged to say where he obtained it. British use since the 1950s? Now also used as an example of a weak excuse about anything.

(the) female form divine In *Iris* (1998), his touching memoir of life with Iris

Murdoch, John Bayley ponders the 'Edwardian archness' of the phrase 'female form divine' – 'a comic but also rather lyrical cliché that had also appealed once to James Joyce'. In fact, it is a little older than that. The earliest *OED2* has is 'form divine' (only) in a female context in 1866. However, in a poem called 'The Caroline' in the *Miscellaneous Works* (1813) of Robert Charles Dallas, a friend of Byron, there is: 'The matchless properties combine / To make the female form divine.'

(the) female of the species (and **deadlier than the male)** Two phrases from a Rudyard Kipling poem, 'The Female of the Species' (1911). The key line is: 'For the female of the species is more deadly than the male.' Hence, the film titles *The Female of the Species* (UK 1917) (a silent version of *The Admirable Crichton*) and (UK 1967), the latter based on Sapper's novel *The Female of the Species* (1927). *Deadlier Than the Male* was also the title of a survey of female crime writers (1981) by Jessica Mann. A much quoted line, though sometimes the quoter takes the teeth out of the remark. In 1989, Margaret Thatcher said: 'The female of the species is rather better than the male.'

(a) femme fatale A fatally attractive woman who lures an unfortunate male into her grasp and then betrays him. It is not clear why this phrase entered the language in French. *'Femme, beauté fatale. Envoyée par le destin pour perdre ou, plus communément, séduire ceux qui l'approchent. Comme elle [la Salomé de Luini] exprime bien la cruauté douce des femmes fatales'* – Théophile Gautier, *Guide Louvre* (1872); *'Cela me gêne, que la Duse aime ce rôle grossier de femme fatale. Serait-elle plus actrice que femme?'* – Jules Renard, *Journal* (1905); 'Here I saw a *Femme Fatale* who was a fine figure of a woman' – Bernard Shaw, letter of 19 August 1912.

(the) ferocious chastity (of Irishwomen) Phrase allegedly to be found in a letter from Karl Marx to Friedrich Engels (who had two Irish mistresses). Hence, *Ferocious Chastity* (1987), a stage recital on the lot of Irish women by Gemma O'Connor. Shaw uses the phrase 'ferocious chastity' in

his preface to *The Dark Lady of the Sonnets* (1910) – though not about Irish women: 'Isabella in Measure for Measure has religious charm, in spite of the conventional theatrical assumption that female religion means an inhumanly ferocious chastity.'

(the) Few Name given to fighter pilots of the RAF at the height of the German air attacks on London and the south-east of England in 1940 during what came to be known as the Battle of Britain. Although greatly outnumbered, they wreaked havoc on the Luftwaffe, with heavy losses to themselves. Paying tribute to these airmen, Winston Churchill, Prime Minister, said in the House of Commons (20 August 1940): 'Never in the field of human conflict was so much owed by so many to so few.' Here we have an echo of Shakespeare's Henry V speaking to his men before the Battle of Agincourt and talking of: 'We few, we happy few, we band of brothers' – *Henry V*, IV.iii.60 (1599). *Benham* (1948) compares Sir John Moore after the fall of Calpi (where Nelson lost an eye): 'Never was so much work done by so few men.' Another pre-echo may be found in Vol. 2 of Churchill's own *A History of the English-Speaking Peoples* (1956, but largely written pre-war). Describing a 1640 Scottish incursion in the run-up to the English Civil War, he writes: 'All the Scots cannon fired and all the English army fled. A contemporary wrote that "Never so many ran from so few with less ado".' In a speech on the Government of Ireland Bill, in the House of Commons (30 April 1912), Churchill himself had said: 'Never before has so little been asked; and never before have so many people asked for it.' It is interesting to find that Harold Nicolson, noting Churchill's 1940 speech in his diary (20 August), slightly misquotes the passage: '[Winston] says, in referring to the RAF, "never in the history of human conflict has so much been owed by so many to so few".' By 22 September, Churchill's daughter, Mary, was uttering a *bon mot* in his hearing about the collapse of France through weak leadership: 'Never before has so much been betrayed for so many by so few' – recorded by John Colville in *The Fringes of Power*, Vol. 1 (1985).

few and far between 'Our semi-tauto-logical phrase "few and far between" is a corrupt formulation by the nineteenth-century Scottish poet Thomas Campbell of an old folk saying to the effect that the visits of angels to our world are "brief and far between"' – *The Observer* (26 June 1988). To be precise, Campbell's reference in *The Pleasures of Hope*, II.372 (1799), is: '. . . my winged hours of bliss have been, / Like angel-visits, few and far between.' This was an echo of what Robert Blair had written in *The Grave* (1743): 'Its Visits Like those of Angels' short, and far between.' Even so, something like the phrase had existed before this. R. Verney wrote a letter in July 1668 saying 'Hedges are few and far between' – *Memoirs of the Verney Family*, IV.iii.89.

(a) few vouchers short of a pop-up toaster Not very clever. First noticed in May 1987. Indeed, one of those phrases used to describe mental shortcomings or 'a deficiency in the marbles' department' of someone who is 'not all there' and has either 'a screw loose' or 'a bit missing'. Other versions of the 'short of' formula include: 'a couple of bales shy of a full trailer load'; 'a couple of ha'pennies short of a shilling'; 'got off two stops short of Cincinnati'; 'not quite enough coupons for the coffee percolator and matching set of cups'; 'one apple short of a full load'; 'one brick/a few bricks short of a (full) load'; 'one can short of a six-pack'; 'one card short of a full deck'; 'one grape short of a bunch'; 'one pork pie/two sandwiches short of a picnic'; 'tuppence short of a shilling'; 'two ants short of a picnic'; 'two sticks short of a bundle'. More venerable idioms for the same thing would include that a person is: 'dumb as a sack of hammers'; 'eleven pence half-penny'; 'fifty cards in the pack'; 'the lift/elevator doesn't go to the top floor/all the way up'; 'the light's on, but no one's in'; 'ninepence to the shilling'; 'not playing with a full deck'; 'not the full shilling'; 'only sixpence in the shilling'; 'operating on cruise control'; 'rowing with one oar in the water'; and, 'the stairs do not reach all the way to the attic'.

fickle See FLYING.

(a) fiddler on the roof An opportunist, one who takes life easy, one who does what he pleases, a happy-go-lucky person. Popularized by *Fiddler on the Roof*, a musical (1964; film US 1971), with a book by Joseph Stein and lyrics by Sheldon Harnick. Based on Sholom Aleichem's collected stories *Tevye and His Daughters*, this tells the story of Tevye, a Jewish milkman in pre-Revolutionary Russia, who cheerfully survives family and political problems before emigrating to America. The title is used allusively to describe the easy-going nature of the hero. The title song merely asks the question, why is the fiddler playing up on the roof all day and in all weathers? It concludes: 'It might not mean a thing / But then again it might!' 'Fiddling on the roof' is, however, one of the proverbial expressions portrayed (literally) in the painting known as 'The Proverbs' by David Teniers the Younger (d. 1690) which hangs in Belvoir Castle, England. In the key to these Flemish proverbs, 'fiddling on the roof' is com-pared to 'eat, drink and be merry'. In Marc Chagall's painting 'The Dead Man' (1908), he shows – literally – a fiddler on a roof. Chagall often drew on Russian folktales in his work, and the character also turns up in his painting 'The Fiddler' (1912–13). Werner Haftmann in his book on the artist calls the fiddler on the roof, 'representative of the artist; a solitary individual, isolated by the strangeness and mystery of his art . . . a metaphorical figure who can be identi-fied with . . . Chagall himself'. It has been asserted that the writers of the musical were definitely thinking of this second picture when they came to settle on their title. A further attempt at explanation can be found in *Gänzl's Book of the Musical Theatre* (1988) where Tevye is described as: 'the epitome of the Jewish people of Anatevka who each scratch out a living, as the fiddler scratches out his tune, while perilously perched on the edge of existence as represented by the unsafe roof'. An-other correspondent is certain that 'fiddler on the roof' is a Jewish euphemism for 'God'.

fiddler's elbow See UP AND DOWN LIKE A.

(to) fiddle while Rome burns Meaning, 'to do something irrelevant while there are important matters to be dealt with'. For example, in early 1979, the Kuwaiti

Ambassador to the UN told the Security Council, referring to Cambodia, 'Rome is burning, children are being orphaned, women widowed, and we haggle.' The allusion is to the Emperor Nero's behaviour when Rome burned for several days and was two-thirds destroyed in AD 64. It is possible that he knew what he was doing, however, and that the fire was started on his orders, as part of what we would now call an 'urban renewal programme'. Nevertheless, being a shrewd politician, he blamed the Christians and persecuted them. As to the fiddling: Suetonius states that Nero watched the conflagration, then put on his tragedian's costume and sang the *Fall of Ilium* from beginning to end. The fiddle as we know it had not been invented, so if he played anything it was probably the lyre. Tacitus says, rather, that Nero went on his private stage and 'sang' of the (comparable) destruction of Troy. The phrase is in English by 1649, when George Daniel wrote in *Trinarchodia*: 'Let Nero fiddle out Rome's obsequies.' Benjamin Haydon (d. 1846) painted a vast canvas with the title 'Nero playing his Lyre while Rome is burning'.

fiddling and fooling Bill matter of the British comedian/violinist Ted Ray (1906–77), by the late 1940s. But the alliteration had appeared long before. Jonathan Swift in *Polite Conversation* has: 'For my Part, I believe the young Gentleman is his Sweetheart; there's such fooling and fiddling betwixt them.'

(the) Fifth Beatle Someone who by association with The Beatles pop group in the 1960s was considered to have earned honorary membership status. Murray the K, the American disc jockey, applied the term to himself, on the basis of his presumed friendship with The Beatles during the group's visit to the USA in 1964 – much to the annoyance of Brian Epstein, their manager. The tale is recounted in an essay entitled 'The Fifth Beatle' in Tom Wolfe's *The Kandy-Kolored Tangerine-Flake Streamline Baby* (1966). Others would more fittingly have merited the title – Stu Sutcliffe, an early member of the group who was eased out and died before fame struck; Pete Best, who was replaced as drummer by Ringo Starr; Neil Aspinall,

road manager, aide and friend; and George Martin, the group's arranger and record producer. And others have had it applied to them with less reason. In addition, even if he wasn't actually called it at the time, the footballer George Best is looked upon as qualifying for the title in retrospect. In his Sixties heyday, Best flourished in Manchester (which is almost Liverpool, after all), had something approximating to a Beatles haircut and was certainly the first British footballer to be accorded pop star status. On an LBC Radio phone-in (1989), a listener cleverly suggested that the 'fifth Beatle' was the Volkswagen Beetle that figures on the group's *Abbey Road* album sleeve. 'Stitched-together . . . scrambled, incoherent . . . All this is the doing of Richard Lester, who still has "Help!" and "A Hard Day's Night" to his credit but hereby forefeits any claim he ever had to being the Fifth Beatle' – review of the Paul McCartney concert movie *Get Back*, directed by Richard Lester, in *The New York Times* (25 October 1991). There is a secondary meaning, referring to someone who has missed out on the success of something he was once a part of. This was certainly true in the case of Stu Sutcliffe and Pete Best. It was applied, for example, by an *Observer* TV critic to Robert Hewison, the writer, who could be said to have missed out on the success of the *Monty Python* TV comedy team. At one time, Hewison worked closely at developing the Python type of humour with some of the other members of the group, though he never profited from it himself. Similarly, both Michael Bentine and Graham Stark have been referred to as 'the Fourth Goon' of the BBC radio *Goon Show* – and with some justification.

(a) fifth column A group of traitors, infiltrators. In October 1936, during the Spanish Civil War, the Nationalist General Emilio Mola was besieging the Republican-held city of Madrid with four columns. He was asked in a broadcast whether this was sufficient to capture the city, and he replied that he was relying on the support of the *quinta columna* [the fifth column], which was already hiding inside the city and which sympathized with his side. *The Fifth Column* was the title of Ernest

Hemingway's only play (1938). Some doubt has been cast on the ascription to Mola. Lance Haward (1996) noted that in the *Daily Express* of 27 October 1936, Moscow Radio was quoted as having attributed the phrase to General Franco. In the *Daily Mail* of 7 November, the Guardia Civile in Madrid, disaffected with the Republican cause, was being referred to as 'General Franco's now famous "Fifth Column".' In Hugh Thomas, *The Spanish Civil War* (1961), it is reported that the expression has been found in *Mundo Obrero* (3 October 1936) and that Lord St Oswald had used the term several weeks earlier in a report to *The Daily Telegraph*.

fifty million Frenchmen can't be wrong
As a slightly grudging expression, this appears to have originated with American servicemen during the First World War, justifying support for their French allies. The precise number of millions varies. *Partridge/Catch Phrases* suggests that it was the last line of a First World War song 'extolling the supreme virtue of copulation, though in veiled terms'. Partridge may, however, have been referring to a song with the title (by Billy Rose, Willy Raskin and Fred Fisher) that was recorded by Sophie Tucker in 1927. Cole Porter's musical *Fifty Million Frenchmen* opened in New York in 1929. An unrelated US film with this three-word title was released in 1931. Where confusion has crept in is that Texas Guinan, the New York nightclub hostess, was refused entry into France with her girls in 1931 and said: 'It goes to show that fifty million Frenchmen *can* be wrong.' She returned to the USA and renamed her show *Too Hot for Paris*. Perversely, the *ODQ* (1979, 1992) has her saying 'Fifty million Frenchmen *can't* be wrong' in the *New York World-Telegram* on 21 March 1931 and seems to be arguing that she originated the phrase, as she had been using it 'six or seven years earlier'. Sometimes it is quoted as '*forty* million Frenchmen . . .' George Bernard Shaw also held out against the phrase. He insisted: 'Fifty million Frenchmen can't be right.'

fifty ways to leave your —— Format phrase for headlines after the title line of Paul Simon's song '50 Ways To Leave Your Lover' (1976). Hence these headlines: 'Nice girls sleep alone: Nifty ways to leave your lover' – *Today* (4 November 1987); '50 Ways to Leave Your Blubber' – *Men's Health* Magazine (September 1994) (about low-fat dining); 'Fuel for Thought: Fifty thousand ways to leave your lawyer' – *Lloyd's List* (16 April 1998).

(to) fight and fight and fight again
Oratorical expression of determination. Hugh Gaitskell, leader of the British Labour Party, used a similar construction memorably at the party conference on 3 October 1960. When, against the wishes of the Party leadership, the conference looked like taking what Gaitskell called the 'suicidal path' of unilateral disarmament 'which will leave our country defenceless and alone', he was faced with making the most important speech of his life – for his leadership was at issue. 'There are some of us, Mr Chairman,' he said, 'who will fight and fight and fight again to save the Party we love.' Many delegates who were free to do so changed their votes, but the Party executive was still defeated. Nevertheless, Gaitskell reduced his opponents to a paper victory and the phrase is often recalled in tribute to a great personal achievement. Earlier, when Austrian armies had threatened France, the revolutionary leader Danton (1759–94) had exhorted his fellow countrymen to: 'Dare! and dare! and dare again!'

(a) fight between two bald men over a comb A proverbial saying, possibly of Russian origin and meaning 'an unnecessary struggle'. The Argentinian novelist Jorge Luis Borges was quoted as saying of the 1982 Falklands War between Britain and Argentina: 'The Falklands thing was a fight between two bald men over a comb.' The *ODMQ* (1991) and *ODQ* (1992) may have caused readers to think that it was Borges who originated the remark. Not so. Borges was quoted by *Time* Magazine on 14 February 1983 as having characterized the previous year's conflict in these words. *Time* is unable to say for sure where it acquired this quotation, though it has had a good rummage among its yellowing files. It may have picked it up from the Spanish paper *La Nación* (28 June 1982), which was apparently quoting from an interview with Borges that had appeared in *Le*

Monde the previous day. But the basic expression about bald men fighting over combs had very definitely been around before 1983. Robert Nye wrote in *The Times* (18 June 1981): 'I think it was Christopher Logue who once characterized the drabness of the English Movement poets of the 1950s as being like the antics of two bald men fighting for possession of a comb.' The saying occurs even earlier in *Mencken* (1942) as 'Two baldheaded men are fighting over a comb' (listed as a 'Russian saying') and in Champion's *Racial Proverbs* (1938).

fighting   See COME OUT.

(the) fight on flab   Term for physical jerks used by the Irish-born disc jockey Terry Wogan (b. 1938) on BBC Radio 2 in the early 1970s. He himself managed to lose two of the sixteen stone he weighed on first arriving in Britain, though whether this achievement was permanent is doubtful.

figure   See FINE.

—— **file**   PHRASES. Format for book, film and television programme titles, to give a spurious sense of fact-gathering and investigativeness. Possibly inspired by the title of Len Deighton's espionage novel *The Ipcress File* (1962; film UK 1965), the cliché was well established by the 1970s. In 1976, TV reporters Anthony Summers and Tom Mangold published *The File on the Tsar*. In 1978, two BBC reporters, Barrie Penrose and Roger Courtior, published a book about plots involving leading British politicians and gave it the curious title *The Pencourt File*.

(to) fill one's boots   To take as much as one likes of a good thing, to take plenty, to take advantage of availability. Known by the 1940s and possibly of Irish origin. The notion, presumably, is that you should fill your boots to the top with beer or food now that you have the opportunity. Perhaps the image is of large sea boots: when packing up to go to sea, a mariner would pack his boots in a kit bag and literally fill them with the little treats that make life at sea bearable: tobacco, chocolate, pictures of loved ones. The more of these treats you could pack in, the better. 'Graham Norton is like a man making up for lost time. An actor until his late twen-

ties, he spent most of his time "resting" . . . Who can really blame him if he's now filling his boots, and hyperactively running around a studio in spangly jackets for five nights of the week' – *The Independent* (14 March 2003).

film   See GETS RID OF.

filthy lucre   Money. From 1 Timothy 3:2–3: 'A bishop then must be blameless, the husband of one wife . . . Not given to wine, no striker, not greedy of filthy lucre.' *The New English Bible* translates 'no striker' as 'not a brawler'. Filthy lucre is 'money', though the original Greek suggests more 'dishonourable gain'. The phrase is also used by Paul, in the same context, in Titus 1:7 and 1:11, and in 1 Peter 5:2. The word 'lucre' also occurs in the Old Testament (1 Samuel 8:3).

final analysis   See IN THE.

finally   See AND FINALLY.

(the) final solution [*Endlösung*]   Euphemistic name given to Adolf Hitler's plan to exterminate the Jews of Europe and used by Nazi officials from the summer of 1941 onwards to disguise the enormity of what they intended. A directive (drafted by Adolf Eichmann) was sent by Hermann Goering to Reinhard Heydrich on 31 July 1941: 'Submit to me as soon as possible a draft showing . . . measures already taken for the execution of the intended final solution of the Jewish question.' Gerald Reitlinger in *The Final Solution* (1953) says that the choice of phrase was probably, though not certainly, Hitler's own. Before then it had been used in a non-specific way to cover other possibilities – like emigration, for example. It is estimated that the 'final solution' led to the deaths of up to six million Jews.

fin de siècle   Meaning, 'end of century'. A phrase employed almost exclusively about the decadent 1890s and hardly used at all about the 1990s. *OED2*'s earliest citation is from the *Daily News* (29 December 1890) – 'The finance of the year has been special – fin de siècle' – unrevealing as to why the French form was used. This is another of those French phrases commonly to be found in English and little used by the French themselves.

fine See HERE'S ANOTHER.

(a) fine figure of a woman Complimentary phrase. The earliest citation found so far is from Samuel Richardson, *Sir Charles Grandison,* Pt 4, Chap. 21 (1754): 'She is a very fine figure of a woman.' 'Here I saw a *Femme Fatale* who was a fine figure of a woman' – Bernard Shaw, letter of 19 August 1912.

fine, fine! Catchphrase from the BBC radio *Goon Show* (1951–60). Exclamation mostly by Spike Milligan as the gormless character Eccles.

fine sets these Ferguson's A curiously memorable slogan for Ferguson radio sets and current in the UK in the 1950s. The advertisements carried what looked like a wood-cut of a pipe-smoking man listening to one of the sets.

(the) Finest Nickname for New York City police, from about 1930 onwards. Later the use became ironic, as in: 'New York's finest – the best that money can buy.'

(their) finest hour Phrase of Winston Churchill's delivered in his notable speech to the House of Commons (18 June 1940): 'Let us therefore brace ourselves to our duties, and so bear ourselves that, if the British Empire and its Commonwealth last for a thousand years, men will say, "This was their finest hour".' *The Finest Hours* was the title of a documentary film (UK 1964) about Churchill's life.

(to go through something with a) fine-tooth comb 'To examine very closely' (known by 1891). Note, it is 'a fine-tooth comb' rather than 'fine tooth-comb' – the comb has fine teeth (enabling the smallest pieces of dirt to be removed) and isn't necessarily excellent.

fine weather See LOVELY WEATHER.

fine words butter no parsnips This standard proverb, known since the 1630s at least, tends to get rattled off with little regard for its meaning or point, which is that 'fine words won't achieve anything on their own.' Or, as the other saying has it, 'Deeds not words.' *Brewer* (1923) translates it well: 'Saying "Be thou fed," will not feed a hungry man.' Quite why parsnips are singled out is a puzzle, except that

they are traditionally buttered before serving. John Taylor, *Epigrammes* (1651), however, has this verse, which shows that parsnips were not the only food mentioned in this regard: 'Words are but wind that do from men proceed, / None but Chamelions on bare Air can feed: / Great men large hopeful promises may utter; / But words did never Fish or Parsnips butter.' Sometimes the word 'fine' is replaced by 'fair' or 'soft'.

finger See BOY WHO PUT HIS; FLYING FICKLE.

(the) finger of suspicion points at you! Humorous way of making an accusation. The notion of a 'finger of suspicion' in more serious vein probably dates back to crime writing in the 19th century. The British singer Dickie Valentine recorded a song, 'Finger of Suspicion', in 1954, referring to matters amatory.

(the) finishing touch The stroke or addition that brings something to a proper conclusion. 'We tire of all the painter's art when it wants these finishing touches' – Horace Walpole, *Anecdotes of Painting,* 'On Gardening' (1771); 'With the finishing touch . . . he completes his picture of that intense depravity' – John Keble, *Sermons,* Chap. 5 (1831/1848). There was a Laurel and Hardy silent film entitled *The Finishing Touch* (US 1928), in which they destroy the house they are building, and also an erotic crime thriller with the title (US 1992).

fire See BAPTISM OF.

fire and ice This word combination has appealed to many over the ages. It is the title of a short poem (1923) by Robert Frost: 'Some say the world will end in fire, / Some say in ice.' Here fire = desire/ice = hate, either of which is strong enough to kill. A. E. Housman in *A Shropshire Lad* (1896) has: 'And fire and ice within me fight / Beneath the suffocating night.' Dante's *Inferno* has: 'Into the eternal darkness, into fire and into ice.' Psalm 148:7 in the Book of Common Prayer has 'fire and hail'. Latterly, the phrase has been used to refer to the death of the planet Earth by atomic warfare or a new ice age. Revlon produced a range of cosmetics called 'Fire and ice' in 1952: 'For you who love to flirt with fire . . . who dare to skate on thin ice.' The ice skaters Jayne Torville and Christopher Dean had a routine with the title in the late 1980s.

fire and water　In origin, an ancient conjunction. From Ovid, *Fasti*, Bk 4, lines 787–790: *'An, quia cunctarum contraria semina rerum sunt duo discordes, ignis et unda, dei, iunxerunt elementa patres, abtumque putarunt ignibus et sparsa tangere corpus aqua* [Are we to suppose that because all things are composed of fire and water – those two discordant deities – therefore our father did conjoin these elements and thought meet to touch the body with fire and sprinkled water]?' Under Roman Law there was the 'interdiction of fire and water' – meaning that the person sentenced could not be supplied with fire and water or the necessaries of life. From Psalms 66:12: 'We went through fire and through water: but thou broughtest us into a wealthy place.' Hence, the expression 'to go through fire and water', meaning 'to encounter great dangers'. Known by 1534 (in a translation of Xenophon). The fire and water colophon of the publishers HarperCollins followed the merger of the publishers Harper&Row (which formerly had a torch symbol) and William Collins (which had a fountain).

first among equals　As *primus inter pares*, this is an anonymous Latin saying. It has been used about the position of politicians in a number of countries and also of the Pope, and has been defined as meaning 'the one of a group who leads or takes special responsibility but who neither feels himself, nor is held by others to be, their superior'. The Round Table in Arthurian legend was meant to show not only that there was no precedence among the knights who sat at it but also that King Arthur was no more than first among equals. Used specifically regarding the British Prime Minister within the Cabinet, the phrase cannot pre-date Sir Robert Walpole (in power 1721–42) who is traditionally the first to have held that position. Lord Morley may have been the first to use the phrase in this context in his life of Walpole (1889) where he says: 'Although in Cabinet all its members stand on an equal footing, speak with equal voice, and, on the rare occasions when a

division is taken, are counted on the fraternal principle of one vote, yet the head of the Cabinet is *primus inter pares*, and occupies a position which, so long as it lasts, is one of exceptional and peculiar authority.' In 1988, Julian Critchley MP was quoted as having referred to Margaret Thatcher as *'prima donna inter pares'*. *First Among Equals* was the title of a novel (1984) by Jeffrey Archer about the pursuit of the British Prime Ministership.

first catch your hare　Proverb indicating that you can't begin to do something until you have acquired a certain necessary element (that may be difficult to acquire). *CODP* finds the equivalent thought in *circa* 1300, translated from the Latin: 'It is commonly said that one must first catch the deer, and afterwards, when he has been caught, skin him.' For a long time, however, the saying was taken to be a piece of practical, blunt good sense to be found in Mrs Beeton's *Book of Household Management* (1851), but it does not appear there. However, in Mrs Hannah Glasse's earlier *The Art of Cookery made plain and easy* (1747), there is the similar: 'Take your hare when it is cased [skinned].' It was known in the familiar form by 1855 when it appeared in Thackeray's *The Rose and the Ring*. From an edition of the *York Herald and County Advertiser* (1808): 'Our new books of cookery are becoming a little more particular than formerly in their directions; one of them, in ordering a species of pudding, begins thus – "Take your maid, and send her for a peck of flour" etc. This is something like Mrs Glasse's receipt for dressing a carp, "First catch your fish".' Similar proverbs include: 'Catch your bear before you sell its skin', 'Never spend your money before you have it' and 'Don't count your chickens before they are hatched'.

(the) firstest with the mostest　To describe anything as 'the mostest' might seem an exclusively US activity. However, *OED2* finds English dialect use in the 1880s and *Partridge/Slang* recognizes it as a jocular superlative without restricting it to the USA. As such, it is a consciously ungrammatical way of expressing extreme degree. Whether this was consciously the case with the Confederate General, Nathan

B. Forrest (d. 1877), is very much in doubt. He could hardly read or write, but he managed to say that the way to win battles was to be 'firstest with the mostest', or that you needed to 'git thar fustest with the mostest'. *Bartlett* gives this last as the usual rendering of the more formally reported words: 'Get there first with the most men.' In Irving Berlin's musical *Call Me Madam* (1950) there is a song with the title 'The Hostess with the Mostes' on the Ball'. One assumes that Berlin's use, like any evocation of 'the mostest' nowadays, refers back to Forrest's remark.

(the) first hundred thousand *The First Hundred Thousand* was the title of a war novel (1915) by Ian Hay, subtitled 'Adventures of a typical regiment in Kitchener's army'. The book begins with a poem (Hay's own, presumably): 'We're off a hundred thousand strong. / And some of us will not come back.' A. J. P. Taylor, in his *English History 1914–45*, describing a period of 'patriotic frenzy' in the Great War, says that the 'spirit of 1915 was best expressed by Ian Hay, a writer of light fiction, in *The First Hundred Thousand* – a book which treated soldiering as a joke, reviving "the best days of our lives" at some imaginary public school'.

first in the field See PROMINENT.

first past the post Electoral arrangements (as in Britain) where the candidate or party with the largest number of votes wins, as compared to the system known as proportional representation. W. P. Brown commented (1993): 'Note how the felicitous phrase attaches the warm glow of Great British Sportsmanship (Derby Day, the Boat Race, *Chariots of Fire*, etc.) to a voting system whose defining characteristic is the absence of anything corresponding to a winning post. It is merely a case of "first past the second" after all.' There was no need for this comforting metaphor until the Westminster system was under attack by the advocates of electoral reform. The earliest citations in the *OED2* date from 1952/65 and come from Australia, one of them referring back to Queensland in 1892.

first up ... best dressed! *Partridge/Catch Phrases* confidently asserts that this is an Australian phrase for circumstances 'where members of a family use each other's [or one another's] clothes'.

(the) First World War Known at first as the 'European War', it became known quite rapidly as **the Great War**. By 10 September 1918, Lieutenant-Colonel C. à Court Repington was referring to it in his diary as the 'First World War', thus: 'I saw Major Johnstone, the Harvard Professor who is here to lay the bases of an American History. We discussed the right name of the war. I said that we called it now *The War*, but that this could not last. The Napoleonic War was *The Great War*. To call it *The German War* was too much flattery for the Boche. I suggested *The World War* as a shade better title, and finally we mutually agreed to call it *The First World War* in order to prevent the millennium folk from forgetting that the history of the world was the history of war.' Repington's book entitled *The First World War 1914–18* was published in 1920. Presumably this helped popularize the name for the war, while ominously suggesting that it was the first of a series.

(the) first —— years are the hardest Format phrase usually employed in connection with marriage or jobs – suggesting, in an ironical way, that the initial stages of anything are the most difficult. It probably derives from the Army saying, 'Cheer up – the first seven years are the worst!' from about the time of the First World War, referring to the term of a regular soldier's service. *Partridge/Catch Phrases* also finds 'the first hundred years are the hardest/worst' from about the same period.

fish See HERE'S A FINE.

(the) fishing fleet Name given to girls who went out to India in search of husbands during the days of the British Raj. If they were unsuccessful they were known as 'Returned Empties'.

fishing in troubled (or muddy) waters Meaning, 'prepared to try to extract advantage from difficult circumstances' or, simply, 'to concern oneself with unpleasant or confused matters' (often used by journalists in a literal sense when writing about fisheries disputes, etc). Known by

1625. 'Fishing in troubled waters' was cited as a 'dying metaphor' by George Orwell in 'Politics and the English Language' (*Horizon*, April 1946). Also the phrase **troubled waters** on its own. 'He was fishing in the muddy waters of race . . . "Racism," he began, "destroys those it touches"' – *The Listener* (25 September 1975); 'The Arts: More troubled waters? – Interview / Charles Laurence talks to singer Paul Simon about his first visit to South Africa since the stormy days of Graceland' – *The Daily Telegraph* (2 January 1992); 'Troubled Waters – Victoria Griffith examines growing concerns about the ecological impact of fish farming' – by-line, *Financial Times* (27 July 1994); '"What all this shows is that Iran is prepared to fish in troubled waters where it can," a senior United States administration official said' – *The Guardian* (28 December 1994); 'Canadian Fisheries Minister Brian Tobin is unrepentant and unyielding. He made it quite clear that the answer to any further attempts to fish in these troubled Newfoundland waters was more gunboats' – *Evening Standard* (London) (10 March 1995);

fit See ALL THE NEWS THAT'S; LOOKING BRONZED AND.

(to be as) fit as a fiddle A fiddler, when playing quickly, has to be so dextrous with his fingers and bow that he is assumed to be especially lively and awake. Could, then, the phrase that we have be a contraction of 'fit as a fiddler'? It was current by 1616.

fit for a king The very best of anything but most applied to a meal or dish. 'For a grant of ale is a dish for a king' – Shakespeare, *The Winter's Tale*, IV.iii.8 (1611); 'Thou art a cure fit for a king' – Shakespeare, *King Henry VIII*, II.ii.75 (1612); '"[Referring to her figure] Fit for a king," she said proudly, and got on with her dressing' – Howard Spring, *Shabby Tiger*, Chap. 17 (1934).

(it) fits where it touches Referring to loose clothing. *Partridge/Catch Phrases* has 'they fit where they touch' as applied originally to *loose-fitting* trousers (with a 1932 citation) but, since the 1960s, to suggestively *tight* clothes, especially trousers.

(to) fit to a T 'To fit perfectly'. A T-square is used by draughtsmen to draw parallel lines and angles, though it seems 'to a T' was in use by 1693 and before the T-square got its name. Perhaps the original expression was 'fit to a tittle' – a tittle being the dot over the letter *i* – so the phrase meant 'to a dot, fine point'. There are other theories, none of them conclusive.

5–4–3–2–1 It is said that the backwards countdown to a rocket launch was originated by the German film director Fritz Lang (1890–1976). He thought it would make things more suspenseful if the count was reversed – 5–4–3–2–1 – so, in his 1928 film *By Rocket to the Moon* (sometimes known as *Frau im Mond* or 'The Woman in the Moon', from the German title), he established the routine for future real-life space shots. The 1931 American novel with the title *By Rocket to the Moon* (by Otto Willi Gail) does not appear to include the phrase.

(the) five senses Traditionally, sight, hearing, taste, smell and touch. Known as such by 1669. Hence, **the sixth sense**: a supposed faculty by which a human being or animal has perceptions without recourse to the familiar five. Discussed in the 17th century. *The Six Sense* was the title of a film (US 1999).

fix See IF IT AIN'T BROKE.

(the) flags are out Meaning, 'the celebrations have already begun', especially in downmarket journalism or in parody thereof. Date of origin unknown. 'The flags are out for the link-up we've waited so long to see; the inauguration of the Channel Tunnel is a real splash of colour for a grey "fin de siècle"' – *The Guardian* (6 May 1994); 'The flags are out for tomorrow's start of the 1994 French Open, and with them comes the Roland Garros magic. It is a quality less easy to grasp than the garden-party aura of Wimbledon, though no less real. It is perhaps just a component of that illogical but romantic phenomenon known as "Paris in the spring"' – *Independent on Sunday* (22 May 1994). Compare, from the *Sunday Express* (25 November 1984): 'If [boxer] Sibson, weaving and bobbing, can find his former big-punch savagery – and Kaylor's chin – the requiems will be in full swing down West Ham way on Tuesday night.'

Flaming Nora See RUDDY NORA.

(a) flanelled fool Phrase from the poem 'The Islanders' (1902) by Rudyard Kipling: 'Flannelled fools at the wicket or the muddied oafs at the goals' – where the 'fools' are, of course, cricketers. *Flannelled Fool* was used as the title of a book (1967), 'a slice of life in the 30s', by the critic, T. C. Worsley.

(a) flash in the pan A short-lived success, failure after a showy attempt. From the irregular firing of a flintlock musket. A hammer was supposed to strike a flint and produce sparks that exploded the charge, but this did not always occur. The powder in the 'pan', a small depression, sometimes flashed but failed to ignite the charge. Figurative sense known by 1741.

(the) flavour of the month Originally a generic advertising phrase aimed at persuading people to try new varieties of ice cream and not just stick to their customary choice (in the USA, as 'flavor', by 1946). Latterly, it has become an idiom for any fad, craze or person that is quickly discarded after a period of being in the news or in demand. From the BBC radio *Goon Show* (3 March 1958): 'Banana – the flavour of the month. Owwwwwwwwww, more!' From the *Longman Register of New Words* (1989): 'The metaphorical possibilities of the word *ambush* are catching on in several areas of activity in the USA, making it the lexical flavour-of-the-month in American English.'

(the) Fleet's lit up Phrase from the most famous British broadcasting boob of all. On the night of 20 May 1937, Lieutenant-Commander Tommy Woodrooffe (1899–1978), a leading BBC radio commentator of the day, was due to give a fifteen-minute description of the 'illumination' of the Fleet after the Coronation Naval Review at Spithead. What he said, in a commentary that was faded out after less than four minutes, began: 'At the present moment, the whole Fleet's lit up. When I say "lit up", I mean lit up by fairy lamps. We've forgotten the whole Royal Review. We've forgotten the Royal Review. The

whole thing is lit up by fairy lamps. It's fantastic. It isn't the Fleet at all. It's just . . . fairy land. The whole fleet is in fairy land . . .' Naturally, many listeners concluded that Woodrooffe himself had been 'lit up' as the result of enjoying too much hospitality from his former shipmates on board HMS *Nelson* before the broadcast. But he denied this. 'I had a kind of nervous blackout. I had been working too hard and my mind just went blank.' He told the *News Chronicle*: 'I was so overcome by the occasion that I literally burst into tears . . . I found I could say no more.' The BBC took a kindly view and the incident did not put paid to Woodrooffe's broadcasting career. But the phrase became so famous that it was used as the title of a 'musical frolic' at the London Hippodrome in 1938 and Bud Flanagan recorded a song written by Vivian Ellis called 'The Fleet's Lit Up'. The Second World War song 'I'm Going to Get Lit Up When the Lights Go Up in London' by Hubert Gregg (1943) probably owes something to the Woodrooffe affair, though use of 'lit up' to mean 'tipsy' dates back to 1914, at least.

flesh and blood Denoting that which is real as opposed to that which is in the mind, or humanity as opposed to disembodied spirit. The phrase is in St Paul's Epistle to the Ephesians 6:12: 'For we wrestle not against flesh and blood, but against principalities, against powers, against the rulers of the darkness of this world, against spiritual wickedness in high places' – but had been written down by 1340. Has become part of the titles of three films: *Flesh and Blood* (UK 1951), *The Flesh and Blood Show* (UK 1972) and *Flesh & Blood* (US 1985). The phrase can also be used to refer to one's blood relatives – 'Fancy something like that happening to one's own flesh and blood . . .'

(the) fleshpots of Egypt Meaning 'any place of comparative luxury', it was originally said by the Israelites (Exodus 16:3): 'Would to God we had died by the hand of the Lord in the land of Egypt, when we sat by the flesh pots, and when we did eat bread to the full.' Clementine Churchill wrote to Winston on 20 December 1910: 'I do so wish I was at Warter with you enjoying the Flesh Pots of Egypt! It sounds a delightful party . . .' – quoted in Mary Soames, *Clementine Churchill* (1979).

flick your Bic Originally a slogan for Bic cigarette lighters, this was coined by US copywriter Charlie Moss in 1975 and occurred in an ad that showed how smart, sophisticated people didn't use lighters – they simply 'flicked their Bics'. The phrase caught on and was picked up by many comedians. During an energy crisis, Bob Hope said: 'Things are getting so bad that the Statue of Liberty doesn't light up any more. She just stands there and flicks her Bic.'

(a) flight from fear (sometimes **of/to fear)** Cliché of journalism, demonstrating the lure of alliteration yet again. Date of origin unknown. 'To Britain on flight from fear. A flight from fear ended at Heathrow Airport yesterday for passengers on the first plane to arrive from Poland since martial law was proclaimed at the weekend' – headline and text in the *Daily Mail* (18 December 1981); 'Flight of fear as families pray for rain' – headline in *The Sunday Telegraph* (9 January 1994); 'Flight To Fear: Pato Tells Of His Israeli Asylum Hell' – headline in the *Daily Mirror* (27 October 1994).

(a) flight of fancy In the basic sense of 'something extravagantly imagined' (in which it has been known since 1687), probably only a borderline cliché. However, when applied to air travel it becomes a part of the 'travel scribes' armoury' compiled from a competition in *The Guardian* (10 April 1993). 'Platt, a most practical man, does not often indulge in flights of fancy. A millionaire already, he needs only to be a winner to fulfil every ambition he has set for himself' – *Daily Mirror* (27 March 1995).

flippin' kids! Catchphrase from the BBC radio show *Educating Archie* (1950–60). Bizarre though the idea of ventriloquism on radio may be, this show, starring Peter Brough and his wooden dummy, Archie Andrews, was a noted breeding ground for young entertainers, and catchphrases abounded. The 'catchphrase of the year' in 1951, according to Brough, was spoken by Tony Hancock as one of the dummy's long line of 'tutors'. Indeed, 'The Lad 'Imself'

was billed as 'Tony (Flippin' Kids) Hancock' before moving on to star in his own shows, which more or less eschewed the use of catchphrases. The word 'flipping' has been the commonest euphemism for 'fucking' when used as an intensifier since about 1920.

flood See DON'T SPIT.

floor See FACE ON.

***Floreat Etona* [may Eton flourish]** Motto of Eton College (founded 1440) in Berkshire. It is spoken by the villain Captain Hook (presumably an Old Etonian) just before he is eaten by a crocodile in J. M. Barrie's play *Peter Pan* (1904). In Barrie's novel *Peter Pan and Wendy* (1911), he merely cries, 'Bad form.' It was earlier used as the title of a painting (1882) by Elizabeth, Lady Butler, depicting a British attack on the Boers in South Africa at Laing's Neck in 1881, after this eyewitness account: 'Poor Elwes fell among the 58th. He shouted to another Eton boy (adjutant of the 58th, whose horse had been shot) "Come along, Monck! Floreat Etona! we must be in the front rank!" and he was shot immediately.'

Flower Power A hippy slogan – formed, no doubt, in emulation of BLACK POWER, to describe the beliefs of the so-called Flower Children. Flowers were used as a love and peace symbol when the phrase came into use *circa* 1967.

(the) flowers of the forest Phrase from a poem (1765 – though believed to have been written twenty years before) by Alison Cockburn, the Scottish poet and songwriter (1713–94): 'For the flowers of the forest are a'wade away'. The poem was apparently inspired by a commercial disaster in which seven local lairds were bankrupted in one year. 'Wade/wede' means 'weeded', but sometimes the phrase is rendered as 'withered away'. The line also appears in 'The Flowers of the Forest' (*circa* 1755) by the Scottish poet and songwriter Jean Elliot (1727–1805). *The Dictionary of Scottish Quotations* (1996) notes: 'Based on a traditional version of which only a fragment survives, this song was written as a lament for the Battle of Flodden (9 September 1513) in which James IV and thousands of his men were slain by the English.' What the connection is between the Cockburn and Elliot versions (so close in time) is not clear. According to the *Oxford Dictionary of Music* (1985), the Cockburn was originally sung to a different tune but is now 'generally sung to an old tune' (i.e. the traditional one used by Elliot for her version), 'the flowers are young men, the Forest a district of Selkirk and Peebles: the poem commemorates their death in battle. The tune, played by pipers, is a regular and moving feature of the Remembrance Day ceremony at the Cenotaph in Whitehall, London.'

fly See AND PIGS MIGHT.

(to) fly by the seat of one's pants To perform any function relying on instinct and experience without scientific support or knowledge. Originally applied to flying (in the USA by 1942) and now used mostly figuratively.

flying See DARING YOUNG MAN ON.

(the) Flying Fickle Finger of Fate Award Catchphrase from NBC TV's *Rowan and Martin's Laugh-In* (1967–73). This was the name of the prize in a mock talent contest segment of the show ('who knows when the Fickle Finger of Fate may beckon *you* to stardom?') According to *Partridge/Slang*, 'fucked by the Fickle Finger of Fate' was a Canadian armed forces' expression in the 1930s.

(a) fly in the ointment Meaning, 'the small thing that spoils everything; an intractable problem (however small).' Curiously, this is a biblical phrase, from Ecclesiastes 10:1: 'Dead flies cause the ointment of the apothecary to send forth a stinking savour; so doth a little folly him that is in reputation for wisdom and honour.'

fly on the wall Adjectival phrase used to describe a type of documentary in which the participants are observed going about their normal lives or work supposedly without too much awareness that a camera crew is following them. Probably in use by 1974 when BBC TV produced *The Family* about a working-class family in Reading (in imitation of the previous year's PBS show *An American Family*). 'The "fly-on-

the-wall" technique, so successful elsewhere, would not overcome this problem' – *The Listener* (10 February 1983).

fog See CONTINENT ISOLATED.

(the) fog of war The confusion of events amid the smoke of battle. This phrase was examined by William Safire in his *New York Times* Magazine 'On Language' column (13 April 2003) when it arose regarding the US invasion of Iraq: 'A reporter began a question to Gen. Tommy Franks with "Mindful of the term 'fog of war . . . ' The general dealt with a "friendly fire" incident and added, "Probably the description you used in your question is as good as any: 'the fog of war.'"' Safire went on to suggest that the phrase was based on an image in *Vom Kriege* (1832) by Karl von Clausewitz: 'All action must be planned in a mere twilight, which – like the effect of a fog or moonshine – gives to things exaggerated dimension and an unnatural appearance.' Von Clausewitz is perhaps too readily cited by all and sundry at times like these, and there are problems in finding a definitive text of what he actually wrote. Neither the phrase *Nebel des Krieg(e)s* (fog of war) nor anything like it actually appears in his work. So quite how the phrase caught on is not yet apparent. In 1938, the British military historian Basil Liddell Hart wrote a book entitled *Through the Fog of War* – a potted history of the First World War to see what lessons could be learned from it 'under the shadow of another "Great War"' – but he does not explain the relevance or provenance of the title. 'The duty of writing from time to time these appreciations, and making forecasts on necessarily imperfect information, is a difficult task. It demands sound knowledge of military service, a trained judgment, assiduous study, and a natural gift for piercing the fog of war' – 'The Literature of the Russo-Japanese War' by a 'British Officer' in *The American Historical Review* (July 1911). So, wherever it came from, it seems to have been an established phrase before the First World War. Perhaps one should conclude that the phrase arose through 19th-century 'war studies' under the influence of Von Clausewitz.

fold See DO NOT.

(to) fold one's tents like the Arabs
Meaning 'to bring to a conclusion
unostentatiously', this expression comes
from Longfellow's 'The Day is Done': 'And
the night shall be filled with music / And
the cares that infest the day / Shall fold
their tents, like the Arabs, / And as silently
steal away.' Alas, at the conclusion of his
case for the defence in the Jeremy Thorpe
trial (1979), George Carman QC said to the
jury: 'I end by saying in the words *of the
Bible* [*sic*]: "Let this prosecution fold up its
tent and quietly creep away."'

follow that! Phrase used inevitably by
the speaker or entertainer who comes after
another who has succeeded exceptionally
in pleasing an audience. Date of origin
unknown. Compare HARD ACT TO FOLLOW.
'[On the man replacing Laurence Olivier at
the National Theatre] Our welcome to
Peter Hall is heartfelt, but we would be
more than human if it were not tinged
with a distinct overtone of "Follow *that*"' –
Kenneth Tynan, *The Diaries of Kenneth
Tynan* (2001) – entry for 16 March 1973.

follow that cab (or **taxi** or **van)!** Said to
a driver by the hero/policeman in pursuit
of a villain. A cliché of the cinema. Few
people can ever have said it in real life. (It
is as much of a cliché as the ability film
actors have, on getting *out* of taxis, to
tender exactly the right amount to the
driver.) 'Follow that cab!' was established
early in cinema history, as in *Top Hat* (US
1935) and *Mr Deeds Goes to Town* (US
1936); James Stewart says it jokily in *The
Philadelphia Story* (US 1940); Fred Astaire
says it in *Let's Dance* (US 1950) in order to
chase Betty Hutton. In *Sabotage* (UK
1936), there is a 'Follow that taxi!' In *Song
of the Thin Man* (US 1947), a taxi driver
says to William Powell and Myrna Loy,
'Follow that cab?' 'Hmmm,' says she. 'A
movie fan.' In *The Moon Is Blue* (US 1953),
William Holden is pursuing a girl who gets
into an elevator. He tells the elevator
operator, 'Follow that car!' In *Arabesque*
(US 1966), Gregory Peck says, 'Follow that
car!' and the cab driver replies: 'All my life
I've waited for somebody to say that!' In *A
Fine Pair* (Italy 1969), Claudia Cardinale
says, 'Follow that car!' and the cabby replies:
'I gave up my career as a stockbroker just
to hear someone say, "Follow that car".'

follow that with your sea lions! A
challenge thrown down by an entertainer
after having pulled off a particularly
gallery-pleasing act in the circus or the
music hall. Or an extension of FOLLOW *THAT!*
In my book *The Gift of the Gab: a Guide to
Sparkling Chat* (1985), it is said of showbiz
folk: 'When recalling an uproarious or
disastrous incident, they should cap it by
saying: "Follow that with the sea lions!"'
The Oldie (January 2002) reported on the
Westminster Abbey memorial service for
the comedian Sir Harry Secombe: 'Jimmy
Tarbuck, ascending the high pulpit after
the beautiful William Mathias setting of
"Let the people praise thee, O God",
opened, as Sir Harry might have done,
with "Follow that with the sea lions".'

(a) fond farewell A cliché by the 1950s,
particularly in connection with funerals
and memorial services. Date of origin
unknown. 'It might have been a day of
double farewells; goodbye to Brian Moore,
and perhaps goodbye to the First Division.
Fond farewell and laughing-stock demo-
tion. Highly charged stuff' – *The Observer*
(30 April 1995); 'Four legs and a fond
farewell – Liz Hurley' – headline in *Today*
(1 May 1995); 'And his [Dudley Moore's]
jokey performance hit the right note with
more than 500 [Peter] Cook admirers who
gathered for the fond farewell in a London
church' – *Daily Mirror* (2 May 1995).

food for thought Something that requires
reflection and consideration. Known by
1825.

food shot from guns Slogan for Quaker
Puffed Wheat and Puffed Rice, current
since the early 1900s. Claude C. Hopkins
(1867–1932), one of the great American
advertising gurus, wrote: 'I watched the
process where the grains were shot from
guns. And I coined the phrase. The idea
aroused ridicule. One of the greatest food
advertisers in the country wrote an article
about it. He said that of all the follies
evolved in food advertising this certainly
was the worst – the idea of appealing on
"Food shot from guns" was the theory of
an imbecile. But the theory proved attractive. It was such a curiosity arouser that it
proved itself the most successful campaign
ever conducted in cereals.'

fool See AS ANY FULE.

fools rush in Bill matter for the British comedians Morecambe and Wise in the early 1950s. A quotation from Alexander Pope, *An Essay on Criticism* (1711): 'For fools rush in where angels fear to tread.'

foot See BEST FOOT.

(to put one's) foot in one's mouth To say something embarrassing. 'Every time he opens his mouth at the Town Hall, he puts his foot in it, so they call him "the foot and mouth disease". Ha. Ha.' – J. B. Priestley, *When We Are Married* (1938); '"Dentopedology" is the science of opening your mouth and putting your foot in it. I've been practising it for years' – Prince Philip, quoted in Herbert V. Prochnow, Snr & Jnr, *A Treasury of Humorous Quotations* (1969). With 'dontopedology', this view is said to have been expressed by Prince Philip in a speech to the (British) General Dental Council and quoted in *Time* Magazine (21 November 1960). Presumably, the expression is a development of the basic **to put one's foot in it**, known by 1798 – of which, according to *Brewer* (1894), a version used to be 'the bishop hath put his foot in it' (when some mess has occurred, not necessarily a verbal one).

for all mankind Portentous phrase for 'everybody' and used, for example, on the plaque left on the moon by the US crew of the Apollo 11 space mission: 'HERE MEN FROM THE PLANET EARTH / FIRST SET FOOT UPON THE MOON / JULY 1969 AD / WE CAME IN PEACE FOR ALL MANKIND.' Known by 1792. 'The two clever ones embracing each other and dissolving into tears of tenderness for all mankind . . .' – Charles Dickens, *Little Dorrit*, Chap. 29 (1857); 'The settlement agreed by Servo Computers with two former women employees was not merely a victory for the sensibilities of women; it was a victory for all mankind' – *The Daily Telegraph* (15 February 1996).

force See DON'T FORCE IT.

(the) forces of darkness Consciously purple phrase to describe opponents, whether evil or not. Date of origin unknown. A parallel phrase to **forces of evil**, which was known by 1862. 'It can scarcely have escaped the notice of thinking men, I think, that the forces of darkness opposed to those of us who like a quiet smoke are gathering momentum daily' – P. G. Wodehouse, *Over Seventy,* Chap. 12 (1957). A cliché by the time the phrase was mocked by Tom Stoppard in his play *Night and Day* (1978): 'Commandeered it as the NERVE CENTRE of Mageeba's victorious drive against the forces of darkness, otherwise known as the Adoma Liberation Front.' 'I've stood by and watched as the Gaelic language is regularly savaged by a prominent Harris-based columnist, by the name of John Macleod. I've listened as the forces of darkness snigger in pubs that more Scots speak Urdu than Gaelic' – *The Scotsman* (20 January 1995); 'Mr Blair's challenge is to push his party in a radical but non-socialist direction when its heart remains wedded to the old tunes, and to keep these forces of darkness at bay when in power' – *The Sunday Times* (19 March 1995).

forearmed See FOREWARNED IS.

forever England Phrase from Rupert Brooke's 1914 poem 'The Soldier': 'If I should die, think only this of me: / That there's some corner of a foreign field / That is for ever England.' *Forever England* was the UK title given to the reissue of the film version of C. S. Forester's novel *Brown on Resolution* (1929; film UK 1935). In the USA, the film had been known all along as *Born for Glory.* A flag-waving anthology, *For Ever England,* edited by Collie Knox, was published in 1943.

(a) foregone conclusion An inevitable pairing for 'predictable outcome'. Known by 1856. 'The privatization of the BBC and the race down-market of ITV would then be a foregone conclusion' – *The Listener* (2 February 1984); 'Investors were looking decidedly punch-drunk after finding themselves on the receiving end of the Government's double whammy. It was a foregone conclusion that the Conservatives would take a beating in the local government elections, but the extent of the rout shocked both brokers and investors alike' – *The Times* (6 May 1995); '"If Celtic Swing doesn't win by eight lengths your reputation is smashed forever," bellowed

McCririck, having taken the gravest exception to Timeform (with which McGrath is closely involved) rating Celtic Swing 15lb ahead of Pennekamp and famously describing the race's outcome as a "foregone conclusion"' – *The Times* (8 May 1995).

forewarned is forearmed Proverbial expression suggesting that if you know about something in advance, you will be better able to deal with it. There is a Latin tag (probably medieval rather than classical): *praemonitus, praemunitus*, which means the same thing. The saying was known in English by 1530 as 'forewarned is *half* armed.' As 'forewarned, forearmed' it was current by 1592. *Forewarned Is Forearmed* was the title of a book (1948) by T. E. Winslow.

for goodness sake Now used as a euphemistic exclamation instead of 'for God's sake', it was originally used as a literal appeal. It occurs twice in Shakespeare, *King Henry VIII* – Prologue, line 23 and III.i.159 – the earliest citations known (1612).

(I've) forgotten more than you're ever likely to know Parent-child put-down. In her book *Daddy, We Hardly Knew You* (1989), Germaine Greer described how she had researched her father's true history to find out the answers to questions about him that had always tantalized her. Along the way, she recorded Reg Greer's way of putting down children's questions. 'At the dinner-table where we children were forbidden to speak,' she wrote, 'he occasionally held forth . . . [but] if I pounced on some statement that seemed to me to reflect however dimly upon the real world [he would say], "I've forgotten more than you're ever likely to know".' Germaine commented: 'This fatuous hyperbole dismayed me . . . but perhaps after all it was literally true. Daddy's whole life was an exercise in forgetting.' This would appear to be a venerable put-down. Something like it has been found in 1685. The proverb 'We have all forgot more than we remember' was known by 1732.

for men of distinction Slogan for Lord Calvert custom-blended whiskey in the USA, current 1945. 'For years,' the copy

ran, 'the most expensive whiskey blended in America, Lord Calvert is intended especially for those who can afford the finest.' Marshall McLuhan wrote in *The Mechanical Bride* (1951): 'Snob appeal might seem to be the most obvious feature of this type of ad, with its submerged syllogism that since all sorts of eminent men drink this whiskey they are eminent because they drink it. Or only this kind of whiskey is suited to the palate of distinguished men, therefore a taste for it confers, or at least displays an affinity for, distinction in those who have not yet achieved greatness.'

Former Naval Person In his wartime cables as Prime Minister to President Roosevelt, Winston Churchill used this code name. He had sent his telegrams to the President as 'Naval Person' when First Lord of the Admiralty at the beginning of the Second World War.

(and) for my next trick . . . ! Catchphrase 'excuse' uttered after some minor mishap, derived from the patter of stage magicians. By the 1950s, if not long before.

for Pete's sake! A mild oath, known in the USA since 1903, possibly derived from 'for pity's sake'.

forth See AND SO FORTH.

fortune See HIS FACE IS HIS.

fortune's fool Just after he has killed Tybalt, Romeo says in Shakespeare's *Romeo and Juliet*, III.1.138 (1594): 'O I am fortune's fool' – meaning, 'I am the helpless victim of Fortune's mockery and abuse.' Hence, the title applied to an English version (Broadway 2002) of a Turgenev play (1846/1852) that was originally called in Russian either 'Insolvency' or 'Impecuniousness' or 'A Poor Gentlemen'.

fortune(s) of war Olivia Manning's 'Balkan' and 'Levant' trilogies of novels form a single narrative. When BBC TV adapted the six books under the title *Fortunes of War* (1985), this became the overall name of the cycle, perhaps inspired by one of the individual titles being *The Great Fortune* (1960). The earliest citation in *OED2* for the plural phrase 'fortunes of the war' is 1880, but it had

---

long been known in the singular: in Caxton's *Aesop* (1484); Charles Dickens, *Sketches by Boz*, Chap. 12 (1833–6), has this cry from a street game: 'All the fortin of war! this time I vin, next time you vin'; a rhyme from the time of the Crimean War goes: 'The fortunes of war I tell you plain / Are a wooden leg, or a golden chain'; the war memorial at the cemetery of El Alamein (following the battle of 1942) is dedicated 'to whom the fortune of war denied a known and honoured grave'.

forty acres and a mule   See TEN ACRES.

forty winks   A nap or brief sleep. Known by 1828. 'Wink' here means 'a short closing of the eyes.'

for you, Tommy, the war is over!   Said by a German capturing a British soldier ('Tommy Atkins' being the traditional nickname for such), presumably in fiction, but few citations are to hand. *Partridge/Catch Phrases* has it as said, rather, by Italians to British prisoners of war 1940–5 and without the 'Tommy'. A correspondent (1995), referring to the Second World War, stated: 'Among the thousands of prisoners I met there was none who had not been greeted with this phrase on his entrance into captivity.' Sam Kydd, the British film character actor, entitled his war memoirs *For You the War Is Over* (1974) and described his own capture by the Germans at Calais in May 1940 after he had been only six days on active service: '[The officer] sported a monocle and with the effort of keeping it in place his face assumed a twisted grin just like Erich Von Stroheim. He announced the immortal words, "For you ze VOR is OVair!"' It was used again as a title in 1983 by the Hon. Philip Kindersley, who was captured at Tunis at Christmas in 1942. Both are pre-dated by Jan Gerstel (*The War for You Is Over*, 1960). Even earlier, in 1946, Martin Jordan published a novel with the title *For You the War Is Over*. In McGowan & Hands's *Don't Cry for Me, Sergeant-Major* (1983) (about the Falklands war), a British radio officer is asked what Spanish voices are saying over the air waves and 'could hardly keep the smile from his lips as he replied in a phoney Spanish accent, "They're saying, 'Buenos dias, senors, for you the war is over!'"' It has also been suggested that this might have been what a doctor or nurse would have said to a British soldier wounded in the First World War and being returned to 'Blighty' for treatment.

foul play   A long-established legal term for a treacherous or violent deed, such as murder. Hence, the police habit of saying, on the discovery of a body that appears to have died naturally, 'foul play is not suspected'. The phrase is used in more than one Shakespeare play, notably *Hamlet*, I.ii.256 (1600–1), where the Prince says: 'My father's spirit in arms! All is not well. / I doubt some foul play.' Hence, also, the title of the film *Foul Play* (US 1978).

four more years!   Slogan in US presidential elections where the incumbent seeks, or is being urged to seek, a further term. His supporters chanted it at the renomination of Richard Nixon in 1972, and look what happened. The transcript of Ronald Reagan's 'Remarks on Accepting the GOP Presidential Nomination, Dallas, Texas, August 23, 1984' is punctuated with: '*The Audience*. Four more years! Four more years! Four more years!' – *Speaking My Mind by Ronald Reagan: Selected Speeches* (1989). Their prayer was answered.

(a) fourpenny one   A blow with a fist (earliest *OED* citation, 1936). *Partridge/Slang* suggests that it is rhyming slang for a fourpenny bit = 'hit', as fourpenny bits – coins – were once in circulation. But, if so, why was the fourpenny one chosen rather than the threepenny or sixpenny? Neil Ewart, *Everyday Phrases* (1983) has a colourful unverifiable theory (as so often): '[This] stems from the days when the wound suffered by a victim was carefully measured and the culprit was fined at the rate of a penny an inch . . .'

(are you) four-square?   Slogan of Aimée Semple McPherson (d. 1944), the Canadian-born revivalist. The Angelus Temple in Los Angeles was the centre for her 'Foursquare Gospel'. The phrase was the greeting and slogan of her followers – and was used to mean 'are you solid, resolute?' Being 'square', in this sense, dates from at least 1300. Compare Theodore Roosevelt's campaign promise in 1901: 'We demand that big business give people a **Square**

Deal . . . If elected I shall see to it that every man has a Square Deal, no more and no less.' Meaning 'a fair deal', this phrase of US origin was current by 1876.

fourteen hundred! Traditional cry at the London Stock Exchange when a stranger is noticed on the trading floor. This apparently dates from the time (*circa* 1700) when the Stock Exchange membership had remained constant at 1,399 members. Accordingly, the appearance of one non-member made it up to the round number.

(the) fourth estate The press (chiefly in Britain). In 1828, Thomas Macaulay wrote of the House of Commons: 'The gallery in which the reporters sit has become the fourth estate of the realm' – that is to say, after the Lords Spiritual, the Lords Temporal and the Commons – and Macaulay has often been credited with coining this expression. But so have a number of others. The phrase was originally used to describe various forces outside Parliament – such as the Army (as by Falkland in 1638) or the Mob (as by Fielding in 1752). When William Hazlitt used it in 'Table Talk' in 1821, he meant not the Press in general but just William Cobbett. Two years later, Lord Brougham is said to have used the phrase in the House of Commons to describe the Press in general. So by the time Macaulay used it in the *Edinburgh Review* in 1828, it was obviously an established usage. Then Thomas Carlyle used it several times – in his article on Boswell's *Life of Johnson* in 1832, in his history of the *The French Revolution* in 1837 and in his lectures 'On Heroes, Hero-Worship, & the Heroic in History' in 1841. But, just to keep the confusion alive, he attributed the phrase to Edmund Burke, who died in 1797 and is said to have pointed at the press gallery and remarked: 'And yonder sits the fourth estate, more important than them all.' It has been suggested that the BBC (or the broadcast media in general) now constitute a *fifth* estate, as also, at one time, the trades unions.

fox See CRAZY LIKE A.

France See BEST SWORDSMAN IN.

frankly, my dear, I don't give a damn In the last scene of the film *Gone With the Wind* (US 1939), Scarlett O'Hara is finally abandoned by her husband, Rhett Butler. Although she believes she can get him back, there occurs the controversial moment when Rhett replies with these words to her entreaty, 'Where shall I go? What shall I do?' They were allowed on to the soundtrack only after months of negotiation with the Hays Office, which controlled film censorship. In those days, the word 'damn' was forbidden in Hollywood under Section V (1) of the Hays Code, even if it was what Margaret Mitchell had written in her novel (though she hadn't included the 'frankly'). In fact, 'damn' had been uttered twice before, not least in the 1938 *Pygmalion* where perhaps it was overshadowed by the 'bloody'. Sidney Howard's original draft was accordingly changed to: 'Frankly, my dear, I don't care.' The scene was shot with both versions of the line, and the producer, David Selznick, argued at great length with the censors over which was to be used. He did this not least because he thought he would look a fool if the famous line was excluded. He also wanted to show how faithful the film was to the novel. Selznick argued that the *Oxford Dictionary* described 'damn' not as an oath but as a vulgarism, that many women's magazines used the word and that preview audiences had expressed disappointment when the line was omitted. The censors suggested 'darn' instead. Selznick finally won the day – but because he was technically in breach of the Hays Code he was fined $5,000. The line still didn't sound quite right: Clark Gable, as Rhett, had to put the emphasis unnaturally on 'give' rather than on 'damn'.

Freddy See ARE YOU READY.

free See BEST THINGS IN LIFE.

Freedom Now In the early 1960s, a black activists' litany went: *Q.* What do you want? / *A.* Freedom! / *Q.* Let me hear it again – what do you want? / *A.* Freedom! / *Q.* When do you want it? / *A.* Now! The format may have arisen from a petition delivered to Governor George Wallace of Alabama in March 1965. On that occasion, the Reverend Martin Luther King Jr and other civil rights' leaders led some 3,000 people in a 50-mile march from Selma to Montgomery. The petition began: 'We have come to you, the Governor of Alabama, to declare that we must have our *freedom now*. We must have the right to vote; we must have equal protection of the law, and an end to police brutality.'

free, gratis and for nothing A double tautology. *Partridge/Slang* quotes Thomas Bridges as saying in 1770 that 'the common people' always put 'free' and 'gratis' together; and notes that the longer version occurs in an 1841 book. In fact, 'free, gratis' was current by 1682 and the longer version occurs a little earlier than 1841. Charles Dickens in *The Pickwick Papers*, Chap. 26 (1836–7) has Sam Weller's father say 'free gratis for nothin''. In *Usage and Abusage* (1947), Partridge decides that it is a cliché, only excusable as a jocularity. 'Another part was the advice of Paul Russell, a Welsh cricketing nut at Andersen Consulting, who persuaded his firm that it would win the goodwill of Welsh businessmen, and so lots of new work, if it could – free, gratis and for nothing – come up with a plan to turn the club from chump into champ' – *The Economist* (14 May 1994); 'It's all tosh, and I can prove it. Did you know (not a lot of people know this) that there are 153 free shows or exhibitions on the fringe? Yes, that's free, gratis, for nothing, zilch, not a bean' – *The Herald* (Glasgow) (10 August 1994).

free the —— All-purpose protest group slogan that came into its own in the 1960s – usually in conjunction with a place name and a number. Hence: 'Free the Chicago 7' (charged with creating disorder during the Democratic Convention in 1968), 'Free the Wilmington 10', and so on. Dignifying protesters with a group name incorporating place and number may have begun with the **Hollywood 10** (protesters against McCarthyite investigations) in 1947. The format has now become a cliché of sloganeering. Various joke slogans from the late 1970s demanded: 'Free the Beethoven 9/the Heinz 57/ the Intercity 125/the Chiltern Hundreds/the Indianapolis 500/the Grecian 2000.'

free, white and 21 'Having reached the age of consent and in charge of one's own life, especially sex life.' Known in the USA

and the UK, the first recorded use of this expression appears to be in John Buchan, *The Courts of the Morning* (1929), where a minor American gangster states that someone is 'free, white, twenty-one and hairy-chested'. A little earlier, *Punch* had the line 'He's fat, fair and forty-one' (1 November 1916), which might be an allusion to a phrase already in existence. Dorothy Parker wrote in *The New Yorker* (11 April 1931): 'Here I am, taking my formal leave of the New York theater, before I go, free, white, and eighty-one, out to battle with the larger and, I can but hope, the kindlier world.' In the film *Dames* (US 1934), Ruby Keeler gets to say the line, 'I'm free, white and twenty-one, and intend to work.'

fresh woods and pastures new (incorrectly **fresh fields . . .)** Probably Hesketh Pearson in his *Common Misquotations* (1937) first identified this as one of the Top Ten Misquotations. As every schoolboy once knew, but now almost certainly doesn't, if you are quoting from Milton's 'Lycidas', you should say 'Tomorrow to fresh *woods* and pastures new' and not 'fresh fields'. That said, someone once remarked that a fresh wood was a curious place for a shepherd to park his flock. Surely they would be liable to get lost in a wood, lose their wool on bushes, eat poisonous plants, and so on? Mike Jones (Principal Lecturer, National School of Forestry, Cumbria) commented (2002): 'Although we think of woods and grazing land being mutually exclusive these days, there was a long tradition dating back to the Middle Ages and beyond of "Woodpasture" – a form of land management that now comes under the more modern title of Agroforestry. Under this system, animals would be grazed in the woods, and the trees would be spaced out widely enough to give shelter but not block out too much light. In this way, a herb-rich layer would develop on the woodland floor, whilst still allowing the harvest of woodland products.'

Friday night is Amami night Slogan for Amami hair products, current in the UK in the 1920s. Presumably this inspired the title of the long-running BBC radio show *Friday Night is Music Night* (1953–).

friend See IS SHE A; IS THAT YOUR.

friendly persuasion Phrase popularized by *Friendly Persuasion* as the title of a film (US 1956), based on a novel by Jessamyn West, and by the accompanying song. 'In business his most obvious talent is sales-manship. "I'm not a foot-in-the-door person, but I believe in persuasion, and friendly persuasion at that," he says. He has also become a good delegator' – *The Sunday Telegraph* (19 June 1994); 'Even without the scandals, selling in the UK had begun a mini-revolution. The time when an irrepressible confidence plus friendly persuasion were the way to earn a fortune in sales is fast fading' – *The Times* (19 October 1994).

friends See EVEN YOUR BEST.

friends … and you are my friends … Catchphrase of Ersil Twing (Pat Patrick) in the American radio show *The Chase and Sanborn Hour* (1937–48).

friends of the earth Name given to a party cake (full of fruits and good things) in the USA, recorded *circa* 1976, but better known as the name of an international lobbying organization of green environ-mentalists. Originating in the USA, the name Friends of the Earth was adopted in Britain in 1970.

friends thought I was mad Journalistic cliché when describing the pursuit of some activity or adventure. Date of origin unknown. Part of the 'travel scribes' armoury' compiled from a competition in the *The Guardian* (10 April 1993) and used particularly in describing unusual holidays, property purchases, and so on. 'After that we started seeing each other, initially quite casually. Some friends thought we were mad to get back to-gether; many were surprised Duncan would even contemplate seeing me again. One friend said we were perfectly matched, we just acted too fast' – *Daily Mail* (10 May 1994); 'Friends thought they were mad. Family shook their heads as they surveyed the mildew-spotted wall, peeling plaster, rusty radiators, and the gull droppings on the parquet floor. Amazingly, all is now restored to its former art deco glory' – *Daily Mail* (28 May 1994); 'His friends apparently thought him mad to

even think about it, but the atmosphere and the surrounding 34 acres of park and woodland not surprisingly appealed to Mackenzie' – *The Herald* (Glasgow) (6 July 1994); 'A 17th-century convent on the edge of the Tuscan Maremma, with wheat plains rolling down to the sea, provided his retreat. When Pollock found the convent, it was a shelter for sheep and goats. There was no electricity, no running water. His friends thought him mad to sink his cash into this enormous pile of crumbling stone but it was a Bohemian idyll' – *The Euro-pean* (12 August 1994).

from a far country Quasi-poetic phrase. *From a Far Country* was the title of a TV film (1981) of dramatized episodes from the early life of Pope John Paul II. The far country from which he came to the Vatican was, of course, Poland. The idea for this would seem to lie in the Old Testament where there are several examples of 'from a far land' and 'from a far country' (Deu-teronomy 29:22, 2 Kings 20:14, Isaiah 39:3, etc.) but, perhaps most felicitously, there is 'good news from a far country' (Proverbs 25:25). Compare *Crowned In a Far Coun-try*, a book (1986) by Princess Michael of Kent about people who married into the British Royal Family. William Caxton, in England's first printed book, *Dictes or Sayengis of the Philosophres* (1477), has: 'Socrates was a Greek born in a far country from here.' H. D. Thoreau, *On the Duty of Civil Disobedience* (1849), has: '[On going to prison] It was like travelling into a far country, such as I had never expected to behold, to lie there for one night.' Poem X in the Edith Sitwell/William Walton entertainment *Façade* (1922) is entitled 'A Man From a Far Countree'.

from a grateful nation (or **country)** Memorial/epitaphic phrase especially popular in the 19th century. At St Deiniol's, W. E. Gladstone's library in the village of Hawarden, Wales, where the British Prime Minister (1809–98) had his family home for almost fifty years, there is a plaque saying it was 'erected to his memory by a grateful nation'. W. M. Thackeray, writing in *The Virginians*, Chap. 35 (1859), has: 'The late lamented O'Connell . . . over whom a grateful country has raised such a magnificent testimonial.' On the statue to General Havelock (1795–1857) in Trafalgar Square, London, is written: 'Soldiers! Your valour will not be forgotten by a grateful country.' The notable Alexander Column in the square outside the Winter Palace at St Petersburg was completed in 1834. On the base was the inscription (in Russian): 'To Alexander the First from a Grateful Russia.' Nowadays, the phrase is invariably used with irony. From *The Independent* (23 July 1992): 'There have been loads of Roy Orbisons and Neil Diamonds and Gene Pitneys, and, after Elvis, the man most often impersonated by a grateful nation . . . Cliff Richard.'

from arse-hole to breakfast time All the time. Date of origin unknown, but recorded from the 1960s on. Often in the sense of 'buggered about . . .' Politer variations include 'from ear'ole to breakfast-time' and 'from Alice Springs to breakfast-time'. 'That Bernadette Shaw? What a chatterbox! Nags away from asshole to breakfast-time but never sees what's staring her in the face' – Peter Nichols, *Privates on Parade*, Act 1 Sc. 5 (1977).

from a view to a death Foxhunting term, as in 'From a view to a death in the morning', a line from the song 'D'ye ken John Peel' (1832) by John Woodcock Graves. In foxhunting terminology, a 'check' is a loss of scent, a 'view (halloo)' is the huntsman's shout when a fox breaks cover, and a 'kill' or a 'death' is self-explanatory. Hence, the title of Anthony Powell's 1933 novel *From a View to a Death*. Compare *A View to a Kill*, title of a James Bond film (UK 1985). The original title of the short story by Ian Fleming (published in 1960 in *For Your Eyes Only*) was '*From* a View To a Kill'. The verse from Graves's song also provided the title of a film (UK 1988) based on a novel by Desmond Lowden, *Bellman and True* (1975). Although **Bellman and True** are mentioned in the list of hounds, the book and film are about a bellman in the criminal sense: that is, a man who disables alarm systems so that robberies can take place.

from each according to his ability (to each according to his needs) Marxist slogan from the 19th century. Usually attributed to Karl Marx but from neither *Das Kapital* nor *The Communist Manifesto*. The slogan appears in his *Critique of the Gotha Programme* (1875) in which Marx says that after the workers have taken power, capitalist thinking must first disappear. Only then will the day come when society can 'inscribe on its banners: from each according to his ability, to each according to his needs'. John Kenneth Galbraith commented in *The Age of Uncertainty* (1977): 'It is possible that these . . . twelve words enlisted for Marx more followers than all the hundreds of thousands in the three volumes of *Das Kapital* combined.' There is some doubt whether Marx originated the slogan or whether he was quoting Louis Blanc, Morelly or Mikhail Bakunin. The latter wrote: 'From each according to his faculties, to each according to his needs' (declaration, 1870, by anarchists on trial after the failure of their uprising in Lyons). Also, Saint-Simon (1760–1825), the French reformer, had earlier said: 'The task of each be according to his capacity, the wealth of each be according to his works.' And, much earlier, Acts 4:34–35 had: 'Neither was there any among them that lacked: for as many as were possessors of lands or houses sold them, and brought the prices of things that were sold, and laid them down at the apostles' feet: and distribution was made unto every man according as he had need.'

—— from Hell Meaning 'ghastly' or 'hellish'. The situation or person being described must be extremely, even exaggeratedly, characteristic of the type but strongly emphasizing the negative qualities. Thus, the grandma from Hell would need to exhibit all the traits that would lead others to describe her as 'a typical grandmother' but only in the pejorative sense. Something or somebody said to be 'the —— from Hell' has not just gone wrong but has done so specifically by inflating the negative characteristics of the species. The origin would seem to lie in the neighbouring fields of horror movies and rock albums. A writer in *The Independent* (24 September 1988) joked about videos with titles like *Mutant Hollywood Chainsaw Hookers From Hell!* Original Sin recorded 'Bitches from Hell' in 1986 and Pantera, 'Cowboys from Hell' in 1990. But the term may go back much farther. In 1902, L. McKee wrote in his exposé of the Alaskan mining industry, *Land of Nome*: 'I felt that I had received a very high compliment . . . when an old-timer in the party . . . told me that I was a "musher from hell".' In the First World War, kilted Scottish regiments were apparently known as 'ladies from hell' – and in the BBC radio show *Round the Horne* (20 March 1966), reference is made to bus-drivers as 'ladies from hell'. *Posse From Hell* was the title of a film (US 1961). In 1968, an American feminist group was founded, going by the name of the Women's International Terrorist Conspiracy from Hell, or WITCH (Robin Morgan, *The Word of a Woman: Selected Prose 1968–1992* (1993). Some more examples from the 1990s' popularity of the expression: '[US figure-skating champion Christopher Bowman] – the Hans Brinker from Hell' – *Hartford Courant* (Connecticut) (7 February 1992); 'Lisa Samalin's painting of grandma from hell' – *The New York Times* (9 May 1993); '[Hillary Clinton] is alternately deified and vilified as nun or Lady Macbeth, Florence Nightingale or Yuppie From Hell' – *The New York Times* (13 June 1993); 'The chief executive of Cunard walked the plank yesterday, taking responsibility for the QE2's Christmas "cruise from hell" which has cost the liner's owner, Trafalgar House, at least £7.5m in compensation payments' – *The Independent* (19 May 1995); 'The settlement agreed . . . with two former women employees was not merely a victory for the sensibilities of women; it was a victory for all mankind. Or at any rate, the substantial section of the population who have, at some time in their working life, had to endure the office party from hell' – *The Daily Telegraph* (15 February 1996).

from Land's End to John o'Groats   The length of the country, from one end of Great Britain to the other. These two points on the mainland of the British Isles are traditionally taken to be the farthest apart. Certainly, they are at the south-west and north-eastern extremities and make suitable points between which people may travel – sometimes on foot – to raise money for charity. 'The weary penman who could send a smile wreathing from Land's End to John o'Groats' – Edmund C. Stedman, *Victorian Poets* (1875). Compare the biblical expression **from Dan to Beersheba**, meaning from one end of the Holy Land to the other.

from log cabin to White House   The title of a biography (1881) of President James Garfield by the Reverend William Thayer was *From Log Cabin to White House*. Earlier US Presidents Henry Harrison and Abraham Lincoln had used the log cabin as a prop in their campaigns. Subsequently almost all presidential aspirants have sought a humble 'log cabin' substitute to help them on their way.

from sea to shining sea   Phrase from the poem 'America the Beautiful' (1893) by Katharine Lee Bates: 'America! America! / God shed his grace on thee / And crown thy good with brotherhood / From sea to shining to shining sea!' These words have also been set to music. The motto of the Dominion of Canada (adopted 1867) is '*A mari usque ad mare*' [from sea to sea], which came from Psalm 72:8: 'He shall have dominion also from sea to sea.'

from the cradle to the grave   The whole of a person's life. The phrase appears to have been coined by Sir Richard Steele in an essay in the *Tatler*, No. 52 (1709): 'A modest Fellow never has a doubt from his Cradle to his Grave'; 'A little rule, a little sway, / A sunbeam in a winter's day, / Is all the proud and mighty have / Between the cradle and the grave' – John Dyer, *Grongar Hill* (1726); 'That betwixt the cradle and the grave / It only once smil'd can be; / And when it once is smil'd; / There's an end to all misery' – William Blake, 'The Smile' (*circa* 1801); *Von der Wiege bis zum Grabe* [From the Cradle to the Grave] – title of a symphonic poem by Franz Liszt (1881–2); Winston Churchill said in a radio broadcast (21 March 1943): 'National compulsory insurance for all classes for all purposes from the cradle to the grave'; 'There's your National Health, friend. Look after you from the cradle to the grave' – Peter Nichols, *The National Health*, Act 2, Sc. 1 (1969); 'The move represents a tacit admission that the National Health Service has in parts of Britain lost sight of its commitment to offer care from the cradle to the grave' – *The Guardian* (28 February 1996).

from truck to kelson Meaning, 'from top to bottom'. The *OED2* gives the nautical definition of 'truck' as 'a circular or square cap of wood fixed on the head of a mast or flag-staff' and 'kelson' as 'a line of timber placed inside a ship along the floor-timbers and parallel with the keel . . . or combination of iron plates in iron vessels'. A report of legal proceedings during the American Civil War on the burning of the ship *Brilliant* by the rebel pirate *Alabama* (1862) contains the sentence: 'Every part of the vessel, from truck to kelson, is accurately and faithfully described.' From an American naval officer's diary (7 September 1907): 'Honolulu. Cleaned ship from truck to *keelson.*' But the words, however spelt, are not solely in American use.

from whence The 'from' is superfluous in this near-tautologous usage, but language is not always logical and the usage has been with us too long. The *OED2*'s earliest citation is from Langland, with Shakespeare among those following suit. One of Milton's memorable lines from *Paradise Lost*, Bk 1, 75 is: 'O how unlike the place from whence they fell!'

from —— with love The obvious inspiration for the title of *From Russia With Love*, Ian Fleming's James Bond novel (1957; film UK 1963) is the simple form of wording used to accompany a present. But, as a format phrase, it has launched any number of allusions of the 'from —— with ——' variety. Compare: *Barcelona, With Love*, a book by Clifford King (1959), *To Paris With Love*, a film (UK 1954) and *To Sir With Love*, a book by E. R. Braithwaite (1959; film UK 1967). In *Keep Taking the Tabloids* (1983), Fritz Spiegl noted these newspaper headlines: 'From the Rush Hour with Love', 'From Maggie without love!'

from your mouth to God's ear Meaning, 'I hope what you say will come true by being acted upon by God'. Probably of American origin, adapted from a Jewish/

Yiddish expression. A character in the film *New York, New York* (US 1977) says 'from my mouth to God's ear' in a context that suggests he means 'What I am saying is the truth.' Lillian Merwin in *The Taste of Yiddish* (1970) has: 'FUN ZAYN MOYL, IN GOTS OYER. *Lit.*, From his mouth into God's ear. May God hear what he has said (and fulfil it)!' Appropriately, the line is uttered in the musical *Fiddler on the Roof* (1964) – as 'from your mouth to God's ears.' As such, it may stem from Psalm 130:2: 'Lord, hear my voice: let thine ears be attentive to the voice of my supplications.' The expression also makes an appearance in the orthodox Jewish prayer book. From the *Evening Standard* (London) (4 October 1995): 'Goldeneye is the best movie in the series since Diamonds Are Forever . . . I told him I thought it would take $30 million in its opening weekend, to which he replied: "From your lips to God's ears".' An Arab version is **from your mouth to the Gates of Heaven**. Arabic also has a sarcastic if vulgar retort when the occasion arises: 'From your mouth to his arsehole', meaning 'like hell it will.'

(to give someone the) frozen mit Meaning, 'to freeze out; give the cold shoulder to someone; exclude' (from 'mit', 'mitten', thence 'hand'). Lady Diana Cooper writing to Duff Cooper on 14 September 1925, from a letter printed in *A Durable Fire* (1983), said: 'Duffy, don't be deathly proud, my darling . . . you probably dish out the frozen mit to all, and I want all men to love and admire you.' *Partridge/Slang* finds the expression in *Punch* in 1915. 'To give someone the mitten', meaning to reject a lover (especially) was known by 1838.

fruit gums See DON'T FORGET.

fruits See BY THEIR.

Fry's chocolate See DESPERATION.

fuck See I SUPPOSE A; BEST FUCKS.

fuck off money (or **fuck you money)** A sizeable amount of money the possession of which enables an individual to turn down work he does not wish to do. Known by the 1970s/80s, especially in media circles. 'Sidney Lumet gave me some good advice . . . You must always have enough money in the bank not to care about being paid. He called this his "fuck you" fund' – Peter Hall, *Making an Exhibition of Myself* (1993).

fuck the army (or FTA) Slogan much used in the US Army, especially as graffiti. *DOAS* adds: 'Since *circa* 1960, as a counter expression to disliked orders, rules etc.' *F.T.A.* was the title of an anti-Vietnam War film made by Jane Fonda in 1972. The 'initial' type of slogan has also been used regarding the Pope ('FTP') and the Queen ('FTQ'), especially in Northern Ireland – both types recorded in Belfast (1971).

fuck this (or that) for a lark! Expression of disgust at some chore or duty imposed. Mostly British use since the 1940s. Laurence Olivier is said to have used a cod French translation: *'Baisez cela pour une alouette.'* Compare SOD THIS FOR A GAME OF SOLDIERS!

fuck you Jack See I'M ALL RIGHT.

(to) fudge and mudge Meaning, 'to produce the appearance of a solution while, in fact, only patching up a compromise'. These verbs (and associated nouns) were often wheeled out in discussions of the Social Democratic and the Liberal parties in Britain in the 1980s. One of the SDP's Gang of Four, Dr David Owen, had used them earlier in his previous incarnation as a member of the Labour Party. He told Labour's Blackpool Conference (2 October 1980): 'We are fed up with fudging and mudging, with mush and slush.'

(to) fulfil a long-felt want To achieve a long desired urge or requirement. From Abraham Lincoln's Annual Message to Congress (December 1862): 'The judicious legislation of Congress . . . has satisfied . . . the long felt want of an uniform circulating medium.' 'I would suggest the following as likely to fulfil a long-felt want of the weekend visitor' – *Punch* (24 February 1915). *Casanova (Frank Finlay)*: 'I'll be perfectly frank with you – I have a long felt want.' *Eric Morecambe*: 'There's no answer to that' – BBC TV, *The Morecambe and Wise Show* (2 February 1973); 'Shots rained in on the Dutch area, but the long felt want of a great international class

finisher was once again the team's failing' – *The Irish Times* (5 July 1994).

full-frontal nudity Nudity that allows a man or woman's sexual parts to be seen. Before the 1960s, naked people when being photographed had a way of holding large beach balls in front of themselves, but with the advent of naked actors in such shows as *Hair* (1967) and *Oh! Calcutta!* (1969), a term obviously had to be invented for this great leap forward in civilized behaviour. *OED2* does not find the term until 1971. But the episode of TV's *Monty Python's Flying Circus* broadcast on 7 December 1969 was entitled 'Full Frontal Nudity', and my diary for 25 March 1970 notes a viewing of Ken Russell's film *Women in Love*: 'Full frontal nudity, too, as they call it, though I don't feel a better man for having seen Oliver Reed's genitals'.

(the) full monty Meaning 'the full amount, everything included' – a phrase suddenly popular in British English in the early 1990s but known since the early 1980s. Its appearance in *Street Talk* (1986) shows that it was established in Lancashire/the North of England by that date. The dictionary explains: 'To avoid the awkwardness of stumbling through an unfamiliar menu, someone might tell the waiter: "We'll have the full monty"' (though the expression 'full house' might just as easily be used in that context). From *The Guardian* (28 September 1989): '"What we're after is a live skeleton – the full monty," said the stage manager.' The somewhat Cockney comedian Jim Davidson entitled his autobiography *The Full Monty* in 1993. The title of the film *The Full Monty* (UK 1997) refers to full-frontal nudity as sported by a team of male strippers. Could it be a corruption of the 'full amount'? Or could it have something to do with 'monty' (from the Spanish *monte*), a card game, or the Australian/ New Zealand term for a horse considered certain to win a race? Or, again, could it have something to do with bales stuffed *full* of wool and imported from Montevideo? Or with Field Marshal Montgomery being kitted out with all his medals? Or, with the word 'mont', meaning 'to pawn', which probably has its origins in the Monti di Pietà, the Italian medieval pawn shops that developed into banks (in pawning an item the customer need not take the full amount of cash offered or he could take the 'full monti')? Or, most convincingly of all, with being dressed in a full complement of jacket, trousers, waistcoat and overcoat from the tailors Montague Burton (first established in Chesterfield in 1904 and later to become Burton Menswear)? A correspondent wrote (1996): 'When I started work in insurance in Manchester in 1949, the full monty was a three-piece suit [from Montague Burton] – *de rigueur* in those circles – [which you could get] for the price of a two-piece at the opposition – the "fifty shilling" tailor, later John Collier.' In fact, the most popular presumed origin for the phrase has something to do with Sir Montague Burton (1885– 1952), founder of Burton menswear stores, and his supplying of a full suit and accessories to purchasers, especially those being demobilized from the forces. As the *DNB* records, a quarter of all uniforms provided in this country in the 1939–45 war were made by 'Monty' Burton's company, as were a third of the clothes issued on demob. But if 'full monty' had anything to do with Montague Burton or demobbed servicemen's clothes, it is surprising that Eric Partridge and his reviser, Paul Beale, had never heard of it. If only someone could turn up a citation for 'the full monty' significantly earlier than the 1986 one above, then this theory might acquire something approaching legs. The second most popular etymology takes us back to Field Marshal Montgomery, not to his medals but to his supposed insistence on a full English breakfast every morning even at the height of battle. The trouble with this one is that tucking into a hearty breakfast was about the last thing he would do. He preferred plain food, did not drink or smoke, so probably did not make a fuss over his breakfast either. Whatever the case, the phrase has given everybody a good deal of fun. A TV commentator on a football match described a player who had flung off his shirt in triumph after scoring as 'Giving the crowd a Half Monty'. Prime Minister Tony Blair further distorted the meaning of the original phrase by saying (30 January 1998): 'I have to say nonetheless,

in terms of getting jobs for people, better education standards, tackling poverty, we do intend to go the full monty . . .' William Safire's 'On Language' column in *The New York Times* (16 November 1997) revealed how the specific interpretation of the phrase in the film seems to be the one catching on in the USA: '*The San Diego Union-Tribune* ran a story about the Carlsbad City Council's zoning restrictions to avert garishness: "Carlsbad has reached the point where it can afford to go the full monty – full frontal snobbery" . . . Fox Searchlight Pictures publicity defines the phrase this way: "1. Naked, nude. 2. To go the Full Monty, vb., to take all one's clothes off, to go the whole way, to be totally naked".' Safire also noted how America was taking gleefully to the new phrase and spawning puns. *Entertainment Week* had referred to *Wuthering Heights* as 'the full Brontë'.

full of Eastern promise Slogan for Fry's Turkish Delight (confectionery), current in the late 1950s. One of the longest-running British TV ads, appealing to escapist fantasies. An early example showed a male slave unrolling a carpet containing a woman captive in front of an eastern potentate. From the *Independent on Sunday* (5 April 1992): 'Benny Hill was fired by Thames in 1989 when ratings slumped after decades of . . . the Crimplene eroticism of Hill's Angels – those willing young ladies with the bee-stung mouths, full of East End promise.'

full of memories Journalistic cliché mostly used in connection with elderly people or the recently departed. Date of origin unknown. Listed in the *Independent* 'DIY travel writers' cliché kit' (31 December 1988): '"Before the tourists came," said Old —, his sad, wet eyes full of memories, "things were different".' 'I happened to be in the speaker's chair presiding over one debate in the union in 1963 when the news of Hugh Gaitskell's premature death came through. Now John himself has gone before his time, perhaps equally cheated of the highest office. The past few days have been full of memories and echoes' – *The Sunday Times* (15 May 1994); 'The sleeves of records like Dylan's Blood on the Tracks, the first two Roxy Music albums, the first Clash album, Bowie's Ziggy Stardust and Diamond Dogs, anything by the Beatles and the Stones, The Best of the Doors with Joel Brodsky's portrait of Jim Morrison as a crucified Adonis are aesthetically beautiful and full of memories in a way that a CD could never be' – *The Daily Telegraph* (16 June 1994).

(a) fully paid-up member of the human race Complimentary phrase to describe a person who has human qualities and is three-dimensional in character terms. Of the British Conservative politician Kenneth Clarke, *The Observer* wrote (31 July 1988): 'He is always well-informed (or anyway well-briefed), always reasonable and equable. He seems to be a fully paid-up member of the human race.'

fumed oak Oak that has been darkened by exposure to ammonia vapour. Furniture made of this wood was popular in the early 1900s especially. The phrase used allusively points to a certain suburban type of household where it would be found. Noël Coward gave the title *Fumed Oak* to one of his playlets in *To-night at 8.30* (1936). '[Of a house called The Beeches in Headington] This is a little half-timbered heaven furnished with "fumed oak" and simple colours' – John Betjeman, *Letters* (1994) – letter of 3 October 1927; 'One of the participants is Dillon himself, a *farouche* young actor-dramatist currently sponging on a suburban family straight out of Mr Coward's *Fumed Oak*' – Kenneth Tynan in a 1958 theatre review, *Curtains* (1961).

fun See IS IT TRUE.

funny! Peter Cook remembered (1979) that this word caught on between himself and Dudley Moore when delivered in a strangulated Pete and Dud voices in BBC2 TV *Not Only . . . But Also*, if not with the public at large. For example, 'At the Art Gallery' (1965) has 'Dud' saying: 'I had the feeling of somebody in the room with me. I thought – funny – you know, and I didn't see no one come in and I thought – funny. And I felt these eyes burning in the back of my head.' Later, Fozzy Bear tried something similar in *The Muppet Show*, pronouncing it 'Fun-neee!'

funny bone The part of the elbow over which the ulnar nerve passes – so called from the peculiar sensation experienced when it is hit. There is some suggestion that the term may be a pun on the Latin *humerus*, the medical name of the long bone in the upper arm. But how would this medical joke have gained common currency? Known by 1867.

funny is money An old Hollywood expression, quoted in Steven M. L. Aronson, *Hype* (1983) – meaning that it is more profitable to deal in comedy than the more serious reaches of dramatic art.

funny papers See SEE YOU IN THE.

funny peculiar Phrase from the basic distinction made clear by Ian Hay in his play *Housemaster*, Act 3 (1936) – not the novel published in the same year, where it does not appear: 'That's funny.' 'What do you mean, funny? Funny-peculiar, or funny ha-ha?' Earlier, however, in the American Meriel Brady's novel *Genevieve Gertrude*, Chap. 7 (1928), there had been: '"I liked that song, myself," he said, "even if it isn't classical. It's funny, anyhow." Genevieve Gertrude raised her hand. "Do you mean funny peculiar, or funny ha-ha?" she inquired politely . . . "'Cause," explained his mentor gravely, "our teacher don't allow us to say funny when we mean peculiar. It's bad English, you know".' There is also a tantalizing play on words to be found in Mary Vivian Hughes, *A London Family Between the Wars*, Chap. 6 (1940) – referring to the 1920s: 'Haven't you brought me any funny stories this time?' 'Not much. There's one thing I heard – "not sunny but pecoola" as you used to say when you were tiny.' The first, if not the second, of these quotes is clear proof that the phrase existed before Ian Hay popularized it further. Mae West in her autobiography, *Goodness Had Nothing To Do With It*, Chap. 9 (1959), writing of the period before her play *Pleasure Man* opened in New York (17 September 1928), quotes a male friend as saying: 'Men can get funny over a woman. Funny peculiar that is.' *Funny Peculiar* was the title of a play (1976) by Mike Stott, and also of an (unrelated) series of compilations of newspaper clangers and oddities by Denys

Parsons beginning with *Funny Ha Ha and Funny Peculiar* (1965).

(a) funny thing happened (to me) on the way to the theatre tonight ... The uninspired comedian's preliminary to telling a joke and dating presumably from music-hall/vaudeville days. Compare the title of a book by Nancy Spain – *A Funny Thing Happened On the Way* (1964) – and of the comedy musical *A Funny Thing Happened on the Way to the Forum* (film US 1966) set in ancient Rome, based on Plautus (but the phrase can't be *quite* as old as that, surely?). Following one of his election defeats in the 1950s, Adlai Stevenson remarked, 'A funny thing happened to me on my way to the White House.'

fur coat See ALL FUR COAT.

fur, feather and fin Phrase for what gets hunted. Ludovic Kennedy, *Truth To Tell* (1991), refers to his great uncle Will as 'a lifelong destroyer of fur, feather and fin.'

G

gaff See BLOW THE.

gag me with a spoon See GRODY TO THE MAX.

(the) gaiety of nations Phrase from one of the finest obituary tributes ever penned – Samuel Johnson's lament for his friend the actor David Garrick (d. 1779). In his 'Life of Edmund Smith', one of the *Lives of the English Poets* (1779), Johnson wrote: 'At this man's table I enjoyed many cheerful and instructive hours . . . with David Garrick, whom I hoped to have gratified with this character of our common friend; but what are the hopes of man! I am disappointed by that stroke of death, which has eclipsed the gaiety of nations, and impoverished the public stock of harmless pleasure.' When Charles Dickens died in 1870, Thomas Carlyle wrote: 'It is an event world-wide, a *unique* of talents suddenly extinct, and has "eclipsed" (we too may say) "the gaiety of nations".' 'At one level, the famous "List of the Good and Great", to which governments resort . . . has added to the gaiety of the nation' – *The Times* (22 January 1983).

gaiters See ALL GAS.

Gallagher See ABSOLUTELY.

game See ANYTHING FOR A.

game of soldiers See SOD THIS.

(it's a) game of two halves Cliché of broadcast and journalistic football commentary in the UK. A reminder that one team may dominate the first half, the other team the second half, so the outcome of a game is not predictable as matters may alter after half time. The first citation (with its 'Brian' denoting the generic name for all TV football pundits/commentators) shows it had already become a recognized phrase by 1985. 'A superb game, but a game of two halves, Brian. Liverpool played brilliant football in the first forty-five minutes with "watch out Atkinson" all over it, and could have been four up' – *The Sunday Times* (27 October 1985); 'It would have been in keeping with the style of this book if she'd borrowed a phrase from her fellow Experts in the world of sports commentary. "A relationship," she could have concluded, "is a game of two halves"' – *Today* (25 May 1986). Fritz Spiegl entitled his book on journalistic clichés, *A Game of Two Halves, Brian* (1996).

(the) game's afoot Phrase from Shakespeare, *Henry V*, III.i.5 (1599), in which the King rallies his troops before Harfleur: 'I see you stand like greyhounds in the slips, / Straining upon the start. The game's afoot: / Follow your spirit.' From this, Sherlock Holmes, in the stories by Sir Arthur Conan Doyle, had a way of saying: 'Come, Watson, come! The game is afoot' – as in 'The Adventure of the Abbey Grange' (1904).

game, set and match Complete victory – as, originally, in lawn tennis. Known in figurative use by 1968. *Game, Set and Match* was the title given to a TV spy drama series (UK 1988) based on a trilogy of novels by Len Deighton – *Berlin Game, Mexico Set* and *London Match*.

(to come on like) gangbusters Meaning 'to perform in a striking manner', this expression comes from the US radio series *Gangbusters*, which ran from *circa* 1945 to 1957 and used to begin with the sound of screeching tyres, machine guns and police sirens, followed by the announcement: '*Gangbusters!* With the co-operation of leading law enforcement officials of the United States, *Gangbusters* presents facts in the relentless war of the police on the underworld, authentic case histories that show the never-ending activity of the police in their work of protecting our citizens.' 'He [counsel investigating Jim Wright, Speaker of the House of Representatives] came in like gangbusters. He came in full of enthusiasm' – *The New York Times* (12 May 1989); 'At the interview, this guy [Anthony Cheetham] was coming across like gangbusters. We told him we'd let him know' – *The Observer* (30 August 1992).

(a/the) gang of four Now meaning 'any group of four people working in concert', the original 'Gang of Four', in China, was led by Jiang Qing, the unscrupulous wife of Chairman Mao Tse-tung and so labelled in the mid-1970s when the four were tried and given the death sentence for treason and other crimes (later commuted to life imprisonment). The other three members were Zhang Chunqiao, a political organizer in the Cultural Revolution; Wang Hogwen, a youthful activist; and Yao Wenyuan, a journalist. Chairman Hua Kuofeng attributed the phrase to his predecessor. Apparently on one occasion, Mao had warned his wife and her colleagues: 'Don't be a gang of four.' The nickname was later applied to the founders of the Social Democratic Party in Britain in 1981 – Roy Jenkins, David Owen, William Rodgers and Shirley Williams.

(the) gang's all here The chorus 'Hail, hail, the gang's all here / What the hell do we care? / What the hell do we care?' is sung to Sir Arthur Sullivan's music for 'Come, friends, who plow the sea' from the *Pirates of Penzance*. It was sung at a Democratic Party Convention in the early

1900s and the words of the American version were copyrighted in 1917. *Hail, Hail, The Gang's All Here!* was used as the title of an Ed McBain novel (1971) and, as *The Gang's All Here*, of films in 1939 and 1943.

garbage in, garbage out A term from computing, known by 1964 (and sometimes abbreviated to **GIGO**, pronounced 'guy-go'). Basically, it means that if you put bad data into a computer, you can come up with anything you want but what comes out will be useless and meaningless. In the wider sense it conveys the simple idea that what you get out of something depends very much on what you put into it.

gardener See AS THE ART.

Garnet See ALL SIR.

gas See ALL.

gate See CREAKING.

——gate PHRASES. Journalistic suffix, used especially to help in the naming of any political and royal scandal in the USA and UK. 'Watergate' was the name given to the scandal in US politics that led to the resignation of President Richard Nixon in 1974. It came from the Watergate apartment block in Washington DC where a bungled burglary by those seeking to re-elect President Nixon led to a cover-up and then the scandal. Among the scores there have been subsequently are: Koreagate, Lancegate, Billygate, Liffeygate, Westlandgate, Contragate, Irangate, Thatchergate, Camillagate and Squidgygate. A cliché really by the time of the third or fourth such coinage.

gates See BARBARIANS ARE AT.

(a) gaudy night The Dorothy L. Sayers detective novel *Gaudy Night* (1935) is set during a 'gaudy' (or 'gaude') at an Oxford college. A 'gaudy' (from Latin *gaudium*, 'joy') is the name given at that university to a feast (often commemorative of the college founder) to which former members are invited. It is hard to think that Sayers with her unrivalled use and knowledge of quotations was unaware that the phrase came from Shakespeare, *Antony and Cleopatra*, III.xiii.183 (1597), in which Antony says: 'Let's have one other gaudy night: call to me / All my sad captains; fill our bowls once more; / Let's mock the midnight bell.' Sayers does not make the connection explicit in her book, though in Chap. 23, Lord Peter Wimsey does say, 'We'll have one other gaudy night.'

geddit? Meaning 'Do you get it?' and said after a poor joke. Popularized from the early 1980s onwards by the Glenda Slag column in *Private Eye*, a parody of feisty women journalists.

geese See ALL ONE'S.

geezer See EE, WOT.

generously See ALL CONTRIBUTIONS.

(a) gentle giant The alliteration is important, and the application to any tall, big, strong person has become a journalistic cliché, especially in obituary writing. A policeman killed by an IRA bomb outside Harrods' store in London (December 1983) was so dubbed. Terry Wogan used the expression allusively in the early 1980s to describe the BBC Radio 2 network. Larry Holmes (b. 1950), a world heavyweight boxing champion, is another to whom the label has been affixed, as also James Randel Matson (b. 1945), the US track and field champion. In 1967 there was an American film entitled *The Gentle Giant*. This was about a small boy in Florida who befriends a bear, which later saves the life of the boy's disapproving father. In the 1930s Pickfords Removals were promoted with the rhyme: 'A note from you, a call from us, / The date is fixed, with no worry or fuss, / A Pickfords van, a gentle giant, / The work is done – a satisfied client.' Going back even farther, the journalist William Howard Russell wrote of Dr Thomas Alexander, a surgeon who served in the Crimean War, as a 'gentle giant of a Scotchman'. 'Rugby: Gentle giant Munro keen to kick the losing habit' – headline in *The Scotsman* (10 June 1994); 'Controversy has stalked the 35-year-old gentle giant nicknamed "Piggy" every step of his dual-international career, resulting in numerous brushes with authority' – *Today* (26 August 1994); 'I speeded up as I left the canal and into the open waters of Coot Bay, a stiff breeze whipping up the surface, only to slow down again on the other side for Tarpon Creek, a habitat of the Florida

manatee, or sea-cow, a gentle giant whose numbers have been decimated by weekend boaters' – *Daily Mail* (15 April 1995).

gentleman See ALMOST.

(a) gentleman and a scholar (or a **scholar and a gentleman)** Paul Beale notes in *Partridge/Catch Phrases* that he was familiar with this compliment in the British army (*circa* 1960) in the form: 'Sir, you are a Christian, a scholar, and a gentleman.' It was 'often used as jocular, fulsome, though quite genuine, thanks for services rendered'. Partridge, earlier, had been tracking down a longer version – 'A gentleman, a scholar, and a fine judge of whiskey' – but had only been able to find the 'gentleman and scholar' in Robert Burns (1786): 'His locked, lettered, braw brass collar / Shew'd him the gentleman an' the scholar.' It looks, however, as though the conjunction goes back even farther. *OED2* has a citation from 1621: 'As becommed a Gentleman and a Scholer'. The phrase was probably born out of a very real respect for anyone who could claim to have both these highest of attributes. Equally as old is the combination 'a gentleman and a soldier'.

(a) gentleman caller A man who calls on a woman and becomes a potential suitor. Also a euphemism for a male lover. The phrase occurs in the script of *Citizen Kane* (US 1941) – 'When I have a gentleman caller . . .' – but the concept is best known from Tennessee Williams's play *The Glass Menagerie* (1944).

(a) gentleman's agreement Meaning, 'an agreement not enforceable at law and only binding as a matter of honour.' Of US origin and not known before the 1920s. A. J. P. Taylor in *English History 1914–1945* (1965) says: 'This absurd phrase was taken by [von] Papen from business usage to describe the agreement between Austria and Germany in July 1936. It was much used hereafter for an agreement with anyone who was obviously not a gentleman and who would obviously not keep his agreement.'

(a) gentleman's gentleman A valet. The phrase was first used in its modern sense by Sheridan in *The Rivals* (1775). In fiction, P. G. Wodehouse's Jeeves is the prime example, and many pedants insist that he is one of these and not a butler. However, note what Wodehouse said in *Bring on the Girls*, Chap. 11 (1954): 'I'm writing some stories about a butler. At least, he's not a butler, he's a valet, but the two species are almost identical.'

gentlemen – be seated!　Stock phrase from the days of black minstrels in the USA, 1840–1900. 'Mr Interlocutor', the white compère, would say this to the minstrels.

gentlemen of the road　Euphemistic name for highwaymen and tramps. In the 18th century, the nickname was used sarcastically as the roads became busy with stage coaches as well as horse-riders and family carriages, but stories were told of certain courtesies during a robbery – a doffed hat to a lady, a wedding ring spared, a helping hand to the infirm. 'Even a highwayman, in the way of trade, may blow out your brains,' writes Hazlitt in *The Fight* (1822), 'but if he uses foul language at the same time, I should say he was no gentleman.' 'Tramps may be costing the National Health Service millions of pounds by flitting from hospital to hospital . . . Gentlemen of the road get first-class accommodation plus medical care, costing up to £100 a week or more' – *The Guardian* (21 April 1975).

gentlemen prefer blondes　*Gentlemen Prefer Blondes* is the title of a novel (1925) by Anita Loos, to which the sequel was *But Gentlemen Marry Brunettes* (1928). Loos is presumed to have originated the phrase, though a lesser-known Irving Berlin song with this title was being performed in 1926, and in the same year there was another song with the title by B. G. De Sylva and Lewis Gensler.

(the) gentle sex　Now non-PC term to describe the female sex. Known by 1583. 'So while fashions may change and student starter packs come and go, no self-respecting young lady need ever find herself unarmed. Parasol or rape alarm, the gentle sex are not what they seem. Let the unsuspecting fresher beware!' – *The Times* (13 March 1995).

gently, Bentley!　Catchphrase spoken by Jimmy Edwards to Dick Bentley in the BBC radio show *Take It From Here* (1948–59).

George – don't do that!　A quotation from Joyce Grenfell's 'Nursery School Sketches' (1953). Grenfell (1910–79), the British monologist, would do entire solo evenings of monologues and songs. This line came from a sketch in which she played a slightly harassed but unflappable teacher. Part of its charm lay in the audience's never knowing precisely what it was that George was being asked not to do. In her book *In Pleasant Places,* Chap. 1 (1979), she noted: 'In my series of nursery-school sketches I always introduced a five-year-old character called George. He is apparently misbehaving and in every sketch I admonish him in that high, bright adult voice that is used to divert attention from some undesirable behaviour . . . "George – don't do that . . ." The misdeed remains unspecified to this day. In America after I had done the sketches on television [on *The Ed Sullivan Show*] I was continually asked what was George doing, but I always answered that I thought it best not to know. And I didn't.'

George, I am a woman with needs　Catchphrase from the ITV sitcom *George and Mildred* (1976–9). Mildred Roper (played by Yootha Joyce) had been in a long-running marriage to George Roper (Brian Murphy), who would go to any lengths to avoid anything of the sort that she was seeking.

George Washington slept here　See QUEEN ELIZABETH.

Germans　See ANOTHER MEAL.

Germany calling, Germany calling!　Call-sign of 'Lord Haw-Haw', nickname of William Joyce, who broadcast Nazi propaganda from Hamburg during the Second World War. He was found guilty of treason (on the technicality that he held a British passport at the beginning of the war) and was hanged in 1946. He had a threatening, sneering, lower-middle-class delivery, which made his call-sign sound more like 'Jarmany calling'. Although Joyce was treated mostly as a joke in wartime Britain, he is credited with giving rise to some unsettling rumours. No one seemed to have heard the particular broadcast in question, but it got about that he had said the clock on Darlington Town Hall was two minutes slow, and so it was supposed to be. The nickname of 'Lord Haw-Haw' was inappropriate as he did not sound the slightest bit aristocratic. *That* sobriquet had originally been applied by Jonah Barrington, the *Daily Express* radio correspondent, to Joyce's predecessor who *did* speak with a cultured accent but lasted only a few weeks from September 1939. This was Norman Baillie-Stewart, who is said to have sounded like the entertainer Claud Hulbert or one of the Western Brothers. An imaginary drawing appeared in the *Daily Express* of a Bertie Woosterish character with a monocle and receding chin. Baillie-Stewart himself said that he understood there was a popular English song called 'We're Going to Hang Out the Washing on the Siegfried Line' which ended 'If the Siegfried Line's still there'. 'Curiously enoff,' he said, 'the Siegfried Line is still they-ah.'

Geronimo! It was during the North African campaign of November 1942 that US paratroopers are said first to have shouted 'Geronimo!' as they jumped out of planes. It then became customary to do so and turned into a popular exclamation akin to 'Eureka!' A number of American Indians in the paratroop units coined and popularized the expression, recalling the actual Apache Geronimo who died in 1909. It is said that when he was being pursued by the army over some steep hills near Fort Sill, Oklahoma, he made a leap on horseback over a sheer cliff into water. As the troops did not dare follow him, he cried 'Geronimo!' as he leapt. Some of the paratroopers who were trained at Fort Bragg and Fort Campbell adopted this shout, not least because it reminded them to breathe deeply during a jump. In 1939, there had been a film entitled *Geronimo*, which may have reminded them. From Christy Brown, *Down All the Days*, Chap. 6 (1970): 'He heard his brothers cry out in unison: "The dirty lousy bastards – hitting a cripple! Geronimo! . . ." And off they flew in maddened pursuit of the ungentlemanly enemy.'

gertcha! This slogan had a burst of popularity in about 1980 when it was used in TV advertisements for Courage Best Bitter in the UK. Various grim-faced drinkers sat around in an East End pub and shouted it out during breaks in the music. Dave Trott, the copywriter responsible for using the word, suggested it derived from 'Get out of it, you!' This is supported by *Partridge/Slang* who was on to it – as 'gercher' – in 1937. The *OED2* has 'get away/along with you' as a 'derisive expression of disbelief'. The line got into the commercial from a song composed by the Cockney singers Chas and Dave. They originally pronounced it 'Wooertcha'.

Gesundheit! Exclamation made when someone sneezes. It is German (and Yiddish) for 'health', but it also has the rhythm of 'God bless you' and of a musical finish (as to a music-hall joke). Recorded as part of English language use by 1914. Sneezing was believed to be the expulsion of an evil spirit, hence the need for such an exclamation. The Romans cried **absit omen [flee, omen]!**

get a life! Admonition suggesting that the person addressed should find him/herself a worthwhile, focused role to play in life. Suddenly popular in the early 1990s, probably from the USA (does it sound a touch Jewish?) The slogan for the film *Thelma and Louise* (US 1991) was: 'Someone Said Get a Life . . . So They Did.' From *The Independent* (27 July 1994): 'Disney is used to taking flak for its cartoons . . . A spokesman said: "These people need to get a life. It's a story. It's fiction."' The title of actor William Shatner's book *Get a Life* (1999) apparently refers to a *Saturday Night Live* skit (date unknown). Also in the form **get yourself a life!** From the *Daily Mail* (27 February 1993): '[Pam Ferris, actress] is not a fan [of the part she plays on TV]. "Ma Larkin," she says, "is a male chauvinist's dream, constantly available and even celebrating her husband's conquests of other women. I'd like to educate Ma a bit. Give her some Germaine Greer to read. Tell her: 'Get yourself a life!' I'd probably split up the Larkins' marriage, be a real cat among the pigeons".'

(to) get along like a house on fire
Meaning to get on together extremely well. One of the clichés cited by Ted Morgan in *Somerset Maugham* (1980) as having been used by the writer in his efforts to achieve

a 'casual style'. 'The two parties express shock, embarrassment, excitement etc, but are soon getting on (or off) like a house on fire. This is all very jolly, but after a short while becomes, like most sex films, unbearably repetitive' – *The Sunday Telegraph* (30 April 1995).

(to) get away from it all Cliché of travel journalism/advertising and meaning 'to have a rest, holiday'. 'Somebody who wants to get away from it all is likely to wind up in a chalet in a Heidi-like village on a mountain' – *National Observer* (USA) (13 March 1976); 'In 1943 where did Churchill go to get away from it all?' – advertisement for the Moroccan National Tourist Office (February 1989).

(the) getaway people Glamorous, dashing folk, akin to the BEAUTIFUL PEOPLE, and so dubbed in an advertising campaign for National Benzole petrol in the UK, from 1963. Bryan Oakes of the London Press Exchange agency told the authors of *The Persuasion Industry* (1965): 'They were the jet set, clean-limbed beautiful girls, the gods and goddesses who did exotic things. We used expensive cars – E-type Jaguars and Aston Martins – and the promise was that, if you get this petrol, you're aligning yourself with those wonderful people, midnight drives on the beach and so on. Of course, it's tough luck – you don't happen to have a Jag just yet, or a girl like that, but any day now . . .'

(to) get away with blue murder (or cry/ scream/yell blue murder) Why is murder blue? It has been suggested that this is a pun on the French exclamation *morbleu!* which sounds as if it means 'blue death' but is actually a version of *mort Dieu* (God's death). The *OED2* notes that blue is 'often made the colour of plagues and things hurtful'. 'Blue murder' as a 'desperate or alarming cry' was recorded by 1859.

(to) get away with something scot-free Not 'scot', as in Scotland, but as in *sceot*, a medieval municipal tax paid to the local bailiff or sheriff – so it means 'tax-free; without penalty'. Known in its modern figurative sense by 1700. 'If we could do that, she might go scot-free for aught I cared' – Charles Dickens, *The Old Curiosity Shop* (1840–1).

get back on your jam jar Said dismissively to someone who is behaving objectionably. This appears to be rhyming slang for 'get back on your tram-car' (i.e. go away). It is not in origin a racial slur alluding to the golliwog figure who appears on jars of Robertson's Jam (although such a use was suggested in 1985).

(to) get laughs merely reading the telephone directory A clichéd compliment to comedy performers who are considered funny whatever their material. 'It has often been said that a comedy team as popular as Kenneth Horne [etc.] . . . can be hilariously funny without the aid of any script at all. "*They'd* get laughs reading the telephone directory!" is a comment often made about them' – *Radio Times* (4 March 1965).

get off my cloud! Leave me alone! Presumably, the image evoked is of someone sitting peacefully on a tuft of cloud in heaven. The phrase was popularized by the song 'Get Off My Cloud', recorded by the Rolling Stones in 1965.

(to) get one's feet under the table Phrase used, especially in trades unions and the business world, to suggest the point at which real work ('substantive negotiations') starts to be done. Date of origin unknown. Identified as a current cliché by Howard Dimmock of Westcliff-on-Sea in a letter to the *Sunday Times* (31 December 1989). 'The Social Affairs Unit has performed a public service by drawing attention, in a pamphlet published today, to the fact that counselling has been allowed to get its feet under the national table without serious examination of its medical or philosophical credentials' – *The Daily Telegraph* (2 May 1994); 'The IRA cessation of violence was announced on 31 August; the historic handshake between Mr Reynolds and Gerry Adams took place on 6 September; and yesterday Sinn Fein got its feet under the political table in Dublin' – *The Independent* (29 October 1994); 'Private sector's feet "under the operating table": MP lists contracts going outside NHS' – headline in *The Herald* (Glasgow) (9 March 1995).

(to) get one's goat To be annoyed by something. 'The way she carries on, that really gets my goat!' Apparently another Americanism that has passed into general use (and current by 1910), this expression can also be found in French as *prendre la chèvre*, 'to take the milch-goat'. One is always suspicious of explanations that go on to explain that, of course, goats were very important to poor people and if anyone were to get a man's goat . . . etc. One is even more unimpressed by the explanation given by *Morris* (1977): 'It used to be a fairly common practice to stable a goat with a thoroughbred [horse], the theory being that the goat's presence would help the high-strung nag to keep its composure. If the goat were stolen the night before a big race, the horse might be expected to lose its poise and blow the race.' Robert L. Shook in *The Book of Why* (1983) wonders, interestingly, whether it has anything to do with a 'goatee' (a beard like a goat's). If you got someone by the 'goat', it would certainly annoy them. All one can do is to point to the number of idioms referring to goats – 'act the goat', 'giddy goat', 'scapegoat' – and, once more, emphasize the alliteration. Another version is 'to get one's nanny-goat'.

(to) get one's kit off To undress, take one's clothes off. Originally from removing one's football kit or other sports gear but, in the early 1990s in the UK, increasingly applied to actors and actresses or any other exhibitionists revealing their naked-ness. 'In the late Sixties and early Seventies directors banged on endlessly about the artistic integrity of their nude scenes, though it was strange, as Bernard Levin perceptively observed, that only pretty women seemed to be required to get their kit off. Chaps still clung cravenly to their Y-fronts, and older, uglier women were generally spared strip-tease duties' – *The Daily Telegraph* (29 April 1994).

(to) get one's oar in (also **to put/stick . . .**) To interfere in an unwelcome fashion with what someone else is doing or to interrupt what they are saying. From an older expression, 'to have an oar in another man's boat'. Known by 1543.

(to) get on (some)one's wick To get on (some)one's nerves. 'You really get on my wick, y'know that?' As *Street Talk* (1986) explained: 'The expression, oddly enough,

comes from "Hampton Wick", an area of London, which became rhyming slang for "prick".' Known by 1945.

(to) get out of one's pram Meaning, 'to get angry, over-excited'. Learned debate over this phrase followed in the wake of Neil Kinnock's use of 'Schultz got out of his pram' to describe US Secretary of State George Schultz during the Labour leader's visit to Washington in February 1984. Mr Kinnock said: 'It's a colloquialism. I believe it is becoming more common in its usage. It means Mr Schultz was departing from his normal diplomatic calm. Nothing so undiplomatic as losing his temper.' Nevertheless, other forms are more widely known. London East End and Glasgow slang both have, 'Don't get out of your pram about it', when someone is 'off his head' about something. A touch of OFF ONE'S TROLLEY seems to be involved, too.

get out of that! What one might say to anyone in a tricky situation but used as part of a 'visual catchphrase' by the British comedians Morecambe and Wise on TV shows starting in the early 1960s. Eric Morecambe would put his hand under Ernie Wise's chin, as in a judo hold, and say the line. The pair's other 'visual catchphrases' included: the 'throttling' of Eric, which appeared to happen as he went through the gap in the theatre curtain but was, of course, self-administered; the imaginary stone that thudded into a paper bag held out to catch it; Eric's spectacles hooked over one ear but under the other; the rapid self-slap on the back of the neck; Eric's two-handed slap of Ernie's cheeks; the shoulder hug; and the characteristic dance with hands alternately behind head and bottom while the pair hopped in deliberate emulation of Groucho Marx.

(to) get someone's number To find out what sort of character a person has or what motivates him/her. Origin obscure. 'Whenever a person proclaims to you "In worldly matters I'm a child" . . . you have got that person's number and it's Number One' – Charles Dickens, *Bleak House*, Chap. 57 (1853). 'Yes, duckie, we've all got your number' – Kenneth Williams in the BBC radio show *Round the Horne* (25 December 1966) and *passim*.

gets rid of film on teeth　Slogan for Pepsodent, current in the USA in the early 1900s. It was another of advertising guru Claude C. Hopkins's great coups – to claim something that every toothpaste could claim and get away with it. In *My Life in Advertising* (1927) he commented: 'People do not want to read of penalties. They want to be told of rewards . . . People want to be told the ways to happiness and cheer . . . I resolved to advertise this toothpaste as a creator of beauty.'

(to) get the bird (or be given the bird) Meaning, 'to be rejected by an audience'. Originally the expression was 'to get the big bird' and has been used as such since the 19th century. What do audiences do when they do not like something? They boo or they hiss, sounding something like a flock of geese, perhaps.

get thee behind me, Satan!　Nowadays an exclamation used in answer to the mildest call to temptation. It comes originally from St Matthew 16:23, where Jesus Christ rebukes Peter with the phrase for something he has said.

getting there is half the fun　This expression sloganizes Robert Louis Stevenson's views: 'I travel not to go anywhere, but to go' and 'to travel hopefully is a better thing than to arrive'. It also reflects 'the journey not the arrival matters' – an expression used as the title of an autobiographical volume by Leonard Woolf (1969). As a slogan, it may have been used to advertise Cunard steamships in the 1920s/30s. It was definitely used to promote the Peter Sellers film *Being There* (US 1980) in the form, 'Getting there is half the fun. Being there is all of it.' In *Up the Organisation* (1970), Robert Townshend commented on getting to the top: 'Getting there isn't half the fun – it's all the fun.'

(to) get under someone's skin　(1) To annoy or upset them greatly. (2) To empathize with them. Presumably the image is of some disease getting under the skin. Known since 1896 and 1927, respectively. In the famous song by Cole Porter 'I've Got You Under My Skin' (1936), the malady of love is, of course, regarded as a benign contagion.

get up them stairs!　A reference to the prospect of sexual intercourse. *Partridge/ Catch Phrases* finds it in 1942 with 'Blossom' added. Denis Gifford in *The Golden Age of Radio* (1985) gives it as comedian Hal Monty's catchphrase (noting that it seems to have escaped the BBC's BLUE PENCIL).

get your coat, you've pulled!　Alleged chat-up line from the late 1990s – 'by conceited but self-confident lothario . . . the assumption [being] that the woman is in search of a sexual partner and has got lucky . . . See also "My name's Chris. I'm telling you that now, so you know what to scream later on"' – John Walsh in *The Independent* (2 December 2000).

(to) get your ducks in a row　To get everything lined up ready to do something, to be prepared. Date of origin unknown but probably by the mid-20th century. The allusion may be to ducks in a shooting gallery or maybe just to the fact that ducks do tend to swim in a line.

—— get your gun　Even if the title of Irving Berlin's 1946 musical *Annie Get Your Gun* was utterly suitable for the tale of Annie Oakley, the gun-toting gal, it does appear to have been an allusion. 'Johnny Get Your Gun', written by 'F. Belasco' (Monroe H. Rosenfeld) was published in New York (1886) and was a popular American song of the First World War. *Punch* (17 February 1915) has the phrase 'Johnny, get your gun', and Dalton Trumbo's film *Johnny Got His Gun* (US 1971) was about a badly mutilated soldier in the 1914–18 war.

get your hair cut!　Catchphrase from British music hall. Some say it was the property of the comedian George Beauchamp (1863–1901) who sang it in a song, 'Johnnie Get Your Hair Cut'. Others would have that it comes from a song popularized by Harry Champion (and written by Fred Murray) (see GINGER, YOU'RE BARMY!) Either way, it seems to have been current in the years 1880–1900, especially so at the end of the period. It was eventually, of course, the sort of thing sergeant-majors would bawl at new recruits, though perhaps originally it might have been addressed to long-haired aesthetes of the 1880s/90s.

get your retaliation in first Expression credited to Carwyn James, British sports coach (1929–83). 'The Government was trying to get its retaliation in first, as we realised it would. The phrase, by the way, comes from the late Carwyn James, the coach to the British Isles rugby team who beat New Zealand in 1971. It is now freely used by people who would be hard to tell the difference between a rugby ball and a boiled egg. James, who liked Chekhov and gin-and-tonic, would have been pleased to be remembered in the dictionaries of quotation as well as in the record books' – Alan Watkins, *Independent on Sunday* (18 February 1996). Also recorded in *The Guardian* (7 November 1989) and applied to other sports, possibly before this.

get your tanks off my lawn The first recorded use of this political metaphor for 'back off, don't threaten me' was by the British Prime Minister, Harold Wilson. According to Peter Jenkins, *The Battle of Downing Street* (1970), Wilson said it to Hugh Scanlon, the trade union leader, at Chequers, the prime ministerial residence, in June 1969, during the battle between the Government and the trade unions over reform. Scanlon was head of Britain's second largest union, the engineers'. Jenkins reports that Wilson was enraged at the intransigence and arrogance of Scanlon and Jack Jones, another union leader. In an exchange of views, Scanlon said, 'Prime Minister, we don't want you to become another Ramsay Macdonald' (that is, betraying the Labour movement). Wilson replied, 'I have no intention of becoming another Ramsay Macdonald. Nor do I intend to become another Dubcek. Get your tanks off my lawn, Hughie!' Subsequently it has entered the lexicon of British politics and journalism. From the *Financial Times* (6 November 1982) on the Harrods/Lonrho dispute: '[Professor Roland Smith, chairman, House of Fraser:] If this is your idea of a game, please play somewhere else in the future . . . To make it absolutely clear: get your tanks off my lawn.' From *The Observer* (14 April 1991): 'It is true, of course, that the Home Secretary does not park his tanks on [BBC Director-General] Checkland's lawn . . . That is not the British way.' From a speech made by John Major to the Conservative Party Conference, 8 October 1993: 'Let me say to some of our European colleagues, "You're playing with fire [on GATT world free trade talks]," or to put it more bluntly, "Get your tractors off our lawn".'

ghastly good taste Title of a book (1933), subtitled 'a depressing story of the Rise and Fall of English Architecture', in which its author, John Betjeman, concludes: 'We have seen in this book how English architecture emerged from the religious unity of Christendom to the reasoned unity of an educated monarchic system, and then to the stranger order of an industrialised community. As soon as it became unsettled, towards the end of the nineteenth century, "architecture" *qua* architecture became self-conscious.' This probably applies equally to design in general.

(the) ghost walks (on Friday) Meaning, 'it's pay day' (for actors). The expression (current by 1833) is said to date from a touring company's production of *Hamlet*. The cast had been unpaid for many weeks and when Hamlet said of his father's ghost: 'Perchance 'twill walk again,' the ghost replied: 'Nay, 'twill walk no more until its salary is paid.' Consequently, a theatrical manager who hands out the pay has sometimes been called a 'ghost'.

giant See HE WAS A BIG.

(to make a) giant stride (forward) Date of origin unknown. 'Britain took a giant stride towards becoming self-supporting in oil yesterday' – *The Guardian* (1 September 1972); 'The Government's rate-capping plan was "yet another giant stride along the path of tight Whitehall control over life in Britain"' – *The Daily Telegraph* (28 September 1983); 'Giant stride forward for a mint Murray' – headline [about athlete], *The Observer* (21 May 1995).

giddy aunt See MY GIDDY.

(the) gift of the gab Eloquence in speech (but usually applied somewhat pejoratively), where 'gab' = 'gob' = 'mouth'. Known by 1785 and, as 'the gift of the gob, by 1695. 'He was perfectly aware that the milkman was a rare one with his jokes . . . The way girls fell for anyone with the gift of the gab – that was what embittered Constable Plimmer' – P. G. Wodehouse, 'The Romance of an Ugly Policeman' (1917); *The Gift of the Gab: a guide to sparkling chat* – title of a book (1985) by Nigel Rees.

(to) gild the lily   Meaning, 'to attempt to improve something that is already attractive and risk spoiling it'. In Shakespeare's *King John*, IV.ii.11 (1596), Salisbury speaks what may be the original form: 'To be possess'd with double pomp, / To guard a title that was rich before, / To gild refined gold, to paint the lily / . . . Is wasteful and ridiculous excess'. The Arden edition notes that 'to gild gold' was a common expression in Shakespeare's time.

Ginger, you're barmy!   Addressed to any male, this street cry merely means he is stupid or crazy. It may date from the early 1900s and most probably originated in the British music-hall song with the title 'Ginger, You're Balmy [the alternative spelling]!' written by Fred Murray and published in 1912. This was sung by Harry Champion (1866–1942). In the song the next phrase is 'Get your hair cut!' Also, in the chorus, there occurs another line sometimes coupled with the 'Ginger, you're barmy!' – 'Why don't you join the army'. *Ginger, You're Barmy* was used as the title of a novel (1962) by David Lodge. Separately, the word 'ginger' has been applied in the UK to male homosexuals (since the 1930s, at least) on account of the rhyming slang, 'ginger beer = queer'. 'Ginger' is also the name given to a red-headed man. But neither of these appears relevant to the song. Ian Gillies commented (1995): 'The plot of "Ginger" is very similar [to another Champion song] "Any Old Iron" – someone who fancies himself well dressed, being shouted at in the one case because of his "old iron" watch-chain, and in the other because he isn't wearing a hat and not, apparently, because he is ginger. Indeed, there is no specific reference to his being ginger.' Here are the lines: '"Don't walk a-bout with your cady [= hat] on; / Ginger, you're balmy! / Get your hair cut!", they all be-gin to cry. / With nothing on your nap-per, oh, you are a pie! / Pies must have a lit-tle bit of crust, / Why don't you join the army? /

If you want to look a don you want a bit of something on – / Ginger, you're balmy!'

(to) gird up one's loins   To prepare for action – especially battle – or for a journey. *Brewer* (1894) explains the biblical origin of this expression thus: 'The Jews wore a girdle [or belt] only when at work or on a journey. Even to the present day, Eastern people, who wear loose dresses, gird them about the loins.' There are several references in the Old Testament, for example: 'Gird up thy loins, and take my staff in thine hand, and go thy way' – 2 Kings 4:29. 'As Britain prepares to help launch the first Western war of the new century, the usual brigade of do-gooders are reflexively girding their anoraks to oppose it' – *The Spectator* (14 December 2002).

(a) girl in every port   Benefit supposedly enjoyed by sailors. The phrase was used as the title of a film (US 1928) with Louise Brooks. The more venerable version of the phrase is **a wife in every port**, which occurs for example in the caption to a *Punch* cartoon (22 May 1907) and as far back as Isaac Bickerstaffe's play *Thomas and Sally* (1761). In Charles Dibdin's 'Jack in his Element' (1790), there is: 'In every mess I find a friend, / In every port a wife.' And in John Gay's *Sweet William's Farewell to Black-Eyed Susan* (1720): 'They'll tell thee, sailors, when away, / In ev'ry port a mistress find.'

gi'us a job, I could do that (or **gizza job . . .)**   Rare example of a catchphrase coming out of a TV *drama* series. Alan Bleasdale's *The Boys from the Blackstuff* (about unemployment in Liverpool) was first shown on BBC TV in 1982 and introduced the character of Yosser Hughes. His plea became a nationally repeated catchphrase, not least because of the political ramifications. It was chanted by football crowds in Liverpool and printed on T-shirts with Yosser confronting Prime Minister Margaret Thatcher. From *The Observer* (30 January 1983): 'At Anfield nowadays whenever the Liverpool goal-keeper makes a save, the Kop affection-ately chants at him the catch-phrase of Yosser Hughes: "We could do that." It's a slogan which might usefully rise to the lips of the chairbound viewer just as often.' In

fact, there were *two* phrases here, sometimes used independently and sometimes
together in a different form, 'I can do that.
Gi'us a job.'

(to) give a dog a bad name   Meaning
'say bad things about a person and they'll
stick', this possibly comes from the longer
'Give a dog a bad name and hang him'
(known by 1818), suggesting that if a dog
has a reputation for ferocity, it might as
well be killed because no one will trust it.

give 'im (or 'er) the money, Barney!
Catchphrase from the BBC radio show
Have A Go (1946–67). This was the cry
when a winner was established (sometimes with a good deal of help from the
host, Wilfred Pickles). The 'Barney' in
question was Barney Colehan, a BBC
producer (d. 1991). Later, Mrs Pickles
supervised the prizes – hence the alternative **give 'im/'er the money, Mabel!** and
the references to **Mabel at the table** and
the query **what's on the table, Mabel?**
Winners of the quiz took away not cars or
consumer goods or holidays abroad but
pots of jam and the odd shilling or two.

(to) give (or grant) no quarter   Not to
concede any ground. Previously, 'give
quarter' meant to spare the life of an
enemy in one's power. Known by 1645.
An old theory that 'quarter' referred to the
share of a soldier's pay that would be
claimed as ransom does not seem to stand
up. Perhaps, rather, it refers to the *quarters*
a prisoner would have to occupy. From
The Times (30 July 1900): [Kaiser Wilhelm
II said at Bremerhaven] 'No quarter will be
given, no prisoners will be taken. Let all
who fall into your hands be at your
mercy.'

give order!   The injunction 'Give order –
thank you, please!' became nationally
known in the UK when Colin Crompton
used it to members of Granada TV's
Wheeltappers' and Shunters' Social Club
(1974–7). 'I had been including the club
chairman character in my variety act for
some years,' Crompton said in 1979,
'before Johnny Hamp of Granada suggested that we build a sketch round it for
inclusion in the stage version of *The
Comedians*. This led to *Wheeltappers*. Like
most successful catchphrases it was

manufactured. It has been used by club
concert chairmen for years – and still is.'
Crompton also used the version **best of
order!** In Christy Brown's novel *Down All
the Days*, Chap. 15 (1970), we have the cry
(at a social gathering): 'Best of order now
for the singer!' Of his phrase, **on behalf of
the committee-ee!**, Crompton said:
'Letters by the score told me my catchphrases were a schoolteacher's nightmare.
And we had so many children outside the
house, shouting them out, that we were
forced to move to a quieter neighbourhood! Although it is several years since the
last programme was transmitted, the
phrases have remained popular and I'm
flattered that most impressionists include
them in their acts.'

give over   See RIGHT MONKEY.

**(to) give someone (or get given) the
sack**   The suggestion is that this expression dates from the days when workers
would carry the tools of their trade around
with them, from job to job, in a bag which
they would leave with their employer.
When their services were no longer
required, they would be given the bag
back. Known in English since 1825, but in
French since the 17th century as '*On luy a
donné son sac*'.

**(to) give someone the topmost brick off
the chimney (stack)**   Metaphorical act of
adoration. *Partridge/Slang* suggests that
the phrase means 'to be the acme of
generosity, with implication that foolish
spoiling, or detriment to the donor would
result, as in "his parents'd give that boy
the . . ." or "she's that soft-hearted, she'd
give you . . ."' Partridge's reviser, Paul
Beale, who inserted this entry, commented
that he had heard the phrase in the early
1980s, but that it was probably in use
much earlier. Indeed, when Anthony
Trollope was standing for parliament in
1868, he described a seat at Westminster as
'the highest object of ambition to every
educated Englishman' and 'the top brick of
the chimney'. *Casson/Grenfell* includes,
'Very particular we are – it's top brick off
the chimney or nothing.' In 1985, Denis
Thatcher, husband of the then Prime
Minister Margaret Thatcher, was quoted as
having said: 'I like everything my beloved

wife likes. If she wants to buy the top brick of St Paul's, then I would buy it.' Presumably, Denis was reworking the chimney-stack version for his own ends. Unconsciously, he may also have been conflating it with another kind of reference, such as is found in Charles Dickens, *Martin Chuzzlewit*, Chap. 38, (1844): 'He would as soon have thought of the cross upon the top of St Paul's Cathedral taking note of what he did . . . as of Nadgett's being engaged in such an occupation.'

(to) give someone (or **be given) the willies** Meaning, 'to frighten (or be frightened)' – as in 'that gave me the willies'. *OED2* suggests a US 19th-century origin. Another possible source is 'wiffle woffle', meaning stomach-ache. Note also that in the ballet *Giselle* (Paris 1841) there are things called *Wilis* – spirits of maidens who die before marriage. The fairy chorus in the Gilbert and Sullivan opera *Iolanthe* (1882) sings: 'Willahalah,! Willaloo', and this has been compared to the wailing of the Rhinedaughters in Wagner's *Das Rheingold* (1869): 'Wag-a-la-weia, Wa-la-la, Wei-la-la, Weia'. Could there be some common thread running through all these wails?

(to) give something more/some welly Meaning, 'to put in more/some effort'. Dates from the 1970s, in British use. 'Wellies' is, of course, a common name for waterproof, rubber (Wellington) boots, so perhaps the image is that of a booted foot being applied to a spade in some digging task that requires a good deal of effort.

give the man a (big) cigar! Give him a prize, reward! Opinion is that this complimentary cry is of American origin and originated when cigars were awarded to the winners of games or of prizes at fairgrounds. The British equivalent seems to have been **give the gentleman a coconut**. There is also the related phrase **close, but no cigar**, perhaps stemming from US sporting use. Did Groucho Marx ever say it (or indeed gave cigars as prizes) on his radio and TV quiz show, *You Bet Your Life*? This ran from 1947 to 1961 (and also ran in London, disastrously, for a season as plain *Groucho*). From the show came the memorable comment when a contestant said the reason for her

bearing twenty-two children was that she loved her husband. Groucho commented: 'Yes, and I like my cigar but I take it out once in a while.' History records that this was cut from the broadcast . . . Chico Marx does say 'And the boy gets a cigar!' in *Duck Soup* (US 1933). In the 1940s, the comedian Charlie Chester had a mildly derisive catchphrase, **give the boy an Oscar**, on his BBC radio show.

Gladly, my cross-eyed bear Mondegreen (mishearing by a child) known widely since the 1950s or 1960s at least. Clearly the phrase must have been used by the time that John Hopkins so entitled an episode of his TV drama *Talking To a Stranger* (1966). The joke rather depends on there having been a line 'gladly my [*or* the] cross I'd bear' in some hymn or other. But which hymn? The one popularly known as 'The Old Rugged Cross', written by the Reverend George Bennard in 1913, contains the lines, 'To the old rugged cross I will ever be true, / Its shame and reproach gladly bear . . .' Ed McBain's thriller entitled *Gladly the Cross-Eyed Bear* (1996) attributes the quotation, however, to 'Keep Thou My Way' by the blind American hymnodist Fanny Crosby (1820–1915), who is credited with writing more than 9,000 of the things . . . The line alluded to occurs in the third stanza, thus: 'Keep Thou my all, O Lord, / Hide my life in Thine; / O let Thy sacred light, / O'er my pathway shine; / Kept by Thy tender care, / Gladly the cross I'll bear, / Hear Thou and grant my prayer, / Hide my life in Thine.'

glasses See BUT MISS.

(the) glass of fashion The dictating of fashion in clothing. A quotation from Shakespeare, *Hamlet*, III.i.152 (1600–1): 'O! what a noble mind is here o'erthrown . . . / The glass of fashion, and the mould of form.' Ophelia is lamenting Hamlet's apparent madness and decline. This is what he once was: a person upon whom others modelled themselves and who dictated what fashion should be. *The Glass of Fashion* was used as the title of a play by Sydney Grundy, first staged at the Globe, London, in the 1880s; also as the title of book (1954) by Cecil Beaton.

(the) glittering prizes Phrase from the Rectorial Address at Glasgow University by F. E. Smith, 1st Earl of Birkenhead (7 November 1923): 'The world continues to offer glittering prizes to those who have stout hearts and sharp swords.' *The Glittering Prizes* was the title of the BBC TV drama series (1976) by Frederic Raphael, about a group of Cambridge graduates.

(all that) glitters is not gold Meaning 'appearances may be deceptive', the allusion is to Shakespeare's *The Merchant of Venice*, II.vii.65 (1596): 'All that *glisters* is not gold, / Often have you heard that told.' As indicated, the proverb was common by Shakespeare's time. *CODP* quotes a Latin version – '*Non omne quod nitet aurum est* [not all that shines is gold]' and also an English one in Chaucer. The now obsolete word 'glisters' rather than 'glitters' or 'glistens' was commonly used in the saying from the 17th century onwards, though in poetic use; Thomas Gray, for example, used 'glisters' in his 'Ode on the Death of A Favourite Cat drowned in a Tub of Gold Fishe' (1748).

(the) global village Phrase from Marshall McLuhan's dictum that: 'The new electronic interdependence recreates the world in the image of a global village' – *The Gutenberg Galaxy* (1962). From 1979, *David Frost's Global Village* was the title of an occasional Yorkshire TV series in which Frost discussed global issues with pundits beamed in by satellite.

(the) Glorious Revolution When King James II was removed from the English throne in 1688 and replaced by William and Mary of Orange, the process came to be variously described as the 'bloodless' and 'glorious' revolution. But by whom first and when? By 1749, Henry Fielding was writing in *Tom Jones* (Bk 8, Chap. 14): 'I remained concealed, til the news of the Glorious Revolution put an end to all my apprehensions of danger.' Before that, *OED2* finds only other epithets: 'great revolution' in 1689 and 'prodigious revolution' in 1688 itself. At about this turn of the century, it was occasionally also called 'the happy revolution'. 'That glorious Revolution' was, however, applied in 1725 to the overthrow of the Rump Parliament in 1660. By

about 1690 a club was founded in Northampton to celebrate the William and Mary 'glorious revolution' and by 1692 'Glorious' had acquired a capital G. If this is true, it would confirm that something like the phrase arose very early on. Indeed, Robert Spencer, Earl of Sunderland (a Secretary of State under Charles II and James II) used the term 'glorious undertaking' in a letter to King William on 8 March 1689.

(the) Glorious Twelfth (or simply **the Twelfth)** Name for the 12th of August, when grouse-shooting legally begins in Britain, was current by 1895 and was possibly devised in emulation of 'The Glorious First of June', a sea battle in the French revolutionary war (and known as such since 1794). Compare 'the Twelfth' (of July), celebrated by Protestants in Northern Ireland to commemorate the Battle of the Boyne (1 July 1690, Old Style) at which William III defeated James II.

(the) gloves are off Phrase used to describe when a dispute becomes serious. By allusion to boxing in which, when the gloves are taken off, one is left with a bare-knuckle fight. Date of origin unknown. 'We've got to take the gloves off and we're in a bare knuckle fight on some of the things we've got to do. Because we've got to have an effective and a prosperous industry, and it matters to the people of this country' – Sir Terence Beckett, speech, Confederation of British Industry conference (November 1980); 'Tottenham chairman Alan Sugar warned his manager Ossie Ardiles today that the gloves are off. The crucial, battling 2–0 win at Oldham has kept Spurs in the Premiership but it is clear that the tough talking is only just beginning' – *Evening Standard* (London) (6 May 1994); 'The European Elections: Gloves are off for main parties as posters paint divisions on Europe with the zeal of an advertising campaign' – headline in *The Independent* (26 May 1994); 'If Murdoch can offer big bucks and get them, then so can we. The gloves are off now. We don't like some of the amounts we are having to offer but, if that is what is necessary, that is what will happen. We are fighting for survival here' – *The Guardian* (29 April 1995). Probably this has grown out of the expression **with**

the gloves off – meaning (figuratively) bare-fisted, ready for a fight, setting to without mercy, in earnest. Known by 1827 in the USA. 'There were now eighteen days left to the campaign, and Mr Nixon was free to take the gloves off and "peak" in his own manner' – Theodore H. White, *The Making of the President 1960* (1961); 'Indications that this latest radio wannabe is ready to take off the gloves in the fight for listeners came this week . . .' – *The Independent* (10 June 1995).

gnarled old fishermen Would-be picturesque phrase from travel writing. Date of origin unknown. Listed in *The Independent* 'DIY travel writers' cliché kit' (31 December 1988). 'A few miles south of Barfleur is St-Vaast-la-Hougue which has the sort of fishing harbour which guidebooks describe as "picturesque" and being full of "gnarled old fishermen" – *The Independent* (1 October 1988); 'Its members were indeed fishermen and "beach boys", who were not what one might expect at Bondi Beach or Malibu, but entrusted with the task of hauling the fishing-boats on to the shingle, and were often as gnarled and weather-beaten as the old, tarred lugger on view in the town's maritime museum' – *The Times* (18 March 1989); 'The traditional view is instantly recognizable on entering Penlee Art Gallery in Penzance, a brief journey away across a windswept moor. Here are the Gnarled Fishwives of Walter Langley, Percy Craft's weary Fishermen and Garstin's evocative The Rain it Raineth Every Day' – *The Independent* (27 November 1990).

(the) Gnomes of Zurich Term used to disparage the tight-fisted speculators in the Swiss financial capital who questioned Britain's creditworthiness and who forced austerity measures on the Labour government of Prime Minister Harold Wilson when it came to power in 1964. George Brown, Secretary of State for Economic Affairs, popularized the term in November of that year. Wilson himself had, however, used it long before in a speech to the House of Commons (12 November 1956), referring to 'all the little gnomes in Zurich and other financial centres'. In 1958, Andrew Shonfield wrote in *British Economic Policy Since the War*: 'Hence the

tragedy of the autumn of 1957, when the Chancellor of the Exchequer [Peter Thorneycroft] adopted as his guide to action the slogan: I must be hard-faced enough to match the mirror-image of an imaginary hard-faced little man in Zurich. It is tough on the Swiss that William Tell should be displaced in English folklore by this new image of a gnome in a bank at the end of a telephone line.' ('Lord Gnome', the wealthy and unscrupulous supposed proprietor of *Private Eye* was presumably named after the 1964 use.)

go See DO NOT PASS.

go ahead, make my day 'Do what you like, see if I care, be my guest' – a laconicism. In March 1985, President Ronald Reagan told the American Business Conference: 'I have my veto pen drawn and ready for any tax increase that Congress might even think of sending up. And I have only one thing to say to the tax increasers. Go ahead – make my day.' For once, he was not quoting from one of his own film roles, or old Hollywood. The line was originally spoken by Clint Eastwood, himself brandishing a .44 Magnum, to a gunman he was holding at bay in *Sudden Impact* (1983). At the end of the film he says (to another villain, similarly armed), 'Come on, make my day.' In neither case does he add 'punk', as is sometimes supposed. (This may come from confusion with *Dirty Harry* in which he holds a .44 Magnum to the temple of a criminal and says 'Well, do ya [feel lucky], punk?') The phrase may have been eased into Reagan's speech by having appeared in a parody of the *New York Post* put together by editors, many of them anti-Reagan, in the autumn of 1984. Reagan was shown starting a nuclear war by throwing down this dare to the Kremlin. Information from *Time Magazine* (25 March 1985).

goat See GET ONE'S.

go (and) boil your head! 'Go away, don't be silly!' Probably known by 1900, especially in Scots use.

(to) go at something baldheaded Meaning, 'to act without regard for the consequences, to go at something full tilt' – e.g. from J. R. Lowell, *The Biglow Papers* (1848): 'I scent what pays the best, an' then / Go into it baldheaded.' This is thought to be an American expression, dating from the 19th century. The suggestion is that of a man who would tackle a problem as though he had just rushed out of the house without putting on his wig, or without wearing a hat. Earlier sources have been suggested – notably that the Marquis of Granby, a colonel of the Blues, led a cavalry charge at the Battle of Warburg (1760) despite his hat and wig falling off. He was an enormously popular figure (hence the number of British pubs named after him), but it is unlikely that his fame was sufficient to have led to the expression being used in the USA. In addition, there is no record of the expression being used in connection with Granby earlier than 1915.

——, God Bless 'er/'im Originally a toast to Royalty, this gradually turned into a more general, genial way of referring to such people and others. From George Eliot, *Felix Holt* (1866): 'You'll rally round the throne – and the King, God bless him, and the usual toasts.' Robert Louis Stevenson in 'Random Memories 1. The Coast of Fife' (1892) has: 'For the sake of the cat, God bless her!' From *Punch*, Vol. 120 (1902): 'The Queen God Bless 'Er.' In *Busman's Honeymoon*, Chap. 7 (1937), Dorothy L. Sayers has 'The ladies. God bless them!' said by a man in a faintly patronizing way, and the American cartoonist Helen Hokinson has one of her collections entitled *The Ladies, God Bless 'Em* (1950). Robert Lacey revived the custom in 1990 with a book entitled *The Queen Mother, God Bless Her*.

God bless the Duke of Argyll! What Scots Highlanders were supposed to exclaim when scratching themselves. Why? Because a Duke of Argyll is said to have erected scratching posts on his estates for cattle and sheep. His herdsmen would use the posts for the same purpose and give this shout by way of thanks for the relief they afforded. Nobody knows which Duke this was or when the saying became established. *Brewer* (1894), while relating the foregoing, spells it 'Argyle'.

God help the poor sailors . . . Exclamation by a land-lubber on a stormy night. 'My grandmother on the North East coast would exclain "heaven help the sailors on a night like this!" when the wind howled around the house' – Ian Forsyth, Co. Durham (2000). Compare, from *Partridge/ Catch Phrases*: 'Pity the poor sailor on a night like this!' and 'God help sailors on a night like this.'

God is an Englishman Saying that became the title of a novel (1970) by R. F. Delderfield and which may derive from an untraced saying of George Bernard Shaw (1856–1950): 'The ordinary Britisher imagines that God is an Englishman.' But the view is of long standing. Harold Nicolson recorded in his diary on 3 June 1942 that three years before, R. S. Hudson, the Minister of Agriculture, was being told by the Yugoslav minister in London of the dangers facing Britain. 'Yes,' replied Hudson, 'you are probably correct and these things may well happen. But you forget that God is English.' Compare (from the address to the new intake of naval ratings at *Royal Arthur* by the camp chaplain, mid-1940s) '"God," he told us in an inane parsonical bray, "is the highest officer in the British Navy"' – George Melly, *Rum, Bum and Concertina*, Chap. 1 (1977).

God is in the details Saying usually stated to have originated with the German-born architect Ludwig Mies Van Der Rohe (1886–1969), sometimes in the form: '[The dear] God is in the details [*der liebe Gott steckt im Detail*].' The architect's obituary in *The New York Times* (1969) attributed this saying to Mies, but it also appears to have been a favourite of the German art historian Aby Warburg (though E. M. Gombrich, his biographer, is not certain that it originated with him). In the form *Le bon Dieu est dans le détail*, it has also been attributed to Gustave Flaubert (1821–80). Compare Arthur Miller: 'Generalisation is the death of art. It is in the details where god resides' – quoted in *The Observer*, 'Sayings of the Week' (9 April 1995). Subsequently, there has arisen the saying **the devil is in the detail**, which has been described as a maxim of the German pop musician Blixa Bargeld. He probably did not invent it himself as it is mentioned in Lutz Röhrich's *Lexikon der sprichwörtlichen Redensarten* (1994) – as '*Der Teufel steckt im Detail*'.

God is not mocked   Favourite text of the super-religious when confronted with any form of blasphemy. From Galatians 6:7: 'Be not deceived; God is not mocked: for whatsoever a man soweth, that shall he also reap.' The New English Bible chooses rather to say that 'God is not to be fooled', which does not convey the same element of abusiveness towards the deity.

Godiva   See PEEPING TOM.

God love you   Famous signing-off line of the Most Reverend Fulton J. Sheen (1895–1979), Auxiliary (Roman Catholic) Bishop of New York. He presented highly popular religious TV shows called *Life Is Worth Living* and *The Bishop Sheen Program* in the period 1952–68.

God moves in a mysterious way   A direct quotation from No. 35 of the *Olney Hymns* (1779) by William Cowper. The hymn continues: '. . . His wonders to perform'.

(to) go down a bomb (or **go a bomb**)   To go over really well, 'with a bang' – though probably 'very fast' was the original image evoked. Known by 1962. This is very much a positive British expression to be compared with the negative American **to bomb**, meaning to fail, crash, come to grief. 'Heller was subsequently distracted by the writing and production of his first stage play – an army comedy called *We Bombed In New Haven*, which, indeed, bombed on Broadway' – *Independent on Sunday* (25 September 1994).

(to) go down like a lead balloon   To fail in an unsuccessful venture. Presumably the image is of something plummeting madly down. *DOAS* has 'lead balloon', in the USA, by 1960: 'A failure; a plan, joke, action or the like that elicits no favorable response; a flop; anything that lays an egg.' By 1968, the variation **lead zeppelin** was known – spelt thus as the title of an unsuccessful TV pilot comedy show (in the UK) – and **Led Zeppelin** as the name of a successful British rock group that was formed in that year, both presumably alluding to the type of airship, named after Count Ferdinand von Zeppelin (d. 1917), the German aeronautical pioneer who designed and built them (*circa* 1900). The spelling of 'led' was designed to reduce

the likelihood of mispronunciation, especially in the USA.

(to) go down the tubes   To be lost, finished, in trouble. An Americanism meaning 'to go down the drain', where 'toob' = 'drain'. First recorded in the early 1960s.

God protect me from my friends   The full expression is: 'I can look after my enemies, but God protect me from my friends.' *CODP* traces it to 1477 in the forms 'God keep/save/defend us from our friends' and says it is now often used in the abbreviated form, 'Save us from our friends.' It appears to be common to many languages. *God Protect Me from My Friends* was the title of a book (1956) by Gavin Maxwell about Salvatore Giuliano, the Sicilian bandit. The diarist Chips Channon (21 February 1938) has: 'This evening a group of excited Communists even invaded the Lobby, demanding Anthony [Eden]'s reinstatement. God preserve us from our friends, they did him harm.' *Morris* seems to confuse the saying with the similar WITH FRIENDS LIKE THESE . . . but finds a quotation from Maréchal Villars who, on leaving Louis XIV, said: 'Defend me from my friends; I can defend myself from my enemies'.

God save the King (or **Queen**)   Title phrase from the British national anthem. Of obscure composition, this was possibly written by Henry Carey – and sung by him as his own composition in 1740 – or by James Hogg, or taken from an old Jacobite drinking song (*circa* 1725), or date back to the 17th century. *Benham* (1948) comments: 'The words of "God Save the King" appear in the *Gentleman's Magazine* (October 1745). John Bull (1563?–1628), composer, singer, and organist at Antwerp Cathedral in 1617, has been credited with composition of the words and music.' *The British Inheritance, A Treasury of Historic Documents* (2000) refers to a document in the British Library (Music Library), which is dated 1745 and contains 'A Loyal Song' with these words: 'God save Great George our King, Long Live our noble King / God save the King. / God save Great George our King, / Long live our noble King / God save the King. / Send him victorious . . .'

The book states: 'The first recorded performances of the National Anthem took place at Drury Lane and Covent Garden in September 1745, when Thomas Arne's arrangement of *God Save the King* was loudly sung on several successive nights until the dangers of the Jacobite rebellion were past.' The phrase 'God save the king' appears several times in the Bible: at 1 Samuel 10:24 (referring to Saul), and at 2 Samuel 16:16, 2 Kings 11:12 and 2 Chronicles 23:11.

God's own country Referring to one's own country, if one is fond of it. There can be few countries that have not elected to call themselves this. *Of the United States*: *OED2* provides an example from 1865 and tags the phrase as being of US origin. *Flexner* (1976) says that in the Civil War the shorter 'God's country' was the Union troops' term for the North, 'especially when battling heat, humidity, and mosquitoes in the South. Not until the 1880s did the term mean any section of the country one loved or the open spaces of the West'. In *Animal Crackers* (1930), Groucho Marx says, 'Africa is God's country and he can have it.' A 1937 US film had the title *God's Country and the Woman*. *Of Australia*: Dr Richard Arthur, a State politician and President of the Immigration League of Australasia, was quoted in *Australia Today* (1 November 1911) as saying: 'This Australia is "God's Own Country" for the brave.' The *Dictionary of Australian Quotations* (1984) notes that at the time 'Australia was frequently referred to as "God's Own Country", the phrase drawing satirical comments from the foreign unenlightened.' *Of South Africa/Ireland*: one has heard both these countries so dubbed informally (in the 1970s), with varying degrees of appropriateness and irony. Also Yorkshiremen describe their homeland as 'God's own *county*'. 'York-shire's natural reluctance to play second fiddle to London has faced some difficulty in the matter of house prices . . . God's own county is at the centre of things yet again' – *The Guardian* (23 January 1989).

God, what a beauty! The British 'Coster Comedian' Leon Cortez (1898–1970) was associated with this cry. Also with **as you may know . . . or as you may not know . . .**

goes See AND SO IT; ANYTHING.

(to) go for a song To be sold very cheaply, if not for free. *Going for a Song* has been the title of a BBC TV antiques programme (from 1968). The expression 'for a song' was proverbial in Shakespeare's day and occurs in *All's Well That Ends Well*, III.ii.8 (1603): 'I know a man that had this trick of melancholy sold a goodly manor for a song.' 'I bought it for a song' occurs in *Regulus* (1694) by John Crowne. Possibly also from the 'trifling cost' of ballad sheets sold in olden days – *Brewer* (1923), favouring the form 'to go for an old song'.

go for (the) gold Slogan meaning, literally, 'aim for a gold medal', and first used by the US Olympic team at the Lake Placid Winter Olympics in 1980, as is alluded to in this report on ice hockey in *The Times* (16 February 1980): 'The United States, now encouraged by the legend "shoot for the gold", took a grip of the game thereafter.' *Going for Gold* became the title of an Emma Lathen thriller set in Lake Placid, published in 1981. Other teams had taken it up by the time of the 1984 Olympics at Los Angeles – the British team recorded a song called 'Go for Gold' (accompanied by the Pangbourne Digital Silver Band). In his stump speech for re-election in that same year, Ronald Reagan repeatedly said: 'And like our Olympic athletes, this nation should set its sights on the stars and go for the gold . . .' A US TV movie, *Going for the Gold*, in 1985 did not have any Olympics connections, however. A BBC TV quiz called *Going for Gold* began in 1987. Just to show, as always, that there is nothing new under the sun: in 1832, there was a political slogan 'To Stop the Duke, Go for Gold' – which was intended, through its alliterative force, to prevent the Duke of Wellington from forming a government in the run-up to the Reform Bill. The slogan was coined by a radical politician, Francis Place, for a poster, on 12 May 1832. It was intended to cause a run on the Bank of England – and succeeded.

go for it! Popular slogan from the early 1980s, mostly in America – though any number of sales managers have encouraged their teams to strive this way in the UK too. In June 1985, President Reagan's call on tax reform was, 'America, go for it!' Victor Kiam, an American razor entrepreneur, entitled his 1986 memoirs *Going For It!*; and 'Go for it, America' was the slogan used by British Airways in the same year to get more US tourists to ignore the terrorist threat and travel to Europe. Lisa Bernbach in *The Official Preppie Handbook* (1980) pointed to a possible US campus origin, giving the phrase as a general exhortation meaning, 'Let's get carried away and act stupid'. At about the same time, the phrase was used in aerobics. Jane Fonda in a work-out book (1981) and video (*circa* 1983) cried, 'Go for it, **go for the burn!**' (where the burn was a sensation felt during exercise). There was also a US beer slogan (current 1981), 'Go for it! Schlitz makes it great'. Media mogul Ted Turner was later called a 'go-for-it guy', and so on. *Partridge/Slang* has 'to go for it' as Australian for being 'extremely eager for sexual intercourse' (*circa* 1925).

go forth and multiply Euphemism for 'fuck off'. You might think it was in the Bible but the King James version of the Old Testament does not contain these words. The nearest is Genesis 1:28: 'Be fruitful and multiply'. Presumably, 'Go forth' is a phrase made up to sound biblical.

(to) go forth to war To go to war. The 1989 BBC TV comedy series *Blackadder Goes Forth* was set during the First World War. The phrase this title embodied was as used by Bishop Heber in his hymn (1812) beginning: 'The Son of God goes forth to war / A kingly crown to gain.' Earlier, it was known in the Bible, occurring in Numbers 1:3 and 2 Chronicles 25:5.

go go See A GO GO.

going, going, gone! Traditional cry of the auctioneer as he allows time for a final bid before banging down his gavel. 'Going' signifies 'on the point of being sold' and 'gone', 'sold'. 'I'll knock 'em down at forty pounds. Going – going – gone' – R. B. Sheridan, *The School for Scandal*, Act 4 Sc. 1 (1777); 'I've never been to an auction before and I always thought the auctioneer

banged his gavel three times and said going, going, gone, so as to give the bidders a last chance' – Ian Fleming, short story 'The Property of a Lady' (1963).

go jump in the lake! Go away, get lost, to hell with you. From the 1910s. Mainly North American.

gold See GO FOR.

golden See MAN WITH THE.

(a/the) golden age The original golden age was that in which, according to ancient Greek and Roman poets, men lived in an ideal state of happiness. It was also applied to the period of Latin literature from Cicero to Ovid (which was followed by the lesser, silver age). Now the phrase is widely used in such clichés as 'the Golden Age of Hollywood' to describe periods when a country or a creative field is considered to have been at the height of its excellence or prosperity. Kenneth Grahame's story *The Golden Age* (1895) refers to childhood. 'The 'eighties and 'nineties were the Golden Age [of music-hall]; and in 1905 the writing was on the wall . . . Musical comedy, the cinema, television all hastened its decline' – *The Listener* (2 December 1965); 'The Golden Age detective story is alive and well' – review in *The Times* of Ruth Rendell's *Put On By Cunning* (1981); 'My generation, the twentysomethings, were fortunate enough to catch the golden age of American TV detectives' – *The Guardian* (3 May 1991); 'Explorers hail 1990s as "golden age of discovery"' – headline in *The independent on Sunday* (30 April 1995).

(the) golden bowl Phrase alluding to Ecclesiastes 12:6: 'Or ever the silver cord be loosed, or the golden bowl be broken, or the pitcher be broken at the fountain, or the wheel broken at the cistern.' Hence, *The Golden Bowl*, title of a novel (1904) by Henry James in which there is an actual golden bowl that is used emblematically. It is not solid gold and contains a flaw.

(a) golden boy Meaning 'a young person with talent', it derives chiefly from its use as the title of a play, *Golden Boy* (1937; film US 1939), by Clifford Odets in which the violinist hero becomes a successful boxer instead. It was also the title of a cinema short (*circa* 1962) about the singer Paul Anka. Possibly influenced by the terms **golden youth** (known by 1844) or **gilded youth** (known by 1882) and Shakespeare's *Cymbeline*, IV.ii.262 (1609): 'Golden lads and girls all must, / As chimney-sweepers, come to dust.'

(the) golden floor Meaning, 'Heaven', and possibly derived from 'threshing floor', as in various Old Testament verses, or from the pure gold street mentioned in Revelation 21:21. Current by 1813 (Shelley, 'Queen Mab'), the phrase also occurs in the Harvest Festival hymn 'Come ye thankful people, come'. The poet A. E. Housman said to the doctor who told him a risqué story to cheer him up before he died: 'That is indeed very good. I shall have to repeat that on the Golden Floor' – quoted in *The Daily Telegraph* (21 February 1984).

(a) golden opportunity Phrase known by 1703. 'With try-scoring so difficult, Wales missed a golden opportunity of taking a decisive lead midway through the first half' – *The Times* (4 February 1974); 'Oxford had thrown away a golden opportunity to finish the day at least on level terms, but they had already done enough to show that they will be a force to be reckoned with in matches to come this season' – *The Times* (15 April 1995); 'One of her tasks is to organise the annual British ABBA day in Bristol – a golden opportunity for hundreds of fanatics who, like Muriel in the film, can forget their real lives, come out of the closet and live out their fantasies as Dancing Queens' – *Daily Mirror* (21 April 1995).

(the) golden rule Nowadays, any guiding principle that the speaker wishes to nominate as especially important. By the 17th century, 'Do as you would be done by' (based on Matthew 7:12, from Christ's Sermon on the Mount) was known as 'The Golden Rule' or 'The Golden Law'. But the 'rule of three' in mathematics was, however, known as the Golden Rule the century before that.

go, man, go! Phrase of encouragement originally shouted at jazz musicians in the 1940s. Then it took on wider use. At the beginning of the number 'It's Too Darn Hot' in Cole Porter's *Kiss Me Kate* (film version, 1953), a dancer cries, 'Go, girl, go!' TV newscaster Walter Cronkite reverted famously to 'Go, baby, go!' when describing the launch of Apollo 11 in 1969, and this form became a fairly standard cry at rocket and missile departures thereafter. *Time* Magazine reported it being shouted at a test firing of a Pershing missile (29 November 1982). **Crazy, man, crazy!** originated at about the same time. One wonders whether T. S. Eliot's 'Go go go said the bird' ('Burnt Norton', *Four Quartets*, 1935) or Hamlet's 'Come, bird, come' (the cry of a falconer recalling his hawk) relate to these cries in any way . . . ?

gone but not forgotten Gravestone and memorial use. The earliest example found (in a far from exhaustive search) is on the grave of William Thomas Till (d. 1892, aged 28 years) in the churchyard of St Michael on Greenhill, Lichfield. Ludovic Kennedy in his autobiography *On My Way to the Club* (1989) suggests that it is an epitaph much found in the English graveyard at Poona, India. The precise origin of the phrase is not known, but it may have been used as the title of a Victorian print showing children at a grave. An earlier appearance in verse is on the headstone of Jane Damerell (d. 26 March 1883 aged 70) at Shaugh Prior in Devon: 'Gone from us but not forgoten / Never shall thy memory fade / Sweetest thoughts shall ever linger / Round the spot where thou art laid.' Also the phrase is reported on its own on the headstone to John Worth (d. 7 June 1879 aged 71) in Princeton churchyard, Devon. Selected editions from the BBC radio *Goon Show* were issued on a commercial record album in 1967 with the title *Goon . . . But Not Forgotten*.

gone for a Burton Dead. Early in the Second World War, an RAF expression arose to describe what had happened to a missing person, presumed dead. He had 'gone for a Burton', meaning that he had gone for a drink (*in* the drink = the sea) or, as another phrase put it, 'he'd bought it'. Folk memory has it that during the 1930s 'Gone for a Burton' had been used in advertisements to promote a Bass beer known in the trade as 'a Burton' (though, in fact, several ales are produced at

Burton-on-Trent). More positive proof is lacking. An advert for Carlsberg in the 1987 Egon Ronay *Good Food in Pubs and Bars* described Burton thus: 'A strong ale, dark in colour, made with a proportion of highly dried or roasted malts. It is not necessarily brewed in Burton and a variety of strong or old ales were given the term.' Other fanciful theories are that RAF casualty records were kept in an office above or near a branch of Burton Menswear in Blackpool and that Morse code instruction for wireless operators/air gunners took place in a converted billiards hall above Burton's in the same town (and failure in tests meant posting off the course – a fairly minor kind of 'death'). Probably no more than a coincidental use of the name Burton, and there are numerous other explanations for this involving other Burtons.

gone to earth Huntsman's traditional cry when the fox has disappeared into the earth or the quarry escapes to its lair. Used as the title of a novel (1917; film UK 1948) by Mary Webb about a Shropshire girl who is pursued by the local squire. In the story, the heroine has a pet fox, a hunting scene is the climax and both the pursued end up down a disused mine shaft.

gone to the big (or **great)** —— **in the sky** Format phrase used to announce lightly that someone has died. Thus, an actor might go to 'the great Green Room in the sky', a surgeon to 'the great operating theatre in the sky', a boozer to 'the great saloon bar in the sky', etc. From *Joe Bob Goes to the Drive-in* (1987): 'Ever since Bruce Lee went to the big Tae Kwon Do Academy in the sky'.

gone with the wind Phrase from Ernest Dowson's poem *'Non Sum Qualis Eram'* (1896): 'I have forgot much, Cynara! Gone with the wind . . .' As the title of Margaret Mitchell's novel *Gone With the Wind* (1936; film US 1939), the phrase refers to the Southern United States before the American Civil War, as is made clear by the on-screen epigraph to the film: 'There was a land of Cavaliers and Cotton Fields called the Old South. Here in this patrician world the Age of Chivalry took its last bows. Here was the last ever seen of the Knights and their Ladies fair, of Master and Slave. Look for it only in books, for it is no more than a dream remembered, a Civilization gone with the wind . . .'

gong See ALL.

go now, pay later Advertising inducement that has developed into a format phrase. Daniel Boorstin in *The Image* (1962) makes oblique reference to travel advertisements using the line 'Go now, pay later'. Was hire purchase ever promoted with 'Buy now, pay later'? It seems likely. These lines – in the USA and UK – seem to be the starting point for a construction much used and adapted since. *Live Now Pay Later* was the title of Jack Trevor Story's 1962 screenplay based on the novel *All on the Never Never* by Jack Lindsay. As a simple graffito, the same line was recorded in Los Angeles (1970), according to *The Encyclopedia of Graffiti* (1974). The same book records a New York subway graffito on a funeral parlour ad: 'Our layaway plan – die now, pay later.' 'Book now, pay later' was used in an ad in the programme of the Royal Opera House, Covent Garden, in 1977.

good See ALL; IT SEEMED LIKE.

(the) good and the great (or **great and the good)** Those who are on a British Government list from which are selected members of Royal Commissions and committees of inquiry. In 1983 the list stood at some 4,500 names. For the previous eight years custodians of the list had sought more women, more people under 40 and more from outside the golden triangle of London and the South-East in an attempt to break the stereotype enshrined in Lord Rothschild's parody of it as containing only 53-year-old men 'who live in the South-East, have the right accent and belong to the Reform Club'. In the 1950s, the Treasury division, which kept the list, was actually known as the 'G and G'. On one occasion, it really did nominate two dead people for service on a public body. 'At one level, the famous "List of the Good and Great", to which governments resort . . . has added to the gaiety of the nation' – *The Times* (22 January 1983). 'A secret tome of *The Great and the Good* is kept, listing everyone who has the right, safe qualifications of worthiness, sound-ness and discretion; and from this tome came the stage army of committee people' – Anthony Sampson, *Anatomy of Britain Today* (1965).

good-bye-ee! Catchphrase of the British music-hall comedian Harry Tate (1872–1940), who is also said to have been the first to sing the song with this title which became very popular during the First World War. The song was written by R. P. Weston and Bert Lee in 1917. Peter Cook and Dudley Moore sang their own song 'Goodbyee' at the end of each edition of *Not Only . . . But Also* on BBC TV (1965–6).

goodbye to all that Phrase popularized by Robert Graves in the title of his auto-biographical volume *Goodbye To All That* (1929) – a farewell to his participation in the First World War and to an unhappy period in his private life.

good career move Ironic comment on an event in a person's life, most often their death. Gore Vidal said it on hearing of Truman Capote's death in 1984 – con-firmed by him in BBC TV *Gore Vidal's Gore Vidal* (1995). According to *Time* Magazine (8 April 1985), the graffito 'Good career move' had earlier appeared follow-ing Elvis Presley's death in 1977.

good cop/bad cop Term for a police interrogation technique aimed at breaking down a suspect's resistance. One police-man adopts a friendly tone, attempting to win the suspect's confidence, while the other one adopts a brusque, if not actually brutal, approach. A concept known by the 1980s. 'Don't pull that good-cop, bad-cop crap. I practically invented it' – line from film *L.A. Confidential* (US 1997). *Good Cop, Bad Cop* was the title of a film (US 1993).

(one's) good deed for the day An act of service for others, usually associated with the Scout Movement though 'good turn' was the original phrase in Lord Baden-Powell's *Scouting for Boys* (first published 1908). Discussing 'The Scout Law . . . 3. A Scout's Duty is to be Useful and to Help Others', he writes: 'And *he must try his best to do at least one good turn* to somebody

every day.' 'This . . . was the spot where the boy scouts were encamped . . . fourteen good deeds were registered' – Ronald Knox, *Footsteps at Lock*, Chap. 5 (1928); 'You've done your Good Deed for the Day, visiting the sick' – J. C. Fennessy, *Sonnet In a Bottle* (1951).

(the) good doctor The epithet 'good' coupled with 'doctor' (of the medical type) appears to have originated in French and *'le bon docteur'*. In English by the 18th century.

good egg! (1) An exclamation of enthusi-astic approbation, known by 1903. (2) term for an excellent person or object, known by 1914. (There is also the oppo-site **bad egg**, known by 1910.) 'Apparently innocuous phrases now frowned on in the Metropolitan Police . . . are "egg and spoon" and "good egg". Egg and spoon is deemed to be a rhyming slang term suggesting "coon" – a racially offensive phrase used towards black people – and good egg is said to be linked to it' – *The Daily Telegraph* (15 May 2002).

good evening, England! – this is Gillie Potter speaking to you in English Customary beginning of BBC radio talks by Gillie Potter (1887–1975), the English humorist. Delivered in an assumed peda-gogic and superior air, Potter's talks recounted the doings of the Marshmallow family of Hogsnorton Towers – a delight from the 1940s and early 50s. He would conclude with **goodbye, England, and good luck!**

good evening, each See MY NAME'S MONICA.

good evening, everyone The customary salutation of A. J. Alan, the BBC radio storyteller of the 1920s and 30s. He was a civil servant (real name Leslie Lambert) who eschewed personal publicity and always broadcast wearing a dinner-jacket. He never went into a BBC studio without having a candle by him in case the lights fused. *Good Evening, Everyone* was the title of a book by him (1928).

good evening, Mr and Mrs North America and all the ships at sea – let's go to press Walter Winchell (1892–1972) was an ex-vaudevillian who became a top radio newscaster. This was how he introduced his zippy fifteen-minute broadcast on Sunday nights, starting in 1932. By 1948 it was the top-rated radio show in the USA with an average audience of 20 million people. A TV version ran 1952–5 in which Winchell entertained viewers by wearing his hat throughout. A variation of his greeting was 'Mr and Mrs North *and South* America'. Winchell also ran a syndicated newspaper gossip column and narrated the TV series *The Untouchables*. Many of his stories were pure fabrication.

(the) good —— guide Format for book titles that is obviously helped by the alliteration. The first in the field was *The Good Food Guide*, edited by Raymond Postgate (1951). Subsequently, there have been Good – Book, Cheese, Hotel, Museums, Pub, Reading, Sex, Skiing, Software, Word – Guides, and many others.

(a) good man fallen among —— Format that would appear to be based on 'a good man fallen among thieves', which may, in turn, allude to Luke 10:30 in the parable of the good Samaritan: 'A certain man went down from Jerusalem to Jericho, and fell among thieves.' Arthur Ransome, *Six Weeks in Russia* (1919), quotes Lenin as having called Bernard Shaw 'A good man fallen among Fabians.' From R. M. Wardle, *Oliver Goldsmith* (1957): 'It was Goldsmith's misfortune that he was a jigger fallen among goons.' John Stonehouse called Edward Heath 'A good man fallen among bureaucrats' – speech, House of Commons (13 May 1964). And when former journalist Michael Foot was leader of the British Labour Party, the *Daily Mirror* described him in an editorial (28 February 1983) as 'a good man fallen among politicians'.

(a) good man is hard to find Is this the same as the proverb 'Good men are scarce' found by *CODP* in 1609? In the present form, it was the title of a song by Eddie Green (1919). Nowadays, it is most frequently encountered in reverse: 'A hard man is good to find' was used, nudgingly, as the slogan for Soloflex body-building equipment in the USA (1985). Ads showed a woman's hand touching the bodies of well-known brawny athletes. In this form the saying is also sometimes attributed to Mae West.

good men and true Descriptive phrase used now only in a consciously archaic fashion. 'Are you good men and true' occurs in Shakespeare's *Much Ado About Nothing*, III.iii.1 (1598). Dogberry puts the question and, being a constable, would naturally use legal terminology, so it presumably relates to the longer '*twelve* good men and true', referring to the composition of a jury. 'It is a maxim of English law that legal memory begins with the accession of Richard I in 1189 . . . with the establishment of royal courts . . . The truth of [witnesses'] testimony [was] weighed not by the judge but by twelve "good men and true"' – Winston Churchill, *A History of the English-Speaking Peoples*, Vol. 1 (1956). More examples: '12 good men and true, glumly spruce, resigned to a long haul and bored, bored out of their skulls' – *The Listener* (7 December 1967); 'Tognazzi's anger at the way good men and true are killed, or sidelined by Italian bureaucracy out of fear of retribution or even complicity with the predatory Mafiosi, comes strongly across. But the movie otherwise doesn't travel too well' – *Evening Standard* (London) (5 May 1994); '"How can this man get a fair trial?" he demanded of the experts. They chorused: "It all comes down to the 12 good men and true, the ladies and gentlemen of the jury." But not just any old jury. No, to ensure a fair trial for OJ [Simpson], it seems, the jury itself must be tried first' – *The Independent* (8 October 1994).

good morning, boys! Catchphrase opening line from the British comedian Will Hay (1888–1949) in his schoolmaster persona. He would say this as the Headmaster of St Michael's. His pupils would reply wearily, 'Good morning, sir!' Used as the title of a film (UK 1937).

good morning . . . nice day! Catchphrase from the BBC radio show *ITMA* (1939–49). Said by Clarence Wright as a commercial traveller who never seemed to sell anything.

good morning, sir! – was there something? Catchphrase from the BBC radio show, *Much Binding in the Marsh* (1947–53). Sam Costa's entry line. He played a kind of batman to Kenneth Horne and Richard Murdoch.

goodness See FOR.

goodness gracious me! Key phrase in Peter Sellers's Indian doctor impersonation – that all citizens of the subcontinent subsequently rushed to emulate. It occurred in a song called 'Goodness Gracious Me' (written by Herbert Kretzmer and Dave Lee), recorded by Sellers and Sophia Loren in 1960 and based on their characters in the film of Shaw's *The Millionairess*. Hence, *Goodness Gracious Me!* – title of a British TV comedy show (1998–) based on the experiences of immigrants from the Indian sub-continent.

(it's) good news for —— and it's good news for —— Cliché slogan of politicians when their strings are being pulled by PR people in the age of the soundbite. Unfortunately reminiscent of the 'good news/bad news' jokes of the 1960s/70s, this format was much used by Norman Lamont, the British Chancellor of the Exchequer (1990–3), when announcing interest rate reductions. 'Transport Minister Lord Whitty has said: "This is good news for motorists and good news for crime fighting. Number plates should be easy to read and easy to remember"' – *The Independent* (10 March 2001).

goodnight See AND A SPECIAL.

goodnight ... and good luck Sign-off by Edward R. Murrow (1908–65), the American broadcaster, particularly on *See It Now*, which has been called 'the prototype of the in-depth quality television documentary' (CBS TV, 1951–8).

goodnight, Chet / goodnight, David Closing exchange between Chet Huntley and David Brinkley, co-anchors on NBC TV News and *The Huntley-Brinkley Report* from *circa* 1956 to Huntley's retirement in 1970. 'It became a national catchphrase' – obituary of Brinkley in *The Independent* (14 June 2003).

goodnight, children ... everywhere! Stock phrase of Derek McCulloch (Uncle Mac) who was one of the original Uncles and Aunts introducing BBC radio *Children's Hour* from the 1920s onwards. He developed this special farewell during the Second World War when many of the programme's listeners were evacuees. Vera Lynn recorded a song and J. B. Priestley wrote a play, both with the title.

goodnight, everybody ... goodnight! Distinctive pay-off at the end of the day's broadcasting from Stuart Hibberd (even in the days when BBC radio announcers were anonymous). Hibberd (1893–1983) would count four after the initial two words in order that listeners could say 'goodnight' back to him if they felt like it. *Punch* alluded to the broadcast use of 'Goodnight, everybody' on 13 January 1937.

goodnight, gentlemen, and good sailing! Another example of informality from a BBC announcer in the otherwise starchier days of presentation – the customary end to a shipping forecast read by Frank Phillips (1901–80).

goodnight ... God bless Comedian Benny Hill (1925–92), as himself, at the end of his TV comedy shows in the UK from 1969 onwards. Latterly, Hill became equally well known in the USA, where this farewell had once been associated with the comedian Red Skelton.

goodnight, good luck, and may your God go with you Customary farewell from Dave Allen (b. 1934), the Irish-born comedian, on British and Australian TV from the 1970s onwards.

goodnight, Mrs Calabash ... wherever you are! Jimmy 'Schnozzle' Durante (1893–1980), the big-nosed American comedian, had a gaggle of phrases – including **I'm mortified** and an exasperated **everybody wants to get into the act!** and (after a successful joke) **I've got a million of 'em!** (also used in the UK by Max Miller and others). He used to sign off his radio and TV shows in the 1940s and 1950s with the Calabash phrase. It was a pet name for his first wife, Maud, who died in 1943. The word comes from an American idiom for 'empty head', taken from the calabash or gourd. For a long time, Durante resisted explaining the phrase. His biographer, Gene Fowler, writing in 1952, could only note: 'When he says that line his manner changes to one of great seriousness, and his voice takes on a tender, emotional depth . . . when asked to explain the Calabash farewells, Jim replied, "That's my secret – I want it to rest where it is".' Of Gary Moore, the MC on American radio's *The Camel Caravan* (1943–7) – and 22 years his junior – Durante would say **dat's my boy dat said dat!** Yet more phrases: **stop da music! stop da music!** and **dem's de conditions dat prevail!** or **dese are de conditions dat prevail!** or **it's da conditions dat prevail!**

goodnight, Vienna! Catchphrase that can be used in a variety of ways but all of them signifying that some outcome will occur, good or bad. 'If we get caught doing this, it'll be goodnight Vienna' or 'I had a few drinks with this bird and then it was goodnight Vienna!' It alludes to the famous operetta *Goodnight Vienna* ('you city of a million melodies') of the 1930s. Which also gave rise to a famous showbiz joke. The show's writer, Eric Maschwitz, is said to have popped into a theatre where the show was playing – variously this is placed in Walthamstow and Lewisham. When he asked how it was doing, the manager replied, 'Just about as well as you would expect "Goodnight in Walthamstow" to be doing in Vienna.'

good old Charlie-ee! Catchphrase from the BBC radio show *Much Binding in the Marsh* (1947–53). This was an interjection by Richard Murdoch, given with especial relish at the birth of Prince Charles in 1948. The phrase was an old one – it is used, for example, in *Punch* (2 February 1910).

good riddance to bad rubbish (or **gentle/ fair riddance . . .)** Phrase aimed at an unwanted departing person. Since the 16th century but in this particular form, the earliest example appears to be from Charles Dickens, *Dombey and Son*, Chap. 44 (1848), precisely as: 'A good riddance *of* bad rubbish.'

(the) good, the bad and the ugly *The Good, the Bad and the Ugly* was the English-language title of the Italian 'spaghetti Western', *Il Buono, il Bruto, il Cattivo* (1966). Colonel Oliver North, giving evidence to the Washington hearings on the Irangate scandal in the summer of 1987, said: 'I came here to tell you the truth – the good, the bad, and the ugly.'

(a) good time was had by all When the poet Stevie Smith entitled a collection of her poems *A Good Time Was Had By All* (1937), Eric Partridge asked her where she had taken the phrase from. She replied: from parish magazines where reports of church picnics or social evenings invariably end with the phrase.

good to the last drop Slogan for Maxwell House coffee, in the USA, from 1907. President Theodore Roosevelt was visiting Joel Cheek, perfector of the Maxwell House blend. After the President had had a cup, he said of it that it was 'Good . . . to the last drop'. It has been used as a slogan ever since, despite those who have inquired what was wrong with the last drop. Professors of English have been called in to consider the problem and ruled that 'to' can be inclusive and not just mean 'up to but not including' – I. E. Lambert, *The Public Accepts* (1941). In 1982, Maxwell House in the USA was still using a logo of a tilted coffee cup with the last drop falling from it. The brand has also used the slogan **tastes as good as it smells** – a slogan that attempts to remedy the age-old complaint, 'Why does coffee never taste as good as it smells?'

(to have a) good war To survive and have experiences that, though testing, add to a person's achievements. Probably first used in relation to combatants in the Second World War. Lord Moran in *Churchill: The Struggle for Survival* made a 1943 allusion: 'But it was [Lord] Wavell who said to me, "I have had a bad war".' In Henry Reed's radio play of 1959, *Not a Drum Was Heard: the War Memoirs of General Gland*, Gland says: 'It was, I think a *good* war, one of the best there have so far been. I've often advanced the view that it was a war deserving of better generalship than it received on either side.' Usually, however, it is a good war in the sense of a personally successful or enjoyable one that is being talked about. Recent uses have been mostly figurative. In his *European Diary*, Roy Jenkins has this entry for 19 February 1979: 'Bill Rodgers . . . clearly thought he had had, as Peter Jenkins put it, "a good war" during the strike period and was exhilarated by having made a public breakthrough.' From Julian Critchley MP in

The Guardian (3 May 1989): 'I well remember some years ago at the Savoy a colleague who had had a good war leaping to his feet (before the Loyal Toast) in order to pull back the curtains which separated the party from the outside world . . .' From *The Independent* (13 July 1989): 'British Rail has not had a good war. The public relations battle in the industrial dispute seems to have been all but lost.'

goody-goody gumdrops! Exclamation used by Humphrey Lestocq, host of the BBC TV children's show *Whirligig* in the early 1950s, though he did not originate it. Harold Acton in his book *Nancy Mitford: a Memoir* (1975) quotes 'goody-goody gumtrees' as being a favourite of Noël Coward in the late 1920s.

(a) goody two-shoes An oppressively well-behaved child. The phrase comes from *The History of Little Goody Two-Shoes* . . . , a children's story (1765) believed to have been written by Oliver Goldsmith. The heroine begins by having only one shoe but when she is given another, she goes round saying, 'Two shoes!'

(the) goose step Name given to the type of march step, used especially by German troops on formal occasions before the Second World War. It takes its name from the exaggerated swinging up of each leg and foot without bending the knee. The term dates from the 18th century at least, when the Germans or Prussians and several other armies were already doing it. Beatrix Potter in *The Tale of Tom Kitten* (1907) reverts to a literal use of the term: 'The three Puddle-ducks came along the hard high road, marching one behind the other and doing the goose-step – pit pat paddle pat! Pit pat waddle pat!'

(to) go postal Meaning, 'to go berserk or to have an outburst.' A coinage reflecting the behaviour of postal workers in the USA who come under pressure, according to *Wired* (February 1994). Used in the film *Clueless* (US 1995). Confirmed by *The Economist* (21 June 1997), saying such workers went on shooting rampages when stressed out.

Gordon Bennett! Euphemistic exclamation suddenly popular – or popular again – in the Britain of the early 1980s. Understandably, people shrink from blaspheming. 'Oh Gawd!' is felt to be less offensive than 'Oh God!' Around 1900, it was natural for people facetiously to water down the exclamation 'God!' by saying 'Gordon!' The name Gordon Bennett was to hand. The initial letters of the name also had the explosive quality found in 'Gor*b*limey! [God blind me!]'. But who was this man? James Gordon Bennett II (1841–1918) was the editor-in-chief of the *New York Herald*, the man who sent Henry Morton Stanley to find Dr Livingstone in Africa and altogether quite a character. He was exiled to Paris after a scandal, but somehow managed to run his New York newspaper from there. He disposed of some $40 million in his lifetime. He offered numerous trophies to stimulate French sport and, when the motor car was in its infancy, presented the Gordon Bennett cup to be competed for. He became, as the *Dictionary of American Biography* puts it, 'one of the most picturesque figures of two continents'. This, if anything does, probably explains why it was *his* name that ended up on people's lips and why they did not go around exclaiming 'Gordon of Khartoum!' or 'Gordon Selfridge!' or anything else. Gordon Bennett was a man with an amazing reputation. A decade or two later, in similar fashion – and with a view to circumventing the strict Hollywood Hay's Code – W. C. Fields would exclaim **Godfrey Daniel!**, a 'minced oath' in place of 'God, damn you!' But who was Godfrey Daniel . . . ? 'The plats de jour were ready, the sauces simmering; [but] not a stove, not a hotplate was free. "Gordon Bennett," said the chef. But the restaurant was in all the guides' – *The Guardian* (24 June 1995).

got See AHA, ME.

gotcha! 'Got you!' – the *OED2* has an example of the phrase in this form from 1966. The headline 'GOTCHA!' was how *The Sun* newspaper 'celebrated' the sinking of the Argentine cruiser *General Belgrano* during the Falklands war – front page (4 May 1982), but it was retained for the first edition only.

Gotham City Name of the city featured in the Batman cartoon strip, possibly deriving from 'Gotham' as the name for New York City in Washington Irving's *Salmagundi* (1807). Could this in turn be derived from the name of a village in Nottinghamshire, England, noted for the (sometimes calculated) folly of its inhabitants? Their reputation was established by the 15th century, as in the nursery rhyme: 'Three wise Men of Gotham / Went to sea in a bowl, / If the bowl had been stronger, / My story would have been longer.'

(to) go the extra mile To make an extra special effort to accomplish something. President Bush used this American military/business expression at the time of the Gulf War (1991) about his attempts to get a peaceful settlement before resorting to arms. That same year, Bush, expressing sorrow for the baseball star Magic Johnson who was HIV-positive, said: 'If there's more I can do to empathize, to make clear what AIDS is and what it isn't, I want to go the extra mile.' The expression had been around long before this, however. Even in a revue song by Joyce Grenfell, 'All We Ask Is Kindness' (1957), there is: 'Working like a beaver / Always with a smile / Ready to take the rough and smooth / To go the extra mile.' A link has been suggested to Matthew 5:41, which, in the New English Bible, has Jesus Christ advising: 'If a man in authority makes you go one mile, go with him two.'

(to) go the whole hog Meaning, 'to go all the way, go into something throughly'. Known in the USA by 1828. One explanation for this phrase is that in 17th-century England, a 'hog' was a shilling, so 'to go the whole hog' was to make a substantial investment (or bet or whatever) at that time. *OED2* compares the expression 'to go the whole coon' but without dating or justification. Possibly introduced into British English by Fanny Trollope through *The Domestic Manners of the Americans* (1832). 'As you are not prepared, as the Americans say, *to go the whole hog*, we will part good friends' – Frederick Marryat, *Japhet in Search of a Father*, Chap. 54 (1836); in a *Beyond the Fringe* revue sketch (1961), when Alan Bennett pointed out that Jonathan Miller was 'a Jew', Miller replied by saying that, rather, he was 'not really a Jew, but Jew*ish* – not the whole

hog'; 'I suggest we go the whole hog and shove them up 1%. No use being namby pamby about it and going for itsy bitsy fractions' – *The Herald* (Glasgow) (6 June 1994); 'Sebastian Coe, as clean-cut and as mother-in-law-friendly as Andrew, has gone the whole hog and become a Conservative MP' – *The Times* (28 September 1994).

Gothic See AMERICAN.

(to) go to Hell in a handbasket (or **handcart** or **bucket)** To decline rapidly. *DOAS* defines this as 'amateurish, small-sized (handbasket-sized) dissipation of the kind indulged in, usually, by the young, as protest against a disappointment or a frustration; driving too fast, drinking too much, and the like, for a fairly short period of time.' The American journalist H. Allen Smith (1907–76) entitled his memoirs *To Hell in a Handbasket* (1962).

go to it! Slogan for a voluntary labour force in wartime. In the summer of 1940, the Minister of Supply, Herbert Morrison, called for such a force in words that echoed the public mood after Dunkirk. The slogan was used in a campaign run by the S. H. Benson agency (which later indulged in self-parody on behalf of Bovril with 'Glow to it' in 1951–2). 'Go to it', meaning 'to act vigorously, set to with a will' dates at least from the early 19th century. In Shakespeare, it means something else, of course: 'Die for adultery! No: / The wren goes to't, and the small gilded fly / Does lecher in my sight' – *King Lear*, IV.vi.112 (1605).

(to) go to pot To go to ruin. This could refer to the custom of putting a dead person's ashes into an urn or pot. After that happens, there is no more to be done. Neil Ewart, *Everyday Phrases* (1983), on the other hand, prefers to think 'the phrase comes from the melting-pots into which broken items of metal, gold and silver, were thrown when they could no longer be used in their original form as they were either damaged, or stolen.' *Morris* (1977) thinks it means left-over meat and vegetables all chopped up and ready for their last appearance as stew or hash in the pot. This is supported by *OED2*, which sees the phrases as shortened from 'go to the pot' (lit. 'to be cut in pieces like meat for the pot'). Known by 1530. Whatever the case, the phrase has nothing whatever to do with the other type of pot, namely marijuana. This word is said to come from the Mexican Spanish word *potiguaya*, meaning marijuana leaves.

(to) go to the dogs To go downhill, down the drain, and end up in a bad state. This form (known by 1619) appears to have grown out of, or alongside, the expression to the effect that something is only fit for 'throwing to the dogs' (which Shakespeare uses on several occasions). The suggestion that it is a corruption of a Dutch business maxim: '*Toe goe, toe de dogs*' [Money gone, credit gone] is probably fanciful.

(to) go to the loo Euphemism for going to the lavatory, established in well-to-do British society by the early 20th century and in general middle-class use after the Second World War. Of the several theories for its origin, perhaps the most well known is that the word comes from the French *gardez l'eau* [mind the water], dating from the days when chamber pots or dirty water were emptied out of the window into the street and recorded by Laurence Sterne as *garde d'eau* in *A Sentimental Journey* (1768). This cry was also rendered 'gardyloo' in old Edinburgh and recorded by Tobias Smollett in *Humphrey Clinker* (1771). However, Professor A. S. C. Ross who examined the various options in a 1974 issue of *Blackwood's Magazine* favoured a derivation, 'in some way which could not be determined', from 'Waterloo'. At one time people probably said: 'I must go to the water-closet' and, wishing not to be explicit, substituted 'Water–loo' as a weak little joke. The name 'Waterloo' was there, waiting to be used, from 1815 onwards.

go to work on an egg Slogan for the British Egg Marketing Board. In 1957, Fay Weldon (b. 1932), later known as a novelist and TV playwright, was a copy-writer on this account at the Mather & Crowther agency. In 1981 she poured a little cold water on the frequent linking of her name to the slogan: 'I was certainly in charge of copy at the time "Go to work on

an egg" was first used as a slogan as the main theme for an advertising campaign. The phrase itself had been in existence for some time and hung about in the middle of paragraphs and was sometimes promoted to base lines. Who invented it, it would be hard to say. It is perfectly possible, indeed probable, that I put those particular six words together in that particular order but I would not swear to it.'

gottle o' geer The standard showbiz way of mocking the inadequacies of many ventriloquial acts. It represents 'bottle of beer', said with teeth tightly clenched. Known by the 1960s, at least.

got your mojo working? Is your spell/charm working? In 1960, Muddy Waters, the American blues singer (1915–83), was singing a song with the refrain, 'Got my mojo workin', but it just don't work on you.' He knew what he was singing about because he had written the song under his real name, McKinley Morganfield. *DOAS* defines 'mojo' simply as 'any narcotic' but a sleeve note to an album entitled *Got My Mojo Workin'* (1966) by the jazz organist Jimmy Smith is perhaps nearer to the meaning of the word in the song. It describes 'mojo' as 'magic – a spell or charm guaranteed to make the user irresistible to the opposite sex'. Known by 1926. Indeed, it seems that 'mojo' could well be a form of the word 'magic' corrupted through Afro-American pronunciation, though the *OED2* finds an African word meaning 'magic, witchcraft' that is similar. The *OED2* derives the narcotic meaning of the word from the Spanish *mojar*, 'to celebrate by drinking'.

(to) go up the aisle To be married (in church) – an erroneous usage. Sir Thomas Bazley fired off a letter to *The Times* in July 1986: 'Sir, You report that Miss Sarah Ferguson will go up the aisle to the strains of Elgar's "Imperial March". Hitherto, brides have always gone up the nave. Yours faithfully . . .' Indeed, the nave is the main route from the west door of a church to the chancel and altar; the aisles are the parallel routes at the side of the building, usually separated from the nave by pillars. 'Film star Julia Roberts got her manager to call actor Kiefer Sutherland to tell him the wedding was off – two weeks before she was due to walk up the aisle' – *Daily Mirror* (28 February 1996).

(to) go west Meaning 'to die', it dates back to the 16th century and alludes to the setting of the sun and may have entered American Indian usage by 1801. However, another theory is that the term alludes to the practice of taking condemned criminals westward out of London to be executed at Tyburn. Additionally, the west gate of Roman and Greek towns led to both the place of execution and the cemetery. The pharaohs were buried on the west bank of the Nile, and it seems that Egyptians referred to death as 'going unto the western land.' There have been two films called simply *Go West*, notably the 1940 one often referred to as *The Marx Brothers Go West*, but these derive from:

go West, young man The saying 'Go west, young man (and grow up with the country)' was originated and popularized by the American editor and Presidential candidate, Horace Greeley, by 1853 (and attested in print in 1872). Frequent attribution of the phrase to John Babson Lane Soule, an Indiana editor, is spurious, based on an apparently fictitious 1890 newspaper article. *Go West Young Man* became the title of a film (1936), which was a vehicle for *Mae* West rather than anything to do with *the* West. *Go West Young Lady* followed in 1940.

gown See ALICE BLUE.

grace See AGE BEFORE; AMAZING.

grace under pressure Definition of 'guts' by Ernest Hemingway in a *New Yorker* article (30 November 1929). It was later invoked by John F. Kennedy in *Profiles in Courage* (1956). Based, perhaps, on the Latin tag '*Suaviter in modo, fortiter in re* [gentle in manner, resolute in action].'

graduate of the college See SCHOOL OF HARD.

grand See AIN'T IT.

grandmother See DON'T TEACH.

Grand Old Man (or GOM) Nickname of W. E. Gladstone – and believed to have been coined by either Sir William Harcourt

or Lord Rosebery or the Earl of Iddesleigh. The latter said in an 1882 speech (when Gladstone was 73): 'Argue as you please, you are nowhere; that grand old man, the Prime Minister, insists on the other thing.' Sometimes also applied (before and after Gladstone) to other venerable figures: 'A sight of the Duke of Wellington at the Chapel Royal (he is a real grand old man)' – Charlotte Brontë, letter of 12 June 1850; '[Thomas Hardy] the stonemason's son . . . who was eventually elevated to the position of GOM of letters' – *The Listener* (5 September 1968).

grape See BEULAH.

(to) grasp the nettle Meaning, 'to summon up the courage to deal with a difficult problem'. Known by 1884, possibly earlier. Compare from Shakespeare, *Henry IV, Part 1*, II.iii.9 (1597): 'I tell you, my lord fool, out of this nettle, danger, we pluck this flower, safety.' 'The difficulty which the EU and Canada are having in coming to an agreement highlights the scale of the task, however, since no nation appears willing to grasp the nettle and act on what everyone knows – namely that there are too many fishermen chasing too few fish' – *The Scotsman* (13 April 1995); 'The fact that individual party membership has now passed the 300,000 mark, the level at which the 1993 constitutional resolution suggested the union's share of conference votes might drop from 70% to 50%, should speed the process. But Mr Blair is unlikely to grasp this particular nettle before the general election' – *The Economist* (29 April 1995).

(to) grasp — with both hands Date of origin unknown. It occurs along with other rhetorical clichés during the 'Party Political Speech' (written by Max Schreiner) on Peter Sellers's comedy album *The Best of Sellers* (1958): 'Grasp, I beseech you, with both hands – oh, I'm sorry, I beg your pardon, Madam – the opportunities that are offered. Let us assume a bold front.' Identified as a current cliché in *The Times* (17 March 1995). 'If there was to be anything resembling a normal childhood ahead of her, Laura Davies demonstrated she was the sort of girl who would grasp it with both hands' – *The Daily Telegraph* (12 November 1993).

(the) grass is greener Short form of the proverb 'The grass is always greener on the other side of the fence', which is ignored by the *ODP* (1970), which prefers to cite a 16th-century translation of a Latin proverb, 'The corn in another man's ground seemeth ever more fertile than doth our own'. By 1956, time of the play *The Grass is Greener* by Hugh and Margaret Williams, the modern form – sometimes ending 'on the other side of the hedge' – was well established. Wolfgang Mieder in *Proverbium* (1993) questioned whether the two proverbs are in fact related but finds an earlier citation of the modern one: an American song with words by Raymond B. Egan and music by Richard A. Whiting entitled 'The Grass is Always Greener (In the Other Fellow's Yard)', published in 1924.

grassroots See AT THE.

(a) grass widow A divorced woman or one apart from her husband because his job or some other preoccupation has taken him elsewhere. It originally meant an unmarried woman who had sexual relations with one or more men – perhaps on the grass rather than in the lawful marriage bed – and had had a child out of wedlock. This sense was known by the 16th century. Later it seems to have been applied to women in British India who were sent up to the cool hill country (where grass grows) during the hottest season of the year. An alternative derivation is from 'grace widow' or even 'Grace Widow', the name of an actual person.

grass will grow in the streets Popular warning of the decay that will inevitably follow the pursuit of certain policies. 'The grass will grow in the streets of a hundred cities, a thousand towns,' said President Hoover in a speech (31 October 1932) on proposals 'to reduce the protective tariff to a competitive tariff for revenue'. The image had earlier been used by William Jennings Bryan in his 'Cross of Gold' speech (1896): 'Burn down your cities and leave our farms, and your cities will spring up again as if by magic; but destroy our farms and the grass will grow in the streets of every city in the country.' Compare, from Anthony Trollope, *Dr Thorne*, Chap. 15 (1858): 'Why, luke at this 'ere town . . .

the grass be a-growing in the very streets; – that can't be no gude.'

grateful See FROM A.

grateful and comforting like Epps's Cocoa Slogan since *circa* 1900. In Noël Coward's play *Peace In Our Time* (1947) one character says, 'One quick brandy, like Epps's Cocoa, would be both grateful and comforting.' When asked, 'Who is Epps?' he replies, 'Epps's cocoa – it's an advertisement I remember when I was a little boy.'

gratefully See ALL CONTRIBUTIONS.

gratis See FREE.

grave See CAUSING; FACE LIKE.

greasepaint See DOCTOR.

(the) greasy pole Politics at a high level. The term comes from a remark made by Benjamin Disraeli to friends when he first became British Prime Minister in 1868: 'Yes, I have climbed to the top of the greasy pole.' The allusion is to the competitive sport, once popular at fairs and games, of climbing up or along a greasy pole without slipping off.

(the) great American novel American novelists are supposed to aspire to writing this work, though some would say that Melville's *Moby-Dick* and Fitzgerald's *The Great Gatsby* already deserve the title. The phrase was coined in 1868 by the American novelist John William DeForest. *The Great American Novel* was the title of a collection of essays (1923) by the American poet William Carlos Williams. Two novels have also used the phrase for a title – by Clyde Davis in 1938 and by Philip Roth in 1973.

great balls of fire! To those who are most familiar with this exclamation from the Jerry Lee Lewis hit song of 1957 (written by Jack Hammer and Otis Blackwell) or the Lewis biopic (1989), it should be pointed out that, of course, it didn't begin there. In fact, it occurs several times in the script of the film *Gone With the Wind* (1939), confirming what might be its distinctly Southern USA origins. While the *OED2* and other dictionaries content themselves with the slang meaning of 'ball of fire' (glass of brandy/a person of great liveliness of spirit), even Partridge/ *Slang* and American slang dictionaries avoid recording the phrase.

(the) great British public Ironical or sarcastic usage. 'Supposing a printer put "h" in the place of "p", by mistake, in that mere word spit? Then the great American public knows that this man has committed an obscenity, an indecency, that his act was lewd, and as a compositor he was pornographical. You can't tamper with the great public, British or American' – D. H. Lawrence, 'Pornography and Obscenity' (1929); 'He learned . . . that if, by the most far-fetched stretch of ingenuity, an indecent meaning could be read into a headline, that was the meaning that the great British Public would infallibly read into it' – Dorothy L. Sayers, *Murder Must Advertise*, Chap. 3 (1933); 'There was a lot more nonsense in this vein [about U and non-U] and the great British public took it seriously' – Mary S. Lovell, *The Mitford Girls* (2001).

(a/the) great debate Politicians like to apply this dignifying label to any period of discussion over policy. The rhyming phrase goes back to 1601, at least. 'The Conservative leaders now decided to bring a vote of no confidence against the Government [on its Defence Programme], and on February 15 [1951] the "Great Debate" as it was known in Tory circles was opened, by Churchill himself' – Martin Gilbert, *Never Despair* (1988). From BBC TV, *Monty Python's Flying Circus* (4 January 1973): '*Stern music as the lights come on.* SUPERIMPOSED CAPTIONS: "THE GREAT DEBATE" "NUMBER 31" "TV4 OR NOT TV4".' In a speech at Ruskin College, Oxford, in October 1976, James Callaghan, as Prime Minister, called for a 'national debate' on education policy which also became known as a 'Great Debate'.

(the) greatest living —— Mostly journalistic tag applied to people since at least the 1850s and latterly with irony. David Lloyd George used to annoy C. P. Scott, editor of the *Manchester Guardian* in the 1910s/20s by always referring to him at public meetings as 'the world's greatest living journalist'. James Agate, writing in *Ego 3* (on 5 December 1936) of King Edward VIII and the Abdication, said: 'Everybody

is impressed by Rothermere's letter saying that Baldwin is in too much of a hurry, and that "the greatest living Englishman cannot be smuggled off his throne in a week-end".' The term 'Greatest Englishman of his Age' was much used of Sir Winston Churchill about the time of his death in 1965 – also ironically of Cyril Connolly, the writer and critic. In the 1970s, Nigel Dempster, the gossip columnist who contributed to *Private Eye* pseudonymously as part of the 'Grovel' column, promoted himself as 'the Greatest Living Englishman' or 'GLE'. In Muriel Box, *Rebel Advocate* (1983), a story is told of Gerald Gardiner, a future Lord Chancellor, who, when he was a schoolboy at Harrow, was asked by his father: 'Tell me, my boy, who d'you think is the greatest living Englishman?' Gardiner replied 'Winston Churchill, I suppose' but this did not go down well at that time. Gardiner's mother said he should have answered, 'You, father!' If there is any truth in this use of the phrase, it must have been spoken some time in the 1910s.

(the) greatest show on earth Slogan used by P. T. Barnum (1810–91) to promote the circus formed by the merger with his rival, Bailey's, in the USA, from 1881. Eventually it became the slogan of what is now Ringling Bros and Barnum & Bailey Circus. The phrase was used as the title of a Cecil B. de Mille circus film in 1952.

(the) greatest thing since sliced bread (sometimes **best/hottest thing . . .**) A 1981 advertisement in the UK declared: 'Sainsbury's bring you the greatest thing since sliced bread. Unsliced bread' – neatly turning an old formula on its head. Quite when the idea that pre-sliced bread was one of the landmark inventions arose is not clear. Sliced bread had first appeared on the market by the 1920s – so a suitable period of time after that.

(the) great game (1) Golf. 'The old golf ball maker's shop is associated in my mind with elevating talks about the "great game"' – letter from J. Blackwood (26 April 1866) in *George Eliot's Letters*, IV.245 (1955); (2) The other use has to do with intelligence and undercover operations between the British Empire in India and the Russian Empire, across the North West Frontier and into the debatable lands of

Central Asia. Indeed, if we are talking about late 19th-century British imperialism, the term takes on the additional aspect of defence of the (British) realm as performed by heroic individuals. This is what Peter Hopkirk's book *The Great Game*: on secret service in High Asia (1990) is all about. The phrase was apparently coined in the 1830s and widely used from the 1870s onwards. 'When he comes to the Great Game he must go alone – alone, and at peril of his head' – Rudyard Kipling, *Kim*, Chap. 7 (1901); 'Some John Buchan hero, busily playing the Great Game for Queen and Country' – *The Guardian* (17 March 1961); 'Originally the Secret Service was entrusted to amateurs who played "the great game", as they romantically called it' – John Welcome, *Hard to Handle*, Chap. 2 (1964); 'The extensive action of *The Mulberry Empire* swirls between two great cities – London and Kabul – in the years that saw Afghanistan first become embroiled in the Great Game' – *The Observer* (2 March 2003).

(the) Great Helmsman Sobriquet for Chairman Mao Tse-tung during the Cultural Revolution in China of the 1960s. It was applied, jokingly, to Edward Heath, when British Prime Minister (1970–76), because of his enthusiasm for yachting.

(the) Great Leap Forward Chairman Mao Tse-tung's phrase for the enforced industrialization in China in 1958. It is now used ironically about any supposed move in the forward direction.

(the) great majority (or simply **the majority)** The dead – since the 18th century (compare SILENT MAJORITY). Edward Yonge's *The Revenge* (1719) has: 'Death joins us to the great majority.' In the Epistle Dedicatory of *Urn-Burial* (1658), Sir Thomas Browne writes of: 'When the living might exceed, and to depart this world could not be properly said to go unto the greatest number.' There is also the Latin phrase *abiit ad plures*. The dying words of Lord Houghton in 1884 were: 'Yes, I am going to join the Majority and you know I have always preferred Minorities.' *Punch* (19 June 1907) carries an exchange between a parson and a parishioner after a funeral: 'Joined the great majority, eh?' 'Oh, I wouldn't like to say

that, Sir. He was a good enough man as far as I know.'

great minds think alike Sometimes self-congratulatory, sometimes mutually congratulatory exclamation, when people agree with each other. Originally 'great wits jump together' (by 1618); in this form perhaps by the 1890s. Can also be applied to others and ironically: 'Lord Riddell considers that Mr H. G. Wells is one of the world's greatest minds. Great minds, as the saying is, think alike' – *Punch* (27 December 1922).

(the) great open (or **wide open) spaces** The place to which an escape is made from the confines of city- or town-dwelling. 'I recall as if I had been there the wide open spaces, the ragged hillsides [of South Africa]' – H. G. Wells, *The New Machiavelli* (1911); 'You will find me somewhere out there in the great open spaces where men are men' – P. G. Wodehouse, *Leave It To Psmith*, Chap. 8 (1924); 'Are you familiar with the expression "the great open spaces"?' – P. G. Wodehouse, *Ice In the Bedroom*, Chap. 1 (1961); 'The spaces are very great and open there, he tells me' – from the same book, Chap. 19; 'If you seek clean fresh air and the wide open spaces (cliché though it is, that phrase is exactly right), this is the place' – *The Times* (8 February 1975).

great Scott! Euphemistic expletive. 'Great Scott!' clearly sounds like 'Great God!' and yet is not blasphemous. *Morris* states that the expression became popular when the American Winfield Scott was the hero of the Mexican War (1847) and 'probably our most admired general between Washington and Lee'. No rival candidate seems to have been proposed, and the origination is almost certainly American. The diary of Private Robert Knox Sneden (published as *Eye of the Storm: a Civil War Odyssey*) (entry for 3 May 1864) has: '"Great Scott," who would have thought that this would be the destiny of the Union Volunteer in 1861–2 while marching down Broadway to the tune of "John Brown's Body".' *OED2*'s earliest British English example dates from 1885.

(the) Great Society Slogan/name of President Lyndon Johnson's policy platform in the USA. In a speech at the

University of Michigan (May 1964) he said: 'In your time, we have the opportunity to move not only toward the rich society and the powerful society but upward to the Great Society.'

(the) Great Train Robbery Journalistic tag given to the spectacular hold-up of a Glasgow-to-London train in Buckinghamshire (1963), when £2,500,000 was stolen from a mail van. Those who committed the robbery were consequently dubbed 'the Great Train Robbers'. *The Great Train Robbery* had earlier been the title of a silent film (US 1903) that is sometimes considered to be the first 'real' movie. The 1963 robbery was, in turn, appropriately 'celebrated' in the films *Robbery* (1967) and *Buster* (1988).

(the) Great Unwashed Meaning, 'working-class people; the lower orders'. This term was originally used by the politician and writer Edmund Burke (d. 1797), perhaps echoing Shakespeare's reference to 'another lean unwash'd artificer' – *King John*, IV.ii.201 (1596). Lytton in *Paul Clifford* (1830) uses the full phrase.

(the) Great Wen London. In *Rural Rides* (1830), William Cobbett asked of London: 'But what is to be the fate of the great wen of all? The monster, called . . . "the metropolis of empire"?' A 'wen' is a lump or protuberance on a body; a wart. Compare MONSTROUS CARBUNCLE.

(the) Great White Way Nickname for Broadway, the main theatre zone of New York City – alluding to the brightness of the illumination and taken from the title of a novel (1901) by Albert Bigelow Paine. For a while, Broadway was also known as 'the Gay White Way', though for understandable reasons this is no longer so. In Vanessa Letts, *New York* (1991), it is confidently stated, however, that the phrase 'Great White Way' was coined by an advertising man called O. J. Gude in 1901, 'and actually referred to the stretch of Broadway *below* 34th Street which was illuminated in 1880 and got its first electricity-driven advertisement . . . in 1891.'

Greeks See BEWARE.

(the) Greeks had a word for it Phrase used, a trifle archly, when one wishes to express disapproval – as one might say: 'There's a name for that sort of behaviour'. From the title of a US play (1930) by Zoë Akins, although, as she said, the 'phrase is original and grew out of the dialogue', but it does not appear anywhere in the text. The 'it' refers to a type of woman. One character thinks that 'tart' is meant, but the other corrects this and says 'free soul' is more to the point.

green See I'M NOT SO.

(the) green-eyed monster Jealousy. From Shakespeare's *Othello*, III.iii.170 (1604), where Iago says to Othello, 'O, beware jealousy; / It is the green-ey'd monster, which doth mock / That meat it feeds on.'

(to have) green fingers To have a natural talent for gardening and for making plants grow. 'A green thumb' may be an American version (by 1943) – and this compares with a miller's 'golden thumb' (though a sign of dishonesty), as mentioned in Chaucer. The title *Green Fingers* was used for a book of gardening poems (1934) by Reginald Arkell. It may have been popularized by C. H. Middleton ('Mr Middleton'), the BBC radio gardening expert from 1931 to 1945.

(a) Green Goddess Alliterative nickname that has been applied variously to Second World War fire engines (painted green), Liverpool trams, a crème de menthe cocktail, a lettuce salad and a lily. In 1983, Diana Moran, a keep-fit demonstrator on a BBC TV breakfast programme, was also so billed. She wore distinctive green exercise clothing. Perhaps all these uses derive from William Archer's play entitled *The Green Goddess* (1923; film US 1930).

green grow the rushes, oh One of the many almost impenetrable phrases from one of the most quoted folk songs. A pamphlet from the English Folk Dance and Song Society (*circa* 1985) remarks: 'This song has appeared in many forms in ancient and modern languages from Hebrew onwards, and it purports in almost all cases to be theological.' *Green Grow the Rushes* was used as the title of a film (UK 1950). Here is what some of the other phrases in the song *may* be about: 'I'll sing you one oh, / Green grow the rushes oh, /

One is one and all alone and evermore shall be so' [refers to God Almighty.] 'Two, two for the **lilywhite boys**, / Clothed all in green oh.' [Christ and St John the Baptist as children (though what the green refers to is not clear). Compare the title of Christopher Logue's 1950s' play *The Lily-White Boys*.] 'Three, three for the rivals [The Trinity? The Three Wise Men?] / Four for the Gospel makers [Matthew, Mark, Luke, and John?] / Five for the **symbol at your door** [the Pentagram or five-pointed star inscribed on the threshold to drive away the evil one.] / Six for the **six proud walkers** [the six *waterpots* used in the miracle of Cana of Galilee. Compare the title of Donald Wilson's detective series on BBC TV (1954, 1964), *The Six Proud Walkers*.] / Seven for the seven stars in the sky [the group in Ursa Major called Charley's Wain; or the seven days of the week; or Revelation 1:16: 'And he had in his right hand seven stars and out of his mouth went a two-edged sword.'] / Eight for the eight bold rainers/rangers/archangels [bold rainers, i.e. angels? But why eight? There are only four archangels, so why double? A 1625 version refers to the people in Noah's Ark who might well be described as 'bold rangers'.] / Nine for the nine bright shiners [the nine choirs of angels? The nine months before birth?] / Ten for the ten commandments [obvious, this one.] / Eleven for the eleven that went up to heaven [the Apostles without Judas Iscariot.] / Twelve for the twelve apostles [or the tribes of Israel].'

green shoots   Phrase used to indicate that something is about to bud or bloom. As Britain's Chancellor of the Exchequer, Norman Lamont was earnestly endeavouring to convince his audience that Britain was coming out of a recession when he used this horticultural metaphor in a speech to the Conservative Party Conference at Blackpool on 9 October 1991: 'The turn of the tide is sometimes difficult to discern. What we are seeing is the return of that vital ingredient – confidence. The green shoots of economic spring are appearing once again.' In a letter to a lover (6 May 1962), the poet Philip Larkin wrote: 'Spring comes with your birthday, and I love to think of you as somehow linked with the tender green shoots I see on all the trees and bushes . . . I wish I could be with you and we could plunge into bed.'

Gregory   See MILK?

grey suits   See MAN IN A GREY.

grievous bodily harm (or GBH)   British legal term for an offence that involves serious injury. Known by 1861. Since the 1950s, the term has been used almost invariably in its initials form, especially outside the legal field. There are other grades – e.g. Actual Bodily Harm.

grind   See AXE TO GRIND.

grinding   See COME TO A.

grinning   See CHESHIRE CAT.

(to be) grist to (someone's) mill   To be capable of being turned to profit or advantage, made use of. Known by 1583 and referring to the saying 'All is grist that comes to his mill', i.e. 'the miller makes profits from any corn that comes to his mill'. Cited as a 'dying metaphor' by George Orwell, 'Politics and the English Language' in *Horizon* (April 1946). 'Local artists often are grist for the critic's malevolent word mill. This isn't fair because area performers are competing with world-class companies that tour here. Good, bad and indifferent, local artists are the heart of a town. It's important for them to perform, but not always pleasant to see' – *The Washington Post* (4 April 1995); 'On the 1992 tribute album "Sweet Relief: A Benefit for Victoria Williams," Williams's songs were interpreted by a wide variety of bands and musicians, including Pearl Jam and Soul Asylum. "Loose" boasts a similarly convivial atmosphere. Folk, country, pop and rock are all grist for the mill' – *The Washington Post* (11 December 1994).

(the) grit in the oyster   The catalyst/agent for change – in the same way that the grit in an oyster delivers improvements and renders the pearl. A fashionable image, say from the late 1990s. 'Leadership is the grit in the oyster that produces real outcomes for students and employers' – Charles Clarke, Secretary of State for Education, speech to the Association of Colleges' annual conference (19 November 2002).

grody to the max 'Vile, grotty, unspeakably awful to the maximum degree' – from American 'Valspeak', the slang of American pubescent teenage girls (aged 13 to 17) of a type first observed and indentified in California's San Fernando Valley in the early 1980s. She is from a fairly well-to-do family, her passions are shopping, junk food, cosmetics, and speaking in a curious language – Valspeak – 'for sure' (pronounced 'fer shurr'), 'totally' (pronounced 'todally' or 'toe-dully'), **gag me with a spoon** (expression of disgust 'you make me feel sick'). The phrases first became known to the outside world in 1982, especially following its inclusion in the record 'Valley Girl', performed by Moon Unit, the 15-year-old daughter of Frank Zappa.

groovy baby! Catchphrase given added impetus *circa* 1968 through its use by the disc jockey Dave Cash on BBC Radio 1. He would play a brief clip of an actual baby boy, referred to as 'Microbe', saying it. As a result, 'Groovy baby' stickers were much in demand and Blue Mink incorporated 'Microbe' saying the phrase on a record with the title (1969). 'Groovy' meaning 'very good' (particularly of music) was, in any case, already popular in the 1960s, although *DOAS* traces it back to the mid-1930s and its use among 'swing' musicians and devotees. It comes from 'in the groove', referring to the way a gramophone or phonograph stylus or needle fits neatly into the groove on a record.

ground-breaking Phrase for any activity that 'breaks new ground'. At the start of building operations there is often a ground-breaking ceremony performed. In the figurative sense, the phrase was known by 1907. 'Such suspicions are, at present, almost completely without foundation, according to Professor Carl McMillan of Carleton University in Ottawa who presented a ground-breaking study to a Nato economic seminar last month' – *Financial Times* (18 May 1983); 'The judge, who made his order under section 4 (2) of the 1981 Contempt of Court Act, said that he did not doubt a sincere attempt would be made to present a balanced picture in what Channel 4 had described as "ground-breaking coverage"

of a trial' – *The Guardian* (29 January 1985); 'Ingram's legal battle to stay alive, defeated in the US Supreme Court last month and again minutes before his death, led to a ground-breaking ruling that jurors' beliefs on whether a death penalty will be imposed or not is legally irrelevant' – Press Association report (8 April 1995); 'Delivering the James MacTaggart Memorial Lecture . . . the creator of ground-breaking shows such as *Network 7, The Vampyr* and the *Def II* youth strand said that British television had been pushed to crisis point' – *The Independent* (26 August 1995).

ground zero The basic position from which you start. This (probably) military and American coinage may date from early in the Second World War. It is occasionally still used in the original sense: 'Burns was advocating that government agencies start from ground zero, as it were, with each year's budget and present their requests for appropriations in such a fashion that all funds can be allocated on the basis of cost/benefit or some similar kind of evaluative analysis' P. A. Pyhrr in *Harvard Business Review* (Nov.–Dec. 1970). The phrase soon took on another meaning: the point of impact or part of the ground immediately under an exploding bomb, especially an atomic one. 'The intense heat of the blast started fires as far as 3,500 feet from "ground zero" (the point on the ground directly under the bomb's explosion in the air)' – *The New York Times* (7 July 1946) – referring to the dropping of atomic bombs on Japan. *Black Scorpion: Ground Zero* was the title of a film (US 1996) about someone trying to steal earthquake relief funds and *Ground Zero* (US 2000) about a woman taking her son to the scene of an earthquake that claimed his father's life and discovering that a sinister company could have caused the tragedy. Following the terrorist attacks on the World Trade Center in New York on 11 September 2001, almost instantly the name 'Ground Zero' was applied to the site of rubble where the devastated twin towers once stood. Perhaps the meaning will change permanently to 'site of massive destruction'.

(the) groves of Academe The world of scholarship; the academic community. A translation of Horace's phrase *silvas Academi*. Popular in its English form since the mid-19th century.

(a) growing experience   Meaning, 'an experience that leads to the positive development of your character'. When the American film people David and Talia Shire were experiencing 'a very loving separation', said she, 'We're going to rotate the house and we even rotate the car. We've been separated for four months and it's a growing experience' – quoted by William Safire in *The New York Times* Magazine (20 January 1980).

guest   See BE MY.

(a) guide, philosopher and friend   Ingratiating form of address (compare GENTLEMAN AND A SCHOLAR), it originally came from Alexander Pope's *An Essay on Man* (1733): 'Shall then this verse to future age pretend / Thou wert my guide, philosopher and friend?'

guilty as sin   See UGLY AS SIN.

gum   See ANY GUM; CAN'T EAT; HE CAN'T; DROP THE; GET YOUR.

gun   See HAVE GUN.

Guinness is good for you   Slogan for Guinness beer. After 170 years without advertising, Arthur Guinness, Son & Company decided to call in the image-makers for their beer in 1929. So, Oswald Greene at the S. H. Benson agency initiated some consumer research (unusual in those days) into why people drank Guinness. It transpired that they thought it did them good. Today, ask British people to give you an example of an advertising slogan and the chances are they are likely to quote 'Guinness is Good for You'. It is etched on the national consciousness although the slogan was discontinued *circa* 1941 and has not been revived since 1963.

gunfire   See ALWAYS STEER.

gung-ho   Meaning 'enthusiastic, if carelessly so', the phrase derives from Chinese *kung* plus *ho*, meaning 'work together'. It became a semi-official slogan of the US Marines during the Second World War –

said to have been chosen by Lieutenant General Evans F. Carlson. Hence, in 1943, a film about the Marines had the title *Gung Ho!* In Geoff Chapple, *Rewi Alley of China* (1980), it is stated that the phrase was coined in 1938 and used as the motto of the Chinese Industrial Co-operatives Association.

guns before butter   Political slogan associated with Joseph Goebbels, the German Nazi leader, though there are other candidates. When a nation is under pressure to choose between material comforts and some kind of war effort, the choice has to be made between 'guns *and* butter'. Some will urge 'guns *before* butter'. From a translation of a speech Goebbels gave in Berlin (17 January 1936): 'We can do without butter, but, despite all our love of peace, not without arms. One cannot shoot with butter, but with guns' Later that same year, however, Hermann Goering said in a broadcast, 'Guns will make us powerful; butter will only make us fat,' so he may also be credited with the 'guns or butter' slogan. But there is a third candidate. Airey Neave in his book *Nuremberg* (1978) stated of Rudolf Hess: 'It was he who urged the German people to make sacrifices and coined the phrase: "Guns before butter".'

gymslip mums   Teenage girls who become pregnant while still attending school – hence the, by now dated, reference to the traditional sleeveless tunic worn by British schoolgirls – the gymslip. Listed (and deplored) by Keith Waterhouse in *Daily Mirror Style* (1981) who wrote that the gymslip: 'Must have given way to jeans and T-shirt mums by now.' No, it hasn't. Not in the minds of out-of-touch journalists at any rate. 'Other vintage episodes being re-run for the first time include the October 1985 teaser which revealed the identity of gymslip mum Michelle's seducer – Dirty Den again' – *The Herald* (Glasgow) (30 January 1995); 'Today, Clare, Chris and Linda open their hearts exclusively to *The People* to reveal how they coped from the moment Linda discovered her daughter was about to become a gymslip mum' – *The People* (30 April 1995).

H

habeas corpus [you have the body]
Legal term. A habeas corpus is a writ
ordering someone who is keeping another
in custody to produce him in court. Its aim
is to stop people being imprisoned on
mere suspicion or kept waiting unduly for
trial. Hence, *Have His Carcase*, the title of
a detective novel (1932) by Dorothy L.
Sayers based on an old joke upon the
Latin legal phrase that Sam Weller makes,
for example, in Charles Dickens, *The
Pickwick Papers*, Chap. 40 (1836–7).

ha bloody ha! Sarcastic response to a
silly remark or a deed that the speaker
does not find funny. From the 1950s?

**(we) had one (of those) but the wheel
fell off** Response to pretentious use of
language or anything unintelligible. By the
late 19th century. More recently: **we had
one (of those) but it died/I lost the pawn
ticket**.

ha! ha! – joke over! Stock phrase of the
British music-hall entertainer Dick
Henderson Snr (1891–1958) after telling an
obvious or failed joke. *Partridge/Catch
Phrases* also has 'joke over' as a sarcastic
catchphrase addressed to the maker of a
feeble witticism from '*circa* 1925'.

ha-harr, Jim, lad! Nowadays used to
indicate how any piratical old sea dog
would talk, but originally an impersonation of Robert Newton as the eye-rolling,
very English West Country Long John
Silver in the film *Treasure Island* (UK
1950). The British comedian Tony
Hancock used an impersonation of Newton in his stage 'Concert Party' routine,
from the early 1950s onwards. This was
carried over to *Hancock's Half-hour* (BBC
radio and TV, later 1950s) in emulation of
bad impressionism.

hair See AFTER I'VE; BAD HAIR.

hair cut See GET YOUR.

(there's a) hair in the gate Joke explanation for almost anything that goes
wrong. It comes from filming, where this is
a frequent setback. J. K. Galbraith in *A Life*

in Our Times (1981), recalling his participation in a documentary film, says: 'A "hair
in the gate" means that, on post-operative
inspection, the camera lens – or something
else shows some defect. A retake is required.
Briefing me on what I could expect in my
new career, David Niven had warned, "Just
remember that when the cameraman or
the technicians bitch up, they will always
say there's a hair in the gate".'

(the) hair of the dog (that bit me)
Meaning, 'another drink of the same to
help cure a hangover'. This comes from
the old belief that a bite from a mad dog
could be cured if you put hair from the
same dog's tail on the wound. Known by
1760, but this unconfirmed couplet is said
to date from 1546: 'I pray thee let me and
my fellow have / A haire of the dog that
bit us last night.'

half of my kingdom See EVEN UNTO.

Halifax See COME HELL.

hallelujah, I'm a bum Title of a song
(1928) by Harry Kirby McClintock, later
popularized by Burl Ives. In 1933, the
song was used as the basis of the US film
Hallelujah, I'm a Bum, which starred Al
Jolson as a tramp. In Britain, a change of
title to *Hallelujah, I'm a Tramp* was forced
upon the distributors. For the film, a new
song with the title was written by Lorenz
Hart (music by Richard Rodgers) which, in
fact, only included the line 'Hallelujah, I'm
a bum again!' Even so, a separate version
had to be made for the sensitive British
censor.

halls See DARLING OF THE.

(the) halt and the blind Phrase for any
group of unfortunate people. From the
parable of the great supper in St Luke
14:21: 'Go out quickly into the streets and
lanes of the city and bring in hither the
poor, and the maimed, and the halt and
the blind.' 'Halt' here means 'lame, crip-
pled, limping'.

***Hamlet* without the Prince** An event
without the leading participant. Byron

wrote in a letter on 26 August 1818: 'My autobiographical essay would resemble the tragedy of Hamlet . . . recited "with the part of Hamlet left out by particular desire".' This and other early uses of the phrase may possibly hark back to a theatrical anecdote as told in the *Morning Post* (21 September 1775): 'Lee Lewes diverts them with the manner of their performing Hamlet in a company that he belonged to, when the hero who was to play the principal character had absconded with an inn-keeper's daughter; and that when he came forward to give out the play, he added, "the part of Hamlet to be left out, for that night".' Compare the title of Philip King's play *Without the Prince* (1946). In 1938, James Agate headed his review of a Ralph Richardson perform-ance: 'Othello Without the Moor'.

(to go at something) hammer and tongs   To do something with great vigour – as a blacksmith hammers the metal that he holds with tongs. By 1708. The original expression may have been 'To live ham-mer and tongs' where the suggestion is that those involved are always quarrelling. 'They beat each other like hammers and are as cross as the tongs' – *Brewer* (1894), which also quotes: 'Both parties went at it hammer and tongs; and hit one another anywhere and with anything' – James Payn.

hand   See CLOUD NO BIGGER.

handbasket   See GO TO HELL.

hand in glove   Meaning, 'going together extremely well or closely, as snugly as a hand in a glove, in close association or partnership'. Sometimes with a suggestion of connivance. Originally 'hand *and* glove', by 1680. Listed in *The Independent* (24 December 1994) as a cliché of newspa-per editorials. 'Architects and builders seldom work hand-in-glove on the kind of housing people can afford to buy' – *The Guardian* (22 February 1975); 'It is a much more smoothly organized system now, almost seamless, and it makes us much more effective in getting our jobs done. Because they have improved their organi-zation, [our customers] are also going to get an improvement, because the two go hand in glove' – *Lloyd's List* (18 October

1994); '"Oh Ireland, my first and only love / Where Christ and Caesar are hand in glove." Those lines by James Joyce seem at first sight, to encapsulate poetically the dramatic developments which have un-folded in Dublin over the last few days' – *Scotland on Sunday* (20 November 1994).

hand over fist   As in 'to make money hand over fist'. A similar expression, 'pulling it in', provides the origin here. If you are pulling in a rope or hoisting a sail on board ship, you pass it between your two hands and, in so doing, unavoidably put one hand over the fist of the other hand. Current by 1825.

hands off cock(s), on with sock(s)   As though delivered as a wake-up call to a men's dormitory (in the army, Boy Scouts, or wherever), this cry was included, for example, in a play called *Is Your Doctor Really Necessary?* at the Theatre Royal, Stratford East in 1973. *Partridge/Catch Phrases* suggests an early 20th-century British Army origin and the slightly more elaborate form: 'Hands off your cocks and pull up your socks!' The female equivalent is: **all hands above the bedclothes, girls**, which Edward V. Marks said (1994) that he overheard said by one of three women in their late twenties who were in a tea-shop in Kensington on their way to an old girls' reunion.

hands   See ALL HANDS; COLD HANDS.

(the) hand that rocks the cradle (is the hand that rules the world)   This tribute to motherhood comes from 'What Rules the World' by the US poet William Ross Wallace (d. 1881). *The Hand That Rocks the Cradle* was the title of a film (US 1992).

(to) hang, draw and quarter   To execute for treason using a method known by the mid-17th century and last carried out in the UK in 1867. The order of procedure is actually 'drawn, hanged, and quartered' as is plain from the words of a British judge sentencing Irish rebels in 1775: 'You are to be *drawn* on hurdles to the place of execution, where you are to be *hanged* by the neck but not until you are dead; for, while you are still living, your bodies are to be taken down, your bowels torn out and burned before your faces; your heads then cut off, and your bodies *divided each* *into four quarters*, and your heads and quarters to be then at the King's disposal; and may the Almighty God have mercy on your souls.' However, if the meaning of 'draw' is taken as 'eviscerate, have your bowels torn out', then this would obviously occur between the hanging and the quartering.

(to) hang fire To be hesitant, hold back. This expression comes from gunnery – when the gun is slow to fire, or there is a delay between the fuse being ignited and the weapon firing. Current by 1781 and, figuratively, by 1801.

(to) hang in the balance To be in a position where an outcome of something is not known – as though one was waiting for a balance to be tipped one way or the other. 'Throughout March his future seemed to hang in the balance' – Arthur Bryant, *Samuel Pepys: The Man in the Making*, Chap. 18 (1933).

(to) hang someone out to dry To punish a person by isolating them from their group. Date of origin unkown. Probably American. '"Nasser has been hung out to dry; he could do nothing about it"' – *The Observer* (16 February 2003). 'Even Mr Blair, America's most trusty ally but in dire political straits at home if he fails to get UN blessing, was hung out to dry' – *The Independent* (8 March 2003). Compare TWIST SLOWLY, SLOWLY IN THE WIND.

hang the Kaiser! Slogan. Given the role played in the First World War by Kaiser Wilhelm II, there was pressure for retribution at the war's end during the 1918 British General Election. The demand was largely fuelled by the press. The Treaty of Versailles (1919) committed the Allies to trying the Kaiser (who was forced to abdicate), but the government of the Netherlands refused to hand him over. He lived until 1941.

hang your knickers on the line Domestic catchphrase. When someone asks, 'What's the time?' and the answer happens to be (as it does, frequently, for some reason), 'Half past nine', the first person says, '(Hang your) knickers on the line.' Known in the UK by the 1950s. In a section called 'Crooked Answers' in *The*

Lore and Language of Schoolchildren (1959), Iona and Peter Opie print two versions of a rhyme from Alton, Hampshire: 'What's the time? / Half past nine / Put the napkins on the line. / When they're dry / Bring them in / And don't forget the safety pin.' And: 'What's the time? / Half past nine / Hang your breeches on the line. / When the copper / Comes along / Pull them off and put them on.'

happen See ACCIDENT WAITING; ANYTHING CAN.

happens See AS IT.

(the) happiest days of one's life The traditional platitude intoned by an old buffer giving away the prizes at school speech days is that his listeners will agree (or will come to realize) that schooldays are 'the happiest days of your life'. The expression of this sentiment pre-dates *The Happiest Days of Your Life*, a famous play by John Dighton (produced in London in 1948; film UK 1950.) However, the schoolchildren in that work may have had special cause to believe the catchphrase as the plot hinges on wartime confusion in which a boys' school and a girls' school are lodged under the same roof. Winston Churchill wrote in *My Early Life* (1930): 'I was told that "school days were the happiest time in one's life".' Lord Berners wrote in *A Distant Prospect* (1945): 'Accounts I had been given of Eton – not by the kind of old gentleman who says that his schooldays were his happiest . . .' Compare **the best years of one's life**, which dates from at least 1827. Groucho Marx says in *Monkey Business* (1931): 'Oh, so that's it. Infatuated with a pretty uniform! We don't count, after we've given you the best years of our lives. You have to have an officer.' 'Mrs Eduardo Acuna' in *You Were Never Lovelier* (US 1942) says: 'I gave you the best twenty-five years of my life'. *The Best Years of Our Lives* is the title of an American film (1946) about what happens to a group of ex-servicemen when they return from the war – presumably having 'given the best years of their lives' to their country. Also, **the best days of our lives** is an expression used in this kind of context. *Days of Our Lives*, the title of the long-running US TV daytime soap opera (current by 1983), could somehow be alluding to one or more of these phrases. 'Days of our lives' is not biblical, though there are any number of near-misses, like 'labours all the days of his life' (Ecclesiastes 8:15).

happily See AND THEY ALL.

happiness is —— Slogan. Samuel Johnson declared in 1766, 'Happiness consists in the multiplicity of agreeable consciousness,' but he was not the first to have a go at defining happiness, nor the last. In 1942, along came E. Y. Harburg with the lyrics to his song 'Happiness is a Thing Called Joe'. However, it was Charles M. Schultz, creator of the Peanuts comic strip, who really launched the 'Happiness is —— ' format. In *circa* 1957 he had drawn a strip 'centring around some kid hugging Snoopy and saying in the fourth panel that "Happiness is a warm puppy".' This became the title of a best-selling book in 1962 and let loose a stream of promotional phrases using the format, including: 'Happiness is egg-shaped', 'Happiness is a cigar called Hamlet', 'Happiness is a warm ear-piece' (UK ad slogans); 'Happiness is being elected team captain – and getting a Bulova watch', 'Happiness is a $49 table' (both US ad slogans); 'Happiness is seeing Lubbock, Texas, in the rear view mirror' (line from a Country and Western song); 'Happiness is a Warm Gun' (song title), 'Happiness is Wren-shaped', and many, many more. By which time one might conclude that 'Happiness is . . . a worn cliché'.

(as) happy as a sandboy (or jolly/merry as . . .) These expressions would seem to refer to the boy who used to hawk sand from door to door, but why he was especially remarkable for his happiness is hard to say. The *OED2* finds a quotation from Pierce Egan (1821): 'As happy as a sandboy who had unexpectedly met with good luck in disposing of his hampers full of the above household commodity.' Dickens in *The Old Curiosity Shop* (1840–1) has 'The Jolly Sandboys' as the name of a pub, with a sign 'representing three Sandboys increasing their jollity with as many jugs of ale and bags of gold'. Angus Easson in his Penguin edition notes: 'Sand was sold for scouring, as a floor cover to absorb liquids, and for bird cages.

Sandboys were proverbially happy people, as indeed they might be in 1840 when they could buy a load of about $2^1/_2$ tons for 3s. 6d. ($17^1/_2$p), and take £6 or £7 in a morning . . . During the century, sawdust tended to replace sand for floors . . . and, by 1851, those in the trade were much less happy.' Indeed, Henry Mayhew, *London Labour and the London Poor* (1861), wrote: 'The trade is inconsiderable to what it was, saw-dust having greatly superseded it in the gin-palace, the tap-room, and the butcher's shop.' Other explanations are that the phrase refers to a type of sand flea known as a 'sandboy' (it looks jolly because of the way it jumps and hops about) or to the jollity that would come from much alcoholic refreshment – of the type that the sandboys, working in a dusty environment, would require. 'One night we went to the theatre, and back to Fred's, had a jolly supper and got as merry as sand-boys' – 'Walter', *My Secret Life*, Vol. 2, Chap. 12 (1888–92).

(as) happy as Larry Meaning, 'extremely happy'. *Brewer* (1999) has it as an Australian expression and supposedly referring to the boxer Larry Foley (1847–1917). The first *OED2* citation (indeed Australian) is from 1905. Another suggestion is that the phrase derives from the Australian 'larrikin', meaning 'lout, hoodlum, mischievous young person'.

(as) happy as the day is long Happy and contented. Current by 1786, this expression was much used, for example, by Charles Dickens who, nevertheless, occasionally varied it. In *David Copperfield*, Chap. 41 (1849–50), he wrote: 'We . . . were happy as the week was long.' In 1820, Lord Norbury joked of Caroline of Brunswick's behaviour with the *dey* (governor) of Algiers: 'She was happy as the dey was long.'

happy birthday to you The most frequently sung phrase in English, according to *The Guinness Book of Records 1985* (which also lists 'For He's a Jolly Good Fellow' and 'Auld Lang Syne' as the most performed songs of all time). It started out as 'Good Morning to All' with words by Patty Smith Hill and music by Mildred J. Hill in *Song Stories for the Kindergarten*

(1893). 'Happy Birthday to You' is the first line of the second stanza, but was not promoted to the title until 1935. The song has had a chequered legal history because of the erroneous belief that it is in the public domain and out of copyright.

(the) happy couple A pair about to be or just joined in matrimony. Known by 1753. '"There were cards and good luck messages for the happy couple," said the insider. "But now things don't look too good, we're getting phone calls blaming Des for everything again"' – *Daily Mirror* (14 January 1995); 'About 40 friends and family joined the happy couple at the church' – *Daily Record* (28 January 1995). Similarly, **the happy pair**. This phrase was known by 1633 and, in the specifically marital sense, by 1697.

(ah,) happy days! Catchphrase from the BBC radio show *Band Waggon* (1938–39). Sighed nostalgically by Arthur Askey and Richard Murdoch in unison when reminiscing about the early days in their flat on the top of Broadcasting House. The phrase is also well known in other contexts. By the early 20th century it was a popular drinker's toast, deriving from the form that Tennyson included in *In Memoriam* (1850): 'Drinking health to bride and groom / We wish them store of happy days.' The song 'Happy Days Are Here Again' appeared in 1930. 'Happy days, happy days!' is a line in J. B. Priestley's play *When We Are Married* (1938). In 1974, *Happy Days* was taken as the title of a long-running US TV series that looked back nostalgically to the 1950s.

(the) happy hunting grounds A translation of the North American Indian name for 'heaven, paradise', the phrase is now used of any field that appears fruitful. H. L. Mencken's *The American Language*, 4th ed. (1947) has: 'There was also some translation of terms supposed to be in use among the Indians, e.g., squaw-man, heap big chief, Great White Father, Father of Waters, and happy hunting-grounds, but most of these, I suspect, owed more to the imagination of the pioneers than to the actual usage of the Indians.' In Supplement I (1945), Mencken adds that 'happy hunting-grounds' was apparently first

introduced by James Fennimore Cooper in his novel *Pathfinder* (1840). In fact, he also has it in *The Pioneers, or the Sources of the Susquehanna*, Chap. 38 (1823): 'Hawk-eye! my fathers call me to the happy hunting-grounds.' There is some doubt as to whether Cooper's Indianisms are genuine, however.

(a) happy medium A compromise, avoiding extremes. Known by 1778.

(a) hard act to follow Meaning, 'my predecessor has been very good and I may not be able to equal him'. Clearly derived from show business, say in the early 1900s, where an act appearing after a particularly successful one might have its work cut out to attract the audience's support.

hard cheese! Tough luck! Known since the late 19th century and possibly linked to the meaning of 'cheese' as 'the best thing'. Hard cheese is not the best.

(a) hard day's night *A Hard Day's Night* – the title of the Beatles' first feature film (UK 1964) – was apparently chosen towards the end of filming when Ringo Starr used the phrase to describe a 'heavy' night – according to Ray Coleman, *John Lennon* (1984). What, in fact, Ringo must have done was to use the title of the Lennon and McCartney song (presumably already written if it was towards the end of filming) in a conversational way. Indeed, Hunter Davies in *The Beatles* (1968) notes: 'Ringo Starr came out with the phrase, though John had used it earlier in a poem.' It certainly sounds like a Lennonism and may have had some limited general use subsequently as a catchphrase meaning that one has had 'a very tiring time'.

hard-faced men who had done well out of the war Members of the House of Commons who had been returned in the 1918 General Election were so described by a 'Conservative politician', according to John Maynard Keynes in *The Economic Consequences of Peace* (1919). In fact, Stanley Baldwin, a future Conservative Prime Minister, was the one who said it. In the biography of Baldwin by Keith Middlemas, he is also quoted as having noted privately on 12 February 1918: 'We have started with the new House of Commons. They look much as usual – not so young as I had expected. The prevailing type is a rather successful-looking business kind which is not very attractive.' The playwright Julian Mitchell, surveying members of Mrs Thatcher's government, remarked that they looked like 'hard-faced men who had done well out of the peace' – BBC Radio, *Quote . . . Unquote* (22 June 1988).

hard knocks See SCHOOL OF HARD.

hardest See FIRST YEARS.

harm can come to a young man like that (or lad . . .)! Fairly frequent cry of the pathetic Bluebottle (Peter Sellers) in the BBC radio *Goon Show* (1951–60). He was much put upon and exploded.

harness See CAME THE DAWN.

has he been in, whack? *Club Night* was a radio comedy series produced in the BBC's North Region in 1955–6 and was hosted by the pebble-lensed 'manager', Dave Morris. He would be pestered repeatedly by an eccentric figure who asked, "'As 'e bin in, whack?' 'E never 'ad, of course. Morris also originated the saying **meet the wife – don't laugh!** What the real Mrs Morris thought of this is something we may perhaps never know.

***hasta la vista*, baby** The Spanish for 'goodbye, au revoir, until we meet again' [literally, 'until the seeing'] was given a distinctive twist by Arnold Schwarzennegger in the film *Terminator II: Judgement Day* (US 1991).

hat See AT THE DROP.

hatband See AS QUEER AS.

hatched, matched and dispatched Nickname given to the births, marriages and deaths column of a newspaper. The phrase was referred to in a *Punch* poem (17 August 1904).

hatchet See BURY THE.

hats off, strangers! Traditional cry in the House of Commons when the Speaker's Procession tramps through the Central Lobby. It tends to be bellowed out by a policeman.

have a banana! Britain became 'banana conscious' in the early years of the 20th century following the appointment of

Roger Ackerley as chief salesman of Elders & Fyffes, banana importers, in 1898. The phrase 'have a banana!' – never a slogan as such – was popularly interpolated at the end of the first line of the song 'Let's All Go Down the Strand', which was published in 1904. It had not been put there by the composer but was so successful that later printings of the song always included it. Every time it was sung, the phrase reinforced the sales campaign free of charge. There is a slight sexual innuendo, of course, in the phrase – as in the song 'Burlington Bertie from Bow' (1914) – 'I've had a banana with Lady Diana'.

have a go Police slogan encouraging public participation in the fight against crime in the UK (1964). Sir Ranulph Bacon, then Assistant Commissioner at Scotland Yard, caused a storm of protest when he urged members of the public to 'have a go' if, say, they saw an armed robbery taking place. His advice was labelled 'madness' and 'suicidal' by the British Safety Council. The phrase was presumably inspired by the title of a long-running BBC radio show (1946–67). *Have A Go* was a folksy, travelling affair – a simple quiz that enabled the host, Wilfred Pickles, accompanied by his wife, Mabel, to indulge in folksy chatting to contestants. Within twelve months of its start, it had an audience of twenty million. The show had, in turn, taken its name from an old phrase known by the early 19th century, meaning 'have a try, make an attempt'.

have a gorilla! A way of offering a cigarette in the BBC radio *Goon Show* (1951–60). To which the reply might be 'No, thank you, I'm trying to give them up' or 'No, thanks, I only smoke baboons!' Many variations on this occur in the edition entitled 'Napoleon's Piano' (11 October 1955).

have a nice day (or good/happy day) Parting remark. William Safire traces the origins of this pervasive American greeting in his book *On Language* (1980). He finds 'Farewell, have good day' occurring twice in Chaucer's *The Canterbury Tales* (*circa* 1387). Then he jumps to 1956 and the Carson/Roberts advertising agency in Los Angeles. 'Our phone was answered "Good morning, Carson/Roberts. Have a happy day,' recalled Ralph Carson. 'We used the salutation on all letters, tie tacks, cuff buttons, beach towels, blazer crests, the works.' Shortly after this, WCBS-TV weather-girl Carol Reed would wave goodbye with 'Have a happy'. In the 1960s, 'Have a good day' was still going strong. Then the early 1970s saw 'Have a nice day' push its insidious way in, although Kirk Douglas had got his tongue around it in the 1948 film *A Letter to Three Wives*. 'Have a nice city' was a slogan in the 1970 Los Angeles mayoral election. From all this, it may be understood that the usage seems likely to have been a Californian imposition upon the rest of the USA (and the world beyond). Similarly **missing you already!** (said to someone parting). Known by 1992, though in the earlier film *When Harry Met Sally* (US 1989), one lover says to the other, 'I'm missing you already.'

have gun, will travel   Advertising line – best known as the title of a TV Western series (US 1957–64) – this led to a format phrase capable of much variation. The hired-gun hero of the series had on his business card, 'Have gun. Will travel. Wire Paladin. San Francisco', and this probably reflects what actually appeared in newspaper personal columns at the end of the 19th century, say. Later, the phrase turned up in many ways – as joke slogans ('Have pill, will'; 'Have wife, must travel') and even as the UK title of another TV series (1981) – *Have Girls, Will Travel* (but known as *The American Girls* in the USA).

have I got news for you!   Be prepared to receive some startling information. Mostly American use since the 1950s? – though there is an example in the BBC radio *Goon Show* (recorded 2 December 1956). 'Have We Got News For You' was the title of a record by the March Hare (including Peter Skellern) *circa* 1969. *Have I Got News for You* has been the title of a BBC TV quiz about the week's news (since 1990).

(the) haves and the have-nots   The advantaged and disadvantaged in society. Motteux's 1700 translation of Cervantes's *Don Quixote* has Sancho Panza saying: 'There are only two families in the world, the Haves and the Have-Nots' (Spanish *el*

tener and *el no tener*). Edward Bulwer-Lytton in *Athens* (1836) wrote: 'The division . . . of the Rich and the Poor – the havenots and the haves.'

have you ever had any embarrassing moments?   Stock phrase from the BBC radio show *Have A Go* (1946–67). The host, Wilfred Pickles (1904–78), spent most of the programme fishing for laughs with questions like 'Have you ever had any embarrassing moments?' One reply he received was from a woman who had been out with a very shy young man. Getting desperate for conversation with him she had said, 'If there's one thing I can't stand, it's people who sit on you and use you as a convenience.'

have your lawyer call my lawyer   Phrase of dismissive unconcern (implying, 'I pay people to look after this sort of thing, I'm not going to spend time dealing with you directly about it'). From the film *Play It Again, Sam* (US 1972) – *Departing wife* (Susan Anspach): 'My lawyer will call your lawyer' – *Husband* (Woody Allen): 'I don't have a lawyer.' A possible variant is: **have my agent call your agent**.

have you met my niece?   Phrase used by an older man when introducing a female companion who is patently not his niece. A well-known British political figure arriving at some function with a nubile young girl on his arm tends to introduce her by asking, 'Have you met my niece?' He is not alone. According to *The Independent*'s obituary of film producer Nat Cohen (11 February 1988), 'He was much loved – not least by the young ladies usually introduced as "Have you met my niece?"' According to *Soho* by Judith Summers (1989), the first Lord Beaverbrook habitually dined upstairs at the French [restaurant] with sundry 'nieces' – 'He had more nieces than any man I've known,' one Gaston confided to the author. The film *Pretty Woman* (1990) contains an entertaining disquisition between a hooker and a hotel manager on 'niece' being used in this sense. Clearly, this is a well-established piece of usage. Working backwards: from BBC radio *Round the Horne* (26 March 1967): [A butler announces] 'Lord Grisley Makeshift and his niece (he says) – Mrs Costello Funf.' In the film *Road to Utopia* (US 1945), an elderly Bing Crosby introduces his two 'nieces' to an equally aged Bob Hope. In James Thurber's story 'Something to Say' (1927), there is this: 'Elliot Vereker . . . arrived about noon on 4th July . . . accompanied by a lady in black velvet whom he introduced as "my niece, Olga Nethersole". She was, it turned out, neither his niece nor Olga Nethersole.' The lines 'Moreover, if you please, a niece of mine / Shall there attend you' – Shakespeare, *Pericles*, III.iv.14 (1609) – are unfortunately not connected.

having a wonderful time See WISH YOU WERE HERE.

hawae the lads! Cry of encouragement (like 'come on!') from the North-East of England, also in the forms 'Haway' (or 'Howay') or 'Away' (or 'A-wee'). According to Frank Graham's *New Geordie Dictionary* (1979), it is a corruption of 'hadaway' as in 'hadaway wi'ye' (which actually means the opposite, 'begone!')

hay See AND THAT AIN'T.

(to be) heading for the rocks To be courting disaster. Date of origin unknown. '[On being sacked as Deputy Foreign Secretary by Margaret Thatcher] It does no harm to throw the occasional man overboard, but it does not do much good if you are steering full speed ahead for the rocks' – (Sir) Ian Gilmour, quoted in *Time* Magazine (September 1981); 'New Leader's bid to steer Labour off rocks. Captain Kinnock sets sail for No 10' – headline in *Sunday People* (2 October 1983); 'The Tory party is split from stem to stern. The captain of the ship has lost his rudder. And now the mate [Mr Clarke] is steering us towards the rocks again' – leading article in *The Sun* (about 9 December 1994); 'To resign now, six months into a new job at Trade, would seem and would be quixotic if this was still an administration heading for victory at the polls. But it isn't. It's an administration heading for the European rocks. Increasingly it's beginning to be every man for himself in the rush for the lifeboats' – *The Guardian* (13 February 1995); 'Another Tory political career looked to be heading for the rocks last

night after five pages of allegations in the *News of the World* about the sex life of Conservative MP Richard Spring, writes Andy McSmith' – *The Observer* (9 April 1995).

heads must (or will) roll Meaning, 'some people will be ousted from their positions of authority for their mistakes or as scapegoats (as if they were being guillotined)'. 'If our movement is victorious there will be a revolutionary tribunal which will punish the crimes of November 1918. Then decapitated heads will roll in the sand' – Adolf Hitler, quoted in *Daily Herald* (26 September 1930). 'Heads must roll' was listed in *The Independent* (24 December 1994) as a cliché of newspaper editorials. 'Wales lost, and heads rolled' – *Rugby World* (April 1978); 'Heads are rolling at Warner Music, the world's most successful record company . . . Gerald Levin, Time Warner's embattled boss, is out to bring the music makers to heel' – *The Economist* (1 July 1995); '"Heads will roll" over intruder . . . The heads of police chiefs were "on the block" for allowing an intruder to gatecrash Prince William's 21st birthday party, David Blunkett, the Home Secretary, said yesterday' – *The Daily Telegraph* (24 June 2003).

(a) heady mixture A potent mixture liable to go to the head (like liquor). Date of origin unknown. 'The inquiry last week of the origins of the word "balderdash" has taken many an intriguing turn, as word inquiries often do. Says Robert Dalgliesh of Cumbria: "The word is obscure in origin and once meant a heady mixture of alcoholic liquids, thereby resulting in slurred speech and unsound opinions"' – *The Herald* (Glasgow) (13 August 1994); 'Artists from the west travelled into the Moslem and Arab world . . . They were drawn inevitably by those living civilizations, no less ancient, through which they had to pass. There they tasted that heady mixture of the exotic and the refined, the cultured and the barbaric, the sympathetic and the alien, that altogether was irresistible' – *Financial Times* (12 November 1994).

he ain't heavy, he's my brother Slogan. King George VI concluded his 1942 Christmas radio broadcast by reflecting on the European allies and the benefits of mutual cooperation, saying: 'A former President of the United States of America used to tell of a boy who was carrying an even smaller child up a hill. Asked whether the heavy burden was not too much for him, the boy answered: "It's not a burden, it's my brother!" So let us welcome the future in a spirit of brotherhood, and thus make a world in which, please God, all may dwell together in justice and peace.' *Benham* (1948) suggests that the American President referred to must have been Lincoln – though it has not been possible to trace a source for the story. In fact, the King's allusion seems rather to have been a dignification of an advertising slogan and a charity's motto. As an advertising headline, 'He ain't heavy . . . he's my brother' the expression may have been used first by Jack Cornelius of the BBD&O agency in a 1936 American advertisement for the 'Community Chest' campaign ('35 appeals in 1'). But it is difficult to tell what relationship this has, if any, with the similar slogan used to promote the Nebraska orphanage and poor boys' home known as 'Boys Town'. In the early 1920s, the Reverend Edward J. Flanagan – Spencer Tracy played him in the film *Boys Town* (1938) – admitted to this home a boy named Howard Loomis who could not walk without the aid of crutches. The larger boys often took turns carrying him about on their backs. One day, Father Flanagan is said to have seen a boy carrying Loomis and asked whether this wasn't a heavy load. The reply: 'He ain't heavy, Father . . . he's m'brother.' In 1943, a 'two brothers' logo (similar to, though not the same as, the drawing used in the Community Chest campaign) was copyrighted for Boys Town's exclusive use. Today, the logo and the motto (in the 'Father/m'brother' form) are registered service marks of Father Flanagan's Boys Home (Boys Town). The saying probably *does* predate the Father Flanagan story, though whether it goes back to Lincoln is anybody's guess. More recent applications have included the song with the title, written by Bob Russell and Bobby Scott, and popularized by the Hollies in 1969. Perhaps the brief Lennon and McCartney song 'Carry that Weight' (September 1969) alludes similarly? – 'Boy – you're gonna

carry that weight, / Carry that weight a long time.'

health See AS LONG AS.

hear See DON'T FORCE IT.

hear all – see all – say nowt The motto of Yorkshiremen is said to be: 'Hear all, see all, say nowt, / Aight all, sup all, pay nowt, / And if ever tha does owt for nowt / Do it for thisen.' A Noel Gay song written in 1938 for Sandy Powell, the Yorkshire comedian, had the title: 'Hear all, see all, say nowt'. Compare **hear no evil, see no evil, speak no evil**, which *Bartlett* describes as a legend related to the Three Wise Monkeys carved over the door of the Sacred Stable, Nikko, Japan in the 17th century. The monkeys are represented having their paws over, respectively, ears, eyes and mouth. 'Hear, see, keep silence' (often accompanied by a sketch of the Three Wise Monkeys) is the motto of the United Grand Lodge of Freemasons – in the form *Audi, Vide, Tace*. Compare also, from the Second Book of Hermas, 2:2 in the Apocryphal New Testament: 'Especially see that thou speak evil of none, nor willingly hear anyone speak evil of any.'

heard nothin' yet See YOU AIN'T SEEN.

(to) hear something on the grapevine Meaning, 'to acquire information by word of mouth, through intermediaries, rather than directly from the original source' – how gossip and rumour usually travel. In the American Civil War, the method was known as 'the grapevine telegraph'. Presumably the allusion is to a network running about the place like the branches of a vine. The soul singer Marvin Gaye had a hit with the song 'I Heard It Through the Grapevine' in 1969. Compare the Australian **bush telegraph**, a name given to the system of unofficial warnings of police movements given by bushrangers to each other (known by 1878), and now used generally.

heart See EAT YOUR; IN THE; IN YOUR.

(a) heartbeat away from the presidency Traditional phrase for the position of the US Vice-President and, as *Safire* (1978) puts it, 'a reminder to voters to examine the shortcomings of a Vice-Presidential

candidate'. The earliest use of the phrase
Safire finds is Adlai Stevenson beginning
an attack on Richard Nixon in 1952 with
'The Republican Vice-Presidential candidate, who asks you to place him a heartbeat from the Presidency'. Or 'The young
man who asks you to set him one heartbeat from the Presidency of the United
States' – speech at Cleveland, Ohio (23
October 1952). Jules Witcover entitled a
book on Vice-President Spiro Agnew's
enforced resignation in 1973, *A Heartbeat
Away*. The phrase was much in evidence
again when George Bush selected Dan
Quayle as his running mate in 1988.

heart(s) of gold Popular phrase, as in
the concept of a 'tart with a heart of gold'
(a prostitute with a generous nature).
'There are hearts of gold among those
Broadbrims' – G. A. Sala, *The Strange
Adventures of Captain Dangerous* (1863).
In the early 1990s, a sentimental BBC TV
series *Hearts of Gold* (hosted by Esther
Rantzen) rewarded members of the public
who had been nominated for their good
deeds. 'Rescued by heart-of-gold Rosie and
endeavouring to rehabilitate herself,
Lorraine realises that she is the only
witness who can recognize the serial killer'
– *The Irish Times* (9 September 1994);
'David James of the Hilliard Ensemble, the
group responsible for performing most of
Pärt's music, explains: "Arvo's the most
lovable guy with a heart of gold and a
wonderful, zany sense of humour"' – *The
Independent* (21 April 1995); 'As Bessie
Burgess, a truly rough-voiced, hard-looking
Aideen O'Kelly valuably restricts the number
of glimpses we get of the heart of gold
beating beneath the battle-axe exterior' –
The Independent (4 May 1995).

hearts and flowers Phrase for anything
of tear-jerking appeal – from the title of a
popular, sentimental song of the early 1900s.
The tune was often played to accompany
the weepy bits of silent movies.

hearts and minds Phrase describing
what had to be won in the Vietnam War
by the US Government and almost of
slogan status. John Pilger, writing on 23
August 1967, reported: 'When Sergeant
Melvin Murrell and his company of United
States Marines drop by helicopter into the

village of Tuylon, west of Danang, with
orders to sell "the basic liberties as outlined on page 233 of the Pacification
Programme Handbook" and at the same
time win the hearts and minds of the
people (see same handbook, page 86
under WHAM) they see no one: not a
child or a chicken' – quoted in *The Faber
Book of Reportage* (1987). The origins of
the phrase go back to Theodore
Roosevelt's day when Douglas MacArthur,
as a young aide, asked him (in 1906) to
what he attributed his popularity. The
President replied: '[My ability] to put into
words what is in their hearts and minds
but not in their mouths.' *Safire* also points
out that, in 1954, Earl Warren ruled in the
case of Brown *v* Board of Education of
Topeka: 'To separate [Negro children] from
others of similar age and qualifications
solely because of their race generates a
feeling of inferiority as to their status in
the community that may affect their hearts
and minds in a way unlikely ever to be
undone.' The Blessing in the Holy Communion service of the Book of Common
Prayer: 'The peace of God, which passeth
all understanding, keep your hearts and
minds in the knowledge and love of God,
and of his Son Jesus Christ Our Lord.' This
is drawn from the Epistle of Paul the
Apostle to the Philippians 4:7. In fact, the
Vietnam use had been anticipated in the
previous decade by the British counter-
insurgency campaign in Malaya. The idea
was formulated by General Sir Harold
Briggs and carried out by his successor
General Sir Gerald Templer who stated
(1952) that to cut off support for the
communist guerrillas, 'the answer lies not
in pouring more troops into the jungle, but
in the hearts and minds of the people.'
This approach was largely successful,
leading to relatively few British casualties
and to Malaya becoming independent in
1957.

hearty See CONDEMNED MAN.

(to) heave a sigh of relief Date of origin
unknown. Listed in *The Independent* (24
December 1994) as a cliché of newspaper
editorials. 'There were plenty [of women]
still to heave a sigh of relief (if their
waspies would let them)' – *The Times* (27
May 1976); 'Is she his mistress? We cer-

tainly presume so until we realise that their arrival at a country hotel is not an indicator of where they'll be spending the night but the setting for a surprise party for his wife. Just as we heave a sigh of relief and begin to think he's a really nice guy he leaves the party and hits the road again' – *The Sunday Times* (22 May 1994); 'With the Booker Bingo over for another year, you might have thought that television would heave a sigh of relief and wave cheerio to all that bookchat' – *The Independent* (28 October 1994).

heaven See ALL THAT; ALL THIS.

(the) heavenly twins Complimentary phrase applied to a well-meaning couple, usually of the same sex. Possibly alluding to the Gemini twins in astrology and perhaps popularized by its use as the title of a novel by 'Sarah Guard' (1893).

heaven on earth Ideal conditions, a pleasant state of affairs. An early use of the precise phrase occurs in the title of Thomas Brooks's *Heaven on Earth, or a Serious Discourse touching a well-grounded Assurance of Mens Everlasting Happiness* (1654). But similar occurrences are plentiful: 'For if heaven be on this earth, and ease to any soul, / It is in cloister or in school' – William Langland, *The Vision of Piers Plowman* (B text, *circa* 1377); 'A heaven on earth I have won by wooing thee' – Shakespeare, *All's Well That Ends Well*, IV.ii.66 (1603); '"In educational terms," he says of his current post, "it's heaven on earth"' – *The Guardian* (3 September 1974); 'The Prime Minister [Mrs Thatcher] yesterday promised her party "a little bit of heaven on earth" produced by further tax cuts' – *The Guardian* (5 June 1986).

heavens, eleven o'clock and not a whore in the house dressed! Domestic cry, acknowledging that progress is not being made in carrying out household duties. British use, possibly of theatrical origin in the 1920s and capable of immense variation. One continues **. . . not a po emptied, and the streets full of Spanish sailors . . .** The time can, of course, vary, as also the precise nature of the potential users of the brothel: 'the street full of sailors', 'the Spanish soldiers in the courtyard', 'a street

full of matelots', 'a troopship in the bay' and 'the Japanese fleet in town'. *Partridge/ Slang* examines only the comparatively simple phrase 'eleven o'clock and no pos emptied' – though **no potatoes peeled** and **no babies scraped** are mentioned as variants. In Paul Beale's revision of *Partridge/Catch Phrases*, there is a 1984 reference to the version used by Terry Wogan on his breakfast radio show (after giving a time-check) – '[It's eight twenty-five] . . . and not a child in the house washed.' In the 1980s, the comedian Les Dawson in drag is reliably reported to have uttered the 'no pos emptied' line. Rupert Hart-Davis in *The Lyttelton Hart-Davis Letters* (Vol.3, 1981) writes in a letter dated 9 June 1958: 'In the words of the harassed theatrical landlady, "Half-past four, and not a po emptied".' The 'whores/ pos/sailors' version is possibly a colourful elaboration of the basic expression. In *The Spectator* (24 April 1959), Patrick Campbell recorded that 'Ten-thirty, and not a strumpet in the house painted!' was a favourite saying, apparently round about the late 1930s, of Robert Smyllie, editor of *The Irish Times*.

heaven's gate The idea of a 'gate to heaven' goes back to the Bible, e.g.: 'This is none other but the house of God, and this is the gate of heaven' (Genesis 28:17) and 'He commanded the clouds from above, and opened the doors of heaven' (Psalm 78:23). Shakespeare twice uses the phrase. In *Cymbeline*, II.iii.20 (1609), there is the song: 'Hark, hark, the lark at heaven's gate sings', and Sonnet 29 (1590s) has: 'Like to the lark at break of day arising / From sullen earth sings hymns at heaven's gate.' In *Heaven's Gate*, the film (US 1980) directed by Michael Cimino, 'Heaven's Gate' is the name of a roller-skating rink used by settlers and immigrants in Wyoming in 1891. Conceivably, the name is meant to be taken as an ironic one for the rough situation many of the characters find themselves in as they arrive to start a new life. Steven Bach in *Final Cut* (1985), a book about the making of the film, cites other possible sources. William Blake in *Jerusalem* (1820) wrote: 'I give you the end of a golden string; / Only wind it into a ball, / It will lead you in at Heaven's gate, / Built in Jerusalem's wall.' Robert Browning also uses the phrase, and there is a poem by Wallace Stevens with the title, 'The Worms at Heaven's Gate'.

heavens to Betsy! Exclamation of American origin, first recorded in 1914. How the phrase arose and caught on is a mystery, though links to Betsy Griscom Ross (1752–1836), seamstress and reported maker of the first American flag, and to 'a Bets(e)y', as the slang name for a frontiersman's gun or pistol (by 1856) are both suggested. The second idea was favoured by Charles Earle Funk, author of books on phrase origins, in *Heavens To Betsy* (1955).

heavens to Murgatroyd! Catchphrase of a rather camp cartoon lion called Snagglepuss, created by the Hannah-Barbera studios in the 1960s. He made his first appearance in *The Yogi Bear Show*. But his catchphrase was apparently not original. An American correspondent noted (1993): 'It was a favorite expression of a favorite uncle of mine in the 1940s, and my wife also remembers it from her growing-up years in the '40s.' 'Very good, Murgatroyd!' says Bing Crosby to Bob Hope (and that is not the character's name) in the film *Road to Bali* (US 1952), which is presumably an allusion to the phrase – and pre-dates Snagglepuss. Murgatroyd and Winterbottom was the name of a double-act (Ronald Frankau and Tommy Handley) on BBC radio in the UK from 1934, but presumably there is no link.

heavy See AND NO.

heavy, man! Stock phrase of the lugubrious, long-haired student Neil (Nigel Planer) in BBC TV's *The Young Ones* (1982–4). This use was a parody of earlier hip/hippie slang. 'Heavy', meaning 'profound, serious, intense, meaningful, important', was established in the jazz world by the 1930s. But, equally, the meaning can be akin to 'it's a drag' and, indeed, the opposite of 'groovy'.

heavy metal The type of music known as heavy metal – very loud, amplified, clashing – was first described as such in the late 1960s following the group Steppenwolf's use of the phrase 'heavy metal thunder' in the song 'Born to be Wild', written by M. Bonfire (1968). This was apparently derived from the writings of the American novelist William Burroughs who wrote, for example, in *Nova Express* (1964) of 'Ukrainian Willy the Heavy Metal Kid'. In science, 'heavy metal' also refers to uranium and the transuranic elements (such as plutonium). There have also been other uses of the phrase: from P. G. Wodehouse, *Summer Lightning*, Chap. 4 (1929): 'Anybody who has ever been bounced from a restaurant knows that commissionaires are heavy metal.'

he can leave his boots (or shoes) under my bed anytime 'I find him sexually attractive'. A reasonably common expression. I recall it being said to me by a small lady of Iranian extraction regarding Robert Redford in April 1970. As far as I know, she still hasn't had a chance to make him the offer.

he can talk the talk, but can he walk the walk? 'He can make all the right noises about something, but has he got the courage to put it into practice?' This probably has its roots in black American street language of the 1960s. It is also the thing black preachers might have said in a spiritual context, meaning 'Can you carry out what you say you will do?' It was taken up by organisational gurus in the 1990s, one of whom stated, 'If you can't walk the talk, how can you talk the walk?' What this means is anybody's guess. In the film *Full Metal Jacket* (US 1987), 'Animal Mother' says to 'Private Joker', 'You talk the talk. Do you walk the walk?'

he can't fart and chew gum at the same time Meaning, 'he's stupid'. This is the correct version – advanced on the authority of John Kenneth Galbraith – of what President Lyndon Johnson once said about Gerald Ford and is rather more colourful than 'He can't *walk* and chew gum at the same time', the version quoted when Ford became President in 1974. Like much of Johnson's earthy speech, it might have been an established Texan expression rather than his own invention.

(a) hectic schedule An inevitable pairing, especially in journalistic use. Date of origin unknown. A cliché by the 1980s.

'Earlier this year Princess Diana took time out of her hectic schedule to sit for this new photographic portrait' – *Hello!* (13 May 1995); 'The acting couple show us the dream farm that's allowed them to put down their roots and provides a break from their hectic film careers' – *Hello!* (13 May 1995); 'With his hectic lifestyle, I asked [Donald] Trump if he found the house relaxing' – British TV programme, *Selina Scott Meets Donald Trump* (18 June 1995).

heel See ACHILLES'.

Heineken refreshes the parts other beers cannot reach Slogan for Heineken lager, chiefly in the UK, and used on and off since 1975. 'I wrote the slogan,' said Terry Lovelock, 'during December 1974 at 3 a.m. at the Hotel Marmounia in Marakesh. After eight weeks of incubation with the agency [Collett, Dickenson, Pearce], it was really a brainstorm. No other lines were written. The trip was to refresh the brain, but it worked.' The resulting sentence – though not tripping easily off the tongue – became one of the most popular advertising slogans ever used in Britain and is still revived from time to time. The refreshing qualities of the lager are always demonstrated with amusing accompanying visuals: the 'droop-snoot' of Concorde raised by an infusion of the brew; a piano tuner's ears sharpened; a policeman's toes refreshed. There has also been a strong topical element. When Chia-Chia, a panda from London Zoo, was sent off in 1981 to mate with Ling-Ling in Washington, a full-page press ad merely said 'Good Luck Chia-Chia from Heineken', the slogan being understood. Much parodied – in graffiti: 'Courage reaches the parts other beers don't bother with', 'Joe Jordan [Scottish footballer] kicks the parts other beers don't reach', 'Hook Norton ale reaches the parts Heineken daren't mention', 'Mavis Brown reaches parts most beers can't reach', 'Vindaloo purges the parts other curries can't reach'; in political speeches: 'When I think of our much travelled Foreign Secretary [Lord Carrington] I am reminded of . . . the peer that reaches those foreign parts other peers cannot reach' – Margaret Thatcher, Conservative Party Conference (1980).

Compare the American proverb first recorded by Gelett Burgess in *Are You a Bromide?* (1907): 'The Salvation Army reaches a class of people that churches never do.'

(a) heinous crime An utterly odious or wicked crime – now an inevitable pairing and mostly used figuratively. Known by 1594. 'In their feeble discussion of the controversy at Brown University and the so-called PC movement, columnists Jonathan Yardley (Style, Feb. 18) and Nat Hentoff (op-ed, Feb. 26) committed perhaps the most heinous crime of all: labeling justice politically correct' – *The Washington Post* (16 March 1991); 'It is lamentable that you . . . find you need to portray the crimes as more heinous than they already are, with conjecture rather than the facts contained in the trial transcripts' – Myra Hindley, quoted in *The Independent* (23 September 1995).

Heinz See BEANZ MEANZ.

he knows whereof he speaks (or knew whereof he wrote) A conscious archaism used in place of 'he knows what he's talking about/he has a particular reason for saying that'. 'I know whereof I speak' – Mark Twain, *The Innocents Abroad*, Chap. 31 (1869); '[Erasmus] had travelled a great deal and knew whereof he wrote' – Hendrik Van Loon, *The Story of Mankind* (1922); 'How could he know whereof he spoke, / When all of his wheels are turning him into a joke?' – song 'Homeward Through the Haze' (1975) by David Crosby and Graham Nash.

hell See ALL; GO TO.

(to go) hell for leather 'To go fast, flat out' – originally on horseback. Known by 1889, this expression is not totally explicable. One suggestion has been that it is a corruption of 'all of a lather', but some association with leather saddles seems likely.

hellish dark, and smells of cheese! Exclamation from Chap. 50 of R. S. Surtees's *Handley Cross* (1843 edition) when a drunken man looking to see what sort of night it is, sticks his nose into a cupboard. In the expanded 1854 edition this becomes Chap. 57.

hello See AND I'M LIKE.

hello birds, hello trees, hello clouds, hello sky! Joke expression of joy in nature, as though spoken by a poet, aesthete or other fey character. Of uncertain origin – possibly in a revue sketch or song – but may have been used in a Warner Bros. cartoon film dating from as early as 1941. An approximate appearance occurs in *How To Be Topp* (1954) by Geoffrey Willans and Ronald Searle, in which the (British) schoolboy character Nigel Molesworth writes: 'There is no better xsample of a goody-goody than fotherington-tomas in the world in space. You kno he is the one who sa Hullo Clouds Hullo Sky and skip about like a girly.' Indeed, the most prominent British use has been in the Molesworth books: from *Back in the Jug Agane* (1959): 'And who is this who skip weedily up to me, eh? "Hullo clouds, hullo sky," he sa. "Hullo birds, hullo poetry books, hullo skool sossages, hullo molesworth 1." You hav guessed it is dere little basil fotherington-tomas.'

hello boys Slogan for Wonderbra in the UK (1994). Posters featured the model Eva Herzigova glancing down at her impressive frontage. Other, less well-remembered captions were 'Look me in the eyes and tell me that you love me' and 'Or are you just pleased to see me?' Various advertising persons have claimed credit for this coinage but, whoever deserves it, he was beaten to it by Mel Brooks in the film *Blazing Saddles* (US 1974). As Governor William J. Le Petomane, Brooks suddenly turns to his bikini-clad secretary and finds he is faced with her cleavage. 'Hello boys,' he says, 'Have a good night's rest? . . . I missed you.'

hello, everybody Not much of a phrase, you may think, but it is still associated with the British radio comedian John Henry. From *The Independent* (2 August 1988): 'Here was the first radio catchphrase, remembered by "Blossom", stagewife of the Yorkshire comedian, John Henry. "I think he said 'Ah Well'. He used to say that a lot. 'Ah Well.' 'Hello, everybody' of course, that became very well known . . . he used to come on, he never had any make-up on at all, always a dinner jacket, and he just said 'Hello, everybody', and as soon as he said that there used to be a round of applause. Just sheer personality – very ugly man – but sheer personality".' Henry is sometimes called 'the first wireless comedian'. **John Henry, come here! / coming, Blossom** is remembered by some as the archetypal exchange between wife and hen-pecked husband. On BBC radio from 1925.

hello, everyone – old ones, new ones, loved ones, neglected ones The pianist Semprini's opening patter (referring to the music he was going to play) on his BBC radio shows in the 1960s and 70s.

hello, folks! Catchphrase of British comedian Tommy Handley from the late 1930s and throughout his *ITMA* show on BBC radio (1939–49). After which, *The Goon Show* took up the cry and gave it a strangulated delivery. Harry Secombe extended this, elsewhere, to **hello, folks, and what about the workers?!** Even later, Eric Morecambe gave it a sexual connotation when he referred to **a touch of hello folks and what about the workers?!** See also under HELLO, PLAYMATES! and also WHAT ABOUT THE WORKERS?!

hello, good evening and welcome! Stock greeting well known on both sides of the Atlantic of the English broadcaster (Sir) David Frost (b. 1939). Its origins lie in the period when he was commuting back and forth to host TV chat shows in London and New York. Frost probably did not use it as host of BBC TV's *That Was the Week That Was* (1962–4) but may have introduced it in *Not So Much a Programme, More a Way of Life* (1964–5). As 'Hello, good evening, welcome', the catchphrase was used in an impersonation of Frost on the *Private Eye* record 'The Rites of Spring' (1 April 1965). The phrase may say three things where only one is needed, but it became an essential part of the Frost impersonator's kit (not to mention the Frost self-impersonator's kit). It was used as the title of a BBC TV 'Wednesday Play' about a TV interrogator (16 October 1968). Frost was still saying it in 1983 when, with a small alteration, it became 'Hello, good *morning* and welcome!' at the debut of TV-am, the breakfast-TV station. For a while, Frost also used a variation on the traditional lead-in to a commercial break – 'We'll be right back after this break / after this word / don't go away' – which was, **we'll be back in a trice!**

hello, hello, and a very good, good morning to you all! Edmundo Ros, the Venezuelan-born band leader who came to Britain in 1937, introduced Latin-American music programmes on BBC radio until the mid-1970s. He would say things like, 'You're listening to a programme of Latin-American music played by my ballroom orchestra – which we most sincerely hope you are enjoying.' Whatever type of dance music he was about to lead the orchestra into, he always seemed to say, 'Ah, three-four!'

hello, honky-tonks! See under OOOH, YOU ARE AWFUL.

hello, I'm Julian and this is my friend Sandy See under OH, HELLO.

hello, it's me – Twinkletoes! Catchphrase from the BBC radio show *Educating Archie* (1950–60). Following his success as the gormless private in ITV's *The Army Game*, Bernard Bresslaw was a natural choice as another of Archie's educators. Preceded by the sound of heavy footsteps, he would arrive and give this greeting in his 'thicko' voice.

hello, Jim (pronounced Jeem**)** Catchphrase with which Jim Spriggs (played by Spike Milligan) introduced himself in the BBC radio *Goon Show* (1951–60). It was often taken up by other characters and repeated many times, as in the edition entitled 'The Red Fort' (11 November 1957).

hello, John, got a new motor? The use of 'John' as a mode of address to any man (in England) was drawn attention to by the comedian Alexei Sayle in about 1980. Compare the use of 'Jimmy' in Scotland and 'Boyo' in Wales. ''Ullo, John, got a new motor?' was the full catchphrase, echoing East End of London and Essex use and, in this form, was the title of a record by Sayle, released in 1984. This, in turn, presumably inspired ''Ello, Tosh, Got A Toshiba?', an advertising slogan for Toshiba electrical products in the UK

(quoted in 1990). Coined by Dave Trott and credited with catapulting Toshiba's brand awareness to equal Sony's and Hitachi's.

hello, me old mates! Stock phrase of presenter/disc jockey Brian Matthew on early BBC radio pop programmes like *Easy Beat* and *Saturday Club* in the 1960s. In 1983, he was still referring to himself on the air as 'Your old mate, Brian Matthew'.

hello, Missus! See under HOW TICKLED.

hello, my darlings! Catchphrase greeting of comedian Charlie Drake (b. 1925) since the early 1950s. Perhaps it was rendered more memorable because of the husky, baby-voiced way in which it is spoken. 'Hullo, My Darlings!' was also used as his bill matter.

hello, playmates! Arthur Askey's catchphrase from the BBC radio show *Band Waggon* (1938–39) and subsequently. As Askey pointed out (1979), this was originally HELLO, FOLKS! When he used 'Hello, folks!' in the first broadcast of *Band Waggon*, he received a call from Tommy Handley telling him to lay off as the other comedian considered it to be *his* catchphrase. So, Askey changed it to 'Hello, playmates!' – with *Hello Playmates!* becoming the title of another of his radio shows in the mid-1950s.

hello, Rodney! / hello, Charles! Introductory exchange between two frightfully correct English types played by Hugh Paddick and Kenneth Williams in the BBC radio show *Beyond Our Ken* (1958–64).

hello, sailor! Catchphrase – originally this must have been something that a prostitute would call out to a potential customer in a port somewhere like Portsmouth, along the lines of, 'Like a nice time, dearie?' Indeed, the phrase must have long been around – with varying degrees of heterosexual and homosexual emphasis – before becoming a camp catchphrase in the early 1970s, reaching a peak in 1975/6 and promoted by various branches of the media. The first appearance of the phrase might be in a reminiscence of Graham Payn singing the song 'Matelot' in Noël Coward's *Sigh No More* in 1945. The chorus is said to have muttered 'Hello, sailor!' whenever Payn appeared. Next, in Spike Milligan's script for 'Tales of Men's Shirts' in the BBC radio *Goon Show* (31 December 1959), 'Hello, sailor!' is spoken, for no very good reason, by Minnie Bannister. Milligan commented in 1978 that he thought he had started the 70s' revival of the phrase in one of his *Q* TV shows. To fill up time, he had just sat and said it a number of times. However, it had already been spoken on BBC TV, *Monty Python's Flying Circus* (12 October 1969), and the title of *Private Eye*'s Christmas record (published 14 December 1969) was 'Hullo Sailor.' The cast of radio's *I'm Sorry I'll Read That Again* also promoted the phrase heavily – perhaps influenced by there being a number of newsworthy sailors about in the early 1970s, including Prince Philip, Prince Charles and the Prime Minister, Edward Heath. It was most often used by the speaker to indicate that the person being addressed was homosexual.

hello there, record-lovers everywhere and welcome to the show Stock phrase/ greeting of the British bandleader Jack Jackson (1906–78) when latterly a disc jockey. His show on BBC Radio 2 chiefly consisted of pop music intercut with extracts from comedy records.

hello, twins! In the very early days of BBC radio's *Children's Hour*, Derek McCulloch and Mary Elizabeth Jenkin were 'Mac' and 'Elizabeth' among the original 'Uncles' and 'Aunts' who presented the programmes. In the 1920s, birthday greetings were read out over the air (until they were dropped in 1932 because they took up nearly half the 'hour') and the joint cry of 'hello . . . twins!' or, less frequently, 'hello . . . triplets!' became a catchphrase.

'Hell!' said the Duchess . . . Exclamation. The opening of Agatha Christie's *The Murder on the Links* (1923): 'I believe that a well-known anecdote exists to the effect that a young writer, determined to make the commencement of his story forcible and original enough to catch the attention of the most blasé of editors, penned the first sentence: "'Hell!' said the Duchess".' Note also, *Hell! Said the Duchess*, 'A Bedtime Story' by Michael Arlen (1934). *Partridge/Catch Phrases* dates the longer

phrase: 'Hell! said the Duchess when she caught her teats in the mangle' to *circa* 1895 (see also I HAVEN'T BEEN SO HAPPY . . .) Compare the suggested newspaper headline containing all the ingredients necessary to capture a reader's attention (sex, royalty, religion, etc.): 'Teenage Sexchange Priest in Mercy Dash to Palace' (a joke current by 1976).

Hell's bells and buckets of blood Expression of annoyance, current by the 1930s. *Partridge/Slang* has this as a 'mock ferocious' extension of the basic 'Hell's bells!' = hell!

(—— has been) helping the police with their inquiries Journalistic stock phrase, now a cliché. When a suspect is being interviewed by the British police but has not yet been charged with any offence, this rather quaint euphemism is trotted out and eagerly passed on by the media. It is quite possible, of course, that the suspect in question is, in fact, being quite unhelpful to the police in their inquiries and that they are being impolite to him in equal measure. Current by 1957. 'A 17-year-old girl . . . was found battered to death . . . Later, a man was helping police with their inquiries' – *The Sunday Times* (14 October 1973); 'Woman knifed to death in garden. A man was arrested close to the scene and was later helping police with their inquiries' – *Evening Standard* (London) (23 November 1994); 'Several hurt in North beatings . . . After a brief chase, three men, were arrested and are now helping police with their inquiries' – *The Irish Times* (13 February 1995).

help yourself – and your friends will like you Bryan Magee, the philosopher and broadcaster, recalled on BBC Radio *Quote . . . Unquote* (26 April 1994) that when his grandfather was offered something with the words, 'Help yourself . . .', he would reply softly: 'And your friends will like you.' This is based on the Scottish proverb 'Help thyself, and God will help thee', which has been known since the 18th century. *Casson/Grenfell* has the nannyism: 'Help yourself and your friends will love you', but this is obviously derived from what we find in Swift's *Polite Conversation* (1738): 'Come, Colonel, help your self, and your Friends will love you the better.'

hen See COCKS MAY CROW.

Henry! Henry Aldrich! / coming, Mother!
The television version of the long-running American radio show *The Aldrich Family* ran from 1949 to 1953. The plots concerned a teenager from a typical American family. This was the opening exchange between mother and son.

here am I, slaving over a hot stove all day (while all you do is ...) Housewife's lament, since the early 1900s. A catchphrase when used ironically or as a joke. Compare the caption to a drawing (*circa* 1912) by Art Young: 'Here am I, standin' over a hot stove all day, and you workin' in a nice, cool sewer!'

here and now, before your very eyes!
Catchphrase of the British comedian Arthur Askey. When he moved from radio to TV in the early 1950s, his first series was called *Before Your Very Eyes*. Indeed, he was one of the first comedians to address the viewer through the camera in an intimate way rather than just do a variety act as if to a theatre audience. Arthur registered the title in conversation with the BBC's Ronnie Waldman, even before he had been given the series – although, in the end, it was made by ITV. He would say the phrase to emphasize that the show was, indeed, done live. The basic expression 'before your very eyes' predates the Askey use – perhaps it comes from the patter of magicians and showmen – and was current by 1835.

here be dragons Notice said to be found on the edges of old maps and, if so, probably in Latin: *Hic sunt dracones*. But an actual example has not been found. The British Library does, however, contain a 10th-century map of the east coast of Asia that bears the legend, '*Hic abundant leones* [here lions abound].'

here come de judge! Catchphrase adopted from vaudeville into NBC TV, *Rowan and Martin's Laugh-In* (1967–73). Dewey 'Pigmeat' Markham, a vaudeville veteran, was brought back to take part in a series of blackout sketches to which the

build-up was the chant 'Here comes de judge!' *Judge*: 'Have you ever been up before me?' – *Defendant*: 'I don't know – what time do you get up?' In July 1968, Pigmeat and an American vocalist called Shorty Long both had records of a song called 'Here Come(s) the Judge' in the US and UK charts.

here is the news – and this is Alvar Liddell reading it Until the Second World War, and for about twenty years after it, newsreaders on BBC radio were anonymous, but for a period during the war they did identify themselves. This was to lessen the possibility of impersonation by English-speaking newsreaders on German propaganda stations or if Britain was invaded. Hence, when Alvar Liddell (1908–81), a regular broadcaster from 1932 to his retirement in 1969, died, it was suggested that it was he who had made the format famous. Indeed, he may well have done so, being the possessor of one of the most famous of the old-style BBC voices and having read the news at some key points in the course of the war.

here's a funny thing ... Stock phrase of the flamboyant British comedian Max Miller (1895–1963) and used as the introduction to a joke. Hence, 'Now this *is* a funny thing. I went home the other night. *There*'s a funny thing!' *Here's a Funny Thing* was the title of a stage show about Miller, written by R. W. Shakespeare, in *circa* 1981. *Partridge/Catch Phrases* has **now there's a funny thing** current by the late 19th century. His bill matter was **The Cheeky Chappie**. Another of his rather ingratiating phrases was **when I'm dead and gone, the game's finished!** as also, 'Miller's the name, lady – **there'll never be another!**' And not forgetting, **you're the kind of people who give me a bad name!** – when an audience perceived a double entendre without him having emphasized it.

here's another nice mess you've gotten me into (or fine mess ...)! The exasperated cry of Oliver Hardy (1892–1957) to Stan Laurel (1890–1965) after yet another example of the latter's ineptitude has come to light. Spoken in several of the comedians' American films, notably *The Laurel-*

Hardy Murder Case (US 1930), *The Sons of the Desert* (US 1933) and *Going Bye-Bye!* (US 1934). Oddly, both *The Oxford Dictionary of Modern Quotations* (1991) and *The Oxford Dictionary of Quotations* (1992) place the saying under Laurel's name while acknowledging that it was always said *to* him. Perhaps they are trying to reflect that Laurel was the prime mover in the partnership. John P. Fennell in *Film Quotes: Great Lines from Famous Films* (1991) goes one step further towards inaccuracy and even has 'Another fine mess you've got us in, *Ollie*.' It is one of the few film catchphrases to register because there was a sufficient number of Laurel and Hardy features through which audiences could become familiar with it. Latterly, it has often been remembered as 'another fine mess', possibly on account of one of Laurel and Hardy's thirty-minute features (released in 1930) being entitled *Another Fine Mess*. *The Independent* (21 January 1994) carried a letter from Darren George of Sheffield – clearly a Laurel and Hardy scholar – which stated that 'nice mess' was what was 'invariably' spoken and in *Another Fine Mess* 'the duo inexplicably misquote themselves'. A graffito, reported during the Falklands war of 1982, declared: 'There's another fine mess you got me into, [Port] Stanley.' The 'nice mess' phrase existed before all this, of course. In W. S. Gilbert, *The Mikado*, Act 2 (1885), Ko-Ko says to Nanki-Pooh: 'Well, a nice mess you've got us into, with your nodding head and the deference due to a man of pedigree.'

here's a pretty kettle of fish! Exclamation at a sorry state of affairs. Established usage by the 1740s, when Henry Fielding used 'pretty kettle of fish' in both *Joseph Andrews* and *Tom Jones*. Brewer (1894) has this explanation: that 'kettle of fish' is an old name for a kind of *fête champêtre*, or riverside picnic, where a newly caught salmon is boiled and eaten. 'The discomfort of this sort of party may have led to the phrase, "A pretty kettle of fish", meaning an awkward state of affairs, a mess, a muddle.' A 'fish kettle' as the name of a cauldron for cooking fish has been a term used since the 17th century, though this appears not to have much to do with

the expression. Rather preferable is the explanation given in *English Idioms*, published by Nelson (*circa* 1912), that kettle comes from 'kiddle' = a net. So all one is saying is 'here is a nice net of fish', as one might on drawing it out of the sea, not being totally sure what it contains. Curiously, *Brewer* (1894) also had '*Kittle* of fish' as an entry, defining it as 'a pretty muddle, a bad job. Corruption of "kiddle of fish." A kiddle is a basket set in the opening of a weir for catching fish. Perhaps the Welsh *hidl* or *hidyl*, a strainer.' This explanation disappeared from *Brewer* and has not been found in it since. That Queen Mary did indeed exclaim 'Here's a pretty kettle of fish' to Prime Minister Stanley Baldwin at the time of the Abdication crisis, is not in doubt. However, a differently worded version has turned up with a precise date. Nancy Dugdale (d. 1969) wrote a diary from data supplied by her husband, Thomas (Parliamentary Private Secretary to Baldwin from 1935 to 1937). On Tuesday 17 November 1936 she wrote: 'Mr Baldwin went today to see the Queen, who enchanted him by the sentence with which she greeted him: "This is a nice kettle of fish, isn't it?" She was naturally very upset . . .'

here's Johnny! Said with a drawn-out, rising inflection on the first word, this was Ed McMahon's introduction to Johnny Carson on NBC's *Tonight* show from its inception in 1961: [*Drum roll*] 'And now . . . heeeeere's Johnny!' It was emulated during Simon Dee's brief reign as a chat-show host in Britain during the 1960s. The studio audience joined in the rising inflection of the announcer's **it's Siiimon Dee!** Jack Nicholson playing a psychopath chops through a door with an axe and cries 'Here's Johnny!' in the film *The Shining* (US 1981).

here's looking at you, kid! From the film *Casablanca* (US 1942), a line based on existing drinking phrases and turned into a catchphrase by Humphrey Bogart impersonators. 'Here's Looking At You' had earlier been the title of one of the first revues transmitted by the BBC from Alexandra Palace in the early days of television (*circa* 1936).

here's one I made earlier (or one I prepared earlier . . .) Curiously popular catchphrase in Britain that originated with 'live' TV cookery demonstrations in the 1950s. It was important that the showing of the finished product was not left to chance. But the phrase was also borrowed by presenters of the BBC TV children's programme *Blue Peter* (from 1963 onwards) who had to explain how to make models of the Taj Mahal out of milk-bottle tops, for example, but wouldn't actually be seen doing so there and then. Headline from *The Independent* (14 December 1991) – over a gardening article – 'And here's one I made earlier . . .'; *Here's Another One I Invaded Earlier* – title of Channel 4 documentary about Afghanistan (31 May 2003).

here's to the next time See THIS IS HENRY HALL.

here's to our next merry meeting! As a catchphrase, this might seem at first to be linked to Henry Hall's signature theme **here's to the next time!** for the BBC Dance Orchestra (that Hall took over in March 1932) and which includes the lines: 'Here's to the next time and a merry meeting, / Here's to the next time, we send you all our greeting, / Set it to music, sing it in rhyme, / Now, all together, Here's to the next time!' This phrase was also Hall's sign-off and, inevitably, the title of his autobiography (1956). Then again, Robin Richmond, for many years presenter of *The Organist Entertains* on BBC Radio, used the phrase 'here's to our next merry meeting!' as his weekly sign-off. But the alliterative lure of 'merry meetings' was in evidence long before these two gentlemen. Sir Thomas More wrote to his daughter on 5 July 1535, the eve of his execution, praying that 'we may merrily meet in heaven'. King Richard III has 'Our stern alarums chang'd to merry meetings' in the famous opening speech to Shakespeare's play (1592). *Punch* for 27 July 1904 has a cartoon accompanying 'Operatic Notes' with the caption 'TO OUR NEXT MERRY MEETING!' Even more significantly, the *Punch Almanack* for 1902 has a cartoon of two foxes drinking in a club, celebrating the fact that all the best hunting horses are away in the Boer War. One fox is saying,

'To our next merry meeting!' Does all this indicate that it was once an established toast? Might it also suggest that the original 'meeting' referred to in the phrase was the kind you have in fox-hunting?

here's your starter for ten (and no conferring) Stock phrases from the British TV quiz *University Challenge* (1962–87, 1994–) and forever associated with the original chairman, Bamber Gascoigne.

here today, gone tomorrow Phrase applied to any short-lived, transitory phenomenon or person. An early use of this old proverbial expression occurs in Aphra Benn's *Luckey Chance* (1687): 'Faith, Sir, we are here to Day and gone to Morrow.' A more recent and notable use occurred in 1982, when Robin Day was interviewing Sir John Nott, Defence Secretary in the Conservative Government, on BBC TV and asked: 'Why should the public on this issue believe you, a transient, here today and, if I may say so, gone tomorrow politician, rather than a senior officer of many years experience?' At which point, Nott unclipped his microphone and walked out, though he later entitled his autobiography *Here Today, Gone Tomorrow: memoirs of an errant politician* (2002).

here we are again! Possibly the oldest catchphrase it is possible to attach to a particular performer. Joseph Grimaldi (d. 1837) used it as 'Joey the Clown' in pantomime, and it has subsequently been used by almost all clowns on entering the circus ring. The line appears in a *Punch* cartoon (10 February 1844).

here we go, here we go, here we go! Chant, sung to the tune of Sousa's 'Stars and Stripes for Ever' and beloved of British football supporters, though it does have other applications. It suddenly became very noticeable at the time of the Mexico World Cup in June 1986. The previous year, the Everton football team had made a record of the chant, arranged and adapted by Tony Hiller and Harold Spiro. This version included an excursion into Offenbach's famous Can-Can tune. It was also the song of Yorkshire miners as they spearheaded their union's year-long strike in 1984–5.

here we go round the mulberry bush
Phrase from the refrain sung in a children's game (first recorded in the mid-19th century, though probably earlier) in which the participants hold hands and dance in a ring. There are numerous variations, using various fruits. One theory of the rhyme's origin is that a mulberry tree stood in the middle of the exercise yard at Wakefield Prison in Yorkshire. The prisoners would have to go round and round it on a 'cold and frosty morning'. This may, however, be no more than a coincidence. *Here We Go, Round the Mulberry Bush* (with a comma inserted) was the title of a novel (1965; film UK 1967) by Hunter Davies.

hern, hern Catchphrase from the BBC radio *Goon Show* (1951–60). Used by Harry Secombe as Lootenant Hern-Hern and by Peter Sellers in reproducing the sound of American (usually military) language (without actually saying anything). An example occurs in 'The Call of the West' (20 January 1959).

(a) hero from zero Rhyming phrase suggesting that a person has risen from humble beginnings. It was used as the title of a document produced in 1988 by the British industrialist Tiny Rowlands in a prolonged war of words with Mohamed Al-Fayed. The Egyptian businessman had been able to gain control of the House of Fraser stores group (which includes Harrods) and thwarted Mr Rowlands's ambitions in that direction. The phrase was derived from an alleged tape recording of a conversation between Fayed (who was presumably talking about himself) and two Indian gurus said to have links with the Sultan of Brunei. In 1994, 'From Zero to Hero' was a promotional line used for the film *The Mask*. 'From zero to hero – how to make £75 a month on interest-free cards' – headline in *The Observer* (2 February 2003).

he said, she said Phrase used in the relating of male/female rows. *He Said, She Said* was the title of a film (US 1991) in which married journalists, played by Kevin Bacon and Elizabeth Perkins, 'bickered in Baltimore'. William Safire took stock of the phrase in *The New York Times* Magazine (12 April 1998): '[The] phrase now dominates the accounts of what lawyers used to call formally *material fact disputes,* and more colloquially *swearing matches* . . . In 1976, a book by the sociolinguists Nancy Henley and Barrie Thorne was titled "*She Said-He Said*" . . . the phrase's meaning then dealt with . . . "cross-gender discourse" – different understandings of the same words.' '[An FBI report on Anita Hill's accusation of Supreme Court nominee Clarence Thomas for verbal impropriety] could not draw any conclusion because of the "*he said, she said*" nature of the allegation and denial' – *The Chicago Trubune* (7 October 1991). Safire concluded: 'Uniform punctuation would clarify the phrase's use as a modifier . . . Treat it thus: "It's one of those classic, unresolvable *he-said, she-said* situations".'

he's back – and he's angry! Slogan – possibly for an untraced film. According to the *Daily Mail* (29 March 1996), this strapline had been borrowed to promote an Edinburgh Festival Fringe show called *Jesus II – The Sequel*, featuring Peter Holmes à Court. The phrase 'He's back' (on its own) was used variously for the films *Halloween 4: The Return of Michael Myers* (1988), *Robocop 2* (1990) and *Robocop 3* (1993). Could the full version have been used for any of these? Or could it be a reference to Arnold Schwarzenegger's famous line in *The Terminator* (see ɪ'ʟʟ ʙᴇ ʙᴀᴄᴋ) or to *Rambo: First Blood Part Two*, or to any of the *Nightmare on Elm Street* or *Halloween* sequels? *A Nightmare on Elm Street Part 2: Freddy's Revenge* (US 1985) was apparently promoted with 'He's back, but he's not happy.' Later, came 'He's back . . . and very angry!' for *The Prophecy II* (US 1998); 'The mink are back . . . and this time they're angry' – headline in *The Independent* (18 September 1998); 'She's back, and she's angry' – billing for Germaine Greer in *The Independent* (No. 3,760 – 1998). Compare — ɪs ʙᴀᴄᴋ ᴀɴᴅ ᴛʜɪs ᴛɪᴍᴇ ɪᴛ's ᴘᴇʀsᴏɴᴀʟ.

he's fallen in the water! One of the most frequently used catchphrases in the BBC radio *Goon Show* (1951–60), usually following the sound of a splash. Spoken by Little Jim (Spike Milligan). *Voice:* 'Oh, dear, children – look what's happened to Uncle Harry!' *Little Jim (helpfully, in simple sing-song voice):* 'He's fallen in the wa-ter!'

he's loo-vely, Mrs Hoskin ... he's loo-oo-vely! Catchphrase of Ivy (Ted Ray) in the BBC radio show, *Ray's a Laugh* (1949–60). The comedian (1909–77) served his apprenticeship around the music halls before becoming one of Britain's great radio comedians. He recalled one of the radio show's most famous catchphrases in his book *Raising the Laughs* (1952). It occurred in sketches between Ivy and Mrs Hoskin (played by Bob Pearson): 'George Inns [the producer] agreed that the climax of their original conversation should be the mention of a mystical "Dr Hardcastle" whom Ivy secretly adored . . . From the moment Bob, in his new role, had spoken the words, "I sent for young Dr Hardcastle", and we heard Ivy's excited little intake of breath, followed by, "He's loo-vely, Mrs Hoskin . . . he's loo-oo-vely!" a new phrase had come into being.' Mrs Hoskin would also say, famously, **Ee, it was agony, Ivy!** – however, it has been suggested that this had earlier origins in music hall.

he's very good, you know! Catchphrase from the BBC radio *Goon Show* (1951–60). Ironic commendation, spoken by various characters or by the announcer, Wallace Greenslade, after a musical performance – as after Max Geldray/Ray Ellington's spots in 'The £1,000,000 Penny' (12 November 1958).

he was a big man (or **a giant among men** or **larger than life) in every sense of the word (**or **in every way)** Clichés mostly of obituary and tribute. Dates of origin not known. 'Roddy was an excellent stockbroker and wonderful friend. His memorial service . . . was a marvellous tribute to a man who was larger than life in every way' – *Money-Brief*, issued by stockbrokers Gerrard Vivian Gray (April 1989); 'Michael Swann, a big man in every way, was a renaissance figure, scholar, scientist, soldier . . .' – Marmaduke Hussey in *The Independent* (24 September 1990); 'John Drummond, a big man in every sense of the word, has protected his fiefdom well' – *Financial Times* (11 July 1994); 'Sean Bean is many things; former welder, giant among men, supporter of Sheffield United and a lovely little thespian when he is in the mood. But above all,

Sean Bean is sexy' – *The Sunday Times* (19 February 1995); '"Absolutely magnificent, a giant among men," was Alan Hansen's verdict on his fellow Scot' – *The Herald* (Glasgow) (3 April 1995); 'Judge Hugh Morton was a big man in every sense of the word. His imposing physical stature was matched by his courage and constant concern for the ordinary people that the law is meant to serve' – *The Herald* (Glasgow) (28 April 1995); 'Arnold Goodman, who has died in London after a long illness at the age of 81, was – in both senses of the phrase – larger than life' – Roy Hattersley in *The Mail on Sunday* (14 May 1995); 'Former prime minister Lord Callaghan described Robert Maxwell as "a very big man". He praised Maxwell's "remarkable gift of leadership"' – *The Independent* (3 June 1995).

he who is not with us is against us Phrase popularly ascribed to the Soviet leader Joseph Stalin. *Time* Magazine (11 August 1986) noted a corollary attributed to the Hungarian Communist Party leader Janos Kadar: 'He who is not against us is with us.' In fact, Stalin was quoting Jesus Christ who said: 'He that is not with me is against me' (Luke 11:23), and Kadar was also quoting Christ in providing the corollary: 'He that is not against us is for us' (Luke 9:50). It is not surprising that Stalin quoted Scripture. He went from a Church school at Guri to the theological seminary at Tiflis to train for the Russian Orthodox priesthood. The day after the terrorist attacks on the USA of 11 September 2001, a senior official of the Bush administration declared, 'Either you are with us or against us', and President George W. Bush himself later declared 'Either you are with us or you are with the terrorists.'

he who loves me follows me Slogan for Jesus Jeans, in various countries, from 1970. In that year, Maglificio Calzificio Torinese, an Italian clothing manufacturer, launched an advertising campaign showing the rear view of a young girl in a tight-fitting pair of the company's new Jesus Jeans, cut very short. The slogan echoed the New Testament, as also did another one, **thou shalt have no other jeans before me**. Later, a spokesman for the company explained in the *International Herald Tribune* (12 January 1982): 'We were not looking for a scandal. It's just that it was the late 1960s and Jesus was emerging increasingly as a sort of cult figure. There was the Jesus generation and *Jesus Christ Superstar*. There was this enormous protest, in Italy and around the world, and Jesus looked to a lot of people like the biggest protester ever . . . It's funny, we had no trouble in Mediterranean countries, but the biggest resistance came in the protestant countries, in North America and northern Europe.' Jesus Jeans were eventually sold only in Italy, Greece and Spain. In Greece, there was a threat of prosecution for 'insulting religion and offending the Christian conscience of the public'. In France, complaints of blasphemy and sacrilege flooded in when the slogan '*Qui m'aime me suive*' was tried out in 1982, similarly located on a girl's behind.

he who runs may read Alteration of Habbakuk 2:2, 'That he may run that readeth it' – but no more easily understandable. The New English Bible translates it as 'ready for a herald to carry it with speed' and provides the alternative 'so that a man may read it easily'. The *OED2* has citations from 1672, 1784 and 1821, but possibly the most famous use is in John Keble's hymn 'Septuagesima' from *The Christian Year* (1827): 'There is a book, who runs may read, / Which heavenly truth imparts, / And all the lore its scholars need, / Pure eyes and Christian hearts.' Given the obscurity, one of the most unlikely uses of the phrase has been as an advertising slogan for *The Golden Book* in the 1920s – according to E. S. Turner, *The Shocking History of Advertising* (1952).

he won't be happy till he gets it Slogan for Pears' soap, current 1888 and coupled with a picture of a baby stretching out of its bath to pick up a cake of the soap. Cartoonists made much play with this idea – changing the baby into the Tsar or Kaiser and the soap into various disputed territories. In early editions of *Scouting for Boys* (*circa* 1908) Robert Baden-Powell used the slogan (with acknowledgement to Pears) to refer to the achievement of a

first-class badge. There was also a companion advertisement with the slogan **he's got it and he's happy now**.

hey, are you putting it around I'm barmy? See I'VE GOT A LETTER.

hey! – Mambo! Irritating call, dating from the late 1950s. Walking quietly along the street (minding your own business) you would be hailed by someone shouting 'Hey!' When you turned round, they added 'Mambo!', alluding to the lyric of the hit record 'Mambo Italiano' recorded by Dean Martin in 1955.

hey, you down there with the glasses (on)! Stock phrase from BBC radio's *The Billy Cotton Band Show* (1949–68) (see WAKEY!-WAKEY!) The words were addressed to Cotton by an American voice that sounded as though it was coming from a plane. This was the opening gambit to some comedy crosstalk.

hey – your back wheel's going round! 'Helpful' comment volunteered by a juvenile pedestrian to a cyclist or motorist with the purpose of distracting or annoying him. Since the early 1900s. Possibly addressed earlier to users of any other form of wheeled transport.

(a/the) hidden agenda The true meaning behind words and actions, often contradicting them. The expression is believed to have emerged following discussions in British educational circles in the late 1960s and early 1970s when the concept of a 'hidden curriculum' in schools (going against the actual curriculum that was taught) was much talked about. The phenomenon is also sometimes referred to as **the subtext**. 'Those who vote Yes for the new constitution will vote ostensibly for reform in South Africa but will in effect be voting for the permanent rejection of the black majority – unless, as the Government repeatedly denies, there is a "hidden agenda" for dramatic new reforms after the vote is won' – *Financial Times* (5 October 1983); in 1990, a UK film about the 'shoot-to-kill' policy of security forces in Northern Ireland was given the title *Hidden Agenda*, as also was an unrelated film (US 2001); 'A Labour government, grabbing vast new powers and dispensing patronage on a scale never seen before, will give [political correctness] impetus, official backing and legislative authority. Here indeed is the hidden agenda, which does not figure in the manifesto because much of it will be enacted by private members' bills in a parliament with a "progressive" majority' – *The Sunday Telegraph* (29 March 1992).

hi-de-hi! Catchphrase deriving from dance band vocals of the 1920s/30s – the 'Hi-de-ho, vo-de-o-do' sort of thing. In particular, Cab Calloway's song 'Minnie the Moocher' (1931) contains the refrain, 'Ho-de-ho, hi-de-hi'. The line 'Hey, ho-de-ho, hi-de-hi!' also occurs in the Ira Gershwin lyrics for the song 'The Lorelei' (1933). In addition, according to Denis Gifford's *The Golden Age of Radio*, 'Hi-de-hi! Ho-de-ho!' was the catchphrase of Christopher Stone, the BBC's first 'disc jockey', when he went off and presented *Post Toasties Radio Corner*, a children's programme for Radio Normandy in 1937. Shortly after this last, the phrase achieved notoriety when a commanding officer in the army faced a court of inquiry or court-martial for making his troops answer 'Ho-de-ho' when he (or his fellow officers) yelled 'Hi-de-hi'. This case was well in the past when *Notes and Queries* got around to it in 1943–4, and there was a revue with the title at the Palace Theatre, London, in 1943. Gerald Kersh referred to army use of the exchange (though not to the specific case) in *They Die with their Boots Clean* in 1941. From 1981 to 1988, BBC TV had a long-running situation comedy series, set in a 1950s' holiday camp, called *Hi-de-Hi!* The title probably came to be used in this way from a campers' song special to Butlin's: 'Tramp, tramp, tramp, tramp, / Here we come, to jolly old Butlin's every year. / All come down to Butlin's, all by the sea. / Never mind the weather, we're as happy as can be. / Hi-de-hi! Ho-de-ho!' – quoted in *The Observer* Magazine (12 June 1983). This may possibly date from the late 1930s also. In May 1937, Stanley Holloway recorded a song called 'Hi-de-hi' (his own composition) on a promotional record for Butlin's Holiday Camps, though the lyrics differ from the above.

(to) hide one's light under a bushel To be modest about one's abilities and achievements. Phrase used in this sense by

1650, though known since 1557. It derives from Matthew 5:15 or, as here, from Luke 11:33: 'No man, when he hath lighted a candle, putteth it in a secret place, neither under a bushel, but on a candlestick, that they which come in may see the light.' A bushel is a vessel for measuring the volume of a grain, especially of corn.

(to be on a) hiding to nothing The origin of the expression is obscure but possibly comes from horse racing. In use by 1905. It means the same as **to be in a no-win situation** (a phrase known by 1962), namely, 'to be confronted with a thrashing without the chance of avoiding it, to face impossible odds'. 'No-win' has been known since 1962. 'Both attack Washington for a "no-win" war policy' – *The Economist* (5 November 1966); 'Under Michael Grade, Channel 4 is in a no-win situation – too commercially successful for its own good and still managing to shock' – *The Observer* (11 Sunday 1995).

hi, gang! Stock greeting from Ben Lyon to the audience of his wartime BBC radio programme of the same name, first broadcast on 26 May 1940. The former Hollywood star would shout, 'Hi gang!' The audience would reply, 'Hi, Ben!' At the end of the show, he would say, 'So long, gang!' and they would reply, 'So long, Ben!' An incidental line of Lyon's, addressed to members of the studio audience was: **not you, momma, siddown!** (once reported as having appeared as a graffito on the underside of a train lavatory seat).

(because the) higher the fewer See under WHY IS A MOUSE WHEN IT SPINS?

highly acclaimed Promotional adjectival phrase, especially in theatre, broadcasting and publishing. As with AWARD-WINNING, this adjective, while not being laden with meaning, is often self-serving and thus depressing. The reason for its use is not hard to discover. During the course of the first series of my BBC Radio show *Quote . . . Unquote* (in 1976), I connived with the producer to have it billed in *Radio Times* as 'the highly acclaimed quiz', even though at that stage it was too early for it to be any such thing (compare publishers' use of 'best-selling' on the jackets of books even before they have been put on sale).

In no time at all, the servile print media took to describing *Quote . . . Unquote* as 'highly acclaimed' in preview columns. 'Anthony Page directed the acclaimed BBC TV production of *Absolute Hell . . . Richard II* reunited the highly-acclaimed director/actor/designer team . . .' – Royal National Theatre brochure (26 June – 28 August 1995).

high noon In the straightforward sense, 'high noon' is simply a way of describing the time when the sun is high in the heavens. John Milton, *Paradise Lost*, Bk V, line 174 (1667) has, 'Sun . . . sound his praise . . . both when thou climb'st, / And when high Noon hast gain'd.' The film Western *High Noon* (US 1951) concerns a sheriff (played by Gary Cooper) who, alone, faces up to four outlaws threatening to take over his town. The climax of the film is a confrontation between the sheriff and the leader of the outlaws in the town square at high noon. Consequently, the phrase 'high noon' is used in situations where anyone is standing up to a fight against lawlessness or where there is a fatal/final confrontation.

(to eat or **live) high off the hog** Meaning, 'to live prosperously, in luxury'. It is an expression, as *Morris* (1977) puts it, 'quite literally accurate, since you have to go pretty high on the hog to get tender – and expensive – loin chops and roasts.' Of American origin and recorded by 1946.

(a) high profile When people are said to be keeping one of these, it means that they are actively seeking publicity or attention and are not hiding away – which would involve, rather, maintaining a **low profile**. It is likely that 'high profile' was created in response to the popularity of 'low profile', which had become a way of describing the Nixon administration's attitude in certain policy matters in about 1970. It is probably of US military origin and soon became incorporated into 'Pentagonese' (the jargon of defence). As *Safire* (1978) points out, in tank warfare, a low vehicle presents less of a target for artillery. He also quotes presidential assistant Leonard Garment as saying in early 1970: 'I've kept my profile so low for so long, I've got a permanent backache.' The use of the British term 'low profile' in

connection with motor-car tyres, a year or two before this, appears to be a coincidental coinage. 'Dean Robinson Replies: "Stinson's high profile at DCSL is Exhibit 1 for the case that there is no rigid political orthodoxy at the school"' – *The Washington Post* (29 September 1991); 'There have been times, however, when the council's politics have dictated that Atwell take a low profile on a controversial issue' – also *The Washington Post* (3 November 1991).

(the) high toby Highway robbery by a mounted thief – where 'toby' was slang for the public highway (18th century). J. B. Priestley wrote a play about highwaymen for Pollock's Toy Theatres. It was called *The High Toby* (1948).

high, wide and handsome *DOAS* defines this as 'easily, pleasantly, and with few worries; in a carefree manner.' One might add: 'going swimmingly, successfully.' *High, Wide and Handsome* was the title of a film (US 1937) about a travelling show-girl. The term was recorded in use by 1907.

hill See AMOUNT TO.

him bad man, kemo sabe! See HI-YO, SILVER!

***hinc illae lacrimae* [hence all those tears]** Said by way of explanation as to the real cause of something. From *Andria* by Terence (d. 159 BC).

hint! hint! Rather obvious way of emphasizing, say, that you have a birthday coming up and that the person you are addressing might take the hint and buy you something you are both looking at, as a present. From the mid-20th century.

his death diminishes us all Cliché of obituaries, this derives from John Donne's *Devotions*, No. 17 (1624): 'Any man's death diminishes me, because I am involved in Mankind: and therefore never send to know for whom the bell tolls; it tolls for thee.' If one can make the distinction, the cliché resides not so much in the words themselves as in the inevitable use of the quotation. 'In some respects, he was a beardless Patrick Geddes. His death diminishes us' – *The Scotsman* (19 July 1993); 'If one person's death diminishes us all, as John Donne believed, the year's crop of celebrated demises has shrunk us to an immoderate degree. Nowhere did the reaper's scythe cut a wider swath than through the arts' – *The Sunday Times* (26 December 1993); 'In our sorrow at his loss we are all united. Our parliamentary life is the poorer; and so is our national life. "No man is an island," said the poet, "each man's death diminishes me"' – *The Scotsman* (13 May 1994); '"Any man's death diminishes me, because I am involved in Mankind", wrote John Donne. The latest death to diminish sport was Simon Prior, a 40-year-old Briton who had been racing as a passenger in motorcycle sidecars for two decades' – *The Sunday Times* (19 June 1994); 'The word the lawyer, and Ingram's mother, kept using was "barbaric". It fitted, twice over. A man had been sentenced not just to death but to 12 years on a knife-edge. "Any man's death diminishes me," Donne wrote. But some more than others; and this one more than most' – *The Independent on Sunday* (9 April 1995).

his face is his fortune (or **her face . . .)** Old saying. 'My face is my fortune' occurs, for example, in the (laundered) sea shanty 'Rio Grande' (trad./anon.) to be found in various students' song-books. 'What is your fortune, my pretty maid? / My face is my fortune, sir, she said' is in a nursery rhyme *circa* 1800 ('Where are you going to, my pretty maid?') which is a version of an earlier, more lubricious, folk song.

his master's voice Occasionally used to describe 'the voice of authority' or the practice of carrying out only what one is instructed to do – or of not revealing one's own thoughts, only those of one's superiors. '"Francesca!" shouted Briggs. She came running . . . "Her Master's Voice," remarked Mr Wilkins' – M. A. von Arnim, *Enchanted April* (1922). 'While the titular chief was little more than echo of "his master's voice", Ludendorff's technical grasp and organizing power ensured that he remained master of his own staff' – Liddell Hart, *Through the Fog of War*, Chap. 10 (1938). The phrase comes from the trademark and brand name of the HMV record company. In 1899, the English painter Francis Barraud approached the Gramophone Company in London to

borrow one of their machines so that he could paint his fox terrier, Nipper, listening to it. Nipper was accustomed, in fact, to hearing a *phonograph* but his master thought that the larger horn of the gramophone would make a better picture. Barraud entitled the finished work, 'His Master's Voice'. Subsequently, the Gramophone Company bought the painting and adapted and adopted it as a trademark. In 1901, the Victor Talking Machine Company ('Loud enough for dancing' was its slogan) acquired the US rights. The company later became RCA Victor and took Nipper with them. Nowadays Britain's EMI owns the trademark in most countries, RCA owns it in North and South America, and JVC owns it in Japan. It was used until 1991.

history See DUSTBIN OF.

(a) history man Following the BBC TV adaptation in 1981 of the novel *The History Man* (1975) by Malcolm Bradbury, the phrase 'history man' has been used to describe a particular type of scheming, unidealistic university lecturer. In fact, the title of the novel describes a character who does not appear, but it was taken to mean the left-wing sociology don 'hero' – and from that, any similar don at a 'new' university.

(to) hitch your wagon to a star To advance by attaching yourself to the ideas of greater people. To aspire to another's admirable example. To set oneself high aspirations. Perhaps now more loosely, 'to climb on to someone else's bandwagon'. The phrase comes from R. W. Emerson's 'Civilization' in *Society and Solitude* (1870): 'To accomplish anything excellent the will must work for catholic and universal ends . . . When his will leans on a principle, when he is the vehicle of ideas, he borrows their omnipotence. Gibraltar may be strong, but ideas are impregnable, and bestow on the hero their invincibility . . . Hitch your wagon to a star.' 'One of the few things in my life of which I am proud is that in all matters of major policy during the past five years I have hitched my waggon to your star' – letter from Robert Boothby to Winston Churchill (27 May 1939). It is said that until his wife pointed it out to him, John F. Kennedy would incorrectly incorporate the phrase into lines by Robert Frost and end speeches on the campaign trail with: 'I'll hitch my wagon to a star / But I have promises to keep . . .' Hence, however, *Hitch Your Wagon*, title of a play (Broadway 1937) by Bernard C. Schoenfeld. Not to be confused with the song, 'When You Wish Upon a Star' from the Disney film *Pinocchio* (US 1940).

hi-tiddly-i-ti, brown bread! Snappy ending from children's singing games, vocalizing the familiar musical phrase 'om-tiddly-om-pom, pom pom', which is said first to have occurred in Fischler's 'Hot Scotch Rag' of 1911. The phrase 'Hi-tidli-i-ti/-i-ti-hi' had already occurred, however, in *Punch* in 1900. Other versions: 'Tripe and bananas, fried fish!' 'Guard to the guard-room, dismiss!' 'Shave and a haircut, five bob/two bits!' Also extended to: '. . . I look at your father's – bald head!' It has been suggested that the most common conclusion to the phrase used in British music hall was '—, cream cheese' and that the comedian Harry Champion (1866–1942) may first have used the 'brown bread' version, either because of the alliteration or through irony – a restaurant or pub advertising brown bread through such a cry would be offering very meagre fare indeed.

hit list See ENEMIES LIST.

(will it be a) hit or a miss? A familiar question posed by David Jacobs, presenter of BBC TV *Juke Box Jury* (original series 1959–67) in which a panel would vote on the likely prospects of new record releases. If it was a hit, Jacobs would ring a bell. If it was a miss, he would sound a klaxon. The whole format was devised by a Hollywood disc jockey called Peter Potter who first introduced *Juke Box Jury* on American radio and in 1953–4 on TV

(to) hit (something) for six Meaning, 'to destroy an opponent or demolish an argument completely'. From cricket, where knocking or hitting a ball over the boundary results in six points (or runs) being won. Identified as a current cliché in *The Times* (17 March 1995). 'I began to wonder if my massive and inexpert administration of chloroform had hit his liver – perhaps not inappropriately – for six' – *The Lancet*

(1 July 1967); 'Conscious of the rightness of our cause, let us knock the enemy for six' – *Punch* (23 October 1974).

(to) hit the ground running To be effective right from the start, to be up to speed immediately. A phrase from the military – leaping from assault craft and helicopters, even landing by parachute, immediately running off, and, without preamble, successfully getting straight on with the business in hand. Current by 1984, probably becoming popular through American business use. '*The Late Show* has so far generated an overwhelmingly favourable response . . . "To hit the ground running with four shows a week," said Alex Graham, editor of *The Media Show* on Channel 4, "that's really impressive"' – *The Independent* (29 March 1989). 'Pentagon-ese has given us infamous little expressions like: "Hell, that guy's good. He hit the ground running." Obviously, the guy got off to a splendid start' – *The Times* (2 April 1984). Compare **up and running**, meaning 'to be under way', current by 1987. 'Party chiefs will tell delegates that a Scottish Parliament will be up and running by 1999' – *Daily Record* (28 February 1996).

hi-yo, Silver (away)! Stock phrase of the Lone Ranger in the various American radio, cinema and TV accounts of his exploits. 'Who *was* that masked man? . . . A fiery horse with the speed of light, a cloud of dust, and a hearty "Hi-yo, Silver!" The Lone Ranger! With his faithful Indian companion Tonto, the daring and re-sourceful masked rider of the plains led the fight for law and order in the early western United States. Nowhere in the pages of history can one find a greater champion of justice. **Return with us now to those thrilling days of yesteryear** . . . From out of the past come the thundering hoofbeats of the great horse Silver. **The Lone Ranger rides again!** "Come on, Silver! Let's go, big fellow! Hi-yo, Silver, away!"' This was more or less the introduction to the masked Lone Ranger and his horse, Silver, especially in the original radio shows – accompanied, of course, by Rossini's *William Tell* overture. Groucho Marx used to say that George Seaton (the first Lone Ranger on radio from 1933) invented the call 'Hi-yo, Silver!' because he was unable to whistle for his horse. It seems, indeed, that the phrase was minted by Seaton and not by Fran Striker, the chief scriptwriter in the early days. The Lone Ranger's Indian friend, Tonto (which is Spanish for 'fool'), wrestled meanwhile with such lines as, **him bad man, kemo sabe!** 'Kemos sabe' – whichever way you spell it – is supposed to mean 'trusty scout' and was derived from the name of a boys' camp at Mullet Lake, Michigan, in 1911.

Hobson's choice   No choice at all. Thomas or Tobias Hobson (d. 1631) hired horses from a livery stable in Cambridge. His customers were always obliged to take the horse nearest the door. The man's fame was considerable, the expression was recorded by 1649, and Hobson was celebrated in two epitaphs by Milton. *Hobson's Choice* was the title of a play (1915; film UK 1953) by Harold Brighouse.

hocus pocus   Trickery, deception. From a 17th-century name for a conjuror or fairground magician, bedazzling the crowds with mock-Latin incantations including these words.

(to) hog the limelight   Meaning, 'to keep the focus of attention upon oneself'. From theatrical use where a spotlight singles out the most prominent performer. Known by 1959. Listed as a cliché in *The Times* (28 May 1984). 'A back injury had compelled him to return from Pakistan's recent tour of New Zealand after the first Test, leaving Shane Warne to hog the limelight in the new world of the wristy men' – *The Independent* (10 May 1994); 'After several seasons when the Italians, the French and even the Americans seemed to hog the limelight . . . the pendulum has swung back as a new generation of talent has grown up to make London swing again' – *TheEuropean* (14 October 1994). It is a development of the phrase **in the lime-light** – the centre of attention – after the type of lighting used in 19th-century theatre following the discovery of the brilliant luminosity of incandescent lime by Thomas Drummond, a British army surveyor, in 1825. Figurative use by 1877. 'The most limelighted person in Europe this morning is Queen Wilhelmina of Holland' – *Daily Chronicle* (10 April 1903).

hog-whimpering   Of drunkenness, in an extreme state. A delightful coinage which, nevertheless, defies plodding definition. Also, figuratively, for anything you think is awful (or which is, so to speak, enough to make a hog whimper). 'Hog-drunk' appears to be either a contraction or, indeed, the original phrase. 'All those Gestapo toughs with their doxies. All of 'em hog-drunk' – Ian Fleming, *Octopussy* (1966); 'Of course people get drunk, absolutely hog-whimpering drunk, and there's lots of straight sex about' – *The Sunday Times* Magazine (8 March 1981); 'I can hardly approve of this blatant pander-ing to the filthy, stinking, hog-whimpering rich, but I can forgive the magazine a lot for its slogan: "Not since the last act of *La Traviata* has consumption been quite so conspicuous"' – *Today* (1 March 1987); 'Blair ducked. "I'll tell him what people will recall," he said, then produced two sound-bites of such hog-whimpering banality that they do not even deserve the name of weasel. They were gerbil soundbites' – *The Times* (1 December 1995).

ho ho, very satirical   Phrase expressing ironical appreciation of a satirical joke. Probably a reaction to the 'satire boom' of the early 1960s but still alive. A 'Mini-Trog' cartoon in *The Observer* (17 July 1988), at a time of long delays at British airports, shows a little man looking at an advertise-ment jokily promoting Gatwick as 'Gatqwick'. He is saying to himself, '*Very* satirical.' In fact, the phrase had its origins on the cover of the fourth issue of *Private Eye* (7 February 1962). It is a comment on a piece of artwork showing the Albert Memorial as 'Britain's first man into space'. Compare this from a letter written by Nancy Mitford on 26 December 1940: 'These ton bombs are [Hitler's] new joke . . . so one has great fun guessing where they will land. Ha ha ha *such* a little comedian.'

(to be) hoist with one's own petard Meaning, 'to be caught in one's own trap' – but, in origin, nothing to do with being stabbed by one's own knife (poniard = dagger) or hanged by one's own rope. The context in which Hamlet uses it in Shake-speare's play, III.iv.209 (1600–1) makes the source clear: 'For 'tis the sport to have the engineer / Hoist with his own petard.' A petard was a newly invented device in Shakespeare's day, used for blowing up walls, etc., with gunpowder. Thus the image is of the operative being blown up into the air by his own device. Compare the more recent expression 'to score an OWN GOAL'.

(unable to) hold a candle to (someone/thing) Not in a position to be compared favourably to someone/thing. In the pre-electric light era, an apprentice might have found himself holding a candle so that a more experienced workman could do his job. Or, in the days before street lighting, a linkboy would carry a torch for another person. Holding a candle, in either of these ways, was a necessary but menial task. If a person was so incompetent that he could not even do that properly, then he really was not fit for anything. There seems to have been no suggestion of anything to do with examining eggs by holding them up to the light (as has been suggested) or even of one person being *compared* with another. The meaning of the phrase is better expressed as 'not fit to hold a candle *for* another'. It has been known since the 16th century. 'Though I be not worthy to hold the candle to Aristotle' – Sir Edward Dering, *The Four Cardinal Virtues of a Carmelite Friar* (1641).

hold back the dawn Would-be poetic title. Not a quotation. *Hold Back the Dawn* as the title of a film (US 1941) is apparently an original phrase, as also are *Hold Back the Night* (US 1956) and *Hold Back Tomorrow* (US 1956), and Barbara Taylor Bradford's novel *Hold the Dream* (1985).

(to be left) holding the bag Meaning, to be left in an incriminating position and having to CARRY THE CAN. But what bag? One suggestion is that, in the 16th century, 'giving the bag' was an expression used to describe a servant who ran off with his master's cash, leaving behind only an empty purse or bag. In time, 'giving' became 'holding'.

hold it gently but firmly (like a schoolgirl holding her first cock) Instruction to embryo pilots as to how to handle a joystick, since the early 1930s.

hold it up to the light, not a stain, and shining bright Slogan for Surf washing

powder and current in the UK in the late 1950s. This was a line from the 'Mrs Bradshaw' series of TV ads in which the eponymous lady never appeared but her male lodger did. Compare: from 'The Scarlet Capsule' edition of the *Goon Show* (2 February 1959): 'This is the BBC – hold it up to the light – not a brain in sight!'

hold my hand and call me Charlie *Partridge/Slang* describes this as 'a mostly derisive catch phrase usually addressed by youth to girl: 1930s.'

hold the fort This phrase has two meanings: 'Look after this place while I'm away' and 'Hang on, relief is at hand'. In the second sense, there is a specific origin. In the American Civil War, General William T. Sherman signalled words to this effect to General John M. Corse at the Battle of Allatoona, Georgia (5 October 1864). What he actually semaphored from Keneshaw Mountain was: 'Sherman says hold fast. We are coming' (*Mencken*) or 'Hold out. Relief is coming' (*Bartlett*). The phrase became popularized in its present form as the first line of a hymn/gospel song written by Philip Paul Bliss in *circa* 1870 ('Ho, My Comrades, See the Signal!' in *The Charm*). This was introduced to Britain by Moody and Sankey during their evangelical tour of the British Isles in 1873 (but not written by them, as is sometimes supposed): '"Hold the fort, for I am coming," Jesus signals still; / Wave the answer back to heaven, / By thy grace we will.' More recently, perhaps thanks to a pun on 'union' (as in the American Civil War and trade union), the song has been adapted as a trade union song in Britain: 'Hold the fort, for we are coming / Union men be strong / Side by side keep pressing onward. / Victory will come.'

hold the front page! That is, 'Don't print what you've got set up but wait for the major news story that's just broken.' Has this supposed editor's cry ever been uttered in a film (or, indeed, in real life)? It is not uttered in the Ben Hecht/Charles MacArthur play *The Front Page* (1928). 'Clear the front page' – Bluebottle in 'The Scarlet Capsule' edition of *The Goon Show* (2 February 1959); 'Mirrorsoft previewed two programs that are bound to get mentioned in a newspaper: Hold the Front Page . . . is a game about journalism' – *The Guardian* (19 September 1985); there was a BBC TV series called *Hold the Back Page* about tabloid sports writers (1985). 'Hold the front page for one of Fleet Street's biggest ever grovels' – headline in *The Observer* (31 May 1998). A near miss occurs in the film *The Finger Points* (US 1931) when a harassed city editor barks into the phone: 'You're going to have to make up a new front page! Stop the presses!' Indeed, the cry **stop the presses!** is more findable. In *Deadline USA* (US 1952), Humphrey Bogart says, 'Stop the presses! I'm going to blow the lid off this town.' Michael Keaton as Henry Hackett, newspaper editor, in *The Paper* (US 1994) says 'Stop the presses!' and Jonathan Pryce as the media tycoon in the James Bond film *Tomorrow Never Dies* (US 1997) shouts, 'Hold the presses!'

hold your horses!   Hold everything, don't jump to conclusions or rush into action! Known in the USA and Australia by the 1940s.

hole   See ACE IN THE.

(the) hole heals up as soon as you leave the car park   Meaning, 'one will not be missed, no one is irreplaceable'. Broadcasting executive Michael Grade said it on leaving the BBC for Channel 4 in November 1987 and called it a 'BBC saying'.

(to need something like a) hole in the head   Meaning, 'not to need something at all'. Leo Rosten in *Hooray for Yiddish* (1982) describes this phrase as 'accepted from Alaska to the Hebrides' and states that it comes directly from the Yiddish *lock in kop*: 'It was propelled into our vernacular by the play *A Hole in the Head* (1957) by Arnold Schulman and more forcibly impressed upon mass consciousness by the Frank Sinatra movie (1959).' *OED2* finds it by 1951.

(a) hole-in-the-wall   In the 19th century, relatives of prisoners would make gifts of food and drink through a hole in the wall of a debtors' prison. It would appear that religious communities had something similar. 'The Gate House, of which . . . the Verger's hole in the wall was an appanage or subsidiary part' – Charles Dickens, *The*

Mystery of Edwin Drood, Chap. 18 (1870). By 1887, in the USA, the term had come to be applied to a place where alcoholic drinks were sold illegally. Hence, adjectivally, 'hole-in-the-wall' came to mean anything that was small, dingy or mean. Then in the mid-1980s, in the UK, the name came into use again for automatic cash dispensing machines set in the walls of banks. 'I must remember to visit the hole-in-the-wall', one might say,

Hollywood Ten   See under FREE THE —.

holy ——!   PHRASES. Use of exclamatory cries was a hallmark of the *Batman* filmed series for TV (US 1966–8), e.g. 'Holy flypaper!' / 'Holy cow!' / 'Holy schizophrenia!' Batman and Robin were characters created by Bob Kane in 1939 and featured in comic books before being portrayed by Adam West and Burt Ward on TV. Also used were: **quick thinking, Batman!** – a typically crawling remark from sidekick Robin – and **boy wonder!** – Batman's commendation in return. The on-screen titles 'Pow!' 'Biff!' 'Thwack!' 'Crunch!' 'Rakkk!' 'Oooofff!' and 'Bonk!' might also be said to be a kind of catchphrase.

holy mackerel   See I'SE REGUSTED.

home   See ARE THERE; DON'T TRY.

(a) home! a home!   Slogan of the Home family from Scotland. The traditional war-cry not only identified it but spurred its soldiers on to action – despite the legend that on hearing it at the Battle of Flodden Field in 1513, they turned tail and headed for home. This anecdote is sometimes advanced as the reason why Home is pronounced 'hume'. 'Mole, black and grim, brandishing his stick and shouting his awful war-cry, "A Mole! A Mole!"' – Kenneth Grahame, *The Wind In the Willows*, Chap. 12 (1908).

home and beauty   See ENGLAND.

home is the sailor, home from sea   In Robert Louis Stevenson's poem 'Requiem' (1887), it is definitely 'home from sea' – without the definite article, but his grave in Samoa has (incorrectly) 'home from *the* sea', as also his memorial in St Giles Cathedral, Edinburgh. 'Home from sea' is also the title of a painting (1862) by Arthur Hughes, showing a young sailor and (probably) his sister at their mother's grave (also known as 'The Sailor Boy' and 'Mother's Grave'). Compare *Home Is the Hero*, the title of a film (UK 1959) based on a play by Walter Macken.

home, James, and don't spare the horses Catchphrase used jocularly, as if talking to a driver, telling someone to proceed or get a move on. From the title of a song (1934) by the American song-writer Fred Hillebrand and recorded by Elsie Carlisle in that year and by Hillebrand himself in 1935. The compo-nent 'Home, James!' had existed long before – in the works of Thackeray, for example.

(even) Homer nods Meaning, 'even the greatest, best and wisest of us can't be perfect all the time, and can make mis-takes'. Current by the 18th century at least: 'Let Homer, who sometimes nods, sleep soundly upon your shelf for three or four years' – letter of Lord Chesterfield to Lord Huntingdon (31 August 1749). *Mencken* has 'even Homer sometimes nods' as an English proverb derived from Horace, *De Arte Poetica* (*circa* 8 BC): 'I am indignant when worthy Homer nods', and familiar since the 17th century. Longinus (*circa* AD 213–273) evidently added: 'They say that Homer sometimes nods. Perhaps he does – but then he dreams as Zeus might dream.' In the original, the criticism was of Homer's occasional lapses of style rather than making factual mistakes.

home rule (for ever) Slogan first used about 1870 in its usual sense of self-government for Ireland, then under British rule. The phrase 'Home Rule' is said to have been coined by a Professor Galbraith, though it had been used incidentally in 1860. It was preferred to the official term 'Home Government'. The Home Rule movement led by Sinn Fein wished to see the whole of Ireland become independent of British rule. The political battles that raged into the 20th century ultimately led to the founding of the Irish Free State, which eventually became the Republic of Ireland – but with Northern Ireland remaining part of the United Kingdom.

home sweet home Title phrase of a song by J. H. Payne, American actor and songwriter (1791–1852) from the opera *Clari, or, The Maid of Milan* (1823). From the same song we get **there's no place like home**. ''Mid pleasures and palaces though we may roam, / Be it ever so humble, there's no place like home.' This appears to build on the earlier proverb (1546), 'Home is home though it's never so homely.' An advertising slogan, quoted in 1982, was: 'Come to Jamaica, it's no place like home' which nicely plays upon the other, derogatory, view of home.

honest See DIGNITY.

honest Injun [honest Indian]! 'Honestly, you can take my word for it!' In the USA and UK by the 1880s/90s and used by Mark Twain in *Tom Sawyer* (1876). As Native Americans were not then consid-ered honest or honourable, the remark carries a hint of sarcasm.

honey, I just forgot to duck! Explanation or excuse derived from a remark made by the American boxer Jack Dempsey to his wife, on losing his World Heavyweight title to Gene Tunney during a fight in Philadel-phia in 1926. The line was recalled by ex-sports commentator, then President, Ronald Reagan when explaining to *his* wife what had happened during an assassination attempt in 1981.

(the) honeymoon is over for —— The period when goodwill shown to a newly arrived person or plan has come to an end. Known in a literal sense since Walter Scott, *The Bride of Lammermoor*, Chap. 21 (1818): 'The women could never bear me and always contrived to trundle me out of favour before the honeymoon was over.' '"Rise and shine, lovebirds!" he shouted. "The honeymoon is over!"' – H. Nielsen, *The Severed Key* (1973); 'The split opposi-tion vote has helped the Tories win the last four general elections; when Blair's honeymoon is over, it could help them win a fifth' – *The Sunday Times* (19 June 1994); 'Five years on, Romania's honey-moon is over and the unresolved affairs of the past have returned, like old lovers, to threaten the future' – *The Daily Telegraph* (4 March 1995).

(to) honk one's chuff To vomit. Known by 1985. To honk = to squeeze has been known in British slang since the 1950s.

However, 'chuff' has been known since the 1940s as 'anus, backside', so perhaps this really means to evacuate/void one's bowels?

hook   See BY HOOK.

(a) Hooray Henry   A loud-mouthed, upper-class twit' (in Britain). The phrase was coined by Jim Godbolt in 1951 to describe the upper-class contingent attracted to a jazz club at 100 Oxford Street, London, by the Old Etonian trumpeter Humphrey Lyttelton. It derives from a character in Damon Runyon's story 'Tight Shoes' who is described as 'strictly a Hurrah Henry'. In his book *Second Chorus* (1958), Lyttelton discusses the habitués of jazz clubs: 'In jazz circles, aggressively "upper-class" characters are known as Hoorays – an adaptation, I believe, of Damon Runyon's "Hooray Henries".'

hoots, mon!   'Mon' = 'man', but the *Collins English Dictionary* describes 'hoot/s' as 'an exclamation of impatience or dissatisfaction; a supposed Scotticism – C17: of unknown origin'. The *OED2* weighs in with the word being 'of Scottish and Northern England use', comparing the Swedish *hut* [begone], the Welsh *hwt* [away] and the Irish *ut* [out], all used in a similar sense. In 1982, I put the phrase to a panel including such noted Scottish word-persons as John Byrne, Cliff Hanley and Jimmy Reid. One thought it was a greeting with the meaning, 'How's it going, man?' Another thought it might mean 'Have a big dram, man' – a 'hoot' being a drink. Finally, Jimmy Reid dismissed it as 'stage Scots . . . bastardized Scots, for the placation of Sassenachs'. The 1958 British hit instrumental record 'Hoots Mon', performed by Lord Rockingham's XI, was punctuated at strategic points by the speaking of the cod Scotticisms, 'Hoots Mon, there's a moose loose aboot this hoose' and **it's a braw bricht moonlicht nicht**. This last phrase also occurs in the song 'Just a wee deoch-an-duoris', which Sir Harry Lauder performed and which he wrote in 1912 in collaboration with G. Grafton, R. F. Morrison and Whit Cunliffe.

hope   See ABANDON.

(I) hope your rabbit dies   A mild curse. Known by the 1920s. In Dorothy L. Sayers, *Have His Carcase*, Chap.7 (1932), Lord Peter Wimsey phones Harriet Vane and during the conversation says: 'All right, and I hope your rabbit dies.' Stella Gibbons, *Cold Comfort Farm*, Chap. 16 (1932) has her doughty heroine apparently adapt the phrase: '"Then you're a crashing bounder," said Flora, vigorously, "and I hope your water-voles die".' Many elaborations have been reported (particularly from Yorkshire): 'Well, all I hope is that his rabbit dies – and he can't sell the hutch'; 'I hope yer rabbit dies an' yer can't sell t' skin'; 'I hope your rabbits die and your rhubarb won't grow'; 'May your rabbits die and your toenails grow inward for evermore.'

Horlicks   See NIGHT STARVATION.

(a) horny-handed son of toil   A labourer bearing the marks of his trade. The expression was popularized by Irish-born Denis Kearney in a speech at San Francisco (*circa* 1878) when he was leading a 'workingman's protest movement against unemployment, unjust taxes, unfair banking laws, and mainly against Chinese labourers' – *Flexner* (1982). Earlier, J. R. Lowell had written in 'A Glance Behind the Curtain' (1843): 'And blessèd are the horny hands of toil', and Lord Salisbury, the British Conservative Prime Minister, had been quoted as using the precise phrase, in the *Quarterly Review* (October 1873).

horse   See BEHOLD A PALE.

(a) horse of another (or different) colour   Meaning, that something is 'of another matter altogether, of a different complexion entirely'. Known in the USA by 1798. Note the related 'horse of the *same* colour', known by 1601. Some etymologists have gone to unnecessary lengths to find an origin for a perfectly simple phrase. One even says it could have grown out of the White Horse of Berkshire, an English archaeological phenomenon, carved in a chalk hillside. From time to time, it was customary for neighbourhood volunteers to clean the weeds away, thus making it 'a horse of a different colour' . . .

horses sweat, men perspire – and women merely glow   A saying used to reprove someone who has spoken of 'sweating'. It is listed as a nanny's reprimand in *Casson/Grenfell* (1972) in the form: 'Horses sweat, gentlemen perspire, but ladies only gently glow.' J. M. Cohen includes it in *More Comic and Curious Verse* (1956) as merely by Anon, in the form: 'Here's a little proverb that you surely ought to know:/ Horses sweat and men perspire, but ladies only glow.'

(a) hostage to fortune What one establishes by delivering one's future into the hands of fate, usually by making some specific move or decision. 'He that hath wife and children, hath given hostages to fortune; for they are impediments to great enterprizes, either of vertue, or of mischief' – Francis Bacon, *Essays*, 'Marriage' (1607–12). Listed in *The Independent* (24 December 1994) as a cliché of newspaper editorials. 'Every manager who indulges in advertising is giving a hostage to fortune in that he is inviting public confidence in his goods and service, and he will rapidly go out of business if he cannot live up to his claims' – *The Listener* (4 November 1965); 'To let a 3–0 lead slip into a narrow 3–2 success as Newcastle had done at St James' Park was always creating a hostage to fortune and the true cost of their slipping concentration became apparent with Ciganda's strike' – *The Independent* (2 November 1994); 'The Political Outlook – Simon Heffer sees the Budget as opportunities missed – with Major giving a hostage to fortune' – by-line in *The Daily Telegraph* (30 November 1994).

hot See AS MANY; BLOW HOT; BY GUM SHE'S A.

(a) hotbed of —— Anywhere that appears to favour the rapid growth of any condition (after the bed of earth used for raising or forcing plants). Known since 1768: 'The seeds of wickedness . . . sprout up every where too fast; but a play-house is the devil's hot-bed' – Isaac Bickerstaffe, *The Hypocrite*, Act 1, Sc. 1. Cited as a 'dying metaphor' in George Orwell, 'Politics and the English Language' – *Horizon* (April 1946); 'It is as though Britain had gone off football or France had tired of haute cuisine. California, that hotbed of new-age political correctness, is beginning to balk at the burden of keeping the globe green'

– *The Sunday Times* (26 April 1992); 'Brisbane, rugby league-wise once the London of Australia and isolated from the game's hotbed of New South Wales, was barren ground for league colonists' – *The Observer* (22 May 1994).

hotly contested Inevitable pairing. Known by 1895. 'Swiss Bank has come in for stinging criticism in some quarters for building up a stake in Northern Electricity which is subject to a hotly contested £1200m bid from Trafalgar House' – *The Herald* (Glasgow) (19 January 1995); 'They have played in some of the most hotly-contested matches to grace the table-top' – *Daily Mail* (31 January 1995); 'Ever since the establishment of the university acts in the mid-1970s which banned political activity on Malaysian campuses, academic freedom has been a hotly contested issue' – *The Times Higher Education Supplement* (17 March 1995).

hot metal Term for the traditional method of newspaper production (before the advent of computer typesetting). Known by 1960. Type would be set up by hand and then, when the page was complete, an impression would be made by pouring molten metal over it. From this, plates would be made for printing the finished newspaper. *Hot Metal* was the title of a TV satire about newspaper production, written by Andrew Marshall and David Renwick in 1986. 'The company also claims that an agreement to reduce National Graphical Association (NGA) composing-room staff from 372 to 186 has been badly held up as a consequence of delays in introducing new coldtype computer setting technology to replace the oldfashioned "hot-metal" system, still used in most of Fleet Street' – *Financial Times* (13 February 1982).

(a) hot potato A subject (or person) that is very difficult and dangerous to handle – thus best dropped. Of American origin and known since 1840. 'This hot potato [a report on a secret meeting] was whizzed to London by teleprinter so that ministers and civil servants should have one more report indicating a possible new area of insecurity' – *The Guardian* (30 January 1975); 'Terry Hooper . . . has compiled hundreds of big cat sightings since the Seventies, [and] said: "Politically it's become a very hot potato"' – *The Observer* (9 February 2003).

hot to trot (1) Eager to be on the move. (2) Eager for sex. *MacMurphy* (*on electric shock treatment*): 'They was giving me ten thousand watts a day, you know, and I'm hot to trot. Next woman takes me on's going to light up like a pinball machine, and playoff in silver dollars' – film, *One Flew Over the Cuckoo's Nest* (US 1975).

hour See COMETH THE HOUR.

(the) hour of the wolf Meaning not clear. It is the English title of Ingmar Bergman's *Vargtimmen,* a Gothic fantasy film (1968) about an artist haunted by demons. On the other hand, Nicholas Freeling has a novel, *Wolfnight* (1982), in which he suggests there is a French saying 'that the country of twilight lies between dog and wolf.' Indeed, *entre chien et loup* means dusk/twilight, when you can't distinguish things very well and might conceivably take a wolf for a dog. 'Littré [19th cent.] says it means "half-light" in the evening or the morning, when the day is so gloomy that one wouldn't know how to distinguish between a dog and a wolf . . . Perhaps also the dog represents daytime, light and activity, and the wolf, night-time, darkness and fear – when you stay at home asleep and also have nightmares [It was in use by 1739]' – Claude Duneton, *La Puce à l'oreille – anthologie des expressions populaires avec leur origine* (1990).

house See EAT SOMEONE; IS THERE A DOCTOR.

(the) house of mirth Phrase from Ecclesiastes 7:3–4: 'Sorrow is better than laughter: for by the sadness of the countenance is the heart made better. The heart of the wise is in the house of mourning; but the heart of fools is in the house of mirth.' Hence, *The House of Mirth*, title of an Edith Wharton novel (1905; film UK 2000) about a failed social climber.

Houston, we have a problem Laconic understatement. The Apollo 13 space mission took off at 13.13 Houston time on 11 April 1970. Two days into the mission – i.e. on the 13th – and 200,000 miles from Earth, an oxygen tank exploded, seriously endangering the crew. What was then said is not very clear. The astronauts did *not* say, 'Houston, we've got a problem', as reported in *The Times* (15 April 1970) and as in the titles of a TV move (US 1974) and a documentary (US 1994) made about the incident. Nor did they say, 'Hey, we've got a problem here . . . Houston, we have a problem', as is suggested in the film *Apollo 13* (US 1995). What in fact crew member John L. Swigert said was: 'OK, Houston, we've had a problem here.' And what the commander, James Lovell, added was: 'Oh, Houston, we've had a problem. We've had a Main B Bus Undervolt' (indicating a fault in the electrical system).

Hovis See DON'T SAY BROWN.

how See AND HOW.

how about that (then)! Probably an American expression of surprise or wonderment dating from the 1930s. Noticed in the UK particularly in the late 1950s and mid-1960s. Before the BBC really began to use disc jockeys, in the modern sense of the word, there were one or two announcers or 'introducers' who developed distinctive ways. Roger Moffatt (1927–86) was a staff announcer in Manchester with the necessary plumy voice for reading the news. He also had a long and fruitful relationship introducing broadcasts by the BBC Northern Dance Orchestra (originally Variety Orchestra). After some dazzlingly impressive instrumental number, he was inclined to exclaim: 'Well, how about that then!' (See also Jimmy Savile's version of the phrase under AS IT HAPPENS.) Incidentally, when introducing a programme called *Make Way for Music* (broadcast simultaneously on radio and TV in the early 1960s), Moffatt had another stock phrase: **wherever you are, whoever you are, why not make way for music?**

how are the mighty fallen! Phrase now used ironically when anyone gets their come-uppance. It is a biblical quotation – from 2 Samuel 1:19 when David laments the deaths of Saul and Jonathan – 'The beauty of Israel is slain upon thy high places; how are the mighty fallen!' And the next verse is the famous, 'Tell it not in Gath, publish it not in the streets of Askelon.' Verse 25 of the same chapter has

'How are the mighty fallen in the midst of the battle!' and verse 27: 'How are the mighty fallen, and the weapons of war perished!'

how did you feel when —-? An appallingly clichéd question from TV newsgathering, especially in the UK – 'How did you feel when your daughter was raped before your eyes / your house was blown up / you forgot to post the pools coupon and lost your next-door neighbour a million pounds?' It may be necessary for the question to be asked in order to elicit a response, but the nearest any of the newsgatherers has come to doing anything about it is to suggest that, while asking the question is a legitimate activity, the question itself shouldn't actually be broadcast – only the answer. Noticed since the mid-1970s. Condemned in *The Times* (31 December 1981) as: 'One of those questions, specialities of television reporting, to which there seems to be no answer that is both rational and polite . . . It was firmly in the category of public interest interrogations which requires Miss Worlds, dismissed football managers and shot policemen to say how they feel about it.' When Thurgood Marshall was retiring from the US Supreme Court in 1992, he was asked at a press conference, 'How do you feel?' He replied, 'With my hands.' Compare: *Amanda (to Doris, accused of shooting her husband)*: 'And after you shot him – how did you feel?' *Doris*: 'Hungry' – film, *Adam's Rib* (US 1949).

how do? North of England greeting. Date of origin unknown. From the first edition of the BBC radio show *Have A Go* (1946): 'Ladies and gentlemen of Bingley, 'ow do, 'ow are yer?'

how do they do that? Question asked about any trick effect on films or TV. A BBC TV programme with the title *How Do They Do That?* (by 1994) was constructed around the subsequent explanations.

how do you do? Traditional polite greeting (established by the 17th century). It has been treated as a catchphrase or stock phrase by a number of entertainers particularly in the Britain of the 1940s and 50s. The comedian Arthur Askey used it as the title of a BBC radio series in 1949 and

a film. Terry-Thomas used the phrase at the start of monologues (and in the early 1950s had a BBC TV show called *How Do You View?*). Carroll Levis had a distinctive variation (see next entry). In any number of editions of BBC Radio's *Desert Island Discs*, Roy Plomley began, 'How do you do, ladies and gentlemen, our castaway this week is . . .' (how old-fashioned). The goofy British comedian Cardew Robinson (1917–92) inevitably had the version **this is Cardew the Cad saying Car-dew do!** See also under I'VE GOT A LETTER FROM A BLOKE IN BOOTLE.

how *do* you do, ladies and gentlemen, how *do* you do? Stock greeting of Carroll Levis, a Canadian-born showman who introduced a talent contest on British radio for a number of years. From a typical edition broadcast in 1946: after a fanfare, the announcer said: 'The Carroll Levis Show! We're back again with our feast of fun for everybody, bringing you the family show which is equally welcome to outlaws and in-laws. The founder of the feast, Carroll Levis!' Levis would then intone his welcome. Along the way he called people 'Brother' and would refer to 'my brother Cyril's favourite comedy couple . . .'. At the end of the show he would say: '**Same day, same time, same spot on the dial** . . . so long, good luck and happy listening.'

how long is a piece of string? Answer to an unanswerable (or poorly posed) question. Date of origin unknown but probably by the 1920s. Suggested answers include, however, 'Twice the length from the end to the middle' or 'Equidistant from the centre.' Used as the title of a book of scientific puzzles by Bob Eastaway (2002). 'BBC staff sign own expenses . . . Asked how many claims for under £100 an employee could make, a spokesman for the corporation said: "How long is a piece of string?"' – *Metro* (London) (15 August 2002). Similar questions (akin to meaningless riddles) are: 'How many legs does a shark have?' '**How high is up?**' and '**How high is the moon?**' – hence the song 'How High the Moon' by Lewis/Hamilton (1940).

how long, O Lord, how long? Question of mock exasperation, based on Isaiah 6:11: 'Then said I, Lord, how long?' The prophet has a vision in which God tells him to do various things, and he reports: 'Then said I, Lord how long?' The more familiar version occurs, for example, in 'The Marriage of Tirzah and Ahirad' (1827) by Macaulay – 'From all the angelic ranks goes forth a groan, / "How long, O Lord, how long"' – and in schoolboy verse by G. K. Chesterton (*circa* 1890): 'Not from the misery of the weak, the madness of the strong, / Goes upward from our lips the cry, "How long, oh Lord, how long?"'

how many beans make five? Joke riddle, but also a catchphrase uttered as an answer to an impossible question. Miss Alice Lloyd was singing a music-hall song in November 1898 that contained these lines: 'You say you've never heard / How many beans make five? / It's time you knew a thing or two – / You don't know you're alive!' The phrase was also re-corded twelve years earlier and seems to come from the heyday of Victorian hu-mour. Possible answers are: 'Two in each hand and one in the mouth'; 'Two beans and a bean, a bean and a half, and half a bean'; 'One and a half, and a half of one, one and three quarters, one quarter and one'; 'Half a bean, bean, bean and a half, two half beans and a bean'; 'A bean, a bean, a bean and a half, half a bean, and a bean'; 'One and another and two and a t'other'; 'A bean and a half, a bean and a half, half a bean, and a bean and half'; 'A bean and a half and half a bean, a bean and a quarter and a quarter of a bean, half a bean and a bean'.

how'm I doin'? Stock phrase of Ed Koch when Mayor of New York City (1977–89). He helped balance the books after a period of bankruptcy on the city's part by drastically cutting services. He would call out this phrase as he ranged round the city. 'You're doing fine, Ed' the people were supposed to shout back. An old song with the title was disinterred in due course. Unfortunately for him, Koch's achievements in NYC did not carry him forward to the State governorship as he had hoped and finally everything turned sour on him. A 1979 cartoon in *The New Yorker* showed a woman answering the phone and saying to her husband: 'It's Ed Koch. He wants to know how he's doin'.'

A booklet of Koch's wit and wisdom had the phrase as its title.

how now, brown cow? Phrase long used as an elocution exercise in the UK and regarded as the chief example thereof. Date of origin unknown, but it is men-tioned in a reminiscence of the Oxford University Dramatic Society in the 1920s by Osbert Lancaster in his book *With an Eye to the Future* (1967). Of an OUDS Last Night party, he writes: 'The principal entertainment was provided by musical members past and present repeating the numbers which they had composed for OUDS smokers, many of which – such as "How now brown cow" – had, after some slight modification of the lyrics at the request of the Lord Chamberlain, reap-peared in West End revues.' Indeed, 'How Now Brown Cow' with words by Rowland Leigh and music by Richard Addinsell was sung by Joyce Barbour in the revue *RSVP* at the Vaudeville theatre on 23 February 1926 and was recorded by her. (Inciden-tally, the *OED2* has an example of the simple interjection 'How now?', meaning 'How goes it?', dating from 1480.) It was not, however, included in the elocution song 'The Rain in Spain' from the musical *My Fair Lady* (1956) but made way for **the rain in Spain stays mainly in the plain** and 'in Hertford, Hereford and Hampshire hurricanes hardly ever happen'. According to Jonathan Cecil (1996), the rain/Spain phrase was invented by Anthony Asquith, director of the 1938 film version of *Pygmalion* and received Shaw's approval. The rhyming of 'rain' and 'Spain' seems a venerable activity, too. In *Polite Conversa-tion* (1738), Jonathan Swift has this ex-change: 'I see 'tis raining again. / Why then, Madam, we must do as they do in Spain. / Pray, my Lord, how is that? / Why, Madam, we must let it rain.' 'Rain, rain, go to Spain' was a proverbial expression current by 1659. Yet another speaking exercise appears in *Little Dorrit* by Charles Dickens (1857). Mrs General opines, 'Papa, potatoes, poultry, prunes and prism, are all very good words for the lips: especially prunes and prism.' Two undated speaking exercises from the schooldays of the actress Eleanor Bron (shall we say 1950s?) went: 'Lippy and Loppy were two little rabbits – lippity, lippity, lippity, lop', and, 'They put the lady in the tar. They said that she was in their power. They left her there for half-an-hour'.

how's your father? Catchphrase associated with the British music-hall comedian Harry Tate (1872–1940). Apparently, he would exclaim it as a way of changing the subject and in order to get out of a difficult situation (compare READ ANY GOOD BOOKS LATELY?). One account tells of a sketch in which he is on a sofa with a young woman. He was just saying something like, 'Let's get together for a bit of . . .' when he saw her father enter the room and hastily said to the girl, 'And how's your dear father?' Possibly this was what gave rise to the phrase's use as a euphemism for sexual activity (as, 'indulging in a spot of how's-your-father'). It has been suggested that another source for the phrase might be George Robey's song 'In Other Words' (written by N. Ayer and C. Grey, 1916), of which some versions may contain these lines: 'A student of nature, I walked down the Strand / And there a fair maiden did see. / I didn't know her, but she seemed to know me, / For she said, "How's your father?" to me.' A comic song performed from the early 1940s by Flanagan and Allen in the character of a First World War veteran and his newly enlisted son contains the lines 'If a grey-haired lady asks "How's your father?", that'll be Madame Moselle' – obviously on the basis that she had been up to some 'how's your father' with the father long ago. This refers to the First World War song 'Madamoiselle from Armentiers', which, in its many versions, does not appear to contain the actual expression 'How's your father?' Whatever the case, the phrase also took on a third use, meaning the same as a 'thingummy' or anything the speaker did not wish to name.

how's your poor old feet? Catchphrase from 19th-century music hall? Referred to by Ted Ray in his book *Raising the Laughs* (1952). *Benham* (1948) has a version without the 'old' dating from *circa* 1851 – 'alleged to have been a jocular saying in allusion to the fatigue resulting from visiting the Great Exhibition [in London] of 1851'. *Partridge/Catch Phrases* suggests

that, as a catchphrase, it was 'rampant' in 1862 and popular until 1870.

how the money rolls in! Phrase from the last line of each verse in a bawdy anonymous song – included, for example, in *Rugby Songs* (1967) – telling of the various fund-raising activities of a family. A typical verse: 'My brother's a poor missionary, / He saves fallen women from sin, / He'll save you a blonde for a guinea, / My God how the money rolls in.' T. R. Ritchie's *The Singing Street* (1964) seems to favour 'By God . . .' in the last line.

how the other half lives Meaning, 'how people live who belong to different social groups, especially the rich.' The expression was used as the title of a book (1890) by Jacob Riis, an American newspaper reporter. He described the conditions in which poor people lived in New York City. Indeed, the expression seems basically to have referred to the poor but has since been used about any 'other half'. Riis alluded to the core saying in these words: 'Long ago it was said that "one half of the world does not know how the other half lives".' *OED2* finds this proverb in 1607 in English, and in French, in *Pantagruel* (1532) by Rabelais. Alan Ayckbourn entitled a play *How the Other Half Loves* (1970).

how tickled I am! Catchphrase of the British comedian Ken Dodd (b. 1927) who commented (1979): 'I was once a salesman and I've always been fascinated by sales techniques and catchphrases are like trade marks – they are attention-getting details which in my case make people exclaim, "Ah yes, Ken Dodd." The disadvantage of catchphrases is that they get worn – like tyres. So I wanted a catchphrase that was better than a catchphrase . . . I narrowed it down to the fact that it had to be a greeting like HELLO, FOLKS or something like Fanny Brice's ARE YOU ALL RIGHT? FANNY'S ALL RIGHT. I thought of the word "tickled" and all the permutations and combinations one could get from that. So I devised "How tickled I am" as a phrase that could be varied by the addition of a joke – "Have you ever been tickled, Mrs?" and so on. But it was out of the need for a catchphrase that the Tickling Stick actually came.' Dodd's greeting **hello, Mrs** is also a hangover from his days as a travelling hardware salesman. Dodd had a whole series of BBC radio comedy shows from 1963 into the 70s. 'Like most performers, I'm always trying out material on friends and relatives. One night after recording my radio show in London [by 1966], we rushed to catch the train back to Knotty Ash [in Liverpool] from Euston. I was trying on various daft voices and saying, "Where's me case? **Where's me shirt?**" and the people who were with me laughed – so it went into the next show.' The Liverpool pronunciation is approximately 'whair's me shairt?' and Dodd recorded a song with the title. From the same source: **I'm a shirt short**. Other Doddisms on stage and on radio included: **diddy** – an adjective used to describe anything 'quaint, small and lovable'. In the 18th century a 'diddy' was a woman's breast or nipple (or that of an animal) – compare 'titty'. 'Diddy Uncle Jack' was how the family used to describe Dodd's great-uncle. 'My family,' he says, 'always impressed on me the importance of being original in my act and I suppose these words I use, like "diddy", **full of plumptiousness** and **tattifalarious**, are an attempt at having something which is mine and nobody else's.' Another one, **discum-knockerating**, means that something bowls you over. On 31 December 1981, the *Liverpool Echo* reported Dodd's reaction to being awarded the OBE: 'I am delighted. It's a great honour and wonderful news. I am full of plumptiousness. The jam butty workers are discumknockerated and the Diddymen are diddy-delighted.' Then there is his nonsense phrase **nikky-nokky-noo**. 'Humour is anarchic, I suppose. So, like a child, from time to time you revolt against the discipline of words and just jabber!' Dodd inherited his form of farewell **tatty-bye (everybody)!** from his father. Another example of a phrase format that allows for variety by the addition of new punchlines is his **what a beautiful day for ——**.

how to succeed in business without really trying Title of a business handbook (1953) by Shepherd Mead – now more widely known as the title of Frank Loesser's musical (1961; film US 1967).

how to win friends and influence people Title of a book (1936) by Dale Carnegie. Carnegie's courses incorporating his self-improvement plan had already been aimed at business people for a quarter of a century before the book came out.

how true that is, even today (or **how true those words are today)!** A plonking remark in response to another such. As it turns out, this catchphrase has a show business origin, but that was by no means clear when I first started investigating it. In 1998, Dr James Atherton noticed my responding to a rather vacuous remark on my radio show with the words, 'How true that is, even today.' He wondered if the phrase came from a sketch or satire upon churchy folk? All I could point to was this from the actor Kenneth Williams's published letters: 'I must say I fell about at your line "Age shall not wither her nor iron bars a cage." I thought "How true that is even today".' This is from a letter dated 2 October 1971 and led to discovering the source: the BBC radio show *Round the Horne* (in which Kenneth Williams appeared, of course). The phrase occurs regularly in the parodies of Eamonn Andrews's inept TV chat shows. On 13 and 20 March 1966, Seamus Android (played by Bill Pertwee) replies to one of his guests: 'How true that is even today.' On 27 March, Williams as Claphanger (a movie producer) says, 'You see, I'm illiterate, too.' Android replies: 'Yes. And how true those words are even today.' On 3 April, movie star Zsa Zsa Poltergeist (Betty Marsden) says, 'I'll get around to all of you in time.' Android comments: 'And how true those words are even today.' So we may say that, rather than stemming from the airy philosophising of church folk in the 1960s, the expression is meant to mock the plonking style of a chat-show host. The scripts were written by Barry Took and Marty Feldman.

how weird is that? An expression that suddenly caught on in about 2002, possibly from the USA.

Hoyle See ACCORDING TO.

ho yuss! 'Oh, yes!' 'Yuss' is a dialect form of 'yes'. In this form, the phrase apparently makes its first appearance in Rudyard

Kipling's chapter-heading poem 'Many Inventions' from the story 'My Lord the Elephant' (1893): 'The bullocks are walkin' two by two, / An' the elephants bring the guns! / Ho! Yuss!'

hubba! hubba! (or hubba! bubba!) Said, echoic of a wolf-whistle, to a pretty girl. Popular in the US military, 1940s, and used by Bob Hope in radio shows of that period. Said to be based on the Chinese cry *how-pu-how*.

Hubert See APPROBATION FROM.

(the) hub of the universe Sobriquet applied to any place that seems at the centre of activity. Bostonians are said to refer to their city as 'The Hub', alluding to its self-proclaimed status as 'The hub of the universe': 'Boston State-House is the hub of the solar system. You couldn't pry that out of a Boston man, if you had the tire of all creation straightened out for a crow-bar' – Oliver Wendell Holmes Sr, *The Autocrat at the Breakfast-table* (1858); 'Monica Dickens is uncompromising about the area of London where she was born. "Notting Hill Gate," she says, "is the hub of the universe"' – quoted in Valerie Grove, *Where I Was Young*, Chap. 5 (1976).

Hull See COME HELL.

human See ALL; FULLY PAID-UP.

(a) human dynamo A person who is tireless in performing any activity. Date of origin probably early 1900s. 'A human dynamo of enormous kilowattage' – *Daily Express* (5 April 1935); 'So badly was the Spaniard being mauled that she received an ovation whenever she won a point, but after recovering another break to level at 2–2 in the second set, the human dynamo finally hummed into action and competed in some fierce baseline rallies' – *Mail on Sunday* (11 September 1994); 'A pensioner, known as the Human Dynamo to her friends, has celebrated her 101st birthday' – *Northern Echo* (14 October 1994); 'Moon in . . . Aries: You're the original human dynamo. Nothing stops you from getting what you want, apart from your occasional lack of foresight or self-restraint' – horoscope in *Daily Mail* (7 December 1994).

humbug See BAH.

(a) humble abode A modest dwelling – self-deprecating term for where one lives and an inevitable pairing. Date of origin unknown. Appropriately, two of the most unctuous characters in literature use it. Mr Collins in Jane Austen's *Pride and Prejudice* (1813) says: 'The garden in which stands my humble abode, is separated only by a lane from Rosings Park, her ladyship's residence.' Uriah Heep in Charles Dickens's *David Copperfield* (1849) says: 'My mother is likewise a very umble person. We live in a numble abode.' 'A mangy pi-dog shared his humble abode' – *The Times* (12 June 1959); 'Only much later, when the price of whatever humble abode they have managed to secure starts to look like telephone numbers, will they, too, begin with calculating eye to look on their home as a property and contemplate the prospects of trading up' – *The Irish Times* (23 July 1993); 'His life revolves around a humble abode on an estate "at the tap o' the hill" in the ancient Scottish border town of Jedburgh' – *Daily Mail* (4 February 1994); 'Venus the artist brings to Cancer the home-lover an ability to make a humble abode into a glorious palace' – horoscope in *Daily Mail* (16 February 1995); 'In the village of Eastwood, 10 miles distant, stands the more humble abode of Nottinghamshire's other world-famous writer, D. H. Lawrence, at 8A Victoria Street' – *The Herald* (Glasgow) (3 April 1995).

(a/the) hundred days Phrase used to refer to a period of intense political action (often immediately upon coming to power). During the 1964 General Election, Harold Wilson said Britain would need a 'programme of a hundred days of dynamic action' such as President Kennedy had promised in 1961. In fact, Kennedy had specifically ruled out a hundred days, saying in his inaugural speech that even 'a thousand days' would be too short – hence the title of Arthur M. Schlesinger's memoir, *A Thousand Days* (1965), referring also to the 1,056 days of Kennedy's presidency. The allusion was to the period during which Napoleon ruled between his escape from Elba and his defeat at the Battle of Waterloo in 1815.

hurry on down The epigraph of John Wain's 1953 novel *Hurry on Down* simply has 'Hurry on down to my place, baby, / Nobody home but me. – *Old Song*'. In fact it was a song (1947) written and performed by Nellie Lutcher, the American entertainer. Wain's novel was lumped together with others in the Angry Young Men school of the early 1950s. It was about a man hurrying down from university and doing rather unlikely jobs.

(this) hurts me more than it hurts you Traditional line spoken by teacher or parent administering corporal punishment to a child. An early occurrence is in Harry Graham's *Ruthless Rhymes* (1899): 'Father, chancing to chastise / His indignant daughter Sue, / Said: 'I hope you realize / That this hurts me more than you.' A *Punch* cartoon (11 April 1905) has the politician Augustine Birrell saying to a boy representing 'the Education Act 1902' (which Birrell was reforming): 'My boy, this can't hurt you more than it's going to hurt me.' Also turned on its head from time to time: from James Agate's *Ego 4* (1940): '*Nouveaux Contes Scabreux*, No. 7. This is a tale of a rosy-cheeked schoolboy who turns his head to the master flogging him and winningly remarks, "Excuse me, sir, but this is pleasing me more than it is hurting you!"'

hush, hush, hush, here comes the bogey man Compton Mackenzie recalled going to pantomimes in the 1890s and, in particular, hearing the Demon King sing: 'Hush, hush, hush! / Here comes the bogey man, / Be on your best behaviour, / For he'll catch you if he can.' He added – in *Echoes* (1925): 'At these words children were fain to clutch parent or nurse or governess in panic, and I remember hearing it debated whether a theatre management was justified in terrifying children with such songs.' A song incorporating the full phrase is on the B-side of the famous Henry Hall recording of 'The Teddy Bears' Picnic' (1932). The golf term 'bogey' apparently was derived from 'bogey-man' (as recounted in *OED2*) on an occasion in 1890. 'Bogey' meaning 'goblin, phantom or sprite' is very old indeed.

hush, keep it dark! See KEEP IT DARK.

hush puppies (1) Deep-fried corn meal batter, often served with fried fish in the Southern USA. The food may have got its name from pieces being tossed to hounds with the admonition, 'Hush, puppy!' (2) Soft shoes, popular in the 1960s in the USA and UK. In 1961, the Wolverine Shoe and Tanning Corp registered 'Hush Puppies' as a trade name in the USA. Adrian Room in his *Dictionary of Trade Name Origins* (1982) suggests the name was adopted because it conjures up softness and suppleness. Pictures of beagle-like dogs were shown on the display material. The only connection between the food and the shoe seems to have been a sort of homeliness.

I

I aim at the stars Which actual rocket scientist was the subject of a biographical film entitled *I Aim At the Stars* (US 1960) with Curt Jurgens in the role? The answer is Wernher von Braun, who after working on German V-2s in the Second World War, went to the USA and participated in the space programme. The title may allude to Virgil's *Aeneid* (as also may the RAF motto *Per ardua ad astra*). Erik Berghast's 1960 biography of von Braun is entitled *Reaching for the Stars. Griff nach den Sternen* (the title of a book on which von Braun collaborated in 1962) is more properly translated as 'reaching/grasping/groping for the stars.' There is, of course, the joke that although von Braun may have been aiming at the stars, he more usually hit London. And then again, there are the lines from Tom Lehrer's song, 'Werner von Braun' (1965), '"Once the rockets are up, who cares where they come down? / That's not my department," says Werner von Braun'.

I always do my best for all my gentlemen
Catchphrase of Mrs Lola Tickle (Maurice
Denham) in the BBC radio show *ITMA*
(1939–49). She appeared within six weeks
of the start of the show as office charlady
to Mr ITMA (Tommy Handley) and was the
precursor by a full year of Mrs Mopp. She
pronounced it *gentlemaine*.

I am the greatest Slogan of Muhammad
Ali, formerly Cassius Clay (b. 1942), who
became world heavyweight boxing
champion in 1964. He admitted that he
copied his 'I am the greatest . . . I am the
prettiest' routine from a wrestler called
Gorgeous George he had once seen in Las
Vegas: 'I noticed they all paid to get in –
and I said, this is a good idea!' In a
moment of unusual modesty, Ali added:
'I'm not really the greatest. I only say I'm
the greatest because it sells tickets.'

**I believe you, (but) thousands
wouldn't** Reassuring statement to a
friend or colleague but possibly implying
that the thousands are quite right in their
unbelief. *Partridge/Catch Phrases* describes
this as 'indicative either of friendship
victorious over incredulity or tactfully
implying that the addressee is a liar' and
finds a citation in R. H. Mottram, *The
Spanish Farm* (1927). It is spoken by both
the Albert Finney and the Rachel Roberts
characters in the film of Alan Sillitoe's
Saturday Night and Sunday Morning (UK
1960).

I bet you say that to all the girls! Said
by a woman to a man in response to
flattery. British use, by the 1930s.

I came to London to seek my fortune 'I
therefore came to London last Tuesday –
as the old saying goes – "to seek my
fortune"' – Tom Driberg in a letter dated 5
June 1955 – quoted in Francis Wheen's
biography (1990). Indeed, it is an old
saying (though more usually applied to
young people) and probably derives from
the same source as STREETS PAVED WITH GOLD
– namely, the legend of Dick Whittington.
Swift wrote *circa* 1745: 'His father dying,
he was driven to London to seek his
fortune.'

I can hear you! See under DON'T FORCE IT,
PHOEBE.

I can't believe I ate the whole thing See
TRY IT YOU LIKE IT.

ice See CUT NO.

ich bin ein Berliner Slogan. On 26 June
1963, President John F. Kennedy proclaimed a stirring slogan outside the City
Hall of West Berlin in the then recently
divided city: 'All free men, wherever they
may live, are citizens of Berlin, and,
therefore, as a free man, I take pride in the
words *Ich bin ein Berliner*.' Ben Bradlee
noted in *Conversations with Kennedy*
(1975) that the President had to spend 'the
better part of an hour' with Frederick
Vreeland and his wife before he could
manage to pronounce this and the other
German phrases he used. It detracts only
slightly to know that the President need
only have said, '*Ich bin Berliner*' to convey
the meaning 'I am a Berliner'. It could be
argued that the '*ein*' adds drama because
he was saying not 'I was born and bred in
Berlin' or 'I live in Berlin', but 'I am one of
you'. But by saying what he did, he drew
attention to the fact that in Germany '*ein
Berliner*' is a doughnut.

(the) icing on the cake What finishes off
something and brings it to perfection
(while at the same time being a bit of an
unnecessary luxury and no more than 'the
trimmings'). This figurative use may date
only from the mid-20th century. Concerning the imprisonment of a dictator: '"A
political jackpot" is how Lee Atwater,
Bush's chief Republican campaign adviser,
sees the outcome of the Panamanian
invasion. "The icing on the cake," was the
description of Dick Cheney, the Defence
Secretary' – *The Observer* (7 January 1990).

**I couldn't fancy him if his arse was
decked with diamonds** For some reason,
I have a note of this expression as having
being said by a 'Welsh woman 1920s/30s',
but no more.

**I counted them all out and I counted
them all back** This was 'an elegant way
of telling the truth without compromising
the exigencies of military censorship,'
according to the BBC's Director-General
Alasdair Milne in *DG: The Memoirs of a
British Broadcaster* (1988). 'I'm not
allowed to say how many planes [Harrier
jets from HMS *Hermes*] joined the raid, but

I counted them all out and I counted them all back,' said Brian Hanrahan, a British journalist, in a report broadcast by BBC Television on 1 May 1982. Hanrahan was attempting to convey the success of a British attack on Port Stanley airport during the Falklands War. The phrase stuck.

I cover the waterfront Title phrase of a film (US 1933) about a newspaper reporter exposing corruption, based on a book (1932) by Max Miller, a 'waterfront reporter' on the *San Diego Sun*. Hence 'cover' is in the journalistic sense. The song with this title (by John W. Green and Ed Heyman), performed notably by Billie Holiday, is unconnected with the film and sounds as if it might be about laying paving stones or some other activity. It was so successful, however, that it was later added to the soundtrack of the film. Since the film, 'to cover the waterfront' has meant 'to cover all aspects of a topic' or merely 'to experience something'. A woman going in to try a new nightclub in the film *Cover Girl* (US, 1944) says: 'This is it. We cover the waterfront.' In *The Wise Wound* (1978) by Penelope Shuttle and Peter Redgrove, 'she's covering the waterfront' is listed among the many slang expressions for menstruation.

idea See IT SEEMED LIKE.

I didn't get where I am today . . . Catchphrase of 'C.J.', the boss (John Barron), in BBC TV's *The Fall and Rise of Reginald Perrin* (1976–9), written by David Nobbs. This popularized a characteristic phrase of the pompous. Nobbs entitled his autobiography *I Didn't Get Where I Am Today* (2003).

I didn't know you cared! Phrase spoken after an unexpected gesture or compliment but, often ironically, when the compliment is double-edged or outright critical. Known by the 1940s. *I Didn't Know You Cared* was taken as the title of a BBC TV comedy series (1975) set in a dour North Country family.

I didn't oughter 'ave et it! Catchphrase of the British actor and entertainer Jack Warner. In his book *Jack of All Trades* (1975), he recounted the occasion when the phrase was born. He was leaving Broadcasting House in London with

Richard Murdoch: 'I had to step over the legs of a couple of fellows who were sitting in the sunshine with their backs against the wall eating their lunches from paper bags. As we passed, I heard one say to the other, "I don't know what my old woman has given me for dinner today but I didn't oughter 'ave et it." I remarked to Dickie, "If that isn't a cue for a song, I don't know what is!" It provided me with my first catchphrase to be picked out by members of the public.'

I didn't recognize you with your clothes on Frisky line addressed to a member of the opposite sex (sometimes in jokes about doctors meeting patients at parties). Compare Groucho Marx's line in *Go West* (US 1940): 'Lulubelle, it's you! I didn't recognize you standing up.'

idle on parade A sergeant-major's phrase for when a soldier makes the slightest wrong movement on the parade ground. Compare **naked on parade**, similar sergeant-major's hyperbole for, say, one button left undone in an otherwise immaculately smart turn-out. Both phrases were probably current in the 1930s. *Idle on Parade* is the title of a film (US 1959) with Anthony Newley as a rock singer in what has been described as a 'kind of folksy British parody of Elvis Presley's controversial drafting into the US Army'.

I'd like to get you on a slow boat to China I would like to get you on your own (for amatory purposes) – a quotation from the song 'On a Slow Boat to China' (1948) by Frank Loesser, which continues '. . . all to myself alone'.

I do/I will When taking marriage vows, which reply is correct? In the Anglican Prayer Book, the response to 'Wilt thou have this man/woman to thy wedded husband/wife . . . ?' is obviously 'I will.' In the Order of Confirmation, to the question: 'Do ye renew the solemn promise and vow that was made . . . at your baptism?' the response is obviously 'I do.' But in some US marriage services, the question is posed: 'Do you take so-and-so . . . ?' to which the response has to be 'I do.' 'Will you . . . ?' is said to be more popular with American clergy, 'Do you . . . ?' at civil ceremonies. Jan de Hartog's play *The Four*

Poster was turned into a musical with the title *I Do! I Do!* (Broadway 1966).

I do not choose to run Phrase associated with President Calvin Coolidge, but it is not quite what he said, and, in any case, he didn't actually *say* it. Having been President since 1923, his words to newsmen at Rapid City, South Dakota, on 2 August 1927 were 'I do not choose to run for President in 1928'. And rather than speak the words, 'Silent Cal' handed slips of paper with these words on them to waiting journalists. For some reason, the unusual wording of the announcement caught people's fancy and the phrase was remembered. In 1928, there was a silly song recorded in New York about a recalcitrant wristwatch. It was performed by Six Jumping Jacks with Tom Stacks (vocal) and was called 'I Do Not Choose To Run'. The dedication of Frank Nicholson's *Favorite Jokes of Famous People* (1928) is to: 'A famous man whose favorite joke is not included in this collection . . . he did not choose to pun.'

I do not like this game! Catchphrase of Bluebottle (Peter Sellers) in the BBC radio *Goon Show* (1951–60), when the truth belatedly dawned on him that he was going to be 'deaded' again. *Seagoon:* 'Now, Bluebottle, take this stick of dynamite.' *Bluebottle:* 'No, I do not like this game!' Another example occurs in '1985' (8 February 1955).

I don't *believe* it! Anybody's exclamation of incredulity but one that achieved catchphrase status from 1993 when spoken in a distinctive, strangulated Scots accent by the actor Richard Wilson as 'Victor Meldrew' in BBC TV's blackish comedy *One Foot In the Grave*, written by David Renwick. Meldrew, coping with enforced retirement, was in a state of permanent exasperation at modern life and at all the extraordinary misfortunes that befell him.

I don't get no respect Catchphrase of Rodney Dangerfield (b. 1921), a comedian popular in the USA during the 1970s/80s.

I don't know much about —— but I know what I like In *Are You a Bromide?* (1907), the American writer Gelett Burgess castigated people who spoke in clichés.

Among the 'Bromidioms' he listed was: 'I don't know much about Art, but I know what I like.' In his novel *Zuleika Dobson* (1911), Max Beerbohm says of the heroine when she is at a college concert: 'She was one of the people who say, "I don't know anything about music really, but I know what I like"'; '[Keith Floyd says: "My] house is full of daft articles I've picked up from all over the place . . . I don't know anything about art or music; I just know what I like"' – *The Irish Times* (11 August 1994).

I don't mind if I do! Catchphrase from the BBC radio show *ITMA* (1939–49). It was the immortal reply of Colonel Chinstrap (Jack Train) whenever an alcoholic drink was even so much as hinted at. The idea first appeared in 1940–41 in the form, 'Thanks, I will!' The Colonel was based on an elderly friend of John Snagge's – a typical ex-Indian Army type, well pleased with himself. The phrase had existed before, of course. *Punch* carried a cartoon in the edition of 25 December 1869: *Railway Porter:* 'Weybridge! Weybridge! Any one for V'rgin'a water!' *Thirsty passenger (waking up at the sound of the last word):* 'Gin 'an water! 'Ere y'are, Porter! Bring 'sh four penn'th!!' Then in ?1880, this reportedly became: *Porter:* 'Virginia Water!' *Bibulous old gentleman (seated in railway carriage):* 'Gin and water! I don't mind if I do!' In the edition of 31 October 1900, there was this: *Hostess:* 'Come and hear a whistling solo by my husband.' *Smith (whose hearing is a trifle indistinct):* 'A whiskey and soda with your husband? Well, thanks, I don't mind if I do have just one!' *ITMA*, however, secured the phrase a place in the language, as the Colonel doggedly turned every hint of liquid refreshment into an offer: *Handley:* 'Hello, what's this group? King John signing the Magna Carta at Runnymede?' *Chinstrap:* 'Rum and mead, sir? I don't mind if I do!'

. . . I *don't* think! Catchphrase reversing the statement that precedes it (compare . . . NOT!) Charles Dickens in *Pickwick Papers*, Chap. 38 (1837) has: '"Amiably disposed . . . I don't think," resumed Mr Weller in a tone of moral reproof.' *Punch* (7 April 1909) refers to it as a 'popular slang phrase'.

I don't wish to know that, kindly leave the stage Traditional response to a corny joke in music hall, variety and, presumably, vaudeville. Usually said by a person who has been interrupted by the joker while engaged in some other activity on stage. Impossible to say when, and with whom, it started, but in the 1950s the phrase was given a new lease of life by *The Goon Show* on BBC radio and by other British entertainers who still owed much to the routines and spirit of music hall. In the 1930s, the phrase was associated with Murray and Mooney (say, 1909–14) (later, Murray and King, to 1948), but may have been used earlier by Dave and Joe O'Gorman (say 1906–55). In similar circumstances, Dan Rowan used to say to Dick Martin on *Laugh-In*, 'I don't want to hear about it.' See also I SAY, I SAY, I SAY!

I dood it Catchphrase of Junior, the Mean Widdle Kid – as portrayed by Red Skelton on American radio in the 1930s. This was how he owned up to mischief (i.e. 'I did it'). Used as the title of a Red Skelton film in 1943. The character also appeared in the *Red Skelton Show* on TV (1951–71).

I dreamed I —— in my Maidenform bra Classic slogan format from the days when bras were not for burning but for dreaming about. The series, devised by the Norman Craig & Kummel agency in the USA, ran for twenty years from 1949. Maidenform offered prizes of up to $10,000 for dream situations that could be used in the advertising, in addition to: 'I dreamed I took the bull by the horns / Went walking / Stopped the traffic/ Was a social butterfly / Rode in a gondola / Was Cleopatra . . . in my Maidenform bra.' 'I dreamed I went to blazes . . . ' was illustrated by a girl in a bra, fireman's helmet and boots, swinging from a fire engine.

I'd walk a mile for a Camel Slogan for Camel cigarettes in the USA, current in the early 1900s and discontinued in 1944. According to Julian Lewis Watkins, *The 100 Greatest Advertisements* (1959 edn): 'A sign painter was painting a billboard one day and a man walked up and asked him if he could give him a cigarette. The painter said "yes" and offered him a Camel. The stranger thanked him with enthusiasm, and said "I'd walk a mile for a camel." The sign painter was smart enough to report the incident as a suggestion for a billboard and from this incident grew one of the best and most familiar slogans in advertising.' In a very early Cole Porter song, 'It Pays to Advertise' (*circa* 1912), there is the allusion: 'I'd walk a mile for that schoolgirl complexion'. '"I'd walk a mile for a Camel," murmured the hungry lion, as he watched a caravan crossing the Sahara' – is a Wellerism from California in *The Pelican*, Vol. 31, No. 1 (1925). Chico Marx says, 'I'd walk a mile for a calomel' in the film *Horse Feathers* (US 1932).

if anything can go wrong, it will Most commonly known as **Murphy's Law** (and indistinguishable from **Sod's Law** or **Spode's Law**), this saying dates back to the 1940s. *The Macquarie Dictionary* (1981) suggests that it was named after a character who always made mistakes in a series of educational cartoons published by the US Navy. *CODP* has that it was invented by George Nichols, a project manager for Northrop, the Californian aviation firm, in 1949. He developed the idea from a remark by a colleague, Captain Edward A. Murphy Jnr of the Wright Field-Aircraft Laboratory, 'If there is a wrong way to do something, then someone will do it.' The most notable demonstration of Murphy's Law is that a piece of bread when dropped on the floor will always fall with its buttered side facing down (otherwise known as the Law of Universal Cussedness). This, however, predates the promulgation of Murphy's Law. In 1867, A. D. Eichardson wrote in *Beyond Mississippi*: 'His bread never fell on the buttered side.' In 1884, James Payn composed the lines: 'I never had a piece of toast / Particularly long and wide, / But fell upon the sanded floor / And always on the buttered side.' The corollary of this aspect of the Law is that bread always falls buttered side down *except when demonstrating the Law*! Some have argued that the point of Captain Murphy's original observation was constructive rather than defeatist – it was a prescription for avoiding mistakes in the design of a valve for an aircraft's hydraulic system. If the valve could be fitted in more than one way, then sooner or later someone would fit it the wrong way. The idea was to design it so that the valve could only be fitted the right way. Film titles have included *Murphy's Law* (US 1986) and *Murphy's War* (UK 1971).

if —— did not exist, it would have to be invented Format phrase originating with Voltaire's remark: '*Si Dieu n'existait pas, il faudrait l'inventer* [if God did not exist, it would be necessary to invent him]' – *Epîtres*, 96 (1770). Other examples include: 'If Austria did not exist it would have to be invented' (Frantisek Palacky, *circa* 1845); 'If he [Auberon Waugh, a literary critic] did not exist, it would be un-necessary to invent him' – Desmond Elliott, literary agent (*circa* 1977); 'What becomes clear is that Olivier developed his own vivid, earthy classical style as a reaction to Gielgud's more ethereal one . . . So if Gielgud did not exist would Olivier have found it necessary to invent himself?' – review in *The Observer* (1988); 'If Tony Benn did not exist, the old Right of the Labour Party would have had to invent him' – *The Observer* (15 October 1989).

I feel no pain! Stock phrase of Major Denis Bloodnok (Peter Sellers) in the BBC radio *Goon Show* (1951–60).

if God had intended us to —— he wouldn't have ... Format phrase used as an argument against doing or using something, especially the aeroplane: 'If God had intended us to fly, He'd never have given us the railways' – Michael Flanders, *At the Drop of Another Hat*, 'By Air' (1963). In the final chapter of David Lodge's novel *Changing Places* (1975), Morris Zapp, after a close air miss, comments: 'I always said, if God had meant us to fly, he'd have given me guts.' Attributed to Mel Brooks is the observation: 'If God had intended us to fly, He would have sent us tickets.' From Lord Berners, *First Childhood* (1934): 'My [model flying machine] elicited a reproof from the Headmaster, who happened to see it [in *circa* 1893]. "Men," he said, "were never meant to fly; otherwise God would have given them wings." The argument was convincing, if not strikingly, having been

used previously, if I am not mistaken, by Mr Chadband.' (Sort of: Charles Dickens, *Bleak House*, Chap. 19 (1853): '[Chadband] "Why can't we not fly, my friends?" [Mr Snagsby] "No wings."') In turn, one can imagine the remark being adjusted to dismiss the railway train and the motor car. From J. B. Priestley's play *When We Are Married*, Act 2 (1938): *Ruby*: 'Me mother says if God had intended men to smoke He'd have put chimneys in their heads.' *Ormonroyd*: 'Tell your mother from me that if God had intended men to wear clothes He'd have put collar studs at back of their necks.'

if in doubt, strike it out Journalist's lore – meaning, 'if you're not sure of a fact or about the wisdom of including an item of information or opinion, leave it out'. It may be that the advice was more specific, originally. Mark Twain in *Pudd'nhead Wilson* (1894) says: 'As to the Adjective: when in doubt strike it out.' Ernest Hemingway is supposed to have recommended striking out adverbs. Compare this with the advice Samuel Johnson quoted from a college tutor (in Boswell's *Life* – for 30 April 1773): 'Read over your compositions, and where ever you meet with a passage which you think is particularly fine, strike it out.' Which might be recommended to journalists also. The precise phrase appears in the notorious 'Green Book' (issued *circa* 1949) to guide BBC Light Entertainment producers as to which jokes were, or were not, then permissible on the radio: 'Material about which a producer has any doubts should, if it cannot be submitted to someone in higher authority, be deleted, and an artist's assurance that it has been previously broadcast is no justification for repeating it. "When in doubt, take it out" is the wisest maxim.' *Partridge/Slang* has 'when/if in doubt, toss it out' as, curiously, a 'pharmaceutical catchphrase C20'. 'When in doubt, do nowt' is a northern English proverb which *CODP* first finds in 1884. Compare KILL YOUR DARLINGS.

if I said you had a beautiful body, would you hold it against me? Chat-up line – a simple punning question that became the title of a hit song by the American duo the Bellamy Brothers in 1979 (though they sang 'have' instead of 'had'). *The Naff Sex Guide* (1984) then listed it among 'Naff Pick-Up Lines'. Earlier, *Monty Python's Flying Circus* used the line on 15 December 1970 (adding 'I am not infected'). But, not unexpectedly, the British comedian Max Miller (1895–1963) seems to have got there first. In a selection of his jokes (once published by the *Sunday Dispatch* and reprinted in *The Last Empires*, ed. Benny Green, 1986), we find: 'I saw a girl who was proud of her figure. Just to make conversation I asked her, "What would you do if a chap criticised your figure?" "Well," she said, "I wouldn't hold it against him".'

if it ain't broke(n), why fix it?   Modern proverb. The earliest citation (if not coinage) is from Bert Lance, President Carter's Director of the Office of Management and Budget, talking about government reorganization and quoted in *The Nation's Business* (27 May 1977). It has also been ascribed to the motor magnate Henry Ford and was later picked up by Margaret Thatcher as an argument against unnecessary governmental intervention. Indeed, the proverb 'caught on' in the late 1980s. A TV reviewer asked it of the Government's plans to deregulate broadcasting in *The Independent* (3 November 1988); 'Tim Rice [the writer of the musical *Chess* said of the changes made after its opening], "The notices were very good and people liked it, so we could have said, 'If it ain't broken, don't fix it.' But we felt that certain aspects weren't quite right"' – *The Independent* (12 November 1988).

if it isn't hurting, it isn't working
Modern proverb. 'The harsh truth is that if the policy isn't hurting it isn't working' – John Major, speech at Northampton (27 October 1989) on suddenly becoming Chancellor of the Exchequer following the resignation of Nigel Lawson. It had probably been written for his predecessor. In 1996, the Conservative Party tried to capitalize on this 'harsh truth' by producing poster advertisements declaring, 'YES, IT HURTS. YES, IT WORKS.' As such, this is a newer version of **no pains, no gains** – perhaps more commonly known in the USA (it dates back at least to 1577). In the form 'no pain, no gain', it was used by

Jane Fonda in her fitness workout videos (by 1984). Adlai Stevenson said in his speech accepting the Democratic presidential nomination (26 July 1952): 'Let's talk sense to the American people. Let's tell them the truth, that there are no gains without pains.'

if it moves, salute it, if it don't, paint it!
Sardonic catchphrase summing up American and British military attitudes, since the 1940s. A longer version is: 'If you can lift it, carry it; if you can't lift it, paint it; if it moves of its own accord, salute it.' Latterly there has been the more vulgar (from the USA), 'If it moves, salute it; if it doesn't move, paint it; if you can't paint it, fuck it!' This links to a sentiment attributed to the well-known bachelor and hi-tech British journalist, Andrew Neil (in 1990): 'If you can't plug it into the mains or fuck it, the editor's not interested.'

if it's going on, it's going in   Slogan for the *Sunday Mail* newspaper, 1983. Ken Bruce commented (1985): 'Because the Scottish *Sunday Mail* was just about the only Sunday newspaper that was not imported from England, the Mirror Group's advertising agents came up with a slogan which, they felt, demonstrated the *Mail*'s ability to carry all the very latest news on its pages. The slogan was "If it's going on, it's going in".' This served well for some months but was quietly withdrawn when it was discovered that some local wits had been going round public houses applying the promotional stickers to contraceptive vending machines . . .'

if it's h-h-hokay with you, it's h-h-hokay with me   The stuttering catchphrase of Tubby Turner (1882-*circa* 1935), the Lancashire-born music-hall performer.

if it's ──, this must be ──   Format phrase for when people are in the midst of some hectic activity, whilst also reflecting on the confused state of many tourists superficially 'doing' the sights without really knowing where they are. Popularized by *If It's Tuesday, This Must be Belgium*, the title of a film (US 1969) about a group of American tourists rushing around Europe. 'If It's Thursday, Then It Must Be Thatcherland' – headline (on a brief visit to London by Mikhail

Gorbachev) in *The Guardian* (7 April 1989). A German magazine dating from before the First World War apparently put a similar phrase in the mouth of an English tourist.

if it was raining ——, I'd ... A series of moans by the terminally miserable/ unfortunate/disaster-prone ('If it was raining pea soup, I'd only have a fork') may date from 1940s' Australia; 'If it was raining palaces I'd end up with a toilet at the bottom of the garden' (heard in 1983); 'If it was raining palaces, I'd be hit on the head with the handle of a dunny [privy] door' (also Australian); 'If it was raining virgins, I'd end up with a poofter'.

I forgot the question! Stock phrase of Goldie Hawn, originally the blonde dum-dum in NBC TV's *Rowan and Martin's Laugh-In* (1967–73). In the middle of a quick exchange, she would giggle and then miaow, 'I forgot the question!' At first her fluffs were a case of misreading cue cards, then they became part of her act.

if seven maids with seven mops ... Phrase indicative of some immense undertaking. In a letter to her daughter, Clementine Churchill described Tunis (23 December 1943): 'It is really a particularly dirty and unattractive town. I do not believe if seven hundred thousand mops "swept it for half a year, that they could get it clean" . . .' – Mary Soames, *Clementine Churchill* (1979). The allusion is to Lewis Carroll, *Through the Looking-Glass* (1872), when the Walrus and the Carpenter are reflecting on 'such quantities of sand': '"If seven maids with seven mops / Swept it for half a year, / Do you suppose," the Walrus said, / "That they could get it clear?"'

if the mountain won't come to Moham-med ... Proverb notably recorded in Francis Bacon's *Essays*, 'Of Boldness' (1625), where it probably made its first appearance in English, as: 'If the hill will not come to Mahomet, Mahomet will go to the hill.' Bacon had it in the form of a Spanish proverb in his commonplace book but the ultimate source is probably the *Hadith* – the traditional sayings of Moham-med but not included in the Koran. Mohammed asked for miraculous proof of

his teaching and ordered Mount Sofa (a hill near Mecca) to come to him. When it did not, he took this as a sign of God's mercy – because if it had moved, he and his fellows would have been buried – so instead he went to the mountain to give thanks.

if wishes were horses, beggars would ride Nannyism in *Casson/Grenfell*. Or rather a proverb that nannies were once much inclined to quote. In this form, the proverb has been in existence since the 18th century (*CODP*).

if you build it, he will come *The Ob-server* (5 June 1994) quoted James Cosgrove of 'telecoms giant AT&T': 'In the movie *Field of Dreams* there is the phrase "If you build it they will come".' Not exactly. In the 1989 US movie, Kevin Costner plays an Iowa farmer who hears a voice (played by 'Himself' according to the credits) that tells him repeatedly, 'If you build it, *he* will come.' So Costner creates a baseball pitch in a field so that 'Shoeless Joe' Jackson, the discredited Chicago White Sox player of SAY IT AIN'T SO, JOE fame, can come back from the dead and be rehabilitated. Subsequent messages received – and too complicated to explain here – are 'Ease his pain' and 'Go the distance'. A neat allusion to the main phrase occurred in the second *Wayne's World* movie (US 1994) in which the ghost of rock star Jim Morrison inspires the teenagers to put on a rock concert called 'Waynestock'. When Morrison is asked whether big name groups will actually show up, he intones, 'If you book them, they will come.'

if you can't beat 'em, join 'em Modern proverb, probably American in origin in the alternative form, 'If you can't lick 'em, join 'em'. The earliest citation in the *CODP* is from Quentin Reynolds, the American writer, in 1941. *Mencken* had it in his dictionary, however, by 1942. *Safire* calls it 'a frequent bit of advice, origin obscure, given in areas dominated by one (political) party . . . The phrase, akin to the Scottish proverb "Better bend than break", carries no connotation of surrender; it is used to indicate that the way to take over the opposition's strength is to adopt their positions and platform'.

if you can't be good, be careful! Nudging farewell remark, sometimes completed with 'and if you can't be careful, name it after me' – or 'buy a pram'. *Mencken* calls it an American proverb, though *CODP*'s pedigree is mostly British, finding its first proper citation in 1903 – from A. M. Binstead, *Pitcher in Paradise*. In 1907, there was an American song called 'Be Good! If You Can't Be Good, be Careful!' written by Harrington Tate. The same sort of farewell remark as **don't do anything I wouldn't do!**

if you can't fight, wear a big hat *Partridge/Catch Phrases* has this as a taunt made to someone who has just bought a new hat. Presumably the implication is that they have bought a big hat of the type that would intimidate potential opponents. A Cockney 1930s' starting point is suggested.

if you can't ride two horses at once, you shouldn't be in the circus Modern proverb, probably originating in a remark attributed to Jimmy Maxton, the Scottish Independent Labour Party politician (1855–1946): 'If my friend cannot ride two horses – what's he doing in the bloody circus?' – said of a man who had proposed disaffiliation of the ILP from the Labour Party – quoted in G. McAllister, *James Maxton* (1935). Maxton had been speaking in a debate at a Scottish conference of the ILP in 1931 and been told he could not be a member of two parties – or ride two horses – at the same time.

if you can't stand the heat, get out of the kitchen Modern proverb, invariably associated with Harry S Truman. In 1960, the former US President said: 'Some men can make decisions and some cannot. Some men fret and delay under criticism. I used to have a saying that applies here, and I note that some people have picked it up.' When Truman announced that he would not stand again as President, *Time* (28 April 1952) had him give a 'down-to-earth reason for his retirement, quoting a favourite expression of his military jester Major General Harry Vaughan', namely, 'If you can't stand the heat, get out of the kitchen.' The attribution is usually given to Truman himself, but it may not be what he said at all. 'Down-to-earth' is not quite how I would describe this remark, but that

would do very nicely for 'If you can't stand the stink, get out of the shit-house'. There is only hearsay evidence for this, but given Truman's reputation for salty expressions, it is not improbable. *Bartlett* quotes Philip D. Lagerquist of the Harry S Truman Library as saying, 'President Truman has used variations of the aphorism . . . for many years, both orally and in his writings' (1966). Note the 'variations'.

if you got it, flaunt it See WHEN YOU GOT IT, FLAUNT IT.

if you know a better 'ole – go to it Philosophical acceptance of one's lot. The catchphrase comes from the caption to a cartoon (1915) by the British cartoonist, Bruce Bairnsfather, depicting 'Old Bill', up to his waist in mud on the Somme during the First World War. Two films (UK 1918; US 1926), based on the strip, were called *The Better 'Ole* and followed a musical with the title staged in London and New York (1917–18).

if you know what I mean See JOE BOB SAYS; NARMEAN?

if you'll excuse the pun! Of the kind used archly by the humourless, when having just committed one. So ghastly, one feels like calling it a cliché, which it isn't really. Alternatives are **pardon the pun** and **no pun intended**. Nothing new about it: in *Pictures from Italy* (1846), Charles Dickens wrote, 'The ten fingers, which are always – I intend no pun – at hand.' 'I begin to think that perhaps there is a point in keeping a foot in both camps [theatre and films]. No pun intended' – Kenneth Williams in *The Kenneth Williams Letters* (1994) – letter of 11 January 1973. 'But these have to be dry cleaned! Apart from the expense, can you imagine men remembering to drop off their underwear (excuse the pun!) at the cleaners' – *Northern Echo* (25 July 1994); 'You could refer to it as a case of cheap sex – just under £1m was used to set up the campaign using the advertising world's favourite tool (no pun intended) i.e. sex' – *Today* (10 August 1994); 'But other headlines suggest that what we have here is an offshoot of *Farmer's Weekly* . . . Alongside the key words "Toronto" and "blessing", all the words and pictures which I have mentioned fall (no pun intended) into place' – *The Independent* (25 February 1995).

if you've never been to Manchester, you've never lived (or perhaps **if you haven't been to Manchester, you haven't lived)** Either way, it was said by Tommy Trafford (Graham Stark) in the BBC radio show *Ray's a Laugh* (1949–60). Probably, one has here another format phrase – 'If/ until you've . . . you haven't lived.' From *The Observer* (15 January 1989) on the George Formby Appreciation Society: 'Until you have seen this herd of wallies, all long past their sell-by dates and playing their ukuleles in time to a film of their diminutive hero, you haven't lived.' Compare, too, the Spanish proverb that *Mencken* records: 'He who has not seen Seville has seen nothing.'

if you want anything, just whistle Seductive catchphrase derived from lines in the film *To Have and Have Not* (US 1945). What Lauren Bacall says to Humphrey Bogart (and not the other way round) is: 'You know you don't have to act with me, Steve. You don't have to say anything, and you don't have to do anything. Not a thing. Oh, maybe just whistle. You know how to whistle, don't you, Steve? You just put your lips together and blow.'

if you want to get ahead, get a hat Slogan for the (British) Hat Council – and curiously memorable. Quoted in 1965, but also remembered from the early 1950s and perhaps even from the 1930s.

I go – I come back! Catchphrase spoken in a hoarse whisper by Ali Oop (Horace Percival), a saucy postcard vendor in the BBC radio show *ITMA* (1939–49). First used in the summer of 1940.

I gotta horse! Ras Prince Monolulu was a British racing tipster who flourished – perhaps the only nationally famous one of his kind – from the 1930s to the 1950s. His real name was Peter Carl McKay, and he used to wander around dressed up like a Masai warrior, or similar. He died in 1965. *Partridge/Catch Phrases* renders his cry as both 'I got an 'orse!' and 'I gotta norse!' and finds that it was coined when Monolulu was trying to outdo a racetrack evangelist

who carried the placard 'I got Heaven'. There seem to be many ways of reproducing the cry. However, there is a record on which he sings it – Regal MR 812 – but I've not been able to trace a copy – and there the title is given as 'I got a 'orse'. *I've Got a Horse* appears to have been the title of a Noel Gay revue in London (1938) and definitely the title of a British film, featuring the singer Billy Fury, in 1965. A black version of Cinderella, originally entitled *I Gotta Shoe*, was presented in London in 1976 and may distantly refer to this phrase.

I hae me doots Scottish pronunciation of 'I have my doubts' – slightly affected, patronizing and irritating. In a Joyce Grenfell sketch, 'Head Girl' from *The Little Revue* (1939): 'It would be great fun to give Miss Torpor a present . . . Mavis suggests silver candlesticks . . . if we get enough £.s.d . . . about which I Hae Me Doots.'

I hate J.R. See WHO SHOT J.R.?

I have a bone in my leg (or **I've got a bone . . .)** All-purpose humorous excuse for non-activity. Sometimes '. . . in my throat/arm/ etc.' It dates back to the 16th century, as *Apperson* makes clear. Anthony Fisher recalled (1997): 'As a child in the early forties I would frequently summon my father to come upstairs to read me a story. He obviously found this a rather tiresome chore and to relieve him of this duty my mother would reply, "He can't come now, he has a bone in his leg". Even at my early age, I thought this a pretty, er, lame excuse as mobility would have been even more difficult without a bone in his leg – but what on earth could have been the origin of this curious expression?' It is fairly pointless seeking a reason for this feeble excuse. The obviousness of the statement – like 'he's got two ears on his head' – is an indication that the excuse is not to be taken in any way seriously. Whatever the case, it is a venerable idiom. Jonathan Swift included it among the conversational clichés in *Polite Conversation* (1738) – which shows it did indeed have whiskers even then: *Neverout*: 'Miss, come be kind for once, and order me a dish of coffee.' *Miss*: 'Pray, go yourself; let us wear out the oldest first. Besides, I can't go, for I have a bone in my leg.'

I have a cunning plan Catchphrase of Baldrick (Tony Robinson), the inept sidekick of Blackadder in the several series of BBC TV *Blackadder* (1983–9). Indeed, he often has, and it is invariably disastrous. First uttered in the second episode, 'Born to Be King', of the first series (22 June 1983). The phrase 'cunning plan' existed before this, of course, but this use cemented the inevitable pairing. 'The cabling of Europe . . . The French then came up with a cunning plan' – *The Economist* (13 August 1983); 'The cunning plan for Charles and Camilla . . . Yet this week's episcopal activity does suggest that someone somewhere has had a cunning plan' – *The Independent* (7 November 1998).

I haven't been so happy (or **laughed so much) since my grandmother caught her tit in a mangle** Daley Thompson, the British athlete, actually had the nerve to say the 'I haven't been so happy . . .' version on winning a gold medal in the decathlon at the 1984 Los Angeles Olympics. The rest can vary. It might be 'mother/aunt' and 'left tit/tits'. *Partridge/ Catch Phrases* dates the similar 'Hell! said the Duchess when she caught her teats in the mangle' to *circa* 1895. There is a version in Nicholas Monsarrat's *The Cruel Sea* (1951), which hints at a probable origin in the services. Alan Bennett in *Forty Years On* (1968) has a victorious rugby team sing: 'I haven't laughed so much since Grandma died / And Aunty Mabel caught her left titty in the mangle / And whitewashed the ceiling.' Nick Bicat recalled (2000) that when he was at school, Snoo Wilson (later a playwright) coined the version: 'Haven't laughed so much since uncle Horace caught his dewlaps in the starter-motor.'

I haven't (got) a thing to wear . . .! Women's catchphrase designed to reduce their partners to helpless silence. Meaning, 'I haven't got a dress suitable for this occasion we're going to and which I haven't worn several times before.' By 1900, probably.

I hear what you say (or **are saying)** Phrase of argument, meaning 'I can see what you are getting at but it is not going to make me alter my opinions.' By the 1970s and listed among 'Naff Expressions' in *The Complete Naff Guide* (1983).

I hear you Scots expression meaning that a remark is not worth considering or is untrue and is certainly not going to be responded to. Notably used by Lord Reith to fob off suggestions by Malcolm Muggeridge in the BBC TV programme *Lord Reith Looks Back* (1967).

I just don't care any more! See SHUT THAT DOOR!

I kid you not! Don't mistake what I say – I mean it. Probably American in origin, from about the 1940s. The phrase occurs in the film of Herman Wouk's *The Caine Mutiny* (US 1954).

I like Ike Slogan. These words began appearing on lapel buttons in 1947 as the Second World War US General Dwight David Eisenhower began to be spoken of as a possible presidential nominee (initially as a Democrat). By 1950, Irving Berlin was including one of his least memorable songs, 'They Like Ike', in *Call Me Madam,* and 15,000 people at a rally in Madison Square Gardens were urging Eisenhower to return from a military posting in Paris and run as the Republican candidate in 1952, with the chant 'We like Ike'. It worked. The three sharp monosyllables, and the effectiveness of the repeated 'i' sound in 'I like Ike', made it an enduring slogan throughout the 1950s.

I like the backing See under I'LL GIVE IT FIVE.

I'll 'ave to ask me Dad Catchphrase of Ancient Mark Time in the BBC radio show *ITMA* (1939–49) who sounded as if he was about a hundred years old. Randolph Churchill, speaking at a General Election meeting in 1945, was heckled with the remark, 'He'll have to ask his Dad!'

(well,) I'll be a dirty bird! Catchphrase of the American comedian George Gobel, star of *The George Gobel Show* (1954–60) on NBC and then CBS TV. According to Brooks & Marsh, *The Complete Directory to Prime Time Network TV Shows* (1981), 'Low-key comedian George Gobel, known affectionately as "Lonesome George" . . . [was] for a time one of TV's top hits, and his familiar sayings ("Well, I'll be a dirty bird!", **"You don't hardly get those no more"**) became bywords.'

I'll be back! Phrase that caught on following its menacing use by Arnold Schwarzenegger in the film *The Terminator* (US 1984), in which he played a time-travelling robot who terminates his opponents with extreme prejudice (ripping their hearts out, etc.). Coincidentally, the last words of the film *Pimpernel Smith* (UK 1941) are: 'I'll be back . . . we'll all be back.' These are spoken by Leslie Howard as a professor of archaeology who goes into war-torn Europe to rescue refugees.

I'll be leaving you now, sir . . . Stock phrase when anticipating a tip – given new life by Claud Snudge (Bill Fraser) in Granada TV's *Bootsie and Snudge* (1960–62). He was a doorman at a London club. The phrase was obviously established by 28 June 1911 when the caption to a *Punch* cartoon read: '*Foreign Waiter (who has forgotten the right formula for the usual hint, "I am leaving you now, Sir," to startled guest. "YOU WILL NEVARE SEE ME NO MORE, SIR".*'

I'll drink to that! 'I agree with what you say or the course of action you propose' – but used only in light-hearted situations. American origin, by the 1950s. It had something of a revival when Dick Martin took to saying it to Dan Rowan in NBC TV's *Rowan and Martin's Laugh-In* (1960s).

illegal, immoral or fattening Alexander Woollcott wrote in *The Knock at the Stage Door* (1933): 'All the things I really like to do are either illegal, immoral, or fattening.' Hence, the song, 'It's Illegal, It's Immoral Or It Makes You Fat' by Griffin, Hecht and Bruce – popularized in the UK by the Beverley Sisters (1950s).

illegitimi non carborundum Cod-Latin phrase – supposed to mean 'Don't let the bastards grind you down' – used by US General 'Vinegar Joe' Stilwell as his motto during the Second World War, though it is not suggested he devised it. *Partridge/Catch Phrases* gives it as '*illegitimis . . .*' and places its origins in British army intelligence very early on in the same war. Something like the phrase has also been

reported from 1929. 'Carborundum' was, in fact, the trade name of a very hard substance composed of silicon carbide, used in grinding. The same meaning is also conveyed by the phrase ***nil carborundum*** . . . (as in the title of a play by Henry Livings (1962) – a pun upon the genuine Latin ***nil desperandum*** [never say die – literally, 'there is nought to be despaired of'] which comes from '*nil desperandum est Teucro duce et auspice Teucro* [nothing is to be despaired of with Teucer as leader and protector]' – Horace, *Odes*, I.vii.27. Perhaps because it is a made-up one, the phrase takes many forms, e.g.: '*nil illegitimis . . .*', '*nil bastardo illegitimi . . .*', '*nil bastardo carborundum . . .*' etc. When the Right Reverend David Jenkins, the Bishop of Durham, was unwise enough to make use of the phrase at a private meeting in March 1985, a cloth-eared journalist reported him as having said, '*Nil desperandum illegitimi . . .*'

I'll forget my own name in a minute Catchphrase of the nameless man from the ministry (Horace Percival) in the BBC radio show *ITMA* (1939–49). This was already an established phrase to show the limits of one's forgetfulness. It occurs in Charles Dickens, *The Chimes* (First Quarter) (1844), as 'I'll forget my own name next.' James Boswell said to Samuel Johnson – recorded in *Journal of a Tour to the Hebrides*, for 19 August 1773): 'A worthy gentleman of my acquaintance actually forgot his own name.' Johnson replied, 'Sir, that was a morbid oblivion.' Even earlier, in the Motteux translation of Cervantes, *Don Quixote* (1605), there is: 'My memory is so bad that many times I forget my own name!'

I'll give it five Catchphrase launched by a member of the British public – something of a rarity. Not that Janice Nicholls, a Birmingham girl conscripted on to the 'Spin-a-Disc' panel of ABC TV's pop show *Thank Your Lucky Stars* in *circa* 1963, could avoid a type of celebrity for long. Awarding points to newly released records in her local dialect ('five' was pronounced 'foyve') and declaring (as if in mitigation for some awful performance) 'but **I like the backing . . .** ', she became a minor celebrity herself. She even made a record called 'I'll Give It Five' (coupled with 'The Wednesbury Madison') – which later she was prepared to admit was worth about *minus* five. When she started appearing, Janice was only sixteen, had just left school and was working as a junior clerk/telephonist at a local factory. She was soon meeting 'all the stars except Elvis' and became the pin-up of three ships, a submarine and a fire station. Janice commented (1980): 'I think it was just the accent really. It's a broad Black Country accent, y'know. I think it must have took the fancy of a lot of people. So they just kept asking me to go back and it ended up being three years before I finished.'

I'll give you the results in reverse order
Eric Morley founded the Miss World beauty contest in 1951. He assured himself a small measure of fame each year by appearing in the TV show and announcing the winners in the order No. 3, No. 2, No. 1 – so building up to the winner. In consequence, whenever anyone has to give similar results in this way, it is said they are being given **in Miss World order**.

I'll go out into the garden and eat worms 'I'll eat humble pie,' often said ironically. An early appearance is in Elsie J. Oxenham, *The Two Form Captains* (1921). *The Sunday Telegraph* (19 March 1989) published a slightly different version: 'Nobody loves me, everybody hates me, / I'll go into the garden and eat worms: / Great big juicy ones, little squiggly-wiggly ones, / Golly, how they wriggles and they squirms.'

I'll go to bed at noon Phrase from the Fool's last words in Shakespeare's *King Lear*, III.vi.83 (1605): 'And I'll go to bed at noon' – after Lear has said: 'We'll go to supper i' th' morning.' Used as the title of a book (1944), subtitled 'A Soldier's Letters to His Sons', by the actor Stephen Haggard, published posthumously. Haggard had played the Fool in the 1940 Old Vic production of *Lear* with John Gielgud.

(well,) I'll go to the foot of our stairs!
An old northern English expression of surprise and amazement or lack of interest in something that has just been said. Presumably, the implication is that the short walk to the place mentioned would

allow the speaker to recover equanimity. Or perhaps it means it is time to go upstairs to bed ('go to the *top* of our stairs' has been reported)? Used by Tommy Handley in BBC radio's *ITMA* (1940s) and elsewhere. Said to have been used by the entertainer George Formby as 'Eeh, I'll go to the foot of our stairs', as also, 'Eeh, I'll go to our 'ouse [pronounced 'our rouse'].' A variation from the North-East, 'I'll go to the bottom of our garden', links it perhaps to I'LL GO OUT INTO THE GARDEN AND EAT WORMS. Professor Ron Leigh commented (2002): 'The saying was very common in Sheffield when I grew up there. As you probably know, Sheffield is very conscious of its proud tradition of being underwhelmed by startling news. So, on being told some amazing story, a typical Sheffielder will dryly respond, "I'll go to the foot of our stairs", indicating, "How very unimpressed I am".'

ill-gotten gains Money or other benefit gained illegally or in any underhand way – an inevitable coupling. Also used loosely with no criminal inference (see first citation). Macaulay used it in his *History of England* (1859). 'The resorts seemed to be full of elderly English derelicts . . . all . . . anxiously searching the Times ordinary share index for news of their ill-gotten gains' – Kenneth Williams in *The Kenneth Williams Letters* (1994) – letter of 12 March 1972). 'Undercover Britain claims to be a "hard-hitting documentary series which exposes injustices", but who is it ultimately aimed at? Not the exploiters, who are far too busy enjoying their ill-gotten gains to watch TV' – *Evening Standard* (London) (28 March 1995); 'Businesses up and down the land are receiving faxes from Lagos sent by one Mr Nko Ezeh, the chairman of the contract award and implementation committee and chief accountant of the corporation who is offering $10 million to anyone prepared to let him use their bank account to transfer ill-gotten gains of 35 million out of Nigeria' – *The Irish Times* (21 April 1995).

I'll have what she's having Quotation hovering on the edge of becoming a catchphrase. In the film *When Harry Met Sally* (US 1989), Meg Ryan fakes an orgasm in the middle of a crowded restaurant. The punch line to the scene is provided by Estelle Reiner as an older woman sitting at a nearby table. When a waiter asks what she would like to order, she says, 'I'll have what she's having.'

I'll see myself out Cliché line of drama. It is what the visiting policeman invariably says after having come to break some bad news. It enables the other participants to continue the scene without a break. Observed by Fritz Spiegl in an article on drama cliché lines in *The Listener* (7 February 1985).

I'll try anything once Meaning, 'there's always a first time' and often said somewhat fatalistically. *Mencken* has 'I am always glad to try anything once' as an 'American saying not recorded before the nineteenth century'. Certainly current by 1921.

(the) illustrious dead Phrase known by 1809 but now a cliché. 'Goethe is in danger of turning into a Nobodaddy – a booming, boring member of that depressed class, the illustrious dead' – *The Listener* (29 November 1962); 'Such illustrious dead as Orpheus and Eurydice, Vermeer and his pearl girl, a swami and an American millionaire couple are repetitively enacting key moments of their lives at the command of the jackal Anubis who feeds off their desires' – *The Sunday Times* (30 October 1994); 'Marie Curie, who discovered radium, was yesterday chosen to be the first woman for burial in the Paris Pantheon, resting place of France's illustrious dead' – *The Herald* (Glasgow) (15 March 1995).

I love —— (or I♥ ——) Slogan format. In June 1977, the New York State Department of Commerce launched a campaign to attract tourists. The first commercial showed people enjoying themselves in outdoor activities – fishing, horseback riding, camping, and so forth. Each one said something like, 'I'm from New Hampshire, but I love New York,' 'I'm from Cape Cod, but I love New York,' and ended with a man in a camping scene saying, 'I'm from Brooklyn, but I loooove New York.' Since then 'I Love New York' has become one of the best-known advertising slogans in the world but has been swamped by the use of the 'I Love —' formula on stickers and T-shirts to promote almost every other place in the world (and much else), particularly with the word 'love' replaced by a heart shape. Charlie Moss at the Wells, Rich, Greene agency is credited with having coined the phrase – though maybe he had heard the song 'How About You?' (lyrics by Ralph Freed, music by Burton Lane), which includes the line 'I like New York in June' and was written for the Garland/Rooney film *Babes on Broadway* (US 1941). Earlier, Cole Porter had written 'I Happen to Like New York' for his show *The New Yorkers* (1930).

I love it but it doesn't love me What people say to soften their refusal of what they have been offered – usually food or drink. Jonathan Swift lists it in *Polite Conversation* (1738): *Lady Smart*: 'Madam, do you love bohea tea?' *Lady Answerall*: 'Why, madam, I must confess I do love it; but it does not love me . . .'

I love my wife, but oh you kid! American expression addressed to an attractive girl – possibly amounting to a not very serious 'pass' but indicating that despite the tug of marital fidelity it is still possible for a married man to dream a little. Popular during the years 1916–40, though *Flexner* (1976) has it by 1908. 'Oh you kid!' has had a life of its own as a rather meaningless exclamation: '[Boxer] Kid Brady . . . Psmith rose to his feet. "Oh, you Kid!" he observed encouragingly' – P. G. Wodehouse, *Psmith Journalist*, Chap. 14 (1915).

——, I love ya! Clark Gable's stock phrase from several films in the 1930s. Celebrated in a sequence in the compilation *That's Entertainment Part Two* (US 1976).

I love you, Alice B. Toklas The film comedy (US 1968) with this title was about a lawyer (Peter Sellers) amid the Flower People of San Francisco in the 1960s. Alice B. Toklas (who also came, as it happens, from San Francisco) was Gertrude Stein's secretary and lover, for whom Stein 'ghosted' *The Autobiography of Alice B. Toklas* (1933). *The Alice B. Toklas Cookbook* (1954) – a mixture of memoirs and culinary hints – was, however, written by Toklas herself. Popular in the 1960s –

perhaps in an 'alternative' edition – it contains, for example, Brian Gysen's recipe for 'haschich fudge'.

ils ne passeront pas [they shall not pass]
Military and political slogan. First said to have been uttered during the First World War (on 26 February 1916) by Marshal Pétain, the man who defended Verdun with great tenacity. The official record appears later in General Nivelle's Order of the Day (23 June 1916) as: '*Vous ne les laisserez pas passer* [you will not let them pass]!' Alternatively, Nivelle is supposed to have said these words to General Castelnau on 23 January 1916. To add further to the mystery, the inscription on the Verdun medal was '*On ne passe pas*'. One suspects that the slogan was coined by Nivelle and used a number of times by him but came to be associated with Pétain, the more famous 'Hero of Verdun'. Subsequently, as **No pasarán**, the phrase was used at the end of a radio speech by Dolores Ibarrurí (*La Pasionaria*) on 18 July 1936, calling for the women of Spain to help defend the Republic: 'Fascism will not pass, the executioners of October will not pass.' It became a Republican watchword in the Spanish Civil War.

I'm a ba-a-a-ad-boy! Admission from chubby American comedian Lou Costello (1906–59) to his partner, Bud Abbott (1895–1974), in their many films of the 1940s. Quoted by Eric Morecambe in *There's No Answer To That* (1981) as 'H'im a bad boy!'

I'm a cop See MY NAME'S.

I'm all right, Jack Phrase representing the selfish, uncaring attitude of any person or group of people. *Partridge/Catch Phrases* suggests, however, that this saying may have arisen *circa* 1880 in the form 'Fuck you, Jack, I'm all right'. Bowdlerized versions 'typified concisely the implied and often explicit arrogance of many senior officers towards the ranks' – this was in the Royal Navy ('Jack' has been the traditional name for a sailor since *circa* 1700). Hence, also, the example included in *The Brassbounder* (1910), one of Sir David Bone's many novels set at sea and based on his own experiences (he rose to be Commodore of the Anchor Line): 'It's

"Damn you, Jack – I'm all right!" with you chaps.' *I'm All Right Jack* was the title of a British film (1959) satirizing labour relations, bosses and the trade unions.

(well) I'm (or I'll be) a monkey's uncle
Expressing astonishment, surprise. *OED2* finds it established in a 1926 'wise-crack' dictionary, which rather rules out one origin that has been given for it – that it had something to do with the famous 'Scopes' or 'Monkey Trial' (of a teacher who taught evolutionary theory in Tennessee). As the trial took place only the year before, the connection is unlikely. As, too, is anything to do with the fact that in London East End slang a 'monkey' = £500 and an 'uncle' = pawnbroker. *Partridge/ Slang* has it of American origin.

I married him for better or worse but not for lunch Said to be an Australian catchphrase used by a woman whose husband has retired, works at home or comes home for his midday meal – dating from the 1940s and known in Britain since the 1960s. This rather pleasing play on words from the Anglican marriage service was also ascribed to the Duchess of Windsor in *The Windsor Story* (1979) by J. Bryan III and Charles J.V. Murphy, in the context: '[The Duke of Windsor] usually lunched alone on a salad while the duchess went out ("I married the Duke for better or worse but not for lunch").'

I'm a shirt short! See HOW TICKLED I AM.

I'm as mad as hell and I'm not taking any more! Political slogan adopted in 1978 by Howard Jarvis (1902–86), a Californian social activist, when campaigning to have property taxes reduced. Jarvis entitled a book *I'm Mad as Hell* but duly credited Paddy Chayevsky with the coinage. Chayevsky wrote the film *Network* (US 1976) in which Peter Finch played a TV pundit-cum-evangelist who exhorted his viewers to get mad: 'I want you to get up right now and go to the window, open it and stick your head out and yell: "I'm as mad as hell, and I'm not going to take this any more!"'

(no, I'm sorry) I'm a stranger here myself Excuse given for inability or unwillingness to be of assistance to someone who comes up to you in the street asking for directions. 'I'm a stranger 'ere myself' occurs in the caption to a *Punch* cartoon (16 July 1881). 'I don't know why-a-no-chicken. I'm a stranger here myself' is a Groucho Marx line from *The Cocoanuts* (US 1929). *I'm a Stranger Here Myself* is the title of a book (1938) by Ogden Nash and also of a later song with lyrics by Nash and music by Kurt Weill from the show *One Touch of Venus* (1943). It is also a line spoken in Nicholas Ray's camp Western *Johnny Guitar* (1953) and the title of books by John Seymour, 'the story of a Welsh farm' (1978), and Deric Longden, 'Huddersfield seen as a foreign country' (1994).

I'm backing Britain Political slogan. The most curious revival of the 'Buy British' theme occurred in January 1968 when, in the wake of the Labour Government's decision to devalue the pound sterling, all kinds of peculiar reactions were observed. In particular, Valerie, Brenda, Joan, Carol and Christine – typists at the Colt Heating and Ventilation offices at Surbiton – responded to a Christmas message from their boss to make some special work-effort. From 1 January they declared they would work half an hour extra each day for no extra pay. Was this spontaneous, or were they pushed? Whatever the case, the media leapt in. The slogan 'I'm Backing Britain' appeared from somewhere, and Prime Minister Harold Wilson added, 'What we want is "Back Britain", not back-biting.' The Industrial Society launched an official campaign on 24 January. Bruce Forsyth recorded a song, 'I'm Backing Britain'. Two million badges and stickers were manufactured. A press ad listed 'three things retired folk could do' to help the economy or 'seven things a manufac-turer could do'. People actually started sending money to the Chancellor of the Exchequer. It was as barmy as that. Then things turned sour. 'Back Britain' T-shirts were found to have been made in Portu-gal. Trade unions objected to the idea of anyone working extra hours for no more pay. A rival 'Help Britain' group, led by Robert Maxwell MP, conflicted with the Industrial Society's effort. The whole thing had fizzled out by August.

I'm black and I'm proud See say it loud.

I'm dreaming, oh, my darling love, of thee! Catchphrase of the British comedy performer Cyril Fletcher (b. 1913) who recalls in *Nice One, Cyril* (1978) how he was persuaded to broadcast Edgar Wallace's poem 'Dreaming of Thee' / 'The Lovesick Tommy's Dream of Home' in 1938. He did it in an extraordinary voice – a Cockney caricature – and the constant refrain of each verse got 'yells of delight'. It 'made' him, he says, and later when he returned to London for a repeat perform-ance he was on a bus and the conductor was saying 'Dreaming of thee' to every passenger, in a passable imitation of Fletcher's funny voice, as he gave them their tickets. 'Dreamin' of thee' became his bill matter. Fletcher's customary cry when embarking on one of his Odd Odes was **pin back your lugholes!** (i.e. 'lend me your ears') (by 1939). Other Fletcherisms have included **thanking you!** (pronounced 'thenking yew' and as *Thanking Yew* used as the title of a BBC radio series, 1940). As 'yerse, thanking yew!', the phrase was first spoken by the character 'Percy Parker' in a mid-1930s series of sketches, *The Lodger*. Also **ours is a nice 'ouse ours is** – from the possibly Cockney and ironic description which *Partridge/Catch Phrases* dates from 1925 – the sort of argument a respectable matron might advance to discourage any behaviour in her home of which she might disapprove. In fact, 'Ours Is a Nice House Ours Is' was the title of a song written by Herbert Rule and Fred Holt (1921) and sung notably by Alfred Lester.

I meanter say! Catchphrase of the British music-hall comedian (Sir) George Robey (1869–1954). Neville Cardus recalled him arriving on a stage filled with girls posing as nude Greek statues: 'I can see now his eyebrows going up and him saying, "Well, I mean to say, I mean to say".' But it is quite a common expression as a kind of slightly exasperated apology or exclama-tion (and spelt this way to emphasize the pronunciation). It is used in a Frank Richards's 'Billy Bunter' story in a 1915 edition of *The Magnet*, and it is spoken by Joe Gargery in Charles Dickens, *Great Expectations*, Chap. 27 (1860–61).

I mean that most sincerely, folks When Hughie Green (1920–97) was introducing

Opportunity Knocks, the British TV talent show (1956–77), he may never have said this (nor 'sincerely, friends'). The point is that everyone thought he had and it seemed typical of his manner. The impressionist Mike Yarwood is said to have claimed on the *Parkinson* TV chat show that he had invented the phrase as part of his take-off of Green.

I'm —, fly me   Slogan for National Airlines in the USA, *circa* 1971 – e.g. 'I'm Margie, fly me', referring to (supposedly actual) air hostesses whose pictures appeared in the advertisements. The campaign aroused the ire of feminist groups (another suggestive line used was 'I'm going to fly you like you've never been flown before'). The group 10 CC had a hit with 'I'm Mandy Fly Me', obviously inspired by the slogan, in 1976. Wall's Sausages later parodied it in Britain with, 'I'm meaty, fry me' (current 1976).

I'm free!   Catchphrase from the BBC TV comedy series *Are You Being Served?* (1974–84): the lilting cry of Mr Humphries (John Inman), a lighter-than-air menswear salesman of Grace Bros. store. In *The Independent* (10 April 1994), it was reported: 'Early on, everyone got to say it. You were meant to look left, look right, then say, "I'm free." But in one episode a colonel turned up and asked for a woman's dress. Inman threw his ties in the air: "*I'm freeeee!!!*" From then on, the writers always gave him the line.'

I'm from Missouri (you'll have to show me)   Phrase showing scepticism and demanding proof. Something said by Willard D. Vandiver, a Congressman (1897–1905) from Columbia, Missouri: 'I come from a state that raises corn and cotton and cockleburs and Democrats, and frothy eloquence neither convinces nor satisfies me. I am from Missouri. You have got to show me.' Inspecting the Navy Yard at Philadelphia in 1899 as a member of the House Naval Committee, Vandiver good-humouredly made the above statement when speaking at a dinner. Missouri, accordingly, became known as the 'Show Me' state.

I'm going down now, sir!   See under DON'T FORGET THE DIVER!

I'm goin' back to the wagon, boys – these shoes are killin' me   Grand Old Opry, the Nashville country and western venue, was featured in network radio broadcasts until 1957. At one time, the *Grand Ole Opry* show featured an MC, Whitey Ford, who was known as the 'Duke of Paducah'. And this was his catchphrase.

I'm going to make him an offer he can't refuse   In 1969, Mario Puzo (1920–99) published his novel about the Mafia, called *The Godfather*. It gave to the language a new expression that, as far as one can tell, was Puzo's invention. Johnny Fontane, a singer, desperately wants a part in a movie and goes to see his godfather, Don Corleone, for help. All the contracts have been signed and there is no chance of the studio chief changing his mind. Still, the godfather promises Fontane he will get him the part. As he says of the studio chief, 'He's a businessman. I'll make him an offer he can't refuse.' In the film (US 1971), this was turned into the following dialogue: 'In a month from now this Hollywood big shot's going to give you what you want.' 'Too late, they start shooting in a week.' 'I'm going to make him an offer he can't refuse.' In 1973, Jimmy Helms had a hit with the song 'Gonna Make You An Offer You Can't Refuse'.

I'm gonna hate myself for this in the morning   Woman's line when rejecting a pass. Film and drama use. Listed by Fritz Spiegl in an article on drama cliché lines in *The Listener* (7 February 1985). Compare **I couldn't, Bill, I'd only feel cheap**. Probably from the 1940s/50s – could Doris Day have said it? Cited in the song 'I Love a Film Cliché' by Dick Vosburgh and Trevor Lyttleton from the show *A Day in Hollywood, A Night in the Ukraine* (1980).

I'm in charge!   Catchphrase of the British entertainer Bruce Forsyth (b. 1928), who first achieved fame as an entertainer when host of the ATV show *Sunday Night at the London Palladium* (from 1958). One night he was supervising 'Beat the Clock', a game involving members of the audience. A young couple was in a muddle, throwing plates at a see-saw table. Forsyth recalled (1980): 'We had a particularly stroppy contestant. In the end I just turned round and told him, "Hold on a minute . . . I'm in charge!" It just happened, but the audience loved it and it caught on.' Lapel badges began appearing with the slogan, foremen had it painted on their hard hats. The phrase suited Forsyth's mock-bossy manner to a tee.

I'm looking for someone to love See under I THINK THE ANSWER LIES . . .

immemorial elms Cliché of quotation – from Alfred Tennyson, *The Princess*, Canto 7, line 206 (1847): 'The moan of doves in immemorial elms'. 'There were weekends at stately homes and country houses, complete with tea on the lawn, cawing of rooks in immemorial elms, and the whack of cricket or tennis balls in the near distance' – Cole Lesley, *The Life of Noël Coward*, Chap. 4 (1976); 'The PM [John Major] . . . dreams of a Britain where we all drink warm beer in the shadow of immemorial elms, and nuns bicycle to church through the mist, and Denis Compton is still at the crease on the final day of the Oval test match' – *The Observer* (19 February 1995); 'I have driven for hours around those winding lagoon-like car parks, lovingly landscaped between clumps of immemorial elms, trying to find the exit' – *The Times Higher Education Supplement* (31 March 1995).

I'm mortified! See under GOODNIGHT, MRS CALABASH . . .

I'm not a number, I'm a free man First shown on British TV in 1967, *The Prisoner*, Patrick McGoohan's unusual series about a man at odds with a *1984*-type world, acquired a new cult following in the late 1970s. The McGoohan character was 'Political Prisoner Number Six'. **Six of one** was another phrase from the series. The Six of One Appreciation Society had 2,000 members in 1982. The saying 'Six of one, half a dozen of the other' – meaning, 'there is nothing to choose between them, they are both/all in the wrong' – had been current by 1836.

I'm not so green as (I'm) cabbage-looking I'm not such a fool [or as inno-cent] as I may appear – i.e. 'I may be cabbage-looking but I'm not green.' This expression appears to have been around since the late 19th century. How about this from James Joyce, *Ulysses* (1922): 'Gob, he's not as green as he's cabbagelooking'?

I'm not well Catchphrase of the British comedian George Williams (1910–95). Denis Gifford in an obituary for *The Independent* (8 May 1995) wrote: 'It was in 1934 that he coined the catchphrase "I'm not well". He played the patient in a hospital sketch. His face chalked white, he was pushed on in a bathchair and got such uproarious laughter that the chap playing the doctor, fed up with the long wait, shouted his feed line at the top of his voice, "What's the matter with you?" The laughter died away and at last Williams spoke, "I'm not well," he said. Again there was audience uproar. It told Williams he had chanced on the gag of a lifetime.' Used as his bill matter. Sometimes recalled as 'I've not been well'.

I'm (or we're) only here for the beer Slogan for Double Diamond beer. In 1971, a visiting American advertising copywriter, Ros Levenstein, contributed this phrase to a British campaign for the Double Dia-mond brand. It passed into the language as an inconsequential catchphrase, though – from the advertiser's point of view – it was not a good slogan because it became detached from the particular brand. The *Oxford Dictionary of Current Idiomatic English* (1985) glossed it thus: 'We don't pretend to be present in order to help, show goodwill, etc. but just to get the drink, or other hospitality.' Indeed, in September 1971, Prince Philip attended a champagne reception at Burghley. 'Don't look at me,' he was quoted as saying, 'I'm only here for the beer.' A. J. P. Taylor, the British historian, was quoted by Peter Vansittart in *Voices 1870–1914* (1984) as having said: 'In my opinion, most of the great men of the past were only there for the beer – the wealth, prestige and gran-deur that went with the power.'

(an) impish grin An inevitable pairing – used by George Eliot in *Romona* (1863). 'The Roux brothers, who have not changed their name or, as far we know, their religion, but simply become more discernibly Albert and Michel, would doubtless agree with that lyric – although an impish grin is a valuable part of their public personae' – *Evening Standard* (London) (26 July 1994); '"Sully in *Nobody's Fool* is about that stubborn, wilful and foolish part of my father that I love so deeply. I guess I may have inherited too many of those qualities," he says with an impish grin' – *Scotland on Sunday* (9 April 1995).

improve   See ADOPT ADAPT.

I'm sorry, I'll read that again   The BBC radio newsreader's traditional apology for a stumble was registered as a cliché when the phrase was taken as the title of a long-running radio comedy show (1964–73) featuring ex-Cambridge Footlights performers.

I must get a little hand on this watch Catchphrase of Hylda Baker in the Granada TV series *Nearest and Dearest* (1968–73). She played Nellie Pledge who inherited a pickle factory.

I must go down to the seas again Opening phrase of John Masefield's poem 'Sea Fever', much quoted and parodied, has for many years had a question mark over it. Should the 'go' be omitted before the 'down'? Is it 'seas' or 'sea'? The original manuscript is lost. An early draft of the poem had 'I must down' – indeed, it pursues a different course, beginning, 'I must down to the roads again, to the vagrant life.' The repeated line was 'I must down' in the first published version of *Salt Water Ballads* in 1902. Heinemann Collected Editions of Masefield's poetry had just 'down' (in 1923, 1932 and 1938) but changed to 'go down' in 1946. *Selected Poems* in 1922 and 1938 both had 'go down'. No one knows why this divergence occurred, but the pull of Psalm 107 ('They that *go down to the sea* in ships, that do their business in great waters') may have been a factor. John Ireland's musical setting of the poem has had the 'go' since its first publication (1915). Some editions of the poem also have a singular '*sea* again'. The *ODQ* has suggested for some time that the 1902 original 'I [. . .] must down to the *seas*' was 'possibly a misprint' (and latterly has opted for a 'go down' and a singular 'sea'). Most of this information is

drawn from an article by Agnes Whitaker in *The Times* (5 December 1980). She commented on 'the inspired economy' of 'I must down' and added: 'It is disconcerting that standard editions, and works of reference which we treat almost like sacred texts, should contradict each other, especially over such an immensely well-known poem.' Reviving the puzzle in 2001 completely resolved the matter. Three people wrote to say that they had approached Masefield about it (before his death in 1967) and received letters back saying that the third word should indeed be 'go'. The reply to June Mack (14 August 1951) stated: 'As to the word "go", in the verses; it was there at first; then, later, somehow, it dropped out; then, later, was restored.' The final proof comes from the Poet Laureate's own reading of 'Sea Fever, Cargoes and other poems' on a Caedmon disc (TC1147). The 'go' is clearly audible, not to mention a plural 'seas'. This version must presumably reflect the poet's own wishes on both points.

I must love you and leave you   See under LOVE ME OR LEAVE ME.

I must, I must, I must improve my bust Women's chant while doing a standard arm and shoulder exercise, known informally as the 'Sweater Filler' – remembered from *circa* 1967 in the USA: 'I must, I must, I must / I must increase my bust / I'd better, I'd better, I'd better / I'd better fill out this sweater.' Note it is 'increase' here rather than 'improve'. There may also have been a 'develop' version. From the early 1960s in the UK is remembered: 'I must, I must, / I must improve my bust. / The bigger the sweater / The tighter the better, / The boys depend on us.' Also from the early 1960s: 'I must, I must, I must improve my bust / Oh dear, I fear, I have overdeveloped my rear!' Others would date the chant back to the mid-1950s. Then there is a reminiscence by the actress Jane Birkin of her short-lived marriage to the composer, John Barry: 'I met John when we did a rather jolly musical called Passion Flower Hotel . . . He got me to sing a song called "I must, I must improve my bust"' – *Scotland on Sunday* (6 April 1997). That would have been in 1965. The musical, written with Trevor Peacock, was a disastrous flop, and the song is not included on the cast album. It was based on a novel (1962) by 'Rosalind Erskine' (Roger Longrigg) but the book does not contain anything like the chant.

I must love you and leave you See LOVE ME OR.

I'm worried about Jim Ellis Powell played the eponymous heroine of BBC radio's domestic soap opera *Mrs Dale's Diary* (1948–69), and this is what she always seemed to be confiding to that diary about her doctor husband, James. Although she may not have spoken the phrase very often, it was essential in parodies of the programme. Her successor in the part, Jessie Matthews, definitely once had the line, 'I'm afraid one thing's never going to change: I shall always worry about you, Jim.'

in and out – like a dog at a fair Irritating – like a child running in and out of the house. The phrase appears in R. H. Barham's poem 'The Jackdaw of Rheims', published with *The Ingoldsby Legends* in 1840. The eponymous bird busies itself on the Cardinal's table: 'In and out / Through the motley rout, / That little jackdaw kept hopping about: / Here and there, / Like a dog at a fair, / Over comfits and cates [dainties], / And dishes and plates . . .' Barham seems, however, to have been using an already established expression. *Apperson* finds 'As sprites in the haire, Or dogges in the ffayre' by 1520. G. L. Gower's *Glossary of Surrey Words* (1893) has the version: 'They didn't keep nothing reg'lar, it was all over the place like a dog at a fair.'

in a nutshell Meaning, 'compactly, in brief'. Known by 1693. Book titles: *The Franco-Prussian War in a Nutshell* by E. Perkins (1871); *Muddling Through, or Britain in a Nutshell* by Betty Askwith and Theodora Benson (1936). 'That, in a nutshell, is the mysterious art of switch trading' – *The Economist* (14 January 1967); 'Management (The Growing Business): British businesses on the rise – in a nutshell' – headline in *Financial Times* (24 January 1995); 'My highest scorer has netted five goals, the next best four. Le

Tissier has scored 29. That's the difference in a nutshell' – *Evening Standard* (London) (4 May 1995).

in anybody's list of the ten most . . . The compiling of lists became in itself a journalistic and publishing cliché in the 1980s – see *Hunter Davies's Book of British Lists* (1980) – and shows little sign of dying out. This particular phrase was listed as part of the 'travel scribes' armoury', compiled from a competition in *The Guardian* (10 April 1993). Heralding the announcement of 'crowded beaches/ unlikely holiday resorts/hazardous safari holidays', it harks back to the original traveller's list of lists: the Seven Wonders of the World. 'A top ten hit list of the most complained about goods has been published by trading standards officers' – *Northern Echo* (7 July 1993); 'In the process he has overtaken Mr Reagan in the polls and has featured seven years running in Good Housekeeping magazine's list of the ten most-admired Americans' – *The Times* (16 June 1994); 'The offer, and the inclusion of the two men on the FBI's Ten Most Wanted Fugitives List, had "the ring of banditry", said Lord Macaulay' – *The Herald* (Glasgow) (19 May 1995).

in a very real sense Rhetorical phrase – and flannel of the worst sort, especially from ecclesiastics. Date of origin unknown. 'What I think is clear is that what Lawrence is trying to do is to portray the sex relationship as something essentially sacred . . . as in a real sense an act of holy communion' – Right Reverend John Robinson on *Lady Chatterley's Lover*, evidence in Regina *v.* Penguin Books Ltd (27 October 1960). In 1970 I wrote a sketch called 'Yes, Folks, It's Obituary Time' that parodied obituary clichés as spoken at a memorial meeting for a recently dead author. This phrase was intoned ritually in turn by about six speakers: 'The death of A. B. Porter has plucked from our midst, in a very real sense, one of the greatest and most significant figures in twentieth-century English literature . . .'; 'You know, when I was preparing this Thought for the Day my glance fell on a painting of The Last Supper, and I couldn't help feeling, in a very real sense, that Jesus and the twelve disciples were much like a prime minister and his cabinet' – Miles Kington in *The Independent* (12 June 1995)

in bed with my favourite Trollope
Archetypal punning joke. Chips Channon, the diarist, wrote on 4 April 1943: 'At Wells we went over the Cathedral, and then to the Palace where we lunched with the Bishop . . . Much talk of Barchester, "there is nothing I like better than to lie on my bed for an hour with my favourite Trollope", the Bishop said, to everybody's consternation.' ('Trollop' has meant a 'slut, morally loose woman' since the 17th century.) Kenneth Horne got into trouble on *Beyond Our Ken* (BBC radio, early 1960s) when he said that there was nothing he liked more of a cold winter's evening than to curl up on the hearth rug with Enid Blyton. Her husband objected.

include me out!　One of the more likely Goldwynisms – that is to say, remarks made by the Hollywood film producer Samuel Goldwyn (1882–1974) – and meaning, 'Leave me out of your plan'. Goldwyn had a habit of massacring the English language in a way that nonetheless conveyed vividly what he wanted to say. This phrase apparently arose when Goldwyn and Jack L. Warner were in disagreement over a labour dispute. Busby Berkeley, who had made his first musical for Goldwyn, was discovered moonlighting for Warner Brothers. Goldwyn said to Warner: 'How can we sit together and deal with this industry if you're going to do things like this to me? If this is the way you do it, gentlemen, include me out!' Many Goldwynisms are invented, but Goldwyn himself might appear to have acknowledged this one when speaking at Balliol College, Oxford, on 1 March 1945: 'For years I have been known for saying "Include me out" but today I am giving it up for ever.'

in cold blood　Meaning, 'with cool deliberateness', especially as in 'murdered in cold blood'. Known by 1711. *In Cold Blood* was the title of a Truman Capote 'non-fiction novel' (1965). '"The obvious motive was payment of money and the act was carried out in cold blood," the Recorder of London, Sir Lawrence Verney,

told Te Rangimaria Ngarimu' – *The Guardian* (23 December 1994); 'It wasn't akin to the actions of a street brawler at pub throwing-out time, it was a case of a highly trained athlete attacking someone in cold blood' – *Today* (26 January 1995).

inconvenience　See DEEPLY REGRETS ANY.

in days of old and knights were bold and monkeys chewed tobacco　A promising start to a story that does not, however, materialize. A series of somewhat frisky playground verses beginning, 'In days of old when knights were bold . . .' was current by the 1950s.

(yes) indeedy-doody!　American affirmative, noted in TV's *The Muppet Show* (1980 series). *DOAS* finds 'indeedy' on its own by 1856, as in 'yes, indeedy' or 'no, indeedy'.

indubitably!　See OH, CALAMITY!

I never promised you a rose garden
Phrase used by Joanne Greenberg ('Hannah Green') as the title of a best-selling (American) novel (1964; film US 1977). Also used as a line in the song 'Rose Garden' in 1968. Presumably meaning: 'It wasn't going to be roses, roses all the way between us – or a bed of roses – but maybe it's still acceptable.' 'I never promised you a rose garden . . . following the example of developed countries, we are also cutting state spending' – Fernando Collor de Mello, President of Brazil, in TV address to his shaken countrymen (reported 26 June 1990).

(an/the) infant phenomenon　Phrase from the stage billing of Ninetta Crummles (who has been ten years old for at least five years) in *Nicholas Nickleby* (1838–9) by Charles Dickens. The term appears earlier in *Pickwick Papers*, Chap. 26 (1836–7) when Sam Weller says to Master Bardwell: 'Tell her I want to speak to her, will you my hinfant fernomenon?' This suggests that the phrase was in general use or was something Dickens had picked up from an actual case. In 1837, the eight-year-old Jean Davenport was merely billed as 'the most celebrated juvenile actress of the day'. George Parker Bidder (b. 1806) who possessed extraordinary arithmetical abilities had been exhibited round the country as a child, billed as 'the calculating phenomenon'.

information See MORE THAN I WISH.

in God we trust – all others pay cash
American saying. After the Washington summit between Mikhail Gorbachev and Ronald Reagan in December 1987, the US Secretary of State George Schultz commented on a Russian slogan that Reagan had made much of: '"Trust but verify" is really an ancient saying in the United States, but in a different guise. Remember the storekeeper who was a little leery of credit, and he had a sign in his store that said, IN GOD WE TRUST – ALL OTHERS CASH?' Referring to the verification procedures over arms reductions signed by the leaders in Washington, Shultz said, 'This is the cash.' *Mencken* in 1942 was listing 'In God we trust; all others must pay cash' as an 'American saying'. 'In God we trust' has been the official national motto of the United States since 1956, when it superseded '*E Pluribus Unum*', but had been known since 1864 when it was first put on a two-cent bronze coin. There is a similar joke in the British Isles – of the type printed on small cards and sold for display in pubs and shops. J. Millar Watt in a 'Pop' cartoon in the *Daily Sketch* (1927) has Pop being told: 'No sir! We don't cash cheques in this restaurant! We've made a special arrangement with the banks. *We* cash no cheques – *they* serve no dinners.' The saying also made an appearance as a quote in the early 1940s in Flann O'Brien's column for *The Irish Times*: 'We have come to an arrangement with our bankers. They have agreed not to sell drink. We, on our part, have agreed not to cash cheques.' In the film *True to Life* (US 1943), Dick Powell asks the owner of a diner if he will take a check. Replies he: 'We got an agreement with the bank. They don't sell no hamburgers; we don't cash no checks.'

in like Flynn Someone who is 'in like Flynn' is a quick seducer – at least, according to the Australian use of the phrase. Appropriately, it is derived from the name of Errol Flynn (1909–59), the Australian-born film actor. It alludes to his legendary bedroom prowess, though the

phrase can also mean that a person simply seizes an offered opportunity (of any kind). According to *The Intimate Sex Lives of Famous People* (Irving Wallace *et al*, 1981), Flynn frowned on the expression when it became popular, especially among servicemen, in the Second World War. It 'implied he was a fun-loving rapist', though 'in fact, Flynn's reputation stemmed partly from his having been charged with statutory rape'. After a celebrated trial, he was acquitted. Nevertheless, he 'boasted that he had spent between 12,000 and 14,000 nights making love'. Rather weakly, a US film of 1967 was entitled *In Like Flint* because the hero, 'Derek Flint' (James Coburn), was surrounded by dolly birds. *Partridge/Catch Phrases* turns up an American version that refers to Ed Flynn, a Democratic machine politician in the Bronx, New York City, in the 1940s. Here the meaning is simply 'to be in automatically' – as his candidates would have been.

in Miss World order See under I'LL GIVE YOU THE RESULTS . . .

in my heart of hearts In my deepest and most hidden thoughts and feelings. Apparently a coinage of Shakespeare. In *Hamlet*, III.ii.73 (1600–1), there is: 'In my heart's core, in my heart of heart.' '"In my heart of hearts, I always know that God comes first," [Dolly Parton] says. "But in my body of bodies, some other urges can be absolutely irresistible"' – *Northern Echo* (7 February 1995).

(Andrews for) inner cleanliness Slogan for Andrews Liver Salts (laxative) in the UK, current from the 1950s. 'To complete your inner cleanliness, Andrews cleans the bowels. It sweeps away troublemaking poisons, relieves constipation, and purifies the blood . . .'

innocence See AGE OF.

in no uncertain terms Phrase used as a filler. Known by 1958. 'Let me forecast in no uncertain terms that this policy can lead only to a severe shortage of high quality reds in five years' time' – *The Age* (Melbourne) (18 January 1977); 'When I asked her to calm down, she informed me, in no uncertain terms, of my place in the scheme of things' – *Today* (15 February

1995); 'I told him in no uncertain terms to go to bed. He just would not listen to reason. He would not listen to the fact he should not do it' – *The Herald* (Glasgow) (4 March 1995).

in office but not in power   When Norman Lamont was sacked as Britain's Chancellor of the Exchequer in June 1993, he caused a slight stir in the House of Commons during his 'resignation' statement, by saying of the Government: 'We give the impression of being in office but not in power.' A shaft, but not a new one. As A. J. P. Taylor noted in his *English History 1914–45* (1965), writing of Ramsay MacDonald as Prime Minister of a minority government in 1924: 'The Labour government recognized that they could make no fundamental changes, even if they knew what to make: they were "in office, but not in power".'

in place of strife   Phrase suggested by the journalist Ted (later Lord) Castle for the title of an ill-fated Labour government White Paper on industrial relations legislation. It was introduced by his wife, Barbara Castle, Secretary of State for Employment, on 17 January 1969. It was clearly modelled on the title of Aneurin Bevan's book about disarmament, *In Place of Fear* (1952).

inquiries   See HELPING THE.

(wants to know the) ins and outs of a Merryman's backside   Phrase for an overly inquisitive person. 'Merryman' here is in the sense of a jester or buffoon, defined by *Grose*'s (1785) as: 'Merry Andrew, or Mr. Merryman, the jack pudding, jester, or zany of a mountebank, usually dressed in a party coloured coat.' Similar expressions are: wanting to know about **the ins and outs of a nag's arse/ mag's arse**   'Mag's' would seem to be a softer substitution for 'nag's' or an abbreviation of 'magpie's'. Indeed, 'you would want to know the ins and outs of a magpie's bottom' has also been recorded.

(to have someone) inside the tent pissing out than outside the tent pissing in   Expression based on President Lyndon Johnson's explanation of why he kept J. Edgar Hoover at the FBI: 'I'd much rather have that fellow inside my tent pissing out, than outside my tent pissing in' – quoted in David Halberstam, *The Best and the Brightest* (1972). Possibly Johnson's coinage or from the earthy Texan vernacular which he used so often. The same sentiment is attributed to Laurence Olivier about employing Kenneth Tynan, a critic, at the National Theatre, in John Dexter, *The Honourable Beast* (1993).

(to be/stand) in someone else's shoes   To be in someone else's place; to know what it feels like to be someone else. Originally, 'to be in someone else's coat'. *Brewer* (1894) adds: 'Among the ancient Northmen, when a man adopted a son, the person adopted put on the shoes of the adopter' – quoting an 1834 source.

in song and story   A somewhat literary tag, probably best known from W. S. Gilbert's lyric for *The Pirates of Penzance* (1879): 'Go, ye heroes, go to glory, / Though you die in combat gory, / Ye shall live in song and story.' An earlier occurrence is in Charles J. Lever, *Jack Hinton the Guardsman* (1843): 'To lighten the road by song and story.'

interrupted   See AS I WAS.

(to be) in the cart   Meaning 'to be in trouble', this expression may come from the fact that prisoners used to be taken in a cart to punishment or execution, or from when a horse was put in a cart (because it was ill or dead), the owner being left in a spot. Probably known in this sense by the late 19th century. 'Emily was left in the cart' – W. Somerset Maugham, *Smith* (1914).

in the club   Pregnant. Known since the 1930s. Hence, 'She's joined the club!', especially when the woman in question is unmarried. The club referred to – with a far from exclusive membership – was known in the 19th century as the 'Pudding' or 'Pudden Club' (where 'pudden' was seminal fluid). This latter expression has also been used to describe a girl's first menstrual period.

in the cold light of day   How things look realistically, as compared to the feverish perceptions of night-time or just after the event has taken place. Date of origin unknown. 'And always in the cold light of the Falklands dawn, the . . . Marines . . . have always been ready to "yomp on"' – *The Daily Telegraph* (3 June 1982); 'The bag follows her everywhere and gets bigger as she asks a number of people for advice, but gets no help. Finally, her grandmother steps in and, slowly and with great care, she pulls out the worries, which seem small in the cold light of day' – *The Scotsman* (21 September 1994); '"In the cold light of day you could not say yesterday was strictly Gold Cup form," Henderson said. "But it was a great race"' – *The Independent* (19 December 1994).

in the country of the blind (the one-eyed man is king)   Phrase often ascribed to H. G. Wells because of its use by him in the story 'The Country of the Blind' (1904) – though he quite clearly labels it an old proverb. As indeed it is, and in many languages. An early appearance is in a book of *Adages* by Erasmus (d. 1536): '*In regione caecorum rex est luscus.*'

in the family way   Pregnant. Known by 1796 as 'being in . . .' and by 1898, 'to put in . . .' *The Family Way* was the title of a film (UK 1966) based on the play *All In Good Time* by Bill Naughton.

in the final/last/ultimate analysis
Venerable construction, now a frightful cliché. 'Ultimate analysis' was known by 1791; 'Last analysis' by 1844; 'Final analysis' by 1944. 'In the final analysis, there are two types of program music . . .' – Willi Apel, *The Harvard Dictionary of Music* (1944); 'In the final analysis, all girls aspire to be beauties' – Vladimir Nabokov, *The Gift* (1963); 'Final analysis' was listed in *The Independent* (24 December 1994) as a cliché of newspaper editorials; 'Poetry . . . is in the last analysis an endeavour to condense . . .' – W. B. Yeats, Preface to *Poems* (1906); *Mencken* contains this translation of a passage from J. M. Charcot, *De l'Expectation en Médecin* (1857): 'In the last analysis, we see only what we are ready to see, what we have been taught to see'; *Fowler's Modern English Usage* (2nd edition, 1965) had earlier concentrated its fire specifically on 'in the ultimate analysis'. More examples: 'Fenella Fielding has rushed into print saying "I feel outraged on behalf of the entire profession" . . . But

really – in the last analysis – who cares?' – Kenneth Williams in *The Kenneth Williams Letters* (1994) – letter of 19 June 1967; 'Which is more "barbaric" in the final analysis? A highly controlled society which deters crime by punitive retribution, or a society where innocent people are subjected to daily torment by vandalism and crime – much of which goes unpunished?' – *Daily Mail* (6 May 1994); 'In Europe, British Airways occupied middle rankings for much of the final analysis, despite having one of the most profitable first-class cabin operations' – *The European* (24 March 1995); 'But in the last analysis a slightly less individualist and slightly more inclusive approach might win greater support within the Government, within the Oireachtas, and among the electorate' – *The Irish Times* (4 May 1995); 'The same kind of audit behaviour that is permissible within the institution and its own staff and students is often totally inappropriate when used upon an external clientele who, in the last analysis, are the university's customers' – *The Times Higher Education Supplement* (5 May 1995).

in the heart of ——   Show business, journalistic use. One recalls writing in a 1966 sketch: 'The well-known male impersonator, Miss Deirdre de la Zouche, has just opened a new cabaret club in the heart of London's theatreland'. 'All Carlton's UK companies were required to use VIP, which operates out of exclusive premises in the heart of London's Mayfair' – *Mail on Sunday* (12 June 1994).

in their death they were not divided
Quotation from 2 Samuel 1:23, referring to Saul and Jonathan: 'They were lovely and pleasant in their lives and in their death they were not divided.' Sometimes used in epitaphs, though not without caution. When an epitaph was being sought for Joseph Severn, the devoted friend of the poet Keats, Walter Severn, his son, suggested that the text should be, 'In their death they were not divided', but the argument was advanced that it 'must seem highly inappropriate to anyone who recollects the original application of the phrase' – Saul and Jonathan who died on the same battlefield – 'as more than sixty years elapsed between Keats's death and

your father's.' So it was not used. It does, however, appear on the memorial plaque to the British-born husband-and-wife actors Dame May Whitty (1865–1948) and Ben Webster (1864–1947) in St Paul's Church, Covent Garden, London. The use of the phrase, though charming, is open to question for a different reason than that advanced regarding Keats and Severn. Here it must be pointed out that the original couple, Saul and Jonathan, were of the same sex and died on the battle-field. However, in *The Mill on the Floss* (1860), George Eliot had put this epitaph on the tomb of Tom and Maggie Tulliver, who were brother and sister.

in the kitty   Money is put in the kitty or 'the pool' in card games, and the expression has been known since 1887. Robert L. Shook in *The Book of Why* (1983) suggests that it comes from 'kit', short for 'kitbag', which was used among soldiers as a receptacle in which to pool their money.

in the land of the living   Meaning, 'alive'. From Jeremiah 11:19: 'Let us cut him off from the land of the living, that his name may be no more remembered.' One might ask of a person referred to: 'Oh, is he still in the land of the living?'

in the lap of luxury   Where (usually) the luxury is being envied. Known by 1802. 'If you just want to be pampered, try . . . the Lap of the Minch in the lap of luxury (£900–£3000 per person)' – *The Herald* (Glasgow) (16 July 1994); 'Shock for our man in the lap of luxury' – headline in *Daily Mail* (21 September 1994); 'Even though judges are living in the lap of luxury, they can still claim £40 a day for meals' – *Daily Mirror* (22 September 1994).

in the lap of the gods   Left to chance – there is nothing can be done about a situation or even known about its out-come. The idea originated in Homer, *The Odyssey*, Bk 1, in which Eurymachus remarks to Telemachus regarding who will take Odysseus's place as King of Ithaca with the words – 'It surely lies on the lap of the gods'. Similar expressions are 'in the lap of Providence' and 'in the lap of the future'.

in the mind's eye   In the imagination. After Shakespeare, *Hamlet*, I.ii.184 (1600–1):

'Methinks I see my father . . . in my mind's eye, Horatio'. However, this is a traditional metaphor dating back to Plato.

in the pink (of condition/health)   In the most perfect state. Presumably because a gentle pinkness of colour nay be indicative of good condition or health in white people. Oliver Goldsmith seems to have coined the phrase 'very pink of perfection' in *She Stoops To Conquer*, Act 1, Sc. 1 (1773). But earlier Mercutio says, 'I am the very pink of courtesie' in Shakespeare's *Romeo and Juliet* (1594) and Romeo links it to 'flower', meaning 'finest example of'. One then recalls that there are flowers known as 'pinks'.

in the pipeline   Meaning, 'in train, on the way'. Known by 1955. 'We have several more [test-tube] babies in the pipeline' – said a doctor on BBC Radio in 1985. 'Evidence of the bulge of higher prices working along the inflation pipeline is shown in Dun & Bradstreet's finding that the proportion of retailers expecting to raise prices climbed from 66.5 to 69.5 per cent' – *The Independent* (19 April 1995); 'The drive in the Mondeo was a tantalizing glimpse of the near future. Renault, Volvo, Volkswagen and other manufacturers have similar systems in the pipeline' – *The Independent* (6 May 1995).

(to be) in the same boat   In the same position – often a difficult one. Known by 1845. This has been traced back to *in eadem es navi*, a Latin tag used in a letter by Cicero in 53 BC. 'They [the Japanese] have attacked us at Pearl Harbor. We are all in the same boat now [December 1941]' – President F. D. Roosevelt quoted by Winston Churchill in *The Second World War*, Vol. 3 (1950).

in the shadowlands   In the writings of C. S. Lewis, there appear to be two meanings to this phrase – death and what has not been achieved in life. 'Then Aslan [the great Lion] turned to them and said: ". . . You are – as you used to call it – in the Shadow Lands – dead. The term is over; the holidays have begun. The dream is ended: this is the morning' – *The Last Battle* (1956) (Lewis's final 'Narnia' book). Hence, the title *Shadowlands* of a BBC TV film (1985), a play (1989) and a film (UK

1993), all by William Nicholson and all about Lewis's late-flowering relationship with the woman who became his wife and died shortly after of cancer. In Act 1 of the play, the meaning of the term 'shadowlands' seems to have been transferred from death to what has not been attained in life: 'For believe me, this world that seems to us so substantial, is no more than the shadowlands. Real life has not begun yet.' In Nicholson's script for the film, the Lewis character says: 'Shadows . . . It's one of my stories. We live in the shadowlands. The sun is always shining, somewhere else, round a bend in the road, over the brow of a hill.'

in the tradition of —— Promotional phrase used mostly in publishing. Possibly since the 1970s and always an obnoxious habit if not quite a cliché. At its worst, the device is used to get the name of a better or more famous author on to the cover of a (usually) paperback edition of a lesser one. So, the new authors are said to be writing 'in the tradition of Catherine Cookson/Dick Francis' or whoever – when what they are really doing is hoping that some of the established authors' gold dust will rub off on them. At its least offensive, as in the first citation, it is just rather pompously self-serving (even if that is what blurbs are supposed to be . . .) 'In the tradition of his best-selling books *Quote . . . Unquote* and *Graffiti Lives, OK* and his popular radio and television shows, Nigel Rees presents another galaxy of quotes and quizzes' – blurb for *The 'Quote . . . Unquote' Book of Love, Death and the Universe* (1980); 'A nostalgic Cockney novel in the Lena Kennedy tradition' – paperback blurb on Harry Bowling, *Conner Street's War* (1987); 'In the grand tradition of Catherine Cookson' – paperback blurb for Josephine Cox, *Alley Urchin* (1992) and other books of hers published by Headline.

in the wrong box *The Oxford Dictionary of Phrase, Saying, and Quotation* (1997) defines this as 'unsuitably or awkwardly placed; in a difficulty, at a disadvantage . . . perhaps originally referring to an apothecary's boxes; a mistaken choice from which might have provided poison instead of medicine.' In use by 1555 but of obscure origins. *Brewer* (1894) states: 'Lord Lyttelton used to say that whenever he went to Vauxhall [pleasure gardens] and heard the mirth of his neighbours, he used to fancy pleasure was in every box but his own. Wherever he went for happiness, he somehow always got into the wrong box.' Hence, possibly, the title of R. L. Stevenson & Lloyd Osborne, *The Wrong Box* (1889) where a box containing a body is misdelivered and so may be said to be the wrong box.

in this day and age Verbal padding, date of origin unknown, though there was a film with the title *This Day and Age* (US 1933). Identified as a still current cliché by Eric Partridge in the preface to the 5th edition of his *A Dictionary of Clichés* (1978). Dating it since 1960, he says the phrase, 'originally possessing sonority and dignity, now implies mental decrepitude and marks a man for the rest of his life'. 'What a comfort it was in this day and age to meet someone obliging' – *The New Yorker* (17 October 1970); 'Given the wonderful, or supposedly so, communications that we have these days, surely this could all have been avoided, or am I the one who needs his head examined for expecting people in this day and age to have some simple, old-fashioned ethics' – *The Herald* (Glasgow) (22 July 1994); 'We knew drug-dealing was going on in one part of it but I thought that, in this day and age, you just had to learn to accept that sort of thing' – *The People* (4 December 1994).

into each life some rain must fall Phrase from 'The Rainy Day' (1842) by H. W. Longfellow: 'Thy fate is the common fate of all, / Into each life some rain must fall, / Some days must be dark and dreary.' Now a quasi-proverbial expression meaning 'unfortunate things happen in life.' Hence, 'Into each life some rain must fall, / But too much is falling in mine' from the song 'Into Each Life a Little Rain Must Fall' (as it is sometimes worded, but which also contains 'some rain' in the lyrics) – written by Allan Roberts and Doris Fisher (1944).

(to vanish) into thin air To disappear completely, without leaving any trace. Probably derived basically from Prospero's speech in Shakespeare, *The Tempest*, IV.i.148 (1612): 'Our revels now are ended. These our actors, / As I foretold you, were all spirits and / Are melted into air, into thin air . . . / And, like this insubstantial pageant faded, / Leave not a rack behind.' Hence, *Into Thin Air*, the title of a book (1997) by John Krakauer about the deaths of eight climbers on Mount Everest where, of course, there is a lack of oxygen at high altitude.

in your face (usually **in yer face)** Adjectival phrase meaning 'upfront, not hidden' and, reflecting aggressive behaviour, perhaps derived from 'I'll shove this fist right in your face'. An 'in yer face' performance at a theatre would be one where the actor confronted the audience directly. A buzz phrase of the early 1990s, it made an early appearance in March 1991 as the title of the theme tune from the Channel 4 TV programme *The Word*, recorded by 808 State. 'This country has never particularly enjoyed its sex "in yer face", as young folk say nowadays. Behind your back, under your heaving stays, beyond the twitching curtains of Bennettland fine, but not explicit' – *The Sunday Times* (28 February 1993); 'In-yer-face investment banking, as practised by Swiss Bank Corporation, is not a pretty sight' – *The Daily Telegraph* (14 January 1995); 'They can be seen pulling their episcopal clobber out of a theatrical wicker skip and making up in hand mirrors. This is in-yer-face bogusness' – *The Independent* (8 September 1995).

in your heart you know I'm (or **he's) right** Senator Barry Goldwater's much parodied slogan when he attempted to unseat President Lyndon Johnson in the 1964 US presidential election. Come-backs included: 'In your guts, you know he's nuts' and 'You know in your heart he's right – far right'.

in your shell-like (ear) Phrase used when asking to have a 'quiet word' with someone: '(Let me have a word) in your ear' is all it means, but it makes gentle fun of a poetic simile. Keats, in 'To —' (1817), has: 'Had I a man's fair form, then might my sighs / Be echoed swiftly through that ivory shell, / Thine ear and find thy gentle heart', and Thomas Hood's *Bianca's Dream* (1827) has: 'Her small and shell-like ear'. 'So, Effie, turn that shell-like ear, / Nor to my sighing close it' – P. G.

Wodehouse, 'The Gourmet's Love-Song' in *Punch* (24 December 1902). *The Complete Naff Guide* (1983) has 'a word in your shell-like ear' among 'naff things schoolmasters say'. Sometimes the word 'ear' is not spoken but understood. From an episode of the BBC radio show *Round the Horne* (31 March 1968): 'I started to whisper endearments into her shell-like.' 'Don't you think you ought to whisper in my shell-like what this is all about?' – Kerry Greenwood, *Murder in Montparnasse*, Chap. 12 (2002).

I only asked! Quite the most popular British catchphrase of the late 1950s. Bernard Bresslaw (1934–93) played a large, gormless army private – 'Popeye' Popplewell – in Granada TV's *The Army Game* from 1957 to 1962. This was his response when anyone put him down, and the phrase occurred in the very first episode. A feature film for the cinema called *I Only Arsked* was made in 1958.

(don't ask/blame me) I only work here Defensive response to any criticism of how an organization is run. British, from the late 1940s.

I rest my case Concluding words of an argument, offered in parody of a barrister's customary sign-off. Date of origin unknown. Frank Muir used to round off his (sometimes invented) definitions of words with it on BBC TV *Call My Bluff* (1970s/80s).

(the) Iron Chancellor Nickname of Prince Otto E. L. Bismarck (1815–98), mainly responsible for making Prussia the most powerful of the German states. When the German Empire was formed in 1871, he became its first Chancellor. He declared his policy to be one of BLOOD AND IRON. He used these words in a speech to the Prussian parliament in 1862, and they seemed also to fit his own warlike and inflexible character. The phrase has subsequently been applied to British Chancellors of the Exchequer who took a strict line on the country's economy. 'It suited Gordon Brown, at least during the Blair government's first term, to be known as the "Iron Chancellor"' – *The Observer* (12 January 2003).

(the) Iron Curtain Imaginary dividing line between East and West blocs in

Europe, caused by the hard-line tactics of the Soviet Union after the Second World War. In a speech at Fulton, Missouri (5 March 1946) Winston Churchill said: 'From Stettin in the Baltic to Trieste in the Adriatic, an iron curtain has descended across the Continent.' The phrase *in this context* dates back to the 1920s, and Churchill had already used it in telegrams to President Truman and in the House of Commons. Before this, when Germany invaded Belgium in 1914, Queen Elisabeth of Belgium, who was the daughter of a German duke and married the later King Albert of Belgium in 1900, is reported to have said that between the Germans and herself *'un rideau de fer'* had descended.

(the) Iron Duke Nickname of Arthur Wellesley, 1st Duke of Wellington (1769–1852), soldier and statesman, as strong and unbending as Bismarck, but in his case the nickname was especially applicable when he erected iron shutters (and two cannons in the gateway) at his home, Apsley House, London, during riots in favour of the Reform Bill. It was appropriate, too, that large iron statues were set up in various parts of the country after his death. Elizabeth Longford in her biography of Wellington (1969–72) comments: '*Punch* may be said to have coined the expression in 1845. Commenting on the regimental brevity of Wellington's epistolary style from which all "small courtesies and minor graces" were omitted, *Punch* said: "We cannot but think that Iron Dukes like Iron Pokers are none the worse for just a little polish." If the term became popular only after the Duke's death, there were plenty of precedents earlier than 1845 for its subsequent adoption – from General Pakenham's admiration for "the iron man", to his own frank pride in his "iron hand". His younger contemporary, the painter Frith, heard that after Waterloo he "shed iron tears".'

(the) iron entered his soul He has become embittered, anguished. From the Prayer Book version of Psalm 105:18: 'Whose feet they hurt in the stocks: the iron entered into his soul.' In the Authorized Version of the Bible, it is: 'Whose feet they hurt with fetters: he was laid in iron.' In fact, 'the iron entered into his soul' is a mistranslation of the Hebrew. It was used notably by David Lloyd George who said about Sir John Simon, who had been Attorney-General and Home Secretary in Asquith's Liberal government but had resigned by the time Lloyd George became PM in 1916: 'Simon has sat on the fence so long that the iron has entered into his soul.' He formed a division of the Liberal Party in the 1920s which Lloyd George scorned – quoted in A. J. P. Taylor, *English History 1914–1945* (1965). The English title of Jean-Paul Sartre's novel *La Mort dans L'âme* (1949) is *Iron in the Soul*.

(an) iron fist (or hand) in a velvet glove Unbending ruthlessness or firmness covered by a veneer of courtesy and gentle manners. Thomas Carlyle in *Latter-Day Pamphlets* (1850) wrote: 'Soft speech and manner, yet with an inflexible rigour of command . . . "iron hand in a velvet glove", as Napoleon defined it.' The Emperor Charles V may have said it earlier. 'Iron fist' was known by 1740. Napoleon is indeed supposed to have said, 'Men must be led by an iron hand in a velvet glove', but this expression is hard to pin down as a quotation. 'Once upon a time, the judiciary was criticised for using an iron fist against the poor and a velvet glove against the wealthy and powerful' – *The Observer* (17 July 1994); 'Hard man in a time of soft-spoken clichés – Ronald Payne sees popular support for the French interior minister's iron fist – but some distrust his political ambitions' – by-line in *The European* (19 August 1994); 'This would have the great merit of ending opposition or indifference to the alliance within Bill Clinton's administration while maintaining America's role as leader. It would, however, mean Nato having to accept becoming the servant of the UN instead of the iron fist of the West' – *The Sunday Times* (2 October 1994).

(the) Iron Lady Nickname of Margaret Thatcher, British Prime Minister from 1979 to 1990. On 19 January 1976, she said in a speech, while she was still Leader of the Opposition: 'The Russians are bent on world dominance . . . the Russians put guns before butter.' Within a few days, the Soviet Defence Ministry newspaper *Red Star* had accused the 'Iron Lady' of seeking to revive the Cold War. The article wrongly suggested that she was known by this nickname in the UK at that time, although the headline over a profile by Marjorie Proops in the *Daily Mirror* of 5 February 1975 had been 'The IRON MAIDEN'.

(the) Iron Maiden 'The Iron Maiden of Nuremberg' was a medieval instrument of torture in the form of a woman-shaped box with spiked doors that closed in on the victim. Hence the name of a British heavy metal group of the 1980s and its application to formidable women (see IRON LADY).

iron resolution Inevitable pairing. Date of origin unknown. Cited as a 'dying metaphor' in George Orwell, 'Politics and the English Language' in *Horizon* (April 1946). 'There is one overriding concern in today's Labour Party. Indeed it is part of John Smith's legacy: an iron resolution not to allow anyone to know what it is thinking' – *Daily Mail* (26 May 1994); 'Cricket: Hick gives England heart . . . Instead, he proceeded to play one of iron resolution, which was equally impressive' – *The Times* (29 November 1994).

—— is —— Cliché of sloganeering, in which actors or singers are promoted as if they were indistinguishable from the characters they portray. The film *You Only Live Twice* (UK 1967) was promoted with the slogan 'Sean Connery *is* James Bond' – surely, a debatable proposition at the best of times and likely only to encourage a regrettable tendency, particularly among journalists, to confuse actors with their roles. Other examples: 'Michael Caine is Alfie is wicked!' – (UK 1966); 'Paul Hogan *is* Crocodile Dundee' – (Australia/US 1987); '*Phil Collins* is *Buster*' – title of video about the making of the film *Buster* (UK 1988); 'Domingo *is* Otello [*sic*]' – advertisement in *Los Angeles* Magazine (March 1989); 'Jessye Norman *is* Carmen' – advertisement on LBC radio, London (August 1989).

—— is back and this time it's personal Slogan format. 'This time . . . it's personal' – *Jaws: The Revenge* (US 1987); 'This time, it's personal' – *Die Hard: With a Vengeance* (US 1995); 'Blur are back! And this time it's personal' – headline in *The*

Observer Magazine (14 March 1999). Compare HE'S BACK – AND HE'S ANGRY.

I said a subtle! See under NOW THERE'S A BEAUT . . .

—— is a long time in —— Format phrase, based on the remark 'A week is a long time in politics', attributed to the British Prime Minister Harold Wilson (1916–95). I asked him in 1977 when he first uttered the much quoted dictum, but uncharacteristically he was unable to remember. He also challenged the accepted interpretation of the words – which most people would think was along the lines of 'What a difference a day makes', 'Wait and see' and 'Don't panic, it'll all blow over'. 'It does not mean I'm living from day to day,' he said, but was intended as 'a prescription for long-term strategic thinking and planning, ignoring the day-to-day issues and pressures which may hit the headlines but which must not be allowed to get out of focus while longer-term policies are taking effect'. Inquiries among political journalists led to the conclusion that in its present form the phrase was probably first used at a meeting between Wilson and the Parliamentary lobby correspondents in the wake of the sterling crisis shortly after he first took office as Prime Minister in 1964. From the late 1980s onwards, Channel Four carried a weekly review with the title *A Week in Politics*, clearly alluding to Wilson's phrase – which provides an easily variable format. From *The Independent* (19 May 1989), on the outgoing editor of the TV programme *Forty Minutes*: 'His successor will have to work hard, though, to keep the formula fresh. 2,400 seconds is a long time in television.'

I say, I say, I say! Catchphrase of music-hall/variety performers. It is hard to know whether Murray and Mooney, the British variety duo, invented this interruption, but they perfected the routine in their act during the 1930s. Mooney would interrupt with, 'I say, I say, I say!' To whatever he had to impart, Murray would reply with the traditional, I DON'T WISH TO KNOW THAT, KINDLY LEAVE THE STAGE. Harry Murray died in 1967; Harry Mooney in 1972.

I say it's spinach Meaning 'nonsense', this phrase comes from a caption devised by Elwyn Brooks White for a cartoon by Carl Rose that appeared in the issue of *The New Yorker* of 8 December 1928. It shows a mother at table saying: 'It's broccoli, dear.' Her little girl replies: 'I say it's spinach, and I say the hell with it.' Ross, then editor of the magazine, remembered that when White asked his opinion of the caption the writer was clearly uncertain that he had hit on the right idea. 'I looked at the drawing and the caption and said, "Yeh, it seems okay to me," but neither of us cracked a smile.' The use of the word 'spinach' to mean 'nonsense' stems from this (mostly in the USA), as in the title of Irving Berlin's song 'I'll Say It's Spinach' from the revue *Face the Music* (1932) and of the book *Fashion is Spinach* by Elizabeth Dawes (1933).

I say, what a smasher!   See under DON'T FORCE IT, PHOEBE.

I say, you fellows!   See under YAROOOO!

'I see', said the blind man (when he couldn't see at all)   *Partridge/Catch Phrases* has this from America by the late 19th century, as also, '"I see," said the blind man, as he picked up his hammer and saw.'

I'se regusted!   When the long-running US radio series *Amos 'n' Andy* (1930s and 40s) was transferred to TV in 1951–53, black actors had to be found to play the characters originally portrayed by whites. The catchphrases and stock phrases were carried over intact, however. They included: '**Holy mackerel, Andy!** We's all got to stick together in dis heah thing . . . remember, we is brothers in that great fraternity, the Mystic Knights of the Sea'; **check and double check**; and **now ain't dat sump'n?**

is everybody happy?   Traditional holiday camp cry and also the rallying call of several entertainers. The American comedian Harry Brown is mentioned as using it *circa* 1906. Ian Whitcomb, *After the Ball* (1972), states: 'Ted Lewis, ex-clarinettist of the Earl Fuller Jazz Band [post 1919], toured as the "Top-Hatted Tragedian of Jazz", the Hamlet of the Halls, posing the eternal question, "Is everybody happy?"' 'Is Everybody Happy Now?' was a popular song in the USA (1927) – was this the one

that Florrie Forde (d. 1940) is said to have sung? – and *Is Everybody Happy?* was the title of an early sound film (US 1929, remade 1943) recounting the life of Ted Lewis and featuring him.

I shall return   Slogan/motto of the American general Douglas MacArthur (1880–1964). MacArthur was forced by the Japanese to pull out of the Philippines and left Corregidor on 11 March 1942. On 20 March he made his commitment to return when he arrived by train at Adelaide, South Australia. He had journeyed southwards across Australia and was just about to set off eastwards for Melbourne. So, although he had talked in these terms before leaving the Philippines, his main statement was delivered not there but on Australian soil. At the station, a crowd awaited him, and he had scrawled a few words on the back of an envelope: 'The President of the United States ordered me to break through the Japanese lines and proceed from Corregidor to Australia for the purpose, as I understand it, of organizing the American offensive against Japan, a primary object of which is the relief of the Philippines. I came through and I shall return.' MacArthur had intended his first words to have the most impact – as a way of getting the war in the Pacific a higher priority – but it was his last three words that caught on. The Office of War Information tried to get him to amend them to '*We* shall return', foreseeing that there would be objections to a slogan which seemed to imply that he was all-important and that his men mattered little. MacArthur refused. In fact, the phrase had first been suggested to a MacArthur aide in the form '*We* shall return' by a Filipino journalist, Carlos Romulo. On 20 October 1944, MacArthur *did* return. Landing at Leyte, he said to a background of still continuing gunfire: 'People of the Philippines, I have returned . . . By the grace of Almighty God, our forces stand again upon Philippine soil.'

is he one of us?   Asked concerning anyone being considered for membership of a select group. I.e. 'does he share our beliefs and concerns?; is he loyal?' Probably since about 1900. In *As We Are*, Chap. 10 (1932), E. F. Benson has: 'She became quite friends with Miss Stevenson who, she ascertained, was of very good parentage (almost "one of us"), for her mother had been the daughter of an Irish peer.' Stock question of Margaret Thatcher, when, as British Prime Minister, reviewing candidates for appointments (by 1985). There is a report that she was heard to say of Labour MP, Geoffrey de Freitas in about 1959, '*What* a nice man . . . *What* a pity he's not one of us.' Hence, *One of Us*, the title of Hugo Young's political study of Mrs Thatcher (1989). From *The Independent* (28 January 1989): 'Mr [Kenneth] Clarke also failed the is-he-one-of-us? test applied by Mrs Thatcher to favoured colleagues.'

I should cocoa! 'Certainly not!' – a slightly dated British English exclamation. Current by 1936. Longman's *Dictionary of English Idioms* (1979) adds a word of caution: 'This phrase is not recommended for use by the foreign student.' But why 'cocoa'? As always when in difficulty with a phrase origin, turn to rhyming slang. 'Cocoa' is from 'coffee and cocoa', almost rhyming slang for 'I should hope so!' Often used ironically.

I should of stood in bed See WE WUZ ROBBED!

is it bigger than a breadbox? Since 1950, the Goodson-Todman production *What's My Line* has remained the archetypal TV panel game. Guessing the jobs of contestants and then donning masks to work out the identity of a visiting celebrity turned panellists into national figures in the USA and UK. Attempting to establish the size of an article made by one contestant, Steve Allen formulated the classic inquiry, 'Is it bigger than a breadbox?' From 'Tinseltown' in Armistead Maupin, *Further Tales of the City* (1982): '"Right . . . how big was his dick again? . . . Bigger than a breadbox?"' Other *What's My Line?* phrases included: **would the next challenger sign in please!** – the chairman inviting a contestant to indicate something or other by the way he or she wrote their name. Then **a spot of mime for the panel** would be largely mystifying. The chairman, trying to get the contestant to answer 'No' to ten of the panel's questions would score: **and that's three down, seven to go!** If ten was scored: **you've beaten the panel!** In the UK, the game ran from 1951

to 1963, with brief revivals in the 1970s and 80s.

is it true . . . blondes have more fun? Slogan for Lady Clairol in the USA from 1957, devised by Shirley Polykoff. Chosen from ten suggestions, including 'Is it true that blondes are never lonesome?' and 'Is it true blondes marry millionaires?' 'Blondes have more fun' entered the language and had great persuasive effect. The artist David Hockney once told on TV of how and why he decided to bleach his hair and become the blond bombshell he is today. It was in response to a television advertisement he saw late one evening in New York City. 'Blondes have more fun,' it said. 'You've only one life. Live it as a Blonde!' He immediately jumped up, left the apartment, found an all-night hairdresser and followed the advice of the advertiser. The TV jingle managed to become a hit in the USSR *circa* 1965.

(an) island paradise Cliché of travel journalism and promotion. Date of origin unknown. 'For the opening programme, Jill reports from the island paradise of Mauritius' – *Daily Record* (1 November 1994); 'As a blood red sun settled across the Pacific Ocean, Brando learned that he had failed his daughter for the last time. She had hanged herself in her bedroom on the South Pacific island paradise of Tahiti' – *Daily Mail* (18 April 1995); 'Even on their wedding day they were to be found exchanging sacred vows on the paradise isle of Fiji' – *Hello!* (13 May 1995).

(the) island race *The Island Race* was the title of a book of poems (1898) by Sir Henry Newbolt. In Newbolt's first book, *Admirals All and other verses* (1897), there is a poem called 'The Guides at Cabul 1879' whose first line is: 'Sons of the Island Race, wherever ye dwell.' The characterization of Britain as an 'island race' understandably reached its apogee in the Second World War, but at big patriotic moments there has always been a tendency to draw attention to the fact of Britain being an island, from John of Gaunt's 'sceptr'd isle' in Shakespeare's *Richard II* onwards. Winston Churchill said, 'We shall defend our Island, whatever the cost may be' in his 'We shall fight on the beaches' speech of 4 June 1940. The flag-waving film *In Which We Serve* (1942) refers specifically to the 'island race'. Churchill used the phrase as the title of Bk 1, Vol. 1 of his *History of the English-Speaking Peoples* (1956). In *The Second World War*, Vol. 5 (1952) he also quotes the 'island *story*' phrase from Tennyson's 'Ode on the Death of the Duke of Wellington' (1852): 'Not once or twice in our rough island story / The path of duty was the way to glory.'

isn't he a panic?   Aside uttered by Fred Harris about Eric Pode of Croydon (Chris Emmett) in the BBC Radio series *The Burkiss Way* (1976–80), usually after Pode had made a tasteless and/or feeble joke. Was this an original coinage? All one can point to is the use of the verb 'to panic', meaning 'to elicit great response, esp. applause from an audience by one's performing; to amuse or entertain well' – American use by 1929 (*DOAS*). Robert L. Chapman, *The New Dictionary of American Slang* (1987), develops the meaning of this verbal use even closer as: 'To get a strong favorable reaction, esp to get loud laughter from an audience.' For the use of panic as a noun, compare these lines from Johnny Mercer's song 'Hooray for Hollywood' (1937): 'Hooray for Hollywood, / That screwy, ballyhooey Hollywood. / Where any office boy or young mechanic can / Be a panic with just a looking pan.' And this passage from Vladimir Nabokov, *Lolita*, Pt 2, Chap. 9 (1955): 'How had the ball been? Oh, it had been a riot. A what? A panic. Terrific, in a word.' Incidentally, when the grotty scumbag introduced himself with the words **Eric Pode of Croydon**, there was always ecstatic cheering, applause, the 'Hallelujah Chorus' and much more.

—— is one's middle name   A (mostly) American way of defining a person's outstanding characteristic (often negatively). From P. G. Wodehouse, *Damsel in Distress* (1919): 'Everyone told me your middle name was Nero.' From Sinclair Lewis, *Main Street* (1920): '"Like fishing?" "Fishing is my middle name".' From Thomas Tryon, *All That Glitters* (1987): 'Belinda Carroll had a middle name, but you never saw it in print or on a theatre marquee. Her middle name was trouble

with a capital "T".' 'Trouble Is My Middle Name' was the title of a song (US 1963) by Nader & Gluck.

I spy   Meaning, simply, 'I've seen/spotted something'. The exclamation 'I spy!' appeared in *Punch* (14 September 1910), and in the 1950s there was a British craze for 'I Spy' which extended the game of train-spotting to other fields. According to the subject of whichever little book was being used, the spotter would score points for having observed different breeds of animal, types of building, and so on. The craze was presided over by 'Big Chief I Spy' in the *Daily Express*. The origin of the phrase probably lies in the simple children's game of 'I spy' or 'Hy-spy' (known in the 18th century), a form of hide and seek. Then there is also the children's game of '**I spy with my little eye** . . . something beginning with [a letter of the alphabet] . . .', in which the guessers have to work out what object this initial letter refers to. Might there also be an allusion to the nursery rhyme 'Who Killed Cock Robin?' (1740s) in which the question 'Who saw him die?' is answered with, 'I said the fly, / With my little eye'?

I spy strangers!   Procedural phrase in the House of Commons that draws attention to the presence of outsiders with a view to having them excluded. This is a bizarre device used to delay controversial legislation or to embarrass the Government by forcing a division. The 'strangers' may be members of the public in the galleries, reporters or journalists. The device can be blocked but has succeeded – for example, on 18 November 1958.

is she a friend of Dorothy?   I.e. 'Is he [*sic*] a homosexual?' Probably this inquiry originated among American homosexuals. It was current by 1984. Dorothy was the put-upon heroine of *The Wizard of Oz* and was played in the film by Judy Garland, a woman much revered in male homosexual circles. A similar expression, probably current from about the same time, is **does he dance at the other end of the ballroom?**

is she ... or isn't she?   Slogan for Harmony hairspray, in the UK, current in 1980. The ad went on: 'Harmony has a ultra-fine spray to leave hair softer and more natural. She *is* wearing a hairspray but with Harmony it's so fine you're the only one that knows for sure.' Nothing to do with DOES SHE . . . OR DOESN'T SHE?, but a deliberate echo of that – as, presumably, also was the line 'Is she or isn't she a phoney?', spoken in the film *Breakfast at Tiffany's* (US 1961).

is that a chicken joke? Catchphrase from NBC TV, *Rowan and Martin's Laugh-In* (1967–73). Posed by Jo Ann Worley and presumably alluding to the age-old type of joke, *Q.* Why did the chicken cross the road? *A.* To get to the other side / For some foul reason, etc.

is that your final answer? Catchphrase from the British TV quiz *Who Wants To Be a Millionaire?* (from 1999) and emulated all over the world. A feature of the quiz was the opportunities it gave for contestants to **phone a friend** and to consult the studio audience before finally coming up with an answer. Hence, the host, Chris Tarrant's, insistence on establishing that this was it.

—— is the cruellest month Format phrase based on use – or rather misuse – of a quotation. 'April is the cruellest month, breeding / Lilacs out of the dead land' – the first five words of T. S. Eliot's *The Waste Land* (1922) are frequently misquoted. Often 'August' is substituted for 'April', possibly out of confusion with *August Is a Wicked Month*, the title of a novel (1965) by Edna O'Brien. But, really, almost any month can be inserted into the format: 'After the highs and lows of Christmas and the winter holidays, February always seems to me the cruellest month' – *The Daily Telegraph* (15 February 1992); 'Sometimes March can be the cruellest month' – *Northern Echo* (18 February 1992); 'August used to be the cruellest month' – *The Times* (25 August 1992); 'June is the cruellest month in politics' – *The Times* (5 June 1993); 'August has always been the cruellest month' – *The Times* (25 August 1993).

—— is the name of the game An overused phrase from the mid-1960s, meaning '. . . is what it's all about/is the essence of the whole thing'. *Partridge/Catch Phrases*

finds an example in 1961. US National Security Adviser McGeorge Bundy talking about foreign policy goals in Europe in 1966 said: 'Settlement is the name of the game.' In time, almost everything was, following the title of an American TV movie called *Fame Is the Name of the Game* (1966). Then came several series of TV's *The Name of the Game* (1968–71). 'The name of the game this week is survival' – *The Times* (29 September 1972). The expression was replaced for a while by —— **is where it's at**.

—— is the new —— Phrase format of epidemic proportions since 1998. Probably a development of the next phrase format (below). 'Why soup is the new sandwich' – headline in *The Independent* (6 November 1998); 'The 1990s are the new 1960s' – *The Sunday Times* (8 November 1998); also observed about this time on the front cover of a DIY magazine: 'Sex is the new decorating.' During TV coverage of Royal Ascot in 1998, the phrase 'Grey is the new black' came up, at which Eve Pollard may have quoted Lady Mountbatten who used to say 'Pink is the navy blue of India'. However, in March 1974, Cecil Beaton quoted in his diary, Diana Vreeland as having said: 'Pink is the blue of India'.

—— is the new rock'n'roll Phrase format from *circa* 1993. Originally, 'comedy is the new rock'n'roll'. In Britain at that time, such was the attention paid to comedy performers and writers in the 'alternative' and 'improvisational' fields, and such was the wealth and fame accrued by young comedy practitioners in the media generally, that the parallel was drawn with the exciting, fashionable phenomenon of an earlier time. The phrase made an early appearance in *The Guardian* (19 October 1991): 'In this age of CDs, Discmasters, videos, prototype virtual reality, handheld computer games, all-night raves, and stand-up comedy as the new rock'n'roll, the gig has become a tedious anachronism.' 'This year's award recognizes the way the arts can reach out and extend into new areas and to a new audience. For many who have seen it, the Citizens' Theatre production of *Trainspotting* is a reminder of how powerful drama can be. *Trainspotting* proves that theatre can be the new rock 'n' roll' – *The Herald* (Glasgow) (21 May 1994); '"Gardening is the new rock 'n' roll. When I was little, it was all fuddy-duddy Percy Thrower. Now it's very social and very, very fashionable" – Ex-supermodel Ali Ward, who has switched careers to become a model gardener' – *The Independent* (13 June 1998).

is the Pope (a) Catholic? *Partridge/ Catch Phrases* lists this as one of its 'American responses to stupid questions', along with: **do chickens have lips?, can snakes do push-ups?, do frogs have watertight assholes?** and **does a bear shit in the woods?** It may date from *circa* 1950. Now quite well established elsewhere: 'Is Melvyn [Bragg] vain? Is the Pope Catholic?' – *The Independent on Sunday* (17 June 1990). In the *Midwestern Journal of Language and Folklore* (1975), Charles Clay Doyle described these phrases as 'sarcastic interrogative affirmatives'. Robert L. Chapman, *New Dictionary of American Slang* (1986), provides further examples in addition to the variations 'Is the Pope Polish/Italian?': **does a wooden horse have a hickory dick?, does a dog have fleas?, is Bismarck a herring?** – as in the film *Blazing Saddles* (US 1974); and **does Muhammad Ali own a mirror?** Compare CAN A BLOODY DUCK SWIM?

is there a doctor in the house? Traditional cry, usually in a theatre or at some other large gathering of people, when a member of the audience is taken ill. One suspects that it dates from the 19th century, if not before. The query appears in a *Punch* cartoon (6 February 1935). Three years before this, in the film *Horse Feathers*, Groucho Marx addresses the crowd at a football game with the question 'Is there a doctor in the stands?' and then, when he finds one, says: 'How do you like the game, Doc?' The *Daily Mirror* (10 October 1984) reported a member of the audience passing out during the film *1984*: 'There was a kerfuffle as people rallied round and an excited rustle as the traditional call went out: "Is there a doctor in the house?" . . . Dr David Owen, a few rows away, continued to be transfixed by the activities on the screen.' Sir Ralph Richardson used

to tell of an actor who was taking part in a very bad play. Halfway through he turned to the audience and asked, 'Is there a doctor in the house?' When one stood up, the actor said, 'Doctor, isn't this show *terrible!*' *Doctor in the House* (1952) was the title of a novel by Richard Gordon (but is also a play on the term 'house doctor').

is there a law against it? Reply to a suggestion the speaker thinks is unreasonable, meaning 'why shouldn't I?' Since the 1950s? In the USA: **is there some kind of law?**

is there life after ——? Presumably derived from the question of life after death, there seems no end to the variations on this theme. The original form of the question was posed, for example, in BBC TV *Monty Python's Flying Circus* (21 December 1972): 'Tonight on "Is There" we examine the question, "Is there a life after death?" And here to discuss it are three dead people.' There were films (US 1971 and 1973) with the titles *Is There Sex After Death?* and *Is There Sex After Marriage?* The variant 'Is there life *before* death?' was recorded as a graffito in Ballymurphy, Ireland, *circa* 1971 and is confirmed by Seamus Heaney's poem 'Whatever You Say Say Nothing' from *North* (1975), which has: 'Is there a life before death? That's chalked up / In Ballymurphy . . .' But as if this underlines the saying's Irish origins too well, bear in mind that 'Is there life before death?' had earlier been the epigraph to Chap. 9 of Stephen Vizinczey's novel *In Praise of Older Women* (1966). There, it is credited to 'Anon. Hungarian'. *Is There Life After Housework?* – title of book (1981) by Don A. Aslett; 'Is there life after redundancy?' – headline in *The Sunday Times* Magazine (14 October 1984); 'Is there life after Wogan?' – headline in the *Sunday People* (14 October 1984).

is there no balm in Gilead? Meaning, 'is there no remedy or consolation?' – comes from Jeremiah 8:22. In the so-called Treacle Bible (1568), it is curiously translated as, 'is there no tryacle in Gilead, is there no phisition there?' 'Balm of Gilead' has also been used as a slang expression for 'money' and 'illicitly distilled whisky'.

... is the right answer! Quizmaster's traditional way of saying 'yes' or 'correct' when a contestant has just come up with it. Possibly imported from the USA? The line was used in a parody on the BBC radio show *The Burkiss Way* (27 December 1977).

is this a record? Traditional cry of people writing to newspapers with claims of various kinds. The line occurs in *Punch* (3 April 1935). A letter to *The Times* (18 September 1951), written from the Reform Club, stated: 'I have just been asked "Any money for the guy?" Is this a record?' 'I draft (but don't send) a letter to *The Times*: Dear Sir, I am in possession of a thin circular disc of what seems to be shellac, bearing faint concentric striations and a label reading: "Down Mexico Way with Dame Clara Butt". Is this a record?' – *The Diaries of Kenneth Tynan* (2001) – entry for 12 April 1971. Bernard Levin recalled a letter he claimed to have sent to *The Times*: 'I have just got a crossed line on which I heard a man getting a wrong number, is this a record?' This was in his preface to a book entitled *The First Cuckoo* (1976), celebrating 'the most witty amusing and memorable letters' sent to *The Times* since 1900. Claiming to have heard **the first cuckoo** of Spring is, or was, a popular pastime of *Times* letter writers. Mr R. Lydekker FRS claimed to have heard one as early as 6 February 1913 (on which day he wrote to the paper), but this turned out to have been a hoax. Whether or not there is earlier correspondence on this subject in *The Times* is not clear, but by a curious coincidence, a piece of music with the title 'On Hearing The First Cuckoo In Spring' by Frederick Delius was given its first performance in Leipzig on 2 October that same year.

is this the party to whom I am speaking? Catchphrase from NBC TV, *Rowan and Martin's Laugh-In* (1967–73). Spoken by Ernestine (Lily Tomlin), the rude, snobbish, nasal switchboard operator, *circa* 1969.

... is unwell Format explaining why a regular contributor's piece is not appearing in a newspaper or magazine (alternatively: '. . . is away'). Popularized when 'Jeffrey Bernard is unwell' appeared so frequently in *The Spectator* that it was used as the title of a London play (1989) by Keith Waterhouse, based on Bernard's writings about his 'low life' adventures in the world of ill-health and alcohol. The English journalist in question was Jeffrey Bernard (1932–97).

I suppose a fuck's out of the question (or **no chance of a fuck, I suppose)?** Sly, sideways chat-up line – perhaps first of all in a cartoon caption, say *circa* 1981? What the precise allusion is, if any, remains unclear. In the film *See No Evil, Hear No Evil* (US 1989), Richard Pryor asks it of a gorgeous murderess, played by Joan Severance. A British cinema commercial (1994) included the obvious reference, 'I suppose a plumber's out of the question?' From *The Independent* (23 July 1994): '[A chat-up from a] man I met at a recent dinner party. "Can I have your home number?" "No." "How about your home address?" "No," I repeated. "Does that mean a fax is out of the question?"'

I swear by Almighty God that the evidence ... There are many versions of the oath sworn by witnesses in courts of law. A composite formed from countless viewings of fictional courts, on TV and film, in the UK and the USA, might be: 'I swear by Almighty God that the evidence I shall give will be the **truth, the whole truth and nothing but the truth. So help me God.**' The last phrase has never been part of the English court oath. However, it is common in the USA and has also occurred in oaths of allegiance to the British Crown. The emphatic repetition of 'the truth' is common to many countries. In Cervantes, *Don Quixote* (1605–15), we find: 'I must speak the truth, and nothing but the truth'. *Nothing But the Truth* has been the title of three films (US 1920, 1929, 1941) based on James Montgomery's play (pre-1920). *The Whole Truth* was also the title of a film (UK 1958).

is your journey really necessary? Slogan first devised in 1939 to discourage evacuated civil servants from going home for Christmas. 'From 1941, the question was constantly addressed to all civilians, for, after considering a scheme for rationing on the "points" principle, or to ban all travel without a permit over more than fifty miles, the government had finally decided to rely on voluntary appeals, and on making travel uncomfortable by reducing the number of trains' – Norman Longmate, *How We Lived Then* (1973).

it all depends what you mean by ... *The Brains Trust* was a discussion programme first broadcast on BBC radio in 1941, taking its title from President Roosevelt's name for his circle of advisers (see BRAIN(S) TRUST). A regular participant, who became a national figure, was C. E. M. Joad (1891–1953) – often called 'Professor', though not entitled to be. His discussion technique was to jump in first and leave the other speakers with little else to say. Alternatively, he would try to undermine arguments by using the phrase for which he became famous. When the chairman once read out a question from a listener, Mr W. E. Jack of Keynsham – 'Are thoughts things or about things?' – Joad inevitably began his answer with 'It all depends what you mean by a "thing".' A more precise dating for when the phrase had 'caught on' is contained in a letter to James Agate, dated 15 October 1943 and included in his *Ego 6*: '"Is *Responsibility* a work of art?" Well, as Joad would say, that depends on your definition of a work of art.' Joad's broadcasting career ended rather abruptly when he was found travelling by rail using a ticket that was not valid. The BBC banished him.

it always rains on Sunday(s) *It Always Rains On Sunday* was the title of a British film (1948, from a novel by Arthur La Bern) – apparently original but having a nice proverbial feel to it. The melodramatic story was about an escaped convict in London's East End. As it happens, the phrase also appeared very shortly afterwards as an English language sub-title in the film *Bicycle Thieves* (Italy 1948).

it beats as it sweeps as it cleans Slogan for Hoover carpet sweepers, in the USA from 1919 and still current in the UK in the 1980s. Coined by Gerald Page-Wood of the Erwin Wasey agency in Cleveland, Ohio. The exclusive feature of Hoovers was that they gently beat or tapped the carpet to loosen dirt and grit embedded in it. An agitator bar performed this function, together with strong suction and revolving brushes – giving the Hoover the 'triple action' enshrined in the slogan. The words 'Hoover' and **to hoover** became generic terms for vacuum cleaners and for vacuuming. Meaning 'to use a vacuum cleaner', the verb is derived from the name of William H. Hoover who marketed, but did not invent, the original Hoover model. James Murray Spengler invented the 'triple action' machine 1908. Alas for him, we don't say we are going to 'spengler' the carpet.

it can't happen here Self-deluding catchphrase. Not unexpectedly for such a short-sighted view of external threats, it appears to have arisen in the 1930s. Sinclair Lewis's novel *It Can't Happen Here* was published in 1935 and adapted for the stage the following year. It warned against fascism in the United States. Appropriately, Kevin Brownlow and Andrew Mollo's film about what would have happened if the Germans had invaded England in 1940 was entitled *It Happened Here* (UK 1963).

it couldn't have happened to a nicer chap (or **guy)** He deserves it – whatever stroke of luck he has received. Since the 1940s? '[To Phil Silvers] How happy I am over your success. You've had it coming . . . Well, it couldn't have happened to a nicer guy' – Groucho Marx, *The Groucho Letters* (1967) – letter of 15 November 1951. Now increasingly used, ironically, when *misfortune* has struck.

it does exactly what it says on the tin Meaning, 'It does, or is, exactly what you would expect it do or be.' 'Stroppy working-class one-liner suggesting a no-frills, no-bullshit, no-marketing-strategy bluntness' – John Walsh in *The Independent* (2 December 2000). This phrase caught on from the concluding sales pitch in a UK TV commercial for a wood-care product from Ronseal. 'What it says on the box, can, packet etc.' may also be substituted. 'I know [Joanne] Harris's work, like most readers, through the seductive film *Chocolat,* and this book does exactly what it says on the tin' – *The Observer* (16 July 2003).

it don't arf make you larf! Favourite phrase of the British comedian Max Wall

(1908–90) – he of the incomparable voice and appearance. By the 1950s.

it fits like a stocking on a chicken's lip I.e. 'No damn good, it doesn't fit at all'. Paul Beale glossed this as 'a traditional carpenter's catchphrase which I first heard from a Loughborough College carpenter and joiner in 1990.'

it floats See 99 44/100 PER CENT . . .

(the) It Girl Nickname of Clara Bow (1905–65), the popular actress of the silent film era who appeared in the film *It* (1928), based on an Elinor Glyn story. 'It' was the word used in billings to describe her vivacious sex appeal. A little earlier, 'It' was the title of a song in *The Desert Song* (1926). Elsewhere 'it' has had more basic sexual connotations such as survive in the expression 'to have it off'. In 1904, Rudyard Kipling wrote in *Traffics and Discoveries*: ''Tisn't beauty, so to speak, nor good talk necessarily. It's just It. Some women'll stay in a man's memory if they once walk down a street.' *Punch* commented on an 'It' craze (18 March 1908), which may be relevant. In the 1990s, the phrase was resurrected and applied, in the UK, to certain young women of minor celebrity status.

it goes without saying . . . Rhetorical filler phrase, always risking the rejoinder, 'Well, don't bother then.' Translated from the French *cela va sans dire* and found in American English by 1878. 'To hold the public's confidence, and take another step towards finding a team that can recapture the Ashes from Australia next winter, it goes without saying that England have to win the series, and ought to win the match' – *Evening Standard* (London) (1 June 1994); 'In our view, the American and French positions can be modified by just listening to the UN demands. It goes without saying that if all the UN member states act consistently and fairly when dealing with world problems, the UN will accordingly succeed as a peace broker worldwide' – *The Guardian* (13 June 1994).

it goes with the territory (sometimes **comes with . . .)** Late-20th-century expression meaning 'It's all part and parcel of something, what is expected, not something that can be avoided'. From *The Washington Post* (13 July 1984): '[Geraldine Ferraro as prospective Vice-President] will have to be judged on her background, training and capacity to do the job. That goes with the territory.' In the film *Father of the Bride* (1991), Steve Martin says: 'I'm a father. Worrying comes with the territory.' From the London *Evening Standard* (London) (17 February 1993): 'Why go on about the latest "award-winning documentary maker"? If you get a documentary on television, you win an award: it goes with the territory.' Since at least 1900, 'territory' has been the American term for the area a salesman covers, and it seems quite likely that the origin of the 'goes with' phrase is the 'Requiem' scene at the end of Arthur Miller's play *Death of a Salesman* (1948): 'For a salesman, there is no rock bottom to the life . . . He's a man way out there in the blue, riding on a smile and a shoeshine . . . A salesman is got to dream, boy. It comes with the territory.' '"These stories come with the territory now, don't they?" With these words, the Prime Minister finally broke his silence on the so-called Cheriegate affair' – *The Observer* (22 December 2002).

I think I go home At one time, 'I tink I go home', spoken in a would-be Swedish accent, was as much part of the impressionist's view of Greta Garbo as I WANT TO BE ALONE. One version of how the line came to be spoken is told by Norman Zierold in *Moguls* (1969): 'After such films as *The Torrent* and *Flesh and the Devil*, Garbo decided to exploit her box-office power and asked Louis B. Mayer for a raise – from three hundred and fifty to five thousand dollars a week. Mayer offered her twenty-five hundred. "I tink I go home," said Garbo. She went back to her hotel and stayed there for a full seven months until Mayer finally gave way.' Alexander Walker in *Garbo* (1980) recalls, rather, what Sven-Hugo Borg, the actress's interpreter, said of the time in 1926 when Mauritz Stiller, who had come with her from Sweden, was fired from directing *The Temptress*: 'She was tired, terrified and lost . . . as she returned to my side after a trying scene, she sank down beside me and said so low it was almost a whisper, "Borg, I think I shall go home now. It isn't worth it, is it?"' Walker. comments: 'That catch-phrase, shortened into "I think I go home", soon passed into the repertoire of a legion of Garbo-imitators and helped publicize her strong-willed temperament.' A caricatured Garbo was shown hugging Mickey Mouse in a cartoon film in the 1930s. 'Ah tahnk ah kees you now' and 'ah tink ah go home', she said. This cartoon was, incidentally, the last item to be shown on British television before the transmitters were closed down on the brink of war on 1 September 1939.

I think that shows we're getting it about right A cliché of argument. For example, when defending itself in the 1980s, the BBC was in the habit of pointing out that half the letters of complaint it received about a particular programme were critical, the other half supportive. A spokesman or mandarin would say, 'I think that shows we're getting it about right . . .' 'Top TV dramatist Andrew Davies is the latest figure to pour scorn on Alan Yentob, embattled head of BBC1 . . . Indeed, so contradictory are the complaints that Mr Yentob probably feels he's getting it about right' – John Naughton, *Evening Standard* (London) (4 January 1995); 'For a man caught in such vitriolic crossfire, the Scottish National Heritage chairman is remarkably sanguine . . . "We get opposition from both sides, which pleases me very much, because it means we're getting it about right. We are going along the line of mediation between them, of the practical, the possible, not just the ideal. We are working towards what we can achieve"' – *The Herald* (Glasgow) (3 May 1995).

I think the answer lies in the soil In the BBC radio show *Beyond Our Ken* (1958–64), Kenneth Williams created a professional countryman figure with a loam-rich voice who appeared in an *Any Questions* spoof. Perhaps based on Ralph Wightman or A. G. Street, he was called 'Arthur Fallowfield', and this was his comment on every problem. He also had the lament, **I'm looking for someone to love**.

I think we should be told By 1980, *Private Eye* was running a regular parody

of the opinion column written by John Junor (1919–97) for the *Sunday Express*. It frequently included the would-be campaigning journalist's line, 'I think we should be told'. In 1985, Sir John – as he was by then – told me that he had never once used the phrase in his column. He did, however, admit to having used the *Eye* parody's other stock phrase – **pass the sick-bag, Alice** (an expression of assumed revulsion) – though only once. As though to confirm this its status, the exact catchphrase was spoken by Morse in the UK TV series *Inspector Morse*, 'Who Killed Harry Field?' (13 March 1991).

I thought —— until I discovered —— Slogan format as in the common advertising notion of a way of life or a belief being swept away by some sudden revelation. From a David Frost/Christopher Booker parody of political advertisements on BBC TV, *That Was the Week That Was* (1962–3 series): 'I was a floating voter until they discovered Wilson – now I'm sunk.' The format was used memorably in the UK (1970–5) in a series of slogans for Smirnoff vodka. The variations included: 'I thought . . . St Tropez was a Spanish monk/ accountancy was my life/the Kama Sutra was an Indian restaurant/I was the mainstay of the public library . . . until I discovered Smirnoff.' David Tree, an art director at the Young & Rubicam agency, recalled how he and John Bacon, the copywriter, had struggled for weeks to get the right idea. One day, after a fruitless session, he was leaving for lunch when he happened to glance at a magazine pin-up adorning the wall of their office. 'If we really get stuck,' he said, 'we can always say, "I was a boring housewife in Southgate until . . ."' (Southgate was where he was living at the time.) The end-line to the ads, which also caught on, was the **effect is shattering**.

it is disgraceful, it ought not to be allowed! A popular ingredient of BBC radio *Children's Hour* between 1929 and 1963 was the dramatizations of S. G. Hulme Beaman's *Tales of Toytown*. Mr Growser's 'It is disgr-r-raceful . . .' (spoken by Ralph de Rohan) and the bleatings of **Laaaa-rry the Laaa-amb!** (played by Derek McCulloch) became famous expressions.

it'll all come out in the wash The truth will emerge in due course, a situation will be resolved. Anthony Trollope was using the expression in 1876: 'The effects which causes will produce, the manner in which this or that will come out in the washing, do not strike even Cabinet Ministers at a glance.' The phrase appears to have been put further into common parlance by Rudyard Kipling through its use as a refrain in his 1903 poem 'Stellenbosch': 'And it all goes into the laundry, / But it never comes out in the wash . . .'

it'll be all right on the night Theatrical phrase, and dating from the late 19th century, at least. In 'Slaves of the Lamp, Part 1', one of Rudyard Kipling's tales of Stalky and Co. – published in *Cosmopolis* (April 1897) – the schoolboys are rehearsing a pantomime: 'Aladdin came to his own at last, Abanazar lay poisoned on the floor, the Widow Twankey danced her dance, and the company decided it would "come all right on the night".' Curiously, when the phrase has to be invoked, things quite often *are* better on the subsequent (first) night. In the same way, a disastrous dress rehearsal is said to betoken a successful first night. It was the title of a song by Alan Melville and Ivor Novello in the musical *Gay's the Word* (1950). In 1954, V. C. Clinton-Baddeley published a book about the Georgian theatre, with the title *All Right on the Night* while Maurice Dolbier called his theatre reminiscences *All Wrong On the Night* (1966). London Weekend Television hi-jacked the full expression for a long-running series of TV 'blooper' programmes, beginning in 1977, though witlessly spelt it 'alright'.

it'll be all right with a bit of doing up Catchphrase from the BBC radio show *Band Waggon* (1938–39). Arthur Askey, as he cleared out his flat at the top of Broadcasting House, when asked, 'Shall we throw this out?', would reply: 'No, it'll be all right with a bit of doing up.'

it'll play in Peoria In about 1968, during Richard Nixon's presidential election campaign, John Ehrlichman is credited with having devised a yardstick for judging whether policies would appeal to voters in 'Middle America'. They had to be judged on whether they would 'play in Peoria'. Ehrlichman later told William Safire, 'Onomatopoeia was the only reason for Peoria, I suppose. And it . . . exemplified a place, far removed from the media centres of the coasts where the national verdict is cast.' Peoria is in Illinois and was earlier the hometown of one of Sergeant Bilko's men in the 1950s' TV series – so was picked on humorously even then.

it looks like something out of Quatermass This phrase alludes to *The Quatermass Experiment* (1953) – first in a series of BBC TV science-fiction drama series by Nigel Kneale involving a certain Professor Quatermass. In this one, viewers were held enthralled by the tale of a British astronaut who returned from a space trip and started turning into a plant. Eventually, he holed up in Poets' Corner at Westminster Abbey, by which time he was a mass of waving fronds. Although the phrase was not used in the programme, it gave rise to an expression still to be heard in the 1990s, and used to describe any peculiar – but especially rambling and leafy – specimen.

it must be hell in there (sometimes **it's hell in there** or **it was hell in there)!** Catchphrase from the BBC radio *Goon Show* (1951–60), usually referring to something like the inside of a person's socks or nightshirt or any place or situation that one is glad to have escaped from. Said on many occasions, principally by Major Bloodnok (Peter Sellers), as for example in 'The Mysterious Punch-up-the-Conker' (7 February 1957).

it must have been something he/she/I ate Reason advanced for a person's mood or behaviour, as though it could be accounted for only in terms of food that has an unsettling effect. Since the 1950s?

it never rains but it pours Meaning, 'misfortunes never come singly'. John Arbuthnot, the pamphleteer, entitled a piece thus in 1726 and since then the phrase has gained proverbial status. A famous US advertising slogan was **when it rains, it pours** – used from 1911 by Morton salt. The logo showed a girl sheltering the salt under her umbrella and capitalized on the fact that the Morton grade ran freely from salt cellars even when the atmosphere was damp. The film *Cocktail* (US 1989), about a barman, was promoted with the line: 'When he pours, he reigns.'

I took my harp to a party (but nobody asked me to play) Meaning, 'I went prepared to do something, but wasn't given the opportunity'. From a song by Desmond Carter and Noel Gay, popularized by Gracie Fields and Phyllis Robins (1933/4).

it pays to advertise Proverbial saying that almost certainly originated in the USA. Indeed, *Mencken* in 1942 lists it simply as an 'American proverb'. *Bartlett* quotes the anonymous (undated) rhyme: 'The codfish lays ten thousand eggs, / The homely hen lays one. / The codfish never cackles / To tell you what she's done. / And so we scorn the codfish, / While the humble hen we prize, / Which only goes to show you / That it pays to advertise.' It is possible to push back the dating of the phrase rather more positively. There was a play co-written by Walter Hackett (1876–1944) that had the phrase for a title in 1914, and this was turned into a film in 1931. Back even earlier, Cole Porter entitled one of his earliest songs 'It Pays to Advertise'. The song alludes to a number of advertising lines that were current when he was a student at Yale (*circa* 1912): 'I'd walk a mile for that schoolgirl complexion, / Palmolive soap will do it every time. / Oh cream, oh best cigar! / Maxwell Motor Car! / Do you have a baby vacuum in your home? / Gum is good for you, / Try our new shampoo, / Flit will always free your home of flies. / If you travel, travel, travel at all, / You know, it pays to advertise' – included in *The Complete Lyrics of Cole Porter*, ed. Robert Kimball (1983). This suggests that the phrase, though not Porter's own, was not too much of cliché by 1912. Ezra Pound wrote in a letter to his father in 1908 about the launch of his poems: 'Sound trumpet. Let rip the drum & swatt the big bassoon. It pays to advertise.' We are probably looking for an origin in the 1870s/90s when advertising really took off in America (as in Britain). Indeed, *Benham* (1960) lists an 'American saying

circa 1870' – 'The man who on his trade relies must either bust or advertise' – and notes that 'Sir Thomas Lipton [d. 1931] is said to have derived inspiration and success through seeing this couplet in New York about 1875.'

it's a bird See FASTER THAN.

it's a braw bricht moonlicht nicht See under HOOTS, MON.

it's absolutely vital both to the character and to the integrity of the script What actresses (and occasionally actors) invariably answer when asked whether there is any nudity in the play or film they are to appear in and whether there is any justification for taking their clothes off. BBC TV *Monty Python's Flying Circus* was already guying the answer on 7 February 1969: a policeman states: 'I would not appear in a frontal nude scene unless it was valid'; and a woman: 'Oh, no, no, no . . . unless it was artistically valid.' When I consulted the actress Glenda Jackson about it in 1983, she suggested that the remark was usually made in reply to a reporter's question, 'Is there any nudity in this film?' – 'Yes, but it is absolutely vital to the character and the part.' *The Naff Sex Guide* (1984) gave as one of the 'naff things starlets say': 'Yes, I would appear nude, as long as I trusted the director and the integrity of the script demanded it.' Other responses to the nudity question include, 'I don't mind if it's *relevant* to the script' or '. . . if it's done in a meaningful way'. Lord Delfont, the impresario, is quoted by Hunter Davies in *The Grades* (1981) as saying: 'I do allow four-letter words and nudity in my films, if they are in the right context, if it has integrity.'

it's a cracker! See IT'S THE WAY I TELL 'EM.

it's a fair cop Traditional British spoken phrase to a policeman when he arrests you. 'Cop' here means 'capture'. Known by 1886. '"It's a fair cop," said the thief' – *Daily News* (24 October 1891); 'It's a fair cop; you have got me all right and no mistake' – from the same paper (13 April 1898). Compare BANG TO RIGHTS.

it's a free country (or this is a . . .)! Argument advanced when trying to assert one's right to do what one likes. Probably since the 19th century and mostly British.

it's a funny game, football Phrase beloved of people associated with football, especially journalists and broadcasters thereon. Date of origin unknown. Listed as a cliché in *The Times* (28 May 1984). 'Funny old game football, as Greavsie might have said . . . even when it's TV's fantasy kind' – *Today* (30 August 1994); 'Almost as darkly comic as they are deeply sinister, Grobbelaar's wasted efforts show that football, to quote one of the game's hoariest clichés, really is a funny old game' – *Scotland on Sunday* (13 November 1994); 'All of which proved once again that football is indeed a funny game because it was Grobbelaar, perhaps inevitably, who did most to bring about the misfiring Gunners' second defeat in 15 games' – *The Irish Times* (21 November 1994).

it's a funny old world Expression reluctantly accepting some blow that fate has delivered. In the 1934 film *You're Telling Me*, W. C. Fields delivers the line, 'It's a funny old world – a man's lucky if he gets out of it alive.' About the same time, the British entertainers Murray and Mooney had a routine where Murray would recite a monologue 'It's a funny old world we live in, but the world's not entirely to blame' and Mooney would interrupt. In *The Independent* (23 November 1990), Margaret Thatcher was reported as having exclaimed 'It's a funny old world' (with tears in her eyes) at the previous day's Cabinet meeting at which she announced she had been ousted from the Prime Ministership. 'Well it's a funny old world. Think of Philby, Profumo, Stonehouse. Strange things do happen. Let's run the story: LOST PREMIER WAS RED SPY' – *The Guardian* (20 May 1985); 'It's a funny old world. Here you have, in his final months of office, that aged American butcher, Mr Ian MacGregor, quietly going about his lawful occasion at Hobart House' – *The Guardian* (7 May 1986).

it's a hard life! Jocular or ironic exclamation, often when the 'hardness' is actually trivial – as when repeatedly one has to

answer the door or the phone. Early 20th century, USA and UK.

it's all done in the best possible taste Catchphrase of the British comedy performer Kenny Everett (1944–95), when (with beard) playing a large-breasted Hollywood actress, 'Cupid Stunt', being 'interviewed' by a cardboard cut-out Michael Parkinson (chat-show host) in *The Kenny Everett Television Show* (after 1981). 'She' was explaining how she justified playing in some forthcoming film of less than award-winning potential (see IT'S ABSOLUTELY VITAL . . .). According to the co-scriptwriter Barry Cryer, 'she' was never intended to be Dolly Parton. He had heard these very words said in an interview with an American actress whose name he has since, fortunately, forgotten. In *Time* Magazine (20 July 1981), John Derek, director of *Tarzan the Ape Man*, did declare almost the same thing: 'The sacrifice scene was done in the finest of taste – taste the Pope would applaud.' Compare Jack Lemmon's line (recalling his days as a TV censor) in the film *Buddy, Buddy* (1981): 'I'm not against a little cleavage . . . if it's done in good taste.' As an illustration of how a good catchphrase is seized upon by the media, there were two separate stories on the same day in one newspaper making use of it: 'Pia [Zadora] . . . in the best possible taste'; 'Spicy Geraldine . . . in the best possible taste' – *Scottish Daily Express* (28 April 1982). Understandably, too, at this time, Wills Tobacco began to promote its Three Castles brand with the slogan 'In the best possible taste'.

it's all gone pear-shaped Out of control, chaotic – because it is a collapse from the perfect sphere. Known by the mid-20th century. Suggested sources for the phrase include the making of lead shot (where molten lead was dropped through a sieve and by the time it reached the bottom of the shot tower it had solidified into a spherical lead shot – or not, in which case it was pear-shaped) or on the potter's wheel, where collapsed clay has this appearance. Compare (and make anything of it, if you can) what W. C. Fields says to Mae West when he is locked out of the bridal suite in the film *My Little Chickadee*

(US 1940): 'Come, my phlox, my flower. I have some very definite pear-shaped ideas I'd like to discuss with thee.'

it's all happening! Rather a 1960s' phrase intended to suggest that life is very exciting, swinging, and what have you. A British film with the title came out in 1963 – it was about a talent scout for a record company and starred Tommy Steele. The title was changed to *The Dream Maker* in the USA. Also in *circa* 1965 there was a BBC TV show called *Gadzooks It's All Happening* (yes, really). In the same period, Norman Vaughan used the stock phrase **it's all been happening this week!** to introduce topical gags when he was compering TV's *Sunday Night at the London Palladium* (from 1962).

it's all in the mind, you know Catchphrase from the BBC radio *Goon Show* (1951–60). Convincing explanation of anything heard in the show – often said as a final word by Wallace Greenslade, the announcer, as in 'The White Neddie Trade' (3 February 1958).

it's all my aunt 'It's all a load of nonsense' – perhaps a combination of 'my aunt Fanny!' and 'my arse!' D. H. Lawrence uses 'it is all my aunt' in his poem 'Last Lesson of the Afternoon' (1928).

it's all part of life's rich pageant Reflective, philosophical phrase. Peter Sellers as Inspector Clouseau has just fallen into a fountain in *A Shot in the Dark* (US 1964) when Elke Sommer commiserates with him: 'You'll catch your death of pneumonia.' Playing it phlegmatically, Clouseau replies, 'It's all part of life's rich pageant.' The origin of this happy phrase – sometimes 'pattern' or 'tapestry' is substituted for 'pageant' – was the subject of an inquiry by Michael Watts of the *Sunday Express* in 1982. The earliest citation he came up with was a record called 'The Games Mistress', written and performed by Arthur Marshall (1910–89) in *circa* 1935. The monologue concludes, 'Never mind, dear – laugh it off, laugh it off. It's all part of life's rich pageant.' Consequently, Arthur called his autobiography, *Life's Rich Pageant* (1984). The alternative phrase, **life's rich tapestry**, appears in BBC radio's *Round the Horne* (16 May 1965). In 1831,

Thomas Carlyle talked earlier of 'the fair tapestry of human life'.

it's all part of the service! Response to an expression of gratitude from a customer. Spoken by a tradesman it suggests that thanks (or further payment) is not necessary as he has 'only been doing his job'. Elevated to a slogan by Austin Reed, the British menswear stores, in 1930, as: **it's just a part of the Austin Reed service**.

it's always August under your armpits See MAKES YOUR ARMPIT . . .

it's a monkey's wedding This is a 20th-century African catchphrase, 'applied to weather characterized by a drizzling rain accompanied by a shining sun' – *Partridge/Catch Phrases*. Known by 1968, it is a direct equivalent of the Zulu *umshado wezinkawu* [wedding for monkeys]. Compare a saying, for the same eventuality, **the devil is beating his wife**. *Apperson* dates from 1666 the proverbial expression 'When it rains and the sun shines at the same time the devil is beating his wife.' Or, '. . . is beating his grandmother . . . he is laughing and she is crying.' And compare 'A fox's wedding and a monkey's dance' – used when it starts to rain but the sun continues to shine, and first heard in a military boarding school at Sanawar, India, by Grace Constable (in the mid-20th century). *Partridge/Slang* also has 'monkey's wedding' as a naval term for an unpleasant smell. Given that foxes are also noted for their smell, could there be something to do with the smell of sun on damp ground going on here? There have been other attempts to describe this phenomenon and in several languages. But quite what the implication of the phrase is remains a bit of a mystery.

it's an old —— custom See OLD SPANISH CUSTOMS.

it's a-one for the money, a-two for the show (three to get ready, now go, cat, go)! The start to the Carl Perkins song 'Blue Suede Shoes' (immortalized by Elvis Presley in 1956) is based on the form of words that children traditionally use to begin races. A version used in Britain and dating from 1888 is 'One for the money, two for the show, three to make ready, and four to go.' Another version, from 1853, is 'One to make ready, and two to prepare; good luck to the rider, and away goes the mare.'

it's a pile of pants   Meaning, 'it stinks' or 'is a load of rubbish', where 'pants' = 'underpants'. In other words, this is the male equivalent of 'knickers' as a term of contempt or exasperation, perhaps vaguely alluding to the similar 'a heap of shit', 'a pile of poo'. Compare also the expression 'to bore the pants off'. It is said that the precise phrase first became popular in the early 1990s, particularly through use by the BBC Radio 1 DJ Simon Mayo. However, Karen Shepherd wrote to say (2001) that when she was at primary school in Glasgow thirty years before, boys *and* girls used the word 'pants' to express dislike or disgust in order to avoid being told off for using bad language. Angela Popham said a friend of hers bought some underwear for her teenage daughter, who took one look at the shopping and declared, 'These bras are pants!' The British TV fund-raising Red Nose Day had the slogan 'Say Pants to Poverty' in March 2001.

it's a wrap   'That's it, we've finished for the day'. From film/TV slang, after the expression 'to wrap it up' = to put an end to something, presumably because wrapping up is the last thing you do when a goods purchase has been completed. Noted by 1974. From Alan Bennett's published diary of filming for TV plays, 'The Writer in Disguise' (entry for 15 March 1978): 'We finish at 11.30 with the customary call, "Right, that's a wrap." The judge could have said the same. "Manslaughter. Seven years. And that's a wrap".'

it says here . . .   Inserted phrase that distances the reader of a document from the contents thereof. Arthur Mullard, the British actor who specialized in 'thicko' parts, would add 'It sez 'ere' after reading with apparent difficulty some definition on TV's *Celebrity Squares* (1976–80).

it's being so cheerful as keeps me going Catchphrase from the BBC radio show *ITMA* (1939–49). Said by Mona Lott (Joan Harben), the gloomy laundrywoman. When told to keep her pecker up by the show's star, Tommy Handley, she would

reply, 'I always do, sir, it's being so cheerful as keeps me going.' Her family was always running into bad luck, so she had plenty upon which to exercise her particular form of fortitude. Something like the phrase had earlier appeared in a *Punch* cartoon by L. Craven Hill (27 September 1916): 'Wot a life! No rest, no beer, no nuffin. It's only us keeping so cheerful as pulls us through.'

it's b'ootiful, really b'ootiful!   Slogan. From *The Sunday Times* (21 December 1980): 'No surer test of fame exists than the school playground . . . Small boys narrow their eyes, flatten their voices to a Norfolk burr like Bernard Matthews's and repeat what Matthews says of his Golden Norfolk turkey, "It's b'ootiful. Really b'ootiful."' It is an axiom of the advertising world that, when in doubt, one should allow the client to appear in the ads for his product. Matthews endured for more than fifteen years, promoting his products – turkey roll, sausages, frankfurters, and so on – in his own distinctive way.

it's dark (or black) over Bill's (or Will's) mother's way . . .   Popular comment on the weather when rain threatens. Paul Beale in his revision of *Partridge/Catch Phrases* mentions the expression 'it's a bit black over Bill's mother's' and gives an East Midlands source. H. S. Middleton, Shropshire, formerly of Leicestershire, and whose brother was called Bill, wrote in 1993 to say how, in the early 1920s, a certain Len Moss had looked through the sitting room window in the direction of Mr Middleton's home and said, 'It looks black over Bill's mother's.' Was this the origin of the phrase? In 1930, the erudite journal *Notes and Queries* carried a query about it in the form 'it looks pretty black over Will's Mother's'. It was described as an 'old Sussex' saying. And there was no response. Barry Day of New York, NY, recalled that 'It's a bit black over Bill's mother's' used to be said a great deal by *his* mother when he was growing up in Derbyshire (1940s). 'It was always said ironically,' he added. 'So I can confirm its Midlands usage.' I first heard about it on a London radio phone-in (June 1990) in the form, 'It looks like rain . . . over Will's mother's way.' In *Verbatim* (Autumn 1993),

Alan Major discussed a number of 'Kentish sayings' and included, 'Out Will's mother's way', meaning 'somewhere else, in the distance, on the horizon'. Major added: 'Who Will's mother was is unknown, but there are several similar expressions, with word variations, used in other English counties. In Gloucestershire, the expression is "It's dark over our Bill's Mum's mind".' The Reverend P. W. Gallup, Hampshire, wrote in 1994 that he had traced the saying in eleven counties and commented on its age: 'I have friends in their late eighties who as children knew it well from their parents and say that it was then widely known and used. This suggests that the saying has been used at least by several generations.' Since 1993, I have received a goodly number of claims from correspondents that they were personally acquainted with the original Bill and his mother.

it seemed like a good idea at the time Limp excuse for something that has gone awry. *Partridge/Catch Phrases* has this as dating back to the 1950s. But the filmographer Leslie Halliwell found it in a 1931 film called *The Last Flight*. In this story of a group of American airmen who remain in Europe after the First World War, one of them is gored to death when he leaps into the arena during a bullfight. Journalists outside the hospital ask his friend why the man should have done such a thing. The friend (played by Richard Barthelmess) replies: 'Because it seemed like a good idea at the time.' 'The best, indeed, that you could really say of the great gesture . . . was that, like so many rash acts, it had seemed like a good idea at the time' – P. G. Wodehouse, *Heavy Weather*, Chap. 11 (1933). *Vin*: 'Like a fellow I once knew in El Paso. One day he just took all his clothes off and jumped into a mess of cactus. I asked him the same question, *Why?' Calvera*: 'And?' *Vin*: 'He said it seemed to be a good idea at the time' – exchange from film *The Magnificent Seven* (US 1960). *It Seemed Like a Good Idea At the Time* – title of the autobiography (1999) of the British television executive, Michael Grade.

it sends me! The 1950s' way for young people to describe the effect of popular music on their souls. But earlier, in a letter to *The Times* (18 December 1945), Evelyn Waugh was writing: 'He [Picasso] can only be treated as crooners are treated by their devotees. In the United States the adolescents, speaking of music, do not ask: "What do you think of So-and-so?" They say: "Does So-and-so *send* you?"' Indeed, *OED2* finds this use in the early 1930s.

it's fingerlickin' good! Slogan for Kentucky Fried Chicken, current by 1958. Several songs/instrumental numbers with the title 'Fingerlickin' Good' appear to have been inspired by this advertising use. In addition, Lonnie Smith had a record album called 'Fingerlickin' Good Soul Organ' in 1968. In 1966, 'Finger Lickin'', on its own, was the title of a (guitar) instrumental by Barbara Clark. But was the word 'fingerlickin'' an established Southern USA/possibly black/musicians' phrase before being made famous by the slogan? 'Licking good', on its own, was a phrase current by the 1890s.

it's for yoo-hoo! Slogan for British Telecom (*circa* 1985). From the familiar phrase of someone answering the phone and finding it is for another, 'It's for you'. But it was pronounced in a distinctive way, and this no doubt led to its catching on. According to *The Guardian* (24 October 1985), detectives seeking a man on assault charges – a man who was known to be a keen Chelsea supporter – put an 'urgent message for Graham Montagu' sign on the electronic scoreboard at Stamford Bridge football ground. Thousands of fans spontaneously sang out, 'Montagu, it's for yoo-hoo!', the man fell for the ruse, and he was arrested.

it's goodnight from me . . . and it's goodnight from him! A cliché of TV presentation was gently sent up when it became the basis for this exchange at the end of the BBC TV comedy series *The Two Ronnies* (1971–88). Ronnie Corbett would feed Ronnie Barker with, 'It's goodnight from me . . .' And Ronnie B. would sabotage this with, 'And it's goodnight from him.'

it's got to get worse before it gets better Pessimistic platitude. Date of origin unknown. Given as an example of a cliché in the *Collins English Dictionary*

(1979). 'Encouraging the kind of dynamic economy in which lots of jobs are created will mean hacking away at policies that have long operated in favour of rigid work rules, high social costs, subsidies and protectionism; and that may mean things getting worse for the poor before they can get better' – *The Economist* (30 July 1994); 'Divisional Commander Mike Currie appealed yesterday for more help in ensnaring the criminals and condemned those who were withholding information. "The situation could get worse before it gets better," he said' – *Daily Mail* (31 March 1995).

it's just a trick of the light Stock phrase of Kenneth Horne on the BBC radio show *Round the Horne* (1965–9) as an amusing way of explaining away almost anything. For example, he used it twice in the edition of 28 March 1965.

it's later than you think Proverb that once used to be found in various forms on sundials, designed to create a sense of urgency in the beholder. A catchphrase since its use in a Robert W. Service poem from *Ballads of a Bohemian* (1923): 'Ah! the clock is always slow; It is later than you think.'

it's life, Jim, but not as we know it Catchphrase associated with the TV series *Star Trek* (US 1966–9) and the subsequent feature films, and thought to have been said by Scotty, the engineer, to Captain James T. Kirk. But patient searching by Trekkies has failed to uncover the line or anything like it in any of these places. Indeed, the phrase entered the language only around 1990 (its first appearance on a UK newspapers' database) whereas BEAM ME UP, SCOTTY and TO BOLDLY GO have long been with us, almost since the TV series was first aired. A 1995 poster advertisement in London stated 'It's direct insurance, but not as we know it, Jim'. A headline from *The Independent* (19 April 1996): 'It's the weekend, Jim, but not as we know it.' So why the delay in the phrase catching on? In fact, it is not from *Star Trek* itself but from 'Star Trekkin', a No. 1 hit record for the UK group The Firm in June 1987. The record consists of a bouncy tune to which impersonators of the main *Star Trek* characters intone five

phrases that sound reasonably like what you might hear in the actual films. Mr Spock's line is this one. That explains why the phrase has only latterly caught on and why these invented *Star Trek* phrases may not be known in the USA. But, not for the first time, one wonders how wise it is for advertisers and journalists to allude to a source as obscure as this that may not be known to the majority they are trying to communicate with.

it's me noives! Catchphrase from the BBC radio show *ITMA* (1939–49). Spoken by the gangster, Lefty (Jack Train), a friend of Sam Scram. An unexpected complaint for a gangster to have.

it's more than my job's worth Defining the word 'jobsworth', Tony Thorne in his *Dictionary of Contemporary Slang* (1990) has: 'An obstinate petty official, especially a doorman, bouncer or car park attendant from their turning down of reasonable requests on the grounds that *"It's more than my job's worth"*. The term was popularized in the rock-music press of the early 1970s when it referred to the officials . . . who prevented music fans from expressing their enthusiasm or meeting their idols.' From 1975, the BBC TV programme *That's Life* featured a Jobsworth Award, a gold peaked cap awarded to the worst example of such behaviour submitted by viewers. A song, written by Jeremy Taylor in 1973, went: 'Jobsworth, jobsworth / It's more than me jobsworth; / I don't mind, rain or snow, / Whatever you want, the answer's no; / I can keep you standing / For hours in a queue, / And if you don't like it, / You know what you can do!' So this, presumably, was the coining moment.

it's not cricket 'It is not fair, proper, the done thing.' An expression suggesting that certain conduct or behaviour is not worthy of an Englishman and a gentleman. It was known in the game of cricket itself by 1851, and by 1900 in other contexts. A *Punch* headline on 15 January 1902: 'AS IT WERE NOT QUITE CRICKET'. In *First Childhood* (1934), Lord Berners comments that it 'came into vogue in the 'nineties' and gives the example: '"I mean to say," he protested. "To kick your wife! And in public too! It's not cricket, is it?"'

it's not fancy, but it's good! Slogan for Horn & Hardart, the American restaurant chain, dispensing meals through vending machines. Current by the 1960s.

it's not for me, it's for my daughter
What people almost invariably say when asking famous people for an autograph. From *The Guardian*'s obituary of Arthur Marshall (28 January 1989): 'One of his favourite stories was about how, on coming out of the BBC TV centre, he was once accosted and asked for an autograph. The woman making the request explained that she wanted it for her daughter . . .'

it's not over till it's over (sometimes **the game isn't over . . .)** A warning comparable to the OPERA AIN'T OVER TILL THE FAT LADY SINGS and of American origin also. Possibly originating with 'Yogi' Berra, the American baseball player and coach (1925–), who may have said, 'The game isn't over till it's over', though reportedly *Sports Illustrated* investigated the matter and found that Berra's actual comment was 'You're not out of it till you're out of it.' 'It ain't over till it's over' is spoken in the film *Moonstruck* (US 1987); '[Tammy Faye Bakker] then added "It isn't over until it's over", confirming that her husband intends to appeal against the decision' – *The Independent* (6 October 1989); 'Brigadier General Richard Neal, the US spokesman in Riyadh, warned "let there be no mistake the [Gulf] war is over. Parts of the Iraqi army are still in Kuwait City" . . . He added: "It's not over until it's over"' – *The Independent* (27 February 1991).

it's not rocket science Meaning, 'it is a simple matter that does not take great intelligence to understand it.' Sometimes **it's not brain surgery** – where no great skill is required. Based on the (somewhat debatable) view that rocket scientists require formidable powers of mind to do what they do – a view that may have gained ground as a result of the achievements of the US space programme in the 1960s/70s. An exchange from the film *Roxanne* (US 1987): *Chris (of Roxanne)*: 'Why am I afraid of her? She's not a rocket scientist.' *Charlie*: 'Actually, she is a rocket scientist.' '"The military is saying that during the day we need more [firefighting services], and during the night we need

less. It is not rocket science," [Tony Blair] said' – *The Independent* (30 November 2002); 'It's not rocket science: free access to museums works' – headline in *The Independent* (1 January 2003).

it's not the cough that carries you off (it's the coffin they carry you off in)
Iona and Peter Opie include this in *The Lore and Language of Schoolchildren* (1959) as a type of ghoulish catchphrase enjoyed by ten-year-olds. But where does it come from? When I heard Billy Cotton's recording of Alan Breeze singing 'It Ain't the Cough' (written by 'Mann', about 1956), I made the assumption that this was based on an earlier song but that it might lead us to the true original. In time, I obtained the music of a comic song called 'The Cough-Drop Shop' written by Leslie Sarony in 1932. It ends: 'When you get to the cough-drop shop, / Remember when you're coughing, / It's not the cough that carries you off, / It's the coffin they carry you off in!' A correspondent, meanwhile, very definitely recalls hearing the last line in 1927, so perhaps both songs are borrowing from something even earlier.

it's not the heat, it's the humidity
Catchphrase explanation of the reason why hot weather is oppressive. An expression certainly current in the Second World War but of earlier and most probably American origin. One of S. J. Perelman's prose pieces had the punning title 'It's Not the Heat, It's the Cupidity'. What was the allusion there? Presumably the same as contained in the title of a revue put on by the British Combined Services Entertainment in the Far East (*circa* 1947) and featuring the young actor Kenneth Williams. It was called 'It's Not So Much the Heat, It's the Humidity', though in his memoirs he simply calls it *Not So Much the Heat*. The case for supporting an American origin is this: in the first paragraph of P. G. Wodehouse's novel *Sam the Sudden* (1925), he describes the inhabitants of New York on a late August afternoon: '[One half] crawling about and asking those they met if this was hot enough for them, the other maintaining that what they minded was not so much the heat as the humidity.' American use of the phrase is further confirmed by Thomas Tryon's novel *The Other* which,

though not published until 1971, is set in the New England of the mid-1930s. Several times it has characters saying, 'It ain't the heat, it's the humidity,' in circumstances suggesting that it was a conversational cliché of the time and place. In addition, Leonard Miall, who was the BBC's first peacetime correspondent in Washington DC after the Second World War, recalls the expression commonly being used in complaints about the climate of the US capital and adds that around 1953, when McCarthyism was at its height, the saying was changed to, 'It's not so much the heat, it's the humiliation.' To Yogi Berra, the professional baseball player and manager (1925–) has been ascribed the typically nonsensical remark, 'It ain't the heat, it's the humility.' The clincher is that in his booklet *Are You a Bromide?* (1907), the American author Gelett Burgess lists 'it isn't so much the heat (or the cold), as the humidity in the air' as the sort of thing a 'bromide' (someone addicted to clichés and platitudes) would say.

it's nothing   What the wounded say, invariably, to the question, '(Are) you hurt?' in plays, films, etc. Observed by Fritz Spiegl in an article on drama cliché lines in *The Listener* (7 February 1985).

it's nourishment I want, not punishment 'Said by a Lancastrian woman in her eighties, when asked why she had not remarried' – according to the historian Michael Wood on BBC Radio *Quote . . . Unquote* (13 July 1985). A letter dated 20 October 1969 from the actor Kenneth Williams, commiserating on the death of a friend's mother, contains this: 'Mine is still going strong, and leaves on the 25th for a cruise in the Med. I told her to be careful. "Keep your hand on your ha'penny dear" I said, "they're all after a bit out there" and she retorted "Don't worry yourself, I want nourishment, not punishment" so I think she knows what she's doing. Certainly at 69 she ought to . . .' – published in *The Kenneth Williams Letters* (1994).

it's only rock'n'roll   Meaning, 'It doesn't matter; the importance should not be exaggerated; it's only a bit of fun'. The title of a Mick Jagger/Keith Richard composition of 1974 has entered the language to a certain extent. In a 1983 *Sunday Express*

interview, Tim Rice was quoted as saying, "It would be nice if [the musical *Blondel*] is a success but I won't be upset if it isn't. It is only rock'n'roll after all and it doesn't really matter a hoot.'

it's page one   'It's elementary, fundamental, what you start from'. Noted in broadcasters' use by 1986. In the film *Wilt* (UK 1989), a police inspector says 'Page one! Page one!', with the same meaning.

it's showtime, folks!   Exclamation used by people in the entertainment business – sometimes to remind themselves that now is the time to get out there on the stage and shine; sometimes a touch sarcastically. Also used in other fields where an element of performance or presentational glitter is required. Just before attempting to blow up a town in *Blazing Saddles* (US 1974), the character played by Cleavon Little says, 'Hold your ears, folks. It's showtime!' In the film *All That Jazz* (US 1979), Roy Scheider playing a choreographer ritually says the line before getting on with whatever has to be done in his life.

it's Siiimon Dee!   See under HERE'S JOHNNY!

it's snowing in Paris   Meaning, that a girl's petticoat is showing below her skirt. Iona and Peter Opie include this in *The Lore and Language of Schoolchildren* (1959) as a 'juvenile corrective', along with **SOS (Slip On Show)** and **is your name Seymour?** To which one might add another, **it's snowing down South**. Compare CHARLIE'S DEAD.

it's so ——   Format phrase through which to condemn something as out of date or out of fashion – 'that is so Joan Collins/ Margaret Thatcher/1980s'. This somewhat camp use of 'so' was especially marked in British speech around the turn of the millennium. The gay, Irish comedian even entitled his Channel 4 TV show *So Graham Norton* (1998–2002). 'Glossy hair, healthy skin, toned bodies – it's all so last century, darling!' – Barbara Ellen in *The Observer* Magazine (3 December 2000).

it's so bracing (or Skegness is so bracing)!   Slogan promoting Skegness, the seaside resort in Lincolnshire, along with the Great Northern Railway company (GNR) in advertisements current from

1909. The company joined the London & North Eastern (LNER) in 1923. The slogan is inseparable from the accompanying portrait of a jolly fisherman drawn by John Hassall (1868–1948). Actually, Hassall did not visit Skegness until twenty-eight years after he drew the poster. His first visit there was when he was made a freeman of the town.

it's still early days Meaning, 'it's too soon to tell what is going to happen'. Now British use only. In 1534, the phrase 'early days' was used in this way by Sir Thomas More.

it's that man again! Late 1930s' catch-phrase, often used in newspaper headlines and referring to Adolf Hitler, who was always bursting into the news with some territorial claim or other. Winston Churchill was to speak often of Hitler as 'that man'. It is appropriate that *ITMA*, the BBC radio programme incorporating more catchphrases per square minute than any other, before or since, should have had as its title an acronym based on a catchphrase. *ITMA* was first broadcast in July 1939 and ran until January 1949, when its star, Tommy Handley, died. What did the show consist of? There would be a knock on the famous *ITMA* door, a charac-ter would engage in a little banter with Tommy Handley, the catchphrase would be delivered (usually receiving a gigantic ovation), and then the next one would be wheeled in. Given this format, it is not easy now to appreciate why the show was so popular. But the laughter undoubtedly took people's minds off the war, and the programmes brought together the whole country, fostering a family feeling and a sense of sharing that in turn encouraged the spread of catchphrases. The writing is not to everyone's taste nowadays (it relied heavily on feeble rather than atrocious puns) but Handley's brisk, cheerful personality was the magic ingredient that held the proceedings together. Characters came and went over the years, the cast fluctuated, and catchphrases changed.

it's the best See READY AYE READY.

it's the business Meaning, 'it's the real thing, the genuine article, not a fake' or 'the very best, the acme of excellence.'

Current in the UK by 1990. 'The business' is also used in phrases referring to a dressing down, a beating up, defecation or a sexual act. Also **to do the business** was an early 1980s' phrase, in Britain at least. This was teenage slang for anything that was particularly good. Paul Beale's *Concise Slang* gives an example: '"They did the business" was about the highest praise you could get from fellow hooligans for a really spectacular display of violence, such as that by the Millwall [football] "fans" at Luton, Spring 1985.' Compare from *A Wonder Book for Girls and Boys* (1892) by Nathaniel Hawthorne – in a re-telling of his labours, Hercules says of the cleansing of the Augean stables: 'It would have taken me all my life to perform it, if I had not luckily thought of turning the channel of a river through the stable-door. That did the business in a very short time!' Clearly, this use of the phrase is more in the way of 'that did the trick', but it is an interest-ing example of a phrase that appears to have been ignored by most dictionary makers – whichever meaning it carries. Thirdly, a use of the phrase where the meaning is apparently in transition be-tween the two already mentioned. From a boxing preview in the *Sunday Express* (25 November 1984): 'I [Tony Sibson] can't even contemplate it [defeat]. I have great respect for Kaylor but, on the night, I'm going out there to do the business.'

it's the economy, stupid! Slogan/motto of the Bill Clinton campaign team in the US presidential election of 1992 – meaning simply that the economy was the issue of most importance to the electorate. It was coined by James Carville, who orchestrated the campaign, and was displayed on a sign in the staff's office to keep them on message.

it's the poor wot gets the blame Catch-phrase that has achieved near proverbial status from the song 'She Was Poor But She Was Honest', hugely popular with British soldiers in the First World War: 'She was poor but she was honest / Victim of a rich man's game. / First he loved her, then he left her, / And she lost her maiden name . . . / It's the same the whole world over, / It's the poor wot gets the blame, / It's the rich wot gets the gravy. / Ain't it all a bleedin' shame?' It is not known who wrote the song.

it's the story of my life (or that's . . .)
Exclamation when relating a piece of personal misfortune – usually fairly minor, like losing a parking space. Meaning, 'This sort of thing is always happening to me.' By the second half of the 20th century.

(ah well) it's the thought that counts
Conventional response when a gift or gesture is considered to be of little value or inappropriate. By the 1960s?

it's the way I tell 'em! Almost any comedian could say this of a joke that has just gone down well (and no doubt most of them would agree with the observation), but Frank Carson, the Ulster comedian (b. 1926), managed to make the catchphrase his own (from the mid-1970s.) In full, the line is perhaps: 'You've heard them all before, but . . . it's the way I tell 'em.' Another of his fillers has been **it's a cracker!** (pronounced 'crocker').

it's turned out nice again! Catchphrase of the British North Country entertainer George Formby (1904–61). He disclaimed any credit for originating the phrase with which he always opened his act. 'It's simply a familiar Lancashire expression,' he once said. 'People use it naturally up there. I used it as part of a gag and have been doing so ever since' – particularly in his films when emerging from some disaster or other. It was used as the title of one of these films in 1941 (as well as being the punch line of it) and as the title of a song. Formby was not exactly a comedian but he exuded personality and, singing slightly naughty songs to a ukelele accompaniment, he became one of the great stars of the variety stage between the wars. He also appeared in a highly successful series of films. In these, there was another catchphrase: **ooh, mother!** – said when scuttling away from trouble.

it's twelve o'clock in London, one o'clock in Cologne – at home and away it's time for Two-Way Family Favourites (or words to that effect) A potent memory of Sunday mornings in the 1950s and early 1960s: the smell of roast and gravy wafting out of the kitchen, and from the radio, these words (or similar), fol-

lowed by the sweeping strings of the signature tune – the André Kostelanetz version of Rodgers and Hart's 'With a Song in My Heart' . . . The BBC radio programme took various forms and had various presenters between its first broadcast on 7 October 1945 and its closing in 1984. The title change to *Two-Way Family Favourites* was in 1960 (giving rise to a slang expression for a type of sexual intercourse). The show's original purpose was to act as a link between home and the British occupying troops in Germany.

it's what it's not that makes it what it is The all-purpose slogan, joked about by advertising creative personnel and quoted to me by one such, Keith Ravenscroft (1981). However, in 1997 the Guernsey Tourist Board was actually using it in advertisements in the form: 'Guernsey. It's what it isn't that makes it what it is.'

it's what your right arm's for Slogan for Courage Tavern (ale), current in the UK by 1972. Although this line became a popular catchphrase, it risks being applied to rival products. Possibly of earlier origin.

it's worse than a crime, it's a blunder!
From a remark uttered in connection with the execution of the Duc d'Enghien in 1804. Napoleon, suspecting the duke of being involved in royalist conspiracies against him, had the Duc captured and executed – an act that hardened opinion against the French Emperor. But who said it? Comte Boulay de la Meurthe (1761–1840) has been credited with the remark, but among other names sometimes linked to it are Talleyrand, Joseph Fouché and Napoleon himself. In French, the remark is usually rendered as: '*C'est pire qu'un crime; c'est une faute!*'

it takes two to tango Modern proverbial expression that appears to derive solely from the song 'Takes Two to Tango' (1952), written by Al Hoffman and Dick Manning and popularized by Pearl Bailey. President Ronald Reagan cited it when commenting (11 November 1982) on the future of Soviet-American relations following the death of Leonid Brezhnev. Possibly based on the earlier proverb, 'It takes two to quarrel' (known by the early 18th century). *Slanguage* glosses it as a: 'Euphemistic expression implying that in any sexual indiscretion both partners take a share of the blame.'

it was a dark and stormy night ... As a scene-setting, opening phrase, this appears to have been irresistible to more than one storyteller over the years and has now become a joke. At some time unknown, this phrase became part of a children's 'circular' storytelling game, 'The tale without an end'. Iona and Peter Opie in *The Lore and Language of Schoolchildren* (1959) describe the workings thus: 'The tale usually begins: "It was a dark and stormy night, and the Captain said to the Bo'sun, 'Bo'sun, tell us a story,' so the Bo'sun began . . ." Or it may be: "It was a dark and stormy night, the rain came down in torrents, there were brigands on the mountains, and thieves, and the chief said unto Antonio: 'Antonio, tell us a story.' And Antonio, in fear and dread of the mighty chief, began his story: 'It was a dark and stormy night, the rain came down in torrents, there were brigands on the mountains, and thieves . . .'" And such is any child's readiness to hear a good story that the tale may be told three times round before the listeners appreciate that they are being diddled.' The Opies note that each of these variations was also current in the USA, 'except that in the first tale American children say: "It was a dark and stormy night, some Indians were sitting around the camp fire when their chief rose and said . . ."' The phrase had been used in all seriousness by the English novelist Edward Bulwer-Lytton at the start of *Paul Clifford* (1830): 'It was a dark and stormy night, the rain falling in torrents – except at occasional intervals, when it was checked by a violent gust of wind which swept up the streets and then (for it is in London that our scene lies), rattling along the housetops, and fiercely agitating the scanty flames of the lamps that struggled against the darkness.' In the 1960s, it became the title of one of Charles M. Schultz's books in which the line is given to the character Snoopy in his doomed attempts to write the Great American Novel. Consequently, the dog is acclaimed as author of the world's greatest one-line novel. Paradoxically, Schultz's own book *It Was a Dark and Stormy Night* was a bestseller. The culmination of all this has been

the Annual Bulwer-Lytton Fiction Contest, founded by Dr Scott Rice, a professor of English literature at San Jose State University, California. Contestants are asked to compose truly atrocious opening sentences to hypothetical bad novels. Rice was quoted in *Time* (21 February 1983) as saying, 'We want the kind of writing that makes readers say, "Don't go on."' Some of the entries have now been published in book form – with the authors given every inducement not to keep on writing . . .

it was going to be a long night Catchphrase that becomes a cliché when used by would-be creative writers. Date of origin not known. In the film *North by Northwest* (US 1959), Eve Marie Saint seducing Cary Grant says, 'It's going to be a long night . . . and I don't particularly like the book I started' – which may indicate how the phrase came to be coined. 'He was doing the crossword from *The Washington Star*. He had finished three clues; it was going to be a long night' – Jeffrey Archer, *Shall We Tell the President* (1977); 'Paul told his mother how he managed to clamber on to a raft and crouched wet and shivering until he saw the lights of a helicopter overhead. As Paul waited to be rescued – he later told his mother – he sighed: "It's going to be a long night"' – *Daily Mirror* (29 September 1994).

it was like an Aladdin's cave (in there)! What – according to the press – ordinary members of the (British) public invariably say when they stumble upon any treasure trove or collection of rare and valuable objects (especially if they have been missing or been recovered after a robbery). 'Aladdin's cave' as a phrase signifying a place of vast stores of wealth was already established by 1922. Alluding to the story of 'Aladdin and the Wonderful Lamp' in *Tales from the Arabian Nights*, in which the hero has a palace built for him by the 'genie in the lamp'. Curiously, however, there is no mention of a cave in the original story. 'With the vivid sunlight streaming in upon thousands of rainbow-coloured glass drops . . . it seemed as unreal as Alladin's [*sic*] Cave' – Rudyard Kipling, in *Civil and Military Gazette* (1884); 'Down in London's Soho is . . . an Aladdin's cave of cotton jerseys, silks, velvets and unusual cloths' – *Good House-keeping* (May 1986); 'There has, after all, been a tantalising, semi-official figure quoted by the Russo-German Commission which sits on this problem of 134,000 paintings and works of art – a fabled Aladdin's cave allegedly kept since 1945 at Zagorsk' – *The Daily Telegraph* (8 April 1995); 'The planning consent envisages the restoration of a working grist-mill. Inside the mill house is an Aladdin's cave of dogs and implements but the only remnants of the mill-wheel outside are a few rusted paddles' – *The Daily Telegraph* (29 April 1995); 'The National Lottery was to have been an Aladdin's cave overflowing with treasures for all' – leading article in *The Independent* (2 May 1995); 'Sybarite's is a veritable Aladdin's Cave of possible gifts!' – advertisement in *Kensington & Chelsea Times* (7 July 1995).

it was worse than the Blitz/World War Two all over again What – according to the press – ordinary members of the (British) public invariably say when involved in bomb incidents, train crashes, etc. 'Mr David Steele . . . in a Volkswagen van which was behind the Mini carrying Mr Waldorf [was asked about the number of police officers he saw]: "I saw one, then two, then it was World War Two all over again"' – *The Daily Telegraph* (14 October 1983); 'Another dewy-eyed heroine hits the screen in an all-guns-blazing wartime weepie. But this one bombs worse than the blitz over Dresden' – *Today* (28 October 1988); 'Palestinian gunmen wilfully killed several of Mann's horses. Twenty-two more died in an Israeli air raid during the 1982 invasion, which Sunnie Mann always described as being worse than the blitz' – *The Times* (1 December 1992); 'What they say: "It's worse than the blitz" – police officer at blast scene' – *Evening Standard* (London) (26 April 1993).

it went from failure to classic without ever passing through success Mostly arts, showbiz use. For example, George Axelrod, writer of the film *The Manchurian Candidate*, said it to *Time* Magazine (21 March 1988). The film was a flop when first launched in 1962, languished in a vault for twenty-five years and then became something of a cult. Compare

Gore Vidal, *Palimpsest* (1995): 'The Best Man [film] went from commercial failure to "classic" without an intervening success.'

it will all be the same in a hundred years (or years' time) Consolatory or dismissive catchphrase – meaning, 'why worry?', 'who will care in time?' As 'it will all be one in a hundred/thousand years', the saying was recorded in various versions between 1611 and 1839. Swift's *Polite Conversation* (1738) has: 'My Comfort is, it will be all one a thousand Years hence.' Ralph Waldo Emerson, *Representative Men*, 'Montaigne; or The Skeptic' (1850) has: 'Keep cool: it will be all one a hundred years hence.' Bill Wilkes told Paul Beale (1994) that his mother, originally from Norfolk, used the expression **by that time you'll all be dead and your arse cold** in the same sense. Compare Samuel Johnson's excellent advice for putting a distressful situation in perspective: 'Consider, Sir, how insignificant this will appear a twelvemonth hence' – Boswell's *Life of Johnson* (1791) – for 6 July 1763.

I've arrived – and to prove it – I'm here! Catchphrase of Max Bygraves in the BBC radio show *Educating Archie* (1950–60). During his period as Archie's tutor, Bygraves made a splash with this catchphrase (which formed part of his bill matter when he appeared at the London Palladium in 1952). There are recollections of the phrase having been used in the 1930s, so perhaps he just popularized it. Also: **a good idea . . . son!** (also incorporated in a song). Bygraves commented (1980): 'None of them were planned. They just came up in the reading. When Archie read a line, it was so stilted, I would ape him. This happened a couple of times and people sensed I was reading the line rather than saying it. They're still saying it today, a lot of people.'

I've been sponned! Catchphrase from the BBC radio *Goon Show* (1951–60). Although this phrase does not actually occur in the episode called 'The Spon Plague' broadcast in March 1958, variations on it occurred in the episode entitled 'Spon' (30 September 1957). Peter Sellers used the exact phrase as the tag line for his recording of 'Any Old Iron' (released August 1957). One clearly remembers running around saying it at school. The symptoms of sponning included bare knees – of which we had quite a few in those days. Later, in 'Tales of Men's Shirts' (December 1959), Sellers's 'Mate' character gets clobbered and says, 'Ow! I've been sponned from the film of the same name' and proceeds to write his memoirs, 'How I was sponned in action.'

I've died and gone to heaven!   I'm in ecstasy, in a state of bliss (but also used ironically in situations where the opposite is the case). Possibly of Afro-American origin and in vogue by the 1980s. 'I feel like we've died and gone to heaven – only we had to climb up' – Neil Simon, screenplay for *Barefoot In the Park* (US 1967); 'In the 1,000 acres of Prince Charles's died-and-gone-to-heaven organic Gloucestershire idyll . . .' – *The Observer* (2 February 2003).

I've failed!   In a Sherlock Holmes sketch (of the 1940s/50s), the Scots comedian Dave Willis would come on stage with a huge magnifying glass. Peering through it, he would go up to an imaginary flower and, without bending his knees, would balance and hover over it, examining it through the glass, getting closer and closer until he fell over. 'I've failed!' he would wail in a wee voice. In a song about wartime air-raids he sang: 'Then all run helter-skelter / But don't run after me, / You'll no' get in my shelter / For it's far too wee!' Hence, he would declare of others, '**You're far too wee!**' From the same source came, 'An aeroplane, an aeroplane, away, way up 'a 'ky' – hence, '**Way up 'a 'ky**' (English: 'Way up in the sky').

I've given you the best years of my life!   What one half of a fictional couple is apt to say when it is splitting up or having a row with the other half. In the film *Monkey Business* (US 1931), Groucho Marx says to a woman: 'Oh, so that's it. Infatuated with a pretty uniform! We don't count, after we've given you the best years of our lives. You have to have an officer.' From J. B. Priestley, *When We Are Married*, Act 2 (1938): 'And after giving you the best years of our life – without a word o' thanks.' The exact line is spoken in the film *Mr and Mrs Smith* (US 1941). Compare *The Best Years of Our Lives* under HAPPIEST DAYS OF YOUR LIFE.

I've got a letter from a bloke in Bootle   This was one of a number of expressions used by the great British comedian Jimmy James (1892–1965). Others he employed on stage, radio and TV were: **excuse me, is this the place, are you the bloke?**; **somebody come** (said by James in his 'drunk' bedroom sketch – though he himself was a teetotaller); **give me a note please . . . er-fa-a-fa-a fah . . . fah . . . fah** (trying to get the note at the start of a song, when drunk); and **how do you do?** – said with a slight nod. One of his team – the splendidly named Hutton Conyers – would say to James: **hey, are you putting it around that I'm barmy?**

I've got a million of 'em!   See under GOODNIGHT, MRS CALABASH . . .

I've got his pecker in my pocket   Meaning 'he is under obligation to me', this was one of President Lyndon B. Johnson's earthy phrases from his time as Senate Majority leader in Washington. 'Pecker' means 'penis' in North America (rather less so in Britain) – though this should not inhibit people from using the old British expression **keep your pecker up**, where the word has been derived from 'peck', meaning appetite. In other words, this second phrase is merely a way of wishing someone good health, though *OED2* has 'pecker' meaning 'courage, resolution' in 1855. Queen Victoria uses it in a letter (2 May 1859): 'As Papa says (the policeman says it to Hawkesley in "Still Waters Run Deep" [play by Tom Taylor 1855]) "Keep up your pecker; that's right" meaning keep up your spirits and don't be downhearted.'

I've got the time if you've got the inclination   Chat-up line – also used in response to an expletive like 'fuck me!' or 'bugger me!' American origin, since the 1950s?

I've heard geese fart before in windy weather   Response to an extravagant or boastful utterance. Date of origin unknown. Also known as 'I've heard ducks fart before'.

I've never believed in anything so much in all my life   Something of a cliché of film scriptwriting, though perhaps not too painful as clichés go. An example occurs in Noël Coward's play *Design for Living* (1932) in the form: 'I've never been so serious in my life'. There is a 'believed' version in the film *Dangerous Moonlight* (UK 1941). Compare what Mickey Rooney says to Judy Garland in *Strike Up the Band* (US 1940): 'Mary, I was never more sure of anything in my life'; and what Fred Astaire says to Rita Hayworth in *You'll Never Get Rich* (US 1941): 'I was never so sure of anything in my life.' But it is an old format. In Henry Fielding's *Tom Jones* (1749) there is: 'D—n me if ever I was more in earnest in my life'. In Boswell, *Life of Johnson* (1791) – for 11 June 1784 – a Dr Adams says, 'I never was more serious about any thing in my life.' In Conan Doyle's 'The Priory School' (1905): 'I was never more earnest in my life'; and in his 'The Cardboard Box' (1917): 'I was never more serious in my life.'

I've only got four minutes . . . Stock phrase of the Australian actor/comedian Bill Kerr at the start of a broadcasting spot. Chiefly remembered now as one of the supporting characters in *Hancock's Half-hour,* he began his career in Britain doing stand-up routines on BBC radio's *Variety Bandbox* (from 1948). **I don't want to worry you . . .** (concerning the imminent collapse of the theatre) was another part of his assumed depressive act.

I've started so I'll finish! In BBC TV's *Mastermind* quiz (1972–97), the chairman, Magnus Magnusson, would say this if one of his questions was interrupted when the time ran out. It became a figure of speech – sometimes also given a double meaning. From the same programme came **Pass!** The word was used by participants in the quiz when they did not know the answer to a question and wished to move on to the next, so as not to waste valuable time. It is not the most obvious of things to say. 'Next question' or 'I dunno' would spring more readily to mind, but so deep has this phrase penetrated the public consciousness that when I was chairing a TV quiz called *Challenge of the South* in 1987/8, I found that contestants automatically reached for 'Pass'. Noted *The Times* (8 November 1977): 'For proof of how . . . *Mastermind* is catching on, I would refer

you to this story sent in by a reader from London NW6. He was accosted by a small lad, asking for a penny for the guy. On being asked if he knew who Guy Fawkes was, the lad replied with engaging honesty, "Pass."' In 1981, London Transport advertisements showed an empty studio chair, of the type used in the programme, with the query, 'How can you save money on bus fares?' The answer was, 'Correct. The London Bus pass.'

(to live in an) ivory tower Meaning, 'to live in intellectual seclusion and protected from the harsh realities of life'. The expression comes from Sainte-Beuve writing in 1837 about the turret room in which the Comte de Vigny, the French poet, dramatist and novelist, worked. He described it as his *tour d'ivoire*, possibly after the Song of Solomon 7:4: 'Thy neck is as a tower of ivory; thine eyes like fishpools . . .'

(the) Ivy League Nickname given to the old north-eastern university colleges in the USA – Harvard, Yale, Princeton and Columbia. Nothing to do with ivy-covered walls but rather with the interscholastic 'Four League', which was always written with Roman numerals as the 'IV League' and pronounced 'I-V League'. 'Ivy' came to be the accepted version in the 1930s and the official 'Ivy League' was formed after the Second World War.

I wanna tell you a story! Launched on a sea of catchphrases in *Educating Archie*, Max Bygraves (b. 1922) later became associated with a phrase wished upon him by an impersonator. It is possible that he may have said of his own accord, 'I wanna tell you a story' (with the appropriate hand gestures – as if shaking water off them), but it was Mike Yarwood who capitalized on it in his impersonation. Bygraves then used the phrase himself in self-parody and chose it as the title of his autobiography (1976). Still, as he says, he once went into a competition for Max Bygraves impressionists – and came fifth. Of having successful catchphrases in general, Bygraves told me (1980): 'It's like having a hit record!'

I want me tea! *The Grove Family* was the first British TV soap opera – or something approaching one – and ran for three years from 1953. It told of a suburban family that included a wonderfully irritable Gran (Nancy Roberts) who used to make this demand. There are still families that consciously repeat her phrase (I belong to one). She used to go on, **I'm faint from lack of nourishment!** In *It's a Great Day!* (UK 1956), a cinema feature, she gets to say rather, 'Where's me cocoa? I'm faint from lack of nourishment.'

I want to be alone   Greta Garbo (1905–90) claimed that what she said was 'I want to be *let* alone' – i.e. she wanted privacy rather than solitude. Oddly, as Alexander Walker observes in *Sex in the Movies* (1968): 'Nowhere in anything she said, either in the lengthy interviews she gave in her Hollywood days when she was perfectly approachable, or in the state-ments on-the-run from the publicity-shy fugitive she later became, has it been possible to find the famous phrase, "I want to be alone". What one can find, in abundance, later on, is "Why don't you let me alone?" and even "I want to be left alone", but neither is redolent of any more exotic order of being than a harassed celebrity. Yet the world prefers to believe the mythical and much more mysterious catchphrase utterance.' What complicates the issue is that Garbo herself *did* use the line several times on the screen. For example, in the 1929 silent film *The Single Standard* she gives the brush-off to a stranger, and the subtitle declares: 'I am walking alone because I want to be alone.' And, as the ageing ballerina who loses her nerve and flees back to her suite in *Grand Hotel* (US 1932), she actually *speaks* it. Walker calls this 'an excellent example of art borrowing its effects from a myth that was reality for millions of people'. The phrase was obviously well established by 1935 when Groucho Marx uttered it in *A Night at the Opera*. Garbo herself says, 'Go to bed, little father. We want to be alone' in *Ninotchka* (US 1939). So it is not surprising that the myth took such a firm hold and particularly since Garbo became a virtual recluse for the second half of her life.

I want to make it perfectly clear
Politicians' cliché. Often said when doing quite the opposite. Much used by William Whitelaw, British Conservative politician – especially when Home Secretary in the early 1980s. '[Of ghosting *Reader's Digest* articles by famous people and assuming their verbal characteristics] When I was Richard Nixon, I began every second sentence with "Let me make one thing perfectly clear"' – Willard R. Espy, *An Almanac of Words at Play* (1975); 'Is it too much to ask the Conservative government here to make it perfectly clear that we do consider Mussolini to be a notorious mass murderer and we hold with contempt all those in Italy who consider him some sort of hero?' – *The Independent* (5 May 1994); 'I want to make it perfectly clear that he was under no pressure from the Argyle board to resign due to the club's poor start' – *Today* (14 September 1994); 'Mr Hamilton said last night: "I entirely refute the allegations and the writ will make that perfectly clear." When asked if there was any grain of truth in the Guardian report Mr Hamilton said: "My writ I think is eloquent testimony to the view that I have as to their veracity. Nobody issues a writ to launch a libel action for fun"' – *The Times* (21 October 1994); 'I want to make it perfectly clear that Lough Derg Yacht Club didn't cancel the regatta, it was cancelled by the ISA' – *The Irish Times* (31 March 1995).

I was amazed!   See under NAY, NAY – THRICE AGAIN NAY!

I was a seven-stone weakling   See YOU, TOO, CAN HAVE A BODY LIKE MINE.

I wasn't born yesterday   Meaning, 'I'm not as innocent as you take me for'. An established saying by 1757. Modern use must have been encouraged by the Garson Kanin play *Born Yesterday* (1946; film US 1951), an excellent vehicle for Judy Holliday, about an ignorant girl who wins out in the end.

I was only obeying orders!   Much parodied self-excusal from responsibility for one's actions. The Charter of the Interna-tional Military Tribunal at Nuremberg (1945–6) specifically excluded the tradi-tional German defence of 'superior orders'. But the plea was, nevertheless, much advanced. As early as 1940, Rex Harrison said in the UK film *Night Train to Munich*: 'Captain Marsen was only obeying orders.' Kenneth Mars as a mad, Nazi-fixated playwright in *The Producers* (US 1967) said, 'I only followed orders!' Not that everyone seemed aware of the parodying. From *The New York Times* (6 July 1983): 'Herbert Bechtold, a German-born officer in the [US] counter-intelligence who became [the "handler" of Klaus Barbie, the Nazi war criminal] was asked if he questioned the morality of hiring a man like Barbie by the United States. "I am not in a position to pass judgement on that," Mr Bechtold replied, "I was just following orders".'

I went to New Zealand but it was closed
A joke remark that gets rediscovered every so often. The Beatles found it in the 1960s; slightly before, Anna Russell, the musical comedienne, said it on one of her records. It has also been attributed to Clement Freud. But William Franklyn, son of the Antipodean actor, Leo Franklyn, tells me that his father was saying it in the 1920s. W. C. Fields probably began saying 'I went to Philadelphia and found that it was closed' about the same time (if indeed he did).

I wonder if they are by any chance related? It is an obsession with some to make assumptions about people being related to one another on the basis that they look similar or have names in common. For many years from the 1970s, *Private Eye* ran a feature in which people would write in, under a pseudonym, drawing attention to facial similarities – almost always ending up with the line, 'I wonder if they are by any chance related?' (e.g. Lyndon Johnson/Mrs Golda Meir; Alfred Brendel/Roy Hudd). The US magazine *Spy* has run a similar feature headed **separated at birth?**

I won't take me coat off – I'm not stopping Catchphrase of Ken Platt (1921–98), the nasal-voiced, somewhat lugubrious British North Country comedian, who was handed it on a plate by Ronnie Taylor, producer of BBC radio's *Variety Fanfare* in January 1951. Platt said (1979): 'I told him rather grudgingly that I thought it was "as good as anything" . . . and I've been stuck with it ever since. People are disappointed if I don't say it.' Also in the show he would comment **hasn't it been a funny day, today?**

I would like to spend more time with my (wife and) family A cliché of political resignations. '[The Duke of Omnium, after deciding to give up the prime ministership, is asked what he will do:] I am a private gentleman who will now be able to devote more of his time to his wife and children than has hitherto been possible with him' – Anthony Trollope, *The Prime Minster*, 'The New Ministry' (1876). *Woodward (to Deep Throat)*: 'John Mitchell resigns as the head of C.R.E.E.P. and says that he wants to spend more time with his family. Sounds like bullshit. We don't exactly believe that' – film *All the President's Men* (US 1976). In March 1990, two of Prime Minister Thatcher's ministers – Norman Fowler and Peter Walker – withdrew from the Cabinet, both giving as their reason for going that they wished to 'spend more time with their families'. Fowler, in his resignation letter, wrote: 'I have a young family and for the next few years I should like to devote more time to them while they are still so young.' Prime Minister Thatcher replied: 'I am naturally very sorry to see you go, but understand your reasons for doing this, particularly your wish to be able to spend more time with your family.' Subsequently, Gordon Brown, the Labour MP, suggested in the House of Commons that Nicholas Ridley might care to follow suit. But the Secretary of State for Industry was having none of it. 'The last thing I want to do,' he said, 'is spend more time with my family' – quoted in *The Independent* (14 July 1990).

I wouldn't kick her out of bed! Male's remark about an attractive woman, since the 1920s? US and UK.

I wouldn't like to meet him in the dark (or on a dark night or up a dark alley or similar) Said of any formidably hefty or ugly man. 'I know few men I would not rather meet in a lonely road than Comrade Repetto. He is one of Nature's sandbaggers. Probably the thing crept upon him slowly. He started, possibly, in a merely tentative way by slugging one of the family circle' – P. G. Wodehouse, *Psmith Journalist*, Chap. 17 (1915); 'For such a game as this, Sam has all his best hustlers . . . The best you will figure them is a lot of guys who are not to be met up with in a dark alley' – Damon Runyon, *More Than Somewhat*, 'Hold 'em, Yale!' (1937); 'Gosh! I'd hate to meet that bird down a lonely alley on a dark night' – P. G. Wodehouse, *Full Moon*, Chap. 9 (1947).

I wouldn't piss on him if he was on fire Expression of extreme dislike, said to be of Australian origin, 1970s. Compare what Rodney Bickerstaffe, the British trade union leader, said at the Labour Party Conference in Blackpool (1992): 'John Major, Norman Lamont – I wouldn't spit in their mouths if their teeth were on fire.' The figure of speech was undoubtedly not original. 'I wasn't going to say "spit" but Willis [TUC General Secretary] made me change it.' He later said it was based on a Scottish insult he had learned in his youth: 'I wouldn't piss down his throat if his chest was on fire.' The same idea can be seen in such pronouncements as this from Carrie Fisher in *Vanity Fair* (August 1990): '[Acting means] ingratiating yourself to people you wouldn't fucking spit on if they were on fire.' In the film *Matewan* (US 1987), David Strathairn as a Sheriff says, 'I wouldn't pee on him if his heart was on fire . . .'

I wouldn't trust him as far as I could throw him 'I wouldn't trust him very far at all.' British use mostly, by the 1870s.

I would walk over my grandmother (to achieve something) When Richard Nixon sought re-election as US president in 1972, he surrounded himself with an unsavoury crew including Charles W. Colson, a special counsel and White House hatchet man. This phrase was a view attributed to Colson rather than anything he ever actually said himself, but he subsequently muddied the water by appearing to endorse the sentiment. An article in *The Wall Street Journal* in 1971 had portrayed Colson as someone who, in the words of another Washington official, would be prepared to walk over his grandmother if he had to. In 1972, when Nixon sought re-election as US President, Colson misguidedly sent a memo to campaign staff that stated: 'I am totally unconcerned about anything other than

getting the job done . . . Just so you understand me, let me point out that the statement . . . "I would walk over my grandmother if necessary" is absolutely accurate.' This was leaked to *The Washington Post*. Subsequently convicted for offences connected with Watergate and then emerging as a born-again Christian, Colson tried unavailingly to point out that he had never really said it. In his book, *Born Again* (1977), he wrote: 'My mother failed to see the humour in the whole affair, convinced that I was disparaging the memory of my father's mother . . . Even though both of my grandmothers had been dead for more than twenty-five years (I was very fond of both).' Such are the penalties for tangling with figures of speech. In an earlier age – the 1880s – the editor of the *Pall Mall Gazette*, W. T. Stead, famous for his exposé of the child prostitution racket, said: 'I would not take libel proceedings if it were stated that I had killed my grandmother and eaten her.' Another even earlier image often invoked was of 'selling one's own grandmother'. In the film *The Philadelphia Story* (US 1940), a character exclaims: 'I'd sell my grandmother for a drink.'

I yam what I yam (and that's all that I yam) Personal philosophy of Popeye, the one-eyed, pipe-smoking, spinach-eating sailor who originally appeared in strip cartoons but is best known through many short animated films made for cinema and TV. Created by Elzie Crisler Sefar, Popeye first appeared in a syndicated strip entitled 'Thimble Theatre' in the 1930s. His slender, shrewish girlfriend was called Olive Oyl.

izzy-wizzy, let's get busy! Catchphrase of Harry Corbett's little bear puppet Sooty, who first appeared on British TV screens in 1952 and has been there ever since, latterly with Harry's son Matthew with his hand up the back. This was the magic spell for conjuring tricks. The programmes invariably ended with Sooty squirting water at, or throwing a custard pie in, Harry's face ('Ooh, 'e's a scamp, 'e is really!'). Harry would then intone the famous farewell in his flat Lancashire vowels, **bye-bye, everyone, bye-bye!**

J

j'accuse **[I accuse]** Campaigning slogan. The Dreyfus Affair in France arose in 1894 when Captain Alfred Dreyfus, who was Jewish, was dismissed from the army on trumped-up charges of treason. Condemned to life imprisonment on Devil's Island, he was not reinstated until 1906. In the meantime, the case had divided France. The writer Émile Zola (1840–1902) came to the defence of Dreyfus with two open letters addressed to the President of the French Republic and printed in the paper *L'Aurore*. In these letters, Zola accused the French military and civil authorities of lying. The first, under the banner headline '*J'Accuse!*', was published on 13 January 1898, each concluding paragraph beginning with the words. For example: 'I accuse Lieutenant Colonel du Paty de Clam of having been the diabolic agent of the judicial error . . . and of having for three years bolstered his dastardly deed with the strangest, most culpable machinations . . . I accuse the three expert graphologists – Messrs. Belhomme, Varinard and Couard – of having prepared fraudulent and deceitful analyses, unless a medical examination should prove them to be afflicted with impaired vision and judgement . . .' The second letter, more moderate in tone, followed on 22 January. As he anticipated, Zola was convicted of libel on the basis of the letters and fled to England. It is a small point, perhaps, but Georges Clemenceau, the future Prime Minister, who played a prominent part in the campaign with Zola, claimed in a letter (19 June 1902) that: 'It was I who gave the title "*J'accuse*" to Zola's letter.' He also said that he had written most of the second letter – source: D. R. Watson, *Clemenceau* (1974.) Uses of the phrase: in 1919, Abel Gance made a film for Charles Pathé with the title *J'Accuse*, but it was not about the Dreyfus Affair. In it, the dead returned en masse from the First World War to accuse the survivors. Another version of the film was made before the outbreak of the Second World War. *I Accuse* became the title of a British film (1958), which was about the case, with José Ferrer as Dreyfus and Emlyn Williams as Zola. In time, an 'I accuse' became a term of limited use given to any kind of crusading writing, especially in a newspaper. Frank Brady wrote in *Citizen Welles*, Chap. 12 (1989) about a statement ascribed to Orson Welles in a magazine called *Friday* that 'Citizen Kane' was based on William Randolph Hearst: 'After giving an outline of what the film was really about, in his opinion, Welles finished up his j'accuse against *Friday* with an interpretation and an attempt at self-protection.' Graham Greene entitled his short book on organized crime in the South of France *J'Accuse: the dark side of Nice* (1982).

Jack See BROTHER OF THE MORE.

(a) jack in office Meaning 'a self-important petty official', this term was known by 1700. Sir Edwin Landseer entitled a painting 'A Jack in Office' (1833), which showed a terrier guarding the barrow of a cat-and-dog-meat salesman while four mangy, obsequious dogs eyed the barrow.

Jack the Lad Name given to a (possibly harmless) ruffian – 'a bit of a lad' – and latterly to a promiscuous young man. Such a venerable-sounding phrase may, however, be of comparatively recent origin – first becoming apparent in the 1970s. 'I was always Jack the Lad – the one everyone liked but nobody wanted to know' – *New Society* (4 June 1981). The phrase is said to have originated in Liverpool working-class argot, referring to an outstanding individual in a group.

Jack was free See WITH ONE BOUND.

(a) Jacob's join Name for a gathering where everyone brings along an item of food or drink. In 1997, Donald H. Stock, having pursued the matter in and around Lytham, Lancashire, without success, asked about this expression. *Partridge/Slang* states that it was gathered from a Lancashire source also and defines it as, 'What is sometimes called a "faith supper" in church circles, i.e. the eating equivalent of a bottle party, each participant making a contribution to the communal meal.' What the connection is with the biblical Jacob, if any, is not clear. Mr Stock later noted that he had heard of the phrase **American pie** being applied to the same sort of gathering.

jam See ALL.

James See HOME.

jam-jar See GET BACK.

jam tomorrow, and never jam today An allusion to Lewis Carroll's *Through the Looking Glass* (1871). The White Queen wants Alice to be her maid and offers her twopence a week and jam every other day, except that she can never actually have any – it's never jam today. I.e. an early version of CATCH-22. The Queen explains: 'The rule is, jam to-morrow and jam yesterday – but never jam *to-day*.' Quite often the phrase is used in connection with the unfulfilled promises of politicians. Could Carroll have adopted an older phrase? Others recall being taught that this was an academic joke. In Latin there are two words meaning 'now': *nunc* and *iam*. The former is used in the present tense, whereas the latter is the correct word for past and future tenses, i.e. yesterday and tomorrow.

JAP (Jewish American Princess) Nickname for a type of upwardly mobile woman who wants to be rich and well married, and believes that there is a formula for achieving this. She is notable, therefore, for wearing the right clothes, for her lacquered hair and carefully tended fingernails, and for her jewellery. Perhaps she would once have liked to emulate that (non-Jewish) princess Jackie Kennedy Onassis – indeed, she does not have to be Jewish or even American. The type occurs in most societies. Identified by 1985, at least. There is a male equivalent but he lacks a nickname.

jazz See AND ALL THAT.

(the) Jazz Age Another sobriquet for the ROARING TWENTIES. This one comes from the title *Tales of the Jazz Age* (1922) by F. Scott Fitzgerald.

(a) Jekyll and Hyde Term for a person displaying two completely different characters, one respectable, the other not. Rather more than 'two-faced'. After the eponymous character in R. L. Stevenson's *The Strange Case of Dr Jekyll and Mr Hyde* (1886) who, by means of a drug, can switch between the good and evil in his own nature. Consequently, a 'Jekyll and Hyde ——' is something that is a mixture of contrasting elements or switches between two such elements. G. K. Chesterton wrote in 1927: 'Jekyll and Hyde have become a proverb and a joke; only it is a proverb read backwards and a joke that nobody sees.'

Jennifer! Catchphrase from the BBC radio show *Ray's a Laugh* (1949–60). This appears to have grown out of an exchange between Ted Ray and a little girl (played by Bob Pearson). Ray would ask what her name was and she would lisp the reply in a special way – 'Jen-nif-er'. In the mid-1950s.

Jerusalem See ALL JAM.

jesting Pilate Phrase from a notable saying in Francis Bacon's essay 'Of Truth' (1625): '*What is Truth?* said jesting Pilate, and would not stay for an answer.' The allusion is to Pilate's question to Jesus Christ, as reported in John 18:38. 'Jesting' is Bacon's additional comment. Hence *Jesting Pilate*, title of a travel book (1926) by Aldous Huxley.

Jesus wept! John 11:35 is the shortest verse in the Bible (the shortest sentence would be 'Amen.'). It occurs in the story of the raising of Lazarus. Jesus is moved by the plight of Mary and Martha, the sisters of Lazarus, who break down and weep when Lazarus is sick. When Jesus sees the dying man he, too, weeps. Like it or not, the phrase has become an expletive to express exasperation. The most notable uttering was by Richard Dimbleby, the British TV commentator, on 27 May 1965. In a broadcast in which everything went wrong during a Royal visit to West Germany, Dimbleby let slip this oath when he thought his words were not being broadcast. A graffito of the 1970s, from the London advertising agency that lost the Schweppes account, was: 'Jesus wepped'.

(a/the) jewel in the crown Meaning, 'a bright feature, an outstanding part of something.' In the space of a single day – 2 March 1988 – one could read in *The Guardian*, 'Poor David Steel. He's bound for Southport on Saturday for a regional conference in what ought to be one of the precious few jewels in the Liberals' dented crown'; in *Harpers & Queen*, 'Annecy is considered to be the jewel in the Savoyard crown'; and in Michael Powell's book *A Life in Movies* (published two years before), 'Sir Thomas Beecham, Bart., conducting the "Ballet of the Red Shoes" would be the final jewel in our crown.' One had to conclude that the 1984 television adaptation of Paul Scott's 'Raj Quartet' of novels had everything to do with the popularity of this phrase. The first of Scott's novels (published in 1966) was called *The Jewel in the Crown* and gave its name to the TV series. 'The Jewel in *Her* Crown' is the title of a 'semi-historical, semi-allegorical' picture referred to early on in the book. It showed Queen Victoria, 'surrounded by representative figures of her Indian Empire: Princes, landowners, merchants, money-lenders, sepoys, farmers, servants, children, mothers, and remarkably clean and tidy beggars . . . An Indian prince, attended by native servants, was approaching the throne bearing a velvet cushion on which he offered a large and sparkling gem'. (In fact, Victoria, like Disraeli, who is also portrayed, never set foot in India.) Children at the school where the picture was displayed had to be told that, 'the gem was simply representative of tribute, and that the jewel of the title was India herself'. The picture must have been painted *after* 1877, the year in which Victoria became Empress of India. One imagines it was an actual picture, no doubt much reproduced, but it has not been found. The *OED2* refers only to the 'jewels of the crown', as a rhetorical phrase for the colonies of the British Empire and has a citation from 1901. The specifying of India as *the* jewel is understandable. The Kohinoor, a very large oval diamond of 108.8 carats, from India, has been part of the British crown jewels since 1849. Many writers have used the phrase in other contexts. In *Dombey and Son*, Chap. 39 (1844–6), Charles Dickens writes: 'Clemency is the brightest jewel in the crown of a Briton's head.' Earlier, in *The*

Pickwick Papers, Chap. 24 (1836–7), he has (of Magna Carta): 'One of the brightest jewels in the British crown.' In the poem 'O Went Thou in the cauld blast', Robert Burns has: 'The brightest jewel in my crown / Wad be my queen.' And then again, Laurence Olivier was quoted in *The Scotsman* (19 July 1957) as saying: 'I have always had the greatest admiration for the work of the BBC . . . By far its most valuable jewel in its crown is the Third Programme, and that is going to be cut up, we are told.'

Jim   See IT'S LIFE.

Jim Crow must go   I.e., racial segregation must be abolished. An early 1960s US chant, with 'clap, clap' between the second and third words. The phrase 'Jim Crow' became common in the 1880s but goes back to the 1730s when blacks were first called 'crows'. By 1835, 'Jim Crow' or 'Jim Crowism' meant segregation.

Jimmy who?   The question was posed when Jimmy Carter (b. 1924) came from nowhere to challenge Gerald Ford, successfully, for the US presidency in 1976. It had almost the force of a slogan. Carter's official slogan, used as the title of a campaign book and song, was **why not the best?** This came from an interview Carter had had with Admiral Hyman Rickover when applying to join the nuclear submarine programme in 1948: 'Did you do your best [at Naval Academy]?' Rickover asked him. 'No, sir, I didn't *always* do my best,' replied Carter. Rickover stared at him for a moment and then asked: 'Why not?'

jingo   See BY JINGO.

job   See DON'T GIVE UP.

(a) Job's comforter   One who seeks to give you comfort but who, by blaming you for what has happened, makes things worse. It comes from the rebukes Job receives from his friends, to whom he says: 'Miserable comforters are ye all' – Job 16:2.

jockstrap   See MOUTH LIKE.

Joe Bob says check it out   Stock phrase of 'Joe Bob Briggs', pseudonymous 'drive-in movie' critic of the *Dallas Times Herald*

1982–5. Written by John Bloom, the reviews represented the views of a self-declared redneck. They frequently caused offence, not least because they tended to rate movies according to the number of 'garbonzas' (breasts) on display. Joe Bob had a battery of stock phrases (not all original to him, by any means), including **no way, José**; **if you know what I mean, and I think you do**; and the inevitable closing comment: 'Joe Bob says check it out'. The column was eventually dropped when Briggs poked fun at efforts to raise money for starving Africans. The columns were published in book form as *Joe Bob Goes to the Drive-In* (1989).

John Bull   See under BULLDOG BREED.

Johnstown   See DON'T SPIT.

John Toy   See LOOK LIKE YOU.

John Willie, come on!   Catchphrase of the British comedian George Formby Snr (1877–1921) who included in his act monologues from a typical Lancashire character called 'John Willie'. The phrase 'John Willie, come on' swept the country. Audiences waited for the line and knew just when it was coming – so they could join in.

joined at the hip   (Of persons) inseparably joined, very closely associated. From the condition of some Siamese twins. A coinage of the late 1980s, apparently. 'Minnick v. Mississippi: Attorney and client joined at the hip' – title of article by Irah Donner in *Case Western Reserve Law Review*, Vol. 41 (1991); *Lewis*: 'You didn't tell me you were going to London.' *Morse*: 'We're not joined at the hip, Lewis' – episode 'Who Killed Harry Field?' in UK TV *Inspector Morse* (13 March 1991).

join the Army (or Navy) and see the world   The Army version of this slogan seems to have been used in both Britain and the USA in the 1920s and 30s. In the song 'Join the Navy' from the musical *Hit the Deck* (1927), there appears the line 'Join the Navy and see the world'. In the film *Duck Soup* (US 1933), Harpo Marx holds up a placard that says, 'Join the Army and See the Navy'. Irving Berlin's song 'We Saw the Sea' from *Follow the Fleet* (US 1936) goes, 'I joined the Navy to

see the world. And what did I see? I saw the sea.' 'I joined the Navy to see the world' is quoted, ironically, by a sailor in the film *In Which We Serve* (UK 1942). *Partridge/Slang* dates the riposte '. . . the next one' as *circa* 1948.

joints   See ALL JOINTS.

joke over (or joke's over)!   Either said by the teller of a joke that has misfired or by the person to whom it has been told. By the 1920s.

jolly good show!   A very English phrase of approbation, recorded by 1934. Terry-Thomas, the gap-toothed comedian (1911–90), used it, as also **oh, good show!** in his late 1940s' and early 1950s' monologues.

jolly hockey sticks!   See MY NAME'S MONICA.

(a) jot and tittle   Meaning 'the least item or detail', these words come from Matthew 5:18: 'Till heaven and earth pass, one jot or one tittle shall in no wise pass from the law, till all be fulfilled.' 'Jot' is *iota*, the smallest Greek letter (compare 'not one iota') and 'tittle' is the dot over the letter *i* (Latin *titulus*).

(a) journey into the unknown   Journalistic cliché. Date of origin not clear, but *Journey To the Unknown* was the title of a TV suspense series (US, produced in England, 1968–9). 'To the strains of "We are Sailing", the ropes were slipped and *Canberra* was off into the unknown' – J. Hands & R. McGowan, *Don't Cry for Me, Sergeant-Major* (1983).

journey's end   The title of R. C. Sherriff's play (1929), set in the trenches of the First World War, might seem to nod towards Shakespeare – 'Journeys end in lovers meeting' – *Twelfth Night*, II.iii.44 (1600) or 'Here is my journey's end' – *Othello*, V.ii.268 (1604) – or towards Dryden's 'Palamon and Arcite': 'The world's an inn, and death the journey's end'. But it is impossible to be certain. In his autobiography, *No Leading Lady* (1968), Sherriff writes of the titles he rejected, like 'Suspense' and 'Waiting', and then adds: 'One night I was reading a book in bed. I got to a chapter that closed with the words: "It was late in the evening when we came at last to our Journey's End". The last two words sprang out as the ones I was looking for. Next night I typed them on a front page for the play, and the thing was done.' He does not say what the book was. It has also been reported that Sherriff once explained that, in need of a title, he saw an advertisement for a whisky that proclaimed, 'Have a dram at your journey's end . . .'

Jove See BY JOVE.

(the) joy of — Cliché format, mostly of book-titling. First on the scene were I. S. Rombauer and M. R. Becker, American cookery experts, with *The Joy of Cooking* (1931). A US film was entitled *Joy of Living* in 1938. Then, in 1972, along came Alex Comfort with *The Joy of Sex* and even *More Joy of Sex*. Then everyone joined in, so that we have had books about the 'joys' of computers, chickens, cheesecake, breast-feeding and geraniums, among many others. In 1984, I published *The Joy of Clichés* – which I thought would be seen to be ironical – though neither Gyles Brandreth seems to have had any compunction in naming a book *The Joy of Lex* (1980) nor Fritz Spiegl, *The Joy of Words* (1986).

joys and sorrows See PARTNER OF ONE'S.

Judas Priest Euphemism for the oath 'Jesus Christ!' Of American origin and recorded by 1914. Judas Priest was taken as the name of a UK pop group of the 1980s.

Judy! . . . Judy! . . . Judy! Impersonators always put this line in the mouth of Cary Grant, but the actor always denied that he had ever said it and had a check made of all his films (in which, presumably, if he was referring to Judy Garland in character, he wouldn't have been calling her by her actual name, anyway). According to Richard Keyes, *Nice Guys Finish Seventh* (1992), Grant once said: 'I vaguely recall that at a party someone introduced Judy by saying, "Judy, Judy, Judy," and it caught on, attributed to me.' There may be another explanation. Impersonators usually seek a key phrase that, through simple repetition, readily gives them the subject's voice. It is possible that one of these impersonators found that saying 'Judy' helped summon up Grant's distinctive tones, and it went on from there. Besides, many an impersonator, rather than ape his

subject, simply impersonates fellow impersonators. Did Bette Davies ever say, similarly, 'Peter . . . Peter . . . Peter!'?

jump See GO.

jumping Jehoshaphat! Mild expletive taking a curious name from the Old Testament and adding an alliterative adjective. Compare 'Holy jumping Jupiter'. It's been around since the mid-19th century and may euphemistically be trying to avoid using the name 'Jesus'. A lot of expletives do try to soften the blow. There's more than one Jehoshaphat in the Old Testament, but in 1 Chronicles 16, he is one of the priests who blows a trumpet before the ark of God. (Not to be confused with Joshua and the battle of Jericho.) W. C. Fields may have used this expression or 'great Jehoshaphat!' as a way to avoid censorship in the early days of film.

jungle fresh A gloriously meaningless advertising line used to promote Golden Wonder salted peanuts in the UK, current late 1970s.

jungle See BACK TO THE; DON'T FORCE IT.

Jungle Jim Nickname for any he-man type of person, derived from a 1930s' American comic-strip character, somewhat derivative, in turn, of Tarzan. In 1948 there began a series of *Jungle Jim* films featuring Johnny Weissmuller (who had previously played Tarzan) in the main role.

(the) jury is (still) out on — A mostly journalistic cliché, noticeable from the late 1980s, meaning that no final conclusion can be drawn, minds are not yet made up. 'The royal family now face an unenviable task in adapting themselves to the challenges of the twenty-first century. The jury is out and it is by no means certain that the verdict will be favourable to the monarchy' – Andrew Morton, *Diana: Her True Story* (1993); 'We no longer give fealty to any institution (or person) simply because of their lineage. Nowadays we rightly want to know whether they perform or not. And on that test, as far as the monarchy is concerned, the jury is out' – Stephen Haseler in the *Daily Mail* (22 May 1993); 'The jury was really out about whether I wanted the marriage to survive' – Hillary Clinton, *Living History* (2003).

(a) just and lasting settlement Cliché of politics. As *Safire* notes, President Eisenhower spoke in Geneva (1955) of 'a just and durable peace' and later said, 'We will make constantly brighter the lamp that will one day guide us to our goal – a just and lasting peace'. The 'settlement' version became boringly popular with regard to the Palestinian problem after 1973. When the IRA announced its 'ceasefire' in Northern Ireland (31 August 1994), its statement managed to include the phrase twice: 'the desire for peace based on a just and lasting settlement cannot be crushed . . . We believe that an opportunity to secure a just and lasting settlement has been created'. Whichever version is used, however, it does come with the Abraham Lincoln seal of approval. He talked of a 'just and lasting peace' in his Second Inaugural address (4 March 1865), referring to the end of the American Civil War.

just deserts Meaning, 'a deserved reward or come-uppance'. An inevitable pairing. So, 'to get one's just deserts' means, 'To suffer the fate or outcome of a situation which one deserves – especially if bad.' The temptation to spell it 'desserts' should be resisted. Known by 1970 but surely of earlier provenance? 'Sentence lengths could be shorter, the only relevant matter being that they should represent a just response to the crime committed. This, broadly, was the doctrine known as "just deserts", on which much of the Criminal Justice Act 1991 was based' – *The Sunday Times* (1 May 1994); 'Biggs [says], "I've managed to avoid the grim grey cells for 30 years. I believe in the power of good. If I keep my nose clean it will be all right." He pauses: "Don't you agree that the villain always gets his just deserts?"' – *The Sunday Telegraph* (5 February 1995); 'The father thumps the yob, pulls out his warrant card to reveal he's a policeman, and arrests him. Just deserts for the yob and cheers for the PC? Not in the Britain we have become' – Andrew Neil in the *Daily Mail* (9 March 1995); 'Sentences must reflect an assessment of the individual circumstances and of the offender's just deserts' – *The Guardian* (2 December 1995).

just do it Slogan for Nike sportswear, especially shoes, current by August 1989.

Hardly meaningful (though it has been glossed as 'If a thing's worth doing, it's worth doing well') but a slogan that 'had become second nature to an entire generation', according to the *International Herald Tribune* (June 1994).

just fancy that! Often ironical exclamation after a revelation has been made which – to the speaker – was eminently predictable given what was known about the person/people involved beforehand. Since the 1880s, and revived as a catchphrase by *Private Eye* in the 1970s – often as a headline over a story of curious malfeasance.

(we're) just good friends Clichéd way for a person being interviewed to express that his or her relationship with another is not sexual or romantic. Usually a fobbing-off phrase and often untruthful. In James Joyce, *Ulysses* (1922), there occurs the original straightforward form: 'They would be just good friends like a big brother and sister without all that other.' The phrase probably established itself in the USA during the 1930s, though in the film of Cole Porter's musical *Silk Stockings* (US 1957), the phrase is used several times as if not clichéd yet. 'The old fathead had got entirely the wrong angle on the relations between his ewe lamb and myself, we being just good friends, as the expression is' – P. G. Wodehouse, *Stiff Upper Lip, Jeeves*, Chap. 2 (1963). From *Vivien: The Life of Vivien Leigh* by Alexander Walker (1987): 'At Cherbourg, Jack [Merivale – Vivien's lover as her marriage to Laurence Olivier was ending in 1960] experienced for the first time the bruising intrusiveness of the British Press who boarded the ship *en masse* to interrogate Vivien's handsome travelling companion. In self-defence, he fell back on the old "just good friends" cliché.' Now used as a consciously humorous evasion, especially when not true. A BBC sitcom current in 1984 was called *Just Good Friends* and several songs about that time also had the title.

just how serious . . . ? Cliché of broadcast journalism, the invariable start to a thrusting, probing question. In the mid-1970s, Michael Leapman, as diarist on *The Times*, invented a character called 'Justow Serious'.

justice   See AND JUSTICE.

justice should be seen to be done   Legal maxim originally expressed by Gordon Hewart (later Viscount Hewart), the British lawyer and politician (1870–1943). His words, 'Justice should not only be done, but should manifestly and undoubtedly be seen to be done', were contained in a ruling in King's Bench Reports (1924). A man named McCarthy in Hastings had been accused of dangerous driving. There had been an accident in which people were injured. He was convicted, but it was later discovered that a partner in the firm of solicitors who had demanded damages against him was also clerk to the Hastings' justices. As Robert Jackson noted in his biography, *The Chief* (1959), no one believed that the clerk had acted improperly during the case, but the circumstances warranted an application by McCarthy's solicitor for the conviction to be quashed in a Divisional Court. Hewart ruled in his favour in the case of Rex *v*. Sussex Justices (9 November 1923). When a fellow-judge joked that 'be seen' was a misprint for 'seem', Hewart made it clear that justice must always be seen to be done in view of the defendant and of the world. J. B. Morton (Beachcomber) commented (1930s?): 'Justice must not only be seen to be done but has to be seen to be believed.'

just in time; or, born in the vestry!
Meaning, 'You are late.' *Partridge/Catch Phrases* notes: 'Obviously, applied [and referring] to a wedding held only just in time to prevent the coming child from being adjudged illegitimate.' Paul Beale adds: 'Perhaps modelled on typical Victorian novel-titles.'

just like that!   Catchphrase of the British comedian Tommy Cooper (1922–84). Said in gruff tones and accompanied by small paddling gestures, this was a gift to mimics. It was not a premeditated catchphrase, he said. He only noticed it when impressionists and others singled it out from his mad 'failed conjuror' act. Inevitably, the phrase was used by Cooper as the title of his autobiography. There is also a song incorporating it.

just one of those things   Meaning, 'something inexplicable or inevitable'. The

OED2 finds the first modern use in John O'Hara's story *Appointment in Samarra* (1934) and in the following year as the title of the Cole Porter song that undoubtedly ensured its enduring place in the language. Five years earlier, however, Porter had used the title for a completely different song, which was published though dropped from the show it was supposed to be in. The form of words had been in existence, however, since 1875.

just say no   Slogan of the anti-drug abuse campaign in the USA, supported by Nancy Reagan when First Lady. From *The Washington Post* (22 February 1985): 'The 8-year-old [Soleil Moon Frye] is honorary national chairperson of the Just Say No Club movement organized by three elementary school youngsters in Oakland to encourage kids to say no to drugs instead of giving in to peer pressure. The program attracted the attention of Mrs Reagan last summer when she visited the participants.'

just what the doctor ordered   Phrase of approval applied to anything that is just right or eminently agreeable – and by no means restricted to medicinal matters, healthy foods, etc. Presumably referring to a course of action that a doctor might recommend to keep you in good health. Known in the USA and UK by the 1910s. C. H. Rolph wrote in *London Particulars* (1980): 'Grandma Hewitt [his grandmother] was a walking repository, rather than a dictionary, of clichés and catchphrases; and I have often wished she could have been known to Mr Eric Partridge during the compilation of his delectable dictionaries. Both she and I . . . could pre-date many of [his] attributions. Here are four examples . . . all of which were common currency in my Edwardian childhood: "Just what the doctor ordered", "Are you kidding?", "Cheats never prosper", and "All behind like a cow's tail".'

just when you thought it was safe to ——
Catchphrase format from a slogan. The film *Jaws 2* (US 1978) – a sequel to the successful shark saga – was promoted with the line, 'Just when you thought it was safe to go back in the water . . .' A graffito reported in 1979 was 'Jaws 3 – just when

you thought it was safe to go to the toilet'. Headline from *The Observer* (16 July 1989):

'Just when you thought it was safe to get back in a bikini . . .'

K

Kaiser See ARF A MO.

(a) kangaroo court The name applied to a self-appointed court that has no proper legal authority – as in the disciplinary proceedings sometimes to be found among prisoners in gaol. Recorded by 1853. Ironically, *Macquarie* (1981), the Australian dictionary, calls this an American and British colloquialism, but surely it must have something to do with the land of the kangaroo? Perhaps it alludes to the vicious streak that such animals sometimes display? The *OED2*'s earliest citation – from the USA – is dated 1853, and this provides a clue to the likely explanation. In W. S. Ransom's *Australian English: An Historical Study of the Vocabulary 1788–1898* (1966), it is stated that over 800 Australians entered California for the 1849 gold rush. They presumably brought with them knowledge of the kangaroo's somewhat vicious nature. On the other hand, between 1852 and 1856, 16,000 miners arrived in Australia from California when gold was found in Victoria. They, likewise, would have taken home knowledge of the beast. In any case, American sealers and whalers had been putting into Sydney from about 1800.

Katy, bar the door (or **Katie . . .)** 'Get ready for trouble, watch out for danger, all hell is about to break loose.' An American expression, though its origins may lie in Perth, Scotland, on 20 February 1437, when some relatives came to assassinate King James I of Scots. The bar to secure the door was missing, and a brave young woman, Catherine Douglas, put her arms through the hasps and held it long enough for the King to escape into a secret passage. She earned the nickname 'Kate Barlass', but it did the King no good as the passage led to the Royal tennis court and the other end had been blocked to stop balls going in, so the King was caught and killed. Michael Brown, *James I* (1994),

suggests that the woman's real name was Elizabeth not Catherine Douglas and that she did not actually bar the door but fell into the passage (or drain) beside the king, and so did delay the onslaught of the attackers, but not for long.

KBO (Keep Buggering On) Informal motto derived from a remark of Winston Churchill in December 1941: 'We must just KBO' – quoted in Martin Gilbert, *Finest Hour* (1983).

keen as mustard Extremely keen. According to *The Independent* (3 November 1993), the Thomas *Keen*, who is buried in West Norwood Cemetery, near London, is the one 'whose family firm made mustard and whose activities led to the phrase "keen as mustard".' A nice thought, but 'the keenest mustard' was a phrase by 1658.

(to) keep body and soul together To keep oneself going – chiefly by eating properly. 'In my late husband's family, a great saying when serving up a substantial snack or full meal was, "There you are, that will keep B. and S. Tog"' – Joan Bell, Clackmannanshire (1992). 'Keeping body [or life] and soul together' is, of course, an old phrase. According to the *OED2*, 'Tate' in *Dryden's Juvenal* (1697) has: 'The Vascons once with Man's Flesh (as 'tis sed) / Kept Life and Soul together'. Jane Collier, *The Art of Tormenting* (1753) has: 'By never letting him see you swallow half enough to keep body and soul together.' *The Century Illustrated Monthly Magazine* (November 1884) has: 'How on earth they managed to keep body and soul together.'

keep Britain tidy Slogan – one of the simplest messages and one of the most enduring. Promoted through the Central Office of Information, it first appeared as a sticker produced for the Ministry of Housing and Local Government in 1952. However, it was probably coined about 1949.

keep death off the road (carelessness kills) Slogan. Nobody knows who created this message – the best-remembered of any used in British government-sponsored advertising campaigns through the Central Office of Information. It was used in the memorable poster by W. Little featuring the so-called 'Black Widow' in 1946. Discussing the pointlessness of the campaign in *Tribune* (8 November 1946), George Orwell referred to 'Keep Death off the *Roads*', though the poster version in fact used the singular.

keep it dark! Security slogan from the Second World War (in the UK). The basic expression, meaning 'keep it secret', had been in use by 1681. As a wartime slogan, it appeared in more than one formulation, also in verse: 'If you've news of our munitions / KEEP IT DARK / Ships or plans or troop positions / KEEP IT DARK / Lives are lost through conversation / Here's a tip for the duration / When you've private information. / KEEP IT DARK.' *Shush, Keep It Dark* was the title of a variety show running in London during September 1940. Later, the naval version of the BBC radio show *Merry Go Round* (1943–8) featured a character called Commander High-Price (Jon Pertwee) whose catchphrase was, 'Hush, keep it dark!' None of this had been forgotten by 1983, apparently, when Anthony Beaumont-Dark, a Tory candidate in the General Election, campaigned successfully for re-election with the slogan, 'Keep it Dark'. 'If my mother told me something she didn't wish me to disclose to anyone else, she would say: "Keep it dark and I'll buy you a lantern"' – Mrs J. Tunnicliff, Worcestershire (1995).

keep it under your hat (or stetson) Security slogans from the Second World War for the UK and USA, respectively. *Under Your Hat* had been the title of a Cicely Courtneidge/Jack Hulbert musical comedy (London 1938).

keep mum, she's not so dumb See BE LIKE DAD, KEEP MUM.

keep on keeping on Injunction/slogan of unknown date and origin. It may have been used as a Salvation Army slogan at some time. George Orwell used the phrase in a 'London Letter' to *Partisan Review* (5 June 1945): 'In the face of terrifying dangers and golden political opportunities, people just keep on keeping on, in a sort of twilight sleep in which they are conscious of nothing except the daily round of work, family life, darts at the pub, exercising the dog, mowing the lawn, bringing home the supper beer, etc. etc.'

keep on truckin' This expression, meaning that you've got to 'persevere' or 'keep on keeping on', is described in *Bartlett* as the 'slogan of a cartoon character' created by Robert Crumb (b. 1943). Crumb drew 'dirty' cartoons for a number of underground periodicals like *Snatch* and created 'Fritz the Cat', later the subject of a full-length cartoon film. There were a number of records with the title by 1970, and there was certainly a vogue for the phrase in the 1960s and 70s. However, there had been a song called simply 'Truckin'' in 1935 (words by Ted Koehler and music by Rube Bloom) and the *OED2* finds 'the truck' or 'trucking' as a jerky dance that came out of Harlem in the summer of 1934. *Partridge/Catch Phrases* plumps for a suggestion that the phrase, while of 'Negro dance origin', came out of the great American dance marathons of the 1930s, though one of Partridge's contributors hotly disputes this. *Flexner* (1982) discussing 'hoboes, tramps and bums' on the American railroad probably gets nearest to the source. He defines 'trucking it' thus: 'Riding or clinging to the trucking hardware between the wheels. This may have contributed to the jitterbug's use of *trucking* (also meaning "to leave or move on" in the 1930s) and to the 1960 students' phrase *keep on trucking*, keep moving, keep trying, keep "doing one's (own) thing" with good cheer.'

keep taking the tablets Traditionally what doctors advise patients to do and what anybody might say particularly to someone who is getting on in years and needs to have medication in order to keep on going. Possibly turned into a catchphrase by the BBC radio *Goon Show*, though this is unverified. Several editions of the BBC radio show *Round the Horne* (including 15 May 1966) do include the remark. There is a lino-cut by Gertrude

Elias, dated 1950, entitled 'Keep on taking the tablets' – reproduced in *Women's Images of Men*, ed. Kent & Morreau (1985). It is also the punch line of a sort of joke. When James Callaghan, the British Labour Prime Minister, was compared by his son-in-law Peter Jay to Moses in 1977, Margaret Thatcher, then Leader of the Opposition, sought to make capital out of it by jesting in her speech to that year's Conservative Party Conference, 'My advice to Moses is: keep taking the tablets.' This was a venerable jest even then. 'What Moses said to David Kossoff was "Continue taking the tablets as before"' was mentioned on BBC Radio *Quote . . . Unquote* (28 March 1976). Even so, according to an account given by Alan Watkins in *The Observer* (27 May 1988), the joke very nearly misfired. When Sir Ronald Millar, Mrs Thatcher's speechwriter, presented her with the effort, she 'pronounced the joke funny but capable of improvement. Would it not be more hilarious for her to say "Keep taking the pill"?' And, indeed, 'Keep taking the Pils' was used as an advertising slogan for Pilsener lager in the late 1970s. The development of the phrase to **keep taking the tabloids** had occurred by 12 May 1968 when it was used in *Round the Horne*. In 1976, this phrase was used as the title of a pilot version of BBC Radio's *News Quiz*.

keep that schoolgirl complexion Slogan used to promote Palmolive soap, in the USA, from 1917. Coined by Charles S. Pearce, a Palmolive executive. Beverley Nichols wrote in *The Star-Spangled Manner* (1928) that in his 'riotous youth' he had been comforted through 'numberless orgies' only by the conviction that if he used a certain soap he would retain his schoolboy complexion: 'It did not matter how much I drank or smoked, how many nameless and exquisite sins I enjoyed – they would all be washed out in the morning by that magical soap . . . I bought it merely because years ago a bright young American sat down in an office on the other side of the Atlantic and thought of a slogan to sell soap. And he certainly sold it.' During the Second World War, Palmolive was still plugging the old line in the UK: 'Driving through blitzes won't spoil that schoolgirl complexion'.

(to) keep the ball rolling To keep something going, especially a conversation. Possibly from an elementary game where this had to be done or from bandy (a type of hockey). If the ball was not kept rolling it was a slow game and uninteresting for the spectators. Known by 1840. *To Keep the Ball Rolling* was the overall title given to Anthony Powell's autobiographical sequence (1976–82). He said it came from Joseph Conrad's *Chance* (1913): 'To keep the ball rolling I asked Marlow if this Powell was remarkable in any way. "He was not exactly remarkable," Marlow answered with his usual nonchalance. "In a general way it's very difficult to become remarkable. People won't take sufficient notice of one, don't you know."'

keep the faith, baby Slogan adopted by black activists in the USA in the 1960s – designed to encourage fellow blacks to carry on the struggle for civil rights whatever the setbacks. Popularized by the Congressman Adam Clayton Powell, then used more generally: 'The rock'n'roll momentoes, the Elvis Presley commemorative plaque . . . album covers pinned to the Ashtons' living-room walls to indicate that, even as they entered middle age, they were still "keeping the faith"' – Gordon Burn, *Somebody's Husband, Somebody's Son*, Chap. 32 (1984). *Keeping the Faith* is the title of a film about a priest and a rabbi both falling for the same woman (US 2000).

(to) keep the wolf from the door Meaning, 'to keep poverty and hunger at bay, to find the elementary necessities needed for survival'. The literal expression occurs in the *OED2* as long ago as 1470. Groucho Marx had a song called 'Toronto', which incorporated an elaborate joke about keeping (Jewish) people called Woolf from the door. In the film *She Done Him Wrong* (US 1933), Mae West has the line: 'The wolf at my door? Why, I remember when he came right into my room and had pups!' 'Compassion fatigue has set in . . . If I gave them anything, I would only have to ask for the money back to keep the wolf from my own door' – *The Independent* (1 June 1994); 'Through it all, Dermody could hardly keep the wolf from the door. Appealing to Owenson for assistance he once wrote: "I have now fasted for a longer time than caused the death of Chatterton'" – *The Irish Times* (11 July 1994).

keep up the good work! Phrase of encouragement, probably current in the UK before 1939. The *OED2* has an American citation, dated 1953, from Eugene O'Neill's *Long Day's Journey Into Night*. I would have plumped for a services' origin myself. Surely, it is the sort of thing likely to be uttered by any officer before, after, or instead of, saying, 'Carry on, Sergeant!'?

(to) keep up with the Joneses Meaning 'to strive not to be outdone by one's neighbours', the expression comes from a comic strip by Arthur R. 'Pop' Momand entitled *Keeping up with the Joneses*, which appeared in the New York *Globe* from 1913 to 1931. It is said that Momand had at first intended to call his strip 'Keeping up with the Smiths' but refrained because his own neighbours were actually of that name and some of the exploits he wished to report had been acted out by them in real life.

keep your hand on your ha'penny Advice to a woman or girl to fend off sexual advances, with the implication that she should 'save' herself 'until the right man turns up'. *Partridge/Catch Phrases* dates it from the 1880s. A letter dated 20 October 1969 from the actor Kenneth Williams, commiserating on the death of a friend's mother, contains this: 'Mine is still going strong, and leaves on the 25th for a cruise in the Med. I told her to be careful "Keep your hand on your ha'penny dear" I said, "they're all after a bit out there . . ."' – from *The Kenneth Williams Letters* (1994).

keep your legs together (or **crossed)!** Jocular advice to a girl or woman in order that she can thwart sexual advances. Mostly in the USA, by the 1930s, though 'Cross your legs' was what Billy Sunday, the American evangelist, used to advise the females in his audience in the 1890s, adding, when they had done so, 'Now the gates of hell are closed'.

keep your pecker up See I'VE GOT HIS PECKER IN MY POCKET.

(to) keep your powder dry The overall idiomatic injunction means 'remain calm and prepared for immediate action', 'be prudent, practical, on the alert'. Perhaps an element of 'not using up your essential supplies until they are needed' has also crept in. The part about keeping one's powder dry is no more than sensible advice from the days when gunpowder had to be kept dry if it was to be used at all. Alluding to: 'Put your trust in God, my boys, and keep your powder dry' – attributed to Oliver Cromwell during his Irish campaign of 1649, but there is some doubt whether he really said it at all, as it was ascribed to him long after his death by a certain Valentine Blacker (1778–1823) in an Orange ballad, *Oliver's Advice* (published 1856). Playing upon the word 'powder', *Keep Your Powder Dry* was the title of a 'female flagwaver' film (US 1945) – about female WACS. 'It is clear that M. Fauré, to judge by what he did not say today, is keeping his powder dry' – *The Times* (6 August 1955).

Kelly See DARBY.

kemo sabe See HI YO.

kettle See HERE'S A.

Keynsham – that's K-E-Y-N-S-H-A-M ... Listeners to Radio Luxembourg in the 1950s and 60s remember the rolling, West Country accent of Horace Batchelor (1898–1977) who appeared in commercials for his own method of winning the football pools. At his death it was said he had netted £12 million for his clients. His usual message was something like: 'Good evening, friends. This is Horace Bachelor at the microphone – the inventor of the Infra-Draw Method for the Treble Chance. I have myself, with my own coupon entries, won 1012 first Treble Chance top dividends. And my ingenious method can help you to win also. Don't send any money – just your name and address.' Then came the high spot of his ads: 'Send now to Horace Batchelor, Department One, Keynsham – spelt K-E-Y-N-S-H-A-M, Keynsham, Bristol.'

kicking See DRAGGED.

(to) kick the bucket (or **dust)** Euphemistic phrases for 'to die' – derived from either the suicide's kicking away the bucket on which he/she is standing, in order to hang him/herself, or from the 'bucket beam' on which pigs were hung *after* being slaughtered. The odd *post mortem* spasm would lead to the 'bucket' being kicked. 'Kick the dust' for 'to die' is nicely illustrated by a passage from Thoreau's *Walden* (1854): 'I was present at the auction of a deacon's effects . . . after lying half a century in his garret and other dust holes . . . When a man dies he kicks the dust.' The *OED2* mentions neither this expression nor 'kiss the dust', though it does find **bite the dust** in 1856. Psalm 72:9 has **lick the dust**: 'They that dwell in the wilderness shall bow before him; and his enemies shall lick the dust' – though this is suggesting humiliation rather than death.

(the) killer instinct The quality of extreme seriousness thought to be re-quired to win in sport and life. Known by 1931 (in a boxing context). 'Already he has given Oxford a lift with his drive, enthusi-asm, attack and killer instinct' – *The Times* (20 February 1973); 'Maybe it's the killer instinct that Seidelman needs to develop. She appears more concerned with keeping her movie politically correct than with making it fun' – *The Washington Post* (10 April 1987).

(the) killing fields Places where mass slaughter is carried out. *The Killing Fields* was the title of a film (UK 1984) concern-ing the mass murders carried out by the Communist Khmer Rouge, under Pol Pot, in Cambodia between 1975 and 1978, when possibly three million were killed. The mass graves were discovered in April 1979. In the film, the phrase was seen to refer, literally, to paddy fields where prisoners were first forced to work and where many of them were then callously shot. The film was based on an article, 'The Death and Life of Dith Pran', by Sydney Schanberg, published in *The New York Times* Magazine (20 January 1980), which tells of the journalist's quest for reunion with his former assistant. The article has the phrase towards the begin-ning, thus: 'In July of 1975 – two months after Pran and I had been forced apart on April 20 – an American diplomat who had known Pran wrote me a consoling letter.

The diplomat, who had served in Phnom Penh, knew the odds of anyone emerging safely from a country that was being transformed into a society of terror and purges and "killing fields".' So it appears that the coinage is due to the unnamed diplomat. William Shawcross, author of two notable books on Cambodia, said (1990) that he had never heard the phrase until the film was in preparation. It is now widely used allusively to describe any place given over to mass executions, e.g. 'How Ridley saved his killing fields' [where a British politician went shooting game] – *The Observer* (23 July 1989); and: 'The killing fields revisited' [headline to a travel article about the battlefield of Waterloo] – *The Observer* (25 February 1990). The phrase **killing ground(s)** has also entered the military vocabulary as a strategic term for an area into which you manoeuvre an enemy force before finishing it off and which has been current since the Second World War. From Ian Fleming, *The Living Daylights* (1966): 'Trouble is, he'll have thirty yards of brightly lit frontier to sprint across. That'll be the killing ground. Right?' In a non-military sense, the phrase was used by Rudyard Kipling in his poem 'The Rhyme of the Three Sealers' (1893) about seal hunting. It is difficult to say whether there is any connection with the US term **killing floor**, originally referring perhaps to an abbatoir but in the 1960s used for a place where sexual intercourse took place.

(to) kill the messenger *Kill the Messen-ger* was the title given to his memoirs (1991) by (Sir) Bernard Ingham, Chief Press Secretary to the Prime Minister, Margaret Thatcher, from 1979 to 1990. The somewhat surprising title was an apparent allusion to what reputedly happened to messengers bringing bad news in classical times. Ingham's implication would seem to be that press officers get blamed for their master's – or in his case, mistress's – doings, just as the media are often blamed for the news that they report rather than initiate. As early as Sophocles, *Antigone* (line 277), a sentinel was saying to Creon: 'None love the messenger who brings bad news.' Compare the maltreatment of messengers in several Shakespeare plays: in *Antony and Cleopatra*, I.ii.92 (1607), a

Liberal Party is dead. Long live the Liberal Party." It was hard to distinguish the wake from the marriage feast' – *The Independent* (25 January 1988).

(the) king of terrors 'Death' – as in Job 18:14. Thomas Carlyle, *The History of French Revolution*, I.i.iv (1837), has: 'Frightful to all men in Death; from of old named King of Terror.' The phrase was used as the title of Henry Scott Holland's sermon (1910) from which the passage beginning 'Death is nothing at all' is taken.

(the) king of the road Slogan for Lucas bicycle lamps in the UK, 1920s. In the song 'A Transport of Delight' (1957), Flanders and Swann refer to a London bus as a 'monarch of the road'. Also used as the title of a song written and performed by Roger Miller (US, 1965), by way of allusion to hoboes and tramps, who have more usually been known as **knights of the road**. In England, 'knight of the road' has also referred to a highwayman since 1665.

(the) king over the water! Toast using the name given to the exiled James II after his departure from the English throne in 1688 (also to his son and grandson, the Old Pretender and the Young Pretender). Jacobites would propose the toast while passing the glass over a water decanter.

kings See AGE OF.

(the) king's English (or, more rarely, **queen's English)** The English language as it is correctly spoken and written. 'Abusing of God's patience, and the King's English' appears in Shakespeare, *The Merry Wives of Windsor*, I.iv.5 (1601). It was apparently a standard phrase even by then and appears in this form although Queen Elizabeth I was on the throne at the time the play was (most probably) written and performed. Hence, *The King's English* – title of H. W. & F. G. Fowler's guide (1906).

(a) king's ransom A huge amount of money – presumably implying an amount sufficient to release a king from captivity. Used by Christopher Marlowe in *Dr Faustus* (1590). 'Venables made a killing on his 23 per cent shareholding, cashing in the blue chips for around £3 million. Part of that has been invested in his London club Scribes West but he would pay a king's

ransom to call off the dogs of war' – *Daily Mirror* (31 October 1994); 'Lawyers acting for the Princess of Wales in any divorce would ask for a king's ransom, says Frances Gibb' – *The Times* (15 November 1994).

kipper's knickers See under BEE'S KNEES.

kiss See CAME THE DAWN; BLARNEY STONE.

kiss and tell As in 'kiss and tell memoirs', used to describe the situation where one half of a couple sells an account of their affair (invariably over by this stage) to a newspaper. An older phrase than you might think: William Congreve in *Love for Love* (1695) has: 'Oh, fie, Miss, you must not kiss and tell.' Bernard Shaw in a letter to Mrs Patrick Campbell (30 December 1921) writes: 'A gentleman does not kiss and tell.' A headline from *The Sunday Telegraph* (17 May 1992): 'Kiss if You Must, But Please Don't Tell'.

kiss-kiss bang-bang Phrase describing a certain type of movie. *Kiss Kiss Bang Bang* was the title of a book of collected criticism (1968) by Pauline Kael. She says the words came from an Italian poster – 'perhaps the briefest statement imaginable on the basic appeal of movies'. Usually, they are taken to refer to the James Bond movies. Indeed, Bond's creator, Ian Fleming, himself described his books in a letter (*circa* 1955) to Raymond Chandler as 'straight pillow fantasies of the bang-bang, kiss-kiss variety'. John Barry, composer of music for most of the Bond films, named one of his themes 'Mr Kiss Kiss Bang Bang', for *Thunderball* (1965). Compare, however, this from the American anthropoligst Hortense Powdermaker in *Hollywood, The Dream Factory* (1951): 'South Sea natives who have been exposed to American movies classify them into two types, "kiss-kiss" and "bang-bang".'

kissed See EVERYBODY TO THEIR LIKING.

kiss me, Hardy Dying words of Horatio Nelson as he lay dying on HMS *Victory* at Trafalgar in 1805, having been severely injured by a shot fired from a French ship. It has been asserted that, according to the Nelson family, he was in the habit of saying 'kismet' (fate) when anything went wrong. It is therefore not *too* unlikely that he said, 'Kismet, Hardy' to his Flag Captain, and that witnesses misheard, but there is no real reason to choose this version. In fact, the recording angel had to work overtime when Nelson lay dying, he said so much. The first reliable report of what went on was by Dr Beatty, the ship's surgeon, included in *Despatches and Letters of Lord Nelson* (ed. Nicholas, 1846): 'Captain Hardy now came to the cockpit to see his Lordship a second time. He then told Captain Hardy that he felt that in a few minutes he should be no more, adding in a low tone, "Don't throw me overboard, Hardy." The Captain answered, "Oh, no, certainly not." Then replied his Lordship, "You know what to do. Take care of my dear Lady Hamilton. Kiss me, Hardy." The Captain now knelt and kissed his cheek, when his Lordship said, "Now I am satisfied. Thank God I have done my duty".' This seems to be quite a reasonable description and, if Hardy did actually kiss him (a gesture that surely couldn't be mistaken), why should Nelson not have asked him to? Was there something wrong with a naval hero asking for this gesture from another man? Robert Southey, in his *Life of Nelson*, published earlier, in 1813, also supports the 'kiss me' version (his account is almost identical to Beatty's). In Ludovic Kennedy's *On My Way to the Club* (1989), he recalls his own investigations into the matter: 'I was delighted to receive further confirmation from a Mr Corbett, writing from Hardy's home town of Portesham [in 1951]. He said that Nelson's grandson by his daughter Horatia had recently paid him a visit, at the age of over ninety. "He told me he had asked his mother what exactly had happened when Nelson was dying. She said she herself had asked Hardy, who replied, 'Nelson said, "Kiss me, Hardy" and I knelt down and kissed him"'.' It is also possible to argue that 'kiss' can mean no more than 'touch' – a reasonable and usual request from a dying man who needs some last physical contact.

kiss me, my fool   See CAME THE DAWN.

kiss my grits!   Meaning, 'to hell with you', a catchphrase from the TV situation comedy *Alice* (US 1976–80). Flo Castelberry, a Southern-born, man-hungry waitress (played by Polly Holliday), uttered the phrase and later had her own series, *Flo* (1980–81). Compare **kiss my chuddies!** from the later British TV comedy show *Goodness Gracious Me!* (1998–) based on the experiences of immigrants from the Indian sub-continent who speak a blend of English and Hindi, called 'Hinglish'. 'Chuddies' is the Hindi word for underpants.

(the) kiss of death (or life)   The 'kiss of death' derives from the kiss of betrayal given by Judas to Christ, which foreshadowed the latter's death. In the Mafia, too, a kiss from the boss is an indication that your time is up. Compare *Kiss of Death* – the title of a gangster film (US 1947). *Safire* defines the political use of the phrase as 'unwelcome support from an unpopular source, occasionally engineered by the opposition'. He suggests that Governor Al Smith popularized the phrase in 1926, when he called William Randolph Hearst's support for Smith's opponent, Ogden Mills, 'the kiss of death'. In Britain, Winston Churchill used the phrase in the House of Commons on 16 November 1948. Nationalization and all its methods were a 'murderous theme'; the remarks of a government spokesman about the control of raw materials, 'about as refreshing to the minor firms as the kiss of death'. **Kiss of life** as the name of a method of mouth-to-mouth artificial respiration was current by the beginning of the 1960s. On one unfortunate occasion, a BBC Radio 4 newsreader confused the two. 'Having been pulled out of the river,' he said, 'the boy did not survive, despite being given the kiss of death by a passing policeman.'

(to) kiss the book   To seal an oath when taking it, by kissing the Bible, the New Testament or the Gospels. A procedure known by 1523. Hence, a catchphrase, 'You can kiss the book on that!' (= 'it's a dead cert!), dating from the 1890s.

kissy-kissy   Come-on of Miss Piggy, the resident porcine vamp of TV's *The Muppet Show* (UK, 1976–81).

kit   See GET ONE'S.

Kite   See BEING FOR THE BENEFIT.

kith and kin   People to whom one is connected by blood or family ties, but including friends also. The alliterative pairing goes back to 1377. Rudyard Kipling, 'The Rupaiyat of Omar Kal'vin' (1886), has the lines: 'So I with begging Dish and ready Tongue / Assail all Men for all that I can get. / . . . Surely my Kith and Kin will not refuse.'

knees up, Mother Brown! Title of a song by R. P. Weston and Bert Lee (1939) that was very popular in the Second World War and led to the term 'knees-up' for a lively celebration. *Collins English Dictionary* (by the 1979 edn) defined the word as: 'A boisterous dance involving the raising of alternate knees.' *Partridge/Catch Phrases* gives the full phrase as a catchphrase meaning 'Courage!' (which seems unlikely).

knickers See ALL FUR; DON'T GET YOUR; HANG YOUR.

knickers off ready when I come home See NORWICH.

knife-box See BACK IN THE.

(the) knight of the doleful countenance [*El Caballero de la Triste Figura*] Sobriquet of Don Quixote in the 1605 novel by Cervantes (Pt 1, Chap. 19), in Motteux's translation (1700–3). Supplied by Sancho Panza. Smollett translates this as 'Knight of the Sorrowful Countenance' and Shelton, 'Knight of the Ill-favoured Face'.

knights of the road See KING OF THE ROAD.

(a) knight of the shires British political term for a type of Conservative backbench member of parliament who is awarded a knighthood simply for long and devoted service. He then continues to represent the safe, conservative interests of 'Middle England' in which perhaps at one time he was also a landowner. From the 15th to the 18th centuries, the phrase was a straightforward way of describing what then became called 'member of parliament'. In *Punch*'s 'political dictionary' (in an 1846 issue), 'knights of the shire' is defined as 'a representative of an English county. He was formerly entitled to four shillings a day for his attendance in Parliament.' 'Those traditional Tory stalwarts, the knights of the shires – and suburbs – may be becoming an endangered species. At least 26 Tories have announced they are going, and this includes 17 with knighthoods' – *Financial Times* (12 May 1983).

knights of the road See under KING OF THE ROAD.

knocker See AS BLACK AS.

knock, knock! (1) Catchphrase said to have been used in the UK by the British music-hall comedian Wee Georgie *Wood* (1895–1979). He used it in a radio programme in 1936. This was possibly an imported American device to warn that a type of joke was coming up. From *Variety* (19 August 1936): 'Manager Russell Bovim of Loew's Broad, Columbus, cashed in handsomely on the "Knock Knock" craze now sweeping the country' – which may, however, refer to: (2) Name given to a type of (usually punning) joke popular especially in the UK and USA by the 1950/60s and re-popularized by *Laugh-In*, e.g.: 'Knock, knock! / Who's there? / Sam and Janet. / Sam and Janet who? / "Sam and Janet evening" . . .'

(to) knock off work I.e. to finish work for the day. *Morris* suggests that this dates from the days of slave galleys. The man who beat time to keep the oarsmen pulling in unison would give a special knock to indicate when there was to be a change of shift. Good try. Not recorded before 1902 (in the UK).

(a) knock-out blow The final thrust that finishes the fight. As Britain's Secretary of State for War, David Lloyd George gave an interview to Roy W. Harris of the United Press of America. It was printed in *The Times* (29 September 1915). Lloyd George was asked to 'give the United Press, in the simplest possible language, the British attitude toward the recent peace talk'. He answered: 'Sporting terms are pretty well understood wherever English is spoken . . . Well, then. The British soldier is a good sportsman . . . Germany elected to make this a finish fight with England . . . The fight must be to a finish – to a knock out.' In his memoirs, Lloyd George entitled one chapter 'The Knock-out Blow' – which is how this notion was popularly expressed. In boxing, the expression had been known since the 1880s.

(to) knock seven bells out of   To beat severely, if not actually knock someone out. It is nautical in origin (and known by 1929), but why seven out of the eight bells available aboard ship? Also figurative use: 'If they [louts] misbehave, the players leave the pitch and kick seven bells out of them' – *People* (19 February 1995); 'There is something reassuringly solid about sculptors, especially those who work on the grand scale. Perhaps belting seven bells out of a ton of granite all day long dispels any high-flown airs and graces' – *Scotland on Sunday* (2 July 1995).

(to) knock something into a cocked hat To change the shape of something completely. A cocked hat was one with the brim turned up (as once worn by bishops and deans) or pointed at the back and in the front (as once was part of military full-dress uniform). Originally an American expression – recorded in the USA by 1833. *Brewer* (1923) comments: 'In the game of ninepins, three pins were set up in the form of a triangle, and when all the pins except these three were knocked down, the set was technically said to be "knocked into a cocked hat".' 'The concussion knocked all the Negro's conditioning into a cocked hat' – Aldous Huxley, *Brave New World*, Chap. 11 (1932); 'English lexicography knocks Johnnie Walker into a tricuspidal fedora. Over four hundred years, and going stronger than ever' – Randolph Quirk, *Style and Communication in the English Language* (1983).

(to) knock spots off (the competition) To do something better than somebody else. American origin, known by 1861. But what spots are alluded to?

know   See ALL I; ANYONE WE; AS WE KNOW; END OF CIVILISATION; FORGOTTEN MORE; I DON'T.

(to) know all the angles   Meaning, 'to have experience, to be professional'. The earliest *OED2* citation is from Nevil Shute's *Pastoral* (1944): 'The old stagers . . . the men who knew all the angles, who had great experience.' But where does the expression come from – geometry/gunnery/snooker/billiards? Compare: Humphrey Bogart saying 'I covered all the angles' in the film *In a Lonely Place* (US 1950). 'The professionals were content to remain extras. They had no acting ambitions. They worked all the angles and were not above slipping a percentage of their daily salaries . . . to guarantee being "called" next day' – David Niven, *The Moon's a Balloon*, Chap. 10 (1971).

(the) knowledge   The process of acquiring and learning the traffic routes around London, which is part of the training of licensed taxi-cab drivers. Celebrated in a TV comedy drama called *The Knowledge* (1979) by Jack Rosenthal.

(not to) know one's arse from a hole in the ground   'To be insufficiently clued up and unable to make this distinction.' Almost certainly American in origin and possibly current by the early 1900s. It is usually presented in the negative and allusive form 'doesn't know – from a hole in the ground', as in the film *Mr Smith Goes to Washington* (US 1939). The 'arse' form in the negative is used by W. H. Auden in 'Shorts II' (1969–71).

(to) know one's onions   To know what you are about, to be knowledgeable in the subject to hand. This would seem to be an American coinage, as shown by the citation (at which there were similar 'knowing' expressions involving oats and other foods). 'Mr Roberts knows his onions, all right' – *Harper's Magazine* (March 1922). Any connection with C. T. Onions, the lexicographer and etymologist (1873–1965), is back-formation etymology of the folk-lore kind.

(to) know the ropes   To understand the procedures to be followed in any situation. From nautical use where, literally, to know the ropes was vital for survival. Recorded in 1874. Hence, also **to show someone the ropes** – to teach someone how to do something or how things are done.

know what I mean, 'Arry?   Post-boxing match interview phrase supposedly used by the British fighter Frank Bruno in reply to Harry Carpenter, for many years BBC TV's chief match commentator. Established by 1986. Carpenter himself commented: 'I only have to walk down the street or stand in a bar to have someone say to me: "Where's Frank?" or "Know what I mean, 'Arry?" (Strange how people always drop the aitch when they say that. Frank never does)' – *The Sunday Times* (19 April 1992). See also NARMEAN?

(to) know where the bodies are buried
To know the secrets of an organization and thus to be in a position where you are not likely to be 'let go'. In the film *Citizen Kane* (US 1941), Susan, Kane's estranged wife, says of the butler at 'Xanadu' that he 'knows where all the bodies are buried.' The expression also occurs in the film *I Am the Law* (US 1938). Particularly popular from the 1980s onwards in the USA and UK. 'A senior member of the PLP [in the Bahamas] said: "If he is sent to America, he will sing like a canary – and this guy knows where the bodies are buried"' – *The Sunday Times* (29 September 1985); 'Like Martha Mitchell, the political wife who spilled the beans, she knows where the bodies are buried in the Rose Garden' – *Financial Times* (9 June 1986); 'Politicians trust John [Cole]. They talk to him because he would never say where the bodies are buried' – *The Independent* Metro (2 June 1995).

(to) knuckle down To get down to doing, to apply oneself seriously to a difficult task. Known by 1740 – from placing the knuckles on the ground in shooting or playing at marbles. '"I play well in some matches but not in others so in my next match I need to knuckle down and produce a good performance," said Henman' – *The Herald* (Glasgow) (17 January 1996).

(to) knuckle under To give in to someone else, to give way to a superior force. Known by 1740. 'Protesters denounced the ban on travel to jobs in Israel and the expansion of Jewish settlements in the West Bank. "No to starvation, no to settlements. We are a people who won't knuckle under," they chanted' – *The Independent* (14 February 1995).

Kookie, Kookie (lend me your comb)
This was the title of a song (1960), featuring Ed Byrnes and Connie Stevens, using a stock phrase from the American TV cop show *77 Sunset Strip* (1958–63). Byrnes played 'Kookie', a fast-talking parking lot attendant who became a teen idol wearing slick shirts, tight pants and a 'wet look' hairstyle. He had a habit of constantly combing his hair, and this was celebrated in the hit song.

(the) Kreutzer sonata Tolstoy's short novel *The Kreutzer Sonata* (1891) is about a man who suspects his wife of having an affair with a neighbour with whom she also plays the 'Kreutzer' violin sonata by Beethoven. The sonata was dedicated to a French violinist called Rodolphe Kreutzer, but he is thought never to have played it. Following Tolstoy's use of the title, Janacek gave it to his String Quartet No. 1 (1923) – and this was definitely a reference to Tolstoy rather than Beethoven, as he was giving the title to a quartet and not to a sonata.

L

labonza See AND AWAY WE GO!

Labour isn't working Slogan of the British Conservative party. It first appeared in 1978 on posters showing a long queue outside an employment office. Created by the Saatchi & Saatchi agency, the poster was later widely used in the 1979 General Election that took Margaret Thatcher to Downing Street. When unemployment continued to rise under the Conservatives, the slogan was, of course, recalled with irony.

(a) labour of love Work undertaken through enjoyment of the work itself rather than for any other reward. Biblical origin: 'Your works of faith and labours of love' – 1 Thessalonians 1:3 (also Hebrews 6:10). Now a cliché. 'Dr Mackay's own personal selection of extracts – the labour of many years and clearly a labour of love'

– Sir Peter Medawar, in foreword to *The Harvest of a Quiet Eye: a selection of scientific quotations* by Alan L. Mackay (1977); '[Congratulating John Lahr on his book *Prick Up Your Ears*] It all reads so effortlessly! Labour of love must be right. The affection shone through the book' – Kenneth Williams in *The Kenneth Williams Letters* (1994) – letter of 3 September 1978; 'What of the future for *Viz*? Thanks to the contract publishing business Brown has created a company that could now run without his labour of love' – *Evening Standard* (London) (16 November 1994); 'They'll write this wonderful tune and a first verse, and then find that the second verse doesn't fit. It drags in all sorts of skills. It's a labour of love and it takes up lots of time' – *Times Educational Supplement* (16 December 1994); 'This book has been for me a labour of love' – Martin Walker, *Words Without Frontiers: The Spread of European English* (1995).

lace See ARSENIC AND OLD.

laddie See ACTOR.

ladies who lunch Rich men's wives (sad and mostly middle-aged) whose chief activity (apart from shopping) is to lunch with each other (or at events devoted to charitable fund-raising) and put away the drinks thereat. An American phenomenon – or at least when the phrase was coined by Stephen Sondheim for his song 'The Ladies Who Lunch' in the musical *Company* (1970).

lady See AND ALL BECAUSE.

(a) lady bountiful Applied (now only ironically) to a woman who is conspicuously generous to others less fortunate than herself (particularly within a small community or village). The expression comes from the name of a character in George Farquhar's play *The Beaux' Stratagem* (1707).

Lady Chatterley (or Lady C) Usually, when this name is invoked, it is not so much the particular character in the novel *Lady Chatterley's Lover* by D. H. Lawrence that is being referred to but the whole phenomenon of the book. She is, of course, an aristocrat who has a sexual affair with her gamekeeper, but in October

1960, when Penguin Books Ltd were cleared of publishing an obscene work in the unexpurgated edition of the novel, a landmark in publishing and sexual freedom was established. Philip Larkin, in his poem 'Annus Mirabilis' (1974), said: 'Sexual intercourse began / In nineteen sixty-three / . . . Between the end of the *Chatterley* ban / And the Beatles' first LP.'

(the) lady's not for turning Phrase from a speech by Margaret Thatcher, when British Prime Minister, to the Conservative Party Conference at Brighton (11 October 1980): 'To those waiting with bated breath for that favourite media catchphrase, the U-turn, I have only one thing to say. You turn if you want to. The lady's not for turning.' Here, Thatcher came up with what is, in a sense, her best-remembered formally spoken 'line'. While not convincing the hearer that she could have alluded unaided to the title of the play *The Lady's Not for Burning* (1948) by Christopher Fry, the cry had the curiously insidious memorability that most effective slogans need to have. Again, one detects the hand of her speechwriter, Sir Ronald Millar, in all this. Indeed, in *The Sunday Times* (23 November 1980), he confirmed that he had coined the phrase but also reported that he would have 'preferred his friend the prime minister to have said "the lady's not for turning" with an elided "'s" exactly as in the original title of Christopher Fry's play.' Which is odd, because any recording of the speech will confirm that she did *not* say, 'The lady is not', but 'the lady's not . . .' (just as she was told).

(the) lady with a lamp (or the Lamp) Nickname given to Florence Nightingale, philanthropist and nursing pioneer, in commemoration of her services to soldiers at Scutari during the Crimean War (1853–6). She inspected hospital wards at night, carrying a lamp – a Turkish lantern consisting of a candle inside a collapsible shade. The phrase 'lady with *a* lamp' appears to have been coined by Longfellow in his poem *Santa Filomena* (1858 – i.e. very shortly after the events described). On her death, Moore Smith & Co. of Moorgate, London, published an anonymous ballad with the title 'The Lady with *the* Lamp'. The film biography (1951), with Anna Neagle as Miss Nightingale, was called *The Lady with a Lamp* and was based on a play (1929) by Reginald Berkeley. Very occasionally one finds 'The Lady *of* a Lamp'.

(a) lager lout A young person in the UK, noted for lager consumption and a tendency to violence, particularly when attending football matches. The species was identified in 1988, the name clearly owing much to alliteration. According to Simon Walters, political correspondent of *The Sun*, in a letter to *The Independent* (13 April 1989): 'It dates back to last August when the Home Office referred to the "lager culture" among young troublemakers . . . from that I coined the term "lager lout" to give it more meaning.'

lake See GO JUMP.

(a) lame duck Referring to someone or something handicapped by misfortune or by incapacity, this was the name originally given to a defaulter on the London Stock Exchange in the 19th century. In William Thackeray's *Vanity Fair*, Chap. 13 (1847–8), the money-conscious Mr Osborne is suspicious of the financial position of Amelia's father: 'I'll have no lame duck's daughter in my family.' It is said that people who could not pay their debts would 'waddle' out of Exchange Alley in the City of London – hence perhaps, the 'duck'. In the USA, the term has come to be applied to a President or other office-holder whose power is diminished because he is about to leave office or because he is handicapped by some scandal. In *circa* 1970, the term came also to be applied by British politicians to industries unable to survive without government financial support.

lamp See AS DIM.

(a) lamp in the window (for my wandering boy) What was Groucho Marx alluding to in *Horse Feathers* (US 1932) when he said, 'There'll always be a lamp in the window for my wandering boy'? Probably this was a bringing together of two clichés from popular fiction and parlour poetry. 'Where is my wand'ring boy tonight?' is the first line of a poem/song written and composed by the (pre-

sumably American) Reverend R. Lowry in 1877. Under the title 'Where Is My Boy Tonight?' it is said to be No. 303 in Ira D. Sankey's *Sacred Songs and Solos*. There was a silent film entitled *Where Is My Wandering Boy Tonight?* (US 1922). No mention of a lamp in the window, however. Putting a light or lamp in a window is, though, a traditional sign of devotion or of showing support for a cause. In a speech in Scotland on 29 November 1880, Lord Rosebery said of Gladstone: 'From his home in Wales to the Metropolis of Scotland there has been no village too small to afford a crowd to greet him – there has been no cottager so humble that could not find a light to put in his window as he passed.'

(to) lance the boil Meaning 'to try and solve a problem by making a bold stroke'. Date of origin of this figurative use, unknown. 'Lebanon has now made it possible to involve other Arab states in the process and therefore to come up with a more comprehensive approach than would have been possible otherwise. That is the boil the Reagan plan has helped lance' – *The Economist* (13 November 1982); 'The Treasury rules should be changed to close this loophole and lance the nasty little boil of councillors awarding themselves poll tax payers' cash without having to account' – *The Sunday Times* (20 August 1989); 'Mr Major at least, and at last, has had enough . . . He has been seeking out his closest friends in the trade to discuss how to "lance the boil"' – *The Independent* (23 June 1995); '"Mr Major has lanced the boil," he reported confidently at 5.23. This, indeed, quickly became the metaphor of the night. Never was a boil more comprehensively lanced' – *The Observer* (25 June 1995).

land See BACK TO THE; IN THE; BLOT ON.

—land PHRASES. Format phrase, as in 'radioland', 'listenerland' 'viewerland' – a suffix construction originating in the USA. 'Hi there, all you folks out their in radioland!' – a presenter might well have said in the 1930s/40s. In the late 1950s/early 1960s, Granada TV in the UK was promoted with a series of print ads giving facts about 'Granadaland', the area covered by the company and then comprising Lancashire and Yorkshire. From the American *Spy* Magazine (February 1989): 'And from the *Spy* mailroom floor: The Unsoliciteds out in Returnenvelopeland continue to ply us with free verse and promises of loose fiction.' It can be argued that the format predates all this. Shaw used the words 'Gilbertland' in 1892 and 'Wagnerland' in 1894. Almost the last words of Thackeray's novel *The Newcomes* (1853–4) are: 'Anything you like happens in Fableland'. In 1827 Coleridge has in his poem 'The Two Founts': "Twas my last waking thought, how it could be / That thou, sweet friend, such anguish should'st endure; / When straight from Dreamland came a Dwarf, and he / Could tell the cause, forsooth, and knew the cure.' Even earlier, in 1682, lines 203–206 of Dryden's 'Mac Flecknoe' offer this advice to minor poets: 'Thy Genius calls thee not to purchase fame / In keen Iambicks, but mild Anagram: / Leave writing Plays, and chuse for thy command / Some peacefull Province in Acrostick Land.'

(a) land fit for heroes (sometimes **country fit for heroes)** Semi-official political slogan in the UK, after the First World War. When the war was over, Prime Minister David Lloyd George gave rise to this slogan in a speech at Wolverhampton on 24 November 1918, the exact words of which were: 'What is our task? To make Britain a fit country for heroes to live in.' By 1921, with wages falling in all industries, the sentiment was frequently recalled and mocked.

(a) land flowing with milk and honey An idyllic, prosperous situation. The origin of the phrase is to be found in Exodus 3:8: 'And I am come to deliver them out of the hand of the Egyptians . . . unto a land flowing with milk and honey.'

(a) land of a thousand contrasts Travel promotion and general advertising cliché. Date of origin unknown. 'Land of contrasts' was included in the 'travel scribes' armoury' compiled from a competition in *The Guardian* (10 April 1993). Any use of 'contrasts' is liable to qualify as a cliché, however. 'A Moroccan Summer. This beautiful land of a thousand contrasts is

the backdrop to the Austin Reed Spring Summer Collections' – Austin Reed's Spring/Summer catalogue (1995); 'In part two, to be shown next Friday, [Jan] Morris will be visiting Manhattan. One suspects that she will find it a city of contrasts' – *The Observer* Magazine (22 December 1996).

land of hope and glory 'Land of Hope and Glory' is the title popularly given to the Finale of Sir Edward Elgar's *Coronation Ode* (1902), originally written for performance at the time of the Coronation of Edward VII. Elgar, having written the basic *Ode*, invited A. C. Benson to fit words to the big tune in the Trio of the 'Pomp and Circumstance March No. 1', which had first been performed the previous year: 'Land of Hope and Glory, Mother of the Free, / How shall we extol thee, who are born of thee? / Wider still and wider shall thy bounds be set; / God who made thee mighty, make thee mightier yet.' It is said that the idea for this came from the King himself. In 1914, Benson recast the words as a war song, but these have not endured in the way the originals have done. Hence, *Hope and Glory*, the title of a film (UK 1987).

(to go into the) land of Nod To fall/be asleep (compare 'to nod off'). Jonathan Swift has the expression in *Polite Conversation* (1738). As such, this is a pun on the land of Nod ('on the East of Eden'), to which Cain was exiled after he had slain Abel (Genesis 4:16).

lang may yer lum reek 'May you have long life', in Scots dialect. A 'lum' is a chimney, 'reek' is smoke – so the phrase literally means: 'long may your chimney smoke'.

language See COUNTRIES SEPARATED.

lantern See CA IRA.

lap See IN THE.

large lumps! Catchphrase of the British comedian Dickie Hassett, who flourished in about 1940. He was even given a BBC radio show with the title. Remembered by some as 'large lumps – they're lovely!' and explained by others as having appeared in a sketch about London street cries: 'Don't fergit yer mohair laces . . . Sarsparillar . . .

Matches, two fer a h'penny!' 'Large lumps' was the cry of the iced coconut man.

larger than life   See HE WAS A BIG MAN.

(the) lark ascending   'The Lark Ascending' is the title of poem (1881) by George Meredith. It was taken by Ralph Vaughan Williams for his noted orchestral piece (1914).

larovers for meddlers and crutches for lame ducks   Fobbing-off phrase – and like all such, this is a way of *not* giving an answer to an inquisitive person, especially a child. If someone asks, 'What have you got there?' this is the reply. Possibly a Northern dialect expression originally but now quite widespread. Could 'meddlers' be 'medlars' (i.e. the fruit – also a term for the female genitals)? There are many variations as to the words involved. Philip N. Wicks, Northamptonshire, recalled (1994): 'When as a small I child I asked my Mother [who hailed from Norfolk], "What's in there?" regarding the contents of any unreadable packet or blank blue grocer's bag, she would reply secretively, "Leerooks for meddlers and beans for gooses eyes". I've wondered for forty years what she meant.' *Partridge/Catch Phrases* finds a version already in use by 1668. *Apperson* explained 'larovers' as 'lay-overs' – things laid over, covered up, to protect them from meddlers – and concluded: 'Almost every county has its variation probably of this phrase. The most common form in which it survives, however, is "Layers for meddler".' A surprising occurrence is in Chap. 32 of Margaret Mitchell's *Gone With the Wind* (1936). Scarlett O'Hara, when asked who is going to lend her money in Atlanta, that she needed to pay the taxes on Tara, avoids answering the question by saying, 'archly': 'Layovers catch meddlers.' *Morris* confirms the American use: '*layover to catch meddlers* is a dialect variant of a very common answer used by adults to evade a direct answer to children's questions. Instead of saying to the child, "It's none of your business," he would be told, "It's *layover to catch meddlers*." So what's a *layover?* you ask. A *layover* is a trap for bears or other unwary animals, made of a pit covered with boughs. And a *meddler*, of course, is a

person who interferes in other people's business. The phrase was recorded in Eastern and Southern states as long ago as 1890. It also appears as *larovers for meddlers, layos to catch meddlers* and even as a single word, *larofamedlers.*' Another explanation is that 'lay-holes for medlars' are what you put the fruit in to ripen. *Partridge* also gives the variant: 'Crutches for meddlers and legs for lame ducks'. No easy solution to this one. Compare WHIM-WHAMS FOR A GOOSE'S BRIDLE.

(the) last best hope of earth   Referring to the act of giving freedom to the slaves by the USA, the phrase comes from Abraham Lincoln's Second Annual Message to Congress (1 December 1862): 'We shall nobly save or meanly lose the last, best hope of earth'.

(a) last chance trendy (or LCT)   Species of male, identified in the UK, who – faced with the onset of his fortieth birthday, or thereabouts – attempts to look and behave younger than he is, with inappropriate results. At the time this man was celebrated (Fred Wedlock's disc 'The Oldest Swinger in Town' was a hit in 1981; Christopher Matthew used the phrase 'Last-Chance Trendy' in his book *How To Survive Middle Age* in 1983), the symptoms of such behaviour included wearing tight trousers, styling long hair carefully to cover bald spots, and sporting gold medallions and other equipment unsuitable for a man of this vintage. The LCT also attempts to pursue younger women, often dumping his wife in the process, and exhibits many of the hallmarks of the mid-life crisis.

(the) last great wilderness   Cliché, especially in travel writing use. Date of origin unknown. Part of the 'travel scribes' armoury' compiled from a competition in *The Guardian* (10 April 1993). 'Each year the Highlands of Scotland, Britain's last great wilderness, attract thousands of people seeking a new way of life' – *The Independent* (30 June 1994); 'The howling of the grey wolf, portrayed for centuries as a bloodthirsty predator to be killed on sight, is being heard in the snow-covered forests of Yellowstone Park this week for the first time in half a century. This is thanks to an enlightened "recovery plan" to restore the balance of nature in one of north America's last great wilderness areas' – *The Irish Times* (20 January 1995); 'A Highland estate regarded as one of Scotland's last great wilderness areas, that of Knoydart, is likely to be sold following an imminent take-over of its present owner, the Dundee-based Titaghur jute company' – *The Herald* (Glasgow) (11 April 1995).

(a/the) last hurrah Phrase for a politician's final flourish or farewell. From *The Last Hurrah*, the title of a novel (1956; film US 1958) by Edwin O'Connor, about an ageing Boston-Irish politician making his last electoral foray.

(the) last of England 'The Last of England' is the title of a painting (1855) by Ford Madox Brown that shows a young man and woman huddled together on a boat, as they emigrate. It was inspired by the departure of Thomas Woolner, the Pre-Raphaelite sculptor, who left England for Australia in order to join the gold rush. 'The Last of England' also became the title poem of a collection (1970) by the Australian poet Peter Porter ('You cannot leave England, it turns / A planet majestically in the mind').

(ah, the) last of the big spenders! Ironic put-down, descriptive of someone who is being tight with his money. American, from the 1920s/30s.

(the) last of the Red-Hot Mommas (or **Mamas)** Stage sobriquet of Sophie Tucker, the singer, taken from the title of a song by Jack Yellen, which was introduced by her in 1928.

(the) last of the (summer) wine *The Last of the Summer Wine* is the title of a BBC TV comedy series (1974 onwards) about a trio of old school friends in a Yorkshire village, finding themselves elderly and unemployed. According to Roy Clarke, the programme's writer, the phrase is 'not a quotation, merely a provisional title which seemed to suit the age group and location. I expected it to be changed but no one ever thought of anything better' – in *Radio Times* (February 1983). The phrase 'last of the wine' had earlier been used to describe things of which there is only a finite amount or of which

the best has gone. From a programme note by composer Nicholas Maw for *The Rising of the Moon*, Glyndebourne Festival Opera, 1970: 'In a recent television interview, Noël Coward was asked if he thought it still possible to write comedy for the stage. Did his own generation not have the "last of the wine"?' In the 1950s, Robert Bolt wrote a radio play with the title *The Last of the Wine* and Mary Renault, a novel (1956).

(a/the) last resort Positively the last place wherein to seek help or the ultimate chance to rescue a situation. Originally a legal expression for the supreme court of appeal. From Sir Walter Scott, *The Bride of Lammermoor*, Chap. 16 (1819): '"No, my lord," answered Underwood; "it is in the House of British Peers, whose honour must be equal to their rank – it is in the court of last resort, that we must parley together".' Probably French in origin – in the 17th century, they talked of *dernier ressort*.

—— lasts the whole —— through The original advertising use of this format occurred in advertisements for Schweppes Tonic Water, created by Ogilvy & Mather in 1955 and current into the 1960s. Commander Edward Whitehead, an actual Royal Navy veteran (with a splendid beard), appeared in ads explaining 'Schweppervescence . . . those patrician little bubbles that always *last your whole drink through*.' From the BBC radio *Goon Show* (1958/9): 'Ray Ellington lasts the whole drink through' / 'Ray Ellington lasts the whole *day* through' etc.

(the) last supper Name given to the meal shared by Jesus Christ and his disciples the night before he was crucified and, thus, the origin of the Eucharist, Lord's Supper, Holy Communion and Mass. The phrase does not appear as such in the Bible, but may have become known chiefly through its use as the English title of the painting (1494–7) by Leonardo da Vinci in Milan. This is known in Italian simply as '*La Cena*' [The Supper], though sometimes '*L'Ultima Cena*'.

(you'd/you'll be) late for your own funeral Admonition to someone who is chronically unpunctual. Origin and date unknown.

(the) late great ―― Cliché, mostly used by disc jockeys and pop promoters. That death can confer status on a pop star, and do wonders for record sales, is certainly true – however, one feels that the use of 'great' here has often rather more to do with the demands of rhyme than truth. Since the 1950s/60s? 'Callaway, 75, earned his spurs as president of textile combine Burlington Industries, subsequently created a vineyard that he sold to Hiram Walker for $14 million, and, as befits a second cousin of the late, great Bobby Jones, turned his talents to golf' – *The Times* (10 November 1994); 'Scottish football will today be given another chance to pay its respects to the late great Davie Cooper – and Hotline callers are anxious for it to be done properly' – *Daily Record* (1 April 1995).

late lamented ―― Referring mostly to the dead who are still missed. Known by 1859. A cliché by the mid-20th century. 'One programme, *Subterranea Britannica* (BBC2), was the stuff of the late-lamented *40 Minutes* and at 50 minutes outstayed its welcome' – *The Herald* (Glasgow) (7 May 1994); 'Like the time when, as a callow 17-year-old during an Edinburgh Festival-time jam session, Travis suggested to the late, lamented alto saxophonist Joe Harriott that they play something up-tempo' – *The Herald* (Glasgow) (19 January 1995).

(the) late unpleasantness Euphemism for the previous war or recent hostilities. It was introduced by the US humorist David Ross Locke in *Ekkoes from Kentucky* (1868). Writing as 'Petroleum V. Nasby', he referred to the recently ended Civil War as 'the late onpleasantniss' and the coinage spread. It still survives: 'Here, for instance, is Dan Rather, America's father-figure, on the hot-line to Panama during the late unpleasantness [an invasion] . . .' – *The Independent* (20 January 1990).

laugh See ANYTHING FOR A; HAS HE BEEN.

laughed See I HAVEN'T BEEN.

(to) laugh haversacks To laugh a great deal. The choice of 'haversacks' is puzzling. Could it mean, 'laugh *loads*', especially when variants include 'laughing kitbags'? Mostly Forces' slang, since the 1930s.

laugh? – I thought I should have died (or **. . . I thought I'd died)** Exaggerated expression to convey appreciation of a joke or, more usually, a comic happening. British use, since the 1880s. The line occurs in Albert Chevalier's song 'Knocked 'Em in the Old Kent Road' (1890s). Variant completions include **. . . I nearly bought my own beer!** and **. . . I nearly fell off the wife!**

(to) laugh like drains To laugh very hard and loud. Probably of British origin in the mid-20th century. Possibly reflecting that, just as drains sometimes gurgle, so that is the way extreme laughter can sound. Recorded by 1948. 'Some people at the screening I went to laughed like drains. Maybe they were Alan Parker's family, or his backers. Most of us sat in pained silence' – *Independent on Sunday* (5 February 1995).

laughter is the best medicine Modern-ish proverb but with no supporting dates or sources. Wolfgang Mieder & Co.'s *A Dictionary of American Proverbs* has it, together with 'Laugh and be well', which states the same thing. Going back a bit further there are other similar proverbs, like 'Time is the best medicine' (Ovid) and 'Patience is the best medicine' (John Florio). The nearest to a sourced version of this one is 'Mirth is God's medicine', which is in *Proverbs from Plymouth Pulpit* by Henry Ward Beecher, the American Congregationalist minister and writer (1813–97). Like Benjamin Franklin's *Poor Richard's Almanac*, this work was a collection rather than an original composition. Still, it confirms the proverbial nature of the target remark. Odd that 'Laughter is the best medicine' is not more specifically recorded before the 20th century and before *Reader's Digest* began running its 'Laughter, the Best Medicine' feature. Of course, there have been a number of studies to show that laughter can have a very positive effect on patients' actual health, especially when conventional medical methods have failed. This does not extend to the Robin Williams's film *Patch Adams* about an excruciating man who entertains terminally ill kids in clown costume. This remark has been ascribed to a 17th-century British physician: 'The arrival of a good clown into a village does more for its health than twenty asses laden down with drugs.' Compare the title of Irvin S. Cobb's joke miscellany: *A Laugh a Day Keeps the Doctor Away* (1921).

law See IS THERE A.

law and order An inevitable coupling, together by 1598 at least. In 1846, the 'Law and Order' Party existed in the USA. The recent cliché status of the phrase dates from 1968 when Richard Nixon was running for the American presidency and decided to pursue the 'law and order vote'. It also became a popular issue in British politics, and so widely was the phrase used – and so sloppily spoken – that people took to referring to 'Laura Norder' as if she were a person. 'Laura Norder is adamant . . . more police means less crime, tougher courts lead to fuller jails equals happiness all round. Or so the theory goes' – George Hume column in *The Herald* (Glasgow) (22 September 1994).

(the) law is an ass Strictly speaking, if one is quoting Dickens, what Mr Bumble says, is not 'the law is *an* ass' but, 'If the law supposes that . . . the law is a ass – a idiot' – *Oliver Twist*, Chap. 51 (1837). He is dismayed that the law holds him responsible for his wife's actions. Earlier, the playwright George Chapman wrote in *Revenge for Honour* (published 1654): 'I am ashamed the law is such an ass.'

lawk-a-mussy (or lawks . . .)! Euphemistic exclamation since the late 19th century. A softening of 'Lord have mercy!'

lawyer See HAVE YOUR LAWYER.

(to) lay an egg To fail, flop. Although the *OED2* says the source is American, *Morris* and other transatlantic sources give the English game of cricket as the origin of this expression meaning 'to fail'. A zero score was called a 'duck's egg' because of the obvious resemblance between the number and the object. In the USA in baseball there developed a similar expression, 'goose egg'. 'Wall Street lays an egg . . . The most dramatic event in the financial history of America is the collapse of the New York Stock Market' – headline and text in *Variety* (30 October 1929).

(to) lay it on with a trowel Benjamin Disraeli is said to have told Matthew Arnold: 'Everyone likes flattery; and when you come to Royalty you should lay it on with a trowel.' But the figure of speech was an old one even in the 19th century. 'That was laid on with a trowel' appears in Shakespeare's *As You Like It*, I.ii.98 (1598), which the Arden edition glosses as 'slapped on thick and without nicety, like mortar'. The trowel in question is not a garden one, but of the kind used by painters for spreading paint thickly.

lazy See AS LAZY AS.

lazy Lawrence (or Larrence or Laurence) 'One of my father's sayings if we said we were too tired to do anything was "You've got Laurence"' – Mrs K.Y. Williams, Herefordshire (1998). This dates back to 1650, by some accounts. The reference may be to the general 'heat around St Lawrence's day (10 August) or to the legend of the martyred St Lawrence being too lazy to move in the flames' – according to *Apperson* and *Partridge/Slang*.

lead balloon See GO DOWN.

lead on, Macduff! Meaning, 'you lead the way!; let's get started!' the expression is from Shakespeare's *Macbeth*, V.iii.33 (1606): '*Lay on*, Macduff; / And damn'd be he that first cries, "Hold enough!"' There has been a change of meaning along the way. Macbeth uses the words 'lay on', defined by *OED2* as: 'to deal blows with vigour, to make vigorous attack, assail'. The shape of the phrase was clearly so appealing that it was adapted to a different purpose.

(a) leap in the dark A venture, an action, a decision, where the outcome is unknown or unknowable. Known by the 17th century. 'I am about to take my last voyage, a great leap in the dark' – last words of Thomas Hobbes (d. 1679), quoted in John Watkins *Anecdotes of Men of Learning* (1808); 'A little before you made a leap into the dark' – Thomas Brown, *Letters from the Dead to the Living* (1702).

(people with) learning difficulties. Substitute phrase for 'mentally handicapped', in deference to political correctness, but this term is rejected by the charity Mencap, which after all has an interest in retaining the well-established phrase alluded to in its name. In July 1992, the charity said the new phrase was 'inaccurate' and that using it in answer to demands from charity and social workers would cost Mencap support because the public 'would not understand it'. Steven Billington, Mencap's director of marketing and appeals, said, 'It is only a matter of time before even the most right-on expression becomes a term of abuse. It has been the same since people talked about village idiots, and "learning difficulties" is no exception. Children are already calling each other LDs as an insult.' 'In cautioning against putting too much emphasis on early French immersion for the majority of children, the report says such programs may harm children with learning difficulties' – *The Globe and Mail* (Toronto) (25 August 1976); 'When I heard that someone had "learning difficulties", I had no idea what it meant . . . If someone has learning difficulties, it could be because their school was burnt down, because they are deaf, because they are in the Tory Cabinet, because all their teachers are talking a foreign language or many other reasons, one of which might be a physical or psychological inability to learn' – *The Independent* (20 January 1992); '[Lord Rix, Mencap's chairman, said:] "learning difficulties" is a misnomer. It implies that mental handicap is all a matter of education . . . My child [born mentally handicapped] is 40 and to describe her as having a learning difficulty is a travesty of the truth"' – *The Independent* (20 July 1992).

(to) leave no stone unturned Meaning, 'to search for something with complete thoroughness, to make every endeavour to find something'. From an anonymously published attack on dice-playing, *circa* 1550: 'He will refuse no labour nor leave no stone unturned, to pick up a penny.' Also known since 1575 in the form 'no straw unturned'. The expression was used by President Johnson in 1963 when announcing the terms of the Warren Commission's investigations into the cause of President Kennedy's assassination. Diana Rigg neatly twisted the phrase for her collection of theatrical reviews – *No*

Turn Unstoned (1982), though Bernard Shaw and Arthur Wimperis had done so before her. It was cited as a 'silly expression' that had recently been 'killed by the jeers of a few journalists' in George Orwell, 'Politics and the English Language' in *Horizon* (April 1946) – obviously a touch prematurely. Listed in *The Independent* (24 December 1994) as a cliché of newspaper editorials. 'Fancy picture of an eminent politician in search of a formula, leaving no stone unturned while exploring every avenue' – caption to cartoon in *Punch* (2 December 1931); 'We won't leave a stone unturned until we bring this animal to justice. We'll catch someone for this because they need to be locked up' – *Daily Mirror* (6 September 1994); 'Police are leaving no stone unturned as they search for a slippery customer who stole a snake' – *Daily Record* (4 May 1995).

(to) leave severely alone Known by 1880. The *Pocket Oxford Dictionary* (1924 edn) gave it as an example of a cliché. 'If the King Street commissars were not so invincibly stupid, they would have insisted that the movement be left severely alone' – Christopher Driver, *The Disarmers* (1964).

left and right See RIGHT AND LEFT.

(a) left-footer A Roman Catholic; 20th-century origin, possibly a coinage of Northern Ireland Protestants. In the Irish Republic it is assumed that a spade is pushed into the ground using the left foot by agricultural labourers. Hence, as anyone from southern Ireland is likely to be a Roman Catholic, then he is likely to be a left-footer. Recorded by 1944.

left hand down a bit A standard instruction to people with their hands on the steering wheel of a vehicle. Meaning, 'to turn in an anti-clockwise direction'. Applied to navigation in many editions of BBC radio's *The Navy Lark* (1960s/70s). Leslie Phillips would say it as a naval officer steering a boat. Jon Pertwee would reply, 'Left hand down it is, sir!'

leg See ARM AND A; BREAK A.

legal, decent, honest, truthful Slogan of the Advertising Standards Authority (founded 1962), reflecting the British Code of Advertising Practice view that the essence of good advertising is that 'all advertisements should be legal, decent, honest and truthful'. Originally, this was 'Legal, *Clean*, Honest, Truthful' – according to J. Pearson and G. Turner, *The Persuasion Industry* (1965). *Legal Decent Honest Truthful* was, accordingly, the title of a BBC Radio 4 comedy series about advertising (mid-1980s).

(a) legal eagle A legal expert. For many years from the 1980s to the early 2000s, the BBC Radio 2 presenter Jimmy Young referred to his visiting legal expert thus. Obviously, the rhyme dictates the 'eagle' bit, though this might be an appropriate epithet for one playing a look-out role. *Partridge/Slang* dates it from 'late 1940s, ex US'. There was a US film with the title *Legal Eagles* in 1986.

(a) legal loophole Meaning, 'a way of getting round the law.' This alliterative phrase was known by 1768. 'Legal loophole allows boy rapist to avoid custody' – headline in *The Independent* (12 November 1994); 'The closure of a legal loophole which lets Europe dump toxic waste on developing countries as "recyclable" material has created a profitable new crime: waste smuggling' – *Independent on Sunday* (1 January 1995).

(a) legend in one's own lifetime (or **living legend)** Both these phrases are now clichés of tribute. A possibility exists that the first person to whom both were applied (and within a couple of pages of each other) actually deserved them. Lytton Strachey in *Eminent Victorians* (1918) wrote of Florence Nightingale: 'She was a legend in her lifetime, and she knew it . . . Once or twice a year, perhaps, but nobody could be quite certain, in deadly secrecy, she went for a drive in the park. Unrecognised, the living legend flitted for a moment before the common gaze.' 'A great many have occupied your chair but it is a measure of your Speakership that you have become a legend in your own lifetime' – Margaret Thatcher, speech marking the retirement of George Thomas, Speaker of the House of Commons (May 1983); '"It's called The Living Legend – The Tony Blackburn Story," he explains more or less tongue-in-cheek. "They call me the

Living Legend at Radio One . . . I'm known as the Survivor around there"' – Tony Blackburn, disc jockey, quoted in *The Guardian* (25 August 1984); 'In 1888 [Robert Louis] Stevenson had set out with his family entourage for the South Seas, becoming a legend in his lifetime' – *The Oxford Companion to English Literature* (1985); '. . . the King of the One-liners, Henny Youngman, who'd befriended me after I'd introduced him on one of the London Palladium shows as "a rumour in his own lifetime"' – Bob Monkhouse, *Crying With Laughter* (1993), referring to the 1950s; 'Leading libel lawyer Peter Carter-Ruck once said of him [Lord Goodman]: "He became a legend in his lifetime"' – *Sunday Express* (14 May 1995). Compare: **legend in his own lunchtime**. In about 1976, Christopher Wordsworth, reviewing a novel by Clifford Makins, a sporting journalist, described the author as having been this. The epithet is now quite frequently applied to other journalists of a certain type. According to Ned Sherrin, *Theatrical Anecdotes* (1991): 'David Climie, the witty revue and comedy writer . . . claims to have invented the phrase "A legend in his own lunchtime" and to have lavished it on the mercurial BBC comedy innovator, Dennis Main Wilson.'

lemon See ANSWER'S A; LIKE A PORK CHOP.

less is more A design statement made by the German-born architect Mies van der Rohe (d. 1969), meaning that less visual clutter makes for a more satisfying living environment. Robert Browning had used the phrase in a different artistic context in the poem 'Andrea del Sarto' (1855). In Philip Johnson's *Mies van der Rohe* (1953 edn, though probably also in the original 1947 one), there is a passage on Mies as an architect of 'exhibition installation' (the Barcelona chair and the like): 'As in architecture, he has always been guided by his personal motto, "less is more".' In June or July 1923 Mies wrote, in the first issue of the magazine *G* (that is the full title), on a *Bürohaus* [office building]: *"Größter Effekt mit geringstem Aufwand an Mitteln* [greatest effect with smallest use of means]"' – which is the very same as the Mies explanation of 'Less is more' that was given in *Time* (14 June 1954).

lest we forget   Phrase from Rudyard Kipling's 'Recessional' (1897), written as a Jubilee Day warning that while empires pass away, God lives on. Kipling himself, however, may have agreed to the adoption of 'Lest we forget' as an epitaph at the time of his work for the Imperial War Graves Commission after the First World War. *Lest We Forget* was the title of the Fritz Lang film *Hangmen Also Die* (US 1943) when it was re-issued.

let   See DON'T CALL.

let bygones be bygones   Let us not dwell on things that have happened in the past. 'Bygones' here means 'things that are past'. A proverbial expression known in English by 1546, but the thought is expressed by the Greek philosopher Epictetus.

let George do it!   Meaning 'let someone else do it, or take the responsibility', this catchphrase was in use by the 1900s and is probably of American origin. It appears on a screen title in *Gertie the Dinosaur*, one of the first movie cartoons (US 1909). A bet is placed in an archaeological museum that a dinosaur cannot be made to move. When it does so, a celebratory dinner is held. The question then is, who will pay? 'Let George do it' is the reply. It seems unlikely that this was the origin of the phrase – merely one of the uses that popularized it. Indeed, H. L. Mencken, *The American Language* (1922), traces it back to the French *laissez faire à Georges*. The phase received a new lease of life with the invention of the autopilot in the Second World War. Inevitably, the autopilot was dubbed 'George'.

let me tell you   See RAMSBOTTOM.

let's —— and see if ——   In business and advertising, this construction has been much used to indicate how an idea should be researched and tested, or rather, simply put to the public to see what the reaction will be. Some of the versions: 'Let's . . . run it up the flagpole and see if anyone salutes it' [apparently used in the film *Twelve Angry Men*, US 1957] / '. . . put it on the porch and see if the cat will eat it' / '. . . put it on the train and see if it gets off at Westchester' / '. . . leave it in the water overnight and see if it springs any leaks.'

Not forgetting: 'Let me just pull something out of the hat here and see if it hops for us.' All these were known by the early 1980s.

let's do the show (right here in the barn)!   Show business and entertainment cliché but always recalled in affectionate parody. This is taken to be a staple line from the films featuring the young Mickey Rooney and Judy Garland from 1939 onwards. It had several forms: 'Hey! I've got it! Why don't we **put on a show?**' / 'Hey kids! We can put on the show in the backyard!' – but a precise example has proved hard to find. In *Babes in Arms* (1939), Rooney and Garland play teenage children (of retired vaudeville players) who decide to put on a big show of their own. Alas, they do not actually say any of the above lines, though they do express their determination to 'put on a show'. In *Strike Up the Band* (1940), Rooney has the line: 'Say, that's not a bad idea. We could put on our own show!' – though he does not say it to Garland. 'Hey, why don't we put on a show?' is cited in the song 'I Love a Film Cliché' by Dick Vosburgh and Trevor Lyttleton from the show *A Day in Hollywood, A Night in the Ukraine* (1980).

let's get America moving again. Slogan. A recurring theme in election slogans is that of promising to move forward after a period of inertia. John F. Kennedy used this one in 1960 – Walt Rostow is credited with suggesting it (sometimes it was '. . . this country moving again'). It is a short step from this to Ronald Reagan's 'Let's make America great again' in 1980. There is also a format phrase: **let's get —— moving again**. The Irish politician Jack Lynch ran under the banner 'Get our country moving'. So, interchangeable slogans and formats that could be made to apply to any politician, party or country.

let's get down to the (real) nitty-gritty   Meaning, 'let's get down to the real basics of a problem or situation' (like 'getting down to brass tacks'). Sheilah Graham, the Hollywood columnist, in her book *Scratch an Actor* (1969) says of Steve McQueen: 'Without a formal education – Steve left school when he was fifteen – he has invented his own vocabulary to express what he means . . . His "Let's get down to the nitty-gritty" has gone into the American language.' All she meant, one feels, is that McQueen popularized the term, for it is generally held to be a Black phrase and was talked about before the film star came on the scene. It seems to have had a particular vogue among Black Power campaigners *circa* 1963, and the first *OED2* citation is from that year. In 1963, Shirley Ellis recorded a song, 'The Nitty Gritty', to launch a new dance (like 'The Locomotion' before it). The opening line of the record was, 'Now let's get down to the real nitty-gritty'. *Flexner* (1982) comments: 'It may have originally referred to the grit-like nits or small lice that are hard to get out of one's hair or scalp, or to a Black English term for the anus.' In May 2002, when the British Home Office minister John Denham used the expression before delegates at the Police Federation annual conference, it was pointed out to him that this was prohibited in the modern police service as being a racist term. It was claimed that 'nitty-gritty' was the name for waste at the bottom of slave ships and would therefore be offensive to Afro-American or Afro-Caribbean sensitivities. How this derivation arose is anybody's guess.

let's get myself comfy! See under NAY, NAY – THRICE AGAIN NAY!

let's get *on* with it! Catchphrase of the British husband and wife entertainers, Nat Mills (1900–93) and Bobbie (d. 1955). They flourished in the 1930s and 1940s portraying 'a gumpish type of lad and his equally gumpish girlfriend'. Nat recalled (in 1979): 'It was during the very early part of the war. We were booked by the BBC to go to South Wales for a *Workers' Playtime*. Long tables had been set up in front of the stage for the workers to have lunch on before the broadcast. On this occasion, a works foreman went round all the tables shouting, "Come on, let's get on with it," to get them to finish their lunch on time. I was informed he used this phrase so many times, the workers would mimic him among themselves. So I said to Bobbie, "You start the broadcast by talking to yourself and I'll interject and say, 'Let's get on with it'." Lo and behold it got such

a yell of laughter we kept it in all our broadcasts. Even Churchill used our slogan to the troops during the early part of the war.'

let's get outta here! Stock phrase from the movies. A survey of 350 feature films, made in the USA between 1938 and 1985, revealed that the cry 'Let's get outta here!' was used at least once in 81 per cent of them and more than once in 17 per cent. In reporting this, the *Guinness Book of Movie Facts and Feats* (1993) adds that a film critic, David McGillivray, had disputed the finding. He asserted that no single phrase had been so overworked in film scripts as **try to get some rest**.

let's get this show on the road Now used as an encouragement to get started on any activity, this phrase was originally from American show business. Perhaps originally from circus and travelling theatre use, it probably moved into the mainstream through the military and business. From J. Blish, *Fallen Star* (1957): '"That's enough," Jayne said at last. "Let's get this show on the road".'

let's not, and say we did! 'While my father would never encourage me to lie, when confronted with something relatively trivial he did not want to do, he would say this' – Richard Paul-Jones, East Sussex (2000). *Partridge/Catch Phrases* has it as American, mainly juvenile, from about 1925 and 'probably long extinct'.

let's put on a show! See under LET'S DO THE SHOW . . .

let's roll! 'Let's get started!' Could this be a version of **wagon's roll!** (popularized in the 1950s' TV series *Wagon* Train) and, indeed, be from the days of wagon trains in the USA? Compare LET'S GET THIS SHOW ON THE ROAD. From *The Independent* (18 December 2001): 'It was a phrase that summed up America's resilience after the attacks of 11 September. "Let's roll" – the final words of Todd Beamer before he and other passengers on United Airlines Flight 93 tackled the hi-jackers – was even adopted by President Bush . . . "But we have our marching orders. My fellow Americans, let's roll".'

(to) let the cat out of the bag Meaning 'to reveal a secret', this saying derives from the trick played on unsuspecting purchasers of sucking pigs at old English country fairs. The pig would be shown to the buyer, then put in a sack while the deal was finalized. A quick substitution of a less valuable *cat* would then be made, and this is what the buyer would take away. When he opened the sack, he would 'let the cat out of the bag' and the subterfuge would be revealed. Known by 1760. 'We are commanded to be silent lest we should let the cat out of the bag. The cat out of the bag! There are in this novel about a hundred cats contained in a hundred bags, all screaming and mewing to be let out. Every new chapter contains a new cat. When we come to the end of it out goes the animal, and there is a new bag put into our hands which it is the object of the subsequent chapter to open. We are very willing to stroke some of these numerous cats, but it is not possible to do it without letting them out' – *The Times* (30 October 1860), reviewing *The Woman in White* by Wilkie Collins.

let the dog see the rabbit 'Said to others when crowding around a fire' – Stella Richardson, Essex (1998). *Partridge/Catch Phrases* gives a less specific meaning – 'get out of the way, get out of the light', from dog-track frequenters.

let them eat cake [*qu'ils mangent de la brioche*] Remark commonly ascribed to Marie-Antoinette, an Austrian disliked by the French people, after she had arrived in France to marry King Louis XVI in 1770. More specifically, she is supposed to have said it during the riots caused by a bread shortage in Paris (October 1789), though no evidence exists that she did. In the form, '*Qu'ils mangent de la brioche*', the saying refers to *brioche*, a type of sponge cake. *Brewer* (1894) has it that the Duchesse de Polignac was the culprit, exclaiming *to* Marie-Antoinette, 'How is it that these silly people are so clamorous for *bread*, when they can buy some nice brioches for a few sous?' And, 'It is said that our own Princess Charlotte avowed "that she would for her part *rather eat beef than starve*," and wondered that the people should be so obstinate as to insist upon having bread when it was so scarce.' The saying is to be found in Book 6 of Rousseau's *Confessions*, published posthumously in 1781–8 but written during the 1760s. Rousseau's version, referring to an incident in Grenoble about 1740, goes: 'At length I recollected the thoughtless saying of a great princess who, on being informed that the country people had no bread, replied, "Let them eat cake".' The *ODQ* (1979) notes that Louis XVIII in his *Relation d'un Voyage à Bruxelles et à Coblentz en 1791* (published 1823) attributes to Marie-Thérèse (1638–83), wife of Louis XIV, 'Why don't they eat pastry? [*Que ne mangent-ils de la croûte de pâté?*]' Tom Burnam, *The Dictionary of Misinformation* (1975), adds that Alphonse Karr, writing in 1843, recorded that a Duchess of Tuscany had said it in 1760 or before. Later, it was circulated to discredit Marie-Antoinette. Similar remarks are said to date back to the 13th century, so if Marie-Antoinette did ever say it, she was quoting.

let the punishment fit the crime Quotation with almost the force of a slogan. 'My object all sublime / I shall achieve in time – / To let the punishment fit the crime – / The punishment fit the crime' – W. S. Gilbert, *The Mikado*, Act 2 (1885).

let us go forward together Political slogan, if not cliché – chiefly made so by Winston Churchill: 'I can only say to you let us go forward together and put these grave matters to the proof' – the conclusion of a speech on Ulster (14 March 1914); 'Let us go forward together in all parts of the Empire, in all parts of the Island' – speaking on the war (27 January 1940); and 'I say, "Come then, let us go forward together with our united strength"' – in his 'Blood, sweat and tears' speech (13 May 1940). It occurs along with other rhetorical clichés during the 'Party Political Speech' (written by Max Schreiner) on the Peter Sellers comedy album *The Best of Sellers* (1958): 'Let us assume a bold front and go forward together.'

let your fingers do the walking Slogan for Yellow Pages (classified phone directories) from American Telephone & Telegraph Co., current from the 1960s. Also used in the UK and elsewhere.

(to start from a) level playing field
Meaning, 'to begin an enterprise with no
participant having an advantage over
another or with no unfairness involved'.
Known in the USA by 1988. Identified as a
current cliché in *The Times* (17 March
1995). 'We would in effect be saying "Here
are the arms: fight it out". That is the
policy of the level killing field' – Douglas
Hurd, British Foreign Secretary, in a letter
to *The Daily Telegraph* (5 April 1993) on
lifting the arms embargo in Bosnia in
favour of Muslims only; 'Tears flowed
when the axe fell. "The programme [TV
soap *Eldorado*] had a lot of baggage
attached to it," said Ms Hollingworth. "We
did not start from a level playing field
because there was so much antipathy"' –
Independent on Sunday (2 May 1993).

**Liberté, Égalité, Fraternité [liberty,
equality, fraternity]** Political slogan or
motto. Of earlier origin than the French
Revolution, it was adopted by the revolutionary Club des Cordeliers as its offical
motto on 30 June 1793. At first, the words
'. . . *Ou la mort* [or death]' were added,
but these were dropped from 1795.

Liberty Hall See ANYTHING GOES.

liberty or death Motto of *The New
Yorker* Magazine in the 1920s. This somewhat unlikely motto for a witty goings-on-
about-town sort of magazine was apparently chosen by the founding editor,
Harold Ross, in 1925. He was undoubtedly
thinking of Patrick Henry's famous speech
in the Virginia Convention (23 March 1775)
which helped carry the vote for independence: 'I know not what course others may
take; but as for me, give me liberty or give
me death!' Compare Joseph Addison, *Cato*,
Act, Sc. 5 (1713): 'Chains or conquest,
liberty or death.' Alexander Woollcott is
supposed to have said to Harold Ross: 'I
think your slogan "Liberty or Death" is
splendid and whichever one you decide
on will be all right with me.'

(a) licence to print money Said of any
enterprise where there is easy money to
be made. Roy Thomson (later Lord
Thomson), the Canadian-born industrialist,
said to a neighbour in Edinburgh just after
the opening of Scottish Television (a
commercial TV company he had founded)
in 1957: 'You know, it's just like having a
licence to print your own money.'

licensed to kill This James Bond label
appears frequently in the works of Ian
Fleming. In *Dr No* (1958): 'The licence to
kill for the Secret Service, the double-0
prefix, was a great honour.' There was a
Bond film with the title *Licence to Kill* (UK
1989). Compare this, by William Godwin
Jnr (son of the philosopher-novelist), in
Blackwood's Magazine (October 1833):
'My Lord of the thirty thousand acres
expired on a couch of down . . . each
moment of his fluctuating existence
watched by an obsequious practitioner,
"licensed to kill", whose trade it is to
assuage the pangs of death . . .' The
quotation marks make it look like an
established joke at the expense of doctors.
In 1881, Arthur Conan Doyle made a
rough sketch of himself on learning that
he had obtained his diploma as a Bachelor
of Medicine. Entitled 'Licensed to kill', it
was reproduced in *The Strand Magazine*
(October 1923). In Saki's posthumously
published short story 'The Cupboard of the
Yesterdays', one character says, 'In old
bygone days we had the wars in the Low
Countries always at our doors, as it were;
there was no need to go far afield into
malaria-stricken wilds if one wanted a life
of boot and saddle and licence to kill and
be killed.'

(to give something a) lick and a promise
A hasty cleaning of the body, especially
the face, with a promise to carry it out
more thoroughly at a later time. Also
applied to a dab of paint or a small
amount of work. Known by 1855.

(to) lick into shape To put the final
touches to something, make it more
presentable or efficient. Known by 1413.
From the belief that bear cubs are born
shapeless and have to be licked into shape
by their mothers. Told in the encyclopaedia compiled by the Arab physician
Avicenna (979–1037). 'Enforced, as a Bear
doth her Whelps, to bring forth this
confused lump, I had not time to lick it
into form' – Robert Burton, *The Anatomy
of Melancholy* (1621); 'A cast of 35, aged
from 11 to 25, will be taking part in the
Lionel Bart musical *Blitz*. They have had

just seven days of intensive rehearsals to lick it into shape' – *Northern Echo* (8 August 1995).

(that) licks hen racing 'My mother aged 90 has a saying. If anything puzzles her – such as mislaying something she had recently handled – she will look round, then stop and say, "Well, that licks hen racing"' – Mrs Gwyneth Harwood, North Yorkshire (1995), who later wrote to say that there had been a Radio 4 talk by Les Woodland on 'one man's efforts to revive the old country tradition of chicken racing' – apparently in Norfolk. A leg pull? 'My mother had a fund of sayings. About anything surprising, she would say: "That caps hen-racing"' – Ethel S. Dowey, North Yorkshire.

lick the dust See KICK THE BUCKET.

lie See CAMERA CANNOT.

lie down, I think I love you This was considered a sufficiently well-established, smart, jokey remark to be listed by *The Sun* (10 October 1984) as one of its 'ten top chat-up lines'. It may also have been used in a song or cartoon just a little before that. Indeed, there was a song entitled 'Lie Down (A Modern Love Song)' written and performed by the British group Whitesnake in 1978. Before that, 'Sit Down I Think I Love You', written by Stills, was performed by The Mojo Men in 1967. An article, 'Down with sex', was published in collected form (1966) by Malcolm Muggeridge in which he wrote: 'I saw scrawled on a wall in Santa Monica in California: "Lie down! I think I love you." Thus stripped, sex becomes an orgasm merely.' And then again, there was Groucho Marx' line to Margaret Dumont (indicating a sofa) from *The Cocoanuts* (US 1929), 'Won't you . . . lie down?' As ever, there is nothing new under the sun. Horace Walpole, in a letter to H. S. Conway on 23 October 1778, wrote: 'This sublime age reduces everything to its quintessence; all periphrases and expletives are so much in disuse, that I suppose soon the only way to making love will be to say "Lie down".'

lies, damn lies – and statistics Although sometimes attributed to Mark Twain – because it appears in his posthumously published *Autobiography* (1924) – this line should more properly be ascribed to Benjamin Disraeli, as indeed Twain took trouble to do: his exact words being, 'The remark attributed to Disraeli would often apply with justice and force: "There are three kinds of lies: lies, damned lies, and statistics".' On the other hand, the remark remains untraced among Disraeli's writings and sayings, and Lord Blake, Disraeli's biographer, does not know of any evidence that Disraeli said any such thing and thinks it most unlikely that he did. So why did Twain make the attribution? Leonard Henry Courtney, the British economist and politician (1832–1918), later Lord Courtney, gave a speech on proportional representation 'To My Fellow-Disciples at Saratoga Springs' (New York) in August 1895, in which this sentence appeared: 'After all, facts are facts, and although we may quote one to another with a chuckle the words of the Wise Statesman, "Lies – damn lies – and statistics," still there are some easy figures the simplest must understand, and the astutest cannot wriggle out of.' It is conceivable that Twain acquired the quotation from this – and also its veiled attribution to a 'Wise Statesman', whom he understood to be Disraeli. The speech was reproduced in *The* (British) *National Review*, No. 26, in the same year. Subsequently, Courtney's comment was reproduced in an article by J. A. Baines on 'Parliamentary Representation in England illustrated by the Elections of 1892 and 1895' in *Journal of the Royal Statistical Society,* No. 59 (1896): 'We may quote to one another with a chuckle the words of the Wise Statesman, lies, damn lies, and statistics, still there are some easy figures which the simplest must understand but the astutest cannot wriggle out of.' It would be a reasonable assumption that Courtney was referring to Disraeli by his use of the phrase 'Wise Statesman', though the context in which this phrase is used is somewhat complicated. For some reason, at this time, allusions to, rather than outright quotations of, Disraeli were the order of the day (he had died in 1881). Compare the fact that the remark to an author who had sent him an unsolicited manuscript – 'Many thanks; I shall lose no time in reading it' – is merely ascribed to an 'eminent man on this side of the Atlantic' by G. W. E. Russell in *Collections and Recollections*, Chap. 31 (1898). Comparable sayings: Dr Halliday Sutherland's autobiographical *A Time to Keep* (1934) has an account of Sir Henry Littlejohn, 'Police Surgeon, Medical Officer of Health and Professor of Forensic Medicine at the University [Edinburgh] . . . Sir Henry's class at 9 a.m. was always crowded, and he told us of the murder trials of the last century in which he had played his part. It was Lord Young [judge] who said, "There are four classes of witnesses – liars, damned liars, expert witnesses, and Sir Henry Littlejohn".' *Lies, Damn Lies, and Some Exclusives* – was the title of a book about British newspapers (1984) by Henry Porter. 'There are lies, damned lies . . . and Fianna Fáil party political broadcasts' – Barry Desmond MEP, (Irish) Labour Party director of elections, in November 1992.

life See ALL HUMAN; IS THERE.

(the) life and soul of the party Description of the person who makes a party go with a swing through force of personality. The words 'life' and 'soul' are together in Milton (1643), and *OED2* finds 'life of every party' in 1797 and 'life and soul of the play' in 1809. The full phrase does not appear before the 20th century. 'They seemed so anxious to make it plain to him, these honest fellows, that in him they recognized not only the life and soul of the party but the Master Mind' – P. G. Wodehouse, 'Archibald and the Masses' (1935); 'Offstage – Dudley doesn't strike you as being the life and soul of the party' – *Melody Maker* (17 July 1965); 'Lady Falkender on impartial obituaries of George Brown who was, for a while, the life and soul of the Party' – BBC Radio, *Stop Press* (7 June 1985); *Life of the Party* – title of biography of Pamela Harriman (1994) by Christopher Ogden.

life begins at forty Motto/modern proverb. In 1932, William B. Pitkin (1878–1953), Professor of Journalism at Columbia University, New York, published a book called *Life Begins at Forty* in which he dealt with 'adult reorientation' at a time when the problems of extended life and leisure were beginning to be recognized.

Based on lectures Pitkin had given, the book was a hearty bit of uplift: 'Every day brings forth some new thing that adds to the joy of life after forty. Work becomes easy and brief. Play grows richer and longer. Leisure lengthens. Life's afternoon is brighter, warmer, fuller of song; and long before shadows stretch, every fruit grows ripe . . . Life begins at forty. This is the revolutionary outcome of our new era . . . TODAY it is half a truth. TOMORROW it will be an axiom.' It is certainly a well-established catchphrase. Helping it along was a song with the title by Jack Yellen and Ted Shapiro (recorded by Sophie Tucker in 1937). *Life Begins at Forty* was the title of a film comedy (US, 1935) about a newspaper editor campaigning to free a man jailed for a bank robbery he did not commit. *Life Begins at Oxford Circus* was the title of a Crazy Gang show at the London Palladium in 1935. *Life Begins at Eight-Thirty* followed as the title of a film (US 1942).

life gits tee-jus, don't it? 'Life Gits Tee-Jus, Don't It?' was the title of a monologue, or 'talking blues', written in the 1940s by the American guitarist/singer/songwriter Carson J. Robison (1890–1957). Robison himself recorded the song in 1947 and had a US hit with it in 1948, though others were also successful, notably Tex Williams, Peter Lind Hayes and Wink Martindale.' 'Spoken ad lib', this is how it begins: 'The sun comes up and the sun goes down, / The hands on the clock keep goin' roun', / I just git up and it's time to lay down, / LIFE GITS TEE-JUS, DON'T IT?'

life is hard This stern text was always quoted to Peter Wood, the theatre director, by what he called his West Country 'Protestant Work Ethic' family. Many years later, he was struggling upstairs with his parrot, Sid, in his cage – when the parrot, too, suddenly said it to him (as he recalled on BBC Radio *Quote . . . Unquote* (31 March 1992). Other forms of this exclamation would include the traditional: 'It's a hard life', 'Life is hell', 'Life is not a bed of roses', LIFE WASN'T MEANT TO BE EASY, 'Life is unfair'.

life is just a bowl of cherries Modern proverbial expression that apparently originated in the song by Lew Brown (music by Ray Henderson), first heard in the American musical *Scandals of 1931*.

life is just one damned thing after another A view of life in which problems and difficulties 'come along in threes', just like buses. Known by the 1920s, when John Masefield even entitled a novel *Odtaa* (1926), an acronym made from the initials of the last five words of the saying.

life isn't all beer and skittles Proverbial expression warning that life does not solely consist of the enjoyment of simple pleasures, such as those of the typical English yeoman in his tavern (compare CAKES AND ALE). This was an established 'saw' by 1857 when it appeared, for example, in Thomas Hughes, *Tom Brown's Schooldays*

life, liberty and the pursuit of happiness Slogan/motto derived from the US Declaration of Independence (4 July 1776) that Thomas Jefferson drafted: 'We hold these truths to be self-evident; that all men are created equal; that they are endowed by their creator with certain unalienable rights; that among these are life, liberty, and the pursuit of happiness.' Note, not 'inalienable'. George Mason had already drafted the Virginia Declaration of Rights (1774), which stated that 'all men are by nature equally free and independent and have certain inherent rights'.

(to live the) life of Reilly (or **O'Reilly** or **Riley)** Meaning, 'to have a high old time, wallow in luxury, live it up, without much effort – have an easy life'. *The Life of Riley* was used as the title of an American TV sitcom with Jackie Gleason (1949–50). *Partridge/Catch Phrases* guesses an Anglo-Irish origin *circa* 1935. In 1939, US adverts for Coronada, 'the air-cooled suit that resists wrinkles', were on the theme 'A Day in the Life of Reilly' (Jim Reilly Jr). In 1919 (also in the USA) there was a song by Harry Pease with the title 'My Name Is Kelly', which went, 'Faith and my name is Kelly, Michael Kelly, / But I'm living the life of Reilly just the same.' This seems to be using an established phrase. *Morris* thinks the name was 'O'Reilly' and that the association arose from a US vaudeville song about such a character, from the

1880s – though it doesn't appear to incorporate the line as we know it. *Bartlett*, however, quotes from the chorus of an 1882 song with the title 'Is That Mr Reilly' and adds that this is the 'assumed origin of "the life of Riley".' It tells of what the hero would do if he struck it rich. Another song sometimes mentioned as a source is from *circa* 1900: 'Best of the House is None Too Good for Reilly'. Yet another origin suggested is that the expression refers to a rustic American poet called James Whitcomb Riley (1849–1916) who worked on the *Indianapolis Journal* from 1877 to 1885, penning cheerful, sentimental verses about such pastimes as sunbathing and swimming in country rivers – pursuits that might be termed the 'life of Riley'.

life's a bitch, and then you die This is a modern proverb of untraced origin, though probably North American. A development of it, known both in the USA and the UK, is 'Life's a bitch, *you marry a bitch*, and then you die.' Citations in print are few. Working backwards: during the summer of 1991, the Body Shop chain in the UK was promoting suntan products with a window display under the punning slogan, 'Life's a beach – and then you fry'. [Another pun: 'Life's a bleach – and then you dye'.] A caption to an article in *The Observer* (23 September 1990) about frozen food was the equally punning, 'Life's a binge and then you diet'. In Caryl Churchill's play about the City, *Serious Money* (first performed March 1987), we find: 'I thought I'd be extremely rich. / You can't be certain what you'll get. / I've heard the young say Life's a bitch.' From *The Sunday Times* (21 December 1986): 'Life is a bitch, then you die. So says the pilot of a flying fuel tank who, last week took off to circumnavigate the globe with his girlfriend.' From an interview with Maya Angelou, *Girl About Town* Magazine (13 October 1986): 'Life's a bitch. You've got to go out and kick ass.' As a slogan, **life's a beach** seems to have taken on a life of its own as a slogan, especially in Australia, but probably developed from 'Life's a bitch' rather than the other way round. *Campaign* (5 May 1989) quoted the view: 'Coke's image is like the kind of

American musical which gets terrible reviews but pulls people in all the same. Life's a beach, basically.' As to the origins of all this, attention might be drawn to *An Essay on Woman* by 'Pego Borewell Esq.', published in about 1763, as a bawdy parody of Alexander Pope's *An Essay on Man*. It is thought to have been written by the politician John 'Friend of Liberty' Wilkes and one Thomas Potter, working in some form of collaboration. Interestingly, it starts like this: 'Let us (since life can little more supply / Than just a few good fucks, and then we die) / Expatiate freely . . .' Something of the same spirit comes through here. Later, *The Observer* Magazine (2 August 1998) told us that when the couturier Balenciaga closed the door of his salon for the last time in 1968, he declared: 'Life's a dog'. As he was Spanish-born and worked in Paris, he might have said this in either Spanish or French. A proverbial expression in either language?

life's better with the Conservatives – don't let Labour ruin it Tory slogan that helped bring the party a further period in office after the 1959 General Election – a poll in which many broadcasting and advertising techniques were applied to UK politics for the first time. There was much to justify the claim: material conditions had improved for most people; the balance of payments surplus, gold and dollar reserves were at a high level; wages were up; and taxation had gone down. The slogan emerged from consultations between Central Office and the Colman, Prentis & Varley agency. In his book *Influencing Voters* (1967), Richard Rose says he knows of four people who claimed to have originated it. Ronald Simms was the PR chief at Central Office from 1957 to 1967. He is said to have come up with 'Life is good with the Conservatives, don't let the Socialists support it'. Lord Hailsham wanted 'better' instead of 'good' and CPV changed 'spoil' to 'ruin'. On the other hand, Maurice Smelt wrote (1981): 'The slogan was so successful that many people have claimed it (that always happens): but it was just a perfectly routine thing I did one afternoon in 1959 as the copywriter on the Conservative account at CPV. The brief from Oliver Poole [party chairman]

was to say something like "YOU'VE NEVER HAD IT SO GOOD" but with less cynicism and more bite. The first five words were the paraphrase: and the whole ten told what I still think was a truth for its time. It's the slogan I am proudest of.'

life's rich pageant See IT'S ALL PART.

life's too short (or ... short enough as it is) An excuse for not doing something. 'Life's too short for chess' occurs in Henry James Byron's play *Our Boys* (1874). 'Life's too short to stuff a mushroom' is the epigraph to Shirley Conran's home-help manual *Superwoman* (1975).

life, the universe and everything From Douglas Adams, *The Hitch Hiker's Guide to the Galaxy*, Chap. 25 (1979): "'O Deep Thought Computer," he said, "the task we have designed for you to perform is this. We want you to tell us . . ." he paused, ". . . the Answer!" "The Answer?" said Deep Thought. "The Answer to what?" "Life!" urged Fook. "The Universe!" said Lunkwill. "Everything!" they said in chorus . . .' The phrase was adapted to form an advertising slogan for *The Daily Telegraph* (current 1988): 'The Earth Dweller's Guide to Life the Universe and Everything'. The format, from an untraced source, is now used to signify 'absolutely everything'. Compare the all-embracing title of my own *The Quote . . . Unquote Book of Love, Death and the Universe* (1980), which may have been suggested to me by the first Douglas Adams book. *Life, the Universe and Everything* became the title of the third novel of four in Adams's 'trilogy' (1982).

lifetime See ALL IN.

life wasn't meant to be easy Proverb. Malcolm Fraser, Prime Minister of Australia (1975–83), was noted, among other things, for having said: 'Life wasn't meant to be easy.' The phrase was used as the title of a book about him by John Edwards in 1977. Fraser replied to a question from *The Times* (16 March 1981), as to whether he had ever actually said it: 'I said something very like it. It's from *Back to Methusaleh* [1918–20] by Bernard Shaw.' Indeed it is: 'Life is not meant to be easy, my child; but take courage: it can be delightful.' In a Deakin lecture on 20 July 1971, which seems to have been his first public use of the phrase, Fraser made no mention of Shaw, however. It is not, anyway, a startlingly original view. In one of A. C. Benson's essays in *The Leaves of the Tree* (1912), he quotes Brooke Foss Westcott, Bishop of Durham, as saying: 'The only people with whom I have no sympathy . . . are those who say that things are easy. Life is not easy, nor was it meant to be.'

lifting See AND NO HEAVY.

(the) light at the end of the tunnel
Meaning, a sign that some long-awaited relief or an end to some problem is at hand. Mostly used in politics, this is an idiom that has become a cliché. The *OED2*'s earliest citation is from 1922 (and in a non-political context), though George Eliot had expressed the idea of coming out of a tunnel of darkness into daylight in a letter of 1879. In June 1983, the diarist of *The Times* tried to find the first *Tory* politician to have used the phrase. Stanley Baldwin in 1929 was the first, it turned out, followed by Neville Chamberlain at a Lord Mayor's banquet in 1937. As for Churchill – well, John Colville, his private secretary, seems to quote a *French* source in his diary for 13 June 1940 ('some gleam of light at the far end of the tunnel'); quotes Paul Reynaud, the French PM on 16 June ('the ray of light at the end of the tunnel'); and himself uses it on 31 May 1952, 'I think it is more that he [Churchill] cannot see the light at the end of the tunnel.' In *The Second World War*, Vol. 2 , Chap. 9 (1949), Churchill quotes Reynaud's phrase in italics as, *'There is no light at the end of the tunnel.'* The old expression was later dusted down and invoked about an end to the Vietnam War. In 1967, New Year's Eve invitations to a function at the American Embassy in Saigon bore the legend: 'Come and see the light at the end of the tunnel.' President Kennedy nearly employed the expression apropos something else at a press conference on 12 December 1962: 'We don't see the end of the tunnel, but I must say I don't think it is darker than it was a year ago, and in some ways lighter.' An earlier use of the expression in an Indo-China context came from French general Henri-Eugene Navarre, quoted in *Time* Magazine (28 September

1953): 'A year ago none of us could see victory. There's wasn't a prayer. Now we can see it clearly – like light at the end of the tunnel.' Somewhere along the way, a joke was added: 'If we see the light at the end of the tunnel, it's the light of the oncoming train.' Though not original to him, the line appears in Robert Lowell's poem 'Day by Day' (1977). In 1988, a graffito in Dublin announced: 'Because of the present economic situation, the light at the end of the tunnel will be switched off at weekends.'

lightning See AJAX DEFYING.

lightning never strikes twice in the same place Taken literally, this is an untrue statement. Lightning is often drawn repeatedly to the same spot. When used as a figurative, superstitious expression, however, it means that you are going to tempt providence because the chances are, you will not suffer a misfortune of the kind (large or small) undergone by a previous doer of what you are about to do. Mostly 20th-century use? 'Presumably operating on the assumption that lightning never strikes twice in the same partnership, Merrill has agreed to take Becker Paribas, the Wall Street securities business, off the hands of the French bank' – *Financial Times* (7 Aug 1984); 'What should the fund manager do now? . . . Lightning never strikes the same place twice, and the interest-rate play may be nearing its finish' – *Financial Times* (5 November 1984); 'They also say that lightning never strikes twice, which makes York Minster a rare sanctuary if you're unlucky enough to be an astrapophobe' – *The Independent* (5 February 1996); '"They say that lightning never strikes twice in the same place but that's exactly what we're all hoping for," said Rush' – Press Association (24 January 1996).

(the) light of one's life The be-all and end-all of one's existence, usually referring to an adored spouse or partner. Date of origin unknown. The epitaph for Thomas Carlyle's wife, Jane, in Haddington church, states: 'For forty years she was the true and ever-loving helpmate of her husband, and, by act and word, unweariedly forwarded him, as none else could, in all of worthy that he did or attempted. She died at London, 21st April 1866, suddenly snatched away from him, and the light of his life as if gone out.'

(to be) light on one's feet To display the attributes of the homosexual, to be camp. A relatively inoffensive characterization. British, mid-20th century? From *Roy Hudd's Book of Music-Hall, Variety and Showbiz Anecdotes* (1993): 'This same infamous loo was, for many years, a meeting place for those who were a bit light on their feet – all right, then – "ginger".'

light the blue touchpaper and retire immediately. Catchphrase from the BBC radio show *Band Waggon* (1938–39). This standard firework instruction was first used by Arthur Askey on a Guy Fawkes's night broadcast and subsequently when he was withdrawing from any confrontation with 'Mrs Bagwash'.

like a bat out of hell With extreme (and desperate) speed. The image is clear. Known by 1921. 'Once I went through Spain, like a bat out of hell, with a party that included . . . a distinguished American of letters' – Dorothy Parker in *The New Yorker* (25 July 1931); 'She'll shoot out of Greenwich like a bat out of hell, if she thinks there's a chance of seeing you' – Dorothy Parker, 'Dusk Before Fireworks' (before 1944).

like a beached whale 'Stranded, high and dry', particularly if any person so described is large and helpless. '[Of R. A. Butler in his later years] He seemed like a benign and decent beached whale washed up on the harder shores of modern Conservatism' – Peter Hennessy in *The Independent* (8 May 1987); 'Beached whale – Michael Billington on a Moby Dick that's all at sea' – headline in *The Guardian* (19 March 1992); 'Here is stalk-chewing Johnny Depp, who divides his days between tending his oversize Momma – "Did yer ever see a beached whale on television?" is how he describes her to strangers – and saving his mentally re-tarded brother Leonardo DiCaprio from suicidal escapades' – *Financial Times* (5 May 1994); 'Holly Wantuch's trembling Sharla is forced to fellate a chicken drumstick, Michael Shannon's Chris spatters the kitchen with his blood, Marc A. Nelson's lumbering Ansel collapses like a beached whale' – *The Times* (24 August 1994).

like a bear garden Consciously archaic phrase to describe any disorderly situation. A bear garden was originally a place set aside for bear baiting and thence the term came (by 1743) to be applied to any disorderly place. 'Squabbles and boxings . . . rendering the place more like a bear-garden than a hall of instruction' – John Bristed, *Anthroplanomenus: Being an Account of a Pedestrian Tour through part of the Highlands of Scotland* (1803). Possibly now used out of some confusion with the term 'beer garden', from the German and in English use in the USA by 1884. 'Whatever follies this country has fallen into since the war, none seems to me nearly so grievous as the hash we have made of our schools. Teaching is, or should be, one of the most rewarding callings anybody can follow; but it has become a bear garden' – Godfrey Smith in *The Sunday Times* (6 June 1993).

like a coiled spring Phrase used in attempts at fine writing to convey tension. Date of origin unknown. 'Each panzer was a coiled spring, oiled / For instant action' – George Macbeth, *A War Quartet* (1969); 'His fingers teased until her nipples hardened to desire, and in a great upsurge of longing, she arched her body to the coiled-spring inflexibility of his' – Anne Hampson, *Stormy Masquerade* (1980); 'Music became metaphor with the terrific surge of self-pride in the playing of the great billowing melody in the first movement; there was a buccaneering, defiant elan in the hectic waltz. There was dignity in the slow movement. And in a crisp and rude version of the witty finale, the tension was as tight as a coiled spring' – Michael Tumelty in *The Herald* (Glasgow) (2 June 1993); 'United will start handsome favour-ites to become the fourth club this century to complete the coveted league and FA Cup double, with every good reason. Seeing them in training this week, they have appeared as a coiled spring, ready to burst into dramatic life in the May sun-shine' – *Daily Mail* (14 May 1994).

like a dream come true What any stroke of luck is to an ordinary member of the public, when reported by journalists, and thus an idiom that has turned into a cliché. Date of origin unknown. 'The advent of the laser would seem to be a chemist's dream come true' – *Scientific American* (May 1979); 'British radio hams are to be able to talk to an astronaut on board the latest US space shuttle . . . Dr Garriott said: "This will be a dream come true. I have had this project on my mind since I first became an astronaut"' – *The Times* (October 1983); 'A club cricket enthusiast has inherited a fortune and his own village cricket club from an elderly widow who was a distant relative he never knew . . . Mr Hews, aged 68, a retired company representative, lives in a semi-detached house in Arnold Avenue, Coventry. "It's like a dream come true," he said' – *The Times* (22 October 1983); 'At the end of May 1985 Brian MacArthur, in the cramped Covent Garden basement, was experiencing an editor's dream come true' – David Goodhart and Patrick Wintour, *Eddie Shah and the Newspaper Revolution* (1986); 'For Susan [George], the purchase of their 17th-century house is a dream come true' – *Hello!* (13 May 1995); 'But the Sheikh's first words after [winning] the race [the Derby] were not for himself. He said: "This is a dream come true, but my thoughts are now of Alex"' – *Independent on Sunday* (11 June 1995).

like a Drury Lane fairy 'I'm 70 years old and was brought up by a grandmother who in turn was brought up by a mother who took in washing at the back of Leicester Square. When I came home crying because I'd fallen over and hurt myself, my grandmother always said, "You're like a Drury Lane fairy – always in trouble." She would never tell me what a Drury Lane fairy was . . .' – Violet Mills, West Sussex (1994). Understandably. J. Redding Ware's *Passing English of the Victorian Era* (1909) defines a 'fairy' as 'a debauched, hideous old woman, especially when drunk'. *Grose* (1785) has 'Drury Lane vestal' = 'harlot'. 'My family always said, "You sound just like a Drury Lane dressmaker" to anyone complaining of various aches and pains, usually trivialities.

Sometimes combined with the maladies there would be a moan about their general life' – Mrs B. Parker, Bedfordshire (2000).

like a fairy tale (princess) The urge to say that everything in sight was 'like a fairy tale' was, of course, rampant at the nuptials of the Prince of Wales and Lady Diana Spencer in July 1981. Tom Fleming, the BBC TV commentator for the fixture, said the bride was 'like a fairy-tale princess'. Even Robert Runcie, Archbishop of Canterbury, began his address at St Paul's: 'Here is the stuff of which fairy tales are made.' Another cliché (current by 1860) is **it was just like a fairy tale**, now put into the mouths of unsuspecting members of the public by popular journalists when they are trying to describe some rather pleasant thing that has happened to them. As Iona and Peter Opie point out, however, in *The Classic Fairy Tales* (1974), this is a very misguided way of looking at such matters: 'When the wonderful happens, when a holiday abroad is a splendid success or an unlikely romance ends happily, we commonly exclaim it was "just like a fairy tale", overlooking that most events in fairy tales are remarkable for their unpleasantness, and that in some of the tales there is no happy ending, not even the hero or heroine escaping with their life.' 'The story from then on is like a fairytale – ending in a link with a fairytale princess. For instead of having to fight for cash and premises, Jackie was handed both on a plate' – *Today* (17 June 1994); 'Diana Spencer chose her own companions. This fairytale princess has not got dainty feet in glass slippers but lumps of clay' – *The Times* (6 October 1994).

like a fart in a colander Indecisive, dithering, all over the place, rushing around. *Partridge/Catch Phrases* suggests an origin sometime in the 1920s. This phrase is also used when describing someone particularly evasive or slippery. I was first introduced to this wonderful expression by Roy Hudd on BBC Radio *Quote . . . Unquote* (24 May 1994). Although I found it hugely amusing, I did not quite understand the mechanics of it until Mrs J. Harrison of Powys wrote that, as she knew it, the phrase was used to describe someone who was indecisive and the complete version was: 'He's like a fart in a colander – can't make up his mind which hole to come out of!' A slightly different version of the same idea: 'My own grandmother used a wealth of descriptive and colourful expressions. One frequently addressed to me was, "Can't you just sit still, child, fidgeting about like a parched pea in a colander!"' – Mrs Stella Mummery, London SW14 (1995).

like a fish out of water Inappropriate for the environment or situation. Known by 1886. Listed as a current cliché in *The Times* (28 May 1984). '"But," added the young Wadhamite . . . "I've heard he's an absolute fish out of water when he's away from the academic world he's accustomed to"' – Anthony Powell, *Infants of the Spring* (1976).

like a pork chop at a Jewish wedding (. . . at a synagogue) Isolated, at a loose end, redundant, useless (because inappropriate). Since the mid-20th century, because pork is a forbidden food as far as Jews are concerned. Compare: **(standing about) like a spare prick at a wedding**. Known by the mid-20th century and certainly by 1971 when John Osborne, in *West of Suez*, has 'like a professional spare prick at a wedding'. Compare the more polite **standing around like a lost lemon**.

like a red rag to a bull Meaning, 'obviously provocative'. Working backwards: Christy Brown in *Down All the Days*, Chap. 13 (1970) has: 'Sure they [breasts] only get you into trouble, woman dear . . . Showing them off to a man is like waving a red cloth at a bull.' Caption from a Du Maurier cartoon in *Punch* (26 July 1879): 'Jordan Jones (to whom a picture by R. Robinson is as a red rag to a bull, as B.B. knows) . . .' There is no example to hand of the phrase in use before 1873, but John Lyly in *Euphues and His England* (1580) has: 'He that cometh before [a bull] will not wear . . . red', based on the belief that bulls are aggravated by the colour. In fact, they are colour-blind. In all probability, if they do react, it is simply the *movement* of material in a bright colour that causes the animal to charge. Charles Dickens in *Bleak House*, Chap. 43 (1853) seems to allude to the saying in: 'You know my old opinion of him . . . An amiable bull, who is determined to make every colour scarlet.'

like a Trojan In a brave, spirited, trustworthy and courageous manner. The inhabitants of Troy have traditionally been held to have these qualities. 'There they say right, and like true Trojans' – Samuel Butler, *Hudibras*, I.1 (1613).

like a trooper Foully and vigorously, as in the military. 'Swear like . . .' seems to be the most common of such phrases (since 1727), though *OED2* has 'eat like . . .' (1812) and 'lie like . . .' (1854). 'Fart like . . .' seems to be a 20th-century innovation.

(makes —— look) like a vicarage tea-party Critical simile and format. Date of origin unknown. One that lingers in my memory is from a *Daily Telegraph* review of Alan Sillitoe's novel *Saturday Night and Sunday Morning* (1958): 'A novel of today, with a freshness and raw fury that makes *Room at the Top* look like a vicarage tea-party.' The quote was used on the cover of the paperback edition. From the BBC radio show *Round the Horne* (14 March 1965): 'That grand old lady of the theatre, whose life story makes *Fanny Hill* sound like *Mary Poppins*.' When Jacqueline Suzanne's *Valley of the Dolls* came out in 1966, a publication called *This Week* noted that it made '*Peyton Place* look like a Bobbsey Twins escapade' (the Bobbsey Twins were nice, clean-cut Americans who got into and out of scrapes in juvenile fiction). 'He surveyed the smoking ruins of . . . a fine old Elizabethan rectory . . . and said: "It makes the dissolution of the Monasteries look like a vicarage tea-party"' – *The Daily Telegraph* (31 January 1984); 'After the Mexican earthquake, they were all jumping up and down saying "Are we prepared?" The next big one here is going to make Mexico look like a Sunday afternoon tea party," Shah said' – *The Washington Post* (19 April 1986); '[Charles Saatchi's advertisements] made previous campaigns look like Mary Poppins' – *The Sunday Times* (21 August 1988), quoting an earlier *Sun* profile; 'The City would grind to a standstill if I spoke out. What I could reveal would make the film *Scandal* look like a teddy bears' picnic' – Pamella Bordes, quoted in *The Sun* (16 March 1989) during a political/sexual scandal.

like Brer Fox he lay low 'He was reticent, kept out of the public eye.' A fairly common conflation of what the American author Joel Chandler Harris actually wrote in 'The Wonderful Tar-Baby Story' from *Uncle Remus and His Legends of the Old Plantation* (1881): 'Tar-baby ain't sayin' nuthin', en Brer Fox, he lay low.' In fact, the phrase 'en Brer Fox, he lay low' is a phrase repeated rhythmically throughout the piece, as Frank Muir once noted, 'like a line in a Blues song'. From Joyce Grenfell, *In Pleasant Places*, Chap. 7 (1979): 'I once spent a happy hour lying full-length along a pew . . . listening to Sir John Barbirolli rehearsing an orchestra in some Haydn . . . I don't know how I happened to be there, but I lay low and, like Brer Fox, I said nuthin'.'

like coming home Meaning, 'what is appropriate for one; what one feels completely natural doing' – an idiom, almost a cliché. Originally, the phrase was used in a near literal fashion: 'I am sure nobody can deny that the house is very small . . . and yet, it feels like coming home again' – Wilkie Collins, *No Name* (1862). Then, more figuratively, Winston Churchill said at a Conservative rally in 1924 (having left the Liberal Party): 'It's all very strange for [his wife]. But to me, of course, it's just like coming home.' In the film *The Garden of Allah* (US 1936), Marlene Dietrich says 'It's like coming home' about returning to a nunnery. A cliché by the 1970s, perhaps as a result of the film title *Coming Home* (US 1978). 'For Douglas Hurd, it was just like coming home . . . [as he] took his place behind the Foreign Secretary's desk' – *The Independent* (31 October 1989); 'Actually I found arriving at the BBC was like arriving home . . . It was a job I knew I wanted to do' – Melvyn Bragg in the *Independent on Sunday* (17 June 1990).

(just) like mother makes (used to make) I.e. like home cooking and very acceptable. This expression seems to have acquired figurative quotation marks around it by the early years of the 20th century. It is of American origin and was soon used by advertisers as a form of slogan (compare the US pop song of the Second World War, 'Ma, I Miss Your Apple Pie'). 'The kind mother used to make' was used as a slogan by New England Mincemeat around 1900. Vance Packard, in *The Hidden Persuaders* (1957), records an example of the phrase's effectiveness when slightly altered: 'When the Mogen David wine people were seeking some way to add magic to their wine's sales appeal, they turned to motivation research via their agency. Psychiatrists and other probers listening to people talk at random about wine found that many related it to old family-centred or festive occasions. The campaign tied home and mother into the selling themes. One line was: "the good old days – the home sweet home wine – the wine that grandma used to make." As a result of these carefully "motivated" slogans, the sales of Mogen David doubled within a year.' So, one of numerous advertising lines playing on assumptions about the goodness of home produce and the good old days, and reminding one of the advertisement that proclaimed: 'BUCK WHEAT CAKES / Like mother used to bake – $1.25 / Like mother thought she made – $2.25.'

like one o'clock half struck Immobile, hesitating. As in 'don't stand there like one o'clock half struck; do something'. Known by 1876.

like opening an oven door Meaning 'it was suddenly, fiercely hot', but especially when referring to the climate. As such, part of the 'travel scribes' armoury' compiled from a competition in *The Guardian* (10 April 1993). '*Wine* magazine writer Stuart Walton knows a vino that "offers a blast of roasting pork, like opening the oven door"' – *Today* (8 May 1995).

like painting the Forth Bridge Phrase used in describing an endless task. It is a popular belief that since it was constructed in the 1880s, the steel rail bridge over the Firth of Forth in Scotland has been continuously repainted. That is to say, when they got to the end of it, the painters immediately started all over again. In 1997, however, it was announced that the bridge was to be given a water-repellent coating of a semi-permanent nature, removing the necessity for perpetual redecoration. Furthermore, a Railtrack project manager was quoted in *The Observer* (25 May 1997) as saying, 'The painters have never started at one end and gone all the way to the other and then started all over again. That was always a myth.' 'Because of the mismatch in the computer criteria used by Western governments and industry, a nightmarish task is now involved in explaining the new CoCom rules to companies . . . There is talk in CoCom of making its list review a continuous process – "like painting the Forth Bridge, the minute you finish, you start again," one official says' – *Financial Times* (25 July 1984); 'In the far future, small free-roaming insectoids could be set to handle continuous tasks such as cleaning the outside of skyscrapers, or painting the Forth Bridge. Miniature versions could be put to work cleaning pavements and gutters, or the inside of your house' – *The Guardian* (2 August 1984); 'Dealing with social security is a bit like the Forth Bridge, [Peter Lilley] says. "I suspect I am only halfway across. But if I do get to the other side, I suspect whoever comes after me will have to start at the beginning and repaint all over again"' – *The Independent* (23 May 1995). As to finding a similar expression in American English or any other language, little progress has been made, except that l'abbayé Raynal in his *Anecdotes littéraires* (1750) gives the response made by a translator when accused of taking too much trouble and time over a piece of work: '*A quoi il appliquait plaisamment ce qui est dit dans Martial de ce barbier qui était si longtemps à faire une barbe qu'avant qu'il l'êut achevée, elle commençait à revenir* . . . [to which he replied what is to be found in Martial of the barber who was so long in shaving off a beard that before he had finished, it was beginning to grow again . . .]' Lawrence H. Summers, Deputy Secretary of the US Treasury, was quoted in March 1999 as having said: 'One is reminded of painting the Brooklyn Bridge: no sooner is one section painted over, than another appears needing work.'

(to sit) like Piffy As when a person is left in an isolated, useless position for some time and asks, 'Why am I sat here like Piffy?' British North Country usage. A longer version is, 'Sitting **like Piffy on a rock-bun**', remembered from the 1930s. And never send to ask who the original Piffy was. 'When I was a lad in Macclesfield, sixty years ago, my mother often said to me: "Shape yourself, don't stand there like Piffey"' – John Heys, letter in *The Guardian* (17 August 1989). 'Waiting here like piffey' – Graham White-head (2000). Compare also: 'In the days before theme parks and garden centres, when it was quite usual to go for a Sunday picnic which included a visit to the family grave, a child in the party fell over and was comforted in these words: "sit on your grand-dad's grave and have a rock-bun". This phrase has been used ever since in our family as slightly mocking comfort, particularly if someone has been making an inordinate fuss about some minor mishap' – Glenys Hopkins, Cheshire (1994). It has been suggested that 'piffy' was a type of icing dolloped on a rock bun but only in small amounts.

like rats deserting (or leaving) a sinking ship I.e. hurriedly, desperately. This comes from the English proverb to the effect that 'rats desert/forsake/leave a falling house/ sinking ship.' *ODP* finds an example of the 'house' version in 1579 and of the 'ship' (in Shakespeare) in 1611. It was an old superstition that rats deserted a ship before she set out on a voyage that was to end in her loss. 'Rat' to mean 'a politician who deserts his party' was used by the 1st Earl of Malmesbury in 1792. In the USA it made its first appearance in the saying 'like a rat deserting a sinking ship' around 1800 – *Safire*. A number of good jokes have grown from this usage. In Malcolm Muggeridge's diary for 14 February 1948 (published 1981), he notes: 'Remark of Churchill's was quoted to me about the Liberal candidature of Air Vice-Marshal Bennett in Croydon. "It was the first time," Churchill said, "that he had heard of a rat actually swimming out to join a sinking ship".' In his diary for 26 January 1941, John Colville noted that Churchill had reflected on the difficulty of 'crossing the floor' (changing parties) in the House of Commons: 'He had done it and he knew. Indeed he had re-done it, which everybody said was impossible. They had said you could rat but you couldn't re-rat.' When TV-am, the British breakfast television company, had a disastrous start in 1983 and was pulled round, in part, by the introduction of a puppet called 'Roland Rat', an unnamed spokesman for the rival BBC said, 'This must be the first time a rat has come to the aid of a sinking ship.'

(looking) like something the cat's brought (or **dragged in)**   Bedraggled, a mess, a sight (sometimes concluded with **. . . on a wet night**). Possibly by the 1920s.

like taking money from blind beggars Meaning, 'achieving something effortlessly, by taking advantage.' Compare, 'as easy as taking/stealing pennies from a blind man' or 'sweets/candy/money from a child.' There are also the expressions **they'd steal the pennies off a dead man's eyes** and **they'd steal the eyes out of your head and come back for the sockets**. 'Like taking candy from a baby' occurs in the film *Mr Smith Goes to Washington* (US 1939). I first heard the head-phrase form in *circa* 1962 – said by my English teacher who had just given a talk to an easily impressed Women's Institute or some such group. But it is an old idea. Charles Dickens in *Nicholas Nickleby*, Chap. 59 (1838–9) has Newman Noggs say: 'If I would sell my soul for drink, why wasn't I a thief, swindler, housebreaker, area sneak, robber of pence out of the trays of blind men's dogs . . .'

like the barber's cat – full of wind and water   Dismissive phrase, used as when the opinion of another is adduced or when an argument is reinforced with 'so and so said', with 'water' pronounced to rhyme with 'hatter'. *Partridge/Slang* has 'like the barber's cat – all wind and piss', and dates it from the late 19th century. John Beaumont, Hertfordshire (2000), added that his grandfather used to say after a good Sunday dinner, 'I'm full of wind and water like a barber's cat.' This was around the time of the Second World War.

(not to) like the cut of someone's jib Meaning 'not to like the look of someone', the expression has a nautical origin – the 'cut' or condition of the 'jib' or foresail signifying the quality of the sailing vessel as a whole. Current by 1823.

like there was no tomorrow   Meaning 'recklessly, with no regard to the future' or 'with desperate vigour' (especially the spending of money), as Paul Beale glosses it in his revision of *Partridge/Slang*. He also suggests that it was adopted from the USA in the late 1970s. However, it has been known since 1862. Identified as a current cliché in *The Times* (17 March 1995). 'The free travel scheme aimed at encouraging cyclists to use trains un- earthed a biking underground which took to the trains like there was no tomorrow' – *Time Out* (4 January 1980); 'Oil supplies that Americans at home continue to consume as though there were no tomor- row' – *Guardian Weekly* (3 February 1980); 'The evidence from the last major redraw- ing of council boundaries is mixed. Some authorities did go for broke, and spent their capital reserves as though there were no tomorrow' – *The Times* (9 June 1994).

like Topsy – she just growed   Rephrased expression from Harriet Beecher Stowe's novel *Uncle Tom's Cabin* (1852). The little slave girl, Topsy, asserting that she has no mother or father, replies thus, on being asked who made her: 'I s'pect I growed. Don't think nobody ever made me.'

like turning a tanker round   Describing any slow, difficult task. 'Clive Leach, managing director, said that reversing the trend on [TV] advertising was rather like "turning a tanker round"' – *The Independ- ent* (24 May 1990). Similarly, in 1988, Dr Billy Graham was quoted as saying of the difficulty of converting China to Christian- ity: 'I think what Winston Churchill or somebody like that said is true: "You can't turn the *Queen Mary* on a dime".'

like —— was going out of style   Meaning, 'was behaving as though this was the last opportunity to do something.' Date of origin unknown, though *Partridge/Catch Phrases* (1977) has 'spends money as if it were going out of fashion/style' as a phrase by *circa* 1930. 'The familiar story is smothered in the stalest of prose, in which principles are "deeply held", people are "eminently suitable" or spend money "as though it were going out of style" and a car is driven "hell for leather". There was a time when an assiduous editor would have chucked out such a bouquet of clichés, or been moved to less demanding employment. Oh well!' – *Mail on Sunday* (11 September 1994); 'And Don Johnson "hands out money like it's going out of style"' – *Daily Mirror* (12 December 1994).

limped into port Journalistic cliché. Date of origin unknown. How a boat without legs can limp is never explained . . . 'Amid the glare of television lights, the panoply of ecstatic family and friends marking their return, and the flotilla of small boats sounding their klaxons, the fact that the women and their yacht, *Heineken*, limped into port behind the 14 other competitors was an irrelevance' – *Mail on Sunday* (12 June 1994); 'The *Lupina C* limped back to her home port of Kilkeel with her gear in tatters' – *The Herald* (Glasgow) (18 January 1995).

(to draw a) line in the sand To fix a boundary beyond which an opponent or foe should not go. To describe limits in order to provide a framework for negotiations. Date of origin not known. Mark Twain, *The Adventures of Tom Sawyer*, Chap. 1 (1876): '[On meeting a new boy in the village] Tom drew a line in the dust with his big toe, and said: "I dare you to step over that, and I'll lick you till you can't stand up".'

lion See BEARD THE.

lions led by donkeys Phrase used when describing incompetent leadership (usually military). In a book called *The Donkeys* (1961), Alan Clark put this epigraph involving two German generals at the time of the First World War: *Ludendorff*: 'The English soldiers fight like lions.' *Hoffman*: 'True. But don't we know that they are lions led by donkeys.' Clark gives the source as Field Marshal von Falkenhayn's memoirs – but the exchange remains untraced. In fact, the phrase seems to predate this occasion. In a book called *Le Siège de Paris* by Francisque Sarcey (1871 – and translated the same year as *Paris During the Siege*), we find: 'Unceasingly they [the French forces] had had drummed into them the utterances of the "Times": "You are lions led by jackasses." Alas! The very lions had lost their manes.' So what we have here is probably a military saying, modified to suit particular circumstances.

Deutsches Sprich-wörter-Lexikon, Vol. 3 (1873) has: '*Hundert Löwen verlieren, wenn ein Schaf sie anführt* [a hundred lions lose, when led by a sheep].' Even earlier, the phrase 'lions led by donkeys' has been attributed to a Russian sergeant in the Crimean War and apparently communicated to a sergeant of the British 46th Regiment of Foot on 18 June 1855, during a ceasefire for the recovery of bodies. It was mentioned in two separate letters home, both dated 25 June 1855, one from Lieutenant Colonel David Wood, Royal Artillery, and the other from Captain George Frederick Dallas, 46th Regiment of Foot. This information is from the *Journal of the Society for Army Historical Research* (Notes and Documents Section). There is a similar proverb, 'An army of stags led by a lion would be more formidable than one of lions led by a stag', cited by W. F. Butler in *Sir Charles Napier* (1890) and which would appear to be based on Plutarch. If there is a connection, it takes the whole matter back to classical times.

(the) lion's share The largest portion of anything. This probably derives from Aesop's fable of the lion, the fox and the ass. They went hunting and killed a stag. The ass divided it into equal proportions, but the lion looked upon this as an insult to his dignity and killed the ass. The fox, more craftily, nibbled a bit and left the 'lion's share' to the bigger beast. In fact, a lion does get the largest share of the food obtained for him by the lionesses in his pride. The expression is recorded by 1790. 'The art of finding a rich friend to make a tour with you in autumn, and of leaving him to bear the lion's share of the expenses' – *Punch* (22 June 1872); 'The lion's share – £215m – would be used to develop distribution networks, said Mr Marcelino Oreja, commissioner for culture' – *The Daily Telegraph* (9 February 1995).

(my) lips are sealed Meaning, 'I am not giving anything away', and deriving originally perhaps from the expression to seal up *another* person's lips, mouth, to prevent him betraying a secret. Known by 1782. 'My lips are not yet unsealed' was said during the Abyssinia Crisis of 1935 by the British Prime Minister, Stanley Baldwin. He was playing for time, with what he subsequently admitted was one of the stupidest things he had ever said. The cartoonist Low portrayed him for weeks afterwards with sticking plaster over his lips.

listen very carefully, I shall say this only once Catchphrase from the BBC TV comedy series *'Allo, 'Allo* (1984–92) about Resistance workers in occupied France during the Second World War (*sic*). Used by Michelle Dubois (Kirsten Cooke), an agent of the Resistance, it somehow contrived to catch on. Jeremy Lloyd, one of the show's co-scriptwriters, used it as the title of his autobiography (1993).

little See EVERY.

(a) little black book There have been many 'black books' over the centuries containing authoritative records or lists of people in disgrace. The 'little' ones, however, are now more usually those containing lists of girls' telephone numbers such as might be kept by a promiscuous male. 'Guess you got back to my name in your little black book' is a line from the song 'Running Out of Fools' (by K. Rogers and R. Ahlert), recorded by Aretha Franklin in 1964. But note: 'Never the most elegant or fastidious of [football] defenders, Jack [Charlton] kept an infamous little black book for noting opponents he "owed one"' – *The Independent* (30 June 1990).

(a) little black dress A simple frock suitable for most social occasions and sometimes abbreviated to 'lbd'. It was popular from the 1920s and 30s onwards. The original, a creation of Coco Chanel, was sold at auction for £1,500 in 1978. In Britain, the designer Molyneux perfected the dress as the ideal cocktail party wear of the between-the-wars years.

Little Egypt Stage name of Catherine Devine who made the Coochee-Coochee dance famous at the Chicago Colombian Exposition in 1893. She had a tendency to dance in the nude and was celebrated in the song 'Little Egypt' (1961) by Lieber and Stoller (sung by The Coasters and Elvis Presley). *Little Egypt* was also the title of a film (US 1951) about a girl posing as an Egyptian princess at the Chicago World Fair. One etymology of the word 'gypsy' is

that it derives from 'Little Egypt', the fictional Middle Eastern homeland of the gypsies.

little fish are sweet See under OIL FOR THE LAMPS OF CHINA.

(the) little gentleman in black velvet! Jacobite toast to the mole whose hillock caused King William III's horse to stumble in 1702. William died soon afterwards, partly from the injuries sustained. Compare KING OVER THE WATER!

(a) little lady A girl – but not a politically correct usage, according to Rosalie Maggio, *The Nonsexist Word Finder: A Dictionary of Gender-Free Usage* (1988): 'The very intent is demeaning. It is also incorrect to refer to a child this way because (1) a child is not an adult and should be allowed to be a child while she is a child and (2) telling a child she is a little lady almost without exception is an attempt to perpetuate some cultural stereotype e.g. sitting quietly and neatly in the background.' An example: 'Now, now little lady, you don't want to believe all those things you read in the newspapers about crisis and upheavals, and the end of civilisation as we know it. Dearie me, not at all' – *The Daily Telegraph* (10 June 1976). This was a *parody* of James Callaghan's style of addressing Margaret Thatcher, when he was Prime Minister, and was written by John O'Sullivan. It was quoted in all seriousness by *Time* Magazine.

(a) little learning Phrase from Alexander Pope's *An Essay on Criticism* (1711): 'A little learning is a dang'rous thing; / Drink deep, or taste not the Pierian Spring.' Pieria was the home of the Greek Muses. Hence, the title of a volume of Evelyn Waugh's autobiography (1964).

little local difficulties Phrase used dismissively to show a lack of concern. In 1958, as British Prime Minister, Harold Macmillan made a characteristically airy reference to the fact that his entire Treasury team, including the Chancellor of the Exchequer, had resigned over disagreement about budget estimates. In a statement at London airport before leaving for a tour of the Commonwealth on 7 January, he said: 'I thought the best thing to do was to settle up these little local difficulties, and then turn to the wider vision of the Commonwealth.'

Little Nell Nickname of Nell Trent, child heroine of *The Old Curiosity Shop* (1840–41) by Charles Dickens. She attempts to look after her inadequate grandfather and to protect him from various threats, but her strength gives out. According to one account, 'Does Little Nell die?' was the cry of 6,000 book-loving Americans who hurried to the docks in New York to ask this question of sailors arriving from England. Another version is that it was longshoremen who demanded 'How is Little Nell?' or 'Is Little Nell dead?' As the novel was serialized, they were waiting for the arrival of the final instalment of the magazine to find out what had happened to the heroine. Little Nell's death came to typify the heights of Victorian sentimental fiction. Oscar Wilde later commented: 'One must have a heart of stone to read the death of Little Nell without laughing.'

(a) little of what you fancy does you good A nudging point of view from a song by Fred W. Leigh and George Arthurs: 'I always hold in having it, if you fancy it, / If you fancy it, that's under-stood. / And suppose it makes you fat, / I don't worry over that / Cos a little of what you fancy does you good.' It was popular-ized, with a wink, by the music-hall singer Marie Lloyd (1870–1922) in the 1890s.

(the) little old lady from Dubuque When Harold Ross founded *The New Yorker* in 1925, he said it would 'not be edited for the old lady from Dubuque' but for caviare sophisticates. Dubuque, Iowa, thus became involved in another of those yardstick phrases of non-cosmopolitanism – like IT'LL PLAY IN PEORIA – on account of it being representative of MIDDLE AMERICA.

Little Orphan Annie Name of the irrepressible, red-haired waif, who stands up to the world, succoured by millionaire 'Daddy Warbucks'. She originally appeared in a poem by J. W. Riley in 1913 ('Little Orphant Annie's come to our house to stay') but then became the heroine of a comic strip created by Harold Gray (in the USA, from 1924) and of versions in virtually every other medium. Conse-quently, any waif-like person is so known.

little pitchers have big ears 'A warning that children are around [who may hear what they should not]' – friend of Marjorie Wild, Devon (2000). *Apperson* finds this in Heywood's *Proverbs* (1546) as: 'Auoyd your children: small pitchers haue wide eares.' *Casson/Grenfell* has the nannyism: 'Little pitchers have long ears, so have donkeys.'

(the) Little Red Book Name given to the collected thoughts of Chairman Mao Tse-tung, which were published in this form (and brandished by Red Guards) during the Chinese Cultural Revolution of the 1960s. An English-language version was published as *Quotations from Mao Tse-tung* by the Foreign Language Press, Peking (1972).

(the) Little Sparrow Sobriquet of Edith Piaf (1915–63), the small French singer. Her real name was Edith Gassion. 'Piaf' is French slang for sparrow or little sparrow.

Little Tich Stage name of Harry Relph (1868–1928), a popular British music-hall comedian. Probably invented by his family when he was a baby, the nickname derived from the sensational Tichborne case – about the claim made in 1866 by a man from Australia that he was the missing heir to a Hampshire baronetcy and for-tune. The Tichborne Claimant (Arthur Orton), who was imprisoned for perjury, was plump – as no doubt was Harry Relph as a little boy. Relph remained small in stature and, at first, called himself 'Little Tichborne'. 'Tich' then became the nick-name for anyone small.

little things please little minds Proverb that *Apperson* finds in Lyly's *Sapho and Phao* (1584), with 'catch' for 'please'. The actress June Whitfield, quoting the proverb on BBC Radio *Quote . . . Unquote* (13 June 1995), added: 'Little trousers fit little behinds.'

(a) little weakness Euphemism for (usually) a drink problem. Date of origin unknown. 'Esau . . . undogcollared because of his little weakness, was scythed to the bone one harvest by mistake' – Dylan Thomas, *Under Milk Mood* (1954).

live and learn Proverbial admonition to learn from experience. Or a philosophical reflection – 'Well, you live and learn . . .' Known by 1620. 'Why then, Miss, you have one wrinkle – more than ever you had before.' 'Well; live and learn' – Swift, *Polite Conversation* (1738).

live and let live A plea for what has come to be known as peaceful co-exist-ence, and recorded by 1622. An obvious play upon the expression is *Live and Let Die*, the title of a James Bond novel by Ian Fleming (1954; film UK 1973).

live horse and you'll eat corn 'When I told my Mum I'd repay her in a couple of days for the tights/perfume/whatever I'd "borrowed", she'd say (wryly, I now know): "Och aye, live horse and you'll eat corn"' – Morag Becker, London SE22 (1996). Presumably derived from: **live horse and you'll get grass**. *Apperson* has, rather, 'Live, horse! And thou shalt have grass' and finds it, in that form, in Swift's *Polite Conversation* (1738). *Partridge/Slang* glosses it as, 'Well, let's wait and see! Later on, we'll see!'

(the) lively arts A curious phrase that must have been used for any number of broadcast programmes about the arts, not all of which needed to be described as other than boring. A possible origin is Billy Rose's stage show *The Seven Lively Arts* (Broadway 1944), which included ballet among its number.

(to) live over the brush (or get married over the brush or jump over the broom-stick) Meaning 'to live together as though married', this expression possibly derives from some form of informal ceremony that involved the couple jumping over a stick.

(he) lives like God in France He lives in ease and comfort. In German: '*Er lebt wie Gott in Frankreich*'; in Dutch: '*Hij leeft als God in Frankrijk.*' Lutz Röhrich has this in German by 1693 and also with *Gods*, plural. A number of origins have been suggested. One is that it is a reference to the comfort-able life of the French clergy in the Middle Ages. Another is that it is a mixture of the older 'To live like a God' and 'To live like a lord in France.' Or is it an allusion to the well-known splendour of the French court under Louis XIV with the older idea that gods lead privileged lives?

livid I was See WE'VE GOT A RIGHT ONE.

living See ALIVE AND.

living legend See LEGEND IN.

lives of quiet desperation Phrase based on a quotation from Henry David Thoreau's *Walden* (1854): 'The mass of men lead lives of quiet desperation.'

living a lie Meaning, 'keeping up a pretence'. 'To live a lie' was known by 1770. A journalistic cliché by the 1960s/ 70s. From the BBC radio show *Round the Horne* (3 April 1966): 'I can live this lie no longer.' 'Zany Kenny Everett's wife kept her love affair secret from the outside world for four years – to save hurting his feelings. Cuddly Ken knew of the affair. But Lee Everett and her lover, Sweeney actor John Atkin, lived a lie to avoid publicity' – *News of the World* (2 October 1983).

living in a fool's paradise Experiencing contentment or happiness based on an incorrect assessment of the circumstances. Known by 1621 (in Robert Burton's *Anatomy of Melancholy*). 'They live in a fool's paradise, for rabies has already visited the British Isles. In the latter part of the 19th century a number of deer in London's Richmond Park died of the disease. In any case, rabies is carried by many animals other than dogs' – *The European* (31 March 1995).

living in sin Cohabiting though not married. Known by 1838. The phrase had earlier been used with slightly different meanings. Margaret Cavendish, Duchess of Newcastle, *Bell in Canpo*, Pt 1, Act 5, Sc. 25 (1662), has the phrase in a rather involved conceit. A twice-married woman is said to 'live in sin herself by Cuckolding both her Husbands, having had two'. 'Think women seek to match with men, / To live in sin and not to saint' occurs in one version of poem 18 in Shakespeare's 'The Passionate Pilgrim', though it is difficult to understand what is meant by this.

living life in the fast lane Cliché of journalism, meaning 'living expensively, indulgently and dangerously'. From the association of such a lifestyle with 'fast cars' and such. Date of origin unknown, but 'The image usually associated with the superjet, "fast lane" set' appeared in the *Detroit Free Press* (16 April 1978). Used with plodding literalness in these: 'Controversial racing car genius Colin Chapman lived life in the fast lane' – *Daily Star* (11 October 1984); 'Jackie Stewart lives life in the fast lane. Like any businessman, really' – advertisement for Toshiba computer (February 1989); '"Life in the fast lane" was how one tabloid newspaper described the short career of Michael VerMeulen, the American editor of *GQ* who died, allegedly of a drug overdose, last week at the age of only 38' – *The Observer* (3 September 1995).

Livingstone See DOCTOR.

Lloyd George knew my father Even before David Lloyd George's death in 1945, Welsh people away from home liked to claim some affinity with the Great Man. In time, this inclination was encapsulated in the singing of the words 'Lloyd George knew my father, my father knew Lloyd George' to the strains of 'Onward Christian Soldiers', which they neatly fit. In Welsh legal and Liberal circles the credit for this happy coinage has been given to Tommy Rhys Roberts QC (1910–75) whose father did indeed know Lloyd George. Arthur Rhys Roberts was a Newport solicitor who set up a London practice with Lloyd George in 1897. The partnership continued for many years, although on two occasions Lloyd George's political activities caused them to lose practically all their clients. The junior Rhys Roberts was a gourmet, a wine-bibber and of enormous girth. Lord (Martin) Thomas QC, a prominent Welsh liberal of the next generation, recalled (1984): 'It was, and is, a tradition of the Welsh circuit that there should be, following the after-dinner speeches, a full-blooded sing-song. For as long as anyone can remember, Rhys Roberts's set-piece was to sing the phrase to the tune of "Onward Christian Soldiers" – it is widely believed that he started the practice . . . By the 50s it had certainly entered the repertoire of Welsh Rugby Clubs. In the 60s, it became customary for Welsh Liberals to hold a Noson Lawen, or sing-song, on the Friday night of the Liberal Assemblies. It became thoroughly adopted in the party. I

recall it as being strikingly daring and new in the late 60s for Young Liberals to sing the so-called second verse, "Lloyd George knew my mother". William Douglas-Home's play *Lloyd George Knew My Father* was produced in London in 1972. One of the leading Welsh Silks recalls persuading Rhys Roberts to see it with him.' From Robert Robinson, *Landscape with Dead Dons* (1956): 'He had displayed a massive indifference to the rollicking scientists who would strike up *Lloyd George Knew My Father* in a spirit of abandoned wickedness.'

(a) load of old cobblers Nonsense – rhyming slang where cobbler's awls = balls. Known by 1955.

loadsamoney! 'Loadsamoney' was the name of a character portrayed by the British comedy performer Harry Enfield, chiefly in the Channel 4 TV series *Friday Night Live* in 1987–8. A 'monster son of the enterprise culture', as he was described, the character waved wads of tenners about, proclaimed his belief in what he referred to as 'dosh' (money) and said 'Loadsamoney!' or **show us your wad!** a lot. A *Guardian* editorial on 30 April 1988 noted that, 'to his horror (for in private life Mr Enfield is a politics graduate of impeccable left-wing persuasions) a creation intended to be a satire of the money-worshipping philistinism of Thatcher's Britain appears to be savoured and loved. Real yobs all over the City, according to eye-witness reports, have begun appearing in pubs brandishing bundles of genuine bank notes and screaming "loadsamoney, loadsamoney".' As sometimes happens, a satirical invention threatened to become a role model instead, and Mr Enfield took steps to abandon the character. The following month, Neil Kinnock, the Labour Party leader, was telling a conference at Tenby, 'We've got the loadsamoney economy – and behind it comes loadsatrouble.' And there were signs of a format phrase in the making: 'Loadsa-sermons won't stop the Thatcherite rot' – headline in *The Sunday Times* (29 May 1988; 'Loadsateachers' – headline in the *Daily Mail* (25 July 1989). Earlier constructions on the same theme have included **big money!** (said by Max Bygraves of what contestants stood to win in the ITV quiz *Family Fortunes*, current 1985) and *Tons of Money*, the title of a long-running stage farce (and film) of the 1920s. In BBC TV shows in the early 1990s, Enfield created a whole series of characters whose names or catchphrases neatly defined them – Mr **You Don't Want To Do That**, a *nouveau riche* Midlands couple who said, **We appear to be considerably richer than you**, the Lovely Wobbly Randy Old Ladies who exclaimed **Young man!**, the pub authoritarian who would tell celebrities when to desist from some action, [**Name of celebrity**], **no!**, and so on.

local boy makes good Journalistic phrase turned into a catchphrase. The story in a local newspaper would typically tell how a young person had had to leave the area in order to find fame and fortune in the big world beyond. Probably American in origin. In the film *Swing Time* (US 1936), the line 'local boy makes *bad*' obviously indicates that the expression was well established by that date. 'Local Boy Makes Good' was the title of a sketch by George S. Kaufman in the revue *The Seven Lively Arts* (New York, 1944).

location, location, location Often described as the (real) estate agents' mantra. In apparent answer to the question, 'What are the three most important factors in determining the selling price of a property?' Established usage in the UK by 1999. A TV programme about property followed shortly afterwards with the title *Location, Location, Location*. As such, this was in a long line of 'three rules' sayings which are all exactly the same, emphasizing the importance of the concept. Working backwards: 'There is a famous quote in theatrical circles . . . the three most important things to get right when embarking on a musical are "book, book and book," the book being the storyline' – Tim Rice, *Oh, What a Circus* (1999); in a speech at the Labour Party conference in 1996 – the year before he became Prime Minister – Tony Blair said, 'Ask me my three main priorities for government, and I tell you: education, education, education'; Michael Heseltine said that the 1992 General Election would be about three issues, 'Tax, tax and tax'; 'The three golden

rules for teaching: Repeat, Repeat and Repeat' – known by the 1990s; and Thomas Hood wrote in 1836: 'There are three things which the public will always clamour for, sooner or later: namely, novelty, novelty, novelty.'

lock stock and barrel Meaning 'the whole lot', this term comes to us from the armoury where the lock (or firing mechanism), stock and barrel are the principal parts of a gun. Known by 1817. 'The whole thing, lock, stock, and barrel, isn't worth one big yellow sea-poppy' – Rudyard Kipling, *The Light That Failed* (1891); 'On November 13th while the going was still good . . . he got his partner to agree to buy him out, lock, stock and barrel, for £500 profit' – Arthur Bryant, *Samuel Pepys: The Man in the Making*, Chap. 13 (1933); 'He went into any game lock, stock and barrel . . . He would get whatever he needed – the best horses, coaches, equipment . . .' – Christopher Ogden, *Life of the Party* (1994); *Lock, Stock and Two Smoking Barrels* – title of film (UK 1998). Compare **hook, line and sinker** – that is, 'completely', as though a fish had swallowed not only the hook but the whole business end of a fishing rod. Known by 1838.

log See AS EASY AS.

London's burning Phrase from a traditional rhyme of which these are two versions: 'London's burning, London's burning / Look it yonder, look it yonder. / Fire, fire, fire, fire / And we have no water' – and – 'London's burning, London's burning / Fetch the engine, fetch the engine. / Fire, fire, fire, fire / Pour on water, pour on water.' The reference is presumably to the Great Fire of London (1666), but the provenance of the rhyme has been little discussed or recorded. *London's Burning* was the title of a TV drama series about the lives of firefighters in London (London Weekend Television, 1988–2001) and which was developed from a TV film (1986) written by Jack Rosenthal.

(it's) lonely at the top An observation that might apply to any leader, prominent politician or show business star. Date of origin uncertain. 'Oh, it's lonely at the top' is the refrain of a song, 'Lonely At the Top', by Randy Newman (1972). Apparently, the German philosopher Arthur Schopenhauer (1788–1860) once wrote, *'Auf der Höhe muss es einsam sein* [at the height it must be lonely].'

lonelyhearts See MISS LONELYHEARTS.

long See HAPPY AS THE; HOW MANY BEANS; IS A.

(the) long and the short and the tall The title of the play *The Long and the Short and the Tall* (1959; film UK 1960) by Willis Hall comes from the song 'Bless 'em all' (1940) by Jimmy Hughes and Frank Lake. This includes the lines: 'Bless 'em all, bless 'em all, / The long and the short and the tall' (though a parody version has 'Sod 'em all . . .'). The film's US title was *Jungle Fighters*.

(the) long and the short of it Meaning 'in brief, in a nutshell' or 'the essence, all that need be said'. Known by *circa* 1330. Inevitably, it became the bill matter of British music-hall entertainers Ethel Revnel and Gracie West (1930s/40s), one of whom was short and one of whom wasn't. The bill matter was also used by Chic Murray and Maidie (active 1945–68), who were similarly endowed.

(the) long arm of the law Phrase suggesting that the law is like a long arm, rooting out the guilty however far away they may hide. Used as the title of a film (UK 1956 – *The Third Key* in the USA) about a Scotland Yard superintendent solving a series of robberies. Charles Dickens in *The Pickwick Papers* (1836–7) has: 'Here was the strong arm of the law, coming down with twenty gold-beater force,' and in *The Mystery of Edwin Drood* (1870): 'The arm of the law is a strong arm, and a long arm.' In Shakespeare's *Richard II*, IV.i.11 (1595), Aumerle is quoted as saying: 'Is not my arm of length, / That reacheth from the restful English court / As far as Callice, to mine uncle's head?' It is possibly a development of the proverb 'Kings have long arms/hands/ many ears and many eyes', found by *ODP* in Ovid, and in English by 1539.

long-felt want See FULFIL A.

(a/the) long hot summer Cliché. *The Long Hot Summer* was the title of a 1958 film based on the stories of William Faulkner and also of a spin-off TV series (1965–6). The film was based on 'The Hamlet', a story published by Faulkner in 1928, which contains the chapter heading 'The Long Summer' (*sic*). Originally, as a literal description, the phrase appears, for example, in the opening chapter of Wilkie Collins, *The Woman in White* (1860): 'It was the last day of July. The long, hot summer was drawing to a close.' But the once bright phrase rapidly turned into a journalist's cliché following the 1967 riots in the ghettos of eighteen US cities, notably Detroit and Newark. In June of that year, the Reverend Dr Martin Luther King Jr warned: 'Everyone is worrying about the long hot summer with its threat of riots. We had a long cold winter when little was done about the conditions that create riots.' Claud Cockburn's *I, Claud* (1967) had a chapter entitled 'Long Cold Winter'. 'It looks as if it will be a long hot summer for the dons of Christ's College, Cambridge, who are once again faced with the tricky business of electing a Master' – Lady Olga Maitland in the *Sunday Express* (11 July 1982); 'Poles face long hot summer of discontent' – headline in *The Independent* (5 June 1995).

long in the tooth Older people suffer from receding of the gums, so their teeth appear to have got longer. The same probably applies to horses, so compare LOOK A GIFT HORSE IN THE MOUTH. Known by 1852 – Thackeray, *Esmond*.

long time no see The *OED2* calls this a 'jocular imitation of broken English' and has citations showing that the phrase was in use, more or less, by 1900. It appears fully formed in Raymond Chandler, *Farewell, My Lovely* (1940), and as a title in Ed McBain's *Long Time No See* (1977).

(the) long walk to freedom 'There is no easy walk-over to freedom anywhere, and many of us will have to pass through the valley of the shadow again and again before we reach the mountain-tops of our desire.' This passage from Jawaharlal Nehru's 'From Lucknow to Tripuri' (1939) is referred to by Nelson Mandela in his book with the title *Long Walk to Freedom* (1994), when discussing a speech that had to be delivered for him (Mandela) when he was banned from political activities in South Africa in the early 1950s: 'In that speech, which subsequently became known as "The No Easy Walk to Freedom" speech, I said that the masses now had to be prepared for new forms of political struggle.'

(to) look a gift horse in the mouth
Meaning, 'to find fault with a gift or spoil an offer by inquiring too closely into it'. This proverb alludes to the fact that the age of horses is commonly assessed by the length of their teeth. If you are offered the gift of a horse, you would be ill-advised to look in its mouth. You might discover information not to your advantage. Known by 1546 (as 'no man ought to looke a geuen [given] hors in the mouth . . .')

(to) look for a needle in a haystack   To attempt to find something that will be extremely difficult if not impossible to find. *Apperson* finds what may be the earliest formulation of this idea in 1532: 'To go looke a nedle in a medow.' In Greene's *A Quip for an Upstart Courtier* (1592) is the closer: 'He gropeth in the dark for a needle in a bottle of hay' ['bottle' here means 'bundle or bunch']. 'Haystack' is a relatively recent development (1855).

looking   See I THINK.

looking bronzed and fit (or tanned and fit)   Cliché of journalism, current by 1961. An inevitable pairing when someone (often a politician) 'returns to the fray' having acquired a suntan, perhaps after earlier being ill, and having enjoyed the inevitable 'well-earned rest.' Alternatively, people in this situation are **looking tanned, rested and fit** or **looking relaxed**. 'In he blew, looking bronzed and fit, and I gave him the scenario' – P. G. Wodehouse, *Very Good, Jeeves*, 'The Love That Purifies' (1930); 'Epitaph. Here lies a Gossip Writer. / Heart Failure Made Him Quit. / He met a Famous Person / Who Didn't Look Tanned and Fit' – Anonymous in *Punch* (6 December 1933); '"Relaxed" has taken the place of the outmoded "bronzed and fit"' – *The Times* (16 March 1961); 'Kennedy arrived . . . looking tanned, rested and fit. My television

adviser, Ted Rodgers, recommended that I use television make-up, but unwisely I refused, permitting only a little "beard stick" on my perpetual five o'clock shadow' – Richard M. Nixon, *Memoirs* (1978); 'He's tanned, he's rested, he's ready: Nixon in '88' – T-shirt slogan quoted in *Time* Magazine (22 February 1988); 'Eric Burdon: Tan, fit and living in the desert' – headline in the *San Diego Union* (25 March 1989); 'Mr Major, looking relaxed and confident, was not going down without a fight. In a warmly appreciated appeal to regional chauvinism, the Prime Minister cast back 1,100 years to the era of King Alfred the Great for reasons to vote Tory in the West Country' – *The Times* (24 May 1994); 'Looking slim, tanned and relaxed [Antonia De Sancha] wore a single white flower in her hair and white high-heeled shoes' – *Sunday Mirror* (4 September 1994); 'Bronzed and fit, Anthony and Paul have travelled across 39 American states, mainly by picking up a car in one state and delivering it to another' – *Daily Mail* (30 September 1994); 'Looking tanned and fit after a two-week break at the renowned St James's Club in Antigua, the petite Miss [Elaine] Paige . . .' – *Hello!* (13 May 1995); 'Princess Anne, suntanned and relaxed after a working visit to Mauritius, looked a picture of happiness as she danced the night away with her husband Cdr. Tim Laurence' – *Hello!* (13 May 1995).

(it's) looking good   Obviously, to say that something 'looks good' is an old expression, but this particular version was popularized by participants in and commentators on the US space programme in the 1960s/70s. The optimism that things are going smoothly is tempered by the unstated addition '. . . so far'. A British TV fitness programme *circa* 1989 was entitled *Looking Good, Feeling Great*.

looking like The Soul's Awakening   'The Soul's Awakening' was the title of a painting by the English artist James Sant (1820–1916) that was exhibited at the Royal Academy in 1888. An engraving (1890) by Henry Scott Bridgewater further increased its popularity. The picture shows a young woman soulfully clutching a book that is probably the Bible and looking up towards the light. 'It impressed her. No mistaking that. She uttered a meditative "Golly!" and stood on one leg, looking like "The Soul's Awakening"' – P. G. Wodehouse, *The Mating Season*, Chap. 12 (1949).

(you) look like you've lost a shilling and found a tanner 'My late father used this saying if he saw an old friend who looked a bit down in the mouth' – Arthur W. Jillions, Essex (1995). 'You look as though you've lost a bob and found a tanner' – father of E. N. Rouse, Worcestershire (2000). A bob/shilling was worth twice a tanner/sixpence, hence the disappointment. This has probably derived from the earlier sayings connected to the name of **John Toy** – as in *Cornish Proverbs* (1864). C. H. Spurgeon, *Ploughman's Pictures* (1880), has: 'The luck that comes to them is like Johnny Toy's, who lost a shilling and found a two-penny loaf.'

look, Ma, no hands! The American version of the British 'look, Mum, no hands!' or 'look, no hands!' cry when a child (usually) is demonstrating some feat to its elders, like riding a bicycle. Now used allusively about any activity to which the doer seeks to draw attention. Lesley Storm's comedy *Look, No Hands!* opened in London in July 1971, but the phrase probably dates back to the 1950s at least (from when I seem to a recall a joke about a German boy shooting his mother and saying to a friend – 'Look, Hans – no Ma!')

looks even better on a man Advertising line for Tootal shirts in the UK, from 1961. The poster featured a girl wearing an oversize man's shirt.

looks like a million dollars Looks extremely attractive, as though a great deal of money has been spent on it (or more usually her). By the 1920s. Compare **I feel like a million dollars** – 'I feel on top of the world, couldn't be better.'

looks like a wet weekend Looks grim, unappealing, about as much fun – and this may be the (Australian?) origin of the phrase – as a woman who is having a period and thus putting the damper on joint sexual activity. Since the 1930s/40s.

look that up in your Funk and Wagnall(s)! Catchphrase from NBC TV, *Rowan and Martin's Laugh-In* (1967–73). Referring to the American dictionary.

look who it isn't! Facetious greeting of the **do you see who I see?** variety, uttered on spotting a friend or acquaintance. Mid-20th century.

look who's talking (or **listen/hark . . .)** Derisive comment on someone who has just said something that they should not, because by their usual behaviour they contradict the sentiment they have just expressed. Mid-20th century. *Look Who's Talking* was the title of a chat-show presented by Derek Batey and produced by Border TV in the UK (current 1983).

(a) looney tune Meaning, 'a mad person' or, as an adjective, 'mad'. President Reagan commented on the hijacking of a US plane by Shi-ite Muslims: 'We are not going to tolerate these attacks from outlaw states run by the strangest collection of misfits, looney tunes, and squalid criminals since the advent of the Third Reich' (8 July 1985). The phrase had earlier been used in the Mel Brooks's film *High Anxiety* (US 1977). The reference is to the cinema cartoon comedies called Looney Tunes, produced by Warner Brothers since the 1940s.

(a) loony bin Now politically incorrect term for the equally unacceptable 'lunatic asylum' and 'madhouse'. The expression does still have a certain self-conscious currency though, even, or especially, among those who administer such places. 'Lunatic asylum' was, however, considered politically correct in the early 19th century when it took over from the previous century's 'lunatic hospital/house' and, especially, was preferred to the 17th century term 'madhouse'. The earliest citation to hand for 'loony bin . . . the facetious term for a mental hospital' is from *My Man Jeeves* (1919) by P. G. Wodehouse. Elsewhere, euphemisms rule. Now 'mental home' and 'mental institution' are still reasonably PC usage, though both frequently undergo a further euphemistic layer when used in such statements as, 'Oh, he's in a home', 'he's in an institution', or even, 'he's had to be sent away.'

(a) loose cannon A person who is not attached to a particular faction and acts independently and, possibly, unreliably.

Of American origin. The reference is either to a cannon that is not properly secured to the deck of a ship or to an artillery man who is working independently during a land battle. 'A subcategory of journalese involves the language used to indicate a powerful or celebrated person who is about to self-destruct or walk the plank . . . Soon Mr Brilliant will be labeled a "loose cannon" and transmute himself into an adviser, the Washington version of self-imposed exile' – *Time* Magazine (1 September 1986); 'Gung-ho, loose cannon, cowboy, Jesus freak – there is already a cottage industry manufacturing Ollie epithets. Lynching [Oliver] North is quickly becoming a national sport' – *The Observer* (26 July 1987); *Loose Cannons* was the title of a comedy cop movie (US 1990).

Lord love a duck! Exclamation of surprise. Perhaps a version of 'Lord love us!' Known by 1917. From T. S. Eliot's 'The Rock' (1934): 'Lor-love-a-duck, it's the missus!' This makes one wonder whether it is a phrase more used in emulation of common, perhaps Cockney, speech than the real thing? 'I had been right in supposing that the information would have a marked effect on her dark mood . . . an ecstatic "Well, Lord love a duck!" escaped her' – P. G. Wodehouse, *Stiff Upper Lip, Jeeves*, Chap. 21 (1963).

lord mayor See AFTER THE.

(the) lord of the dance Sydney Carter's song 'Lord of the Dance' (1967) refers to Jesus Christ and employs the image of life as a dance: 'Dance then, wherever you may be, / I am the Lord of the Dance, said he, / And I'll lead you all wherever you may be, / And I'll lead you all in the dance, said he.' Hence, *Lord of the Dance*, title of a dance show (1996), choreographed by and featuring Michael Flatley.

(the) lord of the flies Phrase from the literal meaning of the Hebrew word 'Beelzebub', the devil. Hence, *The Lord of the Flies* – title of the novel (1954; films UK 1963, US 1990) by William Golding.

(a) lord of words Complimentary title bestowed upon a 'master of language'. It was used to describe the broadcaster, Sir Huw Wheldon, and the playwright, Samuel Beckett, at their deaths in 1986 and 1989,

respectively. 'The Word-Lord' is a heading in *Punch* (9 June 1915). The phrase **lord of language** may be older. In *Ego 8* (for 2 May 1945), James Agate discusses a passage in *De Profundis* in which Oscar Wilde says of himself, 'I summed up all systems in a phrase and all existence in an epigram.' Agate writes: 'The boast about being "a lord of language". Wilde was that very different thing – the fine lady of the purple passage.' Whence, however, the 'lord of language'? In Tennyson's poem 'To Virgil' (1882) – 'written at the request of the Mantuans for the nineteenth centenary of Virgil's death' – the Mantuan poet is described, in a rush of alliteration, as 'landscape-lover, lord of language'.

(a) lorra lorra laffs In *circa* 1987, when the singer Cilla Black was presenting a programme called *Surprise, Surprise* for London Weekend Television, her way of saying, '[There'll be a] lot of, lot of laughs' somehow became the key phrase for impressionists to skewer her very wonderful Liverpool accent.

(to) lose a battle but not the war Charles de Gaulle in his proclamation dated 18 June 1940 and circulated among exiled Frenchmen, said: '*La France a perdu une bataille! Mais la France n'a pas perdu la guerre*' [France has lost a battle, but France has not lost the war!]. Earlier, on 19 May 1940, Winston Churchill, in his first broadcast to the British people as Prime Minister, had said: 'Our task is not only to win the battle – but to win the war' (meaning the battle *for* Britain, which he was later to call the Battle of Britain). Later, in 1962, Harold Macmillan used the formula after a by-election defeat at Orpington: 'We have lost a number of skirmishes, perhaps a battle, but not a campaign.'

(to) lose one's marbles Meaning 'to lose one's mental faculties.' Almost everyone agrees that this expression is American in origin, the *OED2* finding it first recorded in the journal *American Speech* in 1927. *Partridge/Slang* also has it that 'marbles' = testicles, though *DOAS* rates this usage as 'not common'. Partridge also defines the word 'marbles' on its own as meaning 'furniture, movables', derived from the

French *meubles* and dating from 1864. Could one imagine 'to lose one's marbles' coming from the idea of losing one's 'mind furniture' or possessions? *Apperson* lends suport to this account by showing that the English Dialect Society had included in a publication called *West Cornwall Words* (1880): 'Those that have marbles may play, but those that have none must look on.' Surely this admirably conveys the misfortune of those who are without the necessary wherewithal to participate in the game of life? Again, Elizabeth Monkhouse recalled (1997) that in her part of Cheshire, 'He's got all his chairs at home' was an expression used to mean, 'He's all there, alert.' Hence, a home without furniture is empty, so 'lost one's marbles' = empty-headed, no longer at home, no longer 'there'. This was also reported from Lancashire. Meanwhile, Joyce Hanley wrote: 'In Yorkshire, if someone is a bit lacking in the head, we say that they haven't got all their furniture at home.' At the popular level, most people believe the phrase derives from a joke. When Lord Elgin brought back his famous marbles from the Parthenon and they ended up in the British Museum in 1816, the Greeks were hopping mad (and, indeed, remain so). But, with all due respect and however entertaining, this is not an origin to be taken seriously. Dictionary explanations include this from Robert L. Chapman's *New Dictionary of American Slang* (1987): 'From an earlier phrase *let his marbles go with the monkey* from a story about a boy whose marbles were carried off by a monkey.' Chapman, basing himself on *DOAS*, also draws a parallel with the American expression 'to have all one's buttons', meaning 'to be of normal mentality or behavior' (by 1949).

(to) lose the plot   To be in ignorance of or no longer in control of a given situation; to be confused, lose direction. From the late 1990s and possibly referring to 'the plot' of dramas or films. 'Modernise or lose the plot, Scots party told' – headline in *The Guardian* (23 September 1999).

(the) lost generation   This phrase refers to the large number of promising young men who lost their lives in the First World War and also, by extension, to those who were *not* killed in the war but who were part of a generation thought to have lost its values. Gertrude Stein recorded the remark made by a French garage owner in the Midi just after the war. Rebuking an apprentice who had made a shoddy repair to her car, he said: 'All you young people who served in the war' are from 'a lost generation [*une génération perdue*]'. Ernest Hemingway used this as the epigraph to his novel *The Sun Also Rises* (1926) and referred to it again in *A Moveable Feast* (1964). John Keegan's *The First World War* (1998) begins by analysing the casualties and says of the small percentages of national populations killed or wounded: 'Even those smaller proportions left terrible psychic wounds, falling as they did on the youngest and most active sections of society's males. It has, as the war recedes into history, become fashionable to decry the lament for this "Lost Generation" as myth-making.' Here Keegan seems to equate 'The Lost Generation' with those men killed or wounded, rather than all those men who wasted their youth in the war, which is what Gertrude Stein meant. A further redefining of the phrase occurs in an F. Scott Fitzgerald short story 'The Swimmers', published in *The Saturday Evening Post* (19 October 1929): 'There was a lost generation in the saddle at the moment, but it seemed to him that the men coming on, the men of the war, were better.' So that makes the lost generation, the men of *before* the First World War: the old gang, not the new bunch.

lost in the mists of time   Phrase used in explanation for what is lost or forgotten because it happened a very long time ago. Date of origin unknown (or, rather, lost in the . . .) 'Stockton Castle, which stood at the southern end of the town's High Street on the site that is now the Swallow Hotel, was the focus of the action although the details of what happened have been lost in the mists of time' – *Northern Echo* (11 May 1994); 'For centuries, in communities like Sartene, Fozzano and Carbini, fanatical pride dictated that family was pitted against family, sworn to seek revenge for deeds that should have been lost in the mists of time' – *Mail on Sunday* (26 March 1995); 'The origins of Wexford are lost in the mists of time but it is likely that Celtic settlers arrived there in the 2nd century AD' – advertisement brochure, Travel for the Arts, London (Autumn 1995).

(a) lounge lizard Phrase for a type of man who would hang out in hotel lounges waiting to attempt seduction. They would also *lounge* loosely over the furniture. A very 1920s' coinage. 'Where are the Lounge Lizards?' is the caption to a *Punch* cartoon (9 March 1927) featuring the other sort of lizard. 'Makes a chap look a bit of a fool when his mother proposes to give him a twenty-two-year-old lounge lizard for a step-papa' – Dorothy L. Sayers, *Have His Carcase*, Chap. 12 (1932).

love See ALL'S FAIR; I THINK.

love among the —— Format phrase much used in titles, especially **love among the ruins**. The notion of love among classical ruins seems hauntingly appealing, rather as do the reminders of time and decay in Arcadia. 'And found young Love among the roses' is a line from an old ballad alluded to by Charles Dickens in *Barnaby Rudge* (1841); *Love Among the Chickens* is the title of a Ukridge novel by P. G. Wodehouse (1906/1920); and *Love Among the Haystacks* is the title of a collection of short stories (1930) by D. H. Lawrence. Evelyn Waugh entitled one of his shorter novels *Love Among the Ruins: A Romance of the Near Future* (1953), and Angela Thirkell used the title for a novel about the aristocracy in the post-war period, in 1948 (of which only the title was borrowed for a TV movie (1974), with Laurence Olivier and Katharine Hepburn). Earlier than this, there was the painting (so titled) by Sir Edward Burne-Jones where the lover and his lass embrace among fallen pillars and stones with mysterious inscriptions on them, hemmed in by the briar rose that rambles over all, and search for the way to Cythara where in the end they must separate. The subject comes from the Italian romance *Hypnerotomachia* (1499). The painting dates from 1870–3 and hangs in Wightwick Manor. Earlier still is Robert Browning's poem with the title in *Men and Women* (1855).

love in a —— Format used in several titles and phrases. *The Comical Revenge, or Love in a Tub* was the title of a play by George Etherege (1664); *Love In a Wood*, of a play by William Wycherley (1671); and *Love in a Village*, of a comic opera by Isaac Bickerstaffe (1762). Keats has 'love in a hut' in 'Lamia' (1820) and William Thackeray refers to 'love in a cottage' in *Pendennis* (1848–50) – both these deal with the romantic fantasy of love in poverty. *Love In a Mist* (from the popular name for the misty blue plant *Nigella*) was the title of a silent film (1916) with two popular British stars, Stewart Rome and Alma Taylor, and of several popular songs, especially one in the musical comedy *Dear Love* (London 1929). It was also the title of a play by Kenneth Horne (the writer, not the comedian), staged in London (1942). This last is a light comedy about two couples who find themselves fog-bound in a duck farm on Exmoor. *Love in a Cold Climate*, the novel (1949) by Nancy Mitford, caused Evelyn Waugh to write to her (10 October): '[It] has become a phrase. I mean when people want to be witty they say I've caught a cold in a cold climate and everyone understands.' Earlier, Robert Southey, the poet, writing to his brother Thomas (28 April 1797) had said: 'She has made me half in love with a cold climate.' There was also a film, *Love in a Goldfish Bowl* (US 1961).

love is the answer Phrase from John Lennon's song 'Mind Games' (1973), which itself became the title of a song written by Ralph Cole and performed by Island Lighthouse (1974). The line 'Is love the answer?' occurs in Liz Lochhead's poem 'Riddle-Me-Ree' (1984). A much alluded to view: 'Love is the answer, but while you are waiting for the answer, sex raises some pretty good questions' – Woody Allen, 1975; 'If love is the answer, could you rephrase the question?' – Lily Tomlin, 1979; both quoted in Bob Chieger, *Was It Good For You Too?* (1983).

love locked out *Love Locked Out* is the title of a painting (1889) by Anna Lea Merritt in the Tate Gallery, London. It shows a naked young woman trying to gain entrance to a sealed tomb. The artist was widowed in 1877 after only three months of marriage and had originally planned a bronze cast of this image for her husband's tomb. She explained it as showing that 'my love was waiting for the door of death to open and the reunion of the lonely pair.'

lovely grub, lovely grub! Catchphrase from the BBC radio show *ITMA* (1939–49). Said by George Gorge (Fred Yule), the 'greediest man ever to have two ration books'. He used to say it smacking his lips.

lovely jubbly See YER PLONKER!

lovely – tell your mother! Phrase for when things turn out just right. By the mid-20th century. Was often delivered as 'Lovelytellyourmother', with no pause. Ian Forsyth commented (2000): 'The snappiness and inverted word order were the appeal (rather like Jewish "Now he tells me").' Cliff Blake added: 'This was used in S.E. London in the form "It's lovely – tell your Mum!" It was often said to a child delivering something on behalf of its parent, or – jokingly – when someone was passing a minor object to a friend.'

lovely weather for ducks! What you say when it is raining. Although it must be ancient, a citation in this precise form has not been found before 1985. *Partridge/ Catch Phrases* finds 'nice weather for ducks' in Philip Oakes, *Experiment at Proto* (1973). *Apperson* has 'Weather meete to sette paddockes [frogs] abroode in' from Heywood's *Proverbs* (1546) and 'another fine week for the ducks' in Charles Dickens, *The Old Curiosity Shop*, Chap. 2 (1840). He also suggests that the predominant form is 'fine weather for ducks'.

love me, love my dog Meaning 'if you are inclined to take my side in matters generally, you must put up with one or two things you don't like at the same time', it comes from one of St Bernard's sermons: *'Qui me amat, amat et canem meum* [who loves me, also loves my dog]'. Alas, this was a different St Bernard from the one after whom the breed of Alpine dog is named. It was said (or quoted) by St Bernard of Clairvaux (d. 1153) rather than St Bernard of Menthon (d. 1008). A good illustration comes from an article by Valerie Bornstein in *Proverbium* (1991): 'I told my mother that she must love my father a lot because she tolerated his

snoring! . . . She became aggravated with me and stated the proverb *"Aime moi, aime mon chien"*. She told me that when you love someone, you accept all the things that go along with them, their virtues and faults.'

love me, or leave me During the Vietnam War, one of the few memorable patriotic slogans, current from 1969, was 'America, Love It or Leave It'. This was perhaps inspired by the song 'Love Me or Leave Me' (1928, hit version 1955), although since the 19th century there has been the semi-proverbial, semi-jocular farewell, **I must love you and leave you**. *Love 'Em and Leave 'Em* was the title of a Louise Brooks's film (US 1927).

love, pain and the whole damn thing *Love, Pain and the Whole Damn Thing* was the English title of a collection (1989) of four short stories by the German writer and film director Doris Dorrie. Earlier, in 1972, there had been Alan J. Pakula's US film with the title *Love and Pain and the Whole Damn Thing*.

lover See ALL THE WORLD.

love thy neighbour Injunction from Leviticus 19:18: 'Thou shalt love thy neighbour as thyself.' Not one of the Ten Commandments, as might be supposed. However, in Matthew 22:39, Jesus says of 'Thou shalt love thy neighbour as thyself' that it is one of the two commandments upon which 'hang all the law and the prophets'. *Love Thy Neighbour* was the title of an ITV sitcom (1972–6) and spin-off film (UK 1973), concerning English/West Indian families living next door to each other.

love you madly Duke Ellington (1899–1974), the composer, pianist and bandleader, used to say, 'We'd like you to know that the boys in the band all *love you madly!*' It is also the title of one of his songs.

(the) lowest common denominator Mathematical term that is used, rather loosely in a transferred sense, to describe appealing to public taste in the choice of content in popular media. That is, by screening cheap TV programmes or films that appeal to the basic needs of viewers, or 'pander to the masses', it is hoped that large audiences will result. In fact, it should be the 'highest common factor' that relates to the dumbing-down tendency – but this is a lost cause. 'At a time when film-makers, television schedulers and advertisers sometimes appear as if their only aim is to reach the lowest common denominator . . .' – editorial in *The Independent* (1 January 2003).

(the) lowest form of animal life Phrase used in abusive contexts but originally a straightforward descriptive phrase, as in J. R. Greene, *Protozoa* (1859): 'The lowest form of animal life with which we are acquainted . . .' In the film *Mutiny on the Bounty* (US 1935), a midshipman is described as the 'lowest form of animal life in the navy'. 'These are essentially the tic-tac merchants of the business: the lowest form of financial animal whose computer-quick trading minds feed the screens in the great towers occupied by the new networks' – *The Guardian* (18 October 1994).

low profile See HIGH PROFILE.

LS/MFT Slogan for Lucky Strike cigarettes, in the USA, current in the 1940s. The initials, spoken in radio ads, meant 'Lucky Strike Means Finer Tobacco'. A graffito collected in *Graffiti 4* (1982) translated the initials as 'Let's Screw, My Finger's Tired', though this merely reproduces oral tradition.

luck See AND THE BEST; AREN'T YOU.

lucky Jim Title of a US song by Frederick Bowers (d. 1961) and his vaudeville partner, Charles Horwitz (though it is usually ascribed to Anon.). It tells of a man who has to wait for his childhood friend to die before he can marry the girl they were once both after. Then, married to the woman and not enjoying it, he would rather he was dead like his friend: 'Oh, lucky Jim, how I envy him.' *Lucky Jim* became the title of a comic novel (1953) by Kingsley Amis, about a hapless university lecturer, Jim Dixon.

Ludlum See AS LAZY AS.

lulled into a sense of false security Eric Partridge, *A Dictionary of Clichés* (5th edition, 1978), has 'lulled to a false sense of security' and adds 'Politicians, please note!' 'To rock them . . . in the cradle of their false security' – Lord Lytton, *Rienzi*

(1835); 'But the Australians seemed to be lulled into a false sense of security when scrum-half Edwards was dismissed in the first half' – *Daily Mail* (18 November 1994); 'The Ombudsman may hold insurers responsible for failure to collect these premiums if the arrangement has been working well, and the policyholder has been lulled into a false sense of security' – *The Scotsman* (15 February 1995).

(a) lunar landscape Inevitable alliterative pairing to describe any bleak prospect of a physical, geographical kind. Date of origin unknown – 1960s? Part of the 'travel scribes' armoury' compiled from a competition in *The Guardian* (10 April 1993). 'That still left our own 340 yards of lunar landscape for the hearse to negotiate. There was no way the council would pay two-thirds of that, so out came the old tin bath again – and two narrow strips of concrete were laid' – *The Herald* (Glasgow) (18 July 1994); 'The tourists, mostly wealthy Americans, had been drifting through stormy seas for days anticipating their first glimpse of the Antarctic peninsula, and the lunar landscape of dark grey rocky hills patched with snow was not what they had expected' – *The Observer* (26 March 1995).

(the) lunatic fringe Referring to a minority group of extremists, usually in politics, the phrase gained currency after Theodore Roosevelt said in 1913: 'There is apt to be a lunatic fringe among the votaries of any forward movement.'

lunchtime See LEGEND IN.

lush vegetation Inevitable pairing. Date of origin unknown. Part of the 'travel scribes' armoury' compiled from a competition in *The Guardian* (10 April 1993). 'Upland lakes and ranches, rugged peaks and awesome ravines, and dense forests of Ponderosa pine give way to semi-arid plains, vast peach and apple orchards, lush vegetation and areas so remote that they are still unexplored' – *The Herald* (Glasgow) (5 September 1994); 'Even more exhilarating was swimming behind the torrent to stand on a rock ledge and look out through the film of water to the lush vegetation below' – *The Times* (5 November 1994).

Luton Airport See NICE 'ERE.

(a) lynch mob A group of people administering summary justice by execution. There are several candidates for the origin of this name. Most likely is Colonel William Lynch (d. 1820) of Pittsylvania County, Virginia, who certainly took the law into his own hands, formed a vigilante band and devised what became known as the Lynch Laws. However, as Tom Burnam, *More Misinformation* (1980), points out, even he did not really behave in the way 'to lynch' came to mean. There was also an old English word *linch*, meaning punishment by whipping or flogging, and this was sometimes imposed by the 'Lynch' courts of Virginia. The verb 'to lynch' was in use by 1836.

M

(a) machine for living in From the definition of a house by the French architect Le Corbusier (Charles Edouard Jeanneret) (1887–1965) in *Vers une Architecture* (1923): '*La maison est une machine à habiter* [A house is a machine for living in].' Some feel that Le Corbusier's description of the purpose of a house is a rather chilling one but in the context of his expanded explanation, it is not so bleak. He wrote in *Almanach de l'Architecture* (1925): 'The house has [three] aims. First it's a machine for living in, that is, a machine destined to serve as a useful aid for rapidity and precision in our work, a tireless and thoughtful machine to satisfy the needs of the body: comfort. But it is, secondly, a place intended for meditation and thirdly a place whose beauty exists and brings to the soul that calm which is indispensable.' Compare from Leo Tolstoy, *War and Peace*, Bk 10, Chap. 29 (1865–9): '*Notre corps est une machine à vivre* [our body is a machine for living].'

(a) mackerel sky is very wet – or very dry The actress Sian Phillips chose this to illustrate the unhelpfulness of weather proverbs on BBC Radio *Quote . . . Unquote* (13 April 1993). Mrs Barbara Williams, Plymouth, wrote (1993) that the version she grew up with was, 'Mackerel sky, mackerel sky / Neither wet, neither dry.' *Apperson* finds any number of explanations as to what a mackerel sky foretells, and none of them is very helpful. For example from West Somerset (1886): 'Mackerel-sky! not much wet, not much dry.'

Mac the Knife English name of the character 'Mackie Messer' in *The Threepenny Opera* (1928) by Brecht and Weill, derived from the name 'MacHeath' in Gay's *The Beggar's Opera* (1728). It is now a nickname applied to people with a name beginning Mac or Mc who behave ruthlessly, e.g. Harold Macmillan at the time of the NIGHT OF THE LONG KNIVES and Ian MacGregor at the National Coal Board when making large-scale redundancies in the 1980s.

mad See DON'T GET.

mad as a hatter The Hatter in Lewis Carroll's *Alice's Adventures in Wonderland* (1865) is not described as the *Mad* Hatter, though he is undoubtedly potty. His behaviour seems to confirm, however, a once popular belief that people working as hat-makers could suffer brain damage by inhaling the nitrate of mercury used to treat felt. In fact, Carroll may not have been thinking of a hatter at all but rather of a certain Theophilus Carter, a furniture dealer of Oxford, who was notable for the top hat he wore, was also a bit potty and known as the Mad Hatter. And it is the March Hare who is marginally more mad (after the much older expression **mad as a march hare** – known by 1529). *Morris* favours a derivation from the Anglo-Saxon word *atter*, meaning poison (and closely related to the adder, the British snake whose bite can cause fever). The phrase 'mad as a hatter' is not recorded before 1837. On the other hand, by 1609 there was a phrase, 'mad as a weaver', which takes us back to the peculiarities of specific trades people.

mad, bad, and dangerous to know Lady Caroline Lamb's famous encapsulation of Lord Byron appears in her diary entry on first meeting him at a ball in March 1812. Quoted in Elizabeth Jenkins, *Lady Caroline Lamb* (1932). She was the wife of 2nd Viscount Melbourne.

(the) Mad Monk   Nickname of Grigori Efimovich (*circa* 1871–1916), otherwise known as Rasputin. Of Siberian peasant origin, he was a self-styled holy man but was famous for his debauchery and the influence he exercised over Tsarina Alexandra. He was murdered by a group of Russian noblemen. *Rasputin the Mad Monk* was the title used in the UK for the film *Rasputin and the Empress* (US 1932) and also for a new film (UK 1966). In the early 1980s, the nickname was applied by *Private Eye* Magazine to Sir Keith Joseph (1918–94), who was something of an *éminence grise* to Prime Minister Margaret Thatcher.

(the) Mad Mullah   Nickname shared by two Mohammedan leaders of revolt against British rule: one, the 'Mad Mullah of Swat' in the Indian uprisings of 1897–8, the other, the better-known Mohammed bin Abdullah, who created terror for tribes friendly to the British in Somaliland (1899–1920). In the plural, the name was reapplied to Iranian religious leaders in the turmoil following the fall of the Shah (1979) and the rise of Ayatollah Khomeini.

mad woman   See ALL OVER.

(a) mad world, my masters   *A Mad World, My Masters* is the title of a play (written 1604–7) by the Jacobean playwright Thomas Middleton. It has a complicated plot of deceits and disguises. The title was borrowed for a volume of memoirs (2001) by John Simpson, the BBC's World Affairs Editor.

Maggie May   Name of a character in a Liverpool song, dating from at least 1830. She is a prostitute who steals sailors' trousers, but: 'A policeman came and took that girl away. / For she robbed a Yankee whaler, / She won't walk down Lime Street any more'. A number of groups (including The Beatles) revived the song at the time of Liverpool's resurgence in the early 1960s. Lionel Bart and Alun Owen wrote a musical based on her life called *Maggie May* in 1964. Margaret Thatcher unwisely alluded to the song in April 1983 when

wishing to appear coy about whether she would be calling a General Election soon: 'Some say Maggie may, or others say Maggie may not. I can only say that when the time comes, I shall decide.'

magic!   Catchphrase of the title character in Yorkshire Television's comedy series *Oh, No, It's Selwyn Froggit* (1976–8). Bill Maynard in the cheerful role would exclaim this about almost anything he encountered. Now quite a common adjectival exclamation.

(a) magical mystery tour   Name given to a winding journey, caused by the driver not knowing where he is going. A 'Mystery Tour' is a journey undertaken in a coach from a holiday resort when the passengers are not told of the intended destination (and known as such from about the 1920s onwards). The 'magical' derives from The Beatles's title for a largely unsuccessful attempt at making their own film in 1967. 'Climbing with Tom Patey was a kind of Magical Mystery Tour, in which no one, except perhaps himself, knew what was coming next' – Chris Bonington, *Next Horizon* (1973); 'Then at Midnight *Canberra* slipped out, or as Lt Hornby so eloquently put it, "buggered off on the second leg of our magical mystery tour"' – Robert McGowan & Jeremy Hands, *Don't Cry for Me, Sergeant-Major* (1983) (about the Falklands war); 'On and on went the city bus driver's magical mystery tour. Passengers point out their way home – and get a lift to the door' – *Daily Express* (12 April 1989).

(a) magic circle (sometimes . . . of Old Etonians)   In British politics this phrase was introduced by Iain Macleod in an article in *The Spectator* (17 January 1964) about the previous year's struggle for the leadership of the Conservative Party. He was describing the way in which the leader, although supposedly just 'emerging', was in fact the choice of a small group of influential Tory peers and manipulators: 'It is some measure of the tightness of the magic circle on this occasion that neither the Chancellor of the Exchequer nor the Leader of the House of Commons had any inkling of what was happening.' A year or two later, and as a result of this experience, the Tory leadership came to be decided instead by a ballot of Conservative MPs. Presumably, Macleod was influenced in his choice of phrase by the magicians' Magic Circle (founded 1905) and the ancient use of the term in necromancy. The phrase has continued to be applied to other semi-secret cabals to which those wishing to belong are denied access.

Mahomet See IF THE MOUNTAIN.

maiden See ANSWER TO.

(a/the) mailed fist Meaning, 'physical force' or, figuratively, 'tough action'. Known by 1897. 'In Enfield, North London, where Labour ousted the Tories after 26 years, former leader Graham Eustance said: "Local issues didn't come into it. If John Major doesn't want to lose the next election he must produce the mailed fist and start knocking some heads together, starting with the Cabinet"' – *Daily Mail* (7 May 1994); 'The Iraqis should not be allowed to renew this threat when the American and British soldiers have gone home. Unless something is done to prevent this then his mailed fist will still be over Kuwait and her neighbours' – *Financial Times* (15 October 1994).

(the) mail must get through (or go through) Slogan of probable North American origin – as indicated by use of the word 'mail' rather than 'post'. Though 'Royal Mail' is still very much used in the UK, the older term 'post' predominates. There is no citation of the precise slogan being used in Britain. As for the USA, the Longman *Chronicle of America* reports (as for 13 April 1860) the arrival in Sacramento, California, of the first Pony Express delivery – a satchel with forty-nine letters and three newspapers that had left St Joseph, Missouri, eleven days previously. 'The pace is an astounding improvement over the eight-week wagon convoys. But the brave riders, who vow "the mail must get through" despite all kinds of dangers ranging from hostile Indians on the prairie to storms in the mountains, may only be a temporary link [as the Iron Horse makes progress].' The *Chronicle* does not provide a solid basis for invoking the slogan at this point, but the connection

with Pony Express seems very likely. It would be good to have an actual citation from the period. Raymond and Mary Settle in *The Story of the Pony Express* (1955) point out that the organization flourished only in the years 1860–61, soon being overtaken by telegraph and railroad, and add: 'A schedule, as exacting as that of a railroad timetable, was set up, and each rider was under rigid orders to keep it, day and night, fair weather or foul. Allowance was made for nothing, not even attack by Indians. Their motto was, "The mail must go through", and it did except in a very few, rare cases.' Unverified is the suggestion that a Walt Disney cartoon, 'The Mail Pilot' (*circa* 1938), contained a 'stirring patriotic paean' that 'insisted that the mail Must Go Through.'

(a) major setback Inevitable pairing. Date of origin unknown. 'The result is a major setback for USI's hopes of bringing the non-affiliated universities into the fold' – *The Irish Times* (10 May 1994); 'Sir Hugh's sentiments were shared by stunned Ministers. Armed Forces Minister Jeremy Hanley spoke of the major setback of the crash and praised the "brave and talented men" who had saved countless lives over the years with their work in Northern Ireland' – *Daily Mail* (4 June 1994).

(to) make a beeline for Meaning 'to go directly', from the supposition that bees fly in a straight line back to the hive. Possibly American origin; known by 1849.

(to) make a leg A 'leg' is defined by the *OED2* as 'an obeisance made by drawing back one leg and bending the other; a bow, scrape'. It has it by 1589. Hence, 'to make a leg' means to make such a gesture, literally or figuratively. Making a leg to the reader (see citation below) is an indication of respect or request for the indulgence of that person. Shakespeare has it in *Richard II*, III.iii.175 (1592–3). *Brewer* (1923) quotes: 'The pursuivant smiled at their simplicitye, / And making many leggs, tooke their rewards' – from Percy's *Reliques* (The King and the Miller of Mansfield, Pt 2) (1765). In Charles Dickens, *Bleak House*, Chap. 53 (1852–3), Mr Bucket 'makes a leg'. '*Not* the least hint of the Round Table is detectable in the stories

– no sassy showing off, no making a leg at the reader' – Brendan Gill, Introduction to *The Collected Dorothy Parker* (1973).

(to) make a U-turn   The word 'U-turn' was probably first used in the USA (by 1937) to describe the turn a motor car makes when the driver wishes to proceed in an opposite direction to the one he has been travelling in. The political use of the term to denote a reversal of policy was established in the USA by 1961. In British politics, it was in use by the time of the Heath government (1970–4).

make-do and mend   Phrase popularized during the Second World War when there were Make-do-and-Mend sections in some department stores. It was designed to encourage thrift and the repairing of old garments, furniture, etc., rather than expenditure of scarce resources on making new. It was possibly derived from 'make and mend', which was a Royal Navy term for an afternoon free from work and devoted to mending clothes.

make 'em laugh, make 'em cry, make 'em wait   Suggested recipe for writing novels to be published in serial form (as done by Charles Dickens and many others in the 19th century). Charles Reade, who wrote *The Cloister and the Hearth* (1863), came up with it.

make love, not war   A 'peacenik' and 'flower power' slogan of the mid-1960s. It was not just applied to the Vietnam War but was used to express the attitude of a whole generation of protest. It was written up on the walls (in English) at the University of Nanterre during the French student revolution of 1968. Gershon Legman, a sexologist with the Kinsey Institute and an anthologist of erotic humour, may have coined the phrase at the University of Ohio in 1963. In the 1970/80s, it was still current, as part of a well-known car-sticker joke: 'Make love not war – see driver for details'.

make my day   See GO AHEAD.

(to) make no bones about   Meaning 'to get straight to the point; not to conceal anything', the expression refers either to drinking a bowl of soup in which there are no bones, which is easy to swallow and

there is nothing to complain about; or, from 'bones' meaning 'dice'. Here 'making no bones' means not making much of, and not attempting to coax the dice in order to show favour. Known by 1459.

makes you feel like a queen   Slogan for Summer County margarine, current in the UK in the 1960s. Barry Day, vice-chairman of McCann-Erickson Worldwide, pointed out in 1985 that this slogan was originally used in the USA for Imperial Margarine (also a Unilever product): 'The sudden magical appearance of the crown on the mother clever enough to use the brand made more sense. It was considered to be a successful brand property and used on several brands in other markets, irrespective of brand name. In none of the other cases was it markedly successful. The device seems to have been a piece of Americana that did not travel well.' The idea is not new. In November 1864, Tolstoy's wife, Sonya, wrote to him, 'Without you, I am nothing. With you, I feel like a queen' – though this is from a translation for an American edition of a French biography (1967).

(like all great comic creations, he) makes you laugh before he opens his mouth   Phrase used in criticism. 'The test of a real comedian is whether you laugh at him before he opens his mouth' – George Jean Nathan, in *American Mercury* (September 1929); 'Very early on in his stage career Stan [Laurel] had made an interesting discovery: he found that audiences laughed at him before he ever said or did anything' – Fred Lawrence Guiles, *Stan* (1980); Robert McLennan MP said it of Barry Humphries in the character of 'Sir Les Patterson' in November 1987.

make(s) your armpit your charmpit   Slogan for a deodorant spray called Stopette. In about 1953, Lady Barnett, the British TV personality, paid a visit to the United States and came across a most ladylike advertising slogan. It was: 'Make the armpit the charm pit!' – as related in her book, *My Life Line* (1956). Compare this: arriving in Los Angeles after flying on an inaugural flight over the Pole (1940s?), Wynford Vaughan-Thomas, the Welsh broadcaster, was – unusually – rendered speechless by an American colleague. V-T's description of the Greenland icecap apparently made the American broadcaster remember his sponsors, who were makers of deodorants. Said he: 'It may be December outside, but **it's always August under your armpits**' – related in V-T's *Trust to Talk* (1980). However, *News Review* (13 November 1947) reproduced this from the *Evening Standard* (London): 'He [John Snagge] had been against commercial broadcasting ever since he heard a Toscanini radio concert in New York interrupted by the sponsor's slogan "It may be December outside, ladies, but it is always August under your armpits".' According to Miles Kington in *The Independent* (13 May 1994), when W. H. Auden was Professor of Poetry at Oxford (early 1960s), he said in a lecture: 'Never underestimate advertisers. One of the most impressive lines of poetry I have ever come across was contained in an ad for a deodorant. This was the line: "It's always August underneath your arms . . ."'

makes you think   See THIS IS IT.

make the desert bloom   The modern state of Israel has made this injunction come true, but it 'dates from Bible times', according to Daniel J. Boorstin in *The Image* (1960). Adlai Stevenson also alluded to the phrase in a speech at Hartford, Connecticut (18 September 1952): 'Man has wrested from nature the power to make the world a desert or to make the deserts bloom.' The exact phrase does not appear in the Bible, though Isaiah 35:1 has: 'The desert shall rejoice, and blossom as the rose,' and 51:3 has: 'For the Lord shall comfort Zion . . . and he will make . . . her desert like the garden of the Lord.' Cruden's *Concordance* points out: 'In the Bible this word [desert] means a deserted place, wilderness, not desert in the modern usage of the term.'

(to) make the supreme sacrifice
Meaning 'to die for a cause, a friend, etc.', especially in the 1914–18 war. 'These young men . . . have gone down not only to the horror of the battlefield but to the gates of death as they made the supreme sacrifice' – W. M. Clow, *The Evangelist of the Strait Gate* (1916). A (perhaps) forgiv-

able cliché since then. 'Governor Nelson Rockefeller . . . has emerged from the dark night of the soul that afflicts all politicians pondering the supreme sacrifice' – *The Guardian* (22 December 1970); 'Only when we dare to question the necessity for the "supreme" sacrifice, and examine truthfully the quality of life that all the survivors are destined to lead afterwards . . .' – *The Independent* (1 May 1995).

make your mind up time   See OPPORTUNITY KNOCKS.

male chauvinist (pig) (or **MCP)**   Phrase for a man who is sunk in masculine preoccupations and attitudes. It erupted in 1970 at the time of the launch of the women's movement in the USA and elsewhere. The optional use of 'pig' was a reversion to the traditional, fat, porky use of the word after the recent slang borrowing to describe the police (mostly in the USA). **Male chauvinism** was a phrase in the 1950s. 'Chauvinism' itself is a venerable coinage and originally referred to excessive patriotism. Nicolas Chauvin was a French general during Napoleon's campaigns who became famous for his excessive devotion to his leader. 'This has been a good lesson to all concerned that male chauvinism is un-American to the core' – S. J. Perelman, 'Hell Hath No Fury . . . And Saks No Brake' (1951); 'Hello, you male-chauvinist racist pig' – caption to cartoon in *The New Yorker* (5 September 1970).

malice aforethought   English legal term (current by 1670) for a wrongful act carried out against another person *intentionally*, without just cause or excuse (originally Old French *malice prepense*). *Malice Aforethought* was the title of a crime novel (1931) by Francis Iles.

malice in wonderland   An expression obviously playing upon *Alice in Wonderland* – as Lewis Carroll's story is generally called. It has been used as the title of a novel (1940) by 'Nicholas Blake' (C. Day Lewis) and also of an unrelated TV movie (US 1985) about Hollywood gossip columnists. It was also the title of a record album by the UK group Nazareth (1980). In his diary for February 1935, Cecil Beaton, the photographer, wrote: 'Cocteau says I am Malice in Wonderland and I have succeeded in spending my life in an unreality made up of fun.'

man See AM I NOT; ARE YOU A MAN.

man alive! Expression of surprise, a mild expletive and building on the older usage, 'any man alive', when referring to 'any living man whatever'. Swift recorded it in *Polite Conversation* (1738). Ollie exclaims it in *The Laurel-Hardy Murder Case* (US 1930); 'Why, man alive, Laura! Just look about you a little' – Tennessee Williams, *The Glass Menagerie*, Sc. 7 (1944). *Man Alive* was the title of a long-running BBC TV documentary series (1965–82).

man and myth (or the man behind the myth) What biographies and articles often claim to reveal. Date of origin unknown. 'The Man and the Myth' was the title given to a Kenneth Tynan profile of Humphrey Bogart in *Playboy* (June 1966). 'Christopher Dobson and Ronald Payne are looking for the man behind the myth' – Martin Bell reviewing the book *The Carlos Complex* (1977) in *The Listener; P. G. Wodehouse: Man and Myth* – title of book (1982) by Barry Phelps; 'On Saturday night and Sunday, the festival presents The Middleham Requiem in Middleham Church, a new choral work exploring the real man behind the myth of Richard III, whose northern home was Middleham Castle' – *Northern Echo* (27 May 1994).

Manchester See IF YOU'VE NEVER BEEN.

(a) man for all seasons Chiefly promotional and journalistic phrase, to describe an accomplished, adaptable, appealing person. The origin is a description of Sir Thomas More (1478–1535) by a contemporary, Robert Whittington: 'More is a man of angel's wit and singular learning; I know not his fellow. For where is the man of that gentleness, lowliness and affability? And as time requireth, a man of marvellous mirth and pastimes; and sometimes of as sad a gravity: as who say a man for all seasons.' Whittington (*circa* 1480–*circa* 1530) wrote the passage for schoolboys to put into Latin in his book *Vulgaria* (*circa* 1521). It translates a comment on More by Erasmus – who wrote in his preface to *In Praise of Folly* (1509) that More was '*omnium horarum hominem*.' The phrase's

popularity stems from its use as the title of Robert Bolt's play about Sir Thomas More (1960, filmed UK 1967). The cliché formula 'a — for all seasons' was established soon after. '[Ralph Richardson] was warm and what the public might call ordinary and, therefore, quite exceptional. That was his ability, that was his talent; he really was a man for all seasons' – Laurence Olivier, *On Acting* (1986); 'She [Margaret Thatcher] has proved herself not the "best man in Britain" but the "Woman For All Seasons"' – Jean Rook in the *Daily Express* (1982/3).

(the) Man From —— There has been an intermittent tendency to describe US presidents as if they were tall-walking characters from Westerns. Thus Harry Truman was dubbed 'The Man from Missouri', Dwight Eisenhower 'The Man from Abilene', and Jimmy Carter 'The Man from Plains'. John F. Kennedy nominating Adlai Stevenson for the Democratic ticket hailed him as 'The Man from Libertyville'. None of this was very convincing and the craze is best left to the cinema whence we have had *The Man from Bitter Ridge/ Colorado/Dakota/Del Rio/Laramie/the Alamo/Wyoming*, not to mention, any number of 'The Man Who —— 's and 'A Man Called —— 's.

(the) Man from the Pru Slogan for The Prudential Assurance Co. Ltd, which was founded in Britain in 1848. The phrase 'The Man from the Pru' evolved naturally from what people would call the person who came to collect their life-insurance premiums. It had become a music-hall joke by the end of the century, but there was no serious use of it as a company slogan until the late 1940s, when it appeared in ads as 'Ask the Man from the Pru'.

(the) Man from UNCLE *The Man from U.N.C.L.E.* was the title of a US TV series (1964–7) about an international spy organization. The letters stood for 'United Network Command for Law and Enforcement'. Any number of BBC stars have been dubbed 'the Man from Auntie' in consequence.

mangle See I HAVEN'T BEEN.

(a) man in a grey suit (or dark suit) A colourless administrator or technocrat who is probably as grey in his personality as in the colour of his suit. When The Beatles set up the Apple organization in the 1960s, John Lennon said this was an attempt 'to wrest control from the **men in suits**'. Sometimes such people are simply called **suits**. The **men in grey suits** are, however, something a little different. In the November 1990 politicking that saw the British Prime Minister Margaret Thatcher eased out of office by her own party, there was much talk of the 'men in (grey) suits', those senior members of the Tory party who would advise Mrs Thatcher when it was time for her to go. Here, although still referring to faceless administrative types, the term is not quite so pejorative. In *The Observer* (1 December 1990), Alan Watkins adjusted the phrase slightly: 'I claim the paternity of "the men in suits" from an *Observer* column of the mid-1980s. Not you may notice, the men in dark suits, still less those in grey ones, which give quite the wrong idea.' 'With this latest career move can we expect to see the wunder-kind [John Birt] transformed into the proverbial Man In A Grey Suit?' – *Broadcast* Magazine (1987); '[John] Major's spectacular ordinariness – the Treasury is now led by a "man in a suit" whose most distinguishing feature is his spectacles' – *The Observer* (29 October 1989); 'That was more than just a re-assertion of the company's mission statement. It was almost a threat to the new regime of financial "bean counters" from the ousted advertising "suit"' – *The Sunday Times* (8 January 1995).

(the) man in the street Cliché of journalism, as in: 'Let's find out what the man in the street wants to know/really thinks'. Not a modern phrase. Fulke Greville, the English diarist, used it (entry dated 22 March 1830). 'Up to recently, the man in the street might have defined his attitude to animals in terms of coursing, fox hunting, or dogfighting. If he did not spend time watching live animals being torn apart for entertainment or kick the family dog into the kennel at night, he might class himself as an animal lover while contemplating rack of lamb for dinner' – *The Irish Times* (24 October 1994).

man is as God made him Proverb. 'Every man is as God made him, and often even worse [*Cada uno es como Dios le hizo, y aun peor muchas veces*]' – Miguel de Cervantes, *Don Quixote,* Pt 2, Chap. 4 (1615) (Sancho Panza's comment); 'My Lord, I am as God made me' – Swift, *Polite Conversation* (1738); '[On the horribleness of jellyfish] They are as God made them, Mr Reeve' – Henry Reed, *The Primal Scene, As It Were . . .* (1958).

mankind See FOR ALL.

manners makyth man Motto of William of Wykeham, English prelate and statesman (1324–1404), and consequently of his foundations, Winchester College and New College, Oxford. It is unlikely, however, that he coined the phrase: it was a proverbial saying by the mid-14th century.

manners, please – tits first Cry of the seducer's victim, when she considers that foreplay has started in the wrong place. Current in the 1960s and probably earlier.

(the) Man of Destiny Nickname of Napoleon Bonaparte. It was used as the title of a play about him (1895) by George Bernard Shaw. Sir Walter Scott had earlier used the phrase in his *Life of Napoleon Bonaparte* (1827).

(a) man of his time Phrase for a man who exhibits the characteristics of his era – not necessarily complimentary ones – and who may be excused his failings or aspects of his behaviour for this reason. *A Man of His Time* was the title of a play (1923) by H. Simpson. '[Sir Thomas More was] one who wore a hairshirt of exceptional severity, who scourged himself and persecuted others, who wrote charming letters to his daughter and religious pamphlets of the most vicious scurrility. Very much a man of his time, But – a fanatic?' – *Financial Times* (15 January 1983); 'The first Sir John [Ellerman], he described thus: 'Essentially a man of his time, he was an individualist, a commercial giant, and a moneymaker of supreme ability' – *Financial Times* (25 March 1983). Compare *A Child of Our Time* – title of an oratorio (1940) by Michael Tippett.

(a) man of my calibre Phrase used of himself by Tony Hancock in radio and TV series (from 1956). 'Calibre' was pronounced 'cal-aye-ber'.

(the) man of the moment Phrase with alliterative appeal. Known by 1871 when Browning wrote of a 'man o' the moment'. 'The Man of the Moment . . . The Chemist' – title of article in *Punch* (28 January 1914); Used as the title of a Norman Wisdom film (UK 1955). 'Here's our man of the moment . . . Hail the conquering hero comes' – Vincent Brome, *Day of Destruction* (1974); 'What counts is being man of the moment among the solicitors and powerful corporate clients willing to pay for who they believe is the best' – *Mail on Sunday* (22 May 1994); 'Once the final whistle has blown and the floodlights are dimmed, man of the moment Smith will switch his attention to a more difficult task' – *Northern Echo* (26 July 1994).

(a/the) man of the world Originally meaning an irreligious, worldly man, after Psalm 17:14: 'Deliver my soul from the wicked, which is thy sword: From men which are thy hand, O Lord, from men of the world, which have their portion in this life.' From this, the term has come to mean (less pejoratively) one versed in the ways of the world, a sophisticated person, one who has 'been around' and is broad-minded. The phrase has been used as the title of a novel by Henry Mackenzie (1773) and a comedy by Charles Macklin (1871).

(a) man of wrath Sam Weller's father is thrice called 'a man of wrath' in Charles Dickens, *The Pickwick Papers*, Chaps. 27 and 52 (1837). This is an allusion to Proverbs 19:19, 'A man of great wrath shall bear the penalty.'

(a/the) man on a white horse An authoritarian politician. This a development of the earlier **man on horseback** that *Safire* defines as: 'a military figure with political potential; or a would-be dictator; or any strong, authoritarian leader.' The archetypal man on a white horse (and first modern tyrant) was Napoleon Bonaparte, as depicted by Meissonier in his painting '1814', and in several other portraits. Note these citations: J. D. Lorenz's book *Jerry Brown: The Man on the* [sic] *White Horse* (1978) takes its title from a conversation with Brown in late 1974. Brown had mused, 'People want a dictator these days, a man on a white horse. They're looking for a man on a white horse to ride in and tell them what to do. A politician can do anything he wants so long as he manipulates the right symbols'; 'He [Ralph Nader] is, I believe, an authoritarian, a man on a white horse, and I for one hope that he will never ride into the White House' – David Sanford, a former colleague, writing in 1976; 'The citizens of this great nation want leadership – yes – but not a "man on a white horse" demanding obedience to his commands . . . a leader who will unleash their great strength and remove the road-blocks government has put in their way' – Ronald Reagan announcing that he would run for President (13 November 1979).

(the) man on the Clapham omnibus I.e. the ordinary or average person, the MAN IN THE STREET, particularly when his/her point of view is instanced by the courts, newspaper editorials, etc. This person was first evoked (according to a 1903 law report) by Lord Bowen when hearing a case of negligence: 'We must ask ourselves what the man on the Clapham omnibus would think.' Quite why he singled out that particular route we shall never know. It sounds suitably prosaic, of course, and the present 77A to Clapham Junction (1995) does pass though Whitehall and Westminster, thus providing a link between governors and governed. There is evidence to suggest that the 'Clapham omnibus' in itself had already become a figure of speech by the mid-19th century. In 1857, there was talk of the 'occupant of the knife-board of a Clapham omnibus'.

(a) man's gotta do what a man's gotta do *Partridge/Catch Phrases* dates this from *circa* 1945. Donald Hickling recalled hearing it in a wartime concert party, and suggested it came out of some late 1930s' Western (Hopalong Cassidy?) or from an American strip cartoon. The only printed reference to a definite source for the phrase in this precise form is to the Alan Ladd film *Shane* (1953), which was based on a novel by Jack Shaeffer, though – on checking – neither book nor film contains the exact line. Ladd says: 'A man has to be what he is, Joey.' Another male character in the film says: 'I couldn't do what I gotta do if . . .' And a woman notes: 'Shane did what he had to do.' In the novel, we find only: 'A man is what he is, Bob, and there's no breaking the mould.' Perhaps the phrase was used in promotional material for the film? Other suggested residing places of the phrase include *High Noon*, *The Sheepman* and *Stagecoach*. In the latter, John Wayne gets to say something like, 'There are some things a man just has to do.' The BBC radio show *Round the Horne* was using the precise form by the editions of 22 May and 4 June 1967. By the 1970s, several songs had been recorded with the title. So, the origin remains obscure, but an early example has now been found in John Steinbeck's novel *The Grapes of Wrath*, Chap. 18 (1939): 'I know this – a man got to do what he got to do.' It is not in the film (US 1940), though Ma Joad does say, at one point, 'You done what you had to do.'

(the) man they couldn't gag Nickname/by-line of Peter Wilson (1913–81), a sports journalist on the *Daily Mirror* who was famous for his hard-hitting style and outspoken opinions. A line from the BBC radio show *Round the Horne* (19 March 1967) about two camp journalists: 'We're from the *Daily Palare*. He's the man you follow around and I'm the one you can't gag.'

(the) man who —— Format title for a series of cartoons from the 1920s/30s by H. M. Bateman that showed people who had committed some solecism or other. The person singled out was usually represented as red-faced and embarrassed to death by what he/she had just done while those around him/her reacted in a horrified manner. Among the titles are: 'The Man Who Missed the Ball on the First Tee at St Andrews', 'The Man Who Lit His Cigar Before the Royal Toast', 'The Girl Who Ordered a Glass of Milk at the Café Royal' and, 'The Man Who Asked for "A Double Scotch" in the Grand Pump Room at Bath'.

(for the) man who has everything Slogan, ex-US in the 1920s/30s?, promoting some odd luxury gift-item, inessential and overpriced – like a gold remover of fluff from belly buttons, or the like. A salesman at the eponymous jewellery store in

Breakfast at Tiffany's (film US 1961) produces something 'For the lady and gentleman who has everything'. A woman asks of the eponymous millionaire in *The Thomas Crown Affair* (US 1968): 'What do you get for a guy who has everything?' In *Sunday Today* (4 January 1987), Alana Stewart was quoted as saying of her ex-husband, singer Rod: 'What do you give to the man who's had everyone?'

(the) man who was —— Format phrase based on *The Man Who Was Thursday: a Nightmare*, title of a short novel (1908) by G. K. Chesterton – a fantasy with an anarchist background. The seven members of the Central Anarchist Council are named after the days of the week.

(the) man who would be —— Format phrase based on Rudyard Kipling's *The Man Who Would Be King* – title of a story (1888; film US 1975) about two adventurers in India in the 1880s who find themselves accepted as kings by a remote tribe. Compare *The Man Born To Be King* – Jesus Christ – title of a verse drama for radio (1942) by Dorothy L. Sayers (a title already used by William Morris for a part of his poem *The Earthly Paradise*, 1868–70); and 'the lad that's born to be king', referring to Bonnie Prince Charlie, in 'The Skye Boat Song' (1908) by Sir Harold Edwin Boulton.

(the) man with the golden arm (or **flute** or **gun** or **orchid-lined voice** or **trumpet)** A medley of sobriquets. *The Man With the Golden Arm* was the title of a novel by Nelson Algren (1949; film US 1956) about a poker dealer who kicks the drug habit. 'The Man With the Golden Flute' is the sobriquet of the Ulster-born flautist James Galway (b. 1939). *The Man With the Golden Gun* is the title of a James Bond novel by Ian Fleming (1965; film UK 1974). 'The Man With the Orchid-Lined Voice' was a sobriquet of the Italian tenor Enrico Caruso (1873–1921) – a phrase coined by his publicist Edward L. Bernays. 'The Man With the Golden Trumpet' was the British musician Eddie Calvert (1922–78).

(the) man with the plan Political slogan used by the British Labour Party in the 1959 General Election. Posters carried the line under a picture of the party leader, Hugh Gaitskell, who did not win the election.

many a mickle maks a muckle   This supposed Scottish proverb isn't – and it is tautological nonsense into the bargain. In origin it is a very old English proverb (the idea known by 1250) as 'many a little makes a mickle' (= many a small quantity makes a great quantity). In Scots and northern English *mickle* becomes *muckle*, but that would spoil the assonance, so the old Scots word *pickle* (a grain or speck) was used to give a near-rhyme ('many a pickle makes a muckle'). Caught between two cultures, the phrase then became hopelessly muddled, until the meaningless cod-Scots form 'many a mickle maks a muckle' emerged as the most popular version. But it makes no sense in either English or Scots.

many, many times!   Catchphrase of Lady Beatrice Counterblast (née Clissold) (Betty Marsden) in the BBC radio show *Round the Horne* (1965–9) – originally in answer to a query as to how many times she had been married. 'Spasm', her butler (played by Kenneth Williams), would wail **we're all doomed, we all be doomed, I've got a touch of the dooms!** Both these catch-phrases were in position from the very first edition of the show (7 March 1965).

(the) man you love to hate   Billing phrase applied to Erich Von Stroheim (1885–1957), the Hollywood director, in one of his screen acting roles. He ap-peared in the 1918 propaganda film *The Heart of Humanity*. In it, he played an obnoxious German officer who not only attempted to violate the leading lady but nonchalantly tossed a baby out of the window. At the film's premiere in Los Angeles, Von Stroheim was hooted and jeered at when he walked on stage. He had to explain that he was only an actor – and was himself an Austrian. A 1979 tribute film to Von Stroheim was entitled *The Man You Love To Hate*.

March comes in like a lion   Proverbial saying: 'March comes in like a lion and goes out like a lamb,' known by 1625. Some hold that the saying is actually: 'If March comes in like a lion it goes out like a lamb and if it comes in like a lamb it goes out like a lion.' 'March came in like a lion with wild wind and rain and hail' – diary entry (1 March 1876) of the Reverend Francis Kilvert; 'In the fifth round the thing became a certainty. Like the month of March, the Cyclone, who had come in like a lion, was going out like a lamb' – P. G. Wodehouse, *Psmith Journalist*, Chap. 14 (1915).

march hare   See MAD AS A HATTER.

(to find a) mare's nest   To make what appears to be a great discovery but which turns out to be illusory or no discovery at all and a disappointment. Known by 1576. Swift's *Polite Conversation* (1738) has: 'What; you have found a Mare's Nest and laugh at the eggs.'

marital bliss   Phrase for what is supposed to be experienced in marriage, often ironic. Date of origin unknown. Compare **domestic bliss** and NUPTIAL BLISS. *Girls In Their Married Bliss* – title of novel (1964) by Edna O'Brien; 'Their marriage ran for more than 30 years, with periods where that impossible state of "marital bliss" came close to realization' – *The Times* (7 September 1994). 'Joanna Trollope's domestic bliss in Gloucestershire is much chronicled' – Valerie Grove, *The Times* (31 March 1995).

mark twain   'Mark Twain' was the pen name of Samuel Langhorne Clemens (1835–1910). It comes from the cry 'mark twain', meaning 'two fathoms deep', used when taking soundings on the Mississippi steamboats.

marry   See AND THAT MY DEARS.

Mars are marvellous   Slogan for the chocolate-coated soft-toffee bar, manufac-tured in the UK from 1932 and named after Forrest Mars, an American who founded the company that makes it. Another notable advertising line for the product has been **a Mars a day helps you work, rest and play** (since 1960). In the 1960s, Mars Bars became unforgettably associated with Marianne Faithfull, the singer, who was the girlfriend of Mick Jagger 1967–70. For the uses to which one was supposedly put, see Philip Norman, *The Rolling Stones*, Chap. 9 (1984). In

Faithfull (1994), the singer dismisses the myth of the Mars Bar event as 'a very effective piece of demonising that was such a malicious twisting of the facts – a cop's idea of what people do on acid'.

(rather a) Martha Nickname given to a housewifely woman and deriving from the biblical Martha, sister of Lazarus and Mary. While Mary sat listening to Jesus, her sister got on with the housework – 'distracted with much serving' – and Martha complained to Jesus, who nevertheless supported Mary (Luke 10:38–42). A modern example of the word's use occurs in *One of Us* by Hugo Young (1989): 'There was an almost obsessive reluctance to refer to [Margaret Thatcher's mother] . . . If she was alluded to at all, it was under the patronizing designation of "rather a Martha".'

Martin See ALL MY.

(a) Martini – shaken not stirred This example of would-be sophistication became a running joke in the immensely popular James Bond films of the 1960s and 70s. The idea stems from the very first of Ian Fleming's Bond books, *Casino Royale* (1953), in which Bond orders a cocktail of his own devising. It consists of one dry Martini 'in a deep champagne goblet', three measures of Gordon's gin, one of vodka – 'made with grain instead of potatoes' – and half a measure of Kina Lillet. 'Shake it very well until it's ice-cold.' Bond justifies this fussiness a page or two later: 'I take a ridiculous pleasure in what I eat and drink. It comes partly from being a bachelor, but mostly from a habit of taking a lot of trouble over details. It's very pernickety and old-maidish really, but when I'm working I generally have to eat all my meals alone and it makes them more interesting when one takes trouble.' Subsequently came several mentions of Bond's fad: for example, 'The waiter brought the Martinis, shaken and not stirred, as Bond had stipulated' – *Diamonds are Forever* (1956). The characteristic was aped by the writers of the first Bond story to be filmed – *Dr No* (1962). A West Indian servant brings Bond a vodka and Martini, and says: 'Martini like you said, sir, and not stirred.' Dr No also

mentions the fad, though the words are not spoken by Bond. In the third film, *Goldfinger* (1964), Bond (played by Sean Connery) does get to say 'a Martini, shaken not stirred' – he needs a drink after just escaping a laser death ray – and there are references to it in *You Only Live Twice* (1967) and *On Her Majesty's Secret Service* (1969), among others. The phrase was taken up in all the numerous parodies of the Bond phenomenon on film, TV and radio (e.g. *Round the Horne*, 13 March and 17 April 1966), though – curiously enough – it may be a piece of absolute nonsense. According to one expert, shaking a dry Martini 'turns it from something crystal-clear into a dreary frosted drink. It should be stirred quickly with ice in a jug'.

MASH Acronym standing for 'Mobile Army Surgical Hospital' and made famous by the film *M*A*S*H* (US 1970) and the subsequent sardonic TV series (1972–82) about one such American unit in the Korean War.

mask See FACE GROWS.

master See AGE BEFORE BEAUTY.

(the) Master Nickname of Sir Noël Coward (1899–1973), actor and writer, who was known thus throughout the theatrical profession from the 1940s but not by those close to him. He professed to dislike the name (perhaps because it had already been applied to Richard Wagner, Henry James, D. W. Griffith and W. Somerset Maugham, among others) and, when asked to explain it, replied: 'Oh, you know, jack of all trades, master of none . . .' Sir John Mills in his autobiography, *Up In the Clouds, Gentlemen, Please* (1980), claims to have been the first to give Coward the name when they were both involved in a production of *Journey's End*.

(a/the) master mind (1) Since 1720, a term for someone of commanding intellect but also often given to the supposed progenitor of criminal acts who (usually) is not directly involved in their execution – Trollope has one in *The Eustace Diamonds* (1872); 'They seemed so anxious to make it plain to him, these honest fellows, that in him they recognized not only the life and soul of the party but the Master Mind' – P. G. Wodehouse, 'Archibald and the

Masses' (1935). (2) Senior Service cigarettes were promoted in the UK, sometime before 1950, with the curious line **a product of the mastermind**. (3) A sort of catchphrase from the BBC radio comedy series *Ray's a Laugh*. From the edition of 1 April 1954, the home help Mrs Easy (Patricia Hayes): 'Now, don't you take that tone of voice with me, Mastermind!' (4) *Mastermind* – the title of a long-running general and specialist knowledge quiz (1972–97) on BBC TV – see under I'VE STARTED SO I'LL FINISH.

(the) matter is receiving my close personal attention Phrase used in official correspondence, often meaning the reverse. Date of origin unknown. The phrase 'close personal attention' also has a life of its own: 'They said outdoor activities coupled with close personal attention helped the youngsters realise their self worth' – *Northern Echo* (9 September 1994); 'If leaders don't pay close attention to their team members, they will fail: and attention is by definition personal' – *Daily Mail* (24 May 1995).

(a) matter of life and death Meaning that something is of the utmost importance. Often used in an exaggerated, figurative fashion. Known by 1583. *A Matter of Life and Death* was the title of a Powell and Pressburger film (UK 1946; known as *Stairway to Heaven* in the USA). 'Some people think football is a matter of life and death. I don't like that attitude. I can assure them it is much more serious than that' – Bill Shankly, Scottish football manager, quoted in *The Guardian*, 'Sports Quotes of the Year' (24 December 1973); 'For Jane Fonda, it has been the quintessential political correctness dilemma of the American Nineties: should she chop, or should she not chop? For Fonda and Co, it may just be a matter of political correctness in the Nineties. For the Indians, it is a matter of life and death' – *The Observer* (27 October 1991); 'The Foreign Office said it was doing "everything possible" to secure the release of Mr Cowley . . . "It is a very delicate situation, really a matter of life and death. We have to be very careful about how we conduct this matter"' – *The Observer* (27 August 1995).

May See DARLING BUDS.

maybe See AND I DON'T.

(a) May-December romance A relationship in which there is a wide age gap. Probably originating in American show business. *Punch* (5 April 1862) carries what is presumably a parody of an actual marriage break-up between a plebeian girl, May (20), and a 76-year-old aristocrat (called December). The headline is 'May and December', suggesting that the concept may have been a familiar one even then. *May to December* has been the title of a BBC TV situation comedy (1989–94) about such an age-gap relationship: Anton Rodgers with a young-enough-to-be-his-daughter girlfriend. 'Martha Raye's 75, he's 42 . . . as for the romantic side of their May-December matchup, she says, "After all those years, I almost forgot how to "do it"' – *The Washington Post* (28 December 1991); 'In the novel [*Grand Hotel*] the big love affair involves a couple with a big age disparity. But in the movie they cast Garbo and John Barrymore. No May-December' – *The Independent* (5 July 1992). Possible inspiration for the phrase may be: the James Walker/Ernest R. Ball song 'Will You Love Me in December As You Do in May' (1905); the Maxwell Anderson/Kurt Weill 'September Song' (1938): 'Oh, it's a long, long while / From May to December, / But the days grow short / When you reach September.' Compare this, from 'To the most Courteous and Fair Gentlewoman, Mrs Elinor Williams' by Rowland Watkyns (d. 1664): 'For every marriage then is best in tune, / When that the wife is May, the husband June.' In Chaucer's 'The Merchant's Tale', a 60-year-old bachelor called *January* marries a young thing called *May*. She is unfaithful, as is perhaps sometimes the case. There is also the phrase, **a spring and winter romance**. 'She [Coral Browne] showed the same frankness when commenting on a spring and winter romance between Jill Bennett and Sir Godfrey Tearle: "I could never understand what he saw in her," she drawled, "until I saw her eating corn on the cob at the Caprice"' – Ned Sherrin, *Theatrical Anecdotes* (1991).

may I spend a penny? Catchphrase of Private Godfrey (Arnold Ridley) in the BBC

TV comedy series *Dad's Army* (1968–77). See also SPEND A PENNY.

may the Force be with you! This benediction/valediction is a delicious piece of hokum from the film *Star Wars* (US 1977). At one point, 'Obi-Wan "Ben" Kenobi' (Alec Guinness) explains what it means: 'The Force is what gives the Jedi its power. It's an energy field created by all living things. It surrounds us, it penetrates us, it binds the galaxy together.' The phrase turned up in Cornwall a short while after the film was released in Britain – as a police recruiting slogan. Later, President Reagan, promoting his 'Star Wars' weapon system, said: 'It isn't about fear, it's about hope, and in that struggle, if you'll pardon my stealing a film line, "The force is with us".' Compare 'The Lord be with you' from, for example, Morning Prayer in the Anglican Prayer Book.

may you live in interesting times! Said to be an ancient Chinese curse and popular in the UK from the early 1980s.

meal See ANOTHER MEAL; AGE BEFORE BEAUTY.

meaning of the act See PLACE WITHIN THE.

mean! moody! magnificent! Slogan from the most notorious of all film advertising campaigns – for the Howard Hughes production of *The Outlaw* (US 1943). As if 'The Two Great Reasons for Jane Russell's Rise to Stardom' (skilfully supported by the Hughes-designed cantilever bra) were not enough, there were various pictures of the skimpily clad new star. One version had her reclining with a long whip. It's a very tame film, but the campaign has to be an early example of promotional hype.

mean streets Phrase used by Raymond Chandler in 'The Simple Art of Murder' (1950): 'Down these mean streets a man must go who is not himself mean; who is neither tarnished nor afraid' (referring to the heroic qualities a detective should have). However, in 1894, Arthur Morrison had written *Tales of Mean Streets* about impoverished life in the East End of London. *Mean Streets* was also the title of a film (US 1973) about an Italian ghetto in New York.

(a) meaningful dialogue Political use, mainly, but also in business. American

origin in the 1960s? Perhaps a coinage that runs parallel to the use of 'meaningful' in the druggy, alternative artistic sense, also from the 1960s (e.g. a pop song's lyrics might have been described as 'very wonderful and meaningful'). 'We hope that international pressure will be increased and that meaningful dialogue will begin soon in Burma' – letter to the editor in *The Guardian* (22 July 1994).

—— means never having to say you're sorry Adaptation of the dubious sentiment expressed in Erich Segal's film script (and novel) *Love Story* (US 1970) and as a promotional tag for it. Ryan O'Neal says 'Love means never having to say you're sorry', quoting his student wife (Ali MacGraw) who has just died. In the novelization of the story, the line appears as the penultimate sentence, in the form 'Love means *not ever* having to say you're sorry'. A graffito (quoted 1974) stated: 'A vasectomy means never having to say you're sorry'; the film *The Abominable Dr Phibes* (UK 1971) was promoted with the slogan: 'Love means never having to say you're ugly'; '"We tried to introduce scuppies, which are socially conscious yuppies. But . . . nobody wanted to know." Well, of course not. Yuppie means never having to say you're sorry' – in *The Independent* Magazine (in 1992); '"Politicians don't do that sort of thing [admit to having genuine human feelings of regret]", was the dismissive retort of a Conservative MP . . . Politics means never having to say you're sorry' – in *The Spectator* (in 1992).

meanwhile back at the ranch . . . One of the caption/subtitles/intertitles from the days of the silent cinema. It may also have been used in US radio 'horse operas', when recapping the story after a commercial break. Quoted in *Flexner* (1982).

meeting See HERE'S TO.

(to) meet one's Waterloo I.e. to meet one's ultimate challenge and fail, as Napoleon did at the Battle of Waterloo in 1815. An early use of the expression was by the American lawyer Wendell Phillips in the form, 'Every man meets his Waterloo at last', said Brooklyn (1 November 1859). He was referring to the failure of an attack by his fellow abolitionist, John Brown, on an arsenal in Virginia two weeks before. On the other hand, earlier examples in the *OED2* show that, almost from the word go, a 'Waterloo' entered the language in this sense. Byron in 1816 called Armenian 'a Waterloo of an alphabet'; John Aiton in his *Manual of Domestic Economy for Clergymen* (1842) wrote: 'If there must be a Waterloo, let it be a conflict for all the minister's rights, so that he may never require to go to law in his lifetime again.'

meet the wife See HAS HE BEEN IN?

(to) meet with an untimely end Meaning, 'to die'. 'Untimely end' known by 1578; 'meet with . . .' by 1890. Identified as a current cliché in *The Times* (17 March 1995). 'The only way you can benefit from Barclays' offer is to meet an untimely end. The money will then be just enough to pay for a modest funeral' – *The Observer* (19 February 1995).

megaphone diplomacy Referring to political 'dialogue' that consists of shouted sloganeering rather than a genuine meeting of minds, exchange of views, the phrase was used (by 1985) in particular to describe the abusive tone of relations between the USA and the USSR, prior to the *rapprochement* of the late 1980s.

melt See BUTTER WOULDN'T.

melting pot See THROWN INTO.

member See FULLY PAID-UP.

men in white coats Doctors and orderlies (especially from mental hospitals) whose appearance on the scene suggests that someone is about to be taken away for treatment. The cry 'Send for the men in white coats' might have preceded their arrival. *OED2* finds the term 'whitecoat' for such a person in use by 1911.

(oooo arr,) me ol' pal, me ol' beauty! The nearest that BBC Radio's agricultural soap opera *The Archers* (1951–) has come to a catchphrase was said distinctively by Chriss Gittins (d. 1988) in the part of the old yokel Walter Gabriel. No doubt it was adopted from traditional yokel-ese. The phrase was already established by 3 June 1958 when Tony Hancock did an impersonation of Gabriel on the BBC radio show *Hancock's Half-Hour* ('The Sleepless

Night'). Later, in June 1961, in a TV parody called *The Bowmans*, Hancock as Joshua had the line, 'Me old pal, me old beauty.'

(a) merciful release Phrase of condolence, used to suggest that a person's death means that they will not have to suffer bodily any further. Also that the relatives of the deceased will have a burden lifted from them. Known by 1901. A forgivable cliché, though less so in other contexts. 'I have had a grave week as my mother has just died, aged 84. You say the English always say "Happy release" at a death. It was really so in her case' – letter from Evelyn Waugh to Nancy Mitford (18 December 1954); 'He was screaming in such agony that I doubt that I or anyone else who heard him will ever be able to forget it. A British medic ran up, pulled out a pistol, and handed it to a captured Argie medic. The man took it with a nod, leaned down, and shot his own comrade in the head. It was a merciful release for a human being in ultimate pain' – *The Herald* (Glasgow) (4 June 1994); 'The crowd, traditionally one of the most supine in sport, were comatose long before the merciful release of the Croat's third-set collapse' – *The Daily Telegraph* (4 July 1994).

merde! See under BREAK A LEG.

Meredith, we're in! This shout of triumph originated in a music-hall sketch called 'The Bailiff' (or 'Moses and Son'), performed by Fred Kitchen (his dates sometimes given as 1872–1950), the leading comedian with Fred Karno's company. The sketch was first seen in 1907, and the phrase was uttered each time a bailiff and his assistant looked like gaining entrance to the house. Kitchen has the phrase on his gravestone in West Norwood cemetery, south London: 'Fred Kitchen . . . / Passed away / 1 April 1951 / aged 77 years / Beloved by all who knew him / MEREDITH, WE'RE IN'.

meringue See ANIMATED.

merrie England Phrase (so usually spelt) alluding to the supposed rollicking medieval past of the country. Originally not quite so arch or ironic – it was used in a straightforward sense in 1436. 'Thou Saint George shalt called bee, / Saint George of mery England, the signe of victoree' – Spenser, *The Faerie Queene*, I.x.61 (1590); 'Perthshire contains . . . tracts, which may vie with the richness of merry England herself' – Walter Scott, *The Fair Maid of Perth*, Chap. 1 (1828); *Merrie England: a new and original comic opera in two acts* – title of a work by Edward German and Basil Hood (1902).

merry See ALWAYS; HERE'S TO.

(a) merry war In some markets, *A Merry War* was the title given to the film adaptation of George Orwell's *Keep the Aspidistra Flying* (1997). Although not very suggestive of what the film is about, it is a phrase from Chap. 6 of the book: 'Gordon and Rosemary never grew tired of this kind of thing. Each laughed with delight at the other's absurdities. There was a merry war between them.' This is probably an allusion to Shakespeare's *Much Ado About Nothing*, I.i.55 (1598), where Leonato says of his niece (Beatrice), 'There is a kind of merry war betwixt Signior Benedick and her . . .'

mess See HERE'S ANOTHER.

(the) message of —— Cliché of (mostly British) politics, suggesting that the outcome of, say, a by-election should convey a meaning of importance to the leaders of the political parties that have not done well in it. 'The message of Hull [there had been a by-election] is a message for all the world. It is the announcement that this country, whatever its Government may do, will not have a French peace' – *Daily News* (12 April 1919); '"The SDP bubble has burst," crowed Fallon. "That is the message of Darlington"' – *Time* Magazine (4 April 1983).

(a) mess of potage 'To sell one's birthright for a mess of potage', meaning 'to sacrifice something for material comfort', has biblical origins but is not a direct quotation from the Bible. 'Esau selleth his birthright for a mess of potage' appears as a chapter heading for Genesis 25 in one or two early translations of the Bible, though not in the Authorized Version of 1611. The word 'mess' is used in its sense of 'a portion of liquid or pulpy food'. 'Potage' is thick soup (compare French *potage*).

Me, Tarzan – you, Jane Catchphrase from the Tarzan movies. A box-office sensation of 1932 was the first Tarzan film with sound – *Tarzan the Ape Man*. It spawned a long-running series and starred Johnny Weissmuller, an ex-US swimming champion, as Tarzan, and Maureen O'Sullivan as Jane. At one point the ape man whisks Jane away to his tree-top abode and indulges in some elementary conversation with her. Thumping his chest, he says, 'Tarzan!'; pointing at her, he says, 'Jane!' So, in fact, he does not say the catchphrase commonly associated with him – though he may have done in one of the later movies. Interestingly, this great moment of movie dialogue appears to have been 'written' by the British playwright and actor Ivor Novello. In the original novel, *Tarzan of the Apes* (1914), by Edgar Rice Burroughs, the line does not occur – not least because, in the jungle, Tarzan and Jane are only able to communicate by writing notes to each other.

methinks she doth protest too much Gertrude's line from Shakespeare's *Hamlet*, III.ii.225 (1600–1) is often evoked to mean 'there's something suspicious about the way that person is complaining – it's not natural'. However, what Hamlet's mother is actually doing is giving her opinion of 'The Mousetrap', the play-within-a-play. What she means to say is that the Player Queen is overdoing her protestations, and uses the word 'protest' in the sense of 'state formally', not 'complain'.

(a) Mexican wave Stadium crowds have long entertained themselves (and observers) by rising up and down from their seats in an orderly sequence, thus giving the impression (when viewed from a distance) of a rippling wave or flag. The name 'Mexican wave' was given to the practice following much use of it during the football World Cup in Mexico in 1986. Until then it had been known as a 'human wave'.

(a) mickey finn Anything slipped into people's drinks in order to knock them out. *DOAS* claims that, to begin with, the term meant a laxative for horses. The original Mickey Finn may have been a notorious bartender in Chicago (d. 1906) who proceeded to rob his unconscious victims. The term was recorded by 1928.

middle See IS ONE'S; AT THE.

Middle America Originally a geographical expression (by 1898), this phrase was applied to the US conservative middle class in 1968 during Richard Nixon's campaign for the presidency. It corresponded to what he was later to call the SILENT MAJORITY and was what was alluded to in the expression IT'LL PLAY IN PEORIA. The expression is said to have been coined by the journalist Joseph Kraft.

(the) middle of the road The safe option, middle-brow taste (especially in music), the political centre, the middle way, moderate and unadventurous. Known since 1777 in the USA, though not until the 19th century in a political sense. Known since 1958 in connection with music (where latterly it has been sometimes abbreviated to MOR). 'We know what happens to people who stay in the middle of the road. They get run over' – Aneurin Bevan, quoted in *The Observer* (9 December 1953).

(a/the) middle way A middle course in politics, occupying 'the middle ground' between extremes. The concept is an ancient one and also occurs in some religions. Winston Churchill ended an election address on 11 November 1922 by saying: 'What we require now is not a period of turmoil, but a period of stability and recuperation. Let us stand together and tread a sober middle way.' *The Middle Way* was the title of a book (1938) by Harold Macmillan, setting out the arguments for the political approach.

(a) mid-life crisis A crisis of confidence occurring especially in the middle-aged male. It may derive from his perception of the value of the work he does – or his waning sexuality – and may prompt him to try to change his behaviour and the course of his life. Apparently coined by E. Jaques in 'Death and the Mid-life Crisis' (1965), though Erik Erikson is also associated with the phrase. 'Jon Cousins is enjoying a spectacular mid-life crisis, shutting down his £12m-a-year advertising agency and taking a year off to travel the globe' – *The Daily Telegraph* (28 February 1996).

Compare **mid-career crisis**, a specifically work-related malaise. The phrase was used as the title of a book by John Hunt (1983). 'This feeling is contributing to what is being called "mid-career crisis". This used to take place when executives hit their fifties and realised there would be no more promotions. In the past decade it has been spotted in those nearing 40. Now it is starting to affect executives of 30' – *Independent on Sunday* (28 May 1995).

(to take the) midnight express (American?) prison slang for 'to escape'. Hence, *Midnight Express*, the title of a film (UK/US 1978) based on a book by Billy Hayes and William Hoffer about Hayes's experiences in a Turkish gaol to which he had been sent for drug-smuggling.

midsummer See AS I WALKED.

might is right Proverbial expression. In English, this was traced by *Apperson* to 'Might makes right' in about 1311. But the thought, translated, can be found much earlier in Plautus, *Truculentus* (*circa* 190 BC) as 'The more might, the more right' and in Plato, *The Republic* (*circa* 370 BC) as 'Might is right, and justice is the interest of the stronger.'

—— miles from London and still no sign of Dick! Stock phrase from the British pantomime *Dick Whittington* and much enjoyed because of the *double-entendre*. But who is it said by in *Dick Whittington* – Alice Fitzwarren or the cat? From a parody in the BBC radio show *Round the Horne* (3 April 1966): 'Come along, Puss – only six more miles to London'; 'Nine miles from London and still no sign of Dick' – alluded to in 'Nicholas Craig', *I, An Actor*, Chap. 6 (1988); 'Anita Harris, last seen in the Seventies in Puss In Boots [*sic*] (slapping her thigh and saying: "Twenty miles from London and still no sign of Dick")' – *Daily Mirror* (27 April 1996).

Miles's boy told me 'As a small child, many years ago, I used to be puzzled as to how my mother knew about all my dark deeds – or when I'd told a fib. She always knew where I'd been and who I'd been with *and* what I'd been up to. When I asked, she always replied this. How I grew to hate that boy!' – a correspondent (1998). *Partridge/Slang* has 'Miles's boy is spotted' as a printers' catchphrase meaning 'We all know about *that*, addressed to anyone who, in a printing office, begins to spin a yarn: from *circa* 1830. Ex Miles, a Hampstead coach-boy celebrated for his faculty of diverting the passengers with anecdotes and tales.'

milk? Pronounced 'mil-uck' on a rising inflection by Drusilla (Hermione Gingold), making tea for Edmond (Alfred Marks) in a feature called 'Mrs Doom's Diary' on the BBC radio show *Home at Eight* (first broadcast 21 April 1952). According to *The Independent* obituary of the show's scriptwriter, Sid Colin (28 December 1989): 'Sid ingeniously combined Mrs Dale with Charles Addams in a series of sketches . . . [the Dooms] lived in a suburban castle with Fido, their pet alligator, and Trog, their giant speechless servant. At tea-time, people all over Britain were parroting the words that closed every Dooms sketch: "**Tea, Edmond?**" "Yes, thank you, dear – thank you." "Mil-uck?"' When the sketches were included in another radio show, *Grande Gingold* (1955), the phrase became 'Tea, Gregory? . . . Milk?'

milk from contented cows Slogan for Carnation Milk, from 1906. Elbridge A. Stuart launched Carnation evaporated milk in 1899. Seven years later he went to the Mahin agency in Chicago to lay on an advertising campaign. The copywriter was Helen Mar: 'Mr Stuart gave me a description of the conditions under which Carnation was produced . . . the ever-verdant pastures of Washington and Oregon, where grazed the carefully-kept Holstein herds that supplied the raw milk. He described in a manner worthy of Burton Holmes the picturesque background of these pastures from which danced and dashed the pure, sparkling waters to quench the thirst of the herds and render more tender the juicy grasses they fed on. He spoke of the shade of luxuriant trees under which the herds might rest. Remembering my lectures in medical college and recalling that milk produced in mental and physical ease is more readily digested – I involuntarily exclaimed, "Ah! The milk of contented cows!" . . . "That's our slogan" [said Mr Stuart].' And so it has remained or

almost. The words on the can have usually been, '*From* contented cows.' In the film *The Cocoanuts* (US 1929), Groucho Marx gets to say: 'There's more than two hundred dollars worth of milk in those cocoanuts – and *what* milk, milk from contented cow-co-nuts.'

(the) milk of human kindness Compassion. It appears to have originated in Shakespeare, *Macbeth*, I.v.16 (1606): 'Yet do I fear thy nature: / It is too full o'th' milk of human kindness / To catch the nearest way.'

milk's gotta lotta bottle Slogan promoting milk consumption in Britain, *circa* 1982. Milk comes in bottles, of course, but why was the word 'bottle' used to denote courage or guts in this major attempt to get rid of milk's wimpish image? Actually, the word 'bottle' has been used in that sense since the late 1940s at least. To 'bottle out' consequently means to shrink from, e.g. in *Private Eye* (17 December 1982): 'Cowed by the thought of six-figure legal bills and years in the courts, the Dirty Digger has "bottled out" of a confrontation with Sir Jams.' One suggestion is that 'bottle' acquired the meaning through rhyming slang: either 'bottle and glass' = 'class' (said to date from the 1920s, this one); 'bottle and glass' = 'arse'; or, 'bottle of beer' = fear. But the reason for the leap from 'class/arse' to 'courage', and from 'fear' to 'guts', is not terribly obvious, though it has been explained that 'arse' is what you would void your bowels through in an alarming situation. And 'class' is what a boxer has. If he loses it, he has 'lost his bottle'. Other clues? Much earlier, in *Swell's Night Guide* (1846), there had occurred the line: 'She thought it would be no bottle 'cos her rival could go in a buster,' where 'no bottle' = 'no good'. In a play by Frank Norman (1958), there occurs the line: 'What's the matter, Frank? Your bottle fallen out?' There is also an old-established brewer, Courage Ltd, whose products can, of course, be had in bottles. The way forward for the 1982 advertising use was probably cleared by the ITV series *Minder*, which introduced much south London slang to a more general audience.

Milk Tray See AND ALL BECAUSE.

million dollars See LOOKS LIKE A.

(the) mills of God grind slowly (yet they grind exceeding small) Proverb. The meaning of this saying is that the ways in which reforms are brought about, crime is punished, etc., are often slow, but the end result may be perfectly achieved. The saying comes from Longfellow's translation of Friedrich von Logau, a 17th-century German poet.

Milwaukee See BEER THAT MADE.

(the) mind boggles! One is astonished at hearing of such an absurdity! The verb 'to boggle' here means 'to be startled or baffled'. Date of origin unknown. 'The mind boggles . . .' wrote *The Observer* in an editorial headed 'New World' after the death of Stalin in early 1953.

mind how you go! See EVENIN' ALL!

mind my bike! Catchphrase of the British actor and entertainer Jack Warner (1895–1981). He wrote in his autobiography, *Jack of All Trades* (1975): 'When I dropped the phrase for two weeks, I had 3,000 letters from listeners asking why . . . the only other complaint came from a father who wrote, "I am very keen on your *Garrison Theatre* show, but I have spent several hundreds of pounds on my son's education and all he can do is shout "Mind my bike!" in a very raucous Cockney voice. I'm trying to break him of the habit, so will you please stop saying it?"' *Garrison Theatre* was broadcast on BBC radio from 1939 onwards.

(to) mind one's ps and qs Meaning 'to be careful, polite, on one's best behaviour', the phrase has several suggested origins: the letters 'p' and 'q' look so alike, a child might well be admonished to be careful writing them or a printer to take care in setting them; because a well-mannered person has to be careful to remember 'pleases and thankyous'; because in a public house 'pints' and 'quarts' would be chalked up on a blackboard for future payment; and, in the days of wigs, Frenchmen had to be warned not to get their *pieds* [feet] mixed up with their *queues* [wig-tails] when bowing and scraping. Recorded by 1602, as 'For now thou art in thy Pee and Kue.'

mind over matter The influencing of a physical system by the use of the subject's mental effort without any known intermediate action. 'Let us here return to the sublime conjecture of Franklin, that "mind will one day become omnipotent over matter"' – William Godwin, *Social Justice* (1793); 'A Short Cut to Metaphysics. What is Matter? – Never mind. What is Mind? – No matter' – Anonymous (writer) in *Punch* (14 July 1855) (sometimes ascribed to T. H. Key); 'Women represent the triumph of matter over mind, just as men represent the triumph of mind over morals' – Oscar Wilde, *The Picture of Dorian Gray*, Chap. 4 (1891) and, later, in *A Woman of No Importance*, Act 3 (1893); 'The history of mankind is the history of thought – of the gradual ascendancy of mind over matter' – B. H. Liddell Hart, *Thoughts on War* (1944).

mind's eye See IN THE.

mind your own business Rebuke to an inquisitive person. Date of origin unknown. Recorded in *Punch* (1 July 1843).

mine See DON'T GO DOWN.

minions See MOON'S MEN.

ministers decide In the House of Commons (26 October 1989), Prime Minister Margaret Thatcher was commenting on the role of her economic adviser (Alan Walters) in relation to that of her Chancellor of the Exchequer (Nigel Lawson), who resigned next day on this issue. She said: 'The Chancellor's position is unassailable . . . In this party, ministers decide and advisers only advise.' One of her other ministers, Norman Fowler, accordingly entitled his memoirs *Ministers Decide* (1991).

miracles See AGE OF.

mirrors See ALL DONE WITH.

mischief See BE GOOD.

Miss Efficiency (or Mr Efficiency) Compliment bestowed upon someone who has performed a useful task in a very competent manner. Noticed by the 1990s. Origin unknown.

(the) missing link (1) Something missing to complete a series or connection. (2) The supposed connection between man and ape that became the crux of evolutionary theory from *circa* 1860 onwards. Charles Darwin did not use the precise phrase, and certainly not in *On the Origin of Species* (1859), though he did write much of 'links'. Unconfirmed is a statement attributed to him about the Patagonians, that: 'If they are not actually the missing link, they are not far removed from it.'

missing you already   See HAVE A GOOD.

(the) missionary position   The position for sexual intercourse in which the man lies on top of the woman, face-to-face. Possibly also known as the 'Mamma-Papa' position, indicating that it is considered a functional approach to love-making. *Slanguage* suggests that since the 1980s there was been a slang term 'missionary man' for an uninspired lover. The idea that Christian missionaries taught this method may have first been promoted by Alfred C. Kinsey, author of *Sexual Behavior in the Human Male* (1948). This may have been a misreading of the anthropologist Bronislaw Malinowski who, reportedly, wrote that Trobriand Islanders of the western Pacific mocked the sexual technique taught to them by European traders and planters. There is no evidence that any missionary ever promoted the 'missionary position'. 'In six States [in the USA] a woman may still be awarded a divorce if her husband makes love to her in any other than the missionary position' – *The Daily Telegraph* Colour Supplement (10 January 1969); 'The face-to-face "missionary position" (so called because it is virtually unknown in primitive races) is actually said to have been invented by Roman courtesans to hinder conception' – *Vogue* (November 1971).

(a) mission impossible   The title of the US TV series *Mission Impossible* (1966–72) has achieved catchphrase status. The original show dealt with government agents in the Impossible Missions Force. See also SELF-DESTRUCT IN FIVE SECONDS. 'Yet another journalist brought on to the set! He said "I want to write about all the fun that goes on *behind* the scenes . . ." and Kenny Connor said "Mission impossible"' – from *The Diaries of Kenneth Williams*

(1993) – entry for 20 March 1975; 'When Kissinger took the commission post, his associates warned that it was mission impossible' – *The Washington Post* (3 January 1984); 'Hostage rescue is mission impossible' – headline in *The Observer* (19 August 1990).

(a) mission statement   In business and political use, meaning 'a document setting out aims and aspirations'. 1980s' origin? Identified as a current cliché in *The Times* (17 March 1995). 'The fact that the public understanding of science was included in the White Paper, and is now part of the mission statement of the research councils, is a great advance and we applaud this enthusiastically' – *The Daily Telegraph* (1 June 1994); 'That was more than just a re-assertion of the company's mission statement. It was almost a threat to the new regime of financial "bean counters" from the ousted advertising "suit"' – *The Sunday Times* (8 January 1995).

(a) mission to explain   Phrase encapsulating his programme philosophy for the TV-am breakfast television station of which he was the Chief Executive, coined by Peter Jay, the British journalist and diplomat. Said first at an IBA public meeting in Croydon (1980) and many times thereafter. Unfortunately, it did not win him any viewers but the phrase lived on, perhaps as a warning to other programme-makers that high-flown idealistic statements are best avoided.

Miss Lonelyhearts   Name given to writers of advice columns for the lovelorn (chiefly in the USA), taken from the title of a novel (1933) by Nathanael West, about a man who writes such a column under this pen name. In the UK (mostly), the term **lonelyhearts column** has come to mean not an advice column but a listing service for men and women seeking partners.

Missouri   See I'M FROM.

Miss Otis regrets . . .   Parody of a statement of regret as contained in the song 'Miss Otis Regrets She's Unable To Lunch Today' (1934) by Cole Porter, in which a butler catalogues the reasons why this particular woman cannot – chief among which is that she has shot her lover and been hanged for it. In *Graffiti 3* (1981), there appeared this addition to a notice in York: 'LIFT UNDER REPAIR. USE OTHER LIFT – This Otis regrets it is unable to lift today.'

mistake   See AND NO; THIS WEEK'S.

Mis-ter *Chris*-tian . . . I'll have you *hung* from the *high*-est *yard*-arm in the *Navy*! An impersonation of the lines delivered by Charles Laughton as Captain Bligh in the film *Mutiny on the Bounty* (US 1935). The British comedian Tony Hancock made something of a speciality in the impersonation in *Hancock's Half-Hour* on BBC TV and radio, from 1954 onwards. In fact, the nearest Laughton gets to saying this (while addressing Fletcher Christian): 'I'll live to see you – all of you – hanging from the highest yard arm in the British fleet.'

mix and match   A way of selecting clothes for wearing (chiefly by women and in the USA). From *McCall's Sewing* (1964): 'Separates are the answer to the school-girl's needs. Skirts, sweaters, jackets and blouses that can mix and match are ideal.' Sometimes used allusively in other fields.

(to) mix and mingle   To socialize for-mally as part of a programme, especially when a celebrity allots time to meet the public or press. Date of origin unknown. Chiefly an American expression. The line 'mix and a-mingle in the jingling feet' occurs in the lyrics of the song 'Jingle Bell Rock' (known by 1959). 'Reagan will join everybody later at dinner . . . Afterward, forgoing the entertainment by opera singer Grace Bumbry and the "mix and mingle" over after-dinner coffee, he will return to the family quarters' – *The Washington Post* (19 July 1985); 'At Buckingham Palace there's the party within the party. Only those bidden to the royal tea tent actually get to mix and mingle with the royals' – *The Washington Post* (13 July 1986).

Moab is my washpot   Phrase from one of the strangest sentences in the Bible. Psalm 60:8 has: 'Moab is my washpot; over Edom will I cast out my shoe.' The New English Bible translation may make it clearer: '[God speaks from his sanctuary] Gilead and Manasseh are mine; Ephraim is my helmet, Judah my sceptre; Moab is my wash-bowl, I fling my shoes at Edom; Philistia is the target of my anger.' In other words, God is talking about useful objects to throw, in his anger. Moab was an ancient region of Jordan. The actor and writer Stephen Fry entitled his memoirs *Moab Is My Washpot* (1997). In *The Inde-pendent* (18 August 1999) he explained his choice of title as having more to do with the following words ('Philistia, triumph thou because of me' – which he interprets as concerning 'vanquishing the Philistines. My adolescent self saw life as a war between the athlete and the aesthete, the inner life and the outer life. But then, I was something of a wanker.'

(a) Moaning Minnie   A complainer. On 11 September 1985, the British Prime Minister, Margaret Thatcher, paid a visit to Tyneside and was reported as accusing those who complained about the effects of unemployment of being 'Moaning Minnies'. In the ensuing uproar, a Down-ing Street spokesman had to point out that it was the reporters attempting to question her, rather than the unemployed, on whom Mrs Thatcher had bestowed the title. As a nickname, it was not an original alliterative coinage. Anyone who com-plains is a 'moaner', and a 'minnie' can mean a lost lamb that finds itself an adoptive mother. From *The Observer* (20 May 1989): 'Broadcasters are right to complain about the restrictions placed on them for the broadcasting of the House of Commons . . . But the Moaning Minnies have only themselves to blame.' *OED2*'s earliest citation in this sense is 1972. The original 'Moaning Minnie' was something quite different. In the First World War, a 'Minnie' was the slang name for a German *Minenwerfer*, a trench mortar or the shell that came from it, making a distinctive moaning noise. In the Second World War, the name was also applied to air-raid sirens, which were also that way inclined.

(a) modern classic   Phrase in publishing and other promotional use. 'Penguin Modern Classics', for example, were available in the 1960s but the cliché use (often unjustified or too liberally applied) became apparent in the 1970s/80s. Cited in Eric Partridge, *A Dictionary of Clichés* (5th edition, 1978). 'Anna Pasternak, the author of the modern classic *Princess in Love*, has just had the paperback rights to the book returned to her by Bloomsbury. The publisher says the book, about Princess Diana's irresistible romance with James Hewitt, is too downmarket for it' – *Evening Standard* (London) (5 May 1995); 'This was trans-Atlantic publishing co-operation at its best. We provided photographs, [Jackie Kennedy Onassis] offered to produce a map of Tsarist Russia, and jointly we edited a script that turned into a modern classic' – *The Independent* (21 May 1994).

moi non plus Neither do I. Purposely contradictory phrase. In his *Dictionnaire des mots et formules célèbres* (1994), François Dournon writes about the title of the notorious 1969 Serge Gainsbourg disc, *Je t'aime . . . moi non plus* (which means, 'I love you . . . neither do I'). He mentions Salvador Dali having said of Louis Aragon, the French writer and political activist, '*Aragon est communiste et moi non plus.*' There is a hint of this format in the caption to a cartoon by Barry Fantoni in *Private Eye* (15 December 1972). One literary type says to another, 'I'm writing a book' and the other responds, 'Neither am I.'

moment See AT THIS MOMENT.

(the) moment of truth Meaning 'a decisive turning point; a significant moment', the phrase comes from '*el momento de la verdad*' in Spanish bull-fighting – the final sword thrust that kills the animal. *Il Momento della Verità* was the title of an Italian/Spanish film (1964) on a bullfighting theme. In *I, Claud* (1967), Claud Cockburn said of European intellectuals who had fought in the Spanish Civil War: 'They proclaimed, however briefly, that a moment comes when your actions have to bear some kind of relation to your words. This is what is called the Moment of Truth.' From the *Financial Times* (15 September 1986): '"We have 50,000 moments of truth out there every day," said Carlzon, defining a moment of truth as each time a customer came into contact with the company.'

monarch of all one surveys Nowadays used as a light-hearted proprietorial boast, this phrase comes from William Cowper's 'Verses Supposed to be Written by Alexander Selkirk' (the original of 'Robinson Crusoe'), *circa* 1779: 'I am monarch of all I survey, / My right there is none to dispute; / From the centre all round to the sea / I am lord of the fowl and the brute.' Kenneth Tynan, writing about Noël Coward in *Panorama* Magazine (Spring 1952), said: 'He is, if I may test the trope, monocle of all he surveys.'

money for nothing The making or receiving of money that requires no work in return. *Money For Nothing* was the title of a novel (1928) by P. G. Wodehouse. Other similar phrases (but meaning 'easy money/money that requires little effort') are: **money for jam**, which was known by 1919 and might possibly be linked to the huge quantities of jam that were known to be supplied to the British Army during the First World War. And **money for old rope**. Known by 1936. This may have to do with the simple perk of a ship's crew unpicking odd lengths of rope and selling the strands to shipyards. These would then be used to fill gaps in the deck after which they would be covered with pitch.

money is made round to go round Proverb. 'When younger, I was questioned by my grandfather about a spending spree. In justification, I said, "Oh, Grandad, it's made round to go round." He replied, "Aye, lass, but it's made flat to pile up"' – Hylda M. Ball, Cheshire (1995). Another version from Yorkshire: 'Money is made round to go round' – 'Nay, lad, it's made flat to stack.' Neither of these versions is much recorded in proverb books.

money is the root of all evil Misquotation of 1 Timothy 6:10: 'The love of money is the root of all evil.'

money makes the world go (a)round With this phrase, as with TOMORROW BELONGS TO ME, we may have to thank the writers of the musical *Cabaret* (Broadway 1966) for either creating an instant 'saying' or, perhaps in this instance, for introducing to the English language something that has been known in others. 'Money makes the world go around' is clearly built on the well-established proverb ''Tis *love*, that makes the world go round' but is not recorded in either the *ODP* or the *CODP* (the nearest they get is, 'Money makes the mare to go'). The phrase appears in the English-language key to the Flemish proverbs' picture by David Teniers the Younger (1610–90), at Belvoir Castle. The painting shows an obviously wealthy man holding a globe. How odd that it should, apparently, have taken a song in a 1960s' musical to get this expression into English.

money, money, money! Phrase emphasizing the lure of money, as in: 'All she is interested in is money, money, money!' Date of origin unknown. 'Money-money-money – we are all crying for money and might as well cry for the money' – J. B. Fagan, *And So To Bed*, Act 1 (1926); 'I'll be thankful if she sells it [a newspaper] . . . because apart from wearing her to a shadow it's costing me a fortune. Money, money, money, there's no end to it' – P. G. Wodehouse, *Jeeves and the Feudal Spirit*, Chap. 11 (1954); 'Money Money Money' – title of song recorded by Abba (1976).

monkey See AS THE.

monkey business Deceitful, mischievous and foolish conduct, presumably on the basis of what the behaviour of actual monkeys appears to be like. Of American origin. 'There must be no monkey business going on' – G. W. Peck, *Peck's Bad Boy* (1883). 'Monkey Business' is the title of a 'Mr Mulliner' short story (1932) by P. G. Wodehouse. At least two films have been given the title, notably one featuring the Marx Brothers (US 1931) and another with Cary Grant and a chimpanzee (US 1952).

(a) monkey wrench A spanner or wrench with an adjustable jaw – a notable tool that any engineer might possess. But why a *monkey* wrench? It is said that it was invented by Charles Moncke, a London blacksmith, or by a Mr Monk, who was an American (*circa* 1856). Known as such by 1858.

monkey's wedding See IT'S A.

(a) monstrous carbuncle A large protuberance. In June 1984, Prince Charles described a proposed design for a new wing of the National Gallery in London as, 'a kind of vast municipal fire station . . . I would understand better this type of high-tech approach if you demolished the whole of Trafalgar Square, but what is proposed is like a monstrous carbuncle on the face of a much loved and elegant friend.' The Prince of Wales's ventures into architectural criticism have not gone unnoticed, and the image of a 'monstrous carbuncle' ('a red spot or pimple on the nose or face caused by habits of intemperance' – *OED2*) has become part of the critical vocabulary. A report in *The Independent* (1 March 1988) about plans for a new lifeboat station dominating the harbour at Lyme Regis concluded by quoting a local objector: 'They've called this building a design of the age. What we've got here is a Prince Charles Carbuncle, and we don't like carbuncles down on Lyme harbourside.' The Prince's step-mother-in-law, the Countess Spencer, had earlier written in a book called *The Spencers on Spas* (1983) of how 'monstrous carbuncles of concrete have erupted in Gentle Georgian squares'. In *Barnaby Rudge*, Chap. 54 (1841), Charles Dickens writes: 'Old John was so red in the face . . . and lighted up the Maypole Porch wherein they sat together, like a monstrous carbuncle in a fairy tale.' Compare GREAT WEN.

month See IS THE.

(a) month of Sundays A very long time. Known by 1832 in a Captain Marryat novel, *Newton Forster* (1832). Compare: 'I ain't been in church now for more nor a week of Sundays' – R. D. Blackmore, *Cripps the Courier*, Chap. 38 (1877).

(the) moon is made of green cheese One of the most frequently found sayings in 16th- and 17th-century literature. 'You would have us believe that the moon is made of green cheese' is an old riposte to someone inclined to make far-fetched remarks.

moonlight See BY THE PALE.

(the) moon of my delight Phrase from Edward Fitzgerald's *The Rubáiyát of Omar Khayyám*, St. 74 (1859): '. . . Ah, moon of my delight that knows no wane / The moon of heaven is rising once again.' 'L. G. Trotter was a little man with a face like a weasel, who scarcely uttered during the meal because, whenever he tried to, the moon of his delight shut him up' – P. G. Wodehouse, *Jeeves and the Feudal Spirit*, Chap. 3 (1954).

moon's men Thieves and highwaymen operating at night. Falstaff says to Prince Hal in Shakespeare, *Henry IV, Part 1*, I.ii.25 (1597): 'For we that take purses go by the moon', and the Prince plays with the words, remarking that 'the fortune of us that are the moon's men doth ebb and flow like the sea, being governed as the sea is, by the moon.' Similarly, **minions of the moon** (night-time robbers) comes from the same source. Falstaff says to Prince Hal: 'Let not us that are squires of the night's body be called thieves of the day's beauty: let us be Diana's foresters, gentlemen of the shade, minions of the moon.' Hence the film title *Les Favoris de la Lune* (France 1984), which was released in the UK as *Favourites of the Moon*. This was a quirky piece about Parisian crooks, petty and otherwise, whose activities overlapped in one way or another, but the English title hardly seemed relevant to the subject. Not surprisingly, as it was a translation back into English. As a caption acknowledged, the original French title was a translation of the original Shakespearean phrase.

(a) moot point A point that can be argued or is debatable. Known by 1650. 'It is a moot point whether they do much good because, like other party machines, the Conservative local unit functions day-in and day-out pretty successfully' – *Cleethorpes News* (6 May 1977); 'Whether these powerful sounds combined well with Sculthorpe's soppily atmospheric string-quartet writing was a moot point. But it still made quite a change from Mozart at the Wigmore Hall' – *The Daily Telegraph* (30 July 1994); 'A code of conduct could proclaim what good practice and standards should be, but it was a moot point as to whether a trade union was the best organisation to police ethics, said the official' – *The Irish Times* (31 December 1994).

(a) moral obligation Inevitable pairing, known by 1729. 'Institutions are thrilled that they are allowed to invest in South Africa again. But they feel no moral obligation to do so' – *Financial Times* (2

June 1994); 'Kevin Keegan, the Newcastle United manager, felt "morally obliged" to go to Old Trafford and attack. Moral obligation and the Four-man Midfield: a philosophical tract that gave us a belter of a match' – *The Times* (31 October 1994).

more See ALWAYS LEAVE; AND THERE'S; ANY MORE.

more dash than cash Fashion phrase, especially in *Vogue*, for which this slogan appears to have been coined in the 1950s. About clothing which, while stylish, is cheap or – given *Vogue*'s usual standards – cheaper than the norm. It was still being used over *Vogue* features in the 1990s. Also in other contexts: 'The march of Waterstone's bookshops through the 1980s high streets owed more to dash than cash. With their bright staff and "reliable, wide-ranging stock", the stores showed that the marketing flummery of Thatcherism could serve both Mind and Mammon' – *The Observer* (4 September 1994); 'If *Vogue* is a reliable financial sounding board we are in for prosperity and great good sense. In the October issue they have said farewell to the More Dash Than Cash section and welcomed back an old-timer called Great Good Buys' – *The Daily Telegraph* (19 September 1994).

(a) more efficient conduct of the war (sometimes **energetic ...**) This almost became a slogan of the First World War (*circa* 1916) for what was required of the British Government prior to the replacement of Prime Minister Asquith by Lloyd George. However, A. J. P. Taylor in *English History 1914–45* (1965) noted: 'The Coalition government, which Asquith announced on 26 May 1915, claimed to demonstrate national unity and to promote a more efficient conduct of the war.' Writing of the following year (1916) in *Clementine Churchill* (1979), Mary Soames has 'more vigorous and efficient prosecution of the war'. Compare, from Lord Home, *The Way the Wind Blows* (1976): 'Sir Roger Keyes [in 1939] . . . made an impassioned speech in favour of more urgent conduct of the war.'

(to have) more —— in one's little finger than another has in his (or her) whole body 'She has more goodness in her little finger than he has in his whole body' –

cited by Jonathan Swift in *Polite Conversation* (1738). 'You may say what you like, but there is more wit in [Oscar] Wilde's little finger than in the whole of du Maurier's wretched little body!' – Sir Edward Burne-Jones (*circa* 1881), quoted in Richard Ellman, *Oscar Wilde* (1987); '"Mole," said the Badger, in his dry, quiet way, "I perceive you have more sense in your little finger than some other animals have in the whole of their fat bodies"' – Kenneth Grahame, *The Wind In the Willows*, Chap. 11 (1908); 'Hendry was quick to praise O'Sullivan, saying: "He's the most talented young player I've ever seen, with more talent in his little finger than 99 per cent of players have in their entire body"' – *Daily Record* (26 April 1995); 'Benjamin Britten has more genius in his little finger than most of his contemporaries in their whole bodies' – Desmond Shawe-Taylor, *New Statesman* (1 December 1951).

(to do something) more in sorrow than in anger   Meaning, to do something – like meting out punishment – in a rational rather than hot-headed way. An allusion to Shakespeare, *Hamlet*, I.ii.231 (1600), where Horatio explains that the Ghost of Hamlet's father exhibited 'A countenance more in sorrow than in anger.' 'I told an Essex Girl Joke. A young woman turned on me as if I came from another, less advanced planet, and, more in sorrow than in anger, said she didn't think what I'd said was frightfully right-on' – *The Independent* (23 April 1992).

more power to your elbow   Phrase of encouragement (used only when an enterprise is laudable). But where does it come from – archery, gambling, weight-lifting or drinking? As to the latter, there is an obvious link to the beer slogan IT'S WHAT YOUR RIGHT ARM'S FOR. *OED2*'s earliest citation (1832) is Irish: 'More power to your honour's elbow' (which might support the drinking connection). There are also the expressions 'to shake the elbow' for 'to gamble' and 'knight of the elbow' for 'gambler'. The phrase may, however, be no more than a connection between 'elbow' and 'effort', as in the expression 'to apply a little elbow-grease'. One also likes to think that it has some-

thing to do with writing – vigorous movement of the elbow when scribbling in long-hand.

more stars than there are in heaven   Slogan for the MGM studios in Hollywood, and created by Howard Dietz (1896–1983), the writer and film executive, in the 1920s/30s. The slogan appears on a poster for *Broadway Melody* (US 1929), the very first film musical.

more tea, Vicar?   Phrase for use after a fart or to cover any kind of embarrassment. British use, from the 1920s/30s? Paul Beale collected various forms for a revision of *Partridge/Catch Phrases*, including: 'good evening, vicar!'; 'no swearing, please, vicar' (said facetiously to introduce a note of the mock-highbrow into a conversation full of expletives); 'another cucumber sandwich, vicar' (after an involuntary belch); 'speak up, Padre!/Brown/Ginger (you're through)' (as a response to a fart). In *Politics, Prayer and Parliament* (2000), David Rogers declares: 'The phrase, "More tea, Vicar?" has entered the language as shorthand for comfortable suburbia.' Hence these stories: '"More tea, Vicar?" asked Lady Lavinia as she poured the tea with her other hand' and 'One day the young Vicar was visiting two elderly ladies. Whilst he was sitting on the shiny sofa, he passed wind mightily and noisily. As the echoes died away, one of the ladies filled the embarrassing silence by asking, "More tea, Vicar?" "Oh no!" he replied, "It makes me fart!"'

(that's) more than I wish to know about —— (or a little bit more information than I needed)   Dismissive format phrase. Attributed to an unknown schoolchild's essay is: 'This book tells me more about penguins that I am interested in knowing' – quoted in *Handbook of 20th Century Quotations*, ed. Frank S. Pepper (1984). Compare: *Vincent (John Travolta)*: 'I'm gonna take a piss.' *Mia (Uma Thurman)*: 'That's a little bit more information than I needed, Vince, but go right ahead' – *Pulp Fiction* (US 1994).

more —— than one can shake a stick at (sometimes poke a stick at)   I.e. uncountable numbers – as in, 'Hell, there's more deer in those woods than you can shake a stick at.' From the USA, originally – e.g. the *Journal* (Lancaster, Pennsylvania) (5 August 1818): 'We have in Lancaster more Taverns as you can shake a stick at.' In the film *Monkey Business* (US 1931), Groucho Marx says to a sea captain: 'If you were a man you'd go in business for yourself. I know a fella started only last year with just a canoe. Now he's got more women than you could shake a stick at, if that's your idea of a good time.'

more will mean worse Phrase encapsulating a view of the expansion of higher education. In *Encounter* (July 1960), Kingsley Amis wrote on 'the delusion that there are thousands of young people who are capable of benefiting from university training but have somehow failed to find their way there'. He added: 'I wish I could have a little tape-and-loudspeaker arrangement sewn into the binding of this magazine, to be triggered off by the light reflected from the reader's eyes on to this part of the page, and set to bawl out at several bels: MORE WILL MEAN WORSE.' When *The Times* misquoted this as 'more *means* worse' on one occasion, Amis fired off a broadside (22 February 1983): 'I think the difference is substantial, but let that go for now. You show by your misquotation that you couldn't be bothered to look up the reference, thereby ignoring the context, any arguments or evidence put forward, etc. Having garbled my remark you say roundly that in the event I was wrong. Not altogether perhaps. Laziness and incuriosity about sources are familiar symptoms of academic decline.'

(the) more you cry – the less you'll pee
'When we used to cry as children, growing up in the Midlands, my mother would always say, "Stop yer blartin'" – to which my granny once replied, "Let 'em blart, they'll wee all the less"' – Martin Cheek, Broadstairs (1998). *Partridge/Catch Phrases* goes into this quite thoroughly: '"Let her cry: she'll piss the less" was a semi-consolatory catch phrase . . . supposed to have been originally addressed as "the more you cry the less you'll piss", by sailors to their whores – or so *Grose*, 1796, tells us.'

Moriarty See ARE YOU THERE.

morituri te salutant [those who are about to die salute you] Words addressed to the emperor by gladiators in ancient Rome on entering the arena. The practice seems to have been first mentioned in *Claudius* by Suetonius (AD 75–160). In time, the phrase was extended to anyone facing difficulty, and then ironically so.

(the) morning after the night before
Phrase denoting the effects of a drinking bout on the person who is suffering from them. Early 20th century.

morning, all! Catchphrase of (Sir) Jimmy Young (b. 1923), one-time crooner who became an unlikely recruit to BBC Radio 1 as a disc jockey in the late 1960s and became hugely popular with the mainly female morning audience. He would begin with a routine like this: 'Morning, all! I hope you're all leaping about to your entire satisfaction, especially those **sur le continong** . . . and **orft we jolly well go!**' The pronunciation 'continong', approximating to the French, was established by the start of the 20th century. Marie Lloyd had a song called 'The Naughty Continong'. Charles Dickens, in *Little Dorrit*, Bk I, Chap. 2 (1857), wrote '[Marseilles] sent the most insurrectionary tune into the world [the *Marseillaise*]. It couldn't exist without allonging [*allons*] and marshonging [*marchons!*] to something or other.' Young would also frequently wonder **where is it all leading us, I ask myself?** before concluding with **BFN – 'bye for now!** (perhaps harking back to TTFN in *ITMA*). His recipe spot was heralded by a chipmunk-voiced character called 'Raymondo' who asked **what's the recipe today, Jim?** Jim would then recite the ingredients, after which Raymondo would intone **and this is what you do!** Jim would also chat to listeners on the telephone, which he would refer to in curious Euro-lingo as being **sur le telephoneo**. In the mid-1970s, Young transferred to Radio 2, became more involved with current affairs' subjects and virtually dropped all his stock phrases (but see LEGAL EAGLE).

(to apply) Morton's fork To set a kind of test where there is no choice. Dating from England in the 15th century. John Morton (*circa* 1420–1500) was Archbishop of Canterbury and a minister to Henry VII. As a way of raising forced loans he would apply his 'fork' – the argument that if people were obviously rich, then they could afford to pay. And, if people looked poor, then they were obviously holding something back, so could also afford to pay. An early form of CATCH-22. Known by 1889.

(the) most fun I've had without laughing This is how the Woody Allen character compliments the Diane Keaton character in the film *Annie Hall* (US 1977). As a description of sex, it clearly complements the next entry. However, *Mencken* was recording, 'Love [he probably meant sex] is the most fun you can have without laughing' in 1942. 'Nothing beats making love – it's the most fun you can have without laughing' has also been attributed to Humphrey Bogart.

(the) most fun you can have with your clothes on Of something other than sex (naturally). This probably predates the above, though the earliest example to hand is in Jerry Della Femina, *From Those Wonderful Folks Who Gave You Pearl Harbor* (1970): 'Advertising is the most fun you can have with your clothes on.' People are still drawn to play with the phrase: 'Touch Dancing is the closest you can get to making love with a stranger without actually taking your clothes off' – *Evening Standard* (London) (20 October 1987).

(the) *mot de Cambronne* Euphemism for the French expletive '*Merde!*' [= shit!]. At the Battle of Waterloo in 1815, the commander of Napoleon's Old or Imperial Guard is *supposed* to have declined a British request for him to surrender with the words, '*La garde meurt mais ne se rend jamais/pas* [The Guards die but never/do not surrender].' However, it is quite likely that what he said, in fact, was, '*Merde! La garde muert* . . . [shit! The Guards die . . .]' The commander in question was Pierre Jacques Etienne, Count Cambronne (1770–1842). At a banquet in 1835 Cambronne specifically denied saying the more polite version. That may have been invented for him by Rougemont in a newspaper, *L'Indépen-*

dent. In consequence of all this, *merde* is sometimes known in France as *le mot de Cambronne*, a useful euphemism when needed. Unfortunately for Cambronne, the words he denied saying were put on his statue in Nantes, his home town.

mother   See BOY'S BEST FRIEND; CAN YOU HEAR ME; DEAD AND NEVER; DOES YOUR.

(the) mother of all —— The ultimate (anything). Popular in English since the start of the Gulf War (January 1991) when the Iraqi President, Saddam Hussein, said, 'The great, the jewel and the mother of battles has begun.' Although, as a result, 'the mother of ——' became a format phrase in the West, Hussein was simply using the commonplace Arabic 'mother of' construction. A review by Anita Brookner in *The Spectator* (11 May 1991) of Margaret Forster's book *The Battle for Christabel* was headed 'The battle of all mothers'. 'Admire the Cour Carrée and I. M. Pei's Pyramid before entering the mother of all art museums, the Louvre' – *Time Out Paris Guide* (2001).

(the) mother of parliaments Phrase mistakenly applied to Westminster. What John Bright, the English radical politician, said in a speech at Birmingham (18 January 1865) was: '*England* is the mother of parliaments.' Frequently misused, even at the highest levels. Icelanders may well object that they have a prior claim to the title anyway. 'There is a huge complacency about the supposed mother of parliaments. Tradition is of the highest value in things that do not matter but a mathematical nonsense in things that do' – *The Independent* (2 May 1994).

(the) mother of the nation Sobriquet of Winnie Mandela (b. 1934), the South African political activist and second wife of the first black President of that country. A book by Nancy Harrison with the title *Winnie Mandela, Mother of a Nation* was published in 1985. From the *Financial Times* (1 February 1989): 'Mrs Mandela, who earned respect for her dignified resistance to years of official harassment, internal exile and separation from her husband, was given the honorary title "Mother of the Nation" by many in the black community on her defiant return to

Soweto during the 1984–86 township revolt. But she soon gave the impression of being out of her depth and subject to manipulation by feuding factions.' According to Tacitus, the emperor Tiberius refused for his mother, Livia, the title of *Mater Patriae*, which had been offered her by the Senate – *Annales*, line 14.

mothers See SOME MOTHERS.

(at one's) mother's knee At an early and formative stage of one's life, when one learned useful things from one's mother. Known by 1855. 'Mother's Knee' was the title of a story (1920) by P. G. Wodehouse.

(a) mother's little helper Phrase that might once have been applied to a small child literally being of assistance to its mother around the house but then to the 'uppers' that enabled a tired housewife to get through her daily tasks. Celebrated in a song poking fun at such pill addiction – 'Mother's Little Helper', written and performed by the Rolling Stones on the *Aftermath* album (1966).

mother's ruin Gin – and known as such by the late 19th century, according to *Partridge/Slang*. Partridge wondered if it could be (rather poor) rhyming slang, but Paul Beale thought it was just a literal epithet. There was of course the earlier 'mother's milk' to describe the same thing. Quite how and when the coinage arose is not known.

Mother Teresa Public name of Macedonian-born Agnes Gonxha Bojaxhiu (1910–97), a nun who received the Nobel Peace Prize (1979) for her charitable works, notably running a mission among the starving in Calcutta. Her name has now become a byword for goodness. For example, *The Independent* (6 June 1990), quoting a lawyer for arrested Panamanian defendants in the USA: 'If you had Mother Theresa sitting at the table next to [General] Noriega, she'd have trouble getting past the jury.'

(a) motley to the view A fool in public. Harold Nicolson wrote in *The Spectator* (19 March 1948): 'The attention aroused by a bye-election renders even the most sedate candidate a motley to the view.' The allusion is to Shakespeare, Sonnet 110 (1590s): 'Alas 'tis true, I have gone here and there, / And made myself a motley to the view', i.e. 'made a fool of myself in public', 'motley' here meaning 'fool, jester'.

mould See BREAKING THE.

(to) mount a boycott To ostracize someone or thing; to have nothing to do with; to break off all relations. 'The lively Irish have invented a new word; they are saying now to "boycott" someone, meaning to ostracize him' – translated from *Le Figaro* (24 November 1880). Captain Charles Boycott was an ex-British soldier who acted as an agent for absentee landlords in Co. Mayo, Ireland, during the late 19th century. He was extremely hard on the poor tenants and dispossessed them if they fell behind with their rents. By way of retaliation, the tenants isolated him and refused to have any dealings with him or his family. They were encouraged in this by Charles Parnell of the Irish Land League who said that those who grabbed land from people evicted for non-payment of rent should be treated like 'the leper of old'. Eventually, the tenants brought about Boycott's own downfall by leaving his harvest to rot, and he fled back to England where he died in 1897. Note that the verb 'to boycott' describes what was done *to* him rather than what was done *by* him.

mountain-top See BEEN TO THE.

(the) Mounties always get their man The unofficial motto of the Royal Canadian Mounted Police. John J. Healy, editor of the Fort Benton (Montana) *Record*, wrote on 13 April 1877 that the Mounties 'Fetch their man every time'. The official motto since 1873 has been 'Maintain the right [*maintiens le droit*].

mouse See ARE YOU A MAN.

mousetrap See BEAT A PATH.

mouth See ALL.

(to have a) mouth like the bottom of a parrot's cage One of a number of common similes for the effects of a hangover or other form of alcoholic indulgence. Since the 1920s. Another: **like the inside of a Turkish wrestler's jockstrap/Japanese juggler's jockstrap**.

(a) moveable feast In the ecclesiastical world, a moveable feast is one that does not fall on a fixed date but – like Easter – occurs according to certain rules. *A Moveable Feast*, as the title of a book (1964) by Ernest Hemingway, is explained in an epigraph: 'If you are lucky enough to have lived in Paris as a young man, then wherever you go for the rest of your life, it stays with you, for Paris is a moveable feast.' This title was applied posthumously to Hemingway's Paris memoirs after his widow came across the passage in one of his letters. Titles that Hemingway himself had considered for the book included *The Eye and the Ear, To Write It Truly, Love Is Hunger, It Is Different in the Ring* and *The Parts Nobody Knows.*

move 'em on, head 'em up *Rawhide*, the TV Western series (US 1959–66), was notable for its Frankie Laine theme song over the credits: 'Head 'em up, move 'em on, / Move 'em on, head 'em up . . . Rawhide!' From Robert McGowan & Jeremy Hands, *Don't Cry for Me, Sergeant-Major* (1983) (about cattle and sheep in the Falklands war): '"I can just imagine the orders for the Gazelle pilot," smiled an officer as soon as the farmer was out of earshot. "Proceed to grid reference so-and-so, then head 'em on and move 'em on. Most urgent, keep them dogeys movin'."'

movers and shakers People who get things done, innovators and activists. From *The Guardian* (10 November 1986): 'Nancy Reagan, Nancy Kissinger . . . and their friends, the movers and the shakers in fund-raising galas and behind-the-scenes politics.' The phrase comes from Arthur O'Shaughnessy's *Ode* (1874): 'We are the music-makers, / And we are dreamers of dreams . . . / Yet we are the movers and shakers / Of the world for ever, it seems.' Clearly he was thinking of less worldly people than the phrase is nowadays usually applied to.

(to) move the goalposts (or shift . . .) Meaning, 'to change the rules or conditions after something has been started, in order to upset the "players".' 'Barenboim had been appointed under the *ancien régime* of Chirac. Now that Michel Rocard is Prime Minister, the goalposts have been moved and Barenboim has found himself the target of the new order's distrust of the Bastille [Paris opera house] edifice' – *The Independent* (21 January 1989); 'The people of Kent vote solidly for the Conservative Party . . . Why are these people, therefore, trying to attempt to move the goalposts after the football match has started [by imposing a new rail line through the county]?' – *The Guardian* (1 March 1989).

Mr —— Cliché of journalism. Any 'supremo' automatically gets so dubbed. *Private Eye* jokingly pointed to the trend by inventing 'Soccer's Mr Football'. Actual examples: 'Geoffrey Rippon, Britain's "Mr Europe"' – *Punch* (5 August 1970); 'London's new Mr Railway, David Kirby, likes messing about in boats and singing in the choir' – *The Times* (8 December 1981); 'Last week it was disclosed that Newmarch is to be the new chief executive of the Prudential – or, put another way, Mr Insurance UK' – *The Observer* (9 April 1989).

Mr Big Name for the supposed mastermind behind substantial crimes (for example, the Great Train Robbery of 1963). *OED2* finds 'Mr Big' not only in a Groucho Marx letter of 1940 but, more significantly, in Raymond Chandler's *The Long Goodbye* (1953), though it is not clear if either of these uses is specifically criminal. *Mister Big* was the title of a B-movie starring Donald O'Connor (US 1943). In Ian Fleming's second novel, *Live and Let Die* (1954), 'Mr Big', a Black gangster, lives in Harlem: 'Because of the initial letters of his fanciful name, Buonaparte Ignace Gallia, and because of his huge height and bulk, he came to be called, even as a youth "Big Boy" or just "Big". Later this became "The Big Man" or "Mr Big".' From *The Observer* (6 August 1989): '"MR BIG" HELD. Customs officers have arrested a man they believe to be one of London's top criminals.'

Mr Chips Name applied to an elderly schoolmaster, once feared but now revered. It derives from the character in the novel *Goodbye, Mr Chips* (1934) by James Hilton.

Mr Clean Originally the name of an American household cleanser, this has become a fairly generally applied nickname for upright, clean-living people in the public eye. Among those to whom it has been applied are: Pat Boone (b. 1934), the US pop singer and actor noted for his clean image and habits (he would never agree to kiss in films); John Lindsay (1921–2001), Mayor of New York (1965–73); Elliot Richardson (1920–99), US Attorney-General who resigned in 1973 rather than agree to the restrictions President Nixon was then placing on investigations into the Watergate affair. 'The Secretary of State, James Baker, always regarded as Mr Clean among several highly placed roguish officials in Ronald Reagan's administration . . .' – *The Independent* (15 February 1989).

Mr Fixit Nickname for a person who has a reputation for solving problems. Chips Channon wrote of the Abdication crisis, in his diary entry for 30 November 1936: 'Beaverbrook, while enjoying his role of Mr Fixit, and the power he now holds in his horny hands, is now nearly distraught.' *OED2* finds 'Mr and Mrs Fix-It' as the title of a Ring Lardner story in 1925.

Mr Nyet Nickname applied to Andrei Gromyko (1909–89), long-serving Soviet foreign minister (from 1957 almost to his death) because of his liberal use of the veto at the United Nations. Also known by British officials as **Grim Grom** because of his solemn expression.

Mr Sands is in the —— Coded warning – a way of informing the staff and actors in a theatre over a public address system that a fire has broken out but without alarming the audience. Hence, 'Mr Sands is in the scene dock' or, indeed, any mention of 'Mr Sands' should do the trick. Source untraced, but mentioned in *The Independent* (27 July 1992).

Mrs Grundy Meaning, 'a censorious person; an upholder of conventional morality'. The name comes from Thomas Morton's play *Speed the Plough* (1798) in which a character frequently asks: 'What will Mrs Grundy say?' Compare the later names of **Mrs Ormiston Chaunt**, an actual woman who campaigned in the late 19th century against immorality in the music-hall, and **Mrs (Mary) Whitehouse**, who attempted to 'clean up' British TV from 1965 onwards.

Mrs Malaprop Name of a character in *The Rivals* (1775) by Richard Brinsley Sheridan after whom 'malapropisms' are called. 'Her select words [are] so ingeniously *misapplied*, without being *mispronounced*' (II.ii.). Among her misapplied but inspired words are: '*pineapple* of politeness', 'a nice *derangement* of epitaphs' and 'as headstrong as an *allegory* on the banks of the Nile'. She was not the first character to have such an entertaining affliction: Shakespeare's Dogberry and Mistress Quickly are similarly troubled. After the French phrase *mal à propos* ('awkward, inopportune').

Mrs Worthington The name for the archetypal aspiring actress's mother comes from Noël Coward's song 'Mrs Worthington' (1935), which contains the refrain: 'Don't put your daughter on the stage, Mrs Worthington.'

much of a muchness Very much the same or alike; no discernible difference. From Sir John Vanbrugh, *The Provok'd Husband*, Act 1, Sc. 1 (1728): 'I hope you . . . and your good woman agree still?' 'Ay, ay; much of a muchness.' 'You know you say things are "much of a muchness" – did you ever see such a thing as a drawing of a muchness!' – the Dormouse in Lewis Carroll, *Alice's Adventures in Wonderland*, Chap. 7 (1865).

mud See CLEAR AS.

(to keep on) muddling through Supposedly what the British have a great talent for. *Mencken* has 'The English always manage to muddle through' – 'author unidentified; first heard *circa* 1885'. Ira Gershwin celebrated the trait in the song 'Stiff Upper Lip' from *A Damsel in Distress* (1937). He remembered the phrase 'Keep muddling through' from much use at the time of the First World War but knew that it had first been noted in a speech by John Bright MP *circa* 1864 (though, ironically, Bright was talking about the Northern States in the American Civil War).

(does) Muhammad Ali own a mirror? See under IS THE POPE A CATHOLIC?

mum, mum, they are laughing at me!
Catchphrase of the British comedian Arthur English (1919–95) who became famous in the late 1940s for his spiv character with pencil moustache and big tie. Arthur recalled (1979) that this line was ad-libbed in his first broadcast: 'I had my big tie rolled up and proceeded to unfurl it. There was a great laugh and, to cover it, I said, "Mum, mum, they are laughing at me".' A necessary exhortation to audiences from the same spiv character was **sharpen up there, the quick stuff's coming!** It was said that he could talk at a rate of some three hundred words a minute. Before this, at the Windmill Theatre, he had been stuck for a finish to his act: 'So I started rambling on with the senseless chatter I became known for . . . [but] I suddenly realised I had no finish to the chatter. I don't know what made me say it, but I said, "I don't know what the devil I'm talking about. **Play the music and open the cage!**" and ran off.' The phrase stuck, presumably an allusion to the circus?

mum's the word Meaning, 'we are keeping silent on this matter'. No mother is invoked here: 'mum' is just a representation of 'mmmm', the noise made when lips are sealed. The word 'mumble' obviously derives from the same source. Shakespeare has the idea in *Henry VI, Part 2*, I.ii.89 (1590): 'Seal up your lips and give no words but mum.'

(we'll all be) murdered in our beds!
A frequent cry of Minnie Bannister (Spike Milligan) in the BBC radio *Goon Show* (1951–60). Date of origin unknown. '"Why, we may all be murdered in our beds!" he cried. "Front page stuff!" said Roscoe Sherriff, with gleaming eyes' – P. G. Wodehouse, *Uneasy Money*, Chap. 12 (1917).

murder she wrote *Murder She Wrote* has been the title of a US TV series (1984 onwards), with Angela Lansbury as Jessica Fletcher, a widowed best-selling crime writer who becomes involved in solving actual murder cases. Modelled on Miss Marple perhaps, there is another nod in the direction of Agatha Christie in the title. *Murder She Said* was the title given to a film version (UK 1961) of Christie's Miss Marple story *4.50 From Paddington*. In turn, that echoed *Murder He Says* (film US 1945) and 'Murder, He Says', the curious Frank Loesser lyric to music by Jimmy McHugh that was sung by Betty Hutton in the film *Happy Go Lucky* (US 1942).

(a) murky past Inevitable pairing, known by 1917. 'For such a beautiful flower, the tulip has a rather murky past' – headline in *Today* (27 August 1994); 'The sight stirred Chatterjee. "The islands are like that," he said. "They appear beautiful, but they have a very murky past"' – *Financial Times* (29 April 1995).

murmuring judges To 'murmur' a judge is to complain or grumble against his actions. In Scottish law it is still an offence to do this. Hence, the title of a play, *Murmuring Judges* (1991), by David Hare, about the British criminal justice system.

Murphy's Law See IF ANYTHING.

music See ARE YOU SITTING.

music, ho! Command for court music to commence, as in Shakespeare's plays, e.g. Titania's call from *A Midsummer Night's Dream*, IV.i.81 (1594): 'Music ho, music, such as charmeth sleep!', after which 'Soft music' follows. Hence the title of Constant Lambert's book, *Music Ho!*, subtitled 'A Study of Music in Decline' (1934), though here the title is specifically taken from *Antony and Cleopatra*, II.v.1 (1607): *Cleopatra*: 'Give me some music; music, moody food / Of us that trade in love.' *All*: 'The music ho!' [*Enter Mardian the Eunuch*.] *Cleopatra*: 'Let it alone; let's to billiards.' Indeed, this is Lambert's epigraph and in the book he explains: 'It will be observed that Cleopatra emphatically preferred billiards to music. This attitude, though somewhat philistine perhaps, is to be praised in that it recognizes that music and billiards represent two different sides of life. Cleopatra neither confused the functions of the two diversions nor suggested that they were better combined. Today, however, she would either have wireless turned on continually in the billiard room, or else she would have to listen to composers like Hindemith, who reduce music to the spiritual level of billiards, pingpong and clock golf.'

music in the air   Not necessarily the coinage, but the composer Sir Edward Elgar said: 'My idea is that there is music in the air, music all around us, the world is full of it and you simply take as much as you require' – quoted in R. J. Buckley, *Sir Edward Elgar* (1904). The phrase 'music in the air', of which this is, however, an early appearance, was taken as the title of (probably) more than one BBC radio series after the 1920s when music was rather '*on* the air'. *Music in the Air* was also the title of a film (US 1934) about an opera singer, based on a play by Oscar Hammerstein II and Jerome Kern.

music, maestro, please!   Stock phrase of the British band leader Harry Leader (d. 1987), who broadcast on BBC radio from 1933 onwards. Leader had had two signature tunes before he adopted this one while he was resident at the Astoria, Charing Cross Road, in 1943. It appears to have come from a song with the title by Herb Magidson and Allie Wrubel, featured by Flanagan and Allen in the revue *These Foolish Things* (1938).

mustard   See CUT THE.

—— must go!   Slogan format – the sort of thing that is liable to pursue any prominent politician who falls seriously out of favour. To date, A. J. Balfour, Prime Minister 1902–6, is the first British example found. In his case, the cry was sometimes abbreviated to 'BMG'. After losing the 1906 election, Balfour lingered on as leader of his party. Leo Maxse, editor of the *National Review*, wrote an article in the September 1911 edition in the course of which, demonstrating that the Conservative Party needed a new leader, he invented the slogan, 'Balfour must go'. And he went in November. In the months preceding the Munich agreement, *Punch* (1 June 1938) showed a graffitist writing: 'CHAMBER- LAIN MUST G . . .' on a wall. 'Eden Must Go' arose during Sir Anthony Eden's inept premiership (1955–7) when he instigated the disastrous landings in Egypt to 'protect' the Suez canal. On the evening of 4 November 1956, while he met with his Cabinet ministers in 10 Downing Street, he could hear roars of 'Eden Must go!' from an angry mass meeting in Trafalgar Square.

He went under the guise of illness early the following year. The most notable such campaign in British politics was directed at Ernest Marples, an energetic Minister of Transport (1959–64). The slogan arose in October 1962 when he intervened in the build-up of opposition to sweeping cuts in the railway service (announced the following year in the Beeching Report). However, it was because of motoring matters that the slogan was taken up at a more popular level. He introduced various unpopular measures including, in the summer of 1963, a 50 mph speed limit at peak summer weekends in an effort to reduce the number of road accidents. It was this measure that produced a rash of car stickers bearing the cry. It appeared daubed on a bridge over the M1 motorway in August (and remained visible for many years). 'The Saloon Must Go' was the slogan of the Anti-Saloon League in the United States – a temperance movement, organized 18 December 1895, and a precursor of Prohibition.

must surely kiss goodbye to . . .   Journalistic phrase, often used in sporting contexts. Date of origin unknown. 'Brazil were undeniably the better team, but if their finishing is as profligate against Italy in Sunday's final they can surely kiss their hopes of a fourth World Cup goodbye' – *The Scotsman* (14 July 1994); 'Wretched Derby can surely kiss the play-offs goodbye after being out-gunned by Burnley, going down 3–1' – *The People* (16 April 1995).

must you go, can't you stay?   First recorded by G. W. E. Russell in his *Collections and Recollections*, Chap. 24 (1898), this was a helpful remark of Dr Vaughan, Head Master of Harrow, designed to get rid of boys he had entertained at breakfast. 'When the muffins and sausages had been devoured . . . and all possible school-topics discussed, there used to ensue a horrid silence . . . Then the Doctor would approach with cat-like softness, and, extending his hand to the shyest and most loutish boy, would say, "Must you go? Can't you stay?" and the party broke up with magical celerity.' It was later twisted to, 'Must you stay? Can't you go?' – for example, as the caption to a *Punch* cartoon in the edition dated 18 January 1905. The Governor of Madagascar is saying it, referring to the prolonged stay of the Russian Admiral Rodjestvensky when on his way to meet the Japanese Fleet.

mute witnesses (to the passing of time) Especially travel journalism and promotional use, for what buildings and stones (usually) are often described as being. Date of origin unknown, but the idea is old. A French tourist leaflet from Provence in 1959 had the lines (a quotation?): '*Les pierres parlent à ceux qui savent les entendres* [the stones speak to those who know how to hear them]'; 'The old stones of the castle are mute witness to the unrelenting passage of time and the violent forces of history' – listed in *The Independent*'s 'DIY travel writers' cliché kit' (31 December 1988); '"We have been mute witnesses of evil deeds," wrote Pastor Dietrich Bonhoeffer at the end of 1942. "Are we still of any use? Will our spiritual resistance to what is enforced on us still prove strong enough, and will we still be honest enough with ourselves to rediscover the road to simplicity and integrity?"' – *The Independent* (25 August 1994); 'To give the situation an extra spin, the couple are standing inside a prehistoric exhibit at the museum where he's a curator. The mute witnesses to this very modern rite are a pair of neanderthal waxworks' – *The Independent* (6 May 1995).

mutton dressed as lamb Phrase used to describe something old got up to look like something younger – most often a woman wearing clothes that are ridiculously and noticeably too young for her. Since the late 19th century.

my boy is a good boy Cliché phrase from drama – what Italian-American mothers invariably say when told that their sons are, in fact, violent criminals. Observed by Fritz Spiegl in an article on drama cliché lines in *The Listener* (7 February 1985).

my brilliant career To refer to one's or another's 'brilliant career' is a matter of long standing. 'Joe, at the other end, resumed his brilliant career' – P. G. Wodehouse, *Psmith in the City*, Chap. 29 (1910). But the phrase was rendered particularly memorable by *My Brilliant Career*, the title

of a novel (1901; film Australia 1979) by Miles Franklin.

my brother and I See WE BRING YOU.

my captain Affectionate mode of address – not necessarily to a military person. For example, Kenneth Williams writes in his published letters, 'So, goodbye for now, my old Captain' – and uses this expression elsewhere in his published correspondence. Might he have been echoing the Walt Whitman line 'O Captain! my Captain!' (from the poem of that title, 1871)? *Partridge/Slang* lists 'captain' as a 'jesting form of address'. Bluebottle (Peter Sellers) also frequently uses 'my captain' as a form of address in the BBC radio *Goon Show* – in 'The Missing Number 10 Downing Street', for example (3 November 1957). He usually pronounces it *capitaine*, as though French.

my country, right or wrong! Toast originating with the American naval officer Stephen Decatur (1779–1820). Correctly, Decatur's toast at a public dinner in Norfolk, Virginia (April 1816) was: 'Our country! in her intercourse with foreign nations, may she always be in the right; but our country, right or wrong!' This is sometimes referred to as 'Decatur's Toast'. Compare G. K. Chesterton's comment: '"My country, right or wrong" is a thing no patriot would ever think of saying except in a desperate case. It is like saying, "My mother, drunk or sober"' – *The Defendant* (1901).

my dog has fleas Title of a little tune that gives you the tuning notes (A, D, F#, E) for a ukelele or banjo. Has been called the 'international call-sign of the ukelele-player'. Date of origin not known.

my eyes are dim – I cannot see ... (I have not got my specs with me) From the anonymous song 'In the Quartermaster's Stores', date not known though a version was copyrighted in 1940.

my fair lady Phrase little noticed before *My Fair Lady* was used as the title of a musical (1956; film US 1964). It was understandable when Lerner and Loewe wished to make a show out of Shaw's *Pygmalion* that they should seek a new title. After all, not even in Shaw's Preface (only in his Afterword) does he allude to the relevance of the Greek legend to his story of a Covent Garden flower-girl who gets raised up and taught to 'speak proper' just like a Mayfair lady. Lerner and Loewe turned, it seems, to the refrain of a nursery rhyme (first recorded in the 18th century): 'London Bridge is broken down, / Broken down, broken down, / London Bridge is broken down, / My fair lady.' It has also been suggested that they were drawn to the title because 'my fair lady' is how a cockney flower-seller would pronounce the phrase 'Mayfair lady' – at least this a story told by Rex Harrison in his autobiography. One of the titles rejected was 'Lady Liza'.

my fat friend Charles Laurence entitled a play *My Fat Friend* (London 1973). It was about a fat girl (Jennie Linden) and her experiences when she lost weight (it was originally going to be called *The Fat Dress*). As such, one suspected an allusion to Beau Brummell's famous question to Lord Alvanley about the Prince Regent. Brummell, almost a dandy by profession, had fallen out with the Prince of Wales and when they met in London in July 1813, the Prince cut him and greeted his companion instead. As the Prince walked off, Brummell asked in ringing tones, 'Tell me, Alvanley, who is your fat friend?' But the alliterative pairing 'fat friend' also appears in the novel *Handley Cross* (1843) by R. S. Surtees: 'When at length our fat friend got his horse and his hounds . . . together again'; and in Anthony Trollope's *Castle Richmond* (1860): 'Is it not possible that one should have one more game of rounders? Quite impossible, my fat friend.'

my fine feathered friend Form of address – guardedly respectful. Perhaps on finding someone interfering with one's property, one might say: 'And what are you doing, my fine feathered friend?' It is spoken by Burt Lancaster in *The Crimson Pirate* (UK 1952) perhaps as a would-be period phrase. Date of origin unknown. 'Feathered friend', as a sentimental or ironical way of referring to birds was known by 1933.

my friends . . . Clichéd mode of address in politics. It always presumes rather a lot

when politicians make use of this phrase. *Safire* asserts that the first American to do so – noticeably, at any rate – was Franklin D. Roosevelt who acquired the salutation in 1910 from Richard Connell who was running for Congress at the same time. But Abraham Lincoln had used this form of address on occasion. In British politics, during a party political broadcast on 4 June 1945, Winston Churchill said, 'My friends, I must tell you that a Socialist policy is abhorrent to the British idea of freedom.' This was the occasion on which he made the notorious suggestion that a Labour government would require 'some form of Gestapo' to put down criticism. Anthony Eden, in his pained TV broadcast during the Suez crisis (3 November 1956), used the phrase, ingratiatingly, too. But probably no British Prime Minister has done so since. It is hard to imagine Margaret Thatcher ever getting her tongue round it. It occurs along with other rhetorical clichés during the 'Party Political Speech' (written by Max Schreiner) on the Peter Sellers's comedy album *The Best of Sellers* (1958). Identified as a current cliché in *The Times* (17 March 1995). Equally, no British politician has ever tried to find an equivalent of the standard **my fellow Americans**, beloved of US Presidents. Whence, however, *My Fellow Americans*, title of a film comedy about two ex-Presidents (US 1996).

my giddy aunt! One of those trivial exclamations – others include **my sainted aunt!** and **my Aunt Fanny!** or simply **my aunt!** – that seem to have arisen in the mid-19th century. They appear to have been especially popular among school-boys. 'My sainted aunt!' pops up in Chap. 1 of the 1906 edition of P. G. Wodehouse, *Love Among the Chickens*, and quite frequently in the Billy Bunter of Greyfriars stories by Frank Richards (e.g. in *The Magnet*, No. 401 (16 October 1915). In a wry note to *Partridge/Slang*, Paul Beale wonders whether 'My aunt!' was originally a euphemism for *my arse*. He may well be right, though he adds, '. . . or have I been working on this Dictionary too long!'

my hero! Quintessential cry of the female in romantic fiction when her beau has just rescued her or overcome some formidable obstacle to their love. Robert Burns in *The Jolly Beggars* (1785) has a woman say to a soldier: 'But whilst with both hands I can hold the glass steady / Here's to thee, my hero, my sodger laddie!' Perhaps it only really appears in parodies? Raina says it a number of times in Shaw's *Arms and the Man* (1894), hence P. G. Wodehouse's reference in *The Mating Season*, Chap. 22 (1949): 'Muriel Kegley-Bassington stood revealed as a "My Hero" from *The Chocolate Soldier* addict.' And in *Very Good, Jeeves*, 'The Ordeal of Young Tuppy' (1930): 'Unless I am greatly mistaken, the moment they meet, she will exclaim "My hero!" and fall into his bally arms.' Sylvia (Jeff Donnell) says it amusedly in the film *In a Lonely Place* (US 1950) when her husband suddenly appears in a swimsuit.

my husband and I Queen Elizabeth II's father, George VI, had quite naturally spoken the words 'The Queen and I', but something in Elizabeth's drawling delivery turned her version into a joke. It first appeared during her second Christmas radio broadcast (made from New Zealand) in 1953 – 'My husband and I left London a month ago' – and still survived in 1962: 'My husband and I are greatly looking forward to visiting New Zealand and Australia in the New Year.' By 1967, the phrase had become 'Prince Philip and I'. At a Silver Wedding banquet in 1972, the Queen allowed herself a little joke: 'I think on this occasion I may be forgiven for saying "My husband and I".' In 1988, the phrase was used as the title of an ITV comedy series with Mollie Sugden.

my little perforations Phrase from Lyons Quick Brew Tea Bags' commercials in the UK, in the early 1970s: 'It's not me, ma'am, it's me little perforations.' 'You have to admit,' said the British comedian Roy Hudd, who spoke the line, 'that any business which allows a catch-phrase such as "*yer little perforations*" to turn you into a household name, buy you a house in the country and give a certain amount of financial security to you and your family, *has* to be crazy.' He also added: 'For some reason, the tea people thought it sounded too rude. Don't ask me why, but they did' – *Sunday Express* (4 December 1977).

my name is legion 'We/they are many, innumerable.' What the untamed 'man with an unclean spirit' speaking to Jesus in Mark 5:9 actually says is, 'My name is Legion: for we are many'. Jesus has said, 'Come out of the man, thou unclean spirit,' and asked, 'What is thy name?' And this is the answer given. After Jesus expels the devils from the man, he puts them into a herd of swine that jump into the sea. The man is then referred to as 'him that was possessed with the devil, and had the legion'.

my name is mud This exclamation might be uttered as an acknowledgement that one has made a mistake and is held in low esteem. When John Wilkes Booth was escaping from the Washington DC theatre in which he had just assassinated President Lincoln in 1865, he fell and broke his leg. A country doctor called Dr Samuel Mudd tended Booth's wound without realizing the circumstances under which it had been received. When he did realize, he informed the authorities, was charged with being a co-conspirator and sentenced to life imprisonment. As *Morris* points out, however, 'mud' in the sense of scandalous and defamatory charges, goes back to a time well before the Civil War. There had been an expression, 'the mud press', to describe mud-slinging newspapers in the USA before 1846, so it seems most likely that the expression was well established before Dr Mudd met his unhappy fate. Indeed, *OED2* has an 1823 citation from 'Jon Bee' in *Slang* for 'And his name is mud!' as an ejaculation at the end of a silly oration, and also by then from *A Dictionary of the Turf* as a name for a stupid fellow. 'The younger Mosley, a very honourable man, found it hard to cope with the fact that his father's name was mud in polite society' – *Daily Mail* (3 February 1996).

my name's Friday Catchphrase from the American TV series *Dragnet* (1951–8, revived 1967–9). Here is the opening narration from a typical TV episode. Sergeant Joe Friday speaks: 'Ladies and gentlemen, the story you are about to see is true, the names have been changed to protect the innocent . . . **This is the city**. Everything in it is one way or the other.

There's no middle ground – narrow alleys, broad highways; mansions on the hill, shacks in the gullies; people who work for a living and people who steal. These are the ones that cause me trouble. **I'm a cop**. It was Monday April 17. We were working the day-watch on a forgery detail. My partner: Frank Smith. The boss is Captain Welch. My name's Friday . . .'

my name's Monica! Catchphrase from the BBC radio show *Educating Archie* (1950–60). For a while, Beryl Reid (1919–96) played 'Monica' – Archie's posh, toothy, schoolgirl friend, who would introduce herself by saying, 'My name's Monica!' and would declare **Priscilla – she's my best friend and I *hate* her!** [This last is an old idea – a *Punch* cartoon by Stan Terry on 8 September 1920 has this caption: 'Haven't you anyone you can play with, Bobby?' Child: 'I *have* one friend – but I hate him.'] Beryl commented (1979): 'Even though I've done so many other things, straight acting parts and so on, people always remember these little phrases and want me to say them still.' Above all, Beryl's 'Monica' seems to have given rise to the expression **jolly hockey sticks!** – first used as an exclamation and then adjectivally to describe a type of woman – public school, gushing, games-playing and enthusiastic. Beryl claims to have coined it: 'I can't write comedy material . . . but I know what sort of thing my characters should say!' In this case she seems to have lighted upon a masterly phrase that has entered the language. Having established 'Monica', Beryl wanted to find another character from a different social class. This turned out to be 'Marlene' from Birmingham, complete with Brum accent and girlfriend, 'Deirdre'. She helped establish the American import IT SENDS ME! as the archetypical 1950s' phrase for the effect of music on the hearts and minds of the young. She also had a wonderful way of saying **good evening, each!** and **it's terrific!** (pronounced 'turreefeek').

(——'s) my name, ——'s my game
Rhyming phrase of assertion and identification. A format of uncertain origin and date. 'Aardvark's my name, and navigation is my name' – Joseph Heller, *Catch-22*, Chap. 7 (1961).

my old Dutch As in the title of the song 'My Old Dutch' (1911), performed by Albert Chevalier (and written with his brother, Charles Ingle), this phrase refers to the singer's wife. It is not, apparently, derived from rhyming slang – 'Duchess of Fife/wife' – but from the resemblance of the wife's face to an old Dutch clock. *Partridge/Slang* has 'dutch clock' meaning 'wife', soon shortened to 'dutch'.

my postillion has been struck by lightning Said to be a useful expression from an old phrase book. Hence, *A Postillion Struck by Lightning*, title of the first volume of Dirk Bogarde's autobiography (1977). Describing a holiday in early childhood (the 1920s presumably), he mentions an old phrase book (seemingly dated 1898), which contained lines like: 'This muslin is too thin, have you something thicker?'; 'My leg, arm, foot, elbow, nose, finger is broken'; and 'The postillion has been struck by lightning'. Which phrase book is this? Not *English as She is Spoke*, in which the 'postillion' line does not occur. In the third volume of Bogarde's autobiography, *An Orderly Man* (1983), describing the writing of the first, he says: 'My sister-in-law, Cilla, on a wet camping holiday somewhere in northern France . . . once sent me a postcard on which she said . . . she had been forced to learn a little more French than the phrase "Help! My postillion has been struck by lightning!" I took the old phrase for the title of my book.' A similarly untraced Russian/English phrasebook is said to have included: 'Don't bother to unsaddle the horses, lightning has struck the innkeeper.' Karl Baedeker's *The Traveller's Manual of Conversation in Four Languages* (1836 ed.) includes: 'Postilion, stop; we wish to get down; a spoke of one of the wheels is broken.' In an 1886 edition I have found: 'Are the postilions insolent?; the lightning has struck; the coachman is drunk.' From these examples it is quite clear that the preposterous phrase could quite likely have appeared in Baedeker or similar, but where precisely? *More Comic and Curious Verse* (1956) contains the poem 'Ballad of Domestic Calamity' by M. H. Longson, apparently extracted from *Punch*. The last line is 'For our postillion has been struck by lightning' and an introductory note explains: '"Our postillion has been struck by lightning" is one of the "useful Common Phrases" appearing in a Dutch manual on the speaking of English.' One is reminded that Dirk Bogarde was of Dutch ancestry. *Punch* (22 April 1970) contains a headline: 'My postilion has been struck by the vice-consul'. A writer in *The Times*·(30 July 1983) noted: '"Look, the front postillion has been struck by lightning" . . . supposed to feature in a Scandinavian phrase book: but it may well be apocryphal.'

my regiment leaves at dawn   Phrase spoken by Groucho Marx in the film *Monkey Business* (US 1931), preceded by the words, 'Come, Kapellmeister, let the violas throb!' Presumably this was a cliché of operetta, but no precise example has been traced. It was certainly the situation in many romantic tangles, even if the line itself was not actually spoken. However, the writer of the film, S. J. Perelman, is quoted in *Quest* Magazine (November 1978) as saying the following about Groucho: 'I saw him as a verbal clown with literary overtones. For instance, when he kissed Margaret Dumont, I'd have him say: "Goodbye, my little mountain flower. My regiment leaves at dawn." "What's this about a regiment?" he'd say. It's a parody of *The Merry Widow*, I'd say. And he'd worry over the intricacies of the line like a medieval schoolman. "How can an audience laugh at a joke about something they never even heard of?" he would complain.'

(it's) my shout   It's my turn to buy the drinks, stand a round. Known by 1886. 'My shout' is listed among 'Naff Expressions' in *The Complete Naff Guide* (1983). *It's Your Shout* is the title of a British TV audience debate show from the mid-1980s and still current in 2003, when the 'shout' is, of course, literal.

my wife and family are standing by me   Phrase used in (mainly British) politics, when a sacked or disgraced minister issues a resignation statement. Also used when other sorts of people are in difficulties. Date of origin unknown. 'The informal family photographs are very fetching and they will look as good framed on an Islington mantelpiece as they did in print, but they have begun to be as ubiquitous as those of a disgraced Tory minister whose wife has declared that she is standing by him' – *Daily Mail* (3 October 1994); 'Sex attacks PC jailed for three months . . . He added that Turner's wife was standing by him, but the family now faced losing their police home in Forbes Road, Falkirk' – *The Scotsman* (28 October 1994).

my wife doesn't understand me!   Spoken by a man seeking sympathy for the unhappy state of his marriage and – often – seeking solace in the arms of the woman to whom the line is addressed. By the 1920s/30s at least. But compare: '[Try inviting a woman to an irresistible waltz and] she will forthwith impart the embarrassing news that her husband misunderstands her, and drinks too much, and is going to Cleveland, O., on business tomorrow' – H. L. Mencken, *Prejudices, Sixth Series* (1926). 'Nor would the Mrs Mellors and Norrises face public humiliation without some daft, unsisterly bat somewhere believing that a breathy "My wife doesn't understand me" justifies indulging a genital itch' – *The Guardian* (2 May 1994); 'These women are reviled for leading married men astray, when they are often the ones who have been lured into hotel rooms with sweet promises and sympathetic stories about, "how my wife doesn't understand me"' – *Daily Mirror* (10 May 1995).

my word is my bond   Motto of the London Stock Exchange (since 1801), where bargains are made 'on the nod', with no written pledges given and no documents signed. Its Latin form is: '*Dictum meum pactum*'. *Apperson* finds, 'Hir simple recorde / Was founde as trewe as any bond' in Chaucer, *The Book of the Duchesse* (*circa* 1369).

N

naff off! Euphemistic expletive (echoic of 'eff off!') which was once used notably by Princess Anne to press photographers at the Badminton horse trials (April 1982). It was used earlier in Keith Waterhouse's novel *Billy Liar* (1959), where there also appears the participle 'naffing', remembered from his service in the RAF (*circa* 1950). As such, the phrase seems to be derived from the adjective 'naff', meaning 'in poor taste; unfashionable; bad' and largely restricted to British use. This word had a sudden vogue in 1982. Attempts have been made to derive the word 'naff' from 'fanny' in back-slang, from the acronym NAAFI, and from the French '*rien à faire*', none very convincingly. In the BBC radio series *Round the Horne*, the word 'naph' (as it was spelt in the scripts) enjoyed an earlier resurgence as part of camp slang. From the edition of 30 April 1967: 'Don't talk to us about Malaga!' – 'Naph, is it?' – 'He's got the palare off, hasn't he?' – 'I should say it is naph, treashette. Jule had a nasty experience in Malaga . . .'

nah, Luton Airport See NICE 'ERE.

(to) nail a lie Meaning 'to expose and disprove a lie in an obvious fashion'. Date of origin unknown. Identified as a current cliché in *The Times* (17 March 1995). 'The news that yet another independent school is to close down for lack of support should help nail the lie that the better-off in this country are doing better than ever before' – *Daily Telegraph* (29 June 1994); 'I retired in the summer of this year from the headship of Whalley Range High School in Manchester, categorised as the "worst" school for truancy in the country because of its 14 per cent unauthorised absences. Probably no one is in a better position than I am to nail the lie implicit in this simplistic assertion' – *Times Educational Supplement* (9 December 1994).

(the) naked and the dead Phrase used as the title of a novel (1948) by Norman Mailer. It has been said that Mailer first used this title for an unpublished play about an insane asylum based on his experiences during a one-week job he held in such an institution during the summer of 1942. But also told is the story of one Bernard Harlan, who seemed to specialize in providing writers with titles. He reputedly helped Tennessee Williams with most of his play titles and persuaded J. D. Salinger to change the title of his novel from *Growing Pains* to *The Catcher in the Rye*. Mailer reputedly paid him $35 for his help in thinking up this one.

naked as nature intended Phrase used as the title of the most famous British nudist film, in the 1950s – as confirmed by this extract from the sketch 'Naked Films' by Steven Vinaver in the book *That Was the Week That Was*, ed. Frost & Sherrin (1963): 'Two-fifty-eight, entered Gala Royal to see "Naked as Nature Intended". Three-thirty, down to the Cameo Moulin for "My Bare Lady".' Compare 'Stripping as they ran, till, when they touched the sands, they were naked as God had made them, and as happy as He intended them to be' – Rudyard Kipling, 'Propagation of Knowledge' (1926) from *Stalky & Co*. 'But most men will be cringeing in sympathy with Charles. He must have felt like he was caught in one of those terrible nightmares – you know, the ones where you find yourself in the High Street as naked as unforgiving Mother Nature intended' – *Daily Mirror* (8 September 1994).

(the) naked truth Phrase for 'the absolute truth'. It comes from an old fable that tells how Truth and Falsehood went swimming, and Falsehood stole the clothes that Truth had left upon the river bank. Truth declined to wear Falsehood's clothes and went naked. Known in English by 1600. In Latin, as in the works of Horace, the phrase is '*nudas veritas*'. Used as the title of a film (UK 1957).

namby-pamby Meaning 'insipid; wishy-washy; soft', the phrase derives from Ambrose Philips (d. 1749), a writer and politician whom the dramatist Henry Carey ridiculed with this nickname after Philips had written some insipid verses for children.

name See CRAZY NAME; IS ONE'S MIDDLE.

name of the game See IS THE.

name your poison! 'What would you like to drink?' Mostly British use. Recorded by 1951.

(the) nanny state Phrase for over-protective governments. In the 1980s, the derogatory term 'Nanny State' came to be adopted by Thatcherites, who deplored the way in which the (socialist) Welfare State supported a public the Thatcherites believed should be left to sink or swim in the face of the normal forces acting upon society. A coinage of the Conservative politician Iain MacLeod in *The Spectator* (12 February 1965): 'This new victory for the Nanny State represents the wrong approach. It is certainly the duty of ministers to make sure that there is a full knowledge of risks thought to be involved in heavy cigarette smoking – and this duty was discharged by Conservative ministers of health and education. If this is done, the decision to smoke or not is for the indi-vidual, and it should be left to him.'

nanu, nanu! Catchphrase of 'Mork' from the US TV series *Mork and Mindy* (1978–81). Robin Williams played the alien from the planet Ork. This was his phrase for 'farewell'.

narmean? This contraction (in, chiefly, London English and mostly among young people) of the phrase **know what I mean?** was first identified by Alan Coren in about 1981. The longer phrase had been much used by Alfie Elkins (Michael Caine) in his addresses to the camera in the film *Alfie* (UK 1966) – which was derived from Bill Naughton's radio and stage original. There was also notable use in a 1969 sketch in *Monty Python's Flying Circus*. By 1979, the longer version was almost a catchphrase in Jack Rosenthal's TV play about London cab-drivers, *The Knowledge*. 'The WBC heavyweight champion of the world had only a few wishes yesterday. "I want to soak in the vibes of being world cham-pion. I want to be at home, 70 acres of land. It's wicked, know what I mean?" It could only be Frank Bruno' – *The Inde-pendent* (4 September 1995). Use of the infilling phrase **you know?** has also been

much excoriated. Compare: KNOW WHAT I MEAN, 'ARRY?

nasty, brutish and short Much quoted phrase describing life. It was given by Thomas Hobbes in *Leviathan, or the Matter, Form, and Power of a Common-wealth, Ecclesiastical and Civil*, Chap. 13 (1651). In this treatise of political philoso-phy, Hobbes sees man not as a social being but as a selfish creature. The state of nature in which he resides is thus: 'No arts; no letters; no society; and which is worst of all, continual fear and danger of violent death; and the life of man, solitary, poor, nasty, brutish, and short.' The last portion of this bleak view has fallen victim to over-quoting, as Philip Howard, Literary Editor of *The Times*, noted on 15 August 1984. He warned of the danger that: 'We become so fond of hackneyed quotation that we trot it out, without thinking, at every opportunity.' He gave, as his exam-ple, 'the one about the life of man being "solitary, poor, nasty, brutish, and short," just to let everybody know that I am an intellectual sort of chap who reads Hobbes in the bath'. Curiously, later that year, on 1 November, when *The Times* had a first leader on the assassination of Mrs Indira Gandhi, it began by observing that world figures know all too sickeningly well 'the continual fear and danger of violent death' that Thomas Hobbes identified as a condition of man. And added: 'With that awful daily awareness, now goes for some a reminder of his definition of life as nasty, brutish and short.'

nation See FROM A GRATEFUL.

(a/the) nation mourns Catchphrase used ironically when too much importance is attached to some piffling event – the England football team suffers a defeat, for example. Originally used in newspaper headlines at the death of a sovereign or major political leader. On the assassination of the South African politician Hendrik Verwoerd, *Private Eye* ran one of its most memorable covers (17 September 1966): a quartet of gleeful African warriors is shown leaping in the air beneath the headline, 'VERWOERD: A NATION MOURNS'. Still used in some irony-free zones: 'A Nation Mourns' was applied to the death of Princess Margaret in *OK!* Magazine (February 2002).

(a) nation of shopkeepers The British/ the English. Characterization attributed to Napoleon in the form: '*L'Angleterre est une nation de boutiquiers/marchands* [England is a nation of shopkeepers]'. Most of Napoleon's attributed sayings are, like Abraham Lincoln's, impossible to verify now. This remark was quoted by Barry E. O'Meara in *Napoleon in Exile* (1822). Earlier, however, Samuel Adams, the American Revolutionary leader, *may* have said in his *Oration in Philadelphia* (1 August 1776): 'A nation of shop-keepers are very seldom so disinterested.' In the same year, Adam Smith was writing in *The Wealth of Nations*: 'To found a great empire for the sole purpose of raising up a people of customers, may at first sight appear a project fit only for a nation of shopkeepers.' Paoli is also said to have been quoted in this.

nation shall speak peace unto nation Motto of the BBC (since 1927) echoing Micah 4:3: 'Nation shall not lift up a sword against nation.' In 1932, however, it was decided that the BBC's primary mission was to serve the home audience and not that overseas. Hence, **Quaecunque [whatsoever]** was introduced as an alternative, reflecting the Latin inscription (composed by Dr Montague Rendall) in the entrance hall of Broadcasting House, London, and based on Philippians 4:8: 'Whatsoever things are beautiful and honest and of good report . . .' '*Quae-cunque*' was also taken as the motto of Lord Reith, the BBC's first Director-General. In 1948, the BBC's original motto was reintroduced.

(a) nationwide hunt (or search) Journalistic phrase. Date of origin unknown. Listed by Keith Waterhouse in *Daily Mirror Style* (1981) as a phrase to be avoided. 'A citizen's arrest . . . ended the nationwide hunt' – *The Daily Telegraph* (9 November 1978); 'A nationwide hunt has been launched for the vanished strawberries of Britain, the dozens of flavourful old varieties that may be lurking in gardens and country estates' – *The Times* (12 May 1994); '"We can sometimes do a nation-wide search," confesses Ms Ormiston . . . "but it's a nightmare, takes ages, and I only do it if someone is very insistent"' – *The Independent* (9 June 1994); 'To the chagrin of critics of the award, pollution levels and the number of environment-friendly initiatives were not taken into consideration in the nationwide search for the cleanest city' – *The Independent* (4 May 1995).

(the) natives are hostile (or restless)! What someone might say, with literal meaning, in British imperial fiction – but probably best known through parodies of same. Could now be used to convey that any group of people is hostile or impatient or whatever – a queue in a canteen, an audience in a theatre. The 'hostile' version is uttered in *Target for Tonight* (UK 1942), a film about RAF Bomber Command, and the 'restless' version is in *Summer Holiday* (UK 1962). Sometimes the phrase is rendered as: 'The natives are restless tonight, Carruthers.' In the BBC radio *Goon Show*, 'The Red Fort' (set in India) (11 November 1957) is: 'The natives are revolting'. Compare PEASANTS ARE REVOLTING.

nature See ANSWER THE CALL.

(that is the) nature of the beast 'That is the way things are because of the type of person (or situation or circumstance) we are dealing with.' Probably implying there is not much one can do to change it. 'It's the nature o' th' beast' was listed as an English proverbial expression in 1678. From Val Gielgud, *Necessary End* (1969): 'Barry Compayne never made any bones about . . . the number of girls that he had "laid" . . . Anthea had chosen deliberately to put down such exploits to "the nature of the beast".'

(death is) nature's way of telling you to slow down Joke current in the USA by 1960 (as in *Newsweek*, 25 April). It has been specifically attributed to Severn Darden (b. 1937), the American film character actor. It is capable of infinite variation and thus almost a format phrase: from *Punch* (3 January 1962): 'Some neo-Malthusians have been heard to suggest that the bomb is Nature's way . . . of checking . . . the over-spawning of our species.' In 1978, the American cartoon strip 'Garfield' produced a bumper sticker with the slogan: 'My car is God's way of telling you to slow down.' In Robert McGowan & Jeremy Hands, *Don't Cry for Me, Sergeant-Major* (1983) (about the Falklands war), a Marine corporal says, 'This is nature's little way of telling you you are going to die.'

naughty bits Euphemism for the genitals – from a lecture on parts of the body in *Monty Python's Flying Circus* (24 November 1970).

naughty but nice Catchphrase/slogan in which alliteration rules. The catchphrase in full is 'It's naughty but it's nice'. The phrase was used in British advertisements, originated by the Ogilvy & Mather agency, for fresh cream cakes in 1981–4. Also for the National Dairy Council's cream adverts in the late 1980s. But the phrase had already been much used elsewhere. A 1939 US film had the title. It was about a professor of classical music who accidentally wrote a popular song. *Partridge/Slang* glosses it as 'a reference to copulation since *circa* 1900 ex a song that Minnie Schult sang and popularized in the USA, 1890s'. There have since been various songs with the title, notably one by Johnny Mercer and Harry Warren, 'Naughty but Nice', in the film *The Belle of New York* (US 1952). Compare also, 'It's Foolish But It's Fun' (Gus Kahn/Robert Stolz) sung by Deanna Durbin in the film *Spring Parade* (US 1940).

(the) Naughty Nineties (also Gay Nineties) Nicknames referring to the 1890s in England, when VICTORIAN VALUES softened somewhat in the face of hedonism in certain circles. The most characteristic figure was that of Oscar Wilde. *OED2* does not find the term in use until 1925. A play entitled *The Naughty Nineties* by E. Savage Graham and Ronald Simpson was produced in London in September 1931.

(the) Navy's here! Phrase indicating that rescue is at hand, everything is going to be all right, be assured. From an actual use of the words during the Second World War. On the night of 16 February 1940, 299 British seamen were freed from captivity aboard the German ship *Altmark* as it lay in a Norwegian fjord. The destroyer

Cossack, under the command of Captain Philip Vian, had managed to locate the German supply ship, and a boarding party discovered that British prisoners were locked in its hold. As Vian described it, Lieutenant Bradwell Turner, the leader of the boarding party, called out: 'Any British down there?' 'Yes, we're all British,' came the reply. 'Come on up then,' he said, 'The Navy's here.' The identity of the speaker is still in some doubt, however. *The Times* on 19 February 1940 gave a version from the lips of one of those who had been freed and who had actually heard the exchange: 'John Quigley of London said that the first they knew of their rescue was when they heard a shout of "Any Englishmen here?" They shouted "Yes" and immediately came the cheering words, "Well, the Navy is here." Quigley said – "We were all hoarse with cheering when we heard those words".'

nay, nay – thrice again nay! Catchphrase of the British comedian Frankie Howerd (*circa* 1917–92). Towards the end of his life, this emerged as one of the most typical of the stock phrases that he himself referred to as 'verbal punctuation marks'. They did not exactly catch on, but they were certainly characteristic. 'While other shows used catchphrases almost as characters, I was a character who used catchphrases,' was the way he put it. **Ladies and gentle-men!** was an opening phrase to which he gave special emphasis. Howerd explained that when he was starting in radio just after the Second World War he thought a good gimmick would be for him to give unusual emphasis to certain words. Hence **I was a-mazed!** Other Howerdisms included: **not on your Nellie!** *Partridge/Catch Phrases* dates this from the 1930s and says it is abbreviated rhyming slang for 'puff' – breath – as in 'Not on your Nellie Duff!' meaning 'not on your life'. 'Tough Nellie Duff, the Strongarm Schoolmarm' was a cartoon strip character in the *Dandy* or *Beano* magazines of the 1930s. Howerd undoubtedly popularized the expression in the 1940s, however; **no, don't laugh!**; **titter ye not!**; **chilly!**; **'ere, mush!**; **listen!**; **let's get myself comfy!**; **please yourselves!** (also used as the title of a radio series) and **poor soul – she's past it!** (said of his supposedly deaf accompanist), alternatively, **poor old thing – she'll have to go!**, not to be confused with **er, Thing, you know**, when speaking of the person responsible for or in charge of the show. **Shut your face!** perhaps demonstrates what Howerd was all about – taking phrases that are already in circulation (this one was known by 1893) and somehow giving them a special twist. The phrase was also given a going over on a hit single by Joe Dolce, an American singer pretending to be Italian: 'Shaddap Your Face' in 1981.

Nazi jackboots Phrase used to encapsulate the horrors of Nazism in the Second World War. 'Looking back on that visit of the late forties, I had not appreciated just how recently those Nazi jackboots had strutted down the Champs Elysees' – *The Herald* (Glasgow) (23 August 1994); 'We may learn from Janus and Janus that 11 per cent of American men and women have had personal experience of dominance/bondage, but instead of that news satisfying our curiosity, it merely prompts more detailed questions . . . Are Nazi jackboots still in favour?' – *Independent on Sunday* (25 April 1993).

neat but not gaudy Quirky comment coupled with some outlandish image, e.g. 'Neat but not gaudy – like a bull's arse tied up with a bicycle chain' – told by a (sensibly) anonymous correspondent from the Cotswolds in 1994. *Partridge/Catch Phrases* suggests that the initial phrase 'neat but not gaudy' was established by about 1800, though in 1631 there had been the similar 'Comely, not gaudy'. Shakespeare, in *Hamlet*, I.iii.71 (1600), has 'rich, not gaudy; / For the apparel oft proclaims the man . . .' The Reverend Samuel Wesley wrote in 'An Epistle to a Friend concerning Poetry' (1700): 'Style is the dress of thought; a modest dress, / Neat, but not gaudy, will true critics please.' Charles Lamb wrote to William Wordsworth (June 1806), 'A little thin flowery border round, neat not gaudy.' Then variations were introduced – as by John Ruskin, writing in the *Architectural Magazine* (November 1838): 'That admiration of the "neat but gaudy [*sic*]" which is commonly reported to have influenced the devil when he

painted his tail pea green.' Indeed, *Partridge* cites: 'Neat, but not gaudy, as the monkey said, when he painted his tail-sky blue' and '. . . painted his bottom pink and tied up his tail with pea-green'.

nectar See AMBER NECTAR.

needle See EYE OF A.

needle, nardle, noo! Nonsense phrase, spoken by various characters in the BBC radio *Goon Show* (1951–60).

(to) need one's own space Used most often in the context of breaking away from a partnership or marriage in order that the persons involved may be able to grow and flourish independently. From American psycho-babble, perhaps dating from the 1960s/70s. '[Elizabeth Taylor said] that she and Larry Fortensky have agreed to a trial separation. "Larry and I both need our own space now"' – *The Independent* (1 September 1995).

needs no introduction Chairpersons' and presenters' phrase. From my book *Best Behaviour* (1992): 'A good chairman is hard to find, though even a bad one is preferable to professional toastmasters with their noisy gavel-banging, and pompous if not incompetent introductions. The chairman should introduce the speaker with the minimum of words. There is no point in saying that the "speaker needs no introduction" if you then plough through his biography.' Date of origin unknown. 'Elaine Myers needs no introduction to nitelifers' – *The Leader* (Durban) (7 May 1971).

neither fair to you nor true to myself Speechmakers' pompous phrase. It occurs along with other rhetorical clichés during the 'Party Political Speech' (written by Max Schreiner) on the Peter Sellers's comedy album *The Best of Sellers* (1958): 'For if I were to convey to you a spirit of false optimism then I should be neither fair to you nor true to myself.'

neither fish, flesh, nor good red herring Meaning 'neither one thing nor another; suitable to no class of people', the phrase sometimes occurs in the form 'neither fish, flesh, nor fowl', where the origin of the expression (which dates from the Middle

Ages) is that whatever is under discussion is unsuitable food for a monk (fish), for people generally (flesh), or for the poor (red, smoked, herring). A 'red herring' in the sense of a distraction, diversion or false clue, derives from the practice of drawing the strongly smelling fish across the path of foxhounds to put them off the scent. 'Being semi-royal must be tormenting, for one is neither fish, flesh nor good red herring' – James Lees-Milne in *Midway on the Waves* (1985) – diary entry for 24 March 1948.

neither (one thing) nor (the other) Format for a series of expressions giving a sense of 'in-betweenness, indeterminacy, falling between two stools', e.g. **neither arm'ole nor watercress**; **neither breakfast-time nor Wednesday**; (doesn't know whether it's) **Pancake Tuesday or half-past breakfast-time**.

(the) Nelson touch Denoting any action bearing the hallmark of Horatio Nelson, his quality of leadership and seamanship, this term was coined by Nelson himself before the Battle of Trafalgar (1805): 'I am anxious to join the fleet, for it would add to my grief if any other man was to give them the Nelson touch.' The *Oxford Companion to Ships and the Sea* (1976) describes various manoeuvres to which the term could be applied but adds, also: 'It could have meant the magic name of his name among officers and seamen of his fleet, which was always enough to inspire them to great deeds of heroism and endurance.' The British title of the film *Corvette K-225* (US 1943) was *The Nelson Touch*.

ne plus ultra [not more beyond] The supposed inscription on the Pillars of Hercules in the Strait of Gibraltar preventing ships from going further. It subsequently came to mean 'the furthest attainable point; the acme of something'. Other forms of the phrase are *nec plus ultra* and *non plus ultra*. 'No man has the right to say to his country, "Thus far shalt thou go and no further", and we have never attempted to fix the *ne plus ultra* to the progress of Ireland's nationhood and we never shall' – Charles Stewart Parnell, speech at Cork (21 January 1885).

(a/the) nerve centre Meaning, 'the centre of control of any organization.' 'Wall Street is the great nerve centre of all American business' – James Bryce, *The American Commonwealth* (1888); 'A "nerve centre" opens today opposite Victoria Station for cross-Channel steamer car traffic' – *The Daily Telegraph* (30 November 1959); 'Commandeered it as the nerve centre of Mageeba's victorious drive against the forces of darkness, otherwise known as the Adoma Liberation Front' – Tom Stoppard, *Night and Day* (1978); 'Palatable platitudes at the nerve centre of chic – Wet, liberal, self-righteous rap for those who can't stomach the hard stuff. Adam Sweeting on the Disposable Heroes of Hiphoprisy – by-line in *The Guardian* (10 June 1992).

nestling in the valley Cliché of travel journalism. Date of origin unknown. Part of the 'travel scribes' armoury' compiled from a competition in *The Guardian* (10 April 1993). 'For our first night we chose the Hotellerie du Prieuré St Lazare from the Crystal Holidays brochure . . . "Nestling in the Loire Valley, at the crossroads of Anjou, Touraine and Poitou, stands the Royal Abbey of Fontevraud . . ."' – *The Daily Telegraph* (11 June 1994); 'Joanna Trollope's domestic bliss in Gloucestershire is much chronicled. The house of honey-coloured stone, nestling in a valley with roses, wisteria, trout stream, and farmhouse kitchen where she sometimes bops to Elvis and where sits the famous Aga, gibes about which are wearing thin' – Valerie Grove, *The Times* (31 March 1995).

never again! Unofficial slogan used against the Germans during and after the First World War and later. T. F. A. Smith wrote in *Soul of Germany* (1915): 'The oft-quoted phrase is applicable to the case: Never again!' Winston Churchill in his *The Second World War*, Vol. 1 (1948), says of the French: 'With one passionate spasm [they cried] never again'. Later, in the mid-1960s, it became the slogan of the militant Jewish Defence League – referring to the Holocaust. A stone monument erected near the birthplace of Adolf Hitler at Braunau, Austria, in 1989 (the centenary of his birth) bore the lines 'For Peace, Freedom and Democracy – Never Again

Fascism [*Nie wieder Faschismus*] – Millions of Dead are a warning'. Compare NO MORE WAR. The film *Never Say Never Again* (UK 1983), which marked Sean Connery's return to the part of James Bond, was so called because he had reputedly declared 'never again' after playing the secret agent in *Diamonds Are Forever* (UK 1971).

never chase girls or buses (there will always be another one coming along soon) *Partridge/Catch Phrases* dates this to the 1920s and derives it from the early US version, with 'streetcars' instead of 'buses'. Compare this allusion to the saying by Derick Heathcoat-Amory when British Chancellor of the Exchequer (1958–60): 'There are three things not worth running for – a bus, a woman or a new economic panacea; if you wait a bit another one will come along.'

never complain and never explain Motto, variously attributed but especially to Benjamin Disraeli – and quoted in John Morley, *Life of Gladstone* (1903), specifically about attacks in Parliament. The following must have been referring back to, or at least echoing, Disraeli: according to an article in the *Oxford Chronicle* (7 October 1893), a favourite piece of advice given to young men by Benjamin Jowett, who became Master of Balliol College, Oxford, in 1870, was, 'Never regret, never explain, never apologize.' However, in *The Oxford Book of Oxford* this is given as 'Never retreat. Never explain. Get it done and let them howl.' Compare **never explain and never apologize**, said to be a Royal Navy maxim of the early 1900s but known before then. Admiral Lord Fisher wrote to *The Times* (5 September 1919): 'Never contradict. Never explain. Never apologize. (Those are the secrets of a happy life!).'

never darken my door again Meaning, 'never cross the threshold of my house again'. In James Boswell's journal for 5 December 1786 (included in *Boswell: The English Experiment*), he writes: 'Satterthwaite used the expression "Never darkened his door". Lonsdale said he had never heard it before, and he durst say it was not in print. I said, "It is in an Irish song" (see it also in Shadwell's *Hasty*

Wedding, Act III).' Shadwell died in 1692, so that takes us back to the 17th century. Shakespeare does not use the phrase. Nearer to Boswell's time, the *OED2* finds Benjamin Franklin using it in 1729 and Samuel Richardson in his novel *Clarissa* (1749).

never give a sucker an even break Meaning, 'don't pass up the opportunity to take advantage of a fool'. This saying has been attributed to various people (Edward Francis Albee and P. T. Barnum among them) but has largely become associated with the American comedian W. C. Fields. He is believed to have ad-libbed it in the musical *Poppy* (1923) and certainly spoke it in the film version (US 1936). The words are not uttered, however, in the film with the title *Never Give a Sucker an Even Break* (US 1941).

never glad confident morning (again) Much quoted phrase of disappointment with respect to a person's performance. The origin is Robert Browning's poem 'The Lost Leader' (1845) in which William Wordsworth is regretfully portrayed as a man who had lost his revolutionary zeal. A correct – and devastating – use of the phrase came on 17 June 1963 when the British Government under its Prime Minister, Harold Macmillan, was rocking over the Profumo scandal. In the House of Commons, Tory MP Nigel Birch quoted the lines at Macmillan: 'Let him never come back to us! / There would be doubt, hesitation and pain. / Forced praise on our part – the glimmer of twilight, / Never glad confident morning again!' In November 1983, on the twentieth anniversary of President Kennedy's assassination, Lord Harlech, former British Ambassador in Washington, paid tribute thus in *The Observer* Magazine: 'Since 1963 the world has seemed a bleaker place, and for me and I suspect millions of my contemporaries he remains the lost leader – "Never glad confident morning again".' Harlech may have wanted to evoke a leader who had been lost to the world, but surely it was a mistake to quote what is a criticism of one? Also in November 1983, in *The Observer*, Paul Johnson wrote an attack (which he later appeared to regret) on Margaret Thatcher: 'Her courage and sound instincts made her formidable. But if her judgement can no longer be trusted, what is left? A very ordinary woman, occupying a position where ordinary virtues are not enough. For me, I fear it can never be "glad confident morning again".'

never knowingly undersold Promotional line formulated by the founder of the John Lewis Partnership, John Spedan Lewis, in about 1920, to express a pricing policy that originated with his father, who first opened a small shop in Oxford Street, London, in 1864. The quasi-slogan is believed to have been used within the firm before it was given public expression during the 1930s, in the form: 'If you can buy more cheaply elsewhere anything you have just bought from us we will refund the difference.' The firm does not regard the undertaking as an advertising device in the generally accepted sense, although it is displayed on its vans and on sales bills. As John Lewis merchandise is not advertised, the phrase has an almost mystical significance to the Partnership.

never let the facts stand in the way of a good story Journalists' catchphrase. *The Paper* (film US 1994) used the promotional line: 'Never let the truth get in the way of a good story.' To the British journalist James Cameron (1911–85) is attributed the similar: 'It was long ago in my life as a simple reporter that I decided that facts must never get in the way of truth.'

never love a stranger Title of a Harold Robbins's novel (1948; film US 1958). Possibly derived from the English poet Stella Benson (d. 1933). In 'To the Unborn', *This Is the End* (1917) she wrote: 'Call no man foe, but never love a stranger.'

never mind the quality, feel the width Supposedly the sort of thing a street-tradesman (or Jewish tailor) might say. Used as the title of a 'multi-ethnic' TV comedy series (UK 1967–9) about 'Manny Cohen' and 'Patrick Kelly' running a tailoring business in the East End of London. Paul Beale in *Partridge/Catch Phrases* suggests that this 'mid-C20' saying had, by the later 20th century, come to be used in more serious contexts – 'e.g. the

necessity of eking out meagre resources of government aid to cover an impossibly large and neglected field.' Indeed. Headline from an editorial in *The Observer* (29 January 1989) on a National Health Service where 'the pressure will be on to cut overheads and generally sacrifice quality for price' – 'NEVER MIND THE QUALITY'. From *The Independent* (1 March 1989): 'England's senior chief inspector of schools warned . . . "Nor must there be attempts, in trying to reduce shortages, to dilute standards by taking a 'never mind the quality, feel the width' approach".'

(oh well,) never mind, you're a long time dead Consolatory phrase. 'Whenever my mother is regaled with a tale of disastrous experience, or a chain of calamitous events, she always makes this comment' – Nellie Jarvis, Nottinghamshire (2000). This appears in 'Number Two' of John Osborne's play *The Entertainer* (1957). *Partridge/Catch Phrases* has it as a variation of (the mostly 20th century) 'You'll be a long time dead.'

never more (or **nevermore)** In the Courtauld Institute Gallery, London, there is a painting of a nude by Gauguin that has the title 'Nevermore'. What bird would you say features in it? Well, no, not a raven, it is a devil's bird. You might expect it to allude to Edgar Allan Poe's poem 'The Raven' (1845): 'Quoth the Raven "Nevermore"', but Gauguin quite clearly stated that this was not the case.

(the) Never Never (1) The land where the Lost Boys live in J. M. Barrie's *Peter Pan* (1904) – 'Never Never Never Land' in early versions, but simply 'Never Land' in the published text. Not an original coinage: a play by Wilson Barrett was called *The Never Never Land* (1902). Later, Winston Churchill said in the House of Commons (5 April 1906): 'That constitution now passes away into the never never land, into a sort of chilly limbo . . .' 'Never Never Land' was the English title of a song, *Naar de Specituin* (1954), by Beryenberg and Froboess. (2) The Australian outback, known as such by 1882, and as in *We of the Never Never* (1908) by Mrs Aeneas Gunn. (3) Alternative name for hire purchase, as 'the never-never' (by 1926).

never say die! Exclamation, meaning 'never give in'. Much used by Charles Dickens in his writings, starting with 'Greenwich Fair' in *Sketches by Boz* (written 1833–6) – though it may not be original to him. It occurs in *The Pickwick Papers* (1836–7) and is notably the catchphrase of Grip the raven in *Barnaby Rudge* (1841). *Benham* (1907) has, 'Never say die. / Up, man, and try!' in the proverbs section, but undated.

never swap (or **change) horses in mid-stream** Meaning, 'don't alter course in the middle of doing something'. *Mencken* has 'Never swap horses crossing a stream' as an 'American proverb, traced to *circa* 1840'. *CODP*'s earliest citation is Abraham Lincoln saying in 1864: 'I am reminded . . . of a story of an old Dutch farmer, who remarked to a companion once that "it was best not to swap horses when crossing streams".' This would seem to confirm the US origin. 'Don't change barrels going over Niagara' was a slogan attributed (satirically) to the Republicans during the presidential campaign of 1932 and is clearly derived from the foregoing.

never trouble trouble (till trouble troubles you) Nannyism as in *Casson/ Grenfell*. There was a song 'Trouble', written by David Keppel and known by 1916: 'Never trouble trouble/ Till trouble troubles you / For if you trouble trouble / You'll only double trouble / And trouble others too.' *Apperson* has the first two lines recorded as a proverbial saying, in Derby, from the *Folk-Lore Journal* (1884).

never underestimate the power of a woman Slogan for *Ladies' Home Journal*, from *circa* 1941. Gordon Page of the N. W. Ayer agency recalled: 'It came off the back burner of a creative range where ideas simmer while the front burners are preoccupied with meeting closing dates . . . it was just a more direct way of stating the case for the leading woman's magazine of the day. But always believing that you can do things with a twinkle that you can't do with a straight face, it was trotted to Leo Lionni . . . it's largely *his* fault that you can't say "never underestimate the power of *anything*" today without echoing the line.' Even in 1981, the following ad was

appearing in *The New York Times*: 'Ladies' Home Journalism – Never Underestimate Its Power'.

never work with children or animals Well-known piece of show-business lore, from American vaudeville, possibly, and, occasionally, adapted: '"Never work with children, dogs, or Denholm Elliott," British actors are said to advise one another' – *The Guardian* (29 April 1989). Phyllis Hartnoll in *Plays and Players* (1985) has: 'W. C. Fields is quoted as saying, "Never act with animals or children".' Although this line reflects his known views, the attribution may result from confusion with 'Any man who hates dogs and babies can't be all bad' (which he didn't say either: it was said by Leo Rosten *about* him at a dinner in 1939). A similar sentiment is contained in Noël Coward's remark about the child actress Bonnie Langford, who appeared along with a horse in a West End musical version of *Gone With the Wind* in 1972. Inevitably, there came the moment when the horse messed up the stage. Coward said: 'If they'd stuffed the child's head up the horse's arse, they would have solved two problems at once.' Sarah Bernhardt had a pronounced aversion to performing with animals. When she received an offer to appear in music hall in a scene from *L'Aiglon*, she replied, 'Between monkeys, *non!*'

never wrestle with a chimney sweep Don't resort to dirty tricks. From *The Observer* Magazine (4 July 1993) on Tony Benn MP: 'Now he is older he finds himself repeating advice his father offered him as a child like "never wrestle with a chimney sweep", which means don't soil yourself by responding to your opponents' dirty tricks. "The whole wisdom of humanity is summed up in these phrases," he muses.' Benn earlier used the phrase for his own purposes. From Ben Pimlott, *Harold Wilson* (1992): 'For the Labour Party to rub its hands with glee, as Wedgwood Benn put it [about the Profumo Affair, 1963] would be like wrestling with a chimney sweep.' Compare a conversation between Dr Johnson and Dr William Adams in Boswell's *Life of Johnson* (for 20 March 1776): 'JOHNSON: If my antagonist writes bad language, though that may not be essential to the question, I will attack him for his bad language. ADAMS: You would not jostle a chimney-sweeper. JOHNSON: Yes, Sir, if it were necessary to jostle him *down*.'

new See IS THE NEW.

(the) New Deal Slogan of President Franklin D. Roosevelt (though Abraham Lincoln had used it on occasions). To the 1932 Democratic Convention that had just nominated him, Roosevelt said: 'I pledge you, I pledge myself to a New Deal for the American people . . . a new order of competence and courage . . . to restore America to its own people.'

(the) New Frontier Slogan of John F. Kennedy, which he first used on accepting the Democratic nomination in 1960: 'We stand today on the edge of a New Frontier. The frontier of the 1960s . . . is not a set of promises – it is a set of challenges. It sums up not what I intend to offer the American people, but what I intend to ask of them.' In 1964, Harold Wilson said in a speech in Birmingham: 'We want the youth of Britain to storm the new frontiers of knowledge.'

Newgate See AS BLACK AS.

(the) New Journalism Name given to a type of heavily subjective writing practised in the USA by Tom Wolfe and Gay Talese and, in the UK, by Nicholas Tomalin and others during the late 1960s. The term was known by 1970 although, as might be expected, it had been used less specifically before then about other innovative types of journalism. An anthology entitled *The New Journalism*, edited by Tom Wolfe and E. W. Johnson, was published in 1973.

news See ALL THE.

(the) New Wave Name given to a group of young French film-makers in the 1950s. As *Nouvelle vague*, the term was coined by Françoise Giroud, a Swiss-born critic (1916–), in the newspaper *L'Express* (1958), referring to such luminaries as François Truffaut, Jean-Luc Godard and Claude Chabrol. As it so happens, most of the group were originally critics who put their theories to the test as directors. 'It is a film made by one of the old guard rather than by a member of the *nouvelle vague*' – *The Times* (4 September 1959).

(the) new world order Always a rather vague concept. *The New World Order* was the title of a book (1940) by H. G. Wells. 'New Order' had previously been the name given to programmes of Hitler's regime in Germany in the 1930s and of a Japanese Prime Minister in 1938. Additionally, Hitler said in Berlin (30 January 1941): 'I am convinced that 1941 will be the crucial year of a great New Order in Europe. The world will open up for everyone.' The phrase lingers: in an exchange of New Year's greetings with US President Bush in January 1991, President Gorbachev of the Soviet Union spoke of the serious obstacle posed to a 'new world order' by the Iraqi invasion of Kuwait. After the allied victory in the Gulf War, Bush himself proclaimed a New World Order based on law and human rights. New Order was also the name of a British pop vocal/instrumental group from *circa* 1981.

next year in Jerusalem! Familiar Jewish toast. In the Diaspora, it was the eternal hope – expressed particularly at the Feast of the Passover – that all Jews would be reunited, 'next year in Jerusalem'. Passover originally celebrated the exodus of the Jews from Egypt and their deliverance from enslavement some 3,200 years ago. In the centuries of the Diaspora, the central Jewish dream was of being reunited in the land of Israel. In June 1967, following the Six Day War, when the modern state of Israel encompassed once more the old city of Jerusalem, all Jews could, if they were able, end their exile and make this dream more of a reality.

nibble See EVERY TIME A SHEEP.

nice See HERE'S ANOTHER.

nice 'ere, innit? Catchphrase from a British TV advertisement in 1976: on a balcony in Venice, an elegant-looking girl sips Campari and then shatters the atmosphere by saying in a rough Cockney voice, 'Nice 'ere, innit?' In the follow-up ad, a smooth type asks the same girl, 'Were you truly wafted here from Paradise?' She replies: '**Nah ... Luton Airport**.' These nothing phrases were crafted by copywriter Terry Howard and let fall by Lorraine Chase. Campari sales rose by a record 35 per cent in a single year. Lorraine went on to record a song called 'It's Nice 'Ere, Innit?' (1979) and Cats UK recorded 'Luton Airport' the same year. Next step was for the personality to be written into a TV sitcom called *The Other 'Arf* (from 1980).

nice guys finish last During his time as manager of the Brooklyn Dodgers baseball team (1951–4), Leo Durocher (1906–91) became known for this view – also in the form, 'Nice guys don't finish first' or '. . . don't play ball games'. *Partridge/Catch Phrases* dates the popular use of the phrase from July 1946. Used as the title of a book by Paul Gardner, subtitled 'Sport and American Life', in 1974. In his autobiography with the title *Nice Guys Finish Last* (1975), Durocher recalled that what he had said to reporters concerning the New York Giants in July 1946, was: 'All nice guys. They'll finish last. Nice guys. Finish last.' However, Frank Graham of the New York *Journal-American* had written down something slightly different: 'Why, they're the nicest guys in the world! And where are they? In seventh place!' Hence, the title of Ralph Keyes's book on misquotations, *Nice Guys Finish Seventh* (1992).

(a) nice little earner Much used by George Cole in the character of Arthur Daley in British TV's *Minder* series (from the late 1970s on). 'Earner' on its own, for 'money earned' (often shadily), may go back to the 1930s. '[On a large number of claims for tripping over broken paving stones in Northern Ireland] That, said Michael Latham, Tory MP for Rutland, meant that either the state of local pavements was "exceptionally disgraceful . . .", or the locals saw a "nice little earner there and are trying it on"' – *The Independent* (27 April 1989).

nice one, Cyril! Catchphrase from an advertising line. The story of this phrase is a classic instance of a line from an advertisement being taken up by the public, turned into a catchphrase and then as suddenly discarded. Its origins were quite soon obscured and then forgotten. The line, apparently written by Peter Mayle, caught the imagination of British TV viewers in a 1972 advertisement for

Wonderloaf. Two bakers were shown wearing T-shirts labelled 'Nottingham' and 'Liverpool' respectively. 'All our local bakers reckon they can taste a Wonderloaf and tell you who baked it,' purred a voice-over commentary. 'It was oven-baked at one of our local bakeries.' The following exchange then took place between the bakers: *Liverpool*: 'Leeds? High Wycombe? It's one of Cyril's. Mmm. Good texture, nice colour, very fresh . . .' *Nottingham*: 'Cyril . . . I think it's one of Frank's down at Luton . . . it's definitely saying Newcastle to me . . .' The voice-over then intervened: 'The truth is, they can't say for sure. But we can say . . .' *Nottingham*: 'Nice one, Cyril!' As a phrase, why did 'Nice one, Cyril!' catch on? It had a sibilant ease; it was fun to say. More importantly, it could be used in any number of situations, not least sexual ones. In 1973, the phrase was taken up by Tottenham Hotspur football supporters who were fans of the player Cyril Knowles. They even recorded a song about him which went: 'Nice one, Cyril / Nice one, son. / Nice one, Cyril, / Let's have another one.' Comedian Cyril Fletcher inevitably used it as the title of his 1978 autobiography. The following year the word 'Cyril' was observed scrawled on the first kilometre sign outside a certain seaside resort in the south of France. Shortly afterwards the phrase disappeared almost completely from use, although in February 1989 posters appeared for a credit card company, which showed Sir Cyril Smith, the obese politician, attempting to touch his toes. The slogan was: 'Nice one, Sir Cyril . . . but Access is more flexible.' Compare, **nice one, Stew!** from a children's programme on New Zealand TV in the mid-70s. Stew Dennison, the host, wore a schoolboy's cap and would say it to himself. Kids around him would then echo it.

nice place you got here Complimentary and/or threatening phrase from films. Dick Vosburgh and Trevor Lyttleton included it in their delightful catalogue song 'I Love a Film Cliché', which was included in the Broadway hit *A Day in Hollywood, A Night in the Ukraine* (1980). In it, they gave the longer version – the one uttered by a gangster with a lump in his jacket, viz:

'Nice place you got here, blue eyes. Be too bad if something was to . . . happen to it!' At this point, the heavy usually knocks over an ornament, as a warning. Often, one hears the version 'nice *little* place you've got here' – used with equal amounts of irony about a dump or somewhere impressively grand. However, in the film *Breakfast at Tiffany's* (US 1961), it is said almost straight. In *Laura* (1944), Dana Andrews says to Clifton Webb, 'Nice little place you have here, Mr Lydecker' with faint quotation marks round it. *Partridge/Catch Phrases* seems to think it all started in Britain in the 1940s, but one feels sure the film use must have started in the USA in the 1930s. Lana Turner says 'Nice place you got here' in *Ziegfeld Girl* (US 1941), as though it were a well-established phrase. It is also said to have been popularized around 1942 by the BBC radio show *ITMA*, following a visit to Windsor Castle by the star, Tommy Handley. 'To this day [Stevie] Wonder habitually talks about "seeing" and catches out sighted friends by walking into unfamiliar rooms, taking a "look" around and saying: "Hey, nice place you've got here"' – *The Independent* (13 May 1989).

nice ——, shame about the ——   Format phrase launched by 'Nice Legs, Shame About Her Face', the title of a briefly popular song recorded by The Monks in 1979. Hence, 'Nice video, shame about the song', a take-off by TV's *Not the Nine O'Clock News* team, and as an advertising line for Hofmeister lager, 'Great lager, shame about the . . .' (both in 1982). Just before this, Listerine may have run an ad with the slogan 'Nice Face, Shame About the Breath'. 'Good tune, shame about the words' – headline to an article on the hundredth birthday of the 'The Red Flag' in *The Independent* (9 February 1989); 'Nice prints, shame about the books' – headline in *The Observer* (9 April 1989); also used loosely: 'Victoria Wood is almost perfect. Lovely lady, pity about the voice' – *Cosmopolitan* (February 1987); 'Nice Car, But What A Voice!' – headline to a report on puny car horns in *The Observer* (January 1989).

(the) nicest things come in smallest parcels   Nannyism, as in *Casson/Grenfell*. A version of 'the best things come in small

packages', a proverb well established by the late 19th century, according to *CODP*.

nice weather for ducks   See LOVELY WEATHER.

nice work if you can get it!   Approving, if not envious, phrase about a particular type of employment – a job that takes the person addressed to exotic places, for example. Most probably from the title of the song 'Nice Work If You Can Get It' (1937) by George and Ira Gershwin. The latter admitted that he might have found the phrase in the caption to a *Punch* cartoon that had been rejected as not being suitable for publication – in it, two men had been discussing the daughter of a third, who had become a whore.

(in the very) nick of time   Just in time, at the very last moment. *Brewer* (1894) suggests that the 'nick' in question is a notch on a stick used as a tally. Whatever the case, the phrase was in use by 1643. Compare: 'There is a deep nick in Time's restless wheel / For each man's good, when which nick comes, it strikes' – George Chapman, *Bussy D'Ambois*, Act 1, Sc. 1 (written in 1607). '[Mrs Wentworth-Brewster] discovered in the very nick of time that life was for living' – introduction to the song 'A Bar on the Piccola Marina' on the record album *Noël Coward at Las Vegas* (1955); *Nick of Time*, title of film (US 2003).

niece   See HAVE YOU MET.

(a/the) nigger in the woodpile   Meaning, 'something surprising hidden, a concealed factor'. *Mencken* has: 'There's a nigger in the woodpile – American saying, traced by Thornton to 1864, and probably older.' The *OED2* finds it in Kansas in 1852. Nowadays considered an unacceptable usage.

night   See AS NIGHT; DARK NIGHT.

night and fog   Euphemistic phrase. *Nacht und Nebel* was the name of a 1941 decree issued under Adolf Hitler's signature. It described a simple process: anyone suspected of a crime against occupying German forces was to disappear into 'night and fog'. Such people were thrown into the concentration camp system, in most cases never to be heard of again. Alain

Resnais, the French film director, made a cinema short about a concentration camp called *Nuit et Brouillard* (1955). The phrase comes from Wagner's opera *Das Rheingold* (1869): '*Nacht und Nebel niemand gleich*' is the spell that Alberich puts on the magic Tarnhelm, which renders him invisible and omnipresent. It means, approximately, 'In night and fog no one is seen'.

(the) night is young Catchphrase – the sort of thing one says when attempting to justify taking another drink. 'They . . . left the table when the night was yet young, and the bottle just beginning' – Sir Walter Besant, *Dorothy Forster*, Chap. 11 (1884); 'However, the night is yet young. We will . . . cheer ourselves with light refreshments' – P. G. Wodehouse, *Psmith in the City*, Chap. 18 (1910); 'He looked at the clock. I pointed out that the night was young' – Max Beerbohm, *Seven Men* (1919); 'The Night is Young (and You're So Beautiful)' was the title of a song by Billy Rose and Irving Kahal (1936), and the previous year 'The Night Is Young (And So Are We)' had been written by Oscar Hammerstein II and Sigmund Romberg and included in the film *The Night Is Young*; 'At three in the morning, when a few people decided to leave, Orson, stepping into the role of clichéd host from a Grade B movie, would not hear of it: "You're not leaving already, my friends. The night is still young. Play, Gypsies! Play, play, play!"' – Frank Brady, *Citizen Welles* (1989).

(the) night is your friend During the Second World War, resistance movements in occupied Europe were encouraged from London by broadcasts over the BBC. In an English-language broadcast on 31 July 1941, Colonel Britton, *nom de guerre* of Douglas Ritchie, said: 'The night is your friend. The V is your sign.' Compare Cole Porter's song 'All Through the Night' (1934), which had contained the lines: 'The day is my enemy / The night is my friend.' And later, *The Night Was Our Friend*, title of a play (1950) by Michael Pertwee.

nightmare See LIVING HELL.

(the) night of broken glass [*Kristall-nacht*] Euphemism attributed to Walther Funk to describe the Nazi pogrom against Jews in Germany on the night of 9/10 November 1938.

(a/the) night of the long knives Phrase for any kind of surprise purge (but one in which, usually, no actual blood is spilt). It was applied, for example, to Harold Macmillan's wholesale reorganization of his Cabinet in 1962. When Norman St John Stevas was dropped from his Cabinet post in a 1981 reshuffle, one wit described the changes as Mrs Thatcher's 'night of the long hatpin'. The original was *Die Nacht der langen Messer* in Nazi Germany. During the weekend of 29 June/2 July 1934, Hitler, aided by Himmler's black-shirted SS, liquidated the leadership of the brown-shirted SA. These latter undisciplined storm-troopers had helped Hitler gain power but were now getting in the way of his dealings with the German army. Some 83 were murdered on the pretext that they were plotting another revolution. 'It was no secret that this time the revolution would have to be bloody,' Hitler explained to the Reichstag on 13 July. 'When we spoke of it, we called it "The Night of the Long Knives" . . . in every time and place, rebels have been killed . . . I ordered the leaders of the guilty shot. I also ordered the abscesses caused by our internal and external poisons cauterised until the living flesh was burned.' It seems that in using the phrase Hitler may have been quoting from an early Nazi marching song. Compare *Verschwörung der langen Messer* ('conspiracy of the long knives', translating the much older Welsh phrase *twyll y cyllvyll hirion*) that had previously been used as the name of a premeditated massacre of unarmed and unprepared men. To be precise, it described the supposed murder by Hengist and his Saxons of a party of British nobles at a peace conference, as described by Nennius, Geoffrey of Monmouth, and various other pseudo-historical sources. The German phrase is used in Geoffrey of Monmouth's *Historia Regum Britanniae*, ed. San-Marte (1854).

night starvation Horlicks milk drink used the slogan 'Horlicks guards against night starvation' in the UK from 1930. The J. Walter Thompson agency evolved the concept of 'night starvation' to add to the worries of the 20th century – nobody had been aware of it before: 'Right through the night you've been burning up reserves of energy without food to replace it. Breathing alone takes twenty thousand muscular efforts every night.' *Partridge/Slang* records that the phrase became a popular term for sexual deprivation. Horlicks had advertised before this with the memorable picture of a man turning out his suitcase and the slogan **I know I packed it**. During the 1950s, JWT ran comic-strip sagas of the refreshing qualities of Horlicks for tired housewives, run-down executives, etc., which customarily ended with the hero/heroine offering thanks within a think bubble **thinks . . . thanks to Horlicks**. But the idea was an old one. 'Thinks ... . thanks to *Radio Times*' was running in the 1930s.

nighty-night, sleep tight (mind that the fleas don't bite) Nursery valediction. Or 'good night . . . mind the fleas and bugs don't bite.' Date of origin unknown, but probably 19th century. 'I was told on a visit to the American Museum in Bath that early settlers in America built traditional wooden bed frames and then "strung" them, rather like tennis racquets. The most comfortable sleep was deemed to be likely on a bed that had been *tightly* strung. Presumably if a bed were slack, then the occupant might well drop to the floor through the meshing!' – Brian Adams, Berkshire (1997). *Casson/Grenfell* has: 'Good-night, sleep tight, mind the fleas don't bite. If they do, get a shoe and crack their little heads in two.' 'Night night, / Sleep tight, / Mind the fleas don't bite, / Pleasant dreams and sweet repose, / Lie on your back and you won't hurt your nose, / Half the bed and all the clothes, / Mind the mice don't nibble your toes' – grandmother of Chris Gamble, Norfolk (2003). This appears to be an amalgam of various such lines.

nikky-nokky-noo See HOW TICKLED.

nil carborundum See *ILLEGITIMI*.

NIMBY [Not In My BackYard] Acronym describing people who object to having unpleasant developments near their homes but, it is implied, don't mind the developments being sited elsewhere. In 1988, the British Environment Secretary, Nicholas Ridley, was called a 'nimby' when he objected to housing developments near his own home when he had previously criticized people who took this attitude. In fact, 'nimby' was an American coinage, *circa* 1980, for people who had objected to the siting of something like a nuclear waste dumping site or a sewage treatment plant. 'Trendy Diners Turn Nimby Over New York Drugs Clinic' – headline in *The Guardian* (12 November 1991).

(a) nine days' wonder Referring to something of short-lived appeal and expected soon to be forgotten. The expression comes from an old proverb: 'A wonder lasts nine days, and then the puppy's eyes are open' – alluding to the fact that dogs (like cats) are born blind. After nine days, in other words, their eyes are open to see clearly. The saying was known in this form by 1594. Another etymologist finds a link with the old religious practice of selling indulgences, one of which – guaranteeing the purchaser nine days' worth of prayers – was called a *novem*. The indulgence was held to be a bit suspect – rather like this explanation. Chaucer expressed the old proverb thus: 'For wonder last but nine night never in town.' Surely, we need look no further for the origin of an expression of which the truth is self-evident: wonder dies in time. Incidentally, there is an Italian proverb: 'No wonder can last more than three days.'

nine out of ten —— Format beloved of advertisers. 'Nine out of ten screens stars use Lux Toilet Soap for their priceless smooth skins' – so ran a famous campaign that lasted for twenty years from 1927. Among the stars who were listed as Lux users were Fay Wray, Clara Bow and Joan Crawford. The format was also used to promote pet food in the UK in the 1950s/60s? The BBC radio show *Round the Horne* (1 May 1966) called itself 'the show that nine out of ten horses prefer'; a 1987 graffito read, 'Bestiality – nine out of every ten cats said their owners preferred it.' Compare '4 out of 5 people say Big John's Beans taste better' – US ad, quoted in 1977.

ninepence See AS RIGHT.

nines See DRESSED UP TO.

(the) nine tailors In bell-ringing it was possible to indicate the age or sex of a dead person for whom the bells were being tolled. Three times one for a child, three twos for a woman and three threes for a man (hence 'nine tellers' or 'nine tailors' – strokes – meant a man). In Dorothy L. Sayers's novel *The Nine Tailors* (1934), the bell is called 'Tailor Paul' and does indeed toll nine times for a man found dead in the belfry. But the phrase also appears to be from a proverb in contempt of tailors: 'It takes nine tailors to make a man', which apparently came from the French *circa* 1600. The meaning of this seems to be that a man should buy his clothes from various sources. *Apperson* shows that, until the end of the 17th century, there was some uncertainty about the number of tailors mentioned. In *Westward Hoe* by John Webster and Thomas Dekker (1605) it appears as three. Whatever the case, it probably explains why Elizabeth I, on being confronted by a delegation of eighteen tailors, is reputed to have said: 'Good morrow, gentlemen both.'

(to talk) nineteen to the dozen I.e. to talk very quickly. A very literal derivation comes from the Cornish tin mines of the 18th century. When pumps were introduced to get rid of flooding, they were said to pump out 19,000 gallons of water for every twelve bushels of coal needed to operate the engines. But, surely, one can be even more basic than that: to speak nineteen words where only twelve are needed gets across the idea very nicely. Nineteen may be a surprising number to choose. Oddly, however, it sounds right and better than any other number. 'Twenty to the dozen', for example, sounds rather flat. The phrase was in use by 1785.

nine to ninety Cliché of broadcasting, mostly. 'This show will appeal to everyone from nine to ninety.' Sometimes 'nineteen . . .', if the entertainment in question is a touch more adult.

99 44/100 per cent pure Slogan for Ivory Soap, in the USA, from *circa* 1882. One of the clumsiest but most enduring slogans of all. Nobody remembers who first coined this bizarre line but it has stuck, along with the claim that **it floats**.

A story has it that the floating character of the soap was not recognized until a dealer asked for another case of 'that soap that floats'. An advertisement for *Swan* soap in the UK is featured in Vol. 122 of *Punch*, 1902, also using 'it floats'. In 1974, an American gangster film with Richard Harris was entitled *99 And 44/100 Per Cent Dead*. For the benefit of non-Americans who would not understand the allusion, the film was tardily retitled *Call Harry Crown*. But *Variety* opined crisply that even the original version was 'as clumsy as its title'.

(Domestos kills) ninety-nine per cent of all known germs The domestic cleaning agent and disinfectant appears to have used several versions of this slogan. In 1959, 'Domestos kills all known germs in one hour'. In 1967, 'Domestos kills all known germs – dead!' From the BBC radio show *Round the Horne* (13 March 1966): 'Ladies and gentlemen – the programme that contains ninety-nine percent of all known jokes . . .'

ninthlies and lastlies Phrase of pedantry. Ronald Knox's *Juxta Salices* (1910) includes a group of poems he had written when still at Eton and is prefaced with this remark: 'As no less than three of [these poems] wear the aspect of a positively last appearance [i.e. a promise not to write more], they have been called in the words of so many eminent preachers "ninthlies and lastlies".' Earlier, the *OED2* has Thomas B. Aldrich writing in *Prudence Palfrey* (1874–85) of: 'The poor old parson's interminable ninthlies and finallies,' and there is a 'fifthly and lastly' dated 1681. In Sir Walter Scott, *Kenilworth*, Chap. 4 (1821), there is this, of a collection of old books: 'They are popish trash, every one of them, – private studies of the mumping old Abbot of Abingdon. The nineteenthly of a pure gospel sermon were a cart-load of such rakings of the kennel of Rome.' Benjamin Franklin, in 1745, concludes his *Reasons for Preferring an Elderly Mistress* with: 'Eighth and lastly. They are so grateful!!' Ultimately, the origin for all this must be the kind of legal nonsense-talk parodied by Shakespeare's Dogberry in *Much Ado About Nothing* (1598): 'Marry, sir, they have committed false report; moreover, they have spoken untruths; secondarily, they are slanders; *sixthly and lastly*, they have belied a lady; thirdly, they have verified unjust things; and to conclude, they are lying knaves.'

nip and tuck Neck and neck, as in a race. Of American origin. In the 1830s/40s, it was variously 'rip and tuck', 'nip and tack', 'nick and tack' and 'nip and chuck', but it had reached its best-known form by 1857. A suggested origin is from fencing where a 'nip' is a light touch and 'tuck' (from the Italian *tocco*, touch) a heavier one. In the late 20th century, the phrase would appear to have been applied to tailoring or clothes-making, where a nip and tuck represented a small adjustment. From this (by 1978), it was also sometimes used jokingly with reference to what had been done in plastic surgery (an American cable TV show about plastic surgeons was called *Nip/Tuck* from 2003).

nipped in the bud Meaning, 'arrested or checked at the very start'. Known by 1606. Listed in the *The Independent* (24 December 1994) as a cliché of newspaper editorials. 'A promising career was virtually nipped in the bud when the leg-spinner was savaged – chiefly by Aamir Sohail and Javed Miandad – and finished with match figures of 33–0–184–0' – *Daily Mail* (27 June 1994); 'When covering by Pritchard twice nipped danger in the bud, even these worker Bees began to drone in the heat' – *The Observer* (7 May 1995).

(a/the) nipple count The number of pin-ups' nipples shown per issue in 1970s' Britain when *The Sun* and other newspapers began a circulation 'war' in which this was of importance (compare BODY COUNT in the Vietnam War). The American drive-in movie critic Joe Bob Briggs, who wrote for the *Dallas Times Herald* in the 1980s (see JOE BOB SAYS CHECK IT OUT), literally counted the *breasts* he saw and rated the films accordingly. He did not actually use this phrase, though.

'no answer' came the stern reply!
Ironic comment on the fact that no one has replied or said a word. Known by the 1930s but in various forms, including: '"No answer, no answer" came the loud reply' and **'shrieks of silence' was the stern**

reply. If these are quotations, the original source has not been identified. Compare, however, 'But answer came there none – / And this was scarcely odd, because / They'd eaten every one' – Lewis Carroll, *Through the Looking Glass* (1872) – 'The Walrus and the Carpenter' episode. 'But answer came there none' is a phrase that also appears in Scott's *The Bridal of Triermain* (1813) and almost in Shakespeare, 'But answer made it none' – *Hamlet*, I.ii.215(1600–1). It has also been suggested that the phrase might have been a joke response to the opening question in Walter De La Mare's poem 'The Listeners' (1912): '"Is there anybody there?" said the Traveller, / Knocking on the moonlit door.' The actual answer in the poem is '"Tell them I came, and no one answered, / That I kept my word," he said.'

no better than she should be Phrase of understated criticism, established by 1815 and probably much older. Motteux's translation (1712) of Cervantes's *Don Quixote* (Bk III, Chap. 20) has: 'The shepherd fell out with his sweetheart . . . thought her no better than she should be, a little loose in the hilts, and free of her behaviour.' A construction almost invariably applied to women and their morals. Beaumont and Fletcher, *The Coxcomb*, Act 4, Sc. 3 (1612), have: 'You are no better than you should be.' A cartoon caption from James Thurber, *Men, Women and Dogs* (1943), is: 'She used to be no better than she ought to be, but she is now.'

no blade of grass Phrase for a lack of vegetation – with no precise origin. The nearest the Bible gets is Isaiah 15:6: 'The grass faileth, there is no green thing.' Lord Palmerston, quoted in *The Daily Telegraph* (1864), said: 'I had at one time nearly 1,000 acres of blowy sand where no blade of grass grew.' Amelia B. Edwards in *A Thousand Miles Up the Nile* (1877) writes: 'The barren desert hems us in to right and left, with never a blade of green between the rock and the river.' A 1902 citation of an old Turkish proverb in *ODP* is: 'Where the hoof of the Turkish horse treads, no blade of grass ever grows.' From W. H. Auden's poem 'The Shield of Achilles' (1952): 'A plain without a feature, bare and brown, / No blade of grass, no sign of neighbourhood, / Nothing to eat and nowhere to sit down.' Other examples are found in Agatha Christie's *Autobiography* (1977): 'There was no scrap of garden anywhere. All was asphalt. No blade of grass showed green,' and from *The Life of Kenneth Tynan* by Kathleen Tynan (1987): 'I felt there was nothing about the country in Ken at all. Not a blade of grass . . .' *No Blade of Grass* was used as the title of a film (UK 1970) about worldwide food shortages brought about by industrial pollution and based on a book by John Christopher called *The Death of Grass* (1956).

(the) noble science Fencing or boxing. Also 'the noble art of self-defence'. In Beaumont and Fletcher's play *Knight of the Burning Pestle* (1607), there is: 'A bold defiance / Shall meet him, were he of the noble science.' The format 'noble science of —' has been widely applied to other interests.

nobody expects the Spanish Inquisition! Spoken by Cardinal Ximenez of Spain (Michael Palin) as a running gag in BBC TV, *Monty Python's Flying Circus* (22 September 1970). Whenever somebody exclaims, on being questioned closely about something, 'I didn't expect the Spanish Inquisition', the door flies open and a group of cardinals rush in. In turn used as a catchphrase in the film *Sliding Doors* (UK 1998).

nobody's perfect Phrase pleasantly excusing (usually) another's failings. From George Eliot, *Middlemarch*, Chap. 25 (1871–2): '"I'm afraid Fred is not to be trusted, Mary," said the father . . . "Well, well, nobody's perfect, but . . ."' The last lines of the film *Some Like It Hot* (US 1959) have Jack Lemmon (in drag) explaining to a potential husband why they should not marry – 'she' is not a woman. Unflustered by this, Joe E. Brown as an old millionaire says, 'Nobody's perfect.'

nobody tells me anything Lament of the uninformed. It is the stock phrase of James Forsyte in John Galsworthy, *The Man of Property* (1906) and *In Chancery* (1920). James, a brother of Old Jolyon, is an old man even when the Forsyte Saga begins. A solicitor and founder of the firm 'Forsyte,

Bustard and Forsyte', he is the father of Soames, the quasi-villain of the piece, and seeks to distance himself from the uncomfortable goings-on in the family with this phrase. In the form **nobody tells me nothing** (or, possibly, 'nobody tells no one nothing'), it was a catchphrase of Dan Dungeon, the gloomy Liverpudlian (played by Deryck Guyler) in the BBC radio show *ITMA* (1939–49).

no change there then Phrase used by Angus Deayton as chairman of BBC TV, *Have I Got News For You* (1990–2002) as a comment on some assertion that has been reported. '"Jeffrey Archer has no active role in politics these days . . ." No change there then . . .' 'Formerly smug TV face Angus Deayton, said to be making a comeback after revelations about his prostitution and cocaine habit. The show is apparently entitled *Wild Girls On Snow*. So no change there, then . . .' – *Independent on Sunday* (23 February 2003).

no comment Useful phrase, when people in the news are being hounded by journalists, and not quite condemned as a cliché. After all, why should people in such a position be required to find something original to say? Nevertheless, it has come to be used as a consciously inadequate form of evasion, often in an obviously jokey way (compare WE ARE JUST GOOD FRIENDS). The phrase probably arose by way of reaction to the ferretings of Hollywood gossip columnists in the 1920s and 30s, though perhaps it was simply a general reaction to the rise of the popular press in the first half of the 20th century. Winston Churchill appears not to have known it until 1946, so perhaps it was not generally known until then, at least not outside the USA? After a meeting with President Truman, Churchill said, 'I think "No Comment" is a splendid expression. I got it from Sumner Welles.' Also in 1946, critic C. A. Lejeune's entire review of the US film *No Leave, No Love* was 'No comment'. A good example of the phrase in something like straightforward use can be found in a terse broadcast interview conducted with Kim Philby on 10 November 1955 after the diplomat had been cleared of being the 'Third Man' in the Burgess/Maclean spy case. He later defected to Moscow in 1963 and was shown to have been a liar and a spy all along: *Interviewer*: 'Mr Philby, Mr Macmillan, the Foreign Secretary, said there was no evidence that you were the so-called "third man" who allegedly tipped off Burgess and Maclean. Are you satisfied with that clearance that he gave you?' *Philby*: 'Yes, I am.' *Interviewer*: 'Well, if there was a "third man", were you in fact the "third man"?' *Philby*: 'No, I was not.' *Interviewer*: 'Do you think there was one?' *Philby*: 'No comment.' Martha 'The Mouth' Mitchell, the blabber who helped get the Watergate investigations under way and who was the wife of President Nixon's disgraced Attorney-General, once declared: 'I don't believe in that "no comment" business. I always have a comment' (quoted 1979). Desmond Wilcox, a TV executive, came up with a variant for the TV age in 1980. When ducking a question, he said, 'Sorry, your camera's run out of film.' The *Financial Times* for many years has used the slogan 'No *FT*. . . no comment' (current 1982). 'Mr [Norman] Willis [TUC General Secretary at book award ceremony] is not going to rock the boat by descending to literary chat. "No comment," he says vigorously when asked if he has read any of the short-listed books' – *The Guardian* (25 January 1989).

no fear! I.e. 'certainly not, not on your life!' – an emphatic refusal. Known by 1887, but it seems to have grown out of 'there is no fear of something happening . . .'; 'I invite him to dinner! And in his own hotel! No fear!' – Arnold Bennett, *Imperial Palace*, Chap. 12 (1930).

no good deed goes unpunished Consciously ironic rewriting of the older expression 'No *bad* deed goes unpunished' – surely proverbial but unrecorded in *ODP* or *CODP*. Joe Orton recorded in his diary for 13 June 1967: 'Very good line George [Greeves] came out with at dinner: "No good deed ever goes unpunished".' Earlier, before opening in Noël Coward's *Waiting in the Wings*, Marie Lohr went to church and prayed for a good first night. On her way to the theatre she slipped and broke her leg. 'No good deed ever goes unpunished,' was Coward's comment. James Agate in *Ego 3* (for 25 January 1938)

states: '[Isidore Leo] Pavia was in great form today: "Every good deed brings its own punishment".' The remark has also been ascribed to Oscar Wilde and, whether or not it is one of his, it is a perfect example of the inversion technique used in so many of his witticisms.

no guts, no glory It has been reported that when playing golf, people will sometimes say to themselves, before trying a difficult shot, 'No guts, no glory', occasionally followed by 'No failure, no story.' The *Scribner Dictionary of Soldier Talk* (1984) has this as Second World War slang; Mieder & Co.'s *Dictionary of American Proverbs* also has it; and Eric Partridge's *Slang* dictionary has simply 'No guts!' – 'a derisive exhortation' since the 1920s.

no harm in asking Catchphrase in such situations as 'Would you like to go to bed with me? No? Well, no harm in asking' and 'Does she go then? No harm in asking' – *Slanguage* (1984). *Partridge/Catch Phrases* suggests it has been around since the late 19th century.

(the) noise and the people! Mock exclamation of dismay at crowded conditions, derived from what a certain Captain Strahan supposedly said after the Battle of Bastogne (1944): 'Oh, my dear fellow, the noise . . . and the people!' – according to the *ODQ* (1979), quoting the *Hudson Review* (Winter, 1951). Various correspondents have suggested it was earlier in the war than this, however. Roy T. Kendall wrote (1986): 'I heard this phrase used, in a humorous manner, during the early part of 1942. It was related to me as having been said by a young Guards officer, newly returned from Dunkirk, who on being asked what it was like used the expression: the inference being, a blasé attitude to the dangers and a disdain of the common soldiery he was forced to mix with.' Tony Bagnall Smith added that the Guards officer was still properly dressed and equipped when he said it, and that his reply was: 'My dear, the noise and the people – how they smelt!' The *ODQ* (1992) appears to have come round to the earlier use regarding Dunkirk, in the form 'The noise, my dear! And the people!' It finds it already being quoted in Anthony Rhodes,

Sword of Bone, Chap. 22 (1942). Another originator is said to be Lord Sefton, a Guards officer at Dunkirk (suggested in letters in *The London Review of Books* beginning 29 October 1998). In the same correspondence, an assertion reappeared that it was something said by the actor Ernest Thesiger at a dinner party in 1919 regarding his experiences as a soldier in the battle of the Somme.

no likey? oh, crikey! Catchphrase from the BBC radio show *ITMA* (1939–49). Usually said by Ali Oop (Horace Percival), the show's saucy postcard vendor who frequently rhymed English idioms like 'Very jolly – oh golly!' or 'Your hands are grimy' / 'Grimy? Oh, blimey!' Peter Black, the TV critic, once wrote: 'This lunatic exchange sank so deeply into the minds of the girl I was to marry and myself that we still use it thirty years later.'

(there is) no love lost between us Tony Lumpkin says to his mother, Mrs Hardcastle, in Oliver Goldsmith, *She Stoops To Conquer,* Act 4, Sc. 1 (1773): 'As for murmurs, mother, we grumble a little now and then, to be sure. But there's no love lost between us.' The editor of the New Mermaids edition (1979) states that Goldsmith coined the phrase 'No love lost', but this is true neither of the literal sense nor of the modern ironic, opposite one. The *OED2* finds uses of the phrase in both senses over a century before Goldsmith's play.

no man's land Phrase for unowned, waste land (current by 1320) but more recently used to describe the space between entrenched armies (as in the First World War). *No Man's Land* was the title of a play (1974) by Harold Pinter and an unrelated film (US 1987).

no more chance than (or as much chance as) a snowball (or snowflake) in Hell (or Hades) *Mencken* (1942) has the first of these versions listed as an 'American saying'. It had been recorded by 1931. In the form 'Gloom hasn't got a snowball's chance in Hades', the line occurs in Stephen Graham, *London Nights* (1925). Either way, *Partridge/Catch Phrases* thinks the expression dates from about 1900.

no more Latin, no more French (no more sitting on a hard board bench) (or the old school bench) I learnt this rhyme at school in the 1950s – the sort of thing you said before the holidays began. It turns out to be the second half of a verse which – in the USA – begins, 'No more lessons, no more books./ No more teacher's sassy looks' – at least in the 'schoolboy's song, *circa* 1850', quoted by *Mencken*. In the *Lore and Language of Schoolchildren* (1959), Iona and Peter Opie print two lengthy 'breaking up' rhymes current in Britain this century. Both include these two lines.

no more Mr Nice Guy 'Mr Nice Guy' is a nickname applied to 'straight' figures (especially politicians) who may be succeeding someone who is palpably not 'nice' (Gerald Ford after Richard Nixon, for example). They then sometimes feel the need to throw off some of their virtuous image, as presidential challenger Senator Ed Muskie did in 1972 – and his aides declared, 'No more Mr Nice Guy.' In April 1973, Alice Cooper had a song in the British charts entitled 'No More Mr Nice Guy'. *Safire* dates to the 'mid-1950s' the joke about Hitler agreeing to make a comeback with the words, 'But this time – no more Mr Nice Guy.'

no more war Recurring slogan, mostly in the 20th century. At the United Nations in 1965, Pope Paul VI quoted President Kennedy 'four years ago' to the effect that 'mankind must put an end to war, or war will put an end to mankind . . . No more war, never again war.' (He said this in Italian.) Earlier, the phrase was used by Winston Churchill at the end of a letter to Lord Beaverbrook in 1928 (quoted in Martin Gilbert's biography of Churchill, Vol. 5). A. J. P. Taylor in his *English History 1914–45* suggests that the slogan was 'irresistible' at the end of the First World War. In *Goodbye to Berlin* (1939), Christopher Isherwood describes a Nazi book-burning. The books are from a 'small liberal pacifist publisher'. One of the Nazis holds up a book called '*Nie wieder Krieg*' as though it were 'a nasty kind of reptile'. 'No More War!' a fat, well-dressed woman laughs scornfully and savagely, 'What an idea!'

no names, no packdrill I.e., I am not going to betray any confidences by mentioning names. Somehow this alludes to a sometime British army punishment when soldiers were made to march up and down carrying a heavy pack – a very physical punishment for use in the field where fines or confinement to barracks would be meaningless or impossible. It is probably a short way of saying, 'As long as I don't give away any names, I won't get punished for it – that's why I am not telling you.' Recorded by 1923. Paul Beale gave this even lengthier paraphrase (1988): 'I will tell you this discreditable story, because it is a good story and shows the criminal ingenuity, or at least low cunning, of some people I know. But I won't tell you their names (even though you might guess who they are) because I don't want *them* to get into trouble – after all they are my mates, my muckers, and I'm only telling you so that you can admire their cleverness: it's all "off the record".' Beale added: 'Only secondarily was there any implication of "*I* don't want to get punished", except in as far as "the mates" might round on an informant. It's really an expression of the old army muckers-stick-together, and to hell with anyone of any rank higher than private/trooper/gunner/ sapper or effing fusilier.' 'As British Ambassador in Helsinki . . . I once entertained some distinguished Finns and a visiting British bishop (no names, no packdrill) to the Finnish social habit of a sauna' – letter to the editor, *The Times* (14 August 1999).

none but the lonely heart (or weary heart) *None But the Lonely Heart* is the title of a novel (1943; film US 1944) by Richard Llewellyn and is apparently an original coinage, but compare 'None But the Weary Heart', the English title often given to a song by Tchaikovsky (Op. 6, No. 6). The lyrics of this song have been translated into English as 'None but the weary heart can understand how I have suffered and how I am tormented'. It originated as 'Mignon's Song' in the novel *Wilhelm Meister* by Goethe – '*Nur wer die Sehnsucht kennt* [only those who know what longing is]' – which was translated into Russian by Mey.

(she's) no oil painting Phrase for an unattractive woman (rarely of a man). Possibly dating from the 1930s – *Slanguage*.

no one likes us, we don't care Phrase from the new lyrics sung by fans of Millwall football club to the tune of the Rod Stewart song 'Sailing'. Millwall fans are famous in London for their vocal and physical forcefulness. *No One Likes Us, We Don't Care* was, consequently, the title given to a Channel 4 TV documentary about them in January 1990.

no pains See IF IT ISN'T HURTING.

no peace for the wicked (or no rest ...)! Light-hearted exclamation by someone who is being harried by demands from other people or snowed under with work. By the 19th century, possibly in imitation of certain biblical passages, e.g. Isaiah 48:22: 'There is no peace, saith the Lord, unto the wicked' and 57:21: 'There is no peace, saith my God, to the wicked'.

(there are) no pockets in shrouds Rebuke to a person who believes that money is for hoarding, not spending. R. C. Trench, *On Lessons in Proverbs* (1854) refers to an Italian proverb: 'With an image Dantesque in its vigour, that "a man shall carry nothing away with him when he dieth", take this Italian, *Our last robe . . .* is made *without pockets*.' In English nowadays, this proverb is more usually 'Shrouds have no pockets.'

no Popery (no tyranny, no wooden shoes) Slogan. The writer Daniel Defoe (1660– 1731) said that there were a hundred thousand fellows in his time ready to fight to the death against Popery – without knowing whether Popery was a man or a horse. After the initial impact of the Restoration had worn off, this was the cry that came to be heard. The wife of Charles II, Catherine of Braganza, was a Roman Catholic and so was his brother (later James II), and they were surrounded by priests. The Great Fire of London (1666) was said to have been caused by papist action and foreign interference. Hence, the anti-Roman Catholicism of the slogan coupled with a general English distrust of foreigners (wooden shoes = French *sabots*). The variation **no Jews, no wooden**

shoes (obviously rhyming slang) arose in 1753 when an anti-Jewish Bill was before Parliament. The cry 'No Popery' is chiefly associated, however, with the Gordon Riots of 1780, when Lord George Gordon fomented a violent protest against legislation that had lightened penalties on Roman Catholics. The riots in London were put down by George III's troops (and form the background to Charles Dickens's novel *Barnaby Rudge*). The slogan was again used by supporters of the Duke of Portland's government opposed to Catholic Emancipation in 1807.

no problem! Ubiquitous filler phrase, particularly when a request has been put to a worker in the service industries (hotel porters, wait-persons and so on). *American Speech* first noticed it in 1963 when discussing the similar phrase 'no sweat'. It has spread like a virus (since the 1970s?) in place of the straightforward 'I will do that for you', 'Yes' or 'OK'. Sometimes it seems to be the case that the reputation of English as the international language is based on the prolific use of this one phrase. A welcome variation was the cod-Hispanic 'No problemo' in the film *Terminator 2: Judgment Day* (US 1991).

no questions asked Promise of collusion over a deal that probably involves wrongdoing. Apparently, the British Larceny Act of 1861 banned anew the use of this phrase in newspaper personal columns. Modern use is more generally applied in situations where people are being told they will not have to account for their conduct. 'Nine out of ten of them had views on Art which would have admitted them to any looney-bin, and no questions asked' – P. G. Wodehouse, *The Indiscretions of Archie* (1921).

normal See DO NOT ADJUST.

normalcy See BACK TO.

no room at the inn Alluding to the birth of Jesus Christ in Luke 2:7: 'And laid him in a manger; because there was no room for them in the inn.' *No Room at the Inn* was the title of a film (UK 1948), based on a play by Joan Temple, about a woman who mistreats evacuees and turns her house into a brothel.

no room to swing a cat Phrase to describe a confined space. As is well known, the 'cat' was the name given on old sailing vessels to a whip used in discipline. It left scars on the back reminiscent of a cat's scratches. A sailor condemned to be so punished had to be taken up on deck because below deck there literally was no room to swing the whip. Some still believe, however, that the expression merely refers to the amount of space in which you could swing an actual cat around by its tail. This may in fact be the true original. Known by 1665. 'Mrs Crupp had indignantly assured him that there wasn't room to swing a cat there; but, as Mr Dick justly observed to me, sitting down on the foot of the bed, nursing his leg, "You know, Trotwood, I don't want to swing a cat. I never do swing a cat. Therefore, what does that signify to *me*!"' – Charles Dickens, *David Copperfield*, Chap. 35 (1850).

north by northwest Meaning, 'mad', and used obliquely as the title of Alfred Hitchcock's film *North by Northwest* (US 1959) in which Cary Grant feigns madness. The film title may also allude to a slogan of the American airline Northwest. The phrase is a slight adjustment of Hamlet's words in Shakespeare's play, II.ii.374 (1600–1): 'I am but mad north-north-west. When the wind is southerly, I know a hawk from a handsaw.'

(a) Northern fastness Quasi-literary phrase for a stronghold. Always in the North, never the South. Date of origin unknown. 'In four countries – Greenland, Finland, Norway and Sweden – you can visit Santa centres where you can meet the "real" Santa Claus in his "real" Northern fastness' – *Financial Times* (24 December 1994).

north of Watford Meaning 'beyond the edge of civilization' and referring to a town on the northwest of the London conurbation. The *OED2* definition is unbeatable: 'Used with allusion to the view (attributed to Londoners) that north of the metropolis there is nothing of any significance to English national or cultural life.' Recorded by 1973. Compare WOGS BEGIN AT BARNET.

(the) North-South divide Political phrase for (1) the perceived difference in living standards between the developed nations (mostly to be found in the northern hemisphere) and the underdeveloped nations in the southern hemisphere. Recorded by 1980. (2) the division between the prosperous south of England and the rest of the country. In a speech on 4 February 1927, Winston Churchill said: 'I saw a comparison made in the "Nation" newspaper of the conditions prevailing north and south of a line which the writer had drawn across the country from Cardiff to Hull.'

Norwegian Wood Nickname applied to Walter Mondale (b. 1928), US Vice-President (1977–81) during his unsuccessful bid for the presidency in 1984, because of his ancestry and his stiff manner. The name alludes to the title of a John Lennon song where the relevance of the phrase is not easily explained. In an oblique recounting of an affair, perhaps 'Norwegian wood' had some talismanic significance. Maybe it was the wood in the girl's apartment.

NORWICH [(K)Nickers Off Ready When I Come Home] Lovers' acronym for use in correspondence and to avoid military censorship. In use by the First World War?

nose See CUT OFF YOUR.

no sex please – we're British Derived from the title of a long-running farce (London 1971–1987; film UK 1973) by Anthony Marriott and Alistair Foot. Much alluded to by headline writers and such. 'As Ken Livingstone said, "One of the things missing from this election was a sense of humour." No jokes, please, we're British' – *The Independent* (23 April 1992); 'No Opera Please – We're British' – chapter heading in *The State of the Language*, eds Ricks & Michaels (1991); 'No pecks [kisses] please, we're British' – headline in *Harpers & Queen* (September 1994).

(a) nosey parker Meaning, 'an interfering, inquisitive person', from the fact that the nose has long been associated with an inquisitive nature. Traditionally, a link has been suggested with Matthew Parker, Elizabeth I's Archbishop of Canterbury.

But *Partridge/Slang* wonders whether the word 'parker', meaning 'park-keeper', might also have described someone who enjoyed spying on love-making couples in London's Hyde Park. Not found before 1907, however.

no skin off one's nose Phrase suggesting that one is not going to be affected by something; it is a matter of indifference to one. Possibly alluding to a fight in which one has not suffered the injury in question. Probably American in origin and known by 1926 – though the first appearance in a Sinclair Lewis novel (1920) is in the form, 'No skin off my ear'. Charles Dickens, *Hard Times*, Chap. 16 (1854), has: 'If she takes it in the fainting way, I'll have the skin off her nose at all events!' Mr Bounderby has armed himself with a bottle of smelling salts before imparting bad news. The meaning of 'the skin off her nose' is not too clear here. It almost anticipates the later toast, 'Here's to the skin off your nose!' This last has also been described as a theatrical greeting and said to refer to the bad old days of make-up that affected the skin. If you said it to an actor, it meant you wished he be kept in work. However, it was recorded by 1925 as a toast and the actors' use may simply have been a borrowing of this.

nostalgie de la boue Desire for degradation. Literally, a 'longing to be back in the mud'. In the play *Le Mariage d'Olympe* (1855), Émile Augier gave this as an explanation of what happens when you put a duck on a lake with swans. He will miss his own pond and eventually return to it. *Marquis: 'Mettez un canard sur un lac au milieu des cygnes, vous verrez qu'il regrettera sa mare et finira par y retourner.' Montrichard: 'La nostalgie de la boue!'* At the very end of D. H. Lawrence, *Lady Chatterley's Lover* (1928), Sir Clifford says to Lady Connie: 'You're one of those half-insane, perverted women who must run after depravity, the *nostalgie de la boue.*'

(there's) no such thing as a free lunch Old American expression meaning 'There's no getting something for nothing' and dating back to the mid-19th century. *Flexner* (1976) puts an 1840s' date on the supply of a 'free lunch' in saloon bars – even if they were no more than thirst-arousing snacks like pretzels. This was not strictly speaking 'free' because you had to buy beer to obtain it. The precise phrase was quoted by Burton Crane in *The Sophisticated Investor* (1959). It was also attributed to the University of Chicago school of economists by Paul Samuelson in *Newsweek* (29 December 1969). Indeed, the notion was given a new lease of life in the 1970s by the economist Milton Friedman therefrom, and the saying was sometimes ascribed to him by virtue of the fact that he published a book with the title, and wrote articles and gave lectures incorporating the phrase. When Margaret Thatcher and Ronald Reagan attempted to embrace, up to a point, Friedman's monetarist thinking, the phrase was trotted out by their acolytes. (In Thatcher's case, according to press reports, specific instructions were given for ministers to drop it into their speeches.) In July 1989, US Representative Richard Gephardt, commenting on the announcement of a new American goal in space, commented: 'We don't have the economic strength we need to make it a reality . . . there is no such thing as a free launch.'

no surrender! Slogan. In 1689, the year after the Catholic King James II was replaced by the Protestant William of Orange on the British throne, forces still loyal to James maintained a siege against the citizens of Derry in Ulster. The siege was raised after a month or two. 'No surrender!' was the Protestant slogan, and 'Long Live Ulster. No surrender' is still a Loyalist slogan. Another version is: 'No Popery, no surrender.' *No Surrender* was the title of a 1985 film written by Alan Bleasdale about warring Protestant and Roman Catholic factions in Liverpool.

not —— Format used in the TV comedy show *Not the Nine O'Clock News* (UK 1979–82) which was broadcast on BBC2 opposite the *Nine O'Clock News* on BBC1. Accordingly, there were several British derivatives, e.g. *Not Private Eye* (1986), a spoof of the satirical magazine brought out by some of its supposed victims, and *Not Yet the Times* – when the actual newspaper *The Times* was not being published 1978–9.

In fact, the model for all these titles was *Not the New York Times*, a spoof on the newspaper, published in 1978.

——, not! Word tacked on to a statement and instantly negating its meaning. For example, 'I believe you – NOT!' During the 1992 US presidential election, Democrats distributed lapel badges with the slogan 'Vote Republican. Not'. A Nike poster campaign had the slogan: 'Most excellent colours for Wimbledon. Not!' And so on. The usage was introduced by the comedy performer and writer Mike Myers, particularly through his film *Wayne's World* (US 1992; sequel 1994), based on a segment in the NBC TV show *Saturday Night Live* (from 1989) in which Myers and Dana Carvey played Wayne and Garth, urban teenagers who were 'into' various aspects of pop culture, particularly Heavy Metal, and ran their own cable TV show from a basement den. Myers later commented: '"Not" was something my brother used to say to me, to torment me. And suddenly [George] Bush is saying it to torment the whole of the free world.' Catchwords and catchphrases are thick on the ground in *Wayne's World*, including: **Excellent!** and **Party on!** and the call/response **No way?!/Way!** The wail **We're not worthy, we're not worthy!** goes up when the pair fall to their knees before such idols as Madonna, Alice Cooper and Aerosmith. Some of the phrases had earlier appeared in the films *Bill and Ted's Excellent Adventure* (1988) and *Bill and Ted's Bogus Journey* (1991), unconnected with *Wayne's World*, suggesting that all the phrases may have originated in actual teenage slang.

not a dry eye in the house Exaggerated comment on an effective performance or speech that has palpably moved an audience to tears. 'They were deeply affected, and not a dry eye was to be seen in the assembly' – William H. Prescott, *Philip II* (1855); '"Held them spellbound" . . . "Cold," said young Tuppy, "Not a dry eye"' – P. G. Wodehouse, *Very Good, Jeeves!* (1930).

not a happy bunny Comment on a person's miserable state. Possibly of American origin. Remembered by some from the 1960s/70s, though the earliest citation found is only 1991. Maybe alluding to a children's story or to the 'Happy Bunny' character in Energizer battery advertisements whose battery lasted longer than its competitors? 'After being led away in handcuffs for speaking out at a shareholders' meeting, Nigel Watts is not a happy bunny' – *The Sunday Times* (7 November 1993).

not a lot   Catchphrase of the Yorkshire magician and comedian Paul Daniels (b. 1938). In 1979 he recalled finding it early on in his career. He was being heckled by someone who did not like his act. 'A pity,' he said, 'because I like your suit. Not a lot, but I like it.'

not a million miles from ——   Venerable phrase of ironic exaggeration – meaning, 'very close to'. Much used in this form by *Private Eye* since the 1960s, though traditionally the number of miles has been a hundred. Nelson's *English Idioms* (referring to about 1890) explains 'not a hundred miles off/from' thus: 'A phrase often used to avoid a direct reference to any place. The place itself or its immediate neighbourhood is always intended . . . the phrase is also used of events not far distant in time.' The example given is from H. Rider Haggard: 'From all of which wise reflections the reader will gather that our friend Arthur was not a hundred miles off an awkward situation.' 'Mr C's address is not a hundred miles from here, sir' – Charles Dickens, *Bleak House*, Chap. 51 (1853); 'Girls are sometimes inclined to be vain. I know a little girl not a hundred miles from this room who was so proud of her new panties that she ran out in the street in them' – P. G. Wodehouse, 'Portrait of a Disciplinarian' (1927); *Casson/Grenfell* (1972) has the nannyism: 'There's someone not a hundred miles from here who's being rather stupid.' Peter Cook is credited in *The Life and Times of Private Eye* (1971) with introducing 'not a million miles from the truth' to the magazine. Another, almost facetious, variant appears in the *Private Eye* phrase, **a sum not unadjacent to . . .** (meaning, 'a sum very near to . . .')

not a penny more, not a penny less   The exact sum of money being pursued or demanded. The *OED2* finds only the phrase 'not a penny more' in use, on its own, in 1931, but the whole phrase appears in Act 2 of Shaw's *Pygmalion* (1914) (and also in *My Fair Lady*). Alfred Doolittle says to Henry Higgins: 'What's a five-pound note to you? And what's Eliza to me? . . . You give me what I ask you, Governor: not a penny more, and not a penny less.' Before this, it may have been a phrase from market traders' patter. The title of Jeffrey Archer's first novel (1975) was *Not a Penny More, Not a Penny Less* (1975) and told of winning back money from people who had cheated the principal character of it (based on Archer's own experiences).

not a pretty sight   Phrase of understatement for something that looks ugly, horrible, a mess or for simply something the speaker wishes to criticize. Possibly from parodies of old British imperial-speak. Perhaps usually said about the appearance of a body that has been involved in an accident or death. In the BBC radio *Goon Show,* 'The Yehti' (8 March 1955) and, indeed, in most editions. Observed by Fritz Spiegl in an article on drama cliché lines in *The Listener* (7 February 1985). 'The swelling's gone down . . . Not a pretty sight, is it, Fiona?' – BBC radio, *Round the Horne* (15 May 1966); 'Take a long, hard look at this picture. No, it's not a pretty sight but, sad to say, it's the brutal face of Britain, 1994' – *The People* (11 September 1994); 'In-yer-face investment banking, as practised by Swiss Bank Corporation, is not a pretty sight. Swiss Bank has specialised in upsetting the City's establishment, rather as S. G. Warburg did 30 years ago' – *The Daily Telegraph* (14 January 1995).

not as we know it   See IT'S LIFE.

not a word about the pig (and how it died and whose small potatoes it ate)   'My grandmother (92) has this saying – I'd love to know where it comes from' – Kate Pool (1995). The only clue I have found is a headline in *Punch* (20 August 1864) – 'Not a Word About the Pig'. *Partridge/Slang* has 'Not a word of the pudding' = 'say nothing about the matter', dated late 17th century.

not as a stranger   Phrase as in the title of

Morton Thompson's novel *Not As a Stranger* (1954) and the film made from it (US 1955). The song that came out of the film goes, 'Not as a stranger, dear, but my own true love . . .' Possibly derived from the 1928 Episcopal Prayer Book's translation of Job 19:25–27 (in the Burial of the Dead): 'I know that my redeemer liveth . . . and though this body be destroyed, yet shall I see God: whom I shall see for myself, and mine eyes shall behold, and not as a stranger.' The Anglican Prayer Book takes from the Authorized Version of the Bible the less striking 'and not another'. So, perhaps Morton Thompson was familiar with the Episcopal Prayer Book of 1928 (it is not in earlier versions) and took it from there.

no taxation without representation Slogan current before the American War of Independence and, in the form 'Taxation without representation is tyranny', attributed to the lawyer and statesman James Otis in 1763. He opposed British taxation of the American colonies on the grounds that they were not represented in the British House of Commons. Compare Arnold Toynbee's 1947 remark, pressing for a greater British role in the United Nations: 'No annihilation without representation.'

not bloody likely! Phrase of emphatic refusal and a famous quotation from George Bernard Shaw's play *Pygmalion* (1914): *Freddy*: 'Are you walking across the Park, Miss Doolittle? If so —' *Liza*: 'Walk! Not bloody likely.' (*Sensation*)'. The shock of the original was that it was uttered at a polite tea party and the word 'bloody' had rarely, if ever, been uttered on the British stage. The euphemistic 'Not Pygmalion likely' had a certain currency in the 1920s. By the time *My Fair Lady* – the musical version – was filmed in 1964, the shock effect of 'bloody' was so mild that Liza was given the line 'Come on, Dover, move your bloomin' arse!' in the Ascot racing sequence.

not by a long chalk Meaning 'not by any means', this probably refers to the method of making chalk marks on the floor to show the score of a player or team. A 'long chalk' would mean a lot of points, a

great deal. Other explanations refer specifically to keeping the score at darts and to the tally of beers drunk in a public house. Originally, the expression may have been 'by long chalks'. Known by 1835.

not for all the tea in China 'Under no circumstances, not for anything'. A 19th-century phrase that *Partridge/Slang* (1937 edition) seemed to think was Australian in origin, and *OED2* took this up but with no firm evidence. Compare **not for a big clock!** 'I would not do it – not for a big inducement!' – British use by the 1980s.

nothing acts faster than Anadin See TENSE NERVOUS.

nothing in his life became him like the leaving it Phrase in obituary and tribute use. An allusion to Shakespeare, *Macbeth*, I.iv.7 (1606), where Malcolm says it of the murdered Thane of Cawdor, and adds: '. . . he died / As one that had been studied in his death, / To throw away the dearest thing he ow'd, / As 'twere a careless trifle.' Sometimes adapted and used figuratively to describe the way a person has relinquished a position with dignity. 'So farewell then, Kelvin. Nothing became Sydney Carton's life so well as the leaving of it, and that must surely be true of Kelvin's disappearance from the Sky' – *The Guardian* (5 August 1994); 'Yesterday, Reynolds's detractors – Spring, Bruton and Harney included – sang fulsome praises of the man they had just buried [rather, the Irish Prime Minister they had just forced out of office]. 'You have done your best, Taoiseach . . . You have stood up for the family in Irish life . . . Nothing became him so well as his leaving . . . It was his finest hour, and so on' – *The Times* (18 November 1994).

(there is) nothing new under the sun Weary exclamation when something occurs yet again or there is no sign of originality. Based on Ecclesiastes 1:9: 'There is no new thing under the sun.'

nothing over sixpence Slogan. The first British Woolworth's opened in 1909 and was described as a 'threepence and sixpence' store, the equivalent of the 'five-and-ten' (cent) stores in the USA. Hence the phrase 'nothing over sixpence' arose and endured until the Second World War, when prices could no longer be contained below this limit. A song 'There's Nothing Over Sixpence in the Store' (1927), written by W. S. Frank and Frank S. Wilcock, includes the lines: 'To Woolworth's, Hobbs and Sutcliffe always go to get their bats, / Stan Baldwin gets his pipes there, and Winston gets his hats; / And the Prince would never think of going elsewhere for his spats – / And there's nothing over sixpence in the stores!' Aneurin Bevan once said (1930s): 'Listening to a speech by [Neville] Chamberlain is like paying a visit to Woolworth's – everything in its place and nothing above sixpence.'

nothing venture, nothing win Proverb. The first recorded use in this precise form is in Sir Charles Sedley's comedy *The Mulberry Garden* (1668). However, the variants 'nothing venture, nothing gain' and 'nothing venture, nothing have' go back further and may derive from a Latin original. W. S. Gilbert used this form in the 'proverb' song in Act 2 of *Iolanthe* (1882), and Sir Edmund Hillary, the mountaineer, used it as the title of his autobiography (1975).

no tickee, no washee Proverb in the form of a mock Chinese laundry rubric to the effect that you can't collect your laundry when it's done if you haven't got the ticket for it as proof. Hence, in the wider proverbial sense, you can't have something if you don't fulfil some basic condition. Known by 1931. Also as, 'No tickee, no shirtee.'

not in front of the children! Request from one grown-up to another to desist from arguing or making a scene when there are young people present. In use since the 1920s, but now mostly jocularly. When spoken in French, *pas devant les enfants*, as it sometimes is, the phrase is a rather more discreet way of achieving what the speaker wishes.

not in my back yard See NIMBY.

not lost but gone before Condolence and bereavement phrase. According to *Benham* (1907), 'Not lost but gone before' was the title of a song published in Smith's *Edinburgh Harmony* (1829), and it is one of the standard epitaphs now imprinted on countless graves. It may have been popularized by its use as the title of a poem by Caroline Norton (1808–77), which goes: 'For death and life in ceaseless strife, / Beat wild on this world's shore, / And all our calm is in that balm — / Not lost but gone before.' The variant form occurs in *Human Life* (1819) by Samuel Rogers: 'Those whom he loved so long and sees no more, / Loved, and still loves – not dead – but gone before.' However, according to *Mencken* (1942), the phrase occurs in one of Alexander Pope's epitaphs for 'Elijah Fenton, Easthampstead England' (*circa* 1731) – though this one is not included in *Pope's Poetical Works*: 'Weep not, ye mourners, for the dead, / But in this hope your spirits soar, / That ye can say of those ye mourn, / They are not lost but gone before.' And to Philip Henry (1631–96) is ascribed the couplet: 'They are not *amissi*, but *praemissi*; / Not lost but gone before.' Seneca wrote: *Non amittuntur sed praemittuntur* ('They are not lost but sent before'). So the concept is, indeed, a very old one. The simple phrase 'gone before', meaning 'dead', was well established in English by the early 16th century. In *Heaven's Command* (1973), James Morris quotes the epitaph on Lieutenant Christopher Hyland of the 62nd Regiment, who died in Bermuda in 1837: 'Alas, he is not lost, / But is gone before.' In 1982, a woman's gravestone was reported from Canada 'some years ago' that had: 'Dry up your tears, and weep no more, / I am not dead, but gone before, / Remember me, and bear in mind / You have not long to stay behind.'

not many dead In his book *In Time of Trouble* (1956) – incorporated in *I Claud . . .* (1967) – Claud Cockburn claimed to have won a competition for dullness among subeditors on *The Times* with this headline in the late 1920s: 'It had to be a genuine headline, that is to say one which was actually in the next morning's newspaper. I won it only once.' This was it: '**Small earthquake in Chile**. Not many dead.' At Cockburn's death it was said, however, that an exhaustive search had failed to find this particular headline in the paper. It may just have been a smoking-room story. However, the idea lives on. It became (perhaps inevitably) the title of a book (1972) by Alastair Horne about the Allende affair (in Chile). The journalist Michael Green called a volume of memoirs *Nobody Hurt in Small Earthquake* (1990), and the cartoonist Nicholas Garland called his 'Journal of a year in Fleet Street' *Not Many Dead* (1990). In 2000, Mark English made the intriguing discovery that in 1929 (when Cockburn started work on *The Times* in London before becoming its correspondent in New York and Washington), there occurred two similar entries in the paper's 'Telegrams in Brief' column: 'An earthquake was felt yesterday between Illapel, to the north, and Talca, to the south, in Chile. No damage was done' (6 August 1929); 'An earthquake shock was felt in Melilla [which is in Chile] on Wednesday, but no one was injured' (16 August 1929). Could Cockburn have embroidered the story in the telling and asserted that the 'Telegrams in Brief' were in fact headlines?

not many people know that Catch-phrase of the English actor (Sir) Michael Caine (b. 1933). It is rare for a personal catchphrase to catch on (as opposed to phrases in entertainment, films, advertising that are engineered to do so). But it has certainly been the case with the one that will always be associated with Caine. Peter Sellers started the whole thing off when he appeared on BBC TV's *Parkinson* show on 28 October 1972. The edition in question was subsequently released on a disc entitled *Michael Parkinson Meets the Goons*, thus enabling confirmation of what Sellers said: '"Not many people know that" . . . this is my Michael Caine impression . . . You see Mike's always quoting from *The Guinness Book of Records*. At the drop of a hat he'll trot one out. "Did you know that it takes a man in a tweed suit five-and-a-half seconds to fall from the top of Big Ben to the ground? Now there's not many people know that!"' Earlier that year, on 30 April 1972, Sellers apparently ad-libbed a 'There's not many people know that' while doing a Michael Caine accent as a police-man during the recording of the BBC radio show *The Last Goon Show Of All*. It was not until 1981–2 that the remark really caught on. Afterwards, Caine was given

the line to say as an in-joke (in the charac-ter of an inebriated university lecturer) in the film *Educating Rita* (UK 1983), and he put his name to a book of trivial facts for charity with the slight variant, *Not a Lot of People Know That!*, in 1984.

(but/though) not necessarily in that order Mostly humorous (and possibly meaningless) addition to a statement, using an old and rather pedantic formula. 'They married and had a number of children, though not necessarily in that order.' 'With that film is *The Swiss Con-spiracy* which is all about people who tax dodge, and blackmail, are blackmailed and murdered, not necessarily in that order' – *Morecambe Guardian* (7 December 1976); 'The first time someone said, "What are your measurements?" I answered, "Thirty-seven, twenty-four, thirty-eight – but not necessarily in that order' – Carol Burnett, quoted in *American Film* (1982).

not only —— but also —— Traditional sentence format (since the 15th century), now celebrated in its own right as the title of a BBC2 TV series *Not Only . . . But Also* (1965–6; 1970) featuring 'not only Peter Cook but also Dudley Moore.' 'This is the part of the show designed for trendy young moderns – the people who are not only but also, and indeed, scarcely' – BBC radio *Round the Horne* (28 March 1965).

not on your nellie See NAY NAY.

not see the wood for the trees (or . . . wood for trees) Meaning, 'lose sight of the whole because of the multitude of detail.' A proverbial saying by 1546.

not so green See I'M NOT.

not so loud or they'll all want one Phrase used to turn something another has said into a joke (almost in the way AS THE BISHOP SAID TO THE ACTRESS turns something into a *double-entendre*). 'How many of us have said something not particularly amusing, only to have it turned into a joke of sorts by someone else saying, "Not so loud or they'll all want one" . . .' – Miles Kington in *The Independent* (2 May 2000).

not so much a ——, more a —— Format phrase recognized as such and popular-ized by its use in the title of a BBC TV late-night satire-plus-chat show (from 13 November 1964), *Not So Much a Programme, More a Way of Life*. However, earlier in that year, I find in my personal diary for 20 February that an actress at Oxford who was taking part in an undergraduate show, *Hang Down Your Head and Die*, told me that it was going to Stratford-upon-Avon and then on to the West End: 'She concluded, "Not just a show, a way of life".' This would suggest that the construction was a vogue phrase at that time, before the TV show took it up.

not suitable for those of a nervous disposition   Warning phrase used in the 1950s on British television. The announcer would say: 'The programme that follows is not suitable . . .' Used in the BBC radio *Goon Show,* 'The Yehti' (8 March 1955). Curiously, the phrase lingers. A 1982 ad for the video of *Macabre* has 'WARNING. UNSUITABLE FOR THOSE OF A NERVOUS DISPOSITION.' Such phraseology, acting as a come-on, almost amounts to a slogan.

not the marrying kind (or **sort)**   Usually said of men who cling to their bachelor status but only more recently implying that they are homosexual (a similar change has occurred with the now euphemistic term **confirmed bachelor**). 'There were plenty of pretty girls, but none of them caught him, none of them could get hold of his heart; evidently he [Dr Barry] was not a marrying man' – Mark Twain, *Following the Equator* (1897); when Hugh Montefiore, an Anglican clergymen and later a bishop, wondered at a conference in Oxford (26 July 1967) 'Why did He not marry? Could the answer be that Jesus was not by nature the marrying sort?' – people were outraged at the suggestion that Christ might have been a homosexual; in Anthony Powell's autobiographical volume *Infants of the Spring* (1976), he writes of an entertainer called Varda that she 'had been married for a short time to a Greek surrealist painter, Jean Varda, a lively figure . . . but not the marrying sort'. It is not quite clear what is to be inferred from this. Usually encountered in the negative sense, positive use of 'the marrying kind/ sort' has nevertheless existed in its own right. In fact, the phrase may sometimes have originally implied that the man was a

'womaniser – that is to say, not 'homosexual' but '*too* heterosexual'. For example, from Thomas Moore, *M.P., or The Blue-Stocking, a Comic Opera*, Act 3 Sc. 2 (1811): 'So it *is* a hoax, if he told you he / Was going to marry any such thing – La! sir – he is / Not one of your marrying sort'; from Allan Cunningham, *The Maid of Elvar* (1832): 'He wed her? He's none of the marrying kind, – / Let her beware . . .' From Shaw's *Pygmalion* (1916): *Professor Higgins to Liza*: 'All men are not confirmed old bachelors like me and the Colonel. Most men are the marrying sort (poor devils!).' *The Marrying Kind* is the title of a play (1957) by Garson Kanin and Ruth Gordon derived from their film script (US 1952). *Rugby Songs* (1967) contains a ribald piece of verse, entitled 'If I Were the Marrying Kind', that continues '. . . Which thank the Lord I'm not, sir, / The kind of man that I would wed / Would be a rugby full-back . . .', and so on.

not tonight, Josephine   Phrase of refusal – originally to engage in sex. Napoleon did not, as far as we know, ever say the words that have become popularly linked with him. The idea that he had better things to do than satisfy the Empress Josephine's famous appetite, or was not inclined or able to do so, must have grown up during the 19th century. There was also a saying, attributed to Josephine, apparently, '*Bon-a-parte est Bon-à-rien* [Bonaparte is good for nothing]', which may be relevant. The film *I Cover the Waterfront* (US 1933) has been credited with launching the phrase, though it merely popularized it. A knockabout sketch filmed for the Pathé Library in *circa* 1932 has Lupino Lane as Napoleon and Beatrice Lillie as Josephine. After signing a document of divorce (which Napoleon crumples up), Josephine says, 'When you are refreshed, come as usual to my apartment.' Napoleon says (as the tag to the sketch), 'Not tonight, Josephine,' and she throws a custard pie in his face. A British song with the title had appeared in 1915 (sung by Florrie Forde and written by Worton David and Lawrence Wright) and an American one (sung by Ada Jones and Billy Murray) was recorded on an Edison wax cylinder (?1901–10). Neither of these songs is about the historical Josephine: the British one is about a man who has promised his mother he will not kiss his bride before their wedding day and the American one is about a stenographer. The saying may well have been established in music hall and vaudeville by the end of the previous century. Interestingly, a play by W. G. Wills, called *A Royal Divorce* and concerning the divorce of Napoleon and Josephine, was first produced at the Lyceum Theatre, London, in 1891 (and revived at the Scala Theatre in 1906). Ursula Shaw, writing to the *Daily Mail* (18 December 1997), noted that 'Veteran stage director Basil Dean recalled that at the turn of the 19th century, an impresario called W. W. Kelly had been running provincial tours of the [W. G. Wills's] drama, starring his wife as the empress, for so many years "that certain lines, particularly 'Not tonight, Josephine' became bywords with the audience." The catchphrase was profitable enough for Kelly to buy a Liverpool theatre, which he renamed after himself, in the era before World War I.' Where did Basil Dean do this recalling? It is not in either of his two volumes of memoirs. A. E. Wilson's history of the theatre, *The Lyceum* (1952), contains a photo from the 1911 revival of the play with Ethel Warwick and Frank Lister in the leading roles. The caption to the picture is: 'Not tonight, Josephine!' Finally, a text of the play was tracked down in the collection of plays submitted to the Lord Chamberlain for censorship purposes and now lodged in the British Library. As passed for production, the play does *not* contain the famous line, but it might conceivably have been grafted on subsequently. W. G. Wills (1828–91) was an Irish playwright, poet and songwriter who specialized in historical dramas. A film with the title *A Royal Divorce* (UK 1938), produced by Herbert Wilcox and starring Ruth Chatterton and Pierre Blanchar, is said to be based, rather, on the novel *Josephine* by Jacques Thiérry (date unknown, as also whether it contains the catchphrase).

not (to) touch someone (or **something) with a bargepole** Indicating that the speaker will not have anything to do with someone or something, will keep his or her distance and avoid at all costs. From the *length* of the bargepole used to propel a barge. Known by 1893. Eric Partridge, *A Dictionary of Clichés* (5th edition, 1978), dates it as late 19th to 20th century. 'Hideous little beast! I wouldn't touch him with the end of a barge pole' – A. H. Gibbs, *Persistent Lovers* (1915); 'She has begun to campaign on behalf of other badly hit Names concentrated on the so-called "spiral" syndicates – those which provided reinsurance against large-scale losses for other Lloyd's syndicates. "If I knew then what I know now I wouldn't touch (Lloyd's) with a bargepole," she says' – *Financial Times* (1 May 1993); '"Frankly, I wouldn't touch any of the men I have met in nightclubs with a bargepole," says Jane, 23, who lives in Surrey' – *Today* (24 August 1993).

not very good detective, just lucky old Chinaman Catchphrase from the 1930s' American radio series *Charlie Chan*, about a Chinese detective – based on the character created by Earl Derr Biggers in *The House Without a Key* (1925).

not waving but drowning Modern proverbial expression used to describe any sort of situation where a gesture may be misinterpreted. From the poem 'Not Waving, But Drowning' (1957) by Stevie Smith (1902–71): 'Nobody heard him, the dead man, / But still he lay moaning: / I was much further out than you thought / And not waving but drowning.' When Hugh Whitemore's biographical play *Stevie* opened in London (1977), a critic wrote that any poet 'who could encapsulate the whole irony of existence in a poem's title' deserved more than our trifling attention. In a poll to find Britain's favourite poem, conducted by the BBC TV programme *Bookworm* in 1995, this one came fourth.

not with a bang but a whimper Phrase used to express anticlimax – from T. S. Eliot's poem *The Hollow Men* (1925): 'This is the way the world ends / Not with a bang but a whimper'. Frequently alluded to: from Richard Aldington, *The Colonel's Daughter* (1931): 'I wish you'd all shoot yourselves with a bang, instead of continuing to whimper.' From *The Times* (16 December 1959): 'Here the world ends neither with a bang nor a whimper, but with a slow, resigned sigh at its own criminal imbecility.' *Not With a Bang* was the title of an ITV series (1990). *The Observer* reported (8 July 1990): 'After some 70 hours Ernest Saunders finally left the Southwark witness box on Thursday afternoon not with a bang or whimper but more with a chorus of the familiar refrains which had echoed . . .' 'Sussex [cricket team] turn a bang to a whimper' – headline in the *Independent on Sunday* (3 August 2003). The joke variation, 'This is the way to World's End / Not with a Banger but a Wimpy', was ascribed by Michael Flanders to his father-in-law, Professor Robert Gorham Davis of Columbia University, New York, in the introduction to a verse anthology *London Between the Lines* (1973).

not worth a tinker's cuss (or damn) (or simply **a tinker's)** Phrase indicating low worth. The simplest explanation for it is that because tinkers swore so much, one of their cusses would not be worth very much. Or, because tinkers were not exactly outstanding figures, to be damned by one would not bother you. However, there was a thing called a tinker's 'dam' – a piece of bread used to plug a leak in a pot until solder had been poured in. This was not worth anything and was useless afterwards. Given the existence of the 'cuss' version, the expression must involve the idea of swearing and thus the second should be discounted. Emanuel Shinwell, the British Labour politician, said at an ETU Conference, Margate (7 May 1947): 'We know that you, the organised workers of the country, are our friends . . . As for the rest, they do not matter a tinker's curse.'

not worth blacking up for! British show-business expression for anything that is not worth the trouble – but especially an audience that is not worth performing in front of. According to *Roy Hudd's Book of Music-Hall, Variety and Showbiz Anecdotes* (1993), the phrase arose when Billy Bennett was on a variety bill preceding the West Indian entertainer 'Hutch'. As Bennett came off the stage at the end of his act, Hutch asked him what the audience was like. Bennett snorted: 'Not worth blacking up for.' The story has also been given as

though involving Robb Wilton and the Deep River Boys when their act had been cut at the London Palladium – as in Eric Midwinter, *Make 'Em Laugh* (1979).

not you Momma See HI GANG.

(to) nourish a viper in one's bosom Meaning, 'to discover that one has been betrayed by a friend one has supported or encouraged.' The idea occurs in Cicero and Petronius, but the chief reference is to one of Aesop's fables in which a hen hatches some serpent's eggs when she is likely to be their first victim. And the moral is: 'Even the kindest treatment cannot tame a savage nature.'

nourishment See I WANT ME TEA.

now See EVENTUALLY WHY NOT.

now and forever Slogan. The conjunction of words is an old one. Daniel Webster proclaimed: 'Liberty and union, now and forever, one and inseparable' (26 January 1830). '*Et nunc et semper*' at the end of the Gloria in religious services is sometimes translated as 'now and forever [world without end. Amen]' but also (as in the Anglican prayer book) 'now and ever shall be'. Three films have been made with this title: with Gary Cooper (US 1934), Janette Scott (UK 1956) and Cheryl Ladd (US 1983), presumably with 'love' as the thing that was going to be 'now and forever'. Vera Lynn had a hit in 1954 with a song called this, translated from the German. Indeed, the phrase enshrines an idea common to other languages. *Cats*, the longest-running musical in London's West End, used the promotional line from about 1987 until final closure in 2002. Basques demanding that Eta should not keep up its terror campaign (March 1989) bore a banner with the words '*Paz ahora y para* [peace now and forever].'

no way See NOT!

no way! Phrase of short, sharp rejection of a statement or of strongly negative reaction to a request. Of American origin. *Flexner* (1982) dates it from the mid-1960s. Perhaps derived from 'There's no way', which Ann Blyth says to Howard Keel after 'I'll never find him again . . .' – with the expression and emphasis that would now be used today – in the film of *Kismet* (US 1955).

no way, José See JOE BOB.

no wider war Political slogan in the USA. President Lyndon Johnson said in a broadcast address (4 August 1964), referring to the Vietnam War: 'We Americans know, although others appear to forget, the risks of spreading conflict. We still seek no wider war.' 'No wider war' is misleadingly reminiscent of the German phrase *Nie Wieder Krieg* [never again war], a slogan of the 1920s/30s.

no-win See HIDING TO NOTHING.

now is the time for all good men to come to the aid of the party Not a slogan but a typewriter exercise. It was possibly originated in 1867 by Charles E. Weller, a court reporter in Milwaukee, to test the efficiency of the first practical typewriter that his friend Christopher L. Scholes had made. Unfortunately, he did not do a very good job because the phrase contains only 18 letters of the alphabet. **The quick brown fox jumps over the lazy dog**, on the other hand, has all 26 – quoted in R. H. Templeton Jr, *The Quick Brown Fox* (1945). This was once thought to be the shortest sentence in English containing all the letters of the alphabet, but it was superseded by 'Pack my box with five dozen liquor jugs' (which is three letters shorter overall) and 'Quick blowing zephyrs vex daft Jim' (which is even shorter). Even more concise 'pangrams' have been devised but they are also shorter on sense and memorability.

now I've seen everything (or **heard everything)!** Mostly good-humoured expression of wonder or amazement at being told a piece of news. Since the 1940s.

now there's a beaut if ever there was one A failed catchphrase is a contradiction in terms. If a catchphrase does not catch on it is not a catchphrase. Perhaps it should be called a 'drop phrase'. However, here are some phrases that were contrived so that they might take off but lacked some essential ingredient to help them do so. The prominence of Bob Monkhouse in this section is not a criticism – he just had

the courage to remember more than others. He noted (1979): 'As a comedian in the early 1950s, I had one unique aspect. I was without a catchphrase. Radio producers sympathized and made suggestions. Charlie Chester even offered to give me one. "Every time you score a big laugh," he said, "just remember to dance a little jig and say: 'Now there's a beaut if ever there was one!'" I tried it out on a *Variety Ahoy!* down at Portsmouth. I got a big laugh which I killed by suddenly shuffling inexplicably and shouting this catchphrase at the audience who were understandably baffled. So they stopped laughing at once. I politely declined and Charlie, never [one] to waste comic material, repeated it in his next series until its persistent failure to please drove him to ad-lib another line, a plea for audience response – "Speak to Charlee-ee!" – which proved to be a genuine winner.' Monkhouse also tried to launch **I said a subtle** when, for some reason, a joke failed. And another trick that Denis Goodwin and he both used, if a gag really died, was to give a complicated explanation of the joke, ending with, 'That's what the joke means, **and I wish I was dead.**' Later, at the time of his *Golden Shot* appearances on TV, Monkhouse had the idea that a phrase like **hang on to your hollyhocks!** would work. 'During the warm-ups I would tell a joke "I'd been told not to tell" – Lady Chatterley is in bed with a light cold. Through the French windows comes Mellors the gamekeeper, his hands full of hollyhocks, freshly picked from the garden, to present to her ladyship. She says, "Thank you for the hollyhocks. And I would appreciate your attention for I have never been bed-ridden before." "Haven't you?" says Mellors. "Then hang on to your hollyhocks!" I could then place that phrase anywhere in the show with a hundred per cent certainty of getting a roar of laughter . . . and I waited and waited for the nation to be aware of this phrase. A year later I quietly dropped it . . .' Ted Ray recalled two failed catchphrases from *Ray's a Laugh* in about 1950: **what about Rovers?** – as in the exchange, 'Unlucky? – what about Rovers?' 'Unlucky – you don't know you're born.' Also: **he's one of Nature's!** – as in Martha about Albert: 'Don't you insult my husband, he's one of Nature's . . .' Peter Cook remembered (1979) that the exclamation **funny!** – delivered in a strangulated Dud and Pete voice between himself and Dudley in BBC2 TV's *Not Only . . . But Also* (from 1965–) caught on with the performers if not with the public at large. I think he underestimated the extent to which the pronunciation of the word *did* catch on. Later, Fozzy Bear had something similar in *The Muppet Show* (1976–81), pronouncing the word 'fun-neeee!' Max Bygraves told me (1980) that in his 1979 TV series, 'I had Geoff Love keep walking on. He'd get a big laugh and I'd turn to the audience and say **You can't help loving him, can you?** It happened in the studio, but it didn't happen with the public.' On the *Generation Game* in the early 1970s, Bruce Forsyth tried **Tell me – who's to know?**, while Larry Grayson tried unsuccessfully to follow Forsyth's 'Didn't he do well?' with **what a lot you've got!**

(there's) nowt so queer as folks There's nothing so odd as people and the way they behave. 'And not really my mother's – it is still used today all over the North of England – "There's nowt so queer as folks – 'cept folks's childer"' – Margaret Rowden, Somerset (1995). *Partridge/Catch Phrases* dates this from the second half of the 19th century.

now you're cooking with gas! This has come to mean, 'You're on the right track, you're getting there, you're doing the right thing now!' Probably began with American TV commercials of the 1940s promoting the virtues of gas over electricity. In the Broadway musical *On the Town* (1943), the character 'Hildy' sings the song 'I Can Cook Too', which includes the line 'Baby, I'm cooking with gas.' The phrase took some time to catch on in the UK (if it ever really did). From 'The Missing Page' episode (11 March 1960) in BBC TV, *Hancock's Half-Hour*: *Hancock*: 'We're cooking with gas now, man.' *Librarian*: 'Pardon?' *Hancock*: 'Johnny Oxford in the book, that's what he says. I believe it's a phrase employed when one is favourably impressed with the prowess of another chap.'

now you're talking! Meaning, 'now you are saying something worth considering or useful (and not just waffling)'. A develop-

ment of 'Now you talk, indeed!' that occurs in Charles Dickens, *Barnaby Rudge*, Chap. 52 (1841); '"We got to dig him out with the picks and *let on* it's caseknives." "*Now* you're *talking!*" I says; "your head gets leveller and leveller all the time"' – Mark Twain, *The Adventures of Huckleberry Finn*, Chap. 36 (1884).

now you see it, now you don't! Said about anything that quickly disappears, especially as a result of trickery or deception. From conjuror's patter, since the 1930s?

(to the) nth degree I.e. 'to any extent'. This derives from the mathematical use of 'n' to denote an indefinite *number*. Early 20th century? 'In America the film-cutter is a man with a sub-editorial mind developed to the nth degree' – *Sunday Express* (18 March 1928).

nudge-nudge, wink-wink – know what I mean? – say no more! Catchphrases of the prurient character Norman (later known as Nudge) (Eric Idle) who accosted people with remarks like 'Is your wife a goer, then? Eh, eh?' From BBC TV, *Monty Python's Flying Circus* (1969–74). The phrases were spoken in any order (firstly on 19 October 1969).

nuff said See ENOUGH SAID.

number See GET SOMEONE'S.

(one's) number is up Meaning, 'one's time is up, one is doomed to die, one is done for.' Referring to a lottery number being drawn – or any other number (like an army number) – by which one may be identified. Known by 1806.

(the) number one son Nickname for an eldest son, in imitation of Chinese speech. It was popularized in the many American radio shows and films about Charlie Chan, the oriental detective (who had a large family), in the 1930s.

nuptial bliss Slightly facetious or ironical phrase for the supposed contentment of the wedded state. Date of origin unknown. Compare MARITAL BLISS. 'Just when Michael Jackson thought he could enjoy a few quiet weeks as a married man, another expensive lawsuit from a young boy is about to disrupt his nuptial bliss' – *The Sunday Times* (27 November 1994).

oar See GET ONE'S.

object See AND THE NEXT.

O brother, where art thou? The film title *O Brother, Where Art Thou?* (US 2000) is an in-joke, allusive, a bit of a puzzle, call it what you will, but not explained in the film itself. In fact, it alludes to the film-within-a-film of Preston Sturges's *Sullivan's Travels* (1941), in which the comedy director character wishes to produce a serious film to be called 'O Brother, Where Art Thou?'

obscene and not heard See SEEN AND NOT.

(that) obscure object of desire *That Obscure Object of Desire* [*Cet obscur objet du désir*] is the title of a film (France/Spain 1977) written and directed by Luis Buñuel. It was apparently his coinage, as the novel by Pierre Louys upon which the film is based is called *La Femme et le Pantin* [guy/puppet]. The story is about a man whose infatuation with a girl is unrequited.

occur See ACCIDENTS.

— of all time Phrase used whenever a superlative is needlessly heightened. Probably of American origin. Used in this manner by 1900. 'The greatest word-juggler of all time' – *The Month* (January 1901); 'By now we have all learned . . . to substitute "Russia" for the "Soviet Union" in our reporting, our discourse and – increasingly – in our national conscious-ness. The change symbolizes one of the great, transforming, peaceful revolutions of all time' – *The Washington Post* (26 June 1992).

official See AND THAT'S.

(to be) off one's trolley Meaning, 'to be mad'. *DOAS* finds this by 1909 and calls it 'probably the oldest of the "off [one's] —" = crazy terms', but 'off one's head' and 'rocker' are a little older. *OED2* finds it by 1896. An entertaining but coincidental derivation of the phrase comes from the days of the Acoustic Recording Machine (*circa* 1910). The best effects were obtained

not by the use of a volume control, but by physically adjusting the distance between the singer and the machine according to the noise the singer was making. A trolley was employed to effect this. If a singer flounced off from the arrangement, she was said to be 'off her trolley'. There is probably no truth in this . . .

off we go and the colour's pink! Phrase used when restarting some social activity/topic of conversation/fresh round of drinks. In 1980, Anthony Smith of Pinner, Middlesex queried its origin. Many years later, Donald Hickling of Northampton commented: 'I heard this catchphrase in "Metroland" (to the north of Pinner and slightly to the left) in a respectable hos-telry one Saturday lunchtime when the host or master of ceremonies, a WW2 naval officer, was remembering how a liberal supply of pink gins kept him going, and he assumed that everyone in his company appreciated "pinkers". And, in the context of family sayings, I can quote the parent of a friend who was wont to exclaim, "Up she goes and her knickers are pink." Metroland again!'

off we jolly well go See MORNING ALL.

off with his head! Peremptory command as from some king or queen or other, probably most associated with the Queen of Hearts in Lewis Carroll's *Alice's Adven-tures in Wonderland*, Chap. 8 (1865). But Shakespeare, *All's Well That Ends Well*, IV.iii.297 (1603) has: 'Come headsman, off with his head.' Coupled with **so much for Buckingham!** this was a wonderfully dismissive addition by the playwright Colley Cibber to his 1700 edition of Shakespeare's *Richard III*. The extension of Shakespeare's simple 'Off with his head' proved a popular and lasting emendation. In 'Private Theatres' (1835), one of the *Sketches by Boz*, Charles Dickens describes the roles on offer to amateur actors who at that time could pay to take certain roles in plays: 'For instance, the Duke of Glo'ster is well worth two pounds . . . including the "off with his head!" – which is sure to bring down the applause, and it is very easy to do – "Orf with his ed" (very quick and loud; – then slow and sneeringly) – "So much for Bu-u-u-uckingham!" Lay the emphasis on the "uck;" get yourself gradually into a corner, and work with your right hand, while you're saying it, as if you were feeling your way, and it's sure to do.' The extra phrase was included in Laurence Olivier's film of Shakespeare's play (UK 1955).

often a bridesmaid, but never a bride Slogan for Listerine mouthwash, in the USA, from *circa* 1923. One of the best-known lines in advertising, written by Milton Feasley, though there is an echo of the British music-hall song 'Why Am I Always the Bridesmaid?' made famous by Lily Morris (1917). A screen title in the newsreel sequence of *Citizen Kane* (US 1941) states (of Kane): 'In politics – always a bridesmaid, never a bride.'

—— of the century Promotional and advertising format. The *San Francisco Examiner* (13 April 1895) described the murder of two pretty girls by a Sunday school superintendent as 'the crime of a century'. This points to a likely American origin for the format. A review of Amanda M. Ros's novel *Irene Iddesleigh* in the magazine *Black and White* (19 February 1898) was headed 'The Book of the Century'. The Empire Hotel, Bath (opened 1901), had lavatory bowls with the slogan 'The Closet of the Century' written around the rim. The film *Robbery Under Arms* (Australia 1907) was promoted on a Melbourne poster as 'The Picture of the Century'. There were two films, both called *Crime of the Century*, in 1933 and 1946. More recently there was a British TV quiz called *Sale of the Century* (1971–83). The 1981 royal nuptials in the UK were dubbed by *Time* Magazine in a 1983 advertisement as 'the wedding of the century'.

... of which more anon Light-hearted way of closing down a train of thought. Date of origin unknown. 'True, would-be floaters such as TeleWest and General Cable have thought better of it, but that still leaves the likes of 3i and Eurotunnel (of which more anon)' – *Independent on Sunday* (29 May 1994).

—— of yesteryear Consciously quaint and quasi-poetic way of drawing attention to something's age. 'But where are the snows of yester-year?' was coined by D. G. Rossetti to translate '*Mais où sont les neiges d'antan?*' in his version (1870) of the famous line from François Villon's *Grand Testament*. 'Where were the klongs of yesteryear, all those colorful canals, criss-crossing the city?' – *National Geographic Magazine* (July 1967); 'Were progressives of yesteryear any less rigorous in rooting out real or imagined anti-semitic references than the new politically correct bully boys and girls are in rooting out, say, homophobic references?' – *The Sunday Telegraph* (2 February 1992).

oggi, oggi, oggi / oi, oi, oi! Chant at rugby union matches in the late 1970s. It was also featured in the routines of the Welsh comedian (and rugby enthusiast) Max Boyce about the same time. Its use may be much broader than this, especially among children. In 1986, a Thames River police inspector was reported as believing that the shout (as used by children) was similar to that used by watermen to warn their thieving mates of approaching police. A correspondent suggests that it could also be related to the Cornish 'oggy' or 'oggie' or 'tiddy-oggie', nicknames for a pasty. *Partridge/Slang* has this nickname and adds that 'Oggy-land' is a name for Cornwall itself. Another correspondent, also from Cornwall, states that 'oggi-oggi-oggi' was long a rallying cry in those parts before being taken up in Wales and elsewhere. The chant familiar from demonstrations against the Thatcher Government, 'Maggie-Maggie-Maggie, Out-Out-Out!', clearly derives from it.

oh arr (or **oh ah)** Non-commital response to something said when it is considered unlikely or preposterous or dubious. It sounds like an imitation of a country yokel determinedly unimpressed by what he has been told. The examples are all from P. G. Wodehouse: '"Ronald has just announced his intention of marrying a chorus-girl." "Oh, ah?" said Lord Emsworth' – *Summer Lightning*, Chap. 18 (1929); in a letter (24 August 1932) Wodehouse wrote: 'The first time I met him, we had barely finished the initial pip-pippings when he said, apropos of nothing, "My father was a professional cricketer." If there's a good answer to that, you tell me. I thought of saying, "Mine had a white moustache," but finally settled for, "Oh, ah," and we went on to speak of other things'; '"Oh, Mr Wooster," he said meeting me on the stairs . . . "You were good enough to express an interest in this little prize for Good Conduct which I am offering." "Oh, ah?"' – *Very Good, Jeeves*, 'The Love That Purifies' (1930).

oh, calamity! Catchphrase of the comic actor Robertson Hare (1891–1979). It came from an Aldwych farce of long ago – perhaps one in which the put-upon little man lost his trousers – but even he was unable to recall which. His other characteristic utterance was **indubitably!** and he called his autobiography *Yours Indubitably*. In *Up In the Clouds, Gentlemen, Please* (1980), John Mills relates an occasion when Hare had to utter the word – and jump in the air – in the play *Aren't Men Beasts* (1936). Unfortunately, as he did so, Hare let out 'one of the loudest and most spectacular farts it has ever been my pleasure to hear'.

oh! Calcutta! Exclamatory phrase that became the title of Kenneth Tynan's sexually explicit stage revue (Broadway 1969). It derives from a curious piece of word play, being the equivalent of the French '*Oh, quel cul t'as* [oh, what a lovely bum you've got].' French *cul* is derived from the Latin *culus*, 'buttocks', but, according to the context, may be applied to the female vagina or male anus. In her *Life of Kenneth Tynan* (1987), Kathleen Tynan states that she was writing an article on the French surrealist painter Clovis Trouille (1889–1975), one of whose works (1946) showed a naked odalisque lying on her side to reveal a spherical backside. The title was 'Oh! Calcutta! Calcutta!': 'I suggested to Ken that he call his erotic revue *Oh! Calcutta!* . . . I did not know at the time that it had the further advantage of being a French pun.'

oh, get in there, Moreton! Catchphrase of Robert Moreton (1922–1957) who had a brief taste of fame as one of the hero's

tutors in the BBC radio show *Educating Archie* (in the early 1950s). He was noted for his 'Bumper Fun Book', out of which he would quote jokes. '. . . And his Bumper Fun Book' was his bill matter. Alas, he was dropped from the show after only a year, was unable to get other work and committed suicide.

oh, get on with it! Catchphrase of the English comedy performer Kenneth Williams. Off-microphone, he would barrack other performers in the BBC radio show *Round the Horne* (1965–9) with it, though this was all scripted. *Get On With It!* was used as the title of a revue-type show he fronted for BBC Radio (1975–6).

oh, hello, I'm Julian and this is my friend, Sandy Julian (Hugh Paddick) introducing himself and Sandy (Kenneth Williams) at the start of their camp routines in the BBC radio show *Round the Horne*. More or less the same team as in *Beyond Our Ken* manifested itself from 1965 to 1969, this time with somewhat broader and zanier scripts by Marty Feldman (1933–83) and Barry Took (1928–2002). Took recalled (1979): 'Marty and I went all out to avoid catchphrases but the cast kept pencilling them in. Eventually we gave up the unequal struggle.' The new approach was typified by the introduction of two stock figures, the gay ex-chorus boys Julian and Sandy. From their first appearances, they larded their speech with bits of camp *parlare* (talk) from the *omipalomi* (homosexual) subculture of actors and dancers. **Ooh, bold! Very bold!** was their standard exclamation. Also **Fantabulosa!** One of their incarnations was as film producers: *Sandy*: 'Mr Horne, we are in the forefront of your *Nouvelle Vague*. **That's your actual French**.' *Julian*: 'It means we are of the New Wave.' *Sandy*: 'And very nice it looks on you, too.' This last phrase had crept into the show by 27 March 1966. Peter Cook claimed to have launched **your actual** as a turn of phrase, however, and indeed seems to have done so as a member of Cambridge Footlights (1957–60) – according to Harry Thompson, *Peter Cook* (1997).

oh, I say, I rather care for that! hahaha-haa-ha! Catchphrase in the BBC radio show *Waterlogged Spa* (from 1946).

Humphrey Lestocq played Flying Officer Kite, an ex-RAF officer, complete with handlebar moustache and varsity accent. Lestocq recalled (1980): 'When the show started, I'd just left the RAF. I was madly air-force – "Whacko!" "Good-o!" "Bang-on!" . . . all that sort of thing – and this really fascinated Eric Barker [the writer and star of the show]. So he went away and found this character for me.' After many a 'Wizard prang!' Barker would slap Kite down in some way, but Kite would only roar: 'Oh, I say, I rather care for that, hahaha-haa-ha!' The producer, Leslie Bridgmont, once commented: 'When we introduced the character we worked out this pay-off very carefully . . . the rhythm of the laugh, for instance, had to be exactly the same each time. It is this inexorable sameness that establishes a phrase.'

oh, I was livid – livid I was . . . ! See WE'VE GOT A RIGHT ONE 'ERE.

oh, jolly D! Catchphrase of Dudley Davenport (Maurice Denham) in the BBC radio show *Much Binding in the Marsh* (1947–53). The D was short for Decent. Denham (1909–2002) probably took it from public school or RAF usage, though dating from not much earlier than the Second World War. The same character would also cry, **oh, I say, I am a fool!** – followed by a curious chuckle, 'keogh! keogh! keogh!' A Methodist minister in Brighton once advertised it as the title of a sermon. Ken Platt later used the shorter, 'Oh, I am a fool!'

oh joy, oh rapture (oh bliss beyond compare)! A bevy of exclamations. The first pair appears twice in *HMS Pinafore* (1878), though Gilbert and Sullivan operas are stuffed with similar cries. 'What bliss beyond compare' is a phrase from the hymn 'Jerusalem the Golden' by J. M. Neale (1818–66).

oh king, live forever! Traditional cry or toast – see under BANZAI! – but not restricted to that sort of notable figure. A Mr Howells introduced Mark Twain during his seventieth birthday dinner at Delmonico's restaurant, New York City (5 December 1905), with these words: 'I will try not to be greedy on your behalf in wishing the health of our honored and, in view of his great age, our revered guest. I will not say, "Oh King, live forever!" but "Oh King, live as long as you like!"' See also TRUE, O KING!

oh, Moses! Catchphrase of 'Noot', the Bishop's chaplain (Derek Nimmo), in the BBC TV comedy series about clerical folk, *All Gas and Gaiters* (1967–71). Scripted by Pauline Devaney and Edwin Apps who remembered (in 1979): 'Derek Nimmo was always asking for a catchphrase and we always resisted the suggestion until one day a neighbour who was a pillar of the church, discussing something over the garden wall, said "Moses!" and we wrote it into the script. Derek leapt on it and thereafter used it with such frequency that we eventually got a notice to the effect that it was time the writers stopped putting in "Moses" whenever they couldn't think of anything funny!'

oh, my Sunday helmet! Catchphrase of PC 49 (Brian Reece). He was a somewhat silly-ass police constable in the BBC radio series *PC 49* from 1946 onwards. The constable's full name was 'Archibald Berkeley Willoughby'. His exclamation duly occurs in the film *A Case for PC 49* (UK 1951). Reece (1913–62) appears to have died at the age of 49, too.

oh no, there isn't! Catchphrase from British pantomime, where there is always a scene in which an actor speaks to the audience with his back to someone or something that he denies exists. The following kind of ritual exchange then takes place: 'There isn't a bear behind me, is there, children?' Audience: '**Oh yes, there is!**' There will also be cries of '**behind you!**' There is the story of a curtain speech by the manager of a provincial theatre halfway through a panto: 'I'm very sorry, ladies and gentle-men, but we cannot continue the perform-ance as our leading lady has just died.' Children in the audience: 'Oh, no, she hasn't!' The phrase 'Oh, no there isn't!' was also used as bill matter by the Two Pirates variety act.

oh, Ron! / yes, Eth? Immortal exchange between a swooning Eth (June Whitfield) and a gormless Ron (Dick Bentley) in the BBC radio show *Take It From Here* (1948–

59). As the lovers in the segment of the show known as 'The Glums', they had this stock phrase that caught on because of Eth's rising inflection and Ron's flat response.

oh, Sir Jasper, do not touch me! Cry from a ribald, rugby song (current mid-20th century) about a most 'immoral lady / as she lay between the sheets / with nothing on at all'. Presumably this alludes to a vile seducer called Sir Jasper in some actual melodrama. There is a Sir Jasper Fidget in William Wycherley's play *The Country Wife* (1675), but he is quite the reverse of a vile seducer.

oi! Catchphrase of the British comedian Bud Flanagan (1896–1968). He had a way of rounding off a joke or explanation in his routines with Chesney Allen by saying, 'Oi!' Or if he fluffed a line or committed a malapropism, he would at last correct himself with Allen's help, shout, 'Oi!', and the orchestra would repeat it. *Oi!* was used as the title of a biographical show about Flanagan and Allen on the London stage in 1982. The phrase is linked to Flanagan and Allen in Billy Bennett's monologue 'The Foreign Legion' (1934). The phrase was also used by Lupino Lane.

oil and water don't mix Two people with different characteristics will not get on well with each other. A proverbial saying, known especially in the USA since the 1780s but ignored by the main British proverb collections.

oil for the lamps of China Expression said about anything won or received as a windfall. Date of origin unknown. Other similar expressions include **corn in Egypt** and the proverbial (by 1830) **little fish are sweet**, said particularly about receiving a small something. *Oil for the Lamps of China* was the title of a novel by Alice Tisdale Hobart (1933; film US 1935) about an American oil man out East.

OK! The origin of this expression has occasioned more debate than any other in this dictionary. Here are some of the suggested origins, though one probably need go no further than explanations (1) and (2). (1) President Andrew Jackson (d. 1837), when a court clerk in Tennessee, would mark 'OK' on legal documents as

an abbreviation for the illiterate 'Oll Korrect'. The first recorded use in the USA of this jocular form is in the Boston *Morning Post* (23 March 1839). (2) It was used by President Martin van Buren as an election slogan in 1840. The initials stood for 'Old Kinderhook', his nickname, which derived from his birthplace in New York State. (3) Inspectors who weighed and graded bales of cotton as they were delivered to Mississippi river ports for shipment would write *aux quais* on any found faulty (i.e. this meant they were not OK and had to be sent back to the jetty). (4) It comes from Aux Cayes, a port in Haiti famous for its rum. (5) It is an anglicization of the word for 'good' in Ewe or Wolof, the West African language spoken by many of the slaves taken to the Southern USA. (6) It derives from the Greek words *ola kala*, meaning 'all is fine; everything is good'. (7) In the First World War, soldiers would report each night the number of deaths in their group. 'OK' stood for '0 killed'. (8) A railroad freight agent, Obadiah Kelly, used his initials on bills of lading. (9) An Indian chief, Old Keokuk, used his initials on treaties. (10) It stood for 'outer keel' when shipbuilders chalked it on timbers. (11) Teachers used it instead of *omnes korrectes* on perfect exam papers. (12) From boxes of Orrins-Kendall crackers, popular with Union troops in the Civil War. (13) From an English word 'hoacky', meaning 'the last load of a harvest'. (14) From a Finnish word *oikea*, meaning 'correct'. (15) From a Choctaw word *okeh* [it is] or *hoke*. [Footnote: 'Nobody really knows the story of "OK" or "posh" or "bloody" or a great deal else, and all we need is our existing knowledge of what the words mean and how they are used. The rest is small-talk and readers' letters in the "Daily Mail"' – Kingsley Amis, *The King's English* (1997).]

okey-pokey/hokey-pokey Name of an imitation ice cream made from shaved ice mixed with syrup – current by 1900. Perhaps it was thought that the imitation was a form of hocus-pocus or trickery, or else it could have been a corruption of '*ecce, ecce!*', the cry with which Italian street vendors would call attention to their wares. Iona and Peter Opie in *The Lore* *and Language of Schoolchildren* (1959) wonder whether it could derive from Italian '*O che poco* [o how little]!' – though why anyone should say that they do not explain.

OK, yah! Agreeing noise characteristic of the – especially female – Sloane Ranger and remarked upon in the mid-1980s. The London *Evening Standard* wrote of a show called *The Sloane Ranger Revue* at the Duchess Theatre, London, 'OK Yah, that's brill!' – quoted in *Harpers & Queen* Magazine (January 1986).

(as) old as my tongue and a little older than my teeth What nannies (and other older folk) traditionally reply when asked how old they are by inquisitive young persons. Jonathan Swift has it in *Polite Conversation* (1738) as, 'Why, I am as old as my Tongue, and a little older than my teeth'. *Casson/Grenfell* have it reversed as, '(a) little older than my teeth and as old as my tongue.'

(the) Old Bill Nickname for the police – and in particular, the Metropolitan Police of London. So many policemen wore walrus moustaches after the First World War that they reminded people of Bruce Bairnsfather's cartoon character 'Old Bill'. He was the one who said IF YOU KNOW A BETTER 'OLE – GO TO IT. *Partridge/Slang*, providing this explanation, also wonders whether there might have been some connection with the US song 'Won't You Come Home, Bill Bailey' (*circa* 1902) or with the Old Bailey courts. An abbreviation of the name – **the Bill** – was used as the title of a long-running UK TV cops series (from 1984 onwards).

Old Blood 'n' Guts Nickname of George S. Patton (1885–1945), US general and Commander of the Third Army in the Second World War. A brilliantly forceful soldier who liked to be regarded as a 'tough guy' (he was flamboyant and carried a pearl-handled revolver in an open holster); but he could be emotional and friendly – disliked by some, adored by others. The nickname is a tribute to his 'aggressive determination'.

(the) old boy net (or network) British term for the informal system of support given to one another by men who once attended the same school. Not recorded before the 1950s but said to have been known in the Second World War, where the 'old boy *net*' referred to use of the wireless 'net' to organize military support from old friends and colleagues. Here the meaning of 'old boy' seems to move away from that of 'former schoolboy' to anyone you might address using the words, 'I say, old boy . . .' From Claud Cockburn, *In Time of Trouble* (1956): 'My father . . . knew quite enough about the working of what is nowadays called "The Old Boy Net" to realize that as things now stood he had considerably less chance of entering the Indian Civil Service than he did of entering the Church of England and becoming a Bishop.'

(the) Old Contemptibles Nickname gladly taken unto themselves by First World War veterans of the British Expeditionary Force who crossed the English Channel in 1914 to join the French and Belgians against the German advance. It was alleged that Kaiser Wilhelm II had described the army as 'a contemptibly little army' (referring to its *size* rather than its *quality*). The British press was then said to have mistranslated this so that it made him appear to have called them a 'contemptible little army'. The truth is that the whole episode was a propaganda ploy masterminded by the British. Recorded use by 1916.

(the) old grey whistle test There was supposedly a practice in (the British) Tin Pan Alley of trying new pop songs out on the elderly grey-haired doormen. If they could pick up the tune to the extent of being able to whistle it, the song stood a chance of being successful. Hence, *The Old Grey Whistle Test*, title of a BBC TV pop music series (1971–88).

(the) Old Groaner Sobriquet of Harry Lillie Crosby (1904–77), better known by his other nickname **Bing** or (in German) **Der Bingle**. Oddly, he had a smooth, low voice rather than a groaning one (Sinatra had that sort).

(the) Old Hundredth (sometimes Old Hundred) Name given to the tune of the hymn 'All people that on earth do dwell' – words written by William Kethe and first appearing in the Geneva Psalter (1561) – because it is a setting of Psalm 100. In the 1696 Psalter, the name was given to the tune to indicate that the earlier version was being retained.

(the) Old Man of the Sea   Name of a troublesome character in *Tales of the Arabian Nights* who climbed on the back of Sinbad the Sailor and was hard to dislodge, hence, the phrase for 'a burden'. The title of Ernest Hemingway's novel *The Old Man and the Sea* (1952; film US 1958) presumably alludes lightly to him.

Old Nick   One of the oldest nicknames for Satan or The Devil, probably brought by Viking invaders, from a Scandinavian word for a water goblin; or the Anglo-Saxons may have been responsible because of a similar Teutonic word. Recorded by 1643. Also: **Old Harry** (known by 1777), **Auld Clootie**, **Auld Hangie**, **Nickie-ben**, **Old Scratch**, **Satanic Majesty**, **Father of Lies**, etc.

(the) Old Pretender   Nickname of James Francis Edward Stuart (1688–1766), son of James II and claimant to the English throne. He was supported by Louis XIV of France who regarded him as James III, but he spent his life in exile and died in Rome. Another nickname was **the Warming Pan baby**, from the anti-Jacobite rumour that he was smuggled in a warming pan when a baby into the bedroom of his mother (Mary of Modena – second wife of James II) because her own child was stillborn. His Jacobite followers were sneered at as 'Warming Pans'.

(the) old school tie   Symbol of the clannishness and loyalties involving those who attended British public schools (i.e. private schools). One of the features of 'old boys'' associations is that they sell ties, which make the affiliation of the wearer immediately apparent to others of the same background. An early use of the phrase was by Rudyard Kipling in *Limits & Renewals* (1932). The Western Brothers had a monologue entitled 'The Old School Tie' (1934). Often used in a critical sense, hence the more recent expression **strangled by the old school tie**. In Frederic Raphael's script for the film *Nothing But the Best* (UK 1964), the Denholm Elliott

character says to the Alan Bates character, 'From now on, no one will be able to accuse you of being strangled by the old school tie' (this is just a moment before Bates actually strangles Elliott with just such an article of clothing). From the BBC radio show *Round the Horne* (7 April 1968): 'It's painful to be strangled by the old school tie.' *The Times* (27 September 1986) had: '[Trevor Howard] broke new ground, away from the English studio stereotypes of silly-ass eccentrics or decent but wooden chaps strangled by a combination of old school tie and stiff upper lip.' A key use of the term appeared in the politician Norman Tebbit's memoir, *Upwardly Mobile* (1988): 'Some thought my willingness to stand toe to toe against the more thuggish elements of the Labour Party and slug it out blow for blow rather vulgar. Others, especially in the country at large, seemed delighted at the idea of a Tory MP unwilling to be strangled by the old school tie.'

(the) Old Sod   Term for Ireland, more usually spelt **Ould Sod**, to represent the Irish pronunciation. 'Sod' here means a piece of earth to which natives will return and is presumably used because of the close identification between Ireland, green grass and turf. Recorded by 1812.

old soldiers never die, they simply fade away   Notable use of this saying was made by General Douglas MacArthur when, following his dismissal by President Truman, he was allowed to address Congress on 19 April 1951. He ended: 'I still remember the refrain of one of the most popular barrack ballads of that day [turn of the century], which proclaimed, most proudly, that "Old soldiers never die. They just fade away." And like the old soldier of that ballad. I now close my military career and just fade away . . .' The origins of the ballad he quoted lie in a British army parody of the gospel hymn 'Kind Words Can Never Die', which (never mind MacArthur's dating) came out of the First World War. J. Foley copyrighted a version of the parody in 1920. The format has appealed to many jokers over the years. From the early 1980s come these examples: 'Old soldiers never die, just their privates'; 'Old professors . . . just lose their faculties'; 'Old golfers . . . just lose their balls'; 'Old fishermen never die, they just smell that way'.

old Spanish customs The phrase refers to practices that are of long standing but unauthorized. Although the journal *Notes and Queries* was vainly seeking the origin of the phrase in 1932, the term came to prominence in the 1980s to describe the irregular behaviour of British newspaper production workers in Fleet Street (cheating over pay packets, especially). The use seems mainly British, though this does not explain how Groucho Marx came to make the pun 'old Spinach customs' in *Animal Crackers* (US 1930). Why the Spanish are blamed is not clear, except that Spaniards tend to attract pejoratives – not least with regard to working practices (the *mañana* attitude). In Elizabethan times, William Cecil is quoted as saying of Sir Thomas Tresham, architect of Rushton Triangular Lodge, that he was not given to **Spanish practices** (i.e. Roman Catholic ones). In 1584, also, Lord Walsingham referred to 'Spanish practices' in a way that meant they were 'deceitful, perfidious and treacherous'. This could provide us with an origin for the modern phrase. Indeed, latterly (late 1980s), the two have been used interchangeably in the newspaper context. 'Receiving visits . . . when you are from Home, is not consisting with our Spanish Customs' – William R. Chetwood, *The Voyages and Adventures of Captain Robert Boyle* (1724); 'The biggest internal cost is production wages . . . embroidered round with "old Spanish customs", which was regarded as virtually outside management control' – Simon Jenkins, *Newspapers: The Power and the Money* (1979).

(the) Old Vic Name of a famous London theatre. When the Royal Coburg, south of the River Thames in London, was redecorated in 1833, it was renamed the Victoria and was popularly referred to as the 'Vic' by 1858. In time it became known as 'the Old Vic'. In 1914, Lilian Baylis formed the Old Vic Shakespeare Company to perform in the theatre and between then and 1963, when the company was disbanded, the phrase 'the Old Vic' was applied rather more to the distinguished theatrical organization than to the building itself.

Subsequently the building has housed the National Theatre and then other companies.

omnium gatherum Mock Latin term for a gathering of all sorts, a miscellaneous jumble, a mixture. Recorded by 1530. In the novels of Anthony Trollope there is a character called the 'Duke of Omnium' who lives in 'Gatherum Castle'.

on a collision course The original naval use of the term was known by 1944. The figurative use was current by the 1960s. Listed in *The Independent* (24 December 1994) as a cliché of newspaper editorials. 'The great powers are now headed on a collision course over Berlin' – *New Statesman* (21 July 1961); '[The city council's] policies on development and road building . . . set it on a collision course' – *The Times* (8 January 1973); 'The Arts: Collision course on the voyage round Columbus – Two films are planned to celebrate the anniversary of the explorer's famous arrival in America. David Gritten charts progress in the year's hottest clash in film-making' – by-line in *The Daily Telegraph* (8 February 1992).

on a hiding to nothing Facing almost impossible odds; confronted by a beating without any chance of avoiding or escaping it. *Partridge/Slang* dates this from the late 1950s, but his reviser, Paul Beale, suggests that it did not really catch on till the early 1970s. *OED2* finds it by 1905 and offers a horse-racing origin.

on a roll Enjoying a run of success. If this originally American expression came out of surfing, as seems likely, then it would seem appropriate to define it also as 'on the crest of a wave'. Recorded by 1976. 'To give ENO an extra twinge of doubt, the Royal Opera, which was so often compared unfavourably to it in the last decade, is on an artistic roll' – *Independent on Sunday* (18 April 1993).

on a scale of one to ten Popular system of rating things – also used allusively, e.g 'a ten', 'a two'. In the introduction to the song 'Tits and Ass' in the musical *Chorus Line* (1975), a character says (of an audition), 'On a scale of ten, he gave me . . .' In a West Coast party scene in the film *Annie Hall* (US 1977), a character says of a woman, 'She's a ten,' indicating that she is his ideal. This usage was further popularized by the film *10* (US 1979) in which the sexual allure or performance of the hero's girlfriends was so rated. Some people still use it. *The Naff Sex Guide* (1984) quoted an unidentified celebrity as having said: 'On a scale of one to ten I'd give him a two, but that's only because I've never met a one.' An ad in *The New York Times* (26 March 1989) quoted Gary Franklin of KABC-TV as rating the film *Heathers*, 'A 10! Absolutely brilliant, a remarkable film.' Perhaps the usage derives from the Richter scale of measuring the severity of earthquakes (1 to 10), named after Charles F. Richter who began devising the scale in 1932, or simply from the old school habit of marking things out of ten. 'Ten' also equals intercourse on the schoolboy/girl petting scale.

on behalf of the committ-ee! See GIVE ORDER!

on behalf of the working classes . . . At first this was a phrase used literally by people purporting to represent the case of this sector of society; Robert Owen, the social reformer, used the title *Two Memorials on behalf of the Working Classes* in 1816. The phrase later became the bill matter of the British music-hall comedian Billy Russell (1893–1971). His walrus-moustached, pipe-chewing character 'Old Bill' was based on the cartoon character of the First World War – see OLD BILL.

on bended knee Meaning, 'in a suppliant position, deferring to another' – as though to a ruler or other person in high authority. 'With one accord / On castleyard and all around the people sink on bended knee' – Marie A. Brown, *Nadeschda* (1878); 'The offer was met with a hostile reception from Mrs Lennox [Gulf War widow]. "I'm not going on bended knee and expose all my financial details in order to benefit. It's not what my husband gave his life for," she said' – *The Daily Telegraph* (6 May 1994); 'For the first time in his life, or almost the first time (you can never tell with this man), Ballesteros went on bended knee to the USGA to get an invitation' – *The Independent* (7 May 1994).

once a ——, always a —— Format deriving from an old series of proverbs, 'Once a knave/whore/captain, always a . . .' Dr Johnson used 'Once a coxcomb, and always a coxcomb' in an anecdote included in Boswell's *Life of Johnson* (1791) – for the year 1770. S. T. Coleridge wrote an article with the title *Once a Jacobin Always a Jacobin* (21 October 1802). William Cobbett quoted 'Once a parson always a parson' in his *Rural Rides* (for 11 October 1826). Charles Dickens in *Little Dorrit*, Chap. 28 (1857), has, 'Once a gentleman, and always a gentleman.' Mary O'Malley wrote a play called *Once a Catholic* (1971), and 'Once a Catholic always a Catholic' appears in full in a published letter by John Betjeman (28 February 1946) and in Angus Wilson's novel *The Wrong Set* (1949). *Partridge/ Slang* finds more recently, 'Once a teacher/policeman . . .' To which one could add, 'Once a Marine, always a Marine' from the USA (current in 1987) and the joke (noted in 1967): 'Once a knight, always a knight – and **twice a night, you're doing all right!**' *Partridge/ Catch Phrases*, however, finishes the joke off: '. . . twice a night, dead at forty' and dates it *circa* 1950 'but probably from at least fifty years earlier'.

once aboard the lugger and the girl is mine! 'A male catchphrase either joyously or derisively jocular' notes *Partridge/ Catch Phrases*. It came originally from a late Victorian melodrama – either *My Jack and Dorothy* by Ben Landeck (*circa* 1890) or, more likely, from a passage in *The Gypsy Farmer* (performed 1845) by John Benn Johnstone: 'I want you to assist me in forcing her aboard the lugger; once there, I'll frighten her into marriage.' In 1908, A. S. M. Hutchinson called a novel *Once Aboard the Lugger – the History of George and Mary*. The phrase occurs in the music-hall song 'On the Good Ship Yacki-Hicki-Doo-La', written and composed by Billy Merson in 1917, of which the chorus (in the version he recorded himself in 1933) is: 'Then I snap my fingers ha ha ha ha! / Then I snap the other one ho ho ho ho! / I don't care should the lady pine, / Once aboard the lugger and the girl is mine. / Then I set my sails and sail away. / No pirate e'er was cooler. / Wher'er I go I fear no foe. / On the good ship 'Yacki Hicki Doola'. *Benham* (1948) has a different version, as often. According to him: 'Once aboard the lugger and all is well' was said to have been an actor's gag in *Black Eyed Susan*, a nautical melodrama (*circa* 1830).

once again we stop the mighty roar of London's traffic   Stock phrase from the BBC magazine/interview programme *In Town Tonight*. From 1933 to 1960 this was the nearest BBC radio came to a chat show. It was introduced by what now sounds a very quaint montage of 'The Knightsbridge March' by Eric Coates, traffic noises, the voice of a woman selling violets in Piccadilly Circus, and then a stentorian voice – by some people believed (wrongly) to be that of Lord Reith – shouting '**Stopppp!**' Then an announcer would intone: 'Once again we stop the mighty roar of London's traffic and from the great crowds we bring you some of the interesting people who have come by land, sea and air to be "In Town Tonight".'

(the) once and future ——   Format derived from what, according to Sir Thomas Malory in *Le Morte d'Arthur* (1469–70), was written on the tombstone of the legendary King Arthur: '*Hic jacet Arthurus, rex quondam rexque futurus* [Here lies Arthur, the once and future king].' Hence, the title of T. H. White's Arthurian romance, *The Once and Future King* (1958). If a King Arthur did exist (possibly in the sixth century AD), there is a notice in the ruins of Glastonbury Abbey, Somerset, which claims to mark the site of his tomb – but no inscription is apparent.

once every Preston Guild   'Of a rare occurrence, infrequently'. *Partridge/Slang* has this as a Lancashire colloquialism. The fair known as Preston Guild (or Gild) (and more correctly as Preston Guild Merchant) was held irregularly before 1542 and since then has appeared every twenty years. The last was held in 1992, so the next is due in 2012.

once in a blue moon   Meaning, 'very rarely, if ever'. The notion of a 'blue moon' being something you *never* saw and could not believe in was current by 1528. However, given that in some circumstances the moon can appear blue, this

less stringent expression had established itself by 1821. Also, a blue moon is the second full moon within a given month (some say the third . . .). Either way, it is something that happens about once every two years – but still, obviously, a rare event.

(a) once in a lifetime (experience)   Phrase often used in travel promotion and in advertising. Known by 1908. 'The thrill that comes once in a lifetime' – heading in H. T. Webster, *Our Boyhood Thrills* (1915); *Once In a Lifetime* – title of Moss Hart/ George S. Kaufman play (1930; film US 1933); 'Once In a Lifetime' – title of song much performed by Anthony Newley and with lyrics by Leslie Bricusse (1961); 'The *Mail on Sunday* is giving two families of four (two adults, two children) a once-in-a-lifetime chance to experience this spectacular celebration of horsemanship from the comfort of one of Wembley Arena's new fully-catered VIP boxes' – *Mail on Sunday* (4 September 1994); '"It's a once-in-a-lifetime experience," agrees Kate Edwards, who has come with her husband, Nick. "Except we do it every year!"' – *The Independent* (19 December 1994); '"People are going for once-in-a-lifetime experiences which tend to be expensive," says James Daunt of Daunt Books, the . . . travel bookshop that is the scene of much pre-honeymoon browsing' – *The Independent* (15 September 1995).

once upon a time . . .   Traditional start to 'fairy' stories that has existed as a phrase for a very long time. George Peele has the line in his play *The Old Wives' Tale* (1595). The Old Woman begins a story she is telling with, 'Once upon a time there was a King, or a Lord, or a Duke . . .' – which suggests that it was a 'formula' phrase even then. No fewer than thirteen of the twenty-four *Classic Fairy Tales* collected in their earliest English versions by Iona and Peter Opie (1974) begin with the words. Mostly the versions are translations from the French of Charles Perrault's collected *Histories, or Tales of Past Times* (1697). The ready-made English phrase is used to translate his almost invariable '*Il estoit une fois.*' 'There was once upon a time a King and a Queen . . .'; 'Once upon a time, and be sure 'twas a long time ago . . .'; 'Once upon a time, and twice upon a time . . .';

'Once upon a time, and a very good time it was . . .' – all these variants hark back to a mythical past. The Opies comment that fairy stories 'are the space fiction of the past. They describe events that took place when a different range of possibilities operated in the unidentified long ago; and this is part of their attraction . . . The stories would, curiously, not be so believable if the period in which they took place was specified.' 'Never, in all my childhood, did any one address to me the affecting preamble, "Once upon a time!"' – Edmund Gosse, *Father and Son* (1907). The Nelson *English Idioms* (*circa* 1912) calls it 'a somewhat old-fashioned and pedantic phrase used to introduce an incident or story which took place at some indefinite time in the past'.

one   See ALL FOR ONE.

one among the unnumbered dead   Date of origin and source unknown. The phrase 'unnumbered dead' occurs in a 1967 speech (referring to the war in Vietnam) by Martin Luther King and in a modern translation of the *Annals* by Tacitus. Earlier, in a letter (dated 30 July 1863) about the Battle of Gettysburg and written by a certain Sergeant A. P. Carpenter, there is this: 'Two out of every three had fallen. Where are the other fourteen hundred whose names are borne upon our rolls? Some are sleeping on nearly all the Eastern battlefields from 1st Bull Run to Gettysburg. They have gone to rest; they are sleeping in soldiers' graves, among the unknown and unnumbered dead.'

(the) one and only   Promotional phrase about anything or anyone, but Phyllis Dixey (1914–64), the noted British strip-tease artist of the 1940s, was billed as 'The One and Only', as was Max Miller, the comedian. The Gershwins wrote a song 'My One and Only' for *Funny Face* (Broadway 1927).

one brief shining moment   Phrase from the title song of the musical *Camelot* (Broadway 1960): 'Don't let it be forgot / That once there was a spot / For one brief shining moment that was known / As Camelot . . .' *Camelot* was first produced on Broadway in December 1960 just before President Kennedy took office.

Hence, the name 'Camelot' came to be applied to the romantic concept of his presidency. As the lyric writer Alan Jay Lerner wrote in *The Street Where I Live* (1978), when Jackie Kennedy quoted the lines in an interview with *Life* Magazine after her husband's assassination in 1963: '*Camelot* had suddenly become the symbol of those thousand days when people the world over saw a bright new light of hope shining from the White House . . . For myself, I have never been able to see a performance of *Camelot* again.' In 1983, on the twentieth anniversary of President Kennedy's death, William Manchester wrote a memorial volume with the title *One Brief Shining Moment*.

one day all this will be yours, my son   Phrase spoken by a proud father gesturing proprietorially over his property. Date of origin unknown, but note: '"Perfect! By Jove, it's perfect!" Georgie was looking at the round-bosomed woods beyond the home paddock, where the white pheasant-boxes were ranged . . . Georgie felt his father's arm tighten in his. "It's not half bad – but *hodie mihi, eras tibi* [what's mine today will be yours], isn't it? I suppose you'll be turning up some day with a girl under your arm . . ."' – Rudyard Kipling, 'The Brushwood Boy' (1895). Nowadays only in parody? 'One day, son, a little of this will be yours' – caption to a Michael ffolkes's cartoon of a father and son in a wine cellar in *Punch* (11 February 1970); 'One day my son all this might *not* be yours' – headline to Albany Life assurance advertisement (December 1981); 'One day, my boy, all this *won't* be yours' – headline to National Provident life assurance ad (the same month as the previous citation); 'One day, my son, all this will be yours – but not just yet' – Glenmorangie whisky advertisement (December 1982).

one degree under   Phrase from advertising for Aspro headache pills. Current in the UK in the 1960s.

one fine day in the middle of the night   Phrase from a traditional nonsense rhyme. This version comes from Iona and Peter Opie, *I Saw Esau* (1947): 'One fine day in the middle of the night / Two dead men got up to fight. / A blind man came to see fair play, / A dumb man came to shout hurray.' Another version is: 'One fine day in the middle of the night, / Two dead men got up to fight, / Back to back they faced each other, / Drew their swords and shot each other.' Hence, *One Fine Day In the Middle of the Night* – title of a novel (1999) by Christopher Brookmyre.

(to have) one foot in the grave Meaning, 'to be near death'. The earliest citation in the *OED2* is from Burton's *Anatomy of Melancholy* (1621): 'An old acherontic dizzard that hath one foot in his grave.' The idea is older, however, and occurs in Barclay's *Ship of Fools* (1509) and the precise phrase is in J. Case, *Praise of Music* (1586). Swift in *Gulliver's Travels* (1726) uses the phrase in connection with the immortal Struldbruggs of Laputa. There is also a punning inscription upon the grave of the actor and dramatist Samuel Foote (d. 1777) in Westminster Abbey: 'Here lies one Foote, whose death may thousands save, / For death has now one foot within the grave.' David Renwick wrote a popular BBC TV comedy series *One Foot in the Grave* (1990–2000) about a man having to endure premature retirement.

(that's) one for the book Comment on a saying, exaggeration or claim that is so remarkable it ought to be consigned to the book kept for just this purpose in RAF messes since the 1920s. But also said to have been applied to a joke that was so good it deserved putting in the famous book *Joe Miller's Jests* (1739). A somewhat double-edged compliment.

one for the money See IT'S A.

one instinctively knows when something is right Promotional line from advertisements for Croft Original Port. Current in the UK in 1982. It has had some afterlife elsewhere.

one man, one vote Slogan first coined in the 19th century for a campaign led by Major John Cartwright (1740–1824), a radical MP ('the Father of Reform'), in the fight against plural voting. It was possible in those days for a man to cast two votes, one on the basis of residence and the other by virtue of business or university qualifications. This right was not abolished

until 1948. The phrase arose again during the period of the (illegal) Unilateral Declaration of Independence in Rhodesia (1965–80) to indicate a basic condition required by the British government before the breakaway could be legitimized. The phrase has also been used in the USA, in civil rights' contexts. In 1993, when the British Labour Party was trying to over-throw the 'block votes' that gave its trade union membership a disproportionate say in the formulation of policy, the phrase was rendered by the acronym **OMOV**.

one man's —— is another man's —— Format based on the original proverb 'One man's meat is another man's poison' (known in something like this form, in English, by 1576, but the idea dates back to classical times). From meaning, 'what one person likes another person doesn't', the format allows it to be suggested that 'what one man thinks on a subject may not be what another man does.' 'One man's terrorist is another man's freedom fighter' – current by 2001 (but the idea known since 1964); 'At least no one is going to say of him that one man's paedophile is another man's freedom fighter' – *The Independent* (18 January 2003).

one nation under God Phrase from one of the versions of the Pledge of Allegiance to the Flag (USA): 'I pledge allegiance to my flag and the republic for which it stands, one nation indivisible, with liberty and justice for all.' The Pledge was put into this form by Francis Bellamy in 1892 but omitting any mention of God or the United States. A dispute as to who wrote it – he or James Upham – was decided in Bellamy's favour after his death in 1939. In 1923, 'my flag' was changed to 'the flag of the United States', and the words 'of America' were added one year later. 'Under God' was added to 'one nation' in 1954, though this ran counter to the wish of America's founders who opposed the institutionalizing of religion. The wording is now: 'I pledge allegiance to the flag of the United States of America and to the republic for which it stands, one nation under God, indivisible, with liberty and justice for all.' See also AND JUSTICE FOR ALL. 'After a federal appeals court ruled last week that it is unconstitutional to make schoolchildren recite the phrase "one nation under God" in the Pledge of Allegiance, we placed a call to Robin Williams, to hear his thoughts on the decision. "Why don't they change it to 'one nation under Canada'?" he said. "Or 'over Mexico'? That way, everybody's happy'" – *The New Yorker* (8 July 2002).

one never knows, do one? Phrase always associated with the jazz pianist Fats Waller. He speaks the phrase at the end of his recording of 'Your Feet's Too Big' (1939) and seems to have said it on a number of occasions – also in the film *Stormy Weather* (US 1943) in the year he died. But it is also the title of a song written by Harry Revel and Mack Gordon for a film called *Stowaway*, which came earlier, in 1936. And that was a song that was sung later by Billie Holiday.

one of our aircraft is missing Phrase from Second World War news bulletins and, hence, the title of a film (UK 1941). In *A Life in Movies* (1986), Michael Powell writes: 'After I returned from Canada and I had time to listen to the nine o'clock news on the BBC, I had become fascinated by a phrase which occurred only too often: "One of our aircraft failed to return".' He determined to make a film about such a failed bombing mission. 'Our screenplay, which was half-finished, was entitled *One of Our Aircraft is Missing*. We were never too proud to take a tip from distributors, and we saw that the original title, *One of Our Aircraft Failed to Return*, although evocative and euphonious, was downbeat.' Eventually, Walt Disney came up with a film called *One of Our Dinosaurs is Missing* (US 1975).

one of them Derogatory phrase for (usually) a homosexual. Known by the 1950s/60s. Also 'one of those', by 1977. Homosexuals were known to say of their own kind that 'He is one of us', by 1961.

one over the eight This expression for 'drunk' is services' slang but not before the 20th century. For some reason, eight beers was considered to be a reasonable and safe amount for an average man to drink. One more and you were incapable. For a different theory, see under TAKE SOMEONE DOWN A PEG.

one small step for ——, one giant leap for —— Format from quotation. What Neil Armstrong claimed he said when stepping on to the moon's surface for the first time, on 20 July 1969, was 'That's one small step for a man, one giant leap for mankind'. The indefinite article before 'man' was, however, completely inaudible, thus ruining the sense. One suggestion is that, being from Ohio, Armstrong elided 'a man' in such a way that the 'a' appeared to be absent. Many reference books have been thrown into confusion since. Several follow the version – 'One small step for [. . .] man, one *big step* for mankind' (*sic*) – that appeared in the magazine *Nature* in 1974. The *Observer* 'Sayings of the Week' column in the week after the landing had 'That's one small step for [. . .] man, one giant leap for *all* [*sic*] mankind.' The correct version has even been set to music. The Great Mormon Tabernacle Choir sings: 'One small step for a man, one giant leap for mankind – / It shows what a man can do, if he has the will.' Either way, Armstrong launched an imperishable format: 'Small step for non-white mankind' – headline in *The Times* (29 October 1983); 'Up to 10.75% – one small step for your money, one giant leap for your interest rate. You'll be over the moon to discover you only need £1,000 to open a Capital Choice account at the Alliance & Leicester' – advertisement (July 1989); 'A small step for man; a giant leap for plastic frogs' – headline in *The Independent* (9 May 1992); 'Robert Bryhn, of the Swedish advertising agency which dreamt up the idea [of an advertising billboard in space] said in London yesterday: "This is a small step for the people behind the project but a giant leap for modern marketing"' – *The Independent* (12 August 1995); 'One small step is better than a giant leap in cost' – headline in *The Observer* (27 August 1995); *One Giant Leap* – title of film (US 2002).

one step forward, two steps back Phrase describing regression. In 1904, Lenin wrote a book about 'the crisis within our party' under this title [*Shag vpered dva shaga nazad*], but note that in *Conducted Tour* (1981), Bernard Levin refers to Lenin's 'pamphlet' under the title *Four Steps Forward, Three Steps Back*. Vilmos

Voigt pointed out in *Proverbium Yearbook of International Proverb Scholarship* (1984) that just after the publication of his work, Lenin referred to the 'current German form, *Ein Schritt vorwärts, zwei Schritte zurück* [one step forwards, two steps back]', and Voigt wondered what precisely the source of Lenin's phrase was and in what language it had been. 'Gemini. It's been a one-step-forward-two-steps-backwards time' – Russell Grant, astrologer, in the *Chiswick and Brent Gazette* (22 September 1983); 'Alternatively, try retro-dressing. It's here again. One step forward, thirty years back. The Fifties look is determined to make a comeback . . .' – *Cosmopolitan* (February 1987).

(the) one that almost got away Referring to any nearly missed opportunity. Based presumably on the angler's 'this was a fish that almost got away'. 'The biggest fish he ever caught were those that got away' – Eugene Field, American journalist and humorist (1850–95), quoted in *The Treasury of Humorous Quotations*, ed. Evan Esar & Nicolas Bentley (1951); 'Yes, that's the one that got away' – caption, referring to an empty fish tank, of a *Punch* cartoon (12 October 1938) – and one of many *Punch* cartoons using the phrase in that decade; *The One That Got Away* – title of film (UK 1957) (about an escaped prisoner); 'It was the anniversary that almost got away. The *Daily Mail* was the only newspaper to celebrate the opening of the first launderette in Britain 45 years ago last week' – *The Sunday Times* (8 May 1994).

one thing is certain Linking phrase. Date of origin unknown. 'One thing is certain, no matter what asset value Lasmo believes is appropriate, it will play no part in the thinking of Enterprise' – *Lloyd's List* (13 June 1994); 'Whatever happens when [Sibson and Kaylor, boxers] explode into belligerent action . . . at Wembley on Tuesday, one thing is certain: for the loser there will be nothing left except a rubble of wrecked hopes' – *Sunday Express* (25 November 1984); 'Most of these stones are huge and look extremely heavy, being three feet high, two feet wide and over two feet thick. They come in all shapes and sizes but one thing is certain: the

majority could not have been lifted by even two men' – *The Guardian* (11 May 1995).

(a) one-trick pony A person or organization that has only one talent, selling point or reason for existing. Date of origin unknown but American. From a pony in a circus or rodeo that could only perform one trick (and no doubt kept on repeating it monotonously). *One-Trick Pony* was the title of a film (US 1980) in which Paul Simon played a fading rock singer. 'The voguish storyline sees six individuals being legally abducted by a reality-TV show . . . It won an award at Sundance, but it's a one-trick pony' – *The Independent* (25 January 2003).

one wedding brings on another (or **begets/breeds . . .)** Proverbial superstition known since 1634. 'I am glad you are no enemy to matrimony however. Did you ever hear the old song, "Going to one wedding brings on another?"' – Jane Austen, *Northanger Abbey*, Chap. 15 (1818). Compare **one funeral makes many**, a proverb known since 1894.

(an) ongoing situation (or **an — position)** Cliché and format phrase. For several years starting in April 1976, *Private Eye* waged a campaign against the unnecessary addition of the word 'situation' in situations where the speaker thought it added something to the sentence. The column was entitled 'Ongoing situations'. This succeeded in making the matter a well-known joke but did not entirely put an end to the practice. Oddly, as long ago as 22 August 1934, *The Times* had drawn attention to the trend: 'A popular dodge at present is to add the word "situation" or "position" to a noun; by this means, apparently, it has been discovered that the most pregnant meanings can be expressed with the least effort. The "coal situation" remains unchanged; the "herring position" is grave.' A cliché, however, from the 1970s onwards. 'Ongoing situation' was identified as a still current cliché in *The Times* (17 March 1995). 'Whereas a hedge situation at Altwood Road, Maidenhead in Berkshire, belonging to you overhangs the highway known as Altwood Road, Maidenhead aforesaid, so as to endanger or obstruct the passage of pedestrians . . .' – an employee of the Royal Borough of Windsor and Maidenhead wrote to a householder and asked him to trim a hedge in these words (reported 1981); '[John Lennon] asked if I had ever tried [heroin]. I told him that while he was in India with the Maharishi, I had a sniff of it in a party situation . . .' – Yoko Ono, quoted in Peter Brown and Steven Gaines, *The Love You Make* (1983); 'Much has been learned since the first Whitbread [round-the-world yacht race] in 1973/74 when, tragically, three men died in man overboard situations . . .' – *High Life* Magazine (September 1993); 'Whether a conifer will recover from wind burn depends on the severity. If a severe draught is an ongoing situation, then recovery is unlikely' – *The Herald* (Glasgow) (16 July 1994); 'According to the British Airport Authority: "The thing about security is that we review it constantly and we certainly wouldn't be making any reductions. The process of review never stops, it's an ongoing situation"' – *Financial Times* (5 September 1994).

(the) onlooker sees most of the game
Little-recorded proverb, suggesting that when you are in the thick of something you don't get the whole picture. 'It is the onlooker that sees most of the game' – *Macmillan's Magazine* (November 1884).

only connect Phrase summing up the philosophy of the novelist E. M. Forster. It appears as the epigraph to *Howard's End* (1910). Goronwy Rees wrote in *A Chapter of Accidents* (1972): 'It could be said that those two words, so misleading in their ambiguity, had more influence in shaping the emotional attitudes of the English governing class between the two world wars than any other single phrase in the English language.' The words also occur in the body of Forster's book (Chap. 22): 'Only connect! That was the whole of her sermon. Only connect the prose and the passion, and both will be exalted, and human love will be seen at its height. Live in fragments no longer. Only connect, and the beast and the monk, robbed of the isolation that is life to either, will die.' Forster's message was that barriers of all kinds must be dismantled if the harmony

lacking in modern life was to be discovered.

only fools and horses The BBC TV comedy series with the title *Only Fools and Horses*, written by John Sullivan, has been on the air since 1981 and concerns itself with a pair of 'wide boy' brothers sparring together in London. The title must have puzzled many people. Although unrecorded in reference books, it apparently comes from an old Cockney expression, 'Only fools and horses *work*' – though this is also a proverb recorded in the USA. Compare 'Only fools and fiddlers sing at meals,' known by 1813, and observations such as 'Only fools and children believe it' from Dalton Trumbo's script for the film *Spartacus* (US 1960). It has been suggested that it makes more sense if you say, 'Only fools and horses work *for nothing*.' A version remembered from the 1930s goes: 'Only fools and horses work and horses turn their backs on it.' In the book *An tOileánach* [*The Islandman*] written in Irish by Tomás Ó Criomhthain (1856 –1937) and published in 1929, an inhabitant of the Great Blasket island in Kerry is quoted as saying *circa* 1911, '– *ná raibh ag obair sa tsaol seo ach capaill agus amadáin* [only horses and fools work in this world].' In a television documentary (2002) about his show, John Sullivan explained that much of his comic inspiration came from his father, whose family was Irish and were from County Cork. He has only mentioned 'only fools and horses work' as the reason for this title. But an Irish origin of this 'Cockney' saying now seems more than likely.

(the) only good Indian is a dead Indian Quotation to format phrase. Philip Henry Sheridan (1831–88), mostly a cavalry commander on the Federal side in the American Civil War, is supposed to have said this at Fort Cobb in January 1869, but exhaustive study by Wolfgang Mieder (in *The Journal of American Folklore*, No. 106; 1993) has shown that this particular racial slur may already have been proverbial and have been wished on Sheridan unjustly. For example, the previous year, during a debate on an 'Indian Appropriation Bill' in the House of Representatives (28 May 1868), James Michael Cavanagh (1823–79), a congressman from Montana, had said: 'I will say that I like an Indian better dead than living. I have never in my life seen a good Indian (and I have seen thousands) except when I have seen a dead Indian.' Mieder adds that, though Sheridan was known as a bigot and Indian-hater, Charles Nordstrom's account of the Fort Cobb incident in 1869 is of questionable authenticity: 'A chief of the Comanches, on being presented to Sheridan, desired to impress the General in his favor, and striking himself a resounding blow on the breast, he managed to say: "Me, Toch-a-way; me good Injun." A quizzical smile lit up the General's face as he set those standing by in a roar by saying: "The only good Indians I ever saw were dead".' Sheridan repeatedly denied having made any such a statement, but, whatever the case, an imperishable formula had been devised: 'The only good X is a dead X' is still with us.

only her hairdresser knows for sure See DOES SHE . . . OR DOESN'T SHE?

only in America ...! Exclamation meaning 'Only in America is this possible'. Used as the title of a British documentary TV series in 1980. Also of a novel (2002) by Dominic Holland. Leo Rosten wrote in *Hooray for Yiddish!* (1982): 'Not a week passed during my boyhood (or two weeks, since then) without my hearing this exclamation. It is the immigrants' testament, an affirmation of the opportunities imbedded in that Promised Land . . . America. Scarcely a new shop, new product, a new journal or school or fad could appear without ecstatic *Only in America!*s.'

only in the mating season Catchphrase from the BBC radio *Goon Show* (1951–60). A response to the traditional chatting-up line, DO YOU COME HERE OFTEN?

only the names have been changed to protect the innocent Stock phrase from the American TV series *Dragnet* (1951–8, revived 1967–9). The show was largely the creation of Jack Webb (1920–82), who produced, directed and starred in it. As 'Police Sergeant Joe Friday' he had a deadpan style that was much parodied. The show had first appeared on radio in

1949 and was said to draw its stories from actual cases dealt with by the Los Angeles police – hence the famous announcement: 'Ladies and gentlemen, the story you are about to hear is true. Only the names have been changed to protect the innocent.' The signature tune was almost a catchphrase in itself – 'Dum-de-dum-dum'.

only time will tell Cliché, especially of broadcast news journalism, and used by reporters to round off a story when they can't think of anything else to say. The proverbial expression has existed since 1539. 'Time alone can tell' appears in W. S. Gilbert, *HMS Pinafore*, Act 2 (1878). *Time* Magazine (March 1984) quoted Edwin Newman, a former NBC-TV correspondent, on a continuing weakness of TV news: 'There are too many correspondents standing outside buildings and saying, "Time will tell"' (indeed, the 'only' is often omitted). 'One only has to go to any other country to see what happens when the Civil Service is not a bulwark, when it does not have the traditions of our Civil Service. Only time will tell whether that bulwark is now about to be undermined' – *The Scotsman* (14 July 1994); 'Time alone will tell whether the French continue to shop for boys' names on our side of the Channel' – *Mail on Sunday* (11 June 1995).

only when I laugh (or larf) Phrase supposedly derived from an old joke about an English soldier in Africa who gets pinned to a tree by an assegai. When asked if it hurts, he replies with this stiff-upper-lip statement. In the film *Fancy Pants* (US 1950), Bob Hope regales Lucille Ball with an account of an imaginary adventure in Africa. 'There I was, with a spear through my body,' he says. 'Didn't it hurt?' asks Ball. 'Only when I laughed,' he replies. *Only When I Larf* was the title of a novel (1968; film UK 1968) by Len Deighton. As *Only When I Laugh*, it was the title of an ITV comedy series (1979–84), set in a hospital, and of a film (US 1981) that was released in the UK as *It Hurts Only When I Laugh* – which points to its origin.

(to be) on one's tod Meaning, 'to be on one's own'. From rhyming slang: Tod Sloan was a noted US jockey (d. 1933).

The expression was recorded by 1934. In Australia, there is the equivalent, **to be on one's Pat**, meaning to be on one's own, after a certain Pat Malone. Known by 1908.

(to be) on song To be on top form or in top condition. Although recorded in 1971, this phrase suddenly had a vogue in the 1980s, especially among sports commentators and journalists. 'Once the turbo [of a Saab Turbo] is "on song", the power comes in with a blood-tingling rush and catapult acceleration' – *The Daily Telegraph* (2 April 1986). The origin of the phrase would seem to lie in birdsong. Compare, therefore, the line 'then she went *off* song' in the music-hall song 'She Was One of the Early Birds' (*circa* 1900).

(to be) on the carpet (Of a servant or employee) to be reprimanded, hauled over the coals. The 'carpet' here probably refers to the covering on a table at which officials would sit rather than to the floor covering on which the person to be reprimanded might stand. Indeed, 'on the carpet' (*sur le tapis* in French) originally referred to what was up for discussion by, say, members of a council who would be seated at a table. This sense was established by the 18th century. The second (disciplinary) meaning, possibly of American origin, was well known by the early 19th century.

on the nail Promptly, when asked – usually of the making of a payment. Known by the 1590s. The port of Bristol is often given as the source of this saying. Outside the Corn Exchange there, merchants are said to have placed cash on flat-topped pillars (known as 'nails') to settle bargains. The *OED2*, however, points out that the explanations linking the phrase to exchanges at Bristol (and Limerick) are 'too late to be of any authority in deciding the question'. In fact, the phrase *may* have more to do with 'fingernail', as in the French expression *sur l'ongle*, 'precisely, exactly'.

on the road from —— to nowhere Signifying that a place (or a person) is in an obscure position (or is not getting anywhere). Date of origin unknown. Now a mostly journalistic cliché. 'My uncle's farm is on the road to nowhere . . . They often don't see a new face for months on end' – E. Coxhead, *One Green Bottle* (1951); 'People on foot on a hot road . . . walking from nowhere to nowhere' – *The Guardian Weekly* (21 March 1970); 'This time last week Jeddu was a one-horse town on the road from Kamba City to nowhere' – Tom Stoppard, *Night and Day* (1978).

on the toot (or **a toot)** On a drinking spree, from 'toot' or 'tout', meaning a drinking match (known by 1790). Probably an American expression. 'Well, let me tell you, he was out on a toot last night with one of my Nodders' – P. G. Wodehouse, 'The Nodder' (1933).

on the wagon Teetotal, not to be taking alcoholic drink. This phrase probably began in 19th-century America where people who had signed the pledge would say they were 'on the water cart', meaning they would rather drink water from the cart than take the demon drink. This somehow became 'on the wagon'. Perhaps temperance campaigners also invited would-be abstainers to climb aboard their campaign wagon? If they strayed, they would be said to have fallen off the wagon. A colourful theory, said to date back to the early 18th century and the days of public executions at Tyburn (now Marble Arch in west central London), is that when the condemned were being transported there from prison, they were allowed to stop at an inn for a last drink ('one for the road', so to speak). When the drink was over, they climbed back 'on the wagon' and would never drink again.

onwards and upwards! Perhaps this humorously uplifting phrase, designed to encourage, derives from a religious notion of striving onwards and upwards through the everlasting night. In James Russell Lowell's *The Present Crisis* (1844) we find: 'They must upward still, and onward, who would keep abreast of truth.' The first lines of the 19th-century hymn 'Onward! Upward!' (words by F. J. Crosby, music by Ira D. Sankey) are: 'Onward! upward! Christian soldier. / Turn not back nor sheath thy sword; / Let its blade be sharp for conquest / In the battle for the Lord.' Sankey also set the words of Albert

Midlane in 'Onward, Upward, Homeward!' of which the refrain is 'Onward to the glory! / Upward to the prize! / Homeward to the mansions / Far above the skies!' Or could the words be from a motto? The Davies-Colley family of Newfold, Cheshire, have them as such in the form 'Upwards and Onwards'. In 'School Song' from the musical *Passion Flower Hotel* (1965), the opening words are 'Onward and upward and forward and back', suggesting that this might be a common ingredient of such songs. 'Dreyfus' (Herbert Lom) exclaims, 'Onwards and upwards to the top!' in the film *The Pink Panther Strikes Again* (US 1976). The last words of the film *Brighton Beach Memoirs* (US 1986), based on Neil Simon's play, are, 'Puberty is over. Onwards and upwards.' 'Nicholas Craig' in *I, An Actor* (1988) asks of young actors: 'Will you be able to learn the language of the profession and say things like "onwards and upwards", "Oh well, we survive" and "Never stops, love, he *never stops*".' 'Onwards and upwards' as such was recorded by 1901.

on with the motley! *Partridge/Catch Phrases* suggests that this is what one says to start a party or trip to the theatre. It may also mean 'on with the show, in spite of what has happened'. Either way, the allusion is to the Clown's cry – '*vesti la giubba*' – in Leoncavallo's opera *I Pagliacci* (1892). The Clown has to 'carry on with the show' despite having a broken heart. So it might be said jokingly nowadays by anyone who is having to proceed with something in spite of difficulties. The English translation was undoubtedly popularized by Enrico Caruso's 1902 gramophone recording of the song (the first million-selling disc to be made). Laurence Olivier used the phrase in something like its original context when describing a sudden return dash home from Ceylon during a crisis in his marriage to Vivien Leigh: 'I got myself on to a plane . . . and was in Paris on the Saturday afternoon. I went straight on home the next day as I had music sessions for *The Beggar's Opera* from the Monday; and so, on with the motley' – *Confessions of an Actor* (1982). '*Giubba*' in Italian means simply 'jacket' (in the sense of costume),

and 'the motley' is the old English word for an actor or clown's clothes, originally the many-coloured coat worn by a jester or fool (as mentioned several times in Shakespeare's *As You Like It*).

on your bike! Meaning, 'go away' or 'be off with you'. *Partridge/Slang* dates this from *circa* 1960. The saying was unintentionally given a new twist when Norman Tebbit, newly appointed as Britain's Employment Secretary, addressed the Conservative Party conference (15 October 1981). He related how he had grown up in the 1930s when unemployment was all around. '[My father] did not riot. He got on his bike and looked for work. And he kept on looking till he found it.' This caused the pejorative catchphrase 'on your bike' or 'get on your bike' to spring from the lips of Mr Tebbit's opponents. He later pointed out that he had not been suggesting that the unemployed should literally get on their bikes but claimed to find the catchphrase 'fun'.

ooh, an 'e was strong! See under RIGHT MONKEY!

ooh, aah, Cantona! Chanted by supporters of the French footballer Eric Cantona when he was playing for the British teams Leeds United and then Manchester United. Noted from 1992 onwards. At Christmas 1994, Peter Cook composed a trendy church service for *Private* Eye that included this refrain. In 1996, the group 1300 Drums got to No. 11 in the UK record charts with a number entitled 'Ooh! Aah! Cantona' ('Oo . . . Ah . . . Cantona' by Oo La La having made it only to No. 62 in 1992). In 1997, Cantona himself tried to register the phrase as a trademark. Earlier, fans had chanted 'Ooh, aah, Paul McGrath' about the Irish footballer.

ooh, an' 'e was strong See RIGHT MONKEY.

ooh, Betty! Catchphrase of the accident-prone Frank Spencer (Michael Crawford) in the BBC TV series *Some Mothers Do 'Ave 'Em* (1974–9). In particular, the catchphrase was extended to include, 'Ooh, Betty, the cat's done a whoopsie!' when every impressionist in the land took it up.

ooh, I say! Stock exclamation of Dan Maskell in his Wimbledon tennis commentaries for BBC TV during the 1970s and 80s. His voice became an essential part of the occasion. 'Ooh, I say! There's a *dream* volleh!' was remarked on by TV critic Clive James in *The Observer* (1 July 1979) and, a year later, 'Ooh, I *say*! That's as brave a coup as I've seen on the Centre Court in *yers*.' Accordingly, *Ooh, I Say!* became the title of a BBC TV programme to mark Maskell's eightieth birthday in 1988. He died in 1992. He would also use such expressions as 'quite extraordinary!' and 'a peach of a shot'.

ooh-la-la (or oh-la-la)! Phrase, mostly used journalistically, to express the naughtiness commonly associated with the French. Known by 1924 – so possibly a product of the Allies being in France during the First World War. Listed by Keith Waterhouse in *Daily Mirror Style* (1981): 'This foreign-desk phrase, believed to be extinct, was sighted recently in the *Sun*.' 'The ooh-la-la French maid' – *The Spectator* (24 July 1959); 'Those two great standbys of French fashion, quality and a little bit of ooh-la-la' – *The Times* (10 April 1973).

ooh, mother! See under IT'S TURNED OUT NICE AGAIN.

ooh, you are awful . . . but I like you! Catchphrase of the comedian Dick Emery (1917–83) in the character of Mandy, a man-hungry spinster, in several series of BBC TV, *The Dick Emery Show* (started 1963 but mostly in the 1970s). The phrase was followed by a quick bash of her handbag. Also the title of a song and of a feature film (UK 1972). Another of his characters – Hetty, an equally amorous character – would inquire **are you married?**, and Clarence, a camp gentleman, would greet with **hello, honky-tonks!** Either as a result of this, or coincidentally, 'honky-tonk' became one of the names for a homosexual in the Britain of the mid-1970s. Hitherto, of course, the word had described a jangly type of piano or anything that was shoddy, and as plain 'honky' it had been a Black American racist slur against white men (said to derive from the fact that they would honk the horns of their motors when picking up black girlfriends).

oompah, ompah, stick it up your jumper! Dismissive phrase that could be used in response to a stupid suggestion (compare 'why don't you just go and stuff it . . . ?') but really no more than a meaningless exclamation. 'Oompah, oompah' is, of course, imitative of the noise made by a brass musical instrument such as a euphonium or tuba. Known since the 1920s and possibly quoting a line from a song.

opening See ANOTHER.

open sesame! Meaning 'open up (the door)!' or as a mock password, the phrase comes from the tale of 'The Forty Thieves' in the ancient Oriental *Tales of the Arabian Nights*. When it was spoken by Ali Baba, the robbers' door flew open. Sesame seed is also famous for its other opening qualities as a laxative. 'Genius was understood and poetry a sort of "open Sesame" to every noble door' – Mrs Oliphant, *Literary History of England* (1882).

open the box! Contestants in the old British TV quiz *Take Your Pick* – which ran on ITV for almost twenty years from 1955 – were given the option of opening a numbered box (which might contain anything from air-tickets to Ena Sharples's hairnet) or accepting a sum of money which might turn out to be worth more – or less – than what was in the box. The studio audience would chant its advice – 'take the money' or, more usually, 'open the box!' When the host, Michael Miles ('Your Quiz Inquisitor'), died, it was joked that his funeral was interrupted by the congregation shouting, 'Open the box! Open the box! . . .'

open the cage See MUM MUM.

open the door, Richard! Catchphrase from the BBC radio show *ITMA*. It was the title line from a popular American song (1947), first sung in Britain on *ITMA*.

(the) opera ain't over till the fat lady sings Modern proverb. Relatively few modern proverbs have caught on in a big way but, of those that have, this one has produced sharp division over its origin. It is also used with surprising vagueness and lack of perception. If it is a warning 'not to count your chickens before they are hatched', it is too often simply employed to express a generalized view that 'it isn't over till it's over'. So how did the saying come about? A report in *The Washington Post* (13 June 1978) had this version: 'One day three years ago [i.e. 1975], Ralph Carpenter, who was then Texas Tech's sports information director, declared to the press box contingent in Austin, "The rodeo ain't over till the bull riders ride." Stirred to that deep insight, San Antonio sports editor Dan Cook countered with, "The opera ain't over till the fat lady sings".' Two days before this (i.e. 11 June 1978), *The Washington Post* had more precisely quoted Cook as coming up with his version *the previous April*, 'after the basketball playoff game between the San Antonio Spurs and the Washington Bullets, to illustrate that while the Spurs had won once, the series was not over yet. Bullets coach Dick Motta borrowed the phrase later during the Bullets' eventually successful championship drive, and it became widely known and was often mistakenly attributed to him.' Another widely shared view is that the saying refers to Kate Smith, a handsomely proportioned American singer in the 1930s and 1940s. Her rendition of Irving Berlin's 'God Bless America' signified the end of events like the political party conventions and World Series' baseball games. Hence, possibly, the alternative version: the **game's not over till the fat lady sings**. On the other hand, it has been argued that American national anthems ('The Star-Spangled Banner', 'America the Beautiful' among others) are usually sung at the *start* of baseball games, which would remove the point from the saying. If the 'opera' version can actually be said to mean anything, it derives from a hazy view of those sopranos with a 'different body image' who get to sing a big number before they die and thus bring the show to a close. But they do not do this invariably. In *Tosca*, for example, the heroine makes her final death plunge over the battlements without singing a big aria. The end of Wagner's opera *Siegfried* is, however, signalled by the arrival of Brünnhilde who does indeed sing and is often played by a well-proportioned singer. Whatever the case, allusive use of the proverb is widespread – especially just the second part of

it. The Fat Lady Sings was the name of an Irish (pop) band, formed *circa* 1990. After winning the US presidential election in November 1992, Bill Clinton appeared at a victory party in Little Rock bearing a T-shirt with the slogan 'The Fat Lady Sang', which presumably meant no more than 'It's over.' In July 1992, tennis champion Andre Agassi, describing the surprise climax of his Wimbledon final, said, 'I knew that it might just go to 30–30 with two more aces. I didn't hear the fat lady humming yet.' The American singers En Vogue had a song called 'It ain't over till the fat lady sings' about this time, and there were several books with approximate versions of the phrase for their titles. As is to be expected with a proverbial expression, the *idea* behind 'the fat lady' is nothing new. In Eric Maschwitz's memoir, *No Chip on My Shoulder* (1957), he recalled Julian Wylie, 'The Pantomime King': 'He had a number of favourite adages about the Theatre, one of which I have always remembered as a warning against dramatic anti-climax: "Never forget," he used to say "that once the giant is dead, the pantomime is over!"' Which is a corollary if ever there was one. That there were earlier American versions of the saying appears to be confirmed by *A Dictionary of American Proverbs* (1992), which lists both 'The game's not over until the last man strikes out' and 'Church is not out 'til they sing'. *Bartlett* (1992) finds in *Southern Words and Sayings* by F. R. and C. R. Smith, the expression 'Church ain't out till the fat lady sings'. As the Smiths' book was published in 1976, this would seem to confirm that the 'opera' version of the proverb is only a derivative.

opportunity knocks A talent contest with this title ran on British TV from 1956 to 1977. Introducing contestants, the host, Hughie Green (1920–97), would say: **for (***name***) of (***place***), opportunity knocks!** and so characteristic was the pronunciation that the phrase became his. It derives, of course, from the rather more restrictive proverbial expression, 'Opportunity knocks *but once*'. As *CODP* notes, 'fortune' occurs instead of 'opportunity' in earlier forms of the proverb and slightly different ideas are expressed – 'opportunity is said to knock once or more, but in other quotations, once only'. From Sir Geoffrey Fenton's *Bandello* (1567) comes the example: 'Fortune once in the course of our life, doth put into our hands the offer of a good turn.' In the TV show, Green is reported to have said, **this is your show, folks – and I do mean you**. He would also say **it's make-your-mind-up time** when inviting viewers at home to decide who they were going to vote for. First of all, however, the audience in the studio was asked to applaud the various contestants and their support was registered on a 'clapometer'. But it was the postcards from the viewers that really mattered, and **I mean that most sincerely, folks!** 'Sir Jeremy Beecham . . . added that after prolonged discussions and "tweaking" of a potential agreement, there was now a workable basis for a settlement [with firefighters]. "It's make your mind up time," he claimed' – *The Independent* (20 May 2003).

—— or bust! Slogan format light-heartedly expressing that you will accomplish something or die in the attempt. Date of origin unknown. *Monte Carlo or Bust* was the title of a comedy movie about a car race (France/UK/Italy 1969). 'Europe or bust' was a slogan of the Confederation of British Industry at the referendum on EEC membership in 1975. Perhaps derived from 'I must or I'll bust' (i.e. 'burst') that *Partridge/Catch Phrases* gives as what someone desperately heading for the lavatory would say (*circa* 1925).

order, order! Traditional call to order given by the Speaker of the House of Commons. George Thomas (later Viscount Tonypandy) (1909–97) made it very much his own as he was in office when radio broadcasts of the proceedings began for the first time on 3 April 1979. 'George Thomas gave the last Parliament its verbal hallmark. "*Order, order*" was the catchphrase from the Speaker's chair that swept the country – delivered in that soft, distinctive Welsh lilt' – *Sunday Express* (19 June 1983).

orphans of the storm How one might describe, humorously, any bedraggled, rain-soaked people. The phrase was the title of a famous silent film (US 1921), with Lillian and Dorothy Gish as two sisters caught up in the French Revolution (a somewhat different type of storm). Before this, it had been the title of a play by Adolph Ennery.

. . . or words to that effect Mock pedantic phrase spoken when having (perhaps inaccurately) quoted something said by another. Date of origin unknown, but in Isaac D'Israeli, *Commentaries on the Life and Reign of Charles the First* (1830), is: 'Laud . . . turned out Archy, the King's fool, for a pun [viz. for saying as grace "Great praise be to God, and little Laud to the devil", or words to that effect].'

Oscar See GIVE THE MAN AN.

(the) other side of the coin (or penny) I.e. what also exists as part of some situation – and usually less welcome. Date of origin unknown. The implication is that the first matter is inseparable from the other, just as the reverse of a coin is unalterably linked to the obverse. Known by 1904 (as 'the other side of the halfpenny').

OTT See OVER THE TOP.

our day will come Slogan of the Provisional IRA (Irish Republican Army). This is an English translation of the Gaelic '*Tiocfaidh Ar La*'. Relatives of those accused of trying to blow up the British Prime Minister at Brighton in 1984 shouted it out as the defendants were being sentenced in court on 23 June 1986. The phrase had existed independently of this use. It is also the title of a song performed by the American vocal group Ruby and the Romantics (1963). Compare 'Our day is come', as it appeared in Lord Lytton's novel, *Leila* (1838).

our friends in the North *Our Friends in the North* was the title of a BBC TV drama series (1996) tracing the lives of four teenage friends from the 1960s to the 1990s. The phrase has an almost insidious memorability – and it is not a quotation. In Shakespeare's *Richard II,* IV.iv.484 (1595), Stanley says, 'My friends are in the north', but that's not quite it.

our mutual friend Title phrase of the novel (1864) by Charles Dickens and referring to its hero, John Harmon, who feigns death and whose identity is one of the mysteries of the plot. A rare example of Dickens using an established phrase for a title (he usually chose the invented name of a character). 'Our mutual friend' was an expression established by the 17th century, but undoubtedly Dickens encouraged its further use. Some have objected that 'mutual friend' is a solecism, arguing that it is impossible for the reciprocity of friendship to be shared with a third party. Even before Dickens took it for a title, a correspondent was writing to the journal *Notes and Queries* in 1849, asking: 'Is it too late to make an effective stand against the solecistic expression "mutual friend"?' The *Oxford Dictionary for Writers and Editors* (1981) points out that it is an expression used also by Edmund Burke, George Eliot and others, but 'the alternative "common" can be ambiguous'.

our reporter made an excuse and left Journalistic cliché. With the onset of the mass-circulation British newspaper came the rise of a two-faced mode of reporting that sought to depict vice and crime in a titillating way while covering itself with righteous condemnation and crusading zeal. *The People*, which was founded in 1881 as a weekly (and became the *Sunday People* in 1971), was one of those muckraking papers that developed a method of reporting sexual scandals which sometimes involved a reporter setting up a compromising situation – e.g. provoking prostitutes and pimps to reveal their game – and then making it clear that, of course, the journalist had taken no part in what was on offer. Having found out all that was needed, 'our reporter made an excuse and left' – a classic exit line, probably from the 1920s onwards. It was still going strong, more or less, in the *News of the World* (12 March 1989): 'Our investigator declined her [Pamella Bordes's] services and she put her clothes back on.'

ours is a nice 'ouse See I'M DREAMING.

out See BETTER OUT.

(to) out-Herod Herod Literary allusion, often adapted in the format phrase 'to out-something something' and meaning to go beyond the extremes of tyranny (or whatever activity is under consideration)

as usually perceived. The allusion is to Herod's slaughter of all the children of Bethlehem (Matthew 2:16). The precise formulation of the phrase occurs in Shakespeare's *Hamlet*, III.ii.8 (1600), when the Prince is instructing the actors not to go over the top: 'O! it offends me to the soul to hear a robustious periwig-pated fellow tear a passion to tatters . . . I would have such a fellow whipped for o'erdoing Termagant; it out-herods Herod: pray you, avoid it.' (Termagant and Herod both featured in medieval mystery plays as noisy violent types.) Popular in the 19th century, a cliché by the end of it. 'Italian composers essaying the more classical forms are impelled to out-Herod Herod in the seriousness and Teutonicism of their productions' – *Westminster Gazette* (2 October 1901); 'In an act of gross unfairness that even out-Thatchered Thatcher, one-in-four of all workers were sentenced to a three-year standstill. And in an act of gross meanness, that even out-Scrooged Scrooge, the Government's punitive pay policy, unlike any other since the last war, offers no protection whatsoever for the poorest-paid' – *The Herald* (Glasgow) (31 December 1993).

out of —— Format phrase. A small epidemic of 'out of ——s' spread with the release of the film *Out of Africa* (US/UK 1985), based in part on Isak Dinesen's 1938 book (originally, in Danish, *Den Afrikanske Farm*). A series of weekly columns entitled 'Out of Europe/Asia/etc.' was launched by *The Independent* in 1986. In that same year, both Ruth Prawer Jhabvala and Tim Piggot-Smith brought out books called *Out of India*. Perhaps the original had something to do with Pliny's version of a Greek proverb, '*Ex Africa semper aliquid novi* [there is always something new out of Africa]', in his *Natural History*, VIII.17. The title of the Noah Beery film *Out of Singapore* (US 1932) would seem to derive, rather, from the shipping use of 'out of', meaning the port from which a ship has sailed.

out of a clear blue sky Phrase for when something happens completely unexpectedly – as though its approach could not be seen in the sky despite the lack of clouds. Perhaps the combining of 'clear' and 'blue' is recent. Early examples just have 'clear' *or* 'blue' sky. 'So from a clear sky falls the thunderbolt!' – Tennyson, *Queen Mary: A Drama*, V.iii.264 (1875). It was soon remarked upon that the terrorist attacks on New York in September 2001 came, literally, out of a 'clear blue sky'. 'Perhaps the 1993 assault on the buildings should have been taken as a warning that others would want to finish the job, but who would have dreamt that this would come out a clear blue sky? – *The Independent* (15 September 2001).

out of kilter Awry, in a mess, out of condition. Known since 1628 in the USA. Of unknown origin, although the word 'kilter' = 'order, condition' is an old one. 'Mr John Cox, director-general of the Chemical Industries Association, said that this perceived imbalance between the industry's value and its social costs is not only out of kilter but is also a threat to the industry's "licence to operate"' – *Financial Times* (4 February 1995); 'The popular mood and the political mood are out of kilter. None of Sweden's main political parties has publicly campaigned for an end to the monopoly' – *Financial Times* (8 February 1995).

out of the Ark Meaning, 'something that is very old indeed', alluding to the antiquity of Noah's Ark. Thackeray in *Roundabout Papers* (1860–63) has: 'We who lived before railways, and survive out of the ancient world, are like Father Noah and his family out of the Ark.'

out of the closet (and into the street) Slogan for the US homosexual rights organization known as the Gay Liberation Front, *circa* 1969. The starting point was the term 'closet homosexual' or 'closet queen' for one who hid his inclinations away in a closet ('cupboard' in American usage rather than 'lavatory' or 'small room', as in British English).

out of the cradle endlessly rocking Silent film screen title occurring in D. W. Griffith's epic *Intolerance* (US 1916). It accompanies a shot of Lillian Gish rocking a cradle and is repeated many times during the course of the long film. It comes from the title of a poem (1859) by Walt Whitman.

out of the frying pan into the fire Out of one bad situation and into another. Most languages have similar expressions for this predicament: the Italians have 'from the frying pan into the coals', and the ancient Greeks had 'out of the smoke and into the flame'. Known in English by 1532 (Sir Thomas More).

out of the mouths of babes and sucklings . . . Remark when a child or other supposedly innocent person produces a pearl of wisdom. From Psalm 8:2: 'Out of the mouth of babes and sucklings hast thou ordained strength because of thine enemies.' Matthew 21:16 has: 'Out of the mouth of babes and sucklings thou hast perfected praise.' Note 'mouth' not 'mouths' in both cases.

(you must be) out of your tiny Chinese mind Meaning 'mad'. Gratuitously offensive, but one suspects that the only reason for 'Chinese' is because it chimes with 'tiny'. Probably dates from the 1950s, at the earliest. The simpler 'out of your tiny mind' *may* be the older expression, though it is not recorded until 1965. Compare DAMN CLEVER THESE CHINESE! The phrase caused inevitable offence when used by Britain's Chancellor of the Exchequer, Denis Healey, in February 1976 about left-wing opponents of his public expenditure cuts. In his book, *The Time of My Life* (1989), he writes: 'I accused Ian Mikardo of being "out of his tiny Chinese mind" – a phrase of the comedienne Hermione Gingold, with which I thought everyone was familiar. On the contrary, when he leaked it to the press, the Chinese Embassy took it as an insult to the People's Republic.'

out to lunch Mad, barmy. Known by 1955 in the USA. Presumably because the person 'is not *there*' or 'not *all there*', and this is a possible explanation for the phrase.

overpaid, overfed, oversexed and over here Phrase describing American troops in Britain during the Second World War. Ascribed to Tommy Trinder, the English comedian (1909–89) in *The Sunday Times* (4 January 1976). This was Trinder's full-length version of a popular British expression of the early 1940s. He certainly did not invent it although he may have done much to popularize it. *Partridge/Catch Phrases* makes no mention of Trinder and omits the 'overfed'. As 'over-sexed, over-paid and over here' it is said also to have been a popular expression about American troops in Australia 1941–5 – according to *The Dictionary of Australian Quotations* (1984) and to have been revived there during the Vietnam War.

over the garden wall Phrase evoking neighbourliness and especially gossipy conversation. It is the title of a painting by Helen Allingham (*circa* 1880) and was also used to describe particular British variety sketches performed by the comedian Norman Evans (1901–62) in the character of Fanny Fairbottom, a garrulous woman. He also used it as his bill matter.

over the hills and far away Escaped, far distant. One of the most used phrases by poets and songwriters over several centuries – Alfred Tennyson, Robert Louis Stevenson, John Gay among them. In Farquhar's *The Recruiting Officer* (1706), is the exact phrase: 'For now he's free to sing and play, / Over the hills and far away.' The second line occurs slightly altered at the end of each verse. This song reflects the time of Queen Anne and her general, Marlborough, who campaigned in the War of the Spanish Succession in the very early years of the 18th century. But the words were already being alluded to in a ballad, 'The Wind Hath Blown My Plaid Away' (*circa* 1670 and possibly as old as 1549): 'My plaid awa, my plaid awa, / And ore the hill and far awa, / And far awa to Norrowa.' The tune with the title 'Over the Hills and Far Away' dates from about 1706. The song now known by this title was written by John Gay and adorns *The Beggar's Opera* (1728).

over the moon Jubilant, very pleased. In about 1978, two cliché expressions became notorious in Britain if one wished to express either pleasure or dismay at the outcome of anything, but especially of a football match. The speaker was either 'over the moon' or SICK AS A PARROT. It probably all began because of the remorseless post-game analysis by TV football commentators and the consequent need for players and managers to provide pithy comments. Liverpool footballer Phil

Thompson said he felt 'sick as a parrot' after his team's defeat in the 1978 Football League Cup Final. Ironically, *Private Eye* fuelled the cliché by constant mockery, to such an extent that by 1980 an 'instant' BBC Radio play about the European Cup Final (written on the spot by Neville Smith according to the outcome) was given the alternative titles *Over the Moon/Sick as a Parrot*. Some failed to note the cliché. *The Times* (21 January 1982) reported the reaction of M. Albert Roux, the London restaurateur, on gaining three stars in the *Michelin Guide*: '"I am over the moon," M. Roux said yesterday . . . he quickly denied, however, that his brother [another celebrated restaurateur] would be "sick as a parrot".' 'Over the moon' is probably the older of the two phrases. Indeed, in the diaries of May, Lady Cavendish (published 1927) there is an entry for 7 February 1857 saying how she broke the news of her youngest brother's birth to the rest of her siblings: 'I had told the little ones who were first utterly incredulous and then over the moon.' The family of Catherine Gladstone (*née* Gwynne), wife of the Prime Minister, is said to have had its own idiomatic language and originated the phrase. However, the nursery rhyme 'Hey diddle diddle / The cat and the fiddle, / The cow jumped over the moon' dates back to 1765 at least and surely conveys the same meaning. Besides, the Reverend Sydney Smith was reported in 1833 as having said 'I could have jumped over the moon' and in Sir John Vanbrugh's play *The Relapse*, IV.i (1696), Hoyden says: 'O Lord, I could leap over the moon'. The specific application to football was already in evidence in 1962, when Alf Ramsey (a team manager) was quoted as saying, on one occasion, 'I feel like jumping over the moon.'

over the top (or **OTT)** Exaggerated in manner of performance; 'too much'. The expression 'to go over the top' originated in the trenches of the First World War. It was used to describe the method of charging over the parapet and out of the trenches on the attack. In a curious transition, the phrase was later adopted for use by show-business people when describing a performance that had gone beyond the bounds of restraint, possibly to the point of embarrassment: 'They are forced by a dagger, some over the top acting and Don Quixote forcing Lorenzo to bless the union of Kitri and an apparently dying Basilio' – screen title in the film of the ballet *Don Quixote* (Australia 1973). In 1982, a near-the-bone TV series reflected this by calling itself *OTT*. After which, you heard people saying that something was 'a bit OTT' instead of the full expression. On 15 February 1989, *The Independent* quoted from a play called *State of Play* at the Soho Poly theatre: 'Look at sport – I'm sure you'll agree: / It's much more fun when it's OTT.' For 'over the top and the best of luck' see AND THE BEST OF LUCK!

(to score an) own goal In the original football sense (by 1947), this meant a goal scored against one's own side. With grim humour, the phrase was adapted to describe bringing harm upon oneself – most usually, a terrorist being blown up by a bomb that he has made to kill someone else. As such, it originated with the security forces in Northern Ireland and was in use by 1976. A very similar coinage to SHOOT ONESELF IN THE FOOT or HOIST WITH ONE'S OWN PETARD. '[Princess Anne added] "It could be said that the Aids pandemic is a classic own goal, scored by the human race on itself, a self-inflicted wound that

only serves to remind *Homo sapiens* of his fallibility"' – *The Guardian* (27 January 1988); 'Ozal risks own goal in move to kick life into slack election [by attending a Turkish football team's foray into European soccer – when it might have lost the game]' – *The Guardian* (20 March 1989).

owns See ASK THE MAN.

(the) oxygen of publicity Date of origin unknown, though modern use of the phrase stems chiefly from Margaret Thatcher's pronouncement to an American Bar Association meeting in London (15 July 1985): 'We must try to find ways to starve the terrorists of the oxygen of publicity on which they depend.' Coinage of the phrase has been ascribed to Britain's then Chief Rabbi, Lord Jakobovits. Identified as a current cliché in *The Times* (17 March 1995). 'In this ludicrously competitive atmosphere, in which companies deprived of the oxygen of publicity gasp for survival, they resort to ever bolder ways of attracting audiences' – *The Independent* (20 July 1994); 'After 15 years, even parrots get bored, particularly those without the remotest possibility of a larger cage, nor even the prospect of a bell or a mirror to play with. Gasping for the special oxygen, that of publicity, they snatch at any mouthpiece' – *The Independent* (27 November 1994).

P

packed See AND IN A.

(a) packed courtroom Mostly journalistic use. Date of origin unknown. Noted as a cliché in *The Sunday Telegraph* (19 September 1982). 'The chief prosecutor told a packed courtroom that the seven had "actively engaged in preparations to overthrow the lawful government by armed rebellion"' – *Financial Times* (8 February 1983); 'A teenager who spent more than a week in jail for refusing to testify against a US congressman finally took the stand yesterday and said he paid her to have sex with him when she was 16. Beverly Heard, 19, a former campaign worker for Representative Mel Reynolds,

told a packed courtroom she had sexual intercourse many times with the Democrat, who is 43' – *The Herald* (Glasgow) (8 August 1995).

page See ANOTHER PAGE.

(to) paddle one's own canoe To control one's own affairs. American origin – early 19th century, although Captain Marryat's *The Settlers in Canada*, Chap. 8 (1844) has: 'I think it much better that . . . every man paddle his own canoe.' There was a poem with the phrase in *Harper's Magazine* (by Sarah Bolton) in May 1854 and an American 'proverb song' called 'Paddle Your Own Canoe' (*circa* 1871) written by Harry Clifton: 'Then love your neighbor as yourself, / As the world you travel through. / And never sit down with a tear or frown, / But paddle your own canoe.'

(to) paint oneself into a corner To give oneself no route of escape, to reduce the number of options open to one to zero. Date of origin unknown. American origin? Occasionally used transitively (compare 'to drive someone into a corner'): 'Republicans painted them into corners as tax-and-spend democrats' – Christopher Ogden, *Life of the Party*, Chap. 16 (1994), but this misses the point that one has brought the matter upon oneself.

pair See ENOUGH BLUE.

pale See BEHOLD A; BY THE PALE.

(a) pall of fear Journalistic cliché. Date of origin unknown. 'The pall of fear hangs heavy over the strife-torn city today' – cited by Malcolm Bradbury in an article on clichés in *Tatler* (March 1980); 'Nor is it only Hikkaduwa that is living under a pall of fear. The 60-mile road from the capital, Colombo, was deserted last week. It was the same for 100 miles in every direction' – *The Sunday Times* (13 November 1988); 'Despite the massive security force presence at the stadium and a peace pact between police and ANC marshals until midnight tonight, a pall of fear hangs over the country' – *Evening Standard* (London) (19 April 1993).

(wanting the) palm without the dust Wanting a successful outcome without expenditure of effort. It was said of Lord Rosebery, the British Liberal Prime Minister in the 1890s, that 'he wanted the palm without the dust' – an allusion to Horace, the Roman author, who talked of 'the happy state of getting the victor's palm without the dust of racing'. '*Palma non sine pulvere* [no palm without labour]' is a motto of the Earls of Liverpool, among others.

(to open) Pandora's box To let loose a whole stream of difficult problems. In Greek mythology, Pandora – the first mortal woman – kept a box in which were sealed all the evils of the world. They escaped when she opened the box, with only hope remaining. Now, possibly the most used of surviving classical references.

'The favours of Government are like the box of Pandora, with this important difference, that they rarely leave hope at the bottom' – J. E. T. Rogers, *Economic Interpretations of History* (1888); 'Every idea has tended to fall victim to political wrangling between idealists concerned exclusively for the architectural fabric of Venice, environmentalists worried that solving one problem can open up a Pandora's box of others, and trade unionists keen to protect jobs on the mainland' – *The Independent* (1 February 1996).

panel See IS IT BIGGER.

panic See DON'T PANIC.

panic stations! Light-hearted use of the naval term 'be at panic stations', meaning 'be prepared for the worst' (and current from the beginning of the Second World War). Nowadays, it may mean no more than 'don't get in my way, I've got a crisis on!'

pants See FLY BY THE.

papers See ALL I KNOW IS.

(a) paper tiger A person who appears outwardly strong but is, in fact, weak. It was popularized by the Chinese leader Mao Tse-tung, who told a US interviewer in 1946: 'All reactionaries are paper tigers. In appearance, the reactionaries are terrifying, but in reality they are not so powerful.' *Paper Tiger* was used as the title of a film (UK 1975) about a coward who pretends to be otherwise.

parameter PHRASES. This is to say, phrases involving 'limits, boundaries' – from scientific terminology. Date of origin unknown, but given the quotation marks in the first citation, the popular, figurative use may have begun in the 1960s. 'The fact that Nixon was willing to make his chastisement public suggests . . . that the President at least understands "the parameters of the problem"' – *Time* Magazine (3 August 1970); 'Mr Murdoch has made his feelings on this subject very clear to me and I am determined that, as he says, the *News of the World* will strive to maintain the best practices of popular investigative journalism within the agreed parameters of the code of conduct' – *The Times* (12 May 1995); 'Using the simulator, cars can be developed and tested without actually building them: instead, the parameters of suspension design and aerodynamics can be loaded into the computer and proven with a hard drive around the virtual landscape' – *The Daily Telegraph* (13 May 1995).

(of) paramount importance　Pairing known by 1877. 'Bull, of paramount importance to Taylor's promotion plans, limped off after aggravating scar tissue around his hamstring but not before creating the 11th-minute winner' – *The Daily Telegraph* (15 August 1994); 'The executive said: "We will be asking British Gas for evidence that they will be in a position to discharge their duty. Safety is of paramount importance and must not be jeopardised"' – *The Daily Telegraph* (30 December 1994); 'They were of "paramount importance", Mr Ruggiero said, not simply because they covered a big chunk of international commerce but because they were the first test of the credibility of the WTO' – *Financial Times* (4 May 1995).

pardon　See ARE YOU GOING.

pardon me for breathing ...　Response to having been corrected peremptorily (for having said something perhaps) or to generally being made to feel unwanted. Date of origin unknown, though the earlier **pardon me for living** was established usage by 1962. '"Sorry, did I say something wrong?" said Marvin, dragging himself on regardless. "Pardon me for breathing, which I never do anyway so I don't know why I bother to say it, oh God I'm so depressed"' – Douglas Adams, *The Hitch Hiker's Guide to the Galaxy*, Chap. 11 (1979).

(oops,) pardon, Mrs Arden (there's a pig in your garden)!　What you exclaim after belching or burping in order to deflect attention from yourself. In 1997, the *Sunday Telegraph* Magazine started a picture puzzle series under the title 'Pardon, Mrs Arden', but where did the phrase come from? Diligent research unearthed these citations: from the *Daily Mail* (19 March 1994): 'It was blissful to lie in my adjoining single bed, watching her undress down to her vest and pink satin bloomers, averting my gaze while she used what she called the "Edgar Allan", then listening to the crunch of biscuits, the

slurp of gin and tonic and the occasional gentle belch, followed by an apologetic murmur of "Oops! Pardon Mrs Arden!"'; and from *The Daily Telegraph* (29 January 1994): 'Every time you said "pardon" to old Charlie, who worked on the farm, he would answer: "Pardon, Mrs Arden, there's a pig in your garden".' At this point, my wife woke up and added (from her Buckinghamshire childhood) the variant: '. . . there's a pig in your *back* garden', plus the rejoinder, 'That bain't no pig, that be my son, John.' A correspondent whose surname at birth was Arden wrote (2001): 'At my earliest school, a kindergarten in Belsize Park, and at my first Prep School in Croydon, I was often teased with the rhyme: "Ooh beg pardon, Mrs Arden, / For doing nasties/poopoo in your garden." This was almost invariably triggered by someone in the playground breaking wind. The connection between this teasing and my last name made it an easy decision for me to accept my step-father's family name upon my adoption.' But, again, where did the phrase come from? It has been suggested that there was a novelty song with the title 'Pardon, Mrs Arden', continuing, 'There's a kitten in your garden / Saying miaow, miaow, miaow, miaow / Isn't it a pity that it's such a pretty kitty / Saying miaow etc.' I have been unable to trace this but presumably it is the same song as reported having been sung in a show at the Theatre Royal, Manchester, in 1937/8, with the words: 'Pardon, Mrs Arden, / There's a kitty in your garden / And it goes miaow, miaow, miaow, miaow. / All it wants is a saucer full of milk, / Feel her coat for it's just like silk, / So!! Pardon, Mrs Arden, / There's a kitty in your garden, / And it goes miaow, miaow, miaow, miaow.' However, it does seem to be the case that there was an 1870s' music-hall song beginning, 'Beg your parding, Mrs Harding, / Is my kitting in your garding?' It is referred to in Vyvyan Holland's book *Son of Oscar Wilde* (1954): 'Parding Mrs Harding / Is our kitting in your garding, / Eating of a mutting-bone? / No, he's gone to Londing. / How many miles to Londing? / Eleving? I thought it was only seving. / Heavings! *What* a long way from home!' This couplet may also have been included: 'I'm sorry, Missus

Dewsberry / I haven't seen her since last Tuesberry.' H. Montgomery Hyde's *Oscar Wilde* (1976) has the first two lines as, rather: 'Beg your parding, Mrs Harding, / Is my kitting in your garding?'; and Kathleen Strange remembered the first three lines in 1997 when she was 92, as 'I beg your parding, Mrs 'Arding / Is my kitting in your garding / Eating of a herring-bone?' Geoffrey Grigson's anthology *The Cherry Tree* (1959) has yet another version: 'Beg parding, Mrs Harding, / Is my kitting in your garding? / Is your kitting in my garding? / Yes she is, and all alone, / Chewing of a mutting bone.' All in all, it is not hard to see how the expression 'pardon, Mrs Arden' could have developed from this.

pardon my French (or excuse ...) What you say after using bad language in an attempt to lessen its offensiveness. The use of 'French' to mean 'bad language' was known by 1895 when the 'excuse my French' version appeared in *Harper's Magazine*. In the Hecht and MacArthur play *The Front Page*, Act 2 (1928), 'McCue', after saying 'Hell!' adds, 'Excuse my French!' 'Pardon my French' was recorded in 1936. Possibly these phrases had been encouraged by British and American forces being stationed in France during the First World War.

pardon the pun See IF YOU'LL EXCUSE.

par for the course Meaning, 'what you would expect' and derived from golfing parlance. Known by 1947. 'Some midnight assignations, a bit of bonking and a good deal of philosophizing are obviously par for the course' – *Venue* Magazine (26 April 1985).

Paris by night Promotional tag for tourism in the French capital, in use since the 1950s at least. P. J. Kavanagh in *The Perfect Stranger*, Chap. 5 (1966), writes (of the late 1940s): 'We even went to the *Bal Tabarin* together on a "Paris by Night" trip, and I saw my first naked girls.' A London West End revue (with Benny Hill) used the somewhat nudging phrase as its title in 1955, as did a David Hare film (UK 1989). From the 1930s onwards there was a cheap perfume, available from Woolworth and manufactured by Bourjois (*sic*),

called 'Evening in Paris' – also trading, it would seem, on the city's reputation for sophisticated pleasures.

Paris is for lovers Phrase, spoken in Billy Wilder's film *Sabrina* (US 1954 – *Sabrina Fair* in the UK), that almost has the ring of an official slogan, though this was long before the days of such lines as 'I Love New York' (1977) and 'Virginia is for Lovers' (1981). Nor is there a song including the phrase or using it as a title, though Cole Porter's Broadway musical *Silk Stockings* (US 1955) has one called 'Paris Loves Lovers'.

Parker See AS DOROTHY.

(a) parlous state (or parlous times) Inevitable pairings. 'Thou art in a parlous state, shepherd' – Shakespeare, *As You Like It*, III.ii.42 (1598). 'It does not seem like it, but there are 14 other artists at the Serpentine, representing Germany, France and New York, as well as ex-Goldsmiths'. They demonstrate that things are in as parlous a state abroad as here' – *Evening Standard* (London) (15 May 1994); 'Basingstoke council has spent £12 million on it. That is courageous in these parlous times. And the Anvil is not short of surprises' – *The Times* (21 May 1994).

parrots and monkeys Goods and chattels, personal possessions. 'Whenever we were about to embark on a trip my father used to say, "Pick up your monkeys and parrots, fall in facing the boat and don't knock the blooming thing over" – he claims it was common parlance in the Third Hussars but I've never met another Third Hussar to prove it!' – John Brooks, Gloucestershire (1998). *Partridge/Slang* has this as *Army* slang since about 1930 and derives it from the returning *seaman*'s pets and souvenirs.

parsnips See FINE WORDS.

parson See ENOUGH TO MAKE.

part See ANOTHER PART.

(a) parting shot An action or remark usually made dismissively as a last gesture (giving one's opponent no chance to respond). Originally, this was **Parthian shot**, so called from the ancient Parthian horsemen who would turn in flight and fire arrows at their pursuers. 'Bremond had to retire from the battle in good order, getting in a Parthian shot at me . . . by begging Feisal to insist that the British armoured cars in Suez be sent down to Wejh. But even this was a boomerang since they had started!' – T. E. Lawrence, *Seven Pillars of Wisdom*, Chap. 18 (1926/ 35).

partner of one's joys and sorrows
Phrase (usually) for one's spouse and as such a more or less direct quotation from Charles Dickens, *David Copperfield*, Chap. 42 (1849–50). In a letter to David, Mrs Micawber refers somewhat archly to herself, first as 'the bosom of affection – I allude to his wife' and then to 'the partner of his joys and sorrows – I again allude to his wife.' Dickens may, however, have been using an already existing, if looser, formula. Earlier, Scott, in *The Talisman,* Chap. 6 (1825), has: 'The Almighty, who gave the dog to be companion of our pleasures and our toils . . .' and in Motteux's 1703 translation of *Don Quixote*, Sancho Panza refers to his horse Dapple as 'my faithful companion, my friend, and fellow-sharer in my toils and miseries.' A later use: in P. G. Wodehouse, *Ring for Jeeves*, Chap. 9 (1953), Rory refers to Monica (to whom he is indeed married) as 'my old partner of joys and sorrows'.

(a) partridge in a pear tree Lines from the old Christmas carol/nursery rhyme, 'The first day of Christmas, / My true love sent to me / A partridge in a pear tree', have been questioned, chiefly because the game bird is a famously low flyer and is never seen in trees. A popular suggestion (which also explains some of the other gifts listed in the song) is that a 'partridge in a pear tree' is a corruption of the Latin *parturit in aperto* [she gave birth in the open], referring to Mary's delivery of Christ in a stable. Similarly, a mishearing of the Latin for 'the shepherds coming down from the hills' – *descendens de collibus* – could explain the phrases 'three French hens' and 'four colly/calling birds'. The rhyme, which is also known in French, was first recorded in English in *circa* 1780.

party See IS THIS THE.

party on See NOT!

(a) party pooper (or **poop)** Someone who manages to spoil or put a damper on fun by his or her actions or behaviour. American slang originally and known since the mid-1940s. 'No one can call Mr Bulganin and Mr Khrushchev party poopers . . . The Russian leaders demonstrated their suavity and cleverness at the party' – Earl Wilson column (5 July 1956), cited in *DOAS*.

(the) party's over Phrase used to describe the end of absolutely anything but inevitably used in political contexts. On 4 June 1990, the *Daily Express*, *The Sun* and the *Daily Mirror* all used it in headlines regarding the collapse of the British Social Democratic Party. In 1975, Anthony Crosland, the Labour minister, said that local government was 'coming to realize that, for the time being at least, the party is over'. On 12 October 1963, the BBC TV satirical show *That Was the Week That Was* marked the resignation of Prime Minister Harold Macmillan with William Rushton singing the song of this title in a broken-voice. In fact, there are two songs: Noël Coward's 'The Party's Over Now' from *Words and Music* (1932) and 'The Party's Over' from *Bells Are Ringing* (1956) by Comden, Green and Styne.

pas devant les enfants See NOT IN FRONT.

pass See AND THIS TOO; CUT OFF AT THE.

(a/the) passing show Contemporary life seen as a procession, pageant or slowly moving public spectacle. A theatrical 'revue' of such events. Possibly American in origin. 'A whole passing show . . . Your friends grotesquely photographed' – *Sear's Roebuck Catalogue* (1908); *The Passing Show* – title of a revue by Arthur Wimperis (London 1915) and of a show (Broadway 1922). In the 1950s, *The Passing Show* was the title given to a series of BBC TV shows reviewing popular entertainment during the first half of the 20th century. The most notable was that in which Pat Kirkwood portrayed the musical-hall star Marie Lloyd.

passion See ALL PASSION SPENT.

(to) pass the buck Meaning 'to shift responsibility on to someone else', the phrase derives from some card games, where a marker called a 'buck' is put in front of the dealer to remind players who the dealer is. When it is someone else's turn, the 'buck' is 'passed'. The original marker may have been a buckthorn knife or, in the Old West, a silver dollar – hence the modern use of the word 'buck' for a dollar. Known by 1865.

pass the sickbag See I THINK WE SHOULD.

(a) past master A person of acknowledged skill in some activity. From the term applied to a former master of a guild, company or freemasons' lodge. Known by 1868, though in the original sense by 1762.

(to be) past one's sell-by date The phrase 'sell-by date', referring to the date when perishable foodstuffs ought to be sold was known by 1973. In a figurative sense, especially when a person is thought to be 'over the hill', the phrase became popular in the late 1980s. 'I suspect the *Neighbours* phenomenon has reached its peak anyway, though not yet its "sell-by" date' – *The Observer* (4 February 1990); 'Once described by an over-enthusiastic newspaper as "one of London's most eligible bachelors", Stacpoole is now grey, portly and, at 55, looking rather past his sell-by date' – *Today* (1 September 1994); 'Wood and his ilk are well past their sell-by date and it amazes me that they have been able to exert such a huge influence on the sport' – *The Observer* (8 January 1995); 'I'm what they call past my sell-by date, but I've worked at fitness and motivation and that's kept me going longer than most' – Graham Gooch, cricketer, quoted in *Sunday Express* Magazine (14 May 1995).

pat See AMERICA CANNOT STAND.

path See BEAT A PATH.

(the) pathetic fallacy The attribution of human feelings to nature or, to put it another way, the belief that nature reflects human feelings when this is expressed, usually in literature. So, a thunderstorm may be represented as echoing some human drama played out beneath it. Coined by John Ruskin, the English art critic (1819–1900) in *Modern Painters*, Vol. 3 (1856): 'All violent feelings . . . produce . . . a falseness in . . . impressions of external things, which I would generally

characterize as the "Pathetic fallacy".' 'To find a funeral possession proceeding us up the hill to Haworth was a real stroke of what in the theatre is called production. Anything more stagey can hardly be imagined. The pathetic fallacy was working overtime: the sky loured and threatened, the wind wailed and wuthered, gutters wept copiously' – William Plomer, *At Home*, Chap. 10 (1958).

patience and perseverance . . . 'I live in the West Midlands. A few miles from here at Rowley Regis are quarries where they blast a very hard local rock known as Rowley Rag. My Gran used to say that: "Patience and perseverance will saw through Rowley Rag with a feather"' – Patricia M. Rodwell, West Midlands (1995). Compare this with the rhyme recalled by Jim Snell of West Sussex (1998), as said to him in his childhood (around 1918) by his mother: 'Patience and perseverance / Made a bishop of His Reverence'.

(the) patter of tiny feet Phrase indicating that small children are present or that babies are expected in a household. Longfellow has 'patter of little feet' in 1863. 'Going to have little feet pattering about the home?' – P. G. Wodehouse, *Ice In the Bedroom*, Chap. 6 (1961); 'Expectant motherhood these days is marked less by the patter of tiny feet than the tinkling of cash registers' – *The Times* (29 October 1977); 'Newlyweds Nicolas Cage and Patricia Arquette are expecting the patter of tiny feet' – *Hello!* Magazine (13 May 1995).

Paul Pry Name applied to one who pries furtively, a NOSEY PARKER, a PEEPING TOM. Loosely, a nosey, inquisitive person. From an American song (1820). *Paul Pry* was also the title of a comedy (1825) by John Poole and a book (1845) by Thomas Hood. As a result of the play title, several public houses have been called 'The Paul Pry' and their signs show him listening at doors marked 'Private' etc. 'The straitest champion of marital fidelity would, surely, not defend such monstrous Paul Prying' – *The Times* (4 March 1960).

(the) pause that refreshes Slogan used to advertise Coca-Cola from 1929 on. Other Coke slogans, out of scores, include:

thirst knows no season (from 1922); **it's the refreshing thing to do** (current 1937); **things go better with Coke** (from 1963); **I'd like to buy the world a Coke** (from 1971 – the jingle became a hit in its own right when retitled 'I'd Like to Teach the World to Sing'); **Coke adds life** (from 1976); **have a Coke and a smile** (current 1980). See also under COME ALIVE . . . and REAL THING.

pay See CAN'T PAY; EQUAL PAY.

pay freeze See WAGE FREEZE.

(to) pay through the nose Meaning, 'to pay heavily'. One possible explanation for the origin of the phrase lies in the 'nose' tax levied upon the Irish by the Danes in the 9th century. Those who did not pay had their noses slit. Known by 1672. 'TV and radio pay through the nose to cover games live or in highlights packages' – *Daily Record* (1 February 1995); 'A wide smile like Julia Roberts' is much sought after – and some people will pay through the nose for a set of gleaming teeth like hers' – *Sunday Mirror* (26 March 1995).

pay tribute to my long-suffering wife Authors' cliché from the acknowledgements section of their books (compare 'to my wife, without whom . . .') but the phrase 'long-suffering wife' on its own is a cliché also. Known by 1969 – in *Time* Magazine, for example. 'The movie stars John Goodman from TV's Roseanne as larger-than-life Fred and Elizabeth Perkins as his long-suffering wife Wilma' – *Northern Echo* (31 May 1994); 'Its main characters are a hard-drinking, foul-mouthed father, his long-suffering wife (whom he beats regularly) and a family variously embroiled in gangs, tragedy and corrective institutions' – *Independent on Sunday* (16 April 1995); 'I must now pay tribute to the long-suffering good nature of my wife Sally and my two daughters . . . they have lived through this project with me for a number of years' – Martin Walker, *Words Without Frontiers: The Spread of European English* (1995).

PC Plod Like OLD BILL, this is another critical nickname for the British police, perceived as having lumbering ineptitude in the catching of criminals and a plodding walk while on the beat. The most likely allusion is to a character in the 'Noddy' children's books that first appeared in 1949. 'The BBC is reviving Noddy this autumn, but would Enid Blyton recognise the lad? . . . Grumpy old PC Plod will be "less aggressive", while the golliwogs will be replaced by monkeys and gremlins' – *The Independent* (10 April 1992).

peace at any price Slogan. 'Peace at any price; peace and union' was the slogan of the American (Know-Nothing) Party in the 1856 US presidential election. The party supported ex-President Fillmore, and the slogan meant that it was willing to accept slavery for blacks in order to avoid a civil war. Fillmore lost to James Buchanan. It has been suggested that the phrase had been coined earlier (in 1848 or 1820) by Alphonse de Lamartine, the French foreign affairs minister in his *Méditations Poétiques* in the form: '*La paix à tout prix*'. However, the Earl of Clarendon quoted an 'unreasonable calumny' concerning Lord Falkland in his *History of the Rebellion* (written in 1647): 'that he was so enamoured on peace, that he would have been glad the king should have bought it at any price'. When Neville Chamberlain signed his pact with Hitler in 1938, many praised him for trying to obtain 'peace at any price'.

(a) peace dividend A benefit bestowed by the cessation of hostilities – e.g. the fact that savings can be made by the withdrawal of troops and reduction of arms' expenditure when an atmosphere of tension no longer obtains. The phrase was coined at the time of the collapse of communism in eastern Europe in 1989, which meant that, for example, the presence of American troops in western Europe was no longer necessary. It was also applied to Northern Ireland during the IRA ceasefire (1994–6). 'There is only one obvious solution: the long-term diversion of funds from military to peaceful spending; the so-called "peace dividend"' – *The Observer* (24 December 1989); 'He turned to an elegant blonde lady . . . "You must meet this man. He's the most important man in the Government. He's producing the peace dividend"' – Alan Clark, *Diaries* (1993). The idea may have been formulated, though not expressed in this phrase, at the end of the Vietnam War in the early 1970s.

peace for our time (or **in our time**) Slogan. On his return from signing the Munich agreement with Hitler in September 1938, the British Prime Minister, Neville Chamberlain, spoke from a window at 10 Downing Street ('not of design but for the purpose of dispersing the huge multitude below' [according to his biographer Keith Feiling]). He said: 'My good friends, this is the second time in our history that there has come back from Germany to Downing Street PEACE WITH HONOUR. I believe it is peace for [sic] our time. Go home and get a nice quiet sleep.' His phrase 'peace for our time' is often misquoted as 'peace *in* our time' – as by Noël Coward in the title of his 1947 play set in an England after the Germans have conquered. Perhaps Coward, and others, were influenced by the phrase from the Prayer Book: 'Give Peace in our time, O Lord'.

peace is our profession Slogan (by 1962) of the US Strategic Air Command. In 1972, there was a US film called *Lassie: Peace Is Our Profession*.

peace with honour Slogan. When Benjamin Disraeli returned from the Congress of Berlin (1878), which had been called to settle the 'Balkan question' – this was what he claimed to have achieved. Two days before Neville Chamberlain returned from signing the Munich agreement with Hitler, someone had suggested that he might like to use the Disraeli phrase. He impatiently rejected it, but then, according to John Colville, *Footprints in Time* (1976), he used the phrase at the urging of his wife – see PEACE FOR OUR TIME.

pearls before swine Referring to things of quality put before the unappreciative, the source is Matthew 7:6: 'Give not that which is holy unto the dogs, neither cast ye pearls before swine.' See also under AGE BEFORE BEAUTY.

pear-shaped See IT'S ALL GONE.

(they're getting) peas above sticks 'I had an aunt who had an apt and witty saying for every eventuality – sometimes rather sharp and not very kind, but always

apt. Of anyone she knew who had got above themselves, she would say, "The peas have grown above the sticks"' – Doris Humphrey, Grantham (1995).

(the) peasants are revolting! As with the NATIVES ARE HOSTILE!, this is a jocular way of describing almost any form of unrest among people. It also harks back to what imperialist Britons (or medieval tyrants) *might* be supposed to have said, if only in historical fiction. The actual Peasants' Revolt (against taxes) took place in southern England in 1381.

pecker See I'VE GOT HIS.

***pecunia non olet* [money does not smell]** Meaning, 'don't concern yourself with the source of money. Don't look a gift horse in the mouth'. A quotation from the Emperor Vespasian. In about AD 70, when Vespasian imposed a tax on public lavatories, his son Titus objected on the grounds that this was beneath the dignity of the state. The Emperor – according to Suetonius, *Lives of the Ceasars* – took a handful of coins and held them under his son's nose, and asked if they smelt. On being told they didn't, Vespasian said, '*Atque et lotio est* [yes, that's made from urine].' As a result, public urinals in France are still sometimes called *Vespasiennes*.

peel See BEULAH.

(a) peeping Tom Name given to a voyeur of any kind and deriving from Tom the Tailor, who was struck blind because he peeped when **Lady Godiva** rode by. In the legend, Lady Godiva's husband, the Lord of Coventry, agreed to abolish some harsh taxes only if she would ride naked through the town. The townspeople responded to her request that they should stay behind closed doors – all except Peeping Tom. This element of the story was probably grafted on to the record of an actual happening of the 11th century. *Peeping Tom* was the title of a film (UK 1959) about a man who films his victims while murdering them.

penny for the guy See PLEASE TO REMEMBER.

penny plain and twopence coloured Plain and fancy. 'A Penny Plain and Twopence Coloured' was the title of a noted essay (in *The Magazine of Art*, 1884) by Robert Louis Stevenson on the toy theatres or 'juvenile drama' of his youth. The expression referred to the prices of characters and scenery you could buy either already coloured or in black and white to colour yourself. As a phrase, the *Oxford Dictionary of Current Idiomatic English* (1985) has that it means 'in cheap or more expensive (attractive or merely showy) form (from, formerly, paper cut-outs of characters and scenery for toy theatres)'. On the other hand, the *Longman Dictionary of English Idioms* (1979) takes things a little further: '*rather old-fash.*: [meaning] although one of two similar things may be more attractive or bright in appearance than the other, they both basically have the same use or value'. Stevenson popularized the phrase, but it undoubtedly existed before. George Augustus Sala, *Twice Round the Clock* (1859), has: 'The Scala [theatre, Milan] . . . with its rabbit-hutch-like private boxes, whose doors are scrawled over with the penny plain and twopence coloured-like coats of arms of the . . . Lombardian nobility.' *Tuppence Coloured* (on its own) was the title of a theatrical novel by Patrick Hamilton (1927) and of a revue (with Joyce Grenfell and others) in 1947.

(the) penny has dropped Realization has dawned; the implications of a situation have belatedly been understood. Known by the 1940s. From the workings of a slot machine in which it takes a certain amount of time for a coin to operate. 'The penny had begun to drop before the present fuel crisis' – *The Times* (1 December 1973).

people like us See PLU.

people of goodwill Pompous cliché. Date of origin unknown. Listed in *The Independent* (24 December 1994) as a cliché of newspaper editorials. Compare Malcolm Muggeridge on writing leading articles for *The Manchester Guardian* in the 1920s: 'Many an uplifting sentence did I tap out . . . expressing the hope that moderate men of all shades of opinion would draw together, and that wiser counsels would yet prevail.' 'Dr Carey, in his address of welcome, called on people of goodwill to pray that "there may be built a worldwide community where all acknowledge one another as true brothers and sisters, where war shall be no more"' – *The Daily Telegraph* (6 June 1994); 'Failing a guarantee from the RUC that Sunday's parade will be rerouted, LOCC again calls upon all people of goodwill, irrespective of political affiliation, to support our peaceful protests' – *The Irish Times* (22 April 1995).

(the) people's —— Phrase format. The most noted use of this formula in recent years has been British Prime Minister Tony Blair's rapid-response TV statement on hearing of the death of Diana, Princess of Wales (31 August 1997): 'She was the People's Princess, and that is how she will stay . . . in our hearts and in our memories forever.' The phrase was suggested to the PM by his press secretary, Alastair Campbell, though it had already been used regarding the princess by journalists. Also, in 1984, *The People's Princess* had been the title of a book by S. W. Jackman about Princess Mary, Duchess of Teck, the 'crowd-pleasing' mother of Queen Mary. There is, of course, a long history of usage of the formula in egalitarian and/or communistic contexts – we have had the People's Car (*Volkswagen*, known as such by 1938) and then the People's War, not to mention Bureau, Court, Army, and much else. The People's Palace (a London educational institution for the working class) was being referred to as such by 1854 though not formally opened until 1887. Flora Thompson's *Lark Rise* (1939), recalling her Victorian country childhood, tells us that Prime Minister Gladstone was referred to as 'The People's William' – as in the song: 'God bless the people's William, / Long may he lead the van / Of Liberty and Freedom, / God bless the Grand Old Man.'

(a) perfect stranger The phrase 'perfect stranger' – as in 'I'm a perfect stranger to this part of the world' (meaning 'complete, entire' rather than 'possessing perfection') can be found in Vanbrugh, *The False Friend* (1699). From Wilkie Collins, *No Name*, Sc. 2, Chap. 1 (1862–3): '"You are mistaken," she said quietly. "You are a perfect stranger to me".' *The Perfect Stranger* was the title of a volume of autobiography by P. J. Kavanagh (1966), dealing in part with the death of his young wife. He prefaces it with a quotation from Louis MacNeice: 'Or will one's wife also belong to that country / And can one never find the perfect stranger?'

perfick! Kentish pronunciation of 'perfect' as found particularly in H. E. Bates, *The Darling Buds of May* (1958) and subsequent stories. In Chapter 1 of that first book, Pa Larkin talks of 'perfick wevver' for 'perfect weather'. The expression 'perfick!' again had a vogue in the spring of 1991 when the stories were dramatized for British TV with huge success. At that time, 'Perfick' was *The Sun*'s headline over a front-page story about the new council tax (Pa Larkin is a notable income tax dodger); the Family Assurance Society promoted a tax-free investment with the word as a headline in newspaper adverts in May 1991 (revealing, at the same time, that the word had been registered as a trade mark by Yorkshire Television, the programme's producer).

(the) perils of Pauline *The Perils of Pauline* was the name given to a classic cinema serial (1914 onwards) in which Pearl White portrayed a girl, 'Pauline', who was always getting into hair-raising scrapes and then being rescued.

permission to speak, sir! Catchphrase from the BBC TV comedy series *Dad's Army* (1968–77). In the Home Guard platoon, the elderly Lance-Corporal Jones (Clive Dunn) would request 'Permission to speak, sir!', using the correct services' formula. He would also shout **don't panic!** and remark **they don't like it up 'em** (re bayonets).

Persil washes whiter See WHITER THAN WHITE.

personal chemistry See SEXUAL.

(a) person from Porlock A person who, unwittingly, provides reason or excuse for not finishing some task, especially a literary or creative one. From S. T. Coleridge's introductory note to *Kubla Khan* (1816) describing how he, the poet, was interrupted in writing out the two or three hundred lines that had come to him in his sleep, when staying in Somerset: 'On awaking he . . . instantly and eagerly

wrote down the lines that are here preserved. At this moment he was unfortunately called out by a person on business from Porlock.' The incident happened in 1797 after Coleridge had taken opium and fallen asleep.

(a) person of restricted growth Politically correct term for a 'dwarf' or 'midget', though how widely it is used is in doubt. The expression first came to general attention when Lord Snowdon made a TV film on the subject, with the title 'Born To Be Small' (1971). 'An international dwarf-throwing competition in West Germany next month has been cancelled . . . The Hamburg-based Organisation of People of Restricted Growth protested about what it called a macabre spectacle' – *The Daily Telegraph* (18 February 1986); 'Let us get this absolutely clear: Mickey Rooney is not a dwarf, nor a midget, nor a person of stunted nor restricted nor diminished growth, nor is he waist-high to the average grasshopper. Such opening conversational gambits as "Hi there, shortie", or "What's the weather like down in the carpet?" would not be recommended unless you fancy a sharp head-butt in the ankle' – *The Times* (15 March 1992).

Pete See FOR PETE'S SAKE.

phew, what a scorcher! *Private Eye*'s joke headline as over hot-weather reports from tabloid newspapers. This has been current since about 1970 when the magazine published a cartoon showing two Fleet Street journalists sweating under a hot sun with the caption, '60–70–80 – Phew, what a scorcher!' Presumably the phrase did once appear in an actual newspaper. A 'scorcher' was common usage in the 1930s. In Patrick Hamilton's radio play *Money with Menaces* (1937), the events take place in a heat wave: 'Weather hot enough for you, sir?' – 'Yes, it's a scorcher, isn't it?' In fact, *OED2* finds 'scorcher' as early as 1874.

Phoebe See DON'T FORCE IT.

phone a friend See IS THAT YOUR.

(the) phoney war At first, when war was declared in September 1939, nothing happened. Neville Chamberlain talked of a 'Twilight War', and on 22 December

Édouard Daladier, the French Prime Minister, said: '*C'est une drôle de guerre* [it's a phoney war]' – spelt 'phony' in the USA. On 19 January 1940, the *News Chronicle* had a headline: 'This is Not a Phoney War: Paris Envoy.' And Paul Reynaud employed the phrase in a radio speech on 3 April 1940: '"It must be finished", that is the constant theme heard since the beginning. And that means that there will not be any "phoney peace" after a war which is by no means a "phoney war".' Though speaking French, Reynaud used the phrase in English.

(a) photo opportunity An 'event' prepared solely so that it will attract the media cameras and thus publicity for the subject of the photocall. Given the contrivance involved – it is a form of PSEUDO-EVENT – it is surprising how the media invariably fall for it. Said to have been raised to an art form by Ronald Reagan's advisers when he was US President. 'Heseltine['s] visits . . . tend to be one long photo-opportunity . . . Whatever the occasion you could be sure it would produce pictures and copy' – *The Listener* (16 January 1986); 'They operate in the slick new tradition of political handlers, whose job is to reduce a campaign to photo ops and sound bites' – *Time* Magazine (21 November 1988).

Phyllosan fortifies the over-forties Slogan for Phyllosan tonic, current in the UK from the 1940s. This gave rise to the BBC saying of the 1970s, 'Radio 4 over-fortifies the over-forties'.

pianist See DON'T SHOOT.

pick on someone your own size! Advice on how to quarrel, offered to someone who has been picking on an easy victim. Of American origin, since the late 19th century.

(to) pick up the pieces Meaning, 'to try to win some compensation from an apparently hopeless situation'. Known by 1904. 'If anything does go wrong it'll be nice having you around to pick up the pieces' – Rich Perry, *Dead End* (1977); '"There's nothing to be said. It has happened and nothing's going to bring him back," said Ann Ingram [mother of man sentenced to death and electrocuted in the USA]. "Now we must pick up the pieces of

our lives"' – *Independent on Sunday* (9 April 1995).

(a) picture is worth a thousand words Famous observation sometimes said to be a Chinese proverb. However, its origin is more prosaic. It originated in an American paper, *Printers' Ink* (8 December 1921), in the form 'one look is worth a thousand words'. It was later reprinted in the better-known form in the same paper (10 March 1927) and there ascribed by its actual author, Frederick R. Barnard, to a Chinese source ('so that people would take it seriously', he told Burton Stevenson in 1948). But it is still sometimes held to be a Chinese proverb. *Bartlett* (1980) listed it as such in the form 'One picture is worth more than ten thousand words' and compared what Turgenev says in *Fathers and Sons* (1862): 'A picture shows me at a glance what it takes dozens of pages of a book to expound.' The saying is quoted in the song 'If', popularized by Bread in 1971.

piddled See EVERY LITTLE HELPS.

pie See AMERICAN PIE.

(it's a) piece of cake Meaning that something is simple, no bother and easily achieved. Comparisons are inevitable with other food phrases like 'easy as pie' and 'money for jam', but the general assumption seems to be that it is a shortened form of 'it's as easy as eating a piece of cake'. The earliest *OED2* citation is American and from 1936, though the phrase may not be of actual US origin. It was especially popular in the RAF during the Second World War, hence the appropriate title, *Piece of Cake*, applied by Derek Robinson to his novel (1983) about RAF fliers in the Second World War, which was turned into a TV mini-series in 1988. In 1943, C. H. Ward-Jackson published *It's a Piece of Cake*.

pie in the sky An illusory prospect of future happiness, a reward in heaven for virtue or suffering on earth. Apparently coined by Joe Hill (1879–1915), a Swedish-born songwriter and industrial organizer in the USA: 'You will eat, bye and bye, / In that glorious land above the sky; / Work and pray, live on hay, / You'll get pie in the sky when you die' – 'The Preacher and the Slave' in *Songs of the Workers* (1911), published by Industrial Workers of the World. Sung to the tune of 'In the Sweet By and By', this added 'pie in the sky' to the list of common expressions. 'You don't want no pie in the sky when you die, / You want something here on the ground while you're still around' – Muhammad Ali, quoted in 1978.

Piffy/Piffey See LIKE PIFFY.

pig See AS AWKWARD AS.

(to buy a) pig in a poke To buy something sight unseen. 'Poke' here means 'bag' (of which a 'pocket' is a small one, of course). If you bought a pig hidden in a bag you would not know whether it was worth buying or not. Recorded by 1536. From H. G. Wells, *The History of Mr Polly* (1910): 'Never was bachelor married yet that didn't buy a pig in a poke.'

pigs See AND PIGS MIGHT.

pile it high, sell it cheap Slogan. Sir John Cohen (1898–1979), founder of Tesco supermarkets in the UK, built his fortune upon this golden rule, and it became a sort of unofficial slogan for his organization.

pile of pants See IT'S A.

pillars of society People who are the main supporters of church, state, institutions or principles (compare 'pillars of state', 'pillar of faith'). Derived from the English title of Henrik Ibsen's play *Samfundets Støtter* (1877), in the translation by William Archer. When the play was first produced in London in 1880 it was, however, called *Quicksands*. In the play, the 'pillars of society' are described as being 'the spirit of truth and the spirit of freedom'.

(from) pillar to post Originally 'from post to pillar', this expression derives from the game of 'real tennis' and suggests that whoever is being driven or bounced or chased from one place to another is being harassed. In use by 1420. Another more plausible suggestion is that it simply refers to *consecutive* punishments in the pillory and then the whipping post.

pilot See DROPPING THE.

pin See ANGELS DANCING.

pin back your lugholes! See I'M DREAMING...

pink See IN THE.

(a) pink chit Permission granted by wife or partner for a man to go drinking with his chums. 'Formal warning issued to Jack whenever he came over the brow in drink and the worse for wear; a second such episode meant a green chit and then you get your hat for a talk with the bloke [i.e. you'd be up before the Captain as a defaulter]. The expression is now used to denote a wife or girlfriend's prior knowledge of a night out with the boys: "Coming on the section run-ashore? I've got a pink chit from the dragon"' – Surgeon-Commander Rick Jolly, *Jackspeak: the Pusser's Rum Guide to Royal Navy Slanguage* (1989).

pinta See DRINKA.

(from a) pin to an elephant Slogan. Whiteley's, first in Westbourne Grove and later in Queensway, introduced department store shopping to London in 1863. William Whiteley (1831–1907), the self-styled **Universal Provider**, claimed to be able to supply anything, hence his slogan. One morning, as Whiteley described it: 'An eminent pillar of the Church called upon me and said, "Mr Whiteley, I want an elephant." "Certainly, sir. When would you like it?" "Oh, today!" "And where?" "I should like it placed in my stable." "It shall be done!" In four hours, a tuskiana was placed in the reverend gentleman's coach-house. Of course, this was a try-on designed to test our resources, and it originated in a bet. The Vicar confessed himself greatly disconcerted because, as he frankly avowed, he did not think we would execute the order. He displayed the utmost anxiety lest I should hold him to the transaction. But I let him down with a small charge for pilotage and food only, at which he confessed himself deeply grateful' – quoted in R. S. Lambert, *The Universal Provider* (1937).

pipeline See IN THE PIPELINE.

Pip, Squeak and Wilfred Phrase you might apply to any set of three people or things. Derived from the names of cartoon characters in the newspaper strip with this name, featured in the *Daily Mirror* from the 1920 to the 1940s. Pip was a dog, Squeak a female penguin and Wilfred a baby rabbit. Gilbert Harding, the television personality, was invited to the official opening of the BBC Television Centre in London (1960) and observed the Director-General, Hugh Greene, who was talking in a group with two of his predecessors, Sir William Haley and Sir Ian Jacob. 'Ah,' said Harding, 'either the Holy Trinity or Pip, Squeak and Wilfred.' Then he added: 'The latter, I fear' – quoted in Paul Ferris, *Sir Huge* (1990).

piss See ALL PISS AND WIND.

(as) pissed as a newt I.e. 'very drunk', recorded by 1957. *Partridge/Slang* gives various metaphors for drunkenness from the animal kingdom, 'pissed as a coot/rat/parrot' among them. None seems particularly apposite. And why 'newt'? Could it be that the newt, being an amphibious reptile, can submerge itself in liquid as a drunk might do? Or is it because its tight-fitting skin reflects the state of being 'tight'? We may never know, though the alternative (and, according to *Partridge*, original) expression 'tight as a newt' has a pleasing sound to it. Folk expressions have been coined with less reason. (*Partridge's* reviser, Paul Beale, wrote in December 1987: 'The great thing about newts is the characteristic they share with fishes' arse'oles: they are watertight. And you can't get tighter than that!') There is any number of other explanations, most based on mishearings of words.

pistols for two, breakfast for one (or **coffee . . .)!** Parody of duellists' talk, source untraced but known by the 1980s.

pit See BOTTOMLESS PIT.

place See ANY TIME.

(a) place for everything and everything in its place A prescription for orderly domestic arrangements from Isabella Beeton, *The Book of Household Management*, Chap. 2 (1861). One feels that Mrs Beeton was probably more interested in domestic order than in making delicious food. The saying was not original to her, however, as is plain from these earlier uses: George Herbert had the basic idea in his *Outlandish Proverbs* (1640): 'All things

have their place, knew we how to place them.' Captain Marryat in *Masterman Ready*, II.i. (1842), has: 'In a well-conducted man-of-war . . . everything in its place, and there is a place for every thing.' Then there is this Wellerism from *Yankee Blade* (18 May 1848): '"A place for everything in its place",' as an old lady said when she stowed the broom, bellows, balls of yarn, cards, caps, curry-comb, three cats and a gridiron into an old oven.' Samuel Smiles quoted it, notably, in *Thrift*, Chap. 5 (1875), and is sometimes credited with the coinage.

(a) place in the sun Phrase expressing what German colonial ambitions in East Asia were meant to secure. It was coined by Bernard von Bülow, the German Chancellor, in a speech to the Reichstag in 1897: 'In a word, we desire to throw no one into the shade, but we also demand our own place in the sun [*Platz an der Sonne*].' In 1901, Kaiser Wilhelm II took up the theme in a speech at Elbe: 'We have fought for our place in the sun and won it. Our future is on the water.' The notion was much referred to in the run-up to the First World War. An early appearance occurs in the *Pensées* of Blaise Pascal (Walker's translation, 1688): 'This Dog is mine, said those poor Children; That's my place in the Sun. This is the beginning and Image of the Usurpation of all the Earth.' The phrase is now hardly ever used in the precise sense but simply to indicate a rightful piece of good fortune, a desirable situation, e.g.: 'Mr Frisk could bring Aintree punters their place in the sun' – headline in the *Independent on Sunday* (1 April 1990). *A Place in the Sun* was the title given to the film (US 1951) of Theodore Dreiser's *An American Tragedy*.

(a) place within the meaning of the act Legal phrase. The *ODQ* (1979) merely stated that this was from 'the Betting Act', ignoring the fact that there were more than one such. In fact, the phrase comes from Section 2 of the 1853 Betting Act (which banned off-course betting on racehorses). 'A coop within the meaning of the act' – P. G. Wodehouse, *Love Among the Chickens* (1906); 'Folding the girl in my arms, I got home on her right eyebrow. It wasn't one of my best, I will admit, but it was a kiss within the meaning of the act' – same author, *Thank You, Jeeves* (1934).

plague   See AVOID LIKE THE.

planet earth (sometimes **Planet Earth)** Portentous term for the planet on which man lives. Known by 1965. 'Here Men From The Planet Earth / First Set Foot Upon The Moon / July 1969 AD / We Came In Peace For All Mankind' – plaque left on the Moon by the US crew of the Apollo XI space mission. 'We should simply seek to make a mark in the universe . . . that some other civilisation will detect and so know there is . . . sophisticated life on planet Earth' – Len Deighton, *Twinkle, Twinkle, Little Spy*, Chap. 8 (1976).

planks   See AS THICK.

played   See AND THE BAND.

(to) play fast and loose   I.e. to mess another person about, to resort to deceit, to act in a slippery fashion. The expression was known by 1557, as was a game called Fast-and-loose – though which came first is hard to say. The game, also called 'Pricking the Belt', was an old fairground trick akin to 'Find the Lady' (the so-called Three-Card Trick). The victim was incited to pin a folded belt to the table. The operator would then show that the belt was not (held) 'fast' but 'loose'. So the victim would lose the bet. Shakespeare alludes to the game in *Love's Labour's Lost*, III.i.100 (1592–3): 'To sell a bargain well is as cunning as fast and loose.' *Fast and Loose* has been the title of three films (US 1930, 1939 and UK 1954).

(to) play into the hands of . . .   Meaning, 'to act so as to give an advantage to an opponent'. Known by 1705. Cited as a 'dying metaphor' by George Orwell in 'Politics and the English Language', *Horizon* (April 1946). 'In some ways the people who do these things play into our hands. The public are horrified by these actions and become more sympathetic to what we are trying to do' – *The Sunday Times* (29 May 1994); 'The Secretary of State's pre-budget sternness may just be a ploy to deflate expectations and make a small increase in arts funding look like a big one, but the current crisis does play

into the hands of those who say that all the National Lottery will achieve is lots of lovely buildings with nothing going on inside them' – *The Sunday Times* (6 November 1994).

play it again, Sam   Catchphrase based on a misquotation. Humphrey Bogart never actually says this phrase in the film *Casablanca* (US 1941) when talking to Sam, played by Dooley Wilson. Sam is the night-club pianist and reluctant performer of the sentimental song 'As Time Goes By'. At one point Ingrid Bergman, as Ilsa, *does* have this exchange with him: *Ilsa*: 'Play it once, Sam, for old time's sake.' *Sam*: 'I don't know what you mean, Miss Ilsa.' *Ilsa*: 'Play it, Sam. Play, "As Time Goes By".' Later on, Bogart, as 'Rick', also tries to get 'Sam' to play it: *Rick*: 'You know what I want to hear.' *Sam*: 'No, I don't.' *Rick*: 'You played it for her, [and] you can play it for me.' *Sam*: 'Well, I don't think I can remember it.' *Rick*: 'If she can stand it, I can. Play it.' All one can say is that the saying was utterly well established by the time Woody Allen thus entitled his play *Play It Again Sam* (1969; film US 1972) about a film critic who is abandoned by his wife and obtains the help of Bogart's 'shade'. By listing it under Allen's name, *Bartlett* (1980 and 1992) might be thought to suggest that Allen coined the phrase. It would be interesting to know by which year it had really become established. Ian Gillies (1996) recalled that in 1943 the Jack Benny radio programme went to North Africa entertaining the troops. When he returned, two of the shows were based on the idea of a reporter asking him, 'When you toured North Africa, were you in Algiers?' and 'Were you in Casablanca?' Each led to a film parody. In that of *Casablanca*, Benny played the Bogart part ('Ricky') and Rochester (Eddie Anderson), Dooley Wilson. As has now been confirmed with a recording of the original broadcast (17 October 1943), an increasingly inebriated Ricky keeps on saying: 'Go ahead, Sam, play that song. Sam, sing it, boy. Sing it, Sam. Sing it, Sam, sing that song that keeps breaking my heart.' Above all, he exclaims: 'Sam, Sam, play that song for me again, will you?' This is certainly closer to the catchphrase than anything uttered in the film and, to my mind, is reasonable proof that Jack Benny really did help create the phrase. Presumably, rather more people heard the radio show than had seen the film at that point.

play the game, you cads! Stock phrase of the British variety performers The Western Brothers (Kenneth and George – who were in fact cousins). They had an act in which they sang songs to the piano in the 1930s/40s. They played clubbish, bemonocled toffs and would begin with something to the effect: **good evening, cads, your better selves are with you once again!** and end with **cheerio, cads, and happy landings!**

play the music See MUM MUM.

(the) play what I wrote Catchphrase from BBC TV, *The Morecambe and Wise Show* (1968–77). A long-running joke was that Ernie Wise was capable of writing plays in which guest stars would perform during the show. Explaining why the Queen had made him an Earl: 'She gave it to me for those plays what I wrote' (25 December 1973). Hence, *The Play What I Wrote*, title of a tribute entertainment (2001) by Hamish McColl and Sean Foley.

play with fire, pee in the bed Taunt to a child. My wife remembers it from Buckinghamshire in the 1950s and still finds it inexplicable.

please adjust your dress before leaving Phrase from notices in men's British public lavatories (19th century onwards?). 'Adjust' is a perfectly normal word for 'arranging' one's clothes (and has been since the early 18th century), but here it is euphemistic. The 'dress' is a little worrying: Arthur Marshall in *Sunny Side Up* (1987) recalls querying this and other aspects of the wording, possibly in the 1910s. An uncle promised to write to the authorities proposing instead: 'Before leaving please engage all trouser buttons securely and return hands to normal position.' Winston Churchill denied (1941) having said of a long-winded memorandum from Anthony Eden that, 'as far as I can see, you have used every cliché except "God is love" and "Please adjust your dress before leaving".' A graffito (reported 1980): 'Please adjust your dress before leaving – as a refusal often offends.'

pleased See AS PLEASED.

please do not ask for credit as a refusal often offends Notice in shops since the 1920s/30s? A character in the first edition of the British TV soap opera *Coronation Street* (9 December 1960) said, 'I used to have a notice . . . "Please do not ask for credit as a refusal often offends".' A more recent variant, mentioned by Bernard Levin in *The Times* (16 August 1984) and deplored, was taken from a photocopying shop in London W1: 'We do *NOT* give facilities for change, telephone books, or anything not directly pertaining to this business.' From the same decade – a 'Bureau de Change' at Waverley Station, Edinburgh, had a notice in the window, 'We do not give change'.

please to remember / the Fifth of November Continuing: 'Gunpowder treason and plot. / I see no reason / Why gunpowder treason / Should ever be forgot.' Rhyme commemorating the arrest of Guy Fawkes and others who had planned to blow up the House of Parliament at Westminster on the occasion of the opening of parliament by King James I (set for 5 November 1605). In fact, Fawkes was arrested shortly before midnight on the 4 November. He has been burned in effigy on bonfires ever since on the 5 November. Something like the above rhyme was recorded in 1742: 'Don't you remember / The fifth of November / 'Twas Gun-Powder Treason Day . . .' Nowadays, most people would probably say 'Remember, remember, the Fifth of November . . .' Flora Thompson, *Lark Rise*, Chap. 15 (1939), has this full version: 'Remember, remember, the fifth of November, / The gunpowder treason and plot. / A stick or a stake, for King James's sake / Will you please to give us a faggot? / If you won't give us one, we'll take two! / The better for us and the worse for you.' The cry **penny for the guy!** when soliciting contributions ahead of the effigy being burned must date back at least to the 18th century.

(the) plot thickens! Exclamation used seriously in 19th-century melodramas but now jokingly in conversation of any turn of events that appears to be significant or that betrays some complicating feature. In *The Rehearsal* (1671) by George Villiers, a character said, perhaps for the first time, 'Ay, now the plot thickens very much upon us.' Hence, *The Plot That Thickened* – title of a novel (1973) by P. G. Wodehouse.

(a) ploughman's lunch The populariza-tion of this term for a meal of bread, cheese and pickle came as the result of a marketing ploy by the English Country Cheese Council. *The Ploughman's Lunch* was then the title of a film (UK 1983), scripted by Ian McEwan, whose theme was the way that history (especially recent history) tends to get rewritten. The title, unexplained in the film, must have puz-zled many, including those who were familiar with the ploughman's lunch in the other context. The point was that, though redolent of olden days, it had been introduced as a marketing ploy by the English Country Cheese Council in the 1960s. B. H. Axler's *The Cheese Handbook* (1970) has a preface by Sir Richard Trehane, Chairman of the English Country Cheese Council & Milk Marketing Board. He wrote: 'English cheese and beer have for centuries formed a perfect combination enjoyed as the Ploughman's Lunch.' Another source credits Trehane himself with introducing the term as a marketing tool. It is clear, however, that the concept and the name had long existed. In Lock-hart's *Memoirs of the Life of Sir Walter Scott* (1837), there is this: 'The surprised poet swung forth to join them, with an extem-porised sandwich, that looked like a ploughman's luncheon, in his hand.'

(to) plough one's furrow alone To take an independent line, with the loneliness and isolation this may entail. Originally, a political usage. 'I must plough my furrow alone', said Lord Rosebery in a speech at the City Liberal Club, London (19 July 1901), on breaking away from his Liberal Party colleagues. A famous declaration of independence, but it seems likely that the expression had been used by others before him. He added: 'Before I get to the end of that furrow it is possible that I may find myself not alone . . . If it be so, I shall

remain very contented in the society of my books and my home.' So it was to be. *Benham*'s (1948) has this (incorrectly) as: 'I must plough my lonely furrow alone.'

PLU [People Like Us] Social typing phrase, for identifying the kind of people who share one's outlook on life, one's interests and, probably, one's behavioural patterns. British middle-class use – and known by the 1950s? Quoted in Peter Nichols, *A Day in the Death of Joe Egg*, Act 2 (1967).

(la) plume de ma tante As 'the cat sat on the mat' is to learning the English lan-guage, so '*je n'ai pas la plume de ma tante*' is to learning French. It must have occurred in some widely used French grammar in British schools – possibly just prior to the First World War. In Terence Rattigan's play *French Without Tears* (1936) a character says: 'If a Frenchman asked me where the pen of his aunt was, the chances are I could give him a pretty sharp comeback and tell him it was in the pocket of the gardener.' A revue with the title played at the Garrick Theatre, London, in 1955.

plums See AREN'T PLUMS.

plural See ANSWER IS.

pluribus See E PLURIBUS.

plus fours and no breakfast 'My aunts tell me that this was a remark always attributed to the nouveau riche, who wore all they had on their backs. Everything for show and no stability' – Mrs D. E. Thorn, Lincolnshire (1998). 'Speaks rather fancy; truculent; plausible; a bit of a shower-off; plus-fours and no breakfast, you know . . . a gabbing, ambitious, mock-tough, preten-tious young man' – Dylan Thomas charac-terizing himself in a broadcast 'Return Journey' (1947). I suppose the implication is that the 'shower-off' is someone of limited means who spends what he has on flashy clothes and therefore can't afford any breakfast. Then the variations: '"Plus fours and kippers for breakfast" had to do with genteel poverty in upper class Jesmond' – from an 89-year-old in Newcas-tle upon Tyne (1998). 'Fur coats and no breakfast' – Stella Richardson, Essex (1998). '"All crepe sole and bay windows", said in an exaggerated posh voice (with an "h" in "whindows")' – Dave·Hopkins, Kent (1998). Paul Beale commented (1998): '"Plus fours and no breakfast" seems to equate to "(all) bay-windows and no breakfast" = sacrificing everything for the sake of an appearance of social superiority. I heard "bay windows" soon after we came to live in Leicestershire 25 years ago.' Beale also rounded up: 'kippers and curtains', 'brown boots and no breakfast', 'empty bellies and brass doorknobs.'

po See HEAVENS.

poet See AS THE POET.

(the) poetry of motion Phrase known by the 17th century when it referred to dancing (also called **poetry of the foot**) but particularly popular *circa* 1900 in connection with railways and motor vehicles. Near the end of Wilkie Collins, *The Woman in White* (1859–60), the narrator refers to an occasion when he followed the eponymous heroine: 'Studying, behind a convenient waggon which hid me from her, the poetry of motion, as embodied in her walk.' However, **poetry in motion** is nowadays equally, if not more, established. 'Poetry In Motion' was the title of a pop song (1960), recorded by Johnny Tillotson and written by Paul Kaufman and Mike Anthony. 'The style of [American swimmer] Martha Norelius . . . was described by a Parisian as "poetry in motion", and her coach . . . never tired of watching her' – Charles Sprawson, *Haunts of the Black Masseur* (1992).

Poets' Day Phrase from the acronym 'POETS' for 'Piss/Push Off Early Tomorrow's Saturday' – indicating a frequent inclination of workers on Friday afternoons. Perhaps quite recent – by 1960.

(I am a) poet though I didn't know it Traditionally said by a person accidentally making a rhyme. Swift's *Polite Conversation* (1738) has this exchange: *Neverout*: 'Well, miss . . .' *Miss Notable*: 'Ay, ay; many a one says well, that thinks ill.' *Neverout*: 'Well, miss; I'll think of this.' *Miss Notable*: 'That's rhyme, if you take it in time.' *Neverout*: 'What! I see you are a poet.' *Miss Notable*: 'Yes, if I had but the wit to show it.'

(to) point Percy at the porcelain To urinate. An Australian Loophemism (not of his own invention), introduced to Britain by Barry Humphries through the Barry Mackenzie strip in *Private Eye* (before 1971).

point taken! Phrase used to show acceptance of an argument or point of view in conversation. Since the 1940s/50s.

poised between a cliché and an indiscretion Phrase describing a delicate position. Originally said of his role as Foreign Secretary by Harold Macmillan in a speech, House of Commons (27 July 1955): 'And this applies also to a prospective Foreign Secretary – [he] is always faced with this cruel dilemma. Nothing he can say can do very much good, and almost anything he may say may do a great deal of harm. Anything he says that is not obvious is dangerous; whatever is not trite is risky. He is forever poised between the cliché and the indiscretion' – quoted in *Newsweek* Magazine (30 April 1956). Macmillan was also quoted as having said that his life as Foreign Secretary was '*forever* poised between a cliché and an indiscretion.' Compare 'My advice was delicately poised between the cliché and the indiscretion' – Robert Runcie, Archbishop of Canterbury, on discussions with the Prince and Princess of Wales prior to marrying them, quoted in *The Times* (14 July 1981).

poison See BOX-OFFICE POISON.

(to be handed a/the) poisoned chalice To take on a disagreeable responsibility – in particular, to take on a job that nobody else wants and that has probably resulted in defeat for the last person to do it. Known by 1990. From the common occurrence in medieval tales of a chalice being awarded to the winner of some contest – a chalice that then turns out to be poisoned, thus defeating the winner in a foully underhand manner. In Shakespeare, *Hamlet*, Act V (1600–1), the chalice intended to poison Hamlet is mistakenly drunk by Gertrude, and in *Macbeth* (I.vii.11), a 'poison'd chalice' is referred to by name. Modern use of the expression may possibly stem from French use as *cadeau empoisonné*. 'Among those leading the calls for an explanation is Kim Dae-Jung's successor, President Roh Moo-hyun, who has no desire to inherit a poisoned chalice' – *The Independent* (6 February 2003).

(the) poisoned dwarf   Nickname given to any unpleasant person of small stature. According to episode one of the ITV series *The World at War* (1975), it was a popular German nickname in the late 1930s for Hitler's diminutive propaganda chief, Joseph Goebbels. The literal German *Giftzwerg* is defined by the Collins German dictionary as 'poisonous individual; spiteful little devil'. In Wagner's *Das Rheingold* (1869), however, Wellgunde calls Alberich '*Schwefelgezwerg*' (literally 'sulphurous dwarf'). Knowing how a Wagnerian phrase like NIGHT AND FOG was adapted in the Nazi era, this seems a likely source for the phrase. 'The regiment involved in the unhappy events at Minden some 30 years ago, which provoked the local inhabitants to nickname its soldiers "The Poison Dwarves" was The Cameronians (The Scottish Rifles)' – *Independent on Sunday* (5 July 1992). *Circa* 1979, Terry Wogan, the BBC Radio 2 disc jockey, helped ensure the success in Britain of the imported American TV series *Dallas*. He poked fun at it and, in particular, drew attention to the diminutive proportions of the actress Charlene Tilton who played the character Lucy Ewing by referring to her as 'the poison dwarf'. Compare, from John Osborne, *Almost a Gentleman* (1991): 'Ronald Duncan (dubbed "**the Black Dwarf**" by Devine and Richardson, because of his diminutive height and poisonous spirit) . . .' Sir Walter Scott published *The Black Dwarf* in 1816.

poke   See BETTER THAN A POKE.

(to be) in pole position   To be in an advantageous position (though perhaps **poll position** would be a better spelling?) In motor racing, it is the grid position which is on the front row and on the inside of the first bend. Known by 1953. Previously 'to have the pole' meant the same thing in horse racing and was known as such by 1851: 'A horse "has the pole", means that he has drawn the place nearest the inside boundary-fence of the track' –

Frazer's Magazine, No. 93 (1851). More recently, the phrase has been used figuratively in other contexts: 'Ipswich relinquished their hold on the pole position to champions Liverpool' – *News of the World* (17 April 1977); 'Eurovision Song Contest 1995 . . . with Love City Groove's Euro-rap in pole position, Dublin can finally be rid of the whole affair' – *The Independent* Metro (12 May 1995).

police   See HELPING THE.

(a/the) policeman's lot   Phrase from a song in the Gilbert and Sullivan operetta *The Pirates of Penzance*, Act 2 (1879): 'When constabulary duty's to be done, / A policeman's lot is not a happy one.'

(oh I should love to) polish you off   A British actor with the wonderful name of Tod Slaughter (1885–1956) was noted for his performances as Sweeney Todd, 'the demon barber of Fleet Street'. This line came from the rather melodramatic version he performed and which was filmed in 1936. The words were addressed to his victims who, of course, were subsequently turned into meat pies. To 'polish something off', meaning to finish it quickly, began as boxing slang (recorded in 1829) but latterly has often been applied to food. Compare the hangman's phrase for his job in Charles Dickens, *Barnaby Rudge* (1841): he talks of 'working someone off'.

political dynamite   Journalistic cliché. Date of origin not known. 'Spokesmen of the People's Party, aware of the political dynamite involved in any large-scale attack on the nationalized empire, have stressed that their aim is to "de-politicize" rather than de-nationalize' – *The Economist* (9 February 1963); 'He had reason to be cautious for the proposal . . . had been naked, political dynamite' – W. Haggard, *The Hardlines* (1970); 'However innocent his intentions, Atherton must have been aware that every grain of dirt represented a stick of political dynamite. Certainly, England can no longer go on pontificating to Pakistan or any other country in the world now that their captain has been caught with dirt on his hands' – *Daily Mail* (25 July 1994); 'David Hart, general secretary of the National Association of Head Teachers, said the figures confirmed teachers' worst fears: "There is no doubt we are facing the biggest funding crisis in many a long year, maybe since time immemorial and I think Professor Smithers' figures are political dynamite"' – *The Times Educational Supplement* (7 April 1995).

(the) political pendulum (can only swing so far) Journalistic cliché. The idea of a political pendulum swinging one way or the other is often evoked to portray the changing fortunes of the parties. This particular use of it was listed in *The Independent* (24 December 1994) as a cliché of newspaper editorials. A possible origin is the use of 'the pendulum swings' in Fraser, *Disraeli and His day* (1891). 'It is noteworthy that, historically, the swing in the political pendulum away from the direction of full employment and the welfare state, where it pointed in the post-war political climate, has been accompanied by a parallel revival of monetarism' – *The Guardian* (29 August 1994); 'Yet if the political pendulum swing of the 1960s made Cilla famous, she followed its backward sweep. At the last election she came out for Major, whom she swears she still fancies' – *The Observer* (18 December 1994); 'The consequent further economic slowdown in the economy would undermine Mr Major's soothing claim that the economy is coming right and Tory MPs need only hang on for a further year to see the political pendulum swing back their way' – *The Guardian* (2 May 1995).

(to be) politically correct To avoid actions or words that might exclude or reflect badly upon minorities or groups perceived as being disadvantaged. These groups might be identified on the grounds of their race, sex, sexual orientation, class or politics. People in the USA started talking about **political correctness** in the current, specific sense, in about 1984. From *The Washington Post* (12 March 1984): 'Langer . . . is saying that novelists have a duty higher than the one they owe to their art and their private vision of the world; they have a duty to be politically correct . . . In thus construing, Langer reveals herself to be a captive of the assumption, widespread among the academic and literary left, that art exists to serve politics.' By the following year, the phrase in its modern sense is fully formed and stands alone in the same paper (11 March 1985): 'It is the only caffeinated coffee served by the "wait-persons", as they are called, at the politically correct Takoma Cafe in Takoma Park.' Really, 'politically correct' and 'political correctness' are the wrong terms for the idea, in that they may make people think it has to do with Politics with a capital P, whereas it has much more to do with social concerns. Why not 'socially correct', then? – because that would make it sound as though it had something to do with manners and etiquette. 'Ideologically correct' would give the game away, of course, and leads us back to politics. As it is, 'political' hints at the coercion that is all too much part of the PC movement.

pomp and circumstance The title of five marches by Sir Edward Elgar. Nos. 1–4 were composed 1901–7 and No.5 in 1930. The phrase comes from Shakespeare's *Othello*, III.iii.360 (1604): 'O farewell . . . / Pride, pomp, and circumstance of glorious war!'

poodle See BALFOUR'S.

(the) poor are always with you This biblical phrase is to be found in Matthew 26:11, Mark 14:7 and John 12:8: 'For the poor always ye have with you.' Compare: *The Rich Are Always With Us* – title of a film (US 1932) and *The Rich Are With You Always*, title of a novel (1976) by Malcolm Macdonald.

(a) poor little rich girl Phrase used about any young woman whose wealth has not brought her happiness. *The Poor Little Rich Girl* was the title of a novel (1912) by the American writer Eleanor Gates, filmed (US 1917) starring Mary Pickford, remade (US 1936) with Shirley Temple. It is the story of a rich society girl who lives an isolated life and is kept apart from her parents. Later, the title of a song (1925) by Noël Coward.

poor man at his gate See RICH MAN.

(the) poor man's —— Gently derogatory way of indicating that someone is cheaper than (in some sense) and probably inferior to what is named. Hence, 'Joan Collins is the poor man's Marlene Dietrich'; or 'Norman Hunt is the poor man's Robert McKenzie' (broadcasting psephologists) (as the *New Statesman* put it in the early 1970s). William Inge (1860–1954), Dean of St Paul's, is supposed to have described women as 'the poor man's men'; armadillo was known as 'poor man's pork' in the Southern USA (because of its taste); 'In Britain at present mussels are a specialised taste, a sort of poor man's oyster, not an item of general diet at all' – *Financial Times* (4 June 1982); 'The Bank of England is being called in to advise on what controls should be put into place and unless an effective system can be paid for, the Isle of Man could be stuck with the image of a poor man's Jersey' – *Financial Times* (15 July 1982); 'With his burgeoning talent for comic impersonations, scathing one-liners and extravagant predictions of fistic mayhem, [boxer] Riddick Bowe is expanding into a poor man's Cassius Clay. Or rather, in these pay-TV days with $11 million per fight, a rich pretender to being the fastest lip in the ring' – *Daily Mail* (5 November 1993). This continues a tradition going back to the mid-19th century of referring mostly to *things* in this way. In Canada, a plate of dried beans was 'the poor man's piano' – on account of the noise that it provoked. An Italian expression is said to have been, 'Bed is the poor man's opera.'

(a) poor thing but mine own   Self-deprecatory phrase. In 1985, the painter Howard Hodgkin won the £10,000 Turner prize for a work (of art) called 'A Small Thing But My Own'. It was notable that he used the word 'small' rather than 'poor'. Nevertheless, he was presumably alluding to Touchstone's line in Shakespeare's *As You Like It*, V.iv.57 (1598): 'A poor virgin, sir, an ill-favoured thing, sir, but mine own.' Here Touchstone is not talking of art but of Audrey, the country wench he woos. The line is nowadays more likely to be used (in mock modesty) about a thing rather than a person.

Pope   See IS THE POPE.

pop goes the weasel   Exclamation that requires some explanation. At some time in the 19th century, possibly in 1853, W. R.

Mandale may have written the celebrated words: 'Up and down the City Road, / In and out of the Eagle, / That's the way the money goes – / Pop goes the weasel!' He may have put these words to a country dance tune that already existed, but what did he mean by them? What is plain is that 'the Eagle' refers to the Eagle Tavern, then a theatre and pub in the City Road, London (the present tavern was built around 1900). Those who went 'in and out' spent plenty of money and were forced to 'pop', or pawn, something. But what was the 'weasel' they pawned? A kind of tool used by a carpenter or a hatter, a tailor's flat iron, a coat (from rhyming slang 'weasel and stoat') have all been suggested. As for 'pop goes the weasel', meaning an orgasm, this is probably a later play on the established phrase. According to *Morris*, there is an American version of the song that goes: 'Every night when I come home, / The Monkey's on the table. / I take a stick and knock him off / And pop goes the weasel!'

(to) pop one's clogs   Meaning 'to die'. Judging from its absence from *Partridge/Slang* and *OED2*, this must be a fairly recent blending of 'to pop off', to DIE WITH ONE'S BOOTS ON, and possibly 'pop' in the sense of 'to pawn' (see POP GOES THE WEASEL). An unconfirmed 18th-century use has been reported. *Street Talk, the Language of Coronation Street* (1986) has it.

(to do) porridge   To serve time in prison. The term 'porridge' for 'time spent in prison' has been current since the 1950s at least. It is supposedly from rhyming slang, 'borage and thyme' (time). The porridge-stirring connection with the (more American) expressions 'stir' (meaning 'prison'), 'in stir' (in prison) and 'stir crazy' (insane as a result of long imprisonment) may just be coincidental. These terms are said to derive from the Anglo-Saxon word *styr*, meaning 'punishment', reinforced by the Romany *steripen*, meaning 'prison' (*DOAS*). On the other hand, if porridge was once the prisoner's basic food – and it was known as 'stirabout' – it may be more than coincidence that we have here. *Porridge* was the title of a BBC TV comedy series (1974–7) about prison life. In *Something Nasty in the Woodshed* (1976),

Kyril Bonfiglioli provides another angle: '"Porridge" . . . means penal servitude. There is a legend . . . that if . . . on the last morning of your "stretch", you do not eat up all your nice porridge, you will be back in durance vile within the year.'

port See ANY PORT.

POSH [Port Out Starboard Home]
The mythical etymology for the word 'posh', meaning 'smart, grand', is that it is an acronym for 'Port Out Starboard Home', as the requirement for the most desirable staterooms on ships travelling to and from British India. But the P&O Line, which was the principal carrier, has no evidence of a single 'POSH' booking, nor would it have made much difference to the heat of the cabin which side you were on. *OED2* has no citations before the 20th century. However, meaning 'dandy' or 'money', the word was 19th-century thieves' and especially Romany slang. It is not hard to see either of these meanings, or both combined, contributing to what we now mean by 'posh'.

possession is nine points of the law I.e. out of a possible ten points. Meaning, that in a dispute over the ownership of property, the present owner is in the strongest position. An alternative: 'Possession is nine-tenths of the law'. Known by 1809. The original nine points of the law were said to be: 1) a lot of money; 2) a lot of patience; 3) a good cause; 4) a good lawyer; 5) a good counsel; 6) good witnesses; 7) a good jury; 8) a good judge; 9) good luck. Sometimes only eight points have been listed. But an earlier version was: 'Possession is eleven points of the law' (i.e. out of a possible twelve). Known by 1630 and quoted, for example, in Jonathan Swift's *Polite Conversation* (1738).

possible See ART OF THE.

post early for Christmas Slogan of the British Post Office/Royal Mail, intended to reduce the pressure on mail services caused by the numbers of Christmas cards and parcels. Date of inception unknown – possibly 1920s. The simple non-seasonal **Post Early** on its own was apparently new in June 1922. In the Second World War, there was the similar injunction **Post Early**

– before noon, not to mention the very bald **Telegraph less**.

(to find the) pot of gold at the end of the rainbow (or **crock of gold . . .)** The earliest citation of the expression 'Go to the end of the rainbow and you'll find a crock of money' is to be found in W. D. Cooper's *Glossary of the Provincialisms in Use in the County of Sussex 1836* (1853), but the book points out that the association between rainbow and gold goes much further back. There are many legends in different folklores that there is something precious at the end of the rainbow. The key source for information on this topic is Carl B. Boyer's *The Rainbow from Myth to Mathematics* (1987). *Notes and Queries* was discussing the matter in 1850, and it is most often described as a Sussex proverb. Surely it must be more legendary than that? Politicians and the like, looking for the crock, or the rainbow itself, or anything else illusory, were called 'rainbow-chasers' by 1886 (in the USA, originally).

(a/the) pound of flesh Everything to which one is entitled under the terms of an agreement. After the bargain made between Shylock and Antonio in Shakespeare, *The Merchant of Venice* (1596). Shylock was entitled to a pound of Antonio's flesh if he was unable to repay a loan but was foiled when Portia ruled that he could only have the pound of flesh if it was an exact amount and if not a drop of blood was shed. 'That revelatory cri de coeur from Tony Blair to the assembled hacks at the end of the Cherie Booth/Peter Foster imbroglio: "You've had your pound of flesh . . ."' – *The Spectator* (18 January 2003).

pours See IT NEVER.

(the) poverty of aspirations (or **ambition)** 'The real tragedy of the poor is the poverty of their aspirations' is a saying attributed *circa* 1960 to Adam Smith in this form, but unverified. Since 1987, however, it has frequently been attributed to Ernest Bevin, the British Labour minister, though with no precise source as yet (also to Aneurin Bevan, though with even less backing) and any number of subjects – the poor, the working class, Britain, the trade unions. 'There was a marvellous remark by

Ernest Bevin when he said that what characterized Britain was a poverty of aspiration – and it's true' – *The Times* (19 May 1987). Sometimes the word 'ambition' is substituted. 'John Edmonds, secretary of GMB, the general union, recalled Ernest Bevin's observation 50 years ago that the greatest failing of Britain's trade unions was their poverty of ambition which made them set their sights too low' – *The Guardian* (6 September 1990); 'My family were the same as any other working class family in those days; they suffered from what I shall call the poverty of ambition' – Sir Bernard Ingham in *The Times* (18 May 1991); 'Only the Morgan Motor Company refused to follow his advice to expand – a course of action which Sir John [Harvey Jones] cites as evidence of the poverty of ambition of small and medium-sized British companies' – *Financial Times* (21 April 1993).

(to) powder one's nose Euphemism for a woman's going to the lavatory. *OED2* doesn't find it before 1921 when Somerset Maugham daringly put it in his play *The Circle*. Cole Porter put it in *The New Yorkers*, 1930 – though there is some doubt whether the song was actually used in the show: 'The girls today / Have but one thing to say, / "Where can one powder one's nose?"'

power See BALANCE OF POWER.

(the) power and the glory Phrase from the Lord's Prayer in the Book of Common Prayer. Hence, the title of a film, *The Power and the Glory* (US 1933), and Graham Greene's novel (1940). The translation, as found in the service of Morning Prayer (which differs slightly from that in Matthew 6:9–13) has also provided the following titles (among others): *Give Us This Day* (film UK 1949), *Our Daily Bread* (film US 1934); *World Without End* is the title of a film (US 1956); *Deliver Us From Evil* is the title of a book (1953) by Hugh Desmond, and *Thine Is The Kingdom* of unrelated books by Heini Arnold, Thomas Dooley and Paul Marshall. *The Power and the Kingdom* is the title of a novel by Michael Williams (1989), while Gay Talese's book (1971) about *The New York Times* with the title *The Kingdom and the Power* is presumably an allusion.

power to the people Slogan shouted – with clenched fist raised – by the Black Panther movement and publicized as such by its leader, Bobby Seale, in Oakland, California, in July 1969. It was also used by other dissident groups, as illustrated by Eldridge Cleaver: 'We say "All power to the people" – Black Power for Black People, White Power for White People, Brown Power for Brown People, Red Power for Red People, and X Power for any group we've left out.' It was this somewhat generalized view of 'People Power' that John Lennon appeared to promote in the 1971 song 'Power to the People (Right On!)'. 'All Power to the Soviets' was a cry of the Bolsheviks during the Russian Revolution of 1917.

(the) powers that be Phrase now used to describe any form of authority exercising social or political control. It derives from Romans 13:1: 'Let every soul be subject unto the higher powers. For there is no power but of God: the powers that be are ordained of God.' The New English Bible has: 'The existing authorities are instituted by him.' *The Powers That Be* – title of book (1979) by David Halberstam.

pox-doctor See ALL DRESSED.

praise the Lord and pass the ammunition! Phrase of religious pragmatism. Said in 1941 and subsequently used as the title of a song by Frank Loesser (1942); the authorship of this saying is disputed. It may have been said by an American naval chaplain during the Japanese attack on Pearl Harbor. Lieutenant Howell M. Forgy (1908–83) is one candidate. He was on board the US cruiser *New Orleans* on 7 December 1941 and encouraged those around him to to keep up the barrage when under attack. His claim is supported by a report in *The New York Times* (1 November 1942). Another name mentioned is that of Captain W. H. Maguire. At first Captain Maguire did not recall having used the words but a year later said he might have done. Either way, the expression actually dates from the time of the American Civil War.

pram See GET OUT OF ONE'S.

prawn See DON'T COME THE RAW.

prayer See ANSWER TO; COMING IN ON.

prepared See BE PREPARED.

prepare to meet thy God Slogan that, unlike the END IS NIGH, another favourite of placard-bearing religious fanatics, does actually come from the Bible: Amos 4:12.

president See ALL THE PRESIDENT'S.

presses See HOLD THE FRONT PAGE.

pretty See HERE'S A.

pretty amazing! When Lady Diana Spencer (1961–97) was asked in 1981 what her first impression of the Prince of Wales, her intended husband, had been, she replied, 'Pretty amazing!' This innocuous verdict on their encounter in a freshly ploughed field during 1977 briefly achieved catchphrase status.

pretty, please, with a cherry on top Child's phrase when pleading for anything. Sometimes, '. . . with sugar on it'. Sweet emphasis is added in the hope that the plea will be more favourably considered. Jaap Engelsman (2000) commented, 'It reminds me of an American here in Amsterdam, who in his second-hand bookshop put up this note over the *National Geographic* shelves: "Please please please with sugar cream on top put them back in chronological order".' Sylvia Dowling, having come across it in 'various American novels, with and without cherries and other twee additions', added: 'I have always assumed that the "pretty" was a corruption of "prithee", which I believe is itself a corruption of "I pray thee".'

(the) priceless ingredient Slogan for Squibb drug products, in the US, from 1921 (that continued '. . . of every product is the honor and integrity of its maker'.) Before that year, Squibb had never advertised to the public. The problem given to Raymond Rubicam, then a writer at the N. W. Ayer & Son agency, was to produce a series of advertisements that would sell Squibb to the public and not offend the publicity-sensitive medical profession. David Ogilvy commented: 'Raymond Rubicam's famous slogan . . . reminds me of my father's advice: when a company boasts about its integrity, or a woman about her virtue, avoid the former and cultivate the latter.'

price of eggs See WHAT'S THAT GOT TO DO.

prick See LIKE A PORK CHOP.

(to) prick up one's ears To become attentive, as a dog or horse would. Known by 1626. As for *Prick Up Your Ears*, the title of a film (UK 1987) about the life and murder of Joe Orton, the playwright: in his diary for 18 February 1967, Orton wrote: 'Started typing up my final version [of the first draft] of *Up Against It*. Kenneth suggested that I call it *Prick Up Your Ears*. But this is much too good a title to waste on a film.' The 'Kenneth' was Kenneth Halliwell, Orton's flatmate who murdered him later that year. It was indeed too good a title to waste on the abortive *Up Against It*, Orton's planned film for the Beatles. In 1978, John Lahr used the phrase as the title of his biography of Orton. In his edition of *The Orton Diaries* (1986), Lahr noted: 'The title is a triple-pun, "ears" being an anagram of "arse". Orton intended using it as the title for a farce about the backstage goings-on prior to a coronation.' When the film *Prick Up Your Ears* came out, there were reports of enthusiastic punsters in London climbing up to rearrange the lettering of the last word over cinema doors. In *circa* 1974, a *Financial Times* crossword clue is said to have been: 'Listen carefully, or a sexual perversion (5,2,4,4).'

pride and prejudice The title of Jane Austen's novel *Pride and Prejudice* (written as *First Impressions*, 1797, published 1813) has been said to derive from the second chapter of Edward Gibbon's *The Decline and Fall of the Roman Empire* (published 1776). Writing of the enfranchisement of the slaves, Gibbon writes: 'Without destroying the distinction of ranks a distant prospect of freedom and honours was presented, even to those whom pride and prejudice almost disdained to number among the human species.' More to the point, the phrase occurs no fewer than three times, in bold print, towards the end of Fanny Burney's *Cecilia* (1787): '"The whole of this unfortunate business," said Dr Lyster, "has been the result of Pride and Prejudice . . . Yet this, however, remember; if to Pride and Prejudice you owe your miseries, so wonderfully is good and evil balanced, that to Pride and Prejudice you will also owe their termination".' This seems the most likely cue to Jane Austen. On the other hand, *OED2* provides six citations of the phrase 'pride and prejudice' before Burney, one of which has capital Ps.

prime   See BEST PRIME MINISTER.

princess   See COULD MAKE ANY.

print   See ALL THE NEWS.

Priscilla, she's my best friend   See MY NAME'S MONICA.

(a) private eye   Although it is true that a private investigator's job consists of keeping an eye on people, there may be more to the name than that. The term could derive from 'private *i*nvestigator' or from the wide-open 'eye' symbol of the Pinkerton detective agency, founded in Chicago (1850). It went with the slogan WE NEVER SLEEP and was referred to as the 'Eye' by criminals and others. The full phrase seems to have emerged in the 1930s and 40s, particularly through the fiction of Raymond Chandler and others. *Private Eye*, the British satirical fortnightly (founded 1961), seems to have taken the title because of the investigative exposures that have always made up a portion of its contents.

(the) private life of ——   Title format. Although Alexander Korda had directed a film called *The Private Life of Helen of Troy* (1927, based on John Erskine's novel of 1926), the original of all the 'Private Life of . . .' books and films was surely his immensely successful *The Private Life of Henry VIII* (1933). The following year, Julian Huxley with R. M. Lockley produced a natural history film called *The Private Life of Gannets* (which won an Oscar). Since then, in the cinema, we have had private lives of Don Juan (1934), Elizabeth and Essex (1939), Sherlock Holmes (1970), and so on. And, on TV, there have been numerous natural history films since the mid-1960s, e.g. the BBC's *The Private Life of the Kingfisher*. There is, of course, a nudging note to the use of the phrase – as though we are not just being promised a glimpse of domestic happenings, but probably sex life, too.

probably the best lager in the world   Slogan for Carlsberg lager, from 1973. Even if it had not been intoned by Orson Welles in the TV ads, the 'probably' inserted into this hyperbole would still have fascinated. However, it is by no means the first product to be advertised with such caution. Zephyr, imported by A. Gale & Co. Ltd of Glasgow, was called 'Possibly the finest tobacco in the world' in ads current in 1961.

programme   See AND IN A PACKED.

(to be) prominent in one's field   Phrase possibly first used in hunting. Date of origin unknown. Compare **first in the field**. As for 'prominent, mainly because of the flatness of the surrounding countryside', it seems to be a rare joke by Karl Marx. In Vol. 1, Chap. 16 of *Capital* (1867), he writes: 'On a level plain, simple mounds look like hills; and the insipid flatness of our present bourgeoisie is to be measured by the altitude of its "great intellects".' Marx comments thus after having demolished one of John Stuart Mill's arguments.

promises, promises!   Phrase mocking another person's having undertaken to do something or simply producing a *double-entendre*. Dating from at least the 1960s. For example, if one person were to say, 'If you pop round later this evening, I can give you one,' then the other might say . . . From the BBC radio show *Round the Horne* (30 April 1967): 'You swine – you'll feel my crop for this.' 'Promises, promises.' *Promises, Promises* was the title of a musical (Broadway 1968), based on the Billy Wilder film *The Apartment*, and may have further encouraged use of the phrase.

(a) proper Charlie   As with the phrase **right Charlie**, this probably grew out of rhyming slang 'Charlie Hunt', used to describe a fool or simpleton. It may have been a simultaneous British and American coinage during the Second World War. It was commandeered by the comedian Charlie Chester (1914–97) on radio immediately after the war and later used by him as the title of a BBC radio show, *A Proper Charlie* (1956/8). Chester was billed as '**cheerful Charlie** Chester'. 'Cheerful Charlie' is the title of a monologue (1916) by F. Chatterton Hennequin and Phyllis Norman Parker. From *The Guardian* (1 December 1988) concerning a judge, Sir Harold Cassel QC: 'He once gave a robber an hour's bail, warning: "If you do not turn up you will make me look a proper Charlie." The man never returned.'

proper poorly! Catchphrase of the British comedian Reg Dixon (1915–84): 'I didn't feel well, I didn't. I felt poorly – proper poorly'. He was also noted, on early 1950s' radio shows like *Variety Bandbox*, for his theme song, 'Confidentially'.

(a) prophet without honour Phrase from Matthew 13:57: 'A prophet is not without honour, save in his own country, and in his own house.' Usually rendered as 'A prophet is without honour in his own country.' Meaning, you tend not to be appreciated where you usually live or are known.

(to) propose a toast (or **drink a toast)** At one time a piece of spiced toast would be put in a glass of wine in order to improve the flavour or to collect the sediment. From this, the word 'toast' came to be identified with the drink. Equally, the mention of a lady's name to accompany the gesture was supposed to flavour a bumper as spiced toast did a drink. Known by 1700.

prose See DEATHLESS PROSE.

(the) Protestant work ethic An attitude towards business, based on the teachings of Calvin and the analysis of Max Weber in *The Protestant Ethic and the Spirit of Capitalism* (1904). The suggestion is that it is one's duty to be successful through hard work and that the ethic carries with it divine approval. Also known as 'the Puritan ethic' or 'the work ethic', the concept was re-popularized in a speech by President Richard M. Nixon in 1972 – though *Safire* notes that he removed the word 'Protestant' from the phrase. 'The protestant work ethic' was known as such by 1959.

Pseud's Corner A feature of the British satirical magazine *Private Eye* (from 1968 onwards) has been a column listing examples of pretentious writing and thinking culled from the media. This has led to a certain self-consciousness among likely 'pseuds' who are now likely to preface their remarks with, 'I expect this'll land me in Pseud's Corner but . . .' Apparently, the noun 'pseud', referring to a pseudo-intellectual person, was British schoolboy slang among the editors of the *Eye* in the 1950s, but the prefix 'pseudo-' for 'counterfeit; spurious' is very old. The American Daniel J. Boorstin in *The Image* (1960) coined the term **pseudo-event** for an occasion laid on solely for the purpose of attracting news coverage.

PS I Love You Title format. Originally used as the title of song (1934) by Johnny Mercer and Gordon Jenkins, it was revived for a Lennon and McCartney song (1963). Michael Sellers entitled a memoir of his father, the actor Peter Sellers, *PS I Love You* (1981), as has Cecilia Ahern, a novel (2004).

psychological See AT THE.

Public Enemy (No. 1) The term 'Public Enemy' has been attributed to Frank Loesch, President of the Chicago Crime Commission, who had to try to deal with Al Capone's hold over the city in 1923. The idea was to try to dispel the romantic aura such gangsters had been invested with by the popular press. James Cagney starred in a gangster film called *The Public Enemy* in 1931. John Dillinger (1903–34) was the first officially designated 'Public Enemy No. 1' in the USA. He robbed banks and killed people in Illinois, Indiana and Ohio in 1933–4 to such an extent that the Attorney General, Homer Cummings, called him this. In fact, Dillinger was the only person ever so named. The FBI's 'Ten Most Wanted Men' list did not give a ranking. Dillinger's exploits and his escape from capitivity aroused great public interest. He was eventually shot dead by FBI agents outside a cinema in Chicago. The phrase soon passed into general usage. In June 1934, P. G. Wodehouse, referring in a letter to difficulties with US income-tax officials, said: 'I got an offer from Paramount to go to Hollywood at $1,500 a week and had to refuse as I am Public Enemy No. 1 in America, and can't go there.' Other US film titles have been: *Public Hero Number One* (1935), *Public Menace* (1935), and *Public Enemy's Wife* (1936). There was a British musical called *Public Nuisance No. 1* (1935), and in the musical comedy *Seeing Stars* at the Gaiety Theatre, London (1935), Florence Desmond had a hit with the song 'Public Sweetheart Number One'. In *Anything Goes* (1934), Cole Porter had a song 'Public Enemy Number One', and so did Harold Rome for the 1937 *Pins and Needles*. The words have since been applied to any form of supposed undesirable, while Raymond Postgate, founder of the *Good Food Guide*, was dubbed 'Public Stomach No. 1', and Beverley Nichols, the author and journalist, called himself 'Public Anemone No. 1'.

publicity See ALL.

publish and be damned! Meaning, 'Go ahead and write what you want about me!' From the 1st Duke of Wellington's comment to a blackmailer who offered not to publish anecdotes of the Duke and his mistress, Harriet Wilson, in return for payment. *Publish and Be Damned* was the title of a book (1955) by the journalist Hugh Cudlipp. Richard Ingrams declared on several occasions (*circa* 1977) that a suitable motto for *Private Eye*, the British satirical journal of which he was editor, would be: 'Publish and Be Sued'.

publish it not See TELL IT NOT.

(you'd laugh to see a) pudding crawl 'My mother-in-law would say this to children who were having a fit of the giggles for no reason' – Mira Little, Somerset (1999). 'Said when someone laughs at something silly or for no apparent reason' – by the grandmother of the wife of Arthur Haseler, London N22 (2000). Compare: 'What would shock me would make a pudding crawl' – it would take an awful lot to shock me (a female), by 1900, according to *Partridge/Catch Phrases*.

pulled See GET YOUR COAT.

(to) pull out all the stops To execute some task with vigour, energy or emotion, to make every effort. From the action of an organist who, when pulling out all the organ-stops, is enabled to play with the greatest volume of sound. Known by 1865.

pull the other one! 'Do you take me for a fool?' – an expression of disbelief. Part of a longer phrase, 'Pull the other one, it's got bells on', probably referring to the

bells on a jester's, or fool's, costume. Recorded by 1966. A link to the expression 'You're pulling my leg' (i.e. you're teasing me) has also been suggested. In male company, 'Pull the middle one, it's got bells on' would be understood to have a double meaning.

(to) pull the wool over someone's eyes When wigs were commonly worn, they were sometimes referred to as wool (because of the resemblance, particularly the curls). Thus to pull the wool over people's eyes was to pull wigs over their eyes and render them incapable of seeing. Hence also the modern meaning of 'to hoodwink'. 'To pull the wool etc.' would seem to be a phrase of American origin and in use by 1859.

pun See IF YOU'LL EXCUSE THE.

punch See ARE YOU LOOKING.

Punch See AS PLEASED AS.

(to) punch above one's weight Meaning, 'to enter into situations that one might not be considered to have enough strength or fitness for.' From boxing, where fighters are categorized according to their body weights, as heavyweight, flyweight, and so on. The allusive use may not date from much before the 1990s. 'Still, it was felt in Downing Street and in the White House that the Brits mattered, that this was a country punching well above its weight in the global championships' – *The Spectator* (27 September 2003).

pure genius An inevitable pairing. Dryden wrote in 1695: 'Art being strengthened by the knowledge of things may be . . . sublim'd into a pure Genius.' 'Pergolesi's Stabat Mater . . . is a work of pure genius, one for which . . . I would gladly give both of Bach's Passions and feel that I had greatly profited by the exchange' – *Financial Times* (1 December 1983). Used as a slogan for Guinness beer, in the UK, from 1985. Opined *Campaign* (10 January 1986): 'Like it or not, the campaign [from the Ogilvy & Mather agency] put the Guinness name back in the ad industry's consciousness.' A clever stroke by whoever saw the similarity between the words 'genius' and 'Guinness' and laid the foundation of numerous advertising campaigns upon it. 'Who else other than an enormously capable person, would have thought of it? Here we are with some 3 million people for whom every day is much like a May Day and what do we do? We move a Bank Holiday "to August or October". Pure genius' – *The Observer* (11 October 1992); '832 pages of pure genius' – advertisement for John Irving's novel, *A Son of the Circus* in *The Observer* (3 September 1995).

pushed See DID SHE FALL.

(to) push the envelope To take a risk, to expand the possibilities. A phrase suddenly popular in the mid-1990s, though the allusion is not immediately clear. Probably the expression refers to 'envelope' in the sense of the structure containing the gas in an airship or balloon or, more probably, in the sense of the limitations of speed and other technical specifications that dictate an aircraft's performance. It has been suggested that if the aviation context is the original one (dating back to the 1940s), the phrase meant pushing a plane in test flights up to and even beyond its known endurance limits in order to find out its exact capabilities. 'Messrs E & V want you to know that if you thought *Basic Instinct* was pushing the envelope, this year's trendy phrase for taking a risk, *Showgirls* is, according to the publicity material, "pushing the edge of the envelope"' – *The Sunday Times* (10 September 1995); 'This film, set against the background of the Mexican Revolution, aroused enormous controversy over the extent of the violence, which pushed the already bulging envelope out still further' – Simon Rose, *Classic Film Guide* (1995).

put a penny on the drum Stock phrase of the comedian Clay Keyes (a Liverpudlian who pretended to be an American) on a BBC radio show called *The Old Town Hall* in 1941. Members of the studio orchestra had to guess musical riddles sent in by listeners, failing which they paid a forfeit to charity, e.g.: 'Where did the salt and vinegar go?' Musical answer: 'All over the pla(i)ce.' However, the phrase existed before this. Stanley Holloway recorded a song with the title 'Penny on the Drum' in 1937. Written by him, it was on a promotional record made for Butlin's Holiday Camps. Jean Phillips of Henley-on-Thames noted (1994): 'According to my father, who was in the army in the First World War, it constituted among his fellow soldiers an invitation to take part in a game of Crown and Anchor. The person starting the game would call out, "put a penny on the drum", and anyone who did so could then take part in the game. I think the use of an actual drum had been superseded and the game may well have been played on the ground. It was a gambling game, requiring a board and some dice, marked with crown and anchor. I rather fancy that most of the soldiers who innocently put their pennies on the drum never saw them back again.' A Canadian correspondent remembers from the 1940s an irreverent song about the Salvation Army that included the chorus: 'Hallelujah, hallelujah, throw a nickel on the drum and you'll be saved.'

put a sock in it! 'Shut up!' 'Shut your mouth!' addressed to a noisy person. Neil Ewart in *Everyday Phrases* (1983) confidently asserts that this dates from the days of the wind-up, 'acoustic' gramophones where the sound emerged from a horn. With no electronic controls to raise or lower the volume, the only way to regulate the sound was to put in or take out an article of clothing, which deadened it. (Presumably, mutes as stuck in the horns of brass instruments were not supplied.) The *OED2* has a citation from 1919 – an explanation of the term from the *Athenaeum* journal – which suggests the phrase was not widely known even then. The gramophone explanation is not totally convincing. *Partridge/Slang* compares the earlier expression '(to) put a bung in it' – as in a bath or leak. Why shouldn't a sock inserted in the human mouth be the origin? After all, a sock in the jaw would be the next best thing.

(to) put a spoke in someone's wheel Meaning 'to prevent someone from doing something', this is an odd expression if one knows that bicycle wheels already have spokes in them. Here, however, what is evoked is the days when carts had solid wheels and no spokes in the modern sense. The spoke then was a pin that could be inserted into a hole on the wheel to act as a brake. The *OED2* believes that, while the expression has been known since 1583, 'spoke' may be a mistranslation of a Dutch expression including the word *spaak*, meaning 'bar, stave'.

put a tiger in your tank Slogan for Esso petroleum. The Esso Tiger had been around in the USA for a long time before 1964 when a cartoon version was introduced for the first time (a year later in the UK). It became a national craze, with countless tiger tails adorning the petrol caps of the nation's cars. Subsequently, with the slogan 'Put a Tiger in Your Tank', the idea spread even farther afield. *'Pack den Tiger in den Tank'* appeared in Germany. *'Mettez un tigre dans votre moteur'* appeared in France (in Jean-Luc Godard's 1965 film *Pierrot Le Fou*, the Jean-Paul Belmondo character says, 'Put a tiger in my tank' to a Total service station attendant who replies, 'We don't do tigers here.'). In the USA, especially, the slogan gave rise to numerous tiger derivatives: 'If you feel like a tiger is in your throat, reach for Guardets Lozenges . . .' A hamburger stand advertised, 'Put a tiger in your tummy'. Tiger Beer in the Japanese *Times* sloganned, 'Put a tiger in your tankard'. Standard Rochester Beer countered with, 'Put a tankard in your tiger'. The UK campaign ran for two years before it flagged. Perhaps the slogan owed something to the Muddy Waters song '(I Want to Put a) Tiger in Your Tank' (by W. Dixon) which he was performing by 1960 and which gave double meanings to a number of motoring phrases (not least in the title).

put a woman on top for a change Slogan promoting the idea of Margaret Thatcher as Prime Minister, prior to the Conservative election win in 1979. Rob Hayward MP recalled in 1984 that the idea first came up when he was National Vice-Chairman of the Young Conservatives. Originally, 'Have a Woman on Top' (or 'Fuck Me, I'm a Tory'), it was devised by Young Conservatives in 1976 and distributed as a sticker at the Tory Party Conference. The more respectable version was taken up as an official slogan by the party.

(to) put bums on seats Media phrase, referring to the ability that any form of entertainment has to attract an audience. Origin possibly American but date un-

known. 'Bottoms on seats – Sir Peter Hall's policy for the National Theatre' – *The Spectator* (10 May 1980); 'The massed Partick Thistle fans in the audience were ecstatic, everyone else looked a mite baffled. But that's your fragmented postmodern culture, isn't it? It makes no claim to universality; just puts neatly-labelled bums on seats' – *The Guardian* (11 May 1993); 'One guy fronted me up the other week and demanded to know: "What are you going to do about it?" Moi? He suggested that if I gave them a bigger push through the arts page it would put bums on seats' – *The Herald* (Glasgow) (24 February 1994).

(to) put clear blue water between To separate one thing clearly from another – in regulations, policing, conflicts of interest, etc. Specifically in connection with the British Conservative party – an attempt to differentiate its policies from those of its opponents, specifically what right-wing Tories believe they need to put between themselves and Labour. *Clear Blue Water* was the title of a collection of speech extracts published by the Conservative minister Michael Portillo in September 1994. Identified as a current cliché in *The Times* (17 March 1995). Has been explained as: 'From blend of "clear water", the distance between two boats, and "blue water", the open sea, with a play on "blue" as the traditional colour of Conservatism'. 'The anti-European rhetoric of Mr Portillo highlighted the Right's belief that the party has to move in its direction in order to put "clear blue water" between the Conservative Party and the new-look Labour Party of Tony Blair . . . But Mr Major is resisting this, wanting to remain in the centre ground and arguing that "clear blue water" already exists over the minimum wage and Scottish devolution' – *The Scotsman* (13 October 1994); 'Commercial radio . . . took more than half of radio listening hours for the first time. Justin Sampson, head of strategic planning at the Radio Advertising Bureau, said: "There is now clear blue water between commercial and BBC radio"' – *The Independent* (5 August 1995).

(to) put down a marker Meaning, 'to stake a claim, make it obvious what your intentions are or your position is' (often in order to cover yourself in the future). Derived from the use of markers in sports and games. Date of origin unknown. 'The package sets down a marker for the competition' – *The Observer* (20 October 1983); 'Next day he could find not so much as a sentence about his gripe anywhere in the paper . . . Still, he consoled himself with one of his favourite phrases: he had "put down a personal marker"' – Nigel Rees, *The Newsmakers* (1987); 'If the Brazilians put down a marker for the Latin American countries on Monday evening, then Germany and Spain kept the European flag flying bravely yesterday when they served up what many felt was the best match of the tournament so far in their 1–1 draw in the Soldier Field in Chicago' – *The Irish Times* (22 June 1994); 'The IAAF reacted indignantly yesterday to the legal marker put down by Modahl's solicitor, who accused the governing body of prejudicing her forthcoming hearing by failing to release information about her initial test and failing to supply the remains of the sample used for the B test to her medical advisers' – *The Independent* (12 September 1994); 'Anne Simpson, director of PIRC, said: "I believe that if we win, it will bring about a sea-change in pay policies. If we can put down a marker, I think other companies will take note"' – *The Times* (8 April 1995).

put 'em up (or **them up)!** Challenge from someone with a gun, meaning 'put your hands up', but originally in boxing where the challenge meant 'raise your fists' before a fight. Known in the first sense since *circa* 1860 and in the second since 1923. 'The idea of using the Ugly Sisters to represent topical characters or types is by no means new. In 1897, we find a Thisbe who . . . has taken lessons from Eugene Sandow, the strong-man who . . . is "disposed to challenge all and sundry to 'put them up'"' – Gerald Frow, *Oh, Yes It Is!* (1985).

put her down, you don't know where she's been (or **him down ...)!** Jocular remark addressed to a person showing sexual interest in another, since the 1950s. After the domestic catchphrase addressed to a child about an object – 'Put it down,

dear, you don't know where it's been.'

(to) put it about Meaning, 'to be sexually promiscuous'. Date of origin unknown, but whereas *Partridge/Catch Phrases* guesses that it originated in the late 1940s, it does occur much earlier in a letter of Byron's dated 20 January 1817. Speaking of Mary Shelley's sister Claire Clairmont he says, 'I never loved nor pretended to love her – but a man is a man – & if a girl of eighteen comes prancing to you at all hours – there is but one way – the suite of all this is that she was with *child* – & returned to England to assist in peopling that desolate island . . . The next question is is the brat *mine*? – I have reason to think so – for I know as much as one can know such a thing – that she had *not lived* with S[helley] during the time of our acquaintance – & that she had a good deal of that same with me. – This comes of "putting it about" (as Jackson calls it) & be damned to it – and thus people come into the world.' 'Gentleman' John Jackson was a pugilist Byron cultivated. 'The simplest explanation was that he had just got tired of Jacqui . . . He was a man who had always put it about a bit' – Simon Brett, *Cast, In Order of Disappearance* (1975).

put on a show See LET'S DO.

(to) put one's dukes up (or **dooks up)** To put one's fists up as though preparing for a fight. Describing a summit between Soviet and US leaders, *Time* Magazine (20 October 1986) stated: 'Reagan and Gorbachev both came to office not with their hands outstretched but with their dukes up.' If 'dukes' means 'fists', why so? One theory is that because the 1st Duke of Wellington had such a large nose, a 'duke' became a synonym for one. Then, so this theory goes, a man's fist became a 'duke buster'. In time this was shortened, and fists became 'dukes'. *Morris* prefers another theory: that the use derives from Cockney rhyming slang, viz. 'Duke of York's' ('forks' meaning 'fingers' – standing for the whole hand or fist). *OED2* has the expression by 1874. Winston Churchill neatly played on the phrase in a public speech about House of Lords reform on 4 September 1909: 'In the absence of any commanding voice, the Tory party have had to put up their "dooks".' A report of the speech adds: 'Great laughter and a voice: "What about your grandfather?"'. (Churchill's grandfather was the *Duke* of Marlborough).

(to) put on one's thinking cap To take time to think about, and try to resolve, a problem. Known by 1874. Earlier, the phrase was 'to put on one's considering cap' – known by 1657.

(to) put on the dog Meaning, 'to put on airs, fine clothes', this is a US expression dating from the 1870s, probably from among college students (especially at Yale) who had to wear stiff, high collars (jokily known as 'dog-collars') on formal occasions.

(to) put (something) on the back burner (probably less often **on the front burner)** Meaning, either to relegate something or to bring it to the forefront of attention. Derived from cooking. Both versions known since the 1940s. In 1945, 'cooking on the front burner' was American 'jive talk' for 'the tops'. 'With Mr Khruschev showing no interest in the Anglo-American proposals, the test ban . . . will have to be put on the back burner, as the Americans have it' – *The Times* (26 April 1963); 'The whole issue is now on the front burner with the flame turned up high' – *The Times* (26 September 1970); 'After a slow start in July 1991, the G7 nations are finally putting this issue on the front burner. A senior British official said that the problems of refugees would dominate the G7 meetings in July' – *Independent on Sunday* (5 June 1994); 'If it is found that reporters or photographers did practise deception to enter Farm Place in order to expose Lady Spencer no serious person would seek to defend them. The issue of privacy generally will be right back on the political front burner' – *Evening Standard* (London) (5 April 1995); 'The way I see it, anybody thinking of proposing a cooling-off period should pause, hold back, stall, keep it on ice, put it on the back burner, rest on his oar, and desist – at least for a period' – *The Sunday Telegraph* (30 April 1995).

(to) put on the Ritz To put on an air of superiority. Known by 1926. Lines from the title song of the film *Puttin' on the Ritz* (US 1930), written by Irving Berlin, include: 'If you're blue and you don't know where to go / Why don't you go to where fashion sits / Puttin' on the Ritz? . . . Dressed up like a million-dollar trouper / Trying hard to look like Gary Cooper, sooper dooper . . . Come let's mix where Rockefellers / Walk with sticks or umberellas in their mits / Puttin' on the Ritz.' The Ritz Hotel, London, was but one of the hotels with that name opened around the world by César Ritz, the Swiss-born hotelier (1850–1918), at the turn of the 19th/20th century. The first was opened in Paris, London came second (1906) and then New York. Hence: 'ritz(y)' = (1) Smart, glamorous, ostentatiously rich. (2) Flashy, pretentious. Allusions were being made to Ritz's name in such coinages by 1910–11.

(to be) put on the spot See under x MARKS THE SPOT.

(to) put out more flags Hence, *Put Out More Flags* – title of a novel (1942) by Evelyn Waugh. According to Waugh, it comes from a Chinese saying: 'A drunk military man should order gallons and put out more flags in order to increase his military splendour'.

put that in your pipe and smoke it! Retort used after having advanced what the speaker feels is a crushing argument. 'Digest that, if you can!' Since the early 19th century. Possibly alluding to the calming and soothing properties of tobacco.

(to) put the bells and whistles on To make an elaborate fuss about something. From *The Independent* (15 March 1989): '"It's not a story you put the bells and whistles on," says Malcolm Hoddy, the news editor'; 'It's a simple message and I'm leaving out the whistles and bells' – song, 'Birdhouse in Your Soul' (1990), performed by They Might Be Giants. In computing, 'bells and whistles' are additional but not essential features put on hardware and software to make them commercially attractive (and so used by 1984). The same applies to economic products and measures in the money markets. 'Bells and whistles fail to lift stock market gloom' – headline in *The Observer* (9 February 2003). Compare ALL-SINGING, ALL-DANCING. The origin of the phrase in all senses appears to lie in the bells and whistles fixed to fairground organs or (especially) to American railway locomotives. From a song by the American bluesman Blind Willie McTell, 'Broke Down Engine Blues No. 2' (recorded 1933): 'Feel like a broke-down engine, mama, ain't got no whistles or bells. / Feel like a broke-down engine, baby, ain't got no whistles or bells.' Obviously, this has nothing to do with the usage in question but shows that bells and whistles were commonly linked to locomotives. Probably unconnected is the expression 'to souple [soften] the whistle and bells [prick and balls]' that occurs in 'Todlen Hame', a bawdy verse by David McCulloch (collected by Robert Burns). But you never know though . . .

(to) put the kibosh on something Meaning 'to squelch; put an end to; spoil; veto', this expression appears in Charles Dickens, *Sketches by Boz*, 'Seven Dials' (1836): '"Hoo-roar," ejaculates a pot-boy in a parenthesis, "put the kye-bosk [*sic*] on her, Mary!"' An extraordinary (and unverified) explanation is that 'kibosh' was the name of the black cap worn by a British judge when pronouncing sentence of death. It possibly comes from the Gaelic *cie bais*, meaning 'cap of death', but it is also known in Yiddish. 'For Belgium put the kibosh on the Kaiser; / Europe took a stick and made him sore' – song, 'Belgium Put the Kibosh on the Kaiser' (*circa* 1914).

(to) put the screws on Meaning 'to apply pressure on someone to do something', 'screws' here is short for 'thumbscrews', the ancient and medieval method of torturing prisoners. Known by 1834.

This could be why prison guards have been nicknamed 'screws', although another explanation is from screw meaning 'key'. Gaolers were sometimes known as 'turnkeys', as this was their most significant function.

(to) put the tin hat on To finish off completely, in a way that the speaker may find objectionable. Possibly from military use, where tin hat = brass hat. Current by 1919. From P. G. Wodehouse, *Summer Lightning*, Chap. 12 (1929): 'But this was final. This was the end. This put the tin hat on it.'

put up or shut up! 'Either make good your argument or stop talking about it'. In America, this translates as 'put up your money (as though for a bet)' but in Britain, 'put up your fists (as though for a fight)'. Both uses probably dating from the 19th century. A possible third interpretation is 'put up with things or shut up about them', along the lines of the pro-government American slogan in the Vietnam War (1960s): '**America: love it or leave it!**'

(to) put your puddings out for treacle (or **puddens up for treacle**) An encouragement to people to put themselves forward (as though in order to receive sauce on their dessert), though it may be used to suggest a double meaning. In May 1994, Teresa Gorman MP accused the British minister Michael Heseltine of disloyalty to Prime Minister John Major by saying that he was 'putting his puddings out for treacle'. Mrs Gorman subsequently explained her expression to Alan Watkins in the *Independent on Sunday* (12 June 1994): '[It] was used in our neighbourhood about any woman considered to be putting herself forward for attention – or suspected of paying the tradesmen's bills in "kind"!'

Q

(to spend) quality time (together) In family and relationship studies, to spend time in beneficial interaction with a partner or, especially, with a young child.

Of American origin by the 1980s. 'Her mother is an engineer who has read too many articles on quality time and relating to kids' – *San Francisco Sunday Examiner*

& *Chronicle* (12 June 1988); 'As Nathan tells Emery: "People with girlfriends tend to get non-productive. They spend a lot of 'quality time' together; they dawdle. They learn how to make cappuccino; they join AA; they rent *Dances with Wolves* and cry together when Two Socks dies"' – *The Times* (19 May 1994); 'Now I am the last person to look down on Spanish package holidays . . . They allow families to spend quality time together, away from distractions' – *The Herald* (Glasgow) (8 October 1994).

Quatermass See IT LOOKS LIKE SOMETHING.

(a) quantum jump (or **leap)** Meaning, 'a sudden large advance or increase', originally used with a specific scientific meaning. 'Quantum jump' was known by 1927, 'leap' not until the 1970s. In both cases, the use of the word 'quantum' is unnecessary, especially when it is not understood. *Quantum Leap* was the title of a TV series (US 1989–93). 'The imperial Presidency did not begin with Richard Nixon although under him abuses of the office took a quantum leap' – *The New Yorker* Magazine (13 June 1977).

¿qué? In the BBC TV comedy series *Fawlty Towers* (1975–9), Manuel the Spanish waiter (Andrew Sachs) seemed to do very little else but ask 'What?' in Spanish. But then, as Basil Fawlty (John Cleese) would explain, 'You'll have to excuse him – he comes from Barcelona.'

Queen Anne's dead This phrase might be used to put down someone who has just told you some very old news or what you know already. *Mencken* glosses it slightly differently: 'Reply to an inquiry for news, signifying that there is none not stale.' An alternative, **Queen Elizabeth is dead**, is to be found in Swift's *Polite Conversation* (1738). Both forms appear to date from *circa* 1720 – Queen Anne had actually died in 1714. *Apperson* finds, 'He's as dead as Queen Anne the day after she dy'd' (which doesn't seem to convey the modern meaning of the expression). In George Colman the Younger's play *The Heir-at-Law* (1797), there occurs the line: 'Tell 'em Queen Anne's dead.' *Partridge/ Slang* dates 'My Lord Baldwin is dead' to *circa* 1670–1710. A US equivalent is,

'Bryan has carried Texas' – presumably referring to William Jennings Bryan (d. 1925) who stood three times unsuccessfully for the US presidency.

Queen Elizabeth slept here Usually an unsubstantiated claim and a slogan that has been used to promote visits to English stately homes – and some inns – probably since such tourism began in the 18th century. Elizabeth I was an inveterate traveller and guest. By 1847, Thackeray was writing in *Vanity Fair*, Chap. 8: 'I think there are at least twenty bedrooms on the first floor; and one of them has the bed in which Queen Elizabeth slept.' By 1888, Jerome K. Jerome in *Three Men in a Boat* has: 'She was nuts on public houses, was England's Virgin Queen. There's scarcely a pub of any attractions within ten miles of London that she does not seem to have looked in at, stopped at, or slept at, some time or other.' In the USA, the equivalent slogan is **George Washington slept here**, as in the title of Kauffman and Hart's play (1940; film US 1942), which, when adapted by Talbot Rothwell for the Strand Theatre, London, later in the 1940s, was called . . . *Queen Elizabeth Slept Here*.

(a) queen for a day Phrase for a woman who is being given a special treat. It derives from an American radio programme that ran for ten years in the 1940s. According to an informant, 'being a queen for a day didn't mean they gave you a country; you only got your wish, that's what. No one complained.' Adapted as a daytime TV show, it was a big hit 1955–64, but *Halliwell's Television Companion* (1982) calls it 'the nadir of American TV'. When Radio Luxembourg adopted the format (from 1955, introduced by Richard Attenborough, sponsored by Phensic) they changed the title to *Princess for a Day*. Was this because the wishes fulfilled were more modest, the participants younger, or had the word 'queen' become too tainted by that time?

(the) Queen of Spain's legs Phrase for something that should not be mentioned in polite conversation. Known by the mid-19th century, the occasion for the coinage may date back to the end of the 16th century. On her way to be married in

Spain, the future queen (possibly Margaret of Austria who was to marry Philip III), passed through a town where silk stockings were made and the town wanted to present her with a pair. But this was considered an unseemly suggestion, and one of the courtiers declared, 'The Queen of Spain has no legs.' 'Till she came back to give us our cue, we felt that it would be better to consider the engagement in the same light as the Queen of Spain's legs – facts which certainly existed, but the less said about the better' – Elizabeth Gaskell, *Cranford*, Chap. 12 (1853).

Queen's English See KING'S ENGLISH.

queer See AS QUEER AS DICK'S.

(as) queer as a clockwork orange The title of the novel *A Clockwork Orange* (1962; film UK 1971) came, according to its author, Anthony Burgess, from a Cockney expression, 'queer as a clockwork orange' (i.e. homosexual). This had been in use since the mid-1950s, Paul Beale states in *Partridge/Slang*, though few others had heard of it. Perhaps Burgess simply got the location wrong as the phrase was reported from Liverpool in Shaw & Spiegl, *Lern Yerself Scouse* (1966): 'Ee's as queer as clockwerk oringe' – 'He enjoys being hugged after scoring a goal' (this was a year or two after Burgess's novel was published, of course). Another attempt at explaining the title has been that Burgess worked for many years in Malaysia where the word 'orang' means 'human'. As to the title's relevance to the story – which has no overtly homosexual element – this is debatable, unless 'queer' is taken just as 'odd' and without the sexual meaning. The following passage from the novel hints at a possible reason for the choice of title: 'Who ever heard of a clockwork orange? . . . The attempt to impose upon man, a creature of growth and capable of sweetness, to ooze juicily at the last round the bearded lips of God, to attempt to impose, I say, laws and conditions appropriate to a mechanical creation, against this I raise my sword-pen.' The book describes an attempt to punish its criminal hero, Alex, by turning him into a 'mechanical man' through forms of therapy and brainwashing.

queer as a coot This pejorative phrase has been applied to 'queers' in the homosexual sense (and was so recorded in 1958) but is probably no more than an alliterative version of the older 'stupid as a coot'. Coots are probably no stupider or queerer than any other bird, but the name sounds funny. Compare BALD AS A BADGER/BANDICOOT/COOT.

(to be in) Queer Street Meaning, 'to be in debt'. Possibly from the tradesmen's habit of putting a 'query' next to the names of people whose creditworthiness was questionable. The expression has also been used (since 1811) to describe being in any kind of difficulty.

(to) queer the pitch To ruin a plan or prospects. The pitch here is as in 'sales pitch' rather than 'football pitch'. Known by 1846.

question See ASK A SILLY; BEG THE.

(a) question-mark still hangs over . . . Meaning, 'there is still uncertainty or doubt'. Date of origin not known. 'There is uncertainty about what should be done with their sprawling barracks. Many British officers' houses have been put on the market and snapped up, but a question mark hangs over the main complex' – *The Times* (14 May 1994); 'Inkatha envisages a team of "facilitators" rather than arbitrators, but a question mark hangs over the party's course of action if the mediators decide against it. "We will cross that bridge when we come to it," said Chief Buthelezi' – *The Daily Telegraph* (6 March 1995).

(a) question of —— Title format much used in broadcasting and, by now, a cliché of same. As in *A Question of Sport/Confidence/Stars/Politics*, etc. I was responsible for using *A Question of Degree* (about graduate unemployment, BBC Radio 1970) and that particular phrase has been around for a long time – *Punch* (7 December 1910), for example. Other titles are put in the form **the —— in question**, as in *The Body in Question/The Week in Question/Sport In Question*.

quick and dirty Phrase applied to a job or piece of work accomplished fast and with the minimum of fuss – probably not very well done, too, but cheap. Probably American in origin, since the 1950s.

(the) quick and the dead 'Quick' here has the old sense of 'the living', as on several occasions in the Bible, e.g. 'judge of the quick and the dead' (Acts 10:42). Hence, the film title *The Quick and the Dead* (US 1995).

quick brown fox See NOW IS THE TIME FOR.

quick stuff See MUM MUM.

quiet See ALL QUIET ON; ANYTHING FOR A.

(a) quiet revolution A subtle change that does not draw attention to itself. The phrase was written by Barry Day, a speechwriter for the British Prime Minister Edward Heath who, shortly after his election, said in a Conservative Party Conference speech (October 1970): 'If we are to achieve this task we will have to embark on a change so radical, a revolution so quiet and yet so total, that it will go far beyond the programme for a parliament to which we are committed and on which we have already embarked, far beyond the decade and way into the 80s.' 'What we have had is a Quiet Revolution, people starting to tell pollsters that, well, Betty Boothroyd would make a very nice Madam President, and maybe the Royal Family would not be missed after all' – Polly Toynbee in *Radio Times* (22 July 1995).

quite early one morning Dylan Thomas gave a broadcast talk for the BBC Welsh Home Service on 31 August 1945. The opening sentence: 'Quite early one morning in the winter in Wales, by the sea that was lying down still and green as grass after a night of tar-black howling and rolling.' As will be immediately apparent, this concept eventually but directly turned into his masterpiece, the radio play *Under Milk Wood* (first broadcast 21 January 1954, shortly after Thomas's death). This and other broadcasts by Thomas were included in a volume entitled *Quite Early One Morning*, also first published in the wake of his death, in 1954. Hence, *Quite Ugly One Morning*, the title of a novel (1996) by Christopher Brookmyre.

quod me nutrit me destruit When it was noticed in 2001 that the actress Angelina Jolie had a tattoo over her stomach containing this motto (meaning, 'that which nourishes me, destroys me'), it was pointed out that the motto also appears in capital letters at the top left-hand corner of a portrait of a young man that was rescued from builders' rubbish at Corpus Christi College, Cambridge, in the 1950s. On the basis that lettering next to the motto describes him as being aged 21 in 1585, the man is thought to be Christopher Marlowe, the future playwright, who obtained his BA at the college in that year and at that age. The Latin words have not been found in classical texts but bear a resemblance to some lines by Shakespeare (written a few years later): 'Consum'd with that which it was nourish'd by' (Sonnet 73) and 'A burning torch that's turned upside down; / The word, *Qui me alit, me extinguit* [who feeds me extinguishes me]' – *Pericles*, II.ii.33. A. D. Wraight wrote in 1965 that, if the portrait is of Marlowe, then the motto refers to his poetic muse 'which both inspired and nourished him, and yet consumed him with its fiery genius'. But what all this has to do with the stomach of the *Tomb Raider* actress is anybody's guess.

quote See AND I; DON'T.

quote . . . unquote *OED2* defines this phrase rather well as 'a formula used in dictation to introduce a quotation. Frequently in transferred sense, in speech or writing, introducing and terminating words quoted (or ironically imagined to be quoted) from the speech or writing of another.' What is more difficult is to pinpoint when the phrase came into use. The *OED2*'s earliest citation is in a 1935 letter from e. e. cummings in which he uses the formula to highlight a borrowing from James Joyce: 'The Isful ubiquitous wasless&-shallbeless quote scrotum-tightening unquote omnivorously eternal thalassa pelagas or Ocean.' Obviously, for a phrase intended to be spoken, there are not likely to be many written citations. In fact, the only other use of the phrase to hand is in the (slightly earlier) Marx Brothers' film *Animal Crackers* (US 1930): *Jamison (reading from letter Spaulding has dictated)*: 'Quotes, unquotes, and quotes.' *Spaulding*: 'That's three quotes . . . And another quote'll make it a gallon.' Perhaps it all began with the rise of the stenographer in the late 19th century? But the phrase may also have been used by journalists giving spelled-out punctuation when dictating their copy over the telephone or when sending it by cable or telegram: for example, 'HE ADDED COMMA QUOTE MY GOVERNMENT WOULD NOT COMMA ON ANY ACCOUNT COMMA CONSIDER SUCH A SOLUTION UNQUOTE.' From one's own limited experience of these matters, 'open quotes/close quotes' was probably the more usual spoken journalistic method. But, whatever the case, 'quote . . . unquote' seems to have outlasted telegrams and cables and entered popular speech. And it certainly seems to have replaced 'in inverted commas' as a way of signalling that the speaker is quoting.

quo vadis [whither goest thou]?　From the Vulgate (Latin) translation of John 13:36: 'Simon Peter said unto him, Lord, whither goest thou? Jesus answered him, Whither I go, thou canst not follow me now'; and from John 16:5 in which Christ comforts his disciples before the Crucifixion. The words also occur in Genesis 32:17 and in the Acts of St Peter among the New Testament Apocrypha in which, after the Crucifixion, Peter, fleeing Rome, encounters Christ on the Appian Way. He asks Him, '*Domine, quo vadis* [Lord, whither goest thou]' and Christ replies, '*Venio Romam, iterum crucifigi* [I am coming to Rome to be crucified again].' Familiar from the title of a film (US 1951, and two previous Italian ones) and an opera (1909) by Jean Nouguès, all based on the novel *Quo Vadis?* (1896) by the Pole, Henryk Sienkiewicz.

R

rabbit　See I HOPE YOUR.

rabbit, rabbit　The singers Chas and Dave introduced this line to one of their commercials for Courage Best Bitter in the UK, *circa* 1983. It emulates talkative women who interrupt the pleasures of the drinking process. 'To rabbit', meaning 'to talk', comes from rhyming slang ('rabbit and pork').

(the) race to the sea　This phrase dates from the autumn of 1914 and was used during the early months of the First World War. In his *English History 1914–45* (1966), A. J. P. Taylor writes: 'Both combatant lines hung in the air. Some 200 miles of open country separated the German and French armies from the sea. Each side tried to repeat the original German strategy of turning the enemy line. This was not so much a "race to the sea", its usual name, as a race to outflank the other side before the sea was reached. Both sides failed.' Martin Gilbert uses the phrase evocatively of a phase of the Second World War in the official biography of Winston Churchill, Vol. 6, Chap. 21 (1983): 'As dawn broke on May 26 [1940], the news from France dominated Churchill's thoughts, and those of his advisers and staff. The road to Dunkirk was open. The race to the sea was about to begin.' In his own *The Second World War*, Vol. 2, Churchill entitled the chapter dealing with Dunkirk, 'The March to the Sea'.

radical chic　Fashionable espousal of left-wing, radical causes, clothes and lifestyle by people with more money than sense. The phrase was coined in an article by Tom Wolfe when describing a party given by Leonard Bernstein, the American composer and conductor, for members of the Black Panther movement. The article was subsequently collected in Wolfe's book *Radical Chic & Mau-Mauing the Flak Catchers* (1970).

(the) raging moon　The phrase 'raging moon' may be an original coinage of Dylan Thomas. His poem 'In my craft or sullen art' (1945) continues: '. . . Exercised in the still night / When only the moon rages / And the lovers lie abed / With all their griefs in their arms . . . / Not for the proud man apart / From the raging moon I write / On these spindrift pages.' The nearest the *OED2* gets is 'raging *noon*'. *The Raging Moon* was given to the title of a film (UK 1970; from a novel by Peter Marshall) about physically disabled people.

(a) raging torrent An inevitable pairing – the words have been together since at least 1603. 'It is a raging torrent at present, fed by thousands of mountain streams swollen by the wet season' – *Today* (17 May 1994); 'But nobody warned you about the flooding. Come the winds and rains of winter, the water rises and the gurgling stream becomes a raging torrent' – *Daily Mail* (1 April 1995).

rags to riches Name given to a certain type of fiction, often in publishers' blurbs, of which the novels by the American writer Horatio Alger (1832–99) are proto-typical. Sometimes also given to the actual stories of people who have risen from poverty to wealth. The term comes from the story of Cinderella. It was also the title of a popular song (1953) by Adler and Ross. *OED2*'s earliest citation is from 1947.

rain See DAY THAT THE; INTO EACH LIFE.

(to) rain cats and dogs Meaning, 'to rain extremely heavily'. Known by 1738 – Swift, *Polite Conversation* – though there is a 1652 citation: 'Raining dogs and pole-cats'. Shelley wrote 'raining cats and dogs' in a letter to a friend (1819). There is no very convincing explanation for this phrase. According to *Morris* (1977), it comes from the days when street drainage was so poor that a heavy rain storm could easily drown cats and dogs. After the storm people would see the number of dead cats and dogs and think it looked as if they had fallen out of the sky. *Brewer* (1894) suggests, on the other hand, that in northern mythology cats were supposed to have great influence on the weather and dogs were a signal of wind, 'thus cat may be taken as a symbol of the downpouring rain, and the dog of the strong gusts of wind accompanying a rain-storm'.

rain in Spain See HOW NOW.

rain is the best policeman of all Heard from a senior police officer after the London Notting Hill Carnival had been rained off on the Late Summer Bank Holiday in August 1986. Meaning that crime falls when the rain does (as also in cold weather).

rains See IT NEVER.

(to) raise Cain Meaning, 'to make trouble, a fuss, a disturbance'. The allusion here is to the biblical Cain ('the first murderer') who killed his brother, Abel (Genesis 4:2–8). A person who makes trouble, 'raises the spirit' of Cain by doing so. Known by 1840.

(to) raise one's Ebenezer (sometimes **to get one's Ebenezer up)** Meaning 'to be angry', this expression was in American use by the mid-1830s, Ebenezer being a nickname for the devil. It is not to be confused with what is referred to in the hymn: 'Come Thou Fount' (R. Robinson, 1758) – 'Here I raise my Ebenezer', where Ebenezer is the Hebrew 'stone of help', as in the name of a type of chapel. Samuel raised a thanksgiving stone at Ebenezer after the defeat of the Philistines. Plenty of scope for double entendres, of course – especially if the hymn is sung at weddings, as has been known.

(a) raisin in the sun *Raisin in the Sun* was the title of a play (1959) by Lorraine Hansberry, taken from the poem 'Harlem' (1951) by Langston Hughes: 'What happens to a dream deferred? / Does it dry up / Like a raisin in the sun?'

Ramsbottom, Enoch and me During the Second World War, the BBC radio programme *Happidrome* featured Harry Korris as Mr Lovejoy, a theatre manager, Cecil Fredericks as Ramsbottom and Robby Vincent as Enoch, the call-boy. Hence, the phrase from the opening song, 'We three in *Happidrome*, / Ramsbottom, Enoch and me . . .' Also from the show came **take 'im away, Ramsbottom!** and **let me tell you!** Enoch would say this last before revealing some startling fact to Mr Lovejoy.

(the) rank and file Political phrase, referring to the ordinary membership of – particularly – the British Labour Party. Originally, a military term akin to 'foot soldiers' as opposed to the officer class. Date of origin not known, but known in this context by the 1940s, as in the first citation. 'Oratory . . . stratospherically above the plain, blunt, and fairly honest opinions held by the rank and file of Newark Labour' – J. W. Day, *Harvest Adventure* (1946); 'Senior Newham Labour councillor Graham Lane admitted today there had been some annoyance amongst rank and file party members that Mr Kellaway, a Liberal Democrat councillor, had been allowed to return so easily to the Labour fold' – *Evening Standard* (London) (10 June 1994).

rapturous applause An inevitable pairing. Known by 1853. 'No wonder . . . that the first plink of those conciliatory ping-pong balls produced rapturous applause' – *The Daily Telegraph* (3 December 1971); 'The rapturous applause which greeted the voluntary 90-piece orchestra, the 140-strong choir in blue, green, yellow and red, and conductor Noel Tredinnick was enough to make any visitor question whether they had become dislocated in time and found themselves at a concert with the demi-God of rock, Eric Clapton, who had occupied the stage a few weeks earlier' – *The Times* (15 April 1995).

(as) rare as rocking horse shit (or **manure)** That is, rare to the point of being non-existent. By the 1970s and possibly from British forces' slang. A 1986 advertisement for Qantas, the Australian airline, was cajoling passengers with: 'You'll agree a better deal [than Qantas offer] is about as likely as rocking-horse manure'. A modern version of **rare as hen's teeth**.

(a) rash act An inevitable pairing. Known by 1886. 'This helps to explain Pasqua's rash act in lecturing Algerian leaders and initiating contacts with fundamentalists in exile living in Germany' – *The European* (19 August 1994); 'No matter how much sympathy one feels for the sacked drivers, this seems to have been an extraordinarily rash act. What possessed them?' – *The Guardian* (29 April 1995).

raspberry See BLOW A.

(the) ravages of time Slightly literary and self-consciously archaic phrase. 'If Mrs Evergreen does take some pains to repair the ravages of time' occurs in R. B. Sheridan, *The School for Scandal*, II.ii (1777). 'Despite the ravages of time, fine comics for sale still turn up. "I bet there's a whole box of Batman No 1 in someone's attic," Mr McAlpine says' – *The Times* (30

July 1994); 'Reading his great reviews I'm filled with a mixture of admiration and rancorous envy. The writing is so sharp, the detail so illuminating that great performances seem to have been miraculously preserved from the ravages of time' – *Independent on Sunday* (30 October 1994).

raw See DON'T COME THE.

(the) razor's edge The title of the novel by Somerset Maugham *The Razor's Edge* (1944; film US 1946) comes from the Katha-Upanishad: 'The sharp edge of a razor is difficult to pass over; thus the wise say the path to Salvation is hard' – source: Ted Morgan, *Somerset Maugham* (1980).

razor-sharp accuracy (or **analysis** or **wit)** As an adjectival phrase, 'razor-sharp' was known by 1921, but it has now become a cliché. A recent variant has been **laser-sharp**. 'A witty, razor-sharp satire on monogamy' – advertisement in the *New York Review of Books* (25 October 1979); '[Reginald Maudling's] mind was razor-sharp, one of the best I have encountered, and it remained so through all the mistakes and misfortunes of his business life' – John Cole, *As It Seemed To Me* (1995); 'Bill Ashton's charges return with a hustling big-band set, recorded live at Ronnie Scott's. It goes without saying that the section work is laser-sharp; even more welcome is the sensitivity and restraint shown by the soloists' – *The Times* (19 March 1995).

reach for a Lucky instead of a sweet Slogan for Lucky Strike cigarettes, current in the USA from the late 1920s. George Washington Hill of the American Tobacco Company was driving through New York City one day when he noticed a stout woman waiting to cross the street, eating a big piece of candy. Alongside, a taxi pulled up in which a 'nice-looking woman' was smoking a cigarette. The contrast inspired the slogan. Understandably, the confectionery industry wasn't very pleased, but it is said that this campaign created more women smokers than any other promotion.

reach for the sky (or **stars) (**and sometimes just **reach for it)!** This is what a character in a Western movie says when, pointing a gun at an opponent, he wants him to 'put his hands up' and thus away from any weapons the opponent may have. However, when Paul Brickhill entitled his biography of Douglas Bader, the legless flying ace, *Reach for the Sky* (1954) he was no doubt alluding to the RAF motto '*per ardua ad astra* [through striving to the stars]'. 'Reach for the *Star*' was a line used in promoting the British newspaper (current February 1989). Compare I AIM AT THE STARS.

(to) reach the point of no return (or **pass the point . . .)** Phrase from aviation where, at such a point, there is not enough fuel available to cover the same distance home again. Known by 1941. Now almost exclusively figurative use only. 'Scholars may well "have passed the point of no return" in this matter' – *Oxford Diocesan Magazine* (20 October 1977); 'Schumacher's View: Monaco could have been my point of no return' – headline in *The European* (27 May 1994).

read See ALL I KNOW IS.

read all about it! Traditional newspaper vendor's cry. In the UK since 1900? The phrase follows the shouting of the main headline story: 'King to abdicate . . . Bishop elopes with nun . . . read all about it!' By extension applied to books and, hence, *Read All About It*, title of a BBC TV review of new paperback books (1974–9).

read any good books lately? Presumably this phrase was once used in all seriousness as a conversational gambit. 'Have you read any good books lately?' is the caption to a cartoon (showing two lovers on a sofa) by Peter Arno and included in his *Parade* (1931). But it became something that you would say to distract attention away from something. Or it became something you might say to someone who, for no obvious reason, was staring at you. It occurs in the Marx Brothers' *Horse Feathers* (US 1932) and *A Night at the Opera* (US 1935), and was used in the BBC radio show *Band Waggon* (1938–9). Later, in the BBC radio show *Much Binding in the Marsh* (1947–53), it became Richard Murdoch's way of changing the subject: *Kenneth Horne*: 'One of the nicest sandwiches I've ever had. What was in it, Murdoch?' *Murdoch*: 'Well, there was – er

– have you read any good books lately?' *Horne*: 'I thought it tasted something like that.'

(to) read between the lines To discern a hidden or unstated meaning in a written document (or, figuratively) in any form of words. Known by 1866 and possibly referring to the cryptographic method whereby only alternate lines are read in order to discover the meaning of a text. 'Personal inclination as well as the discretion required by his position seems to have led him to evolve a method of writing for the student who can "read between the lines", and of conveying the more sensational facts by delicate implication' – Liddell Hart, *Through the Fog of War,* Chap. 19 (1938).

read, mark, learn and inwardly digest An injunction from the Book of Common Prayer. It is in the Collect for the second Sunday after Advent.

read my lips 'Listen to what I am saying – I mean it.' Although popularized by George Bush in his speech accepting the Republican nomination on 19 August 1988, the phrase was not new. Bush wanted to emphasize his pledge not to raise taxes, whatever pressure Congress applied, so what he said was, 'I'll say no, and they'll push, and I'll say no, and they'll push again, and I'll say to them, "Read my lips, no new taxes."' According to William Safire, in an article in *The New York Times* Magazine (September 1988), the phrase is rooted in 1970s' rock music (despite there being a song with the title copyrighted by Joe Greene in 1957). The British actor/ singer Tim Curry used the phrase as the title of an album of songs in 1978. Curry said he took it from an Italian-American recording engineer who used it to mean, 'Listen and listen very hard, because I want you to hear what I've got to say.' Several lyricists in the 1980s used the phrase for song titles. A football coach with the Chicago Bears became nicknamed Mike 'Read My Lips' Ditka. There has been a thoroughbred race horse so named. Safire also cites a number of American politicians using the phrase before Bush, also in the 1980s. In 2002, the film *Sur mes lèvres* (France 2001), about a deaf secretary who uses her lip-reading skills to help a criminal, was given the English-language title *Read My Lips*.

(to) read the riot act The meaning of this phrase is 'to make strong representations about something; express forcibly that something must cease'. The actual Riot Act passed by the British Parliament in 1714 (and finally repealed in 1973) provided for the dispersal of crowds (defined as being of more than twelve persons) by those in authority. The method used was for someone to stand up and, literally, read out the terms of the Act so that the rioters knew what law they were breaking. Known by 1795.

ready See ARE YOU READY.

ready, aye, ready Slogan for Camp coffee, in the UK from *circa* 1883. This is almost a slogan in the old sense of a war-cry. In fact, it has been used as such by several Scots clans, including the Johnstons, Stewarts, Napiers and Scotts. Various institutions use it as a motto, too – Merchiston Castle School, Edinburgh, is one. But it has travelled farthest on the distinctive label for Camp coffee, manufactured by R. Paterson & Sons of Glasgow. The label remained virtually unchanged for nearly a hundred years. Today the basic elements are still in place: a Scots officer being served coffee by a turbanned attendant with the slogan up a flagpole. Additional phrases have adjured: **Drink Camp – It's The Best!** and **Don't Be Misled!!!**

ready when you are, Mr De Mille! Punchline of a rather lengthy joke, current by the 1960s at least, alluded to in a *Punch* headline (25 March 1970) and quoted in Leslie Halliwell, *The Filmgoers Book of Quotes* (1973). In short, the joke tells of the day when Cecil B. De Mille, the famed producer of biblical epics for the cinema, was directing a battle scene that involved thousands of extras and animals and probably ended with the destruction of the set. Whatever the case, it would only be possible for there to be one 'take'. So, C.B. covered himself by having the scene filmed by four cameras. When the action was completed, the destruction wrought, and any chance of repeating the matter had been lost for all time, Mr De Mille checked with each cameraman that he had filmed the scene successfully. No, said the first, the film had jammed in the camera. No, said the second, 'There's a HAIR IN THE GATE'. No, said the third, the sun had shone into the lens . . . until, in desperation, the director turned to the last cameraman, who said brightly, 'Ready when you are, Mr De Mille!' (or '. . . C.B.!') Presumably this joke is popular because it portrays innocence in the face of dire calamity. The punchline hangs in the air almost joyfully. *Ready When You Are, Mr McGill* became the title of a British TV play (1976) by Jack Rosenthal about how a TV production is ruined by an actor who can't remember his (two) lines. Compare the line spoken by Gloria Swanson as a faded movie star in *Sunset Boulevard* (US 1950): 'Right, Mr De Mille, I'm ready for my close-up.'

(the) real — Travel journalistic cliché – with 'the real Spain' being by far the most common construction. Meaning 'the part of a traveller's destination away from the artificial life of the tourist resorts'. Part of the 'travel scribes' armoury' compiled from a competition in *The Guardian* (10 April 1993). 'The tourist authorities are certainly conscious of the potential of inland Spain – "real" Spain' – *The Guardian* (21 April 1986); 'Consisting of two tiers of arches running for more than half a mile and more than 90 ft high in places, it is just one of the extraordinary sights to be found in the city and a shining example of the real Spain' – *The Guardian* (6 March 1987); 'Another tick on the mental Filofax inscribed "The Real Spain." But then, the whole journey from Malaga had been the real Spain, as if constructed ahead of me in Potemkin Village style by Ministry of Tourism workmen eager to dispel the old image of paella-and-chips' – *The Guardian* (2 June 1990); 'The Costa Brava was named 76 years ago by poet and journalist Ferran Agullo in recognition of its ruggedness. It is also known as "The Gateway to Spain", but those who treat it as such, hurtling down the A17 autopista in search of "the real Spain" further south, miss out on the best bit of all' – *The Sunday Telegraph* (10 July 1994); 'The few tourists who make it as far as Santa Cruz identify themselves by noisily slurping Fanta, and carrying the air of having stumbled upon the real Spain. But economically, the real Tenerife is back there on the beach' – *The Independent* (15 April 1995).

(the) really useful —— Alluding to the story of *Thomas the Tank Engine* (1946) by the Reverend W(ilbert) Awdry, English clergyman and author (1911–97): 'After pushing [trucks] about here for a few weeks you'll know almost as much about them as Edward. Then you'll be a Really Useful Engine.' Accordingly, since the 1980s, the composer Andrew Lloyd Webber has presided over a business empire called the Really Useful Group.

(the) real McCoy Meaning 'the real thing', the genuine article', the phrase *possibly* derives from 'Kid' McCoy, a US welterweight boxing champion in the late 1890s. When challenged by a man in a bar to prove he was who he said he was, McCoy flattened him. When the man came round, he declared that this was indeed the 'real' McCoy. As *Burnam* (1980) notes, 'Kid' McCoy promoted this story about himself. However, Messrs G. Mackay, the Scottish whisky distillers, were apparently promoting their product as 'the real *Mackay*' in 1870, as though alluding to an established expression. This could have derived from the Mackays of Reay in Sutherland claiming to be the principal branch of the Mackay clan. Robert Louis Stevenson used this version in an 1883 letter.

real men don't eat quiche Phrase used as the title of a book (1983) by Bruce Feirstein, following an article by him in *Playboy* (1982). This became a jokey yardstick of manliness of the type popular in journalistic sociological discussions. Compare the film title *Dead Men Don't Wear Plaid* (US 1981).

(it's the) real thing Slogan. There have been so many rivals to the Coca-Cola drink that there has been a continuing necessity to maintain that 'Coke' is the 'real' one. This idea appeared in 1942 in the form, 'The only thing like Coca-Cola is Coca-Cola itself.' 'It's the real thing' followed in 1970 and has proved one of the most

enduring of the Coca-Cola slogans. Tom Stoppard's play *The Real Thing* (1982) was more about love (as in 'it's the real thing this time') but could hardly fail to remind one of the slogan. *OED2* has an example of this use – i.e. true love as distinct from infatuation – in 1857.

reappraisal See AGONIZING.

rearrange the following (words) into a well-known phrase or saying Instruction often to be found in competitions and puzzles. The actual game of re-ordering the words on a board to make up a sentence was almost certainly played in the 'Beat the Clock' segment of the ITV show *Sunday Night at the London Palladium* (1950s/60s). From the 1970s, a graffito: 'Arrange the following words into a well-known phrase or saying: Off Piss.'

—— rears its ugly head Meaning, '(usually something unpleasant) happens or appears'. Anthony Trollope in *Barchester Towers* (1857) has: 'Rebellion had already raised her hideous head within the [bishop's] palace.' In P. G. Wodehouse, *The Heart of a Goof*, Chap. 5 (1926), there is: 'The moment he entered the club-house Disaffection reared its ugly head.' '"It is wildly implausible that the spectre of negative equity will not rise [*sic*] its ugly head in the near future," said Andrew Oswald, professor [of] economics' – *The Observer* (16 February 2003). The image is presumably of a Loch Ness-type monster, emerging from the deep. But as for *sex* raising or rearing its ugly head, why? Because the penis rises? If so, then why ugly? The 'sex' version is used both as an explanation for people's behaviour (like '*cherchez la femme*') and as a complaint of the intrusion of sex in books, TV programmes, etc., where the speaker would rather not find it. It has been current since at least 1930 when James R. Quirk used it in a *Photoplay* editorial about the film *Hell's Angels*. Margery Allingham has 'Once sex rears its ugly 'ead it's time to steer clear' in *Flowers for the Judge*, Chap. 4 (1936) and 'Sex rearin' its ugly 'ead again, eh?' in *The Fashion in Shrouds*, Chap. 6 (1938). In Alan Ayckbourn's play *Bedroom Farce* (1975), Delia comments: 'My mother used to say, Delia, if S-E-X ever rears its ugly head, close your eyes before you see the rest of it.'

reason   See AGE OF.

(a) rebel without a cause   According to the *Oxford Dictionary of Modern Quotations* (1991), the film title *Rebel Without a Cause* (US 1955) was originally the title of a book, subtitled 'The hypnoanalysis of a criminal psychopath', published by the American psychologist R. M. Lindner in 1944. In the *Oxford Dictionary of Quotations* (1992), Lindner is described as a 'novelist'. The screenplay credit, however, is given to Stewart Stern 'from an original story by the director, Nicholas Ray'. Even so, *The Motion Picture Guide* (1990) gives the provenance of the script as 'based on an adaptation by Irving Shulman of a story line by Ray inspired by the story *The Blind Run* by Dr Robert M. Lindner.' The film's study of adolescent misbehaviour had little to do with what one would now think of as psychopathic, but it helped popularize the phrase 'rebel without a cause' to describe a certain type of alienated youth of the period. It was the film that projected its star, James Dean, to status of chief 1950s' rebel, a position confirmed when he met his premature end soon after.

rebuilding one's life   Journalistic cliché, describing the process of coming to terms with a divorce or separation or with a death. Very much part of the *Hello!* Magazine vocabulary, where it almost acquires euphemistic force in putting a positive angle on something that may, in reality, be wretched. Date of origin not known. 'Bitterness is not an emotion Joan understands and she began rebuilding her life with the help of the decent Irish people who showered her with letters of sympathy and gifts' – *Daily Mail* (1 September 1994); 'As the Princess has matured, so she has worn her hair ever shorter. Last year, busy rebuilding her life, she tried out a more severe look in her second Vogue cover' – *Daily Mail* (1 February 1995); 'It seemed everyone except me was part of a happy couple. I dealt with it by burying myself in my work. Although I went on a few blind dates, I wasn't ready for romance so I concentrated on rebuilding my life' – *Daily Mail* (20 April 1995).

(a) recipe for disaster   Date of origin not known. '"The track will have to be open for extensive schooling beforehand and I'm not happy about the incorporation of three regulation fences including an open ditch," said Nicholson. "I think they should stick to cross-country fences, otherwise it could be a recipe for disaster"' – *The Guardian* (24 November 1994); 'He said the suggestion that the Government might grant recognition to the breakaway Garda Federation, which he referred to as an "illegal organization", was a "recipe for disaster"' – *The Irish Times* (10 May 1995).

record   See IS THIS A.

(the) Recording Angel   An angel who keeps a record of every person's good and bad deeds. This was a concept known by 1761 (in Sterne's *Tristram Shandy*) but is not mentioned as such in the Bible. 'She had not convinced me. If the recording angel had come down from heaven to confirm her, and had opened his book to my mortal eyes, the recording angel would not have convinced me' – Wilkie Collins, *The Woman in White*, First Epoch, Chap. 11 (1860).

red   See BETTER RED.

(a) redeeming feature   An inevitable pairing. Known by 1901. 'The state was ruled not by Britain but by the Diwan of Travancore, Sir Ramaswamy Iyer, of whom it could truly be said that he was an unmitigated scoundrel with no redeeming features' – *The Times* (26 November 1993); 'He was barely gracious in his parting remarks afterwards. Wimbledon, for him, did not have one redeeming feature, he said' – *The Times* (28 June 1994); 'The redeeming feature of this tiresome pro-gramme was Evening Songs, to Dvorak, by Smok's fellow-Czech choreographer Jiri Kylian gentle, soft, lyrical, folksy and short' – *The Sunday Times* (9 April 1995).

(a) red herring   A diversionary or mis-leading device to divert attention from the real question, especially (say) in a fictional murder hunt. From the device used to encourage dogs to follow a scent (1686). 'To draw a herring across the track/trail' was an expression known in the USA and UK by the 1880s.

red in tooth and claw Nature, as described in Tennyson, *In Memoriam A.H.H.*, Canto 56 (1850): 'Though Nature, red in tooth and claw / With ravine, shrieked against his creed.'

(a) red-letter day Denoting a special day, because in almanacs and old calendars, feast days and saints' days were often printed in red rather than black ink. *OED2*'s earliest citation is from 1704 in the US.

(to) re-draw the map of —— To make a fundamental change. Date of origin unknown. 'Singlehandedly she has re-drawn the political map of Britain' – a satirical reference to Margaret Thatcher or Shirley Williams in *Private Eye* (4 December 1981); 'But the theatrical legacy [of *Cats*] was to redraw the map of the West End' – *The Independent* (30 January 1996).

Reds under the bed A watchword of anti-Bolshevik scares and current within a few years of the 1917 October Revolution in Russia. A red flag was used in the 1789 French Revolution, and the colour had come to be associated with revolutionary movements during the 19th century before being adopted by Communists and their sympathizers. It was said that originally the flag had been dipped in the blood of victims of oppression.

red tape Referring to delay caused by bureaucrats; the allusion, dating from the 18th century, is to the ribbons that lawyers and other public officials still use to bind up their papers (although they look more pink than red).

references See ALWAYS VERIFY.

refuse all substitutes Advertising phrase and, in particular, associated with it the picture of a 'fawning grocer offering a lady some product, which she is rejecting with upraised arm as an affront either to her virtue or her intelligence'. While this ad remains untraced, various other uses have been found. A book with the title *Accept No Substitutes: The History of American Advertising* (2000) by Christina B. Merau suggests that 'Accept no substitutes' is the preferred version. It was in use for Coca-Cola as early as 1909 and then later for Jell-O, Baker's Chocolate and General Foods. Indeed, one of the features of all Coca-Cola advertising has been to distinguish the product from the numerous other Colas. One early ad read: 'Demand the Genuine by full title. Drink Coca-Cola – Nick-names encourage substitution.' Other variations in the USA include 'Refuse all imitations' for Pearline and, in the UK, 'There is no substitute' for Dr Collis Browne's Compound. Undoubtedly, however, the 'Refuse all substitutes' version has been used in the USA – as in an ad dating from 1909 for the Gillette Safety Razor: 'Refuse all substitutes and write us today for our free trial offer.'

regal splendour An inevitable pairing. Date of origin not known. 'Sitting in the regal splendour of the Foreign Office, Hurd explains . . .' – *The Daily Telegraph* (1 June 1994); 'To crown the occasion, there was the royal yacht Britannia – her days now numbered – moored in regal splendour in front of the Tower of London' – *The Guardian* (1 July 1994).

(to) reinvent the wheel To go back to basics, with a view to doing things better or more freshly. Often used pejoratively of someone who is doing so unnecessarily or out of ignorance. Or, in the form, 'let's not reinvent the wheel', as an injunction not to waste time by going over the obvious. Probably of American origin, since the 1970s. '"It used to be you almost had to reinvent the wheel to get funding," said Daniel Cobb, dean of the faculty at the small liberal arts college in West Virginia' – *The Washington Post* (16 July 1984); '"I don't think a leader of the western world can run a foreign policy that isn't consistent without great danger," says Eagleburger, "You can't reinvent the wheel every time because people have got to have some sense of continuity"' – *The Washington Post* (12 August 1984). The notion of 'reinventing' can also be applied to almost anything apart from the wheel: 'The blurb says of the *Vox* characters [in a novel by Nicholson Baker] that in their 166 pages of conversation they are "re-inventing sex"' – *The Independent* (7 March 1992).

rejoice! rejoice! Margaret Thatcher, the British Prime Minister, is sometimes reported as having said this to newsmen outside 10 Downing Street on 25 April

1982 following the recapture of South Georgia by British forces during the Falklands War. What she actually said was: 'Just rejoice at that news and congratulate our forces and the Marines. Goodnight. Rejoice!' Either way, can one detect signs of her Methodist upbringing? Although 'Rejoice, rejoice!' is quite a common expression, each verse of Charles Wesley's hymn 'Rejoice! the Lord is King' ends: 'Rejoice, again I say, rejoice'. This is derived from Philippians 4:4: 'Rejoice in the Lord alway: and again I say, Rejoice.' The phrase also occurs in Handel's oratorio *Messiah* ('Rejoice, rejoice, rejoice greatly, O daughter of Zion') based on Zechariah 9:9. There is also a 19th-century hymn (words by Grace J. Frances), 'Rejoice, Rejoice, Believer!'

relaxed See LOOKING BRONZED.

remember the ——! A common form of sloganeering, particularly as a way of starting conflicts or keeping them alive, especially in the USA. Probably the first was **remember the River Raisin!** – a warcry of Kentucky soldiers dating from the War of 1812. In the Raisin River massacre, 700 Kentuckians, badly wounded trying to capture Detroit, were scalped and butchered by Indians who were allies of the British. Then came **remember the Alamo!**: the Alamo Mission in San Antonio, Texas, was used as a fort during the rebellion against Mexico in 1836. A garrison of 100 or so Texans, including Davy Crockett, was wiped out by a force of 3,000 Mexicans after a 13-day siege. 'Remember the Alamo' was the war-cry with which Sam Houston subsequently led the Texans to victory over the Mexicans. **Remember Goliad!** comes from the same Texas/Mexican conflict. **Remember the Maine!** helped turn the sinking of the battleship *Maine* in Havana harbour (1898) into an excuse for the Spanish-American War (as well as for the contemporary graffito: 'Remember the Maine /To hell with Spain / Don't forget to pull the chain'). **Remember the Lusitania!** followed the sinking of another ship (in 1915). **Remember Belgium!** was originally a recruiting slogan of the First World War. It eventually re-emerged with ironic emphasis amid the mud of Ypres, encouraging the rejoinder: 'As if I'm ever likely to forget the bloody place!' **Remember Pearl Harbor!** followed from the 1941 incident, and **remember the Pueblo!** commemorated the capture of the USS *Pueblo* by North Korea in 1968.

remembrance of things past The title given to C. K. Scott Moncrieff's 1922 translation of Proust's *À la Recherche du Temps Perdu* was *Remembrance of Things Past*. In parenthesis one might point out that this is not an accurate translation of the French title – which means 'in quest/search of lost *time*'. Presumably, Moncrieff chose it because it was a near-enough, resonant, ready-made phrase. He took it from Shakespeare's Sonnet 30, which begins: 'When to the Sessions of sweet silent thought, / I summon up remembrance of things past . . .' Evidently, Proust did not approve of the English title but was somewhat mollified when told that it came from Shakespeare. Perhaps Shakespeare took the phrase from the Wisdom of Solomon in the Apocrypha 11:12: 'For a double grief came upon them, and a groaning for the remembrance of things past.' This is the translation that accompanied the Authorized Version (1611), though separated from it. Was this translation of the phrase used in earlier English translations of the Bible and would Shakespeare have had access to them (as it is, his references to Old and New Testament are few and far between)? The exact phrase may have predated him, however. *George Lyttelton's Commonplace Book* (2002) quotes: 'Man without learninge and the rememberance of things past, falls into a beastly sottishness and his life is noe better to be accounted of than to be buryed alive' and attributes this to Gavin Douglas, presumably the Bishop of Dunkeld (and poet) of that name (*circa* 1474–1522), though the wording has not been confirmed.

(a) Renaissance man Used to describe anyone who is accomplished in more than one field but (these days) rather less than a polymath. Originally used to describe anyone who displayed the educated, civilized, practical virtues of the idealized Renaissance man. Now a cliché. Kenneth Tynan in *Show* (October 1961): 'Young people in their teens and twenties for whom [Orson] Welles was Renaissance man reborn.' From *Time* Magazine (8 August 1977): 'At 50, Hood is the Renaissance man of sailing; he designed, cut the sails and outfitted *Independence*, the first man in history to control every aspect of a 12-tonner from drawing-board to helm.' From a letter in *Radio Times* (11 February 1989): 'I once told him [actor David Buck] that he was "the Renaissance man of radio". He thought that uproarious.' From Marmaduke Hussey's appreciation of Sir Michael Swann in *The Independent* (24 September 1990): 'Michael Swann, a big man in every way, was a Renaissance figure, scholar, scientist, soldier . . .' A BBC Radio 2 trailer was heard for 'Renaissance man, Humphrey Lyttelton'. While Humph's ability to play the trumpet and write and talk wittily (though not, of course, simultaneously) is well known, this may have been pushing it a bit.

rendezvous with destiny   Phrase from a speech made by President Franklin D. Roosevelt to the Democratic convention (1936): 'There is a mysterious cycle in human events. To some generations much is given. Of other generations much is expected. This generation of Americans has a rendezvous with destiny.' Many years later, in a TV address on behalf of Senator Barry Goldwater (27 October 1964), Ronald Reagan told viewers: 'You and I have a rendezvous with destiny. We will preserve for our children this, the last best hope of man on earth'; 'All Mr Heath's justified complacency as he watches the Labour Party destroying itself will avail him little if, come the next General Election, his own rendezvous with destiny turns out to be an appointment in Samarra' – *The Times* (28 June 1973). Indeed, any phrase incorporating the word 'destiny', especially in alliterative couplings, sounds like a cliché as soon as it is coined. Compare DATE WITH DESTINY. In late 1980s' Britain, a number of funeral directors flirted with the slogan **dignity in destiny**. Then there is **day of destiny**. '[Tony] Blair was in no doubt about the historical significance of yesterday's event. In an impromptu speech after the vote was declared, Blair hoped it would be "a day

of destiny for our party and our country"' – *The Sunday Times* (30 April 1995).

reservoir   See AU RESERVOIR.

reservoir dogs   The title of the film *Reservoir Dogs* (US 1991) has never been satisfactorily explained. One theory is that it derives from the screenwriter/director Quentin Tarantino's inability to pronounce the title of the French film *Au Revoir les Enfants* when working as a clerk in a video store . . .

rested and fit   See LOOKING BRONZED.

(the) rest is history   An ending to a biographical anecdote, now a cliché. It is spoken in the film *Blazing Saddles* (US 1974). 'There across all the papers was the photograph of me presenting the Queen Mother with her chart, under the caption "Astrologer Royal". Well, the rest, as they say, is history' – Russell Grant in *TV Times* (15 October 1983); Alan Bennett played delightfully on the phrase in *Oxford Today* (Michaelmas 1988), having described his transition from Oxford history don to Broadway revue artist: 'The rest, one might say pompously, is history. Except that in my case the opposite was true. What it had been was history. What it was to be was not history at all.'

(to) rest on one's oars   Meaning, 'to suspend efforts, to take things easy, to glide along without doing anything' – as in rowing when oars are lifted out of the water and the arms rested upon them. As 'to lie on one's oars', known by 1726. Listed in *The Independent* (24 December 1994) as a cliché of newspaper editorials. 'They also know that they cannot afford to rest on their oars because Hungary, whose population is only one-quarter of Poland's, has pulled in twice as much foreign investment' – *The Herald* (Glasgow) (4 July 1994).

(to) restore political capital   The phrase 'political capital' was known by 1818. Listed in the *The Independent* (24 December 1994) as a cliché of newspaper editorials. 'While hardliners have made political capital out of the Central Bank's rouble debacle, the Russian President has remained cocooned in his Kremlin offices, offering no reassurance to the people and making no concerted attempt to restore confidence in the leadership' – *The Daily Telegraph* (31 July 1993).

retaliation See GET YOUR.

retreat? hell, no! we just got here! A remark attributed to Captain Lloyd S. William, an American soldier (he existed in 1918), and made by him when advised by the French to retreat, shortly after his arrival at the Western Front in the First World War. Or, specifically referring to the retreat from Belloar (5 June 1918). Margaret Thatcher quoted it at a Confederation of British Industry dinner in 1980, a year after she had become British Prime Minister. Compare: 'Retreat, hell! We're just fighting in another direction' – attributed to General Oliver Prince Smith, US Marine Corps, at Changjin Reservoir, North Korea (1950). When trapped by eight divisions of Chinese Communists in North Korea he led the 20,000-man 1st Division on a bloody, 13-day, 70-mile breakthrough to the sea and rescue. However, when the title *Retreat, Hell!* was bestowed on a film of this event (US 1952), a different ascription was given by the screenwriters, Milton Sperling and Ted Sherdeman. 'The Colonel' says: 'We've been ordered to withdraw.' Soldier: 'You mean retreat?' Colonel: 'Retreat? Hell, we're just attacking in another direction.'

return See AND WITH THAT.

(to) return to the fray Meaning, 'to resume work or activity'. Derived from the Middle English word 'fray', meaning 'conflict, fighting', but now used only in a figurative way. 'Happily, the mechanism in the form of Rule 19 is in place to do that if the club deem fit, but to protect both the good reputation of players like Gary who are keen to return to the fray and the competitive prospects of his clubmates, it would seem that a change is in order' – *The Herald* (Glasgow) (19 July 1994); 'Scotland consider a return to the fray' – headline in *The Sunday Times* (25 September 1994).

revenons à ces moutons [let's get back to these sheep] Sometimes quoted as '*retournons à nos moutons*', as by Rabelais in *Pantagruel* (1545). The meaning is, 'let us get back to the subject'. From an anonymous 15th-century play entitled *La Farce de Maître Pierre Pathelin*. A woollen draper charges a shepherd with maltreating his sheep but continually wanders from the point in court. The judge attempts to bring him back with this phrase. Alluding perhaps to Martial: '*Jam dic, Postume, de tribus capellis*'?

—— revisited PHRASES. Frequently used title format. In January 1989, Channel 4 showed a programme marking the fiftieth anniversary of the publication of a John Steinbeck novel, with the title '*The Grapes of Wrath' Revisited*. In 1989, the South Bank Centre ran a commemoration of the 200th anniversary of the French Revolution under the blanket title 'Revolution Revisited'. All such uses now owe something to the title of Evelyn Waugh's novel *Brideshead Revisited* (1945) and especially to the TV adaptation in 1981, though the format was well established before Waugh got hold of it. A book by E. V. Lucas (1916) has the title *London Revisited*. Chap. 11 of Harrison Ainsworth's novel *Jack Sheppard* (1836) is entitled 'Dollis Hill Revisited'. William Wordsworth wrote poems entitled 'Yarrow Unvisited' (1803), 'Yarrow Visited' (1814) and 'Yarrow Revisited' (1831).

revolution See COME THE.

rhubarb, rhubarb! Actors mumble this in crowd scenes to give the impression of speech, as a background noise, without actually producing coherent sentences. Some unwise actors might think they could actually get away with saying 'rhubarb', but the idea is to repeat a word, which uttered by various voices, adds together to sound like the noise a crowd makes. Does the custom date from much before this century? But it is a well-known concept now, as demonstrated by the use of the verb 'to rhubarb', meaning to talk nonsense. Another phrase said to have been repeated by actors in this situation is 'My fiddle, my fiddle, my fiddle'. There is supposedly a phrase used by Russian actors meaning, literally, 'I speak and I don't speak'. One wonders whether the adoption of the word 'rhubarb' in the English version has anything to do with its slang use to denote the male (and occasionally female) genitals. Or could there have been some rhyming slang phrase, i.e. rhubarb (tart) = fart (akin to raspberry tart = fart)? Rhyming slang books consulted do not support this, however.

rib　See ADAM'S RIB.

rice　See COULDN'T KNOCK THE SKIN.

rich　See DO YOU SINCERELY.

rich and famous　Designated a cliché on the basis that the words are always and inevitably put together. The first example I have noted is in Truman Capote's novella *Breakfast at Tiffany's* (1958). In Neil Simon's *Barefoot in the Park* (1964), a character asks, 'You want me to be rich and famous, don't you?' 'We shall all be rich and famous' –Thames TV, *Rock Follies* (2 March 1976). The usage has become completely set in concrete since a film with the title *Rich and Famous* (US 1981). An American TV series *Lifestyles of the Rich and Famous* was established by 1986. 'The [Press] Council's assistant director, said yesterday that lawyers acting for the rich and famous were becoming aware of the fast track system for getting speedy corrections of untruths' – *The Independent* (4 April 1989); 'Miss Navratilova is extraordinarily rich and famous and can, therefore, do pretty much as she likes. However, it is alarming when such prominent people do such silly things, because they only encourage deviant behaviour in other, more impressionable people' – *Daily Mail* (23 June 1994).

(as) rich as Rockefeller　Extremely rich. An updating of the proverbial 'rich as Croesus' that referred to Croesus, King of Lydia (560–546 BC), who became a byword for his wealth (known by the 1750s). *Flexner* (1982) suggests that in the USA, 'rich as/richer than Astor' also became established. But the main phrase is the one alluding to John D. Rockefeller (1839–1937), the world's first billionaire (in the sense of being worth in excess of one thousand million dollars). At one point he owned 90 per cent of all American oil refineries. Hence, 'I'll be rich as Rockefeller / Gold dust at my feet' – in the Dorothy Fields lyric for the song 'On The Sunny Side of the Street' (1930); 'He's as rich as Rockefeller' – spoken in the film *Written*

On the Wind (US 1956). Compare: **who do you think I am – Rockefeller?**, a catchphrase meaning 'I'm not made of money, you know' – a claim to poverty. At any time since the 1930s but, curiously, still heard in the 1980s.

rich beyond the dreams of avarice　Consciously archaic phrase. 'Dream of avarice' on its own was known by 1678. Dr Samuel Johnson used 'growing rich beyond the dreams of avarice' in 1781. 'Brazil's social conditions still have a long way to go, as do even its advanced industries. The vast gap between rich and poor, which has widened in recent years, seems to many (not just the left) offensive in itself. Yet it does not matter greatly, if at all, that a few are rich beyond the dreams of avarice' – *The Economist* (29 April 1995).

rich man　See EYE OF A NEEDLE.

(the) rich man in his castle (the poor man at his gate)　Controversial phrases from the hymn 'All Things Bright and Beautiful' (1848) by Mrs C. F. Alexander: 'The rich man in his castle, / The poor man at his gate. / God made them, high or lowly, / And ordered their estate.' Mrs Alexander's hymn is in danger of becoming known as the one from which a verse – the third – had to be dropped because of its apparent acceptance of an unacceptable *status quo*. From Barbara Pym's novel *No Fond Return of Love* (1961): 'Dulcie sang in a loud indignant voice, waiting for the lines . . . but they never came. Then she saw that the verse had been left out. She sat down, feeling cheated of her indignation.' Most modern hymnbook compilers omit the verse, and they started doing so about 1930. *Songs of Praise Discussed* (1933) calls it an 'appalling verse . . . She must have forgotten Dives, and how Lazarus lay "at his gate"; but then she had been brought up in the atmosphere of a land-agent on an Irish estate. The *English Hymnal* led the way in obliterating this verse from the Anglican mind.' It remains in *Hymns Ancient and Modern* (Standard Edition, reprinted 1986), but it has disappeared from the *Irish Hymnal*. The authors of *The Houses of Ireland* (1975) note that by the present century 'the ecclesiastical authorities had decided that God's intentions are not to preclude movement within the social system. However, few of her contemporaries doubted that Mrs Alexander's interpretation was correct.'

(the) riddle of the Sphinx The riddle is: 'What animal walks on four feet in the morning, two feet at noon, and on three feet in the evening – but has only one voice; its feet vary, and when it has most it is weakest.' The answer is: Man – because he crawls on all fours as an infant, walks on two feet when full grown, but in old age moves upon his feet and a staff. As mentioned in *Oedipus Rex* by Sophocles, Oedipus answered the riddle correctly when he encountered the Sphinx on the road to Thebes. The Sphinx killed herself in despair, and the Thebans made Oedipus their king out of gratitude. If he had not answered correctly, the Sphinx would have killed him.

riding See AS SURE AS.

(to) ride roughshod over Meaning, 'to tyrannize, domineer, treat roughly'. Derived from the type of horseshoe that has nails projecting from it to enable the horse to gain a firm foothold on difficult ground. Known in the literal sense by 1688 and figuratively by 1813. 'Sociologists are notorious for their use of generalizing terms that ride roughshod over the particularities of history' – *Times Literary Supplement* (11 February 1977); '*The Client* isn't as well made as Peter Weir's *Witness*, but it's a lot dirtier. Schumacher shows how the authorities ride roughshod over the poor, ignoring their civil rights, caring nothing for their safety' – *The Observer* (23 October 1994)

(to) ride the whirlwind Meaning 'to be in a commanding position especially in time of trouble'. Possibly coined by Joseph Addison when writing about the 1st Duke of Marlborough in *The Campaign* (1705), a celebration of the Battle of Blenheim: 'And pleas'd th' Almighty's orders to perform, / Rides in the whirlwind, and directs the storm.' William Cowper in 'The Retirement' (1782) had: ''Till he that rides the whirlwind checks the rein / Then all the world of waters sleeps again.' Henry Buckle in his *History of Civilisation in England* (1857) had: 'To see whether they who had

raised the storm could ride the whirlwind.' 'With his overall Commons majority already down to 18 and his Government fighting on several other damaging policy fronts, Mr Major is riding a whirlwind' – *Daily Mail* (21 May 1993).

(you could) ride to York on that lip 'To a sulking person' – Stella Richardson, Essex (1998). Because the drooping lip looked like a saddle? *Casson/Grenfell* has the nannyism: 'I could ride to London on that lip.'

right See ALL; AM I; AS RIGHT.

(a) right and left A shot fired at game using both barrels of a double-barrelled shotgun. Also used figuratively for a powerful blow or shock. From Josephine Tey, *The Singing Sands* (1952): 'His reply contained a right-and-left.' A **left and right** may also be used to describe a feat in shooting whereby two birds from the same group in flight are brought down with successive shots from the left and right barrels. Possibly this is what Ian Fleming is alluding to when he writes in *Thunderball*, Chap. 5 (1961): '[James Bond] had left for London after, the night before, scoring a most satisfactory left and right of Spaghetti Bolognese and Chianti at Lucien's in Brighton and of Miss Patricia Fearing on the squab seats from her bubble car high up on the Downs . . .' 'Left and right' has also been suggested as rhyming slang for 'fight', where fists are being talked about, of course.

right Charlie See PROPER CHARLIE.

right monkey! Catchphrase of Al Read (1909–87), the northern English comedian, who was big on radio in the 1950s and then disappeared almost completely. His speciality was monologues – or, rather, dialogues – with him playing all the parts. He used a number of standard Lancashire expressions and made them for a while his own – **give over!**; **you'll be lucky . . . I say, you'll be lucky**; **ooh, an' 'e was strong!** and **we've soopped soom stooff tonight** – the last as a drunk staggering homeward and shouting through his neighbours' letter boxes. But compare Frank Randle's similar phrase under BY GUM, SHE'S A HOT 'UN. Above all, Read was known for two catchphrases

– 'right monkey!' and **cheeky monkey!** For example: 'She said, "Did he say anything about the check suit?" and I thought, "Right monkey!"' 'Right, Monkey!' was used as his bill matter. From a theatre poster once seen in Blackpool: 'Henry Hall Presents Al Read In *Right Monkey*'.

right on! Phrase signifying enthusiastic agreement. In the view of *Flexner* (1976), this phrase replaced TELL IT LIKE IT IS! as the American Civil Rights shout of encouragement to speakers at demonstrations, in about 1967. It became 'a general term meaning "you're absolutely right, you tell 'em"' and by no means restricted to Blacks, among whom nevertheless, the saying originated. The practice of calling out agreement to a speaker or preacher – sometimes regularly, rhythmically, in response to his statements – is deeply rooted. In *The Negro and His Songs* (1925) by Odum and Johnson, we find: 'Railroad Bill was a mighty sport. / Shot all button of the high sheriff's coat. / Den hollered, "Right on, Desperado Bill!"' More recently, the phrase has been used adjectivally for attitudes that might equally qualify for the designation POLITICALLY CORRECT. 'My play takes a sledgehammer to the "right on" clichés that have debilitated recent radical theatre in Britain' – *The Guardian* (7 April 1992).

(the) right one Slogan for Martini in the UK from 1970. In a conscious attempt to switch Martini from being a 'woman's drink' to a 'his and hers' drink, the McCann-Erickson agency created a romantic, high-life world full of young, beautiful people engaged in skiing, speedboating, even ballooning. Not the least ingredient was the song composed by Chris Gunning: 'Try a taste of Martini / The most beautiful drink in the world, / It's the bright one, the right one. / There's much more to the world than you guess, / And you taste it the day you say yes / To the bright taste, the right taste / Of Martini . . .' In 1981, Barry Day claimed to have coined the phrase 'The Right One'.

rights See BANG TO.

rights of passage See *RITES DE PASSAGE*.

(the) right stuff The right personal qualities required to carry out some exacting task or function. Tom Wolfe helped re-popularize the phrase when he chose to use it as the title of his book (1979; film US 1983). He employed it to describe the qualities needed by test pilots and would-be astronauts in the early years of the US space programme. But the 'right (sort of) stuff' had been applied much earlier to qualities of manly virtue, of good officer material and even of good cannon fodder. *Partridge/Slang* has an example from the 1880s. In this sense, the phrase was used by Ian Hay as the title of a novel – 'some episodes in the career of a North Briton' – in 1908. It is now a handy journalistic device. An *Independent* headline over a story about the ballet *Ondine* (13 May 1988) was 'The Sprite Stuff'; in the same month, *The Magazine* had 'The Right Stuff' as the title of an article on furnishing fabrics; in 1989, there was an ITV book programme called *The Write Stuff*. It has also been used as an expression for alcohol (compare 'the hard stuff').

(a) ring of steel Journalistic cliché, used to describe something that is surrounded by armaments, preventing escape. Adolf Hitler said in a speech on the Italian armistice in 1943: 'Tactical necessity may compel us once again to give up something on some front in this gigantic fateful struggle, but it will never break the ring of steel that protects the Reich' – translation from *Hitler's Words*, ed. Gordon W. Prange (1944.) 'The place [Warsaw] is just a ring of steel' – reporter on BBC TV *Nine O'clock News* (17 December 1981); 'Ring of steel around islands' – headline over report on the Falklands War, *The Times* (30 April 1982); 'Syrian steel rings Arafat' – *Sunday Express* (8 October 1983); 'The [White House] mansion's £20 million "ring of steel" security, including ground-to-air missiles, failed to stop a Cessna smashing into the south lawn' – *Daily Record* (13 September 1994); 'Tony Blair' ordered a "ring of steel" around Heathrow airport after the cabinet's emergency Cobra meeting' – *The Observer* (16 Ferbuary 2003).

ring round the moon Christopher Fry's adaptation of Jean Anouilh's play *L'Invitation au château* [*The Invitation to the Castle/Château*] was first performed in 1950 (following the Paris production of

1947). The English title, *Ring Round the Moon*, alludes to the proverb 'Ring around the moon, brings a storm soon' (sometimes, '. . . rain comes soon'). This is a modern version of 'When round the moon there is a brugh [halo], the weather will be cold and rough' that *ODP* has by 1631. In Longfellow's 'The Wreck of the Hesperus', there is the line, 'Last night the moon had a golden ring, and tonight no moon we see!' as though this presages bad weather (as indeed it does in the poem).

(to) ring the changes (on) To go through all the variations. Derived from bell-ringing. Known by 1614. 'I prefer to keep all walls as free as possible of electric wiring by having everything at roof level. This isn't as limiting as it sounds. You can still ring the changes between spots, chandeliers, rise-and-fall pendants to suit decor or mood and with the minimum of work' – *The Herald* (Glasgow) (18 June 1994).

(a) ringing declaration (of principle) Mostly political and journalistic use. Date of origin not known. Listed in *The Independent* (24 December 1994) as a cliché of newspaper editorials. 'It seems to have become clear to Mr Heffer that it would be folly to present a predominantly right wing Cabinet with some kind of ringing declaration of radical socialist principle. In his view, a severely practical document was needed, in which the radicalism was presented as realism' – *The Guardian* (28 March 1988).

rise and shine Lest it be thought that this phrase occurred only in the army cry 'Wakey-wakey, rise and shine!' – meaning, 'get up and polish your boots' – there is a, probably earlier, appearance in the poem 'On a Naval Officer Buried in the Atlantic' by H. F. Lyte (1793–1847), the English clergyman and hymnwriter: 'And when the last trump shall sound, / And tombs are asunder riven, / Like the morning sun from the wave thou'lt bound / To rise and shine in heaven.' Compare also 'Arise, shine; for thy light is come, and the glory of the Lord is risen upon thee' – Isaiah 60:1. See also WAKEY-WAKEY!

(to) rise like a rocket and come down like the stick To have rapid success that turns quickly to failure. Tom Paine said of Edmund Burke, 'As he rose like the rocket, he fell like the stick' – *Letter to the Addressers on the late Proclamation* (1792). Abraham Hayward, reviewing *The Pickwick Papers* for *The Quarterly Review* (October 1838), said of Charles Dickens: 'He writes too often and too fast . . . If he persists much longer in this course, it requires no gift of prophecy to foretell his fate – he has risen like a rocket, and he will come down like a stick.'

(the) rise of the meritocracy *The Rise of the Meritocracy* was the title of a book by Michael Young (1958), who thereby coined the word 'meritocracy' for government by those thought to possess merit. Consequently, these people attain positions of power not through inherited privilege but by intense educational effort, passing exams and acquiring qualifications. Oliver Stallybrass in *The Fontana Dictionary of Modern Thought* (1977) notes 'the particular grisly features or ultimately self-destroying character of Young's apocalyptic vision.'

(the) rising of the moon Phrase for Irish opposition to British imperial domination. *The Rising of the Moon* was the title of a one-act play (1907) by Lady (Augusta) Gregory. Shared by a film (Ireland 1957) and by an opera (Glyndebourne 1970) with libretto by Beverley Cross and music by Nicholas Maw. All these works (with Irish themes) borrow the title of an Irish patriotic song. This was written by John Keegan Casey (1846–70) and called, precisely, 'The Rising of the Moon A.D. 1798': 'And a thousand blades were flashing / At the risin' of the moon'.

(a) risky business An inevitable pairing. Date of origin unknown. The phrase occurs in the film *Life Begins at Forty* (US 1935), and *Risky Business* has been used twice as the title of films (US 1939 and 1983).

rites of passage As *rites de passage*, this was a coinage of Arnold van Gennep in the title of a book (1909) about the transitional stages through which man passes between birth and death. The most notable *rite de passage* is probably some experience (maybe of a ritual nature) that a boy has to go through before achieving manhood. It might have to do with a demonstration of his physical skills or involve some confirmation of his sexual maturity. The concept is now well known, especially as the name given to a genre of films. From *Flicks* Magazine (April 1994): 'Brad Pitt and Craig Sheffer play Paul and Norman in Robert Redford's *A River Runs Through It*, a nostalgic "rites of passage" drama . . . it's only when they're fishing that they find the true harmony that eludes them elsewhere.' *Rites of Passage* was the title of a novel (1980) by William Golding.

rivers of blood   On 20 April 1968, Enoch Powell, the Conservative opposition spokesman for Defence, made a speech in Birmingham on the subject of immigration. He concluded with the words: 'As I look ahead, I am filled with foreboding. Like the Roman, I seem to see "the River Tiber foaming with much blood".' Later, Powell said that he should have quoted the remark in Latin to emphasize that he was only evoking a classical prophecy of doom and not actually predicting a bloodbath. In Vergil's *Aeneid*, VI:87, the Sibyl of Cumae prophesies: '*Et Thybrim multo spumantem sanguine cerno.*' 'Rivers of blood' was thus quite a common turn of phrase before Powell made it notorious. Thomas Jefferson in a letter to John Adams (4 September 1823) wrote: 'To attain all this [universal republicanism], however, rivers of blood must yet flow, and years of desolation pass over; yet the object is worth rivers of blood, and years of desolation.' Speaking on European unity (14 February 1948), Winston Churchill said: 'We are asking the nations of Europe between whom rivers of blood have flowed, to forget the feuds of a thousand years.'

(the) road less travelled   Phrase from Robert Frost's poem 'The Road Not Taken' in *Mountain Interval* (1916): 'Two roads diverged in a wood, and I – / I took the one less travelled by, / And that has made all the difference.' Hence, *The Road Less Travelled* – title of a popular work of psychotherapy by M. Scott Peck (1978).

road rage   Phrase for the phenomenon of ordinary drivers of motor vehicles being transformed into violent and abusive people by the behaviour of other motorists on the road. The phrase was apparently coined by a writer in the *Los Angeles Times* in 1984 when a pick-up truck driver shot dead the driver of a Cadillac car who cut him up on the main 405 freeway in Los Angeles. The term became widely known in the UK in 1995–6 when measures to combat it were urged – including roadside counselling by psychotherapists.

roads   See ALL ROADS LEAD.

(the) road to Damascus   The occasion of a change of heart, conversion or sudden realization; a turning point. From St Paul's conversion, on the road to Damascus, to a fervent belief in Christ, as described in Acts 22 – the occasion when he **saw the light**. Previously he had been a Pharisee persecuting the Christians. The precise words in the Authorized Version are: 'As I made my journey, and was come nigh unto Damascus about noon, suddenly there shone from heaven a great light round about me'. The term 'road to Damascus' took some time to enter the language. It was in English by 1879 and in French by 1842 – as *le chemin de Damas* in Sainte-Beuve, *Port-Royal*, Vol. 2 (1842). A less common derivative is 'Damascene conversion'. 'To see the light' was being used (not as an allusion to the St Paul's event) by 1687. 'It is easy to imagine Madonna's biographer, poring over her possessions, years after her death, hoping to arrive at a biographical Damascus . . . and finds no porn at all' – *The Independent on Sunday* (11 April 1993); 'Traffic jam to Damascus. Everyone should try it at least once. The trendiest have several. Conversions, that is. Peter Popham reports' – headline and byline in *The Independent* (20 October 1995).

(the) Roaring 20s   Decade label for the 1920s, itself established by 1939, reflecting the heady buoyant atmosphere in certain sections of society following the horrors of the First World War. The adjective 'roaring', meaning 'boisterous, riotous, noisy', had previously been applied to the 1850s and, in Australia, to the 'roaring days' of the gold-rush. The same meaning occurs in the expression 'roaring drunk'. The 1940s do not appear to have been given a label, least of all **Roaring Forties** – that term had already been applied to parts of the oceans between 40 degrees and 50 degrees south where strong westerly winds blow. Compare SWINGING SIXTIES.

(the) roar of the greasepaint (the smell of the crowd) *The Roar of the Grease-paint – the Smell of the Crowd* – title of a musical (New York 1965) by Leslie Bricusse and Anthony Newley – nicely confuses two standard concepts: the 'roar of the crowd' and 'the smell of grease-paint'. From Vicente Blaco-Ibáñez, *Blood and Sand* (1908): 'It was the roar of the real, the only beast [the crowd in the arena].' The American heavyweight boxer Gentleman Jim Corbett entitled his autobiography *The Roar of the Crowd* (1925). From Margery Allingham, *Dancers in Mourning* (1937): 'Still gives me a thrill, you know, this sort of thing. *Vie de bohème*, lights, far-off music, smell of the grease-paint, women and so on.' From David Piper, *The Companion Guide to London* (1965): 'Other theatres cling still to real live actors and a waft of greasepaint over the footlights.'

(Jack) Robinson See BEFORE ONE CAN SAY.

rock See BETWEEN A ROCK.

rocket science See IT'S NOT.

rock 'n' roll Name for a type of popular music first popularized by Alan Freed, the US disc jockey, who is generally credited with first discovering and promoting it. In 1951, he was hosting *Moondog's Rock'n'Roll Party* on a radio station in Cleveland, Ohio. It was not until he moved to New York City in 1954, however, that the term took hold. Earlier, in 1934, there had been a song by Sidney Clare and Richard Whiting with the title 'Rock and Roll' in the film *Transatlantic Merry-Go-Round*, referring to a ship's movements: 'Rock and roll like a rockin' chair, / Laugh and smile while we drown each care in the tide. / As we glide to the roll-in' rock-in' rhy-thm of the sea.' Earlier, the phrase may also have been Black English slang for the sexual act.

(the) Rock of Ages Epithet for Jesus Christ from a hymn first published in *The Gospel Magazine* (1775) by the English clergyman, Augustus Montague Toplady: 'Rock of Ages, cleft for me, / Let me hide myself in Thee.' *Brewer* (1923) recounts two stories of its composition: one, that it was written while seated by a great cleft in the rock near Cheddar, Somerset; two, that it was written on the ten of diamonds between two rubbers of whist at Bath. The phrase 'rock of ages' is said to be the actual meaning in Hebrew of the words 'everlasting strength' at Isaiah 26:4.

(to do by) rock-of-eye and rule of thumb 'My mother was trained to be a tailoress and in the work-rooms they always referred to things cut out without a pattern as "rock-of-eye". This word is also used in our family when cakes etc. are made without a recipe' – Betty Butcher, Wiltshire (1995). This is more widely known in the full expression (as in the headphrase). *Partridge/Slang* explains that it describes guessing instead of measuring precisely and suggests it originated in the tailoring trade in the mid-19th century. 'Rock' here means 'a movement to an fro'.

rock on, Tommy! Catchphrase of Bobby Ball (b. 1944) of the British comedy partnership Cannon and Ball. The precise origin goes unremembered but Ball thinks it probably arose in a place like Oldham or Wigan when he was spurring on Tommy Cannon (b. 1938). Depending on which of them is telling the story, it may also have occurred when Cannon was singing and be related to the David Essex song 'Rock On' (1973). Ball recalled (1980): 'About three years ago, Tommy was singing a rock'n'roll number. I was fooling about and just happened to say it. To my astonishment it got a big laugh, such a tremendous response that we decided to try it again.' Cannon added: 'After a couple of years we thought of dropping it because it might be losing its impact. But we decided to keep it in for our TV show. We could never drop it now.'

(a) rodent officer (or operator or operative) An early form of political correctness was presumably at work when a 'rat-catcher' was so renamed. 'Westminster City Council's rat-catcher is in future to be called Rodent Officer' – *The Liverpool Echo* (31 January 1944); 'When it comes to official jargon, can you beat turning our old friend the rat-catcher into a "Rodent Operative"?' – *The Sunday Times* (5 November 1944); 'Euphemisms . . . *rodent operator* for *rat-catcher*' – *Word Study* (May 1946); 'It happened to the rat-catcher (he's now a rodent operator), the dustman (refuse collector), and the sweeper (street orderly)' – *Daily Mail* (25 October 1958).

(a/the) rogues' gallery Phrase for a group of disreputable people as shown in a photograph or picture (e.g. wanted criminals) but also used humorously of quite inoffensive people so portrayed. The criminal use was prevalent in the USA in the mid- to late 19th century. The allusive 20th-century UK use may derive, in part, from a Latin school textbook, *The Rogues' Gallery* (current by the 1950s, at least), which included classical descriptions of notable Roman villains. From an *Independent* report of a speech in the House of Lords by Lord Stevens of Ludgate (on 26 April 1989): 'For most people, the *Sun* and the *News of the World* were the starring exhibits in the Rogues Gallery of the Press, but each paper appeared to thrive on its notoriety, he said.'

(a) rogue trader The film *Rogue Trader* (UK/US 1998) is about Nick Leeson, who brought Barings Bank crashing down and is based on his book of that title. He got it from Kenneth Clarke, the Chancellor of the Exchequer, at the time of the collapse. In February 1995, Clarke said: 'This failure is of course a blow to the City of London. But it appears to be a specific incident unique to Barings centred on one rogue trader in Singapore.' *Rogue Traders* became the title of a BBC TV documentary series exposing the selling and other methods of humbler traders on the domestic front (current in 2003).

(a) —— roller-coaster Phrase used to describe anything that is chaotic or frenetic in its progress. After the kind of switchback railway in amusement parks, which were known by this name by 1888. Used figuratively by 1957. 'It might follow from this that budget 2 is just a storm in a commons tea-room tea-cup, a one-day wonder to be easily forgotten as the political rollercoaster buckets onwards' – *The Guardian* (9 December 1994); 'After

Michael Foot defeated Denis Healey for the leadership of the Labour Party in November 1980, Her Majesty's opposition was on a dizzying roller-coaster, and so was I' – John Cole, *As It Seemed To Me* (1995); 'Most defectors appear to come unstuck. Only a few – like Churchill – have ridden the rollercoaster with aplomb' – *The Independent* (9 October 1995).

(the) Rolling Stones Name of an enduring British pop group (formed 1962). It does not directly come from the proverb 'a rolling stone gathers no moss' (known by 1546) but via the title of the Muddy Waters song 'Rollin' Stone' (1950).

(to) roll out the red carpet To make an impressive display out of welcoming somebody, from the literal red carpet laid out for royalty or other distinguished persons to walk on. A folk-origin that has had some circulation goes: 'The architect of the Tate Gallery, just before it was opened by Queen Victoria, looked up at the handsome sculpture of Britannia and realised to his horror, shock and shame, that the shield and the sword were in the wrong hands. Mortified, he went to the top of the building and threw himself off a high point, landing on the long flight of steps outside, just a short time before Queen Victoria was due. His remains having been gathered up, there was still a fair number of bloodstains and an order went out hurriedly for some carpet to cover it up. Red arrived, in a length sufficient to take it up the stairs, and the tradition of greeting royalty and other VIPs on a red carpet started.' Well, a charming tale, but it was in fact the Prince of Wales who opened the Tate in 1897; the building's designer, Sidney R. J. Smith, did not die until 1913; and, more to the point, the expression was in use *before* the occasion described . . . Mark Twain described the reception of the Empress of Germany and the Grand Duchess of Baden at a hotel in Heidelberg in *A Tramp Abroad*, Chap. 2 (1879): 'At this stage of the proceedings, a narrow bright red carpet was unrolled and stretched from the top of the marble steps to the curbstone, along the center of the black carpet [that had been laid just before]. This red path cost the *portier* more trouble than even the black one had done.

But he patiently fixed and re-fixed it until it was exactly right and lay precisely in the middle of the black carpet.' 'The sight of the staff of the Madeleine stretching a broad red carpet down the lofty flight of steps overlooking the Rue Royale caused passersby to pause, and announced to the people of Paris that an important ceremony was about to take place' – Guy de Maupassant, *Bel-Ami*, Pt 2, Chap. 10 (1885) (translated). It is clear from these two examples that the custom (if not the metaphorical expression) was certainly established before the incident described in the Tate anecdote.

(a) Roman holiday Phrase from Byron's poem *Childe Harold's Pilgrimage*, Canto 4, St. 141 (1818): 'Butchered to make a Roman holiday' – referring to gladiators. Mark Twain seemed to think it a cliché of travel writing in *The Innocents Abroad*, Chap 27 (1869). *Punch* uses the phrase 'butchered to make a Spanish holiday', presumably referring to bull-fighting, in the edition of 19 August 1882. Given the provenance of the phrase, the title of the film *Roman Holiday* (US 1953) was not entirely appropriate for the charming story of a journalist falling for a princess.

room at the top *CODP* lists this as a proverbial expression 'commonly used to encourage competition' but doesn't record the occasion when Daniel Webster (d. 1852), the US politician, said it. Responding to a suggestion that he shouldn't become a lawyer because the profession was overcrowded, he said: 'There is always room at the top.' At one point in John Braine's novel *Room At the Top* (1957; film UK 1958), the hero 'Joe Lampton' is told: 'You're the sort of young man we want. There's always room at the top.'

Rome See ALL ROADS LEAD TO.

(a) room of one's own Title of a feminist essay (1929) by Virginia Woolf, arguing that women will not be able to succeed in writing fiction until they have the independence demonstrated by having a room of their own to write in.

Room 101 In George Orwell's novel *Nineteen Eighty-Four* (1949), 'Room 101' is the menacing phrase spoken at the end of Part 3, Chap. 4, presaging unmentionable horrors to be faced by Winston Smith. Indeed, in the next chapter, rats and electrodes feature prominently and O'Brien says to Smith: '"You asked me once . . . what was in Room 101. I told you that you knew the answer already. Everyone knows it. The thing that is in Room 101 is the worst thing in the world.' It has sometimes been suggested that, for this, Orwell used the number of his room in Broadcasting House, London, that he occupied when working for the BBC. From 1994, *Room 101* was used, a touch misleadingly, as the title of a BBC TV programme in which guests described their dislikes. These were then symbolically banished to 'Room 101' as though this was a place of outer darkness from which they could not possibly return.

(a) room with a view The hotel guest's popular requirement. Used as the title of a novel (1908; film UK 1985) by E. M. Forster. Noël Coward's song with the same title did not appear until *This Year of Grace* (1928).

root, hog or die A proverbial expression that was once described (in 1944) as the 'American national motto'. Davy Crockett used it in his memoirs (1834). It affirms the necessity of hard work and exertion to maintain life and prosperity. Here 'root' is used in the sense of rooting around and 'hog', as in 'to appropriate'.

(a) rooted objection An inevitable pairing. Known by 1810. 'Surprisingly, the most rooted objection to donated eggs and to ovarian transplants comes from Lady Warnock, former mistress of Girton College and the guiding light behind the Warnock Report on Human Fertilization' – *The Daily Telegraph* (26 July 1994); 'Polling confirms what anecdote and personal experience suggest, which is that so far, most English voters have no rooted objection to Scottish Home Rule and are, if anything, mildly in favour' – *The Independent* (17 January 1995).

rootless cosmopolitans A Stalinist euphemism for 'Jews' from 1948 onwards. The basic Russian is '*bezrodnye kosmopolity*' ('*bezrodnyi*' literally means 'homeless' or 'stateless') and was used with reference to Soviet Jews, particularly those who supported the newly emerging Zionist movement in Israel, at a time when the Soviet Union was once more insulating itself from the West, after the relatively relaxed relationship with its allies during the war. 'Kosmopolit' on its own had been in use by the 1930s, and Hitler spoke of '*eine wurzellose internationale Clique* [a rootless international clique]' in a speech (also broadcast on radio) at Berlin-Siemensstadt on 11 November 1933. The Russian phrase seems first to have been used by Anatoly Sofronov in an article ('For the Further Development of Soviet Dramaturgy') in *Pravda* (23 December 1948). At Stalin's behest, his henchman Andrey Zhdanov had, in 1948, launched an official attack on Jewish artistic figures, including the internationally famous Yiddish actor Solomon Mikhoels who was murdered that year, probably by Soviet secret police. But the term became a derogatory tag for anyone who did not toe the official party line and was thus perceived as being unpatriotic.

rose is a rose is a rose The poem 'Sacred Emily' (1922) by Gertrude Stein (d. 1946) does not include the line 'a rose is a rose is a rose', but rather: 'Rose is a rose is a rose is a rose' (i.e. upper case 'R', no indefinite article at the start, and three, not two, repetitions). The Rose in question was not a flower but an allusion to the English painter Sir Francis Rose 'whom she and I regarded', wrote Constantine Fitzgibbon, 'as the peer of Matisse and Picasso, and whose paintings – or at least painting – hung in her Paris drawing-room while a Gauguin was relegated to the lavatory' – letter to *The Sunday Telegraph* (7 July 1978). Stein also refers to a 'Jack Rose' (not a 'Jack' rose) earlier in the poem. The format is now a commonplace: 'Bad reviews are bad reviews are bad reviews are bad reviews' – 'Nicholas Craig', *I, An Actor* (1989); 'A Tory is a Tory is a Tory, whatever he might think' – Hugo Young, *One of Us* (1990).

roses See EVERYTHING'S COMING UP.

(it was) roses, roses all the way It was a happy, joyous, carefree, successful time or situation. 'It was roses, roses, all the way' is a direct quotation from Robert Browning's poem 'The Patriot' (1855).

(a) rough old trade Not to be confused with 'rough trade' in the homosexual sense (sadistic, violent), this tag has principally been applied in recent years to politics. Date of origin unknown. 'Terry departs to Provence with more friends and fewer enemies than anyone I know in our rough old trade [literary journalism]' – *The Sunday Telegraph* (4 January 1987); 'Berg, now 79 but still sprightly enough to climb unassisted into the ring and still a handsome and lucid advertisement for a rough old trade [boxing]' – *The Independent* (1 December 1988); 'I have often remarked – it may perhaps have become something of a cliché – that politics is a rough old trade. But not since we ceased executing Ministers some time in the late seventeenth century has it been quite as rough as it is under Mrs Margaret Thatcher' – Alan Watkins in *The Observer* (21 January 1990).

(she has got) round heels She is loose sexually, she's anybody's, she's an easy lay. American origin, current by 1957. A sharp image, suggesting that a woman's heels are so curved that the slightest push from a man would put her on her back and in a position to have sexual intercourse. Compare: **she's got slippery heels**. 'Of a girl of easy virtue – a hussy (said with a sniff)' – UK, 20th century.

(a) round Robin Name for a letter where the responsibility for sending it is shared by all the signatories (known in the British Navy by 1730). In France, in the same century, petitioners would sign their names on a ribbon whose top was joined to its bottom. This was to prevent a situation where the first signatory on the list might be singled out for punishment. Nowadays, the term is often applied to a letter of protest with signatures not arranged in any special way, except perhaps alphabetically. The term has nothing to do with the bird. 'Round' is from French *rond* and 'Robin' is a corruption of French *ruban*, meaning ribbon.

(the) round up the usual suspects Meaning, 'round up the people you would expect, the customary lot'. An allusion to the line 'Round up the usual suspects', spoken by Claude Rains as Captain Louis Renaud in the film *Casablanca* (US 1942).

The Vichy French police chief in the Moroccan city is, in his cynical way, appearing to act responsibly in the light of the fact that a German officer, Major Strasser, has been shot. In 1992 Howard Koch appeared to have conceded the writing of this line to his co-scriptwriters, Julius J. Epstein and Philip G. Epstein. It did not, however, catch on as early as some of the film's other lines. 'Since the bombing, a Korean has been shot dead by Burmese policemen and two Koreans have been arrested . . . If they are from North Korea, the case against the Kim Il Sung government is indeed strong. But it was not clear whether the Burmese security forces were seriously on to something, or whether this was part of a placatory "Casablanca"-style round-up of "the usual suspects"' – *The Economist* (15 October 1983); 'The rumour is worth taking seriously for two reasons. The first is that someone is buying Xerox shares aggressively in the market. That might be Hanson, though the mention of the name had an element of "round up the usual suspects" about it' – *The Guardian* (10 February 1989); 'After half-time, Hastings kicked two more penalties and Bachop dropped a goal before another of Scotland's irresistible forward drives orchestrated by Armstrong and involving all the usual suspects – Allen, Weir and White – gave Jeffrey the chance to snatch the ball and dive over from five yards' – *The Independent on Sunday* (20 October 1991); 'All the usual suspects will be out at Fontwell tomorrow, when the figure-of-eight chase course will throw up its usual quota of specialist [racing] winners' – *Independent on Sunday* (17 January 1993); *The Usual Suspects* – title of film (US 1995); 'Orton's script [contained] . . . a lot of clumsy, predictable sniping at the Church, politicians, small-town mentality – the usual suspects' – *The Independent* (1 September 1995).

roundabouts and swings (or swings and roundabouts) An expression of acceptance of life's fluctuating fortunes, from the modern proverb 'What you lose on the swings you gain on the roundabouts' – a fairground metaphor, sometimes said to have been formulated by the English poet Patrick R. Chalmers in 'Roundabouts and Swings' in *Green Days & Blue Days* (1912). When asked during a stopover at Framlingham in Norfolk how the fairground trade is prospering, a travelling showman philosophizes, 'What's lost upon the roundabouts we pulls up on the swings.' However, a little earlier there had been this in P. G. Wodehouse, *Psmith in the City*, Chap. 26 (1910): 'What you lose on the swings, you make up on the roundabouts.'

Route 66 A major US highway immortalized in the song 'Route 66' (1946) by Bobby Troup: 'If you ever plan to motor west, / Travel my way, take the highway, that's the best, / Get your kicks on Route 66.' From *TV Times* (19 October 1985): 'For years, the 2,200-odd miles of black-top, running from Chicago to Los Angeles, conjured up visions of romance and adventure.' Allusive use: 'Winding through a grim, polluted landscape of new wrecks, new graffiti, new drug dealers and new prostitutes, Europastrasse-55 is the Route 66 of the lands that communism betrayed' – *Independent on Sunday* (21 June 1992).

row See GET YOUR DUCKS.

rowed See ALL ROWED.

(the) royal 'we' King Richard I is believed to have been the first monarch to use the royal 'we' (in Latin) – as a way of showing that he did not simply rule for himself but on behalf of his people. Before this, when Roman consuls *shared* power, it was appropriate for each of them to speak in this collective manner. Some monarchs seem to have been more prone to using it than others. As is obvious from her alleged expression, 'We are not amused', Queen Victoria was one who did, but nevertheless her letters and journals are just as full of the first person singular. However, when non-royals like Margaret Thatcher start saying things like 'We have become a grandmother' (as she did to widespread guffaws in March 1989), it is clearly time for the rest of us to desist. The actual term 'royal we', as opposed to the usage, is comparatively recent (by 1931).

rubber chicken Name given to the circuit around which professional speakers go in the USA. The meal provided is usually chicken, and it usually tastes of rubber. So called by about 1985. In the UK, when the Conservative minister Michael Heseltine resigned from Margaret Thatcher's government, he embarked on a rigorous speaking programme all over the country, addressing constituency associations. In 1990, he was given the nickname 'Rubber chicken' for his pains.

Rubicon See CROSS THE.

Ruddy Nora! A delightful expletive, current in the UK by the late 1970s. It is not known whence it came or to whom, if anyone in particular, it refers. *Street Talk, the Language of Coronation Street* (1986) prefers **Flaming Nora!** and defines it as 'Flipping 'eck!' or, as Americans put it, 'Holy cow!' The operators of the TV soap have no idea who the red-haired Nora was, either. In the BBC radio show *The Burkiss Way*, **Bloody Nora!** was exclaimed (29 November 1977) and 'Ruddy Nora!' (10 January 1978).

rule, Britannia Phrase that originated in *Alfred: a Masque* (1740). It had another author called Mallet, but James Thomson is thought to have written this bit (the music was by Dr Thomas Arne): 'When Britain first, at Heaven's command, / Arose from out the azure main, / This was the charter of the land, / And guardian angels sung this strain: / "Rule, Britannia, rule the waves; / Britons never will be slaves".' Invariably misquoted. Of the several recordings of this famous patriotic song, few can match that by Cilla Black (on PCS 7103). I suspect it was recorded when Swinging London was at its height and the Union Jack flag was plastered patriotically over everything from mini-skirts to tea mugs. Anyway, what she is heard to sing is: 'Rule, Britannia, / Britannia rules the waves. / Britons never, never, never / Shall be slaves.' Of course, Cilla Black is not alone in preferring to sing 'rules' and 'shall'. Annually, at the Last Night of the Proms, several hundred other people can be heard singing her version – and drowning out those who may feel like sticking to Thomson. There is a difference, however, between a poetic exhortation – 'rule' – and a boastful assertion 'rules'. As for the difference between 'will' and 'shall', life is

really too short to go on about that at any length. But an interesting defence of the Cilla Black reading comes from Kingsley Amis and James Cochrane in *The Great British Songbook* (1986): 'When what a poet or lyric-writer wrote differs from what is habitually sung, we have generally preferred the latter . . . Britons never "shall" be slaves here, not "will" as James Thomson, a Scot following Scottish usage, naturally had them.'

(to) rule nothing out and (to rule) nothing in Political phrase meaning that options are still open and no decision has been made one way or another. When John Cartwright was considering whether to stand as leader of the SDP: 'Asked last night if it was the case that he was ruling nothing out and ruling nothing in, he replied: "That's fair"' – *The Guardian* (18 August 1987); when talking about replacements for the poll tax, the British government minister, Michael Heseltine, said: 'In that context, we rule nothing out and nothing in' – *The Daily Telegraph* (6 December 1990).

(a) rule of thumb A rule taken from experience, not theory. This refers either to the use of a thumb's width as a rough and ready means of measurement or to the use of a thumb for dipping into liquids to test them. Known by 1692.

— rules, OK PHRASES. This curious affirmative is said to have begun in gang-speak of the late 1960s in Scotland and Northern Ireland, though some would say it dates back to the 1930s. Either a gang or a football team or the Provisional IRA would be said to 'rule OK'. Later, around 1976, this was turned into a joke with numerous variations – 'Queen Elizabeth rules UK', 'Rodgers and Hammerstein rule OK, lahoma', and so on. It soon became an all but unstoppable cliché. In 1981, Virginian rubbed tobacco was advertised beneath the slogan, 'Virginian Rolls OK', and a French cigarette beneath '*Gauloises à rouler, OK*'. In 1982, I was asked by BBC Radio to present a series on local government. 'Yes,' I said, 'I will – as long as you don't call it "Town Hall Rules OK".' Two weeks later, they rang back to say, 'We've chosen that title you suggested.' And they had. I only spoke it through gritted teeth. 'Golf Rules OK?' appeared as an *Observer* headline (13 November 1983).

(to) rule the roost Meaning 'to lord it over others', this possibly derives from the image of a cock's behaviour towards hens on the roosting perch. The existence of the earlier expression '**to rule the roast**', presiding as the head of the dinner table – as in Shakespeare, *Henry VI, Part 2*, I.i.108 (1590) – may point to a more likely source. However, just possibly the two phrases developed side by side, as the word 'roste' that appears in early citations is a now obsolete form of both 'roost' and 'roast'.

rum, bum and concertina The title of a volume of British jazz singer George Melly's autobiography (1977) alludes to the old naval saying: 'Ashore it's wine, women and song, aboard it's rum, bum and concertina.' Winston Churchill's version in response to a remark about naval tradition – recounted in Harold Nicolson's diary (17 August 1950) was: 'Naval tradition? Monstrous. Nothing but rum, sodomy, prayers and the lash.'

rumour hath it Consciously archaic phrase to introduce information that one has heard. Used in a literal way by 1705. 'Shakespearian scenarios: rumour hath it that Deborah Warner is writing a screenplay of *Measure for Measure* while Ian McKellen has been working on a potential screen adaptation of *Richard III* . . .' – *The Independent* (26 April 1994).

(a) rumour of angels *Rumors of Angels* was the title of a book (1994) by John Vincent Coniglio. The source of the phrase would seem to lie with *A Rumor of Angels: modern society and the rediscovery of the supernatural*, which was the title of a book (1969) by Peter L. Berger. In the closing chapter, Berger explains that he is only trying to keep alive the rumour of angels (that is, some sort of supernatural element in the increasingly secular world). He then tells a story about an (unnamed) priest in an (unnamed) slum who said that he devoted his life to working there, 'So that the rumor of God should not disappear completely.'

(a) runaway success Perhaps the most common example of the 'runaway ——'

format. Date of origin unknown but certainly in use by 1976. 'Runaway sale' and 'runaway best-seller' were in use by 1953 (both in connection with books). 'His plan was a runaway success' – Botham & Donnelly, *Valentino* (1976); '*Q* has taken on the weeklies and won, and in doing so has changed the face of rock journalism in Britain . . . Arguably, its runaway success owes much to its purging of rock-press habits that have alienated generations of weekly readers' – *The Guardian* (28 November 1994).

runneth See CUP RUNNETH.

running dogs Phrase meaning 'lackeys' and popularized by Chairman Mao Tsetung. In a 'Statement Supporting the People of the Congo Against US Aggression' (28 November 1964), he said: 'People of the world, unite and defeat the US aggressors and all their running dogs!' This provided a vivid weapon for use against the 'lackeys' of the USA during the Vietnam War. Edgar Snow had earlier recorded Mao using the term in 1937.

(it) runs in the family like wooden legs 'My wife had an unusual expression, which she would use when we might be discussing peculiarities of a certain family, such as the way they all walk in the same manner, or talk in a similar way. She would say, "It runs in the family like wooden legs"' – Neil G. Clark, South Yorkshire (1996). *Apperson* finds this in Bridge, *Cheshire Proverbs* (1917): '*It runs in the blood like wooden legs.* I heard this saying from the mouth of an Ulsterman, in Surrey, in the sixties of the last century.'

(to) run the gauntlet Expression meaning 'to endure something of a prolonged, testing nature, to be attacked on all sides', this has nothing to do with the type of glove but is from the Swedish *gatlop* or *gatloppe* which means 'lane run'. It carries the idea of someone having to run as a punishment (in the military) between two lines of tormentors. The literal use was recorded in English in 1676, but the transferred sense fifteen years earlier. From Oliver Goldsmith, *She Stoops to Conquer* (1773): 'He claps not only himself but his old-fashioned wife on my back . . . and then, I suppose we are to run the gauntlet through all the rest of the family.'

(a) rush to judgement An over-hasty reaching of conclusions. The phrase was famously used as the title of Mark Lane's book *Rush To Judgement* (1966) in which he challenged the findings of the Warren Commission into the assassination of President John F. Kennedy.

Russians with snow on their boots In September 1914, within a month of war being declared, there was an unfounded rumour that a million Russian troops had landed at Aberdeen in Scotland and passed through England on their way to the Western Front. The detail that they were seen to have had 'snow on their boots' was supposed to add credence to the report. It had to be officially denied by the War Office. Arnold Bennett was one of several people who noted the rumour at the time. In his *Journals* (for 31 August 1914), he wrote: 'The girls came home with a positive statement from the camp that 160,000 Russians were being landed in Britain, to be taken to France . . . The statement was so positive that at first I almost believed it . . . In the end I dismissed it, and yet could not help hoping . . . The most curious embroidery on this rumour was from Mrs A.W., who told Mrs W. that the Russians were coming via us to France, where they would turn treacherous to France and join Germans in taking Paris . . . This rumour I think took the cake.' In Osbert Sitwell's *Great Morning* (1951), he records how his 'unusually wise and cautious' sixteen-year-old brother Sacheverell had written to tell him: 'They saw the Russians pass through the station last night . . . and Miss Vasalt telephoned to Mother this afternoon and said trains in great number had passed through Grantham

Station all day with the blinds down. So there must, I think, be some truth in it, don't you?' In *Falsehood in War-Time* (1928), Arthur Ponsonby said of the phrase 'Russians with snow on their boots', that 'nothing illustrates better the credulity of the public mind in wartime and what favourable soil it becomes for the cultivation of falsehood'. Several suggestions have been made as to how this false information caught hold: that the Secret Service had intercepted a telegram to the effect that '100,000 Russians are on their way from Aberdeen to London' (without realizing that this referred to a consignment of Russian eggs); that a tall, bearded fellow had declared in a train that he came from 'Ross-shire', and so on. In fact, the British Ambassador to Russia *had* requested the dispatch of a complete army corps, but the request was never acceded to. Ponsonby commented: 'As the rumour had undoubted military value, the authorities took no steps to deny it . . . [but] an official War Office denial of the rumour was noted by the *Daily News* on September 16, 1914.' A *Punch* cartoon (23 September 1914) had the caption: *Porter*. 'Do I know if the Rooshuns has really come through England? Well, Sir, if this don't prove it, I don't know what do. A train went through here full, and when it come back I knowed there'd bin Rooshuns in it, 'cause the cushions and floors was covered with snow.'

(the) rustle of spring *Frühlingsrauchen* [Rustle of Spring] is the title of a famous piano piece written in 1896 by the Norwegian composer and pianist Christian Sinding. 'The music of the spheres is heard distinctly over Milk Wood. It is "The Rustle of Spring"' – Dylan Thomas, *Under Milk Wood* (1953).

S

Sabrina Fair The film *Sabrina* (US 1954) was adapted from a play entitled *Sabrina Fair* by Samuel Taylor. The film was originally known as *Sabrina Fair* in the UK. Why was it given the more allusive

title in the UK? This could have been because the distributors thought that British cinemagoers would relish an allusion to the poetic name for the river Severn, as applied to the nymph in

Milton's masque *Comus*. On the other hand, might the distributors have been sending them a message that the film had nothing at all to do with Sabrina, a busty (41–18–36) model, who featured on TV shows with Arthur Askey, the comedian, in the 1950s? Alas, this second theory does not fit, as Norma Sykes (her real name) did not start appearing until 1955 and, in fact, actually took her stage name from the title of the film. So, it must have been the allusion to Milton after all.

sack See BACK US OR; GIVE SOMEONE THE.

(the) sacred art of healing This is a phrase that first appeared in Longfellow's *The Song of Hiawatha* (1855): 'Forth then issued Hiawatha, / Wandered eastward, wandered westward, / Teaching men the use of simples / And the antidotes for poisons . . . / All the mystery of medamin, / All the sacred art of healing.' Much used in medical writings and also much alluded to. Hence, *The Sacred Art of Stealing*, title of a novel (2002) by Christopher Brookmyre, who was prompted by a song, 'The Sacred Art of Leaving'.

(a) sadder and wiser man An allusion to 'The Rime of the Ancient Mariner' (1798) by Samuel Taylor Coleridge: 'He [the Wedding-Guest] went like one that hath been stunned, / And is of sense forlorn: / A sadder and a wiser man, / He rose the morrow morn.' 'The Sadder and Wiser Beaver' was the title of a sketch by Peter Cook in *Beyond the Fringe* (1961) in which an employee of the newspaper proprietor Lord Beaverbrook tried to justify himself.

(a) safe pair of hands In political circles, a person who can be relied upon to perform a task without mistakes and without bringing down opprobrium upon a government. This expression may derive from sporting use and in particular from cricket. In 1851, someone was described as having 'the safest pair of hands in England' (meaning, presumably, that he would not drop the ball or miss a catch). From Colin Clark, *The Prince, the Showgirl and Me* (1995) – diary entry for 26 July 1956: 'Jack Harris is . . . what politicians used to call "a safe pair of hands".' From *The Times* (24 March 1969): 'The late Hugh Gaitskell years ago made an assessment of

Michael Stewart that still stands: "He has a safe pair of hands".' From Ben Pimlott, *Harold Wilson* (1992): 'In London, morning press conferences [during the 1966 General Election] were taken by [James] Callaghan, whom Wilson considered (as he flatteringly told the Chancellor) "a safe pair of hands".' From *The Sunday Telegraph* (1 August 1993): '[Sir Norman Fowler] does the job because he had supported Mr Major's candidature (later acting as his minder during the General Election), and because he was reputed to be "a safe pair of hands".'

safety first A slogan apparently first used in the USA in connection with railroad safety – according to the *Encyclopaedia Britannica*, 13th edn (1926). In the UK of the 1890s, a railway notice had declared: 'The Safety of the Passengers is our First Concern'. First recorded use of the phrase in the UK was, however, in 1873 – 'A system that would go on the motto of safety first' (*Cassell's Magazine*). In 1915, it became the motto of the National Council for Industrial Safety in the USA. In 1916, the London General Bus Company formed a London 'Safety First Council'. The 1922 British General Election saw the phrase in use as a political slogan for the Conservatives. Again, in 1929, it was the Tory slogan under which Stanley Baldwin fought for re-election, but it proved a loser. In 1934, the National Safety First Association was formed, concerned with road and industrial safety, and it is in this connection that the slogan has endured.

sailor See ENOUGH BLUE.

sainted aunt See MY GIDDY AUNT.

salad days Phrase from Shakespeare, *Antony and Cleopatra,* I.v.73 (1607). Cleopatra: 'My salad days, / When I was green in judgement, cold in blood, / To say as I said then!' Hence, *Salad Days*, title of a musical (London 1954) by Julian Slade and Dorothy Reynolds.

(a) salient point Meaning, 'a prominent point or one of conspicuous relevance in argument'. Known by 1838. 'He also misses one salient point in his argument' – Bryan Forbes in letter to the editor, *The Independent* (13 June 1995).

saloon   See DRINKING IN.

(a) saloon-bar Tory   'There is in Britain a political animal known as a "saloon-bar Tory". He sits in the most comfortable bar of his local pub, sipping gin and tonic, bemoaning the state of the nation and saying how much better everything would be if only managements and everyone else would stand up to the dreadful unions' – Michael Leapman, *Barefaced Cheek* (1983).

(the) salt of the earth   Meaning, 'the best of mankind'. This expression comes from Jesus Christ's description of his disciples in Matthew 5:13: 'Ye are the salt of the earth: but if the salt have lost his savour, wherewith shall it be salted?' Which suggests, rather, that they should give the world an interesting flavour, be a ginger group, and not that they were simply jolly good chaps. The New English Bible conveys this meaning better as 'you are salt to the world'. 'My message is not the one I would have liked to send on my retirement from the health service. Those who work in it are the salt of the earth but have been let down by politicians in the grip of dogma' – *The Independent* (20 January 1995).

Samarra   See APPOINTMENT IN.

same boat   See IN THE.

same day   See HOW DO YOU DO.

sandwiches   See BEER AND.

san fairy ann   This expression meaning 'it doesn't matter; why worry?' dates from the First World War and is a corruption of the French *ça ne fait rien* [that's nothing, makes no odds].

***sans peur et sans reproche* [without fear and without reproach]**   The Chevalier de Bayard (d. 1524), a French knight, was known as *le chevalier sans peur et sans reproche*. Mark Twain once proposed '*sans peur et sans culottes*' [knee britches] as the motto of a gentlemen's dining club and Harry Graham of *Punch* proposed '*sans beurre et sans brioche*' [butter/brioche].

sapristi!   Exclamation (also in phrases such as 'sapristi knockoes/nuckoes!' etc) from the BBC radio *Goon Show* (1951–60). Count Jim Moriarty (Spike Milligan) used this fairly traditional exclamation of

surprise – for example, in 'Napoleon's Piano' (11 October 1955). It is a corruption of the French '*sacristi*' and was current by 1839. Some will remember it being said, also, by Corporal Trenet, friend of 'Luck of the Legion' in the boys' paper *Eagle*, also in the 1950s.

(a) sardonic grin   An inevitable pairing. Date of origin unknown, but it is one of the clichés cited by Ted Morgan in *Somerset Maugham* (1980) as having been used by the writer in his efforts to achieve a 'casual style'. 'The idea that by the end of the century it could regularly be turning out large-scale films for the international market, and even drawing talent away from the West Coast . . . this is almost enough to remove that sardonic grin from the Hollywood mogul' – *The Times* (25 March 1995).

Satan   See GET THEE BEHIND.

(like being) savaged by a dead sheep   Abusive phrase, chiefly known as used by Denis Healey, when British Chancellor of the Exchequer, in a House of Commons speech (14 June 1978). On being attacked by Sir Geoffrey Howe in a debate over his Budget proposals, Healey responded: 'That part of his speech was rather like being savaged by a dead sheep.' In 1987, Alan Watkins of *The Observer* suggested that Sir Roy Welensky, of Central African Federation fame, had earlier likened an attack by Iain Macleod to being *bitten* by a sheep. We had to wait until 1989 and the publication of Healey's memoirs to be told that, 'the phrase came to me while I was actually on my feet; it was an adaptation of Churchill's remark that an attack by Attlee was "like being savaged by a pet lamb". Such banter can often enliven a dull afternoon.' The Churchill version remains untraced, but he was noted for his Attlee jokes (and busily denied that he had ever said most of them. In 1990, the victim of Healey's phrase, Geoffrey Howe, also claimed that it wasn't original. 'It came from a play', he said sheepishly. A profile of Healey in *The Sunday Telegraph* (3 November 1996) suggested that he had appropriated the phrase 'savaged by a dead sheep' without acknowledgement from the journalist Andrew Alexander (probably in *The Daily Telegraph* with reference to Howe during the Arab/Israeli war of 1967).

(a) savage story of lust and ambition Cliché phrase of the type used to promote films and books. This one was actually used on posters for the film *Room at the Top* (UK 1958). The combination of 'lust and ambition' was known by 1681.

saw the light See ROAD TO DAMASCUS.

say See ANYTHING YOU SAY.

say goodnight, Dick / goodnight, Dick! Catchphrase from NBC TV, *Rowan and Martin's Laugh-In* (1967–73). Rowan and Martin's concluding exchange was a straight lift from the old George Burns and Gracie Allen sign-off on *The Burns and Allen Show* (1950–58): *Burns*: 'Say goodnight, Gracie.' *Allen*: 'Goodnight, Gracie!'

say hey! Characteristic expression of Willie Mays, the American baseball star of the 1950s/60s. He would say it when he was excited and it somehow caught on.

saying See AS THE SAYING.

say it ain't so, Joe! Phrase used when expressing pained disbelief – the archetypal remark when youthful innocence is confronted with the possibility of corruption in an admired hero. It originated with the question reputedly addressed by a small boy to the American baseball player 'Shoeless Joe' Jackson as he came out of a grand jury session in 1920 about corruption in the 1919 World Series. Jackson, of the Chicago White Sox, had been accused with others of deliberately losing the Series at the behest of gamblers. A journalist reported a boy asking, 'It ain't so, Joe. Is it?' and Jackson's reply, 'Yes, kid, I'm afraid it is'. Over the years, the words re-arranged themselves into the more euphonious order. Ironically, Jackson denied that the exchange had ever taken place – using any set of words.

say it, don't spray it See SPRAY IT AGAIN.

say it loud ... 'Say it loud, **we're gay and we're proud**' was a slogan of the Gay Liberation Front in the USA, *circa* 1970. It was clearly derived from the James Brown song 'Say it loud, **I'm black and I'm proud**' with which he had had a hit in 1968. From *The Encyclopedia of Graffiti* (1974): 'Say it loud, I'm yellow and I'm mellow' (New York City).

say it with flowers This slogan was originally devised for the Society of American Florists and invented in 1917 for its chairman, Henry Penn of Boston, Massachusetts. Major Patrick O'Keefe, head of an advertising agency, suggested: 'Flowers are words that even a babe can understand' – a line he had found in a poetry book. Penn considered that too long. O'Keefe, agreeing, rejoined: 'Why, you can say it with flowers in so many ways' – quoted in I. E. Lambert, *The Public Accepts* (1941). Later came several songs with the title. This little rhyme was known by 1941: 'Say it with flowers / Say it with sweets / Say it with kisses / Say it with eats. / Say it with diamonds / Say it with a drink, / But for Lord's sake / Don't say it with ink.'

says See ALTHOUGH I.

(he/she) says anything but his (or her) prayers Dismissive phrase for when the opinion of another person is adduced. *Apperson* finds, 'He says anything but his prayers and then he whistles', in 1732; six years later, Jonathan Swift has it in *Polite Conversation* as, 'Miss will say anything but her prayers, and those she whistles.'

(a) scarlet woman (or whore or lady) A harlot. Also used as an abusive nickname by Protestants for the Roman Catholic church (known by the mid-19th century), selecting a phrase from Revelation 17:1–5, where a whore is described as 'arrayed in purple and scarlet colour'.

scene See CRIMINALS RETURN TO.

scenery See BECAUSE THE.

schoolboy See AS EVERY.

(the) school of hard knocks I.e. experience or hardship considered as an educative force. The *OED2* calls this 'US Slang' and finds it in 1912. *The Complete Naff Guide* (1983) has as a 'naff boast': 'But then, of course, I left university without a degree. I like to think I have a First from the School of Hard Knocks.' Receiving an honorary doctorate in the humanities from the University of Nevada in May 1976,

Frank Sinatra said, 'I am a graduate of the school of hard knocks.' In losing his job as chairman of Mecca in October 1978, Eric Morley said: 'I went to the College of Hard Knocks and last week I got my doctorate.' At least, he didn't say he had attended **the university of life**. *Partridge/Slang* prefers 'the university of hard knocks' and dates it from *circa* 1910. Robert Louis Stevenson writing in *Memories and Portraits* (1887) had: 'A man, besides, who had taken his degree in life and knew a thing or two about the age we live in.' Horatio Bottomley, addressing the Oxford Union on 2 December 1920, said: 'Gentlemen: I have not had your advantages. What poor education I have received has been gained from the University of Life.' Lord Baden-Powell wrote a book called *Lessons from the 'Varsity' of Life* (1933).

science and tenacity Phrase that lingers from the introduction to a modest detective series, *Fabian of Scotland Yard*, based on the work of an actual detective and first aired on British TV in 1954–6. The opening sequence began with Bruce Seton saying, 'This is Fabian of Scotland Yard,' then an American voice took over: 'In a nation's war on crime, Scotland Yard is the brain of Great Britain's man-hunting machine. Routine, detail, science and tenacity – these are the weapons used by squads of highly-trained men. Men like former Inspector Robert Fabian, hailed by the press as one of England's greatest detectives.' Then Seton came on again and said, 'My name is Fabian. Detective Inspector Robert Fabian.'

scot free See GET AWAY.

Scotland See CURSE OF.

Scots wha hae It sounds like an exclamation – of the wu–hey! or hawae the lads! sort – but it is the title of a battle song by Robert Burns (which is also known as 'Robert Bruce's March to Bannockburn'). The poem begins: 'Scots, wha hae [literally 'who have'] wi' Wallace bled, / Scots, wham Bruce has often led, / Welcome to your gory bed, / Or to victorie.' 'Wham' in the next line means 'whom'. A further comment, from James Murray (creator of the *OED*) in 1912: 'Even Burns thought that Scotch was defiled by "bad grammar" and tried to conform his Scotch to *English* grammar! Transforming e.g. the Scotch *"Scots 'at hae"* to *Scots wha hae* which no sober Scotch man in his senses ever naturally said.'

(the) Scottish play Theatrical superstition is understandable in a profession so dependent on luck. However, the euphemism 'Scottish play', invariably used for Shakespeare's *Macbeth* (1606), is based on a well-documented history of bad luck associated with productions of the play. Merely to utter the name of the play would be enough to invoke misfortune. Date of origin unknown.

Scotty See BEAM ME UP.

Scout's honour! 'Honestly, I'm telling the truth!' – possibly said with an accompanying two-fingered (together) salute to the forehead. Joining the Boy Scout movement, founded by Robert Baden-Powell in 1908, involved a simple oath-taking ceremony, after which it was assumed that a Scout would not lie. The first item of the ten-point 'Scout Law' is 'A Scout's honour is to be trusted'. 'Sam' says it in the film *Ghost* (US 1990).

scratch my back See YOU SCRATCH MY.

scratch'n'sniff Name of a gimmick used originally in the cinema whereby audience members scratched cards to release smells appropriate for the scene they were watching. The first 'scratch'n'sniff' opera production may have been *The Love for Three Oranges* at the English National Opera in 1989. The term is also applied to the kind of perfume samples supplied with magazines. From *Today* (1 April 1987): 'Using the latest refinements in tasteless high technology, Revlon is bringing out a new scratch'n'sniff range of advertisements in America's national women's magazines, under the copy line, "Where does Joan Collins become a Scoundrel?"' From *The Daily Telegraph* (8 September 1989): 'New products can be the answer and Reckitts' latest is an air freshener in a pseudo cut-glass container packaged with a scratch'n'sniff panel.'

screaming See DRAGGED KICKING.

scripture See DEVIL CAN CITE.

(the) scum of the earth The 1st Duke of Wellington said of his men, in a dispatch to Lord Bathurst, the War Minister (July 1813): 'We have in the service the scum of the earth as common soldiers.' This was after the battle of Vittoria, when Wellington's troops ('our vagabond soldiers') were 'totally knocked up' after a night of looting.' On more than one occasion, however, Wellington did speak in complimentary terms about the common soldiers under his command. The expression predates Wellington. Dr John Arbuthnot in *John Bull*, III.vi.25 (1712) has: 'Scoundrels! Dogs! the Scum of the Earth!' *The Scum of the Earth* is the title of a novel by Arthur Koestler (1941).

sea See EVERY LITTLE HELPS.

sea lions See FOLLOW THAT.

(a) seamless robe Phrase from John 19:23: 'The soldiers, when they had crucified Jesus, took . . . his coat: now the coat was without seam, woven from the top throughout.' Used as the title of a book, subtitled 'Broadcasting Philosophy and Practice' (1979) by Sir Charles Curran, a former Director-General of the BBC, it was meant to describe 'the impossibility of separating out any one strand of the job from another . . . It was impossible to disentangle, in the whole pattern, one thread from another'.

(a) sea of upturned faces Literary and journalistic cliché. From Mrs Radcliffe, *The Italian* (1797): 'The thousand upturned faces of the gazing crowd'; from Sir Walter Scott, *Rob Roy*, Chap. 20 (1817): 'I next strained my eyes, with equally bad success, to see if, among the sea of upturned faces which bent their eyes on the pulpit as a common centre, I could discover the sober and businesslike physiognomy of Owen'; from Harriet Martineau, *French Wines and Politics* (1833): 'A heaving ocean of upturned faces.' 'Among literary and journalistic clichés, "a sea of upturned faces" must rival "the PACKED COURTROOM" for frequency of appearance in print' – *The Sunday Telegraph* (19 September 1982). 'In reality, celebrities doubtless clambered wild over upturned faces for a chance of a guest spot on Morecambe and Wise, but to know this for a fact would spoil an important illusion' – *The Times* (16 May 1994); 'From the roof of the guild hall, fireworks scatter burning embers on upturned faces. Those of us in the portico rush out into the crowds to get a glimpse of all those angels in the sky' – *Financial Times* (24 December 1994); 'Welles enthusiastically accepted the new title [*Citizen Kane* in 1939/40]; apart from anything else, no one had been able to think of a suitable one (his secretary's proposal of *A Sea of Upturned Faces* being only the least satisfactory)' – Simon Callow, *Orson Welles: The Road to Xanadu* (1995).

(the) sea shall not have them Motto of Coastal Command's Air-Sea Rescue Service during the Second World War. In John Harris, *The Sea Shall Not Have Them* (1953; film UK 1954), it is mentioned as, rather, 'the motto of Air-Sea Rescue High-Speed Launch Flotillas'.

seat See FLY BY THE.

(the) sea, the sea! Cry taken from Xenophon's story (in *Anabasis*, IV.vii.24) of how his Greek mercenaries retreated to the Black Sea following their defeat in battle (401 BC). When they reached it, the soldiers cried: '*Thalatta, thalatta!*' – an Attic form of the Greek '*Thalassa, thalassa!*' Used as the title of a novel (1978) by Iris Murdoch.

Second Front Now Slogan promoting a demand of the Beaverbrook press (and chalked on walls) in the UK during 1942–3, calling for an invasion of the European mainland, particularly one in collaboration with the Soviet Union. The Allied military command disagreed with this proposal and preferred to drive Axis troops out of North Africa and the Mediterranean first. Churchill's argument against a second front was that Britain's resources were fully stretched already.

(to go and) see a man about a dog To go and urinate; to go for an illicit drink; (providing an excuse) to leave the scene. A caption to a Ghilchik cartoon in *Punch* (22 January 1930) is: 'The Age Old Excuse. Cave-dweller. "I won't be long, dear. I've just got to see a man about a brontosaurus."' But to which of the three meanings does this refer? A little strangely, *Partridge/Catch Phrases* seems to suggest that the phrase originally indicated that the man was about to 'visit a woman – sexually', then that he was 'going out for a drink', and then that he gave it 'in answer to an inconvenient question'. Only fourthly, does it list 'go to the water-closet, usually to "the gents", merely to urinate.' At one time, *Brewer* also preferred the 'concealing one's destination' purpose of this phrase, suggesting that it was a late 19th-century American expression and giving an example of its use during Prohibition as disguising the fact that the speaker was going to buy illegal alcohol from a bootlegger. A later edition suggested that the phrase meant that the speaker was pretending that he would see a man about placing a bet on a dog race. Sticking to what one takes to be the primary meaning: it has been suggested that 'dog' is some sort of rhyming slang for 'bog', a well-known term for a lavatory, but this is not true rhyming slang and does not convince. To unravel this a little: the earliest citation for the phrase, in any meaning, is Dion Boucicault's play *The Flying Scud, or a Four-legged Fortune*, Act 1 (1866), where a character says: 'Excuse me Mr Quail, I can't stop; I've got to see a man about a dog.' Here the meaning would appear to be that he is providing a limp excuse for absenting himself. This does not support an American origin for the phrase, for Boucicault was Irish and working mostly in London. There does seem to have been a US origin for the Prohibition meaning. '*See a man about a dog*, to go out and buy liquor' – *American Speech*, Vol. 3 (1927). Early citations are lacking for the 'go and take a leak' application, in any country.

see America first Slogan for the Great Northern Railway Co., from *circa* 1914. It was splashed all over the USA and helped turn the tide of travel from the east to the west coast. By 1916, the phrase was being used as the title of a show and a song by Cole Porter.

seeds See CONTAINING THE.

(to) see how the cat jumps 'As a child of the 1930s, money was very scarce. Whenever I asked my mother for something – sweets, clothes, bus ride, shoes, etc. – her answer was always the same: "I shall have to see how the cat jumps". Needless to say, I was always watching the cat' – Mrs I. N. Knight, Surrey (1998). *Partridge/Slang* defines this as 'watching the course of events before committing oneself to decision or action' and dates it from about 1820. *Apperson* finds it in Sir Walter Scott's *Journal* (7 October 1826).

seeing is believing Proverb by 1639 and clearly derived from John 20:25 where DOUBTING THOMAS refuses to believe in Christ's resurrection until he sees him: 'Except I shall see in his hands the print of the nails . . . I will not believe.' A modern addition to the proverb – by 1879 – is **. . . but feeling is the truth**. 'Seeing's Believing' is a Harry Warren/Johnny Mercer song from *The Belle of New York* (1952) and 'Seeing Is Believing' a song from Andrew Lloyd Webber's *Aspects of Love* (1989).

seen and not heard Phrase derived from the proverbial expression 'children should be seen and not heard', which has been in existence since *circa* 1400, originally with regard to young women: 'It is an old English saw [proverb]: "A maid should be seen, but not heard"' [modern spelling]. Hence, **obscene and not heard** – this pun is recorded in *Graffiti 2* (1980) as 'Graffiti should be obscene and not heard' and, from New York, in Reisner & Wechsler's *Encyclopedia of Graffiti* (1974) as: 'Women should be obscene and not heard.' Well, nothing new, etc.: in his 1976 biography, H. Montgomery Hyde has Oscar Wilde saying: 'Little boys should be obscene and not heard.'

see Naples and die Old Italian saying suggesting that once you have been to Naples there is nothing more beautiful to be seen on earth or, more ominously, a warning dating from the time when the city was a notorious centre for typhoid, cholera and other diseases. This extract dated 3 March 1787 from Goethe's *Italian Journey* would seem to support the first origin: 'I won't say another word about the beauties of the city and its situation, which have been described and praised so often. As they say here, "*Vedi Napoli e poi muori!*" "See Naples and die!" A story is sometimes told that because, in Roman times, Naples had a neighbouring town or island called More or Mori, visitors were advised to *'vedi Napoli e More/i'*, but this seems more likely to be a later joke.

seen one ——, seen 'em all Blasé format phrase of dismissal. A development of 'when you've seen one, you've seen the lot' – said about members of the opposite sex (and possibly their sexual equipment). From Thomas Tryon, *All That Glitters* (1987): 'I guess I needn't describe the "Community Room" [in an asylum]. Seen one community room, seen 'em all.'

(to) see the colour of someone's money To see a person's money, especially when one is doubtful that he or she really has it and is going to pay one. Also figuratively, to see or obtain proof of the actual existence of anything. Known since 1718. What is slightly curious is the use of the word 'colour', as money in the 18th century had no colour to speak of. Notes were printed in black on white paper.

(to) see the elephant To see what there is to see, gain experience. According to John D. Unruh Jr, *The Plains Across: The Overland Emigrants and the Trans-Mississippi West, 1840–60* (1979), 'seeing the elephant' was a popular expression in the USA, 'connoting, in the main, experiencing hardship and difficulty and somehow surviving'. The source of a longer version – 'I've seen the elephant, and I've heard the owl, and I've been to the other side of the mountain' – is untraced. Another unidentified source suggests that at the time of the American Civil War, the expression 'I've seen the elephant' was used by both Union and Confederate troops to mean that the speaker was an experienced soldier who had seen active service and not a gullible raw recruit. In other words, it was an expression of seniority. *Brewer* defines 'to see the elephant' as 'to see all there is to see'. Edwin Radford, *To Coin a Phrase* (1974), suggests that the original form, dating from the 1830s, was: '"That's sufficient," as Tom Haynes said when he saw the elephant.' J. M. Dixon, *English Idioms* (*circa* 1912), has the definition: 'To be acquainted with all the latest movements; to be knowing', which sharpens the idea somewhat. *Partridge/Slang* has, 'To see the world; gain worldly experience' and dates it to *circa* 1840 in the USA, 1860 in the UK.

Should there be any doubt as to why an elephant is chosen as the defining thing to see, the Lancashire squire Nicholas Blundell wrote in his diary for 6 March 1705: 'My wife rid behind me to Liverpool. She saw the elephant.'

(to) see the sky through the trees To have sex – as though one of the participants was lying on his/her back with this particular view (*al fresco*, naturally). Noted in 1985. Compare the jocular suggestion that a woman (usually) has been **studying the ceilings** in the promiscuous pursuit of sex.

(a) seething cauldron (or **sizzling ...)** Mostly journalistic inevitable pairing. Date of origin not known. 'Plucky British athletes . . . who ran their lion hearts into the ground in the sizzling cauldron that is Perth' – BBC TV *That Was the Week That Was* (1962–3 series); 'The Turks are not averse to reminding their allies on occasion of their strategic value, especially now that political developments in neighbouring countries have emphasised Turkey's relative stability. Compared with the seething cauldron in the Middle East, Turkey is a "still centre" of solidity' – *Financial Times* (17 January 1986); 'Yet Brett has again begun to prise the lid off this gently seething cauldron when he writes that "danger as well as beauty stalks through this score, and it is never quite exorcised by those fairies"' – *The Observer* (28 October 1990); 'In the abyss there seethes a giant cauldron, with the Conservative Party in meltdown' – *Mail on Sunday* (26 June 1995).

see you in church Jocular farewell – usually among *non*-churchgoers. American origin, by the mid-20th century. Compare **see you in court**, a rather more menacing farewell, perhaps hinting that someone is up to no good. Also American, by the 1920s/30s.

see you in the funny pictures (or **papers)!** Valedictory cry, of American origin, referring to newspaper comics. According to Mitford M. Mathews, *A Dictionary of Americanisms On Historical Principles* (1951), 'funny pictures' are 'pictures as appear in the funny papers' (citations from 1857 and 1910). 'Funny paper' is defined as 'a paper largely or entirely devoted to fun or humor'. Lester V. Berrey & Melvin Van Den Bark, *The American Thesaurus of Slang* (1942), list 'see you in the funny papers!' or '. . . the funnies!' as one of many joking expressions meaning 'good-bye'. No explanation is given as to how the expression arose. In Frank Capra's film *It's a Wonderful Life* (US 1947), a departing hearty youth says, 'See you in the funny pictures!'

see you later, alligator Note how a phrase develops: according to *Flexner* (1976), the simple 'See you later', as a form of farewell, entered American speech in the 1870s. By the 1930s, it had some 'jive use' as 'see you later, alligator'. To this was added the response, 'In a while, crocodile.' The exchange became known to a wider public through the song 'See You Later, Alligator', sung by Bill Haley and his Comets in the film *Rock Around the Clock* (1956), which recorded the origins of rock'n'roll. Princess Margaret and her set became keen users. There was even a sudden vogue for keeping pet alligators. The next stage was for the front and back of the phrase to be dropped off, leaving the simple 'Lay-tuh' as a way to say goodbye.

see you on the Christmas tree! Valedictory remark. British origin, 20th century, but why – what is the implication?

see you on the green A theatrical slang expression meaning 'I'll see you on the stage'. Has it something to do with GREEN ROOM? Apparently not, it is simple rhyming slang: 'greengage' = stage. Recorded by 1931. Sometimes 'the greengage' is used in full to mean 'the stage'.

see you on the ice! Phrase wishing someone good luck – mainly theatrical? (Dame) Judi Dench is reported as saying it as an alternative to BREAK A LEG before going on stage – and perhaps it is simply a variation on that expression. Tony Hancock says it in the TV comedy episode 'The Blood Donor' (1961). Could Bernard Shaw have been on to the same thing when he wrote in the Induction to *Fanny's First Play* (1911): 'You cannot learn to skate without being ridiculous . . . The ice of life is slippery'?

see you Wednesday! At the end of the British TV pop show, *Cool for Cats* (late 1950s), the host, Kent Walton, would spin round in his chair and say, 'Happy Monday, Tuesday, see you Wednesday!' Some, however, remember it as **see you Friday!** The confusion may come about because Canadian-born Walton was also famous for his all-in wrestling commentaries on Wednesdays and Saturdays. Hence, on Saturday he would say, 'See you Wednesday' and on Wednesday 'See you Saturday'. Obviously, he had a sign-off that could be adapted to any day of the week, whatever the show.

(a/the) select few An inevitable pairing. Known by 1817. 'For a select few in the field, the season started anew yesterday. Of the 150 players competing in the Canon European Masters, fewer than a fifth can have realistic hopes of making the 1995 Ryder Cup team, but for them yesterday may have been the start of something big' – *The Guardian* (2 September 1994); 'Since Jim's shop Fish Alive became one of a select few British tropical fish importers to get his hands on the rare but beautiful fish, they have been making a name for themselves in North-East fish fancying circles' – *Northern Echo* (4 May 1995).

(this tape will) self-destruct in ten seconds Stock phrase from the TV spy thriller *Mission Impossible* (US 1966–72), though some remember it as *five* seconds. Each episode began with the leader of the Impossible Missions Force listening to tape-recorded instructions for an assignment. The voice on the tape would say: 'Your mission, Dan, should you decide to accept it, is . . . As always, should you or any member of your IM Force be caught or killed, the secretary will disavow any knowledge of your actions. This tape will self-destruct . . .' 'This cubicle will self-destruct in ten seconds which will make your mission impossible' – lavatorial graffito quoted from West Germany in *Graffiti Lives OK* (1979).

(a) self-fulfilling prophecy Anticipation of an outcome that serves only to bring it about. Coined by R. K. Merton in *Social Theory and Social Structure* (1949): 'The self-fulfilling prophecy is, in the beginning, a *false* definition of the situation evoking a new behavior which makes the originally false conception come *true*.' 'Panic buying of spirits . . . caused largely by forecasts of the shortage – a self-fulfilling prophecy' – *The Times* (7 December 1973).

(a/the) sell-by date   A date marked on perishable products, especially foodstuffs, by which time they should have been sold or else they would be unfit for consumption. Used in shops and markets in the UK from 1972. Also figuratively to describe anything that is old or out-of-date. 'Socialism: the package that's passed its sell-by date' – *The Daily Telegraph* (13 March 1987).

(to) sell off the family silver   Meaning 'to dispose of valuable assets which, once gone, cannot be retrieved', this allusion was memorably used in a speech to the Tory Reform Group by the 1st Earl of Stockton (Harold Macmillan) on 8 November 1985. Questioning the British government's policy of privatizing profitable nationalized industries, he said: 'First of all the Georgian silver goes, and then all that nice furniture that used to be in the saloon. Then the Canalettos go.' This was summarized as 'selling off the family silver'.

sell the pig and buy me out   'My father, a hard-working man, was always on the go, muttering such things as, "Must soldier on,"or "Sell the pig," or "Dear mother, it's a bugger." He told me that when men became soldiers they had to serve a minimum time and if they wanted out sooner, they had to pay to leave the army: hence the following correspondence from unhappy son (in army), "Dear mother, sell the pig and buy me out." And from mother to son, "Dear son, pig's dead. Soldier on"' – Mrs Jay Carlyle, Edinburgh (1998). *Partridge/Catch Phrases* dates this saying to about 1910. Hence, the title of W. F. N. Watson, *Sell the Pig and Buy Me Out: Humorous Aspects of Military Life, History and Tradition* (1998).

(a) seminal classic (or work)   Date of origin not known. 'Now that the CUTTING EDGE of British folk humour no longer lies with the seaside postcard, the onus has long since passed to the T-shirt. The lavatory is no longer the prime mirth-maker it was. Much use, however, is made

of language taboos "Same s——, different day", or the seminal classic, "Brits On The Piss Tour 90" (or whichever year)' – *The Sunday Times* (21 August 1994); 'Though this dish has a long history in Burgundy, it was not really introduced to Britain until 1960, by Elizabeth David in her seminal work, *French Provincial Cooking*' – *Independent on Sunday* Magazine (14 May 1995); 'David Finegold and David Soskice reported in a seminal article in 1988 . . .' – Will Hutton, *The State We're In* (1995); 'Kenneth Arrow conceded in a seminal article in the *Guardian* . . .' – same author, same book.

semper perdrix [always partridge]   Meaning, 'too much of a good thing'. When the French King Henri IV (Henri of Navarre) (1553–1610) was reproved by his confessor for marital infidelities, he ordered the priest to be fed on nothing but partridge. When the priest complained that it was 'always partridge' (in French, *toujours perdrix*), the King replied it was the same if you had only one mistress.

(to) send a coded message   Journalistic and political cliché when used as explained in the citation, i.e. not in the literal sense. 'Political speeches described as coded are . . . not speeches in code but euphemisms designed to express disagreeable sentiments about something or somebody in terms less distasteful and more face-saving to the somebody in question than the blunt statement of fact would be' – *The Times* (31 December 1981).

send in the clowns (or send on . . .)   The tradition that the SHOW MUST GO ON grew out of circus. Whatever mishap occurred, the band was told to go on playing and the cry went up 'send in/on the clowns' – for the simple reason that panic had to be avoided, the audience's attention had to be diverted, and the livelihood of everybody in the circus depended on not having to give the audience its money back. Stephen Sondheim chose the 'Send *in* . . .' form as the title of a song in *A Little Night Music* (1974). Perhaps 'send in' was right for the circus, 'send on' for the stage?

(to) send someone to Coventry   Meaning 'to refuse to speak to a person', this expression may have originated in the old story of soldiers stationed in Coventry who were so unwelcome that the citizens carried on as if they did not exist; alternatively, that if women talked to the soldiers, they were ostracized. Another version comes from the Civil War in England in the 17th century. When captured Royalists were sent to Coventry, a strongly Roundhead (Parliamentary) town, they were bound to be ignored. Evidently, the Roundheads sent doubtful or useless officers or soldiers to the garrison at Coventry. 'The expression is used also in America: "Send them into everlasting Coventry" – Emerson's essay, "Manners"' – *Benham* (1948). This is possibly supported by a passage in Clarendon's *History of the Rebellion*, VI:83 (1702–4): '[Birmingham] a town so wicked that it had risen upon small parties of the King's [men], and killed or taken them prisoners and sent them to Coventry.' In use by 1765. 'I seemed to be the person marked for displeasure, and was almost literally sent to Coventry' – in a letter from the actor David Garrick (1777); 'The expression is used also in America: "Send them into everlasting Coventry" – Emerson's essay, "Manners"' – *Benham* (1948).

send someone to the showers See UP AND UNDER.

(to) send someone up the river To imprison. Because Sing Sing gaol lies up the Hudson River from New York City. Known by 1891. 'I done it. Send me up the river. Give me the hot seat' – *Chicago Daily News* (5 March 1946).

(a) senior moment Known by 1997 and probably of American origin, this phrase is used by baby-boomers in middle age to describe failures of memory that can't be blamed on anything but age. It may derive ultimately from the euphemistic term 'Senior Citizen' for an old, retired person – a term that originated in the USA in about 1938. It has been suggested that referring to experiences as '— moments' may have been encouraged by the 'Kodak Moments' in actual Kodak film advertising, later used with or without irony to mean any heart-warming moment. 'The senior moments don't freak me out as much as the "Death in Venice" moments' – caption to cartoon

(showing a group of elderly people) in *The New Yorker* (7 July 2003).

separated See COUNTRIES.

separated at birth See I WONDER IF.

serious PHRASES. For example, 'serious money', meaning 'money in excessive amounts'. The *Longman Register of New Words* (1979) correctly surmises that this 'facetious usage seems to have started life among the fast-burning earners of the post-BIG BANG, pre-Bust city of London, who when speaking of salaries in the six-figure bracket would concede that this was "serious money".' The phrase was popularized when used as the title of Caryl Churchill's satirical play *Serious Money*, about the City (London 1987). The *Register* also noted that the usage was likely to spread to other areas: 'Annie's – a bar favoured by serious drinkers' – *The Sunday Times* (28 August 1988). As indeed it did.

seriously, though, he's doing a grand job After a satirical attack on a person in BBC TV's *That Was The Week That Was* (1962–3), David Frost would proffer this pretend conciliation. It was taken up by clergymen and others, but Ned Sherrin, the show's producer, claims that the phrase was used in the programme no more than half a dozen times in all.

(a) servant of two masters *The Servant of Two Masters* is the English title of Carlo Goldoni's play *Il Servitore Di Due Padroni* (1745). The presumed origin is 'No man can serve two masters' (Matthew 6:24 and Luke 16:13). Compare: 'He who serves two masters has to lie to one of them' – Portuguese proverb; 'It is better to obey the laws of one master than to seek to please several' – Catherine the Great; 'Not bound to swear allegiance to any master, wherever the wind takes me I travel as a visitor' – Horace.

serve that lady with a crusty loaf! Catchphrase of Arthur Askey's from the BBC radio show *Band Waggon* (1938–39). 'Why I said that, I've no idea,' Arthur Askey remarked (1979): 'It came out of the blue when some woman was laughing very loud in the studio audience. Perhaps it goes back to the days when I used to do the shopping for my mum in Liverpool and picked it up then.'

(to) set alarm bells ringing Journalistic cliché, meaning 'to alert'. Date of origin not known. 'The trio moved off in a yellow Mini and as they drove west the resemblance between Mr Waldorf and Martin began to ring alarm bells among the police' – *The Times* (20 October 1983); 'The committee chairman, Mr Sam Nunn . . . interrupted a committee hearing on nuclear weapons to make the announce-ment, immediately setting off alarm bells in Washington' – *The Guardian* (3 Febru-ary 1989); 'The decision early this summer to cut the price from £1.5m to £750,000, however, sent alarm bells ringing through the business. Is English wine facing a crisis?' – *Independent on Sunday* (14 August 1994); 'A very middle class murder . . . She thinks something else Roger said to her that morning set alarm bells ringing. He had said that his parents had decided to visit friends in the South of England and had left him in charge of the house' – *Daily Mail* (16 February 1995); 'He said he "certainly hoped" Saddam would be deposed within the year. His words set alarm bells ringing in London – *The Observer* (4 August 2002); 'A doubling of bad debt provisions in the first half of 2002 to nearly $1 billion, sending alarm bells ringing about the financial health of big business around the globe' – same paper, same date.

set 'em up high, then knock 'em down hard A modern proverb in the making? 'Just ten years after they entered the public consciousness as the "alternative comedi-ans", most of our brightest young perform-ers and writers of the eighties seem to be inexorably passing into the second stage of that old British showbiz tradition, "Set 'em up high, then knock 'em down hard"' – *The Guardian* (25 May 1992). Compare Melvyn Bragg on the actor Richard Burton: 'There's nothing the British like better than a bloke who comes from nowhere, makes it and then gets clobbered' – quoted in *The Observer* (1 January 1989).

(to) set one's cap at To try earnestly to attract someone's favours, especially romantic or sexual ones. Possibly a reference to a woman wearing beguiling

headgear with a view to getting her man. Or possibly a mistranslation of the French nautical expression *mettre le cap à* [to head towards]. Known by the early 19th century. '"You will be setting your cap at him now, and never think of poor Brandon." "That is an expression, Sir John," said Marianne warmly, "which I particularly dislike. I abhor every common-place phrase by which wit is intended; and 'setting one's cap at a man' and 'making a conquest,' are the most odious of all"' – Jane Austen, *Sense and Sensibility* (1811).

sets See EMPIRE UPON WHICH.

(to) set the agenda Meaning, 'to estab-lish the important issues to be dealt with'. Identified as a current cliché in *The Times* (17 March 1995). 'In those days the media approached their role as servants of democracy with more self-effacement. They were less determined to set the agenda than is the case thirty years later' – John Cole, *As It Seemed To Me* (1995); 'Radio 4's *Today*, which has been under fire from the Cabinet, won the speech-based breakfast show award, remaining "the most authoritative, agenda-setting programme available on British radio"' – *The Guardian* (27 April 1995); '"Setting the agenda" has become one of the sacred phrases of the age, especially among politicians . . . [seeming] to mean "getting oneself, or one's thoughts, talked about" – or "being the first to come out with some mindless nonsense or opinion, which is so controversial that people are forced to take it seriously' – *The Observer* (24 September 1995).

set the people free Slogan used by the British Conservative Party, which helped it regain power, with Winston Churchill as Prime Minister, in the 1951 General Election. In a radio broadcast (3 May 1952), Churchill returned to the theme: 'We think it is a good idea to set the people free, as much as is possible in our complicated modern society, from the trammels of state control and bureaucratic management.' Many years later, in a House of Commons debate on the Rates Bill, Edward Heath recalled how he had entered the House in 1950 having fought an election on Mr Churchill's theme that Conservatives were to set the people free.

'It was not a theme,' he said, 'that we were to set the people free to do what we tell them' (17 January 1984). The slogan was taken from the lyrics of a patriotic song of the Second World War. In 'Song of Liberty' (1940), A. P. Herbert put words to the *nobilmente* theme from Edward Elgar's 'Pomp and Circumstance March No. 4': 'All men must be free / March for liberty with me / Brutes and braggarts may have their little day, / We shall never bow the knee. / God is drawing His sword / We are marching with the Lord / Sing, then, brother, sing, giving ev'ry thing, / All you are and hope to be, / To set the peoples free.'

(to) set the Thames on fire To make an impression. Versions of this saying date back to the 18th century, and similar things have been said about the Rhine, Seine and Liffey in the appropriate languages. The Romans had the expression: *'Tiberium accendere nequaquam potest'* [it isn't at all possible to set the Tiber on fire]. The Thames, famously, once used to freeze over, which would serve only to increase the achievement should anyone manage to set it on fire. W. S. Gilbert in *Princess Ida* (1884) has: 'They intend to send a wire? To the moon – to the moon / And they'll set the Thames on fire / Very soon – very soon.' The expression is often used in the negative: 'Well, he didn't exactly set the Thames on fire' – meaning 'he failed to make an impression'.

settle down, now, settle down Catchphrase of the British comedian Ken Goodwin (b. 1933). His diffident phrase was based on the observation that if you tell people not to laugh, they will only do so the more (compare George Robey's DESIST!). 'Settle down now, settle down! I don't want you to make a noise, I've got a headache,' was Goodwin's attempt to quieten laughter at his own jokes. He recalled (1979): 'I first said "Settle down" in a working men's club after the so-called compère/chairman had announced me to the audience. They didn't hear him and they didn't known I was on stage till I let them know. They were so noisy that, to get attention, I said, "Come on, you lot, settle down now." One or two began to smile and say to themselves, "What's this unknown commodity?" They were all waiting

for bingo! It really took off after I did the Royal Variety Show, a summer season at the Palladium and *The Comedians* on TV.'

seven See DANCE OF THE.

seven-leagued boots (or seven-league boots) Very large boots that enable the wearer to stride vast distances in a short space of time. In the traditional fairy tale of 'Little Poucet' (or 'Hop O' My Thumb' or 'The Seven-leagued Boots'), a pace taken in them measures seven leagues. They also appear in 'The Sleeping Beauty in the Wood'. In general use, in English, by 1793. '"How far is it, please Sir?" "O a long way off . . . You must borrow the seven-leagued boots to get to him"' – George Eliot, *The Mill on the Floss*, Chap. 3 (1860).

(in) seventh heaven In a state of ecstasy or supreme bliss. This term occurs in Sir Walter Scott's novel *Heart of Midlothian*, Chap. 33 (1818) – 'You may go to the seventh heaven' – and may also have been popularized as *Seventh Heaven*, the title of a Janet Gaynor/Charles Farrell silent movie (US 1927). But the concept of a seventh heaven is an ancient one. In the Jewish and Muslim religions there are seven heavens. The Jews also call it 'the heaven of heavens', where God and the most exalted angels reside. The division probably derives from an ancient Babylonian theory of astronomy in which the seventh ring of stars was the highest and represented supreme bliss.

(the) seven year itch I.e. the urge to be unfaithful to a spouse after a certain period of matrimony. The *OED2* provides various examples of this phrase going back from the mid-20th to the mid-19th century, but without the specific matrimonial context. For example, the 'seven year itch' describes a rash from poison ivy that was believed to recur every year for a seven-year period. Then one has to recall that since biblical days seven-year periods (of lean or fat) have had special significance, and there has also been the Army saying, 'Cheer up – the first seven years are the worst!' But the specific matrimonial meaning was not popularized until the phrase was used as the title of George Axelrod's play (1952) and then film (US 1955). 'Itch' had long been used for the sexual urge but, as Axelrod commented on BBC Radio *Quote . . . Unquote* (15 June 1979): 'There was a phrase which referred to a somewhat unpleasant disease but nobody had used it in a sexual [he meant 'matrimonial'] context before. I do believe I invented it in that sense.' 'Itch', oddly, does not seem to have been used in connection with venereal diseases. Nonetheless, note the following remark in *W. C. Fields: His Follies and Fortunes* (1950) by Robert Lewis Taylor: 'Bill exchanged women every seven years, as some people get rid of the itch.'

seven years dead Meaning, 'dead for an indefinite period' or just 'dead for a long time'. In Charles Dickens, *A Christmas Carol*, Stave 1 (1843), Marley's ghost is described as 'seven years dead' but this *could* refer to a specific period. 'Mummers', a traditional play/ballad has a doctor in it who claims he can cure a woman 'seven years dead'. The reason why 'seven years' was chosen may relate to its standing as a semi-mystical period, as in the other 'seven' phrases above.

seven years of bad luck The penalty for breaking a mirror. According to Robert L. Shook in *The Book of Why* (1983), this superstition began with the Romans, who believed life renewed itself every seven years (one is also told that the skin on the human body renews itself every seven years). 'Since a mirror held a person's image, when it was broken, the health of the breaker – the last person to look into it – was also broken.' The specific term of seven years for this accident has been recorded as a superstition since the mid-19th century.

sex and the single —— Journalistic headline format derived from the book *Sex and the Single Girl* (1962; film US 1964) by Helen Gurley Brown. Fritz Spiegl, *Keep Taking the Tabloids!* (1983), identified it in the following actual headlines: 'Sex and the single Siberian', 'Sex and the kindly atheist', 'Sex and the girl reporter' and 'Sex and the parish priest'.

sex, lies and —— Journalistic format phrase. After the film title *Sex, Lies and Videotape* (US 1989), which has proved irresistible to headline writers. 'Fury At "Sex, Lies And Stereotypes": Gay Protesters

Threaten To Disrupt Oscars Ceremony Over New Movie' – headline in *The Sunday Telegraph* (29 March 1992); *Sex, Guys and Videotape* – title of a Channel 5 programme about men prosecuted for having gay sex in the privacy of their own homes (5 July 1998); 'Sex, lies and Louise Woodward's lawyer' – headline in *The Independent* (30 May 1998); 'Sickies, lies, videos and tapes' [about private eyes] – headline in *The Independent* (17 July 1998); 'Sex, lies and a cover-up: the case against William Jefferson Clinton' – headline in *The Independent* (12 September 1998).

sex'n'drugs'n'rock'n'roll I.e. what young people are supposed to be preoccupied with. From a 1977 song by Ian Dury and Chaz Jankel (written as 'Sex & Drugs & Rock & Roll'), which continues, '. . . is [*sic*] all my brain and body need . . . is very good indeed'. 'Nostalgia for the 1960s, call it sex and drugs and rock and roll (and high purpose) is rife in *Hot Flashes*' – *The Guardian* (25 January 1989); 'Aurum Press is shortly to publish [Lord Whitelaw's] memoirs . . . "It's not exactly sex, drugs and rock-and-roll," Aurum's Tim Chadwick tells me' – *The Observer* (26 February 1989).

sexual chemistry In the period prior to the start of TV-am, the British breakfast television station, in 1983, David Frost talked about hoped-for new approaches to on-screen presentation. He either invented the phrase 'sexual chemistry' (doubtful), or merely endorsed it when it was suggested to him by a reporter, to describe what it was important for Frost and his colleagues to have: 'The chemistry thing is really important . . . chemistry – sexual or otherwise – that is important.' 'Personal chemistry', to describe the attraction between two people, had long been remarked where it existed in other walks of life. 'Remember the nauseating way Margaret Thatcher turned into a lovesick girl during Gorbachev's visit here and all that talk in the press of "personal chemistry"?' – *The Guardian* (7 June 1989). George Bernard Shaw in *You Never Can Tell* (1898) had earlier had: 'Not love: we know better than that. Let's call it chemistry . . . Well, you're attracting me irresistibly – chemically.'

shades of the prison-house A phrase from William Wordsworth, 'Ode, Intimations of Immortality' (1807): 'Heaven lies about us in our infancy! / Shades of the prison-house begin to close / Upon the growing boy.' Title of a book about prison life by 'S. Wood' (1932). Note also the opening lines of 'Marlborough', a poem written about his old school by John Betjeman for a TV programme (1962): 'Shades of my prison house, they come to view, / Just as they were in 1922:/The stone flag passages, the iron bars . . .'

shadow See AVOID FIVE O'CLOCK.

shadowlands See IN THE.

(to) shake a leg (or **show a leg)** 'Shake a leg' means either 'to dance' (by 1881) or (in the USA) 'to hurry up' (by 1904). 'Show a leg' (meaning 'to get up out of bed in the morning or get a move on') dates from the days when women were allowed to spend the night on board when ships of the Navy were in port. Next morning at the cry, 'Show a leg!', if a woman's leg was stuck out of a hammock, she was allowed to sleep on. If it was a man's, he had to get up and on with his duties. No citation for this use before 1854, however.

(to go and) shake hands with the wife's best friend Loophemism – date of origin unknown, although it was associated with the Australian cartoon character Barry McKenzie in *Private Eye* Magazine by 1971. *Partridge/Catch Phrases* also lists the variations: '. . . with my best friend', '. . . with an old friend', '. . . with the unemployed'. Also: 'I am just going to shake hands with the father of my son.'

shame See AIN'T IT A.

(the) shame of our —— Journalistic cliché. Date of origin not known. 'The shame of our prisons' – headline in *The Observer* (3 May 1981); 'Not the shame of football hooligans, not the shame of our Government, not the shame of permanent sleaze, but the shame of almost a thousand years, years defiled in an instant' – *The Times* (5 May 1995).

shampooed See AFTER I'VE.

sharp See BACK IN THE.

sharpen up there See MUM MUM.

(a) sharp intake of breath (or **short . . .)** I.e. something like a reverse whistle used to invoke scepticism. *A Sharp Intake of Breath* was the title of an ATV comedy series (1977–81) about a man fighting against bureaucrats who would make this noise when asked to do anything. It is also common among household builders and handymen whenever they are asked to give an opinion on the viability of any project or repair.

shattering See I THOUGHT.

she See DOES SHE.

Shean See ABSOLUTELY.

(to) shed a tear for Nelson Loophemism. Date of origin unknown. Variations include 'I'm just going to shed a tear for the widows and orphans' or, simply, 'I'm going to shed a tear . . .'

she done him wrong Phrase from the refrain of the anonymous US ballad 'Frankie and Johnny' that *Mencken* dates *circa* 1875 and which is sung in the film entitled *She Done Him Wrong* (US 1933), based on Mae West's play *Diamond Lil*. There are numerous versions of the ballad (200 is one estimate) and it may be of black origin. 'Frankie and Johnnie were lovers' [or husband and wife] but he [Johnnie] does her wrong by going off with other women – 'He was her man, but he done her wrong'. So, to equal the score, Frankie shoots him, and has to be punished for it (in some versions in the electric chair): 'Frankie walked up to the scaffold, as / Calm as a girl could be, / She turned her eyes to Heaven and said / "Good Lord, I'm coming to Thee; / He was my man, but I done him wrong".' *Bartlett* (1980) draws a comparison with Shakespeare, *The Rape of Lucrece* (line 1462): 'Lucrece swears he did her wrong' and *King Lear* (I.ii.161): 'Some villain hath done me wrong.'

sheep See EVERY TIME A.

shell-like See IN YOUR.

she knows, you know! Catchphrase of the diminutive northern English comedienne Hylda Baker (1908–86) who had a vulgar voice and an utterly distinctive routine. She used to say this in sketches about Cynthia, her mute giraffe-like partner (played by a man). Her other phrase, **be soon!** (said to Cynthia and pronounced 'Be soooooon!'), was used as the title of a TV series in the 1950s.

she's got legs right up to her bum
Admiring description of an attractive girl whose long legs are her main feature. Since the 1950s? Later variations might include, **she's got legs that go on for ever** and (even) **she's got legs that go right up to her armpits/ the lobes of her ears**.

she should lie back and enjoy it　Best described – as it is in Paul Scott's novel *The Jewel in the Crown* (1966) – as 'that old, disreputable saying'. Daphne Manners, upon whose 'rape' the story hinges, adds: 'I can't say, Auntie, that I lay back and enjoyed mine.' It is no more than a saying – a 'mock-Confucianism' is how *Partridge/Slang* describes it, giving a date (*circa* 1950) – and one is unlikely ever to learn when, or from whom, it first arose. A word of caution to anyone thinking of using it. An American broadcaster, Tex Antoine, said in 1975: 'With rape so predominant in the news lately, it is well to remember the words of Confucius: "If rape is inevitable, lie back and enjoy it."' ABC News suspended Antoine for this remark, then demoted him to working in the weather department and prohibited him from appearing on air.

she was only the —–'s daughter　A series of mildly bawdy jokes – presented as though the first line of a song. Perhaps suggested by an original that hasn't been found . . . In an advertisement for the Canada Life Assurance Co. in *The Performer* (2 May 1935) is this: 'She was only the Baggage Man's daughter, but she took out a policy here . . .'; 'She was only the Town Clerk's daughter, but she let the Borough Surveyor'/'She was only a Red Indian's daughter, but she certainly knew how'/'She was only a fisherman's daughter, but when she saw my rod she reeled' – included in John S. Crosbie, *Crosbie's Dictionary of Puns* (1977); 'She was only the road-maker's daughter, but she liked her asphalt' – included in *Graffiti 5* (1986).

she who must be obeyed　The original 'she' in the novel *She* (1887) by H. Rider

Haggard was the all-powerful 'Ayesha', 'who from century to century sat alone, clothed with unchanging loveliness, waiting till her lost love is born again'. But also, 'she was obeyed throughout the length and breadth of the land, and to question her command was certain death'. From the second of these two quotations we get the use of the phrase by barrister Horace Rumpole with regard to his formidable wife in the 'Rumpole of the Bailey' stories by John Mortimer (in TV plays since 1978 and novelizations therefrom). Hence, too, one of the many nicknames applied to Margaret Thatcher when British Prime Minister – 'The great she-elephant, she who-must-be-obeyed' – Denis Healey, speaking in the House of Commons (27 February 1984) – but in the 'elephant' epithet quoting Conservative MP Julian Critchley.

(to) shine like a tanner on a sweep's arse　Peter Foulds of Darlington, County Durham, wrote (1994): 'A Cockney cousin of mine once told me of her pleasure at receiving, from her husband, the gift of a baby grand piano. She described the beautiful lustre of the instrument with these words.' *Partridge/Slang* has 'shine like a shilling up a sweep's arse' – which is a touch more alliterative – and dates it 'early C20'. Compare **(to) shine like shit on a barn door**. Shining admirably (as, say, after a good polishing). *Partridge/Slang* has 'shine like a shitten barn door' and finds an allusion to the phrase in Jonathan Swift's *Polite Conversation* (1738): 'Why, Miss, you shine this Morning like a sh— Barn-Door'.

shine on harvest moon　This was the title of a song (1908) by Nora Bayes and Jack Norworth. The harvest moon seems particularly bright between 15 and 20 September, thus enabling farmers to bring in their crops by moonlight, should they need to. An ITV series (1982–5) was entitled *Shine on, Harvey Moon*.

shipping　See ATTENTION ALL.

shipshape and Bristol-fashion　Neat and methodically arranged as things must be (in the limited space) on board ship. At one time, Bristol was the largest seaport in Britain. Possibly antedating this citation from R. H. Dana's *Two Years Before the Mast*, Chap. 20 (1840): 'Everything on board "ship-shape and Bristol fashion"'.

ships that pass in the night Acquaint-anceship (with people) that is of only short duration – especially regarding brief affairs. From Longfellow, 'The Theologian's Tale: Elizabeth', Pt 4 in *Tales of a Wayside Inn* Pt 3 (1874): 'Ships that pass in the night, and speak each other in passing; / Only a signal shown and a distant voice in the darkness; / So on the ocean of life we pass and speak one another, / Only a look and a voice; then darkness again and silence.'

shirt See HOW TICKLED I AM.

shit cart See AFTER THE LORD MAYOR'S.

(when the) shit hits the fan Probably a 1930s/40s forces' phrase for when the reckoning is due in any situation – when, for example, a person in authority discovers some misdeed and erupts with terrible temper (and, to mix metaphors, **there'll be blood all over the walls**). A colourful and much used image. Alluded to delightfully in January 1989 when the Nottingham Forest football manager, Brian Clough, administered buffets, clouts and clips round the ear to his team's fans who had invaded the pitch (and got into trouble for it). 'The Sh*t Hits the Fan!' was a headline in the *Daily Star* (1995) when the footballer Eric Cantona kicked a Crystal Palace fan during a match and was subsequently arrested.

shit list See ENEMIES LIST.

shit on a barn door See SHINE LIKE A TANNER.

shiver my timbers (also simply **my timbers)!** A mock oath in seafaring fiction, most notably in Robert Louis Stevenson, *Treasure Island* (1883). 'Israel Hands', the coxswain says it (and also 'Long John Silver') referring to a drink of strong spirits. The word 'timbers' alludes to the days of wooden ships. The oath also appears earlier in the works of Captain Marryat and Thomas Dibdin.

shock and awe The US Pentagon's term for instilling fear and doubt in the minds of Iraqis while their country was being invaded by American forces for regime-change purposes in 2003. The phrase first appeared publicly in a book entitled *Shock and Awe* (1996) by Harlan Ullman and James Wade, which came out of a report by the Rapid Dominance Study Group, an informal association of mainly ex-military men. 'It is all part of the administration's basic approach toward foreign policy, which is best described by the phrase used for its war plan – "shock and awe". The notion is that the United States needs to intimidate countries with its power and assertiveness, always threatening, always denouncing, never showing weakness' – *Newsweek* Magazine (March 2003).

shock, horror! Reaction expressed in parody of tabloid newspaper-speak, from the 1970s onwards. In form it is, of course, similar to 'Shock, horror, probe, sensation!' promoted since the 1960s by *Private Eye* as a stock sensational newspaper headline. **Shock probe** was probably a *News of the World* headline phrase.

shocking pink Coinage of the Italian fashion designer Elsa Schiaparelli (1896–1973). She used it in 1938 to describe a lurid pink she had created. As such it made a pleasant change from alliterative coinages and has undoubtedly stuck. In her autobiography, entitled, understandably, *Shocking Life*, Chap. 9 (1954) she notes that her friends and executives warned her off creating a 'nigger pink' but 'the colour "shocking" established itself for ever as a classic. Even Dali dyed an enormous stuffed bear in shocking pink'.

(the) shock of recognition Possibly a coinage of Herman Melville in *Hawthorne and His Mosses* (1850): 'Genius all over the world stands hand in hand, and one shock of recognition runs the whole circle round'. Melville may have been referring to an experiment with electricity, with a circle of soldiers holding hands and getting one collective shock. *The Shock of Recognition: the development of literature in the United States, recorded by the men who made it* – title of a book (1943), edited by Edmund Wilson.

(the) shock of the new *The Shock of the New* was the title of a TV series and a book (1980) by the art critic Robert Hughes. The phrase came – as acknowledged – from Ian Dunlop's 1972 book on 'seven historic exhibitions of modern art'. Compare Thomas Crawford's use of the idea in *Longer Scottish Poems* (1987), in connection with the best efforts of Robert Burns – which represent, 'the perfection of the old achieving the shock and immediacy of the new'.

shock waves were felt Known in its original scientific use – concerning explosions – by 1907. In the figurative sense, the phrase became a cliché by the mid-20th century. 'When the Biba empire finally toppled, the shock waves were felt so far abroad that it seemed unbelievable that they were caused by what was really only a smallish shop in a smallish city' – Sally Brompton, *The Observer* (4 September 1983); 'Here, eleven Japanese photographers respond to the shockwaves felt in a country at present seemingly locked in an identity crisis' – *The Guardian* (14 June 1994); 'When it happens, the cost in lives and property will be many times that of this week's disaster – and the economic shockwaves will be felt all over the world, including Britain' – *Daily Mail* (19 January 1995).

shoe See ACT YOUR; DROP THE OTHER.

shoes See DEAD MEN'S; HE CAN LEAVE.

shome mistake shurely (or shurely shome mistake?) Written as such and interpolated as an editorial query in *Private Eye* copy (from the 1980s), this reproduces the spraying vocal style of William Deedes, editor of the *Daily Telegraph* from 1974 to 1986.

shoot See DON'T.

shoot first and ask afterwards Cynical instruction to, say, soldiers on sentry duty or to policemen in riot situations. The epitome of rough and summary justice – but all too often leading to injustice. Since the 19th century, in the Wild West perhaps? *Bartlett* has 'Shoot first and inquire afterwards, and if you make mistakes, I will protect you' as Hermann Goering's instruction for the Prussian Police (1933). *Shoot First: a Cop's Vengeance* – title of a film (US 1991) presumably alludes.

(to) shoot oneself in the foot Carelessly to mar one's argument or to spoil one's case or to do oneself a figurative injury. Date of origin unknown but in the 20th century. An origin has been suggested in the practice of *deliberately* inflicting such an injury on oneself in the First World War to necessitate treatment in hospital and thus escape from the horror of the trenches.

(to) shoot the moon A chiefly American expression meaning 'to do a moonlight flit', i.e. to leave without paying your bills, rent, etc. or to remove your goods at night in order to cheat the bailiff'. Current by 1869 when it was discussed in *Notes and Queries*. G. K. Chesterton alludes to it in *The Club of Queer Trades*, Chap. 4 (1904): 'His slangier acquaintances were of opinion that "the moon" had been not infrequently amid the victims of his victorious rifle.' '"Mr Ukridge owes a considerable amount of money round about here to tradesmen . . . Well, when they find out he has – er – " "Shot the moon, sir," suggested the Hired Retainer helpfully' – P. G. Wodehouse, *Love Among the Chickens* (1906). *Shoot the Moon* was the title of a film (US 1981). 'To shoot the moon' can also mean 'to go for broke' in card playing.

shopping and fucking See S'N'F.

—— shopping days to Christmas Advertising line. This may have been one of the coinages of H. Gordon Selfridge (1856–1947), American-born creator of Selfridges department store in London. At least, when he was still in Chicago he sent out an instruction to heads of departments and assistants at the Marshall Field store there: 'The Christmas season has begun and but twenty-three more shopping days remain in which to make our holiday sales record.'

shop till you drop Rhyming phrase for the process of seeking out and making purchases until you are exhausted. Popular since the 1980s. But in the screenplay for Noël Coward's *Brief Encounter* (UK 1945 – based on his play), Dolly says, interrupting a tryst, 'I've been shopping till I'm dropping.'

short See BY THE SHORT.

short and sweet like a jackass's gallop Very short. *Apperson* has 'short and sweet like a donkey's gallop' from *Lancs Sayings* (1901), which makes rather more sense. Perhaps 'jackass's' is from 'ass's' out of 'donkey's'?

short, fat, hairy legs Catchphrase of the double-act of comedians on BBC TV, *The Morecambe and Wise Show* (1968–77). The essence of their cross-talk was the inconsequentiality of Eric Morecambe's interruptions of the relatively 'straight' Ernie Wise's posturings. This phrase was applied by Eric to Ernie's legs, in contrast to his own supposedly long, elegant ones. Ernie said that this emerged, like most of their phrases, during rehearsals – particularly during their earlier spell on ITV. Indeed, it was established by the time The Beatles appeared on the ITV show and referred to it (2 December 1963). It has been suggested that some people refer to short trousers that reveal hairy legs as 'Morecambes'.

short of See FEW VOUCHERS.

(a) short, sharp shock Phrase used by William Whitelaw, the British Home Secretary, in a speech to the Conservative Party Conference (10 October 1979) when describing a new method of hard treatment for young offenders. The expression had been used by other Home Secretaries before him and is a quotation (referring to execution) from W. S. Gilbert's lyrics for *The Mikado* (1885). Used as the title of a play (1980) by Howard Brenton and Tony Howard (originally called *Ditch the Bitch* and referring to Margaret Thatcher).

shot See BEST SHOT.

(the) shot heard round the world The one that started the American War of Independence. Coined by R. W. Emerson in the 'Concord Hymn' (1837), written for the opening of the battle monument at Concord, Mass., site of the first armed resistance to the British: 'By the rude bridge that arched the flood, / Their flag to April's breeze unfurled, / Here once the embattled farmers stood, / And fired the shot heard round the world.'

(a) shot in the dark A haphazard guess, a random attempt. After all, a shot fired in the dark is unlikely to hit its target. Known by 1895, though there may be an earlier

allusion in William Cowper, 'Mutual Forbearance' (1782): 'Sir Humphrey, shooting in the dark, / Makes answer quite beside the mark.' The film entitled *A Shot in the Dark* (US 1964) not only refers to literal shots in the dark but also to the bumbling detective work of 'Inspector Clouseau'.

shoulder See CHIP ON ONE'S; COLD.

(to stand/fight) shoulder to shoulder with Date of origin not known. 'Stand shoulder to shoulder' cited as a 'dying metaphor' in George Orwell's 'Politics and the English Language', *Horizon* (April 1946). 'I like seeing my political opponents standing shoulder to shoulder on a burning deck' – Iain Macleod, quoted in *The Observer* (18 December 1967); 'In any other era, Pete Sampras would be celebrated simply as the most brilliant tennis player of his generation. A man able to stand shoulder to shoulder across the ages with Laver, Hoad, McEnroe or Borg' – *Today* (30 June 1994); 'Like entertainment-starved squaddies attending some up-country ENSA concert party, we sweated shoulder-to-shoulder, desperate to have Massive Attack's hipness conferred upon us' – *The Herald* (Glasgow) (10 December 1994).

(to put one's) shoulder to the wheel To make extra effort to start and/or complete a task – obviously from the acting of shifting a wheeled vehicle that has become stuck and requires, in addition to any horse-drawn effort, a human shove to free it. Known by 1692. 'Putting your shoulder to the wheel when the coach gets into the mud. That's what I've been doing all my life' – Anthony Trollope, *The Small House at Allington*, Chap. 46 (1864).

shouting See ALL OVER BAR THE.

show See ANOTHER OPENING; LET'S DO THE.

show a leg See SHAKE A LEG.

(the) show must go on Show-business phrase, also used figuratively in other situations. This seems to have been originally a circus saying, though no one seems able to turn up a written reference much before 1930. *The Show Must Go On* was the title of a film in 1937 and of an Ira Gershwin/Jerome Kern song in *Cover Girl*

(1944). *Punch* (13 April 1938) showed a reluctant bridegroom in the church porch, with the caption: 'Come, come Benedict – the show must go on!' In 1950 the phrase was spoken in the film *All About Eve* and, in the same decade, Noël Coward wrote a song that posed the question '*Why* Must the Show Go On?' 'The day that my heart bled for the Queen: Pride, dignity and a passionate belief that the show must go on' – headline in the *Daily Mail* (19 October 1994); 'Manager Lucy Watson, 27, decided the show must go on and offered reduced-price tickets to punters as they left' – *Daily Record* (5 April 1995).

show someone the ropes See KNOW THE ROPES.

show us your rabbit! Curious but inspired phrase used by the British comedians (Raymond) Bennett and (Harry) Moreny in their variety act of the 1930s/40s.

show us your wad See LOADSAMONEY.

(a) shrinking violet A timid, shy person. From the customary role of the violet flower symbolizing modesty. Known by 1915.

shut that door! Catchphrase of the British comedian Larry Grayson (1923–95) who came to prominence on British TV in the 1970s. The first time he used this phrase was on stage at the Theatre Royal, Brighton in 1970, 'when I felt a terrible draught up my trouser legs. I turned to the wings and said it. I really meant it, but the only response was giggles from the wings and a roar of laughter from the audience. So I kept it in my act. I can't go anywhere now without taxi-drivers or shopkeepers telling me to "shut that door".' Another version has him saying it for the first time when appearing in pantomine at the Kidderminster Playhouse in the 1960s. In the 1970s, Grayson also had any number of camp phrases like **what a gay day!**, **the place is alive!** and **I just don't care any more!** Plus **she seems like a nice girl, doesn't she?** (or **he seems like a nice boy, doesn't he?**) – from when he was presenting BBC TV, *The Generation Game* (1978–82). This was a stock phrase when chatting to contestants. Said Grayson: 'It's the expression mothers always use when

they describe their daughter's boyfriend and I never dreamt it would catch on like it did.'

shut up, Eccles! Catchphrase from the BBC radio *Goon Show* (1951–60). Usually said by Neddie Seagoon (Harry Secombe), repeated by Eccles himself (Spike Milligan), and then taken up by everyone.

shut your cake-hole Meaning 'shut up, be quiet', this phrase was recorded among schoolchildren by 1959. 'Cake-hole' for mouth was British servicemen's slang by 1943. Compare **shut your face**, known by 1893, and **shut your mouth**, known by the 13th century and used by Shakespeare in *King Lear* (1605).

shut your mouth, here comes a bus What you say to a child who has his/her mouth open. 'When I was a child my grandmother, if I had my mouth open in a typically idiotic gape, would say this' – Peter Toye (2000). 'Close your mouth, there's a bus coming' – in script of ITV, *Inspector Morse*, 'The Remorseful Day' (15 November 2000).

sick and tired Why are these two words always put together? Known by 1783. In May 1988, Terry Dicks, a Conservative MP and self-proclaimed tribune of the plebs, spoke during a House of Commons debate on the arts, and said: 'Ordinary people are sick and tired of people who can well afford to pay the full going rate for attendance at the theatre and ballet getting away with being subsidized by the rest of us.' This seems a fairly classic context for the phrase to be used – and spoken by just the type of person one would expect to use it. 'President Bush complained he was "sick and tired" of attacks on Defense Secretary-designate John Tower' – *The Independent* (7 March 1989); 'The 94-year-old Dame Pattie responded by describing Keating as a "disgrace" and a "monster." "He has spoiled my faith in everything we had and I'm sick and tired of it," she said' – *The Independent* (7 September 1995).

sick as a parrot Meaning, 'very disappointed (at losing something)'. Often used in contrast to OVER THE MOON. *Private Eye* had it between quotation marks on 16 February 1979, and this was probably at the start of an epidemic of use of the phrase. What may be an early version appears in Robert Southey's Cumbrian dialect poem *The Terrible Knitters e' Dent* (1834). There, 'sick as a peeate' (pronounced 'pee-at') means a feeling like a heavy lump of peat in the stomach – the equivalent of having a heart feeling 'as heavy as lead' perhaps? A more likely origin is in connection with psittacosis or parrot disease/fever. In about 1973, there were a number of cases of people dying of this in West Africa. It is basically a viral disease of parrots (and other birds) but can be transmitted to humans. Even so, there may be an older source. In the 17th and 18th centuries, there was an expression 'as melancholy as a (sick) parrot' –in the play *False Count* (1682) by Aphra Behn, for example. And Desmond Morris in *Catwatching* (1986) claims that the original expression was 'as sick as a parrot with a rubber beak', meaning that the animal was incapacitated without a sharp weapon, as also in the saying, 'no more chance than a cat in hell with no claws'. Another use for the phrase is to describe post-alcoholic dejection. Parrots will eagerly feed on rotting – and therefore alcoholic – fruit or fruit pulp. Hence 'pissed as a parrot' and, next day, 'sick as a parrot'.

sickbag　See I THINK WE SHOULD.

sic transit gloria mundi　Meaning, 'so passes away the glory of the world' – perhaps now mostly used ironically when something has failed. It is an allusion to *Of the Imitation of Christ* (*circa* 1420) by Thomas à Kempis: '*O quam cito transit gloria mundi* [O, how quickly the world's glory passes away].' It is used at the coronation ceremony of Popes when a reed surmounted with flax is burned and a chaplain intones: '*Pater sancte, sic transit gloria mundi*' to remind the new 'Holy Father' of the transitory nature of human vanity. *ODQ*, however, says it was used at the crowning of Alexander V at Pisa in July 1409 and is of earlier origin, which, if so, would mean that it was à Kempis who was doing the quoting.

Sidi Barrani　See DID I EVER TELL.

(a) sight for sore eyes　Something that is pleasant or welcome to look at. In *Are You*

a Bromide? (1907), the American writer Gelett Burgess castigated people who spoke in clichés. Among the 'Bromidioms' he listed was: 'You're a sight for sore eyes!' Jonathan Swift had earlier included it among the clichés in his *Polite Conversation* (1738). 'He has legs that don't quite match, a lolloping stride, an ungainly style, and a name that gives him no chance, but Kevin Twaddle was a sight for sore eyes as he did his own thing for St Johnstone in their 2–2 draw with St Mirren in Paisley' – *The Herald* (Glasgow) (14 November 1994); 'Here's a sight for sore eyes: the winners of the Spectacle Wearer of the Year Awards' – *Daily Record* (15 February 1995).

(a) significant other　The person with whom one is having a relationship or to whom one is actually married – though whom, for some reason of political correctness, one does not wish to describe in terms of dependency or dominance. Of American origin, since the mid-1980s. 'We are envious when we feel that the significant other has all the power. We feel envy in a relationship of one to one, jealousy in a relationship of one to two. When one partner in an alliance has all the power the other, however apparently loved and cherished, feels envy' – *The Sunday Times* (19 January 1986); 'After all, the business is becoming much more dangerous with Aids. But it seemed a little tactless to take this up with Sharon as she was by now heavily entangled with my significant other person' – *The Sunday Times* (2 November 1986); 'If there's anything I can stand less than the term Significant Other it's hearing its defence mounted in unblushing terms of political correctness' – *The Times* (14 May 1992).

(a) sign of the times　A portent or general indication of current trends. From Christ's words in Matthew 16:3: 'The sky is red and lowring. O ye hypocrites, ye can discern the face of the sky; but can ye not discern the signs of the times?' Hence, an expression used by everyone from Thomas Carlyle – as a book title, *Signs of the Times* (1829) – to the pop singer Prince, as an album title 'Sign 'o' the Times' (1987).

silence is golden　This encouragement to silence is from a Swiss inscription written in German and best known in the English translation by Thomas Carlyle: '*Sprechen ist silbern, Schweigen ist golden* [speech is silver(n), silence is golden].'

(the) silence of the lambs *The Silence of the Lambs* is the title of a novel (1989; film US 1990) by Thomas Harris. It comes from the childhood memories of Clarice Starling, a police investigator, who recalls lambs being rounded up for slaughter on the farm where she lived and her relief when the cries could no longer be heard. After dealing with the cannibal Hannibal Lecter, she 'sleeps deeply, sweetly in the silence of the lambs'.

silent but deadly (or **SBD)** Of a type of fart. Date of origin not known but probably not from before the 1990s. From Helen Fielding, *Bridget Jones: The Edge of Reason*, Chap. 11 (1999): 'In aeroplane in sky. Having to pretend to be very busy wearing walkman and writing as ghastly man next to self in pale brown synthetic-type suit keeps trying to talk to me in between silent but deadly farting.'

(the) silent majority Political phrase. An inevitable pairing. On 3 November 1969 President Richard Nixon gave a TV address on Vietnam and called for the support of a particular section of US opinion – 'the great silent majority of my fellow Americans', by which he meant Middle America or, at least, that part of the USA not involved in the vociferous anti-war protest movement. The previous year, in his speech accepting the Republican nomination, Nixon had already addressed this theme: 'The quiet voice in the tumult and the shouting . . . the voice of the great majority of Americans, the forgotten Americans – the non-shouters.' Earlier, the phrase had been used in the 19th century to describe the dead, as also the GREAT MAJORITY.

(a) silent witness Known by the time of William Cowper's poem *The Task* (1784): 'Act as a silent witness to countless invasions . . .' Compare MUTE WITNESSES. 'There weren't many other people around, and no one said a thing, though one or two mothers looked disapproving. Finally, I couldn't bear being a silent witness any longer, so I went over and asked her to stop. "I'm her nanny," she said angrily.

"It's none of your business what I do"' – *Independent on Sunday* (2 October 1994); 'More than anything, now, Taggart wanted to meet the man who had found the body. For everything in this case came down to the footprints. Snow was the silent witness' – *Daily Record* (24 December 1994).

silly See ASK A SILLY.

silly! Catchphrase of a bossy colonel (Graham Chapman) in BBC TV, *Monty Python's Flying Circus* (1969–74) – as in the edition of 7 December 1969. He would interrupt sketches, sometimes provide them with an ending and say that they were 'Silly!' His tenor, two-note enunciation of this word was much imitated at the time.

silly Billy Nickname for a foolish person. The most notable person to be given it as a nickname was William Frederick, 2nd Duke of Gloucester (1776–1834), uncle of William IV – though it was also applied to the king himself. In the wrangles between Whigs and Tories, when the king supported the former, Gloucester is reported to have asked, 'Who's Silly Billy now?' *Partridge/Slang* has Henry Mayhew in 1851 finding 'Silly Billy . . . very popular with the audience at the fairs' (as a clown's name for his stooge). In the 1970s, Mike Yarwood, the TV impressionist, put it in the mouth of the Labour politician Denis Healey, because it went rather well with the Healey persona and distinctive vocal delivery. Healey then imitated art by saying it himself. According to Alan Watkins in *The Observer* (13 January 1985), Randolph Churchill, the Conservative politician (and son of Winston), was also noted for using the expression.

silly (old) moo! Catchphrase of Alf Garnett (Warren Mitchell) in the BBC TV comedy series *Till Death Us Do Part* (1964–74). He would say either form of the phrase to his wife (Dandy Nichols). 'Moo' is a euphemism for 'cow'. Dandy Nichols said that people used to call it out to her in the street – affectionately, nonetheless.

(the) silly season Period of time around August/September when, for lack of hard news, newspapers traditionally fill their pages with frivolities. Although Parliament and the law courts are in recess and Britain (like France) increasingly seems to stop work for the month of August, the fact is that important news does *not* cease happening. The Soviet invasion of Czechoslovakia took place then, as did the resignation of President Nixon and the 1990 Gulf Crisis, not to mention the start of two world wars. The phrase was in use by 1861.

(the) silver screen The cinema screen – so called because of the light-reflecting coating that has traditionally been applied to it and that might be said to look silvery. But from the early 1920s the phrase was used to describe the whole phenomenon of the movies. The lyric for Noël Coward's song 'Mad About the Boy' (1932) includes the lines: 'I'm so ashamed of it / But must admit / The sleepless nights I've had about the boy. / On the Silver Screen / He melts my foolish heart in every single scene.' By 1936, there was a magazine with the title *Silver Screen.*

since Hector was a pup A very long time ago, way back when. Of American origin and mostly usage. Known by 1912. *Partridge/Catch Phrases* gives it as the 'US equivalent' of the various 'since . . .' expressions he lists, such as 'since Pontius was a pilot', and dates it '*circa* 1920'. *Morris* suggests that W. C. Fields spoke it in a film (unidentified) and that it was popularized by a 1920s' comic strip called *Polly and Her Pals.* It seems to be the case that, in the USA, large dogs were often named 'Hector' at the turn of the 19th/20th century. But it could also be an allusion to Hector in Homer's *Iliad* (when all schoolchildren knew who he was) and 'pup', as the once popular colloquialism for 'kid'. *Partridge* in mentioning an alleged Canadian version 'since Caesar was a pup' might seem to support this. Earlier, in James Fenimore Cooper's novel *The Prairie* (1828), there occurs the phrase, 'The dam of Hector was then a pup', but the relevance of this is not clear.

since time immemorial (or from . . .) For a very long time. Known by 1775 in the USA. 'It's been the custom here from time immemorial or thereabouts' – cartoon caption in *Punch* (29 April 1925); 'David Hart, general secretary of the National Association of Head Teachers, said the figures confirmed teachers' worst fears:

"There is no doubt we are facing the biggest funding crisis in many a long year, maybe since time immemorial and I think Professor Smithers' figures are political dynamite"' – *Times Educational Supplement* (7 April 1995).

since when I have used no other . . . Slogan for Pears' Soap in the UK, 1880s/ 90s. At one time, Pears' advertised through a signed testimonial (with picture) from Lillie Langtry, the actress and mistress of King Edward VII (when he was Prince of Wales): 'Since using Pears' Soap for the hands and complexion *I have discarded all others.*' This ad is undated and may have come before the cartoon parody of such testimonials drawn by Harry Furniss that appeared in *Punch* (26 April 1884). This showed a grubby tramp penning his own testimonial with the caption: 'Good Advertisement. I used your soap two years ago; since then I have used no other.' Not missing a trick, Pears, with permission from *Punch*, rearranged the words, added the firm's name to the cartoon and issued it as one of thousands of handbills distributed in the last two decades of the 19th century. The slogan was changed slightly to: 'Two years ago I used your soap *since when* I have used no other!'

(the) sinews of peace (or war) Winston Churchill's speech at Fulton, Missouri, on 5 March 1946, which introduced the old phrase IRON CURTAIN to a wider audience, was entitled 'The Sinews of Peace'. This was an allusion to the phrase '*nervi belli pecunia*' from Cicero's *Philippics* where the 'sinews of war' means 'money'. The 'sinews of peace' recommended by Churchill in dealing with the Soviet Union amounted to recourse to the newly formed United Nations Organization.

(the) singer not the song I.e. the conduit and not the thing itself. *The Singer Not the Song* was the title of novel (1959) by Audrey Erskine Lindop (film UK 1960) in which a relationship is depicted between a bandit and a priest. The bandit is able to accept the priest but not his message (the singer not the song . . .). Lindop acknowledged that the phrase came from a West Indian calypso. This turned out to be 'Come With Me My Honey', credited to David/Whitney/Kramer and recorded, for example, by Edmundo Ros (in 1944). It contains the line: 'The singer not the song, that's the sound of calypso Joe.' Compare, from W. S. Gilbert, *Iolanthe*, Act 1 (1882): 'Thou the singer; I the song' from Strephon and Phyllis's duet, 'None Shall Part Us From Each Other'.

(to) sing from the same sheet of music (or ... song sheet) 'To operate according to the same plan or agreement, to act according to the same set of principles'. A phrase from British industrial and trade union parlance, possibly influenced by the Welsh choral tradition. 'Parker sums it up: "At Belfast shipyard we have only lost 0.05% of our man hours over the last 10 years. We are all singing from the same sheet of music' – *The Sunday Times* (20 October 1985); 'So the next time a dispute breaks out, both sides could be singing from the same convoluted hymn book' – *Independent on Sunday* (23 February 2003).

singing See ALL-SINGING.

(the) singing sands Long-established term for sands that appear to make a noise. The caption to a cartoon in *Punch* (22 August 1923): 'Lord Curzon's forthcoming book of travel, his publishers state, will contain "a full and picturesque study of the Singing Sands, i.e. the sand slopes and dunes which in remote and often inaccessible parts of Asia, Arabia and even America, give forth sounds which resemble the noise of trumpets and drums".' *The Singing Sands* is the title of a Josephine Tey crime novel (1952) in which the whole plot hinges on a fragment of verse scribbled on a newspaper by a dying man: 'The beasts that talk, / The streams that stand, / The stones that walk, / The singing sand, . . . / That guard the way / To Paradise.' The detective in question – Inspector Grant – is reduced to putting an advert in *The Times* to find the source and thinks: 'It will serve me right if someone writes to say that the thing is one of the best-known lines of some Xanadu concoction of Coleridge's, and that I must be illiterate not to have known it.' But it does not appear to be an actual quotation.

sinking See BOVRIL PREVENTS.

sister See AGONY SISTER.

sir, you are speaking of the woman I love! Pompous assertion on behalf of a woman who has been spoken ill of. From dramas (almost melodramas) of the 1880s/90s and now used as a conscious archaism. 'Gad, my wife looks terrible tonight!' 'Sir, you are speaking of the woman I love!' – caption to a cartoon by Peter Arno, included in *Parade* (1931).

(to) sit about like Joe Egg From Peter Nichols, *A Day in the Death of Joe Egg*, Act 2 (1967): 'My grandma used to say, "Sitting about like Joe Egg," when she meant she had nothing to do.' Hence, the title of the play.

(to) sit in the cat-bird seat To be sitting pretty. James Thurber investigated this phrase in a story entitled 'The Catbird Seat' in *The Thurber Carnival* (1945). A mild-mannered accountant contemplates murdering a colleague because she is always using quaint but obscure American phrases like these. It turns out that she took them from Red Barber, an actual baseball commentator on the Brooklyn Dodgers' team games *circa* 1945–55, who got them 'down South'. In a letter to the *Saturday Review* in 1976, Barber described how he had encountered the expression in a stud poker game where another player, who had a pair of aces, had described himself as 'sitting in the cat-bird seat'. A catbird is an American thrush that chooses to sing from a lofty perch, prominent, advantageous and away from all danger.

sitting See ARE YOU SITTING.

situation See ONGOING.

situation hopeless but not serious The basic format here is 'situation — but not – –'. The film *Situation Hopeless But Not Serious* (US 1965) derived its title from what has been called an Austrian saying: 'The situation in Germany is serious but not hopeless; the situation in Austria is hopeless but not serious.' Conan Doyle in 'The Second Stain', *The Return of Sherlock Holmes* (1905), has the basic saying, 'The situation is desperate, but not hopeless.'

situation normal all fucked up See SNAFU.

(to be at) sixes and sevens Meaning, 'to be confused; in an unresolved situation'; the usual origin given for this expression is that in the days when the medieval guilds of London took pride in their order of precedence, the Merchant Taylors and the Skinners could not agree who should be sixth, and who seventh. After an intervention by the Lord Mayor, they agreed to take it in turns – as they do to this day. *Apperson*, on the other hand, supports the theory that the idiom dates from a dice game (as mentioned by Chaucer in one of his poems) in which the dice bore marks up to seven, if not further: 'Only a confused or disorganized person would roll for this point' (i.e. a 'six and seven'). This is the origin favoured by *OED2*. Shakespeare's only use of the phrase occurs in *Richard II*, II.ii.122 (1595): 'All is uneven, / And everything is left at six and seven.' In *Pericles*, IV.vi.74 (1609), Shakespeare may be making a punning allusion to it when (in a sexual context) Lysimachus says: 'Did you go to't [copulate] young? Were you a gamester at five or at seven?'

six of one and half a dozen of the other Phrase describing a situation where there is no difference, especially where blame is to be laid. Wilkie Collins, *No Name* (1862), has: 'Six of one, and half a dozen of the other; and mine are the biggest – that's all!' The Reverend Francis Kilvert, the English diarist, wrote (6 September 1878): 'There was a great deal of talk at that time in London about the quarrel between the King [George IV] and the Queen [Caroline]. There was about six for one and half a dozen for the other'.

sixpence See BANG GOES.

(the) sixty-four (thousand) dollar question 'Ah, that's the sixty-four dollar question, isn't it?' some people will exclaim, when surely they mean 'sixty-four *thousand*'. Or do they? Put it down to inflation. *Webster's Dictionary* says that $64 *was* the highest award in a CBS radio quiz called *Take It or Leave It*, which ran from 1941 to 1948 and in which the value of the prize doubled every time the contestant got a right answer (in the progression 1–2–4–8–16–32–64 – hence the title *Double Your Money* given to the first of the British TV versions). This is how the saying entered common parlance, meaning 'that is the question which would solve all our problems if only we knew the answer

to it'. An example of the original use in the 1950s is contained in a *Daily Express* article about P. G. Wodehouse written by Rene McColl (undated): '"Wodehouse, Esq.", I observed, "Could I, to use the vernacular of this our host nation, pop the jolly old 64-dollar question? If you were back in Germany, a prisoner, and you had it all to do again – would you do it?"' Subsequently, in the US TV version of the show (1955–7), the top prize did go up to $64,000 – though, cunningly, when ITV imported the show for British viewers shortly afterwards (1956–8), the title was simply *The 64,000 Question* or *Challenge*, making no mention of the denomination of currency involved. In February 1989, I heard a female weather forecaster on ITV being asked, 'Is the mild weather going to continue?' She replied, 'That's the sixty-four million dollar question.' So inflation is still rampant.

size does matter (or doesn't matter) Phrase alluding to the old question of whether 'penis size is unimportant', which is described as a 'Naff sexual myth' in *The Complete Naff Guide* (1983). From Alex Comfort, *The Joy of Sex* (1972): 'The irrational male preoccupation with penile size. Size has absolutely nothing to do with their physical serviceability in intercourse . . . though many women are turned on by the idea of a large one . . . Smaller ones work equally well in most positions . . . Excessive preoccupation with size is an irrational anxiety.' The idea is much played with. 'The programme's handling of sex . . . [includes] one planned item [looking] at things people say to each afterwards ("You were fantastic; of course size doesn't matter")' – *The Times* (30 May 1990); 'Does this prove once and for all that size does matter?' – James Cameron, director of the film *Titanic* on winning an award, quoted in *The Observer* (25 January 1998); 'Where size doesn't have to matter' – headline over article on charities in *The Independent* (11 May 1998); 'Size does matter' – slogan for film *Godzilla* (US 1998); 'Size matters' – slogan for Renault Clio motorcar, in the UK (1998).

skin See COULDN'T KNOCK THE; GET UNDER.

sky-blue pink with a finny haddy border Fobbing-off phrase. 'This was my mother's invariable answer to any question when we were children' – Julie Hickson (2000). Compare 'sky-blue tail', 'bottom pink' and 'little thin flowery border' under NEAT BUT NOT GAUDY. Marjorie Wild, Devon (2000), recalled 'sky-blue-pink' and 'sandy-grey-russet' as nonsense descriptions. 'As a small child, when I asked an Aunt what was the colour of something, she would teasingly reply, "Sky-blue scarlet, the colour of a mouse's fart" – to the annoyance of other adults. I have never heard this from anyone else, and have no idea whether or not it was my Aunt's original' – Mrs J. Jones, Shropshire (1993). Well, *Partridge/Slang* has 'sky-blue pink' for 'colour unknown or indeterminate', since about 1885. *Casson/Grenfell* has, in answer to the question, 'What shall I wear?' – 'Sky blue pink.'

skylark See ANY MORE FOR.

(the) sky's the limit There is no upper limit of opportunity, especially of money to be earned or spent. There are no constraints on any activity. In Motteux's 1700–3 translation of Cervantes, *Don Quixote*, there is 'No limits but the sky' (Pt 1, Bk 3, Chap. 3). *The Sky's the Limit* became the title of a TV quiz in the UK (from 1971) where air miles and spending money were awarded to would-be tourists. 'Mr Bryhn said it was up to the successful bidder exactly how to gain most benefit from their space advertisement. "The sky's the limit, there are endless possibilities," he said' – *The Independent* (12 August 1995); '"I would never do anything involving children being beaten or people suffering from Aids or cancer," De Caunes says in his defence. "But otherwise I'd say the sky's the limit"' –*The Independent* (17 February 1996).

slap See BETTER THAN A SLAP.

slaving See HERE AM I.

(a) sleeping giant (or lion) Something that should not be disturbed lest it provoke dreadful consequences. 'Wake not a sleeping lion' is a proverbial view known by 1580; the fairy tale 'Jack and the Beanstalk' (1730s) turns very much on what happens when a giant is asleep and is then woken. 'China? There lies a sleeping giant. Let him sleep! For when he wakes he will move the world' – is a

saying attributed to Napoleon; 'Australian Sydney, with a magic like sleep . . . a vast, endless, sun-hot, afternoon sleep with the world a mirage . . . But surely a place that will some day wake terribly from this sleep' – D. H. Lawrence, *Kangaroo*, Chap. 16 (1923); 'I fear all we have done is to awaken a sleeping giant, and filled him with a terrible resolve' – attributed to Admiral Yamamoto, commander of the Japanese forces that attacked Pearl Harbor, though the only suggestion that he said any such thing is in the screenplay of *Tora! Tora! Tora!* (US 1970).

(a) sleeping policeman (or dead policeman) Phrases conveying a dead weight (from the fact that policeman traditionally are burly, solid persons). 'Of course we were dead tired, and slept like policemen' – Mark Twain, *A Tramp Abroad*, Chap. 28 (1880); 'Well, it's better than a night in bed with a dead policeman' – included in my book *The Gift of the Gab* (1985); 'Better than sleeping with a dead policeman/better than a drowned policeman' – included in *Partridge/Catch Phrases* (1985), the second phrase known by 1932. A 'sleeping policeman' has been the name used in the UK for a raised hump in the road for traffic-slowing purposes since 1973.

sleeping with the enemy Originally, this phrase was used by lesbian separatists to describe their 'sisters' who persisted in heterosexual dalliances, hence the enemy was 'men'. From Jill Johnston, *Lesbian Nation: The Feminist Solution* (1973): 'Feminists who still sleep with men are delivering their most vital energies to the oppressor.' Used as the title of a film (US 1991), about marital violence, in which the 'enemy' was an individual man. A Mexican proverb is said to observe that 'Marriage is the only war where one sleeps with the enemy.'

(to) sleep the sleep of the just To sleep very soundly, as though one's conscience is not keeping one awake. Date and source unknown. *'Elle s'endormit du sommeil des justes* [she fell asleep and slept the sleep of the just]' – Jean Racine, *Abrége de l'Histoire de Port Royal* (written *circa* 1699); 'Sir Michael was sleeping the sleep of the just' – William Thackeray, *Vanity Fair*, Chap. 43 (1847–8).

sleeve See ACE IN.

sliced bread See GREATEST THING SINCE.

(a) slice off a cut loaf is never missed In other words, it doesn't matter having a bit on the side once you've taken the plunge and got married. In her autobiography, *Billie Whitelaw: Who He?* (1995), the actress recounts how her mother drew her aside when she was about to get married for the first time and told her to remember this bit of advice. 'After forty years I'm still trying to work out what she meant.' Well, I took it upon myself to tell her. One has to say that it was an extraordinary thing for a mother to say on such an occasion. But it is a very old saying indeed. *Apperson* has it as, 'It is safe taking a shive [= slice] of a cut loaf' and traces it back to Shakespeare, *Titus Andronicus* (II.i.87): 'What, man! more water glideth by the mill / Than wots the miller of; and easy it is / Of a cut loaf to steal a shive, we know.' *Partridge/Slang* has it that 'to take a slice' means 'to intrigue, particularly with a married woman'.

(a) slice of life Phrase used to describe a realistic and detailed portrait in novels, plays, paintings, etc., of incidents from everyday life. Apparently derived from the French *tranche de la vie*, used to describe French naturalist literature by J. Jullien in *Art et Critique* (9 August 1890). In English by 1895. 'A Slice of Life' is the title of a story (1926) by P. G. Wodehouse.

slightly foxed Term used in second-hand bookselling to denote a work for sale that is slightly soiled by discoloration but has no major damage to it. From the original use of the phrase to describe reddish-brown or brownish-yellow stains on a book or print. In use by 1847. Also figuratively about anything less than good. 'The rest of the concert consisted of Elgar's "Cockaigne" Overture and the quintessential Holst, Egdon Heath – both carefully sympathetic, a bit over-literal and prosaic, slightly foxed by small fluffs – and the Brahms Double Concerto' – *Financial Times* (12 September 1983).

(to) sling one's hook To go/run away. 'Sling your hook' has been defined as 'a polite invitation to move on'. This British slang expression dates from the 19th century (recorded by 1874), but no one seems too sure where it comes from. One reasonable explanation is that 'hook' in this context means 'anchor', so it means the equivalent of slipping or weighing anchor. *The ABZ of Scouse* (1966) suggests rather that the reference is to a Liverpool docker's loading hook.

(to) slip into something more comfortable To change into more sexually alluring clothes. After the line spoken by Helen (Jean Harlow) to Monte (Ben Lyon) in the film *Hell's Angels* (US 1930): 'Would you be shocked if I put on something more comfortable?' Invariably misquoted – e.g. 'Do you mind if I put on something more comfortable?' or 'Excuse me while I slip into something more comfortable'. 'Pardon me while I slip into something more comfortable' was perpetrated by Denis Gifford in *The Independent* (22 July 1995). What 'Helen' says is, of course, by way of a proposition, and she duly exchanges her fur wrap for a dressing gown.

slippery heels See ROUND HEELS.

slow, slow, quick, quick, slow Dance tempo spoken by Victor Sylvester (1902–78), the British ballroom dance instructor and band leader, on radio from 1941 and on TV from the 1950s. It became associated with him like a catchphrase. The tempo is for the quickstep. In December 1988, poster advertisements for the Rover 200 series compared start-up speeds for two Rover models and a BMW under the heading, 'Quick, Quick, Slow'.

small beer Something unimportant, inconsequential, trivial. Originally this meant 'weak' beer, but the newer meaning derives from a number of references in Shakespeare, notably *Othello*, II.i.160 (1604): 'She was a wight, if ever such wight were . . . / To suckle fools, and chronicle small beer.'

small, but perfectly formed When first encountered in the 1960s/70s, this was thought to be of theatrical, possibly American show-biz, origin. In the BBC radio show *Round the Horne* there was a 'tiny but perfect' (17 April 1966), 'tiny but perfect in every detail' (5 March 1967) and 'tiny but perfectly proportioned' (22 May and 4 June 1967). Then in 1973 there was a 'small but perfectly proportioned' in Alan

Bennett's play *Habeas Corpus*, Act 2 (1973). Citations from earlier than this, however, seemed to suggest it was a phrase from social small-talk and gossip. James Lees-Milne in his diary entry for 21 June 1949 (published in *Midway on the Waves*, 1985) wrote of Princess Margaret: 'In size she is a midget but perfectly made.' In 1983, when Artemis Cooper published *A Durable Fire – The Letters of Duff and Diana Cooper* [her grandparents] *1913–50*, a letter was revealed from Duff to Diana in October 1914 in which he wrote: 'That is the sort of party I like . . . You must think I have enjoyed it too, with your two stout lovers frowning at one another across the hearth rug, while your small, but perfectly formed one kept the party in a roar.' From the use of fashionable slang elsewhere in the letters, I would suppose that this coinage was not original to Cooper but drawn from the smart talk of the period. But could it have come from anywhere else? The 'small, but . . .' construction appears earlier in the German saying '*klein, aber mein* [small, but my own]' and in the line from 'Ode to Evening' (1747) by William Collins: 'Or where the beetle winds / His small but sullen horn' (where 'sullen' = 'of a deep, dull or mournful tone'). A search in the works of Charles Darwin (whose favourite adverb is 'perfectly') produced a 'small but perfect' and an 'extraordinarily small but perfect'. The exact phrase *does* occur, however, in Henry David Thoreau's 'The Allegash and East Branch' (an essay on which he was working when he died in 1862) in *The Maine Woods*: 'I now first began to be seriously molested by the black-fly, a very small but perfectly formed fly of that color, about one-tenth of an inch long.' Obviously, the phrase is not applied here to a person, as is usual in our own time. John Julius Norwich (Duff Cooper's son) commented on this revelation: 'I can't think my Papa was consciously quoting Thoreau – a thing he very seldom did – but he was surely quoting a quoter.'

small earthquake in Chile See NOT MANY DEAD.

(to go to the) smallest room Loophemism. The *OED2*'s earliest citation for this phrase also contains another loophemism: 'It is all very baffling for the uninitiated foreigner, who when his host offers to "show him the geography of the house" finds that his tour begins and ends with the smallest room' – A. Lyall, *It Isn't Done* (1930).

small is beautiful The title of a book published in 1973 by Professor E. F. Schumacher (1911–77) provided a catchphrase and a slogan for those who were opposed to an expansionist trend in business and organizations that was very apparent in the 1960s and 70s and who wanted 'economics on a human scale'. It appears, however, that he very nearly didn't come up with the phrase. According to his daughter and another correspondent writing to *The Observer* (29 April/6 June 1984), the book was going to be called 'The Homecomers'. His publisher, Anthony Blond, suggested 'Small*ness* is Beautiful', and then Desmond Briggs, the co-publisher, came up with the eventual wording.

smarter than the average bear, (Booboo) Said of himself by Yogi Bear to his sidekick, Booboo, in the American Yogi Bear cartoon TV series (started 1958). The character was voiced by Charles 'Daws' Butler. At his death in May 1988, it was suggested, perhaps mistakenly, that he had coined the phrase as well.

(a) smarty boots Derogatory term for a clever person. It was Virginia Woolf's nickname for the critic and writer Cyril Connolly and referred to by Evelyn Waugh in a published letter (5 January 1946). Of US origin and probably preceded by **smarty pants** (recorded by 1941).

smasher See DON'T FORCE IT.

smashing, lovely, super! A *real* catchphrase based on the enthusiastic mutterings of the British comedian Jim Bowen (b. 1937) when hosting a darts-orientated TV game called *Bullseye* (since 1981). In other words, it was not calculated as a catchphrase but was noticed by the audience and it just caught on . . . The order of the words was variable and when Bowen appeared in poster ads for Skol Lager (1993–4), the copy line was 'Great, smashing, super'. From *The Independent* (4 December 1992): 'Jim Bowen is a student hero. In common rooms across the country, they hunker down to watch his show . . . to see if Jim will engage his guests in the small talk beloved of his *Spitting Image* puppet: "Just look at what you could have won! Lovely, smashing, super".' According to an anecdote, Bowen admits himself to having enthused similarly when a female contestant on the TV show informed him that her husband had died.

smelling of roses See EVERYTHING'S COMING UP.

(to) smell of the lamp (Of literary composition) to appear to be the result of laborious, effortful nocturnal study. Oil lamps had a characteristic smell so, in the original circumstances, this might be transferred to the paper and give the game away. North's translation of Plutarch's 'Demosthenes' (1579) has Pytheas taunting Demosthenes with the charge that 'his reasons smelled of the lampe.' In Laurence Sterne, *Tristram Shandy*, Chap. 23 (1759–67), has: 'I should have no objection to this method, but that I think it must smell too strong of the lamp.'

smile, you're on *Candid Camera*! The American broadcaster Allen Funt translated his practical joke radio programme *Candid Microphone* to TV, and it ran from 1948 to 1978 (there was a British version, too). On revealing to members of the public that they had been hoaxed, this was his somewhat hopeful greeting – hopeful that they would not take it badly.

smoke and mirrors Trickery and illusion in politics. From William Safire, *New Political Dictionary* (1993): 'Jimmy Breslin coined the term in a 1975 book, *How the Good Guys Finally Won,* about House Speaker Tip O'Neill's involvement in the removal of Richard Nixon from the Presidency. Quoting Thomas Hobbes's "The reputation of power is power," Breslin opined that political power is primarily an illusion: "Mirrors and blue smoke, beautiful blue smoke rolling over the surface of highly polished mirrors, first a thin veil of blue smoke, then a thick cloud that suddenly dissolves into wisps of blue smoke, the mirrors catching it all, bouncing it back and forth. If somebody tells you how to look, there can be seen in the smoke great, magnificent shapes, castles and kingdoms, and maybe they can be yours."' 'The "blue smoke and mirrors" of Reaganomics, said Mr Mondale, had caused industrial blight to descend on once prosperous states' – *The Economist* (12 May 1984).

(a) smoke-filled room Traditional site of American political wheeler-dealing – a vivid phrase evoking cigar-smoking political bosses coming to a decision after much horse-trading. Suite 408–409–410 (previously rooms 804–5) of the Blackstone Hotel in Chicago was the original 'smoke-filled room' in which Warren Harding was selected as the Republican Party's Presidential candidate in June 1920. Although he denied saying it, the phrase seems to have come out of a prediction by Harding's chief supporter, Harry Daugherty (1860–1941). He foresaw that the convention would not be able to decide between the two obvious candidates and that a group of senators 'bleary-eyed for lack of sleep [would have to] sit down about two o'clock in the morning around a table in a smoke-filled room in some hotel and decide the nomination' – *The New York Times* (21 February 1920). This was precisely what happened and Harding duly emerged as the candidate. *ODMQ* (1991) cites a news report dated 12 June 1920 from Kirke Simpson of the Associated Press: '[Warren] Harding of Ohio was chosen by a group of men in a smoke-filled room early today as Republican candidate for President.' But this is clearly alluding to an already established phrase.

(a) smoking gun (or **pistol)** Meaning 'incriminating evidence', as though a person holding a smoking gun could be assumed to have committed an offence with it – as in Conan Doyle's Sherlock Holmes story 'The "Gloria Scott"' (1894): 'Then we rushed on into the captain's cabin . . . and there he lay . . . while the chaplain stood, with a smoking pistol in his hand.' The term was popularized during Watergate. For example, Representative Barber Conable said of a tape of President Nixon's conversation with H. R. Haldeman, his chief of staff, on 23 June 1972, containing discussion of how the FBI's investigation of the Watergate burglary could be limited,

'I guess we have found the smoking pistol, haven't we?' 'As President Bush so vividly says, "The smoking gun will be a mushroom cloud"' – *The Spectator* (14/21 December 2002).

SNAFU Acronym for 'Situation Normal All Fouled/Fucked Up'. American origin, probably from the services, by early in the Second World War.

snap! crackle! pop! Slogan for Kellogg's Rice Krispies, in the USA from *circa* 1928, later in the UK, supposedly from the noises caused when milk is poured over the cereal. There has been more than one version. An early one: 'It pops! It snaps! It crackles!' Something of a red herring has been raised by H. R. F. Keating, the crime writer, who in an introduction to a reprint of *Epitaph for a Spy* by Eric Ambler, wrote that the immortal phrase had been coined by Ambler when working in advertising before becoming a thriller writer (in the great tradition of copywriters-turned-novelists). But no, Ambler said it was someone else at the agency he worked for. As Ambler worked in advertising 1929–35, it would seem likely that the slogan had been coined before he started anyway. It is certain, too, that the slogan was coined in the USA rather than in the UK.

(to) snatch victory from the jaws of defeat A picturesque expression, date of origin unknown but certainly in use at the time of the American Civil War. From the *Valley Spirit* (Virginia) (1 April 1863): 'Let us take courage, then. With a vigorous, concerted campaign, the mismanagement of the last two years may yet be retrieved. We may yet snatch victory from the jaws of defeat. The armed power of the rebellion may be broken, and the conservative sentiment of the country, discarding alike the radicalism of the Secessionists and the Abolitionists, may yet save the country.' The reverse expression, that so-and-so 'snatched defeat out of the jaws of victory', also seems to date from the American Civil War. Although no precise record of the phrase being used has been found, it is often claimed that Abraham Lincoln said it of General Ambrose Everett Burnside whose Fredericksburg campaign for the Union Army was a disaster. Lincoln relieved him of his command in January 1863.

s'n'f (or **shopping and fucking)** Term for a type of pulp fiction wherein the heroines devote their lives to these activities (though not simultaneously, as a rule). Sometimes known as **s'n's** – for 'sex and shopping'. In fact, shopping is not really the other activity – it is more the author's lingering descriptions of clothes and property, often with the designer labels still attached. 'These Sidney Sheldon, Judith Krantz, Jackie Collins, Shirley Conran books have the generic title of s'n'f' – *The Guardian* (6 February 1986). A play by Mark Ravenhill was entitled *Shopping and Fucking* (though often abbreviated to *Shopping and F***ing*) in 1996.

snippy See YOU DON'T HAVE TO BE.

snobbery with violence In its obituary for Colin Watson, the detective story writer (21 January 1983), *The Times* mentioned his book *Snobbery with Violence* (1971) – a survey of the modern crime story – 'from which the phrase comes'. As usual, there is an earlier example of the phrase in use: 'Sapper, Buchan, Dornford Yates, practitioners in that school of Snobbery with Violence that runs like a thread of good-class tweed through twentieth-century literature' – Alan Bennett, *Forty Years On*, Act 2 (1969). In his preface to the published text of *Forty Years On and Other Plays* (1991), Bennett states that he thought he *had* invented the phrase but was then told it had been used even before him: it was the title of a pamphlet by the New Zealand eccentric, Count Potocki de Montalk. *Snobbery with Violence. A Poet in Gaol* was published in 1932.

'sno use (i.e. **it's no use)** Catchphrase of the British music-hall performer Harry Weldon (1881–1930). From a Matthew Norgate theatre programme article *circa* 1980: '[Weldon's] catch-phrase was "Sno use" with the "s" uttered in an ear-drum-piercing whistle without which Weldon could pronounce no "s". But unlike [Fred] Kitchen's [MEREDITH, WE'RE IN], his catch-phrase was appropriate, and used appropriately, to every situation in which he found himself, and indicative of his claim . . . to be an artist as well as an artiste.'

snow-capped mountains (or **peaks)** Both versions known by the 1870s. Part of the 'travel scribes' armoury' compiled from a competition in *The Guardian* (10 April 1993). 'On a four-day official visit to Morocco, the indomitable Ms Boothroyd had travelled from Marrakesh with a friend on Easter Saturday high into the snow-capped Atlas Mountains for lunch' – *The Guardian* (19 April 1995); 'The plants look quite at home in North Wales. Behind looms the northern edge of the Welsh mountains, presided over by the snow-capped mass of Snowdon' – *The Daily Telegraph* (29 April 1995).

snowing down south See IT'S.

snug as a bug in a rug Meaning, 'well-fitting and/or extremely warm and comfortable'. Usually ascribed to Benjamin Franklin, the American writer and philosopher, who mentioned a type of epitaph in a letter to Miss Georgiana Shipley (26 September 1772) on the death of her pet squirrel, 'Skugg': 'Here Skugg lies snug / As a bug in a rug.' But there are earlier uses. In an anonymous work, *Stratford Jubilee* (commemorating David Garrick's Shakespeare festival in 1769), is: 'If she [a rich widow] has the mopus's [money] / I'll have her, as snug as a bug in a rug.' Probably, however, it was an established expression even by that date, if only because in 1706 Edward Ward in *The Wooden World Dissected* had the similar 'He sits as snug a Bee in a Box' and in Thomas Heywood's play *A Woman Killed with Kindness* (1603) there is 'Let us sleep as snug as pigs in pease-straw.'

sob sister See AGONY AUNT.

(a/the) social contract Jean-Jacques Rousseau's *Du contrat social* was published in 1762 and his, Hobbes's and Locke's use of the phrase 'social contract' was in terms of a compact between a government and a whole people, rather than with just one section of it. Nevertheless, while it was in Opposition from 1970 to 1974, the British Labour Party developed an idea of a social 'compact' between government and trades unions. In return for certain 'social' measures, like price subsidies, the unions would moderate their wage demands. This, in turn, meant that unpopular voluntary or statutory incomes' policies could be aban-

doned. Coinage of the term 'social contract', in this specific sense, has been credited to Dennis (later Lord) Lyons, a public relations consultant who advised the Labour Party in five general elections. 'We say that what Britain needs is a new Social Contract. That is what this document is all about' – James Callaghan, British Prime Minister, referring to *Labour's Programme* at the Labour Party Conference (2 October 1972). Anthony Wedgwood Benn had earlier used the term in a Fabian pamphlet, *The New Politics* (1970).

society See AFFLUENT.

sock it to me! Catchphrase from NBC TV, *Rowan and Martin's Laugh-In* (1967–73). Spoken by the English actress Judy Carne (b. 1939) who became known as the Sock-It-To-Me Girl. She would appear and chant the phrase until – ever unsuspecting – something dreadful happened to her. She would be drenched with a bucket of water, fall through a trap door, get blown up or find herself shot from a cannon. The phrase 'to sock it to someone' originally meant 'to put something bluntly' (and was used as such by Mark Twain). Black jazz musicians gave it a sexual meaning, as in 'I'd like to sock it to *her*'. The precise way in which this old phrase came to be adopted by *Laugh-In* was described by Judy Carne in 1980: 'George Schlatter, the producer, had had great success in America with a show starring Ernie Kovacs in the 1950s. The wife on that show used to get a pie in the face every week and got enormous sympathy mail as a result. So George wanted a spot where an actress would have *horrendous* things done to her each week – a sort of "PERILS OF PAULINE" thing – and then find a catchphrase to fit it.' In the summer of 1967, Aretha Franklin had a hit record with 'Respect', which featured a chorus repeating 'Sock it to me' quite rapidly in the background. The same thing occurred subsequently in her 1970 recording of 'Son of a Preacher Man'. The previous year there had also been a disc called 'Sock it to 'em, J.B.' by Rex Garvin with Mighty Craven, and in February 1967 an LP entitled 'Sock it to me, baby' had come from Mitch Ryder and the Detroit Wheels. But Aretha Franklin's record was where the *Laugh-In* catchphrase came from, Carne insisted. 'George came up with the idea of making it literal. I said, "Well it should be Cockney." He said, "How far are you prepared to go?" And I said, "I'll do anything for a laugh. If I'm safe, I don't mind what you do to me." It all happened very fast . . . in about three weeks we were No. 1 with 50 million people watching. The sayings caught on at exactly the same time the show did . . . It had a dirty connotation and it was also very clean and was great for the kids. That's why I think that it took off the way it did – because it appealed to everyone at one level or another.' On being known as the Sock-It-To-Me Girl, Carne said: 'It got in the way for a while. You have to go through a period of living a tag like that down, and proving that you are not just a saying. The main thing is not to identify with it, not to sit about worrying that people think of you as a saying. But better they think of you as a saying than not at all.' Among the guests on the show who spoke the line were John Wayne, Mae West, Jack Lemmon, Jimmy Durante, Marcel Marceau (even) and Richard Nixon. The latter, running for the US presidency, said it on the broadcast of 16 September 1968. He pronounced it in a perplexed manner: 'Sock it to *me?*' And, lo, they finally did.

socks See BLESS HIS LITTLE.

sod this for a game of soldiers (or **beggar this . . .** or **blow that . . .** or **fuck this . . .)** Expression signifying that one is giving up some activity through exhaustion or disillusionment. 'Beggar' is, of course, a soft form of 'bugger', but quite what is meant by a 'game of soldiers' in either version of the expression is not totally clear. Perhaps the speaker considers the activity being abandoned as pointless as a game of toy soldiers or as futile as the 'ARMY GAME' (life as a professional soldier). Compare FUCK THIS (OR THAT) FOR A LARK! Perhaps none of these date from before the Second World War. 'I met him in the pub one summer. I'd just been stood up by a man I was having a relationship with. Blow that for a game of soldiers, I thought, when suddenly Jim appeared from one corner of the pub and offered me a drink' – *Independent on Sunday* (13 February 1994).

so, farewell then Stock phrase from the drab poems of 'E. J. Thribb' that have graced *Private Eye*'s 'Poetry Corner' since the 1970s. Most of them celebrate, in an off-hand way, the recent deaths of famous people, and usually begin, 'So, farewell then . . .' 'So farewell then Kenneth Williams . . .' – headline in *The Observer* (17 April 1988).

soft as a brush See DAFT AS A BRUSH.

softly, softly catchee monkee Said by *Benham* (1948) to be a 'Negro proverb'. Hence, the title of a BBC TV police drama series *Softly Softly* (1966–76), which came, more particularly, from the motto of the Lancashire Constabulary Training School that had inspired it.

(a) soft-shoe shuffle A kind of gliding dance in which the performer gently scrapes the floor with the sole of the shoe. An alliterative invention, building upon the adjectival 'soft-shoe' to describe a type of tap-dance without metal plates on the shoe. The latter phrase may have been in use by about 1905.

(the) soft underbelly The vulnerable part of something. Speaking to the House of Commons on 11 November 1942, Winston Churchill said: 'We make this wide encircling movement in the Mediterranean . . . having for its object the exposure of the under-belly of the Axis, especially Italy, to heavy attack.' In his *The Second World War*, Vol. 4, Churchill describes a meeting with Stalin before this, in August 1942, at which he had outlined the same plan: 'To illustrate my point I had meanwhile drawn a picture of a crocodile, and explained to Stalin with the help of this picture how it was our intention to attack the soft belly of the crocodile as we attacked his hard snout.' Somewhere, subsequently, the 'soft' and the 'underbelly' must have joined together to produce the phrase in the form in which it is now used.

so help me God See I SWEAR.

(to be) sold a pup To be sold something that is worthless, to be cheated. Presumably from the act of selling a small dog when a larger, trained animal is expected, a fairground practice well established by 1901. Compare LET THE CAT OUT OF THE BAG.

(to be) sold down the river   Meaning 'to be betrayed', this expression is of American origin. In the South, after 1808, it was illegal to import slaves, so they were brought down the Mississippi to the slave markets of Natchez and New Orleans. Hence, if a slave was 'sold down the river', he lost his home and family. The saying particularly relates to the practice of selling troublesome slaves to the owners of plantations on the lower Mississippi where conditions were harsher than in the Northern slave states. Mark Twain's novel *Pudd'nhead Wilson* (1894) is dominated by this theme and the expression occurs in it some fifteen times, e.g.: '"Very good," said the master, putting up his watch, "I will sell you *here*, though you don't deserve it. You ought to be sold down the river".' In British, though not American, English there is the comparable expression '**down** (or **up**) the **Swanee**', which *Partridge/Catch Phrases* defines as 'on the slippery slope, or already gone to perdition, bankruptcy and ruin'. Gordon B. Chamberlain commented (2001): 'Americans can be sold down the (Mississippi) river, sent up the (Hudson) to Sing Sing, or trapped up a creek without a paddle, but "way down upon the Swanee river", like "that Swanee shore", refers to the banks of this river, not its waters.' Indeed, it would seem that this is a British reconstruction of the phrase 'sold down the river', incorporating the name of an actual river (known from the Stephen Foster song 'The Old Folks at Home/Swanee River', 1851), though actually the name is Suwannee river (it runs from Georgia through Florida to the Gulf of Mexico).

soldier   See THAT IS WHAT THE.

(a) soldier's farewell   An insulting farewell that takes various forms, e.g. 'Goodbye and fuck you!' Known since before the First World War. By the Second World War a 'soldier's farewell' was also used to describe maintenance payments payable by the father of an illegitimate child . . .

somebody bawl for Beulah?   This was the cry of Beulah, the cheery Black housemaid who was a supporting character in the American radio series *Fibber McGee and Molly* but went on to have her own radio show – *Beulah* – and TV series

in the period 1944–54. Five people played her over the years – originally she was played by a white *man*. She would also say **on the con-positively-trary!** and **love that man!** (after laughing uproariously at one of Fibber McGee's jokes). From the same show came wife Molly's response to jokes: **t'ain't funny, McGee!** and next-door neighbour Gildersleeve's **you're a hard man, McGee!** When Harold Peary, the actor, died aged 76, *Time* Magazine (15 April 1985) noted that, 'as "The Great Gildersleeve", the pompous windbag with a heart of gold well hidden behind a wall of bluster . . . [he had] made "You're a ha-a-ard man, McGee" and his trademark oily giggle national crazes.'

somebody got out of bed the wrong side today!   That is, 'you *are* in a temper/ bad mood'. Why this should have anything to do with the way you got out of bed is not clear, though it was held to be unlucky to put the left foot on the ground first when getting out of bed. The superstition was commented on by 1540. 'You rose o' the wrong side to-day' – Richard Brome, *The Court Beggar* (1632); 'You have got up on the wrong side, this morning, George' – Anon., *Marvellous Love-Story* (1801); 'Why, brother Nixon, thou art angry this morning . . . hast risen from thy wrong side, I think' – Walter Scott, *Redgauntlet* (1824); 'Miss had got out of bed the wrong side' – Henry Kingsley, *Silcote of Silcotes* (1867).

somebody pinched me puddin'!   Catchphrase of the British variety act Collinson and Breen (1930s/40s). The explanation was that, 'Somebody said "All put your puddins out for treacle", and I put mine out and somebody pinched it!' Relevant to this or not, compare PUT YOUR PUDDINGS OUT FOR TREACLE.

somebody up there likes me   Explanatory phrase for when one has a piece of good fortune. *Somebody Up There Likes Me* was the title of a 1956 film written by Ernest Lehman. It starred Paul Newman and was based on the life of the World Middleweight Boxing Champion of 1947–8, Rocky Graziano (not to be confused with Rocky Marciano). I believe Graziano's autobiography had the same title. There was a title song from the film – also, in 1957, a song called 'Somebody Up There

Digs Me'. Shortly before he was elected leader of the British Labour Party in 1983, Neil Kinnock emerged unscathed from his car when it inexplicably turned over on the M4 motorway. He remarked, 'My escape was miraculous. It's a word which is somewhat overused, but I know what it means. Someone up there likes me.'

some like it hot Phrase chiefly familiar as the title of a film (US 1959) about two unemployed musicians who are accidental witnesses of the St Valentine's Day Massacre and flee to Miami disguised as members of an all-girls jazz band. So the 'hotness' may come from the jazz or the position they find themselves in. In fact, the phrase does actually occur in the film – *Tony Curtis*: 'Syncopators? Does that mean you play very fast music . . . er . . . jazzz?' *Marilyn Monroe*: 'Yeah . . . real hot!' *Tony Curtis*: 'Oh, well, I guess some like it hot. I personally prefer classical music.' There had been an unrelated US film with the same title in 1939 (starring Bob Hope). The allusion is apparently to the nursery rhyme 'Pease porridge hot' (first recorded about 1750), of which the second verse goes: 'Some like it hot / Some like it cold / Some like it in the pot / Nine days old.' This is such nonsense that it is sometimes ended with a riddle: 'Spell me that without a P' ('that' being quite easy to spell without a P). Ring Lardner's story 'Some Like Them Cold' (*circa* 1926, collected 1935) contains a song, referring to women: 'Some like them hot, some like them cold / Some like them fat, some like them lean.'

some mothers do 'ave 'em See DON'T SOME MOTHERS HAVE 'EM.

some of my best friends are —— (most commonly **Jews/Jewish)** A self-conscious (and occasionally jokey) disclaimer of prejudice. In a May 1946 letter, Somerset Maugham replied to charges that he was anti-Semitic and said: 'God knows I have never been that; some of my best friends in England and America are Jews . . .' So, clearly, at that date the phrase could be used without irony. However, the line may – according to one source – have been rejected as a cartoon caption by the *New Yorker* prior to the Second World War and presumably dates, in any case, from the Nazi persecution of the Jews from the 1930s on. In the (Jewish) Marx Brothers' film *Monkey Business* (as early as 1931), there is the line, 'Some of my best friends are *housewives.*' The Russian Prime Minister Alexei Kosygin was apparently unaware of the phrase's near-cliché status in 1971 when he said, 'There is no anti-semitism in Russia. Some of my best friends are Jews.' The expression may be adapted, jokingly, to accommodate any group to which the speaker may be thought to be apart or aloof from.

someone had blundered Phrase from Lord Tennyson's poem 'The Charge of the Light Brigade' (1854): 'Forward the Light Brigade! / Was there a man dismay'd? / Not tho' the soldier knew / Someone had blundered.' The Charge of the Light Brigade took place at Balaclava, near Sebastopol, on 25 October 1854, during the Crimean War. Owing to a misunderstood order, 247 officers and men out of 637 were killed or wounded. Tennyson's famous poem about it was published in *The Examiner* newspaper on 9 December that same year. According to Christopher Ricks's edition of the poems, Tennyson wrote this on 2 December 1854, 'in a few minutes, after reading . . . *The Times* in which occurred the phrase *someone had blundered*, and this was the origin of the metre of his poem'. In fact, *The Times* had spoken rather (in a leader on 13 November) of 'some hideous blunder'. Advised to be careful because controversy would offend the War Office, Tennyson allowed the 'someone had blundered' line to be deleted when his next collection of poems was published (*Maud, and Other Poems*, 1855). But when he heard that the Society for the Propagation of the Gospel intended to circulate this *revised* poem to the troops, he had copies of the *uncut* version printed and sent to the Crimea.

someone isn't using Amplex See EVEN YOUR BEST FRIENDS . . .

someone's mother See WHITER THAN WHITE.

(there is) someone walking on my grave What you say when you shiver or shudder or feel goose-pimples. It is an old superstition that when you shiver, someone is walking over the place of your future grave. Jonathan Swift has it in his list of conversational clichés, *Polite Conversation* (1738).

someone, somewhere, wants a letter from you   Slogan for the British Post Office, current in the early 1960s.

—— something PHRASES. The title of a US TV drama series (from 1987–92) was *thirtysomething*. There was nothing new about giving someone's age as 'twenty something' or 'thirty something', when you didn't know the exact figure, but the TV series about couples around that age helped popularize the usage. 'Eighties pop for the thirtysomethings' said an ad in *Barclay-card Magazine* (1989); 'Judy is a successful and attractive businesswoman toward the far end of her thirtysomething decade. Yet she feels frustrated, alone and angry about her failed relationships with men' – *The Washington Post* (13 March 1990). Adaptable, of course: 'My generation, the twentysomethings, were fortunate enough to catch the golden age of American TV detectives' – *The Guardian* (3 May 1991).

something else A way of complimenting the indefinable. Probably from American, as in, 'Hey, lady, you're something else.' 1960s/70s. From Derek Taylor, *It Was Twenty Years Ago Today* (1987): 'Across the decreasing divide between America and Britain good things were happening . . . It wasn't pop, it wasn't poetry, it wasn't politics. It was . . . Something Else.'

something for the weekend, sir (or anything . . .)? The traditional parting question from British barbers (in the days before they were called men's hairdressers) inviting customers to stock up with condoms (which, for no very obvious reason, they sold). 1930s to 1950s, at a guess.

something in the City Phrase used to describe in the vaguest possible terms what job a person held in banking or the financial world. By 1863, when it appears in *Punch* and in the novel *The Ticket-of-Leave Man* by T. Taylor.

something is rotten in the state of Denmark All is not well in this country or in this organization. A quotation from Shakespeare's *Hamlet*, I.iv.90 (1600–1),

where the line is spoken by Marcellus concerning the corruption that is spreading out from the royal court at Elsinore.

something must be done Phrase associated with King Edward VIII. In November 1936, he went to South Wales to tour the depressed areas and moved the public with his expressions of concern. At the Bessemer steel works at Dowlais, where 9,000 men had been made unemployed, hundreds sang an old Welsh hymn. Afterwards the King was heard to say to an official: 'These works brought all these people here. Something must be done to find them work' [or 'get them at work again']. Occasionally quoted as 'something ought to be done' and followed the next day by the promise, 'You may be sure that all I can do for you, I will', the King's words were taken as an indication of his concern for ordinary people and of his impatience with established authority. Although his distress at what he saw in South Wales was no doubt genuine, the King's assurances might look less hollow if we did not now know that by then he had already informed his family and the Prime Minister of his decision to abdicate. 'Memel was today ceded to Germany . . . not in itself very important, [but] it is the camel-breaking straw and the Cabinet is now unanimous that "something must be done"' – entry for 22 March 1939, *Chips, The Diaries of Sir Henry Channon* (1967).

something nasty in the woodshed Phrase for an unnamed unpleasantness, coined by the British novelist Stella Gibbons in *Cold Comfort Farm* (1933). In that novel, the phrase is used *passim* to refer to a traumatic experience in someone's background, e.g. from Chap. 10: 'When you were very small . . . you had seen something nasty in the woodshed.' Hence, from Beryl Bainbridge's novel *Another Part of the Wood* (1968): 'They had all, Joseph, brother Trevor, the younger sister . . . come across something nasty in the woodshed, mother or father or both, having it off with someone else.' Kyril Bonfiglioli entitled a novel *Something Nasty in the Woodshed* (1976).

something of the night Something dark/evil/mysterious in a situation or in a person's character. *Something of the Night* is the title of a crime novel (1980) by the American writer Mary McMullen. The British politician Ann Widdecombe MP famously used the phrase to describe her former Home Office colleague, Michael Howard, in May 1997, and thus helped scupper his chances as a contender for the leadership of the Conservative Party.

something old, something new, something borrowed, something blue (and silver sixpence in your shoe) The traditional ingredients of a bride's clothes, not recorded in this full form until 1883. However, blue has long been associated with truth in women (and the Virgin Mary is often clothed in this colour). If married in white, the bride usually wears a blue garter. There is also a proverbial expression, 'Married in blue, love ever true'. The 'silver sixpence' in your shoe is a good-luck token with a long history and related to the one in Christmas puddings. The wearing of things old and borrowed also appears designed to bring good fortune. *Something Borrowed, Something Blue* was the title of a film (US 1997).

(to hear) something to one's advantage I.e. good news – for example, that money has been left to one in somebody's will. Traditionally, when executors are not able to contact a beneficiary, a small advertisement has been placed in newspapers asking that so-and-so should contact such-and-such solicitors 'where he will hear something to his advantage'. In *Punch* by 1847. But as this citation shows, the newspaper notices were not solely concerned with wills: 'If the Gentleman who travelled from Yeovil Junction . . . with a violin case, will send his address he will hear of something to his advantage' – *Daily News* (3 November 1882).

something understood *Something Understood* was the title of an autobiography (1986) by Gerald Priestland, the former BBC religious affairs correspondent. It then became the title of a Radio 4 programme about the 'whole universe of religious sensation'. The source is a 1633 sonnet by George Herbert: 'Church-bells beyond the stars heard, the soul's blood, / The land of spices; something understood.'

somewhere in England The construction 'somewhere in —' originated in the First World War, for security reasons – e.g. 'somewhere in France', as in *Punch* (21 April 1915) and in a letter from J. B. Priestley to his father (27 September 1915), and its use came to be broadened to anywhere one cannot, or one does not want to, be too precise about. On 24 August 1941, Winston Churchill broadcast a report on his meeting with President Roosevelt: 'Exactly where we met is secret, but I don't think I shall be indiscreet if I go so far as to say that it was "somewhere in the Atlantic".' There was a film *Somewhere in England* (1940) that begot a series of British regional comedies with titles like *Somewhere in Camp/on Leave/in Civvies* and *in Politics*.

somewhere to the right of Genghis Khan Cliché description of someone's politics, if they are deemed to be right-wing or fascist. Genghis Khan (*circa* 1162–1227) was a Mongol ruler who conquered large parts of Asia, and, rightly or not, his name is always equated with terror, devastation and butchery. A variation evokes the similarly charming Attila the Hun. From Tim Rice's song 'The Lady's Got Potential' in *Evita* (1976 – record album only) about the leaders of an Argentinian military coup: 'They thought that Hitler had the war as good as won / They were slightly to the right of Attila the Hun.' 'Of course, in those days, the union leaders were well to the right of Genghis Khan' – Arthur Scargill, president of the National Union of Mineworkers, quoted by John Mortimer in *The Sunday Times* (10 January 1982); 'Close friends say he [Kenneth Clarke] has been an emollient force behind the doors of the Department of Health, but Genghis Khan would have looked like a calming influence alongside his ebullient ministers David Mellor and Edwina Currie' – *The Independent* (28 January 1989).

so much for Buckingham See OFF WITH HIS HEAD.

(the) son and heir Phrase now used only jokingly to describe an eldest son. Charles Dickens has 'together with the information that the Son and Heir would sail in a fortnight' in *Dombey and Son*, Chap. 17

(1846–8). Shakespeare has 'the son and heir to that same Faulconbridge' – *King John*, I.i.56 (1596) – and 'son and heir of a mongrel bitch' – *King Lear*, II.ii.20 (1606), but here the quotation marks are not yet quite around the phrase.

son et lumière [sound and light] A type of entertainment, usually performed in a historical setting, in which the story of the place is told through the use of a (re-corded) soundtrack and lighting effects. It is said to have been devised by a French architect, Paul Robert-Houdin, and first presented at Chambord in 1952. The first place to be given the treatment in Britain was the Royal Naval College at Greenwich in 1957. Now it would be hard to find any major tourist site around the world that has not been subjected to this frequently disappointing but sometimes evocative procedure.

song See GO FOR A.

(a) song, a smile and a piano Bill matter of the British comedian Norman Long, particularly on the radio in the 1920s/30s. The BBC apparently changed his billing to 'A Song, a Joke and a Piano' on the basis that you could not broadcast a smile on radio. Much alluded to: in BBC Radio, *The Last Goon Show of All* (1972): 'That demon-stration of Mr Secombe's senility – "A smile, a song, a wheelchair" . . .'; *Punch* (13 July 1977) referred to an odd BBC breakfast-time radio rag-bag called *Up To the Hour* as, 'A prayer, a joke, a song, a chat, a cup of tea and a quick cigarette . . .'

son of —— Used, particularly, as the title of sequels to American films and emphasizing how they are the derivatives of (usually) superior originals. The first such *book* may have been *Son of Tarzan* (1917; filmed 1921) by Edgar Rice Burroughs. The first such *film* was probably *Son of the Sheik* (1926), with Rudolph Valentino, following *The Sheik* (1921). Then *Son of Kong* (1933) followed *King Kong*. Others have been: *Son of . . . Ali Baba/Captain Blood/Dr Jekyll/Dracula/Frankenstein/Geronimo/ Lassie/Monte Cristo/Paleface/ Robin Hood/ the Sheik/Zorro*. Alternatively, you could stage a return: *The Return of . . . Dracula / the Scarlet Pimpernel/a Man Called Horse*. Or merely add a number. An early exam-ple of this format came from TV: the BBC's *Quatermass Experiment* (1953) was followed by *Quatermass II* (1955). In the cinema, since *The Godfather, Part II* (1974), we have had not only *Rocky II–V* but also *Jaws II* and *French Connection II/ Death Wish II/Damien: Omen II/ Friday the Thirteenth, Part II/Crocodile Dundee 2*, and so on. There are exceptions, of course. The sequel to *American Graffiti* was *More American Graffiti*. Forswearing 'Pink Panther 2', etc., Blake Edwards gave us *The Pink Panther Strikes Again, The Revenge of the Pink Panther* and *The Return of the Pink Panther*. The *Airport* sequels followed their own peculiar numerology – from *Airport 1975* to *Airport '77* and then *Airport '80 – The Concorde*.

(a) son of a bitch (or SOB) A very old term of abuse. 'Bitch-son' was in use by 1330. Shakespeare has 'son and heir of a mongrel bitch' in *King Lear*, II.ii.20 (1606). The fully formed phrase was with us by 1707. The abbreviation was known by 1918. *S.O.B.* was the title of a film (US 1981) where it was delicately said to stand for 'Standard Operational Bullshit'. Other translations have included 'Silly Old Bastard'.

(a) son of a gun Nowadays, an inoffen-sively jocular way of addressing someone: 'You son of a gun!' However, in seafaring days, if a pregnant woman somehow found herself upon a warship and was ready to go into labour, the place tradition-ally made available to her was between two guns. If the father was unknown, the child could be described as a 'son of a gun'. *Partridge/Slang*, however, quoting an 1823 source, defines the term as meaning a '*soldier*'s bastard', so perhaps there was an Army equivalent of the space made available.

sonnets See DARK LADY.

(she was) so poor she didn't have a pot to piss in Self-explanatory North Ameri-can phrase, sometimes extended to include: '. . . **and not even a window to throw it out of**.' 1980s, and the likely source of the word 'potless' to describe the poverty-stricken.

(a) soppy date A soft, silly, foolish person. Known since at least the 1930s and much used by the British comedian Cyril Fletcher (whose first broadcast was in 1936). An extension of the word 'date', meaning the same, known since 1914. Could 'soppy' come from 'sopping wet'?

(the) sordid topic of coin Term for the question of payment (usually in cash). Not from any sketch by the British monologist Joyce Grenfell but mentioned by her in discussing a woman who inspired the creation of one of her characters. In *Joyce Grenfell Requests the Pleasure* (1976), she writes about the 'wife of an Oxbridge vice chancellor who featured in three monologues called 'Eng. Lit.'. The character was based partly on Grenfell's own expression while cleaning her teeth, partly on the playwright Clemence Dane (Winifred Ashton) and partly on the idiosyncratic speech patterns of Hester Alington, wife of the Dean of Durham and a distant relative of Grenfell's husband. 'On a postcard addressed to a shoe-shop in Sloane Street she had written: "Gently fussed about non-appearance of dim pair of shoes sent to you for heeling" . . . And when Viola [Tunnard, Grenfell's accompanist] and I went to Durham to perform in aid of one of her charities she introduced the paying of our expenses: "My dears, we have not yet touched on the sordid topic of coin . . .'''

sorely missed Obituary phrase, and as forgivable as any other cliché of bereavement. Date of origin unknown. Less forgivable in other contexts. 'Those members, including The Rev. Francis Moss, who died during the year under review will all be sorely missed' – Annual Report and Accounts, The Prayer Book Society (December 1994); 'Shahbaz missed the England game and Wednesday's final qualifying match against Belarus and his team has sorely missed his leadership, and skill' – *The Irish Times* (2 December 1994); 'But it is steaming up the Hudson that the QE2 makes her connection with New York. The sight of a liner docking on the piers, a sight available from countless Manhattan windows, stirs a collective memory, and the QE2 would be sorely missed' – *The Daily Telegraph* (2 January 1995); 'With 7,484 runs in 116 Tests Haynes's experience may be sorely missed

in the six-match series' – *The Daily Telegraph* (26 April 1995).

sorry about that! Ironic, understated apology as when one has been responsible for a big mistake. A catchphrase of Don Adams as the inept secret agent Maxwell Smart in the American TV series *Get Smart* (1965–7). He would say, 'Sorry about that, Chief' to Thaddeus, his boss.

sorts See ALL SORTS.

SOS The emergency Morse Code signal, represented by the dots and dashes for the letters SOS, does not actually stand for anything, least of all 'Save Our Souls', as commonly supposed. The letters were chosen because they were easy to send in an emergency. Until about 1910, the Morse cry for help was 'C, Q, D'. Other acronyms have been devised to suit the letters SOS: e.g., '*Si Opus Sit* [which, in medicine, means 'give relief where necessary']', 'Slip On Show', 'Same Old Slush/Story/Stuff' and 'Short Of Sugar'.

so that's all right then . . . Comment when a feeble or self-serving explanation has been advanced for some state of affairs. Probably popularized by the satirical magazine *Private Eye*. '"In summary, therefore, TV-am's failure to achieve all of its starting aims by March 1983, came down simply and solely to the very bad audience ratings in the first few weeks and the effect of this on the nerves of some of those whose money was at stake. Those poor ratings were not due to any flaw in the conception of the franchises, or TV-am's application for it, or the role and talent of the original presenters." So that's all right then. But who says? Peter Jay himself' – *The Guardian* (5 November 1984); 'A charming letter from Teddy Tinling, the tennis person, corrects a terrible error I made recently when I quoted him as saying of Gabriela Sabatini: "She's beautiful but she walks like John Wayne." Mr Tinling tells me he said that Sabatini walks likes Robert Mitchum. That's all right, then' – *The Times* (18 June 1988).

soul See EYES AS WINDOWS.

(the) sound and the fury Probably an echo of the lines from Shakespeare, *Macbeth,* V.v.19 (1606) – 'It is a tale / Told by an idiot, full of sound and fury, / Signifying nothing.' Hence, perhaps, the title of William Faulkner's novel *The Sound and The Fury* (1929).

sound as a pound   Good, excellent, OK. Probably from North of England slang and known by 1992. Incorporated by Mike Myers in the film *Austin Powers: International Man of Mystery* (US 1997) when Austin, frozen in the 1960s, awakes in the 1990s: 'As long as people are still having premarital sex with many anonymous partners while at the same time experimenting with mind-expanding drugs in a consequence-free environment, I'll be sound as pound!'

(a/the) sound of revelry by night   Phrase from Byron, *Childe Harold's Pilgrimage*, Canto 3, St. 11 (1818): 'There was a sound of revelry by night.' Referring to the Duchess of Richmond's ball in Brussels on the night before the Battle of Waterloo (1815) – or rather, as Lord Wavell points out in *Other Men's Flowers* (1944), on Thursday 15 June, which was on the eve of the battles of Ligny and Quatre Bras and three days before Waterloo. *Sounds of Revelry* is the title of a painting (1886) by Augustus E. Mulready, showing poor children in the snow peering into a warmly lit house where some merrymaking is in progress. 'There was a sound of revelry by night, for the first Saturday in June had arrived and the Golf Club was holding its monthly dance' – P. G. Wodehouse, *The Heart of a Goof*, Chap. 7 (1926).

sour grapes   Explanatory phrase given for the behaviour of anyone who affects to despise something because he knows he cannot have it. The source is Aesop's fable of 'The Fox and the Grapes' in which a fox tries very hard to reach some grapes but, when he is unable to do so, says they looked sour anyway. Phrase known by 1760, though the story was being quoted by the 13th century.

South   See BUT NOT IN THE.

(the) South will rise again   Slogan referring to the aftermath of the American Civil War and which presumably came out of the period that followed it, known as Reconstruction. Meaning, 'the (American) South is not finished yet and has a future'.

Somewhat tainted in that it has also been used as a rallying cry of segregationists. But did any particular person say it originally? Was it an actual slogan? Curiously little information is to hand on these points. It has been suggested that Southerners started making the promise as General Sherman marched through Georgia in April 1865 – the month that President Lincoln was assassinated. Modern allusions: 'President Reagan himself took some giant steps backward in race relations during the campaign . . . telling an audience in Macon, Ga., that "the South will rise again!", a rallying cry of segregationists in an earlier era' – *The Washington Post* (11 November 1984); 'Along the 100-mile highway that now links the two old civil war capitals – Washington (The Union) and Richmond (The Confederacy) – you can stop and buy a tee-shirt that bears the proud slogan "Save your Confederate money, the South will rise again"'– *Financial Times* (7 June 1985); 'Jubilant [George Bush, seeking re-election], told cheering supporters on Tuesday night: "I feel I have a lot in common with Mark Twain: reports of my death were greatly exaggerated." He said he was now going on to the South, "where we will rise again"' – *The Times* (18 February 1988).

so what's new?   See 'TWAS EVER THUS.

(to) sow one's wild oats   A wild oat is a common weed, so for anyone to sow it means that (usually) he is doing something useless or worthless. Hence, the expression is employed to describe behaviour prior to a man's 'settling down'. In use by 1576. Quite how much implication there is of him wasting his semen in unfruitful couplings is hard to judge, though the expression often has reference to sexual dissipation. Perhaps this connotation has increased with the popularity of such expressions as 'getting one's oats' (for having sex). To **feel one's oats**, however, has nothing to do with this. It means to act in an important way as though pleased with oneself, to be lively, and seems to have originated in the USA about 1830. It referred, literally at first, to the way a horse was thought to feel friskier and more energetic after it had eaten oats.

spade See CALL A.

(a) spaghetti Western A film about the American West made by an Italian director (and often filmed in Spain . . .). Chiefly made in the 1960s, these cheaply produced Westerns were principally directed by Sergio Leone, through whom Clint Eastwood achieved international stardom in such films as *A Fistful of Dollars* (1964) and *The Good, the Bad and the Ugly* (1967). The coinage of the term – in use by 1969 – has been ascribed to the British writer Christopher Frayling. The term 'Sukiyaki Western' for Japanese-made films of this type does not seem to have caught on. 'I've heard of Spaghetti Westerns but never of Spaghetti Scotsmen' – Margaret Thatcher (on David Steel's candidacy for an Italian seat in the European Parliament), quoted in *The Independent* (17 June 1989).

Spain See HOW NOW BROWN COW.

Spanish practices See OLD SPANISH CUSTOMS.

spare prick See LIKE A PORK CHOP.

spare rib The title of the British feminist magazine *Spare Rib* (founded 1972) is a punning reference to the cuts of meat known as 'spareribs' and also to ADAM'S RIB.

sparrow's fart Dawn. Often mistakenly taken to be an Australian coinage. It is included in Carr's *Craven Dialect* (1828) – from Yorkshire – and the definition given as 'break of day'.

speak as you find, that's my motto In a 1950s' BBC radio series *Hello Playmates!* featuring Arthur Askey, this catchphrase was spoken not by him but by Nola Purvis (Pat Coombs), the daughter of the studio cleaner (Irene Handl). This was her smug excuse for the appalling insults she hurled. In 1955, *Hello Playmates!* won the *Daily Mail* Radio Award as the year's top show and the catchphrase was inscribed on the presentation silver microphone – which didn't go down too well with Askey, who had never uttered it. (Source Bob Monkhouse, who, with Denis Goodwin, wrote the show.) *Apperson* finds a proverb 'speak of a man as you find him' by 1875. Perhaps she just meant, 'I say what I have to say according to circumstances'.

speak for England The British politician Leo S. Amery made the famous interjection, 'Speak for England, Arthur!' in the House of Commons (2 September 1939). On the eve of war, Prime Minister Neville Chamberlain appeared in the Commons and held out the prospect of a further Munich-type peace conference and did not announce any ultimatum to Germany. When the acting Labour leader, Arthur Greenwood, rose to respond, a Conservative MP shouted, 'Speak for England, Arthur!' For many years, it was generally accepted that the MP was Amery and, indeed, he wrote in *My Political Life* (Vol. 3, 1955): 'It was essential that someone should . . . voice the feelings of the House and of the whole country. Arthur Greenwood rose . . . I dreaded a purely partisan speech, and called out to him across the floor of the House, Speak for England.' (Note, no 'Arthur'.) By October 30, James Agate was writing in his diary (published in *Ego 4*) of the anthology for the forces he had been busy compiling called *Speak for England*: 'Clemence Dane gave me the title; it is the phrase shouted in the House the other day when Arthur Greenwood got up to speak on the declaration of the war.' However, writing up an account of the session in *his* diary, Harold Nicolson (whose usual habit was to make his record first thing the following morning) wrote: 'Bob Boothby cried out, "*You* speak for Britain".' Boothby confirmed that he had said this when shown the diary passage in 1964. The explanation would seem to be that after Amery spoke, his cry was taken up not only by Boothby but by others on the Tory benches. From the Labour benches came cries of 'What about Britain?' and 'Speak for the working classes!' Interestingly, nobody claims to have said the exact words as popularly remembered. The intervention went unrecorded in *Hansard*. *Speak for England* later became the title of a book (1976) by Melvyn Bragg – 'an oral history of England since 1900'.

speaks See HE KNOWS WHEREOF.

speak softly and carry a big stick Political slogan that seems to have started life as a West African proverb. Speaking at the Minnesota State Fair in September 1901, President Theodore Roosevelt gave strength to the idea of backing negotiations with threats of military force when he said: 'There is a homely adage which runs "Speak softly and carry a big stick; you will go far". If the American nation will speak softly and yet build up and keep at a pitch of the highest training a thoroughly efficient navy, the Monroe Doctrine will go far.'

(the) special relationship Term used to describe affiliations between countries (the earliest *OED2* citation is for one between Britain and Galicia in 1929) but particularly referring to that supposed to exist between Britain and the USA on the basis of historical ties and a common language. The notion was principally promoted by Winston Churchill in his attempts to draw the USA into the Second World War, though whether he used the phrase prior to 1941 is not clear. In the House of Commons on 7 November 1945, Churchill said: 'We should not abandon our special relationship with the United States and Canada about the atomic bomb.' In his 1946 IRON CURTAIN speech at Fulton, Missouri, he asked: 'Would a special relationship between the United States and the British Commonwealth be inconsistent with our overriding loyalties to the World Organization [the UN]?'

(a/the) spectre at the feast An embarrassing reminder of something that one would rather have forgotten. Presumably, the allusion is to the appearance of Banquo's ghost in Shakespeare's *Macbeth*, III.iv (1606), where the man whom Macbeth has just had murdered comes back to haunt him during what is specifically called a 'feast'. But similar things happen in Mozart's *Don Giovanni* when a statue of the Commendatore (a man Don Giovanni has murdered) appears during supper and drags him off to Hell. And then there is the WRITING ON THE WALL at Belshazzar's Feast in the Book of Daniel. There is presumably some link to the phrase 'skeleton at the feast/banquet' that *OED2* defines as a 'reminder of serious or saddening things in the midst of enjoyment . . . An allusion to the practice of the ancient Greeks as recounted by Plutarch in his *Moralia*' (i.e. when an actual skeleton was propped up at a feast or banquet). The earliest citations are, however, from only the mid-19th century. The earliest use found of the actual expression is Charles

Dickens's reference to a 'spectre at their licentious feasts' in *Barnaby Rudge*, Chap. 16 (1840). 'Snowdon's just a spectre at Linley's feast' – headline from gossip item in *Today* (16 April 1988); '"There was just one nomination for spectre at the feast," said one of the contributors to . . . BBC1's chocolate box recollection of Coronation Day. He had the Duke of Windsor in mind (who didn't turn up in the end, to everyone's relief)' – *The Independent* (3 June 1993).

(a) spectre is haunting Europe The opening words of *The Communist Manifesto* (1848), written by Karl Marx and Friedrich Engels, are now usually given as: 'A spectre is haunting Europe – the spectre of communism.' However, when the tract was first translated into English this was not the case. The weekly magazine *The Red Republican* serialized the manifesto from 9 to 30 November 1850 and said it was written by 'Citizens *Charles Marx* and *Frederic Engels*'. The translation – actually rather a good one by Helen MacFarlane, a Chartist – nevertheless gets off to a wobbly start with: 'A frightful hobgoblin stalks throughout Europe. We are haunted by a ghost, the ghost of Communism.'

speculation was rife An inevitable pairing. Date of origin unknown. 'Mr Clinton is so weak that Washington is already rife with speculation about which Democrat might take him on, but as he moves sharply to the Right, he is working hard to protect his left flank' – *The Times* (26 January 1995); 'Speculation had been rife that Dr Kohl would have been forced into a grand coalition with the opposition SPD later this year if the liberals had lost in the Hesse election and a second poll scheduled in the state of North Rhine-Westphalia in May' – *The Guardian* (20 February 1995).

speed the plough (or **plow)** A very old phrase indeed: in the form 'God speed the plough', it was what one would say when wishing someone luck in any venture (and not just an agricultural one). The phrase was in use by 1500 at least and is also the title of a traditional song and dance. *Speed the Plough* was the title of a play (1798) by Thomas Morton that introduced the unseen character of MRS GRUNDY. *Speed-The-Plow* was the title of a play (1988) by

David Mamet, about two Hollywood producers trying to get a project off the ground.

Speedy Gonzales A person who moves fast – though sometimes used ironically of someone who is completely the reverse. Most people would think that this name originated in the pop song with which Pat Boone had a hit in 1962, but in fact the film cartoon character Speedy Gonzales ('the fastest mouse in all Mexico') came out of Warner Brothers in 1955. *The Guardian*'s 'Notes and Queries' was asked in late 1992, 'Was there ever a *real* Speedy Gonzales?', but answer came there none. One wonders whether the fact that Pancho Gonzales, the tennis player, was all the rage in the 1950s had anything to do with the naming of the mouse?

spell See ALL PUBLICITY.

(a) spelling bee An innocent game to do with spelling, from the days when people had to make their own entertainment. A 'bee' is the American word (since 1769) for when a group of neighbours gathers to do something communally – hence, a 'harvest bee', even a 'lynching bee' – and so named after the social character of the insect.

(to) spend a penny A euphemism for 'to go to the lavatory'. The first public convenience to charge one penny opened in London in 1855. One is curious about this from Chap. 6 of Charles Dickens's *Dombey and Son* (1846–8): 'The young Toodles, victims of a pious fraud, were deluded into repairing in a body to a chandler's shop in the neighbourhood, for the ostensible purpose of spending a penny.' *OED2* does not have a citation for the phrase before 1945. See also under MAY I SPEND A PENNY?

(a) spending spree Alliteratively inevitable phrase. Known by 1956. 'Ladbroke . . . aside from the £50m spending spree planned on hotels, is quite happy to welcome no-limit betting' – *The Times* (12 April 1973); 'But Roma, anxious to recoup some of the cash spent on a 15 player close season spending spree, have slapped a transfer fee of at least $5 million on his head' – *The Irish Times* (4 July 1994); 'According to the IFS, the Chancellor should not be cutting taxes, nor could he risk raising them to make sure the public do not raid their piggy banks for a spending spree' – *The Times* (13 October 1994).

(I'm going to) spend, spend, spend! Viv Nicholson (b. 1936) and her husband, Keith, a trainee miner, were bringing up three children on a weekly wage of £7 in Castleford, Yorkshire. Then, in September 1961, they won £152,000 on Littlewoods football pools. Arriving by train to collect their prize – as Viv recalled in her autobiography, *Spend, Spend, Spend* (1977), they were confronted by reporters. One asked: 'What are you going to do when you get all this money?' Viv said, 'I'm going to spend, spend, spend, that's what I'm going to do.' She says it was just an off-the-cuff remark, but it made newspaper headlines and was later the title of her book. As a phrase it still lingers, not least because of the tragic overtones to Viv's use of it. Keith died in a car crash, and Viv worked her way through a series of husbands until the money had all gone. *Spend, Spend, Spend* was also the title of a TV play about Viv's win and of a stage musical about it (London 1999). From the *Daily Mail* (4 March 1989): 'The Sixties were indeed "a low dishonest decade" . . . We thought the great post-war boom would go on for ever, that both individuals and the state could spend, spend, spend without the smallest concern for tomorrow.'

spider See ALONG CAME A.

(the) spider and the fly Phrase used regarding entrapment. It comes from Mary Howitt's poem 'The Spider and the Fly' (1834): '"Will you walk into my parlour?" said the spider to the fly. / "'Tis the prettiest little parlour that ever you did spy".' Sometimes it has been insisted that the original was 'said *a* spider to *a* fly' (as in *ODQ* 1941–92) but this appears not to have been the case. A *Punch* parody of the poem (4 July 1868) is quite clearly entitled 'The Spider and the Fly'. There have been several musical settings of this poem. The Rolling Stones's song called 'The Spider and the Fly' (written by Nanker and Phelge, recorded 1971) contains, however: 'Don't say Hi! like a spider to a fly' and 'I said my, my, my, like a spider to a fly, / Jump right ahead in my web.' Films entitled *The Spider and the Fly* (UK 1949; US 1995) have concerned themselves with policeman/thief pursuit and rival mystery writers.

(to) spill the beans To divulge information inadvertently. This has been traced back to the ancient Greeks who held secret ballots for membership of clubs by using beans. A white bean was a 'yes' vote, a brown bean a 'no' vote. The beans were counted in secrecy so that a prospective member would not how many people voted for or against him. If the jar containing the beans was knocked over, that secret might get out. This is a very elaborate explanation, but the phrase entered American speech (from whence it passed into English generally) only in the early 20th century. Why did it take so long? Another possible explanation is that gypsy fortune tellers in Turkey do not have crystal balls, neither do they read tea leaves. One of the many ways they tell fortunes is to spill beans out of a cup and interpret the resulting pattern.

spindle See DO NOT.

(a) spin doctor A public relations practitioner or political aide who puts a positive interpretation upon events, usually in the political sphere, by briefing journalists and correspondents. Out of the USA in the mid-1980s, particularly during the 1988 Presidential election, and taken from the game of baseball where spin has to be put on the ball by a pitcher to make it go where it is wanted. 'The spin doctors, the PR generals, argued after the Reykjavik talks that Reagan still stands by Star Wars and within reach' – *Newsweek* (27 October 1986); 'The theme of the two men having talked bluntly yet courteously . . . is likely to be stressed further by Reagan Administration "spin doctors" who will try to present the summit in a favourable light in the days to come' – *The Daily Telegraph* (11 December 1987).

(the) spirit of —— Political format phrase. 'The Spirit of '76' came into use soon after the American Revolution in the 18th century and was used as the name of several newspapers in the United States. In 1972, it was the name of the plane (Air Force One) that carried President Nixon on his visit to China. President Eisenhower was very fond of the format, speaking of 'the Spirit of Geneva' in 1955, and 'the Spirit of Camp David' in 1959. Michael Foot, the British Labour politician, combined it with another political cliché following a by-election victory in April 1983, and said that Labour would, 'get the spirit of Darlington UP AND DOWN THE COUNTRY'. (The Darlington win was reversed at the General Election the following month . . .)

(the) spirit of the age The distinctive thoughts and feelings that characterize a particular period. Probably a direct translation of the German *Zeitgeist* that was an outcrop of German Romanticism of the 1770s. David Hume had, however, used the phrase in English by 1752. The poet Shelley wrote in a letter of 1820: 'It is the spirit of the age, and we are all infected with it.' William Hazlitt's book of essays *The Spirit of the Age* (1825) was devoted to examinations of the work and characters of contemporary writers. 'The Spirit of the Age is against those who put party or programme before human needs' – *The Pall Mall Gazette* (6 August 1891). In 1975 the title *Spirit of the Age* was given to a BBC TV series on the history of architecture, with Alec Clifton-Taylor.

spit See DOESN'T IT MAKE; DON'T.

(a/the) spitting image An exact likeness. Used as the title of a British TV comedy series (1984–96) using puppets to satirize current events. Given the venom involved in *Spitting Image*, it might be thought that any spitting had to do with saliva. The theories are, however, that the phrase is a corruption of 'speaking image' or 'splitting image' (two split halves of the same tree, which provide an exact likeness), or a Black southern US pronunciation of 'spirit and image' (which a true likeness might have). Current by 1901 and – as 'the spit of someone' – by 1894.

splash it all over Slogan for Brut aftershave in the UK, *circa* 1974. TV ads featured the popular ex-boxer Henry Cooper – to show that using the product was somehow not an unmanly thing to do.

splendid isolation A speech in the Canadian House of Commons (16 January 1896) was the occasion of the coining of the phrase 'splendid isolation', which was the headline in the London *Times* over its subsequent account. Sir George Foster, MP for North Toronto, said: 'In these somewhat troublesome days when the great Mother Empire stands splendidly isolated in Europe . . .' The 1st Lord Goschen picked up the phrase in a speech at Lewes (26 February 1896): 'We have stood here alone in what is called isolation – our splendid isolation, as one of our colonial friends was good enough to call it.' James Morris in *Farewell the Trumpets* (1978) describes it as, 'A flattering Canadian conception of Britain's lonely magnificence.'

splendour in the grass In the film *Splendor in the Grass* (US 1961), Wilma (Natalie Wood) twice speaks the following lines – first in class when she is made to read them aloud and suddenly understands their relevance to her present position: 'Though nothing can bring back the hour / Of splendour in the grass, of glory in the flower; / We will grieve not, rather find / Strength in what remains behind.' She realises for the first time that her relationship with a young man is over and that the ideals of youth have to give way in time to something else. She also recites them as the last lines in the film. They are from William Wordsworth's 'Ode, Intimations of Immortality from Recollections of Early Childhood', St. 10 (1807).

(to) splice the main brace Meaning 'to have a drink', the expression comes from a comparison between the reviving effect of alcoholic drink and repairing or strengthening the mainbrace on board ship, where the mainbrace is the rope for holding or turning one of the sails. As used in the Navy itself, the expression refers to the rare occurrence of an extra tot of rum all round – and known in this sense by 1805.

spoke See HE KNOWS WHEREOF.

sponsor See AND NOW A WORD.

spooky See WAVE YOUR GLADDIES.

spoon See GRODY TO THE MAX.

(the) sport of kings In the 17th century it was war-making. William Somerville described hunting as 'the sport of kings' in *The Chase* (1735). But in the 20th century horse racing has tended to be the sport so described. So, too, has surf-riding.

(a) spot of homely fun, presenting the people to the people Stock phrase from the BBC radio show *Have A Go* (1946–67). This was indeed what the programme set out to provide.

(a) spotty Herbert A simple, unappealing person – usually a young man afflicted by spots on his skin. 1950s' usage, though the derogatory use of 'Herbert' or ''Erbert' predates this. The character Bluebottle in the BBC radio *Goon Show* (1951–60) is a prime example of the type. The term was used in 'The Tay Bridge' (9 February 1959) and 'The Last Goon Show of All' (5 October 1972). It also appeared in the BBC radio show *Hancock's Half-Hour*, 'The Junk Man' (6 May 1958), as: 'Some spotty-faced little Herbert'.

(a) sprat to catch a mackerel Something offered as a small concession in order to gain an important advantage. *Apperson* has 'giving a sprat to catch a herring' by 1827, and 'never to throw away sprats, but as bait for whales' in Charles Dickens, *Martin Chuzzlewit*, Chap. 8 (1850).

spray it again, will you? Pointed remark to the sort of person who 'sprays' when speaking – i.e. produces spittle and saliva on pronouncing certain letters of the alphabet. Since the 1940s. Also **say it, don't spray it!** – which has also been seen as an anti-graffiti graffito in London, early 1980s.

(to) spread alarm and despondency Meaning, 'to have a destabilizing effect, purposely or not'. The phrase goes back to the Army Act of 1879: 'Every person subject to military law who . . . spreads reports calculated to create unnecessary alarm or despondency . . . shall . . . be liable to suffer penal servitude.' When a German invasion was thought to be imminent at the beginning of July 1940, Winston Churchill had issued an 'admonition' to 'His Majesty's servants in high places . . . to report, or if necessary remove, any officers or officials who are found to be consciously exercising a disturbing or depressing influence, and whose talk is calculated to spread alarm and despondency'. Prosecutions for doing this did indeed follow. Also during the

Second World War, Lieutenant-Colonel Vladimir Peniakoff ran a small raiding and reconnaissance force on the British side which became known as 'Popski's Private Army'. In his book *Private Army* (1950), he wrote: 'A message came on the wireless for me. It said 'Spread alarm and despondency . . . The date was, I think, May 18th, 1942.'

spread out like a map (below) Date of origin not known. A cliché by the 1960s/70s. Part of the 'travel scribes' armoury' compiled from a competition in *The Guardian* (10 April 1993). 'After a night at the welcoming Il Nationale hotel, we headed out of town on a marked footpath beside the castle. Steps led upwards until Levanto looked like a map far below' – *The Sunday Telegraph* (15 May 1994); 'His vertiginous perspectives were new, and look how the tracery of the balcony itself becomes the near-abstract subject of the picture. Look down at the island refuge in the middle of the carrefour. Look down upon the tree below, and the circular grating at its base, and the bench beside it, set out like a map' – *Financial Times* (11 October 1994).

spring See WITH ONE BOUND.

spring and winter See MAY-DECEMBER.

square See BACK TO.

(a/the) square deal Just, equitable and fair treatment – in the USA by 1876. Also a political slogan in the USA (1901). Theodore Roosevelt succeeded to the presidency on the assassination of President McKinley. For some US presidents it is not enough to attain the White House, they have to dignify their policies with a resounding label, so Roosevelt declared: 'We demand that big business give people a Square Deal' and 'If elected I shall see to it that every man has a Square Deal, no more and no less.' He was still using the slogan in 1913, with specific reference to its original use regarding big business.

(a) square peg in a round hole Meaning, 'someone badly suited to his job or position'. Known by 1836. However, Sydney Smith, *Lectures on Moral Philosophy* (1804), has: 'If you choose to represent the various parts in life by holes upon a table, of different shapes, – some circular, some triangular, some square, some oblong, – and the persons acting these parts by bits of wood of similar shapes, we shall generally find that the triangular person has got into the square hole, and a square person has squeezed himself into the round hole.' James Agate in *Ego 5* (1942) writes: 'Will somebody please tell me the address of the Ministry for Round Pegs in Square Holes?'

squeak See BAT'S SQUEAK.

(to) squeeze (something) till the pips squeak Meaning, 'to extract the most [usually, money] from anything or anyone'. Apparently coined by Sir Eric Geddes, a British Conservative politician, shortly after the end of the First World War. On the question of reparations, Geddes said in an election speech in Cambridge (10 December 1918): 'The Germans, if this Government is returned, are going to pay every penny; they are going to be squeezed as a lemon is squeezed – until the pips squeak. My only doubt is not whether we can squeeze hard enough, but whether there is enough juice.' The previous night, Geddes, who had lately been First Lord of the Admiralty, said the same thing in a slightly different way as part of what was obviously a stump speech: 'I have personally no doubt we will get everything out of her that you can squeeze out of a lemon and a bit more . . . I will squeeze her until you can hear the pips squeak . . . I would strip Germany as she has stripped Belgium.'

(a/the) stag at bay 'At bay' means 'cornered, unable to escape', so this image may be evoked when someone is in a like position. 'A Stag at Bay' is the title of a painting (1846) and of a sculpture (1866) by Sir Edwin Landseer.

stage See I DON'T WISH.

stairs See GET UP.

(a) stalking horse A device used in hunting to get close to game, which apparently sees no danger in a four-legged beast (and recorded since 1519). The wooden horse at Troy was an even more devastating form of equine deception. Also used figuratively: 'He uses his folly like a stalking horse and under the presentation of that he shoots his wit' – Shakespeare, *As You Like It*, V.iv.105 (1598). Since the mid-1800s in the United States, the phrase has been used in politics about a candidate put forward to test the water on behalf of another candidate. In Britain (from about 1989), the term came to be applied to an MP who stood for election as leader of a party with no hope of getting the job. The stalking horse's role was to test the water on behalf of other stronger candidates and to see whether the incumbent leader was challengeable.

(a/the) standard by which all —— will be measured Cliché of approval. Known by 1878. 'A new standard by which all thoroughbred driving machines will be measured' – *Time* Magazine (14 December 1981).

stand See AMERICA CANNOT; DON'T JUST.

(to) stand head and shoulders above ... Meaning, 'to be distinctly superior in achievement'. Date of origin not known. Listed as a cliché in *The Times* (28 May 1984). '*Life* was more than head and shoulders above the other news magazines. It was a legend' – *Punch* (16 October 1974); 'This is particularly disconcerting news for those of us who, at 5ft 6in, have always secretly relished the idea that, if magically transported back to the days of Good Queen Bess, we would have stood head and shoulders above the riffraff' – *The Sunday Times* (22 May 1994); 'Burgess, who might be described as a Shankill Road socialist, brings a personal passion to his subject that lifts it head and shoulders above the usual sludge of academic sociology' – *The Sunday Times* (14 August 1994).

(to) stand on the shoulders of giants To build upon the achievements of one's greater predecessors. In 1159, Bernard of Chartres, the French philosopher, said, 'We are like dwarfs on the shoulders of giants, so that we can see more than they . . . not by virtue of any sharpness of sight on our part . . . but because we are carried high and raised up by their giant size.' The proverbial expression 'A dwarf on a giant's shoulders sees the further of the two' appears to have been established by the 14th century. Isaac Newton wrote in a letter to Robert Hooke (5 February 1676): 'If I have seen further it is by standing on the shoulders of giants.' Hooke had claimed to have discovered first the gravitational law of inverse squares, and Newton was attempting to conciliate him. However, it has also been interpreted as an insult to Hooke, one of Newton's bitterest enemies, whose main crime seems to have been to criticize Newton's work. Hooke was very short, if not actually a dwarf, and unprepossessing in appearance (he was described by John Aubrey as '. . . but of middling stature, something crooked . . . his eye full and popping . . .'). Newton's reference to giants was (according to this interpretation) to make it clear, albeit in outwardly courteous terms, his utter contempt for Hooke and his complete lack of any intellectual debt to him. 'Standing on the shoulders of giants' appeared on the rim of the British £2 coin from 1998 – apparently because of the Newton use but not knowing that it was proverbial.

stands See BEHIND EVERY.

(to) stand up and be counted To declare openly one's allegiance or beliefs. Of American origin. From the *Hartford Courant* (Connecticut) (12 August 1904): 'Another democratic paper, the "Sacramento Bee", follows the example of the "Chicago Chronicle" and stands up to be counted for Roosevelt.' *Stand Up and Be Counted* was the title of a film (US 1971) about a woman journalist who becomes involved in Women's Lib. In 1976, the British-based entertainer Hughie Green brought out a record entitled 'Stand Up and be Counted' in which he quoted Winston Churchill, lambasted the then Labour Government (by implication) and told the nation to pull its socks up.

Stanley See APPROBATION FROM.

stap my vitals! An oath or expression of surprise, meaning 'stop my breath!' but using the affected pronunciation of Lord Foppington in Sir John Vanbrugh's play *The Relapse*, Act 1, Sc. 3 (1696): 'Well, 'tis Ten Thousand Pawnd well given – stap my Vitals.' Sometimes shortened to just 'Stap me!'

star and garter The Star and Garter is a name given to several British pubs, especially those at Windsor and Putney. It alludes to the Most Noble Order of the Garter, the highest order of knighthood (founded by Edward III in about 1348), and to the star that is an important feature of the insignia. The Royal Star and Garter Homes at Richmond, Surrey, were originally established for wounded war veterans. *Stars and Garters* was the name of an ITV series (1963–6) that presented variety acts in a (fake) pub setting. *Partridge/Slang* reports that 'my star and garter' or 'my stars and garters' were elaborations of the exclamation 'my stars!' and current by the mid-19th century, and probably adopted as though in response to the brightness of breast-worn decorations.

stark staring bonkers A rather English expression for 'mad' and, indeed, a version of 'stark raving mad'. Mid-20th century. The Conservative politician Lord Hailsham, speaking on Labour policies at a General Election press conference (12 October 1964), declared: 'If the British public falls for this, I say it will be stark, staring bonkers.'

(the) stars and bars Nickname for the flag of the Confederate States of the USA (1861), which differed from the 'Stars and Stripes'. Used as the title of a novel, *Stars and Bars* (1984; film US 1988) by William Boyd, in which the bars were of a more alcoholic nature.

starvation in the midst of plenty In *The Book of Cloyne* (1993), concerning the town and former seat of a Protestant bishopric in Co. Cork, Ireland, a certain George Cooper is quoted as having written in 1799: 'The peasant starves in the midst of plenty,' while George Berkeley (1685–1753), the philosopher and one-time Bishop of Cloyne, is also credited with being the first to say this. The *OED2*'s earliest citation (in a different context) is from 1703, and Florence Nightingale is found writing in her *Notes of Nursing* (1861): 'Thousands of patients are annually starved in the midst of plenty.'

star wars The title of the popular sci-fi film *Star Wars* (US 1977) was adopted as a political catchphrase following President Reagan's speech (23 March 1983) proposing to extend the nuclear battleground into space. The President did not use the term 'Star Wars' himself, but it was an inevitable tag to be applied by the media given Reagan's own fondness for adapting lines from the movies. The proposal, properly known by its initials, SDI (for Strategic Defense Initiative), eventually came to nothing.

stately as a galleon Phrase from a song 'Stately As a Galleon' (1962), written and performed by Joyce Grenfell, describing two elderly women in an 'Old Thyme Dance Club' who have to dance together because of the shortage of men partners. Compare Handel's oratorio *Samson*, Act 2, Sc. 2 (1741–2) when Dalila 'attended by her virgins' is greeted by Micah, 'But who is this? That so bedeck'd and gay / Comes this way sailing like a stately ship?' – words based on Milton's *Samson Agonistes*, lines 710–14. In William Congreve, *The Way of the World*, Act 2, Sc. 1 (1700), Mirabell watches the approach of Millamant and comments: 'Here she comes, i'faith, full sail, and with her fan spread and her streamers out, and a shoal of fools for tenders.'

(the) stately homes of England Phrase from the ballad 'The Homes of England' (1827) by Mrs Felicia Dorothea Hemans: 'The stately homes of England, / How beautiful they stand! / Amidst their tall, ancestral trees, / O'er all the pleasant land.' However, it is probably best known as used in one of Noël Coward's most famous songs, from the show *Operette* (1938): 'The Stately Homes of England / How beautiful they stand, / To prove the upper classes / Have still the upper hand.' Quentin Crisp, the English homosexual celebrity (1908–99), wrote in *The Naked Civil Servant* (1968): 'I became one of the stately homos of England.'

(a) stately pleasure dome Phrase in journalistic and popular media use, alluding to the poet Samuel Taylor Coleridge's lines from *Kubla Khan* (1816): 'In Xanadu did Kubla Khan / A stately pleasure-dome decree.' Part of the 'travel scribes' armoury' compiled from a competition in *The Guardian* (10 April 1993). *The Pleasure Dome* – title of a collection of Graham Greene's film criticism (1972); *Welcome to the Pleasure Dome* – title of an album and song by Frankie Goes to Hollywood (1985); 'We would be turning ourselves into not just a non-reproductive society but an unproductive, hedonistic society. Here comes the stately pleasure dome. What kind of beings emerge from a society that does away with all consequences of sexual behaviour?' – *The Sunday Times* (1 May 1994); 'Politics govern artistic activity in France and Italy. President Mitterrand a stately pleasure dome decreed, and thence stem all the Bastille's problems' – *The Times* (12 September 1994); 'Ihilani means "heavenly splendour", and my idea of a decent five-star heaven would definitely include this stately pleasure dome overlooking a tranquil, translucent lagoon' – *The Guardian* (14 January 1995).

state of the art Adjectival phrase describing something that is up-to-the-minute and has the latest features available. Originally used in connection with scientific and technological subjects (by 1955). Latterly, more generally used to describe the newest, latest and most advanced version of anything.

(the) state of the nation Used as the title of British ITV current affairs' specials (from 1966), this phrase might seem to have been devised in emulation of the US President's **state of the Union** message – his annual report to Congress reviewing the way things stand and his intended legislation. This is required of him by the 1787 Constitution: '[The President] shall from time to time give to the Congress information of the state of the union, and recommend to their consideration such measures as he shall judge necessary and expedient . . .' Accordingly, George Washington was the first President to send such a message. It was being referred to as 'the state of the union' by 1945. However, in John Aubrey's plans for a 'Register Generall of People' that he devised *circa* 1684, he writes: 'The design is to have Abstracts of all the above particulars . . . so as to give the King a true State of the Nation at all times' – which may suggest that the concept was known in the 17th century. Edmund Burke wrote *Observations on . . . 'the Present State of the Nation'* in 1769.

states See ALTERED.

***sta viator* [stop, traveller]** The form of epitaph writing that begins or includes 'Stop, stranger/traveller/passer-by' is of ancient origin. A common British epitaphic rhyme is: 'Stop stranger as you pass by / As you are now so once was I / As I am now so will you be / So be prepared to follow me.' James Morris in *Farewell the Trumpets* (1978) records that a Turkish poet, Mehmet Akif Ersoy, is quoted on a memorial above Kilid Bahr at Gallipoli (recalling the debacle of 1915): 'Stop, passer-by! The earth you have just unknowingly trodden is the spot where an era ended and where the heart of a nation beats.' In Gustave Flaubert's novel *Madame Bovary* (1857), the conventional Latin inscription *Sta viator: amabilem conjugem calcas* [hold your step, wayfarer, for you tread on a beloved wife] is put on the grave of Emma Bovary. It is chosen by Homais, the dull chemist, when Emma, a doctor's wife, has taken her own life after committing adultery.

steady, Barker! When Sub-Lieutenant Eric 'Heartthrob' Barker (1912–90) starred in the Royal Navy version of the BBC radio comedy show *Merry Go Round* (*circa* 1945), this was his command to himself. It was later carried over to his other show, *Just Fancy* (1951–61), and became the title of his autobiography in 1956. In that book, Barker writes of the phrase: 'It could be used on so many occasions . . . it almost passed into the language. Also each time it was quoted it gave me the all-vital personal publicity . . . I have had letters from those who have said it helped them to cure a lifelong habit of swearing, as they were able to use it instead. One old lady who shared a flat with an awkward sister in Cheltenham said they had been in danger of drifting apart, but that now, lo! when they reached a point when it seemed neither could endure the bickering a moment longer, they both said, "Steady, Barker!" and it cleared the air. I also learned it was sent as a naval signal from a C-in-C to a ship whose gunfire was a little wide of the mark.'

steady the Buffs! Self-admonitory phrase, meaning 'brace up, be careful, hold on, keep calm'. The Buffs was the name given to the Royal East Kent Regiment (on account of the white facings on their tunics that had got dirty – buff-coloured – during the course of the Battle of Dettingen, 27 June 1743). This was the last battle to be commanded by an English king (George II) in person. It was he who, supposedly, cried out 'Steady the buffs!' as they passed him. However, the phrase may originally have been a military command given to them to hold their position and not to fire. Commonly used by the 1880s.

(to) steal a march on someone To gain an advantage over someone by acting earlier than expected. If one army wished to gain advantage over another, it could march while the other one slept, hence it would 'steal a march' on its opponent. Known by 1771.

(to) steal another's thunder Meaning, 'to get in first and do whatever the other wanted to make a big impression with', particularly with regard to ideas and policies. Known by 1900. The expression is said to derive from an incident involving the dramatist John Dennis (1657–1734). He had invented a device for making the sound of thunder in plays and had used it in an unsuccessful one of his own at the Drury Lane Theatre, London. Subsequently, at the same theatre, he saw a performance of *Macbeth* and noted that the thunder was being produced in his special way. So he said: 'See how the rascals use me! They will not let my play run and yet they steal my thunder!' – quoted in William S. Walsh, *A Handy-Book of Literary Curiosities* (1893). Another version of what he said is: 'That is *my* thunder, by God; the villains will play my thunder, but not my play.'

steam radio This pejorative term for sound broadcasting (in Britain) is said to have been coined by Norman Collins in the early 1950s when, as a broadcasting executive, he transferred his attentions to television. The implicit allusion is to the rivalry between steam and electric trains.

(a) steel magnolia *Steel Magnolias* was the title of a film (US 1990) based on Robert Harling's off-Broadway stage play, revolving round a beauty parlour and the friendship of six women who form the backbone of society in a small Louisiana town. The women share their secrets and, presumably, the title was chosen to suggest their underlying strengths. Earlier, Rosalynn Carter, wife of President Jimmy Carter, had been nicknamed 'the Steel Magnolia'. This First Lady's role (1977–81) apparently went further than holding hands with her husband in public. He consulted her on policy matters, and she seems to have had some influence over his decisions. The magnolia is a flower particularly associated with Southern US areas.

steer See ALWAYS STEER.

stern reply See NO ANSWER CAME.

stick See BETTER THAN A POKE.

stickers See BILL STICKERS.

stick it, Jerry! A phrase from a sketch involving Lew Luke, the Cockney comedian. Playing a burglar, he would say it to his companion when they were throwing missiles at policemen pursuing them. Hence, the phrase of encouragement (i.e. 'stick at it . . .'), originating in the early years of the 20th century. It was popular during the First World War but, apparently, this is not how the name 'Jerry' came to be applied to refer to Germans. As simply 'Stick It!' the phrase appears in a *Punch* cartoon on 2 January 1918.

sticks nix hick pix Phrase meaning that cinema-goers in rural areas are not attracted to films with bucolic themes. It appeared as a headline in *Variety* (17 July 1935) and is credited to Abel Green (1900–73), editor of the showbiz paper at the time. In the film *Yankee Doodle Dandy* (US 1942), James Cagney, playing George M. Cohan, rattles it off about three times, clearly sounding as if he is saying '*hicks* pix'. Even if this version makes the saying flow better, it is not what was actually printed, which was: 'Sticks Nix Hick Pix'.

(a) stiff prick has no conscience This proverbial view was ascribed confidently to St Augustine by John Osborne in *Almost a Gentleman* (1991). This would not be surprising given Augustine's interesting activities prior to conversion. After all, he did write '*Da mihi castitatem et continentiam, sed noli modo* [give me chastity and continence – but not yet]' in his *Confessions* (AD 397–8). The proverbial status of the remark was, however, evident by the 1880s when 'Walter' in *My Secret Life*, Vol. 1, Chap. 12, wrote: 'I thought how unfair it was to her sister, who was in the family way by me . . . but a standing prick stifles all conscience.' Indeed, 'a *standing* prick has no conscience' is an equally well-known variant. *Partridge/Catch Phrases* adds that this proverbial view is sometimes completed with, '. . . and an itching c*** feels no shame', just to even out the matter. Further confirmation of the proverbial nature of this kind of saying is to be found in the diary of Samuel Pepys where, on 15 May 1663, he writes of hearing from Sir Thomas Crew that: 'The King [Charles II] doth mind nothing but pleasures and hates the very sight or thoughts of business. That my Lady Castlemayne rules him; who he says hath all the tricks of Aretin [erotic writer Pietro Aretino] that are to be practised to give pleasure – in which he is too able, hav[ing] a large — [Pepys's blank]; but that which is the unhappiness is that, as the Italian proverb says, *Cazzo dritto non vuolt consiglio* [a stiff prick doesn't want any advice].' Compare: 'Another writer whom [Wilde] did not spare was his old teacher J. P. Mahaffy, two of whose books Wilde reviewed . . . [he] might have treated Mahaffy nostalgically, but the erect pen has no conscience' – Richard Ellman, *Oscar Wilde* (1987).

(to keep, carry, have a) stiff upper lip To be courageous and unflappable. Although once very much associated with the British, the phrase is of American origin: 'I kept a stiff upper lip, and bought [a] license to sell my goods' – *Massachussetts Spy* (14 June 1815). 'And though hard be the task, / "Keep a stiff upper lip"' – Phoebe Cary (American poet, 1824–71), 'Keep a Stiff Upper Lip'. The specific application to the British had obviously occurred by the time of Ira Gershwin's lyric for the song 'Stiff Upper Lip' in *A Damsel in Distress* (1937) where it is sung by the secretary and girlfriend of an American press agent in England: 'What made Good Queen Bess / Such a great success? / What made Wellington do / What he did at Waterloo? . . . / It isn't roast beef or ale or home or mother; / It's just a little thing they say to one another: / . . . Stiff upper lip! Stout fella! / When the going's rough.' *Stiff Upper Lip* has also been the title of a novel (1963) by P. G. Wodehouse and *Stiff Upper Lips* of a film (UK 1997) parodying recent British 'white flannel' screenplays like *Chariots of Fire* and *Brideshead Revisited*.

still See BE STILL.

still —— after all these years Format phrase based on 'Still Crazy After All These Years', the song and album title (1975) by Paul Simon. Writing in *The Hartford Courant* (Connecticut, 30 April 1998), Henry McNulty made the claim that Simon's song had been the inspiration for more headlines than virtually any other song lyric. His explanation: 'Journalists and presumably readers love where-are-they-now stories on people and events of the past. A whole lot of the time, what the reporter finds out is that not much has changed over time. And what could fit the story better than a headline proclaiming "Still [fill the blank] After All These Years"?' As if to oblige, a few days later the *Courant* ran 'Still Clueless After All These Years' over a story about images of women in advertising. 'Stiletto After All These Years' – *Interview* Magazine (June 1994); 'Still Painful After All These Years' – *Harvard Health Letter* (June 1995) (about gout); 'Still Hazy After All These Years' – *The New England Journal of Medicine* (6 October 1994) (about difficult diagnoses), and so on and so on. Hence, also, the title of the film *Still Crazy* (US/UK 1998) (about ageing rock stars) presumably refers.

stinking See CRY.

(to) stir one's stumps To walk or dance briskly – and latterly to bestir oneself to action of any kind. Known since 1559. 'Stump' here means leg, as it has done since at least the 15th century.

(a) stitch in time saves nine A small repair to clothing now may avoid the necessity of having to make a larger repair at a later date; or, figuratively, prompt action now will save serious trouble later on. A proverbial expression known by 1732. *CODP* suggests that 'nine' is merely to give assonance to a couplet (in which form the saying is sometimes displayed).

stolen kisses   *Baisers Volés* was the title of a film (France 1968) by François Truffaut and, as such, is taken from a phrase in the song, '*Que Reste-t-il de Nos Amours*' (1943), written and performed by Charles Trenet (and which is featured in the film). The phrase suggests perhaps that filched, fleeting moments of happiness are the most that can be hoped for in life. In English, there had earlier been a song, 'A Stolen Kiss' (1923), by R. Penso; also a ballad, undated, by F. Buckley, 'Stolen Kisses are the Sweetest'. The proverbial 'stolen kisses are sweet' had appeared, for example, in R. H. Barham's *The Ingoldsby Legends* (1840). Most probably this last saying derives from the proverb **stolen fruit is sweet**, established by the early 17th century and often used alluding to the temptation of Eve with the apple in Genesis 3:6. Also current in the 17th century was **stolen pleasures are sweetest**, perhaps reflecting Proverbs 9:17: 'Stolen waters are sweet.'

stone me!   Mild oath or exclamation. *Partridge/Catch Phrases* suggests that it has been around since the 1920s. Tony Hancock used it often in his BBC radio and TV shows *Hancock's Half-Hour* (1954–61. Possibly a blend of STONE THE CROWS and 'Stap me!'

stone the crows!   Mild oath or exclamation – of no obvious origin, except to state the obvious: expressions of disgust usually contain jabbing, explosive opening consonants that help the utterer get things off his chest. The *OED2* has citations going back to 1930. G. A. Wilkes, *A Dictionary of Australian Colloquialisms* (1978), comments, 'Sometimes "stiffen the crows" or "stone the crows and stiffen the lizards", occurring most frequently in comic strip Australian', and offers a 1918 citation as '"Starve the crows," howled Bluey in that agonised screech of his.' Another suggestion: might it be a euphemistic way of saying 'Stone the cross!' (i.e. 'croze' as in 'crozier' and suitably blasphemous-

sounding). Or might it come from 'holy-stoning' – cleaning decks with soft sand-stone – coupled with an allusion to 'crow's nest'?

(a) stool pigeon   A police spy or decoy. American origin, from the original meaning of the term, a decoy-bird – after the practice of tying or fixing a pigeon to a stool in order to attract other pigeons to it. They were then shot. First sense known by 1825, second by 1906.

stop da music!   See under GOODNIGHT, MRS CALABASH . . .

stop – look – listen   Slogan, said to have been devised in 1912 by Ralph R. Upton, an American engineer, for use on notices at railway crossings in place of the earlier 'Look out for the locomotive'. Certainly, a show called *Stop! Look! Listen!* opened a show (with music by Cole Porter) at the Globe Theater, New York (27 December 1915). A George Robey song from *The Bing Boys Are Here* (1916) was entitled, 'I Stopped, I Looked, I Listened', and by 1936, an advertisement for H. H. Sullivan Inc 'Technical merchandise' (Rochester, New York) was playing with the phrase to the extent of 'Stop, look and kiss 'em' to accompany the picture of a leggy girl in cheesecake pose.

stop me and buy one   Slogan for Wall's ice cream in the UK, from 1923. The phrase is believed to have been invented by Lionel and Charles Rodd, who were on the board of T. Wall & Sons. With the slogan on their tricycles, 8,500 salesmen then pedalled round Britain out of a national network of 136 depots. One salesman whose brakes failed as he descended a very steep hill introduced a slight variation as he hurtled to destruction: 'If you can stop me, you can have the lot.' In the 1970s, there followed the graffito on contraceptive vending machines, 'Buy me and stop one.'

stop me if you've heard it (or this one . . .)   Apologetic preamble to a joke. Since the 1920s. 'Stop me if you've heard it before, won't you?' – *Punch* Magazine (28 January 1925); 'Surely, if Mr Lewis in outlining his plot to some friend, had only said, "Stop me if you've heard this," more than two hundred pages of *Dodsworth* need never have been written' – Dorothy Parker, in *The New Yorker* (16 March 1929); "'It is the custom in Bongo-Bongo to hunt the rhinoceros, and this friend of mine . . . George Bates his name was . . . by the way, stop me if I've told you this before . . .'" – P. G. Wodehouse, 'The Code of the Mulliners' (1935).

stop messin' abaht! Catchphrase of Kenneth Williams, the English comedy actor (1926–88), in the BBC radio show *Hancock's Half-Hour* and subsequently. Co-scriptwriter Ray Galton has said of this BBC radio show's start in 1954: 'Alan Simpson and I wanted a show without breaks, guest singers and catchphrases – something that hadn't been done before. After the first week with Kenneth Williams in the show, bang went out the idea of no funny voices and no catchphrases!' Although Williams's cameos occupied a very tiny part of the show, they were enough to start him on an outrageous career. His 'stop messin' abaht!' began with the Hancock show – indeed, in 'The Bequest' (2 November 1955) Hancock uses the phrase himself and then Williams says it. *Stop Messing About* was later used as the title of a radio show of which Williams, by that time, was the star (1969–70). Williams also had an expression, **it's a disgrace!**, that he used personally all the time – see *The Kenneth Williams Diaries* (1993), *passim* – but also in character, particularly on *Round the Horne*.

stop the world I want to get off! Meaning, 'I'm tired of life' and taken from the title of a musical written by Anthony Newley and Leslie Bricusse (1961; filmed UK 1966). They, in turn, apparently took it from a graffito.

stoppp! See ONCE AGAIN WE STOP.

stop the presses See HOLD THE FRONT PAGE.

Stork See CAN YOU TELL.

storm See ANY PORT.

(a) storm in a teacup Meaning, 'a short-lived dispute about nothing of importance'. Date of origin not known, but *Apperson* finds 'Our skirmish . . . is but a storm in a cream bowl' in 1678 and compares Cicero's *fluctus excitare in*

simpulo where this means to make much ado about nothing 'in a ladle'. Other versions are 'in a wash-hand basin' and 'slop-basin'. The now standard 'teacup' version seems to have begun with *A Storm in a Teacup*, the title of a farce (1854) by W. B. Bernard, an American playwright. Listed as a cliché in *The Times* (28 May 1984). 'Shadow Foreign Secretary Geoffrey Rippon said he was astonished by the angry reaction to his call for a force of citizen volunteers . . . he insisted that the row was a "storm in a teacup"' – *Daily Mirror* (9 September 1974); 'Village hit by storm in tea cup' – headline in *The Times* (26 July 1994); 'Storm in Bradford tea cup' – headline in *The Times* (26 September 1994); 'It might follow from this that Budget 2 is just a storm in a Commons tea-room tea-cup, a one-day wonder to be easily forgotten as the political roller-coaster buckets onwards' – *The Guardian* (9 December 1994).

story See AND THIS IS WHERE; BUT THAT'S ANOTHER; EVERYDAY.

stout See COLLAPSE OF.

stove See HERE AM I.

(the) straight and narrow Meaning, the path of law-abiding behaviour or goodness from which it is easy to wander. From Matthew 7:14: 'Strait is the gate, and narrow is the way, which leadeth unto life, and few there be that find it.'

(to get something) straight from the horse's mouth To hear something directly from the person concerned and not garbled by an intermediary. The horse itself is not doing any speaking, of course. A horse's age can be judged best by looking at its teeth (which grow according to a strict system). So, if you are buying a horse, you do better to look at its teeth than rely on any information about its age that the vendor might give you. Known by 1928. 'Meanwhile, it was a privilege. Straight from the horse's mouth into the note-book. The boys scribbled like mad' – Aldous Huxley, *Brave New World*, Chap. 1 (1932). *The Horse's Mouth* was the title of a novel by Joyce Cary (1944).

straight out of Central Casting Meaning, 'a person who conforms totally to type, or to what you would expect'. Central Casting was set up in 1926 and maintained by all major Hollywood studios as a pool for supplying extras for films. David Niven, for example, claimed to have been listed on their books in the mid-1930s as 'Anglo-Saxon Type No. 2008'. 'If you had asked Central Casting, or Equity, to provide an archetypal bigot, it's unlikely they could come up with someone as perfect as Jan van der Berg . . . owner of one of the better restaurants in Windhoek, the capital of Namibia' – *The Observer* (19 March 1989).

strange but true   The contrasting conjunction of these two adjectives was recorded by 1594 and remains a potent combination. From Anon., *Collection of Epitaphs* (1806): 'Here lies one *Strange*, no *Pagan*, *Turk*, nor *Jew*, / 'Tis *Strange*, but so *Strange* as it is true.' The first line of the song 'So In Love' from Cole Porter's *Kiss Me Kate* (1948) is 'Strange, dear, but true, dear.' *Strange But True* was the title of a book of odd newspaper stories, edited by Tim Healey (1983). 'Interesting If True' was the title of a gossip column in the *Independent on Sunday* in 1990. Compare the proverbial **truth is stranger than fiction**. In Edmund Burke's *On Conciliation with America* (1775), this appears as 'Fiction lags after truth'. In Byron's *Don Juan*, xiv.ci (1819–24), he uses both forms : ''Tis strange, but true; for truth is always strange – / Stranger than fiction.' By the mid-19th century, the version 'Fact is stranger than fiction' had also emerged.

streets paved with gold   What traditionally lures people to seek their fortune in the big city. But where did this near-cliché originate? In the story of Dick Whittington, he makes his way to London from Gloucestershire because he hears the streets are paved with gold and silver. The actual Dick Whittington was thrice Lord Mayor of London in the late 14th and early 15th centuries. The popular legend does not appear to have been told before 1605. *Benham* (1948) comments on the proverbial expression 'London streets are paved with gold' – 'A doubtful story or tradition alleges that this saying was due to the fact that *circa* 1470, a number of members of the Goldsmiths' Company, London, joined the Paviors' Company.' George Colman the Younger wrote in *The Heir-at-Law* (1797): 'Oh, London is a fine town, / A very famous city, / Where all the streets are paved with gold, / And all the maidens pretty'; The Percy French song 'The Mountains of Mourne' (1896) mentions 'Diggin' for gold in the streets [of London]'; 'He had played the traditional part of the country boy who comes up to London where the streets are paved with gold' – G. K. Chesterton, *William Cobbett* (1925); in the Marx Brothers' film *Go West* (US 1940), Chico says: 'He's goin' West, and when he gets off the train he's gonna pick up some gold and send it to me. They say that the gold is layin' all over the streets.' When Hollywood was in its heyday, many writers were reluctant to go there, fearing how badly they would be treated. According to Arthur Marx in *Son of Groucho* (1973), his father tried very hard to persuade the dramatist George S. Kaufman to join him out on the West Coast. 'No, no,' said Kaufman. 'I don't care how much they pay me. I hate it out there.' 'But, George,' pleaded Groucho, 'the streets out here are paved with gold.' There was a moment's pause, and then Kaufman said, 'You mean, you have to bend down and pick it up?' The streets of heaven are also sometimes said to be paved with gold – though not specifically as such in the Bible. There is, however, a 'Negro' spiritual where the 'streets in heaven am paved with gold' and Revelation 21:21 has: 'The street of the city was pure gold'.

strictly for the birds   Meaning 'of no consequence', this is a US expression (by 1951), alluding to horse manure that is good only for picking over by small birds. It was the title of a Dudley Moore instrumental number (1961), and also, rather oddly, given its origin, was used in a Rexona soap advertisement (1968).

strife-torn ——   Journalistic cliché known by 1884. 'The pall of fear hangs heavy over the strife-torn city today' – cited by Malcolm Bradbury in an article on clichés in *Tatler* (March 1980); 'The 36-year-old pacifist leader from strife-torn Northern Ireland declared . . .' – *Arab Times* (14 December 1977); 'For strife-torn Cambodia, that is understandable – for Scotland it is to our shame that we do not set a better example in how we legally protect our natural inheritance in perpetuity for the benefits and enjoyment of present and future generations' – letter to the editor in *The Scotsman* (23 May 1994).

(to) strike the mother lode To find whatever it is that guarantees a supply of (usually) wealth or success. From mining, where the 'mother lode' is the main vein. 'Son of a bitch! We struck the mother-lode' – woman TV executive in the film *Network* (US 1976) when news comes in that the TV evangelist is making viewers imitate him and his madness.

stripped, washed and brought to my tent The singer and actress Cher spent a certain amount of time in March 1988 denying, apropos some toy-boy lover, that she had ever ordered him, metaphorically speaking, to be stripped, washed and brought to her tent. The allusion here was not very precise. Presumably, the suggestion was that she had behaved as, say, an Arab prince might to an underling (either male or female). Perhaps she acquired the line from some film about sheikhs and harems? Compare from Christopher Marlowe, *Tamburlaine the Great*, Pt 2, Act 4, Sc. 1 (1590): 'Then bring those Turkish harlots to my tent / And I'll dispose them as it likes me best.'

striving mightily A florid expression for great endeavour. It appears to have originated in Shakespeare, *The Taming of the Shrew*, I.ii.276 (1592–3): 'And do as adversaries do in law, / Strive mightily, but eat and drink as friends.'

stroke See ALL ROWED; AT A STROKE.

strokes See DIFFERENT.

(a) stroking session An informal meeting at which an attempt is made to persuade and win over somebody – a political opponent, say – to your cause. The term emerged from the White House occupancy of President Richard Nixon and was known by 1973. The choice of the word 'stroking' may have a sexual connotation. Sometimes envoys would be sent on a **stroking mission**. 'President Nixon, revolted by such direct methods, preferred what he called "stroking," a process of

jawboning so sweet to the strokee's earbones that the victim fell into a hypnotic state in which he could be deboned without realizing it' – Russell Baker, *The New York Times* (4 April 1978); 'As if the "stroking missions" were not enough, Nixon began to write Lon Nol a series of warm optimistic letters' – William Shawcross, *Sideshow* (1986).

strong enough to trot a mouse on 'My father, who was in the army for much of his life, always enjoyed a cup of tea but didn't like it too strong. If it was, he would remark that it was "strong enough to trot a mouse on"' – J. G. Hills, Hampshire (1994). The film director Bryan Forbes remembered this (1998) from Lincolnshire as, 'strong enough for a mouse to skate on'.

struck all of a heap Astounded. Gerald du Maurier, as a schoolboy, wrote to his sister about her getting engaged (30 March 1890): 'My Darling Sylvia, I am so sorry I haven't written to congratulate you, but I was "struck all of a 'eap!"' Sir Walter Scott was calling it 'that vulgar phrase' in 1817. 'Struck of a heap' was current by 1741 and Shakespeare has 'all on a heap'.

studio See AND WITH THAT.

(a) stuffed shirt A stiff, pompous person. There seems to be an urge among obituary writers to credit the recently deceased with the coining of phrases, even where the facts do not really support it. Patrick Brogan writing of Mrs Clare Boothe Luce in *The Independent* (12 October 1987) stated: 'She wrote a series of articles poking fun at the rich and pompous, coining for them the descriptive phrase "stuffed shirts", a title she used for her first book.' That book was published in 1933, but the *OED2* has an example of the phrase dating from 1913 (when Luce was a mere ten), which makes it clear that by then it was already current US usage. So though she may have repopularized the phrase she certainly didn't coin it.

stupid boy! Right from the first episode of the BBC TV comedy series *Dad's Army* (1968–77), Captain Mainwaring (Arthur Lowe) was apt to exclaim, 'Stupid boy!' to Private Pike (Ian Lavender). When Lowe died in 1982, the *Daily Mail* reported: 'The

Captain did try to go unrecognised in private life, but found it increasingly difficult. Often people would come up to him in the street or in restaurants and ask him to say "Stupid boy!" just once.'

Sturm und Drang [storm and stress]
Name given to the German literary movement of the late 18th century that chiefly consisted of violently passionate dramas by the likes of Goethe and Schiller. Said to have been applied by Goethe himself. It came from the title of a play (1777) by Friedrich Maximilian von Klinger, German playwright (1752–1831).

(from the) sublime to the ridiculous
This phrase usually comes now without the additional qualifying phrase: '. . . there is but one step'. Napoleon is said to have uttered on one occasion (probably to the Polish ambassador, De Pradt, after the retreat from Moscow in 1812): '*Du sublime au ridicule il n'y a qu'un pas.*' However, Thomas Paine had already written in *The Age of Reason* (1795): 'The sublime and the ridiculous are often so nearly related, that is difficult to class them separately. One step above the sublime, makes the ridiculous; and one step above the ridiculous, makes the sublime again.' Indeed, the chances are that 'from the sublime to the ridiculous' may have been a standard turn of phrase in the late 18th century. 'Dante, Petrarch, Boccacio, Ariosto, make very sudden transitions from the sublime to the ridiculous' – Joseph Warton, *Essay on the Genius and Writings of Pope*, Vol. 2 (1772).

success   See BITCH-GODDESS.

such is life!   A reflective expression of the inevitable. Recorded by 1796 in William Temple's diary: 'This interruption is very teasing; but such is life'. From a George Eliot letter (20 December 1860): 'Our curtains are not up and our oil-cloth is not down. Such is life, seen from the furnishing point of view.' The last words of Ned Kelly, the Australian outlaw who was hanged in Melbourne in 1880 at the age of twenty-five, are said to have been: 'Ah well, I suppose it has come to this! . . . Such is life!' The British pop singer and political clown 'Lord' David Sutch felicitously entitled his autobiography *Life as Sutch* (1992).

such stuff as dreams are made on   If one is quoting Prospero's words from Shakespeare, *The Tempest*, IV.i.156 (1612): 'We are such stuff / As dreams are made on' – it is definitely 'on' not 'of' (though Shakespeare did use the 'of' form elsewhere). Humphrey Bogart as Sam Spade in *The Maltese Falcon* (1941) is asked: 'What is it?' before speaking the last line of the picture, and replies: 'The stuff that dreams are made of.' The title of the 1964 Cambridge Footlights revue was *Stuff What Dreams Are Made Of.* 'Stuff that dreams are made on' – headline in *The Guardian* (9 May 1988).

such were the joys   George Orwell entitled a long essay on his prep school days *Such, Such Were the Joys.* Presumably, he was being ironic. It was written in 1947 and published in *The Partisan Review* (September/October 1952). Also used as the title of a collection of his essays published in New York (1953). The phrase comes from *Songs of Innocence,* 'The Ecchoing Green' (1789) by William Blake: 'Such, such were the joys, / When we all, girls & boys, / In our youth time were seen / On the Ecchoing Green.'

suck   See DON'T TEACH.

(a) sucker punch   A punch (or metaphorical blow) that takes a person by surprise. So named because the person is taken to be a sucker for allowing this to happen. Originally from boxing use in the USA and recorded by 1947. 'Exploited since childhood, the poor man [Michael Jackson] still hasn't managed to reach the stage when he can see the next sucker punch coming' – *The Independent* (7 February 2003).

(to) suffer a sea change   Grandiloquent and irrelevant way of saying 'change'. The phrase alludes to a line from Shakespeare, *The Tempest*, I.ii.401 (1612). However, when Ariel sings 'Suffer a sea-change into something rich and strange', he does actually mean a change caused by the sea. 'I sensed, as apparently Jim Callaghan also sensed in the course of the campaign, that a sea change had occurred in the political sensibility of the British people. They had given up on socialism – the thirty-year experiment had plainly failed – and were ready to try something else. The sea change was our mandate' – Margaret Thatcher, *The Downing Street Years* (1993); 'The shares bounced briefly, but are already almost back to where they were before the figures were released. Yet there are signs of a sea-change in investor behaviour, with funds flowing strongly into unit trusts even when shares generally are not doing well' – *Independent on Sunday* (5 June 1994); 'Anne Simpson, director of PIRC, said: "I believe that if we win, it will bring about a sea-change in pay policies. If we can put down a marker, I think other companies will take note' – *The Times* (8 April 1995); 'Today the [Oxford Union's] finances stand on a solid footing . . . This sea-change is due in large part to the wise guidance of Lord Goodman' – Harvey McGregor in *The Independent* (27 May 1995); 'Interest rates have reached their peak . . . according to Roger Bootle, a leading City economist. His forecast marks a sea-change in the sentiment sweeping through the markets' – *Independent on Sunday* (4 June 1995).

sugar See DOES HE TAKE.

suitable for children of all ages Promotional phrase in the UK since the 1950s/ 60s and an instant cliché. 'Obscenities are so frequently used on television that they are regarded as acceptable parlance; children of all ages and classes use obscene language in public' – letter to the editor in *The Daily Telegraph* (16 May 1994); 'Top of the toys . . . It will occupy children of all ages for hours on end and might well produce the next era of construction engineers' – *Daily Record* (2 December 1994).

suits you, sir! Catchphrase from BBC TV comedy series *The Fast Show* (1994–2000), spoken by Paul Whitehouse as a slimey, nudging tailor. But NB: 'Writer Charlie Higson . . . told us that one of the nation's most famous and beloved comedy catchphrases has been horribly misrepresented for the past few years, not just by the media but in school playgrounds and, almost certainly at thousands of tedious dinner parties. "There isn't an S," he sighed. 'We've been doing it for years and you think people would have noticed

that." We must hang our heads in collective shame for, apparently, it was never "SUITS YOU, SIR!" but "SUIT YOU"' – *The Observer* (28 October 2001). *The Fast Show* also gave rise to **. . . which was nice!** and to **does my bum look big in this?** This last was spoken by Arabella Weir, trying on clothes in a shop, and also caught on considerably. Weir, inevitably, wrote a book with the title.

(the) summer game Cricket. Date of origin unknown, but it is referred to as such in the Billy Bunter stories by Frank Richards (from 1908 onwards) and in Peter Tinniswood's *Tales From a Long Room* (in TV and book form in the 1980s). From the 14th century onwards, 'summer-game' was the name given to a festival held in midsummer.

(the) summer of a dormouse A very short time. The phrase originated in Byron's journal (7 December 1813): 'When one subtracts from life infancy (which is vegetation), – sleep, eating, and swilling – buttoning and unbuttoning – how much remains of downright existence? The summer of a dormouse.' 'If I ever write an autobiography, Byron has found me the title' – Kenneth Tynan in a letter (17 November 1972), also in his diary entry for the same date. Hence, *The Summer of a Dormouse*, title of a novel (1967) by Monica Stirling and title of memoirs (2000) by John Mortimer. [*ODQ* (1992) has 'all this buttoning and unbuttoning' from an anonymous '18th-century suicide note'.]

(the) summer of love The summer of 1967 and so known at the time. It was the high point of the Sixties, at least in terms of the Hippie, Flower Power, 'Love' generation, concerned with drugs and pop music. The chief event of the summer in the world of pop culture was the release of the album *Sgt. Pepper's Lonely Hearts Club Band* by The Beatles. In the same month, June, they sang 'All You Need Is Love' on the first world TV satellite hook-up. 'Another strand was the emergence of an overt philosophy of "love and peace". In San Francisco, indeed, a Summer of Love had been proclaimed by the committee representing Haight-Ashbury' – Derek Taylor, *It Was Twenty Years Ago Today*,

Chap. 3 (1987). This book also contains a photo of The Charlatans performing in the Panhandle, Golden Gate Park, San Francisco. Behind them is a banner (with flower motifs) bearing the words 'Council for Summer of Love'.

(a) summit conference (or **meeting)** A meeting of the chief representatives of anything, usually political leaders of major world powers. 'It is not easy to see how things could be worsened by a parley at the summit, if such a thing were possible' – Winston Churchill, quoted in *The Times* (15 February 1950). This is apparently the genesis of the 'summit' concept, though earlier Walter Bagehot had written in *The English Constitution* (1867): 'Nations touch at their summits.'

sum not unadjacent See NOT A MILLION.

(the) sun also rises Famous as the title of an Ernest Hemingway novel, *The Sun Also Rises*, about expatriates in Europe (1926; film US 1957) (also known as *Fiesta* in the UK), the phrase comes from Ecclesiastes 1:5: 'The sun also ariseth, and the sun goeth down, and hasteth to his place where he arose.' It promoted a Hollywood joke, 'The son-in-law also rises', possibly when Louis B. Mayer promoted his daughter's husband, William Goetz, to a key position at MGM – quoted in Leslie Halliwell, *The Filmgoer's Book of Quotes* (1973). More recently, there has been a book about the Japanese economy called *The Sun Also Sets* (1990) by Bill Emmott.

Sunday See ANOTHER; BLOODY.

(the) sun in splendour *The Sun in Splendour* makes a wonderful book title – as both Jean Plaidy (1983) and Colin Maxwell (1985) have shown – but is it a quotation? It is not quite in Shakespeare, but in 1960 when BBC TV fashioned a series called *An Age of Kings* out of the English history plays from *Richard II* to *Richard III*, the fifteen fortnightly episodes had individual titles such as 'The Hollow Crown', 'The Road to Shrewsbury', 'The Band of Brothers', 'The Boar Hunt', 'The Morning's War' (some quotations, some not). Another was 'The Sun in Splendour'. The exact phrase is not to be found in

Shakespeare, but it alludes to *Henry VI, Part 3* (II.i.21) when Richard, Duke of Gloucester, says: 'See how the morning opes her golden gates, / And takes her farewell of the glorious sun!' A stage direction indicates at this point that no fewer than *three suns appear in the air*. This is an allusion to an occurrence before the actual battle of Mortimer's Cross (in 1461), when Edward IV saw three suns 'sodainly joined all together in one'. In consequence, according to Hall, the chronicler, he 'toke suche courage that he fiercely set on his enemies, & them shortly discomfited: for which cause, men imagined, that he gave the sunne in his full brightness for his cognisaunce or badge.' Indeed, he did, and the 'sun in splendour' or 'in his glory' or 'in his brightness' became a feature of heraldry. The symbol is always shown with surrounding rays and sometimes with a human face on it. So well known was this, that Shakespeare could assume that his audience knew what he was on about when, in the opening lines of *Richard III*, he has Gloucester state punningly: 'Now is the winter of our discontent / Made glorious summer by this *sun* of York.'

Sunny Jim Term applied to a cheerful person. One might say, 'Ah, there you are . . . I've been looking for you, Sunny Jim' – even if the person isn't called Jim. From *Lady Cynthia Asquith's Diary* (for 13 July 1918): 'I like McKenna. He is such a "Sunny Jim" and ripples on so easily.' But it can also be a slightly patronizing expression, and thus was aptly applied to James Callaghan, when Prime Minister, who was nothing if not patronizing in return with his air of a bank manager who knew best – an *Observer* headline of 18 March 1979 stated, 'Sunny Jim tires of wheeler-dealing'. Few who use the term know that it originated with a character who appeared in ads for Force breakfast cereal from about 1903. He was the invention of two young American women, a Miss Ficken and Minnie Maud Hanff (usually credited with the phrase), who came up with a jingle and rough sketch of the character for the Force Food Company.

(the) sunrise industries New and expanding industries. These were much talked about in the 1980s in comparison with 'sunset industries'. The image is a simple one. Sunrise industries are on the way up, sunset industries are on the way down. The term 'sunrise' does not mean that people have to get up early to go to work in them. President Reagan, in his January 1984 State of the Union message, paid tribute to the 'entrepreneurs and risk-takers in the "sunrise industries" of high tech'. The quotation marks in the *Washington Post* report indicate that it must still have been a newish phrase. The *Economist* had, however, been using it in February 1980.

sun, sand and sea Travel journalistic and promotional slogan/cliché. In the 1939 film version of *The Four Feathers* the Sudan is referred to, with similar alliteration, as 'sun, sweat and sunstroke'. In 1972, I interviewed a group of children born in London of West Indian parents, who were about to pay their first visit to Barbados. When I asked one of them what he expected to find there, he quite spontaneously said: 'All I know is, it's sun, sand and sea.' We used this line as the title of a BBC Radio programme that reported their reactions before and after the visit. Clearly, the child had absorbed the phrase at an early age. It is never very far away. Several songs have the title. Part of the 'travel scribes' armoury' compiled from a competition in *The Guardian* (10 April 1993). Increasingly, a fourth S (for sex) has crept into the phrase. 'Sun, sand and sea are no longer enough for the Yuppie generation of fun-seekers' – photo caption in *The Observer* (26 June 1988); 'We bought the beachfront land [in Barbados] a couple of years ago. Sunshine, sand and sea, it's the stuff that dreams and travel brochures are made of' – Bob Monkhouse, *Crying With Laughter* (1993); 'Sea, sand and celebration: a guide to the Brighton Festival' – *Big Issue* (1–7 May, 1995).

sunset See DRIVE OFF INTO THE.

(the) sun sinks slowly in the west Cliché of the cinema travelogue, though it has not been confirmed as being in the 'Fitzpatrick Traveltalks' (1930s – see AND SO WE SAY FAREWELL).

—— **Superstar** PHRASES. This suffix became fashionable following the success of the musical *Jesus Christ Superstar* (1970). Tim Rice, its lyricist, says that he and the composer, Andrew Lloyd Webber, settled on the title after seeing a 1960s' Las Vegas billing for 'Tom Jones – Superstar'. The showbiz use of the term 'superstar' although very much a 1960s' thing – it was also used by Andy Warhol – has been traced back to 1925 by the *OED2* which finds in that year talk of 'cinema superstars'.

supporters of the status quo Date of origin not known. Listed in *The Independent* (24 December 1994) as a cliché of newspaper editorials. 'Sebastian Coe, as clean-cut and as mother-in-law-friendly as Andrew, has gone the whole hog and become a Conservative MP. How far does this reflect a trend? Have the moral leaders become young fogeys; or pillars of the Establishment; or supporters of the status quo?' – *The Times* (28 September 1994). The Latin phrase *status quo* itself, literally meaning 'the state in which' but referring to 'the existing state of affairs', has been known since at least the 1830s. Precisely how the phrase was introduced into the language is not known, but it appears to be neither classical nor medieval Latin.

support your local —— A slogan format, almost certainly from the USA. Established before the film *Support Your Local Sheriff* (US 1968), which was followed three years later by *Support Your Local Gunfighter*. In 1969 there was a police bumper sticker in the USA, 'Support your local police, keep them independent.'

sure See AS SURE.

(a) surfeit of lampreys What King Henry I of England died of in 1135. Or, at least, according to Robert Fabyan, *The New Chronicles of England and France* (1516): 'King Henry being in Normandy, after some writers [i.e. according to some accounts], fell from or with his horse, whereof he took his death; but Ranulphe says he took a surfeit by eating of a lamprey, and thereof died.' A lamprey is a fish that looks a bit like an eel. A surfeit does not necessarily mean an excess. Hence, *A Surfeit of Lampreys*, title of a detective novel (1941) by Ngaio Marsh. Compare Sellar & Yeatman, *1066 and All That*, Chap 13 (1930): 'Henry tried to console himself [for the loss of his son] by eating a surfeit of palfreys. This was a Bad Thing since he died of it and *never smiled again.*'

sur le continong   See MORNING, ALL.

surprise, surprise! What you say when giving someone an unexpected present or when arriving unexpectedly to see him or her or when commenting ironically on what is thought to be an obvious fact. Possibly of American origin, 1950s. In the 1990s, a British TV show with the title *Surprise, Surprise* was built on the premise of surprising members of the public who had merited this treatment. 'The new middle-class voters and the manual workers who had moved into the income tax-paying brackets did not – surprise, surprise! – like high taxation when it applied to them' – John Cole, *As It Seemed To Me* (1995); 'Franz Welser-Möst will doubtless have seen the irony in stepping down as music director of the London Philharmonic with a Requiem . . . But there is an old theatrical adage that says "Always leave them wanting more". And – surprise, surprise – I do believe he has' – *The Independent* (8 May 1996).

(the) survival of the fittest Phrase coined by Herbert Spencer in *Principles of Biology* (1864–7): 'This survival of the fittest which I have here sought to express in mechanical terms is that which Mr Darwin has called "natural selection, or the preservation of favoured races in the struggle for life".' In other words, Spencer, in talking of evolution and the 'survival of the fittest', was pointing to the survival of the most suitable, not of the most physically fit. George John Douglas Campbell commented on the coinage in *Organic Evolution Cross-examined* (1898): 'Nothing could be happier than this invention for . . . giving vogue to whatever it might be supposed to mean . . . It is the fittest of all phrases to survive.'

SWALK Lover's acronym in correspondence, meaning 'Sealed With A Loving Kiss'. Possibly dating from the days of military censorship of letters in the First World War.

S.W.A.L.K. was the alternative title of the film *Melody* (UK 1971).

Swanee   See SOLD DOWN THE RIVER.

swans   See ALL ONE'S.

(a) swan song Meaning, 'a farewell action, the last work or performance of a writer or actor or musician'. From the erroneous belief that swans sing just before they die. Not known in this figurative sense until the 1890s. Cited as a 'dying metaphor' in George Orwell's 'Politics and the English Language', *Horizon* (April 1946). 'A swansong for Martina, the finest there ever was' – headline in *The Sunday Times* (19 June 1994); '*Red*, unlike *Blue* or *White*, failed to carry off a major film festival prize, but is easily the most entertaining and accessible of the trilogy. The director has announced his retirement, so it is also quite possibly his swansong' – *The Sunday Telegraph* (13 November 1994).

swear   See ENOUGH TO MAKE; I SWEAR.

swearing   See AS NEAR AS.

sweat   See HORSES.

(the) Sweeney The title of a British TV drama series, *The Sweeney* (1974–8), about Scotland Yard's Flying Squad comes from rhyming slang: Sweeney Todd = Flying Squad. Sweeney Todd, 'the demon barber of Fleet Street', murdered his customers in the play sometimes called *A String of Pearls, or, The Fiend of Fleet Street* (1847) by George Dibden-Pitt, though the title *Sweeney Todd, the Barber of Fleet Street* seems to have originated with a play (on the same theme) by F. Hazelton in 1865.

sweeping changes Date of origin not known. 'This is a case where the sweeping changes taking place in building societies should be made fully transparent' – *The Observer* (10 July 1994); 'Lady Howe's report on the future of our cathedrals recommends sweeping changes, including the introduction of walkie-talkies for vergers and a new system of counting admissions electronically' – *The Sunday Times* (16 October 1994).

sweeping powers Meaning, 'the taking of measures that are wide in effect'. Date of origin not known. Compare 'drastic powers' and 'draconian powers'. 'There is nothing like a clean sweep, and Berge's successor, Hugues Gall, decided to remove the music director Myung-Whun Chung, who, as the only successful employee of the Bastille, had acquired sweeping artistic powers' – *The Times* (12 September 1994).

sweet See ANOTHER SUNDAY.

sweet as the moment when the pod went 'pop' Slogan for Birds Eye frozen peas, in the UK, from *circa* 1956. Sometimes remembered as 'fresh as the moment when . . .' Written by Len Heath at the Lintas agency.

sweet bird of youth Phrase coined by Tennessee Williams for the title of his play *Sweet Bird of Youth* (1959) and not a quotation. The University of Delaware Library, where the Tennessee Williams's papers are kept, commented: 'The motto in the front of the play is a quote from Hart Crane which is taken from the poem "Legend" in the work *White City* ["Relentless caper for all those who step / The legend of their youth into the noon"]. Some authors make reference to the title as echoing the legendary bird in T.W.'s later *Orpheus Descending*.' A line recalled as, 'Sweet bird of youth, where art thou flown?' appears to be a misremembering of 'To the Nightingale' from *Poems* (1802) by Mrs John Hunter: 'Why from these shades, sweet bird of eve / Art thou to other regions wildly fled? . . . Oh, simple bird! where art thou flown? / What distant woodland now receives thy nest?'

sweet Fanny Adams (or sweet FA or sweet fuck-all) Nothing. There actually was a person called Fanny Adams, from Alton in Hampshire, who was murdered, aged eight, in 1867. At about the same time, tinned meat was introduced to the Royal Navy, and sailors – unimpressed – said it was probably made up from the remains of the murdered girl. 'Fanny Adams' became the naval nickname for mutton or stew, and then the meaning was extended to cover anything that was worthless. The abbreviation, 'Sweet FA', being re-translated as 'Sweet Fuck-All' is a more recent coinage.

(the) sweet smell of success The title of a film *Sweet Smell of Success* (US 1957) is apparently an original coinage of the screenwriters Clifford Odetts and Ernest Lehman. Lehman's short story, on which it is based, was entitled 'Tell Me About It'. Subsequently, Laurence Olivier was quoted as saying that 'Success smells like Brighton'.

swingeing cuts Cuts (i.e. economies, reductions in manpower, etc.) that are wide ranging and also severe. Date of origin not known. 'The threat to the Eurofighter comes with the RAF expecting to feel the full force of swingeing cuts' – *Daily Mail* (11 July 1994); 'Film-makers have been ordered to make swingeing cuts to the thriller *The Color Of Night* if they want it to get a lucrative 15 certificate' – *Today* (2 August 1994).

swinging PHRASES. 'Swinging' had been a musician's commendation for many years before it was adopted to describe the free-wheeling, uninhibited atmosphere associated with **the Swinging Sixties**. By extension, 'swinging' came to denote sexual promiscuity. 'A swinger' was one who indulged in such activity. One suggestion is that 'swinging' in the sense of changing partners derives from the caller's use of words in square dancing. How the phrase caught on is not totally clear. In the early 1960s, the comedian Norman Vaughan would say it – see under DODGY! But Frank Sinatra had had an album entitled *Songs for Swinging Lovers* (1958), Peter Sellers, *Songs for Swinging Sellers* (1959), and Diana Dors, *Swinging Dors*. Could the square-dancing use of 'swing your partners' have contributed to this? The coming together of 'swinging' and 'London' in **swinging London** may first have occurred in an edition of the *Weekend Telegraph* Magazine on 30 April 1965 in which the words of the American fashion journalist Diana Vreeland (*circa* 1903–89) were quoted: 'I love London. It is the most swinging city in the world at the moment.' In addition, a picture caption declared, 'London is a swinging city.' Almost exactly one year later, *Time* Magazine picked up the angle and devoted a cover story to the concept of 'London: The Swinging City' (edition dated

15 April 1966). The 'Swinging Sixties' label was being applied by 1967.

(a) swingometer A 'swingometer' was a device for demonstrating the swing (transfer of votes from one party to another) in British general elections, as used by Robert McKenzie in BBC TV election night broadcasts (from 1959). The suffix '-ometer', for a measuring device (as in 'barometer') was not new, however. Egyptologists of the 18th century were using the name 'Nilometer' for a device found in ancient temples and used to measure the height of the Nile. In the 1960s, the ITV talent show *Opportunity Knocks* had a 'clapometer', which gave a visual indication of the loudness of applause given to individual acts. Hence, from the *Evening Standard* (London) (12 October 1989): 'Nigel Lawson's speech registered well on the clapometer', and other variations of the same: 'Even recent [architecture], like a sheltered housing scheme, would score highly on the Prince Charlesometer' – *The Independent*, (20 January 1990).

swoop See AT ONE FELL.

sword See BY THE SWORD.

swordsman See BEST.

syndrome PHRASES. A somewhat unnecessary elaborative suffix, applied to any set of actions, behaviour or opinions. Originally a medical term for a concurrence of several symptoms (as in Down's syndrome), though the Greek-based word has been known in English since the 1540s), the clichéd use has been around since the 1950s. Recent use was perhaps encouraged by the film title *The China Syndrome* (US 1979). 'Robert Harris, he of massive global sales for his "what if?" novel, *Fatherland*, gets to further hype his latest *Enigma*, using the excuse of a film on the problems of "second-novel syndrome"' – *The Independent* (25 September 1995).

T

table See ALL JOINTS; GET ONE'S FEET.

tacit approval An inevitable pairing, meaning 'unspoken or understated approval'. Date of origin unknown. 'Protected by stringent privacy laws (of which Pythoud approves), married French politicians, businessmen and ordinary citizens enjoy affairs with the tacit approval of society in general, and often that of women, too' – *The European* (19 August 1994).

tacit support Meaning, 'unspoken or understated support'. An inevitable pairing. Date of origin unknown. 'They accuse [the Communist Party] of . . . soft-lining tacit support of Premier Giulio Andreotti's minority government' – *Time* Magazine (28 March 1977); 'Sources close to President Mageeba are conceding that the peasant army of the ALF has the tacit support of the indigenous population of the interior' – cliché mocked by Tom Stoppard in the play *Night and Day* (1978); 'His target is the Party of Democratic Socialism (PDS), reformed rump of the former East German communist party, which he denounces as "red-painted fascists". And the message is that the SPD can only hope to unseat him in Bonn with the tacit support of those communists' – *Financial Times* (26 September 1994).

tacks See BRASS TACKS.

(the) Taffia Nickname applied to a group of Welshmen looking after their own interests, since the 1970s. For example, in the media, one might have said that the founders of Harlech TV in 1968 were members of the Taffia. They included Richard Burton, Sir Geraint Evans, John Morgan and Wynford Vaughan-Thomas. The word is an obvious combination of 'Taffy' (the traditional nickname for a Welshman, from the supposed Welsh pronunciation of Davy = David) and *mafia*, the Sicilian-Italian word that means 'bragging', applied to the organized body

tag, rag and bobtail

646

of criminals among Italian immigrants in the USA. From *The Sun* (2 April 1979): 'Terror of the Taffia! The militants who'll black out your telly for their cause' – though is a reference to Welsh Nationalist activists (rather the opposite of the above-described HTV mob). Similar light-hearted coinages are the **Murphia** (from Murphy, the typical Irish name and nickname of a potato), applied to the band of Irish broadcasters in the UK headed by Terry Wogan, and **kosher nostra**, for the Jewish 'mafia'.

tag, rag and bobtail The common herd, the rabble. Known since the 16th century and in various forms and word orders. A 'bobtail' was the word for a contemptible fellow, a cur, by 1619. 'The dining-room was full of tag, rag, and bobtail, dancing, singing, and drinking' – Samuel Pepys, diary entry (6 March 1659). *Rag, Tag and Bobtail* (1953–5) was the title of part of the BBC TV children's series *Watch With Mother*. The glove puppet 'Rag' was a hedgehog, 'Tag' a wood mouse and 'Bobtail' a rabbit.

tail See ALL BEHIND; CASE OF THE TAIL.

t'ain't a fit night out for man nor beast Repeated phrase from the film *The Fatal Glass of Beer* (US 1933), written by and starring W.C. Fields. In a letter (8 February 1944) reproduced in *W. C. Fields by Himself* (1974), Fields states that the catchphrase was first used by him in a sketch in Earl Carroll's *Vanities* and then as the *title* of the picture he made from it for Mack Sennett. He concludes: 'I do not claim to be the originator of this line as it was probably used long before I was born in some old melodrama.'

take See DOES HE.

take a kick in the pants Catchphrase of the British comedian George Doonan (d. 1973). He also was wont to ask **smatter wit chew [what's the matter with you]?**

(to) take a light-hearted look (back) at ... Media cliché, as in the promotion of satirical radio programmes so as to suggest that they will not give offence. 'He can afford now to take a light-hearted look back at his numerous disasters. "There were times my car was bogged up to the

axles and I knew I wouldn't be found for ages. It pissed down for days, my booze and food ran out"' – *The Sunday Telegraph* (15 May 1994); 'Skits, I suppose, though I don't like the word; humour, though I don't like that very much either – too close to the BBC's "light-hearted look at"' – Alan Bennett, *Writing Home* (1994).

take a pew Meaning, 'take a seat'. Recorded by 1898 and facetiously alluding to the sort of seating you would find in a church. Alan Bennett's archetypal Anglican sermon in the revue *Beyond the Fringe* (1961) was entitled 'Take a Pew'.

(to) take a principled stand Listed in *The Independent* (24 December 1994) as a cliché of newspaper editorials. 'Mr Howard said this hardly squared with claims of a principled stand against his party's anti-Europe policy at the time. Roy Hattersley had chosen not to mention Labour's commitment to withdrawal in his 1983 election address and Mr Howard asked why Mr Blair did not do the same' – *Evening Standard* (London) (7 July 1994); 'We weren't being puritanical about it, nor did we have a principled stand against advertising as such, but the *News of the World*, for God's sake. In the event the campaign went ahead, without our involvement, and we had an expensive meeting with a lawyer who explained in the nicest possible way that there was little we could do about it' – *The Guardian* (28 April 1995).

(to) take a rain-check Originally, in the USA, a rain-check (or -cheque) was a ticket for re-admission to a sporting event when the event had had to be postponed because of rain. The person to whom it was given would be able to produce it at a later date and claim free admission. Now broadened, the expression is used to mean 'let's put this "on hold", let's not make any arrangements about this until the time is more opportune'. Obviously, the phrase can be used as a polite way of postponing something indefinitely, but basically there is some kind of commitment to 'renegoti-ate' at a later date. Known by the 1950s – 'I want a rain-check' is spoken in the film *All That Heaven Allows* (US 1955), 'I'll take a rain-check' in the film *Lolita* (US 1961).

An Australian source states that 'rain-check' was used of someone's action in putting a licked finger on a cake to reserve it for later – 'Unhygienic, but I am talking about perhaps the late 1930s, when I was but a teenager.'

(to) take a shufty To take a look. Probably after the Arab word *shufti* which also occurs in phrases like *shufti bint*, an available woman. Known since 1943. Hence, in military slang, a 'shuftiscope' was the name given to a telescope or similar instrument for looking through.

take back the night An American slogan from the campaign to make it possible for women to go out in the dark without fear of attack or rape (by the late 1970s). The similar **women reclaim the night** was probably better known in the UK.

(to) take French leave To do something without permission. Originally, to leave a reception without announcing one's departure. In Smollett's *Humphrey Clinker* by 1771. One of several coinages that exist to snub the French (compare 'French gout' = venereal disease).

take 'im away See RAMSBOTTOM.

(to) take in one another's washing The joke saying that some people '. . . earned a precarious living by taking in one another's washing' is customarily ascribed (but with slight hesitancy) to Mark Twain. In *The Commonweal* (6 August 1887) an article entitled 'Bourgeois Versus Socialist' signed by William Morris ends: 'A bourgeois paradise will supervene, in which everyone will be free to exploit – but there will be no one to exploit . . . On the whole, one must suppose that the type of it would be that town (surely in America and in the neighbourhood of Mark Twain) that I have heard of, whose inhabitants lived by taking in each other's washing.' Two years later, George Bernard Shaw wrote that 'The inhabitants [of Bayreuth] either live in villas on independent incomes or else by taking in one another's washing and selling confectionery, scrap books and photographs' – in *The Hawk* (13 August 1889). Slightly after this, 'E.W.C.' wrote in *Cornish Notes & Queries* (First Series) (1906): 'I have certainly heard the phrase in connection with the Scilly Islands. And

some go so far, and are so rude, as to suggest "Hence their name".' Similarly, in the forward to his *Poems 1938–1945*) (1946), Robert Graves declared: 'I write poems for poets, and satires or grotesques for wits . . . The moral of the Scilly Islanders who earned a precarious livelihood by taking in one another's washing is that they never upset their carefully balanced island economy by trying to horn into the laundry trade of the mainland; and that nowhere in the Western Hemisphere was washing so well done.' *Benham* (1960) lists the well-known joke with the attribution 'origin unknown', and adds: 'It is said that a society was formed (*circa* 1900) for the purpose of discovering the origin of the phrase, but without result.'

take me back to dear old Blighty
Soldiers serving abroad during the First World War referred to England or home as Blighty. There was a song 'Take me back to dear old Blighty, put me on the train for London town'. It is said to derive from slightly earlier usage when the British were in India. 'Bilayati' is Hindustani for 'foreign' and is thus applied to the place where you are not.

take me to your leader Traditional line spoken in cartoons by Martians having just landed on earth, or in science fiction by earth persons landing on some other planet. Echoing what explorers or invaders might have said when encountering a tribe in some distant land in imperial days. No citations, alas, but very 1950s. The Steve Allen Orchestra seems to have recorded a piece entitled 'Take Me To Your Leader' in the 1950s, perhaps combining a reference to the orchestra leader with an allusion to an already existing phrase. An allusive cartoon by the Scotsman, Alex S. Graham, appeared in *The New Yorker* (21 March 1953) and is captioned, 'Kindly take us to your President.' This remark is addressed to a horse by two aliens with a flying saucer parked in the field behind them. Subsequently, a novel by Leonard Wibberley was entitled *Take Me To Your President* (1957). Then, in 1958, came a swimsuit ad in *Women's Wear Daily* (3 June), headlined 'Take me to your leader' and, in the same year, more than half a dozen songs with this title, plus one 'Take me To Your Leader' and one 'Take Me To Your Leader Cha Cha Cha' . . . Louise and Leslie Waller co-authored a book, *Take Me To Your Leader* (categorized as 'American wit and humor') (1961). In the song 'Whatever Became of Hubert?' (1965), Tom Lehrer puns, 'Take me to your *lieder.*'

take my wife – please! Catchphrase of Henny Youngman (1906–98), comic much on American TV in the 1970s. It is said that the joke was first delivered by accident. Nervous before a radio appearance, he asked an usher to seat his wife, Sadie, with the words, 'Take my wife – please.' (She got used to being the butt of his most famous joke). However, in *Roy Hudd's Book of Music-Hall, Variety and Showbiz Anecdotes* (1993), the inventor of this gag is given as the earlier Canadian music-hall comedian, R.G. Knowles. Either way, the phrase became inextricably linked to Youngman, was used as the title of his autobiography (1973) and appeared under his name in *Bartlett* (1992).

(to) take no prisoners To be utterly ruthless and not take on any liabilities. From *The Times* (30 July 1900): '[Kaiser Wilhelm II said at Bremerhaven] "No quarter will be given, no prisoners will be taken. Let all who fall into your hands be at your mercy".' 'The history of her [Catherine Zeta Jones] career resembles a military campaign in which no prisoners are taken' – *The Independent* (12 February 2003).

(to) take one's breath away Meaning, 'to be astonished – in a way that impresses one or the reverse'. Known by 1900. One of the clichés cited by Ted Morgan in *Somerset Maugham* (1980) as having been used by the writer in his efforts to achieve a 'casual style'. 'Two years ago my husband and I went to southern Corsica and fell in love with it. Bonifacio – with its tall, thin renaissance houses on top of a rock – took our breath away, just as it did Corsica's most famous son, Napoleon' – *Daily Mail* (15 October 1994).

(to) take one's hat off to someone (or cap) To express gratitude or admiration to someone. The literal doffing or removing of a hat as a sign of respect is a traditional gesture. Metaphorically, too, the gesture is well established. *Punch* (5 January 1856) defines a Quaker as, 'a friend who, in the art of making inflammatory speeches, takes his hat off to no man.' The 'cap off' preceded the 'hat off' version. *OED2* has it by 1565, as well as in such a linked expression as 'to come with cap in hand'. An anecdotal (but inaccurate) origin for the phrase can be found in Keith Hayhurst, *The Pictorial History of Lancashire County Cricket Club*: 'In 1884, the North of England team played the Australians on a poor wicket at Trent Bridge. Barlow scored a century and took 10 wickets in the match. Murdoch, the Australian captain was so impressed with Barlow's performance he approached him leaving the field and said, "I take my cap off to you" and presented it to Barlow. It became headlines in the press and the saying "I take my hat off to you" comes from this incident.'

(to) take someone down a peg Meaning, 'to humble; reduce in self-esteem', the expression derives from nautical use, in connection with flags which were raised and lowered with pegs. A flag flying high would carry more honour than one lower down. Known by 1664. An alternative explanation dates from the days when ale was served to students and fellows at the older universities. It was served in tankards with eight indentations at regular intervals horizontally. In his first term, an undergraduate would have his tankard filled with ale to the first mark (known as a peg) and then topped up with water to the eighth. As he progressed, he was 'put up a peg'. Fellows, naturally, were given neat ale up to the eighth peg. Hence, when anyone was drunk he was said to be ONE OVER THE EIGHT. As one of the penalties for infringement of college rules was further dilution of the ale ration, this accounts for the phrase 'to take down a peg.' This sounds quite convincing, especially as the word 'peg' was certainly in use by the 18th century to describe one of a set of *pins* fixed at 'intervals in a drinking vessel to measure the quantity which each drinker was to drink' – *OED2*.

(to) take someone for a ride (1) To deceive or trick a gullible person. (2) To entice a person to their death – US underworld expression. Those who fell foul of gangsters were invited to 'take a ride' with the boss in his car. Flattered they might have been, but it was possible they might not return (another form of the phrase is 'taken for a *one-way* ride'). Both meanings known by 1925.

(to) take someone's ideas on board To receive and accept new ideas. Obviously from the original sense of taking material on board a ship. Known by 1984. Probably in business language at first.

(to) take something with a grain of salt Meaning, 'to treat something sceptically', just as food is sometimes made more palatable by the addition of a pinch of salt. This comes from the Latin *cum grano selis*. Known in English by 1647.

(it) takes one to know one Trick phrase, seizing on people's *awareness* of some interest to accuse them of being rather more involved in it than they might care to admit. Usually with reference to homo-sexuality, though for joking effect it can arise about almost anything. Echoic of the proverbial 'it takes a thief to catch a thief'. From Stephen Fry, *The Liar*, Chap. 3 (1991): '"Only you would know about something as disgusting as the Biscuit Game." "Takes one to know one".' Originally, perhaps, a straightforward recognition of a quality in a person. In the film *The Crimson Fighter* (UK 1952), Burt Lancaster gets to deliver the line as a compliment from one fighter to another.

(to) take the biscuit To take the hon-ours, usually through an act of impudence or effrontery. 'Well, that really takes the biscuit!' is the ironic comment after such an occurrence. Known by 1907 in the UK. One story is that, in the straightforward sense of being 'the best', the phrase was written in 17th century Latin beside the name of a beautiful innkeeper's daughter, '*Ista capit biscottum*'. The American equivalent **to take the cake(s)** – alluding to the awarding of a cake as prize at a fair or *to the horse* after winning a horse race – was known by 1847.

(to) take the bull by the horns Meaning, 'to seize the initiative and not to shrink from dealing with a difficult problem'. Known by 1711. '"What we need is

someone on the park to take the bull by the horns and shout and motivate." Celtic go into the Hampden clash reflecting on the difference two months have made' – *Daily Record* (9 November 1994).

(to) take the mickey Meaning, 'to send up, tease'. Possibly from rhyming slang, 'Mickey Bliss' = 'piss', in the 1950s. But who was Mickey Bliss to be so honoured? We may never know. The Revd Geoffrey Knee wrote to *Radio Times* (in April 1994) thus: 'I have long understood that the phrase is a less vulgar form of "Taking the p***" [his asterisks] and that it's derived from the term "p*** proud", meaning an erection caused by pressure in the bladder and not, therefore a sign of sexual prow-ess; hence, someone who is "p*** proud" has an exaggerated sense of his own importance. Such a one might be to told to "p*** off", meaning, not "go away", but "get rid of the p***" and stop boasting. Thus, to "take the p*** out of someone" means to deride him into lowering his self-esteem.' However, with respect to the reverend etymologist, an earlier form – **to take the Mike** – is remembered by some from the 1920s and would seem to demol-ish his suggested origin. More recently, the verbose and grandiose 'are you by any chance **extracting the Michael?**', and '**extracting the urine**' have become reasonably common. Another explanation is that the 'mickey' = 'piss' derives from the word 'micturition' (the overwhelming desire to urinate frequently).

(to) take the money and run Meaning 'to settle for what you've got and not hang about', as though advice was being given to a bank robber to take what he'd got rather than look for more and risk being caught. Or it might be advice given to a person worried about the value of a job. In which case, one might say, 'I should just take the money and run, if I were you.' *Take the Money and Run* was the title of a Woody Allen film (US 1968).

(to) take up the cudgels (on behalf of) Meaning, figuratively, 'to fight on behalf of'. Known by 1869. Cited as a 'dying metaphor' by George Orwell in 'Politics and the English Language' in *Horizon* (April 1946). 'Already, Christopher Columbus has emerged as the villain of the piece: the man who set the tone for the vandalism that followed. But both the man, and what followed, have been misrepresented. A Columbus scholar at Oxford takes up the cudgels' – by-line in *The Economist* (21 December 1991).

tale See AND THEREBY HANGS.

(a) talent to amuse A phrase from Noël Coward's song 'If Love Were All' in *Bitter Sweet* (1932): 'I believe that since my life began / The most I've had is just/A talent to amuse.' *A Talent To Amuse* became the title of Sheridan Morley's biography of Coward in 1969. But compare this in Byron's *Don Juan*, Canto 13, verse 36 (1819–24): 'There was the *preux Chevalier de la Ruse*, / Whom France and Fortune lately deign'd to waft here, / Whose chiefly harmless talent was to amuse.'

tales See DEAD MEN TELL NO.

talk See HE CAN TALK.

talking heads British broadcasting term for the type of TV programme that is composed mainly of people talking, shown in 'head and shoulder' shots and sometimes addressing the camera directly. Often used critically by those who would prefer a programme to show more physical action or to get out of the confines of the studio. Granada TV's booklet *Some Technical Terms and Slang* (1976) defined the term solely as 'a documentary programme which uses the technique of people talking directly to the camera'. Earlier (*circa* 1968), the term 'talking head' seems to have been applied to anyone addressing the TV camera in a presenter's role. The US/UK pop group with the name Talking Heads performed from 1981. Alan Bennett wrote a series of dramatic monologues for TV called *Talking Heads* in 1988.

talk of the devil! What you say to greet someone who has just joined your company – as though you had just been talking about him. The long version is: 'Talk of the devil and he'll appear'. From a proverbial expression that first appears in a Terence and Cicero. 'The English say, "Talk of the devil, and he's presently at your elbow" – G. Torriano, *Piazza Universale di Proverbi Italiani* (1666).

(to) talk telephone numbers To negotiate about money where the sums involved are extremely large, perhaps in the millions and thus looking like seven-number phone numbers. Probably from American show business usage, by the 1980s. A British ITV game show, based on viewers' telephone numbers and called *Talking Telephone Numbers* had a short run from 1994.

(to) talk the hind leg off a donkey To talk with unflagging and wearying persistence, or to have the power to persuade through eloquent speech. A donkey is noted for its stubbornness, so it would indeed take an enormous amount of persistence or persuasion to remove its hind leg. But, interestingly, the donkey is not important – in 1808 William Cobbett used the expression involving the hind leg of a *horse*. There is an Australian citation from 1879 incorporating the hind leg of a *dog*. There are also versions citing a *bird's leg* (understandably not hind-leg), 'the leg off an *iron pot*' and, from Lancashire, 'the leg off a *brass pan*' . . . Described as a nannyism in *Casson/Grenfell* (which also has 'you'll *eat* the hind leg off a donkey').

(to) talk turkey To get down to business, to talk seriously. Although a widely used expression, this originated in the US and was known by 1824. Robert L. Shook in *The Book of Why* (1983) says it first appeared in American colonial days when the Pilgrim Fathers always seemed to want turkeys when they traded with the Indians. So familiar did their requests become that the Indians would greet them with the words, 'You come to talk turkey?' This seems rather more to the point than the tale usually given as the origin of the phrase: in colonial days, a white hunter and an Indian made a pact that they would share equally between them anything they caught. However, at the end of the day, when they came to share out what they had bagged – three crows and two turkeys – the white man first handed a crow to the Indian and a second turkey to himself. At which point the Indian is said to have remarked, 'You talk all turkey for you. Only talk crow for Indian.'

tall, dark and handsome This description of a romantic hero's attributes (as likely to be found especially in women's fiction) had surfaced by 1906. *Flexner* (1976) puts it in the late 1920s as a Hollywood term referring to Rudolph Valentino (though, in fact, he was not particularly tall). Sophie Tucker recorded a song called 'He's Tall, Dark and Handsome' (by Tobias & Sherman) in 1928. Cesar Romero played the lead in the 1941 film *Tall, Dark and Handsome* which no doubt helped fix the phrase in popular use. However, in a piece called 'Loverboy of the Bourgeoisie' (collected in 1965), Tom Wolfe writes: 'It was Cary Grant that Mae West was talking about when she launched the phrase "tall, dark and handsome" in *She Done Him Wrong* (1933).' This appears to be inaccurate. What Lady Lou says in the film to the character Serge (not played by Cary Grant), after he has just kissed her on the hand, is 'Warm, dark and handsome' – as though playing upon an already established phrase.

tanks　See GET YOUR.

tanned and fit　See LOOKING BRONZED.

(a) tart's boudoir　Usually preceded by 'looking like . . .' or 'smelling like . . .' I.e. whatever is being described is fancy but cheap, such as one would find in a prostitute's work-place. Date of origin unknown.

(a) task force　'An armed force organized for a special operation under a unified command, hence . . . any group of persons organized for a special task' – *OED2*. Known by 1941, possibly of American origin. A film called *Task Force* (US 1949) was a 'flag-waver' (according to *Halliwell's Film Guide*) portraying an admiral about to retire recalling his struggle to promote the cause of aircraft carriers. In the early 1970s (according to *Halliwell's Television Companion*), there was a BBC TV series 'rather clumsily' entitled *Softly, Softly: Task Force*. Then, in 1982, the Falkland Islands were liberated from the Argentinians by what was widely referred to as the British Task Force.

taste　See IT'S ALL DONE.

(a) taste of honey　Shelagh Delaney's play *A Taste of Honey* (1958; film UK 1961) concerns a girl called Jo who finds herself

pregnant after a brief affair with a black sailor. It has been suggested that the title vaguely alludes to 1 Samuel 14:43: 'I did but taste a little honey with the end of the rod that was in mine hand, and, lo, I must die.' The New English Bible renders this as (Jonathan to Saul): 'True, I did taste a little honey on the tip of my stick. Here I am; I am ready to die.' If Shelagh Delaney was thinking of this, then perhaps her 'taste of honey' refers to the brief moment of love or human contact in Jo's bleak life that enables her to survive.

tea and sympathy　Caring behaviour towards a troubled person. In Robert Anderson's play *Tea and Sympathy* (1953; film US 1956), it is provided towards a teenage boy at a New England boarding school by the housemaster's wife. To sort out his possible homosexuality, she goes to bed with him, and is reprimanded with: 'All you're supposed to do is every once in a while give the boys a little tea and sympathy.' The phrase undoubtedly predates the Anderson use, however.

(to) teach the senators wisdom　Sir John Masterman wrote a book entitled *To Teach the Senators Wisdom, or, an Oxford Guidebook*, published in 1952. This is a reference to Psalm 105:22: 'To bind his princes at his pleasure; and teach his senators wisdom.' John Wesley notably alluded to this in his journal (4 July 1787) when recording a visit to the Irish parliament building in Dublin. He was appalled by its splendour at a time when Ireland was suffering. 'But what surprised me above all, were the kitchens of the house, and the large apparatus for good eating. Tables were placed from one end of a large hall to the other; which, it seems, while the parliament sits, are daily covered with meat at four or five o'clock, for the accommodation of the members. Alas, poor Ireland! Who shall teach thy very senators wisdom? War is ceased; *Sed saevior armis, / Luxuria incubuit!* [but luxury, more direful than war, oppresses thee!]'

tea, Edmond?　See MILK?

tear 'em up　See EYAYDON.

teeth　See ARMED TO THE; DARKNESS AND GNASHING OF.

telegrams and anger Phrase from E. M. Forster, *Howard's End*, Chap. 19 (1910): 'Personal relations are the important thing for ever and ever, and not this outer life of telegrams and anger.' 'Jenny and Christopher to Paris to see their mother. The holidays feel over. Back into the world of telegrams and anger . . .' – *Peter Hall's Diaries* (1983) – entry for 30 December 1973.

telephone See GET LAUGHS READING.

telephoneo See MORNING ALL.

tell it like it is! Injunction to tell the truth or as you see things, popular in the 1960s addressed to speakers at American Civil Rights' demonstrations. *Flexner* (1976) has it by 1965 and replaced by RIGHT ON! in 1967.

tell it not in Gath Phrase from 2 Samuel 1:19–20: 'The beauty of Israel is slain upon thy high places: how are the mighty fallen! Tell it not in Gath, **publish it not** in the streets of Askelon; lest the daughters of the Philistines rejoice.' This is part of David's lamentation over the deaths of Saul and Jonathan, his son. *Publish It Not . . .* was the title of a book (1975) by Christopher Mayhew and Michael Adams and subtitled 'the Middle East cover-up'.

tell it to the judge Laconic, dismissive comment on something boasted. From the song 'Gee, Officer Krupke' in *West Side Story* (1957): 'That's a touchin' good story' 'Lemme tell it to the world!' 'Just tell it to the judge.' Compare from Laurence Sterne, *A Sentimental Journey*, 'In the Street – Calais' (1768): 'I popp'd upon Smelfungus again at Turin, in his return home; and a sad tale of sorrowful adventures he had to tell . . . I'll tell it, cried Smelfungus, to the world. You had better tell it, said I, to your physician.'

tell it to the Marines (or tell that . . .) Meaning, 'don't expect us to believe that'. This apparently dates from the days, in Britain, when Marines were looked down upon by ordinary sailors and soldiers. Working on land and sea, the Marines were clearly neither one thing nor the other, and thus stupid. So perhaps they would believe a piece of unbelievable information. The phrase was current by 1806. In 1867, *Notes and Queries* discussed it in the form, 'Tell that to the Marines for the sailors won't believe it.' *Brewer* (1999) continues to derive it from an occasion when Samuel Pepys was regaling Charles I with stories from the Navy. An officer of the Maritime Regiment of Foot (the precursors of the Marines) gave his support to Pepys when doubt was cast on the existence of flying fish. Said the King, 'Henceforeward ere ever we cast doubts upon a tale that lacks likelihood we first "Tell it to the Marines".' In fact, this story was originated by Major W. P. Drury in *The Tadpole of an Archangel* (1904). He subsequently admitted that it was an invention and a 'leg pull of my youth'. The phrase is also well known in the USA. Sometimes it takes the form, 'Tell *that* to the Marines'; sometimes, 'Tell that to the *horse*-marines.'

(to) tell more lies than Tom Pepper 'When I was younger, my mother used to say of certain people that they "told more lies than Tom Pepper". I have never found a reference for this insult' – Peter Dawson (1999). *Partridge/Slang* has a citation for this nautical name for a liar, dating from 1818. Tom Pepper was, apparently, 'the sailor who was kicked out of Hell for lying.' *Apperson* has from *Dialect of Leeds* (1862): 'A noted propagator of untruths is "as big a liar as Tom Pepper".'

(a) tell-tale tit A person who reports discreditable facts about another. The noun 'tell-tale' on its own goes back to the 16th century. As Iona and Peter Opie record in *The Lore and Language of Schoolchildren* (1977), the rhyme: 'Tell tale tit / Your tongue shall be slit, / And all the dogs in the town / Shall have a little bit' has been 'stinging in the ears of blabbers for more than two hundred years' (or since 1780, at least). *Tell-Tale Tits* was the title of the autobiography (1987) of the British soft-porn actress Fiona Richmond.

ten acres and a mule A slogan for what was sought by American slaves from 1862 onwards. They thought that their masters' plantations would be divided up to their benefit after the Civil War. However, this demand escalated to **forty acres and a mule** when, in January 1865, General Sherman stated that 'Every family shall have a plot of not more than forty acres of tillable ground' – a promise that had nothing to do with the Federal government. Consequently, this Reconstruction slogan dwindled to **three acres and a cow**. *That* phrase had originated in John Stuart Mill's *Principles of Political Economy* (1848) – 'When the land is cultivated entirely by the spade and no horses are kept, a cow is kept for every three acres of land.' In Britain, Jesse Collings (1831–1920), a henchman of Joseph Chamberlain in the 1880s, proposed that every smallholder should have these things. He was an advocate of radical agrarian policies and the smallholding movement. He became known as 'Three Acres and a Cow Collings'. Noël Coward once described Edith, Osbert and Sacheverell Sitwell as 'two wiseacres and a cow'.

tender is the night   Phrase from John Keats, 'Ode to a Nightingale' (1820): 'Already with thee! tender is the night.' Hence, *Tender is the Night*, title of a novel (1943; filmed US 1961) by F. Scott Fitzgerald.

tender loving care   Understandably, this is a phrase that appears irresistible to song-writers. The catalogue of the BBC Gramophone Library reveals a considerable list: as 'TLC', there is a song by Lehman, Lebowsky, C. Parker dating from 1960 (and translated as 'Tender loving *and* care). Also with this title, there is a Motown song by Jones, Sawer, Jerome (1971), an instrumental by R. L. Martin, Norman Harris (1975); and a song by the Average White band and Alan Gorrie. As 'Tender Lovin' Care', there is a song written by Brooks, Stillman (1966) and one written and performed by Ronnie Dyson (1983). As 'Tender Loving Care', there is a song written by Mercer, Bright, Wilson, and recorded in 1966 by Nancy Wilson. It was also used as the title of an album by her. The song 'Music To Watch Girls By' (1967) includes the lines: 'Eyes watch / Girls walk / With tender loving care'. It has also been suggested that 't.l.c.' was used in advertisements for BUPA, the British medical insurance scheme, or for Nuffield Hospitals, or for a washing powder. The *OED2* recognizes the phrase as a colloquialism denoting 'especially

solicitous care such as is given by nurses' and cites *The Listener* (12 May 1977): 'It is in a nurse's nature and in her tradition to give the sick what is well called "TLC", "tender loving care", some constant little service to the sick.' The earliest use found of the phrase, in this sense, occurs in the final chapter, 'TLC Treatment', of Ian Fleming's novel *Goldfinger* (1959). 'James Bond' says to 'Pussy Galore', 'All you need is a course of TLC.' 'What's TLC,' she asks. 'Short for Tender Loving Care Treatment,' Bond replies. 'It's what they write on most papers when a waif gets brought in to a children's clinic.' '*T.L.C.*, abbreviation for tender loving care' is to be found in I. A. Staunton, *Dictionary for Medical Secretaries* (1960). The phrase may be of American origin. A correspondent in the USA recalls being told in the 1940s that there was a study done in foundling hospitals where the death rate was very high, which showed that when nurses picked up the babies and cuddled them more frequently, the death rate went down. This led to the prescription 'TLC *t.i.d.*' (including the Latin abbreviation for three times a day). Compare Shakespeare, *Henry VI, Part 2*, III.ii.277/9 (1590): *Commons. (Within)* [i.e. a rabble offstage]: 'An answer from the King, or we will all break in!' *King:* 'Go, Salisbury, and tell them all from me, / I thank them for their tender loving care.'

tender mercies   Ironic phrase for attention and care thought unlikely to be in the patient's best interest. But also as a slightly facetious or old-fashioned way of referring to someone's care. A biblical phrase from Proverbs 12:10. 'Smaller . . . traders and manufacturers . . . left to the tender mercies of the open property market' – *The Listener* (17 June 1965); 'From Miss Aitken's tender mercies in his father's primary school he went to the junior high, a short bus ride away in Lochgilphead, and then on to the greater glory of the old grammar school at Dunoon on the far tip of the Cowal peninsula' – *The Sunday Times* (15 May 1994).

ten-four!   In the American TV cop series *Highway Patrol* (1955–9), Chief Dan Matthews (Broderick Crawford) was always bellowing this into his radio. It signifies agreement and conforms to the 'ten-code' of radio communication used by US police.

ten little Indians Because it contained a word then (and still) considered to be offensive, Agatha Christie's novel *Ten Little Niggers* (1939) became *Ten Little Indians* when published in the USA. But now that 'Indian' is itself considered non-PC usage there does not seem to have been a further change. Christie's novel has been dramatized and thrice filmed. The first of the films (US 1945) was *And Then There Were None*, but it was known as *Ten Little Niggers* in the UK. The 1966 re-make, *Ten Little Niggers*, was called *Ten Little Indians* in the USA. The 1974 UK re-make was known as *And Then There Were None* in both markets. In fact, the title of the *original* song, written by the US song-writer Septimus Winner (*circa* 1868) and the source of both the phrases, was 'Ten Little Injuns'. It seems that Christie was familiar only with Frank Green's British version, 'Ten Little Niggers', published in 1869. This begins: 'Ten little nigger boys went out to dine; / One choked his little self, and then there were nine.' It ends: 'One little nigger boy living all alone; / He got married, and there there were none.'

tennis See ANYONE FOR.

tense, nervous headache? Advertising phrase for Anadin analgesic tablets in the UK. From TV ads (1960s?) came the full slogan: 'Headache? Tense, nervous head-ache? Take Anadin.' Probably this formula originated in the USA. Reisner & Wechsler, *Encyclopedia of Graffiti* (1974), records from 'New York City, 1966': 'Are you nervous, tense? Try my 8-inch relaxer'. Also **nothing acts faster than Anadin**, current in the UK from 1960s, inspired the graffiti retort: 'Then why not use Nothing?'

tents See FOLD ONE'S.

(to) terminate with extreme prejudice To kill, execute, assassinate in American CIA parlance – also, in a weaker sense, simply to dispose of, get rid of. It became known to a wider audience in 1972 and was used in the film *Apocalypse Now* (US 1979). 'Taylor is the design supremo who stood at the right hand of Harold Evans for 15 years, accompanying him from the Sunday Times to refashion the Times. His

relations with Times Newspapers termi-nated with extreme prejudice after he had collected a staff petition in support of the sacked Evans' – *The Guardian* (31 August 1985).

(a) terminological inexactitude A humorously long-winded way of indicating a 'lie', but the original context of the coinage shows that this is not the mean-ing. In 1906, the status of Chinese workers in South Africa was mentioned in the King's speech to Parliament as 'slavery'. An Opposition amendment of 22 February of the same year was tabled regretting, 'That Your Majesty's ministers should have brought the reputation of this country into contempt by describing the employment of Chinese indentured labour as slavery'. Winston Churchill, as Under-Secretary at the Colonial Office, replied by quoting what he had said in the previous election campaign. He went on: 'The conditions of the Transvaal ordinance under which Chinese Labour is now being carried on do not, in my opinion, constitute a state of slavery. A labour contract into which men enter voluntarily for a limited and for a brief period, under which they are paid wages which they consider adequate, under which they are not bought or sold and from which they can obtain relief on payment of seventeen pounds ten shillings may not be a desirable contract . . . but it cannot in the opinion of His Majesty's Government be classified as slavery in the extreme acceptance of the word without some risk of terminological inexactitude.' One of the first to misunderstand Church-ill's phrase was Joseph Chamberlain. Of 'terminological inexactitude' he said: 'Eleven syllables, many of them of Latin or Greek derivation, when one good English word, a Saxon word of a single syllable, would do!' Following Churchill's coinage, *Punch* Magazine ran a series of 'termino-logical exactitudes' from 6 May 1908.

terrific See MY NAME'S MONICA.

territory See IT GOES WITH.

test See ACID TEST.

testimony See BEARS ELOQUENT.

(a) test of credibility Date of origin not known. Listed in *The Independent* (24

December 1994) as a cliché of newspaper editorials. 'World Bank sees Nepal project as test of credibility' – *The Guardian* (7 November 1994); 'Clifford has published a guide which lists all the vanity publishers in Britain, and gives an indication of their relative share of hoodwinking. To test the credibility of each firm, he compiled a collection of poems and submitted these for comment' – *Scotland on Sunday* (5 February 1995); 'On a weekend that was meant to test the credibility of the Doncaster Panthers as Budweiser League title challengers they lost twice' – *The Guardian* (13 March 1995); 'OJ prosecutors test credibility of a psychedelic Nobel laureate' – headline in *The Guardian* (11 April 1995); 'They were "of paramount importance", Mr Ruggiero said, not simply because they covered a big chunk of international commerce but because they were the first test of the credibility of the WTO which superseded the General Agreement on Tariffs and Trade in January' – *Financial Times* (4 May 1995).

thank See AY THANG YEW.

thank God it's Friday (or **TGIF)** An expression of relief, especially among office workers and schoolteachers. Reportedly current in the 1940s. It is amusing to see how broadcasters have shrunk from spelling it out when using it for Friday night programmes. Granada TV in Manchester had *At Last It's Friday* in 1968 and Capital Radio, *T.G.I.F.* in 1983. On the other hand, BBC TV did have *Thank God It's Sunday*, appropriately, in the early 1970s. Visiting Dallas, Texas, in December 1980, one noticed there was a singles bar called Thank God It's Friday – and the name appears to have been adopted subsequently by more than one club or restaurant (e.g. T.G.I. Friday's) in the USA and elsewhere.

thanks, but no thanks! Polite refusal, but perhaps indicating that the offer is not worth much anyway. Mostly American use, since the 1950s.

thank you for sharing that with us!
Mild and ironic put-down after being told an unwelcome piece of news or a poor joke. Mostly American use, since the 1960s.

thank you for those few kind words!
Slightly ironic acceptance of a complimentary remark – especially if it was somewhat double-edged. By the 1910s.

thank you, music-lovers! The American musician Spike Jones (1911–64) specialized in comedy arrangements on radio, records and films from the late 1930s onwards. After massacring some well-known piece of music like 'The Dance of the Hours' he would come forward and acknowledge applause with these words.

thank you, Thing 'Thing' was a disembodied hand that kept popping out of a black box in the live-action American TV series *The Addams Family* (based on the cartoons of Charles Addams) (US 1964–6).

that and a —— will get you a —— An American format for saying that what you are referring to is worthless. So, 'that, and a token, will get you on the subway' or 'that, and a dollar, will get you a cup of coffee'. Noted by 1990. Compare Shakespeare, *A Midsummer Night's Dream*, V.i.277 (1594): 'This passion and the death of a dear friend, would go near to make a man look sad.'

(a/the) —— that gives —— a bad name A quite frequent format where the missing words are ironically inserted. 'It is the sort of play that gives failures a bad name' – critic Walter Kerr on *Hook and Ladder* (1950s) in the *New York Herald*; 'There are interesting failures. There are prestige failures, and there are financial failures, but this is the sort of failure that gives failures a bad name' – line from film *Please Don't Eat the Daisies* (US 1960), spoken by Lawrence Mackay (David Niven); 'This is the kind of show that gives pornography a dirty name' – critic Clive Barnes on the revue *Oh! Calcutta!* in *The New York Times* (18 June 1969).

(the) —— that is —— Portentous cliché format perhaps derived from the notable lines by Edgar Allan Poe in *To Helen* (1831): 'The glory that was Greece / And the grandeur that was Rome.' Identified as a cliché in a BBC TV *That Was the Week That Was* sketch about sports journalist 'Desmond Packet' (1962–3 series): 'Plucky British athletes . . . who ran their lion hearts into the ground in the sizzling cauldron that is Perth.' 'This is a unique opportunity to see these classic films and either re-live or experience for the first time the genius that is Hitchcock' – advertisement for an old Alfred Hitchcock film shown in London (November 1983); 'These are of course the dog days, when news is scarce, when sane human beings do anything to escape the sub-tropical steambath that is Washington DC in late August' – *The Independent* (23 August 1995).

that is what the soldier said A throw-away humorous tag, like **that is what the girl said (at the picnic)**. These are probably earlier versions of the more recent **as/like the man said** or **as the girl said to the sailor**, which are also both throw-away remarks, though not quite to the subversive extent of AS THE BISHOP SAID TO THE ACTRESS. *Partridge/Catch Phrases* suggests that the origin is the passage from Charles Dickens, *The Pickwick Papers*, Chap. 34 (1835–7), where Sam Weller remarks during the trial of Mr Pickwick, 'Oh, quite enough to get, Sir, as the soldier said ven they ordered him three hundred and fifty lashes' – and the judge interposes with – 'You must not tell us what the soldier, or any other man, said, Sir . . . it's not evidence.'

that'll be the day! Response to a statement or promise that something unlikely is going to occur. 'He says he's going to buy us all a drink this time' – 'That'll be the day . . .' Since the 1910s? 'That'll Be the Day' later became the title of a song made famous by Buddy Holly (1957) and, from that, a film (UK 1973).

that'll do nicely, sir A fawning line from an American Express TV ad of the late 1970s, especially in the UK. It was in answer to an inquiry as to whether the establishment accepted the credit card in question. In the early 1980s, another phrase used in advertising for the AmEx card was **do you know me?** Celebrities like Robert Ludlum and Stephen King, known for what they did but not easily recognizable from how they looked, explained that relative celebrity could have its drawbacks . . . but not when you carried the card.

that'll stop you farting in church (or laughing . . .) Phrase used, say, when a father is obliged to act in order to prevent youngsters from meddling with anything dangerous or from straying beyond control. He places something beyond their reach or locks it away. Or, when a person has put right another who has chanced his arm with him. *Partridge/Catch Phrases* suggests that the original was the less polite 'that will teach you to fart in chapel (i.e. 'stop taking liberties') and was possibly an English public school expression of the 1930s.

that's a H**l of a way to run a railroad! Slogan for the Boston & Maine railroad in the USA, 1930s? The inspiration for this slogan may have been the caption to a cartoon said to have appeared in the American *Collier's* Magazine (though *Ballyhoo* in 1932 has also been suggested) that shows two trains about to collide. A signalman is looking out of his box and the caption is: 'Tch-tch, what a way to run a railroad!' The Boston & Maine railroad picked up this line when it sought 'a statement which would explain some of the problems of the railroad in times of inclement weather'. It took the 'stock railroad phrase', derived from the cartoon, and put it between each paragraph of the advertisement in the above form. Added at the foot of the ad was the line, 'But the railroad always runs.' Thus was reinforced (rather than coined) the popular expression 'What a way [*or* hell of a way] to run a railroad/railway!' – or simply **what a way to run a ——**, used as an exclamation concerning mismanagement or chaos of any kind. Echoes or developments of this construction occur (in the UK) in the title of G. F. Fiennes's *I Tried To Run a Railway* (1967) – he had worked for British Rail – and the Conservative Party 1968 poster: 'Higher unemployment . . . Higher taxation . . . Higher prices . . . What a way to run a country!' And from *The Independent* Magazine (4 February 1989): 'The shop told me that it only had demonstration [satellite TV] dishes and suggested I call back in a fortnight. This is, surely, no way to run a revolution!'

that's a joke, son Senator Claghorn in the American radio feature called 'Allen's Alley' (with Fred Allen) in *Town Hall Tonight* (1934–49). Became a national catchphrase.

that's all, folks! Stammered sign-off line of 'Porky Pig' in the Warner Brothers' cartoon series *Merrie Melodies* and *Looney Tunes* from the 1930s onwards. Also written on the screen. Coinage variously ascribed to Fritz Frelang, cartoon director (1906–) and Rudolf C. Ising (recalled at his death in 1992). Voiced by Mel Blanc (1908–89), who when asked for an epitaph, plumped for the following 'in joined-up handwriting' – 'That's All, Folks!'

—— that says it all Journalistic phrase, most usually in a photo caption describing a look or smile. A cliché by the 1960s/70s.

that's life! Exclamation of the *c'est la vie/* SUCH IS LIFE/THAT'S SHOWBIZ!-type, used to cover disappointment at the inevitable happening. Probably established by the 1950s. 'I'm for it. Well-meaning, not to be blamed, the victim of the sort of accident that might have happened to anyone when lit up as I was lit, but nevertheless for it. That's life' – P. G. Wodehouse, 'George and Alfred' (1967). *That's Life* was the title of a BBC TV programme (1975–94) that combined folksy human-interest items with consumerist campaigning.

that's my story and I'm sticking to it! 'I really mean it' – but am also indicating a stubborn unwillingness to drop whatever explanation is at issue. By the 1940s.

(the) —— that spelled —— Journalistic cliché by the 1960s/70s. 'The Ding-Ding special that spelled love for Sid and Jan Parker will take a trip down memory lane . . . to celebrate their 25th wedding anniversary. The happy couple will kiss and cuddle on the top deck of the No. 44 bus, just like they did when they were courting' – *The Sun* (15 October 1983).

that's right – you're wrong! Kay Keyser (who died aged 79 in 1985) was a bandleader and self-styled 'Old Perfessor' of American radio's *Kollege of Musical Knowledge* (1933 to 1949). His weekly mix of dance music, comedy and quiz questions is said to have drawn as many as twenty million listeners. This phrase was said in the quiz part. Also used as the title of a film (US 1939).

that's Shell – that was! Slogan for Shell petrol in the UK, from the late 1930s. Two one-headed men with the slogan 'That's Shell – that is!' (current in 1929) were developed into one seemingly two-headed man (his head sweeping from left profile to right) with the more widely known slogan. A possibly apocryphal story is that the two-headed man was devised by a member of the public called Horsfield, who received £100 for his trouble.

(well) that's show biz (or show business)! Exclamation used to cover disappointment at bad luck or at the failure of anything, and as such no longer limited to the world of entertainment. Certainly in use by the early 1960s, the expression is akin to THAT'S LIFE! 'Ah well, as Jeremy Thorpe said when the Queen came back alive from Ghana, "that's showbiz . . ."' – in a *Private Eye* cartoon feature entitled 'Wh*ch looks for the next Tory Leader', *circa* 1962; at the end of an article on theatrical auditions: 'That, as they say, is show business' – *The Independent* (23 May 1990); in a letter dated 27 September 1973, P. G. Wodehouse wrote to Tim Rice: 'I am of course sad at the thought that your Jeeves show has fallen through, but, as the fellow said, that's show business' – quoted in Rice's *Oh, What a Circus* (1999). The similar-sounding 'That's Entertainment' was used by Howard Dietz and Arthur Schwarz as the title of a song in the film *Band Wagon* (1953) and as the title of two films (US 1974; 1976).

that's the stuff to give the troops Welcoming remark as food is placed on the table or after consuming it. *Partridge/Slang* dates this from the First World War but defines it simply as 'that's the idea, that's what we want', and not necessarily about food. There is an obvious allusion in P. G. Wodehouse, *Carry On, Jeeves*, 'The Spot of Art' (1930): 'Forgive me, old man, for asking you not to raise your voice. A hushed whisper is the stuff to give the troops.'

that's the ticket! Meaning, 'That's just what suits' or 'just what I wanted' or 'exactly right'. The origin (it dates from the early 19th century) is in dispute. Either it refers to a price ticket on a garment or to a lottery ticket or, even, has to do with *etiquette* (the correct form). There may. also be a connection with ticket in the American political sense of the winning line-up of candidates at an election (see DREAM TICKET). The title of a Sid Field film comedy (UK 1940) was *That's the Ticket!*

that's the way the cookie crumbles
Meaning, 'that's the way it is, there's no escaping it'. *Bartlett* (1980) describes this basic form as an anonymous phrase from the 1950s. It was, however, given a memorable twist in Billy Wilder's film *The Apartment* (1960). The main characters make much use of the suffix '–wise', as in 'promotion-wise' and 'gracious-living-wise'. Then Miss Kubelik (Shirley MacLaine) says to C. C. Baxter (Jack Lemmon): 'Why can't I ever fall in love with somebody nice like you?' Replies Baxter: 'Yeah, well, **that's the way it crumbles, cookie-wise.**' A joke translation of the original phrase – '*Sic biscuitus disintegrat*' – occurred in an unidentified Iris Murdoch novel before 1978. In Avram Davidson's fantasy novel *Peregrine: Primus* (1971), there is: '*Sic friatur crustulum*, as Ovid puts it; "Thus," or, "In that manner does the cookie crumble".' A showbiz variant heard in 1988 was **that's the way the mop flops**.

that's what —— is all about A journalistic cliché appearing most frequently in sporting contexts. The basic notion is '*winning* is what it's all about' (and never mind all that nonsense of the Olympic motto). Often ascribed to Vince Lombardi, coach and general manger of the Green Bay Packers pro-football team from 1959, in the form 'Winning isn't everything, it's the only thing'; it had nevertheless been said earlier by John Wayne as a football coach in the 1953 movie *Trouble Along the Way*. President Nixon's notorious Committee to Re-Elect the President in 1972 had as its motto: 'Winning in politics isn't everything; it's the only thing.' Compare 'That's what love is all about', a line in the song 'The Love Bug Will Bite You' by Pinky Tomlin (1937). The format can be used in any sport. 'Football is a physical game. It's about stamina and strength and players battling for each other. A lot of people knock those qualities – but that's what English football is all about' – Ron

Saunders, Aston Villa manager on the League title in 1981, quoted in Ball & Shaw, *The Book of Football Quotations* (1984); 'Whoever plays best is going to win . . . this is what the game is all about' – Peter Purves, commentating on BBC TV *Championship Darts* (22 September 1983); 'Air France's Concorde. Rediscover what flying is all about' – advertisement in the UK (*circa* 1983).

that's what you think! With the inference that the person addressed is wrong and that the speaker knows best. Mid-20th century.

that's you and me Ingratiating parenthetical phrase that some British broadcasters use to involve the listener or viewer. E.g. 'The Chancellor of the Exchequer today imposed a swingeing new tax on everybody whoever downed a well-earned pint, put a pony on a gee-gee, or lit up a Christmas cigar – that's you and me.' Noted by 1980.

(the) —— that time forgot Journalistic cliché by the 1960s/70s. After *The Land That Time Forgot*, the title of a novel by Edgar Rice Burroughs (1924; film UK 1974). 'Campaign for the children that time forgot' – headline in *The Observer* (30 April 1995); 'Tedious? That's the way we like it . . . Angela Pertusini goes to Frinton, the town that time forgot' – by-line in *The Independent* (12 May 1995); 'Male, white millionaire supremacists only need apply to play on this stretch of land time forgot' – *The Daily Telegraph* (7 April 1995).

(the) —— that was once —— Journalistic use: 'The blazing ruin that was once . . .', etc. A cliché by the 1960s/70s.

that was the —— that was The BBC TV satire show *That Was The Week That Was* (1962–3) popularized this format. The programme's title (also used in the USA) was apparently modelled on THAT'S SHELL – THAT WAS! and the producer Ned Sherrin in *A Small Thing – Like an Earthquake* (1983) credits the coinage to the actor John Bird who was originally going to take part. Customarily abbreviated to *TW3*. Headline in the *Evening Standard* (London) (25 January 1989) about a programme to mark the tenth anniversary of Mrs Thatcher's government: 'That Was the Ten Years That Was'.

——: the Movie Format phrase. Probably the first film to be so labelled was *Abba: The Movie* in 1977. In these days of 'concepts' and 'merchandising' in pop music, perhaps the idea was to distinguish the film product from 'the tour', 'the TV series', 'the book' and 'the album' – and in 1978 *Abba: The Album* did, indeed, appear. The format has subsequently been used to poke fun at exploitation, self-promotion and self-aggrandizement. For example, a Cambridge Footlights' show in the mid-1980s was entitled *Ian Botham: The Movie* (referring to the English cricketer and his non-sporting activities). In 1985, Michael Rogin, a professor of political science at Berkeley, California, entitled his exploration of President Reagan's (sometimes) unattributed borrowings of film quotes, 'Ronald Reagan: The Movie'. Headline over an article in *The Observer* (30 April 1989) suggesting that a film would one day be made of a certain actress's life: 'Meryl Streep: The Movie?' Along the same lines, in 1990, a novel by the film critic Iain Johnstone was published with the title *Cannes: the Novel*, and a short-lived West End musical about Martin Luther King was dubbed *King – The Musical*.

(a) theatre piece A theatrical work that is not substantial enough to be called a 'play' or which its devisers feel requires something other than the conventional name. Rather an irritating coinage. Or, in ballet and musical concerts, a dramatic rather than abstract work. Current by the early 1980s. A similar term is **dance work** for something that is not a ballet. 'Isadora arrived and sent a quiver through many very delicate sensibilities. It might seem that Kenneth MacMillan was mounting a Red Brigade assault on the fairy-fanciers, but Isadora was an attempt at a theatre piece to break the mould of balletic traditionalism (and, like dance works here and in New York, it suggested a renewed interest in the forms and possibilities of narrative)' – *Financial Times* (7 January 1982); 'Thea Musgrave's The Last Twilight, a theatre piece for large chorus, semichorus, 12 brasses and percussion, a

setting of D. H. Lawrence's 'Men in New Mexico,' was not well performed (in the Brooklyn Academy of Music), but not so badly as to conceal a large, romantic vision' – *Financial Times* (1 July 1982).

there See GETTING THERE.

there ain't gonna be no war! An optimistic catchphrase or anti-war slogan. As Foreign Secretary to British Prime Minister Eden, Harold Macmillan attended a four-power summit conference at Geneva where the chief topic for discussion was German reunification. Nothing much was achieved, but the 'Geneva spirit' was optimistic, and on his return to London he breezily told a press conference on 24 July 1955, 'There ain't gonna be no war.' Was this a conscious Americanism? There had been, at some time prior to December 1941, an American song (by Frankl) called, precisely, 'There Ain't Gonna Be No War': 'We're going to have peace and quiet / And if they start a riot / We'll just sit back and keep score. / The only place you'll go marching to / Will be the corner grocery store. / So rock-a-bye, my baby / There ain't gonna be no war.' But Macmillan was, without doubt, quoting directly from a *circa* 1910 music-hall song, which was sung in a raucous cockney accent by a certain Mr Pélissier (1879–1913) in a show called 'Pélissier's Follies' during the reign of Edward VII: 'There ain't going to be no waar / So long as we've a king like Good King Edward. / 'E won't 'ave it, 'cos 'e 'ates that sort of fing. / Muvvers, don't worry, / Not wiv a king like Good King Edward. / Peace wiv honour is 'is motter [*snort*] – / Gawd save the King!'

there are more ways of killing a cat than choking it with cream This proverb was recorded by the mid-19th century (*CODP*). It appears as a nannyism in *Casson/ Grenfell*. Compare 'There's more ways of killing a cat than choking it with strawberries' – contributed to BBC Radio *Quote . . . Unquote* (by 1980). 'My old dad used to say when tackling a building or electrical project, when the obvious approach was pointed out to him, "Aah, there's more ways of chokin' a pig than stuffin' it wi' butter"' – Austen Mitchell (2000). 'I was warned by a physiotherapist to take it easy with regard to sexual activity with the words, "There are more ways of killing a pig than blowing in its ear"' – Paul Jennings, Isle of Wight (2000).

there are two kinds of —— In *Are You a Bromide?* (1907), the American writer Gelett Burgess castigated people who spoke in clichés. He drew attention to the tiresome attempt to classify acquaintances – a 'common sport of the thinker' – in such sayings as: 'There are two kinds of persons – those who like olives and those who don't'; 'there are two kinds of women – Daisy, and the Other Kind.' 'There are two kinds of people in the world – those who divide the world into two kinds of people and those who don't' – graffito from the University of Texas, in Haan & Hammerstrom, *Graffiti in the Southwest Conference* (1981); 'The world, he said, was divided into two groups of people: those who went about "throwing bricks through windows" and producing memorable phrases, and the glaziers and window cleaners. His wife fell into the latter camp, who received less attention but tended to do more good' – *The Times* (7 April 1995).

there but for the grace of God, go I Proverbial rendering of the remark made by John Bradford (who died in 1555) on seeing criminals going to their execution: 'There, but for the grace of God, goes John Bradford.' Winston Churchill did not deny having made the remark, 'There, but for the grace of God goes God' about the Labour politician Sir Stafford Cripps. It was quoted in Willans & Roetter, *The Wit of Winston Churchill* (1954) but had already been noted by Geoffrey Madan who died in July 1947 (see his *Notebooks*, published in 1981).

thereby See AND THEREBY HANGS.

there is no alternative When asked in 1984 for the origin of Margaret Thatcher's famously nannyish phrase, her then political secretary replied: 'I am not sure that the British Prime Minister ever actually used the phrase . . . and my suspicion, shared by others, is that TINA was coined by those who were pressing for a change of policy.' Not so. On 21 May 1980, Mrs Thatcher made a speech to the Conservative Women's Conference, marking the end of her first year in office. Describing the harsh economic measures already set in train by her government, she said: 'There is no easy popularity in that, but I believe people accept *there is no alternative*.' Whether this was the first time she used the phrase is not clear. The acronym, **TINA**, said to have been coined by Young Conservatives, was flourishing by the time of the Party Conference in September 1981. A correspondent suggests a comparison to it is an old Hebrew catchphrase, *'ain breira'* ('there is no choice').

there is no substitute Slogan format. One of the lines promoting Dr Collis Browne's Compound (stomach medicine) in the UK, since *circa* 1900? Compare one of several rhymes used to advertise wool generically, by the International Wool Secretariat (1950s): 'Jonah deep inside the whale / Seemed cheerful, hearty, even hale. / The whale, visibly annoyed / Asked "Aren't you cold in this damp void?" / Said Jonah, with a careless shrug, / "My woolly gown keeps me quite snug." / With that the whale told his school, / "There is no substitute for wool".'

there'll be dancing in the streets tonight Journalistic cliché – to signify celebration of, or elation at, some victory. 'There'll be dancing in the streets of Colombo tonight' – sketch, 'Stop Press', in BBC TV *That Was The Week That Was* (1962–3 series); Tom Stoppard in an extended parody of sports journalism in his play *Professional Foul* (1978) has: 'There'll be Czechs bouncing in the streets of Prague tonight as bankruptcy stares English football in the face.' 'Hoots hombre! They'll be dancing in the streets of Tenerife when a swinging, singing band of Highlanders jets in next month' – *Sunday Mail* (19 February 1995); 'The city registered that, against the expectations of many, the ceasefire had lasted a full 12 months; but still nobody danced in the streets' – *The Independent* (1 September 1995); 'I shall be dancing in the streets when hunting is banned by a Labour government because it will be the first attack on this rotten lifestyle' – Alan Amos in *The Independent* (6 September 1995). Compare: 'There'll be joy bells in the NAAFI tonight' – BBC radio *Goon Show*, 'Under the Floorboards' (25 January 1955).

there'll be some changes made Sometimes erroneously followed with, '. . . as Duke Ellington used to say'. The point is that Duke Ellington never recorded the song with this title (which was written by Overstreet and Higgins in 1929.) Most likely there is confusion with the Mercer Ellington/Ted Person's 1939 composition 'Things Ain't What They Used To Be'.

there must be easier ways of making a living! Exasperated comment made in the midst of carrying out a difficult or distasteful or ludicrous task. By the 1940s.

there must be some mistake, officer What middle-class people say on being challenged or arrested by a police officer – or at least in plays and films it is. Observed by Fritz Spiegl in an article on drama cliché lines in *The Listener* (7 February 1985).

there never were such times since Old Leather Arse died! 'When Grandma was alive, she would say this on auspicious occasions. As we all thought it rather rude, this later became "Never were such times . . . you know, since when!" No idea who Old Leather Arse was' – Jean Ford, Devon (1992). 'My aunt, from Framlingham, Suffolk, despite being quite proper, would say, "I hadn't laughed (or, enjoyed myself) so much since old leather arse died' – E. Spratt, Hampshire (1998). Roger Trail, Dorset, subsequently recalled the version used by his grandfather, E. W. Westbrook (d. 1956): 'There never were such times since old Leather-arse fell out of the brake and busted the beano.' Mr Trail thought this must refer to an annual works outing of some kind (beano) by coach (brake): 'I suspect that the manager or some other member of the office staff would have been the natural target of such ribaldry. This is further reinforced by the definition of "leather-bottom" ("a Civil Servant tied to his desk") and "shiny-bum" ("to have a desk-job") in Eric Partridge's slang dictionary.' It is curious that the nickname 'Leather Arse' does not seem to have been applied to a historical character. The phrase 'Since old Leather Ass died' occurs in Brian Friel's play *Philadelphia Here I Come!* (1964).

there's a cheque in the post Customary unbelieved response to a demand for payment. Used as a running gag in *Q8*, a Spike Milligan BBC TV comedy series in 1979.

there's a lot of it about Useful, but fairly meaningless and facetious, rejoinder. Originally, perhaps, what you would say when someone remarked 'I've got the 'flu' (or some other medical complaint). Title of, and running gag in, a Spike Milligan series on BBC TV in 1982.

there's a sucker born every minute (or **there's one born every minute)** Meaning, 'there are lots of fools waiting to be taken advantage of'. There is no evidence that P. T. Barnum, the American circus magnate (1810–91), ever used this expression – not least, it is said, because 'sucker' was not a common term in his day. He did, however, express the view that, 'The people like to be humbugged', which conveys the same idea. There was also a song of the period, 'There's a New Jay Born Every Day' (where 'jay' = 'gullible hick'). By whatever route, Barnum took the attribution. A. H. Saxon in his *P.T. Barnum: The Legend and the Man* (1889) reportedly ascribes the saying to Joseph 'Paper Collar Joe' Bessimer, the American con man of the 1880s. Going further back, '*Populus vult decipi* [people wish to be deceived]' is attributed to Cardinal Carafa (d. 1591), Legate of Pope Paul IV. Understandably, in the musical *Barnum* (Broadway 1980), there is a rousing song 'There's a Sucker Born Ev'ry Minute'.

there's gold in them thar hills Meaning, 'there are opportunities where indicated'. Presumably this phrase was established literally in US gold-mining by the end of the 19th century. It seems to have had a resurgence in the 1930s/40s, probably through use in Western films. Frank Marvin wrote and performed a song with the title in the 1930s. A Laurel and Hardy short called *Them Thar Hills* appeared in 1934. The melodrama *Gold in the Hills* by J. Frank Davis has been performed every season since 1936 by the Vicksburg Theatre Guild in Mississippi. *OED2*'s earliest citation is from 1941. The Hays Office reputedly forbade Marlene Dietrich to utter the line after stuffing money down her cleavage in the film *Destry Rides Again* (US 1939). The phrase now has a jokey application to any enterprise that contains more than a hint of promise.

there's hair (or **'air)!** Street cry aimed at a girl with a lot of hair. Current approximately 1900–1910 in the UK. *Punch* Magazine (8 August 1900) had a poem on 'the latest catchword' and also referred to as 'this fatuous catchword'. W. Buchanan-Taylor, *One More Shake* (1944), suggests that it originated in music hall.

there's life in the old dog yet This expression of wonder may be uttered at the unexpected possession of some power by someone or some thing thought to be 'past it' (especially when referring to the person's love life). It was used as the title of a painting (1838) – precisely 'The Life's in the Old Dog Yet' – by Sir Edwin Landseer, which shows a Scottish ghillie rescuing a deerhound which, unlike a stag and two other hunting dogs, has not just plunged to its death over a precipice.

there's many a tune played on an old fiddle Said about an old man seen in the company of a young woman. This proverb is probably better known in the form, 'There's many a *good* tune played on an old fiddle', which *CODP* finds first with a somewhat different slant: 'Beyond a haricot vein in one of my legs I'm as young as ever I was. Old indeed! There's many a good tune played on an old fiddle' – Samuel Butler, *The Way of All Flesh*, Chap. 61 (1902).

there's more knows Tom Fool than Tom Fool knows As 'more know Tom Fool than Tom Fool knows' this is quoted as 'the old English proverb' in Daniel Defoe, *Colonel Jack*, Chap. 17 (1723). 'When my children were small and wondered how we knew some of the things that they did, the conversation would go: "How do you know?" – "There's a lot of people know Joe what Joe don't know"' – Mrs K. Polond, London SE23 (1995).

there's no answer to that! Catchphrase of Eric Morecambe in the BBC TV *Morecambe and Wise Show* (1968–77). 'How many of us have said something not particularly amusing, only to have it turned into a joke of sorts by someone else saying, "There's no answer to that"?' – Miles Kington in *The Independent* (2 May 2000). As such, it was Eric's standard innuendo-laden response to such comments as: *Casanova (Frank Finlay)*: 'I'll be perfectly frank with you – I have a long felt want' – in the edition of 2 February 1973.

there's no business like show business This was the title of a song written by Irving Berlin for the musical *Annie Get Your Gun* (1946). It later became the title of a musical film (US 1954) and was the origin of a quasi-proverbial modern expression.

there you go! Phrase of excuse, approbation or thanks, known in the USA by 1844. Very common also in Australia. In Britain, *circa* 1979, it was noticed as a fairly meaningless filler phrase used by Tony Blackburn, the disc jockey. A *Guardian* reader suggested that this might be his reaction to yet another disaffected listener switching off. An *Independent* Magazine profile (9 July 1994) noted that Blackburn was still punctuating his speech with the phrase in the form 'there yego'.

there you go again! In a TV debate with President Carter in 1980, the Republican challenger, Ronald Reagan, laughed off Carter's charge that he would dismantle federal health support for the elderly, saying: 'There you go again!' The phrase stuck with the voters and became a campaign refrain.

these are dynamite (or **it's dynamite)!** The sort of thing journalists think real people say, or which people say because journalists expect it of them. 'I call it goddam urgent. It's dynamite' – Peter Cheyney, *I'll Say She Does* (1945); '"These are dynamite in terms of brand names," said Mr Alan Woltz, LRC's American born chief executive of the past five years. "To us they make a good fit"' – *Financial Times* (29 September 1984); 'Mr Little rushed to the Sun offices to study the photographs and said: "These are dynamite"' – *The Sun* (10 December 1984); 'Wait till you see the set and the titles we've designed [for a TV current-affairs show] . . . It's dynamite' – Andrew Neil, sometime editor of *The Sunday Times*, quoted in the *Independent on Sunday* (25 September 1994). See also POLITICAL DYNAMITE.

these foolish things Best known as the title of a popular song ('These foolish things / Remind me of you'), lyrics by Eric Maschwitz (1936); picked up by Michael Sadleir for a book called *These Foolish Things* (1937) and by the Crazy Gang for a stage show (London 1940s?); and by Bertrand Tavernier as the title of a film (France 1990) that included the song on the soundtrack.

thews and sinews Thews = muscular strength/development. Sir Walter Scott may have been the first to put the two words together, as in *Rob Roy*, Chap. 3 (1817). 'He had a certain weediness and lack of thews and sinews' – P. G. Wodehouse, *Bill the Conqueror*, Chap. 5(1924); 'I had never looked on old Chuffy as a fellow of very swift intelligence, he having always run rather to thews and sinews than the grey cells' – *Thank You, Jeeves*, Chap. 14 (1934).

(the ——) they call (or are calling ——) Whoever 'they' may be, they certainly do a lot of it and are most helpful to journalists in search of a tag. '[Of a mining disaster] . . . in what they are calling the South African Aberfan' – Martyn Lewis in ITN, *The Making of '81*; 'Alfredo Astiz drank free champagne in seat 9A of the executive suite on a British Caledonian DC10 flight to Rio yesterday. The man they call Captain Death was being returned to his homeland via Brazil' – *Daily Mail* (12 June 1982); 'They call it paradise. Now burnt-out cars litter the roads, some the tombs of drivers who could not beat the flames' – *The Times* (19 February 1983); 'They called him [Bjorn Borg] "The Iceberg"' – ITN report (7 February 1989); 'Strange goings-on behind the closed doors of that exotic building just off Great Queen Street, Covent Garden . . . Freemasons' Hall they call it, a secret world, a world of secrets' – *The Independent* (19 May 1995); 'In Hong Kong, they are calling the political retirement of Lydia Dunn the end of an era' – *The Independent* (16 June 1995).

they came . . . Cliché of funeral journalism. The chief thing is to start with the word 'They'. From the opening of the *Observer* report on the funeral of Jennie Lee (27 November 1988): 'They scattered the ashes of a proud Scots lassie yesterday on a cold Welsh hillside . . .' But much better to put 'They came . . .'. From *The Times* (11 April 1983): 'They came, 541 of them, across half a world [to the Falklands] to dedicate the war memorial on a treeless hillside above Blue Beach, where British forces first stepped ashore.' Also useful in this context: **they buried their own . . .**

they do not like it up 'em See PERMISSION TO SPEAK.

they don't make —— like that any more 'They don't write tunes like that any more' – BBC radio *Goon Show*, 'Rommel's Treasure' (25 October 1955). In the musical *Phil the Fluter* (London 1969), Evelyn Laye sang a song entitled 'They Don't Make Them Like That Any More' (referring to a type of man known in her youth). From an *Independent* obituary (26 January 1989): '"They don't make them like that any more" said Danny La Rue of Freddie Carpenter, a director who was equally at home with both the traditional and the modern musical.' From *The Guardian* (30 January 1989): 'Paying the keenest attention to the oil painting, when he delivered his judgement it was one that carried enormous authority. "They don't," he said, "make pigs like that any more".' Especially applied to songs in the form, 'They don't write 'em like that any more!' – to which the joke response is, 'Thank goodness!'

they laughed when I sat down at the piano, but when I started to play . . . ! Slogan for the US School of Music piano tutor, from 1925. The copy underneath this headline includes the following: 'As the last notes of the Moonlight Sonata died away, the room resounded with a sudden roar of applause . . . Men shook my hand – wildly congratulated me – pounded me on the back in their enthusiasm! . . . And then I explained [how] I saw an interesting ad for the US School of Music . . .' This ad gave rise to various jokes: 'They laughed when I sat down to play – someone had taken away the stool / how did I know the bathroom door was open, etc.' John

Caples, the copywriter, also came up with, 'They grinned when the waiter spoke to me in French – but their laughter changed to amazement at my reply' (presumably for another client). In *Lyrics On Several Occasions* . . . (1959), Ira Gershwin declared that the song 'They All Laughed' ('. . . at Christopher Columbus / When he said the world was round; / They all laughed when Edison recorded sound)' (1937) was inspired by the piano tutor ad: 'Along this line, I recall writing a postcard from Paris to Gilbert Gabriel, the drama critic, saying: "They all laughed at the Tour d'Argent last night when I said I would order in French." So the phrase "they all laughed" hibernated and estivated in the back of my mind for a dozen years until the right climate and tune popped it out as a title.' In the film *Much Too Shy* (UK 1942) there is a song 'They Laughed When I Sat Down at the Piano', also inspired by the slogan.

they might be giants A film (US 1972) was made from the play with the title *They Might Be Giants* (1961) by James Goldman about a man who thinks he is Sherlock Holmes. He recruits a female Dr Watson who says (in the film): 'You're just like Don Quixote, you think that everything is always something else.' 'Holmes' replies: 'He had a point – of course, he carried it a bit too far, that's all. He thought that every windmill was a giant . . . If we never looked at things and thought what they *might* be we'd still all be in the tall grass with the apes.' A US band took the name They Might Be Giants in *circa* 1989 and also recorded a song with the phrase as title.

they're playing our tune, darling A phrase from romantic fiction when (presumably married and ageing) lovers hear a tune that makes them nostalgic. There is a joke about the Queen saying it to Prince Philip when the National Anthem struck up. A musical, *They're Playing Our Song*, by Marvin Hamlisch and Carole Bayer Sager, was presented in New York in 1979.

they're working well tonight Comment on gags in terms of an audience's response to them. A stock phrase of 'Monsewer' Eddie Gray (1898–1978) of the British Crazy Gang. Other Crazy Gang phrases

included **aye, aye, taxi!** and **shut up, Cecil!** – both usually said by Jimmy Nervo – and SUCK IT AND SEE.

they shoot horses, don't they? Meaning, 'Well, if he was horse, they'd shoot him, such is his condition.' The title of a novel (1935; film US 1969) by Horace McCoy is apparently the source of this now quasi-proverbial expression.

they think it's all over Commentating for BBC Television on the World Cup Final at Wembley between England and West Germany on 30 July 1966, Kenneth Wolstenholme ad-libbed what has come to be regarded as the 'most famous quote in British sport'. After a disputed third goal, the England team was 3–2 in the lead as the game continued in extra time. 'Some people are on the pitch,' Wolstenholme began before the final whistle, 'They think it's all over.' Then Geoff Hurst scored England's fourth goal (and his third) and decisively won the game. So that was why Wolstenholme added, 'It is now!' It took until the 1990s for the phrase really to catch on. By 1992, a jokey BBC Radio sports quiz had the title *They Think It's All Over* and this transferred to TV in 1995. Some accounts have the commentator saying, '*Well*, it is now. It's four.' According to *The Guardian* (30 July 1991), Wolstenholme himself used to complain if the 'well' was omitted but then a replay of his commentary showed that he had not said the word after all.

they went thataway! Stock phrase from movie Westerns – since the 1940s?

thick See AS THICK AS

thin See INTO THIN AIR.

things ain't what they used to be Title of a song by Mercer Ellington and Ted Persons, published in 1939. The thought is an old one. In Charles Dickens, *Sketches By Boz* (1836) – 'A Christmas Dinner': 'There are people who will tell you that Christmas is not to them what it used to be.' *Punch* (9 March 1921) had a cartoon showing two elderly huntsmen, one of whom was complaining: 'Things ain't what they used to be.' The title of the Frank Norman/Lionel Bart's musical *Fings Ain't Wot They Used T'be* (London 1959) – which popularized an already existing catchphrase in a particular form – gave rise to a juxtaposition joke. In an edition of the *Liverpool Echo, circa* 1960, an advertisement for the Royal Court Theatre announced: 'THIS WEEK & NEXT / THEATRE CLOSED FOR ALTERATIONS / Box Office Now Open for / Lionel Bart's Smash Hit Musical / 'FINGS AIN'T WOT THEY USED T'BE'.'

things better left unsaid Title of a regular feature in *Punch* Magazine that recorded verbal infelicities and clangers. At 29 March 1884, it was known as 'Things One Would Rather Have Left Unsaid', but by 10 January 1900 this had been shortened to 'Things better left unsaid'. By 13 January 1904 this had become 'Things that are better left unsaid'.

things can only get better There has been more than one song with that title, but the particular one written and performed by D-Ream that got to No 1 in the UK charts about three years before the 1997 General Election became a sort of theme song and was famously played at the Labour Party's victory celebrations. Subsequently, John O'Farrell wrote a book (1998) with the title *Things Can Only Get Better: Eighteen Miserable Years in the Life of a Labour Supporter 1979–1997*. A *Daily Telegraph* headline in September 1998 was 'Things Can Only Get Worse'.

things fall apart Phrase from 'The Second Coming' (1921) by W. B. Yeats: 'Things fall apart; the centre cannot hold; / Mere anarchy is loosed upon the world . . . / The best lack all conviction, while the worst / Are full of passionate intensity.' Hence, *Things Fall Apart*, title of a novel (1958) by Chinua Achebe. Of all the quotations used by and about politicians, the most common by far in recent years in Britain has been this one. The trend was probably started by Kenneth Clark, the art historian, at the conclusion of his TV series *Civilisation: a Personal View* (1969). Roy Jenkins in his BBC TV Dimbleby Lecture of 23 November 1979 (which pointed towards the setting up of the centrist Social Democratic Party) followed suit. In *The Listener* (14 December 1979), Professor Bernard Crick threatened to horsewhip the next politician who quoted the poem. On

the very next page, Neil Kinnock (later to become Labour Party leader) could be found doing so. The threat has had no lasting effect, either.

(the) things I've done for England In Sir Alexander Korda's film *The Private Life of Henry VIII* (1933), Charles Laughton as the King is just about to get into bed with one of his many wives when, alluding to her ugliness, he sighs: 'The things I've done for England.' The screenplay was written by Lajos Biro and Arthur Wimperis. This became a catchphrase, to be used ironically by anyone when confronted with an unpleasant task. In 1979, Prince Charles on a visit to Hong Kong sampled curried snake meat and, with a polite nod towards his forebear (however fictionalized), exclaimed, 'Boy, the things I do for England . . .' (indeed, this is how it is popularly misquoted).

think See CLOSE YOUR EYES AND.

think globally, act locally Slogan of Friends of the Earth (environmental lobby) by 1985 in the UK. Meaning, 'Do your bit where you can – personal action counts – test ideas on your own doorstep.' The phrase was originated by René Dubos, a French-born US bacteriologist (1901–82) who was an adviser to the UN Conference on the Human Environment in 1972. He put it as 'Think Globally, But Act Locally' as the title of Chap. 3 in his *Celebrations of Life* (1981). There are those who feel, however, that he may have taken it from something said by the anthropologist Margaret Mead – but so much attributed to her is untraced. Later adopted as a maxim in business and other areas. In *The Independent* (15 July 1995), Paul McCartney described his four-year campaign to save Rye Memorial Hospital near where he lives in Sussex. He talked of using a slogan to do 'with the environment, but it might as well have been to do with health. It was, "Think globally, act locally". It was a Friends of the Earth slogan, actually. I nicked it. You do your bit.'

(the) thinking man's (or **person's** or **woman's) ——** As long ago as 1931, Pebeco toothpaste in the USA was being promoted as 'The Toothpaste for Thinking People'. However, it was Frank Muir who set the more recent trend (now almost a cliché) when he talked of British broadcaster Joan Bakewell as 'the thinking man's crumpet'. That was in the 1960s. Much later, Chantal Cuer, a French-born broadcaster in Britain, said she had been described as 'the thinking man's croissant'. And how about these for originality? 'Frank Delaney – the thinking man's Russell Harty' – *The Sunday Times* (16 October 1983); 'Frank Delaney – the thinking man's Terry Wogan' – *The Guardian* (17 October 1983); 'the thinking woman's Terry Wogan, TV's Frank Delaney' – *Sunday Express* (30 October 1983). And still it goes on. Janet Suzman, the actress, says she has been described as 'the thinking man's Barbara Windsor'. From *The Independent* (28 January 1989): 'One member of the Government said: "[Kenneth Clarke's] the thinking man's lager lout".' From *The Observer* (29 January 1989): 'It was chaired by Nick Ross, the thinking woman's newspaper boy.' Also, from *The Observer* (13 September 1987): 'His performance as a trendy and hung-up LA painter in *Heartbreakers* made him the thinking woman's West Coast crumpet' – which brings us back more or less to where we started. In February 1989, the American magazine *Spy* drew up a long list of examples of American variations on the theme: *Hobbies* Magazine in 1977 had described Descartes as 'The thinking man's philosopher'; *Boating Magazine* (1984) described the Mansfield TDC portable toilet as 'the thinking man's head'; *Horizon* (1965) called Lake Geneva, 'the thinking man's lake'; and *Esquire* (1986) had called actor William Hurt, 'the thinking man's asshole'.

(to) think one's shit doesn't stink To be superior or stuck-up without reason. *Partridge/Catch Phrases* suggests that this expression has been with us since about 1870. 'She thinks her shit don't stink, but it do!' – grandmother of Graham Martin, Ceredigion (2000).

(to) think out of the box To brainstorm, think creatively beyond what is considered usual. Known by the 1990s. 'It started in advertising circles, the "box" being the standard rectangular advertisement hoarding. It also alludes to the box-like "enve-lope" – the known limit of an aircraft's range and power, as it appears on a graph – in the 1970s phrase PUSH THE ENVELOPE' – John Walsh in *The Independent* (2 December 2000).

thinks See NIGHT STARVATION.

(the) thin red line A report by William Howard Russell in *The Times* (25 October 1854) described the first stage of the Battle of Balaclava in the Crimean War (the Charge of the Light Brigade followed a few hours later). Of the Russian charge repulsed by the British 93rd Highlanders, he wrote: 'The ground lies beneath their horses' feet; gathering speed at every stride, they dash on towards that thin red streak topped with a line of steel.' By the time he was writing *The British Expedition to the Crimea* (1877), Russell put: 'The Russians dashed on towards *that thin red line tipped with steel*' [his italics]. Thus was created the jingoistic Victorian phrase 'the thin red line', standing for the supposed invincibility of British infantry tactics. Compare Kipling's poem 'Tommy' from *Departmental Ditties* (1890) which goes: 'But it's "Thin red line of 'eroes" when the drums begin to roll.' 'The Thin Red Line' was the title given to one of the paintings of military scenes by Robert Gibb (1881). It showed the 93rd Highlanders at the Battle of Balaclava. In the 1939 version of the film *The Four Feathers*, the character played by C. Aubrey Smith is always reminiscing about it and draws the 'thin red line' in red wine on the dinner table. Someone asks him, 'Were they hungry?' A TV comedy series (UK 1995–6) about an incompetent police inspector and his team was entitled *The Thin Blue Line*.

(the) third age Polite euphemism for 'old age'. Of French origin (*troisième âge*), the phrase can also be used specifically to refer to retirement. The University of the Third Age – set up for retired people in France by Pierre Vellus in 1973 – has also been introduced to the UK. Learning is for pleasure: there are no qualifications, examinations or age limits. The phrase 'the third age of your life' had been used much earlier – in 1446, in English.

(a/the) third man A fielding position in cricket. However, in the film *The Third*

Man (UK 1949) – about the black market in post-war Vienna – he is supposed to be one of three witnesses to a traffic accident that has taken the life of Harry Lime, a 'pusher', played by Orson Welles. It turns out that Lime himself is the Third Man and that he is very much alive. The film probably led to the use of 'Third Man', 'Fourth Man' and even 'Fifth Man' to describe those who were suspected of having tipped off the spies Burgess and Maclean to defect to Moscow in 1954. The 'Third Man' was later identified as Kim Philby and the 'Fourth Man' as Anthony Blunt.

(the) Third World   Phrase for those developing nations generally not aligned with the Communist and non-Communist blocs. Hence also, to describe the same phenomenon, the term 'non-aligned nations'. Coined in French in 1956.

thirteen wasted years (or thirteen years of Tory misrule)   With the force of slogans, these phrases were uttered in the run-up to the 1964 British General Election, which Labour won. So they may be said to have had some effect. From the 1964 Labour Party manifesto: 'A New Britain . . . reversing the decline of thirteen wasted years.' In his maiden speech to the House of Lords as the Earl of Stockton, Harold Macmillan recalled his days as (Conservative) Prime Minister (for six of the years in question): 'Of course, politics being politics, the Socialist party naturally called those years the "thirteen years of Tory misrule". But nobody seemed to mind very much.' Compare Winston Churchill's remark to Denis Kelly, in private conversation (1949), about 'four wasted years of Labour Government' – quoted in Martin Gilbert, *Never Despair* (1988).

thirty-five years!   Catchphrase from the BBC radio show *Beyond Our Ken* (1958–64). Kenneth Williams played an ancient gentleman who, when asked how long he had been doing anything, would give this reply, forthrightly. This catchphrase was obviously well established by the edition broadcast on 15 July 1960 – the audience joined in with it.

this ad insults women   Slogan of the women's movement in the 1970s. Usually attached to the offending sexist ad (in the UK) with a sticker. Compare: an Elliott shoe shop ad in 1979 that showed a pair of models wearing woollen thigh boots – upon which a graffitist had written, 'This insults and degrades sheep'.

this great movement of ours   A British Labour Party phrase, noted in the early 1980s. Sometimes abbreviated to 'THIGMOU'. Compare from a speech by Harold Wilson in Huddersfield (May 1951): 'This Party of ours, this Movement of ours . . . is based on principles and ideals . . . This movement of ours is bigger than any individual or group of individuals.' 'This is not the first time that "Ginger Jack" had placed himself at the services of Thigmoo – This Great Movement of Ours. Four years previously, he signalled his determination to run against the Communist Jack Adams as deputy general secretary of the TGWU' – *Independent on Sunday* (7 May 1995); 'In those days (not so long ago) the [Building Societies Association]'s monthly lunches would be followed by a proclamation of the mortgage rate. It was at such post-prandial moments that the societies liked to refer to themselves as this great movement of ours' – *The Daily Telegraph* (19 May 1995).

this green and pleasant land   An over-loved phrase from William Blake's short preface to his poem *Milton* (1804–10) which has come to be called 'Jerusalem' as a result of the immensely popular musical setting under the title (1916) by Sir Hubert Parry. The song has become an alternative British national anthem: 'I will not cease from mental fight, / Nor shall my sword sleep in my hand, / Till we have built Jerusalem, / In England's green and pleasant land.' 'Up and down our green and pleasant land' is included in a parody of sportswriters' clichés included in the book *That Was The Week That Was* (1963); 'How is it that, if the New Zealand flat-worm's habit of slurping up the good old British earthworm will devastate this green and pleasant land, New Zealand seems a very green and pleasant land, far from an arid wasteland?' – letter to the editor in *The Independent* (17 January 1995); 'Thomas, who regards himself as an immigrant in the so-called green and pleasant land, asserts that the Co-op movement "has always had an ethical position. It has been one of the congress resolutions for years. The bank has always had a desire to live up to these standards but we never publicised the fact"' – *The Observer* (9 April 1995); 'As the environment is increasingly threatened by developers, the concerned classes are rising up to save our green and pleasant land. Sheila Hale reports from the front line' – by-line in *Harpers & Queen* Magazine (May 1995); '[The] Young call for green and pleasant land' – headline in *The Independent* (15 May 1995).

this has restored my faith in British justice   What members of the British public invariably say, when prompted by journalists, after winning a court case. A cliché noted by 1987. 'Mrs Dallaglio, of Barnes, south-west London, who lost her 19-year-old daughter Francesca, said after the ruling: "This has restored my faith in British justice. I am overwhelmed"' – *The Independent* (11 June 1994); 'A jubilant Mr Chichester said his faith in British justice had been restored. "I was very glad that the cloud hanging over my head for five months has been conclusively removed by the court"' – *The Independent* (12 November 1994).

this is a free country (or **it's a . . .)** *Partridge/Slang* dates this as 'late C19' and calls it 'expressive of tolerance (or apathy, depending on points of view)'.

this is a local shop for local people Catchphrase from the BBC TV comedy series *The League of Gentlemen* (1999–). Set in the North of England village of 'Royston Vasey' and populated by weird characters, the series has a major landmark in The Local Shop, whose proprietors are apt to ask of customers, 'Are you local?' If the reply is negative, they are told: 'This is a local shop for local people, there's nothing for you here'.

this is beautiful downtown Burbank Catchphrase from NBC TV, *Rowan and Martin's Laugh-In* (1967–73). A quintessential late 1960s' sound was announcer Gary Owens, with hand cupped to ear, intoning, 'This is beautiful downtown Burbank' – an ironic compliment to the area of Los

Angeles where NBC TV's studios are located and where *Laugh-in* was recorded. An enormous hit on US television from its inception in 1967, *Laugh-In* lasted until 1973 and was briefly revived, without Rowan and Martin, and with little success, in 1977. The original was a brightly coloured, fast-moving series of sketches and gags, with a wide range of stock characters, linked together by the relaxed charm of Dan Rowan (1922–87) and Dick Martin (b. 1923). For a while, the whole of America was ringing to the programme's catchphrases.

this is Funf speaking!   Catchphrase from the BBC radio show *ITMA* (1939–49). Spoken sideways into a glass tumbler, this phrase was 'the embodiment of the nation's spy neurosis', according to the show's producer, Francis Worsley. The first time 'Funf' (Jack Train) appeared was in the second edition of the show on 26 September 1939, just after the outbreak of the Second World War. Initially, he said, 'Dees ees Foonf, your favourite shpy!' Train recalled that when Worsley was searching for a name for the spy, he overheard his six-year-old son, Roger, trying to count in German: '*Ein, zwei, drei, vier, funf*' – and that's where he always got stuck. For a while it became a craze to start phone conversations with the words.

this *is* Henry Hall speaking and tonight is my guest night   Stock phrase of Henry Hall (1899–1989), conductor of light music radio shows on the BBC from the 1930s onwards. But what was the reason for the peculiar emphasis on 'is'? In 1934, the BBC Dance Orchestra had been playing while Hall was away in America and yet it was still announced as 'directed by Henry Hall'. A journalist wrote: 'Why do the BBC allow this to happen? How can Henry Hall possibly be conducting the orchestra when we know for a fact that at this moment he is on the high seas?' Hence, on his return, he said, 'Hello, everyone, this *is* Henry Hall speaking!' and it stayed with him for the rest of his long broadcasting career. See also under HERE'S TO OUR NEXT MERRY MEETING!

this is it!   Phrase of agreement. Noted by Paul Beale in 1974 as occurring where a simple 'yes' or 'I agree' would do. Previously it may have been heard more at points in conversation when something significant had happened. Kenneth Tynan reviewing an idiomatic modern translation (1948) of *Medea* by Euripides noted Medea's reaction to Creon's notice of expulsion, 'This is *it*.' The agreement version acquired catchphrase status through BBC Radio's satirical *Week Ending* show from about 1977 when two pub bores (played by David Jason and Bill Wallis) conversed on current topics. One would ritually say it, followed by **makes you think!**

this ... is ... London! A greeting that became familiar to American radio listeners to reports given by Edward R. Murrow from London during the Second World War. It was a natural borrowing from BBC announcers who had been saying **this is London calling** from the earliest days of station 2LO in the 1920s. One of them, Stuart Hibberd, entitled a book of his broadcasting diaries, *This Is London* (1950).

this is the age of the train See WE'RE GETTING THERE.

this is the city See MY NAME'S.

this is war! Meaning, 'this is very serious, and justifies the particular course adopted'. In a dispatch to Earl Russell (5 September 1863), Charles Francis Adams, the American diplomat, wrote: 'It would be superfluous in me to point out to your lordship that this is war.' 'This is war' – *The Chicago Herald and Examiner* (November 1924); 'Hildy, this is war!' – in the film *His Girl Friday* (US 1940); 'We are all in it together. This is a war. We take a few shots and it will be over . . . I wouldn't want to be on the other side right now. Would you?' – President Nixon on 15 September 1972, quoted in *The White House Transcripts* (1974). 'The President looked at each man in turn. "Gentlemen, this is war. I want to know how we get rid of Harry Perkins and his government"' – Chris Mullin, *A Very British Coup*, Chap. 14 (1982); 'This was not child's play. This was war' – Wilson Goode, Mayor of Philadelphia, defending a police fire-bombing raid that had gone disastrously wrong, quoted in *Time* Magazine (15 May 1985); 'Drug menace:

now it's WAR' – front-page headline in the *Daily Express* (24 May 1985); '[after the Heysel football stadium disaster,] said a Belgian Red Cross rescue worker: "This is not sport. This is war"' – *Time* Magazine (10 June 1985); 'THIS TIME IT'S WAR. TYSON VS. BRUNO' – sign outside the Las Vegas Hilton promoting a big fight (February 1989). Compare **this means war!** – a dramatic cliché mostly in Hollywood films. Ambassador Trentino (Louis Calhern) says it more than once in the Marx Brothers' film *Duck Soup* (US 1933) when his country has been provoked. Later Bugs Bunny frequently used the phrase in his cartoon series (1937–63).

this is where we came in Meaning, 'I am/you are beginning to repeat myself/yourself. This is where we should stop whatever it is we are doing'. Or 'we have been here (to this point) before, haven't we?' From the remark uttered in cinemas when continuous performances were the order of the day – from the 1920s to the 1970s. In *Punch* (9 March 1938), there is a cartoon of a couple at a boxing match. The ring is covered with bodies and the caption is, 'Isn't this where we came in?' – which rather suggests that the expression was well enough established even then for it to be used in a transferred situation. From 'Cato', *Guilty Men* (1940): 'When the news of the appointment [of Sir Samuel Hoare reappointed as Minister of Air in 1940] became known, an aged opponent of the administration rose from his seat, "This is where I came in," he said.'

—— ——, this is your life! Ralph Edwards hosted the original 1950s' US TV series *This Is Your Life* in which a subject's life was told (*without* the warts and all) after he or she had been taken by surprise. The idea has since been taken up in many countries. Largely sentimental, the shows are notable for tearful reunions between the subject and long-lost relatives and friends. Edwards also hosted the first British edition when the BBC took up the idea in 1955. The first UK 'victim' to be hailed with the cry was Eamonn Andrews who went on to become the presenter of the long-running series with the BBC and then with Thames TV. He was still presenting it at his death in 1987, when Michael

Aspel took over the role. When surprised by Eamonn and his 'big Red Book', the victim heard him intone in his Irish drawl something like: 'Fred Pincushion, all-round-entertainer and mass-murderer, this is your loif!' (to which the victim all too rarely replied, 'Push off!')

this one will run and run Promotional cliché from *Private Eye*'s collection of phrases – this one (said of anything, but especially of a political dispute or a strike) was originally the sort of extract taken from critics' notices that theatrical manage-ments liked to display outside their theatres to promote shows. Said originally to have derived from a review of a 1960s' thriller that closed within a month, by Fergus Cashin of *The Sun*. Identified as a cliché in the 1970s and thus rendered unusable again in its original context. 'So this one will run and run. And why not? It has already been running for 18 months since the Downing Street Declaration and for nine since the IRA ceasefire' – *The Guardian* (27 May 1995); 'And, like the best soap operas, this one will run and run. The 35-year-old Tan has been acquit-ted of that charge – although found guilty of uttering a death threat. Boland is now launching a civil suit against her. "I have to keep this case alive," he said. "I hope something will come out of it – but I have to do this, as a mission"' – *The Observer* (28 May 1995).

this (thing) is bigger than both of us 'This (thing)' = 'our love', of course. A whopping film cliché that one can hardly believe was ever uttered in all seriousness. Said to have been popularized, satirically, by Milton Berle in his American radio and TV shows of the 1940s and 50s. In Britain, Frank Muir and Denis Norden did a similar job in their scripts for the BBC radio show *Take It From Here* (1947–58). For example, in this extract from their *Hamlet* with Hollywood subtitles: 'Oh, dear Ophelia, I have not art to reckon my groans but that I love thee best. ("DON'T FIGHT THIS THING, KID, IT'S BIGGER THAN BOTH OF US").' 'This is bigger than both of us' is spoken in the BBC radio *Goon Show*, 'Tales of Montmartre' (17 January 1956), and 'Tales of Men's Shirts' (31 December 1959). In the remake of *King Kong* (US

1976), with the giant ape brushing against the side of the house they are sheltering in, Jack Prescott (Jeff Bridges) says to Dwan (Jessica Lange), 'He's bigger than both of us, know what I mean?' 'And would Ackroyd have died for Brian? He shakes his head. "Because I'm quite a hard person and there was something else that was bigger than both of us and that was my work. I lived for that and Brian lived for me"' – *The Times* (12 September 1994); 'The advocacy of these young players is almost defiantly assertive. There are no rules of engagement here: just an impassioned, up-front manner with dynamic, larger-than-life contrasts between action and repose, and an overriding sense that "this music is bigger than both of us"' – *The Independent* (16 December 1994); 'Hugo Young's heart is in the right place, and mine is there too. But this thing is bigger than both of us' – letter to the editor in *The Guardian* (11 February 1995).

this town ain't big enough for the both of us (or the two of us)! In Western films, it might be said by the villain to the sheriff or to anyone else who is trying to bring him to book. He is, of course, suggesting that the *other person* will have to get out of town in order to make the room. The baddy (played by Charles King) says it to cowboy Tex Ritter in a 1936 film made by Grand National Pictures in the *Boots and Saddles* series. 'Bugs Bunny' says it to his enemy 'Yosemite Sam' in the cartoon *Bugs Bunny Rides Again* (US 1948). The US/UK group Sparks had a hit with their recording of 'This Town Ain't Big Enough for Both of Us' in 1974. 'When the cop discovers that Landry has designs on his wife, the scene is set for a violent showdown. This town ain't big enough for the two of 'em' – *The Herald* (Glasgow) (8 April 1995).

this —— will not change our lives Referring to a win/stroke of good fortune/ luck. What members of the public invari-ably tell journalists. 'Man [a boozer prop-ping up the bar] who has drawn a runner in the Irish Sweep (to reporter): "Put dahn as 'ow, if I win, it won't make no differ-ence to my way o' life"' – caption to a cartoon by Chas Grave in *Punch* (16 March 1932); 'The two men [National

Lottery winners], wearing newly bought clothes, adopted the time-honoured approach of saying the enormous win would not change their lives' – *Daily Mail* (13 June 1995).

this won't bathe the baby 'My mother, a *very* busy lady would sometimes sit down for a few minutes. Feeling guilty she would arise to these words (even though our baby days were long past). I still use it when there are things to be done' – Mrs Elizabeth Durham, Cheshire (1995). Compare: 'From my mother about time-wasting, "This won't get the children boots, or the baby a new bonnet"' – Deborah Chesshire, Somerset (1998). *Casson/Grenfell* has the nannyism: 'Now I must get on, this will never get the baby a new coat.'

this year, next year, now, never Phrase from a children's counting-out game – like 'Tinker, tailor, soldier, sailor . . .' – that enables the player to find out when something is going to happen. In E. M. Forster, *A Room With a View*, Chap. 13 (1908), a young character does it with plum stones. 'The Piglet was sitting on the ground at the door of his house blowing happily at a dandelion, and wondering whether it would be this year, next year, sometime, or never' – A. A. Milne, *Winnie-the-Pooh*, Chap. 8 (1926). *This Year, Next Year* was the title of a TV drama series (UK 1977) written by John Finch.

those were the days An expression of regret for times having past. From Wordsworth, *The Prelude*, Bk 6, line 52 (1850), referring to his time at Cambridge: 'Those were the days / Which also first embold-ened me to trust / With firmness . . . / that I might leave / Some monument behind me which pure hearts / Should reverence.' *Those Were the Days* became the title of: a BBC radio show of old-time dance music (1943–74); of a compilation of books by A. A. Milne (1929); of a song sung by Mary Hopkin in 1968; of the title of a film (UK 1934) about 1890s' music hall; also of a film (US 1940) about looking back to college days.

(a) thousand a year or a handsome husband Said when offering the last portion of food, last sandwich or last cake on a plate. Current in the 1950s, this saying now seems to promise rather slight remuneration for accepting the offer. Iona Opie and Moira Tatem in *A Dictionary of Superstitions* (1992) find various benefits linked to taking the last piece of food on a plate. Their earliest is a 'Lancashire legend' recalled in 1873. From 1923, in Kent: 'The person who, uninvited, takes the last slice of bread and butter from the plate will die unmarried. But the person who takes the last slice upon invitation will have a handsome spouse and an income of thousands amounting to the number of people at the table.' Sylvia Dowling, Lancashire (1998), wrote that in the 1950s it usually attracted the smart reply: 'I'll take the thousand a year and then I'll have my choice of handsome husbands.'

(a) thousand points of light Phrase associated with George Bush who used it many times throughout the 1988 US Presidential election campaign. In his speech accepting the Republican nomina-tion at New Orleans on 18 August 1988, he said: 'I will keep America moving forward, always forward – for a better America, for an endless enduring dream and a thou-sand points of light.' The words were written by his speechwriter, Peggy Noonan, but what did they mean? The phrase was said to symbolize individual endeavour, voluntary charity efforts, across the country (later, in June 1989, President Bush announced details of his 'Points of Light Program, costing $25 million, to encourage a voluntary crusade to fight poverty, drugs and homelessness). But Bush never seemed too sure what he was saying. On one occasion, he called it '1,000 points of life'. Herblock, the car-toonist, drew a drunk at a bar pledging his vote to Bush because he had promised '1,000 pints of Lite'. Perhaps it was sup-posed to echo Shakespeare, *The Merchant of Venice*, V.i.90: 'How far that little candle throws his beams! / So shines a good deed in a naughty world.' In her memoir, *What I Saw at the Revolution* (1990), Noonan makes mention of several earlier uses of the phrase or parts of it. She does not appear to have been aware of C. S. Lewis's *The Magician's Nephew* (1955): 'One moment there had been nothing but darkness, next moment a thousand points of light leaped out . . .', or of Thomas Wolfe's *The Web and the Rock* (1939): 'Instantly he could see the town below now, coiling in a thousand fumes of homely smoke, now winking into a thousand points of friendly light its glorious small design', though she had read it as a teenager. A speech by a turn-of-the-century engineer was also found urging the electrification of Venice so that it would be filled with 'a thousand points of light'. Oddly, Noonan does not draw attention to one possible point of inspiration. Having admitted earlier that she is a fan of Auden's poem 'September 1, 1939' ('We must love one another or die'), she overlooks the lines: 'Defenceless under the night / Our world in stupor lies; / Yet, dotted everywhere, / Ironic points of light / Flash out wherever the Just / Exchange their messages . . .'

(as) thousands cheered A natural enough phrase found in newspaper reports but sometimes echoic of the title *As Thousands Cheer*, a show with words and music by Irving Berlin (New York 1933). Hence, *As Thousands Cheer: The Life of Irving Berlin*, the title of a book (1990) by Laurence Bugneer. 'When Maiden returned to Southampton in 1990, the triumph was enormous. A band played Tina Turner's "You're Simply The Best" as the girls sailed into the marina and thousands cheered and wept' – *Daily Mail* (18 December 1993); '. . . So when Paul O'Callaghan laid into an impersonation of Noel Edmonds's brain, thousands cheered' – *Mail on Sunday* (27 February 1994).

three acres and a cow See TEN ACRES.

(the) three Rs Reading, writing and arithmetic. *Brewer* (1999): 'The phrase is said to have been originated by Sir William Curtis (1752–1829), an illiterate alderman and lord mayor of London, who gave this as a toast, i.e. "Riting, Reading and Rithmetic".' *Brewer* (1894): 'Sir William Curtis being asked to give a toast, said, "I will give you the three R's – writing, reading, and arithmetic". "The House is aware that no payment is made except on the 'three R's'" – Mr Cory MP in the House of Commons (28 February 1867).'

three sheets in the wind Drunk. The 'sheets' in question are not, as you might expect, sails but the ropes or chains attached to sails to trim them with. If the sheet is free, the sail is unrestrained. As Robert L. Shook in *The Book of Why* (1983) puts it, 'if these sheets are loose, the ship will be as unstable on the water as a thoroughly drunk man is on his feet'. Sometimes 'three sheets *to* the wind'. Known by 1821.

three strikes and you're out Encapsulation of a law that was voted for in California in 1994 which meant that people who were convicted of three felonies could end up facing life imprisonment. The phrase comes from baseball where a batter wo allows three strikes – that is, three pitches past him in the strike zone – is out. It can be heard in the title song from the film *Take Me Out To the Ball Game* (US 1949). Adopted elsewhere in the general sense of, 'Three offences/misdemeanours and you'll get no more leniency.'

thrilling days See HI YO SILVER.

throat See AT YOUR.

(the) throbbing metropolis A journalistic cliché by the mid-20th century. Date of origin not known. 'In his view Auchtermuchty . . . is an outpost of human decency in a world festering with immorality: in a word, Brigadoon. But fleeting through its sleepy streets en route to the throbbing metropolis of Cupar, visitors may detect that beneath its douce exterior lurks another, darker, Auchtermuchty' – *Scotland on Sunday* (4 September 1994); 'Miles from the throbbing metropolis where bands blithely go about their hearty pop business, a slumbering beast is rousing itself from its morose torpor' – *The Scotsman* (30 November 1994).

(to look as if one has been dragged) through a hedge backwards To look extremely dishevelled. Date of origin unknown. '"You are a man of very wide literary cognisance. Have you ever encountered the expression, 'It was like being pulled through a hedge, backwards'?" – "Oh, yes, indeed . . . very . . . very racy"' – Henry Reed, BBC radio play, *A Hedge Backwards* (29 February 1956).

through the keyhole A phrase for how one obtains information about a person or household secretly or illicitly. Known by 1592 – in Christopher Marlowe, *The Jew of Malta. Through the Keyhole* has been used as the title of a feature on British TV since 1983 in which the homes of celebrities are revealed to the camera's gaze.

(to) throw in the towel To give up some enterprise, usually in disgust or frustration. To admit defeat. From the traditional gesture by the losing participant in a boxing match. Whether the towel was originally thrown into the ring or into the wash-bucket is not clear. Known by 1915.

throw away your babies See KILL YOUR DARLINGS.

(to) throw money around like snuff at a wake 'My elderly Irish aunt used to say this about people overly generous with their money' – Marie Hartshorne, Dorset (1994). Indeed, this is a pretty standard Irish expression. *Partridge/Catch Phrases* suggests it has been around since about 1910. Compare the opposite expression: **(to) throw money about like a man with no arms** – the traditional way of describing a mean person. *Partridge/Catch Phrases* has it as British/Australian since about 1930. Also 'flinging his money around . . .'

(to be) thrown into the melting-pot To be scrapped and a new beginning made, suggesting that ideas are going to be put into an imaginary 'pool' and mixed together. From the image of the process of making things from metals that have been melted down. 'The jackboot is thrown into the melting-pot' is cited in George Orwell, 'Politics and the English Language', in *Horizon* (April 1946) as a metaphor where the images clash. Known by 1887 in the non-literal sense. In a figurative sense, the image of a melting pot has been used to describe the United States where members of different races and many nationalities have been blended together to form a new society. 'America is God's Crucible, the great Melting-Pot where all the races of Europe are melting and re-forming!' – Israel Zangwill, *The Melting Pot*, Act 1 (1908); 'He said the whole question would be thrown into the melting pot in an "audit" of EU legislation which he secured as part of the Maastricht Treaty package' – *Daily Mail* (9 June 1994); 'Many of today's artists . . . have used the millennium as a metaphor for the post-nuclear, post-Aids culture in which politics, economics, sexual identity, and religion have been thrown up into a melting pot of uncertainties' – *The Guardian* (8 April 1995).

(to) throw one's hat in the ring To join an enterprise or at least show that you intend to. To pick up a challenge. From the days when a challenge to a prizefighter at a showground or fair was delivered in this manner. Known since 1847. 'Mr Secretary Hoover has been forced to throw his hat into the ring for the Presidency, but he does not mean to follow it there' – *The Observer* (4 March 1928).

(a) thumbnail sketch A small drawing or sketch that is the size of a thumbnail (not as though drawn using one's thumbnail). Known by 1852. Figuratively, meaning 'a brief word picture', by 1901. 'There is also a thumbnail sketch of each club's activities' – *Lloyd's List* (14 July 1994); 'Sir, Tim Dickson's piece on W. Edwards Deming . . . gave a sensitive and accurate thumbnail sketch of a man whose ideas and achievements are often misunderstood and hence often misrepresented' – letter to the editor in the *Financial Times* (7 January 1995).

(to give the) thumbs down To indicate disapproval, rejection or failure. From the traditional gesture supposedly made by members of the crowd at Roman gladiatoral combats. This meant that the gladiator was to die. Known by 1906.

(The) Thunderer Sobriquet of *The Times* newspaper. It was known as such from the 1830s onwards, because of its magisterial leading articles. An assistant editor, Edward Sterling (d. 1847), wrote on one occasion: 'We thundered forth the other day in an article on the subject of social and political reform.' Louis Heren, writing in *Memories of Times Past*, Chap. 1 (1988), states rather that 'the nickname "The Thunderer" was earned by a leading article urging the country to "thunder for reform"', under the first editor, Thomas Barnes.

(the) Thundering Herd In stock-market lingo, this is one of the nicknames of Merrill Lynch, the US brokerage firm, and may reflect its large number of clients and brokers. Kathleen Odean's *High Steppers, Fallen Angels, and Lollipops: Wall Street Slang* (1988) quotes the *Wall Street Journal* (14 April 1983): 'Merrill originally used the bull as a symbol of "the thundering herd," the nickname for the firm. When strategists decided that this insulted both brokers and investors by suggesting that they merely followed the crowd, Merrill brought in a new ad agency. The bull stayed on to convey the opposite message – the current "breed apart" campaign.' Any connection with the slogan 'Merrill Lynch is bullish about America' is probably coincidental – the nickname had been coined long before.

thunderous applause Known by 1892. Compare **rapturous applause** (known by 1853) and **tumultuous applause** (known by 1942). 'Mr Mandela arrived at parliament led by a police motorcycle escort. He walked into the chamber to thunderous applause' – *The Independent* (10 May 1994); 'The most vituperative contribution, widely televised, came from a gentleman who turned out to have travelled from Glasgow to stir the pot at what was supposedly a meeting for locals to question the candidates under Christian auspices. There was no doubt whose interests his efforts were intended to serve, and the FoC coalition rewarded him with tumultuous applause' – *The Herald* (Glasgow) (29 June 1994); 'Salle earned himself tumultuous applause on a victory lap but there was no doubt that it was Sally who was the crowd's favourite as the meeting started' – *Daily Mail* (10 September 1994).

thus far shalt thou go and no further Limit-setting phrase. Charles Stewart Parnell, the champion of Irish Home Rule, said in Cork in 1885: 'No man has a right to fix the boundary of the march of a nation; no man has a right to say to his country, Thus far shalt thou go and no further.' On the other hand, George Farquhar, the (Irish-born) playwright has this in *The Beaux' Stratagem*, III.ii (1707): 'And thus far I am a captain, and no farther.' And then again, the Book of Job 38:11 has: 'Hitherto shalt thou come, but no further: and here shall thy proud waves be stayed?'

(to be) tickled pink To be delighted; to be overcome with pleasure or amusement. Presumably, the pinkness would indicate that one was enjoying something. Known by 1922. 'To be tickled to death' is earlier and may be of American origin. Known by 1834.

(the) ties that bind (or tie that binds) This proverbial phrase may possibly have originated in a hymn written by John Fawcett, an English Baptist minister, in 1782: 'Blest be the tie that binds / Our hearts in Christian love: / The fellowship of kindred minds / Is like to that above.' The story goes that Fawcett had already set out on the road leaving a chapel where he had been minister, but his congregation prevailed on him to return. When he got back to his manse he sat down right away and wrote the hymn. It is used prominently in Thornton Wilder's play *Our Town* (1938) and occasioned a parody (probably American): 'Blest be the tie that binds / Our collar to our shirt, / For it is the only things that hides / A little rim of dirt.' Other references: in *Punch* (20 May 1843) there is a cartoon of two dogs tethered by their kennels and the caption: 'There is a tie that binds us to our homes'. In the journal *Lux Mundi* (1889): 'The ties which bind men in the relation of brotherhood and sonhood are the noblest.' Title of a book by P. G. Wodehouse: *Jeeves and the Tie That Binds* (1971). A film about adoption (US 1996), with Keith Carradine and Daryl Hannah, had the title *The Tie That Binds*.

(as) tight as a duck's arse and that's watertight Mean. Date of origin unknown. Discussing the expression 'pissed as a newt' and, according to *Partridge*, the original form, 'tight as a newt', Paul Beale wrote (1987): 'The great thing about newts is the characteristic they share with fishes' arse'oles: they are watertight. And you can't get tighter than that!' One gets the drift.

tightly knit See CLOSELY KNIT.

till death us do part From the marriage vow in the Solemnization of Matrimony in the Book of Common Prayer, where mistakes are often made in the wording. I.e. it is *not* 'till death do us part'. Originally, the phrase was 'till death us depart' = 'separate completely'. The full vow is: 'To have and to hold from this day forward, for better for worse, for richer for poorer, in sickness and in health, to love and to cherish, till death us do part, according to God's holy ordinance' – and this has produced further much used phrases. Hence, the titles of the films *To Have and to Hold* (UK 1963, US 1998), *From This Day Forward* (US 1946, UK 2000), *For Better For Worse* (UK 1954) and *Till Death Us Do Part* (UK 1968), the latter based on the notable British TV comedy series (1964–74). This last also resulted in a sequel, *In Sickness and in Health* (from 1985). *For Richer, For Poorer* was the title of a romance novel by Barbara Goolden (1959) and *To Love and To Cherish*, of a romance novel by Patricia Gaffney (1995).

till the cows come home I.e. for a very long time. Recorded by 1610. Probably makes more sense when 'till the cows come home *unbidden*' is understood. One might say, 'We could end up waiting here till the cows come home' or, like Groucho Marx in *Duck Soup* (1933), say to a woman: 'I could dance with you till the cows come home. On second thoughts I'd rather dance with the cows till you come home.'

(to) tilt at windmills Meaning, 'to try and overcome imaginary obstacles'. From Don Quixote's belief that windmills were giants and needed to be fought in the novel (1605–15) by Cervantes. Compare THEY MIGHT BE GIANTS.

timber-r-r! A sawyer's traditional cry of warning during tree-felling, recorded in Canada by 1912. However, from *The New York Times* (30 March 1992): 'Loggers don't say "timmmmmmber", when a 200-foot Douglas fir comes crashing down . . . They never did, as far as anyone on the Olympic Peninsula [Washington State] can remember.'

time See ANY TIME; COME IN NUMBER; DOESN'T TIME FLY.

(a) time bomb waiting to go off Journalistic cliché by the mid-20th century to describe a serious problem or situation

that is bound to arise. 'Hugh Pennington, professor of bacteriology at Aberdeen University, described the spread of E. coli 0157 as "A time bomb waiting to go off"' – *The Independent* (20 June 1995); 'A senior detective said: "We believe Wardell was a time bomb waiting to explode but managed to control his sexual fantasies by seeing prostitutes"' – *The Daily Telegraph* (21 December 1995).

time for a change Political slogan. Used by the Republican Party in campaigns for the US presidency in 1944, 1948 and – finally, successfully – in 1952. Thomas E. Dewey, the candidate, declared, 'That's why it's time for a change' in a campaign speech at San Francisco (21 September 1944).

'time for bed,' said Zebedee Stock phrase from *Magic Roundabout*, the English version of a French series using stop-action puppets, on BBC TV 1965–77. The English commentary was written and spoken by Eric Thompson.

time has passed by —— Cliché of travel writing and advertising, and especially of film travelogues. Memorably completed in the commentary to Frank Muir and Denis Norden's sketch 'Balham, Gateway to the South' (1948): 'Time has passed by this remote corner. So shall we.' Compare **time has stood still**: 'In this fishing village, where a jumble of neat white-washed houses tumble down the tangle of cobbled streets towards the busy harbour, time seems to have stood still for centuries' – listed in *The Independent* 'DIY travel writers' cliché kit' (31 December 1988). Replaced latterly with the suggestion that the place is **in a time warp** – part of the 'travel scribes' armoury' compiled from a competition in *The Guardian* (10 April 1993).

(a) time-honoured ritual Date of origin not known. A cliché by the mid-20th century. 'For the BBC, Tom Fleming could find clichés of his own. He gave us "the time-honoured ritual of a British royal occasion"' – *The Times* (30 July 1981); 'Time-honoured ritual comes under threat: The confusing arguments for and against British Summertime' – headline in *The Herald* (Glasgow) (22 October 1994).

time is money An ancient encouragement not to waste money. Antiphon is said to have expressed it in Greek, 'The most costly outlay is time.' Benjamin Franklin wrote in 1748: 'Remember that Time is Money. He that can earn Ten Shillings a Day . . . and . . . sits idle one half of that Day . . . has really . . . thrown away Five Shillings.'

time is of the essence Getting this thing done (or started) soon is of the utmost importance. Proverbial expression, not recorded before 1931, though it was contained in the old legal phrase 'time is of the essence of the contract'.

time marches on Meaning, 'It's getting on, time is moving forward, time flies . . .' 'Time . . . Marches On' was a line used in – and to promote – the 'March of Time' news-documentary-dramas that ran on American radio for 14 years from 1931. The programmes were sponsored by *Time* Magazine. To what extent the phrase existed before then is not clear. The phrase 'march of time' itself was known by 1833.

(the) time ——, the place ——, the —— Format probably originating with the staccato narratives of American crime fiction of the 1940s/50s: 'The year, 1934; the place, Fresno, California . . .' In *The Philadelphia Story* (US 1940), James Stewart, as a (tipsy) journalist, invents a very newspapery account of an incident, saying: 'The time: May 1938; the place, Boston, a hotel . . .' In 1961, Bernard Braden was fronting a British TV show called *The Time, The Place and The Camera*. By *circa* 1966, a British TV ad for Players Weights Tipped cigarettes had the line: 'The time . . . the pace [*sic*] . . . the cigarette.' 'The Time: Now/The Place: Kings Road, Chelsea /The Killer: Count Dracula' – film poster for *Dracula AD 1972* (UK 1972). A 1977 biography of Rita Hayworth by John Kobal was entitled *The Time, The Place and The Woman*. The title of an itinerant audience debate series on British TV (from 1987) was *The Time . . . The Place*. However, before all of that, there had been the opening couplet of Robert Browning's poem, 'Never the time and the place / And the loved one all

together!' (1883); 'The time, the place, the circumstances under which we now stood face to face in the evening stillness of that dreary valley . . .' – Wilkie Collins, *The Woman in White*, First Epoch, Chap. 13 (1860); and Shakespeare, *Othello*, V.ii.370 (1604): 'The time, the place, the torture.' Even more significantly, 'The Time, the Place and the Girl' was the title of a song by Victor Herbert/Henry Blosssom in the show *Mlle. Modiste* (Broadway 1905). Then, *The Time, The Place and the Girl* was the title given to a stage musical (Chicago 1906) and two unrelated film musicals (US 1929 and 1946). This last probably provoked the allusion in P. G. Wodehouse, *Leave It To Psmith*, Chap. 9 (1923): 'The time and the place were both above criticism, but, as so often happens in this life of ours, he had been let down by the girl.'

time to re-tire Slogan for Fisk Rubber Co. tyres, in the USA from 1907. Burr Griffin did the original sketch for this long-running pun of an ad which showed a yawning youngster with candle, nightshirt – and tyre. The original slogan was, 'When it's time to re-tire, buy a Fisk'.

time to spare? go by air Saying, perhaps dating from the days when air travel was subject to lengthier delays than it is now and suited the more leisurely traveller. Quoted in 1989.

tin See IT DOES EXACTLY.

tinker, tailor, soldier, sailor From the children's fortune-telling rhyme: 'Tinker, tailor, soldier, sailor, rich man, poor man, beggar man, thief', first recorded in something like this form in 1883. Hence, *Tinker Tailor Soldier Spy* – the title of a spy novel (1974) by John Le Carré. Note also, *Rich Man, Poor Man*, the title of a novel (1970) by Irwin Shaw, to which the sequel was *Beggarman, Thief* (1977).

(a/the) Tin Lizzie Nickname of Henry Ford's Model T motor-car, the first mass-produced vehicle, inelegant but efficient and comparatively cheap. Fifteen million were produced between 1908 and discontinuation of the model in 1927. Ford is said to have encouraged jokes about them for the sake of publicity as they rattled around the world. 'Lizzie' may be a contraction of 'limousine' or be from the name applied to a domestic servant. The term 'Lady Lizzie' was used about the car in a 1913 advertisement. 'Tin Lizzie' was known by 1915, the 'tin' probably referring to the fact it was produced for the masses. The Irish pop group Thin Lizzy (which, being Irish, pronounced itself 'Tin Lizzy') performed 1973–83.

Tin Pan Alley Name given, by 1908, to the area in Manhattan where most music publishers worked – so called because the noise of countless pianos being tinkled must have sounded like tin pans being bashed. A 'tin pan' was also (*circa* 1900) the name given to a cheap tinny piano. It is said that 'Tin Pan Alley' was the title of a New York newspaper article about the music-publishing business written by Monroe H. Rosenfield in *circa* 1892. In London, the equivalent area around Denmark Street, off the Charing Cross Road, was so known by 1934.

(a) tin-pot dictator As a dismissive adjectival phrase referring to the cheap quality or noise of something, 'tin-pot' has been around since the 1830s. The *Daily News* (23 March 1897) used the phrase 'tin-pot politicians'. The inevitable linkage to dictators probably has more to do with the repetition sound of the 't' sound. 'Severn Trent was also attacked by the Labour Party for behaving like a "Third World tin pot dictatorship" over the issue' – *The Independent* (1 September 1995); 'Iain Duncan Smith, the Tory leader, accused the Prime Minister of "behaving like a tinpot dictator" and treating the British constitution as "his own personal plaything"' – *The Independent* (14 June 2003).

(the) tip of the iceberg An indication that a greater and more significant amount of something remains hidden. Based on the well-known fact that only one-ninth of an iceberg projects above the water level. A relatively modern expression, there is an allusion to it in the film *The Band Wagon* (US 1953). 'This situation is similar to that of poliomyelitis or viral hepatitis, where the cases of illness represent only the tip of the iceberg, with a much larger number of persons carrying the infection and spreading it unknowingly' – *Scientific*

American, 8/71 (1963); '[The Sixties] – "The Violent Decade", I'm calling it. Of course, the outstanding instances were the ghetto riots and the assassinations of public figures . . . But I have a theory that they were only the tip of the iceberg' – *Cosmopolitan* (November 1974); 'It will deepen the hole that the Government is in, because it makes it look as though Ridley's outburst was the tip of the iceberg. People are now aware it was not just a rash outburst by one Cabinet eccentric, but reflected deep prejudice within the Cabinet' – *The Independent* (16 July 1990); 'The assistant chief constable said the fraud may also have involved organised crime. "We're just at the tip of the iceberg," Mr Albon added' – *The Independent* (7 September 1995).

(to) tip the scales To decide the outcome of something that is in doubt by adding a little weight to some element of it. From the use of scales in weighing objects. Listed as a cliché in *The Times* (28 May 1984). 'Women tip the scales against diet dictators' – *The Times* (13 April 1992); 'Instead, as has happened before, the factor that may tip the scales in favour of an increase will be the fear that the Government will lose credibility with the markets by doing nothing' – *The Guardian* (1 May 1995); 'A 1lb swing in the weights this time is unlikely to be enough to tip the scales in favour of Shambo, three lengths further adrift in [the] third at Newbury' – *The Irish Times* (11 May 1995).

(to be) tired and emotional Meaning, 'drunk'. A pleasant euphemism, ideally suited to British newspapers, which have to operate under libel laws effectively preventing any direct statement of a person's fondness for the bottle. The expression 't. and e.' (to which it is sometimes abbreviated) is said to have arisen when *Private Eye* printed a spoof Foreign Office memo suggesting it was a useful way of describing the antics of George Brown when he was Foreign Secretary (1966–8). On 29 September 1967, the *Eye* described him as 'tired and overwrought on many occasions' and a cover showed him gesticulating while Harold Wilson explained to General de Gaulle: *'George est un peu fatigué, votre Majesté.'*

There was never any question that Brown *did* get drunk. Peter Paterson entitled his biography of Brown *Tired and Emotional* (1993). *Private Eye* may not actually have coined the phrase, though it undoubtedly popularized it. It has been suggested that a BBC spokesman said of Brown 'He was very tired and emotional' after the much criticized appearance he made on TV on the night of President Kennedy's death in November 1963. In fact, it was ITV Brown appeared on and the remark, even if it was made, has not been traced.

(are you) tired, depressed, irritable? A seemingly standard ingredient in headache advertising, in both the UK and USA by the 1960s, but hard to pin on a particular brand. In BBC TV, *Monty Python's Flying Circus* (28 December 1969), an undertaker says: 'Are you nervy, irritable, depressed, tired of life? Keep it up.'

(a) tissue of lies Meaning, a sequence of falsehoods or misrepresentations. Date of origin not known but probably 19th century. 'In 1911 he died, having months before in an apoplectic outburst from the Bench accused those in the House of Commons who had sought to criticise him five years earlier of "a tissue of lies"' – *The Herald* (Glasgow) (1 June 1994).

tiswas See ALL OF A.

tit See I HAVEN'T BEEN.

titter ye not See NAY NAY.

tit, tote and television In the days when British newspapers were still produced in Fleet Street, tabloid hacks would remind themselves that the chief preoccupations were encapsulated in this phrase (quoted in 1984). An alternative recipe (heard in 1985) was: 'Bosoms, QPR [Queen's Park Rangers, football team] and "where are they now?"' In 1978, Derek Jameson, then editor-in-chief of Express Newspapers (though he denied saying it), was quoted as remarking of the launch of the *Daily Star*: 'It'll be all tits, bums, QPR and roll your own fags.'

(to live like a) toad beneath a harrow To live in an extreme state of wretchedness. The image goes back to the 13th century. 'At ten he was apprenticed to a shoemaker, and while in this employment

he endured much hardship – living as he used to say, "like a toad under a harrow"' – Samuel Smiles, *Self-Help,* Chap. 4 (1859); 'The toad beneath the harrow knows / Exactly where each tooth-point goes' – Rudyard Kipling, 'Pagett, MP' (1886).

to boldly go where no man has gone before! The TV science-fiction series *Star Trek* (US 1966–9), though short-lived, nevertheless acquired a considerable after-life through countless repeats (not least in the UK) and the activities of 'trekky' fans. It was the series whose spoken introduction announced: 'Space – the final frontier. These are the voyages of the starship *Enterprise*. Its five-year mission: to explore strange new worlds, to seek out new life and new civilizations, to boldly go where no man has gone before.' In one of the feature films (US 1988) that belatedly spun off from the series, the split infinitive remained but feminism, presumably, had decreed that it should become 'to boldly go where no *one* has gone before'.

to boot In addition, besides, moreover. Not a verb but a little phrase that gives added emphasis. 'He is a very good friend of mine, to boot'. This has nothing to do with footwear but more to do with 'boot' meaning 'advantage, good'. Known in Old English *circa* 1000. 'Grace to boot!' – Shakespeare, *The Winter's Tale*, I.ii.80 (1611).

Toc H See AS DIM AS.

to coin a phrase Meaning, to invent a phrase or to give it 'currency', and known by 1840. But, in the 20th century, people started saying the whole phrase as an ironic way of excusing a cliché or banal statement they have just uttered.

tod See ON ONE'S.

today is the first day of the rest of your life Attributed to one Charles Dederich, founder of anti-heroin centres in the USA, *circa* 1969, this may also have occurred in the form '*tomorrow* is the first . . .' and as a wall slogan, graffito, etc. 'Today Is the First Day of the Rest of My Life' was apparently sung in a late 1960s' musical *The Love Match* (by Maltby & Shire).

today ——, tomorrow —— Slogan format, as in 'Today Germany, Tomorrow the

World [*Heute gehört uns Deutschland – morgen die ganze Welt*]!' – literally, 'Today Germany belongs to us – tomorrow the whole world'. This was a Nazi political slogan in Germany by the mid-1930s. Although John Colville, *The Fringes of Power* (Vol. 1, 1985), states that by 3 September 1939, Hitler 'had already . . . proclaimed that "Today Germany is ours; tomorrow the whole world"', an example of Hitler actually saying this has yet to be found. However, in *Mein Kampf* (1925), Hitler had written: 'If the German people, in their historic development, had possessed tribal unity like other nations, the German Reich today would be the master of the entire world.' The concept can be glimpsed in embryo in the slogan for the National Socialist Press in Germany of the early 1930s: '*Heute Presse der National-sozialisten, Morgen Presse der Nation* [Today the press of the Nazis, tomorrow the nation's press].' As also in the chorus of a song in the Hitler Youth 'songbook': '*Wir werden weiter marschieren / Wenn alles in Scherben fällt / Denn heute gehört uns Deutschland / Und morgen die ganze Welt*' – which may be roughly translated as: 'We shall keep marching on / Even if everything breaks into fragments, / For today Germany belongs to us / And tomorrow the whole world.' Another version replaces the second line with '*Wenn Scheiße vom Himmel fällt* [when shit from Heaven falls].' Sir David Hunt recalled hearing the song in 1933 or possibly 1934. By the outbreak of the Second World War, the format was sufficiently well known, as John Osborne recalled in *A Better Class of Person* (1981), for an English school magazine to be declaring: 'Now soon it will be our turn to take a hand in the destinies of Empire. Today, scholars; tomorrow, the Empire.' In the film *Forty-Ninth Parallel* (UK 1941), Eric Portman as a German U-boat commander gets to say, 'Today, Europe . . . tomorrow the whole world!' Interestingly, the format does seem to have existed outside Germany in the 1930s. In 1932, William B. Pitkin (1878–1953), Professor of Journalism at Columbia University, New York, published a book called *Life Begins at Forty* in which he dealt with 'adult reorientation' at a time when the problems

of extended life and leisure were beginning to be recognized: 'Life begins at forty. This is the revolutionary outcome of our new era . . . TODAY it is half a truth. TOMORROW it will be an axiom.' The construction became so common that a New York graffito stated: 'Today Hollywood, tomorrow the world' (recorded in 1974); and one from El Salvador (March 1982) ran: '*Ayer Nicaragua, hoy El Salvador, mañana Guatemala* [yesterday Nicaragua, today El Salvador, tomorrow Guatemala]!' *The Guardian* (6 July 1982) carried an advertisement with the unwieldy headline: 'Self-managing Socialism: Today, France – Tomorrow, the World?' A variation: from the British MP Paul Boateng's election victory speech in the Brent South constituency (June 1987): 'Brent South today – Soweto tomorrow!'

—— **to die for** As a verb meaning 'to desire keenly or excessively', 'to die for' has been around since 1591 at least. But as an adjectival expression meaning 'something of great worth', it dates from the early 1980s, although there is an isolated instance in the *1890s* – '"Oh! and to 'top off' with, a mince-pie to die for"' – E. N. Westcott, *David Harum* (1898). 'A tad overweight, but violet eyes to die for' – G. B. Trudeau (1980); a character in the film *Splash* (US 1984) says: 'That outfit is to die for'; Michelle Pfeiffer gets to say it as 'Catwoman' in the film *Batman Returns* (US 1992); *To Die For* was the title of a film (US 1995).

(to) toe the line Meaning, 'to conform to the defined standard of any group' (as though lining up at the starting line of a race or in military drill). Known by 1813. Cited as a 'dying metaphor' by George Orwell in 'Politics and the English Language', *Horizon* (April 1946). 'Germany agrees to toe line on Bosnia: Chancellor puts unity before his "moral" position against blanket arms embargo' – headline in the *Financial Times* (1 December 1994).

toil See DIGNITY OF LABOUR.

toiling upward in the night Inspirational phrase that must have adorned many a motivational speech-day or commencement address. From Longfellow, 'The Ladder of St Augustine' (1858): 'The heights by great men reached and kept / Were not attained by sudden flight, / But they, while their companions slept, / Were toiling upward in the night.'

to infinity and beyond A meaningless slogan from the films *Toy Story* and *Toy Story 2* (US 1999, 2000). It is voiced by Tim Allen as the astronaut figure 'Buzz Lightyear'. Earlier, there had been a book with the title *To Infinity and Beyond: A Cultural History of the Infinite* (1987). In the Preface to his book, Eli Maor states: 'I took the title *To Infinity and Beyond*, from a telescope manual that listed among the many virtues of the instrument the following: "The range of focus of your telescope is from fifteen feet to infinity and beyond".'

(a) token gesture Meaning, 'an action or contribution that is mostly symbolic and does not significantly materially help'. Date of origin unknown. 'Britain made a token gesture, with doctors boarding planes arriving from India to spray cabin and cargo areas with disinfectant and question crews about passengers' health' – *Daily Mail* (30 September 1994).

Tom and Jerry (1) Characters in Pierce Egan, *Life in London; or, The Day and Night Scenes of Jerry Hawthorn, Esq., and his Elegant Friend Corinthian Tom* (1821) – riotous young men about town. (2) The cat (Tom) and mouse (Jerry) featuring in many short cartoon films (US, from the late 1930s). In the early 1930s, Amedee Van Beuren made live-action shorts and cartoons and used the names Tom and Jerry for two human characters – presumably because (1) had led to their being inseparably linked. When William Hanna and Joe Barbera created the animated cat and mouse in *Puss Gets the Boot* (1939), the cat was named Jasper. When they came to make the second cartoon, *Midnight Snack* (1940), the cat was still Jasper but he was renamed Tom in mid-production, and the mouse was then given the name Jerry. The official start of the Tom and Jerry series is usually given as 1941.

Tom, Dick and Harry Any man – or body of men – taken from the common stock (indicated by the popularity of the names). Known by 1734, though more than a century previously, Shakespeare has 'Tom, Dick and Francis' in *Henry IV, Part 1*, II.iv.8 (1597).

Tommy See FOR YOU.

tomorrow See AS THOUGH THERE.

tomorrow belongs to me (or us) Political *quasi*-slogan, chiefly remembered from the musical *Cabaret* (1968, film US 1972) in which Fred Ebb (words) and John Kander (music) wrote a convincing pastiche of a Hitler Youth song: 'The babe in his cradle is closing his eyes, the blossom embraces the bee, / But soon says a whisper, "Arise, arise", Tomorrow belongs to me. / O Fatherland, Fatherland, show us the sign your children have waited to see, / The morning will come when the world is mine, Tomorrow belongs to me.' The idea definitely seems to have been current in Nazi Germany. A popular song, '*Jawohl, mein Herr*', featured in the '1943' episode of the German film chronicle *Heimat* (1984), includes the line, 'For from today, the world belongs to us.' Earlier, Saint-Simon, the French social reformer (1760–1825), once said: 'The future belongs to us. In order to do things one must be enthusiastic.' Harold Wilson in his final broadcast before the 1964 British General Election said, 'If the past belongs to the Tories, the future belongs to us – all of us.' One suspects that most recent use of the phrase has been influenced by the *Cabaret* song. At a Young Conservatives' rally before the 1983 General Election, Margaret Thatcher asked, 'Could Labour have organized a rally like this? In the old days perhaps, but not now. For they are the Party of Yesterday, Tomorrow is ours.' 'Contra leader Adolfo Calero . . . was entertained to dinner on Wednesday by Oxford University's Freedom Society, a clutch of hoorays . . . A coach-load of diners . . . got "hog-whimpering" drunk . . . and songs like "Tomorrow Belongs To Us" and "Miner, Cross that Picket Line" were sung on the return coach trip' – *The Guardian* (30 October 1987). 'Down, sit down, he [the SDP leader, Dr David Owen] eventually gestured; his eyes saying Up, stay up. It reminded you of nothing so much as a Conservative Party conference in one of its

most Tomorrow-belongs-to-us moods' –
The Guardian (1 February 1988).

tomorrow is another day   The last words
of the film *Gone With the Wind* (US 1939),
spoken by Vivien Leigh as 'Scarlett
O'Hara', are: 'Tara! Home! I'll go home,
and I'll think of some way to get him
back. After all, tomorrow is another day!'
The last phrase is as it appears in Margaret
Mitchell's novel, but the idea behind it is
proverbial. In Rastell's *Calisto & Melebea*
(*circa* 1527) there occurs the line: 'Well,
mother, to morrow is a new day.'

tomorrow never dies   After *Never Say
Never Again*, *Tomorrow Never Dies* was the
first James Bond film (US/UK 1997) not to
have a title taken from an Ian Fleming
story nor to have any other Fleming
association (*Goldeneye* was the name of
Fleming's house in Jamaica). Whether this
title has any meaning is, of course, another
matter: the villain of the piece is a media
mogul and *Tomorrow* is on the masthead
of one of his publications. The plot hinges
on the mogul's creation of wars and other
news events so that his paper can get
scoops on them. Presumably, the title also
alludes lightly to the proverb 'Tomorrow
never comes' (a warning against procrasti-
nation because 'tomorrow' is always the
day after today), known since 1523.

tomorrow will be Friday   'If as a child,
disappointed over something, I gave a wail
of "Ooh!", my father would join in with,
"Ooh! Tomorrow will be Friday and we've
caught no fish today"' – Joan Bell,
Clackmannanshire (1992). A song about
monks failing to catch fish for Friday
consumption and resorting to the bottle
instead has the title 'Tomorrow Will Be
Friday'. It has words by Fred E. Weatherly
and music by James Lyman Molloy, who
died in 1900, thereby putting its composition sometime in the 1890s: 'They fish'd
the stream till the moon was high, / But
never a fish came wand'ring by . . . / And
the abbot said "It seems to me, / These
rascally fish are all gone to sea! / And
tomorrow will be Friday, / But we've
caught no fish today" . . .' There are also
paintings by the English artist Walter
Dendy Sadler (1854–1923) entitled 'Thursday' and 'Friday', depicting comparable

events. The first of these (in the Tate
Britain gallery) *may* also have been known
as 'Tomorrow Will Be Friday', though it
was painted in 1880 and thus precedes the
song.

to my wife, without whom . . .   Book
dedication and acknowledgements cliché.
Date of origin unknown. P. G. Wodehouse
was already poking fun at the style in his
dedication to *The Heart of a Goof* (1926):
'To my daughter Leonora without whose
never-failing sympathy and encouragement
this book would have been finished in half
the time.' These days, knowing that it is a
cliché, the writer often substitutes some
jokey variant. But that is almost a cliché,
too. 'To Jill, Without whom, Whose, Who
has been my constant, Who has always,
Who . . .' – Peter Spence, *Some of Our Best
Friends Are Animals* (1976). (However,
every word between the second and the
last is crossed out.) 'To Kerry, without
whom I would probably never have begun
this book, and to Walter, without whom I
would certainly never have finished it' –
Maria Zimmer Bradley, *The Catch Tray*
(1979); 'For Jeffrey, to whom, without this
book . . .' – Brian Innes, *The Red Baron*
(1983); 'This book is dedicated to Alexander (356–23BC) without whom, nothing' –
Alison Spedding, *The Road and the Hills*
(1986); 'For the three mothers in my life,
ladies without whom . . .' – Stephen
Sheppard, *For All the Tea in China* (1988);
'And finally, my thanks to Jean Aitchison,
without whom . . .' – John Ayto, *The
Longman Register of New Words* (1989);
'Plenty of male writers have been, and are,
surrounded by facilitating women (the
cleaner, the cook, the typist, the fender-
off-of-callers, the muse) although usually
just one woman plays all the roles, rewarded by the usual sentence in the
acknowledgements that begins, "Finally,
thanks to my wife, without whom . . ."' –
The Independent (29 June 1994).

tonight   See AND THE NEXT.

tonight's the night!   'Something important is about to happen!' Used as the title
of a musical 'sketch' show (1900) by
George Le Brunn, this phrase has also
been used to indicate that a sexual conquest is imminent.

too clever by half To say that someone is 'too clever by half' is to indicate that you think they are more clever than wise and are overreaching themselves. As such, this is a fairly common idiom. The most notable political use of the phrase was by the 5th Marquess of Salisbury (1893–1972), a prominent Conservative, about another such, Iain Macleod. In a speech to the House of Lords in 1961, he said: 'The present Colonial Secretary has been too clever by half. I believe he is a very fine bridge player. It is not considered immoral, or even bad form to outwit one's opponents at bridge. It almost seems to me as if the Colonial Secretary, when he abandoned the sphere of bridge for the sphere of politics, brought his bridge technique with him.' The remark seems to run in the family. The 3rd Marquess had anticipated him in a debate on the Irish Church Resolutions in the House of Commons on 30 March 1868, when he said of an amendment moved by Disraeli: 'I know that with a certain number of Gentlemen on this side of the House this Amendment is popular. I have heard it spoken of as being very clever. It is clever, Sir; it is too clever by half.' Rodney Ackland's version of an Alexander Ostrovsky play was presented as *Too Clever by Half* at the Old Vic, London, in 1988. Previously, the Russian title had been translated as *The Diary of a Scoundrel* and *Even the Wise Can Err, Even a Wise Man Stumbles* and *Enough Stupidity in Every Wise Man*. Of Jonathan Miller, the polymath, in the mid-1970s, it was said, 'He's too clever by three-quarters.'

too close to call Too difficult to predict – of an outcome – because it could go either way. As with 'close call', meaning 'a narrow escape', this derives from baseball where a decision is 'called' by the umpire.

toodeloo! Parting cry. Possibly connected with 'toot', as though one were to go 'toot, toot', like a horn, on leaving. Or perhaps it has something to do with 'toddling off' or 'tootling off'. Could 'I must tootle-o' have led to it? A much better idea is that the word derives from the French *à tout à l'heure* ('see you soon').

'too late, too late!' shall be the cry . . . This seems to be the basis of a series of fairly nonsensical expressions, uttered when some opportunity has been missed. 'Too late, too late, shall be the cry, / Arnold the ice-cream man's gone by' is to be found in the Peter Nichols play *The Freeway*, Act 1, Scene 3 (1974). 'My father, who is from the West of Ireland, says: "Too late, too late, will be the cry, / When the man with the oranges has passed by"' – from an anonymous correspondent (1995). Alison Klenar (2000) recalled from her childhood, '"Too late, too late," the maiden cried, / "I'd rather have my haddock fried!"' Compare what *Partridge/Catch Phrases* calls originally a military catchphrase – 'Too late! too late!' spoken in a high falsetto, after the story of 'that luckless fellow who lost his manhood in a shark-infested sea very soon after he had summoned help.' Another possible origin: John Gray of Sutton wanted to know (1993) the source and correct form of a couplet that his father used to quote at him when he was a boy: 'Too late, too late, shall be the cry / When you see — passing by.' Sir David Hunt suggested that this was probably a corruption of a hymn to be found in the Sankey and Moody hymnal. Indeed, the final couplet of the concluding verse of 'Jesus of Nazareth passeth by' by Miss Etta Campbell and T. E. Perkins is: '"Too late! too late!" will be the cry – / Jesus of Nazareth *has passed by*.'

'too late, too late!' the —— cried and waved (his) wooden leg Obviously related to the previous phrase. T. A. Dyer, London SW12, noted (1993) that his father used to say (in the 1940s): '"It's come too late!" the lady cried, as she waved her wooden leg – and passed out.' In about 1984, an American professor queried the saying '"Aha!" cried she, as she waved her wooden leg, and died' – which is clearly linked. '"Too late, too late," the maiden cried / Lifted her wooden leg, and died' – Mrs. K.W. Kent, Lancaster (1994). Donald Hickling, Northamptonshire, recalled a nonsense poem that his father brought back from the First World War which included the phrase 'Waving her wooden leg in dire despair.' He added that his family would exclaim it whenever a disaster-prone neighbour hammered on the party wall. P. S. Falla, the translator, wrote (1996): 'There is, "Ha, ha" she cried in Portuguese / And waved her wooden leg." I have heard the first line of this in French also!' 'This saying I have only heard via my mother, and she is 86: '"Oh good,' she said, as she swung her wooden leg, 'only one boot to clean'"' – from Margaret Addicott, Hertfordshire (1996). Remembered by Rip Bulkeley, Oxfordshire (1998), from an American source: 'Ha Ha! she cried, waving her wooden leg. Only one shoe to clean.' But also from his Yorkshire Granny fifty years ago: '"Help! Help!" she cried, and waved her wooden leg.' '"Aha! cried the Duchess, as she waved her wooden leg", also the variant, "Oho! she cried, as the cock flew at her" were both used as jokey exclamations by our Nanny (born 1897), and we were so used to hearing them as children in the 1950s that we never questioned her about where they came from' – Nick Bicat, Oxfordshire (2000). 'Too late! Too late! the Captain cried, and shook his wooden leg' – Tom Doyle, Madrid, Spain. Adam Wilkins, St Albans (2000), remembered from his grandfather, '"Too late, too late," she cried as she waved her wooden leg three times in the air.' '"Too late, too late", the maiden cried, as she waved her timber limber' – remembered by the mother of Marjorie Wild, Devon (2000). '"Oh, thank you, sir,' she said, as with a smile she waved her wooden leg" – heard from my father and only once heard from another man at work' – Derek Armstrong (2000). Clearly, the cry is not 'too late, too late' in all versions, but the emphasis remains upon the wooden leg, as in these citations from the USA: '"Aha!" she cried, as she waved her wooden leg and died' – Anonymous, 'Some Wellerisms from Idaho' in *Western Folklore*, No. 25 (1966); '"Hurrah!" as the old maid shouted waving her wooden leg' – Herbert Halpert, 'Some Wellerisms from Kentucky and Tennessee' in *Journal of American Folklore*, No. 69 (1956).

too little, too late The American Professor Allan Nevins wrote in an article in *Current History* (May 1935): 'The former allies had blundered in the past by offering Germany too little and offering even that too late, until finally Nazi Germany

had become a menace to all mankind.' That was where the phrase began. On 13 March 1940, the former Prime Minister David Lloyd George said in the House of Commons: 'It is the old trouble – too late. Too late with Czechoslovakia, too late with Poland, certainly too late with Finland. It is always too late, or too little, or both.' From there the phrase passed into more general use, though still often political. 'Junior Transport Minister, Peter Bottomley, came to West London last week to unveil plans for a £250m. relief road that will cut a swathe through the heart of the area . . . But Hammersmith and Fulham councillors are furious about the government consultation exercise which they claim is "too little too late"' – *Notting Hill & Paddington Recorder* (25 January 1989); 'The Home Office is preparing a video to warn prisoners of the dangers [of AIDs] – but is it too little, too late?' – *The Guardian* (30 January 1989).

too many chiefs and not enough Indians Phrase suggesting that in some confused situation there are too many leaders and not enough led, or that there are too many people giving orders and instructions but not enough people to carry them out. An alternative title of the film *Who Is Killing the Great Chefs of Europe?* (US/West Germany 1978) was *Too Many Chefs* – which also neatly alludes to the proverb 'too many cooks spoil the broth'.

(out of the) top drawer Of high social standing. 'Such boys as a rule don't come out of the top drawer' – H. A. Vachell, *The Hill*, Chap 1 (1905). Also adjectivally: 'The Potter family, however respectable now, wasn't really "top-drawer"' – Rose Macaulay, *Potterism*, Chap. 1 (1920).

top hole! Excellent. Probably referring to holes or notches cut in a board to record the points scored in some games. The top hole represents the highest, best score. Known by 1899.

top people take *The Times* In the mid-1950s, *The Times* was shedding circulation, the end of post-war newsprint rationing was in sight, and an era of renewed competition in Fleet Street was about to begin. In 1954, the paper's agency, the

London Press Exchange, commissioned a survey to discover people's attitudes to 'The THUNDERER'. They chiefly found it dull, but the management was not going to change anything, least of all allow contributors to be identified by name. The paper would have to be promoted for what it was. A pilot campaign in provincial newspapers included one ad showing a top hat and pair of gloves with the slogan 'Men who make opinion read *The Times*'. It was not the London Press Exchange but an outsider who finally encapsulated that superior view in a memorable way. G. H. Saxon Mills was one of the old school of advertising copywriters. But he was out of a job when he bumped into Stanley Morison of *The Times*. As a favour, Mills was asked to produce a brochure for visitors to the paper's offices. When finished, it contained a series of people who were supposed to read the paper – a barrister, a trade-union official, and so on. Each was supported by the phrase 'Top People take *The Times*'. The idea was adopted for a more public promotional campaign and first appeared on posters during 1957, running into immediate criticism of its snob-appeal. But sales went up and, however toe-curling it may have been, the slogan won attention for the paper and was allowed to run on into the early 1960s.

topsy-turvy (or -turvey) A very old coinage for 'upside down' – *OED2* has it by the 16th century and is unable to explain the etymology of the word. Although it occurs only once in the Gilbert and Sullivan operas, it is certainly a very Gilbertian word and can be found several times in his *Bab Ballads*. This is from 'My Dream' (first published 1870): 'The other night, from cares exempt, / I slept – and what d'you think I dreamt? / I dreamt that somehow I had come / To dwell in Topsy-Turveydom / Where vice is virtue – virtue, vice: / Where nice is nasty – nasty, nice: / Where right is wrong and wrong is right – / Where white is black and black is white.' Hence, *Topsy-Turvy*, the title of a film (UK/US 1999) about the Gilbert and Sullivan partnership, which would appear to have something to do with an (actual?) incident when *The Times* dubbed Gilbert

'The King of Topsy-Turvydom'. Notoriously touchy on all subjects, Gilbert apparently took this as an insult. He wished to be taken *seriously* as a comic writer.

torch See CARRY A.

(a) torch song A love song (usually performed by a woman) that tells of unrequited love or an affair that has ended. Presumably, it comes from the expression CARRY A TORCH FOR SOMEONE, meaning to express unreciprocated admiration or love – the torch representing the flame of love. American origin by 1927. The film *Torch Singer* was released in 1933 and was about an unwed mother who sang in nightclubs. *Torch Song Trilogy* was the title of a play by Harvey Fierstein (1982; film US 1988).

torpedoes See DAMN THE.

(the) Tory Party at prayer A descriptive phrase for the Church of England often attributed to Benjamin Disraeli. However, Robert Blake, the historian and author of *Disraeli* (1966), told the *Observer* (14 April 1985) that he could not say who had said it first and that a correspondence in *The Times* some years before had failed to find an answer. Agnes Maude Royden, the social reformer and preacher, said in an address at the City Temple, London (1917): 'The Church should no longer be satisfied to represent only the Conservative Party at prayer' – but this sounds rather as though it is alluding to an already established saying.

(the) total depravity of inanimate things Phrase attributed to the American teacher, essayist and journalist 'Gail Hamilton' (Mary Abigail Dodge). She was referring to the way in which inanimate things can thwart, trip up and generally obstruct the fulfilment of expectations in normal life. In fact, she wrote of 'total depravity' only when describing the behaviour of a veil in *Gala-Days* (1863). The following year, however, in the *Atlantic Monthly* (September 1864), Katherine K. C. Walker wrote an article on the subject under the heading 'The Total Depravity of Inanimate Things' but made no mention of Hamilton as having first come up with the idea.

to the manner born From Shakespeare, *Hamlet,* I.iv.14 (1600–1): 'Though I am native here / And to the manner born.' Hence, *To the Manor Born*, the title of a BBC TV comedy series (1979–81), created by Peter Spence, about a lady of the manor. Shakespeare may have intended a play on the word 'manor', too.

to the negotiating table Political and journalistic phrase for where negotiations take place. Date of origin unknown. 'The poverty -ridden grape pickers, most of them semi-literate Mexican-Americans, have brought the wealthy grape growers to the negotiating table' – *The Times* (14 July 1970); 'The EU leaders had been called back to the negotiating table after an 8–3–1 split, with Mr Major alone in promoting Sir Leon' – *The Independent* (25 June 1994).

Toto, I have a feeling we're not in Kansas any more! A line from the film *The Wizard of Oz* (US 1939) rather than from Frank L. Baum's original book, but one that has achieved catchphrase status. Judy Garland as Dorothy says it on arrival in the Land of Oz, concluding, 'We must be over the rainbow.' It is used when speakers want to express bewilderment at whatever new circumstances they find themselves in. From the film *The Matrix* (US 1999): *Morpheus*: 'The pill you took is part of a trace program. It's designed to disrupt your input/output carrier signal so we can pinpoint your location.' *Neo*: 'What does that mean?' *Cypher*: 'It means buckle your seatbelt, Dorothy, 'cause Kansas is going bye-bye.'

(to) touch all the right buttons (or **press ...)** To produce all the desired responses. Presumably, from what you would do to make a piece of machinery or equipment perform correctly. Date of origin unknown. '[President Clinton's] speech was just perfect. It was measured, easy, elegant, he touched all the right buttons' – Gyles Brandreth, *Breaking the Code* (1999) – diary entry for 29 November 1995.

tough on —— and tough on the causes of —— Political catchphrase format. From a speech by Tony Blair, as Shadow Home Secretary, to the Labour Party conference (30 September 1993): 'Labour is the party

of law and order in Britain today. Tough on crime and tough on the causes of crime.' The 'tough' phrase had been used by Blair for the first time earlier in the year and had been supplied by his colleague Gordon Brown. When he became the Labour leader in the summer of 1994, there followed any number of 'tough on . . . tough on the causes of . . .' imitations and parodies. '[On cleaning up historic buildings] We're tough on grime and tough on the causes of grime' – Chris Smith MP, quoted in *The Independent* (6 October 1994).

(a) tower of strength Someone who is a great help or encouragement. A possible origin lies in Shakespeare, *King Richard III*, V.iii.12 (1592–3): 'Besides, the King's name is a tower of strength.' Compare: Tennyson, *Ode on the Death of the Duke of Wellington* (1852): 'O fall'n at length that tower of strength.' In the Bible, God is often called a 'strong tower'. 'Special mention must be made of Miss Dorothy Swerdlove who . . . has proved a tower of strength on the details of the American theatre' – Phyllis Hartnoll, *Oxford Companion to the Theatre* (Preface to 1983 edn); 'Though doubtless willing to swap his personal triumphs for the right result, Simon Langford, the veteran full-back, was a tower of strength, scoring all Orrell's points and defusing just about everything that Catt kicked at him' – *The Daily Telegraph* (30 January 1995).

toy! toy! Theatrical good-luck wish. Before the opening of his production of *Don Giovanni* at the English National Opera in 1985, Jonathan Miller explained that 'the cry is age-old, either from kissing or spitting, no one seems really sure'. A correspondent in the Netherlands tells me that 'toi toi' or 'toi toi toi' are common in the Dutch theatre world. Dutch dictionaries explain them as an onomatopoeic reference to knocking on wood (touch wood) to ward off evil. Some suggest a Jewish or Yiddish origin. In German *toi* is apotropaic and the word means 'good luck' – the explanation is as simple as that. Indeed, Lutz Röhrich in his *Lexikon des sprichwörtlichen Redensarten* (1973) gives *Unberufen, toi-toi-toi!* as meaning 'touch wood . . .' and says it was popularized by a song in 1930 (though current since 1900). The word *toi!* may represent the sound of spitting – which has the same superstitious function. However, in *Apperson* there are two mentions of the phrase 'John Toy'. *Notes and Queries* in 1856 had 'Like lucky John Toy' among 'Cornish Proverbs'. And C. H. Spurgeon in *John Ploughman's Pictures* (1880) had: 'The luck that comes to them is like Johnny Toy's, who lost a shilling and found a two-penny loaf.' Surely too much of a coincidence for there not to be some connection. (See under LOOK LIKE YOU'VE LOST A SHILLING AND FOUND A TANNER.)

tradition of   See IN THE.

(a) tragedy queen (or **drama queen)** A woman who makes a fuss/a drama out of a crisis. In Shelagh Delaney's play *A Taste of Honey* (1958), one character appears to quote, 'Poor little Josephine, the tragedy queen, hasn't life been hard on her?' From literal comparisons: 'Just as were at our merriest, in sailed Madam —, like a tragedy queen' – M. R. Mitford, in a letter of 18 March 1819; 'She bowed me out of the room like a tragedy queen' – William Thackeray, *Vanity Fair*, Chap. 46 (1848).

tragedy struck when . . .   Date of origin not known. Listed as a cliché to be avoided, by Keith Waterhouse in *Daily Mirror Style* (1981). 'Para's fatal mistake . . . tragedy struck when, as a safety measure, Captain Kelly switched on his torch to show his position' – *Today* (12 May 1994); 'Since then the Mondeo has covered around 1,700 miles without complaint, although tragedy struck when a strong wind tore off some garage roofing, which clouted the car, denting a wing and cracking the windscreen' – *The Daily Telegraph* (6 August 1994).

(a) transport of delight   Date of origin not known for the original sense of what you get carried away in when ecstatic. Flanders and Swann then gave the title 'A Transport of Delight' to a song about a London bus (1960) in *At the Drop of a Hat*. Subsequently it became a cliché of travel writers and other journalists when dealing with transport arrangements. Part of the 'travel scribes' armoury' compiled from a competition in *The Guardian* (10 April

1993). 'One great thing about running an event on your own estate is being invited to drive or ride all manner of rare machines. Last year's transports of delight were a Maserati A6GCM grand prix car and a Manx Norton' – *The Independent* (18 June 1994); 'Few transports of delight at tramline plan for Grafton Street: Too much to lose in a thoroughfare that inspires strong affection? A CIE project team has proposed running a modern tram line down Grafton Street' – headline in *The Irish Times* (29 October 1994); 'In the pink on transport of delight . . . This is the Beauty Express, a new alternative transport mode . . . [where] Michelle caresses your feet as part of her special herbal-wrap pedicure' – headline and text in *The Independent* (21 June 1995).

trapeze   See DARING YOUNG MAN.

treat 'em mean and keep 'em keen
Recipe for men's hold over women. Donald Hickling wrote (1995): 'A wartime "Wren" remembers this catchphrase from a concert-party in her Plymouth days. And she mentions something similar in the contemporaneous MGM musical *Girl Crazy* (US 1943) in which June Allyson and Mickey Rooney performed the duet "Treat Me Rough" (words by Ira Gershwin).' *Partridge/Catch Phrases* has the similar, 'Catch 'em young, treat 'em rough, tell 'em nothing.'

tree   See ALL DRESSED UP.

(a) tree fell on him   Stock phrase from one of Spike Milligan's *Q* comedy series on BBC TV, in the early 1980s. For example: 'Q. Are you Jewish?' 'A. No, a tree fell on me.' In fact, this originated in Milligan's scripts for the BBC radio *Goon Show*. In 'The Moriarty Murder Mystery' (2 December 1957) is this exchange: *Eccles*: 'He died in bed.' *Bluebottle*: 'What happened?' *Eccles*: 'A tree fell on him.'

trials and tribulations   An inevitable pairing. Date of origin not known. The Australian *Macquarie Dictionary*'s example of a cliché (1981). 'The phantom pilots go up with an instructor for a twice-yearly check-out in the trials and tribulations of spinning' – *RAF News* (27 April 1977); 'Only 10 of the party were in New Zealand – its own indication of the vast difference between the position that obtained then and now. But for all the trials and tribulations of that tour two years ago and Ireland should have won the first Test some benefits of real consequence emerged as a result of it' – *The Irish Times* (14 May 1994).

tributes are pouring in (or flooding in) Journalistic cliché employed in reports of reaction to a notable death. Date of origin unknown. 'According to the BBC, "Tributes are flooding in for Dr Phil Williams" . . . I wonder if tributes would have flooded in for a Tory politician if . . . he'd died in a massage parlour?' – *Daily Mail* (13 June 2003); 'Tributes for Dr Williams poured in from across the political spectrum' – same paper, same edition.

(the) trickle-down theory (of economics) By which is meant the idea that governmental aid to large corporations will 'trickle down' to employees and irrigate the economy. The phrase seems to have arisen in the 1930s in the USA when a policy advanced by Herbert Hoover was derided as a 'trickle-down theory' aimed at feeding the sparrows by feeding the horses. J. K. Galbraith explained this 'less than elegant metaphor' in *The Culture of Contentment* (1992): 'If one feeds the horse enough oats, some will pass through to the road for sparrows.'

trick of the light See IT'S JUST A.

trick or treat? One of the least welcome imports to Britain from the USA in recent years has been the Hallowe'en custom of children, suitably dressed up, knocking on the doors of complete strangers and demanding a 'trick or treat' – i.e. that the house owners should hand over some small present (sweets, money) or have a trick played on them (a message written on the front door in shaving foam, for example). Fairly harmless in essence, the practice soon led to horror stories reaching the UK of children playing 'tricks' which did real damage and of their being given poisoned sweets as 'treats'. The American origins of the custom seem somewhat obscure – *OED2* does not find the phrase before 1947. In the North of England, the traditional Mischief Night may have given rise to the same sort of demands, and may

also have given rise to the jingle ending: 'If you haven't got a penny, a ha'penny will do, / If you haven't got a ha'penny, your door's going through' – though, on the other hand, that appears to be a version of 'Christmas is coming'. In January 1989, a British ITV quiz show was launched called *Trick or Treat* that aimed to do one or the other to its contestants. *Trick or Treats* (US 1992) was a low-budget horror picture.

tricky Dick(y) Nickname of Richard Milhous Nixon (1913–94), US President (1969–74), who resigned after the Watergate scandal. So dubbed at the start of his career by Helen Gahagan Douglas in 1950. During an election campaign in California he had hinted that she was a fellow traveller. Despite his many later achievements, the nickname was generally adopted to indicate Nixon's art of political manipulation and evasion.

(to) trip the light fantastic To dance. Alluding to the lines from Milton's 'L'Allegro' (1645) – 'Come, and trip it as ye go / On the light fantastic toe' and possibly also to his 'Comus' (1637) – 'Come, knit hands, and beat the ground / In a light fantastic round'. 'Fine warblings and trippings on the light fantastic toe' – Thomas Carlyle, *Misc.*, *Goethe's Helena* (1828); '"You dance very nicely," she murmurs. "Yes, for a man who has not tripped the light fantastic for years"' – A. C. Gunter, *Miss Dividends*, Chap. 9 (1892); 'The inlaid sprung floor would still have supported a light fantastic or two' – Len Deighton, *Spy Story*, Chap. 6 (1974). When we get to the song 'A Whiter Shade of Pale' (1967), this has become: 'We skipped the light fandango'.

Trivial Pursuit There had been a quiz game called 'Trivia' in the 1960s, but this was the title under which a hugely successful board game, using trivia questions, was launched from Canada in 1979. The devisers were Scott Abbott, John and Chris Haney, the first game was sold in Canada in 1981, and worldwide popularity reached its worldwide peak *circa* 1985. Quite why it was given this name is a mystery, as describing something as a 'trivial pursuit' was hardly an established figure of speech – except that the two words did sometimes get put together: from Somerset Maugham's *A Writer's Notebook* (1949), this sentence written in 1917: 'You do not admire a man who uses infinite patience to collect postage stamps; the exercise of this quality does not save it from being a trivial pursuit.'

trouble at t'mill A key phrase supposedly taken from English North Country dramas (especially set in the 19th century) but best known as a humorous allusion to the kind of line thought to be uttered in same. It might be used now by someone who is departing to sort out some problem but does not wish to spell it out what it is. Allusively, the phrase was known by 1962 and, according to Frank Muir in *A Kentish Lad* (1997), was used in the BBC radio show *Take It From Here* (which ran from 1948–59). An actual example, though not as it happens from a North Country novel, can be found in *John Halifax, Gentleman*, Chap. 26 (1856) by Dinah Maria Mulock: '"Unless you will consent to let me go alone to Enderley!" She shook her head. "What, with those troubles at the mills?"'

trouble flared when . . . Journalistic cliché. Known by 1913 in the USA. Condemned by Keith Waterhouse in *Daily Mirror Style* (1981). 'Trouble flared when police took loudspeakers off a truck which had been prepared for use at a rally by the militant Hamas Islamic Resistance Movement and Islamic Jihad' – *Daily Mail* (19 November 1994); 'Trouble flared when the two sets of fans descended on the pub for drinks before the tie at Villa Park, Birmingham. Insults were traded before fighting broke out' – *Daily Mail* (10 April 1995).

trousers See ALL MOUTH; ENOUGH BLUE.

true See ALWAYS TRUE.

true, O king! Response made to an obvious statement or a pompous one. Probably from the story of Nebuchadnezzar and the gentlemen who were cast into the burning fiery furnace (Daniel 3:24). 'Did not we cast three men bound into the midst of fire?' Nebuchadnezzar asks. 'They answered and said unto the king, True, O king.' The nearest Shakespeare gets is the ironical '"True"? O God!' in *Much Ado About Nothing*, IV.i.68 (1598), though he has any number of near

misses like 'true, my liege', 'too true, my lord' and 'true, noble prince'. Mrs H. Joan Langdale of Tunbridge Wells wrote to me (1988) to say, 'My father, a Classical Scholar and an Anglican priest, used to use the quotation "True, O King!" and always added, "Live for ever"' – the last phrase of which comes from Daniel 6:21. The phrase occurs in the Billy Bunter stories by Frank Richards (1875–1961). In the published *Diaries* of Kenneth Williams (entry for 5 January 1971), the comedian recounts being told by an Irishman that he was a bore on TV: 'I smiled acquiescence and said "How true, O King!"' "True, O Queen. Live for ever" [said Lord Peter Wimsey]' – Dorothy L. Sayers, *Have His Carcase*, Chap. 9 (1932). In the same novel, Harriet Vane manages a 'True, O king' in Chap. 25. See also OH KING, LIVE FOREVER!

(a) true patriot Known by 1809. 'Marshal Pétain was a true patriot' is cited as a 'meaningless' or 'consciously dishonest' phrase in George Orwell, 'Politics and the English Language', *Horizon* (April 1946): 'The person who uses [this kind of phrase] has his own private definition, but allows his hearer to think he means something quite different.' 'The country's reputation has also been denigrated in an insulting and demeaning manner. No true patriot would talk of their country in some of the terms that have been used, Mr Reynolds said' – *The Irish Times* (3 June 1994); 'He was a true patriot. He was strong for Korea and I was terribly upset by his death,' said Nahomi Kim, a North Korean who lives in Tokyo' – *The Daily Telegraph* (20 July 1994).

trumpet See BLOW ONE'S OWN.

trust me, I'm a doctor Origin not known. First found on the Internet in May 1989, and, as 'Trust us, we're doctors' in July 1996). 'Trust us, we're doctors!' was used (2002) to promote a DVD edition of the film *M*A*S*H* (US 1970), but it is not spoken in the film. Perhaps in the subsequent TV series?

(a) trusty sword Phrase now in consciously archaic use. Known by 1558. Also in Shakespeare, *A Midsummer Night's Dream*, V.i.330 (1594): 'Come, trusty sword, / Come, blade, my breast imbrue!';

and in Spenser: 'His trusty sword, the servant of his might' (1596). The most recent citation might appear to be an attempt to break away from the cliché by rearranging it: 'If it falls to me [to] start a fight to cut out the cancer of bent and twisted journalism in our country with the simple sword of truth and the trusty shield of British fair play, so be it' – Jonathan Aitken MP, statement (10 April 1995). Compare the inevitableness of **trusty steed** (date of origin unknown, possibly from Hollywood?) 'He [an American] actually wrote "Send me a photo of you, and your car, so I can see you standing beside your trusty steed"' – in *The Kenneth Williams Letters* (1994) – letter of 9 November 1971.

truth   See ECONOMICAL WITH; I SWEAR.

truth is stranger   See STRANGE BUT TRUE.

try it – you'll like it!   Slogan for Alka-Seltzer in the USA in 1971 – 'used by every comic, every mother, and certainly every waiter for the entire year of the campaign', according to the agency that wrote it. A year later, another line on the 'morning-after' theme of the agonies of overindulgence was **I can't believe I ate the whole thing**.

try to get some sleep   See LET'S GET OUTTA.

TTFN [Ta-Ta For Now]   Catchphrase from the BBC radio show *ITMA* (1939–49). It was the farewell cry of Mrs Mopp (Dorothy Summers) after having presented her weekly gift to the Mayor (Tommy Handley). It is said that during the Second World War, quite a few people died with the phrase on their lips. Still quite widely used.

tubes   See GO DOWN.

(a) tug of love   Meaning, 'a conflict of affections', especially in relation to disputes between parents over the custody of their children. *The Tug of Love* was the title of a comedy by Israel Zangwill (1907). Also **love-tug**, listed by Keith Waterhouse in *Daily Mirror Style* (1981). 'Back home in the arms of her mother, a tiny tug-of-love girl sleeps peacefully. The girl . . . had been taken to California after being snatched by her father' – *Daily Mirror* (21

March 1977); 'A Scots tug-of-love mum is on the run with her baby daughter after walking out on her American husband' – *Daily Record* (22 September 1994); 'Tug-of-love mother Sarah Dodds is today looking forward to moving into a new home and starting a new life with her two-year-old daughter' – *Daily Mail* (24 April 1995).

(that's the) tune the old cow died of   'Of a poorly sung song' – Stella Richardson, Essex (1998). *Partridge/Catch Phrases* interprets this as 'that's a damned unpleasant noise!' and finds it in Captain Marryat, *Mr Midshipman Easy* (1836), and later in Mark Twain, *Life On the Mississippi* (1883). *Apperson*, as ever, finds it even earlier, in Thomas Fuller, *Gnomologia*, No. 4360 (1732): 'The tune the old cow died of, that is the old tune upon the bag-pipe.'

Turkish wrestler   See MOUTH LIKE.

(a) turning point   Meaning 'a key moment in a person's career, a crisis', this phrase seems to have arisen in religious writings. *OED2*'s earliest citation is from John Keble in 1836. On the other hand, the Reverend Francis Kilvert, the English diarist (entry for 19 May 1873), found it as the title of a painting that impressed him at a Royal Academy exhibition: 'The beautiful face and eyes of the wife looking up to her husband's stern sullen countenance as she leans on his breast, beseeching him, pleading with him, oh so earnestly and imploringly, to give up drinking.' From *The Independent* (20 October 1995): 'Conservative MPs were milling about afterwards in a state of rare over-excitement, informing anyone who passed that Tony Blair had peaked, that this was the turning-point.' *The Turning Point* has been the title of two unrelated films (US 1952 and 1977), though the latter is about ballet (so a pun of sorts).

(the) turn of the century   The earliest citation in *OED2* is from 1926 and refers to that of the 18th/19th, but in the majority of cases the phrase relates to the 19th/20th changeover. So far it has been little applied to the turn of the 20th/21st.

turn on, tune in, drop out   Meaning, 'Tune in to my values, reject those of your parents, turn on [drug] yourself; deal with your problems and those of society by running away from them.' Hippie slogan from the USA, *circa* 1967, possibly created by one of the movement's gurus, Dr Timothy Leary (1920–96). It was used as the title of a lecture by him in 1967, and the theme was explored further in his book *The Politics of Ecstasy*. Towards the end of his life, Leary took to attributing the origin of the phrase to Marshall McLuhan. A joke variant of what was also known as 'the LSD motto', was: 'Turn on, tune in, drop dead'.

(to) turn over in one's grave Meaning, '[for a dead person] to demonstrate horror at what has just happened or been proposed by someone living'. *Mencken* has, 'It is enough to make — turn over in his grave' as an 'English saying, not recorded before the nineteenth century'. William Thackeray has: '"Enough to make poor Mr Pendennis turn in his grave," said Mrs Wapshot' – *Pendennis*, Chap. 16 (1848). In about 1976, one of the idiocies attributed to President Gerald Ford was: 'If Abraham Lincoln was alive today, he'd be turning in his grave.'

(to) turn the tables on someone To obtain advantage over someone, bring a complete reversal in a state of affairs. This derives from playing games (like chess or draughts) that require the use of marked boards or the moving of pieces about on table-tops. If one player is not doing well, then were he to 'turn the table' on his opponent, he would be in the winning position. Known by 1634.

(what a) turn-up for the book(s)! I.e. what an unexpected outcome, what a surprise! The 'books' here are those kept by bookies to maintain a record of bets placed on a race. Does the bookie have to turn up the corner of a page if a race has an unexpected outcome? No, the phrase merely means that something unexpected has 'turned up'. Known by 1873.

tutti-frutti Meaning 'all the fruits' in Italian, this phrase was first applied early in 19th-century America to ice cream containing pieces of various chopped-up fruits. Then it became the name of a proprietary brand of fruit-flavoured chewing gum. More recently, it has been immortalized as the title of a rock'n'roll number written and sung by Little Richard (from 1957). Alas, the lyrics are impenetrable and almost certainly have nothing to do with ice cream or chewing gum.

'twas ever thus An exclamation meaning almost the same as the more modern **so what's new?** and used nowadays as a self-conscious anachronism. It does not occur in Shakespeare or the Bible. In fact, the only examples turned up so far are: as the first line of 'Disaster' by C. S. Calverley (1831–84): ''Twas ever thus from childhood's hour!' (a parody of lines from Thomas Moore's 'The Fire Worshippers' in *Lalla Rookh* (1817): 'Oh! ever thus from childhood's hour!'); and, as the title, ''Twas Ever Thus' given to the parody of the same poem by Henry S. Leigh (1837–83). His version begins, 'I never rear'd a young gazelle.' Ollie does, however, exclaim it in *The Laurel-Hardy Murder Case* (US 1930).

twelve good men and true 'It is a maxim of English law that legal memory begins with the accession of Richard I in 1189 . . . with the establishment of royal courts, giving the same justice all over the country, the old diversity of local law was rapidly broken down, and a law common to the whole land and to all men soon took its place . . . The truth of [witnesses'] testimony [was] weighed not by the judge but by twelve "good men and true"' – Winston Churchill, *A History of the English-Speaking Peoples*, Vol.1 (1956). 'In the 1360s unanimous verdicts were to be welcomed and unwieldy juries were out of date. Enter the twelve good men and true' – Trevor Grove, *The Juryman's Tale* (1998). Probably there were twelve members of a jury because that was the number of Christ's disciples (or the tribes of Israel or the signs of the zodiac). Lord Devlin once suggested the number 12 was chosen as 'an early English abhorrence of the decimal system.' The overall phrase seems to have been established by the 16th century. 'Are you good men and true' occurs on its own in Shakespeare's *Much Ado About Nothing*, III.iii.1 (1598). Dogberry puts the question and, being a constable, would naturally use legal terminology.

twenty things you didn't know about — A much imitated journalistic format derived from a regular *Sun* newspaper feature of the 1980s (said to have been devised by Wendy Henry) in which trivia was listed about celebrities. '20 Things You Didn't Know About Mrs T.' – *The Independent* (24 April 1989).

twice a night   See ONCE A NIGHT.

(the) twilight of empire   This phrase refers to Britain at any time after the death of Queen Victoria in 1901, but particularly when its colonies started moving towards independence. In Malcolm Muggeridge's diary (21 December 1947) he calls it a 'phrase which occurred to me long ago'. One suspects it is after 'twilight of the gods' – German '*Götterdämmerung*'.

(the) twilight zone   The phrase had existed in the early 1900s for an 'indistinct boundary area' but undoubtedly *The Twilight Zone*, a TV series about the supernatural (US 1959–65), reinforced it, e.g.: 'Several key officials charged with formulating foreign policy remain in a bureaucratic twilight zone one hundred days after Reagan's inauguration' – *The Washington Post* (26 April 1981); 'Musicians are not normal human beings. They are a species out of the Twilight Zone with something different in their brains' – Bob Monkhouse, *Crying With Laughter* (1993).

twin peaks   *Twin Peaks* was the title of a seriously weird TV series (US 1990–91) directed by David Lynch. As a phrase it has a certain resonance. Tennyson wrote of 'Twin peaks shadow'd with pine' in his poem 'Leonine Elegiacs' (1830). 'One of Mozart's great masses is usually enough for a choir to tackle in a single concert. But on Friday John Eliot Gardiner and the Monteverdi Choir and Orchestra paired the C minor mass K427 with the Requiem K626, traversing the twin peaks of Mozart's church music in a single effort' – *Financial Times* (1 February 1982); 'Undies that bring you out on top . . . she warned that the "twin peaks" bust that accompanied the fuller figure of the Fifties and Sixties is definitely out. Its place will be taken by a more natural look that completes the circle as we go back to the future' – *Today* (26 April 1990).

twist   See DON'T GET YOUR KNICKERS.

twisted   See ALL BITTER AND.

(to let someone) twist slowly, slowly in the wind   Richard Nixon's henchmen may have acted wrongly and, for much of the time, spoken sleazily. Occasionally, however, they minted political phrases that have lingered on. John D. Ehrlichman, Nixon's Assistant for Domestic Affairs until he was forced to resign over Watergate in 1973, came up with one saying that caught people's imagination. In a telephone conversation with John Dean (Counsel to the President) on 7/8 March 1973 he was speaking about Patrick Gray (Acting Director of the FBI). Gray's nomination to take over the FBI post had been withdrawn by Nixon during Judiciary Committee hearings – though Gray had not been told of this. Ehrlichman said: 'I think we ought to let him hang there. Let him twist slowly, slowly in the wind.' 'The foreign press observed with admiration the way President Bush stressed in words that he was not ditching the beleaguered Mikhail Gorbachev by playing his China card, while making it clear he was doing exactly that, and leaving the Soviet leader to twist a little longer in the wind' – *The Guardian* (28 January 1989).

(one's) two cents' worth   Meaning, 'one's humble opinion, small contribution'. It is clear that in the 19th century, 'two-cent' was used in the USA for a 'derisory amount', so this was a self-deprecatory way of offering one's bit. There was from 1864 a two-cent coin, even. The British version would be **two pennyworth**. A radio commentator was heard using 'sixpence worth' but he was either trying to avoid a cliché or simply allowing for inflation . . .

2–4–6–8, who do we appreciate? / ——!   This widely used chant was popularized by the BBC radio *Goon Show*. In 'Ye Bandit of Sherwood Forest' (28 December 1954), members of the 'Wallace Greenslade Fan Club' [he was the show's chief announcer] had to cry: '2–4–6–8, who do we appreciate? GREENSLADE!' Compare '2–4–6–8, gay is just as good as straight, 3–5–7–9, lesbians are mighty fine' – a chant of the Gay Liberation Front in the 1970s. Also '2–4–6–8, Motorway', the title of a song recorded by the British Tom Robinson Band in 1977.

(to have) two left feet To be a clumsy person – and, perhaps especially, awkward in movement as a dancer. Known by 1915: 'Mr Dawson . . . gave it as his opinion that one of the lady dancers had two left feet' – P. G. Wodehouse, *Psmith Journalist*, Chap. 18. *The Man With Two Left Feet* became the title of a Wodehouse book (1917).

two minds with but a single thought Phrase derived from near the end of Act 2 of *Der Sohn der Wildnis*, a play by Friedrich Halm (Baron von Münch-Bellinghausen) (1806–71): 'Two minds with but a single thought, / Two hearts that beat as one.' What Halm actually wrote was, 'Two *souls* with but a single thought . . .' – as in Maria Lovell's translation of the play, *Ingomar the Barbarian* (1854). The original German is, indeed, '*Zwei Seelen und ein Gedanke*'. But the 'two minds' version is the one that entered the English language. *Partridge/Catch Phrases* draws attention to the similar phrase 'Great minds think alike' – which may have influenced the English form. The British music-hall mind-reading act The Zancigs (the wife died in 1916, the hus-band in 1929) had as bill matter: 'Two Minds With But a Single Thought'. Compare the variation 'two minds with *not* a single thought': Kenneth Horne contributed an article entitled 'TMWNAST' to the *Radio Times Annual* (1954): 'The title of this article is how Murdoch and I would write it in our script if it were a catchphrase . . . It is quite true that when Murdoch and I get together to write our epic stuff we are two minds with not a single thought.'

(in) two shakes of a lamb's tail Very quickly, in no time at all – as in the script of the film *Pulp Fiction* (US 1994): 'I'll be with you in two shakes of a lamb's tail.' Known since 1840. Possibly an elaboration of the simpler 'in two shakes' (of a dice or a cloth or whatever) and often simply abbreviated to that even now. A Norfolk vet wrote (2000): 'The reference is to lamb's tails which lambs shake very rapidly while sucking from their mother's teat or from a bottle, as any shepherd will have observed. Quite why lambs shake their tails while sucking is another question – foals, calves and piglets certainly don't. I reckon the speed of shaking to be about 300 wags per minute.'

two-six See DO A.

U

ugly as sin Very ugly. From Sir Walter Scott, *Kenilworth*, Chap. 10 (1821): 'Though I am as ugly as sin, I would not have you think me an ass.' The 'as sin' construction can also be applied elsewhere, as in **guilty as sin**, etc. Perhaps the comparison is as 'like the devil'. *Guilty As Sin* was the title of a film (US 1993).

'ullo, 'ullo, 'ullo, what's this? Catchphrase of Pa Glum (Jimmy Edwards) in the BBC radio show *Take It From Here* (1948–59). Usually uttered when he interrupted son Ron as he attempted to kiss fiancée Eth. Co-writer Frank Muir commented (1979): 'It was not meant to be a catchphrase but as Pa Glum always said it on his entrance – and it was so useful a phrase in every-day life – it caught on.' It also, of course, echoes the traditional inquiry of a policeman encountering something suspicious going on. This last was established by the time of P. G. Wodehouse, *The Man With Two Left Feet and Other Stories*, 'The Romance of an Ugly Policeman' (1917).

(the) unacceptable face of —— Format phrase. In 1973, it was revealed that a former Tory Cabinet minister, Duncan Sandys, had been paid £130,000 in compensation for giving up his £50,000-a-year consultancy with the Lonrho company. The money was to be paid, quite legally, into an account in the Cayman Islands to avoid British tax. This kind of activity did not seem appropriate when the Government was promoting a counter-inflation policy. Replying to a question from Jo Grimond MP in the House of Commons on 15 May, Edward Heath, the Prime Minister, created a format phrase that has since been used to describe almost anything. He said, 'It is the unpleasant and unacceptable face of capitalism, but one should not suggest that the whole of British industry consists of practices of this kind.' In the text from which he spoke – said to have been prepared by his then aide, Douglas Hurd – it apparently had 'facet'.

unaccustomed as I am to public speaking A long-established speechmaking cliché and still with us. Coleridge was writing 'Unaccustomed to address such an Audience . . .' by 1808. From R. S. Surtees, *Jorrocks's Jaunts and Jollities*, No. 12 (1838): 'Gentlemen, unaccustomed as I am to public speaking . . .' From William Thackeray, *Pendennis*, Chap. 71 (1848–50): 'I'd like to read a speech of yours in the *Times* before I go – "Mr Pendennis said: Unaccustomed as I am to public speaking" – hey, sir?' In 1856, as Lord Dufferin explains in Letter VI of his *Letters from High Latitudes* (1857), he addressed a group of Icelanders in Latin: '*Viri illustres,* I began, *insolitis ut sum ad publicum loquendum.*' On 26 July 1897, Winston Churchill made his first political speech at a Primrose League gathering near Bath: 'If it were pardonable in any speaker to begin with the well worn and time honoured apology, "Unaccustomed as I am to public speaking," it would be pardonable in my case, for the honour I am enjoying at this moment of addressing an audience of my fellow countrymen and women is the first honour of the kind I have ever received.' In *circa* 1940, Noël Coward opened a Red Cross bazaar at Oxford, beginning: 'Desperately *accustomed* as I am to public speaking . . .'

unbridled passion An inevitable pairing. Date of origin not known. 'It looks, to be honest, like a rather humdrum post-war mansion block, not at all the place for unbridled passion and the reckless disregard for decorum and propriety which lies at the heart of A Greater Love: Charles and Camilla' – *The Observer* (7 August 1994); 'A couple of Wednesdays ago I spent a

morning with Bill Giles, the weather man, and an afternoon with Gary Rhodes, the chef, and I realised what it is that carries men of such differing personalities to the top of their respective professions. It's unbridled passion for the job. Lust, almost' – *Mail on Sunday* (30 April 1995).

uncertainty See AGE OF.

unchained from a lunatic Someone asked Sophocles, 'How is your sex-life now? Are you still able to have a woman?' He replied, 'Hush, man; most gladly am I rid of it all, as though I had been unchained from a lunatic.' This remark was reported by Plato in *The Republic*, Bk. 1, line 329b. It all depends on the translation from the Greek, of course. Another is: 'I have left it behind me and escaped from the madness and slavery of passion . . . a release from slavery to all your many passions.'

uncle See BOB'S YOUR.

Uncle Sam The personification of the United States and known as such since 1813. It is no coincidence that Uncle Sam's initials are the same as those of the United States. *Flexner* (1976) precisely locates the origin with Samuel Wilson, an inspecting superintendent at Troy on the Hudson river, New York, during the War of 1812. He was known as 'Uncle Sam', but the initials of his nickname were jokingly interpreted as standing for 'United States'. Uncle Sam did not appear visually – with his goatee beard, top hat and red, white and blue striped suit – until 1868.

unconditional surrender In almost every conflict a time arrives when one of the combatants decides that it will not be enough for the other side to stop fighting, there will have to be 'unconditional surrender': (1) In the American Civil War, General Ulysses S. Grant sent a message to General Simon B. Buckner at Fort Donelson on 16 February 1862: 'No terms except an unconditional and immediate surrender can be accepted. I propose to move immediately upon your works.' (The capture of Fort Donelson was the first major Union victory.) One of Grant's nicknames became 'Unconditional Surrender', matching his initials, US. (2) Prior to the Armistice in the First World War, the

US General Pershing, in defiance of President Wilson, proposed to fight on until the Germans agreed to 'unconditional surrender'. (3) In the 1926 General Strike, Winston Churchill, as Chancellor of the Exchequer, brought out an official government newspaper, the *British Gazette*, in which he denounced British working men as 'the enemy' and demanded 'unconditional surrender'. (4) At the Casablanca conference of January 1943, President F. D. Roosevelt produced his terms for ending the Second World War, including the 'unconditional surrender' of Germany and Italy, a phrase he had used to his military advisers before leaving Washington and which was endorsed by Churchill (though the British would have preferred to exclude Italy). It was a controversial policy and later blamed for prolonging the war. According to Churchill's own account in Vol. 4 of *The Second World War*, Roosevelt admitted he had consciously been echoing U. S. Grant, though the phrase had been used even before Grant in both the US and UK.

underachiever See EAT MY SHORTS.

underclothes See ALL OVER.

under the glare of powerful arc lamps Journalistic cliché. In fact, no matter how glaring or powerful the lamps in question may be, they will certainly not be of the arc variety. E. J. Hatch of Sittingbourne, Kent, advised (1984): 'The last widespread use of arc lamps was for aircraft searchlights during the 1939–45 war; they have been used as theatre spotlights; the other main use is for cinema projectors.' 'He [Dr Christian Barnard] sat facing the glare of arc lamps, six television and newsreel cameras, and 10 microphones' – *Cape Times* (6 January 1968); 'Sydney Airport in November. An expectant crowd jostles for the best vantage point and the arc lamps for the TV cameras blaze away' – *The Observer* (4 December 1994); 'Huge arc lamps are lighting up every one of the course's 16 jumps' – *Daily Record* (6 April 1995). Compare **amid the glare of television lights**. 'Amid the glare of television lights, the panoply of ecstatic family and friends marking their return, and the flotilla of small boats sounding their

klaxons, the fact that the women and their yacht, *Heineken*, limped into port behind the 14 other competitors was an irrelevance' – *Mail on Sunday* (12 June 1994).

unhand me, villain! A jocular version of 'take your hands off me!', echoing the appeal made by a lady to a villain in late 19th-century melodrama. Alternatively, **unhand me, sir!**

unimpeachable authority Date of origin not known. Identified as a current cliché in *The Times* (17 March 1995). 'The argument of Dr Duffy that drinking more than the "safe limit" reduces the risk of heart disease, and the suggestion by Dr Duffy and his colleague Professor Plant that it is healthier to drink than to abstain, are supported by the results of research carried out under the unimpeachable authority of Professor Sir Richard Doll at the Cancer Studies Unit in Oxford' – *The Independent* (7 December 1994); 'At this season, the peace-dreamers like to press the Christmas message into the service of their causes, with the apparently unimpeachable authority of the words which the angels proclaimed to the shepherds: "on earth peace, good will toward men"' – *The Sunday Telegraph* (18 December 1994).

(a) unique selling proposition (or **USP)** Advertising term coined by Rosser Reeves (1910–84) at the Ted Bates & Company agency which he helped found in 1940 and turn into one of the largest in the world. He described the term USP as 'a theory of the ideal selling concept . . . a verbal shorthand of what makes a campaign work.' In his book *Reality in Advertising* (1960), he defined it in some detail: 'Each advertisement must say to each reader: "Buy *this* product, and you will get *this specific benefit*" . . .The proposition must be one that the competition either cannot, or does not, offer. It must be unique . . . The proposition must be so strong that it can move the mass millions . . . These three points are summed up in the phrase: "UNIQUE SELLING PROPOSITION." This is a U.S.P.' 'Derek Luke, Age: 20, Unique Selling Point: He's the new Denzel Washington, with a whiff of danger' – *The Observer* (15 December 2002).

Universal Provider See PIN TO AN ELEPHANT.

universe See AT ONE WITH THE; CENTRE OF THE.

university of life See SCHOOL OF HARD KNOCKS.

unknown See CALL OF THE.

(the) Unknown Soldier (or Warrior)
The 'Unknown Warrior' was buried in
Westminster Abbey on Armistice Day,
1920. The choice of the word 'warrior' was
explained by the need to leave unspecified
which branch of the Services he belonged
to. On the tombstone, set into the floor of
the Nave, is an inscription, written by
Dean Ryle, concluding with the words:
'They buried him among the kings because
he had done good toward God and toward
his house.' This is based on 2 Chronicles
24:16 (concerning Jehoiada, a 130-year-old
man): 'And they buried him in the city of
David among the kings, because he had
done good in Israel, both toward God, and
toward his house.' The idea of such a
burial first came to a chaplain at the Front
in 1916 after he had seen a grave in a back
garden in Armentières, at the head of
which was a rough wooden cross and the
pencilled words: 'An unknown British
Soldier'. The US 'Unknown Soldier' was
buried on 11 November 1921 at Arlington
National Cemetery and lies under the
inscription: 'Here Rests in Honored Glory
an American Soldier Known But to God'.
Over the graves of most of the unknown
dead, in Europe, had been put the simple
inscription: 'A Soldier of the Great War
Known unto God'.

(an) unmitigated scoundrel Date of
origin not known. Cited by Ted Morgan in
Somerset Maugham (1980) as having been
used by the writer in his efforts to achieve
a 'casual style'. 'The state was ruled not by
Britain but by the Diwan of Travancore, Sir
Ramaswamy Iyer, of whom it could truly
be said that he was an unmitigated scoundrel with no redeeming features' – *The
Times* (26 November 1993).

unwell See IS UNWELL.

unzipp a banana Advertising slogan used
by the Mather & Crowther agency in 1959
when it launched a joint promotion on
behalf of the three main UK banana
importers. Sometimes remembered as
'unzipp your banana', it underlies the
sexual suggestiveness of the product,
which no doubt explains some of its
popular appeal and the humour surrounding it.

up a gum tree Stuck, isolated, in a
difficult position. Presumably because not
only could a person (or animal) be
trapped by pursuers if he went up a tree,
but his position would be made doubly
difficult if the tree was of the type he
would stick to. Known in the USA by
1829. The phrase is also used in Australia,
which must have more gum trees to the
square mile than anywhere else. A correspondent writes: 'The characteristic of
many gum trees, as opposed to other
Australian trees, is that it is a long way to
the first branch, and therefore difficult to
climb, either up or down.'

up and down like a fiddler's elbow
'Mum, exasperated with her small son
(me), who would keep running in and out
and chasing up and down stairs, "Stay put,
dammit. Up and down like a fiddler's
elbow"' – Ray Dudley, London E17 (1994).
Indeed, 'like a fiddler's elbow' was quite a
general expression and had been recorded
by 1887. Martin Ward, Norfolk (1994),
commented: 'The richness of this simile is
its more metaphorical (and more common)
use. I have always heard it used to describe something which is *not* in motion –
for instance, the uneven ridge of a house –
something which deviates from the
horizontal plane. Other builders' expressions include: "Hard as a whore's heart"
(e.g. concrete, wood) and, for things
which do actually move up and down,
"Up and down like a whore's drawers".'

up and down the country Political
phrase. Date of origin not known. Edward
Heath, when British Prime Minister 1970–
74, would wrap his vowels around the
phrase. Michael Foot, the British Labour
politician, combined it with another
political catchphrase following a by-
election victory in April 1983 and said that
Labour would 'Get the spirit of Darlington
up and down the country'. 'As she did so,
a fanfare sounded which was the signal to
begin lighting beacons to form a blazing
chain up and down the country . . . The

airwaves also fell silent as radio stations up and down the country joined the hush' – *The Scotsman* (9 May 1995); 'The recognition of winning the award shows that we have been successful in highlighting the efforts of road protesters up and down the country'– *The Herald* (Glasgow) (10 May 1995); 'Those battles are likely to be fought up and down the country, as Mr Cavallo cajoles provinces into slimming their state structures and re-activating moribund private sectors' – *Financial Times* (16 May 1995).

up and down the railway lines Phrase from a monologue first recited by Jack Warner on the BBC radio programme *Monday Night at Eight* (late 1930s). It was about a wheel-tapper who won the pools and continued to refer to his old calling in a mixed Cockney and Mayfair drawl. Hence this phrase was pronounced distinctively as something like, 'Hup hand dahn the rawlaway lanes'.

up and under A rugby football term for a short, high kick that sends the ball high in the air, enabling the kicker and his teammates to run forward and regain possession of the ball. But to British TV viewers it was inseparably linked to the rugby league commentator Eddie Waring (1909–86). He broadcast commentaries, in his distinctive and highly imitable voice, for twenty years before he retired in 1981. Another of his expressions was **to take an early bath** – for a player being sent off the field early. This is the same as the American expression **to send someone to the showers**, in baseball or football, when a player is sent off early for disciplinary reasons.

up guards and at 'em! Popular short form of what the 1st Duke of Wellington is supposed to have said at Waterloo, namely, 'Up Guards and at them *again*'. The longer version was reported in a letter from a certain Captain Batty of the Foot Guards on 22 June 1815, four days after the battle. *Benham* (1980) has this: 'In A. Tels's guide-book, *Excursions to the Lion of Waterloo* (2nd ed. 1904), a Belgian publication, this is improved as follows: "Wellington cried, 'Upright, guards! prepare for battle'." In *The Times* (15 October 1841),

appeared an "anecdote which may be relied on" quoted from *Britannia*, to the effect that lately the Duke had sat for his bust to "one of the most distinguished of living sculptors," who stated "that it would be popular and effective if it could represent his Grace at the moment when he uttered the memorable words . . . at Waterloo. The Duke laughed very good-humouredly at this observation and said 'Ah! the old story. People will invent words for me . . . but really I don't know what I said. I saw that the moment for action was come, and I gave the command for attack. I suppose the words were brief and homely enough, for they ran through the ranks and were obeyed on the instant . . . but I'm sure I don't recollect them, and I very much doubt whether anyone else can'".' Again, in 1852, the Duke commented to J. W. Croker: 'What I must have said and probably did say was, Stand up, Guards! and then gave the commanding officers the order to attack.' The following year, *Notes and Queries* was already puzzling over the matter.

(it's) up in Annie's room behind the clock (or . . . behind the wallpaper) Explanation for when something disappears unaccountably. *Partridge/Slang* simply has 'Up in Annie's room' as a services' catchphrase from before the First World War, in reply to a query concerning someone's whereabouts. *Partridge/Catch Phrases* has 'Up in Annie's room behind the clock' as the civilian version of this.

up Shit Creek without a paddle Irretrievably stuck or in any sort of difficult quandary. Since the 1920s. Possibly an elaboration of the phrase **up the creek**, popular especially in the USA.

upstairs, downstairs In the USA, 'upstairs, downstairs' has become an expression for class and privilege differences, following on from *Upstairs, Downstairs*, the title of a British drama series from London Weekend Television (1970–75) about the lives of family and servants (i.e. 'above and below stairs') in a London house between 1900 and 1930. From *Newsweek* Magazine (4 January 1988): 'The upstairs-downstairs relationship between Jews and Arabs is conspicuous in Nazareth

. . . the 20,000 Jews live in Upper Nazareth, where the schools are spacious and the streets are well maintained.' Compare the names of two linked nightclubs (or discos) in New York City in the 1960s: 'Upstairs at the Downstairs' and 'Downstairs at the Upstairs'. Also, *Up the Down Staircase*, title of a film (US 1967) about a teacher assigned to a school in a slum area.

(to lead someone) up the garden path (or down . . .) Meaning, 'to trick or deceive' and current by the 1920s, certainly. One origin is that it dates from the 19th century, when you would take a person up or down the garden path to a shady bower which provided cover for seduction. Sue Limb, who entitled a newspaper column and book *Up the Garden Path*, commented (2000): 'The friend who suggested the title to me thought it encapsulated ideas of fruitfulness and deception. I suppose in the past the garden was the only place where courting couples could attain a degree of privacy. Jane Austen's hero and heroine always adjourn to the shrubbery at moments of maximum amorous tension. The absence of witnesses or eavesdroppers also means, I suppose, that heartless seducers could get away with breaking promises made in rosy bowers – hence, "He's leading you up the garden path". I wonder if it is related to the Primrose Path of Dalliance? Or, indeed, Tip-toeing through the Tulips?' However, there is strong support for the idea that the trick was originally being played on a *pig*. 'I have always understood the phrase originated in the days when what would then have been regarded as the lower orders kept a domestic pig or two. When it came time for slaughter – away from the eyes of the children – the luckless pig would be led, quite literally, up the garden path to the shed or other out-house to meet its fate – thus the impression conveyed by the expression that one was being led in complete innocence toward something highly undesirable' – Laurence Fowler (2000). 'When I was evacuated to a farm labourer's cottage in Oxfordshire in 1940, I was told by a slaughterman that "Led by the nose, up the garden path and over the garden wall" had regard to the

last five minutes of a pig's life – a performance which I witnessed. No humane killing then!' – Roy Bartlett (2000). A description of the somewhat messy procedure is to be found in Thomas Hardy, *Jude the Obscure*, Chap. 10 (1895), though the phrase is not used.

up there, Cazaly! Roy Cazaly (1893–1963) was an Australian Rules footballer who played for the South Melbourne team from 1921 onwards and formed a 'ruck' combination with 'Skeeter' Fleiter and Mark Tandy, i.e. they were players who worked together but did not have fixed positions. According to the *Australian Dictionary of Biography*: 'Though only 5ft 11ins and twelve and a half stone, Cazaly was a brilliant high-mark; he daily practised leaping for a ball suspended from the roof of a shed at his home. He could mark and turn in mid-air, land and in a few strides send forward a long, accurate drop-kick or stab-pass. Fleiter's constant cry "Up there, Cazaly!" was taken up by the crowds. It entered the Australian idiom, was used by infantry men in North Africa in World War II and became part of folklore.' The phrase was also incorporated in song.

up the Swanee See SOLD DOWN.

up the wooden hill to Bedfordshire Up the stairs to bed. Originally a nursery euphemism, this has become part of grown-up 'golf-club slang', as someone once termed it – i.e. a conversational cliché. Sir Hugh Casson and Joyce Grenfell included it in their *Nanny Says* (1972), together with 'Come on, up wooden hill, down sheet lane'. 'Up the Wooden Hill to Bedfordshire' was the title of the first song recorded by Vera Lynn, in 1936. The 'bedfordshire' joke occurs in a synopsis of *Ali Baba and the Forty Thieves; or, Harlequin and the Magic Donkey* staged at the Alexandra Theatre, Liverpool, in 1868. Indeed, as so often, Jonathan Swift found it even earlier. In *Polite Conversation* (1738), the Colonel says, 'I'm going to the Land of Nod.' Neverout replies: 'Faith, I'm for *Bedfordshire*.' But then again, the poet Charles Cotton had used it in 1665.

up to a point, Lord Copper This phrase is employed when disagreeing with someone it is prudent not to differ with, or when simply disagreeing without being objectionable about it. It comes from Evelyn Waugh's novel about journalists, *Scoop*, Chap. 3, Pt 3 (1938): 'Mr Salter's side of the conversation was limited to expressions of assent. When Lord Copper [a newspaper proprietor] was right he said, "Definitely, Lord Copper"; when he was wrong, "Up to a point".' 'We are told that [Norman Tebbit] was only trying to help . . . he was out to "stop Heseltine". Well, up to a point, Lord Whitelaw' – *The Independent* (4 April 1990).

up to my neck in muck and bullets
Phrase used by the British comedian

Arthur Haynes (1914–66), in his tramp character on TV shows of the 1960s. Sometimes remembered as 'mud and bullets'.

(to be) up to snuff To be of a proper standard or quality. Perhaps literally, if a person is up to snuff it means he is able to follow a scent. Known by 1811. As for the similar **up to scratch**, this has a probable sporting origin – from the line scratched on the ground, especially in boxing, to which contestants are brought ready to start. Known by 1821.

up up and away See FASTER THAN.

useful See DIGNITY OF LABOUR.

V

vacuum See ABHORS.

(the) vagaries of the English climate
The formula (but with 'Spanish climate') was known by 1962. 'Sir, Are weather forecasters an unnecessary luxury? Now being a senior citizen, I survived the vagaries of the English climate long before weather forecasters came to such prominence' – *The Times* (31 July 1993); 'Running an English vineyard these days may well mean diversifying to make ends meet . . . because of the vagaries of the English climate, which mean that the average annual yield is about 20,000 hecto-litres, are unlikely to be directly affected by the ban' – *The Daily Telegraph* (29 September 1993).

(a) vale of tears Phrase for life seen as composed of woe and sorrow. Known by 1554, though earlier as 'vale of troubles', 'vale of misery'. The anonymous 11th-century prayer '*Salve, regina, mater misericordiae*' contains the phrase '*in hac lacrimarum valle*', which may be translated as 'weeping in this vale of tears'. The Bible's 'Valley of Baca' (Psalm 84:6) is translated in the Book of Common Prayer as 'the vale of misery' and in the Revised Version as the 'valley of weeping'. 'Do I view the world as a vale of tears? / Ah, reverend sir, not I!' – Browning, 'Confessions' (1864)

(a) valiant effort An inevitable pairing. Date of origin not known. 'In a valiant effort to find a kinder term than handicapped, the Democratic National Committee has coined differently abled. The committee itself shows signs of being differently abled in the use of English' – *Los Angeles Times* (9 April 1985).

vanities See BONFIRE OF THE.

vanity fair Phrase from John Bunyan, *The Pilgrim's Progress* (1684): 'It beareth the name of Vanity-Fair, because the town where 'tis kept, is lighter than vanity.' Hence, *Vanity Fair*, title of the novel (1847–8) by William Thackeray. John Sutherland in his introduction to the World's Classics' edition says of Thackeray's title that it, 'came upon him unawares in the middle of the night.' He 'jumped out of bed and ran three times round his room, uttering as he went, "Vanity Fair, Vanity Fair, Vanity Fair".' Before this, he had referred to the book as *Novel Without a Hero* and *Pen and Pencil Sketches of English Soicety* – both of which survive as sub-titles in the final version. *Vanity Fair* has also been used as the title of magazines, notably the one published in New York 1914–36.

vas you dere, Sharlie [was you there, Charlie]? Hungarian-born Jack Pearl used to tell stories as 'Baron Munchausen' on American radio in the early 1930s. If his straight man, Charlie, expressed doubts on any aspect of the stories, Pearl would say, 'Vas you dere, Charlie?' It is spoken by James Cagney as the last line of the film *Picture Snatcher* (US 1933).

(the) Velvet Fog Sobriquet but also unofficial bill matter for the American singer Mel Tormé (1925–99). He was noted for his ultra-smooth crooning style. In 1983, he commented: 'By the age of 18, I'd been labelled "the Singer's Singer" and, although I agree it's a lovely label, I'm anti-labels . . . I was known as The Velvet Fog. I was a little churlish about it at first but later I realised it was an affectionate thing.' 'Readers of early editions on June 7 may be glad to know that his nickname which appeared in a headline as the Velvet Frog was corrected in later editions' – *The Guardian* (9 June 1999).

(the) velvet revolution Name for the process that led to the end of Communist rule in Czechoslovakia at the end of 1989. It signifies a non-violent transition and was apparently originally coined in French. The Czechs themselves had talked of a 'gentle revolution'. 'Even in Czechoslovakia's "velvet revolution", the most peaceful and perhaps the most complete of all the transformations, the middle ranks of the new order are staffed by those who kept their heads down during the long nights of normalisation' – *The Observer* (21 January 1990).

veni, vidi, vici [I came, I saw, I conquered] According to Suetonius, *Lives of the Caesars*, this was an inscription displayed in Latin after Julius Caesar's triumph over Pontus (a part of modern Turkey) in 47 BC – a campaign that lasted only five days. 'This referred not to the events of the war . . . but to the speed with which it had been won.' Plutarch states that it was written in a letter by Caesar, announcing the victory of Zela (in Asia Minor), which concluded the Pontic (Black Sea) campaign. In North's 1579 translation of Plutarch, it says: 'Julius Caesar fought a great battle with King Pharnaces and because he would advertise one of his friends of the suddenness of this victory, he only wrote three words unto Anicius at Rome: *Veni, Vidi, Vici*: to wit, I came, saw,

and overcame. These three words ending all with like sound and letters in the Latin, have a certain short grace, more pleasant to the ear, than can well be expressed in any other tongue.' Shakespeare alludes to Caesar's 'thrasonical brag' in four plays, including *Love's Labour's Lost* (IV.i.68) and *As You Like It* (V.ii.30).

verify See ALWAYS VERIFY.

veritable PHRASES. For example, **veritable pot-pourri**, **veritable minefield**, **veritable inferno** – the last cited as a 'lump of verbal refuse' by George Orwell in 'Politics and the English Language', *Horizon* (April 1946). Date of origin for this construction not known. 'For the BBC, Tom Fleming could find clichés of his own. He gave us "the time-honoured ritual of a British royal occasion" . . . and, in front of the Palace balcony, "a veritable sea" of people' – *The Times* (30 July 1981); 'It was while she searched through Reggie's wardrobe that she came upon a veritable bonanza in the form of a Marks and Spencer bag containing an assortment of shirts, underwear and socks' – Gemma O'Connor, *Sins of Omission* (1995).

very interesting . . . Catchphrase of Arte Johnson as a bespectacled German soldier wearing a helmet in *Rowan and Martin's Laugh-In* (1967–73). He would clasp a cigarette between his fingers, peer through the leaves of a potted plant, say the phrase and add '. . . but it stinks/but stupid' or some such comment. 'Verrry Interesting . . . but Wild' was the title of *Time* Magazine's cover story on *Laugh-In* (11 October 1968). My own first book on this subject was entitled *Very Interesting . . . But Stupid! – a book of catchphrases from the world of entertainment* (1980). It seemed to describe the contents very accurately . . .

very tasty . . . very sweet! The British radio comedy couple Kenway and Young (Nan Kenway and Douglas Young) used to say this, smacking their lips, in the 1930s/ 40s. E.g. *Kenway*: 'My nephew's getting on well in the Navy. He's a ship's carpenter. They say he's a very efficient chips.' *Young*: 'Fish and chips? I like them with a dollop of the old vinegar and a sprinkle of old salt. Goes down a treat I reckon. Very tasty, very sweet!' Or: *Young*: 'Ah! (*Pause*.)

I likes that. (*Pause to suck teeth.*) Jolly good grub, I reckon . . . very tasty, very sweet!'

(a/the) vexed question   An inevitable pairing. Known by 1657 in English. Translation of Latin *quaestio vexata*. 'Environment: Throwaway lines – The hour is late and the party's nearly over when Joseph Pisani finds his guests have turned to the vexed question of household waste' – headline in *The Guardian* (22 May 1992).

V for victory   The 'V for Victory' slogan of the Second World War started as a piece of officially encouraged graffiti inscribed on walls in occupied Belgium by members of the anti-German 'freedom movement'. The Flemish word for freedom begins with a V – *Vrijheid* – and the French word for victory is, of course, *Victoire*. The idea came from Victor de Laveleye, the BBC's Belgian Programme Organizer, who, in a broadcast on 14 January 1941, suggested that listeners should adopt the letter 'V' as 'a symbol of their belief in the ultimate victory of the allies'. They were to go out and chalk it up wherever they could. From Belgium, the idea spread into the Netherlands and France, and 'multitudes' of little Vs started appearing on walls in those countries. Winston Churchill spoke of the 'V' sign as a symbol of the 'the unconquerable will of the people of the occupied territories'. The symbol was expressed in other ways, too. The opening three notes of Beethoven's Fifth Symphony corresponded to the '···–' of the 'V' in Morse Code and, accordingly, the music was used in BBC broadcasts to occupied Europe. People gave the 'V for Victory' salute with parted middle index fingers – though Winston Churchill confused matters by presenting his fingers the wrong way round in a manner akin to the traditionally obscene gesture. Churchill's Private Secretary, John Colville, noted in his diary on 26 September 1941: 'The PM *will* give the V sign with two fingers in spite of the representations repeatedly made to him that this gesture has quite another significance'.

(a) Vicar of Bray   Meaning, 'a person who changes allegiance according to the way the wind blows; a turncoat.' So named after a vicar of Bray, Berkshire, in the 16th century who is supposed to have changed his religious affiliation from Roman Catholic to Protestant more than once during the reigns of Henry VIII to Elizabeth I. However, there was more than one vicar in this period. Whatever the case, by the time of Thomas Fuller's *Worthies* (1662) there was a proverb: 'The Vicar of Bray will be Vicar of Bray still.' As for the song beginning 'In Good King Charles's Golden Days . . .', it was probably written at the beginning of the 18th century and describes a different (perhaps completely fictional) vicar of Bray who changed his religion to suit the different faiths of monarchs from Charles II to George I. Can there have been two such turncoat vicars – or was the song merely an updating of the circumstances of the actual first vicar?

(le) vice anglais [the English vice]   Often thought to be the French term for the Englishman's predilection for homosexual over heterosexual behaviour. But originally it applied to the Englishman's supposed love of flagellation (derived in turn from his supposed enjoyment of corporal punishment during his schooldays). *OED2* does not find the original use until 1942. On the other hand, Sir Richard Burton's 'Terminal Essay' in his translation of the *Arabian Nights* (1885) includes the observation on homosexuality, that: 'In our modern capitals, London, Berlin and Paris for instance, the Vice seems subject to periodical outbreaks. For many years, also, England sent her pederasts to Italy, and especially to Naples whence originated the term "*Il vizio Inglese*".'

vices   See ANCESTRAL VICES.

(a) vicious circle   Meaning, 'reciprocal aggravation as in argument and discussion'. Or a self-perpetuating cycle of aggravation. A term used in logic and known by 1792. Compare the film title *Mrs Parker and the Vicious Circle* (US 1995), referring to the witty members of the Algonquin Round Table in the 1930s. 'We must end the vicious circle of low skill, poor wages, unemployment and national economic decline. Instead for the computer age we must create a new virtue circle of education, productivity, high earning power and national prosperity' – *Evening Standard* (London) (12 July 1994).

Victorian values In the General Election of 1983 and thereafter, the British Prime Minister, Margaret Thatcher, and some of her Cabinet ministers frequently commended the virtue of a return to Victorian values. The phrase appears to have been coined by Brian Walden in a TV interview with Mrs Thatcher on ITV's *Weekend World* on 17 January 1983. It was *he* who suggested to *her* that she was trying to restore 'Victorian values'. She replied: 'Very much so. Those were the values when our country became great. But not only did our country become great internationally, also much advance was made in this country – through voluntary rather than state action.' Mrs Thatcher also said in an LBC radio interview on 15 April: 'I was brought up by a Victorian grandmother. We were taught to work jolly hard. We were taught to prove ourselves; we were taught self-reliance; we were taught to live within our income . . . You were taught that cleanliness is next to godliness. You were taught self-respect. You were taught always to give a hand to your neighbour. You were taught tremendous pride in your country. All of these things are Victorian values. They are also perennial values.' On 23 April, the *Daily Telegraph* quoted Dr Rhodes Boyson, the Minister for Schools, as saying: 'Good old-fashioned order, even Victorian order, is far superior to illiterate disorder and innumerate chaos in the classroom,' and Neil Kinnock, then Chief Opposition spokesman on education, as saying: 'Victorian Britain was a place where a few got rich and most got hell. The "Victorian values" that ruled were cruelty, misery, drudgery, squalor and ignorance.' In a speech to the British Jewish Community (21 July 1983), Thatcher said: 'I was asked whether I was trying to restore Victorian values. I said straight out I was. And I am.' In her book, *The Downing Street Years* (1993), Thatcher comments: 'I never felt uneasy about praising "Victorian values" or – the phrase I originally used – "Victorian virtues".'

(a) village tyrant An oppressive person in a small and petty context. Denis Hills, an English teacher and writer (1913–2004), was sentenced to death for treason for describing President Idi Amin of Uganda as 'a village tyrant . . . a black Nero' in his book *The White Pumpkin* (1975). He was pardoned and freed only after the intervention of the Queen and the Foreign Secretary. The 'village tyrant' taunt was not new, however. In his biography *Aneurin Bevan*, Vol. 2 (1975), Michael Foot describes the setting up of the National Health Service in the late 1940s and quotes Dr Roland Cockshut, one of the leading spokesmen on the BMA Council, as saying: 'We might have been going to meet Adolf Hitler . . . [but] he is no village tyrant, but a big man on a big errand.'

(a) virtual standstill Eric Partridge, *A Dictionary of Clichés* (5th edition, 1978), has 'Traffic is (or was) at a virtual standstill' as an American newspaper reporters' cliché, 'dating from ca. 1905'. 'Road traffic between Hungary and Austria came to a virtual standstill on Saturday as Hungarian border guards stepped up passport and customs checks following a bomb blast in Budapest' – *Financial Times* (25 July 1994); 'The railways came to a virtual standstill yesterday as train drivers staged the first of six 24-hour stoppages. Union leaders said there was worse to come' – *The Independent* (15 July 1995).

visible panty line (or VPL) Phrase for an unsightly feature of women's clothing when underwear shows through the outerwear. Known by the 1970s (there is a reference in Woody Allen's film *Annie Hall* – US 1977) and presumably coined in the garment industry or among fashion journalists.

(a/the) vital spark The vital or animating principle in man; a trace of life or vitality. Known by the 15th century. 'The Vital Spark' was the bill matter of the British music-hall entertainer Jenny Hill (1849/50–96).

vive la différence Phrase approving the difference between men and women. An untraced reference has Anatole France sitting next to a 'modern' woman of the 1890s who said to him, 'Monsieur France, there is almost no difference between men and women today', to which he made his famous remark. 'Frenchmen may well cry "Vive la différence", for it is cultivated unceasingly in all aspects of life' – Germaine Greer, *The Female Eunuch*, Chap. 29 (1970).

(a) voice crying in the wilderness A person whose warnings and observations are ignored. After Isaiah 40:3: 'The voice of him that crieth in the wilderness, Prepare ye the way of the Lord, make straight in the desert a highway for our God.' Also Numbers 14:33. It is from this also that one derives the expression that a politician is 'in the wilderness' when he is out of office because of the unpopularity of his views. An example would be Winston Churchill in the 1930s, warning of German rearmament. Hence, *Winston Churchill – The Wilderness Years*, a TV play about this period (UK 1975).

(a) voice from the past A slightly ominous phrase used, perhaps on the telephone, when one introduces oneself to another person with whom one has long been out of touch. Date of origin unknown. 'The Voice from the Past' is the title of a short story (1931) by P. G. Wodehou se.

voices See ANCESTRAL VOICES.

***Vorsprung durch Technik* [advancement ahead/in the lead/through technology]** Slogan for Audi cars in the UK from 1982. The use of a German phrase (which few could understand) was apparently designed to bring home to British buyers that the Audi was, indeed, a German car (and hence a reliable, quality product). The phrase was the company's own exhortation to its workforce to be found written up over the factory gates in Germany. In no sense can it be described as a catchphrase, as it did not catch on, but it certainly intrigued and tantalized and was noticed.

vote early and vote often A cynical political catchphrase of certain American origin. 'Josh Billings' (pseudonym of Henry Wheeler Shaw, the American humorist 1818–85) wrote that it was 'the Politishun's golden rule' in *Josh Billings' Wit and Humour* (1874), and seems merely to be recalling an adage. Indeed, earlier, William Porcher Miles had said in a speech to the House of Representatives (31 March 1858): '"Vote early and vote often", the advice openly displayed on the election banners in one of our northern cities.' Another version is that the original jokester was John Van Buren, a New York lawyer (d. 1866), who was the son of President Martin Van Buren.

votes for women Women's suffrage slogan in the UK (1906–14). If a slogan is judged purely by its effectiveness, 'Votes For Women' is a very good slogan. The words may not sparkle, but they achieved their end. Both Emmeline and Christabel Pankhurst, founders of the Women's Social and Political Union, have described how this particular battle cry emerged. In October 1905, a large meeting at the Free Trade Hall, Manchester, was due to be addressed by Sir Edward Grey, who was likely to attain ministerial office if the Liberals won the forthcoming General Election. The WSPU was thus keen to challenge him in public on his party's attitude to women's suffrage in Britain. 'Good seats were secured for the Free Trade Hall meeting. The question was painted on a banner in large letters, in case it should not be made clear enough by vocal utterance. How should we word it? "Will you give women suffrage?" – we rejected that form, for the word "suffrage" suggested to some unlettered or jesting folk the idea of suffering. "Let them suffer away!" – we had heard the taunt. We must find another wording and we did! It was so obvious and yet, strange to say, quite new. Our banners bore this terse device: "WILL YOU GIVE VOTES FOR WOMEN?"' The plan had been to let down a banner from the gallery as soon as Sir Edward Grey stood up to speak. Unfortunately, the WSPU failed to obtain the requisite tickets. It had to abandon the large banner and cut out the three words that would fit on a small placard. 'Thus quite accidentally came into existence the slogan of the suffrage movement around the world.' Alas, Sir Edward Grey did not answer the question, and it took rather more than this slogan – hunger-strikes, suicide, the First World War – before women first got the vote in 1918. Other uses to which the slogan was put: a newspaper with the title

Votes for Women was launched in October 1907. At a meeting in the Royal Albert Hall, someone boomed 'Votes for Women' down an organ pipe. The Independent Labour Party used to refer to it as 'Votes for Ladies'. Other slogans employed were 'Deeds, Not Words'; 'Arise! Go Forth And Conquer'; and 'The Bill, The Whole Bill, And Nothing But The Bill'. In the USA, the Nineteenth Amendment, extending female franchise on a national scale, was ratified in time for the 1920 elections. In due course, some feminists were to campaign with the slogan 'Orgasms For Women'.

***vouz pouvez cracher* [you may spit]** Catchphrase from the BBC radio show *ITMA* (1939–49). *ITMA* did skits on pre-war Radio Luxembourg and called it 'Radio Fakenburg'. 'Ici Radio Fakenburg,' the announcer would say, 'mesdames et messieurs, défense de cracher' (no spitting). Each episode would end: 'Mesdames et messieurs, vous pouvez cracher!'

***vox populi* [voice of the people]** In British broadcasting of the 1950s/60s there was a vogue for what was known in the business as **vox pops** – namely, street interviews with passers-by presenting views on issues of the day which, with luck, were amusingly expressed and – for reasons of balance – effectively cancelled each other out. The abbreviation *Vox Pop* was also the title of an American radio show in the early 1940s. In full, '*Vox populi*' is of venerable origin. Alcuin wrote in a letter to the Emperor Charlemagne in AD 800: '*Nec audiendi sunt qui solent dicere, "Vox populi, vox Dei"; cum tumult-uositas vulgi semper insaniae proxima sit*'

[Nor should we listen to those who say, "The voice of the people is the voice of God", for the turbulence of the mob is always close to insanity]'. 'The people's voice is odd, / It is, and it is not, the voice of God' – Alexander Pope, 'The First Epistle of the Second Book of Horace Imitated' (1737). 'Fox populi' was a nickname given to Abraham Lincoln (presumably on account of his looks or his populism) by *Vanity Fair* Magazine, London, in 1863. The same year, the US General W. T. Sherman wrote in a letter to his wife: 'Vox populi, vox humbug' – by which he meant 'the voice of the people is humbug'.

(a) voyage of discovery Known by the mid-19th century in both the literal and figurative senses. 'Around The World In Masterpieces; The National Gallery's "Circa 1492", A Grand Voyage Of Discovery' – headline in *The Washington Post* (12 October 1991); 'The prospect of writing a book about myself had been depressing me. Now I realised that it could be a voyage of discovery' – Bob Monkhouse, *Crying With Laughter* (1993).

(a) V sign The obscene gesture so easily confused with Churchill's V FOR VICTORY may have come about as described by Anthony Sher in *Year of the King* (1985): 'The two-fingered sod-off sign comes from Agincourt. The French, certain of victory, had threatened to cut off the bow-fingers of all the English archers [this is attested for in a contemporary French account of the battle]. When the English were victorious, the archers held up their fingers in defiance'.

(a) wage freeze The concept of 'freezing' wages – holding them at a stated level – was current in the USA in the 1930s and 1940s. The term 'wage-freeze' itself had been formed by 1942 and also occurs in the film *To Catch a Thief* (US 1955). It was later popularized in the UK by the Chancellor of the Exchequer Selwyn Lloyd: 'Do you think the unions are going to respond

to what amounts to a wage freeze in the public sector?' – radio broadcast (25 July 1961). This was also termed (in the UK only) a **pay freeze** and a **pay pause**.

(the) wages of sin Punishment or retribution for one's actions – now often jocularly used. After Romans 6:23, St Paul speaking: 'For the wages of sin is death;

but the gift of God is eternal life through Jesus Christ our Lord.' 'For sin pays a wage, and the wage is death', is the New English Bible's version. The strength of expression derives from the perfectly correct singular verb 'is', where the hearer might be more comfortable with 'are'. There may possibly be an allusion in *The Wages of Fear*, English title of the film *Le Salaire de la Peur* (France/Italy 1953).

(a) wagger pagger bagger (sometimes just **wagger** or **wagger pagger)** A wastepaper basket. This is an example of the (now rather dated) slang popular at the University of Oxford in the early years of the 20th century. A whole range of words was transformed into different ones ending in '-agger'. The Prince of Wales (who studied at the university for a while) was the 'Pragger Wagger'. Jesus College was known as 'Jaggers'. And a curious working-class character who used to hang around Oxford and was known as 'the British Workman' came, inevitably, to be called the 'Bragger Wagger'. The whole scheme is a variant upon the old English Public School custom of adding '-er' to everything: rugby becoming 'rugger', football becoming 'footer', and so on. Silly, but rather fun. 'If you don't mind, there-fore, I shall deposit them in the wagger-pagger-bagger [*He drops the flowers into the wastepaper basket*]' – John Dighton, *The Happiest Days Of Your Life*, Act 2 (1948).

wagging See CASE OF THE TAIL.

wagons roll See LET'S ROLL.

wait and see Be patient. 'However, we had no remedy, but to wait and see what the issue of things might present' – Daniel Defoe, *Robinson Crusoe* (1719). Famously attached to H. H. Asquith who told a persistent inquirer about the Parliament Act Procedure Bill, in the House of Commons (4 April 1910): 'You had better wait and see.' In fact, this was the fourth occasion on which Asquith had said 'Wait and see'. On 3 March he had replied 'We had better wait and see' to Lord Helmsey concerning the government's intentions over the Budget and whether the House of Lords would be flooded with Liberal peers to ensure the passage of the Finance Bill.

So he was clearly deliberate in his use of the words. His intention was not to delay making an answer but to warn people off. Roy Jenkins commented in *Asquith* (1964): 'It was a use for which he was to pay dearly in the last years of his premiership when the phrase came to be erected by his enemies as a symbol of his alleged inactivity.' In consequence of all this, Asquith acquired the nickname 'Old Wait and See', and during the First World War French matches that failed to ignite were known either as 'Asquiths' or 'Wait and sees'.

waiting See ACCIDENT.

wake up and smell the coffee Meaning, 'stop dreaming, face reality'. A catchphrase that has been around since at least the 1960s and probably of American origin. Possibly based on a line in a coffee commercial of long ago. 'Asked if he had a message for [Tony] Blair, he [Tim Robbins] said: "Wake up and smell the democracy"' – *The Observer* (16 February 2003); 'Wake up and smell the cliché' – headline in *The Independent* (22 February 2003).

wake up at the back there! Catchphrase of Jimmy Edwards in the BBC radio show *Take It From Here* (1948–59). Co-writer Frank Muir commented (1979): 'This was a line I always used in writing Jim's school-master acts. It was technically very useful in breaking up his first line and getting audience attention.' *Jim*: 'They laughed at Suez, but he went right ahead and built his canal – wake up at the back there!'

wake up, England! A reprimand deliv-ered by the speaker to himself for not having spotted something fairly obvious. Also, according to Iona and Peter Opie, *The Lore and Language of Schoolchildren* (1959), a phrase used to greet a bearer of bad news. In origin it is a misquotation or, rather, a phrase that was not actually spoken. The future King George V made a speech at the Guildhall, London, on 5 December 1901, when Duke of York (but four days before he was created Prince of Wales). Returning from an Empire tour, he warned against taking the Empire for granted: 'To the distinguished representa-tives of the commercial interests of the Empire . . . I venture to allude to the impression which seemed generally to prevail among our brethren overseas, that the old country must wake up if she intends to maintain her old position of pre-eminence in her Colonial trade against foreign competitors.' This statement was encapsulated by the popular press in the phrase 'Wake up, England!' but George did not say precisely that himself.

wakey-wakey! *The Billy Cotton Band Show* ran on BBC radio and TV for over twenty years from the late 1940s. For one seven-year period it was broadcast on radio without a break for fifty-two weeks of the year. First would come a fanfare, then Billy Cotton's cry (without any 'rise and shine') would be followed by a brisk, noisy rendering of 'Somebody Stole My Gal'. The programme was first broadcast on Sunday 6 February 1949 at 10.30 a.m. Because of this unsocial hour, rehearsals had to begin at 8.45 – not the best time to enthuse a band that had just spent six days on the road. 'Oi, come on,' said Cotton, on one occasion, 'Wakey-wakey!' It worked, and eventually led to such a cheerful atmosphere that the producer said the show might as well start with it. Said Cotton (1899–1969): 'I thought of all those people lying in their beds and I remembered the sergeant who used to kick my bottom when I was a kid – and out came the catchword.' So it remained – even when the radio programme moved to its better-remembered spot at Sunday lunchtime. See also RISE AND SHINE.

walk See HE CAN TALK.

walked See AS I WALKED.

walkies! If proof were needed that life can begin at seventy, it was provided by Barbara Woodhouse (1910–88). In 1980, after much badgering, she persuaded the BBC that she should present a programme called *Training Dogs the Woodhouse Way* (which involved training the owners, too). She instantly became a national figure of the eccentric kind the British like to have from time to time, and also found fame in the USA. Her authoritative delivery of such commands as 'Walkies!' and 'Ssssit!' were widely imitated. However, by December 1981 she was telling a newspaper that she was going to retreat a fraction from the public eye: 'It's just that I'm getting tired of people saying "Walkies!" to me wherever I go. Even in a village of 300 inhabitants in Queensland.' The childish diminutive of 'walk' was not, of course, her coinage. It was in use by the 1930s.

(a) walk in the woods Name given to a negotiating tactic employed by high officials in Strategic Arms Limitation Talks (SALT) between the United States and the USSR. A play inspired by the compromise achieved on a specific occasion by negotiators in 1982 and showing how they might have talked through their personal and political differences was accordingly entitled *A Walk in the Woods*. Written by Lee Blessing, it was first performed on Broadway in 1988. 'The package that Mr Nitze and Mr Kvitsinsky worked out in their now famous "walk in the woods" near Geneva last July involved equal ceilings for both sides' medium-range nuclear weapons in Europe' – *Financial Times* (9 March 1983); 'In the summer of 1982 Perle sabotaged the formula agreed between Nitze and the Soviet negotiator, Kvitsinsky, during their famous "walk in the woods"' – Denis Healey, *The Time of My Life* (1989).

wall See BACKS TO THE.

(a) wall of silence Journalistic cliché. Date of origin not known. 'Wall of silence over murder in prison' – headline in *The Observer* (30 April 1995).

wallpaper See UP IN ANNIE'S ROOM.

wallop, Mrs Cox! Exclamation popular in Birmingham and the English Midlands in the mid-20th century – akin to 'Cor blimey!' or STONE ME! or GORDON BENNETT! Used when expressing surprise or amazement or when reacting to a noise or sudden happening. The phrase has also been reported as an alternative to saying 'Cheers!' or 'Bottoms up!' before taking a sip: 'Up she goes and down she goes, and wallops Mrs Cox!' 'Wallop' is an old word (possibly Australian) for beer or alcohol in general, which may be relevant, but 'to wallop' something is to give it a blow. 'To wallop' has also been explained as 'to keel over and die'. Hence, the title of a musical celebration of life in Birmingham, *Wallop Mrs Cox* (2000) by Euan Rose and Laurie

Hornsby, in which the principal character is called Mrs Cox and the show starts with her funeral. There is even a song entitled 'Wallop Mrs Cox'. As to who the original Mrs Cox might have been (apart from it being a common working-class name in the Birmingham area), the suggestion has been made that it refers to a notorious unresolved Victorian murder mystery, the Bravo case. In 1876, a London barrister called Charles Bravo died of poisoning, and his wife, Florence, was the chief suspect, although she was neither charged nor convicted. Florence had a companion who lived in the Bravo household and her name was Mrs Jane Cannon Cox. She was present in the house when Charles cried out for help, and she went to his aid although it was later revealed how she had had many arguments with him. At a second inquest into the poisoning – virtually a trial of Florence and Mrs Cox – a verdict of wilful murder was returned, but there was insufficient evidence to proceed to a proper trial. The whole case is described in James Ruddick's book *Murder At the Priory* (2001). Could this possibly be the origin of a phrase that brings together a 'Mrs Cox' and a situation where someone does drop down dead?

walls have ears A security slogan in the Second World War, but the idea of inanimate objects being able to hear is a very old one. From W. S. Gilbert's *Rozenkrantz and Guildenstern* (1891): 'We know that walls have ears. I gave them tongues – / And they were eloquent with promises.' In 1727, Jonathan Swift wrote: 'Walls have tongues, and hedges ears.' In Vitzentzos Kornaros's epic poem *Erotokritos* (*circa* 1645) there is the following couplet (here translated from the Greek): 'For the halls of our masters have ears and hear, / And the walls of the palace have eyes and watch.' Even earlier, the phrase is to be found in Rabbinical writings of the 11th century – for example, in commentaries on Genesis 31:4 where Jacob calls for his wives to confer in the privacy of a field. According to 'Rashi' (Rabbi Shlomo Yitzschaki), this was because 'walls have ears'.

(a) Walter Mitty The name of a fantasist who daydreams of achievements that are beyond him in real life (compare the

character 'Billy Liar' in the 1959 novel of that name by Keith Waterhouse). It comes from the short story 'The Secret Life of Walter Mitty' (1939; film US 1947) by James Thurber. 'The Government has abandoned its intention to attack the credibility of [scientist Dr] David Kelly after the furore caused by the revelation that Tom Kelly, Tony Blair's official spokesman, denigrated him as a "Walter Mitty"' – *The Independent* (6 August 2003).

wanna buy a duck? Catchphrase of Joe Penner (1904–41), a Hungarian-American, rocketed to fame on American radio in 1934 with rapid-fire one-liners and a number of catchphrases including this one and **you naaasty man!** He carried a real duck, called 'Goo Goo', in a basket.

wandering boy See LAMP IN THE WINDOW.

want See AHA, ME.

war See DAY WAR; DON'T MENTION THE; HARD-FACED MEN.

war and peace The title of Tolstoy's novel *War and Peace* (1865–8) was not decided on until very late in the writing process, according to Henry Troyat's biography. '*The Year 1805* would not do for a book that ended in 1812. He had chosen *All's Well That Ends Well*, thinking that would give the book the casual, romantic tone of a long English novel'. Finally, the title was 'borrowed from Proudhon' – *La Guerre et la Paix* (1862).

(the) war between the states This term for the American Civil War (1861–5), like 'the War Between the North and the South', did not catch on until the conflict was well over (1867 for 'between the States', popular with Southerners, and possibly not until the 1890s for 'between North and South'). 'The Civil War' was an earlier Northern name for it (1861). Southerners had called it 'the Revolution', 'the War of Independence', 'the Second War of Independence', or 'the War of Secession'. Hence, *The War Between the Tates*, punning title for a novel of family feuding (1974) by Alison Lurie.

war is over See FOR YOU TOMMY.

(a) warring faction Known by 1972. 'The central district came under fire from all sides during the fighting and was devastated – though the Riad Solh and the Stock Exchange remain almost undamaged. This was the Wall Street of Beirut, and each warring faction was evidently anxious to preserve its bank accounts' – *Mail on Sunday* (6 November 1994).

(the) war's over, you know Said to someone who is being noticeably and unnecessarily careful about wasting food, electricity, etc. Current since the Second World War and a natural replacement for DON'T YOU KNOW THERE'S A WAR ON?

(the) war to end wars Slogan of the First World War (on the British and Allied side), derived from *The War That Will End War*, the title of a book (1914) by H. G. Wells. It was not an original cry, having been raised in other wars, but by the end of this one it was popularly rendered as 'the war to end wars'. On the afternoon of 11 November 1918, David Lloyd George announced the terms of the Armistice to the House of Commons and concluded: 'I hope we may say that thus, this fateful morning, came to an end all wars.' Later, Wells commented ruefully: 'I launched the phrase "the war to end war" and that was not the least of my crimes' – quoted in Geoffrey West, *H. G. Wells* (1930). Sometimes it is said – for example, in *The Observer* Magazine (2 May 1993) – that it was a phrase of the 1930s and that there is no evidence the words were used at the time of the First World War. Clearly not the case.

warts and all This phrase about a portrait or written description means 'including all the details that someone might prefer to have left out'. Traditionally, it is what Oliver Cromwell is said to have instructed Sir Peter Lely who was painting his portrait: 'Remark all these roughnesses, pimples, warts, and everything as you see, otherwise I will never pay a farthing for it.' It is now thought more likely that Cromwell made the remark to the miniaturist Samuel Cooper (whom Lely copied). The anecdote was first recorded in 1721.

washed See AFTER I'VE.

was it good for you, too (or all right or OK . . .)? What the male lover was supposed to say to his sexual partner after intercourse to show that her needs and feelings were not being ignored (after the rise of feminism in the 1960s/70s). Now a cliché. Indications that the phrase had 'arrived' came when Bob Chieger entitled a book of quotations about love and sex *Was It Good For You Too* (1983). Earlier it had been the title of a sketch by Dan Greenburg in *Oh! Calcutta!* (1969). From the sketch 'Worms' in BBC2 TV *Not Only . . . But Also* (1970): 'Worms aren't in the habit of having a great deal to eat and drink, staggering upstairs, getting into bed and taking all their clothes off and muttering "I love you" and "was it alright for you, darling?"' Compare DID THE EARTH MOVE FOR YOU?

watch See I MUST GET A LITTLE HAND.

—watch PHRASES. The '—watch' suffix is now a cliché – designed, apparently, to add dignity and status to almost any vigil, regular study or observation. Perhaps one should distinguish between two families of '—watch' phrases. In one family, the second element of the phrase means 'an organization set up to police something' and the first element tells you what it is that is being policed (town-watch, night-watch, fire-watch, and so on). In the other family, the second element means an 'organized and continued act of watching, a keeping vigilant to observe something' (though sometimes with an admixture of the policing sense), and the first element tells us what is being looked out for. The fashion may have been set by the BBC TV drama series *Doomwatch*, which ran from 1970 to 1972. The *OED2* shows the word quickly escaping from the TV listings and being used in such phrases as 'his latest piece of political doomwatch' – *The Times* (3 July 1973). The addition of the suffix to signify any kind of regular attention to something began in earnest in the UK about 1985. It stemmed from Neighbourhood Watch (sometimes Home Watch) schemes, which had been started by police in the UK a year or two before this – schemes in which residents are encouraged to 'police' their own and each other's properties. The coinage originated in the USA in the early 1970s, but as early as 6 July 1975, the *Observer* TV critic could write, 'Camden Council employs a lone inspector to walk the pavement on the lookout for citizens allowing their dogs to foul it. In a sane society he would command a department called Shitwatch.' The comedian Les Dawson had a BBC TV series entitled *The Dawson Watch* by 1980. In 1985, there were TV programmes with titles like *Drugwatch*, *Nature Watch*, *Newswatch*, *Crimewatch UK*, *Firewatch*, not to mention a feature called 'Wincey's Animal Watch' on TV-am. In 1986 came *Birdwatch UK* and *Childwatch* (on TV). Since then there has been *Railwatch* on BBC TV (1989), *Weather Watch* on ITV (1989), 'Longman Wordwatch', a scheme for readers to contribute to the *Longman Register of New Words*, and something called the Worldwatch Institute in Washington – which seems to be the ultimate in — watches. 'I'm fed up with Agewatch and Childwatch. I'm thinking of founding a society against potential suicide called Wristwatch' – Russell Harty, quoted by Alan Bennett in a memorial address (14 October 1988).

watchman, what of the night? Not a street cry but a quotation from the Bible. In Isaiah 21:11 the watchman replies, unhelpfully: 'The morning cometh, and also the night.' Used as the title of a Bernard Partridge cartoon in *Punch* (3 January 1900). Set to music several times, notably by Sir Arthur Sullivan.

watch the birdie (also **watch the dicky bird)!** What photographers say to gain the attention of those they are photographing (especially children) and to make them look at the same point. Originally they may have held a toy bird near the camera lens. A song, 'Watch the Birdie', appeared in the film *Hellzapoppin'* (1942). To obtain the semblance of a smile, the photographer says, 'Smile, please!' or 'Say "cheese!"' Cecil Beaton is reported to have encouraged (some of) his subjects to, 'Say "lesbian!"' 'Smile, please – watch the birdie!' was adopted as one of the many *ITMA* catchphrases on the BBC radio show (1939–49).

watch the skies Last words of the film *The Thing* (US 1951) were: 'Watch everywhere, keep looking, watch the skies!' This phrase was subsequently used to promote the film *Close Encounters of the Third Kind* (US 1977) and, indeed, was its original title. Another slogan for the film was **we are not alone**.

watch this space A light-hearted way of saying 'further details will follow'. How did this arise and when? Perhaps it would be put on advertisement hoardings to await the arrival of a new poster? From there transferred to newspaper, even broadcasting, use – meaning 'pay attention to this slot'? The *OED2*'s earliest example is taken from an advertisement in the *B.E.F. Times* [British Expeditionary Force] in 1917.

watch your language! Correctional phrase addressed at someone using bad language, swearing, etc. Known by 1977. 'At the climax of [a play entitled] Gabriel, a man lies bleeding to death amid rising panic. He turns for help but, receiving none, cries: "This bitch would watch me die!" The doughty housekeeper with a heart of gold scolds, "There's a child! Watch your language!" Not a line you hear much nowadays' – *The Independent* (9 May 1997).

water See COME HELL.

Watergate PHRASES. The name 'Watergate' for the scandal in US politics that led to the resignation of President Richard Nixon in 1974 came from the Watergate apartment block in Washington DC where a bungled burglary by those seeking to re-elect the president led to a cover-up and then the scandal. Consequently, it has become standard practice to apply the suffix **——gate** to any political and Royal scandal in the USA and UK. Among the scores there have been are: Koreagate, Lancegate, Billygate, Liffeygate, Westlandgate, Contragate, Irangate, Thatchergate and Squidgygate. For other Watergate phrases see: ALL THE PRESIDENT'S MEN; CUT OFF AT THE PASS; DEEP-SIX; DEEP THROAT; EXPLETIVE DELETED; I WOULD WALK OVER MY GRANDMOTHER; SMOKING GUN; TWIST SLOWLY, SLOWLY IN THE WIND.

waters See CAST ONE'S BREAD.

(that's all) water under the bridge (or ... **over the dam** or **under the dyke** or **under the mill)** Dismissive phrase of anything that it is no longer worth worrying about or spending time over because it happened a long time ago. Date of origin uncertain. 'Water under the bridge' can also simply be used to express the fact that a lot of time has gone by. There is this exchange from the film *Casablanca* (US 1942): *Ilsa*: 'It's been a long time.' *Sam*: 'Yes, ma'am. A lot of water under the bridge.'

(a) watery grave 'Wat'ry grave' occurs in Shakespeare, *Pericles*, II.i.10 (1609), where it is meant literally. Latterly, it has mostly been used jocularly for getting wet and/or in descriptions of being saved from drowning. 'The fact that the rescue was arranged oughtn't to matter . . . and you were genuinely saved from a watery grave and all that sort of thing' – P. G. Wodehouse, *Love Among the Chickens*, Chap. 19 (1906). '[He] was in two bunkers for a double bogey at the eighth. He had a watery grave at the last when he pulled his seven-iron approach into the duck pond' – *The Irish Times* (9 May 1994); 'Political "photo opportunities" are not supposed to be life-or-death affairs. But the Socialist candidate in the French presidential election, Lionel Jospin, broke the rule on Sunday when he very nearly fell into a watery grave while attempting to board a fishing boat in the Breton port of Concarneau' – *Evening Standard* (London) (19 April 1995).

Watson, the needle! 'Quick, Watson, the needle!' is not uttered by Sherlock Holmes in the books by Conan Doyle, but it does occur in the film *The Hound of the Baskervilles* (US 1939). Known as a catchphrase before this, though. P. G. Wodehouse in a letter (22 December 1922) wrote: 'I wonder what an osteopath does if a patient suddenly comes apart in his hands. ("Quick, Watson, the seccotine!")'

wave your gladdies, possums! A stock phrase of 'Dame Edna Everage, the Housewife Superstar' from Australia. Barry Humphries (b. 1934) has been playing this character since the 1950s. The somewhat phallic gladiolus-waving ritual in which he encouraged his audiences was certainly a feature of his stage show by the mid-1970s. Edna's use of the adjective **spooky!** in British TV shows of the 1980s was also noticeable.

(to) wax lyrical To speak effusively about something. Of American origin.

Recorded by 1965. Wax Lyrical was the name given to a chain of stores selling just candles in the UK. It folded in 2003.

way See AND THAT'S THE.

(to see which) way the wind blows To wait before acting or making a decision in order to see whether the circumstances are going to be favourable. 'To know which way the wind blows' means 'to be aware of a tendency or change in affairs or conditions.' Use of this concept goes back to 1400 at least. A proverbial expression of 1546 was 'I knew which way the wind blew'. *The Way the Wind Blows* was the title of memoirs by Lord Home (1976), which his opening words explain. 'When I succeeded Mr Harold Macmillan as Prime Minister in 1963, an inquisitive journalist sought out our head-keeper and asked him, "What do you know about the Homes?" He was probably bamboozled by the reply: "Oh, the Home boys always seem to know which way the wind blows." Our game-keeper was not thinking of me as a political trimmer, but simply stating a fact of our family life; for my father was a countryman, and a naturalist, and on the right interpretation of wind or weather depended the action of the day.' Compare **when the wind blows**, as in 'When the wind blows the cradle will rock' from the nursery rhyme 'Hush-a-bye, baby', known by *circa* 1765. *When the Wind Blows* is the title of a book (1982) by Raymond Briggs about the aftermath of a nuclear holocaust. There is also the proverb, 'Grass never grows when the wind blows' (known by 1836).

we aim to please Slogan of the sort that used automatically to be inscribed over British shops or any institution offering a service. From the 1920s/30s. Not long after, there arrived the graffito written up in men's urinals: 'We aim to please; you aim, too, please.'

(the) weaker vessel A wife. From 1 Peter 3:7: 'Wives, be in subjection to your husbands . . . husbands, giving honour unto the wife, as unto the weaker vessel.' Hence, *The Weaker Vessel*, title of a book (1984) by Antonia Fraser about 'woman's lot in seventeenth-century England'.

(the) weakest go to the wall A proverbial expression established by the early 16th century. A play, possibly by John Webster, was entitled *Weakest Goeth to the Wall* (1600). For a fanciful origin, see *The Book of Cloyne* (1993): 'Welcome to Cloyne Cathedral [in Ireland] . . . In the middle ages . . . there were no pews . . . [and] possibly the only seating in this part of the building would be around the walls for the benefit of the sick and infirm, hence the well known expression: "The weakest go to the wall".'

weaned on a pickle The American political hostess Alice Roosevelt Longworth (1884–1980) is supposed to have said of Calvin Coolidge that he 'looked as if he had been weaned on a pickle.' In fact, she admitted hearing this from someone else 'at my dentist's office. The last patient had said it to him and I just seized on it. I didn't originate it – but didn't it describe him exactly?' – *The New York Times* (25 February 1980). It first appeared as an 'anonymous remark' quoted in Longworth's *Crowded Hours* (1933).

we are all —— now Format for humorous observations of a social and political bent. Edward VII is supposed to have said, 'We are all socialists nowadays' when, as Prince of Wales, he gave a speech at the Mansion House, London, on 5 November 1895. However, no record exists of him making any such speech on that day. His biographer, Sir Philip Magnus, makes no mention of him doing so either. The *ODQ* dropped the entry after pointing out in the Corrigenda to the 1941 edition that the saying should more correctly be ascribed to Sir William Harcourt (1827–1904). Harcourt is quoted as saying it in *Fabian Essays*, ed. Bernard Shaw (1889) – i.e., six years before the supposed 1895 speech. Harcourt was Lord Rosebery's (Liberal) Chancellor of the Exchequer and an impassioned enemy of the House of Lords. He introduced estate duty tax in his Budget of 1894. Also before Edward VII's supposed speech, Oscar Wilde told an interviewer in the spring of 1894: 'We are all of us more or less Socialists nowadays' – Almy, 'New Views of Mr O. W.' in *Theatre* (1894). After a general election had resulted in no party having a clear majority, Jeremy Thorpe said in a speech to the House of Commons (6 March 1974): 'Looking around the House, one realises that we are all minorities now.'

we are not alone See WATCH THE SKIES.

we are not amused The subject of whether Queen Victoria ever uttered this famous put-down was raised in the *Notebooks of a Spinster Lady* (1919) by Miss Caroline Holland: '[The Queen's] remarks can freeze as well as crystallize . . . there is a tale of the unfortunate equerry who ventured during dinner at Windsor to tell a story with a spice of scandal or impropriety in it. "We are not amused," said the Queen when he had finished.' The equerry in question appears to have been the Honourable Alexander Yorke. Unfortunately, the German he had told the story to laughed so loud that the Queen's attention was drawn to it. Another contender for the snub is Admiral Maxse whom she commanded to give his well-known imitation of her which he did by putting a handkerchief on his head and blowing out his cheeks. Earlier than Miss Holland, J. M. Barrie had alluded to the phrase thus in *The Little White Bird* (1902 – just after Victoria had died): 'He was like the child queen who, when the great joke was explained to her, said coldly, "We are not amused".' The subject was explored in a book (1977) by Alan Hardy entitled *Queen Victoria Was Amused.* Interviewed in 1978, Princess Alice, Countess of Athlone, said she had once asked her grandmother about the phrase and she had denied ever having said it.

we are the masters now! The boast of Sir Hartley Shawcross (later Lord Shawcross), Attorney-General in Britain's first postwar Labour Government, in the House of Commons on 2 April 1946. It might have seemed in poor taste for a Labour minister to crow this. After all, it had been into the mouth of an imperialist that George Orwell had earlier put these words in his novel *Burmese Days* (1934): 'No natives in this Club! It's by constantly giving way over small things like that that we've ruined the Empire . . . The only possible policy is to treat 'em like the dirt they are . . . We've got to hang together and say, "We are the masters, and you beggars . . . keep your place".' So quite why Shawcross did say something like it bears some examination. For a start, it was not said, as one might expect, on the day new Labour MPs swarmed into the House of Commons just after their sweeping election victory in 1945. It was said on 2 April 1946, almost nine months later. Then again, what Shawcross said was, 'We are the masters at the moment' – though understandably the more pungent variant has passed into the language. A look at Hansard reveals precisely why he chose this form of words. He was winding up for the Government in the third reading of the Trade Disputes and Trade Unions Bill and drew attention to what he saw as the Conservative Opposition's lack of support for a measure it had promised to introduce if it won the election: '[We made this an issue at the election] when he invited us to submit this matter to the verdict of the people . . . I realise that the right hon. Member for Woodford [Winston Churchill] is such a master of the English language that he has put himself very much in the position of Humpty-Dumpty in *Alice* . . . "When I use a word," said Humpty-Dumpty, "it means just what I intend it to mean, and neither more nor less." "But," said Alice, "the question is whether you can make a word mean different things." "Not so," said Humpty-Dumpty, "the question is which is to be the master. That's all". We are the masters at the moment, and not only at the moment, but for a very long time to come, and as hon. Members opposite are not prepared to implement the pledge which was given by their leader in regard to this matter at the General Election, we are going to implement it for them.' At the end of the debate, the votes cast were: Ayes 349; Noes 182. When the House met again after the 1950 General Election – at which the Conservatives just failed to oust Labour – Winston Churchill commented: 'I like the appearance of these benches better than what we had to look at during the last four and a half years. It is certainly refreshing to feel, at any rate, that this is a Parliament where half the nation will not be able to ride rough-shod over the other half . . . I do not see the Attorney-General in his place,

but no one will be able to boast "We are the masters now".' So, by this time, the popular version of the words had already emerged.

weary   See ART THOU.

weather   See DELIGHTFUL.

weathermen say (or **warn)**   British journalistic stand-bys. When snow and ice engulf us, 'There's more to come, warn weathermen.' And when sun and heat smother us, 'Make the most of it, say weathermen.' By 1976.

—— weaves its own magic (or **spell)**   Journalistic and promotional cliché. Date of origin not known. 'Wembley may indeed be old and cramped, but it carries capital city clout and there is a certain magic about the place that weaves a spell over players and spectators alike' – *Evening Standard* (London) (7 February 1995); 'Life is relaxed. The living is easy. The warm breeze of Morocco weaves its own magic' – Austin Reed Spring Summer (clothing) catalogue (1995).

web . See CAUGHT IN A.

we bring you melodies from out of the sky – my brother and I   From the signature tune of the British entertainers Bob and Alf Pearson. Bob (1907–86) and Alf (b. 1910) would sing comic songs at the piano and were popular on radio into the 1950s. 'My Brother and I' was used as their bill matter.

we can't go on meeting like this!   Possibly a line taken from a fictional love story where the lovers are able to meet only under difficult conditions but now only used as a joking comment when two non-lovers meet again within a short space of time or encounter each other again in the same unromantic situation like a bus queue or public convenience. Since the 1920s?

weed!   High-pitched and squeaky cry of 'Weed' in the BBC TV series *The Flowerpot Men* (1950s).

(the) weekend starts here   Associated-Rediffusion TV's pop show *Ready, Steady, Go* was transmitted live on Friday evenings in the UK from 1963. This slogan for it was current by 1964. For some reason it stuck, and has been used by other programmes since.

weeks rather than months Meaning, 'sooner rather than later.' For example, 'Sir Simon Gourlay, President of the NFU, said the Government had to restore market confidence in "weeks rather than months", or farmers would go "needlessly out of business"' – *The Independent* (21 May 1990). This echoes the British Prime Minister Harold Wilson's use of the phrase at the Commonwealth Prime Ministers' Conference (January 1966): 'The cumulative effect of . . . sanctions [against Rhodesia] might well bring the rebellion to an end within a matter of weeks rather than months.'

weeping See ALEXANDER.

we have lift-off 'We have made a successful start'. From the announcement made by Mission Control at the start of American space flights (from the 1960s) – meaning that the rocket motors have successfully ignited and that the space vehicle is rising above the launch-pad.

we have met the enemy and he is us (or **they are us)** 'One's own faults are the cause of one's lack of success.' The American cartoonist Walt Kelly's syndicated comic strip featured an opossum called Pogo. This phrase was included in a 1970 Pogo cartoon used on the 1971 Earth Day poster. Kelly had taken some time to get round to this formulation. In his introduction to *The Pogo Papers* (1953), he had earlier written: 'Resolve then, that on this very ground, with small flags waving and tinny blasts on tiny trumpets, we shall meet the enemy, and not only may he be ours, he may be us.'

we have ways (and means) of making you talk The threat by evil inquisitor to victim appears to have come originally from 1930s' Hollywood villains and was then handed on to Nazi characters from the 1940s onwards. Douglass Dumbrille, as the evil Mohammed Khan, says, 'We have ways to make men talk' in the film *The Lives of a Bengal Lancer* (US 1934). He means by forcing slivers of wood under the fingernails and setting fire to them . . . A typical 'film Nazi' use can be found in the film *Odette* (UK 1950) in which the

French Resistance worker (Anna Neagle) is threatened with unmentioned nastiness by one of her captors. Says he: 'We have ways and means of making you talk.' Then, after a little stoking of the fire with a poker, he urges her on with: 'We have ways and means of making a woman talk.' Later, used in caricature, the phrase saw further action in programmes like the BBC radio show *Round the Horne* (e.g. 18 April 1965) and *Laugh-In* (*circa* 1968) – invariably pronounced with a German accent. Frank Muir presented a comedy series for London Weekend Television with the title *We Have Ways of Making You Laugh* (1968).

(a) weighty tome Semi-archaic, for a heavy and/or learned book. Date of origin not known. 'Recently, book store displays were joined by a weighty tome about little grey aliens with blank eyes abducting large numbers of Americans and forcing them to have sex inside spaceships, followed by lectures on ecology' – *Financial Times* (23 July 1994); 'I run from the house, chaotic basket of beach equipment in hand . . . A guilty impulse invariably causes me to snatch some weighty tome with which (in theory) to salve my conscience and (in practice) to muddy the enjoyment of the afternoon' – *The Times Higher Education Supplement* (12 May 1995).

we know where you live Has come to be associated with secret police, protest groups and so on, to the extent that the latest Amnesty International Gala (held in London on 3 June 2001) was entitled *We Know Where You Live. Live!* A story from *The Sunday Press*, Dublin (25 August 1991), neatly establishes what an old phrase this is: 'In case you're wondering what will become of all the unemployed KGB men in the event of a change of regime in the USSR, I was talking to a German friend recently and asked him what had become of all the former Stasi secret policemen of East Germany. "Oh, they're all taxi drivers now," he said. "It was the obvious solution." "Why is that?" I asked. "Simple," he said, "you just give them your name – and they know where you live".' In John Mortimer's memoir *The Summer of a Dormouse*, Chap. 9 (2000), he tells of an answering machine message he received relating to his pro-fox-hunting stance: 'Animal Murderer John Mortimer QC. We know where you live and we're coming to get you.'

well   See ALIVE AND; ALL'S; DIDN'T HE DO.

well, Brian   A phrase associated with British TV sports interviews and post-game analysis – because the interviewer of verbally challenged players and managers on ITV football coverage for many years from 1967 was Brian Moore. However, it may have caught on independently as a result of a sketch on *Monty Python's Flying Circus* (28 December 1969) when a very thick footballer replied either 'Good evening, Brian' or 'Well, Brian' to every question he was asked by a pretentious TV interviewer.

well-deserved rest   See ENJOYING A.

we'll get married just as soon as my divorce comes through   A cliché of seduction, probably more apparent in fiction (and parodies of same) than in real life. Registered as a cliché in *Time* (14 December 1981).

well, he would, wouldn't he?   An innocuous enough phrase but one still used allusively because of the way it was spoken by Mandy Rice-Davies (b. 1944) in 1963. A 'good-time girl' and friend of Christine Keeler's, she was called as a witness when Stephen Ward, the pimp figure in the Profumo Affair (British Secretary of State for War, John Profumo, carried on with Keeler who was allegedly sharing her favours with the Soviet military attaché) was charged under the Sexual Offences Act. During the preliminary Magistrates' Court hearing on 28 June 1963, Rice-Davies was questioned about the men she had had sex with. When told by Ward's defence counsel that Lord Astor – one of the names on the list – had categorically denied any involvement with her, she replied, chirpily: 'Well, he would, wouldn't he?' The court burst into laughter, the expression passed into the language and is still resorted to because – as a good catchphrase ought to be – it is bright, useful in various circumstances and tinged with innuendo. 'Oscar Wilde said the Alps were objects of appallingly bad taste. He

would, wouldn't he,' – Russell Harty, *Mr Harty's Grand Tour* (1988).

well-kept   See FACE LIKE A.

well, now then, sir, Miss Bankhead!
Catchphrase from American radio in the 1930s. Thomas Millstead of Chicago wrote (1993): 'The phrase was used by the composer and orchestra leader Meredith Willson on actress Tallulah Bankhead's radio program *The Big Show* (mid to late 1940s). It was called "big" because it was a one and one-half hour variety show, very long for radio in those days. Mr Willson (who later wrote the famous Broadway show *The Music Man*) led the orchestra and also had many speaking opportunities. Miss Bankhead, of course, had an exceptionally deep voice. Thus Mr Willson's frequently addressing her as "sir".'

welly   See GIVE SOMETHING.

we must stamp out this evil in our midst   Journalistic cliché, in campaigning and editorializing. Date of origin not known. In June 1967 Chris Welch of *Melody Maker* wrote: 'We can expect a deluge of drivel about the new people [proponents of Flower Power, peace and love] any day now from the Sunday papers, with demands to "stamp out this evil in our midst".' So, a cliché by that time. 'For each person who advised taking to drink or moving house, there were at least five victors. The tearful letters and the rants about "the jackboot of ground elder" and the "evil in our midst" were far outweighed by vigorous calls to action' – *The Daily Telegraph* (8 May 1993); 'For it was the ability to look the other way when evil was at liberty in society that allowed the monster to grow in Germany in the thirties. It is no less a danger for us, even if evil in our midst has no uniform and is not organised behind a common banner' – *The Herald* (Glasgow) (31 July 1993).

wen   See MONSTROUS CARBUNCLE.

we name the guilty men   Journalistic and authorial use. *Guilty Men* was the title of a tract 'which may rank as literature' (A. J. P. Taylor). It was written by Michael Foot, Frank Owen and Peter Howard, using the pseudonym 'Cato'. Published in July 1940, it taunted the appeasers who had brought about the situation whereby Britain had had to go to war with Germany. The preface contains this anecdote: 'On a spring day in 1793 a crowd of angry men burst their way through the doors of the assembly room where the French Convention was in session. A discomforted figure addressed them from the rostrum. "What do the people desire?" he asked. "The Convention has only their welfare at heart." The leader of the angry crowd replied, "The people haven't come here to be given a lot of phrases. They demand a dozen guilty men."' The phrase 'We *name* the guilty men' subsequently became a cliché of popular 'investigative' journalism. Equally popular was the similar, 'We name these *evil* men.' 'Like all the best Sunday journalists, I name the guilty men, and one guilty woman, if we include Mrs Shirley Williams' – *The Observer* (16 April 1989); 'In this era of "open government" it is left to Michael Heseltine's department to maintain Whitehall standards and not name the guilty men' – *The Guardian* (23 June 1994); 'Bates is still fuming about the pitch invasion which followed his side's FA Cup defeat by Millwall ten days ago and has appealed to the public to name the guilty men. "There will be no hiding place for these people," he raged. "Not at Chelsea, not at home, and not even in their local pub"' – *Daily Mirror* (18 February 1995).

we never closed A slogan coined by Vivien Van Damm, proprietor of the Windmill Theatre, London – a venerable comedy and strip venue – that was the only West End showplace to remain open during the Blitz in the Second World War. An obvious variant: 'We never clothed.'

we never sleep Slogan of Pinkerton's national detective agency, which opened its first office in Chicago, 1850 (and which – through its open-eye symbol *may* have given us the term 'private eye'). Was there an echo of this in the line chosen to promote US Citibank's new 24-hour service in 1977: 'The Citi Never Sleeps' – apart, that is, from an allusion to *City That Never Sleeps*, the title of a film (US 1953) that was indeed set in Chicago? *Nunquam dormio* [I never sleep] has been used as the motto of various organizations and was

(at some later stage) put under the original open-eye logo of the London *Observer* newspaper (founded 1791).

went the day well? 'Went the day well? / We died and never knew. / But, well or ill, / Freedom, we died for you.' This verse appears as the anonymous epigraph on screen at the start of the 1942 British film *Went the Day Well?* (re-titled *48 Hours* in the USA). At the time the film was released, some thought the lines were a version of a Greek epitaph. Based on a story by Graham Greene, entitled *The Lieutenant Died Last*, the film tells of a typical English village managing to repel Nazi invaders. The epigraph thus presumably refers to the villagers who die defending 'Bramley End'. Penelope Houston in her 1992 British Film Institute monograph on the film describes it as a quotation from an anonymous poem that appeared in an anthology of tributes to people killed in the war to which Michael Balcon, head of Ealing Studios, contributed a memoir of the dead director Pen Tennyson. But the poet was J. M. Edmonds, an English poet and academic (1875–1958). It is said that it was based on a suggestion given him by Sir Arthur Quiller-Couch who in turn got it from a Romanian folksong. The original text was: 'Went the day well? we died and never knew; / But well or ill, England we died for you' – 'On Some who died early in the Day of Battle' in 'Four Epitaphs', published in *The Times* (6 February 1918).

we're all doomed See MANY MANY TIMES.

we really move our tails for you A slogan for Continental Airlines in the USA, current 1975. In that year some of the airline's stewardesses threatened to sue over the 'bad taste' it had shown in selecting this slogan.

we're doomed! From BBC TV's comedy series *Dad's Army* (1968–77). John Laurie as Private Fraser (a Scots undertaker when out of uniform) would wail this, or **doomed I am, doomed**.

we're gay and we're proud See SAY IT LOUD.

we're getting there A rather debatable slogan for British Rail, current 1985. In 1980, the organization had been promoted by the even more questionable **this is the age of the train**, which it undoubtedly wasn't (attracting the comments: 'Yes, it takes an age to catch one', 'Ours was 104', etc.).

we're not worthy See NOT!

we're on a mission from God Line spoken frequently by Dan Aykroyd as Elwood Blues in the film *The Blues Brothers* (US 1980). The eponymous brothers justify their various activities with the suggestion that they are working on behalf of a Mother Superior who has been robbed.

we're with the Woolwich A slogan for the Woolwich Equitable Building Society in the UK. In the late 1970s, there was a series of TV ads that posed the question 'Are you with the Woolwich?' More than most advertising lines, this one managed to work its way into jokes and sketches. Perhaps more correctly rendered as, 'No, I'm with the Woolwich' – in answer to such questions as, 'Are you with me?'

we's all live till we die, unless dogs worries us 'This was used by my mother – a Yorkshire West Riding lady – usually after some minor disaster in the home' – Kit Blease, Merseyside (1992). Anne Gledhill, West Yorkshire, added (1993): 'It was part of my background, too (born and brought up in Dewsbury in the West Riding). My version: "We shall live till we dee – if t'dogs doesn't worry us" (the second part given an ironic twist).' *Apperson* finds this particular expression in *Lancashire Sayings* (1901): 'We shan o live till we dee'n – iv th' dogs dunno wory us', but in Richard Jefferies, *Field and Hedgerow* (1889): 'The old country proverb, "Ah, well, we shall live till we die if the pigs don't eat us, and then we shall go acorning.'

we shall not be moved Chant of defiance. According to *Bartlett* (1980), it came originally from a spiritual (echoing more than one psalm): 'Just like a tree that's standing by the water / We shall not be moved.' Later widely taken up as a song of the Civil Rights' and labour movements in the USA from the 1960s. In the UK, mostly the simple slogan was chanted, not the whole spiritual.

we shall not see his like again. A cliché of obituaries and alluding to Shakespeare, *Hamlet*, I.ii.187 (1600–1), where the Prince says of his late father: 'A was a man, take him for all in all; / I shall not look upon his like again.' Dorothy Parker on Isadora Duncan's book *My Life* in *The New Yorker* (14 January 1928): 'She does not whine, nor seek pity. She was a brave woman. We shall not look upon her like again.' In *Joyce Grenfell Requests the Pleasure* (1976), the actress recalls being rung by the United Press for a comment on the death of Ruth Draper, the monologist: 'My diary records: "I said we should not see her like again. She was a genius." Without time to think, clichés take over and often, because that is why they have become clichés, they tell the truth.' 'And if Khamaseen gallops to a glorious tenth for Lester, those famous, famished features will be wreathed in the biggest smile the old place has ever seen. Khamaseen supporter or not, we wish him nothing less. We will assuredly never see his like again' – *The Sunday Times* (29 May 1994); 'Football: The End Of Rushie: We'll Never See The Like Of This Super Hitman Again Says Emlyn Hughes: Farewell Wembley Appearance For Ian Rush' – headline in the *Sunday Mirror* (2 April 1995).

we shall overcome Phrase from the song that became the main American Civil Rights' anthem of the early 1960s. It originated in pre-Civil War times, was adapted as a Baptist hymn called 'I'll Overcome Some Day' (*circa* 1900) by C. Albert Hindley, and first became famous when sung by Black workers on a picket line in Charleston, South Carolina (1946). In the Spanish Civil War, there was a Republican chant, '*¡venceremos!*', which means the same. Pete Seeger and others added verses, including: 'Oh, deep in my heart, I know that I do believe / We shall overcome some day.'

western front See ALL QUIET.

Westward Ho! Name bestowed on a Devon seaside resort in the 1860s, replacing 'Northam Burrows', despite the misgivings of Charles Kingsley whose novel *Westward Ho!* had been published in 1855. Earlier, there had been a play, *Westward*

Ho!, by Webster and Dekker (*circa* 1600). *Westward Ha! or Around the World in 80 Clichés* was the title of a book (1948) by S. J. Perelman.

wet and warm On being offered a drink, one might say, 'I don't mind what it is, as long as it's wet and warm.' Almost a conversational cliché. *Mencken* cites a 'Dutch proverb': 'Coffee has two virtues: it is wet and warm.' In Kenya, *circa* 1950, there was a saying, 'Wet and warm like a honeymoon in Aden.'

we the people These are the opening words of the Preamble to the 1787 Constitution of the United States: 'We the people of the United States . . . do ordain and establish this Constitution for the United States of America.'

(to) wet one's whistle To take some liquid refreshment. Known by 1611.

we've got a right one 'ere! Towards the end of the run of the BBC radio show *Educating Archie* (1950–60), Dick Emery made his mark as more than one character in the show. As Mr Monty, he would say, 'We've got a right one 'ere!' – a familiar phrase also employed at one time or another by Tony Hancock, Frankie Howerd and Bruce Forsyth. In 1959, as Grimble, Emery was saying, **oh, I was livid – livid I was – I wasn't half livid!**

we will get a result Sporting, especially football, cliché – as in 'If we play, we will get a result'. Modern origin. Professor Harold Carter in a letter to *The Sunday Times* (14 January 1990) wondered: 'Presumably if a game is played a result will ensue. Why has "We will win" disappeared? Or, if only a draw is envisaged, "We will not lose"?'

we wuz robbed! A notable reaction to sporting defeat came from the lips of Joe Jacobs (1896–1940), American manager of the boxer Max Schmeling. Believing his man to have been cheated of the heavyweight title in a fight against Jack Sharkey on 21 June 1932, Jacobs shouted his protest into a microphone – 'We wuz robbed!' Quoted in Peter Heller, *In This Corner* (1975). Compare Jack Dempsey's 'I was robbed of the championship' when defeated controversially by Gene Tunney

in 1927. On another occasion, in October 1935, Jacobs left his sick bed to attend the World Series (ball game) for the one and only time. Having bet on the losers, he opined: **I should of stood in bed**. Quoted in John Lardner, *Strong Cigars and Lovely Women* (1951). Leo Rosten in *Hooray for Yiddish* (1983) puts his own gloss on the expression: 'The most celebrated instance of this usage was when Mike [*sic*] Jacobs, the fight promoter, observing the small line at his ticket window, moaned, "I should of stood in bed!" *Stood* is a calque for the Yiddish *geshtanen*, which can mean both "stood" and "remained". Mr Jacobs' use of "of" simply followed the speech pattern of his childhood.'

wham, bam, thank you ma'am! Phrase representing the style of a man who heartlessly and/or perfunctorily has sex with a woman and then throws her over. Probably from American forces' use in the 1940s.

what about the workers?! Usually written 'Wot abaht . . .', this is the traditional proletarian heckler's cry during a political speech. It is almost a slogan in its own right but is now only used satirically. It occurs along with other rhetorical clichés during the 'Party Political Speech' (written by Max Schreiner) on the Peter Sellers's comedy album *The Best of Sellers* (1958). Also in the 1950s, Harry Secombe as Neddie Seagoon on the BBC radio *Goon Show* would sometimes exclaim (for no very good reason), 'Hello, folks, and what about the workers?!' Later, in the 1970s BBC TV *Morecambe and Wise Show*, Eric Morecambe incorporated it in a nonsense phrase of sexual innuendo when referring to 'a touch of hello-folks-and-what-about-the-workers!' In a TV programme to mark his hundredth birthday (1984), Manny Shinwell, the veteran Labour MP, appeared to be claiming that he had been asking 'What about the workers?' – seriously – in 1904, but whether he meant literally or figuratively wasn't clear. He told John Mortimer in *Character Parts* (1986): 'I remember Bonar Law, future Prime Minister and Conservative Member of Parliament for the Gorbals, giving a speech in Glasgow, and it was all about Free Trade or something and they were applauding him! Unemployed men were applauding Bonar Law! So I shouted out, "What about the workers!" . . . I got my picture in the papers.'

what a difference a day makes!   Almost proverbial, yet not listed in any proverb books. The phrase either expresses surprise at someone's rapid recovery from a mood that has laid them low or expresses the old thought that time is a great healer. Did it begin in a song? 'What a Difference a Day *Made*' was a hit for Esther Phillips in 1975 (though adapted from a Mexican lyric in 1934).

what a dump!   Exclamation at the poor condition of a dwelling or of a town. It was used by Bette Davis in *Beyond the Forest* (US 1949) in which she plays the discontented wife of a small-town doctor, has an affair and comes to a sticky end. She also says of the small town: 'If I don't get out of here, I'll just die! Living here is like waiting for the funeral to begin.' This use is memorably quoted by Elizabeth Taylor in the film of Edward Albee's *Who's Afraid of Virginia Woolf?* (US 1966) as coming from a Bette Davis movie. Indeed, a discussion of the phrase's film origins also occupies the opening minutes of the stage play (1962). Even earlier, the phrase had already been used in Otto Preminger's film *Fallen Angel* (US 1945). Dana Andrews, suspected of murdering Linda Darnell, holes up in a seedy San Francisco hotel with his wife. Andrews exclaims, 'What a dump!' without, it must be admitted, the memorably explosive consonants of both Miss Davis and Miss Taylor. But how much farther back can we take the phrase? *Partridge/Catch Phrases* with his famously iffy dating suggests *circa* 1919. A more definite indication comes from Eugene O'Neill's play *Ah Wilderness!* where at III.i.84 there occurs a 'Christ, what a dump!' That was in 1933.

what a name to go to bed with!   Comment on an unusual name – but not intended as a proposition, despite the experience of Mrs D. M. Heigham of Aldershot, Hampshire (1994): 'It was New Year's Eve 1943. I was a Cypher Officer W.R.N.S. on watch at midnight. I was introduced to a man called Worthington Edridge. "Oh," I said, "What a name to go to bed with" (current remark at the time). He said, "Nobody asked you." I don't think you can beat that for a put-down.' *Partridge/Slang* has '. . . a *nice* name to go to bed with' – meaning 'an ugly name' – dating from 1887 and compares the French expression '*un nom à coucher dehors*'.

what a performance!   Catchphrase of the British comedian Sid Field (1904–50), spoken in 'sullen, flattened tones'. Used as the title of a play celebrating Field, written by William Humble and featuring David Suchet in the old routines (London 1994).

what are the wild waves saying?   This is the title of a Victorian song with words by J. E. Carpenter and music by Stephen Glover: 'What are the wild waves saying, / Sister, the whole day long: / That ever amid our playing, / I hear but their low, lone song?' The song is a duet between Paul and Florence Dombey and based on an incident in *Dombey and Son* (1848) by Charles Dickens. Nowhere in the novel does Dickens use the words, 'What are the *wild* waves saying?' though the book is fairly awash with the idea of a 'dark and unknown sea that rolls round all the world' (Chap. 1). The title of Chapter 16 is 'What the Waves were always saying'. An advertisement for Igranic wireless coils, dating from the early 1920s, plays upon the idea of radio waves and asks, 'What are the wild waves saying?'

what are you doing after the show?   A chat-up line, presumably of show-business origin. *What Are You Doing After the Show?* was the title of a long-forgotten British ITV comedy show (1971). The previous year's Swedish film *Rötmanad* had been given the English title *What Are You Doing After the Orgy?*

what a smell of broken glass!   'When driving in the country pre-war, with its appropriate smells around farms, my father always used to say this' – Jocelyn Linter, Essex (1998). *Partridge/Slang* has 'smell of broken glass – a strong body-odour, e.g. in a Rugby footballers' changing-room after a game . . . earlier C20' and compares 'there's a smell of gunpowder – someone has broken wind, late C19.' But how does glass come into it? Patrick Hughes (2002) suggested that 'broken glass' was a form of Cockney rhyming slang for 'the smell of my dirty arse'.

what a turn-up for the book(s)! See TURN-UP FOR THE BOOKS.

what a way to run a —— See THAT'S A HELL OF A WAY.

what a world it is for woossit (or **worsted)** Mrs F. Smith of Adel, Leeds, wrote (1994): 'I had a country-bred Grandmother and her sayings are now part of family lore. One, especially, was "What a world it is for woossit, and nobody knows how to knit" (and all are baffled by the word "woossit").' Vera Geddis of Eastleigh, Hampshire, misheard this last as 'What a world this is for *worsted*' and was reminded of a saying of her mother's: **what a world this is for worsted, four- teen balls of cotton for a penny!** She added: 'I cannot recall my mother ever explaining her saying – I am not certain whether the number of balls was fourteen or sixteen – but I assume that the point of it was that when tempted to bewail the state of the world, one cheered oneself up by changing it into a statement about the amazing cheapness of worsted.' Indeed, Wright's *English Dialect Dictionary* (*circa* 1900) gives 'worset' as a form of 'worsted', so there seems to be more than the glimmer of an explanation here.

what becomes a legend most? Slogan for Blackglama mink in the USA, current 1976. This was the headline from a series of advertisements showing mink coats being worn by dozens of 'legendary' figures, including the likes of Margot Fonteyn, Martha Graham, Rudolf Nureyev (all three together in one ad), Shirley Maclaine, Ethel Merman and Lillian Hellman.

what did Gladstone say in ——? A good-humouredly meaningless heckle aimed at political speakers in the late 19th/early 20th century. J. B. Priestley in his *English Journey* (1934) chooses '1884' to complete the catchphrase.

what did Horace say? Harry Hemsley was a British entertainer who found fame as that contradiction in terms, a radio ventriloquist (though Edgar Bergen was to

have great success on American radio with 'Charlie McCarthy' and Peter Brough had 'Archie Andrews'). He first broadcast in 1923 and was still going in 1949. Hemsley conducted dialogues with his family – two girls, Winnie and Elsie, a boy, Johnny, and a baby, Horace, who spoke gibberish that only Winnie could translate. Hence, 'what did Horace say?'

what did you do in the Great War, Daddy? Catchphrase version of a slogan used on recruiting posters in the First World War. The actual wording was: 'Daddy, what did YOU do in the Great War?' and the accompanying picture showed an understandably appalled family man puzzling over what to reply to the daughter on his knee. It gave rise to such responses as 'Shut up, you little bastard. Get the Bluebell and go and clean my medals', according to *Partridge/Catch Phrases*. 'What did you do in the Great War, Daddy?' was the title of a monologue (recounting actually what various other people did), written by Greatrex Newman and Tom Clare (1919). *What Did You Do in the War, Daddy?* was the title of a film (US 1966).

what do we do now? / we wait Catchphrase from films – as in *Rough Cut* (US 1980), *Beverley Hills Cop* (US 1984) and *Ghost* (US 1990) (where the line is changed to 'Just wait'). The exchange seems to have been routinely written into episodes of TV crime series for decades. It was used in *The Professionals* and in a 1967 episode of *The Champions*. Inevita-bly, the exchange *does* appear in Samuel Beckett's play *Waiting for Godot* (1954), in the form: *Vladimir*: 'What do we do now?' *Estragon*: 'Wait.'

what do women want? 'The great question that has never been answered and which I have not yet been able to answer, despite my thirty years of research into the feminine soul, is "What does a woman want?"' – Sigmund Freud in a letter to Marie Bonaparte, quoted in Ernest Jones, *Sigmund Freud: Life and Work* (1955). The question became a rallying cry in the resurgence of feminism from the 1970s onwards. *What Do Women Want? Exploding the Myth of Dependency* was the title of a book by Luise Eichenbaum and

Susie Orbach (1983). The same question is posed to the protagonist of Chaucer's 'The Wife of Bath's Tale' when the answer is: 'Wommen desiren to have sovereynetee / As wel over hir housbond as hir love, / And for to been in maistrie hym above.'

(well) what do you know! Exclamation on being told something inevitable and not at all surprising, or something far-fetched. Perhaps originally a straightforward inquiry along the lines of 'What's new?' 'Then you can laugh, and call out to a neighbor, or even to the man's wife: "Hey, what do you know? Steve here thinks he's going to get some corn up in this soil!"' – Robert Benchley, *Love Conquers All*, 'Watching a Spring Planting' (1923). *What Do You Know* was the title of a BBC radio 'programme of problems and brain-teasers' (1953–67). It eventually turned into *Brain of Britain*. The title sequence included some interesting facts, followed by the query, 'Well, what do you know? What do *you* know . . .' An earlier series with the same title (which started in 1951) was a transatlantic quiz between British and American universities.

what do you think of the show so far? / rubbish! Eric Morecambe's customary inquiry of audiences animate or inanimate on BBC TV's *The Morecambe and Wise Show* (1968–77) – and their response. He said he got the idea from his family, and it was first put into a famous sketch about Antony and Cleopatra (featuring Glenda Jackson) in 1971. Eric recalled (1980): 'I said it during rehearsals in a sketch with a ventriloquist's dummy. It got such a laugh that we kept it in . . . but it's bounced back on me more than once. When I was a director of Luton Town, I dreaded going to see away games. If we were down at half time, home fans would shout up to me, "What do you think of it so far?"'

whatever else it will be, it will be well and truly – all your own BBC TV's *All Your Own* in the 1950s was a showcase for young viewers who had some interesting hobby and could be seen to enjoy themselves doing it. Introduced by an avuncular Huw Wheldon, the programme would close with him looking forward to the next edition and intoning these words.

whatever happened to ——? Journalistic question. The original type of conversational query occurs in Noël Coward's song 'I Wonder What Happened to Him?' – from *Sigh No More* (1945) – in the form, 'Whatever became of old Bagot . . . ?' But the film title *Whatever Happened to Baby Jane?* (1962) fixed the phrase in the way most usually employed by journalists. Like WHERE ARE THEY NOW?, this became a standard formula for feature-writing on a slack day. In the early 1980s, the *Sunday Express* ran a weekly column disinterring the stars of yesteryear, sometimes under the heading 'Where are they now . . . ?' but more usually, 'What ever happened to . . . ?' *Whatever Happened to . . . ? The Great Rock and Pop Nostalgia Book* – title of a book by Howard Elson and John Brunton (1981); 'Whatever Happened to Romance?' – advertising line for Coty Perfume (*circa* 1983).

whatever turns you on Latterly a jokey response to the announcement of some (slightly odd or, conceivably, sexy) enthusiasm. 'I like bathing in warm ass's milk' – 'Whatever turns you on, dear.' Originally, in the 1960s, it was part of an encouragement to pursue one's own enthusiasms, particularly with regard to the drugs that succeeded in 'turning you on' best: 'You should do whatever turns you on.'

what fresh hell is this? Exclamation when confronted by some horror of modern life or even minor but irritating things, e.g. rain, crowds of people, etc. Very much associated with Dorothy Parker. A book *about* her was indeed given the title *What Fresh Hell Is This?* by Marion Meade in 1988. This derives from what Parker would say on hearing the door bell or telephone ringing – although Vincent Sheean, a foreign correspondent, quoted by John Keats in his Parker biography, *You Might As Well Live*, Chap. 7 (1970), remembered, rather, that, 'If the doorbell rang in her apartment, she would say "What fresh hell *can this be*?" – and it wasn't funny; she meant it.' If Parker herself was quoting, a search through Shakespeare turns up nothing. Nor does the phrase occur in *The Duchess of Malfi* or *The White Devil* (although the latter has 'O me! this place is hell').

what in the Sam Hill . . . ? What in Hell's name . . . ? This euphemistic expression enrols the name of Sam Hill, a 19th-century American politician, to avoid having to say the worst. Known since the early 20th century. 'Characters [in 1936 production] are given to Will Rogerisms like "What in Sam Hills is the matter with her?" and "Creeping Jesus!" (which got them into hot water with the censors)' – Simon Callow, *Orson Welles: The Road to Xanadu* (1995); 'What the Sam Hill you yelling for, George?' – film soundtrack, *It's A Wonderful Life* (US 1946).

what is a Mum? See WHITER THAN WHITE.

what larks, Pip! Exclamation derived from the novel *Great Expectations* (1860–61) by Charles Dickens. It is a characteristic phrase of Joe Gargery, the blacksmith who looks after his brother-in-law and apprentice, Pip, in the boy's youth. Chapter 13 has him saying 'calc'lated to lead to larks' and Chapter 57, 'And when you're well enough to go out for a ride – what larks!' The recent use of the phrase probably has more to do with the 1946 film of the book in which Bernard Miles played Joe. As he sees Pip off on a stage coach, he says, 'One day I'll come to see you in London and then, what larks, eh?' and similarly, after Pip's breakdown, 'You'll soon be well enough to go out again, and then – what larks!' Even here, the name Pip is not actually included in the phrase. In *The Kenneth Williams Diaries* (1993) – entry for 30 August 1970 – the actor writes: 'Tom played the piano and all the girls danced with us & I stuck me bum out and oh! what larks Pip!' Ned Sherrin dedicates his *Theatrical Anecdotes* (1991), 'For Judi [Dench] and Michael [Williams]: "What larks!"'

what me – in my state of health? Catchphrase of Charles Atlas (Fred Yule) from the BBC radio show *ITMA* (1939–49).

what, me worry? Catchphrase of Alfred E. Newman, the cheerfully ignorant character in the US magazine *Mad* (founded 1952).

what price ――? Format phrase, questioning the sacrifices and compromises that may be made in order to carry out any sort of mission. Known by 1893. From

George Bernard Shaw, *Major Barbara* (1907): 'What prawce Selvytion nah?' The phrase was firmly established by *What Price Glory?* – the title of a play about the stupidity of war, by Laurence Stallings and Maxwell Anderson (1924; film US 1952). *What Price Hollywood?* was the title of a film (US 1932).

what's a nice girl like you doing in a joint like this (or **place . . .)?** Cliché of conversation/chatting up and now used only in a consciously arch way. It is listed among the 'naff pick-up lines' in *The Naff Sex Guide* (1984). Did it first arise in Hollywood Westerns of the 1930s? It was certainly established as a film cliché by the 1950s when Frank Muir and Denis Norden included this version in a *Take It From Here* parody on BBC radio: 'Thanks, Kitty. Say, why does a swell girl like you have to work in a saloon like this?' In the film *Kiss Me Stupid* (US 1964) Dean Martin retells a joke: 'There was the one about this doctor, you see. He was examining a girl's knee and he said, "What's a joint like this doing in a pretty girl like you?"' – thus 'reducing the age-old seducer's spiel, while telling the same old story' – as Walter Redfern comments in *Puns* (1984). James Bond says it more or less straight to Helga Brandt in *You Only Live Twice* (UK 1967). In 1973, *Private Eye* carried a cartoon of a male marijuana-smoker with a female, and the caption, 'What's a nice joint like you . . . ?'

what's bred in the bone Meaning 'what's part of one's nature', this was the title of a novel (1985) by Robertson Davies, who cited 'what's bred in the bone will not out of the flesh' as an 'English proverb from the Latin, 1290'. The implication is that one's nature can't be repressed or cured. An English Midlands' version is 'What's bred in the bone comes out in the marrow' and, from County Durham, 'What's bred in the bone can't be brayed [beaten] out of the flesh.'

what's it all about? 'What is the meaning of life?' T. S. Eliot's widow, Valerie, wrote a letter to *The Times* (7 February 1970) telling a tale that the poet himself 'loved to recount'. A taxi-driver had said to the poet, 'You're T. S. Eliot . . . I've got an eye for a celebrity. Only the other evening I picked up Bertrand Russell . . . And I asked him, "What's it all about, guv?" – and, d'you know, he couldn't tell me!' The phrase gained additional resonance from its use in Bill Naughton's *Alfie*, the 1966 film script of his stage and radio play: 'It seems to me if they ain't got you one way then they've got you another. So what's it all about, that's what I keep asking myself, what's it all about?' Subsequently, the phrase 'What's it all about, Alfie?' was popularized by Burt Bacharach and Hal David's song of that title. This was not written for the film, which had a jazz score, with no songs, by Sonny Rollins, but Cher recorded it and this version was added to the soundtrack for the American release of the picture. Cilla Black then recorded it in Britain and Dionne Warwick in the USA. When Michael Caine, who played Alfie in the film, published his autobiography in 1992, it was naturally entitled *What's It All About?* – as was Cilla Black's in 2003.

what's new, pussycat?   Of Warren Beatty, the film actor, Sheilah Graham wrote in *Scratch an Actor* (1969): 'He uses the telephone as a weapon of seduction. He curls up with it, cuddles it, whispers into it, "What's new, pussycat?" (He coined the phrase, and the picture was originally written for him.)' The film with the title (and the Tom Jones's song therefrom) came out in 1965. Perhaps Graham was right. Whatever the case, one would guess that the use of 'pussycat' to describe someone, particularly a woman, as 'attractive, amiable, submissive' (*OED2*) probably emanates from the USA, if not precisely from Hollywood.

what's that got to do with the ——?
Meaning, 'what you have just said is irrelevant.' 'What has that to do with Bacchus?' which *Brewer* (1894) finds in classical literature. 'T. S. Eliot at one point said he doubted that Mr Coward had ever spent one hour in the study of ethics; "What has that got to do with the price of eggs?" Noel wanted to know' – Cole Lesley, *The Life of Noel Coward*, Chap. 15 (1976). Sir Joh Bjelke-Peterson, Premier of Queensland, was reported in *The Australian* (1 May 1985) as saying of something he thought was irrelevant, 'That's got nothing to do with the price of butter.'

'What's that got to do with the price of carrots?' – Nigel Rees, *The Gift of the Gab* (1985). 'What's that got to do with the Prince of Wales?' – told on an LBC radio phone-in, London (1990), but otherwise untraced and unconfirmed. And which Prince of Wales was being talked about, unless this is a simple price/prince play on words? *Partridge/Catch Phrases* has 'What's that got to do with the price of eggs?' as being of American origin. Indeed, it is uttered in the film *While You Were Sleeping* (US 1998). 'When my children were young and far from clean and tidy, I would say, "The state of you and the price of fish!"' – Patricia Harrison, Hertfordshire (1999). 'What's that got to do with the price of fish?' – Jane Bird, North Yorkshire (2000) quoting a friend. 'When I was a child in Canada, the expression commonly used was, "What's that got to do with the price of tea in China?"' – Reg Norman, Somerset (2000).

what's that man *for*?   'Mummy, what's that man *for*?' is the caption to a cartoon in *Punch* Magazine, Vol. 131 (14 November 1906). Drawn by F. H. Townsend, who was art editor of the magazine at the time, it shows the remark being made by a small boy to his mother about a man carrying a bag of golf clubs. This is probably the origin of the widely used jibe, 'What is that lady/gentleman *for*?' – a remark, out of the mouth of a not-quite babe or suckling, which becomes a convenient stick with which to beat anyone the speaker wishes to reduce in importance. It is particularly useful when taunting politicians. For example, 'It was an anonymous little girl who, on first catching sight of Charles James Fox, is supposed to have asked her mother: "what is that gentleman for?" One asks the same question of Mr [Douglas] Hurd. Why is he where he is in this particular government? He has never been wholly in sympathy either with Mrs Thatcher or with her version of Conservatism.' – Alan Watkins, *The Observer* (29 May 1988). Compare 'I am reminded of the small boy who once pointed at Hermione Gingold and asked, "Mummy, what's that lady for?"' – Michael Billington (possibly quoting Kenneth Tynan) in *The Guardian* (21 July 1988). This is probably what

Russell Harty refers to in *Mr Harty's Grand Tour*, Chap. 2 (1988): 'It reminds me of the story one rather famous English actress tells about herself. She was, she says, sitting in a railway carriage . . . A child opposite stared at her for quite a time and then turned to the accompanying mother and said, "What's that lady for?"' '"What," a little girl is supposed to have asked her mother, pointing at Sir John Simon, a pre-war Chancellor, "is that man for?" What, she might now ask, pointing at the Labour faithful assembling in Brighton today, is that party for?' – editorial in the *Independent on Sunday* (29 September 1991).

what's that when it's at home?　Question asked about an unusual name, for example. *Partridge/Catch Phrases* has this as a tag 'implying either derision or incredulity' and has a citation from 1914.

what's the damage?　Phrase used when asking how much the bill is (e.g. for drinks) or establishing who should pay it. *The Hallamshire Glossary* by the Reverend Joseph Hunter (b. 1784) records that this was in common use in the Sheffield area between 1790 and 1810. In fact, the *OED2* has the word 'damage' = 'cost, expense' in 1755, and in 1852, 'What's the damage, as they say in Kentucky' appears in Harriet Beecher Stowe's *Uncle Tom's Cabin* (though not concerning drink). Presumably, the use derives from legal damages.

what's the recipe today?　See MORNING ALL.

what's up, doc?　The characteristic inquiry of Bugs Bunny, the cartoon character, in the US film series that ran from 1937 to 1963, addressed to Elmer Fudd, the doctor who devotes his life to attempting to destroy the rabbit. In full, the phrase is 'Er, what's up, Doc?' followed by a carrot crunch. Its origins may lie in an old Texan expression introduced to the films by one of the animators, Tex Avery. The voices of both Bugs and Elmer were done by Mel Blanc (1908–89) who, on emerging from a coma in 1983, inevitably put the question to his physician. The phrase was used as the title of a film starring Barbra Streisand and Ryan O'Neal (US 1972).

what the butler saw　'What the Butler Saw' was the name given to a type of penny-in-the-slot machine introduced in Britain *circa* 1880. It was a frisky development of the very old peep show. The female so observed was probably doing something fairly mild in corsets and, if this was an early version of soft porn, it wasn't exactly decadent. The Museum of the Moving Image in London contains a Mutoscope as invented by Herman Casler in 1897 and links it to the arrival of 'What the Butler Saw', although there had been earlier machines through which pictures on cards were flipped to give an impression of movement. The museum notes that these penny-in-the-slot machines were in Britain for some seventy years, finally disappearing with the arrival of decimal coinage in 1971. *What the Butler Saw* was used as the title of a comedy first performed at Wyndham's Theatre on 2 August 1905. An advertising postcard for the show shows a girl complaining to her parents, 'My dolly has been and broke itself!' which suggests that any butler in the piece was unlikely to have had his voyeuristic urge gratified. S. J. Perelman referred in one of his *New Yorker* pieces (reprinted 1978) to 'those penny-arcade tableaux called "What the Butler Saw Through the Keyhole"' which, presumably, indicates that the machines were known in the USA. *What the Butler Saw* was again used as a title by Joe Orton for his posthumously produced farce about goings-on in a psychiatric clinic (1969). In this play, a butler definitely makes no appearance, though the characters do tend to wander about in their underpants, or less. Other uses include: as the title for an instrumental number recorded by Lord Rockingham's XI (in 1958) and for a song recorded by Squeeze (in 1980). Very much earlier than both these, Florrie Forde, the music-hall star, recorded a song called 'What the Curate Saw', which is clearly an allusion. An unlikely, though entertaining, suggestion about the phrase's origin concerns the spectacularly naughty 1884 judicial separation of Lord and Lady Colin Campbell, in which the case hinged on the evidence of a butler who claimed he saw goings-on through a keyhole. Piers Compton in his book *Victorian Vortex* (1977) describes how Lord Colin, son of the Duke of Argyll, accused his wife of adultery with any number of chaps ranging from members of the aristocracy to the chief of the Metropolitan Fire Brigade. At the trial, Lady C. countered that the husband had seduced her maid, and it was the maid, not the butler, who, in turn, testified that she had spied upon her Ladyship and the fire chief *in flagrante*. 'At that,' Compton informs us, 'the jury streamed out of the box and tramped to the Campbell residence in Cadogan Square, where they took turns in applying their judicial eyes to the keyhole, to see if the maid could have indeed witnessed such a *coup de théâtre* . . .' 'What the Butler Didn't See' – headline to book review in *The Observer* (20 May 1989).

what the dickens! Exclamation of incredulity. 'Dickens' has nothing to do with the novelist but is a euphemistic way of saying 'What the *devil!*' (and is perhaps a watered-down version of 'devilkin', though that is not certain). Shakespeare has, 'I cannot tell what the dickens his name is' in *The Merry Wives of Windsor*, III.ii.16 (1601).

what the punters want Business and journalistic phrase, referring to purchasers of goods, newspapers, tickets for various forms of entertainment. Date of origin unknown. Identified as a current cliché in *The Times* (17 March 1995). 'The punters were well pleased . . . [but] as far as I was concerned I played crap that night' – *Record Mirror* (7 May 1977); 'This, after all their radical predictions and experiments, is what constitutes a brand-new house as we head towards the start of the third millennium but it is what the punters want, although the punters have little choice anyway' – *The Sunday Times* (12 February 1995); 'For Duncan, his gizmo is pure fantasy. "It is what the punters want," he declared. "There are 2000 people looking up at you – they want something larger than life"' – *The Guardian* (18 May 1995).

what the well-dressed —— is wearing General clothing – and fashion journalistic – slogan in the UK/USA, since 1900? Nowadays an ironical subject like 'tramp' or 'cart horse' is inserted where once something like 'man about town' might have been in a tailor's or couturier's advertisement. Applied to any eccentric or scruffy choice of clothing, by the mid-20th century. 'I had always had a soft spot in my heart for *Milady's Boudoir* ever since I contributed that article to it on What the Well-Dressed Man is Wearing' – P. G. Wodehouse, *Right Ho, Jeeves*, Chap. 7 (1934); 'What the well-dressed expectant mother is wearing this year' – Shelagh Delaney, *A Taste of Honey*, Act 2, Scene 2 (1958).

what —— thinks today, —— will think tomorrow Manchester was the original city nominated as the thought-setter for England as a whole when, in the 19th century, it was indeed a hub of industrial activity and innovation and the capital of free trade. The saying may date back to the 1840s. Quoting it in *English Journey* (1934), J. B. Priestley added: 'We still see some of the results . . . of what Manchester thought in what has been left to us, to mourn over, by the vast, greedy, slovenly, dirty process of industrialization for quick profits.' *Punch* (22 January 1913) joked 'What Manchester squeaks today, &c.' On the other hand, *Notes and Queries* in 1908 discussed the phrase as 'What Lancashire thinks (or says) today, England will think (or say) tomorrow' and also found 'What Birmingham says today, England will say tomorrow'. *Punch* (18 September 1918) has the caption to a cartoon: 'What Lancashire gives you to-day, she looks to you to give to Europe to-morrow.' Whatever the place mentioned, the formula was obviously a truism by 1897 when Rudyard Kipling put in *The Jungle Book*: 'What the *Bandar-log* think now the jungle will think later.' The earliest appearance found so far is in a speech by M. E. Grant Duff MP at a Liberal election campaign meeting in Great Harwood, Lancashire, on 8 August 1868: 'What Lancashire thinks today, England thinks tomorrow.' This was reported in the *Manchester Guardian* two days later.

what we've got here is failure to communicate In the film *Cool Hand Luke* (US 1967), Strother Martin (as a prison officer) says to Paul Newman (as a rebellious prisoner), 'What we've got here is failure to communicate. Some men you just can't reach.' The line was also used to promote the film.

what would you do, chums? Catchphrase from the BBC radio show *Band Waggon* (1938–39). A regular feature was a tale told by the actor Syd Walker (1887–1945) in the character of a junkman. He would pose some everyday dilemma and end with this query – or a variation upon it. It was used as the title of a film in 1939. George Orwell in his essay on 'The Art of Donald McGill' (1942) mentions a comic postcard he had seen that showed Hitler 'with the usual hypertrophied backside' bending down to pick a flower. The caption was: 'What would *you* do, chums?' 'It is wiser for us not to attack the Government too hard at this moment. The people are sick of the Government, anyway . . . What they want is a clear answer to the question: "What would you do, chum?"' – Tony Benn's diary entry for 23 January 1958, published in *Years of Hope* (1994).

wheel See DON'T SPEAK; HAD ONE OF THOSE.

(the) wheel has come full circle (or **turned . . .)** The origin is plainly a passage in Shakespeare, *King Lear*, V.iii.173 (1605) in which Edmund the Bastard says, 'The wheel is come full circle', referring to the wheel of Fortune, being at that moment back down at the bottom where he was before it began to revolve. 'I turned on the wireless and heard the official announcement of Italy's declaration of war on Germany. So now the wheel has turned full circle' – Chips Channon MP's diary entry for 13 October 1943, published in *Chips: The Diaries of Sir Henry Channon* (1967); *Full Circle* – title of memoirs by Sir Anthony Eden (1960); 'The Vixen in Hytner's production is caught by the Forester as a cub while she is entranced watching a dragonfly; at the end, another cub is doing the same. So it comes full circle . . . It was full circle, too, for some of us at Covent Garden on Tuesday when the original four-act version of Britten's Billy Budd returned there for the first time since it was toured in 1952, six months after its world premiere' – *The Sunday Telegraph* (4 June 1995); 'But we could come full circle. Twenty years after Britain voted clearly in favour of being part of Europe, pressure is growing to involve all the Union's voters in a referendum on whatever proposed changes come out of the IGC' – *The Scotsman* (5 June 1995); 'With this, the wheel my father started comes full circle. His mild hero-worship for the likes of PV Doyle has been turned upside down' – *The Irish Times* (5 June 1995).

whelk-stall See COULDN'T RUN A.

when all is said and done . . . Known by the mid-19th century in the USA. Identified as a current cliché in *The Times* (17 March 1995). *When All Is Said and Done* – title of autobiography (1962) by Rose Franken (popular novelist of the 'Claudia' books); 'And when all is said and done, that [cricket] cap belongs to all of us. The England team of our imaginations, of our dreams, represents the whole of England from the top to the bottom' – *The Sunday Times* (31 July 1994); 'To spice up the winter go for a little bit of animal. PVC may be doing a turn with the under 25s but when all is said and done it is very sticky, hot and uncomfortable' – *The Herald* (Glasgow) (20 September 1994).

when are you going to finish off that dress? Cliché used in chatting up, flirting. Addressed to a woman with low *décolletage*. Tom Jones can be heard so addressing a member of the audience on the record album *Tom Jones – Live at Caesar's Palace, Las Vegas* (1971).

when did you stop beating your wife? An example of a leading question (because by attempting to start answering it you admit that you *did* once beat your wife). So, an example, too, of an unanswerable question?

when in Rome – do as the Romans do This maxim suggests that one should adapt to prevalent customs. Its probable source is St Ambrose (d. 397): '*Si fueris Romae, Romano vivito more; / Si fueris alibi, vivito sicut ibi*[if you are at Rome, live in the Roman style; if you live elsewhere, live as they live elsewhere].'

when it's night-time in Italy, it's Wednesday over here Title of a nonsense song written by the Americans James Kendis and Lew Brown in about 1923. It includes the nonsense riddles, 'Why does a fly? When does a bee?/How does a wasp sit down to have its tea?'

when I was in Patagonia ...   A regular participant in the BBC radio *Brains Trust* discussions of the 1940s was Commander A. B. Campbell. His stock phrase arose in an earlier version of the programme when it was still called *Any Questions* (in 1941). Donald McCullough, the chairman, said: 'Mr Edwards of Balham wants to know if the members of the Brains Trust agree with the practice of sending missionaries to foreign lands.' Professor Joad and Julian Huxley gave their answers and then Campbell began, 'When I was in Patagonia . . .' In a book that used the phrase as its title, Campbell recalled: 'I got no further, for Joad burst into a roar of laughter and the other members of the session joined in. For some time the feature was held up while the hilarity spent itself. For the life of me I could not see the joke . . . Even today (1951), years after, I can raise a laugh if I am on a public platform and make an allusion to it.'

when I was in Poona ...   Phrase typical of an old British India hand. Included in *Partridge/Catch Phrases* as 'Gad, sir, when I was in Poona'. It can be found in the story 'Reginald' (1901) by 'Saki' as, 'When I was at Poona in '76 . . .'

when one door closes another door closes   A cynical variant (heard in 1969) of the old 'Irish proverb' (according to *Mencken*), 'God never shuts one door but He opens another.' Whether Irish or not, *CODP* has it as already proverbial by 1586. The cynical variant also comes – perhaps more usually – in the form **as one door closes, another door shuts**.

when people are starving in India ...   Nanny's phrase encouraging little people to eat up their food, though the nearest thing recorded in *Casson/Grenfell* (1972) is, 'Think of all the poor starving children who'd be grateful for that nice plain bread and butter.' Wasn't it also advised that it was polite to leave a little food on the side of the plate 'for the starving in India' if not for 'Mr Manners'? Paul Beale in *Partridge/Catch Phrases*, commenting on the American phrase 'Remember the starving Armenians', notes: 'The one used to exhort me as a child, late 1930s, to clear up my plate or to tackle something I found unpalatable was "think of all the poor starving children

in China!"' According to *The Complete Directory to Prime Time Network TV Shows* (1981), when a proposed US series called *B.A.D. Cats* crashed in 1980, Everett Chambers, its executive producer, said, 'We bought $40,000 worth of cars to smash up, and we never got a chance to smash them up. I think that's kind of immoral, $40,000 worth of cars to smash up when people are starving in India.'

when push comes to shove   At the critical moment, when action must back up words, when matters become serious or crucial. When you really have to start imposing your will and where 'push' is seen as less forceful than 'shove'. Known in the USA by 1958. Especially in American business language of the 1970s. 'We used to say rude things about them and they used to say rude things about us but, when push came to shove, they waded in when we were in the shit and I've got to thank them for it' – *The Independent* Magazine (9 September 1995).

when the going gets tough, the tough get going   One of several axioms said to have come from the Boston-Irish political jungle or, more precisely, from President Kennedy's father, Joseph P. Kennedy (1888–1969). At this distance, it is impossible to say for sure whether this wealthy, ambitious businessman/ambassador/ politician originated the expression, but he certainly instilled it in his sons. Subsequently, it was used as a slogan for the film *The Jewel of the Nile* (US 1985), and a song with the title sung by Billy Ocean and the stars of the film was a No. 1 hit in 1986. The joke slogan **when the going gets tough, the tough go shopping** had appeared on T-shirts in the USA by 1982.

when the — had to stop   Format phrase and journalistic cliché derived from *When the Kissing Had to Stop*, the title of a novel (1960) by Constantine Fitzgibbon about a Russian takeover of Britain, and adapted for TV in 1962. That title derives in turn from Robert Browning's poem 'A Toccata of Galuppi's' (1855): 'What of soul was left, I wonder, / When the kissing had to stop?' In *Keep Taking the Tabloids* (1983), Fritz Spiegl noted these headline uses: 'When the Music had to Stop', 'When the Talking had to Stop'.

when the wind blows Seé WAY THE WIND BLOWS.

when the world was young A wistful expression about 'long ago' and a time more innocent than the present. Also the English title of a song (1952) by Johnny Mercer, based on the French *'Le Chevalier de Paris'* or *'Ah! Les Pommiers Doux'* (1950). The phrase may derive ultimately from a verse in the Apocrypha: 'For the world has lost his youth, and the times begin to wax old' (2 Esdras 14:10). Precisely as 'When the World Was Young', it is the title of a painting (1891) by Sir E. J. Poynter PRA, which shows three young girls in a classical setting, relaxing by a pool. Compare the lines from 'Young and Old' in the *Water Babies* (1863) by Charles Kingsley: 'When all the world is young, lad, / And all the trees are green / . . . Young blood must have its course, lad, / And every dog his day.'

when you are in a hole, stop digging Modern proverb – quoted in September 1983 by Denis Healey (Lord Healey), the British politician. Earlier, however, on 7 January 1983, the *Financial Times* had quoted Kenneth Mayland, an economist with the First Pennsylvania Bank, as saying: 'The first rule of holes; when you're in one, stop digging.'

when you could —— and still have change for —— Format for evoking times past. 'It seems like only yesterday – those dear dead days when a packet of fags was only 4/6, when a pint and a box of matches still cost little more than half-a-crown, when you could have the night of your life down the Tottenham Court Road and still come home with change from a five-pound note' – *Private Eye* advertisement, 'The Week's Good Cause', *circa* 1962; 'Mind you, six bob was six bob in them days. You could buy three pennyworth of chips and still have change from sixpence' – Alan Bennett sketch 'A Writer's World' in BBC TV, *On the Margin* (1966).

when you got it, flaunt it The Braniff Airline in the USA used this headline over ads in *circa* 1969 featuring celebrities such as Sonny Liston, Andy Warhol and Joe Namath. Probably the line was acquired from the 1967 Mel Brooks's movie *The Producers* in which Zero Mostel as 'Max Bialystock' says to the owner of a large white limo: 'That's it, baby! When you got it, flaunt it! Flaunt it!' Later in the film he says, 'Take it when you can get it. Flaunt it! Flaunt it!' The idea was obviously very much around at this time. From an episode of the BBC radio show *Round the Horne* (15 May 1966): 'The physique of a young Greek god and profile of classical perfection . . . Still, what I say is if you've got it, you may as well show it.'

when you hear the gong . . . From Radio Luxembourg in the 1950s and 60s (popular music service beamed at Britain): 'The time now – when you hear the gong – is six o'clock.' And they really did use a gong for the time signal.

where are they now? A popular journalistic formula when resurrecting people who have passed out of the headlines – compare WHATEVER HAPPENED TO ——? The rhetorical question occurs rather differently in Wordsworth's ode 'Intimations of Immortality' (1807): 'Whither is fled the visionary gleam? / Where is it now, the glory and the dream?' *Where Are They Now?* was the title of a radio play by Tom Stoppard in 1970. 'Still, this appears to be the week for national treasures so there is no ignoring Roy Hudd. Full Steam A-Hudd (Radio 2, today, Saturday, 7.33pm) features Hudd, the BBC Big Band and a where-are-they-now line-up which includes Frankie Vaughan, June Whitfield, Marion Montgomery, Pam Ayres and Bonnie Langford' – *The Times* (3 June 1995); 'Sport: Where are they now? – Nicola Pietrangeli' – headline in *The Independent* (6 June 1995).

——, where are you now? Usually employed as an ironical plea to someone who has long since departed because one finds that present circumstances are as bad as – or worse than – when the person was around. And so, one might have said during the Reagan Irangate scandal, 'Richard Nixon, where are you now?' As such, it is a truncation of '. . . where are you now that your country needs you?' and an equivalent of **come back ——, all is forgiven** which, once upon a time, might have been said to some prodigal son or about a warrior who had retired to his farm and fallen out of favour. The graffito 'Lee Harvey Oswald, where are you now that your country needs you?' appeared during the presidencies of both Lyndon Johnson and Richard Nixon. 'Come back all is forgiven' appeared as a phrase in *Punch* (1 November 1939) and doubtless long before that. *Partridge/Catch Phrases* traces this format back to newspaper personal column advertisements and finds a (probably fake entry) in the *Daily Mail* (4 May 1896): 'Uncle Jim, come back at once, all is forgiven. Bring the pawn ticket with you.' Compare — COME HOME, ALL IS FORGIVEN.

where did we go wrong?   What parents say when their offspring commit offences that attract the attention of the popular newspapers. Often preceded by 'we gave him/her everything . . .' All this is reflected in: 'Oh, Rosie, Rosie my darling, my doll, my sweetheart. Where did we go wrong? Where did we go wrong?' – punch-line of sketch 'Father and Son' in BBC2 TV *Not Only . . . But Also* (1966); the Lennon and McCartney song 'She's Leaving Home' from the album *Sergeant Pepper's Lonely Heart's Club Band* (1967) has: 'We gave her most of our lives . . . We gave her everything money could buy . . . What did we do that was wrong.' '"When a Jewish child marries a non-Jew, the parents see it as a rejection of their own values and beliefs," he says. "They may also feel stigmatised in the Jewish community and angry at their child for shaming them." But the overriding emotion is guilt. Rabbi Romain says parents often ask, where did we go wrong?' – *The Guardian* (26 July 1994); '"We don't understand it, we gave him everything," say parents to me when they discover that their son has gone off the rails. By "everything" they mean computer games, video recorders and so forth. They do not mean time, attention or affection' – *Daily Mail* (24 May 1995).

where did you get that hat?   A catch-phrase of the 1890s originating in a comic song with the title (1888), variously attributed to J. J. Sullivan and J. Rolmaz. Hence, the cartoon in *Punch's Almanack for 1911* in which a professor is saying: 'I really think there must be something peculiar about my hat, for this morning

some little boys enquired where I had purchased it, and do you know, Marion, for the life of me I could not remember.'

where did you learn to kiss like that? Catchphrase from the BBC radio show *Calling All Forces* (1950–2). Bob Monkhouse noted in 1979: 'In my script-writing partnership with Denis Goodwin I must confess to the deliberate confecting of catchphrases. From our first major radio success, came "Where did you learn to kiss like that?" But it was what we called a "vehicle phrase", not really constructed to catch on but to carry a fresh joke each week.' It was not actually very original. In an edition of the Jewel and Warriss radio show *Up the Pole* broadcast in November 1948 (script by Ronnie Hanbury), the answer to this same question was 'Siphoning petrol.' By 1959, Tony Curtis was asking it of Marilyn Monroe in the film *Some Like It Hot*.

where do we find such men?   In 1984, on the fortieth anniversary of the D-Day landings, President Reagan visited Europe and made a speech in which he eulogized those who had taken part in the event. 'Where do we find such men?' he asked. On an earlier occasion he had said: 'Many years ago in one of the four wars in my lifetime, an admiral stood on the bridge of a carrier watching the planes take off and out into the darkness bent on a night combat mission and then found himself asking, with no one there to answer – just himself to hear his own voice – "Where do we find such men?"' But the very first time he had used the line he had made it clear where it came from. The story comes from James Michener's novel *Bridges at Toko-Ri*, later filmed (US 1954) with William Holden who asks: 'Where do we get such men?'

where do we go from here?   A clichéd and pompous way of rounding off broad-casting discussions about the future of almost anything. 'Where Do We Go From Here?' was the title of a song of the 1940s, popular for a while in the Army. A cliché by 1967 when it was used as the title of a book by the Reverend Dr Martin Luther King Jr – and the next year when it was the title of a BBC TV programme inquiry in Scotland. 'And now, Winkler, we come to rather a moot point – to wit. Where do we go from here?' – P. G. Wodehouse, *Over Seventy*, Chap. 6 (1957). A possible source was hinted at by Winston Churchill when, in a broadcast to the USA from London on 8 August 1939, he said: 'And now it is holiday again, and where are we now? Or, as you sometimes ask in the United States – where do we go from here?' Alternatively, the question can be put to an individual (who has just been interviewed about his life and works) in the form, 'Well, where do you go from here?' In politics, as a theme for debates, it tends to be put even more pompously (though now, with luck, only jokingly) in the form **whither ——?** (e.g. 'Whither Democracy?' 'Whither Europe?' 'Whither the Labour Party?'). In a joke letterhead (24 August 1952), John Betjeman described himself as 'Author of . . . *Whither Albania? Whither Democracy? Whither the Future?* A sketch from BBC TV *That Was the Week That Was* (1962–3 series) began: 'Question of the year, the future of our leader. How soon if ever will he be eased out of Admiralty House and into the Earldom of Bromley. After Macmillan – whither?' The first episode of BBC TV's *Monty Python's Flying Circus* (1969) was subtitled 'Whither Canada?' 'Whither the BBC?' – headline on leading article in the *The Times* (14 January 1985).

where have all the —— gone? Format phrase based on the title of the song 'Where Have All the Flowers Gone' by Pete Seeger (1961). In *Keep Taking the Tabloids* (1983), Fritz Spiegl noted these headline uses: 'Where Have All the Guitars Gone', 'Where Have All the Letters Gone'

where have you been all my life? Exaggerated question asked by a man of a woman whom he has just met and decided to woo. Since the 1920s. It is hard to believe it was ever said straightforwardly as a chatting-up line, but stranger things have been known. Now only utterable as an obviously over-the-top bid for attention.

where McGregor sits is the head o' the table The fable has it that McGregor, who was head of the Scottish clan, was invited to an important function. At dinner, his host apologized for not placing him at the head of the table. To which McGregor responded, 'Where McGregor sits *is* the

head o' the table.' There are various versions of this. In a letter from Lord Chesterfield to Lord Huntingdon (19 May 1756), Chesterfield quoted 'what the late Duke of Somerset [said] absurdly, when accidentally placed below himself one day at table, *the best place is wherever I sit*'. A footnote to the 1923 publication of this letter states: 'The Highland Chief, The McNab, also said: "Where the McNab sits, there is the Head of the Table.'

where men are men Date of origin unknown. 'You will find me somewhere out there in the great open spaces where men are men' – P. G. Wodehouse, *Leave It To Psmith*, Chap. 8 (1923); 'Australia: where men are men and sheep are nervous' – included in *Graffiti 4* (1982).

where's George? – he's gone to Lyonch Slogan for Lyons Corner Houses in the UK, current 1936. W. Buchanan-Taylor, advertising chief at Lyons, recalled in *One More Shake* (1944): 'I resorted to the unforgivable and invented "Lyonch" as a descriptive of lunch at Lyons . . . then I heard a story within the office of how a man on the advertising staff of *The Times* called one day a little later than was his wont to pick up his pal, George Warner, the head of my studio. He was so much later than usual that when he looked into the room and asked "Where's George?" the artist replied, without looking up from his work, "Gone to Lyonch, you fool." I made a note on my desk pad . . . and I sent one of the staff to Somerset House to tot up the number of registered Georges in the country.' When the count had reached more than a million, the slogan was adopted. It had to be carefully obliterated during the funeral of King George V in 1936.

where's the beef? A classic example of an advertising slogan turning into a political catchphrase. The Wendy International hamburger chain promoted its wares in the USA from 1984 with TV commercials, one of which showed three elderly women eyeing a small hamburger on a huge bun – a Wendy competitor's product. 'It certainly is a big bun,' asserted one. 'It's a very big fluffy bun,' the second agreed. But the third asked, 'Where's the beef?' The line caught on hugely. Walter

Mondale, running for the Democratic nomination in the same year, used it to question the substance of his rival Gary Hart's policies.

where's your Willie Shakespeare now? Pronounced 'Whaur's yer Wullie Shakespeare noo?', in 1756, it was the reported cry of a member of the audience at the first Edinburgh (or possibly first London) performance of a tragedy called *Douglas* by the Scottish playwright John Home. There were those who thought the play marked a resurgence of Scots drama and far superior to anything Shakespeare had written. Referred to in *Punch* (4 September 1869).

where the elite meet to eat Fictional slogan from the American radio series *Duffy's Tavern*, starring Ed Gardner (1940s), also on UK radio (1944) and in a film (US 1945). Later, it was spoken by Bette Davis in the film *All About Eve* (US 1950). On British radio, *Duffy's Tavern* made a further appearance as *Finkel's Café*, starring Peter Sellers (1956). Hence, the headline from *The Wall Street Journal* (8 October 1981): 'For The Democrats Pam's [Pamela Harriman's] Is The Place For The Elite To Meet.'

where the heart is The title of the film *Where the Heart Is* (US 1990), directed by John Boorman, comes from the proverb 'Home is where the heart is.' Its first appearance may well have been in an 1870 play by J. J. McCloskey, but even then it was 'Home, *they say*, is where the heart is', so it was obviously an established saying by then. *Mencken* claims it as an 'American saying, author unidentified'.

where the money is When the American bank robber Willie Sutton (1901–80) was asked why he kept on robbing banks, he reputedly replied, 'Because that's where the money is.' Philip French touched on this topic in *The Observer* (8 October 2000): 'There is a mysterious kind of movie title that is not explained in the film itself and demands some special knowledge. *A Clockwork Orange, Straw Dogs* and *O Brother, Where Art Thou?* are examples. The amiable *Where the Money Is* . . . belongs in this category. Nobody uses the phrase in the film and, surprisingly, it

is not in any dictionary of quotations that I possess. But it is generally attributed to the legendary American criminal Willie Sutton, who spent most of his life in jail and the rest of it planning heists . . . and it is clear that Henry, the elderly thief played by Paul Newman, is modelled on Willie Sutton.' Not having seen the film, one might have assumed that the title referred, rather, to the modern proverb, 'If you want to make money, go where the money is', which is one of a number of savvy sayings attributed to Joseph P. Kennedy, father of the President, though he almost certainly did not coin them. The Willie Sutton allusion is surely meant, however. 'The most publicized bank robber since Jesse James' did tell CBS TV's *Sixty Minutes* (8 August 1976) that, in fact, a reporter made it up and attributed it to him. His book *I, Willie Sutton* (1953) apparently does contain the observation: 'It is a rather pleasant experience to be alone in a bank at night.' Compare the similar-sounding saying, 'Marry for love, but love where there is money' or 'Never marry for money, but marry where money is', though this seems to be ignored by proverb books. Tennyson's dialect poem 'Northern Farmer, New Style' also contains this: 'But I knaw'd a Quaäker feller as often 'as towd ma this: / "Doänt thou marry for munny, but goä wheer munny is!"' According to *Quotations for Our Time*, ed. Laurence J. Peter (1977), John F. Kennedy when asked why he wanted to be President, replied: 'Because that's where the power is!'

where there's muck there's brass The idea behind this proverb has long been known. Ray's book of proverbs in the 17th century had it as: 'Muck and money go together.'

. . . wherever you are A tag usually referring to a dead person (i.e. either in heaven or hell). From the record album *The Muppet Show* (1977) – when Zoot is about to prostitute his talents as a saxophonist by playing a number of which he disapproves, he says: 'Forgive me, Charlie Parker, wherever you are.'

where've you been, who've you been with, what've you been doing, and why? Catchphrase from the British music-hall act of Old Mother Riley and her daughter in the 1930s/40s. Riley was played by Arthur Lucan and the daughter by his wife, Kitty McShane. Another of Riley's lines was 'Oh, did you hear that, **Mrs Girochie? SOS!** Me daughter's at it again!', though I have seen this presented as 'Mrs Ginocchi, SOS.'

where was Moses? See WHERE WERE YOU WHEN.

whereof See HE KNOWS.

where were you in '62? *Where Were You In '62?* was the title of a 1950s/60s nostalgia and trivia quiz on BBC Radio 2 (1983–5). As acknowledged, it was taken from the promotional slogan for the film *American Graffiti* (US 1973).

where were you when the lights went out? The US 1968 film *Where Were You When the Lights Went Out?* was inspired by the great New York blackout of 1965 when the electricity supply failed and – or so it was popularly believed – the birth rate shot up nine months later. The phrase echoes an old music-hall song and perhaps also the American nonsense rhyme 'Where was Moses when the light went out? / Down in the cellar eating sauerkraut.' This last appears to have developed from the 'almost proverbial' riddle – as the Opies call it in *The Lore and Language of Schoolchildren* (1959): Q. 'Where was Moses when the light went out?' A. 'In the dark.' The Opies find this in *The Riddler's Oracle, circa* 1821. *Punch* in its *Almanack for 1873* (17 December 1872) has a 'comic chronology' in which AD 1220 marked the 'First asking of the question, "Where was Moses when the candle went out?"' Another response, current in the 1920s, was: 'Running round the table with his shirt hanging out.'

which comes first, the music or the words? An interviewer's cliché question when faced with a lyricist, composer or songwriter. Having so designated it in my book *The Gift of the Gab* (1985), I found myself interviewing one of the breed on television and was dreadfully conscious of the error I could commit. And so I asked him, 'Which comes first, the words or the lyrics?' Ah, well. When Sammy Cahn, the American lyricist who died in 1993, was posed the question, he would ritually answer: 'First comes the phone call.'

which twin has the Toni? An advertising headline that asks a question, a slogan that contains the brand name, and an idea that was dotty enough to be much copied. In the UK of the early 1950s, Toni home perms advertising featured pairs of identical twins (real ones) who also toured doing promotional work for the product. One twin had a Toni home perm, the other a more expensive perm – a footnote explained which was which in answer to the question. During the 1970 British General Election, the Liberal Party produced a poster showing pictures of Harold Wilson and Edward Heath with the slogan 'Which twin is the Tory?'

which was nice See SUITS YOU SIR.

(a) whiff of grapeshot A warning shot, a hint of force sufficient to impress. Thomas Carlyle uses the phrase as a chapter title and on two other occasions (one apparently quoting Napoleon) in his *History of the French Revolution* (1837): 'The whiff of grapeshot can, if needful, become a blast and tempest' refers to the ease with which Napoleon and the military dispersed the Paris insurrection of the Vendémiaire in 1795.

(a) whimwam for a goose's bridle (or **for ducks to perch on** or **for a treacle mill** or **to wind the sun up)** Fobbing-off phrases. 'In my childhood there was one particular saying my mother used, which I have never heard anywhere else. If she was making something and I became too inquisitive and asked what it was, it was always the same answer: "It's a wimwam for a duck's bridle." In other words, mind your own business' – Mrs E. James, Somerset (1995). 'When we came home from school and asked hungrily "What's for lunch?" our mother replied curtly, "Whimwams for ducks to peak on"' – Owen Wainwright, Guernsey (1996). Graham Aldred said (1998) that his mother would always use this same phrase when she couldn't be bothered to give a full explanation in answer to the question 'Mum, what's that?' or 'What's it for?' 'When I asked what something was, my mother would say: "They are wim-wams for goose's bridles to run through"' – Mike Killen (1998). 'My mum always said (and said that her mum always said), "Wig-wams, for ducks to pee upon" when asked, "What's for tea?", or "What are you doing?", or anything she couldn't be bothered to answer' – Steve McGuigan (2000). 'My mother used to say, "A wigwam to wind the sun up" or "Layalls for meddlers"' – John Alexander, Cheshire (2000). Indeed, compare LAROVERS FOR MEDDLERS . . . *Apperson* has 'A whim-wam from Yocketon. A whim-wham to wind the sun up. [Answers by old folk to inquisitive young people who interrupt them]' – from *Cheshire Proverbs* (1917).

whip it in, whip it out and wipe it
Injunction to practise an early form of safe sex. From British services' use, mid-20th century. 'We . . . were shown a film about the effects of VD – "You're off to the pictures now to learn how to whip it in, whip it out and wipe it!" – George Melly, *Rum, Bum and Concertina*, Chap. 1 (1977).

whippet See DON'T FORCE IT.

(a) whipping boy A person punished because of another person's mistakes. From the custom of having a boy educated at the same time as a royal prince, who received the prince's punishments because it was not allowed for a tutor to strike a royal prince. Known by 1647. 'The superintendents claim that their present reports are not designed for reading by other than experienced senior police officers. They also fear that they will become the whipping boys in any change of procedure' – *The Guardian* (10 September 1974).

(a) whirlwind romance Journalistic cliché to describe an engagement or marriage following a brief courtship. Known by 1969. 'He ended his letter asking his parents to look after his fiancée, Debbie Turley, whom he planned to marry after a whirlwind 10-day romance' – *Today* (10 March 1989).

Whispering Grass Nickname given to Shaw Taylor (b. 1924), presenter of *Police Five* programmes on UK TV from the 1960s to the 1980s. Asking the public to come forward with information to help solve crimes, Taylor reportedly attracted this nickname in the underworld. 'Whispering Grass' is the title of a popular song

(1940) and a 'grass' is underworld slang for an informer.

whistle See BLOW THE.

(to) whistle down the wind Meaning, either (1) to abandon or to cast off lightly – after the releasing of a hawk down wind, from the fist, by whistling, as in Shakespeare's *Othello*, III.iii.266 (1604): 'I'ld whistle her off, and let her down the wind'. This is what you do in falconry when you are turning a hawk loose. You send it into or against the wind when it is pursuing prey. Or (2) 'to defame a person . . . The cognate phrase "blown upon" is more familiar. The idea is to whistle down the wind that the person may be blown upon' – *Brewer* (1894). Or (3) To vanish. From J. M. Barrie, *What Every Woman Knows*, Act 3 (1908): 'Where's your marrying now? . . . all gone whistling down the wind.' Noël Coward was quoted in *Panorama* Magazine (Spring 1952) as saying: 'I marched down to the footlights and screamed: "I gave you my youth! Where is it now? Whistling down the wind! *où song les neiges d'antan?*" . . . And I went madly on in French and Italian.' Or (4) Something to be avoided on board ship. The superstition is that whistling, because it sounds like the wind, can raise the wind, as if by magic – though this may more properly be 'whistle up the wind', as in 'to whistle for something'. (Whistling backstage at the theatre is also said to bring bad luck.) Nevertheless, in the seafaring novels (1970/90s) of Patrick O'Brian, the hero, 'Lucky' Jack Aubrey, is sometimes said to 'whistle down the wind' in order to raise wind to fill his sails. So perhaps there is also the meaning (5) 'to summon' – as also here from Frank Harris, *Oscar Wilde, His Life and Confessions*, Chap. 21 (1930): 'A man should be able to whistle happiness and hope down the wind and take despair to his bed and heart, and win courage from his harsh companion.' Notably, *Whistle Down the Wind* was the title of a novel by Mary Hayley Bell (1958; film UK 1961; musical London 1998). In 1980, Bell said that she had not been aware of the Shakespeare use until Len Deighton pointed it out to her. The relevance of the title to a story of children who believe that a murderer on the run is Jesus Christ may not be immediately apparent, though perhaps (2) might apply here.

(a) whistle stop This was originally the name given to a place in the USA too small to have a scheduled train calling at it. If a passenger did want to alight, the conductor would signal to the engineer/driver and he would respond by pulling the whistle. As a political term for a short train visit to a place by a campaigning politician, it was introduced by Robert Taft (1948) in remarks about President Truman who had been criticizing Congress from the platform of a train in journeys about the country. A 'whistle-stop tour' might now be used of any series of quick visits, not necessarily by a politician or by train.

(a) white Christmas The film *White Christmas* (US 1954), inspired by Irving Berlin's '(I'm Dreaming of a) White Christmas' (1942), has combined with classic song to ensure that the phrase and concept of a white Christmas (i.e. when it has snowed or is snowing) endures. An early use occurs in Charles Kingsley, *Two Years Ago* (1857): 'We shall have a white Christmas, I expect. Snow's coming.'

(a) white elephant Something that turns out to be of no value or an expensive mistake. From Siam/Thailand where elephants were sacred. The king would bestow one on awkward courtiers who then had the bother of its upkeep. Known by 1851.

(a) (great) white hope A great hope. Jack Johnson was the first black boxer to be the World Heavyweight Champion (1908–15). A 'white hope' was, originally, a white boxer who might have been hoped to be able to beat Johnson. From there, the phrase came to refer to anyone who might be able to bring about a much desired end and upon whom hopes were centred. Known by 1911.

(a) white knight A corporation that comes to the aid of another in a takeover fight. Known as Stock Exchange jargon by 1981. 'The knight rescues the embattled firm by agreeing to acquire it on better terms than the pursuer would provide. The improved provisions can include a higher purchase price for the company's stock, and assurances that executives of the acquired corporation will not be forced to use their golden parachutes' – *Time* Magazine (4 March 1985).

(the) white man's burden Phrase for the responsibility of the white race for non-white races. Coined by Rudyard Kipling in 'The White Man's Burden' (1899), subtitled 'The United States and the Philippine Islands': 'Take up the White Man's burden – / Send forth the best ye breed – / Go bind your sons to exile / To serve your captives' need.'

white man speak with forked tongue Supposedly the way an American Indian chief would pronounce on the duplicitous ways of the White man, in Western movies. In the film *Yukon Vengeance* (US 1954), Carol Thurston as Princess Yellow Flower gets to say: 'White man's tongue is forked.' From the BBC radio show *Round the Horne* (28 April 1968): 'He speaks with forked tongue.'

(a) whited sepulchre Meaning, a person 'coated in white' who pretends to be morally better than he, in fact, is – also 'holier than thou'. Alluding to Matthew 23:27: 'Woe unto you, scribes and Pharisees, hypocrites! for ye are like unto whited sepulchres, which indeed appear beautiful outward, but which are full of dead men's bones, and of all uncleanness.' 'If the ombudsman cannot do what seems right in circumstances where the courts themselves would regret having to give judgment for the undeserving party, there is no point in having one at all. Worse, the office would be a whited sepulchre' – *The Times* (21 May 1994).

(a) whiter shade of pale Phrase from the song 'A Whiter Shade of Pale' (1967), lyrics by Keith Reid and music by Gary Brooker. The song was performed by their group, Procul Harum (sometimes spelt 'Procol Harum'): 'And so it was that later / As the miller told his tale / That her face just ghostly / Turned a whiter shade of pale . . .' The song as a whole – and especially the title phrase – is representative of the drug-influenced creativity of the 1960s. The title – according to Reid in *Melody Maker* (3 June 1967) was overheard at a gathering:

'Some guy looked at a chick and said to her, "You've gone a whiter shade of pale".'

whiter than white Meaning 'absolutely pure', this phrase was in use by 1924. Latterly, it was taken up and used as a slogan for Persil washing powder in the UK – quoted in 1976 but probably current a decade or two earlier. Later: 'Town That's Whiter Than White' – headline in *The Guardian* (19 March 1992). Psalm 51:7 has: 'Wash me, and I shall be whiter than snow.' Persil also popularized the theme of **someone's mother**, current in 1940 ('Aha . . . someone's mother isn't using Persil yet'). George Orwell records 'Somebody's Mother isn't Using Persil' in his diary for 13 April 1941. This was carried forward from posters and press ads to TV in the 1950s: 'What someone's mum really ought to know, / So someone's mum better get to know. / That Persil washes whiter, whiter – / **Persil washes whiter.**' The theme **what is a mum?** featured in a series of Persil TV ads from 1961.

whites See DON'T FIRE.

(a) white-water ride An exciting, dangerous experience. Current since the 1990s? White water is the kind that foams in shallows or rapids in sea or river. 'In wrestling myself with some of the great seismic movements of the period, I enjoyed a white-water ride of tumbles and excitements, a great twentieth-century adventure, which these pages attempt to capture and to chronicle' – John Birt, *The Harder Path*, Preface (2002).

whither? See WHERE DO WE GO FROM HERE?

who are the Beatles? The archetypal British judge's remark – often, of course, a question posed when the judge knows the answer, in order to further his reputation for fustiness and aloofness from the concerns of ordinary citizens. But did any judge actually ever pose the question? At the height of Beatlemania in the '60s, when the newspapers were daily full of pieces about the Fab Four, a judge in the High Court is said to have lifted the flap of his wig quizzically and inquired of counsel, 'Who *are* the Beatles?' What probably happened was that an assumption was made, when the Beatles came along, that judges *would* ask that sort of question –

just as they had always done and still do. More recently, for example, in 1990, the year of the football World Cup, Mr Justice Harman actually asked, 'Who is Gazza? Isn't there an operetta called *La Gazza Ladra?*' Indeed, there is – but that has nothing to do with the footballer Paul 'Gazza' Gascoigne. A century before, in 1889, Mr Justice Stephen had asked, 'What is the Grand National?' (but *he* was eventually committed to a lunatic asylum, so perhaps that doesn't count). In *Geoffrey Madan's Notebooks*, edited by Gere and Sparrow (1981), Lord Hewart (1870–1943) is credited with: 'Precedent compels me to ask: what is jazz?' Another query is reputedly, 'What is a G-string? Has it something to do with Bach?' *Punch* indicated the well-established position of such queries (30 December 1936): 'A daily paper says that the "Knock-Knock" craze is gradually dying out in this country. So it will soon be time for some up-to-the-minute member of the Bench to inquire "what is 'knock-knock'?"' In fiction, A. P. Herbert's Mr Justice Snubb asked 'What is a crossword?' An episode of the 'Flook' comic strip dating from 1963 had a judge asking: 'What does darling mean? What is a darling?' And there may have been a cartoon by 'Vicky' just after the war that had a judge asking: 'What is a banana?' In the late 1940s a judge was supposed to have asked, 'What is oomph?' In the next issue of the *News of the World* there was a cartoon of a very curvaceous young woman saying, 'What is a judge?' The apocryphal nature of the Beatles query may be confirmed by a report in *The Guardian* on 10 December 1963 (when Beatlemania was rampant). A Queen's Counsel representing the Performing Right Society at a London tribunal in a case concerning copyright fees at pop concerts objected to a suggestion that tribunal members should attend such a concert in order to see and hear what it was like. Instead, they listened to a recording of a Beatles' concert. Another QC remarked to the court: 'You will only have to suffer two or three minutes.' *The Guardian* headline over its report of all this was: 'What is a Beatle?' – which simply appears to be a case of the old question being applied to a new phenomenon. But it does not appear to have been asked by an actual judge. It should perhaps be allowed that when a judge asks a question like this, he often knows the answer and is merely asking so that things may be clarified for the jury.

who breaks a butterfly upon a wheel?

Meaning, 'who goes to great lengths to accomplish something trifling?' The expression comes from the 'Epistle to Dr Arbuthnot' (1735) by Alexander Pope. As 'Who Breaks a Butterfly on a Wheel', it was used as the headline to a leader in *The Times* (1 July 1967) when Mick Jagger, the pop singer, was given a three month gaol term on drugs charges.

(the) —— who came in from the cold

A journalistic format derived from the title of John Le Carré's novel *The Spy Who Came In From the Cold* (1963), about a spy from the West getting even with his East German counterpart around the time of the erection of the Berlin Wall. From then on, any people or any thing coming in from any kind of exposed position, or returning to favour, might be described as 'coming in from the cold'. In *Keep Taking the Tabloids* (1983), Fritz Spiegl noted these much earlier headline uses: 'Explorer comes in from cold', 'Stranger who flew in from the cold', 'Spy who came in from the Cold War', 'Dartmoor sheep come in from the cold', 'Quarter that came in from the cold'. '[London Stock Exchange] Oils and leading Engineerings were well to the fore. Stores also joined in the recovery, while Life Insurances came in from the cold after a particularly depressing spell before and after abolition of Life Assurance premium relief' – *Financial Times* (21 March 1984); 'We should not forget the reason for which Checkpoint Charlie stood here for so many years but no one can be sorry that it is going. At long last we, we are bringing "Charlie" in from the cold' – Douglas Hurd, British Foreign Secretary, speaking in Berlin (22 June 1990); *The Cat Who Came In From the Cold* – title of book (1991) by Deric Longden; 'Baritone who came in from the cold' – headline about Dmitri Hvorostovsky (who hails from Siberia) in *The Independent* (19 January 1998).

who dares wins

The British SAS (Special Air Service) regiment was founded by Colonel David Stirling in 1950 although its origins lay in the Second World War. Its motto became famous after members of the crack regiment shot their way into the Iranian embassy in London, in May 1980, to end a siege – when wags suggested the motto should really be, 'Who dares use it [fire-power], wins'. A feature film about the supposed exploits of the SAS was made, using the motto as its title, in 1982, and the *Daily Mirror* labelled its 'Win a Million' bingo promotion 'Who Dares Wins' in 1984. The motto appears to have been borrowed from the Alvingham barony, created in 1929.

. . . who did very nicely out of it, thank you

Date of origin not known. A cliché by the 1970s/80s. Gerald Priestland said it in a Channel 4 TV series *Priestland Right and Wrong* (1983).

who do I have to fuck to get out of this ——?

Presumably from show business. Having, as legend would have it, had to fuck to get cast in a show or picture, the speaker is wondering how the process can be reversed – because the show or film is having problems or turns out to be no good. Bob Chieger in *Was It Good For You, Too?* (1983) ascribes to 'Shirley Wood, talent coordinator for NBC's *The Tonight Show* in the 1960s', the quote: 'Who do you have to fuck to get *out* of show business?' The line 'Listen, who do I have to fuck to get *off* this picture?' occurs in Terry Southern's *Blue Movie* (1970). Steve Bach in *Final Cut* (1985) ascribes 'Who do I fuck to get off this picture?' simply to 'Anonymous Hollywood starlet (circa 1930)'. When Stephen Sondheim had the question put to him by Larry Kert during a technical rehearsal for the London production of *Company* (1972), he is said to have replied: 'Same person you fucked to get in!'

who do you think you are: Stirling Moss?

This appeared as a headline in the *Independent on Sunday* (3 August 2003) and is included here to commemorate a remarkable fact – that although the British motor racing champion (Sir) Stirling Moss (b. 1929) has not participated in Formula One racing since he crashed in 1962 and although he never won the World Championship title, his name continues to be alluded to as that of the archetypal fast driver. Many successful racing drivers have followed in his wake but he was the first notable one (ten times British champion) and the label has stuck.

who goes home? The cry that goes up in the House of Commons, echoed by policemen, when the House has finished a sitting and is about to close its doors. It dates from the days when, to protect themselves against robbers, MPs would form small groups for mutual protection on the way home. Chips Channon wrote in his diary (17 March 1937) on Stanley Baldwin's tribute to the late Austen Chamberlain: 'His closing sentence "Austen has at last gone home" made us all think of the attendant's call "Who goes home?"' On the same day, Harold Nicolson wrote in his diary: 'The Prime Minister makes an adequate oration but rather spoils it by introducing at the end a somewhat unsuccessful play on the phrase "Who Goes Home?"'

who he? Editorial interjection after a little-known person's name shows some signs of catching on, popularized by *Private Eye* in the 1980s. Perhaps Richard Ingrams, then editor, consciously borrowed the phrase from Harold Ross (1892–1951), editor of *The New Yorker*. James Thurber in *The Years with Ross* (1959) describes how Ross would customarily add this query to manuscripts on finding a name he did not know (sometimes betraying his ignorance). He said the only two names everyone knew were Houdini and Sherlock Holmes. The phrase echoes the Duke of Wellington's peremptory 'Who? Who?' on hearing the names of ministers in Lord Derby's new administration (1852). A book with the title *Who He? Goodman's Dictionary of the Unknown Famous* was published in 1984. 'This month, for instance, has been the time for remembering the 110th anniversary of the birth of Grigori Petrovsky. Who he?' – *New Statesman* (26 February 1988).

who is to —— what —— is to —— Comparison format usually enabling one (if not both) of the people mentioned to be slighted. The format may also vary. 'This

[Labour Party policy] has as much to do with socialism as Cyril Smith [hugely sized politician] has to do with hang-gliding' – included in *Graffiti 2* (1980); 'Eddie Waring [TV commentator] has done for Rugby League what Cyril Smith has done for hang-gliding' – comment by Reggie Bowden quoted in *A Year of Stings and Squelches* (1985); '[Bobby] Charlton, who is to tact what Charlie Drake is to nuclear physics, found the Pontiff "smaller than I expected"' – *The Independent* (30 June 1990).

whole See I SWEAR.

(the) whole ball of wax Everything. Of American origin and recorded by 1953. Various derivations have been suggested – including one that it is a corruption of 'bailiwick', meaning an area of land supervised by a bailiff – but it seems most probable that it first arose in US advertising/business language. Shepherd Meade's science-fiction novel *The Big Ball of Wax* (1954) was a satire on big business and advertising in America (he had earlier written *How To Succeed In Business Without Really Trying*). The narrator, a market researcher, says about the story to come: 'well, why don't we go back to the beginning and roll it all up, as the fellow says, into one big ball of wax?' Compare BALL OF CLAY.

whole hog See GO THE.

(a) whole new ball game A state of affairs where new factors come into play. From American business jargon and established by the 1960s. 'Mr Gerry Fernback, chairman of ABTA's retail travel agents' council, said last week: "For the first time British Airways is making the right noises. It's a whole new ball game now . . . it's in their interest and ours that cheap tickets are available to the public"' – *The Observer* (26 September 1983).

(the) whole nine yards The entire problem – so defined in an article about Pentagonese in *The Times* (2 April 1984). Everything, the whole lot. Of American origin and known by 1970. A consensus has developed that the phrase comes from concrete mixing – presumably the distance it would be possible to cover using one truckload, or the cubic contents of one cement truck. Sand is sold by the yard and the whole nine yards would be a substantial amount. As a form of measurement, it is quite normal to describe a load in these terms. From Terry Major-Ball, *Major Major* (1994): 'Whenever a truck came with a delivery of sand, usually five or six yards at a time, it simply dumped it in the road leaving me to cart it away.' A film was entitled *The Whole Nine Yards* (US 2000). Another suggestion is that the phrase comes from the days of sailing ships. A website devoted to the novelist Patrick O'Brian states: 'If you look at a typical square-rigger you will see that there are three masts with three yards on each mast. So if you had all of the square sails a-flying on board, you would have the whole nine yards in operation, i.e. everything.' But is there a citation of the phrase being used in this context? Other theories include that it derives from the length of material required for a good suit or of wool to make a 'great kilt' or 'full kilt' and that it has to do with the length of fighter-plane machine-gun belts/bomb racks. An American World War II pilot remembers it being used thus.

(the) whole shooting match Everything; an all-encompassing event. *DOAS* (1987) dates the origin of this American expression to the late 19th century and suggests that it probably comes from the crowd that would gather at a frontier shooting match, hence 'the whole crowd' – 'perhaps influenced by the earlier British "the whole shoot" of the same meaning, from "the whole shoot" meaning "the whole cost or price".' *OED2* has 'to go the whole shoot' meaning 'to risk all', by 1884. *Partridge/Slang,* on the other hand, suggests that it arose or was popularized by the First World War. Now *that* was about as big a 'shooting match' as you could get and would be a useful image when the speaker was trying to evoke 'everything, the whole thing'.

who loves ya, baby? Telly Savalas created a vogue for this phrase, as the lollipop-sucking New York police lieutenant in the TV series *Kojak* (US 1973–7). Inevitably, he also recorded a song with the title (1975).

whore See HEAVENS.

(the) —— who redefined —— Mostly journalistic cliché of compliment on achievement. Date of origin not known. 'Edward Thompson, who died last year, was an intellectual giant . . . Here was a man who redefined history, rescuing from obscurity a host of ordinary people who, in the early nineteenth century, laid the basis for modern democracy' – *The Observer* (8 May 1994); 'The book doesn't follow Elvis into the bedroom . . . This would be a flaw in any serious biography. For a performer who redefined male sexuality with an infusion of narcissism, and whose work was based largely on carnal energy, it borders on the barmy' – *The Sunday Telegraph* (23 October 1994); 'The knives are out for Macaulay Culkin. The child star who redefined mischief in *Home Alone* might only be 14 years old, but already his days in Hollywood are numbered' – *Today* (16 December 1994); 'If Foley, the charming smallholder who has redefined the meaning of humility, was looking for obscurity and peace he has found it. Except that as the trainer of Danoli, Ireland's new Arkle, he is never more than a telephone call away from contact with the outside world' – *Daily Mail* (3 January 1995).

whore's drawers See UP AND DOWN LIKE A.

who's afraid of Virginia Woolf? Joke question. Edward Albee reportedly took the title of his play *Who's Afraid of Virginia Woolf?* (1962; film US 1966) from a graffito seen in Greenwich Village. The character Martha sings it in the play to the tune of 'Who's Afraid of the Big Bad Wolf?' – that is her little joke.

whose finger on the trigger? Political quasi-slogan. In fact, the *Daily Mirror*'s actual front-page headline on 25 October 1951 – General Election day – was 'Whose Finger?' This was the culmination of a campaign to ensure that the Labour Government was re-elected and the Conservatives under Winston Churchill not allowed back. Earlier, on 21 September, the paper had asked, 'Whose finger do you want on the trigger when the world situation is so delicate?' The choice was between Churchill and Clement Attlee. Churchill's response (in a speech, 6

October 1951) was: 'I am sure we do not want any fingers upon any trigger. Least of all do we want a fumbling finger . . . But I must tell you that in any case it will not be a British finger that will pull the trigger of a Third World War. It may be a Russian finger or an American finger, or a United Nations Organization finger, but it cannot be a British finger . . . the control and decision and the timing of that terrible event would not rest with us. Our influence in the world is not what it was in bygone days.' As it happens, the *Mirror* was unable to stir the electorate and the Conservatives duly came back to power under Churchill. The Prime Minister then issued a writ for libel against the newspaper because he took the view that the slogan implied that he was a warmonger. The case was settled out of court.

whose —— is it anyway? Format phrase derived from *Whose Life Is It Anyway?*, the title of a play (1978; film US 1981) by Brian Clark. The theme was about a paralysed patient's right to die. Later a BBC Radio/Channel 4 TV improvisatory game was given the title *Whose Line Is It Anyway?* (from 1988). By 1993, *The Independent* Magazine was campaigning for the abolition of it as a headline cliché. Among a blizzard of examples, it cited: 'Whose womb is it anyway?' – *Northern Echo* (9 November 1992); 'Whose Queen is it anyway?' – *Evening Standard* (London) (18 March 1993).

who shot J.R.? The hero/villain J. R. Ewing (played by Larry Hagman) of the top-rated US TV soap opera *Dallas* was shot in the cliffhanging last episode of the programme's 1979–80 season. For reasons not entirely clear, the question of who had inflicted this far from mortal wound caused a sensation in the USA and UK. Consequently, the first episode of the next series attracted 53.3 per cent of the American viewing audience, the highest ever rating. All those who had posed the question, or who had even sported bumper-stickers declaring **I hate J.R.**, discovered that the guilty party was a jilted lover.

who's she – the cat's aunt? 'My mother had a dislike of the pronoun "she". As a child, if ever I referred to her as "she" in

the course of conversation, she would immediately interject: "Who's she, the cat's aunt?" – Barry Gayton, Norfolk (1996). From Stella Gibbons, *Cold Comfort Farm*, Chap. 6 (1932): '"She comes from up at the farm" . . . "Who's 'she'? The cat's mother?" snapped the shawl. "Speak properly to the young lady".'

who wants to be a millionaire? Title phrase from a song by Cole Porter written for the film musical *High Society* (US 1956). Later the title of a highly successful British TV quiz (1999–) where the top prize is a million pounds and which has been replicated all over the world.

who was that lady I saw you with last night? A stock part of an American vaudeville routine in which the expected answer was, **that was no lady – that was my wife!** It seems generally agreed that the first comedians to perform this exchange were Joseph Weber (1867–1942) and Lew Fields (1867–1941). *Bartlett* (1992) dates this from 1887 and has the riposte in the form: 'She ain't no lady; she's my wife.'

who would have thought it? An expression of amazement. John Day wrote a play with the title *Law-Trickes or who would have thought it* (1608). 'Good lack-a-day! why there now, who would have thought it!' – Henry Fielding, *Tom Jones*, Bk 10, Chap. 9 (1719). John Major is alleged to have said, 'Well – who would have thought it?' when opening his first Cabinet meeting in 1990 when, to his and everyone else's surprise, he succeeded Margaret Thatcher as leader of the Conservative Party and British Prime Minister.

who you lookin' at? The yobbo or lout's challenge that caught on in the UK in the early 1990s. It was already being noted by a humorous columnist in *The Times* (8 August 1990): 'At the turn of the century, when civility was still the rule, people would introduce themselves to strangers with a cheery, "Who are you lookin' at, then?", to which the correct reply would be, "What's your problem?" One would then be invited by one's new acquaintance to "Come outside and say that".' The phrase was used as the title of a short-lived ITV comedy series in 1993. Whether this has anything to do with the famous line '**you talkin' to me?**' from the film *Taxi Driver* (US 1976) is anybody's guess. Robert De Niro as 'Travis' famously says to himself in the mirror: 'You talkin' to me? You talkin' to me? You talkin' to me? Well, who the hell else are you talkin' to? You talkin' to me? Well, I'm the only one here. Who the fuck do you think you're talkin' to?' Originally, the script said, 'Travis speaks to himself in the mirror', but De Niro ad-libbed the speech after consulting with the screenwriter. The line had been growled thirty years earlier by Alan Ladd to Veronica Lake in *The Blue Dahlia*, written by Raymond Chandler, and this film can be glimpsed on TV in *Taxi Driver*.

why are you telling me all this?   Drama cliché use. The agricultural soap opera *The Archers* has been running on BBC national radio since 1951. In 1983, Norman Painting, who has written many of the episodes as well as playing Phil Archer throughout the existence of the series, admitted that a number of expository clichés had crept in, including this one. The line is also mocked in the BBC radio *Goon Show*, 'Lurgi Strikes Britain' (9 November 1954).

why is a mouse when it spins?   A nonsense riddle to which the usual answer is **because the higher, the fewer**. Remembered from the 1920s/30s. John Mack of Surbiton suggested (1987) that it originated in repartee between Jasper Maskelyne and Oswald Williams in magic shows at the St George's Hall in Langham Place, London, in about 1930. However, the phrase 'The Higher the Fewer' occurs as a caption title in *Punch* (18 October 1922). Mrs Jean E. French of Finchampstead suggested that it might not be nonsensical if you substituted the word 'when' for 'why' in posing the riddle. From this I wondered whether it had anything to with 'Hickory, dickory, dock, the mouse ran up the clock, the clock struck one, the mouse fell down . . .' A variation of the riddle (which doesn't help either) is: *Q*. 'Why is a mouse when it's spinning its web?' *A*. 'Because the more the fewer the quicker.' Other phrases from nonsensical riddles: *Q*. '**How is a man when he's out?**' *A*. 'The sooner he does, the much.' *Q*. '**What is the difference between a chicken/duck?**' *A*. 'One of its

legs is both the same.' *Q*. '**Which would you rather, or go fishing** [or swimming/ hunting]?' *A*. 'One rode a horse and the other rhododendron.' This last may not be a riddle at all and the answer may belong elsewhere. *Partridge/Slang* gives 'What shall we do, or go fishing' as a 'trick elaboration' of the straightforward 'What shall we do now?' It occurs in Susan Coolidge, *What Katy Did at School* (1873), and is quoted in Dorothy L. Sayers, *The Nine Tailors*, Chap. 6 (1934). And compare: **which would you rather be – or a wasp?**

why keep a cow when you can buy a bottle of milk?   A common justification for not getting married. Hence, the comic confusion of the version: 'Why go out for a pint of milk when you've got an old cow at home?' *Partridge/Slang* also finds this 'cynical male gibe at marriage' in the forms 'why buy a book when you can join a library?' and 'you don't have to buy a cow merely because you are fond of milk', dating them from the late 19th century. He also suggests that the 'milk/cow' argument features in John Bunyan's *The Life and Death of Mr Badman* (1680), though this has not been verified and is probably not used in connection with marriage. *Apperson* finds the simple expression 'Who would keep a cow when he may have a quart of milk for a penny?' by 1659.

why not the best?   See JIMMY WHO.

why-oh-why?   Catchphrase of exasperated complaint, known since 1865. '[Of a collection by Saki] Why, oh, why, can we see no humour in these stories?' – *New Age* (1912). It was featured in the BBC radio show *Take It From Here* (1948–59). 'My improvisations [in the 1950s] on the why-oh-why school of correspondence were state of the art . . . "Why-oh-why do not Britain's old age pensioners wear a red light fore and aft during the hours of darkness?"' – Robert Robinson, *Skip All That* (1997). By the 1980s, recognized as the customary cry of letter writers to newspapers and of certain hand-wringing columnists. 'Why oh why won't they appreciate that industry is not interested in constantly fluctuating price situation, but stability' – letter to the editor, *Financial*

Times (26 June 1982); 'In the run-up to each Edinburgh Festival, comedians begin to sound like the viewers who write to Anne Robinson on Points of View. Why, oh, why, they say, must we pack our threadbare routines into suitcases for the annual exodus from London? – *The Independent* (21 February 1989).

why-y-y-y, Daddy?   Stock phrase of Fanny Brice playing the part of Baby Snooks on American radio from 1936.

wick   See GET ON ONE'S.

wickedly funny   Publishing and promotional use cliché phrase. 'It is a wickedly funny book, too. The mock lists in "Etymology" and "Extracts" guy any too solemn an encyclopaedist. The fart in "Loomings" confirms the touch of Smollett in Melville, as does his send-up of sabbatarian probity in the Pequod's owners, Peleg and Bildad' – *The Times Higher Education Supplement* (28 April 1995); 'A wickedly funny satire on the English legal system, the comic strip Queen's Counsel has been a regular feature on the Law pages of *The Times* for several years' – new books catalogue, Robson Books Ltd (August–December 1995).

(the) Wicked Witch of the West   Name of a character in *The Wonderful Wizard of Oz* (1900) by L. Frank Baum. Allan Massie, writing on Margaret Thatcher: 'It would not convert those for whom she is SHE WHO MUST BE OBEYED and the Wicked Witch of the West rolled into one' – quoted in Michael Cockerell, *Live From Number 10* (1989).

wide-eyed and legless   'Too drunk to stand' – phrase from the song with this title, written and performed by Andy Fairweather-Low (1976). There is no suggestion of any love interest anywhere in the lyrics. The phrase 'the rhythm of the glass' quite clearly indicates that the song is about the excessive consumption of alcohol and the inability to control such consumption. Paul Beale (1998) commented: '"Legless" was certainly the popular in-word during my last army posting 1972–4 – but Andy Fairweather-Low might have added the "wide-eyed" to make it more colourful/emphatic. It

sounds like a bimbo who's been plied with gin (aka leg-opener).'

wide Sargasso Sea   *Wide Sargasso Sea* is the title of a novel (1966) by Jean Rhys. This, in modern parlance, is a 'prequel' to Charlotte Brontë's *Jane Eyre*. It recounts the previous history of Mr Rochester's mad wife before she was incarcerated in Thornfield Hall. She is described as being Antoinette Cosway, a Creole heiress from the West Indies. The Sargasso Sea, in the North Atlantic, is made up of masses of floating seaweed, creating sluggish waters. 'When I was last at Marvis Bay, the hotel links were a sort of Sargasso Sea into which had drifted all the pitiful flotsam and jetsam of golf' – P. G. Wodehouse, *The Heart of a Goof*, Chap. 1 (1926).

wife   See ALL THE WORLD; CAESAR'S; HAS HE BEEN.

Wigan   See BORED STIFF.

Wigan Pier   An imaginary focus of jokes (compare 'the Swiss Navy'), in this case, the creation of the music-hall comedian George Formby Snr (1876–1921). Wigan, an industrial town in Lancashire, is not a seaside resort but is one of those places dear to the British, the mere mention of whose name is sufficient to provoke laughter (compare Basingstoke, Scunthorpe, Chipping Sodbury, Neasden). A non-fiction book by George Orwell about 'unemployment and the proletarian life' was entitled *The Road To Wigan Pier* (1937). In the 1980s, a derelict warehouse alongside a basin of the Leeds-Liverpool canal, at Wigan, was renovated and given the name.

wigs on the green   'My wife's mother used to say over her shoulder as she left the house, "Don't let the cat get the tongs or wigs will be on the green"' – Peter Tatton-Brown, Devon (1998). Nothing to do with the theatrical 'see you on the green', this one. It is apparently of Irish origin. In the days when people wore wigs, they were likely to end up on the grass if there was a fight. *OED2* has this from *Chambers Journal* (1 March 1856): 'If a quarrel is foreseen as a probable contingency, it is predicted that "there'll be wigs on the green".' *Wigs On the Green* became the title of a novel (1935) by Nancy Mitford.

(the) wilder shores of —— Format phrase. *The Wilder Shores of Love* was the title of a biographical study (1954) in which Lesley Blanch described four 19th-century women 'who found fulfilment as women along wilder *Eastern* shores'. Describing Jane Digby (whose fourth husband was an Arab sheikh), Blanch wrote: 'She was an Amazon. Her whole life was spent riding at breakneck speed towards the wilder shores of love.' Hence, presumably, such usages as: 'The wilder shores of PC [political correctness]' – *The Independent* (21 July 1992); 'The consultant, alone in triumph upon the wilder shores of dermatology, raised his eye-glass to me and averred . . .' – Duncan Fallowell, *One Hot Summer in St Petersburg* (1994); 'Gladstone's third major excursion to the wilder shores of political rashness came in May 1864' – Roy Jenkins, *Gladstone* (1995).

(a) wild-goose chase A pursuit of something that it is impossible to capture or find; a hopeless enterprise. From a 16th-century horse race in which each horse had to follow the leader on an erratic course. But also a wild goose is very difficult to follow. Shakespeare uses the term in its figurative sense in *Romeo and Juliet*, II.iv.72 (1594).

wild horses wouldn't drag it out of me An absolute refusal to divulge information. Referring to the old practice of a person being tied to horses pulling in different directions in order to make him reveal information. Date of origin not known. 'Wild horses would not make me tell you anything more about [the Book Prize for Fiction result]' – Libby Purves in *The Listener* (September 1983).

(looking like the) wild woman of Borneo Looking a terrible mess. A variation on 'Wild *Man* of Borneo' as the name for the somewhat hairy and unkempt orang-outang. Indeed, the meaning of that animal's name, however you spell it, is either 'wild man' or 'man of the woods'. Marjorie Wild, Devon (2001) commented; 'This was one of my mother's oft-used expressions. It got me into trouble once when I was nursing at a nursing home in Croydon in the 60s. Going into the room

of an elderly lady, to give her a "wash and brush up" in the early morning, I exclaimed, "Oh, Mrs —, you look like the wild woman of Borneo!" Soon after, I was summoned to the Matron, to whom Mrs — had complained. She'd spent years in India and felt I'd likened her to the natives. She'd have been even more upset if she'd known I was likening her to an orang-utang!' W. A. R. Hamilton, Wiltshire (2001), recalled an Edwardian popular song along the lines of 'Old Macdonald had a farm'. The first verse consisted of the line 'The Wild Man of Borneo has just come to town' (repeated four times), the second verse, 'The wife of the Wild Man of Borneo . . .', the third verse, 'The son of the Wild Man of Borneo . . .', and so on through the family. There was also a song, 'Wild Men of Borneo' (1922), written by Archibald De Bear to music by Melville Gideon. Could either of these have encouraged use of the expression? As to whether the 'wild *man* of Borneo' was invoked when referring to males, Eric Dunkley (2001) commented that when he was young and had a good head of hair, his mother used to tell him to comb it 'otherwise you'll look like the wild man from Borneo'. This masculine version also appears in the novel *Thin Ice* by Compton Mackenzie (1956). Compare: the **wild man of the woods**, as used as the title of an episode in the BBC radio show *Hancock's Half Hour* (27 January 1957).

willies See GIVE SOMEONE THE.

(the) willing suspension of belief This is Samuel Taylor Coleridge's phrase for what is an essential part of much artistic experience, not just in poetry. It has been called 'one of the most famous phrases ever coined' and describes the state of receptiveness and credulity required by the reader or 'receiver' of a work of literature, as well as the acceptance of dramatic and poetic conventions. In the original context, *Biographia Literaria*, Chap. 14 (1817), Coleridge was writing of two possible subjects for poetry: 'In this idea originated the plan of the Lyrical Ballads; in which it was agreed, that my endeavours should be directed to persons and characters supernatural, or at least romantic; yet so as to transfer from our inward nature a human interest and a semblance of truth sufficient to procure from these shadows of imagination that willing suspension of disbelief for the moment, which constitutes poetic faith.'

(the) —— will never be the same again Any change, however unremarkable, requires this plonking, journalistic cliché phrase. 'ONE THING IS CERTAIN. Things will never be the same again' – cited by Malcolm Bradbury in an article on clichés in *Tatler* (March 1980); 'Politics as we know it will never be the same again' – *Private Eye* (4 December 1981); 'The Broadway musical would never be the same again' – TV promo, New York (1983); 'Life for George Bush will never be the same again' – Tim Ewart, ITN *News at 5.45* (20 January 1989), the day of the president's inauguration; '[Keith Joseph] was irreplaceable; somehow politics would never be the same again' – Margaret Thatcher, *The Downing Street Years* (1993); 'Many families were faced with the fact that someone they loved would not return home. Life would never be the same again' – Reverend Pat Crashaw, *Kensington and Chelsea Post* (4 May 1995); 'Rugby union's backdrop looked much the same as ever . . . It was Day One, though, of the new order – the game would never be the same again' – *The Observer* (25 June 1995).

—— will out A modern proverbial format, meaning that if a person has some quality or has done something, it will emerge. An advertisement for Lloyds Bank Young Theatre Challenge (June 1988) had: 'Talent will out, they say. But only under the right conditions.' Philip Larkin in a letter to Barbara Pym (28 October 1979) wrote: 'I really am delighted that all your lovely books have come to life again . . . Talent *will* out.' From the BBC radio show *Round the Horne* (7 April 1968): 'After all, talent will out.' 'Aye, indeed, money like murder, will out' – J. B. Fagan, *And So To Bed*, Act 1 (1926). The young Beatrix Potter in her diary for 5 June 1891 mentioned: 'A theory I have seen – that genius – like murder – will out – its bent being simply a matter of circumstance.' The proverb 'murder will out' (i.e. will be found out, will reveal itself) goes back at least to 1325, and 'truth will out' to 1439. William Congreve in The

Double Dealer (1694) has: 'See how love and murder will out'; Hannah Cowley in *The Belle's Stratagem* (1782) has: 'Vanity, like murder, will out.'

will the last person to leave —— please turn out the lights Journalistic format phrase. 'Would the last person to leave the country please switch off the lights' – included in *Graffiti 2* (1980). On 9 April 1992, this line suffered a revival when on the day of the British General Election, *The Sun* newspaper's front page headline was: 'If Kinnock wins today will the last person in Britain please turn out the lights.' 'Will the last person to leave Broadway, please turn out the lights' – headline in *The Independent* (10 June 1995).

will the real —— ——, please stand up? In the American TV game *To Tell the Truth*, devised by Goodson-Todman Productions and shown from 1956 to 1966, a panel had to decide which of three contestants, all claiming to be a certain person, was telling the truth. After the panellists had interrogated the challenger and the 'impostors', they had to declare which person they thought was the real one. The MC, Bud Collyer, would then say: 'Will the real —— ——, please stand up!' and he or she did so. The game was revived in the UK as *Tell the Truth* in the 1980s. Ian Carmichael, the actor, entitled his autobiography *Will the Real Ian Carmichael . . .* (1979). In March 1984, Elizabeth Taylor, the actress, was quoted as saying: 'I'm still trying to find the real Elizabeth Taylor and make her stand up.'

wind See ALL PISS AND; CANDLE IN THE.

wind and water See LIKE THE BARBER'S CAT.

windmill See BONNET OVER THE.

(a/the) wind of change A cliché since 1945, states Eric Partridge in *A Dictionary of Clichés* (5th edition, 1978). Speaking to both Houses of the South African parliament on 3 February 1960, the British Prime Minister, Harold Macmillan, gave his hosts a message they cannot have wanted to hear: 'The most striking of all the impressions I have formed since I left London a month ago is of the strength of this African national consciousness. In different places it may take different forms, but it is happening everywhere. The wind of change is blowing through this continent. Whether we like it or not, this growth of national consciousness is a political fact.' The phrase 'wind of change' – though not, of course, original – was contributed to the speechwriting team by the diplomat (later Sir) David Hunt. The *OED2* acknowledges that use of the phrase 'wind(s) of change' increased markedly after the speech. When Macmillan sought a title for one of his volumes of memoirs he plumped for the more common, plural, usage – *Winds of Change*. In a similar windy metaphor, Stanley Baldwin had said in 1934: 'There is a wind of nationalism and freedom round the world, and blowing as strongly in Asia as elsewhere.' President George Bush made 'a new breeze is blowing' the theme of his inauguration speech on 20 January 1989.

(a/the) wind of heaven (or **winds . . .)** This phrase might seem to suggest the movements and changes in our lives, as directed by heaven, but it may simply be poetic usage for 'winds' rather than religious. From George Eliot, *Silas Marner* (1861): 'Life . . . when it is spread over a various surface, and breathed on variously by the multitudinous currents from the winds of heaven to the thoughts of men.' Eliot is also quoted as having said in 1840: 'O how luxuriously joyous to have the wind of heaven blow on one after being stived in a human atmosphere.' *The Wind of Heaven* was a drama by Emlyn Williams, first performed in 1945.

(a) window of opportunity (sometimes just **window)** A period of limited duration in which a task may be attempted. From the US space programme in the 1960s when a 'launch window' was the period of time during which a rocket had to be launched if it was to reach the correct orbit. Weather conditions and technical faults sometimes militated against the window being used. The figurative sense, in other fields of endeavour, was common by 1987.

windows See EYES AS.

(the) winds of war Phrase of uncertain origin (though compare WINDS OF HEAVEN). Used as the title of a US TV series (1983) based on the novel *The Winds of War* (1971) by Herman Wouk. Compare

Winston Churchill's speech to the House of Commons, 3 September 1939: 'Outside, the storms of war may blow and the lands may be lashed with the fury of its gales, but in our own hearts this Sunday morning there is peace.'

wine, women and —— Proverb format. As Wolfgang Mieder describes in *Proverbs Are Never Out of Season*, Chap. 4 (1993), although Martin Luther is often credited with the saying, 'Who does not love wine, woman and song, / Remains a fool his whole life long', there is not the slightest evidence that he did. Besides, it was not until 1775 that the attribution was made, and there are many proverbs in Latin and German using the proverb format: 'Night, women, wine are for the adolescent man', 'Dice, wine, love are three things that have made me destitute', 'Three things make much joy: / Wine, women and, strumming', among them. 'Wine, Women and Loud Happy Songs' is the title of a track written by Larry Kingston on Ringo Starr's record album *Beaucoup of Blues* (1970).

wing See COMING IN ON A.

(the) wings of a dove 'O for the wings of a dove' is the title of a song by Mendelssohn and derives from Psalm 55:6: 'And I said, Oh that I had wings like a dove! for then would I fly away, and be at rest.' A novel by Henry James had the title *The Wings of the Dove* (1902). It was adapted for the stage by Christopher Taylor (1966).

winning isn't everything, it's the only thing A sporting catchphrase or slogan (but also common in American business and politics). Various versions of this oft-repeated statement exist. Vince Lombardi, the football coach and general manager of the Green Bay Packers team from 1959 onwards, claimed *not* to have said it in this form but, rather, 'Winning is not everything – but making the effort to win is' (interview 1962). The first version of Lombardi's remarks to appear in print was in the form, 'Winning is not the most important thing, it's everything.' One Bill Veeck is reported to have said something similar. Henry 'Red' Sanders, a football coach at Vanderbilt University, *does* seem to have said it, however, *circa* 1948, and was so quoted in *Sports Illustrated* (26 December 1955). John Wayne, playing a football coach, delivered the line in the 1953 film *Trouble Along the Way*. Compare 'Winning in politics isn't everything; it's the only thing' – a slogan for the infamous 'Committee to Re-Elect the President' (Nixon) in 1972.

winter holds —— in its icy grip   Described as an American journalistic cliché by one Frank Sullivan, and included by Eric Partridge in *A Dictionary of Clichés* (5th edition, 1978). 'Pickets mount lonely vigils at pit gates down leafy lanes resplendent in the golds and russet-reds of autumn, but soon to be in the icy grip of an Appalachian winter' – *Daily Telegraph* (1 November 1993); 'Sweden ran out of influenza vaccine this month, well before winter had exerted its icy grip' – *Financial Times* (8 November 1993); 'As Britain shivers in the icy grip of winter, people's thoughts have inevitably turned to that annual pilgrimage to the holiday sun' – *Today* (3 January 1995).

(a/the) winter of discontent   Shakespeare's *Richard III* (1592) begins, famously, with Gloucester's punning and original metaphor: 'Now is the winter of our discontent / Made glorious summer by this son of York; / And all the clouds that lour'd upon our House / In the deep bosom of the ocean buried' – even if the editor of the Arden edition does describe the entire image as 'almost proverbial'. The phrase 'winter of discontent' suffered the unpleasant fate of becoming a politicians' and journalists' cliché following the winter of 1978/9 when British life was disrupted by all kinds of industrial protests against the Labour Government's attempts to keep down pay rises. The first actual use found is in *The Sun* (30 April 1979). As part of a series on the issues in the forthcoming election, in the week before polling, the paper splashed across two pages the words: 'Winter Of Discontent. Lest we forget . . . the *Sun* recalls the long, cold months of industrial chaos that brought Britain to its knees.' (Sir) Larry Lamb, editor at the time, suggested in a Channel 4 TV programme, *Benn Diaries II* (29 October 1989), that he had introduced the phrase 'in a small way' during the winter

itself (it was imitated by others), then 'in a big way' during the election. James Callaghan, the Prime Minister who was destroyed by the phrase, seems to have claimed that he used it first (recalled in a TV programme, December 1991). There is little new under the *Sun*, of course. J. B. Priestley, writing of earlier much harder times in *English Journey* (1934), ended his fourth chapter with: 'The delegates have seen one England, Mayfair in the season. Let them see another England next time, West Bromwich out of season. Out of all seasons except the winter of discontent.' Compare: 'Poles face LONG HOT SUMMER of discontent' – headline in *The Independent* (5 June 1995).

win this one for the Gipper   A slogan made very much his own by Ronald Reagan throughout his political career. It refers to George Gipp, a character he had played in *Knute Rockne – All-American* (1940). Gipp was a real-life football star who died young. At half-time in a 1928 Army game, Rockne, the team coach, recalled something Gipp had said to him: 'Rock, someday when things look real tough for Notre Dame, ask the boys to go out there and win one for me.' Reagan used the slogan countless times. One of the last was at a campaign rally for his would-be successor, George Bush, in San Diego, California, on 7 November 1988. His peroration included these words: 'So, now we come to the end of this last campaign . . . And I hope that someday your children and grandchildren will tell of the time that a certain President came to town at the end of a long journey and asked their parents and grandparents to join him in setting America on the course to the new millenium . . . So, if I could ask you just one last time. Tomorrow, when mountains greet the dawn, would you go out there and win one for the Gipper? Thank you, and God bless you all.' Interestingly, Richard Nixon included an allusion to the Reagan/Gipp phrase in his speech accepting the Republican nomination in 1968. Former President Eisenhower was critically ill in hospital, and Nixon said, 'There is nothing that would lift him more than for us to win in November. And I say, let us win this one for Ike.'

wish you were here! This cliché of holiday correspondence has been used as the title of songs (reaching the charts in 1953 and 1984) and of a TV travel series (UK, from 1973 onwards). In the full form, **'having a wonderful time**, wish you were here,' *Partridge/Catch Phrases* suggests a beginning in Edwardian times. But why not earlier, at any time since the introduction of the postcard in Britain, which was in 1870? To be sure, cards on which you wrote your own message did not come on the scene until 1894 and the heyday of the picture postcard was in Edwardian times. In the early days, perhaps the message was already printed on the card by the manufacturer? Nowadays, probably, the wording is used only in jest or ironically. 'Let's just slip off and get married quietly and send her a picture postcard from Venice or somewhere, with a cross and a "This is our room. Wish you were here with us" on it' – P. G. Wodehouse, 'Strychnine in the Soup' (1932). *Having Wonderful Time*, a play about a holiday hotel in the Catskills, by Arthur Kober (1937), became, in an exchange of phrases, the musical *Wish You Were Here* in 1952. 'Wish you were here' appeared in a *Punch* cartoon on 30 May 1938. *Wish You Were Here* was also used in 1987 as the title of a British film about sexual awakenings in a seaside resort.

wit and wisdom An inevitable, alliterative conjunction – with a long pedigree. As long ago as 1297 the two words were put together in this combination. In his *Life of Johnson* (1791), James Boswell writes, 'In progress of time . . . I could . . . carry in my memory and commit to paper the exuberant variety of his wisdom and wit' and also of 'Johnsonian wit and wisdom'. In Edgar Allan Poe's tale 'The Fall of the House of Usher' (1845), there is a poem including the line, 'To sing, / In voices of surpassing beauty, / The wit and wisdom of their king.' The earliest use, in the literary sense, of a collection of examples of the two things may be Sir Richard Burton's *Wit and Wisdom from West Africa* (1865). In the modern publishing sense, the first example may be *The Wit and Wisdom of Lloyd George* (1917), edited by D. Rider.

(the) witching hour This cliché seems to have grown out of a blend of such lines as: ''Tis now the very witching time of night, / When churchyards yawn . . .' – Shakespeare, *Hamlet* III.ii.379 (1600–1) and 'It was now the witching hour consecrated to ghost and spirit' – Lord Lytton, *Rienzi* (1835). *The Witching Hour* was the title of a play by Augustus Thomas (*circa* 1915; film US 1921 and 1934). If a precise hour is being suggested, then it tends to be midnight, though this was probably not specified until the Romantic movement got on to it. There is a sonnet addressed to Mrs Siddons, the actress, written by either Coleridge or Lamb or both and published in the *Morning Chronicle* (29 December 1794), which includes these lines: 'Strange tales of fearful dark decrees / Mutter'd to wretch by necromantic spell; / or of those hags, who at the witching time / Of murky Midnight ride the air sublime . . .' In 1796, Walter Scott published his 'The Wild Huntsman', which includes: '. . . By day, they scour earth's cavern'd space, / At midnight's witching hour, ascend.' 'Drop in to The Midnight Shop (223 Brompton Road, SW3), which, as its name suggests, stays open until the witching hour. It claims to be London's original late-night store, and is a well-stocked grocer's and delicatessen' – *Daily Mirror* (3 December 1994).

—— with a difference Promotional use – as in 'the club/disco/hotel/car/anything . . . with a difference'. The phrase was current in the 19th century: 'So also at Westminster – with a difference' – Anthony Trollope, *The Three Clerks* (1857). '*Earth in Orbit* is a geography book with a difference. It is the first programmed textbook of English origin' – *The Guardian* (15 January 1963); 'On Sunday there is to be a sponsored pub crawl with a difference' – presenter on Radio Clyde (1983).

with a little help from —— friends A suggestion as to how the world operates in terms of help from the 'old boy network', relatives, and old friends. But also hinting at how a person may 'get by' or 'cope' through use of drugs, alcohol and financial assistance. The phrase 'with a little help from my friends' (alluding specifically to drugs – ''I get high with a little help from my friends') was the title of a song written by Lennon and McCartney and included on the *Sgt. Pepper's Lonely Hearts Club Band* album (1967).

with a name like Smuckers it must be good   Slogan for Smucker's preserves in the USA, from *circa* 1960. Lois Wyse of Wyse Advertising, New York, recalled (1981): 'Slogans come and go but [this one] has become a part of the language. I wrote it for a company with an unusual name in answer to a challenge from Marc Wyse who said he didn't feel our Smucker advertising differed from the competition. The real job, however, was not thinking up the slogan but selling it to Paul Smucker. The then sales manager said, "If you run that line, Paul, we'll be out of business in six months"! But it's still in use after twenty years.'

. . . with difficulty!   Jocular reply to questions beginning with 'How . . . ?' Since the 1950s/60s. 'Tell me, my dear, how did you manage to get into those jeans?' – 'With difficulty!' 'How do porcupines make love?' – 'With difficulty! (or perhaps, rather, 'Very carefully . . .')

with flying colours   With triumphant ease, great outward success. From the naval use of colours to mean flags. A victorious ship might sail into harbour with all its flags still flying. Known by 1706 (in Farquhar's *The Beaux' Stratagem*). '"We've come off with flying colors," as the ensign said when he ran from the enemy' – *Yankee Notions* (1854); 'Not only did he pass that test with flying colours, but he also found a trump lead, an essential prerequisite for his side extracting the maximum penalty' – *The Daily Telegraph* (24 February 1996).

with friends like these who needs enemies?   A phrase that may be used in desperation after one has been betrayed by a supporter – the earliest example to hand is of something Richard Crossman said of certain Labour MPs in 1969 – or ironically to others in difficulty. A Mahood cartoon caption (*Punch*, 7 January 1970) has dogs in Battersea Dogs Home saying, 'With best friends like that, who needs enemies?' *The Daily Telegraph* used the version in bold above as the headline over a picture spread of Richard Nixon's henchmen on 9 August 1974. But it is of much older provenance. Charlotte Brontë said it, in a letter, concerning the patronizing reviewer of one of her books. *Partridge/Slang* compares it to the proverb: 'With a Hungarian for a friend, who needs an enemy.' George Canning, the 19th-century British politician, wrote a verse ending: 'Save, save, Oh, save me from the candid friend.'

within a hair's breadth   Meaning, 'within a very short distance, very close indeed'. Known by 1584. 'Black was beaten by a hairsbreadth in a blanket finish for the silver and bronze medals' – *The Times* (1 September 1960); 'The first half ended with Brian McLaughlin missing a Hay cross by a hairbreadth and then Andy Walker forcing a great save from Snelders. Immediately, a Billy Dodds run and shot forced Bonner to give away a corner' – *The Herald* (Glasgow) (27 December 1994); 'A further reason why Mr Blair is wise not to tolerate any complacency among his supporters is the formidable, but often underestimated, height of the electoral hurdle facing Labour. The party needs a swing of 4.5% to achieve even a hairsbreadth overall majority; – *The Economist* (6 May 1995).

with knobs on   As in the similar phrases, **with bells on** and **with brass knobs on**, this is a way of saying (somewhat ironically) that something comes with embellishments. British use only. *OED2* has a 1931 citation from J. J. Farjeon. There is also a 1932 one in a theatre review by Herbert Farjeon (perhaps, if they were related, it was a family expression?). It goes: 'A massive company has been assembled at His Majesty's Theatre to restore what is called "the Tree tradition" with an overwhelming production of *Julius Caesar*, which I need hardly tell anyone who knows anything about the Tree tradition means plenty of lictors and vestal virgins or, to sum the matter up in the base vernacular, *Julius Caesar* with knobs on.' 'Same 'ere, wi' knobs on!' occurs in a *Punch* cartoon (17 July 1918). '"Oh, hullo," she said. "Oh, hullo, yourself, with knobs on," retorted Brancepeth. "Never mind the 'Oh, hullo.' I want an explanation"' – P. G. Wodehouse, 'Buried Treasure' (1936).

with malice towards none Phrase taken from Abraham Lincoln's Second Inaugural (1865), after the Civil War: 'With malice toward none; with charity for all; with firmness in the right . . . let us strive on to finish the work we are in.' Hence, the title of a book (1938) about the British by an American, Margaret Halsey.

with one bound he was free (or **with one spring** or **Jack was free)** Said now of anyone who escapes miraculously from a tricky situation or tight corner. The phrase underlines the preposterousness of the adventures in which such lines can be 'spoken'. At first hearing, this construction would seem to come either from cartoon strips, subtitles to silent films, or from *Boy's Own Paper*-type serials of the early 20th century where the hero would frequently escape from seemingly impossible situations, most usually after he had been condemned to them in a 'cliff-hanger' situation. Other suggestions were that the phrase might have originated with Jack Sheppard, the notorious 18th-century robber who was always escaping from Newgate prison, or with 'Springheeled Jack', a legendary Superman-type hero (by 1840) who was supposed to have springs in the heels of his boots. But no citations were to hand. Then it began to seem as if it was from a comedy send-up of boys' adventure stories rather than the real thing. Well, almost. As E. S. Turner notes in *Boys Will Be Boys* (1948): 'There is a delightful story, attributed to more than one publishing house, of the serial writer who disappears in the middle of a story. As he shows no sign of turning up, it is decided to carry on without him. Unfortunately he has left his hero bound to a stake, with lions circling him, and an avalanche about to fall for good measure (or some such situation). Relays of writers try to think of a way out, and give it up. Then at the eleventh hour the missing author returns. He takes the briefest look at the previous instalment and then, without a moment's hesitation, writes: "With one bound Jack was free".' Author Barbara Newman, writing from Washington DC to *The Observer* (29 October 1989), said of TV correspondent and former Beirut hostage Charles Glass: 'His motivation is to keep alive the fiction that he miraculously escaped from his Hizbollah capturers, offering a Ramboesque picture of himself amounting to "and with one spring Jack was free"'; Anthony Powell, in his published journal (for 22 May 1991), discussing the novel *Dracula*, uses a different version: 'Quite how Harker escapes is not clear, rather in the manner of "with a leap Carruthers freed himself".'

without causing a ripple Date of origin not known. Identified as a current cliché in *The Times* (17 March 1995). 'All the same it is difficult to raise the question of constitutional status in any part of the UK without causing a ripple effect elsewhere' – *The Herald* (Glasgow) (22 September 1994); 'Picture, if you please, a swan, gliding serenely across the water, barely causing a ripple. That's presenters Richard Keays and Andy Gray grinning at the camera. Underneath the water, the other 78 bods are paddling away like the Waverley with a turbo charger' – *Sunday Mail* (1 January 1995).

without further ado Meaning, 'without further delay or messing about'. Often used when speaking aloud in public, and consciously archaic, although it appears to be a modern version of 'without more ado' (known since the 14th century). 'At the airport he was stopped by a pimply young border guard who demanded who he was. "I am Rostropovich," the great cellist replied imperiously. After disappearing to consult a superior, the nervous guard let him through without further ado, and Rostropovich went straight to join Boris Yeltsin on the barricades' – *The Independent* (17 June 1994); 'For a change, I thought I would review the events of the last 12 months and give my own awards for achievements great and small . . . I am sadly not joined today by Kim Basinger to present the awards with me. So without further ado, here are the results: Best British Success of the Year . . .' – *The Daily Telegraph* (31 December 1994).

without hesitation, deviation or repetition In the BBC Radio panel game *Just a Minute* (1967–), devised by Ian Messiter, and versions of which have been played in fifty-seven countries, guests have to speak for one minute 'without hesitation, deviation or repetition'. In 1982, an MP stood up in the House of Commons and said, of a guillotine motion, that he thought all speeches on the Bill should be 'like those in that radio game "without deviation, repetition and . . . what was the other?"' Prompts of 'Hesitation!' from other MPs. 'There is no protective, guiding commentary in Radio 1's new four-parter, in which youth speaks without hesitation, deviation or interruption about the things that really matter' – *The Independent* (6 September 1988).

—— without tears Format phrase, maybe slogan, for something out of which the difficulty has been taken (e.g. learning a language) or generally where the pursuit of something is said to be a pleasurable experience and no hardship is involved. Hence, books with titles including *Shakespeare, Knitting, Topology, Latin, Greek, Toilet Training, Federalism, Capitalism . . . Without Tears*. 'A generation which wishes for a religion without tears must find it difficult to adjust its beliefs to the teaching of the New Testament and of the facts of life' – attributed to Dean W. R. Inge (1860–1954); 'Christianity without tears' – Aldous Huxley, *Brave New World*, Chap. 17 (1932); *French Without Tears* – title of a play (1937) by Terence Rattigan.

with respect . . . A somewhat weasel-like softening of a question or piece of point-making, most commonly in British TV political interviews. Sir Robin Day, the TV interviewer, entitled a selection of his greatest hits . . . *But With Respect* (1993), but it is more often than not the politicians themselves who use the phrase. Most notable was Denis Healey when in power as a Labour minister in the 1970s. The phrase is used in a joke told by Lord Geddes of Epsom (President of the TUC, 1954–5) in *Pass the Port* (1976). From 'Things to be wary of' in *The Pillow Book of Eleanor Bron* (1985): 'People who start their sentences with the words "with respect", in order to sound less abrasive and to conceal, even from themselves, their own arrogance. Far from being respectful or deferential it signals contempt for an unworthy opponent and intellectual inferior. Politicians use it frequently, and deliberately, for this very reason.'

with the added bonus of —— An almost tautological inevitable pairing. Date of origin not known. '*The Gossamer Cord . . .* is the latest in Philippa Carr's Daughters of England series, "a sweeping saga of the history of England" and the fiction equivalent of painting by numbers . . . Grab volume five and you can bone up on "the tumult of Restoration, Plague and Fire" with the added bonus of being right-on and politically correct' – *The Sunday Times* (12 July 1992); 'The changes wrought in Compass will "simply be replicated in the US", says Mackay, with the added bonus of acquiring new catering franchises with the Canteen acquisition' – *Evening Standard* (London) (3 May 1994); 'Game wardens feed the crocodiles every night – it is an entertaining distraction for the tourists before dinner – but this time the leopard was an added bonus' – *Evening Standard* (London) (3 May 1994).

with your thumb in your bum and your mind in neutral Idle, vacant, not thinking. Heard from a military sort of person in 1960. As 'thumb in bum, mind in neutral', it has been suggested as dating back to Second World War usage.

wogs begin at Barnet An ironic view of the North/South divide in Britain (Barnet being on the outer edge of northwest London) and clearly based on the old insular, foreigner-distrusting view that **wogs begin at Calais** (known by 1958). The Barnet version appeared in a motion for debate at the Oxford Union (1964) in the form, 'When going North, the wogs begin at Barnet'. Compare NORTH OF WATFORD.

(the) woman in red The 'woman/lady in red' was a phrase used to describe the mysterious girlfriend of the criminal John Dillinger (PUBLIC ENEMY NO. 1). She alerted the FBI to his whereabouts and was herself the subject of a film (US 1979) called *The Lady in Red*. The day after Dillinger was shot by the FBI in 1934, this graffiti verse appeared on a wall nearby: 'Stranger, stop and wish me well, / Just say a prayer for my soul in Hell. / I was a good fellow, most people said, / Betrayed by a woman all dressed in red.' *The Woman in Red* has also been the title of two unrelated films (US 1935 and 1984).

women See ALL.

women and children first! Catchphrase used jokingly in a situation where people might appear to be behaving as though caught in a shipwreck (in a crowded bus or train perhaps). It originated in the incident involving HMS *Birkenhead*, one of the first ships to have a hull of iron, in 1852. She was taking 476 British soldiers to the eighth 'Kaffir War' in the Eastern Cape of South Africa when she ran aground fifty miles off the Cape of Good Hope. It was clear that the ship would go under but only three of the eight lifeboats could be used and these were rapidly filled with the twenty women and children on board. According to tradition, soldiers remained calm and did not even break ranks when the funnel and mast crashed down on to the deck, with the loss of 445 lives. Thus was born the tradition of 'women and children' first. In naval circles, this is still known as the Birkenhead Drill. Somerset Maugham said he always chose to sail on French ships: 'Because there's none of that nonsense about women and children first!' In 1968, Lord Egremont, writing his family history, gave details of the exploits his forbears were prepared to perpetrate in order to obtain land and titles. The zeal of his ancestors for their aggrandizement at the expense of others, coupled with his family name which he used as the author, John Wyndham, gave him the title, *Wyndham and Children First*.

women are like buses (or **streetcars): there'll be another coming along soon** An observation from the USA around 1900, slightly later in the UK. Compare this allusion to the saying by Derick Heathcoat-Amory when British Chancellor of the Exchequer (1958–60): 'There are three things not worth running for – a bus, a woman or a new economic panacea; if you wait a bit another one will come along.'

women reclaim the night See TAKE BACK.

wonderland See ALICE IN.

wonders will never cease! Exclamation of surprise at an unexpected outcome. Known by 1828. Used as a headline in *Punch* Magazine (14 September 1844).

wood See ANOTHER PART OF THE.

Woodbine See AH.

(a) woolly pully A weekend driver in the UK, from his or her habit of wearing woollen pullovers. *Partridge/Slang* has the term applied simply to the pullover itself, from *circa* 1960.

word See AND NOW A.

(a) word in edgeways Phrase often used when complaining that one has been left out of the conversation by an over-talkative other. 'I couldn't get a word in edgeways,' one might say. Originally, 'edgewise'. 'As if it were possible for any of us to slide in a word edgewise' – Nancy Russell Mitford, *Our Village*, (1832). A long-running discussion programme on the BBC Home Service/Radio 4 (from 1965 to the 1980s) had the title *A Word in Edgeways*.

(by) word of mouth One person telling another by speech, not by writing. Usually applied to a recommendation to see some entertainment or other. Known by 1553; the secondary use by 1951. 'Of the three chances in her favour, on which she had reckoned at the outset of the struggle – the chance of entrapping Magdalen by word of mouth . . .' – Wilkie Collins, *No Name* (1862–3); 'Back to the subject of reviews. I believe the only thing that matters to an author is word-of-mouth advertising' – P. G. Wodehouse in a letter (7 March 1946); 'An award-winning Glasgow hotelier and restaurateur who is expanding east . . . Eventually the problem was solved by word of mouth recommendations by well-known people' – *The Scotsman* (1 February 1994); 'The life of the impresario is not all bouquets and sell-out shows . . . For real exposure, though, you need to rely on more than friends and word of mouth' – *The Independent* (2 February 1994).

workers See BLACK-COATED; HELLO FOLKS.

workers of the world, unite! Political slogan in the UK and elsewhere. Latterly the slogan of Industrial Workers of the World. It is taken from the closing words of *The Communist Manifesto* (1848) by Karl Marx and Friedrich Engels: 'Let the ruling classes tremble at a communist revolution. The proletarians [*or* workers] have nothing to lose in this [revolution] but their chains. They have a world to gain. Workers of the world, unite!' Whether it was Marx or Engels or another who actually coined the slogan, it is difficult to say. The League of the Just held a party congress in London 2–9 June 1847. On June 9, the congress produced draft articles, changing the name to League of Communists. These draft articles – that were rediscovered only in 1968 – are headed by the motto *Proletarier aller Länder, vereinigt Euch* [proletarians of all countries, unite]! This is the earliest-known instance of the slogan. The first public use of the slogan dates from September 1847, when it served as motto to a trial issue of the *Kommunistische Zeitschrift*, edited by Karl Schapper. Marx is an unlikely candidate for authorship, as he was not present at the congress. Friedrich Engels was present but when, in 1885, he described the history of the movement, he merely stated that the old slogan had been replaced by the new one.

world See ALL THE.

(the) world is not enough When a James Bond film was entitled *The World Is Not Enough* (UK/US 1999), it harked back to an earlier one in the series, *On Her Majesty's Secret Service* (UK 1060). In that film, a member of the College of Heralds shows the Bond family coat of arms on which the Latin motto is '*Orbis non sufficie*'. Only the English is given in Fleming's novel, but it would appear that he had done his research. '*Non sufficit orbis*' is the motto of the Bond family of Dorset and, in this form, would appear to be a quotation from Juvenal's *Satires*, No. 10, line 168, where the satirist is illustrating the folly of military glory. The once great Hannibal is reduced to living in exile and finally committing suicide at the arrival of Roman troops at his desert hideaway: 'Whilst one globe seemed too small for the youthful Alexander [*unus pellaeo iuveni non sufficit orbis*], yet a small coffin was enough to contain him when he died of a fever at Babylon.' *The World Is Not Enough* was also used as the title of a 1948 translation of *Argile et cendres* (1946) by the novelist Zoé Oldenbourg.

(to believe the) world owes one a living
Walt Disney's film *The Grasshopper and the Ants* (US 1934), in the 'Silly Symphonies' series, was based on the Aesop fable 'Of the ant and the grasshopper' – as it is called in Caxton's first English translation (1484), which tells of a grasshopper asking an ant for corn to eat in winter. The ant asks, 'What have you done all the summer past?' and the grasshopper can only answer, 'I have sung.' The moral is that you should provide yourself in the summer with what you need in winter. Disney turns the grasshopper into a fiddler and gives him a song to sing – 'Oh! the world owes me a living.' This became quite well known and presumably helped John Llewellyn Rhys choose *The World Owes Me a Living* for his 1939 novel about a redundant Royal Flying Corps hero who tries to make a living with a flying circus (filmed 1944). It is a little odd rendered in this form, because on the whole it is not something people say about themselves. More usually, another would say, pejoratively, 'The trouble with you is you think the world owes you a living.' The proverbial seems not to have been much known before Disney. In W. G. Sumner's *Earth Hunger* (1896), the American author writes: 'The men who start out with the notion that the world owes them a living generally find that the world pays its debt in the penitentiary or the poorhouse.'

worlds See ALEXANDER WEEPING.

(the) world, the flesh and the devil
Phrase from the Litany in the Book of Common Prayer: 'From fornication, and all other deadly sins; and from all the deceits of the world, the flesh, and the devil, *Good Lord, deliver us*.' Hence the expression 'The world, the flesh, and the devil' with the words in the order given – as used, for example, as a film title (UK 1914 and US 1959). There was also a film (US 1927) called *Flesh and the Devil*. Again, in the Collect for the Eighteenth Sunday after Trinity, we find: 'Lord, we beseech thee, grant thy people grace to withstand the temptations of the world, the flesh, and the devil.' The same combination also occurs in the Catechism, where the confirmee is asked what his Godfathers and Godmothers had promised for him at

his baptism: 'First, that I should renounce the *devil* and all his works, the pomps and vanity of this wicked *world*, and all the sinful lusts of the *flesh.*' In the 16th and 17th centuries, the words were also grouped together in a different order to denote 'our ghostly enemies' – as, for example, 'the devil, the world, and the flesh' (1530).

(the) world turned upside down (1) A popular name for English inns. (2) The title of an American tune played when the English surrendered at Yorktown (1781). (3) A figure of speech, as in Robert Burton's *The Anatomy of Melancholy* (1621–51): 'Women wear the breeches . . . in a word, the world turned upside downward'. (4) The title of a well-known tract dating from the English Civil War concerning ridiculous fashions (1646). The origin for all these is possibly biblical: 'Behold, the Lord maketh the earth empty, and maketh it waste, and turneth it upside down' (Isaiah 24:1); 'These that have turned the world upside down are come hither also' (Acts 17:6). Compare the French expression *la vie à l'envers* [life upside down/ the wrong way round], used as the title of a film (1964).

World War II (or Two) After the FIRST WORLD WAR, what could be more natural than to have the **Second World War**? But, of course, it was not immediately recognized as such by all. At first, in 1939, some tried to refer to it as 'the war in Europe', but *Time* Magazine was quick off the mark: 'World War II began last week at 5:20 am (Polish time) Friday, September 1, when a German bombing plane dropped a projectile on Puck, fishing village and air base in the armpit of the Hel Peninsula . . .' Soon after this, Duff Cooper published a book of his collected newspaper articles entitled *The Second World War*. When it quite clearly *was* a world war, in 1942, President Roosevelt tried to find an alternative appellation. After rejecting 'Teutonic Plague' and 'Tyrants' War', he settled for 'The War of Survival'. But this did not catch on. Finally, in 1945, the US *Federal Register* announced that, with the approval of President Truman, the LATE UNPLEASANTNESS was to be known as 'World War II'. (In other less global conflicts, the name of a war depends on which side you are on: the Vietnam War is known to the Vietnamese as 'the American War'.) In the Soviet Union, the Second World War was known as *Velikaya Otechestvennaya Voyna* – **the Great Fatherland (or Patriotic) War**.

worms See CAN OF.

(a) worm's eye view (1) a view as a worm would see it, i.e. the subject is viewed from below rather than above (which would be a 'bird's eye view'). (2) a revealing perspective and understanding of a subject or problem – and one that may be based on actual knowledge of the details or people involved. Known by 1933 in a straightforward architectural sense. 'I write from the worm's-eye point of view' – Ernie Pyle, *Here Is Your War* (1943). *Worm's Eye View* was the title of a play by R. F. Delderfield (London 1945; filmed UK 1951) about a group of RAF billetees.

(the) worm turns Phrase alluding to the proverb, 'Tread on a worm and it will turn', meaning that even the humblest won't take ill-treatment and may eventually rise up and take revenge. A proverb by the 16th century.

worse things happen at sea This consolatory phrase was first recorded in 1829 as 'Worse accidents occur at sea!' – Pierce Egan, *Boxiana*. Casson/Grenfell has it as a nannyism. *Worse Things Happen at Sea* was the title of a play by Keith Winter, presented in London in April 1935.

worth See BECAUSE I'M WORTH IT.

worth a guinea a box Slogan for Beecham's pills (for stomach disorders and headaches) in the UK from 1859. This slogan appeared in the first advertisement Thomas Beecham ever placed in a newspaper, the *St Helens Intelligencer*, on 6 August 1859. Family tradition has it that the saying was inspired by a woman in St Helens market who approached Thomas and asked for another box, saying: 'They're worth a guinea to me, lad.' But in 1897 Thomas stated categorically that he himself had 'struck out from the metal anvil that spark of wit which has made the pills a household word in every quarter of the globe'.

(to be) worth one's salt To be of worth, of strong character and worth employing on any task or in any job. Neil Ewart in *Everyday Phrases* (1983) suggests that 'before money was introduced, soldiers and workers in ancient Roman times had their wages paid in salt'. One wonders whether they really liked this procedure. After all, what did they put the salt on if they did not have the money to buy food? A *salarium* was what was paid to soldiers *for the purchase of* salt. From *salarium* we get our word, 'salary'. If a man was not worth his salt, therefore, he was not worth his salary. *Brewer* takes a middle course and says that a *salarium* was a salt ration that was later replaced by money but retained the same name.

wotalotigot! Slogan for Smarties chocolates, used in the UK from *circa* 1958 to 1964. The slogan was found by the advertising agency's taping children playing with and chattering about the product. At the end of the TV ads came the curious tag, **buy some for Lulu!**

wot no ——? The most common graffito of the past 100 years in Britain – apart from KILROY WAS HERE (with which it was sometimes combined) – is the so-called figure of 'Chad', 'Mr Chad' or 'The Chad'. In Britain at least, there is no doubt that Chad made his first appearance in the early stages of the Second World War, accompanied by protests about shortages of the time, such as 'Wot no cake?', 'Wot no char?', 'Wot no beer?' The format was then used by Watneys London Ltd, the brewers, to promote their beer sometime in the 1940s or 50s. The slogan 'Wot no Watneys?' was shown written on a brick wall – or so everybody says. Possibly, however, they may be confusing this with the famous poster that showed graffiti on a brick wall declaring 'What we want is Watneys' or 'We want Watneys'? Alas, Watneys themselves have no copy of any of these adverts in their archives. In 1933, at the end of Prohibition, Buster Keaton had played in an American film farce with the title *What, No Beer?* As always, there's nothing new . . .

would you believe . . . ? Used when making some exaggerated suggestion.

'One of the cringe-phrases of the age . . . You couldn't go an hour without hearing someone say it in Los Angeles' – Derek Taylor, *It Was Twenty Years Ago Today* (1987). He attributes its popularity to the *Get Smart* TV show (1965–70), created by Buck Henry and Mel Brooks and starring Don Adams. *The Complete Directory to Prime Time Network TV Shows* (1981) adds: 'Used whenever [a secret agent] of K.A.O.S. or someone on [Maxwell Smart's] own side didn't seem to accept one of his fabrications and he was trying to come up with a more acceptable alternative. That catch-phrase became very popular with young people in the late 1960s.'

would you be more careful if it was you that got pregnant? Headline of a (British) Health Education Council poster showing a pregnant *male* (1970) and written by Jeremy Sinclair. *The Sun* commented that it 'made previous campaigns look like Mary Poppins'.

would you be shocked . . . ? See SLIP INTO SOMETHING MORE COMFORTABLE.

would you buy a used car from this man? Although attributed by some to Mort Sahl and by others to Lenny Bruce, and though the cartoonist Herblock had to deny that he was responsible for it – in *The Guardian* (24 December 1975) – this is just a joke and one is no more going to find an origin for it than for most such. The line dates from 1952 at least (before any of the above-named humorists really got going). Hugh Brogan, writing in *New Society* (4 November 1982): 'Nixon is a double-barrelled, treble-shotted twister, as my old history master would have remarked; and the fact has been a matter of universal knowledge since at least 1952, when, if I remember aright the joke, "Would you buy a second-hand car from this man?" began to circulate.' It was a very effective slur, and by 1968 – when Nixon was running (successfully) for president, a poster was in circulation bearing a shifty-looking picture of him and the line. One might use the phrase now about anybody one has doubts about. The *Encyclopedia of Graffiti* (1974) even finds: 'Governor Romney – would you buy a *new* car from this man?' In August 1984,

John de Lorean said of himself – after being acquitted of drug-dealing – 'I have aged 600 years and my life as a hard-working industrialist is in tatters. Would you buy a used car from me?'

wreckage See CLINGING TO THE.

(you look like the) wreck of the Hesperus 'A family saying that I did not resolve for almost fifty years was why, if I came in untidy or windswept, my mother always said, "You look like the Wreck of the Hesperus!"' – Janet M. Carr, Isle of Wight (1997). In fact, this used to be a common expression for 'in a mess, in a sad state'. The reference is to 'The Wreck of the Hesperus', title of Longfellow's poem (1839), much recited in Victorian days and relating the actual shipwreck of a schooner off the coast of New England. It contains such immortal lines as: 'The skipper he stood beside the helm, / His pipe was in his mouth.' The skipper has unfortunately taken his daughter along with him and when a hurricane blows up, he lashes her to the mast – and that's where she's found washed up the next morning. *Partridge/Catch Phrases* dates the use of this to the late 19th century. 'He looked and behaved like the Wreck of the *Hesperus*' – P. G. Wodehouse, *The Code of the Woosters*, Chap. 10 (1938). 'The Wreck of the Hesperus' is also referred to in the song 'Lydia, the Tattooed Lady' – lyrics by E. Y. Harburg, music by Harold Arlen (1939) as though it were commonly known as a picture.

writ large Meaning, 'in enlarged, grand, more prominent form'. John Milton's 'On the New Forcers of Conscience under the Long Parliament' (1646) has 'New *Presbyter* is but Old *Priest* writ Large'. 'In her spring or even summer, one might easily have penned the Thatcher speech: simple virtues, simple prescriptions, Great Britain plc as the family grocery writ large. But yesterday – in a speech no ghost could have written for her – there was a new autumnal, even elegiac Thatcher' – *The Guardian* (27 September 1989); 'The Royal Family is an ordinary family writ large. That has always been its attraction . . . They provide a universal topic of conversation, a frame of reference, and offer proof that, even though they live in bigger houses, wear better clothes and take more glamorous holidays, they are as prone as the rest of us to making mistakes' – *The Independent* (7 January 1995); 'The British documentary tradition . . . became more accessible to the general public when fused with the melodrama of everyday life in a succession of wartime films like *Millions Like Us* and *This Happy Breed*, which created an image of an integrated community – the family writ large – characterised by distinctively British virtues: service and sacrifice, restraint, tolerance and decency' – *Sunday Telegraph* (23 April 1995).

(the) writing (is) on the wall A hint, sign or portent, often doom-laden. The idea – though not the phrase – comes from the Bible (Daniel 5) where King Belshazzar is informed of the forthcoming destruction of the Babylonian Empire through the appearance of a man's hand-writing on a wall. Jonathan Swift was using the precise phrase by *circa* 1720. Note also: 'Here, while the national prosperity feasts, like another Belshazzar, on the spectacle of its own magnificence, is the Writing on the Wall, which warns the monarch, Money, that his glory is weighed in the balance, and his power found wanting' – Wilkie Collins, *No Name* (1862). In a BBC broadcast to resistance workers in Europe (31 July 1941), 'Colonel Britton' (Douglas Ritchie) talked of the V for Victory sign that was being chalked up in occupied countries: 'All over Europe the V sign is seen by the Germans and to the Germans and the Quislings it is indeed the writing on the wall . . .' 'The 'eighties and 'nineties were the GOLDEN AGE [of music-hall]; and in 1905 the writing was on the wall . . . Musical comedy, the cinema, television all hastened its decline' – *The Listener* (2 December 1965). Listed by Keith Waterhouse in *Daily Mirror Style* (1981) as a phrase to be avoided. Listed in *The Independent* (24 December 1994) as a cliché of newspaper editorials. 'And it was about this time that Nigel Rees saw the writing on the wall [as graffiti collector] . . .' – Derek Batey on Border TV, *Look Who's Talking* (30 November 1983).

wrong box See IN THE.

(he was the) wrong side of the hedge when the brains were given away
Meaning, 'he is brainless or stupid'. Known since the 19th century in the UK and USA. Compare **she wasn't around when the looks were given out** (said of an unattractive person).

(on/from the) wrong side of the tracks
Living or born in the less respectable part of town – where the poorer, socially inferior people live. Of American origin, and the concept, if not the phrase, was current by 1929. The main railway tracks are often an important dividing line in an American community. 'We're just two little girls from Little Rock / We lived on the wrong side of the tracks' – lyric by Jule Styne, 'A Little Girl from Little Rock', *Gentlemen Prefer Blondes* (1949); 'Eva Duarte Peron . . . came from the wrong side of the tracks' – *The Listener* (13 October 1977).

wu-hey! For his character of Alf Ippititi-mus, the British comedy performer Jack Douglas (b. 1927) created what for me is one of the most compelling verbal and *visual* catchphrases of all. The bodily twitch that accompanies this phrase defies description. It was based on the nervous spasm of Eric Winstone, the bandleader, but arose when Douglas was appearing in a double-act with Joe Baker at a holiday camp. Baker managed to get himself locked out of the theatre and Douglas found himself alone on stage. 'My mind went completely blank and in sheer desperation I began twitching and falling about.' I recall seeing him in pantomime with Des O'Connor at Oxford in the mid-60s. The audience just waited for him to come on again and do his twitch.

WYSIWYG [What You See Is What You Get] An acronym from computing, meant to suggest that what the operator sees on the computer screen is exactly how the material will appear when printed out (i.e. with correct typefaces, artwork, etc.). It rapidly became a way of expressing that a person was not deceiving by appearances. The full version appears in the lyrics of *Jesus Christ Superstar!* (1970). President Bush spoke the full version on the first day of the Gulf War (16 January 1991) when asked how he was feeling.

X

X marks the spot From the use of the letter X or a cross to show the location of something (buried treasure perhaps) on a map. The *OED2*'s earliest citation is in a letter from Maria Edgeworth (16 May 1813): 'The three crosses X mark the three places where we were let in.' By 1923, P. G. Wodehouse was writing about the producer of a disastrous amateur theatrical event in *The Inimitable Jeeves*, Chap. 15: 'Sitting on a box in the wings perspiring pretty freely and looking more or less like the spot marked with a cross where the accident happened.' The actual phrase 'X marks the spot' appears to have originated with Chicago newspapers in the early days of gangsterism. Here, the 'X' indicated the position of a dead body in a photo of the scene of a murder. At that time, taste dictated that the actual corpse was not shown. Then when the corpses left by the St Valentine's Day Massacre (1929) *were* shown in the press, the graphic shot affected public perception of the gangsters, and the hope was that this would help prevent any glamorising of the gangsters and sway public opinion against them. As a result, in slang of the time, 'spotted' came to mean 'murdered' and '**to be put on the spot**' took on a specific implication. Some time in the 1920s there was a silent film (US) with the title *X Marks the Spot*. A booklet published in Chicago by The Spot Publishing Company (1930) had the title *Chicago Gang Wars in Pictures, X Marks the Spot*.

Y

yabba-dabba-doo! Cry of delight from the US TV cartoon series *The Flintstones* (1960–66), which was a parody of suburban life set in the Stone Age and came from the Hanna-Barbera studios. *Partridge/Catch Phrases* has it popular with Australian surfers and British servicemen overseas in the early 1960s. It was used substantially in the promotion of the feature film *The Flintstones* (US 1994), which used real actors in the cartoon roles. More than one critic of this film when advising audiences whether to go and see it, wrote, 'Yabba-dabba-don't!' But surely the phrase must have predated *The Flintstones* – in jazz perhaps? The American novelty song 'Aba Daba Honeymoon' (telling of the love affair between a monkey and a chimpanzee) was published in 1914. And then there is the British expression '(to have the) screaming abdabs', meaning '(to be in) a state of extreme agitation, enraged frustration' and current by the 1940s.

(to) yakkety-yak To chatter non-stop. 'To ya(c)k' is American slang for 'to chatter' and was current by 1950. Made famous by the song 'Yakkety-Yak', written by Lieber and Stoller and recorded by the Coasters in 1958.

Yanks go home Anti-US slogan; wherever there was unwanted American military and/or business presence, after the Second World War. 'Yankee/Yanqui Go Home' was widely used throughout Latin America from 1950 on.

yaroooo! When Billy Bunter, the famous fat boy created by Frank Richards, came to be recreated for BBC TV (1952–62), he was played memorably by Gerald Campion. The actor gave a memorably metallic ring to this phrase and to **I say, you fellows!** Among the other pupils at Greyfriars School, the Indian boy, Hurree Jamset Ram (known as 'Inky'), had a format phrase, **the ——fulness is terrific!**, as in 'the rottenfulness is terrific' or as in this example from one of the original stories by Richards. '"Are we not in a state of warfulness?" [asked Inky]. Bob Cherry

chuckled: "The warfulness is terrific, as terrific as your variety of the English language, Inky"' – in *The Magnet*, No. 401 (October 1915).

(a) yawning gap An inevitable word pairing. Date of origin not known. Listed in *The Independent* (24 December 1994) as a cliché of newspaper editorials. 'A reflation stimulus is urgently needed now to fill the yawning gap in consumer demand' – *New Scientist* (10 June 1971); 'Mr Norman Ireland, of Reuters Business Information, said the results showed a "yawning gap" between the recognised value of information and the way in which it was managed as a proper asset' – *Financial Times* (16 May 1995); 'Nevertheless there is a yawning gap between the visionary "guiding idea" of the production, nurtured presumably by Crowley, and the actual monologues (each supported by the other actors in indifferent impersonations), which are mostly student humour about the vicissitudes of innocents abroad' – *Financial Times* (16 May 1995).

(the) year of living dangerously Title of a film (Australia 1982) based on a novel, *The Year of Living Dangerously*, by Christopher Koch. In the novel, President Sukarno of Indonesia is quoted as having declared 1960-something to be 'the Year of Living Dangerously'. Much alluded to. 'Ross Perot is the untested wild man [in the Presidential election] . . . admirers say in this political year of living dangerously, anything is possible' – *The New York Times* (29 March 1992); 'Well, this was always destined to be the year of behaving strangely' – Martin Amis, *London Fields*, Prologue (1989); 'Year of living cautiously' – headline in *The Observer* (4 December 1994).

years See FIRST; HAPPIEST.

—— years young Disc jockey and radio presenter use – 'She is 97 years young', etc. Slightly facetious and self-conscious avoidance of '—— years old'. 'To be fair they also twice worked a player free with nobody between him and the line 60 metres away; unfortunately the player was Jeff Probyn, 38 years young and not, at the best of times, built for speed' – *The Times* (10 October 1994).

year zero Term used *circa* 1975 by the Khmer Rouge during their takeover of Cambodia – meaning that the past had been obliterated, nothing had come before. *Cambodia: Year Zero* is the title of a relevant book (1978) by François Ponchaud. The phrase has also been applied to other 'starting from scratch' positions: an Italian/West German film (1947) set in postwar Berlin was entitled *Germania, Anno Zero [Germany, Year Zero]*; a film (US 1962) set in Los Angeles after a nuclear attack was called *Panic in Year Zero*.

ye gods and little fishes! Mock-heroic exclamation of contempt or indignation, possibly derived from 19th-century drama. 'But out of school, – Ye gods and little fishes! how Tommy did carouse!' – Louisa M. Alcott, *Little Men*, Chap. 2 (1871).

yeh, yeh, yeh 'Yeh' as a common corruption of 'yes' has been current (and derived from the USA) since the 1920s. But whether spelt 'yeh-yeh-yeh', as in the published lyrics, or 'yeah-yeah-yeah' (which captures the Liverpudlian pronunciation better), this phrase became a hallmark of the Beatles after its use in their song 'She Loves You'. The record they made of the song was in the UK charts for thirty-one weeks from August 1963 and was for fourteen years Britain's all-time best-selling 45 rpm record. Though most commonly associated with the Beatles, the phrase was not new. Some of the spade-work in Britain had been done by the non-Liverpudlian singer Helen Shapiro who had a hit in September 1961 with 'Walking Back to Happiness', which included the refrain 'Whoop Bah Oh Yeah Yeah'. The Beatles had toured with Shapiro topping the bill before their own careers took off. Following the Beatles' use, there was a French expression in the early 1960s – '*yé yé*' – to describe fashionable clothing.

(the) yellow peril Phrase, first recorded in the 1890s, describing the supposed threat to White people or to the world generally from Asiatic peoples and especially the Chinese. On 4 September 1909, Winston Churchill said in a speech: 'It [the worst threat to Britain] is not in the Yellow Peril, or the Black Peril, or any danger in the wide circuit of colonial and foreign affairs. It is here in our midst.'

ye olde tea shoppe The form 'ye olde' (pronounced 'yee oldee') has become the conventional way of evoking and repro-ducing the speech and writing of English earlier than, say, 1600. It is, however, based on a misconception that the letter '**Þ**' appearing on old manuscripts is the equivalent of the modern 'y'. In fact '**Þ**' – known to Old English and Icelandic philologists as the letter 'thorn' – is pro-nounced with a 'th' sound. Thus, even in Anglo-Saxon times – however peculiar some pronunciations might have been – '**Þe**' would have been pronounced like modern 'the'. 'Ye' did, of course, exist as the second person pronoun. The modern mispronunciation was recorded by 1925.

yeoman service Meaning, 'useful service as rendered by a faithful servant'. 'It did me yeoman's service' – Shakespeare, *Hamlet* V.ii.36 (1600–1). 'Sir, – Your correspondent, Frank McDonald, who has given yeoman service to the protection of our environment, has been misinformed to a degree in regard to the objections to the High Speed Service (HSS) scheme for Dun Laoghaire Harbour' – letter to the editor in *The Irish Times* (9 June 1994).

yer darn tootin' General catchphrase taken to himself by George 'Gabby' Hayes in almost all the films he made with William Boyd ('Hopalong Cassidy'), e.g., *Hills of Old Wyoming* (US 1937). A Laurel and Hardy film had the title *You're Darn' Tootin'* (US 1928). An early allusion is in P. G. Wodehouse's Hollywood story 'The Nodder' (1933), where its meaning is made clear in this exchange: '"Spurned your love, did she?" "You're dern tooting she spurned my love," said Wilmot. "Spurned it good and hard".' The phrase also occurs in *Destry Rides Again* (US 1939).

yer plonker! Abusive epithet ('you idiot!') popularized by Del Boy (David Jason) when referring to his younger brother, Rodney, in the BBC TV comedy series

Only Fools and Horses and current by 1986. In London dialect, 'plonker' = 'penis' (compare the epithets 'prick' and 'schmuck'). From the same series came the other abusive epithets **dipstick** (probably because rhyming with 'prick'), **noofter** and **woofter** (the last two rhyming with 'poofter' = homosexual). The term **lovely jubbly** for money, also used in the series, is derived from a post-Second World War advertisement for a soft drink called Jubbly.

yes, I think so! Catchphrase of the Reverend Vivian Foster, 'The Vicar of Mirth' (1868–1945), who delivered mock sermons in a parsonical voice in British music halls. In the 1920s/30s, he transferred his act to wireless and gramophone records. From a 1933 recorded sermon: 'You know, there are three kinds of untruths: fibs, lies and statistics. Statistics can say anything! I read the other week that in the heavy traffic a man was knocked down in the streets every twenty minutes and I wondered how long it would take to get home . . . yes, I think so!'

yesterdays See ALL OUR.

yesterday's men Political slogan that had to be scrapped during the 1970 British General Election campaign, before which the phrase had been an established idiom applied to any 'has-been' – a song with the title 'Yesterday Man' was a hit for Chris Andrews in the British charts (1965). The Labour Party had issued a poster showing crudely coloured models of Conservative politicians (Edward Heath, Iain Macleod, Lord Hailsham and others) and the additional line 'They failed before'. It was considered to be in poor taste. In fact, Labour lost the election to the men it had ridiculed as 'yesterday's' and the phrase continued to cause trouble. In 1971 it was used as the title of a BBC TV programme about how the defeated Labour leaders were faring in Opposition. This soured relations between the BBC and the Labour Party for a long while afterwards.

yesteryear See HI YO.

yes, we have no bananas Phrase from the song 'Yes, We Have No Bananas' (1923), written by Irving Cohn to music by Frank Silver: 'Yes, we have no bananas, / We have no bananas today.' According to Ian Whitcomb in *After the Ball* (1972), the title line came from a cartoon strip by Tad Dorgan and not, as the composers were wont to claim, from a Greek fruit-store owner on Long Island. Alternatively, it was a saying picked up by US troops in the Philippines from a Greek pedlar. In Britain, Elders & Fyffes, the banana importers, embraced the song and distributed 10,000 hands of bananas to music-sellers with the slogan: 'Yes! we have no bananas! On sale here'.

(to) yield to public pressure The phrase 'public pressure' on its own was known by 1815. Listed in *The Independent* (24 December 1994) as a cliché of newspaper editorials. 'Montgomery later said his forces were short of ammunition and troops . . . "It would have been very easy for me to yield to public criticism and American pressure and to have made greater efforts to gain ground on this flank"' – *The Independent* (3 June 1994); 'It brought it into their living rooms, and with the protests, people saw that public pressure, people power, can yield results. They have realized that they can make a difference' – *The Herald* (Glasgow) (8 February 1995).

ying-tong-iddle-i-po! Catchphrase from the BBC radio *Goon Show* (1951–60). All-purpose nonsense phrase, notably incorporated in 'The Ying Tong Song'.

you ain't seen nothin' yet! President Ronald Reagan appropriated this catchphrase as a kind of slogan in his successful 1984 bid for re-election. He used it repeatedly during the campaign and, on 7 November, in his victory speech. *Partridge/Catch Phrases* has a combined entry for 'you ain't seen nothin' yet' and **you ain't heard nothin' yet**, in which 'seen' is described as the commoner of the two versions. Both are said to date from the 1920s. One could add that Bachman-Turner Overdrive, the Canadian pop group, had a hit with a song called 'You Ain't Seen Nothin' Yet' in 1974. As for 'you ain't heard . . .', it seems that when Al Jolson exclaimed 'You ain't heard nothin' yet!' in the first full-length talking picture, *The Jazz Singer* (US 1927), he wasn't just ad-libbing as is usually supposed. He was promoting the title of one of his songs. He had recorded 'You Ain't Heard Nothing Yet', written by Gus Kahn and Buddy de Sylva, in 1919, and had also used the words as a catchphrase in his act before making the film.

you and whose army? An illustration of how this taunt was used in the 1950s: 'Two boys are arguing. One of the lads – A – has sweets which he refuses to share with the other – B. B: "Give us a sweet." A: "No, they're mine." B: "I'll take one from you." A: "Oh yes, you and who's army?" The last reply implies that B is not up to the job of confiscation without a lot of help.' *Partridge/Slang* has this version dated 1944 and 'You – and who else?' from about 1925 – 'a catchphrase of derisive defiance addressed to a belligerent opponent.' *Lou, to man who says she needs smacking*: 'Yeh, and who's going to do the smacking? You and what militia?' – line from film *Two Girls And a Guy* (US 1997).

you and yours Phrase embracing a person's relatives and dependents, in use since 1300. A long-running BBC Radio programme *You and Yours* has dealt with family and personal matters since 1970.

you are Mr Lobby Lud and I claim ... A circulation-raising stunt for British newspapers in the 1920s took the form of a challenge readers were encouraged to put to a man they were told would be in a certain place (usually a seaside resort) on a particular day. His description and a photograph were given in the paper, and 'You are so-and-so and I claim my £10' (or whatever the prize was) became the formula. The reader had, of course, to be carrying a copy of that day's paper. The first in the field was the *Westminster Gazette* in August 1927, and the correct challenge was: 'You are Mr Lobby Lud – I claim the *Westminster Gazette* prize' (which was initially £50, though if it was unclaimed it increased weekly). The name 'Lobby Lud' came from the *Gazette*'s telegraphic address – 'Lobby' because of the Westminster connection and 'Lud' from Ludgate Circus off Fleet Street. The stunt did nothing for the paper, which closed the following year, but the idea was taken up by the *Daily News* and the *News Chronicle* and ran on for several years. In

the film of Graham Greene's novel *Brighton Rock* (UK 1947), the name becomes 'Kolley Kibber' and has to be challenged with the words, 'You are Kolley Kibber and I claim the *Daily Messenger* prize.'

you are the weakest link – goodbye Stock phrase from the BBC TV general knowledge quiz *The Weakest Link* (since 2000 and in other versions around the world). The presenter, Anne Robinson, assumes a schoolmistressy air and chastises contestants who have performed badly. Contestants vote to eject the person they consider to be 'The Weakest Link' from the competition. This loser is then sent down the 'Walk of Shame' with this phrase ringing in his or her ears. All very odd.

you are what you eat This neat encapsulation of a sensible attitude to diet (known in the USA by 1941) was used as the title of an 'alternative' American film that was first shown in Britain in 1969. The idea behind the phrase has been around for many a year, however. Compare Brillat-Savarin in *La Physiologie du goût*: 'Tell me what you eat and I will tell you what you are' and L. A. Feuerbach: 'Man is what he eats [*Der Mensch ist, was er ißt*]' – in a review of Moleschott's *Lehre der Nahrungsmittel für das Volk* (1850). The German film chronicle *Heimat* (1984) included the version, '*Wie der Mensch ißt, so ist er* [as a man eats, so he is].'

you('d) better believe it! An emphatic 'yes'. Known in the USA by 1865.

you bet your sweet bippy! Catchphrase from NBC TV, *Rowan and Martin's Laugh-In* (1967–73), usually spoken by Dick Martin.

you can always look down and pick nothing up Meaning, 'try to better yourself rather than take the easy option'. *Partridge/Slang* has this as 'You can always stoop and pick up nothing!' and considers it mostly of Cockney use and a 'remark made by a friend after a "row" or by a parent concerning a child's intended husband (or wife)'.

you cannot be serious! By 1980, John McEnroe, the American tennis player and Wimbledon champion, had become celebrated for his 'Superbrat' behaviour towards umpires and linesmen – telling them 'You are the pits', and such like. 'You cannot be serious!' was elevated to catchphrase status through various show-biz take-offs, including Roger Kitter's record, 'Chalk Dust – The Umpire Strikes Back' (UK 1982).

you can run but you can't hide In the wake of the hijacking of a TWA airliner to Beirut in the summer of 1985, President Reagan issued a number of warnings to international terrorists. In October, he said that America had 'sent a message to terrorists everywhere. The message: "You can run, but you can't hide".' He was alluding to an utterance of the boxer Joe Louis who said of an opponent in a World Heavyweight Championship fight in June 1946, 'He can run, but he can't hide.' The opponent was Billy Conn – who was a fast mover – and Louis won the fight on a knock-out.

you can take the —— out of ——, but you can't take the —— out of —— A modern proverbial observation, current in the late 20th century, e.g. 'You can take a boy out of the slums but not the slums out of the boy' (attributed to Arthur 'Bugs' Baer in 1969); 'You can take Salem out of the country . . . but you can't take the country out of Salem' (US cigarette advertisement, quoted 1985); 'You can take the man out of Essex but you can't take the Essex out of the man' – *Ned Sherrin In His Anecdotage* (1993). Origin unknown. 'You can take the girl out of the chorus, but you can't take the chorus out of the girl' – attributed to Dorothy Parker; 'Though Collins was taken out of West Cork, West Cork was never taken out of him' – Tim Pat Coogan, *Michael Collins* (1990); 'You can take the girl out of Richard Shops, but maroon me in Harrods' Cruisewear Department and a congenital reluctance to splash out £275 on diaper-sized designer sarongs proves irrefutably that you can never quite take Richard Shops out of the girl' – Vanessa Feltz, *Mail on Sunday* Review (14 May 1995); 'You can take me out of Europe but you can't take Europe out of me. I have to have my cappuccino every morning' – Isabella Rossellini in 'Milk. What a surprise!' advertising (US 1995);

'You may be able to take the man out of Fife . . .' – headline in *The Scotsman* (13 August 2001).

you can't do that there 'ere! *Partridge/ Catch Phrases* suggests that this arose from comical derision of the sort of thing a lumbering policeman might say. However, the cause of the phrase catching on was probably the song 'You Can't Do That There 'Ere' by Jack Rolls and Raymond Wallace (1935), recorded by Jack Jackson and Jack Payne and their respective bands. Police persons do feature in this song. George Orwell commented (of this song), 'It struck me that perhaps this was the English answer to Fascism' – *The English People* (1947).

you can't get the wood, you know! Catchphrase from the BBC radio *The Goon Show* (1951–60). Said chiefly by Minnie Bannister (Spike Milligan) and Henry Crun (Peter Sellers).

you can't make an omelette without breaking eggs You cannot achieve something worthwhile without hurting or offending somebody. Possibly based on a French proverb (and a saying that has been ascribed to Robespierre), but known in English by 1859. To the Nazi Hermann Goering in 1933 is attributed: 'If people say that here and there someone has been taken away and maltreated, then I can only reply: "You can't make an omelette without breaking eggs."'

you can't make a soufflé rise twice Meaning, 'It is pointless to try and make something happen again if it is unrepeatable.' Alice Roosevelt Longworth is supposed to have said it of Thomas E. Dewey's nomination as the Republican challenger in 1948 (Dewey previously stood against F. D. Roosevelt in 1944) – quoted in James T. Patterson, *Mr Republican, a biography of Robert A. Taft* (1972). 'Paul McCartney has more than once used the phrase to discount the possibility of a Beatles reunion – or in the form 'You cannot reheat a soufflé' – L. Botts, *Loose Talk* (1980). Some say that making a soufflé rise twice is not actually as impossible as it sounds.

you can't see the join Catchphrase from BBC TV, *The Morecambe and Wise Show*

(1968–77). Eric Morecambe would say it to Ernie Wise concerning his (presumed) hairpiece. Ernie recalled (1979) the origin of this: 'We shared digs in Chiswick with an American acrobat who had a toupee which – like all toupees – was perfectly obvious as such. We would whisper to each other, out of the side of our mouths, "You can hardly see the join!"'

you can't take it with you There is no point in holding on to money as it will be no good to you when you are dead. Possibly an allusion to Psalms 49:16–17: 'Be not thou afraid when one is made rich, when the glory of his house is increased; for when he dieth he shall carry nothing away: his glory shall not descend after him'; or to 1 Timothy 6:7: 'For we brought nothing into this world, and it is certain we can carry nothing out.' An early appearance is in Captain Marryat's *Masterman Ready* (1841). *You Can't Take It With You* is the title of a play (1936; film US 1938) by George S. Kaufman and Moss Hart. Another American version is 'You can't take your dough when you go.' Bob Hope is supposed to have said of Bing Crosby, 'If he can't take it with him, he's not going.' 'You can always take one with you' was a slogan suggested by Winston Churchill when invasion by the Germans threatened in 1940.

you can't win 'em all! Self-consolatory phrase after defeat. Of American origin, by the 1940s.

you'd better come in Standard line to a visiting policeman, observed by Fritz Spiegl in an article on drama cliché lines in *The Listener* (7 February 1985).

you'd better try and get some sleep After receiving bad news, a character is invariably told this. Observed by Fritz Spiegl in an article on drama cliché lines in *The Listener* (7 February 1985). See also LET'S GET OUTTA HERE!

you dirty rat! Although impersonators of James Cagney (1899–1986) always have him saying 'You dirty rat!', it may be that he never said it like that himself. In *Blonde Crazy* (US 1931) he does call someone a 'dirty, double-crossing rat', which amounts to much the same thing. In Joan Wyndham's wartime diaries, *Love Lessons* (1985), her

entry for 1 October 1940 begins: 'Double bill at the Forum with Rupert. *Elizabeth and Essex*, and a gangster film where somebody actually *did* say "Stool on me would ya, ya doity rat!"' Note her surprise that the line was uttered at all. Although it was a strange double bill, I think she must have been watching a revival of *Taxi* (US 1931), which is about cabbies fighting off a Mob-controlled fleet. Cagney's exact words in that film are: 'Come out and take it, you dirty yellow-bellied rat, or I'll give it to you through the door.' During a speech to an American Film Institute banquet on 13 March 1974, Cagney said to Frank Gorshin, a well-known impersonator: 'Oh, Frankie, just in passing: I never said [in any film] "Mmm, you dirty rat!" What I actually did say was "Judy! Judy! Judy!"'

you (dirty) rotten swine, you! Catchphrase from the BBC radio *Goon Show* (1951–60). Said by Bluebottle (Peter Sellers) on being visited by some punishment or disaster. Also, 'you have deaded me', and similar expostulations.

you don't have to be Jewish (to love Levy's Real Jewish Rye) Slogan current in the USA in 1967. The point was reinforced by the words being set next to pictures of patently non-Jewish people (Indians, Chinese, Eskimos). There had been a show of Jewish humour with the title *You Don't Have to be Jewish* running on Broadway in 1965, which is probably where it all started. Informal additions to the Levy bread posters were many. They included: '. . . to be offended by this ad/ . . . to be called one/. . . to go to Columbia University, but it helps/. . . to wear Levis/. . . to be circumcised . . .'

you don't rewrite a hit Meaning, 'you don't tamper with what is already established as successful'. This showbiz adage was quoted by Michael Grade in November 1987 when taking charge of the (rather unshowbiz) Channel 4 on British TV.

you give us twenty minutes, we'll give you the world More than one all-news radio station in the USA has used this slogan (e.g. KYW in Philadelphia in 1972). Ten years later, a TV satellite news channel was declaring: 'Give us *18* minutes. We'll give you the world.' In the film *Robocop*

(US 1987), the shout of a TV news team is, 'You give us 3 minutes, and we'll give you the world.'

you gotta go oww! Catchphrase from the BBC radio *Goon Show* (1951–60). Exclaimed by Count 'Jim' Moriarty (Spike Milligan), as in 'Wings Over Dagenham' (10 January 1957).

you have been warned See FAMOUS LAST WORDS.

you have either been listening to – or have just missed ... Announcer Douglas Smith's closing words on the BBC radio show *Beyond Our Ken* (1958–64). This was basically a sketch show, scripted by Eric Merriman and, latterly, Barry Took, and performed by some able supporting actors, but its star was Kenneth Horne (1900–69), a bald, benign and urbane figure who had little of show business about him. He was not a stand-up comedian. He seemed to have drifted into the radio studio from a busy life elsewhere as a company director (and until ill-health forced him to choose broadcasting in favour of business, this was indeed the case).

you have to spend a buck to make a buck An American business maxim (and very sensible) dating from, say, the 1920s/ 30s but curiously unrecorded in US reference works. 'The Opposition rejected the simplistic view that there was always merit in reducing public spending as a percentage of national income. Public spending should be judged on a balanced assessment of need and what prudently could be afforded, bearing in mind "that you have to spend a buck to make a buck"' – *The Times* (14 February 1990).

you know it makes sense This was the end-line to all British road safety advertisements from 1968 to 1970, but the phrase had been used with emphasis on BBC TV's *That Was The Week That Was* in 1963, so it must have been used somewhere else before this . . .

you know what comes between me and my Calvins? – nothing Brooke Shields, all of fifteen years of age, said this in a Calvin Klein jeans ad in the USA in 1980 and the line is remembered for its mild suggestiveness.

you know what thought did – killed the cat and only thought he did it 'When as children we said we "thought something", my Yorkshire Grandma would say: "You know what thought did – killed the cat and only thought he did it". My Edinburgh husband knows the expression as, ". . . planted a chicken thinking it would grow a hen"' – Margaret Barrow, Buckinghamshire (1995). Compare: 'Do you know what thought did? It followed a donkey-cart and thought it was at a funeral' – said by the paternal grandmother of Kathleen B. Crossen, Belfast (1997). Or '. . . he followed a muck cart and thought it was a wedding' – Stella Richardson, Essex (1998). *Partridge/Slang* also lists these continuations: 'Ran away with another man's wife', 'Lay in bed and beshit himself, and thought he was up', and 'No, 'e never! 'E only thought 'e did!'

you'll be lucky See RIGHT MONKEY.

you'll have to take pot-luck ... In *Are You a Bromide?* (1907), the American writer Gelett Burgess castigated people who spoke in clichés. Among the 'Bromidioms' he listed was: 'Come up and see us any time. You'll have to take pot-luck, but you're always welcome.'

you'll look a little lovelier each day (with fabulous Pink Camay) One of the catchiest slogans from the early days of British TV advertising, this one for Camay soap was around in *circa* 1960. A year or two later, the BBC's *That Was The Week That Was* had a parody of it, concerning a Labour politician: 'You'll look a little lovelier each day / With fabulous Douglas Jay.'

you'll wonder where the yellow went when you brush your teeth with Pepsodent Slogan for Pepsodent toothpaste, current in the 1950s. An appeal to vanity rather than health but curiously memorable. From a David Frost/ Christopher Booker parody of political advertisements in BBC TV, *That Was the Week That Was* (1962–3 series): 'You'll wonder where the George Brown went / When Harold forms his Government.'

you lucky people! The British comedian Tommy Trinder (1909–89) rode on a wave of publicity in the early 1940s. He even took space on advertising hoardings to declare, 'If it's laughter you're after, Trinder's the name. You lucky people!' The phrase (which came up first in concert-party work) was also used as the title of a film (UK 1954).

you might think that; I couldn't possibly comment Said to journalists by the fictitious British politician and Prime Minister Francis Urquhart (played by Ian Richardson) in the political thrillers *House of Cards* and *To Play the King* by Michael Dobbs, adapted for television in 1990 and 1993, respectively, by Andrew Davies. The stock phrase, used repeatedly in the adaptations, was taken from the sort of comment politicians in government tend to make to inquisitive lobby journalists at Westminster. As a result of the serialization, actual politicians and prime ministers 'poached' the phrase and used it self-consciously all the more.

you must have seen a lot of changes in your time? Conversation-starter supposedly much used by members of the British Royal Family. Noted by the early 1980s.

you must suffer in order to be beautiful [*il faut souffrir pour être belle*] Date and origin not known. *Casson/Grenfell* has the English words, suggesting them to be a nannyism (from the first half of the 20th century). The French phrase is given as the title of a George Du Maurier cartoon in *Punch* (29 May 1880). The caption explains: 'The scene depicted above is not so tragic as one might suppose. It merely represents that best of husbands, Jones, helping the lovely Mrs J. to divest herself of her jersey.'

you must watch these points! Catchphrase from the BBC radio *Goon Show* (1951–60). Spike Milligan would sometimes interpose himself with a rather schoolmasterly English accent and demand, 'Listeners, have you noticed [some minor plot development] . . .' and then adjure, 'You must watch these points!' – as in 'The Last Tram (from Clapham)' (23 November 1954).

. . . you name it A closing phrase to prevent a list from going on too long. Date of origin not known. American? 'They – or, more likely, producer David Morales (of New York club fame) – loaded the songs with bells, beeping brass, you name it, arranging the lot around sultry basslines' – *The Guardian* (5 May 1995); 'We're in a very competitive environment now, for our ears and our eyes, there's TV, video, cinema, tapes, you name it, it's available and for live music to compete with that, we have to promote what we're doing' – *The Irish Times* (11 May 1995).

you nasty man See WANNA BUY A DUCK.

(a) young fogey A man below the age of 40 who dresses and behaves as if he were prematurely middle-aged. The species was fashionable in Britain from 1984 onwards although observed and commented on as early as 1909 (by the philosopher C. S. Peirce). Obviously, a play upon the phrase 'old fogey' (a Scots word from the 1780s), applied to a person displaying all the attitudes of old age. From Howard Fast, *Spartacus*, Chap. 5, Pt 1 (1951): 'When Antonius Caius asked him his opinion of Cicero, Gracchus replied shortly, "A young fogey"'; 'How far does this reflect a trend? Have the moral leaders become young fogeys; or pillars of the Establishment; or supporters of the status quo?' – *The Times* (28 September 1994).

young, gifted and —— From a remark by the black US playwright Lorraine Hansberry to entrants in the United Negro College Fund writers' competition (1969): 'Though it be a thrilling and marvelous thing to be merely young and gifted in such times, it is doubly so – doubly dynamic – to be young, gifted and black.' *Young, Gifted and Black* was the title of her autobiography (1969) and, thence, 'Young, Gifted and Black', the title of a hit song recorded by the Jamaican duo Bob and Marcia in 1970. The words were by Weldon J. Irvine and the music by Nina Simone. From *The Observer* (16 April 1989): 'They're young, gifted, and the hippest fun things since . . . CFC-free aerosols.' In June 1989, ITV was showing a comedy yarn about five young lads working on a Youth Training Scheme and called *Young, Gifted and Broke*.

(a) young Lochinvar A dashing knight in Sir Walter Scott's poem *Marmion* (1808). He attends the wedding of the woman he loves, sweeps her up on to his horse and rides away with her. 'O young Lochinvar is come out of the west, / Through all the wide border his steed was the best . . . So faithful in love, and so dauntless in war, / There never was knight like young Lochinvar.' Hence, any dashing young lover. 'It took Katie some time to convince him that, just because he had the licence in his pocket, he could not snatch her up on the saddle-bow and carry her off to the nearest clergyman after the manner of young Lochinvar' – P. G. Wodehouse, 'Crowned Heads' (1917).

(the) Young Pretender Nickname of Charles Edward Stuart (1722–88), also **the Young Chevalier**, elder son of James – the OLD PRETENDER – claimant to the English throne who led the unsuccessful uprising in 1745. He was a brave and romantic figure to the Highlanders when young – their **Bonnie Prince Charlie** – and was supported by the French until he became an embarrassment to their government. He wandered through Europe on behalf of a hopeless cause and lapsed into drunkenness and debauchery. Also affectionately known as **the Highland Laddie**.

(a) Young Turk An up-and-coming politician within a party who is keen to take over from the tired old leaders and introduce new ideas and change. The name comes from a reform party in Turkey itself in the 1890s that included Kemal Ataturk and that tried to turn the decadent Ottoman Empire into a modern European state.

you only want me for my body (as opposed to **my mind)** Lovers' use, possibly only in fiction. Date of origin not known. 'But, Mortimer, you're going to love me for my mind, too?' – Elaine Harper (Priscilla Lane) to Mortimer Brewster (Cary Grant) in the film *Arsenic and Old Lace* (US 1944); 'Oh, Mama, all they want is my body' – Jean (Carroll Baker) to Mama (Angela Lansbury) in the film *Harlow* (US 1965); 'And I said, "You don't love me. You don't love me – you only love my body"' – Kate Palmer (Lee Remick) in the film *No Way To Treat a Lady* (US 1967).

you 'orrible little man! Regimental Sergeant-Major Ronald Brittain (*circa*

1899–1981) was reputed to have one of the loudest voices in the British Army. As his obituary in *The Times* put it: 'With his stentorian voice and massive parade ground presence [he] came to epitomise the British Army sergeant. Though he himself denied ever saying it, he was associated with the celebrated parade ground expression "You 'orrible little man" – in some quarters, indeed, was reputed to have coined it . . . His "**wake up there!**" to the somnolent after a command had in his opinion been inadequately executed was legendary – doubtless the ancestor of all the Wake Up Theres which have succeeded it.'

you pays your money and you takes your choice 'It's up to you, the choice is yours' – proverbial expression current in the UK by the 1840s.

you play ball with me and I'll play ball with you Coercive talk from headmasters, policemen, sergeant majors and similar. Recorded by 1944. 'Play ball!' is something that baseball umpires say, but I do not think there is an American influence on this British phrase. It is the child's game of simple catching that is being evoked. In the film *The Loneliness of the Long-distance Runner* (UK 1962), the Governor of a Borstal (young offenders' institution) greets newcomers with, 'We are here to turn you into industrious and honest citizens. If you'll play ball with us, we'll play ball with you.'

you press the button – we do the rest Slogan for Kodak cameras, current 1890. 'It was literally edited out of a long piece of copy by George Eastman himself – one of the greatest advertising ideas' – Julian Lewis Watkins, *The 100 Greatest Advertisements* (1959).

your actual French See OH HELLO.

(hey,) your back wheel's going round! 'Helpful' comment volunteered by a juvenile pedestrian to a cyclist or motorist with the purpose of distracting or annoying him. Since the early 1900s. Possibly addressed earlier to users of any form of wheeled transport.

your beer is sour Although it has taken the rise of the mass media to encourage the spread of catchphrases on a vast scale, it is quite clear that they did exist in the days of music hall and vaudeville. Going back even further, it appears that Shakespeare was familiar with something akin to the phenomenon. In the First Quarto version of *Hamlet*, III.ii. (1603 – but not in the 1623 First Folio), the Prince's advice to the players ('Speak the speech, I pray you . . .') is extended to include: 'Let not your Clown speak / More than is set down . . . / And then you have some again, that keeps one suit / Of jests, as a man is known by one suit of / Apparel, and gentlemen quote his jests down / In their tables, before they come to the play, as thus: / cannot you stay till I eat my porridge? and, you owe me / A quarter's wages: . . . / And, Your beer is sour.'

your cock's on the block British business phrase (noticed in 1988), meaning, 'You're on the line, this is the testing moment. If you fail in this one, you'll be out of a job.'

your country needs you The caption to Alfred Leete's famous First World War recruiting poster showing Field Marshal Lord Kitchener pointing at *you* is a brilliant example of a slogan that is inseparable from a visual. It first appeared on the cover of *London Opinion* on 5 September 1914 and was taken up for poster use the following week. Earlier, a more formal advertisement bearing the words 'Your King and Country need you' with the royal coat of arms had been used. The idea was widely imitated abroad. In the USA, James Montgomery Flagg's poster of a pointing Uncle Sam bore the legend 'I want *you* for the US army'. There was also a version by Howard Chandler Christy featuring a woman with a mildly come-hither look saying, 'I want you for the Navy'. 'Your country needs you' became a catchphrase used in telling a man he had been selected for a dangerous or disgusting task.

you're a brick, Angela! *You're a Brick, Angela!* was the title of a survey of girls' school stories by Mary Cadogan and Patricia Craig (1976). Perhaps it is a line from one of them – perhaps there is also a nod towards the name of Angela Brazil, the writer of many such stories.

you're an absolute shower! Military rebuke to Other Ranks, best spoken in a very English upper-class voice, as by Terry-Thomas in the film *Private's Progress* (UK 1956). He also said of the workers in *I'm All Right Jack* (UK 1959): 'I can tell you, they're an absolute shower – a positive shower.' In this film he was playing a personnel officer. *Partridge/ Catch Phrases* suggests that the original expression was 'What a shower!' (RAF, 1930s), short for 'a shower of shit'.

(at) your earliest convenience A cliché of correspondence – especially formal, business letter writing – since the 19th century. 'You will perhaps oblige me with a line at your earliest convenience' – Charles Dickens, letter (30 July 1832).

you're a star An expression used when complimenting someone and meaning, 'You have done something out of the way for which I am exceedingly grateful!' Noted in 1995. Probably of American origin. Possibly an extension of the literal (show business) sense as in the title of a song (1979) and in the refrain of the two separate songs entitled 'Superstar', recorded by The Carpenters and by Murray Head in 1971/2. The latter is from the musical *Jesus Christ Superstar*. 'He was . . . boasting of securing a discount of £35,000 on one flat and offering to handle the paperwork. She emailed back: "You're a star"' – *The Observer* (8 December 2002).

you're damned if you do and damned if you don't! 'On the horns of a dilemma; torn both ways; in a "Catch-22" situation' – probably American, early 20th century.

you're famous when they can spell your name in Karachi This observation comes from American show biz and is quoted by Steve Aronson in *Hype* (1983). In David Brown, *Star Billing* (1985), 'You're not a star until they can spell your name in Karachi', is ascribed to Humphrey Bogart.

you're going out a youngster – but you've got to come back a star! Not a cliché when new-minted in the film *42nd Street* (1933). Warner Baxter as a theatrical producer says the line to Ruby Keeler as the chorus girl who takes over at short notice from an indisposed star.

you're never alone with a Strand
Slogan from a classic British ad for a brand of cigarettes from W. D. & H. O. Wills that caught the public imagination and yet failed to sell the product. Devised in 1960 by John May of the S. H. Benson agency, the campaign was to launch a new, cheap, filter cigarette called Strand. May decided to appeal to the youth market by associating the product not with sex or social ease but with 'the loneliness and rejection of youth'. 'The young Sinatra was the prototype of the man I had in mind,' says May. 'Loneliness had made him a millionaire. I didn't see why it shouldn't sell us some cigarettes.' And so, a Sinatra clone was found in the 28-year-old actor, Terence Brook, who was also said to bear a resemblance to James Dean. He was shown mooching about lonely locations in raincoat and hat. In no time at all he had his own fan club and the music from the TV ad – 'The Lonely Man Theme' – became a hit in its own right. But the ads did not work. Viewers apparently revised the slogan in their own minds to mean, 'If you buy Strand, then you'll be alone.' However much the young may have wanted to identify with the figure, they did not want to buy him or his aura. Or perhaps it simply wasn't a very good cigarette? Either way, it hasn't been forgotten.

you're only as good as your last —— A film/TV industry adage dating from the 1960s, maybe. Sometimes adapted to fit other professions where past reputation counts for little. Leslie Halliwell in *The Filmgoers Book of Quotes* (1973) gives the originator as the Canadian-born actress Marie Dressler (1869–1934) in the form: 'You're only as good as your last picture.' Compare: 'Hollywood is a place where there is no definition of your worth earlier than your last picture' – Murray Kempton, *Part of Our Time*, 'The Day of the Locust' (1955). From *Jean Shrimpton: An Autobiography* (1990): 'Any photographer is only as good as his last photograph, and the results of every session must appear fresh and innovative.'

you're only young once Modern proverbial expression, often employed to excuse an aspect of behaviour or taking part in an activity that would be frowned upon in anyone older. Recorded by 1941 in the USA.

you're the expert! 'I'll take your word for it' – a phrase respectful of someone who appears to be an authority on any subject. Since the 1930s/40s – like **you're the doctor!**

your friendly neighbourhood ——
'Usually ironic or facetious' notes the *Oxford Dictionary of Current Idiomatic English* (1985) of this construction and says it is derived from the slogan 'Your friendly neighbourhood policeman' in a police public-relations campaign of the 1960s. Of American origin (compare SUPPORT YOUR LOCAL ——).

your future is in your hands Slogan for the British Conservative Party in the 1950 General Election. The Conservatives were returned to power under Winston Churchill the following year. Churchill himself had used the idea in an address to Canadian troops aboard RMS *Queen Elizabeth* in January 1946: 'Our future is in our hands. Our lives are what we choose to make of them.' The slogan led to an inevitably lavatorial joke, as in Keith Waterhouse, *Billy Liar* (1959): '"No writing mucky words on the walls!" he called. I did not reply. Stamp began quoting, "*Gentlemen, you have the future of England in your hands*".'

your money or your life! The highwayman's/robber's challenge. In one of Jack Benny's most celebrated gags (playing on his legendary meanness), when the robber said this, Benny paused for a long time and then replied, 'I'm thinking it over'. This was on American radio in the 1930s/40s. 'Your money *and* your life!' was an anti-smoking slogan in the UK in 1981.

your mother wouldn't like it Ironic warning, used as the title of a rock music programme on London's Capital Radio, presented by Nicky Horne, from 1973. The phrase seems to have been very much around at the time. The slogan 'Mother wouldn't like it' was used in MG motor advertisements (by April 1972) and W. H. Auden is reported by Stephen Spender to have said 'Naughty! Naughty! Mother wouldn't like it!' to Philip Larkin, also in 1972. However, in Margaret Mitchell, *Gone With the Wind* (1936): 'There, [Scarlett] thought, I've said "nigger" and Mother wouldn't like that at all.' Even earlier, J. M. Barrie's play *The Admirable Crichton*, Act 1, Sc.1 (1902) has both 'Mother don't like it' and 'Mother wouldn't like it.'

your own, your very own Old-time music hall from the Leeds City Varieties in *The Good Old Days* was a long-running BBC TV favourite from 1953–83. As its chairman, Leonard Sachs (1909–90) spoke in a florid way, presumably reproducing traditional music-hall phrases. Before banging his gavel to bring on the next act, he would describe 'your own, your very own' artistes with alluring alliteration. At the end, the audience (all in period costume) would join in a sing-song: 'To conclude, we assemble the entire company, ladies and gentlemen – the entire company, the orchestra, but this time, ladies and gentlemen, **chiefly yourselves!**'

your place or mine? Chat-up line, included under 'Naff Expressions' in *The Complete Naff Guide* (1983).

your policemen are wonderful What visitors (especially American ones) traditionally say to the British. A cliché by the mid-20th century but note the dates of the first citations: *Magistrate*: 'Have you anything to say for yourself?' *Prisoner*: 'Yus, I fink your London police are wonderful' – caption to cartoon by Edmund J. Sullivan in *Punch* (25 January 1933); 'Oh, but we're not so *very* wonderful, really!' – bashful London policeman to tourists in *Punch* cartoon (30 May 1938); '. . . and I think your archers are wonderful!' – woman to ancient [Egyptian] potentate in George Morrow cartoon, *Punch* (9 February 1944); 'And what are your first impressions of our city?' 'I think our policemen are wonderful' – city resident to (possibly) invading soldier on park bench in Fougasse cartoon, *Punch* (19 April 1944); '"Oh," said Elizabeth quietly [as she goes into a police station], "aren't our police wonderful?"' – Chris Mullin, *A Very British Coup*, Chap. 15 (1982); 'When Kristina Wayborn [actress in James Bond film] said that she loved British fish and chips it

seemed a simple kindness to ask what she thought of our policemen. "They are so wonderful. They make you feel so secure," she replied in the best possible taste' – *The Guardian* (4 June 1983); 'Thriller writer, Max Byrd . . . almost said that our policemen are wonderful, but stopped himself and touched his shoulder holster' – *The Guardian* (13 July 1985); 'I have yet to see one of your crazy drivers pulled over for a traffic violation. Your policemen are wonderful, but why don't they throw away that halo and get on to a little ticket-writing?' – letter to the editor in *Today* (20 January 1987); 'The British are hypocritical, racist, secretive, arrogant, violent and boorish in drink. They treat old people abominably . . . They have the best and the worst press in the world, the silliest scandals and the most honest taxi drivers. Their policemen are wonderful – up to a point' – *The Guardian* (3 April 1989); '"Your policemen are wonderful" is the stock remark of all visitors to London, to all interviewers; but our own policemen, the Garda Siochana are equally deserving of praise' – *The Irish Times* (26 January 1994).

your slip is showing! 'You are giving yourself away by saying or doing that' – a warning, current since the 1920s, indicating that a person is betraying himself (in however trivial a matter) just as woman 'reveals' herself by letting her slip show under her dress.

yours to enjoy in the privacy of your own home A traditional advertising line, probably ex-US? *Private Eye,* in 1964, ran a spoof advertisement for a part-work, including the lure: 'Now experience the First World War in the privacy of your own home.'

your trumpeter's dead Rebuke to an egoist or to a person who will BLOW [HIS] OWN TRUMPET. *Apperson* finds the expression in use by 1729. From Baker's *Northamptonshire Glossary* (1854): 'Sometime it is said [again to an egotist], "your trumpeter's dead", i.e. no one sounds your praises, so you are compelled to extol yourself.'

you scratch my back and I'll scratch yours! Promise of support in return for a favour. This occurs in Anthony Trollope's novel *The Way We Live Now* (1875) in the form: 'If I scratch their back, I mean them to scratch mine.' There have been several proverbial expressions of this idea, including 'scratch my breech and I'll claw your elbow' and 'scratch me and I'll scratch thee.'

you *shall* go to the ball, Cinders Said by the Fairy Godmother to Cinderella in the fairy tale, but in the pantomime versions rather than the original telling of the tale in Perrault's 1697 edition. 'When Cinderella's fairy god-mother promised "you shall go to the ball", all she had to do was wave a magic wand' – *The Sunday Times* (3 November 1985); '"Fear not, Cinders," she trilled, "You shall go to the ball; I shall fetch you first a fairy coach." "Oh yes?" asked a jaded Cinders, "and what is he supposed to teach me?"' – *Mail on Sunday* (28 December 1997).

you should get out more Admonition to someone who displays ignorance or lack of awareness as to what life is really like. Since the 1980s? Comedy performer Donna McPhail said it to author Salman Rushdie on BBC TV, *Have I Got News For You* (10 June 1994). 'Ministers tell Prince Charles: you should get out more. Ministers want the Prince of Wales to recruit a much wider circle of advisers to ensure that he gets a broader picture of the state of Britain today' – headline and text from *The Independent* (27 September 2002).

you should use stronger elastic! Catchphrase of Ted Ray, the first host of a BBC radio comedy show called *Calling All Forces* (1950–2). In the first show he had as guest Freddie Mills, then world light heavyweight boxing champion. Mills – departing from his script – told of one punch he received when he momentarily lowered his boxing gloves: 'My trainer nearly fainted when he saw me drop 'em. I didn't mean to drop 'em.' Ted Ray immediately responded, 'You should use stronger elastic!' Bob Monkhouse, the show's co-scriptwriter, soon engineered the return of this phrase that certainly did catch on. Ray kept it in his stage act for many years.

you silly little man! Catchphrase from the BBC radio show *Band Waggon* (1938–

39). As, for example: *Richard Murdoch (instructing Arthur Askey how to court 'Nausea Bagwash', with whom he was supposed to be in love)*: 'You say, "Darling Nausea, your lips are like petals . . ."' *Askey*: 'Nausea, darling, your lips are like petals. Bicycle petals.' *Murdoch*: 'No, no, no, you silly little man!'

you silly twisted boy! Catchphrase from the BBC radio *Goon Show* (1951–60). Frequently spoken by Hercules Grytpype-Thynne (Peter Sellers) to Neddie Seagoon (Harry Secombe) after he has done something foolish, as in 'China Story' (18 January 1955).

(what are you) you some kind of nut? Derisive question put to anyone who is acting or speaking strangely. American usage, especially since the 1910s.

you talkin' to me? See WHO YOU LOOKING AT?

you, too, can have a body like mine Slogan of 'Charles Atlas' who was born Angelo Siciliano in Italy in 1894 and died in America in 1972. He won the title of 'The World's Most Perfectly Developed Man' in a 1922 contest sponsored by Bernarr Macfadden and his *Physical Culture* Magazine. Then he started giving mail-order body-building lessons. A famous promotional strip cartoon showed 'How Joe's body brought him FAME instead of SHAME.' 'Hey! Quit kicking sand in our face,' Joe says to a bully on the beach. Then he takes a Charles Atlas course and ends up with a girl by his side who says, 'Oh, Joe! You are a real man after all!' Like Joe, Atlas had himself been 'a skinny, timid weakling of only seven stone' (hence the expression **I was a seven stone weakling**). 'I didn't know what real health and strength were. I was afraid to fight – ashamed to be seen in a bathing costume.' But after watching a lion rippling its muscles at the zoo, he developed a method of pitting one muscle against another, which he called 'Dynamic Tension'.

you've come a long way, baby (to get where you got to today) Slogan for Virginia Slims cigarettes, in the USA, from 1968. A slogan that rode on the feminist mood of the times in selling to women